The Springer Series on Human Exceptionality

Series Editors

Donald H. Saklofske, Ph.D.
Division of Applied Psychology
University of Calgary, Canada

Moshe Zeidner, Ph.D.
Center for Interdisciplinary Research on Emotions
Department of Human Development and Counseling
Haifa University, Israel

For other titles published in this series, go to
www.springer.com/series/6450

Aleksandra Gruszka · Gerald Matthews
Błażej Szymura
Editors

Handbook of Individual Differences in Cognition

Attention, Memory, and Executive Control

Editors
Aleksandra Gruszka
Institute of Psychology
Jagiellonian University
Cracow
Poland
rusalka@apple.phils.uj.edu.pl

Gerald Matthews
Department of Psychology
University of Cincinnati
Cincinnati, OH
USA
gerald.matthews@uc.edu

Błazej Szymura
Institute of Psychology
Jagiellonian University
Cracow
Poland

ISBN 978-1-4419-1209-1 (hardcover)   e-ISBN 978-1-4419-1210-7
ISBN 978-1-4614-3217-3 (softcover)
DOI 10.1007/978-1-4419-1210-7
Springer New York Dordrecht Heidelberg London

Library of Congress Control Number: 2010925383

© Springer Science+Business Media, LLC 2010, First softcover printing 2012
All rights reserved. This work may not be translated or copied in whole or in part without the written permission of the publisher (Springer Science+Business Media, LLC, 233 Spring Street, New York, NY 10013, USA), except for brief excerpts in connection with reviews or scholarly analysis. Use in connection with any form of information storage and retrieval, electronic adaptation, computer software, or by similar or dissimilar methodology now known or hereafter developed is forbidden.
The use in this publication of trade names, trademarks, service marks, and similar terms, even if they are not identified as such, is not to be taken as an expression of opinion as to whether or not they are subject to proprietary rights.

Printed on acid-free paper

Springer is part of Springer Science+Business Media (www.springer.com)

It was a beautiful sunny September day, when some of the authors of the chapters of this book met up in Krakow during the conference on Individual Differences in Cognition (IDIC: Kraków, Poland, September 15–17, 2006). Błażej Szymura, an assistant professor at the time, initiated and organized this meeting and managed to convince the Polish Scientific Research Committee (KBN) to grant financing of a research program to study the individual differences in cognition, of which the conference was an integral part.

The meeting was a great success, for it is rare that such a high number of world experts in a specific field gather together in conditions that are so conducive to the sincere and stimulating exchange of thoughts and ideas as was the case here. It was then that the idea of the book that you have in front of you was born. The book turned out to be an undertaking on a still larger scale than the Krakow get-together. To obtain systematic coverage of the field, new experts working on individual differences in cognition were drafted in to contribute to the project. Throughout the process the driving force was Błażej, who in the meantime obtained his "habilitation" to the role of Principal Investigator.

Błażej had the central role in the IDIC project. So, it has been very difficult for us to come to terms with the tragic event that occurred when we were finalizing editorial works before sending the book off to the Publishers – unexpectedly Błażej passed away.

Our friend and colleague was a special person. Intellectually very gifted, he was full of energy, eagerness and motivation for work that allowed him to undertake remarkable projects. His work ethos and intrinsic scientific curiosity lead him to perform experiments involving large number of studied groups and many research procedures. Obviously, the questions that he tried to answer had a universal dimension and importance. He was interested in cognitive psychology, psychology of individual differences and psychology of creativity. Despite his young age, he was well recognized in the field, he won many grants, published or contributed to numerous books, and peer-reviewed scientific articles.

Błażej was a talented organizer characterized by an extraordinary sense of duty and responsibility. Hence, at a relatively early point of his career, he found himself involved in many administrative functions. Since 1998, he was an assistant professor in the Laboratory of Experimental Psychology at Jagiellonian University in Krakow and (since 2008) a chair of the Department of Psychology of Individual Differences and Personality at the Warsaw School of Social Sciences and Humanities, Faculty in Sopot. He was a member of many associations: European Society for Cognitive Psychology (ESCoP), European Association of Personality Psychology (EAPP) and International Society for the Study of Individual Differences (ISSID). In recognition to his contribution, ISSID founded 'The Błażej Szymura ISSID Conference Travel Award'.

Błażej was a very generous man, generous in his contacts with others, regardless of who they were: colleagues or collaborators, friends or mere students. The teaching of psychology constituted a very important part of his work. Błażej was very well-liked and respected by all of the students, who felt inspired to fulfill his high expectations.

Here we are, left by Błażej. We will always miss his creative imagination, energy and friendship. He left us with a list of tasks to complete necessary to conclude this handbook. We have followed his directions step by step as witnessed by the existence of this book.

This book is dedicated to Professor Błażej Szymura.

Contents

Part I   General Models of Individual Differences in Cognition

1 **Individual Differences in Cognition: in Search of a General Model of Behaviour Control** 3
   Philip J. Corr

2 **Individual Differences in Cognition: New Methods for Examining the Personality-Cognition Link** 27
   William Revelle, Joshua Wilt, and Allen Rosenthal

3 **The Relationship Between Intelligence and Pavlovian Temperament Traits: The Role of Gender and Level of Intelligence** 51
   Magdalena Kaczmarek, Jan Strelau, and Agnieszka Miklewska

4 **General Models of Individual Differences in Cognition: The Commentaries** 63
   Philip Corr, William Revelle, Joshua Wilt, and Allen Rosenthal

Part II   Individual Differences in Cognition from a Neurophysiological Perspective

5 **Neuroscientific Approaches to the Study of Individual Differences in Cognition and Personality** 73
   Aljoscha C. Neubauer and Andreas Fink

6 **Cognitive Neuroscience Approaches to Individual Differences in Working Memory and Executive Control: Conceptual and Methodological Issues** 87
   Tal Yarkoni and Todd S. Braver

7 **Emotional Intelligence and Gender: A Neurophysiological Perspective** 109
   Norbert Jaušovec and Ksenija Jaušovec

8 **Learned Irrelevance Revisited: Pathology-Based Individual Differences, Normal Variation and Neural Correlates** 127
   Aleksandra Gruszka, Adam Hampshire, and Adrian M. Owen

9 **Post-Soviet Psychology and Individual Differences in Cognition: A Psychophysiological Perspective** 145
   Almira Kustubayeva

| 10 | **Individual Differences in Cognition from a Neurophysiological Perspective: The Commentaries** | 169 |

Todd S. Braver, Tal Yarkoni, Aleksandra Gruszka, Adam Hampshire, Adrian M. Owen, Norbert Jaušovec, Almira Kustubayeva, Aljoscha C. Neubauer, and Andreas Fink

Part III Individual Differences in Attentional Mechanisms

| 11 | **Psychopathology and Individual Differences in Latent Inhibition: Schizophrenia and Schizotypality** | 181 |

R.E. Lubow and Oren Kaplan

| 12 | **Attentional Control Theory of Anxiety: Recent Developments** | 195 |

Michael W. Eysenck

| 13 | **Task Engagement, Attention, and Executive Control** | 205 |

Gerald Matthews, Joel S. Warm, Lauren E. Reinerman, Lisa K. Langheim, and Dyani J. Saxby

| 14 | **Individual Differences in Resource Allocation Policy** | 231 |

Błażej Szymura

| 15 | **The Relationship of Attention and Intelligence** | 247 |

Karl Schweizer

| 16 | **Intelligence and Cognitive Control** | 263 |

Adam Chuderski and Edward Nęcka

| 17 | **Individual Differences in Attention: The Commentaries** | 283 |

Michael W. Eysenck, Gerald Matthews, Edward Nęcka, Adam Chuderski, Karl Schweizer, and Błażej Szymura

Part IV Individual Differences in Working Memory Functioning and Higher-Order Processing

| 18 | **Trait and State Differences in Working Memory Capacity** | 295 |

Małgorzata Ilkowska and Randall W. Engle

| 19 | **Adrift in the Stream of Thought: The Effects of Mind Wandering on Executive Control and Working Memory Capacity** | 321 |

Jennifer C. McVay and Michael J. Kane

| 20 | **The Unique Cognitive Limitation in Subclinical Depression: The Impairment of Mental Model Construction** | 335 |

Grzegorz Sedek, Aneta Brzezicka, and Ulrich von Hecker

| 21 | **Working Memory Capacity and Individual Differences in Higher-Level Cognition** | 353 |

Jarosław Orzechowski

Contents

**22 Motivation Towards Closure and Cognitive Resources:
An Individual Differences Approach** 369
Małgorzata Kossowska, Edward Orehek, and Arie W. Kruglanski

23 Mood as Information: The Regulatory Role of Personality 383
Magdalena Marszał-Wiśniewska and Dominika Zajusz

**24 Autobiographical Memory: Individual Differences
and Developmental Course** 403
Mary L. Courage and Mark L. Howe

**25 Individual Differences in Working Memory
and Higher-Ordered Processing: The Commentaries** 419
Mary L. Courage, Mark L. Howe, Małgorzata Ilkowska, Randall W. Engle,
Małgorzata Kossowska, Edward Orehek, Arie W. Kruglanski, Jennifer C. McVay,
Michael J. Kane, Magdalena Marszał-Wiśniewska, Dominika Zajusz,
Jarosław Orzechowski, Grzegorz Sedek, and Aneta Brzezicka

**26 Conclusion: The State of the Art in Research on Individual
Differences in Executive Control and Cognition** 437
Gerald Matthews, Aleksandra Gruszka, and Błażej Szymura

Author Index 463

Subject Index 487

Introduction

Aleksandra Gruszka, Gerald Matthews, and Błażej Szymura

Aims of This Volume

Exceptionality in cognition has typically been understood in terms of general intelligence, as an overarching factor of cognitive aptitude. However, information-processing analyses of human performance suggest a more differentiated view of individual variation in cognitive aptitude and competencies. This book aims to explore exceptionality in two key cognitive functions: attention and working memory. There are pronounced individual differences in attentional selectivity, dual task performance, endurance, and other aspects of attention, as well as in memory span, search strategies, and other aspects of working memory. At least in part, differences between people in these facets of attention and memory may relate to cognitive control. Converging evidence from experimental and neuroscientific studies increasingly suggests that an executive control system or systems localized in the frontal lobes is critical for effortful processing in both task domains.

Individual differences in attention, working memory, and control may be important in accounting for human performance in a variety of cognitive tasks, including real-world skills. Also, one can ask whether people who are characterized by different levels of intelligence, cognitive styles, extraversion, neuroticism, and other dimensions of individual differences differ in the specificity of functioning of their attentional and memory mechanisms. Knowledge of such relationships increases our understanding of the cognitive mechanisms of human intelligence and personality. It is also helpful in creating integrated models of performance, which take into account both general principles of cognition and their interindividual variability.

A review of research in this area is timely for the three following reasons. Firstly, cognitive models of individual differences in complex behavior are becoming more sophisticated, due to both the progressive refinement of existing models, and to the influx of ideas and data from neurological studies. Secondly, psychobiological theories of personality and intellectual traits have for a long time been directed toward specific biological mechanisms for individual differences in performance. Only recently though have such theories engaged with cognitive neuroscience, and a synthesis of approaches is urgently needed. Thirdly, recent work on mechanisms for executive control may provide an important unifying principle for interrelating the often rather fragmented and disconnected data from studies of personality and diverse information-processing tasks.

Thus, the present book aims to review recent research on individual differences in attention and memory, and to assess the prospects for an integrated theory of individual differences in this field. To do so, the book integrates contributions from cognitive psychologists, cognitive neuroscientists, and personality and intelligence researchers. Research on temperament also provides a developmental perspective. Reviews in this area have so far focused on the attentional working memory and other information processing correlates of single individual difference factors such as general intelligence or anxiety. What is lacking from the research literature is a more comprehensive survey that would relate multiple individual difference factors to a well-defined set of information-processing mechanisms (i.e., executive control). Furthermore, such a survey needs to interrelate cognitive mechanisms with existing knowledge of the biological bases of intelligence and personality traits.

In the same volume, we present chapters on some recent achievements of North American and European research teams fostering innovative experimental investigations at the frontier of two scientific paradigms: cognition and individual differences. The idea of publishing this volume was inspired by the small group conference in Kraków (Poland, September 15–17, 2006) entitled "Individual Differences in Cognition" that brought together some of the authors of the presented book. However, this volume is designed to provide a comprehensive handbook for this research field, and so includes chapters from additional contributors. Conference presentations were altered where necessary to provide systematic coverage of the main issues in the field.

Outline of the Book

The book comes in five parts and is structured to present perspectives from both cognitive psychology (including cognitive neuroscience) and from differential psychology. Part I addresses general models of the relationship between cognition and individual differences. Part II reviews individual differences in cognition from neurophysiological perspectives. Part III concentrates on individual differences in attentional mechanisms. Part IV focuses on individual differences in working memory functioning and higher-order processing. Part V is an editorial summary of the state of the art in the field.

Each part of the book (except the last) ends with a commentary section. We asked all the contributors for informal opinions on what they think are the key issues and priorities for future research in the area covered by this part of the book, in the light of the chapters making up the section. The questions were provided by the editors to give some structure to the commentaries, but general commentaries that do not make direct reference to the questions have also been accepted.

Part I: General Models of Individual Differences in Cognition

Chapter 1, by Philip Corr, deals with the still unresolved "unification of psychology" problem. Corr argues that the search for systematic individual differences in cognition is confounded by a number of unrecognized or unappreciated problems. These include the nature of the relationship between on-line (reflexive) and off-line (reflective) processes and the question of the lateness of conscious awareness relative to related cognitive processes. Corr's Reinforcement Sensitivity Theory (RST) relates personality traits to variations in the operating parameters of brain motivation systems such as the Fight-Flight-Freeze system. (FFFS). Traits may then correspond to the basic properties of the cognitive functions that support these neural systems (e.g., reflexive versus reflective cognitive processes, conscientiousness of the cognitive processing, inhibition as the main mechanism of executive control). After raising some fundamental problems that anyone considering individual differences in cognition must confront, referring to Jeffrey Gray's functional model of consciousness, Corr outlines a sketch of the general model of behavior control.

In Chap. 2, Revelle, Wilt, and Rosenthal present a new technique of "Synthetic Aperture Personality Assessment" (SAPA) that allows the examination of the relationship between noncognitive and cognitive aspects of personality, taking advantage of the opportunity to test a large group of subjects via the web. The authors describe the SAPA technique in detail, particularly taking into account item pool and statistical procedures for data analysis. Moreover, the results of the first seven studies relating selectively various dimensions of personality, abilities, and interests (e.g., personality, music preference and cognition; cognitive and noncognitive measures of personality) with the use of the SAPA technique are briefly described. These outcomes are frequently comparable to existing results obtained in laboratory studies on the structure of personality and on the relationship between personality traits and intellectual abilities. SAPA may be the most promising technique in future researches that integrate the study of several personality dimensions in both cognitive and noncognitive domains (e.g., cognition, emotion, and motivation).

In Chap. 3, Kaczmarek, Strelau, and Miklewska attempt to establish the links between temperamental traits and intellectual abilities, with regard to gender and age variables as moderators. The authors describe three ideas that justify their expectations of intelligence/temperament correlation. One of these, the idea of "common ground," may be particularly promising for understanding individual differences in cognition. Temperamental traits and intellectual abilities may be linked due to common cognitive (speed/tempo of information processing) and biological (arousal and arousability) bases. The authors present the outcomes of correlational analyses of a large sample study. Intelligence (IQ) appears to be related mostly to the mobility of the nervous system and, to a lesser extent, to strength of excitation. Surprisingly, Kaczmarek, Strelau, and Miklewska do not reveal any correlation between IQ and strength of inhibition. According to them, the weak relationship between strength of inhibition and intelligence suggests that the concept of control is heterogeneous and cognitive control is weakly predicted by temperament.

Chapter 4 is made up of two short commentaries on models of individual differences in cognition by Corr and by Revelle with his colleagues. Firstly, the commentators take up the problem of brain systems that are critical for understanding systematic individual differences in cognition. They then discuss the question of direction of causation: do individual differences in traits (personality and ability) influence cognitive processes or do variations in cognition determine the traits? Next, Corr and Revelle try to determine to what extent cognition may constitute a missing link between temperamental and abilities facets of personality. They then compare individual differences in trait and state variables as predictors of cognitive performance. Finally, they address the problem of differences in the models of individual differences in cognition with regard to conscious and unconscious information processing.

Part II: Individual Differences in Cognition from a Neurophysiological Perspective

Chapter 5, by Neubauer and Fink, tackles the neurobiology of individual differences in cognition and personality. In their review, the authors link intelligence and creativity to differential brain activation patterns in response to the performance of cognitive tasks employing a broad range of different demands. Neuroscientific data on individual differences in personality traits (with special focus on the extraversion–introversion dimension) presented by Neubauer and Fink indicates that normal-based variation in personality accounts for variability in brain activity during the performance of classic cognitive tasks (e.g., mental speed, reasoning or working memory). In their concluding remarks, Neubauer and Fink argue for the idea of personality and ability as interplaying with one another rather than being independent domains.

The last decade was characterized by a rapid development in cognitive neuroscience studies of executive control and working memory. In response to these interests, Yarkoni and Braver, in Chap. 6, review important conceptual and methodological issues associated with the use of individual difference measures to explain brain activation patterns related to executive functioning. Firstly, they selectively review the existing literature, highlighting common individual differences, approaches to the study of working memory as well as recently emerging trends. Secondly, Yarkoni and Braver discuss conceptual issues that arise when attempting to integrate individual differences analyses with the intraindividual approaches more common in cognitive neuroscience and cognitive psychology. Thirdly, they review several statistical and methodological problems (e.g., lack of power in functional neuroimaging studies, the potential for effect size inflation, etc.). In conclusion, the authors offer useful suggestions for dealing with the issues raised, and discuss possible implications for cognitive neuroscience research on executive control and working memory.

Chapter 7, by Jaušovec and Jaušovec, offers an overview of the neurophysiology of gender differences in mental abilities: general intelligence and emotional intelligence. The authors suggest that general and emotional intelligence represent distinct components of the cognitive architecture, although some phenomena are similar in both systems (e.g., neural efficiency is present in both verbal/performance and emotional intelligence). Males and females, having different levels of emotional intelligence, reveal differences in their brain activity while performing emotional intelligence tasks.

Chapter 8, by Gruszka, Hampshire, and Owen, offers a review of recent behavioral and neuroimaging findings on normal and pathology-based variation in attentional set-shifting, with a special focus on learned irrelevance. Their approach combines information derived from cognitive psychology, clinical neuropsychology, and neuroimaging in the study of individual differences in attentional control. The first part of the chapter attempts to fractionate the various components of attentional control using the intra- and extradimension set-shifting paradigm modeled after the Wisconsin Card Sorting Task. In the second part of the chapter, it is shown how the outcomes of such a detailed analysis can inspire neuroimaging studies of attentional set-shifting. The results of the studies reported by the authors show that – due to a high "psychological resolution" of tasks at hand – lateral prefrontal, orbital and parietal regions may be fractionated in terms of their specific contributions to attentional control.

In Chap. 9, Kustubayeva offers a unique opportunity for an insight into the program of psychophysiological research originally established by Ivan Mikhailovitch Setchenov and Ivan Petrovich Pavlov and followed by B. M. Teplov, V. D. Nebilicin, V. M. Rusalov, and others, unknown to many Western readers due to political and cultural circumstances. The central idea is that specific EEG parameters which index functional brain systems may be identified and measured in the individual. The chapter reviews research which links EEG parameters to individual differences in personality, cognitive abilities and processes, and adaptability. Special attention is given to Soroko's brain plasticity theory as the first attempt to classify individual differences in cortical plasticity, which, in turn, relate to adaptability, stress vulnerability, and cognitive abilities. The author outlines her own ongoing research on how differences in brain plasticity may relate to cognitive processes.

Chapter 10 presents short commentaries by all of the part II contributors on individual differences in cognition from a neurophysiological perspective. Firstly, they consider whether or not the concept of general arousal holds a central place in modern neuroscience theory. Then, they suggest which advances in methods may be critical for future individual differences research. Next, they try to decide whether ability and personality can be assigned to separate brain systems. They then deal with the question of discrimination between mechanisms for attention and mechanisms for executive control of attention on the basis of neuroscientific data. Finally, they tackle the problem of how work on brain motivation systems contributes to understanding individual differences in executive control.

Part III: Individual Differences in Attentional Mechanisms

Chapter 11, by Lubow and Kaplan, reviews the findings on pathology-based individual differences in latent inhibition (LI). They analyze the outcomes of a broad set of studies that have examined individual differences in LI related to: schizophrenia, schizotypia, the administration of drugs known to provoke symptoms of schizophrenia and a variety of other, apparently unrelated, pathologies (anxiety, Obsessive-Compulsive Disorder, Attention Deficit and Hyperactivity Disorder, Parkinson's Disease). After reviewing experimental data, Lubow and Kaplan present two main theories (A-theory and R-theory) that allow the explanation of the phenomenon under consideration. The chapter ends with an attempt to relate LI abnormalities in schizophrenia to specific underlying cognitive mechanisms. The authors conclude that abnormal LI effects in those patients with schizophrenia appear to reflect the inability of schizophrenics to limit the contents of consciousness, with attenuated LI being associated with positive symptoms, and potentiated LI with negative symptoms of the condition.

In Chap. 12, Eysenck takes up the problem of the relationship between anxiety and cognitive performance, from the perspective of his Attentional Control Theory. Eysenck begins with an historical overview of theories of anxiety and performance (e.g., cognitive interference theory, processing efficiency theory). Next, he differentiates negative (as related to the inhibition executive function) from positive (as related to the shifting executive function) attentional control. Eysenck presents data from his own lab which support the Attentional Control Theory; the results reveal a strong and consistent relationship between anxiety and the strength of either positive or negative attentional control. In conclusion, Eysenck suggests that we use our knowledge on correlations between individual differences traits and executive function to revise and reshape the construct of executive functions. For example, the strength of inhibition and the shifting correlate with temperamental traits – mainly anxiety – suggesting that the two functions are not independent, whereas the effectiveness of updating correlates selectively with intelligence and not with anxiety, suggesting that this function is independent.

In Chap. 13, Matthews, Warm, Reinerman, Langheim, and Saxby examine the relationship between task engagement and attentional control. They start by reviewing research that identifies energetic arousal ("energy") as a marker of the availability of attentional resources. Next, Matthews and his colleagues define task engagement as a mode of adaptation to task demands, manifested as an investment of effort in task performance. In their view, task engagement is a biologically influenced factor that is much broader than arousal itself and consists of affective (energetic arousal), motivational (task motivation), and cognitive (task concentration) components. Analyzing the relationship between task engagement and information processing, the authors suggest its bidirectionality. On one hand, changes in engagement reflect self-regulative processes, including appraisal and coping, while on the other hand differences in engagement influence executive control over attention. Matthews et al. outline a cognitive architecture for the regulation and control of attention that may interact with subjective engagement. They conclude that individual differences in task engagement are critical for attention, but that multileveled explanations of engagement are needed.

Chapter 14, by Szymura, deals with the problem of individual differences in dual task coordination as one of the four executive functions that enable control of information processing. First, Szymura describes the capacity theory of attention and its basic assumption that the quality of dual task coordination depends on the arousal level and the arousability of the cognitive system. Next, he indicates individual differences in arousal characteristics as being the main biological basis of many personality traits (extraversion, neuroticism, psychoticism) and intellectual (intelligence, creativity). Concluding his theoretical consideration, Szymura suggests that the effectiveness of dual task coordination should be related in a predictable way to the specific individual difference traits. In the empirical part of his paper, he presents the outcomes of a set of studies with the use of the DIV(ided)A(ttention) test. These results suggest that personality dimensions influence the effectiveness of dual task coordination in various experimental conditions, whereas the nature of these conditions does not influence the positive impact of general abilities on dual task coordination.

In Chap. 15, Schweizer analyzes the relationship between attention and intelligence. He first presents attention as a heterogenic construct, including its aspects, types, and modes. He also highlights those "attentions" that are related (e.g., divided attention) and those that are not, in his opinion, related to intelligence (e.g., vigilance). Next, Schweizer reviews experimental data on the structure of attention that suggest the existence of a hierarchical, three-level (or three strata) structure of attention with one first-order factor (general attention), two second-order factors (perception control and executive control), and several third-order factors related to different, specific aspects of attention (e.g., spatial, sustained, selective, divided, etc.). After focusing on the structure of attention, Schweizer presents supporting evidence that both general attention and second-order attentional factors are moderately correlated with intellectual abilities, mainly fluid intelligence. He concludes that intelligence is related rather to higher-order attentional factors since it can be best predicted by the nonnested, hierarchical three-level model of structure of attention.

In Chap. 16, Chuderski and Nęcka discuss the relationship between intelligence and cognitive control. First, on the basis of a comprehensive review of existing theories of cognitive control, the authors distinguish four of the most important executive functions (shifting, inhibition, updating, dual task coordination). Subsequently, they reveal the existing evidence for the important role of cognitive control (i.e., specific executive functions) in intelligence (mainly fluid intelligence). They conclude their theoretical account by highlighting the need for more research on the control functions that support dual-tasking. Next, Chuderski and Nęcka present empirical data from their own lab to explore relations between cognitive control and intelligence. Summarizing the outcomes, they suggest that when control is involved to a lesser extent, the dual-tasking situation is not sensitive to the subject's intelligence, whereas when control is required, intelligence is strongly related to effectiveness of dual-tasking performance.

Chapter 17 presents short commentaries on individual differences in attentional mechanisms by Eysenck, Matthews, Nęcka, and Chuderski, Schweizer and Szymura. Eysenck and Matthews offer general commentaries on the key issues and priorities for future research in the area of individual differences in attention in the light of the section's chapters, addressing, between the lines, the problems indicated by the questions. Nęcka and Chuderski, Schweizer and Szymura provide responses structured as follows. These commentators all, firstly, take up the problem of mapping the multiple dimensions of individual differences onto the multiple functions of attention. Then, they discuss the question of the relationship between attention and intelligence with regard to task difficulty and complexity. Next, they try to determine to what extent abnormality in attentional functioning explains individual differences in traits related to psychopathology. Then, they deal with the problem of the relation between negative emotionality traits and focus of attention. Finally, they try to decide the optimal attentional tasks for investigating individual differences in attention.

Part IV: Individual Differences in Working Memory Functioning and Higher-Order Processing

Chapter 18, by Ilkowska and Engle, presents a thorough revision of the research on individual differences in working memory capacity (WMC). After a description of current models of working memory, Ilkowska and Engle offer their conceptualization of WMC. According to them, research has shown that there are substantial individual differences in the ability to control attention across a variety of complex tasks and that these differences reflect abiding trait aspects of the individual as well as moment-to-moment changes resulting from such factors as sleep deprivation, fatigue, and stress. Then, the authors introduce a further differentiation of the processes important for state- and trait-WMC. Next, they discuss how the execution of effortful control influences the resources used for temporary states and those determined by biological factors. Finally, they look at genetic influences, neurotransmitters, and brain structures important in higher-order cognition, as well as biological and personality situational factors influencing cognitive abilities in a temporary fashion.

Introduction   xvii

The "executive attention" theory proposed by Engle, Kane, et al. argues that much of the shared variance between WMC and higher-order cognition reflects variation in lower-order attention-control processes. Chapter 19, by McVay and Kane, reviews briefly the behavioral and neurophysiological evidence for and against the executive-attention view, with particular focus on the phenomena of goal neglect and mind wandering. McVay and Kane argue that many goal-neglect errors are due to mind wandering, or the phenomenological experience of task-unrelated thought. They offer an analysis of how empirical studies of mind wandering may apply to our understanding of WMC and executive control, and the role of goal pursuit in controlled cognitive processing.

Chapter 20, by Sedek, Brzezicka, and von Hecker, reviews the current literature and main results of the authors' own international research program on specific cognitive deficits in depression in comparison to cognitive limitations observable in anxiety and normal aging. Subclinical depression specifically impairs integrative reasoning processes, affecting a variety of related cognitive activities (e.g., social mental models construction, linear order reasoning, evaluation of categorical syllogisms, and text comprehension). Sedek et al., have shown that some – but not all – of these deficits are mediated by working memory capacities that operate as a mediator between depression and reasoning. That is, high WMC acts as a buffer, preventing the negative influence of depression to affect higher order cognitive processes.

In Chap. 21, Orzechowski offers a very comprehensive review of behavioral research on the relationship between working memory (WM) and higher level cognition, as exemplified by deductive and inductive reasoning. Following a thorough revision of existing definitions and approaches to the concept of WM, Orzechowski describes studies on individual differences in reasoning and WM, considering various factors that may mediate the relationship (e.g., types of reasoning and types of task content, WM functions). The revision leads the author to the interesting conclusion that it seems that the concept of WM capacity is no longer the first choice when researchers look for a memory correlate of relational reasoning. Indeed, some researchers now prefer the concept of cognitive control, which is rather of an attentional nature.

Chapter 22, by Kossowska, Orehek, and Kruglansky, ties together two separate strands of research on motivation and cognitive capacities. The authors review a set of their own studies which aimed to examine the relationship between epistemic motivation (need for closure; NFC) and WMC. The results consistently indicate that high NFC may be related to certain cognitive deficits (e.g., slower rate of speed of working memory processing or lower WMC). According to Kossowska, Orehek, and Kruglansky, this consistent pattern of results supports the notion that stable individual differences in the need for cognitive closure are linked to (and possibly represent the consequences of) identifiable individual differences in cognitive ability, specifically working memory functioning.

In Chap. 23, Marszał-Wiśniewska and Zajusz discuss the relationship between mood, personality and situational variables, integrating correlational and experimental approaches to the research on mood, behavior and cognition. After reviewing studies on the basic trends in the mood research, Marszał-Wiśniewska and Zajusz present the mood-as-input model (Martin, 2001). According to this model, moods operate much like any other information being processed in parallel with the target and contextual information. Thus, the influence of mood on one's evaluations, motivations, and behavior depends on the interaction of mood and situational conditions. However, the question remains whether this so-called "context-dependent effect of mood" is additionally mediated by personality factors. Studies conducted and reported here by Marszał-Wiśniewska and Zajusz have revealed that the context-dependent motivational implications of mood are modified not only by temperamental factors or volitional traits as such, but also by their mutual relations.

Chapter 24, by Courage and Howe, focuses on individual differences that affect the onset, development, and expression of autobiographical memory. According to Courage and Howe, the necessary

– though insufficient – foundation for autobiographical memory is the emergence of the cognitive self that becomes stable at about 2 years of age. Subsequently, developments in language and other aspects of social cognition serve to refine self-characteristics and to reshape the nature and durability of event recall. Other factors such as age, cognitive (e.g., language), demographic (e.g., gender, SES), socio-emotional (e.g., mother–child interaction, stress, attachment), and cultural (e.g., Asian, Euro-American) variables are shown to affect the recollection and reporting of personally experienced events.

Chapter 25 presents short commentaries on individual differences in attentional mechanisms provided by all contributors of the section. Courage and Howe, Ilkowska and Engle, and Sedek, Brzezicka and Ulrich von Hecker offer general commentaries on the key issues and priorities for future research in the area of individual differences in working memory and higher-order processes in the light of the chapters making up the section, addressing between the lines problems indicated in the questions asked. Kossowska, Orehek and Kruglanski, Marszał-Wiśniewska and Zajusz, McVay and Kane, and Orzechowski answer the chosen questions in a more selective, structured way. The contributors were firstly asked to attempt to indicate the brain mechanisms which determine the various constraints on working memory and short-term recall (e.g., limited capacity, limited time of maintenance, etc.). They then discuss the question of which trait and state factors are critical for understanding individual differences in working memory functioning. Next, they try to show any individual difference factors that affect WM but do not affect attention, and vice versa. Then, they were asked to describe the most important recent methodological developments in the field of WM research, and how these advances can be applied to the study of individual differences in WM. Finally, they were asked to indicate those personality- or ability-related factors that have differential effects on various forms of long-term memory (e.g., autobiographical memory, semantic memory, episodic memory).

Part V: Concluding Summary

Chapter 26 presents the editors' summary of the state of the art in research on individual differences in executive control, and its contribution to the study of exceptionality in cognition. It would be premature to attempt any grand theoretical synthesis of this fast-developing research area. Instead, the editors aim to identify the main themes of current research and to outline major lines of research, especially as exemplified by the chapter contributors. Research depends on progress in the basis cognitive neuroscience of executive functioning, and on advances in models of intelligence and personality. Significant challenges here include the elusive nature of volition and consciousness, as well as accommodating new evidence on implicit personality processes. Turning to work that relates specific ability and personality factors to executive processes, the editors find encouraging signs of emerging consensus on key issues. The rather different research traditions represented by neuroscience, cognitive psychology, and studies of self-regulation provide complementary accounts of how ability and major personality traits relate to individual differences in executive control, expressed in attention, working memory and other domains of cognition. However, some issues familiar to differential psychologists remain to be resolved, including tensions between structural and process models, finding an appropriate "grain-size" for models, and the treatment of personality and ability factors as causal constructs. Various methodological issues in psychometrics, neuroscience, and experimental psychology must also be confronted. On balance, we conclude that this emerging research field is both illuminating the nature of exceptionality in cognition, and advancing theoretical understanding of ability and personality.

The Gratefully Acknowledged

We are grateful to many for their unfailing support throughout this project. The idea of publishing this volume was inspired by a conference entitled *Individual Differences in Cognition* (IDIC: Kraków, Poland, September 15–17, 2006). This meeting had been supported by grant No. PB 1H01F001 27 (4103/27) from the Scientific Research Committee (KBN), given to Błażej Szymura. Without KBN's support the idea of IDIC would have had no chance of being promoted.

Next, thanks are due to the group of distinguished key speakers of that symposium: Philip Corr, Michael W. Eysenck, Małgorzata Kossowska, Almira Kustubayeva, Magdalena Marszał-Wisniewska, Aljoscha Neubauer, Edward Nęcka, Jarosław Orzechowski, Jan Strelau, and William Revelle. Together with the editors of this volume (as well as speakers from the symposium), they decided to publish IDIC not as conference materials, but as a handbook which would also include papers by those who, whilst having been unable to attend the conference, are nonetheless key figures in the domain of individual difference in cognition research,. Thanks to Todd Braver, Randall Engle, Mark Howe, Norbert Jaušovec, Michael Kane, Robert Lubow, Karl Schweizer, and Grzegorz Sedek who accepted this invitation and enthusiastically took part in the project. We also give thanks to the many distinguished contributors who became the coauthors and sometimes even the primary authors of several chapters and whose excellent studies could therefore be presented within our volume. With such a short notice, it is impossible to mention all of them.

We are also grateful for the speedy publication facilitated through the professional assistance of Judy Jones, the senior publishing editor of Springer, and for support from the series editors of the Springer Exceptionality Series, Don Saklofske and Moshe Zeidner.

Contributors

Todd S. Braver
Departments of Psychology & Radiology, Washington University, Campus Box 1125, St. Louis, MO 63130, USA
tbraver@wustl.edu

Aneta Brzezicka
Interdisciplinary Center for Applied Cognitive Studies, Warsaw School of Social Sciences and Humanities, Chodakowska 19/31, 03-815 Warsaw, Poland

Adam Chuderski
Institute of Psychology, Jagiellonian University, Al. Mickiewicza 3, 31-120, Krakow, Poland
adam.chuderski@gmail.com

Phillip J. Corr
School of Social Work and Psychology, University of East Anglia, Norwich NR4 7TJ, UK
p.corr@uea.ac.uk

Mary L. Courage
Memorial University, St. John's, NF, Canada

Randall W. Engle
School of Psychology, Georgia Institute of Technology, 654 Cherry Street, Atlanta, GA 30332-0170, USA

Michael W. Eysenck
Department of Psychology, Royal Holloway University of London, Egham, Surrey, TW20 0EX, UK
m.eysenck@rhul.ac.uk

Andreas Fink
Institute of Psychology, Karl-Franzens-University Graz, Maiffredygasse 12b, A-8010 Graz, Austria

Aleksandra Gruszka
Institute of Psychology, Jagiellonian University, Al. Mickiewicza 3, 31-120 Cracow, Poland
rusalka@apple.phils.uj.edu.pl

Adam Hampshire
MRC Cognition and Brain Sciences Unit, 15 Chaucer Road, Cambridge, CB2 7EF, UK

Ulrich von Hecker
School of Psychology, Cardiff University, Cardiff, Wales, UK

Mark L. Howe
Department of Psychology, Lancaster University, Lancaster, LA1 4YF, UK
mark.howe@lancaster.ac.uk

Małgorzata Ilkowska
School of Psychology, Georgia Institute of Technology, 654 Cherry Street,
Atlanta, GA 30332-0170, USA
ilkowska@gatech.edu

Ksenija Jaušovec
Faculty of Philosophy, University of Maribor, Koroška 160, 2000 Maribor, Slovenia

Norbert Jaušovec
Faculty of Philosophy, University of Maribor, Koroška 160, 2000 Maribor, Slovenia
norbert.jausovec@uni-mb.si

Magdalena Kaczmarek
Interdisciplinary Center for Behavior-Genetic Research, University of Warsaw, ul. Stawki 5/7,
00-183 Warsaw, Poland

Michael J. Kane
Department of Psychology, University of North Carolina at Greensboro,
Greensboro, P.O. Box 26170, NC 27402-6170, USA
mjkane@uncg.edu

Oren Kaplan
The College of Management, Rishon Lezion, Israel

Małgorzata Kossowska
Institute of Psychology, Jagiellonian University, Al. Mickiewicza 3, 31-120 Cracow, Poland
malgosia@apple.phils.uj.edu.pl

Arie W. Kruglanski
University of Maryland, College Park, MD, USA

Almira Kustubayeva
Department of Psychology, Al-Farabi Kazakh National University, Almaty,
Al-Farabi 71, Kazakhstan 480078
kustubayeva@yahoo.com

Lisa K. Langheim
Department of Psychology, University of Cincinnati, Cincinnati, OH 45221, USA

R.E. Lubow
Department of Psychology, Tel Aviv University, Ramat Aviv 69978, Israel
lubow@freud.tau.ac.il

Magdalena Marszał-Wiśniewska
Institute of Psychology, Polish Academy of Sciences, ul. Chodakowska 19/31,
03-815 Warsaw, Poland
marszal@psychpan.waw.pl

Gerald Matthews
Department of Psychology, University of Cincinnati, Cincinnati, OH 45221, USA
gerald.matthews@uc.edu

Jennifer C. McVay
Department of Psychology, University of North Carolina at Greensboro,
Greensboro, P.O. Box 26170, NC 27402-6170, USA

Agnieszka Miklewska
Jan Długosz Academy, Czestochowa, Poland

Edward Nęcka
The Warsaw School of Social Sciences and Humanities, Warsaw, Poland

Aljoscha C. Neubauer
Institute of Psychology, Karl-Franzens-University Graz, Maiffredygasse 12b, A-8010 Graz, Austria
aljoscha.neubauer@uni-graz.at

Edward Orehek
University of Maryland, College Park, MD, USA

Jarosław Orzechowski
Institute of Psychology, Jagiellonian University, Al. Mickiewicza 3, 31-120 Cracow, Poland
jarek@apple.phils.uj.edu.pl

Adrian M. Owen
MRC Cognition and Brain Sciences Unit, 15 Chaucer Road, Cambridge, CB2 7EF, UK

Lauren E. Reinerman
Applied Cognition and Training Immersive Virtual Environments Lab (ACTIVE),
University of Central Florida, 3100 Technology Parkway, Orlando, FL 32826, USA

William Revelle
Department of Psychology, Northwestern University, 633 Clark Street, Evanston, IL, USA 60208
revelle@northwestern.edu

Allen Rosenthal
Department of Psychology, Northwestern University, 633 Clark Street, Evanston, IL, USA 60208

Dyani J. Saxby
Department of Psychology, University of Cincinnati, Cincinnati, OH 45221, USA

Karl Schweizer
Department of Psychology, Goethe University Frankfurt, Mertonstr. 17,
60054 Frankfurt a. M., Germany
k.schweizer@psych.uni-frankfurt.de

Grzegorz Sedek
Interdisciplinary Center for Applied Cognitive Studies, Warsaw School of Social Sciences
and Humanities, Chodakowska 19/31, 03-815 Warsaw, Poland
gsedek@swps.edu.pl

Jan Strelau
Faculty of Psychology, Warsaw School of Social Psychology, Chodakowska 19/31,
03-815 Warsaw, Poland
jan.strelau@swps.edu.pl

Błażej Szymura
Jagiellonian University, Cracow, Poland

Joel S. Warm
Senior Scientist (ST), Warfighter Interface Division, Air Force Research Laboratory,
Wright-Patterson AFB, Ohio, USA

Joshua Wilt
Department of Psychology, Northwestern University, 633 Clark Street, Evanston, IL, USA 60208

Tal Yarkoni
Departments of Psychology & Radiology, Washington University,
Campus Box 1125, St. Louis, MO 63130, USA

Dominika Zajusz
Warsaw School of Social Sciences and Humanities, Warsaw, Poland

Part I
General Models of Individual Differences in Cognition

Chapter 1
Individual Differences in Cognition: in Search of a General Model of Behaviour Control

Philip J. Corr

Introduction

Individual differences in cognition are important for both theories of cognition and for theories of differential psychology. Furthermore, this topic is important for the unification and future development of psychology that runs the risk of fragmenting into a disparate number of loosely connected disciplines with no central theoretical core. The aim of this chapter is to provide an overview of some fundamental, but thorny, issues that need to be acknowledged and addressed before we can start to lay the firm foundations upon which to build the integration of the two great traditions of experimental/cognitive and differential psychology. Specifically, this chapter focuses on how to build a general model of behaviour control, which would provide the theoretical hub around which the particular issues revolve.

This chapter is in the form of a theoretical itch, which the presented material and discussion are intended to scratch. I have one overriding aim: to stimulate thinking about the relationship between systematic individual differences and cognition; however, I cannot claim a priori completeness or, even, correctness, so I will have to be content with receiving succour from Dennett's (1991, p. xi) dictum,

…we often learn more from bold mistakes than from cautious equivocation.

Unification of Psychology

Before embarking on our journey, which will take many winding roads towards our final destination, we should first survey what is at stake, in terms of scientific theories as well as the future development of psychology as a coherent discipline. Forging closer links between cognitive processes and individual differences (principally, but not exclusively, personality and intelligence/abilities) would serve to achieve one of the major goals in psychology, *viz.* the unification of the differential and experimental/cognitive traditions (Corr, 2007). This problem is not new – indeed, it is now rather hackneyed – but it still remains important. It was famously articulated by Cronbach (1957, p. 671) in his APA Presidential Address,

This chapter is dedicated to the memory of Błażej Szymura

P.J. Corr (✉)
School of Social Work and Psychology, University of East Anglia, Norwich, NR4 7TJ, UK
e-mail: p.corr@uea.ac.uk

> Psychology continues to this day to be limited by the dedication of its investigators to one or the other method of inquiry rather than to scientific psychology as a whole

Cronbach's call was echoed by Hans Eysenck (1965, p. 8) who wrote,

> Individuals do differ....and it seems to me that psychology will never advance very far without a recognition of the complexities which are produced by this fact of personality

Later Eysenck (1997, p. 1224) was to reiterate his call in his final published paper,

> It is suggested that the scientific status of psychology is put in danger by the lack of paradigms in many of its fields, and by the failure to achieve unification, psychology is breaking up into many different disciplines. One important cause was suggested by Lee Cronbach...: the continuing failure of the two scientific disciplines of psychology – the experimental and the correlational – to come together and mutually support each other

As discussed by Corr (2007), the work of Hans Eysenck provided a new way of thinking about individual differences. Rather than viewing them as yet more separate faculties of mind (located in a trait box, and rarely brought out in experimental/cognitive research), he conceived of them as reflecting fundamental brain–behavioural systems that have the following characteristics:

1. They show (systematic) variation in the population.
2. They have pervasive effects on cognition, emotion and behaviour.
3. They show stability over time.

Which brain–behavioural systems are implicated in important individual differences? Well, according to this formulation, *any* and *all* that show the above characteristics. Taking this line of argument, we can see that individual differences and behavioural/cognitive processes are reflections of the same thing – opposite sides of the same coin. Therefore, to understand fully the functioning of cognitive and behavioural processes, it is necessary to consider individual differences; and vice versa.

For those of us with interests in differential psychology, it would be tempting to blame this lack of progress on the failure of cognitive psychology to recognise the importance of differential variables and processes. However, this would be a mistake, for as noted by Revelle and Oehlberg (2008, p. 1390) in their review of personality research,

> The unfortunate conclusion from this brief review of publication practices is that the use of experimental techniques is uncommon in current research. This suggests that the desired unification of the correlational/observational with the experimental disciplines called for by Cronbach and Eysenck has not yet occurred

It is timely that the current volume does a volte-face in tackling this issue.

Defining Cognition

Attempts to integrate individual differences and cognition are fraught with problems (e.g. see McNaughton & Corr, 2008a; Matthews, 2008). For this reason, it may be useful to define what I mean, and do not mean, by "cognition" – this will also serve the purpose of avoiding "straw-man" arguments that generate more emotional heat than intellectual light.

Throughout this chapter, I assume that what is generally meant by "cognition" is the capacity to know and to have knowledge, and this rubric encompasses the structures and processes that support knowing/knowledge. Cognition entails many processes: sensory registration, perception, appraisal, decision making, memory, learning, concept formation, perceptual organisations, language, and many more. This knowledge and the process of "knowing" are embedded in structures, beliefs and operations (e.g. decision making) that, in a fundamental conceptual sense, exist independently of nervous activity (although, of course, they are instantiated in this activity). In principle, knowledge can change as a result of "information" and is not determined, or constrained, by the activity of cell assemblies. However, before we run away with the idea of "pure" knowledge, we should recognise two things: (a) specific neural systems in the brain are dedicated to organising and processing specific forms of information (e.g. visual and linguistic); and (b) evolutionary pressures may have shaped neural structures to bias the selection of information and the formation of knowledge (e.g. social knowledge in the form of cheating strategies, see Corr, 2006). Here, emotion seems particularly pertinent, biasing cognitive processing in specific ways that are consistent with the prevailing reinforcement properties of the source of information (see McNaughton & Corr, 2009).

With these caveats in mind, the theoretical arguments proposed in this chapter are framed within the standard definitions of cognition, some of which are given below.

According to Harnish (2002, p. 4),

> Construed narrowly, cognitive science is not an area but a *doctrine*, and the doctrine is basically that of the computational theory of mind (CTM) – the mind/brain is a type of computer

According to Matthews (2008):

> The key issue is the role of symbolic information-processing in human behavior. From the cognitive science standpoint (e.g., Pylyshyn, 1999) processing requires computations performed on discrete symbolic representations, so that, just as in a digital computer, we can distinguish the mental software from the (neural) hardware that supports it (p. 485)
>
> A particular challenge in this respect is the cognitive-psychological view that much of behavior is controlled by symbolic information-processing, rather than being direct by contingent upon activation level of neural systems (p. 484)
>
> Within cognitive science, symbolic, "cognitive" processes are very much different in principle from neural processes that use no symbolic representation. Cognitive science models, in addition to "hardware" and "software" levels, also differentiate a third type of explanation, referred to as the "knowledge" (Newall, 1982) or "semantic" level (Pylyshyn, 1999) (p. 486)
>
> Behavior may be explained by reference to the meanings that the person attributes to stimuli, in relation to personal goals (p. 486)
>
> Lack of conscious awareness does not imply subcortical and/or non-symbolic processing, and symbolic cognition is not obliged to be slow and deliberative (p. 489)

These beliefs are not endorsed by all cognitive scientists though. Jackendorff (1987, p. 35) states,

> In the brain, by contrast, there is far less clear-cut division between "software" and "hardware" change. If the reactivity of a synapse changes, is this a change in the "program" or "wiring"? If a neuron grows new connections, as happens at least during growth, is this a change in "program" as well as in "wiring"? And so forth. In addition, computational functions in the brain are affected by blood flow, hormonal action, and the like, which have no counterpart in computer function. Thus the brain undergoes a great deal of "hardware" change with corresponding effects on the mind. This means that ultimately it is less feasible to separate computational considerations entirely from their physical instantiation in the brain and might be expected from the computer analogy

The theoretical arguments presented below do not depend on any special form of knowledge structures/processes: I am content to proceed as if knowledge is hardware free and represented symbolically (elsewhere, I have argued that this assumption is open to challenge (McNaughton & Corr, 2008a), but for present purposes it shall suffice). To anticipant any subsequent confusion, I am explicitly *not* saying "cognition" is synonymous with conscious awareness, and nor am I assuming that cognition is always slow in operation.

Now, in terms of cybernetic control systems, these knowledge structures/processes must interface with behavioural control systems in some form in order to set the weights at critical points in the self-regulatory feedback system that choreographs behaviour. Somehow, and in some form, this is how symbolic-laden knowledge structure/processes *must* work; otherwise, they could never gain control of behavioural reactions, which we shall see below are orchestrated at a pre-conscious level.

Thus one major problem that *any* theory of cognition and behaviour must address is how knowledge level structures/processes (likened to computer "software") interface with biological structures/processes (likened to computer "hardware") of the neuroendocrine system.

Dual Process Models

The problem of how knowledge structures/processes ("software") interface (or fail to) with behaviour control systems ("hardware") is a real one, as evidenced by the plethora of dual-process models in the literature (for a review, see Carver, 2005). As noted by Toates (1998, 2006), standard psychology textbooks continue to contrast "learning theories" and "cognitive theories"; and this approach follows the long-fought territorial battles between stimulus-response (S-R) theorists (e.g. Skinner), who argued for automatic bonds between eliciting stimuli and responses, and cognitive theorists (e.g. Tolman), who argued for intervening variables between stimuli and responses entailing some form of knowledge structure/process.

The necessity of assuming (at least) two relatively autonomous systems further suggests that evolution had to negotiate conflicting demands; that is, how to achieve adaptive "fast and dirty" behavioural responses, especially in defensive reactions that require reflex-like reactions, as well as "slow and clean" behavioural responses that require deliberate and controlled cognitive processes (for example, as seen in reflective cognition).

Most dual-process models contain some combination of the following features.

1. *Reflexive*: fast, coarse-grained, automatic, ballistic (implicit/procedural learning), and pre/non-conscious.
2. *Reflective*: slow, fine-grained, deliberative, controlled (explicit/declarative learning), and often open to conscious awareness.

The variety of applications of dual process models is shown in the (non-exhaustive) list below.

1. Automatic vs. controlled processing: distinction between automatic processing (unconscious, fast inflexible, parallel, effortless) and controlled processing (conscious, slow, flexible, serial, effortful).
2. Implicit and explicit memory.
3. Procedural and declarative learning.
4. Top-down (concept) processing vs. bottom-up (data) processing.
5. Fast-dirty (subcortical) and slow-refined (cortical) fear processing.
6. "Action system" (dorsal stream) and "perception system" (ventral stream).
7. Neuropsychology (e.g. "blindsight" and "touchsight").
8. Emotion literature: Zajonc–Lazarus debate (emotion triggered by stimulus features of appraisal).
9. Personality: impulsivity vs. constraint.

In terms of specific theories, the following (again non-exhaustive) list illustrates their wide application. (It is perhaps too simplistic to present reflexive and reflective as separate processes, but they do seem to be sufficiently distinct, although maybe overlapping or on a continuum, for us to enquire as to how they interface.)

1. Epstein's (1973, 1994). Rational–experiential model posits that the rational system is mostly conscious, uses logical rules, is verbal and deliberative, and slow; in contrast, the experiential system is intuitive, associative, and uses "quick and dirty" automatic processes.
2. Hirsh (1974). S-R and cognitive systems (hippocampal lesions convert animal to S-R automaton; see below Gray's, 2004, BIS-hippocampal link with consciousness).
3. Toates (1998). "On-line" (fast S-R automatic responses) and "off-line" (slow reflective deliberate responses); extended by Toates (2006) to include emotion changing the weights of "on-line processes" (e.g. background valence on the on-line startle reflex).
4. Rothbart (from the 1980s onwards; see Rothbart & Bates, 2006). Positive and negative affective systems, and "*effortful control*", which is similar to *Constraint* in Tellegen's model. *Effortful control* is concerned with attentional management and inhibitory control – this is superordinate to the affective systems in that he can exercise executive control.

5. Carver (2005). Level of control in impulsivity and constraint.
6. Metcalfe and Mischel (1999). Model comes out of the "delay of gratification" literature, relating to impulsivity vs. restraint. The "hot" system is emotional, impulsive and reflexive; the "cool" system is strategic, flexible, slower and unemotional.
7. Eisenberg (2002). Extended Rothbart's model to the regulation of emotion.
8. Rolls (1999). The first system is based on implicit stimulus-reinforcement learning that accommodates reinforcement history, current motivational state and other factors influencing the reward value of the outcome. The second, explicit route to action is explicitly language based, supported by cortical language, motor and planning areas.
9. Lieberman, Gaunt, Gilbert, and Trope (2002). Attribution model has *reflexive* and *reflective* modes of working.
10. Evans (2003). Thinking and reasoning, referring to a range of biases in logical inferences.
11. Ortony, Norman, and Revelle (2005). Model of three levels of control: reactive, routine, reflective, each with affect (feelings), motivation (needs/wants), cognition (knowledge, thought and beliefs), and behaviour (action). The reactive and routine levels are comparable to on-line and fast, reflexive system, while the reflective level is comparable to slower and more deliberate forms of cognitive control.

Velmans (1991) reviewed a large experimental literature from which he concluded that all of the following processes are capable of being, and normally are, completed pre-consciously – that is before there is any conscious awareness of what has been carried out: (a) analysis of sensory input; (b) analysis of emotion content and input; (c) phonological and semantic analysis of heard speech; (d) phonological and semantic analysis of one's own spoken words and sentences; (e) learning; (f) formation of memories; (g) choice and preparation of voluntary acts. (For a detailed discussion of the implications of these findings for consciousness studies, see Velmans, 2000.) At the point of response *preparation and execution*, Velmans is surely correct in stating that processes are pre-conscious – this is now widely accepted amongst consciousness researchers, as shown by the consensus amongst discussants (which included Velmans) at a meeting of the *British Psychological Society* Consciousness and Experiential Psychology Section (London, 22nd November, 2008).

The Lateness of Conscious Experience

The conclusions reached by Velmans' analysis of pre-conscious processing is strengthened by work on the timing of conscious experience. The importance of this work is to show that conscious awareness comes too late causally speaking to influence the process it *re*presents – this is of importance because many of the variables of interest to the differential psychologist are represented in consciousness, but we still believe that they have, in some way, causal influence on behaviour.

Since the 1950s, Benjamin Libet (1985; for a summary, see Libet, 2004) has conducted a series of experiments, which show that it takes some 200–500 ms of brain activity for consciousness to be generated: this is the "lateness" of conscious experience. Libet has conducted a variety of experiments. In some experiments, the sensory cortex of awake patients was directly stimulated (Libet, 1982) – these patients were undergoing neurosurgery during which the surgeon stimulates parts of the cortex to localise functions. In one series of studies, the somatosensory cortex was stimulated with trains of pulses – such stimulation leads to the sensory perception (e.g. being touched). What was intriguing about these studies was the finding that there appeared to be a necessary period of "neuronal adequacy", that is, some 300–500 ms of stimulation is required before consciousness is experienced – any less stimulation than this figure does not lead to conscious awareness. This period of time would suggest that complex processes are engaged in the generation of consciousness; it may also indicate that a lesser length of time does not lead to conscious awareness because the eliciting stimulus was not sufficiently important.

A number of different types of experiments were conducted to test whether, indeed, conscious awareness lags 300–500 ms behind the initial sensory stimulation. In one such experiment, Libet stimulated the skin and, then, between 200 and 500 ms later stimulated the somatosensory cortex. If skin stimulation takes 500 ms to generate consciousness, then stimulating the cortex after 200 ms should abolish the conscious experience of the touch. This is what was found.

Such findings pose a problem for any adaptive theory of consciousness because long before 300–500 ms, motor actions have already been initiated (e.g. the removal of the hand from a hot stove occurs before awareness of the hand touching the stove). In this specific case, removal of the hand is involuntary and not controlled by conscious processes. However, a further twist of these findings is that events are not experienced as if they happened 300–500 ms ago: consciousness appears to refer to what is happening *now*. Libet suggests that the conscious experience of a stimulus is "referred back in time" once neuronal adequacy has been achieved to make it *seem* as if there was no delay – however, this intriguing finding is not central to the theoretical position advanced in this chapter.

Concerning the volition of will, in later experiments, Libet explored absolute timing using conscious intentions. Briefly, the typical experiment required participants to note the instant they experienced the wish to perform a "voluntary" action (e.g. simple flexion of finger) – that is, the instant they were consciously aware of this wish to act. To record this time, participants remembered the position of a revolving spot on a cathode ray oscilloscope, which swept the periphery of a face like the second hand of a clock (one sweep took 3 s). During this time, the "readiness potential" from the motor cortex was recorded by EEG. This procedure allowed Libet to calculate the precise moment at which the participant "decided" to make the movement. Libet then compared this moment with the timing of events in their brains. He found evidence that these "conscious decisions" lagged between 350 and 400 ms behind the onset of "readiness potentials" recorded from scalp electrodes – once again, the conscious wish comes a long time *after* the brain started to initiate the action, but subjectively it does not feel this way. There are criticisms of Libet's experiments as well as his interpretation of his data (e.g. Libet, 2003; Zhu, 2003; for an overview of this, and related consciousness, literature, see Blackmore, 2003), but the basic finding of the lateness of conscious awareness has withstood attempts at refutation.

What is important for us is the puzzling finding that conscious experience comes so late after the initial stimulation, and often long after brain–behavioural actions have been initiated. Thus, any theory of consciousness needs to take account of these findings. As noted by Gray (2004, p.23),

The scandal of Libet's findings is that they show *the conscious awareness of volition to be illusory*

It would be a mistake to believe that these effects have only limited generalisability, or are oddities of the specific experimental methods employed by Libet's and others. As noted by Gray (2004), we can reduce these experimental effects to something simpler: it *must* be the case that brain events precede conscious events, including the conscious state of free-will. Such effects relate to *all* cognitions and behaviours that have a representation in conscious awareness. Now, for computational models of cognition that do not include an off-line conscious component, these findings are irrelevant; however, this possible theoretical salvage is accompanied by its own problem: such pre-conscious cognitive processes can be no different to brain–behavioural on-line processes.

In everyday life, we routinely experience these illusions of *conscious awareness of volition*. For example, braking hard to avoid hitting another car which we do (thankfully!) automatically; only hundreds of milliseconds later do we (re)experience the event in conscious awareness (we might be fooled sometimes into thinking we consciously "willed" the breaking action). A different example makes the same point more persuasively. When international tennis players are on the Centre Court at Wimbledon, they prepare their return of the ball in a completely non-conscious (i.e. on-line) fashion: the speed of the ball is simply too fast for their brains to have enough time to use conscious processing to prepare their return – certainly, their prior conscious experience of the subtle cues of their opponent's body position, etc., is important, but this conscious awareness is not directly involved in the fast, on-line behaviour needed in returning the ball. As we build the general model of behavioural control below, we might want to keep in mind this tennis player example.

The Direction of Causation

The work of Velmans, Libet and others point to a fundamental issue: we are consciously aware only *after* the brain–behavioural event – that is, on a millisecond-by-millisecond basis, the *re*presentation in conscious awareness of the behaviour to which it relates *must* lag behind the brain execution of the behaviour itself. In addition, only the *results* of the process are accessible to conscious awareness, not of how the behaviour was executed (the production of language is perhaps the most obvious example of this distinction). It is important to note that this realisation is not limited to only some mental events, but to all, even including conscious awareness, which must itself be preceded by necessary brain activation in consciousness-generating circuits.

Now, it is easy to confuse the causal processes – of which we have no direct access – with the *display* in conscious mind of their outputs. As discussed in detail below, this *re*presentation comes after the brain–behavioural processes that cause the behaviours and cognitions displayed. Yet, it is the contents of the *re*presented display that dominates our thinking – indeed, this statement runs the risk of being tautological because so much of our "thinking" is conscious. This begs the question of what are the causal cognitive processes, and how do these cognitive processes differ from more reflexive processes involved in behaviour.

A further moment's thought reveals that, at the point of preparation and excitation of a response, processing is not, and indeed cannot, be accessible to consciousness: that is, *at the very moment* of brain–behaviour execution, behaviour *must* be reflexive – and *not* influenced by simultaneous (conscious) cognitive activity, which itself only becomes accessible to consciousness hundreds of milliseconds after the brain–behavioural causal processes have happened. To deny this flow of causation requires slippage into a scientifically futile Cartesian position (see McNaughton and Corr, 2008a). We will see below that off-line conscious awareness can, and indeed does, exert an important regulatory control function on behaviour, *but not* on the behaviour it immediately *re*presents in the consciously experienced display medium.

I have already conceded that cognition can be automatic, fast, and fine; yet, much of what concerns personality psychology contains constructs that are amenable to conscious awareness; indeed, most cognitive tasks involve, at least some, conscious awareness of the task. Clearly, self-belief, meta-cognition, etc., are largely conscious. So the problem is: how do we relate reflexive and reflective processes? But note that this problem does not dissolve when we consider pre/non-conscious cognitive processes; here too, at the moment of the execution of cognitive routines, etc., everything is reflexive *even* highly sophisticated "cognitive" ones that have been previously "compiled" into brain-executable behavioural control routines.

Martians, Phantoms and Zombies

In this section, we see evidence of the fundamental construction of cognition of the external world and of our concept and experience of the "self", and the implications of this construction for individual differences and cognitive research. This material is presented in order to build the argument that there is a problem to be solved, namely, how reflexive (on-line) processes and reflective (off-line) processes interface in the control of behaviour.

Martians

If Martians were to land on Earth, fairly soon after they turned their attention to understanding human psychology, what would they have to say about the phenomenon of conscious awareness? I doubt that they would dismiss it as of no scientific importance – the behaviourist's stance – or of no causal significance – the epiphenomenalist's stance. They would surely be intrigued by it and would probably hold off final judgement until it was investigated fully. They should surely be interested in the following observations:

1. Human beings report *having* qualia (e.g. "redness" of the rose)[1];
2. Human beings report *being* conscious of outputs of cognition processes but not of the processes themselves;
3. Human beings behave *as if* conscious awareness is important to them, emphasising such constructs as:
   (a) Values
   (b) Beliefs
   (c) Meta-cognitions
   (d) "Self"
   (e) Volition

They may also consult personality psychology books and learn that many of the concepts that dominate the thinking of psychologists involve a high degree of conscious awareness. They would also be aware of Libet's work and may, quite naturally, wonder how cognitive consciousness relates to automatic (on-line) behavioural routines, which they know precedes conscious awareness.

Martians would, in all probability, conclude that there is a problem to be solved. A great help in the Martian's scientific quest would be the lack of philosophical baggage concerning venerable debates over the mind–body problem, which has been taken place historically within a religious or quasi-religious context. Being good scientists, they might look for a biological solution to the "problem of consciousness" – and that is where we too might look.

In the case of phantoms, we are here less concerned with ghostly apparitions than with the neurological variety. We often learn much from clinical neuropsychology, where we find bizarre cognitions and behaviours associated with specific neurological damage. Such conditions include: cortical colour blindness, unilateral neglect, alien hand, prosopagnosia ("face blindness"), blindsight, Capgras ("imposter") delusion, synesthesia (e.g. numbers elicit the experience of colours – it is perhaps no coincidence that the number and colour representations in the brain are next to one another, causing "cross-sparking"), and phantom limb pain. What many of these conditions show is that there are multiple levels of control, and that our representation and experience of the body and external world are not always veridical – indeed, sometimes, they may not even approximate the true reality.

Phantom Limb Sensations/Pain

Phantom limb pain is of special significance. It provides us with one of the best pieces of evidence for the hypothesis that our perception of the external world is, really, constructed between our ears, and is not "out there" in the naïve sense suggested by our perceptions. Even the intact body is a

---

[1] Qualia (singular is "quale") is a term used in philosophy to denote the subjective quality of mind, referring to the way things seem to us (from the Latin "what sort" or "what kind") in the form of properties of sensory experience such as sensations (e.g., pain) and percepts (e.g., colour).

phantom – it is still real, but our subjective representation of it is not determined by its physical properties.

V. Ramachandran (2003, p. 2) notes,

> Your conscious life, in short, is nothing but an elaborate post-hoc rationalisation of things you really do for other reasons

He goes on to say (Ramachandran, 2005, p. 58),

> *Your own body* is a phantom, one that your brain has temporarily constructed purely for convenience

Although the essential construction of conscious experience is not new, its implications are widely ignored in empirical research; for this reason, it may be useful to consider another example in the form of visual illusions.

Illusory Visual Illusions

We shall see soon how such phantoms of the mind are not found only in the neurological clinic but are part-and-parcel of the normal brain–mind. In particular, we shall see that much of our conscious experience is *illusory* – by which I mean is it not what it seems. If you look at Fig. 1.1, you will probably be able to discern the edges of an *apparent* triangle; but no edges exist in terms of differences in the electromagnetic energy reflected off the page. A perhaps more remarkable demonstration of the construction of perception can be seen in Fig. 1.2. Most people (although not all) report some of wheels moving in their peripheral vision, which on a piece of paper they clearly cannot – as this example demonstrates, "seeing may be believing", but it is a false belief!

What is interesting about visual illusions is not that they show how our visual system (there are also similar auditory, olfactory and haptic examples) can be "tricked" by ambiguous stimuli, or how our system has design flaws. Instead, illusions give us some of the most obvious and direct evidence of something much more theoretically compelling: *all* of our experience is *constructed* in the brain. The crucial point here is not so much that experience is constructed in the brain – after all, this "constructivist" position is neither new nor widely challenged – but the implications of this view for understanding how different levels of behavioural control interact. In the arena of personality psychology, this point is nowhere more important than in the construction of the "self".

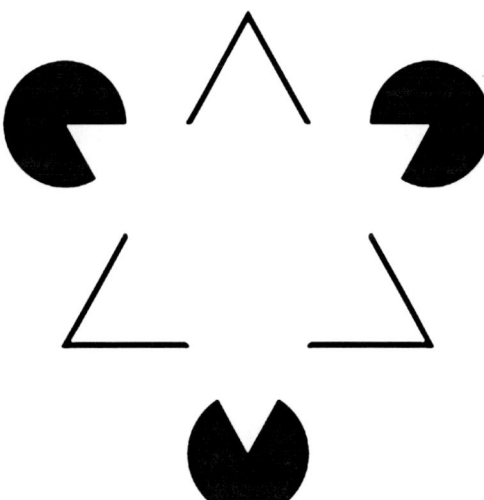

Fig. 1.1 The Kanizsa triangle showing illusory contours where contours are perceived without a luminance or colour change across the contour

Fig. 1.2 The peripheral drift illusion. Movement is experienced on the periphery, although the *circles* are not moving at all (and they cannot on a magic-free plain sheet of paper). Focusing on one particular part of the display shows that it is stationary; yet, the parts in peripheral vision seem to be moving, until focus is shifted to them. This phenomenon was discovered by Akiyoshi Kitaoka and Hiroshi Ashida, of Department of Psychology, Ritsumeikan University, Kyoto, Japan

The perception of apparent colour in the world is perhaps the best example of this fact: objects in the external world are not coloured, but they do reflect "light" energy from a very narrow part of the electromagnetic spectrum, which gets transduced into electrochemical nerve impulses, which then, somehow, lead to the subjective experience of the qualia of colour. Neurological damage shows that these qualia can be selectively lesioned by, for example, accidental poisoning – then the world may be black and white. It is also possible that other animals may "hear" the energy that we "see" as colours – Richard Dawkins hypothesises that this might be how bats "see" in the dark. Certainly, other animals are sensitive to a far wider range of the electromagnetic spectrum than us, and thereby experience a much richer perceptual world. The problem of constructing conscious awareness (e.g. "redness") from raw physical data (e.g. the patterns of electromagnetic energy reflected off an apple) is a major one for evolution to solve; however, as argued by Gray (2004), the close alignment of the *physical* world and our *psychological* construction of it ("physical–psychological correspondence"; Corr, 2006) provides perhaps the best argument for a natural selection pressure on the evolution of consciousness – if this were not the case, then indifferent "genetic drift" would lead to each of us having our own unique idiosyncratic perceptual experiences, including distance and speed perception, which would have immediate consequences for our survival (whether on the African Savannah or the busy highway).

Zombies

The concept of the zombie is a thought-device used by philosophers to allow for the possibility that there may exist people who look, sound and behave like you and I, but who are completely unconscious – that is, they have no subjective experience of the external world and nor of themselves within that world (they would resemble, in psychological terms, current-day "mindless" robots).[2] Our ignorance of consciousness is so great we do not even know whether zombies could, or indeed do, exist.

But hold on for one moment. As a matter of empirical fact, we know that they do exist, at least to some extent: all of us are part-zombie. Much of our behaviour is controlled by nonconscious processes of which we remain blissfully unaware (e.g. speech production, and the "action" visual system that is intact in consciously blind "blindsight" patients; see Weiskrantz, 1986). I am part-zombie in writing these words, and you are part-zombie in reading them: I know what I want to say to you in this chapter (I have rehearsed this in my conscious mind), but I do not have the faintest idea as to how this writing is being generated as I tap the letters on the keyboard (syntax of sentences, semantics, etc.), and even if I engaged in conscious processing, I would probably not be too much the wiser; and you do not have much idea of the brain–cognitive processes required to read and understand these words, and nor do you have to have much, or any, idea because your reflexive system is in control of the cognition/behaviour needed to read understand what I have written (they are then *re*presented in your conscious mind for reflection, analysis, criticism and judgement).

Neurological and normal zombie examples provide clear evidence of the multiple levels of behavioural control that exist, as well as showing that much of our behaviour does not even involve consciousness ("zombie processing"); but, importantly, of those behaviours that do find representation in conscious awareness, their *preparation* and *execution* is no less zombie-like.

The Problem to Be Solved

We are now in a position to state the problem to be addressed in the remainder of this chapter. If we are conscious only of the *products* of cognitive processes, and these are *re*presented *after* their causal influence, then how do off-line *reflective* processes exert any influence (if they do) on on-line *reflexive* processes? This question is central to the understanding of individual differences in cognition.

For example, we may assume that individual differences exist in the extent to which information is taken off-line for further (reflective) processing. As discussed below, individual differences in a behavioural inhibition system (BIS), which detects conflict between stimuli or between responses, should be expected to be closely coupled with the content of conscious awareness (e.g. threat-dominated rumination of anxious patients). Furthermore, the BIS-related contents of consciousness should be expected to influence the amount and quality of cognitive processing, for example, cognitive efficiency and semantic priming. As much of individual differences concepts are found at the off-line level (e.g. verbally expressed self-concepts), the generation of conscious awareness, from individual differences in on-line systems (e.g. the BIS), is clearly important. Later in this chapter, we will see further examples of the importance of this problem for understanding individual differences in on-line and off-line processes.

Once again, for the purpose of this argument, it does not matter whether cognition is fully conscious or not: either it is completely an on-line reflexive process – comprising "pre-compiled" automated brain–behavioural routines – or it has off-line reflective (although not necessarily conscious) qualities. The problem resides in the latter case.

---

[2] However, the zombie may think and feel that they *are* conscious: this raises the interesting possibility of what *we* non-zombies think and feel as consciousness is nothing really of the sort, but a grand illusion of the brain (for further discussion, see Corr, 2006). This possibility need not detract us from the use of the term zombie here: clearly, some of our behaviours can be shown experimentally to be zombie-like, and these stand apart from those behaviours to which we assign conscious awareness.

Recall the important conclusion reached above. At the point of execution, *all* brain–behavioural processes are controlled by the reflexive system. We can *never* be aware of the process of execution (including, of course, the execution of processes that lead to conscious awareness). Brain (reflexive) events *must* precede mind (reflective) events, *always*.

Is There Really a Problem to Be Addressed?

You may well be starting to wonder whether there is a problem at all and that, to the extent that there is one, it is more apparent than real. Presenting the contents of this chapter at various gatherings of academic psychologists has convinced me that the issues raised are not easily appreciated – indeed, they are typically not even acknowledged. Among many psychologists – and certainly amongst the vast majority of the general population who hold explicitly Cartesian views of the mind–body relationship – there is still the sense that consciousness, especially free-will expressed in consciousness, is in charge of the behaviour to which it immediately relates. Naively, we think: "I'm thirsty, so I shall go to get water". The causal chain runs in order of: recognition of some bodily state ("thirsty"), free-will to address state ("I"), and behaviour to achieve this end-goal ("get water"). This is how the causal chain of events *appears* to us. To argue against this perceived chain of events is deeply upsetting to the naïve observer, and equally discommoding to the many psychologists who still, albeit tacitly, adopt a Cartesian view of the mind–body, or at least believe that such argument is simply irrelevant to the day-to-day business of differential or cognitive psychology.

Other researchers have noted a similar reluctance to accept the causal priority of pre-conscious events. For example, in relation to action (dorsal stream) and perception (ventral stream) visual systems, Goodale and Milner (2006, p. 663) note,

> The most difficult aspect of our ideas for many people to accept has been the notion that what we are consciously seeing is not what is in direct control of our visually guided actions. The idea seems to fly in the face of common sense. After all our actions are themselves (usually) voluntary, apparently under the direct control of the will; and the will seems intuitively to be governed by what we consciously experience. So when we claimed that a visual illusion of object size (the Ebbinghaus illusion) did not deceive the hand when people reached out to pick up objects that appeared to be larger or smaller that they really were, vision scientists around the world embarked on a series of experiments to prove that this could not possibly be true

This is not surprising at all. We all find it difficult to abandon beliefs about the world when our beliefs seem to be based on "fact" – "I look at the world and I see that it is coloured!" We also have to contend with the realisation that our beliefs, etc., are, themselves, the product of off-line processes and, as such, do not provide a veridical reflection of the external (or internal) world. Although not of central concern to this chapter, the finding of Libet that conscious experience is back-dated to the brain initiation of cognition/behaviour further strengthens the illusion that our experience is very real in a naïve causal sense.

The Function of Consciousness and Its Role in Cognition

In this section, I sketch a model of the functions of conscious awareness, and then in later sections show how this model can be put to use in explaining the role of individual differences in behaviour and cognition.

To start with, it is somewhat surprising that the nature of consciousness is all too rarely discussed alongside individual differences research. However, this is not unique to the field of individual differences as the problems of consciousness, especially those that seem so scientifically intractable, have, at least until the recent past, been largely ignored by psychology in general – until not too recently, even considering this subject was seen as sign of some kind of (never stated) epistemological flaw in one's thought processes. We are, therefore, fortunate that Jeffrey Gray's (2004) last book, *Consciousness: Creeping up on the Hard Problem*, addressed the problems of consciousness. His work is important for psychology in general – especially the problem of the relationship between systems controlling behaviour and conscious awareness – as well as for understanding individual differences in cognition.

First, Gray does not offer an account of the "Hard Problem" (Chalmers, 1995), which is, the *why* and *how* of conscious experience, especially how the brain *generates* conscious awareness. He instead addresses the *function* of consciousness: what is it *for* and *how* it is implemented?

The data of Libet, summarised above, shows that conscious awareness of emotion, volition, behaviour, etc., does not play any direct (i.e. immediately proximal) role in the brain–behavioural routines *to which they refer* – but we shall shortly see it does exert causal (distal) effects on *subsequent* behaviour.

Gray's (2004) model of consciousness posits three linked functions.

1. It contains a model of the relatively enduring features of the external world; and the model is experienced as though it *is* the external world;
2. Within the framework afforded by this model, features that are particularly relevant to ongoing motor programmes or which depart from expectation are monitored and emphasised;
3. Within the framework of the model, the controlled variables and set-points of the brain's unconscious servomechanisms can be juxtaposed, combined and modified; in this way, error can be corrected.

To understand these functions, imagine you are confronted by a dangerous snake and your fear system fires-off an automated (on-line) brain–behavioural routine (e.g. simple fleeing reaction): all this happens long (i.e. hundreds of milliseconds) before you are consciously aware of (i.e. "see" and "feel") the snake. (Charles Darwin made the point that he could not stop himself flinching from an attacking snake even though it was safely behind glass in a zoo.) It would now be highly adaptive to "replay" the immediate past in order to analyse its contents, especially at those times when the on-line fear behaviour did not achieve its goal (e.g. avoiding the snake in the first place).

Central to Gray's model of conscious awareness is a "comparator", which serves to compare actual stimuli with expected stimuli – these latter stimuli are based on "plans", and related expectations, of the future state of the world (Gray, 1982). When there is no discrepancy, and "all is going to plan", the comparator is said to be in "just checking mode"; however, when there is a mismatch between the expected and actual states of the world, then the comparator goes into "control mode". According to Gray, in this control mode, the *contents* of consciousness are generated.

This general approach is compatible with other models of consciousness, for example, Baars' (1997) theory of global workspace. Within the terms of off-line simulation of the world, working memory is important as it has the putative function of disseminating information to various modules throughout the brain – indeed, the latter is necessary in order for off-line processing to affect on-line reactions. Upon the workspace "backboard" of Baars' model, error-prone information, which has been taken off-line, is written and subjected to further processing. According to Baars, consciousness is similar to a bright spot on the theatre stage of Working Memory (WM), directed by a spotlight of attention under executive guidance (Baddeley, 1986). Continuing with this metaphor, the rest of the theatre is dark and unconscious. Gray's theory proposes *why* information is subjected to the spot-light of working memory and cognitive processing that often leads to conscious experience.

It is interesting to note that Jackendorff (1987, p. 327), when discussing language, noted,

> One possible answer to these questions [i.e., the apparent pointlessness of consciousness] is that the Privileged Representations serve as a kind of "early warning system" for comprehension: it might be crucial to have introspection processors in order to compare what is detected with what is understood, so that attention can be directed to the problematic portions of the field

Jackendorff (1987) provides an elegant explanation for the existence of conscious awareness, at least the qualia aspect of it. His "intermediate level theory" argues that the brain–mind has a fundamental problem to solve: how to organise incoming raw, physical information into cognitively meaningful categories. He contends that it is at the juncture of this data-concept boundary that qualia are generated. In this sense, there is a continuous "error" signal being generated at this boundary. One, possibly counter-intuitive, corollary of this argument is that with closer matches between data and concepts, the less conscious awareness would be generated. Although, this prediction may seem a tad fanciful, it corresponds with much of every-day life, as well as the training/learning literature: early stages of skill acquisition require slow, controlled and deliberate processes that are prone to many errors, but with practise comes fast, automated and attentionally effortless processes that are, largely, error-free (remind yourself of the cognitive effort required to learn to drive a car and how once easier it become with extended practise, which no longer involved the necessity of conscious awareness to change gears, steer, etc).

Reinforcement Sensitivity Theory

Before developing the argument for how off-line reflective processes interface with on-line reflexive processes, it would first be useful to define the two defensive systems and the one approach system that defines reinforcement sensitivity theory (RST) (Gray & McNaughton, 2000; McNaughton & Corr, 2004, 2008b), which, in the rest of this chapter, will be used to illustrate the role played by on-line processes.[3]

1. The *Fight–Flight–Freeze System* (FFFS) mediates reactions to aversive stimuli of all kinds, conditioned *and* unconditioned. It is insubstantiated by a hierarchical array of neural modules, responsible for avoidance and escape behaviours. The FFFS is associated with the emotion of fear and the associated personality trait factor of fear-proneness and avoidance, which is clinically mapped onto such disorders as phobia and panic.
2. The *Behavioural Inhibition System* (BIS) mediates the resolution of *goal conflict* in general (e.g. between BAS-approach and FFFS-avoidance), and is insubstantiated by a hierarchical array of neural modules, responsible for the inhibition of pre-potent conflicting behaviours, the engagement of risk assessment processes, and the scanning of memory and the environment to help resolve concurrent goal conflict. The BIS is associated with the emotion of anxiety and the associated personality trait factor of anxiety proneness, which maps clinically onto the classic anxiety disorders.
3. The *Behavioural Approach System* (BAS) mediates reactions to *all* appetitive stimuli, conditioned and unconditioned. This is the system that generates the emotion of "anticipatory pleasure", and hope. The associated personality comprises optimism, reward-orientation and impulsiveness, which clinically maps onto various varieties of high-risk, impulsive behaviour.

"Late Error Detector" and the Inhibition of Pre-potent Behaviour

The BIS detection of error in the cognitive/motor program, and the generation of an error-signal, leads to the interruption of automatic brain–behaviour routines ("reflexes"). The salient features of this error-triggering environment are then *re*presented (in fact, constructed in a display medium that we

---

[3]The systems of RST are not exclusively "on-line" (reflexive) as they have representations at all levels of the behavioural hierarchy. However, they embody many on-line features, especially at the lower and more primitive levels of defensive reactions.

experience in the form of conscious awareness) and subjected to careful analysis. This mechanism solves one major evolutionary problem: how to ensure that on-line automatic responses are appropriately activated – recall above, that all behaviours, *at the point of neural execution*, are on-line and reflexive. Off-line control is invoked only at critical junctures, when a definite choice has to be made, and where the continuation of automatic, on-line behavioural routines would be inappropriate (e.g. continuing to forage in a field populated by predators). (This process is similar to Libet's idea of "free won't"; that is, the interruption of already-initiated on-line program.) In terms of Gray's notion of the BIS (Gray & McNaughton, 2000; for a summary, see Corr, 2008), this off-line display medium is highly adaptive – but, as seen in clinical conditions, it can also be maladaptive. At these critical junctures, and after analysis of the display medium, cybernetic adjustments can then be made to the on-line system, such that when the same (or similar) stimulus (e.g. snake) is encountered in the future the reflexive behaviour would be more appropriate. By this mechanism, conscious awareness exerts a causal influence, but on *future* on-line behaviours ("future" in this context can be within seconds). By this mechanism, the fine bodily adjustments required by high-ranking professional tennis players are achieved (see above).

The BIS achieves this function by recursively increasing the negative valence of the goals – held in memory stores and cortical processing centres – creating the conflict, via activation of the FFFS, until resolution is achieved either in favour of FFFS avoidance/escape of, or BAS approach to, the stimuli. For this reason, BIS activation is associated with worry, rumination and the engagement of working memory resources, the contents of which are accessible to, and often come to dominate, conscious awareness.

Defensive Systems of Behaviour

We can further illustrate the problem faced by evolution in relation to defensive systems of behaviour. According to Gray and McNaughton (2000; McNaughton & Corr, 2008b), avoidance and escape behaviours are arranged according to a hierarchical system of defence, distributed across brain systems that mediate specific defensive behaviours associated with level of threat experienced, ranging from the pre-frontal cortex, at the highest level, to the periaqueductal grey, at the lowest level (see Fig. 1.3). It is a reasonable guess that the evolution of these separate systems, which in combination comprise the whole defensive system, evolved by a "rules of thumb" (ROT) approach (McNaughton & Corr, 2009), according to which separate emotions (e.g. fear, panic, etc.) may be seen as reflecting the evolution of specific neural modules to deal with specific environmental demands (e.g. flee in the face of a predator) and, as these separate systems evolved and started to work together, some form of regulatory process (e.g. when one module is active, others are inactivated) evolved. The resulting hierarchical nature of the defence system reflects the fact that simpler systems must have evolved before more complex ones, which provides a solution to the problem of conflicting action systems: the later systems evolved to have inhibitory control on lower-level systems. The inhibitory functions of consciousness seem well placed to serve this purpose.

Now, one important consequence of modifying behavioural weights attached to on-line processes is to inhibit inappropriate pre-potent responses. Automatic routines are well suited to predictable stimuli, but they are not so good for tasks requiring a departure from fixed routines (e.g. a novel task) or when automatic performance is not going to plan, which would be the case in most complex environments. The higher level (off-line) systems in the hierarchical arrangement are charged with controlling behaviours appropriate to these complex and unpredictable environments; while behaviours in more simpler and predictable environments are controlled by lower level (on-line) systems that fire-off species-specific reactions. For this reason, the higher level systems entail complex cognition, entailing modelling, planning, etc. We see this operation in Obsessional-Compulsive

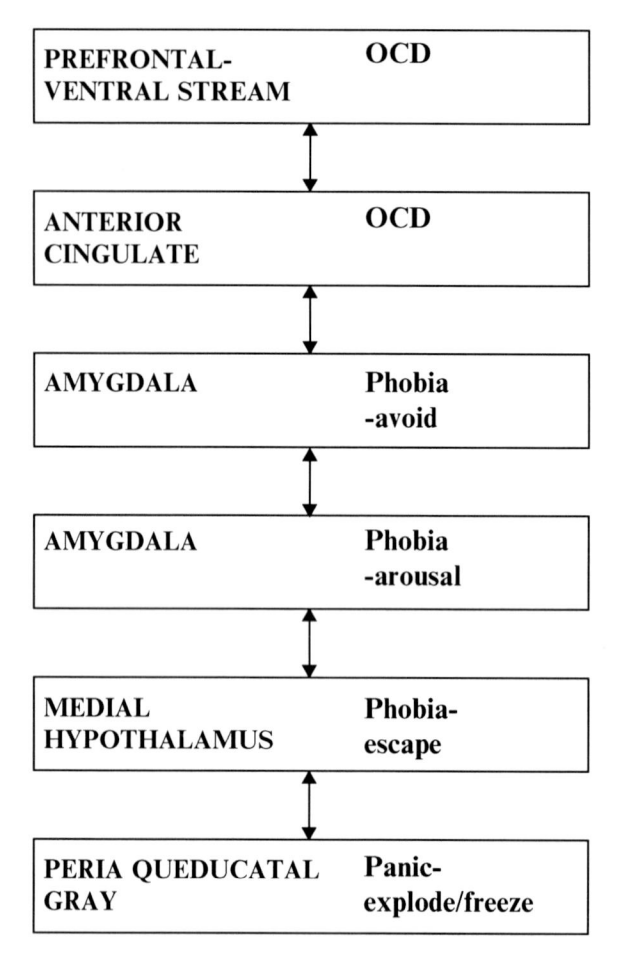

```
┌─────────────────────────┐
│ PREFRONTAL-      OCD    │
│ VENTRAL STREAM          │
└───────────▲─────────────┘
            ▼
┌─────────────────────────┐
│ ANTERIOR         OCD    │
│ CINGULATE               │
└───────────▲─────────────┘
            ▼
┌─────────────────────────┐
│ AMYGDALA       Phobia   │
│                -avoid   │
└───────────▲─────────────┘
            ▼
┌─────────────────────────┐
│ AMYGDALA       Phobia   │
│                -arousal │
└───────────▲─────────────┘
            ▼
┌─────────────────────────┐
│ MEDIAL         Phobia-  │
│ HYPOTHALAMUS   escape   │
└───────────▲─────────────┘
            ▼
┌─────────────────────────┐
│ PERIA QUEDUCATAL Panic- │
│ GRAY          explode/  │
│               freeze    │
└─────────────────────────┘
```

Fig. 1.3 The Fight–Flight–Freeze System (FFFS) comprises a hierarchical array of neural models, each relating to specific cytoarchitectonic complexity, functional level, and emotion. Complexity and sophistication increases up the hierarchy, and each module has the capacity to inhibit the action of modules below it (Modified from McNaughton and Corr, 2008b)

Disorder (OCD) where pathological worry consumes working memory and attentional resources and pervade conscious awareness. As the case of defensive systems show, much of cognitive processing must involve inhibitory functions, and the "late error detection mechanism", activated when things are not going to plan, serves this function.

Jacoby Exclusion Task

An experimental demonstration of the power of conscious awareness to inhibit pre-potent (automatic) responses is seen in the "Jacoby exclusion task" (Debner & Jacoby, 1994). In this task, words are presented either too fast for conscious recognition (i.e. 50 ms) or slow enough for recognition (i.e. 150 ms); backward masking is used to ensure these precise presentation times. In this experimental paradigm, participants are presented with the prime-word, for example:

HOUSE
They are given a stem-completion task, for example:
HOU _ _
A possible stem completion is to add S and E to form "HOUSE".

Now, the crucial manipulation in this task is the instruction to participants *not* to complete the word-stem with a prime-word. In the above example, you might complete it with the N and D to form "HOUND".

This task is trivially easy for most people, but *only* when the word is presented above the threshold of awareness (at 150 ms). What happens when the prime-word is presented *below* the threshold of consciousness? In this case, there is an inability to follow the instruction not to complete the word-stem with the presented prime-word. In fact, what happens is that the word-stem is completed *more often* with the covertly presented prime-word, HOUSE rather HOUND (or some other word completion). It, thus, seems that the default reaction to a word-prime presented covertly is to prime the word-stem, and that the generation of conscious awareness is needed to prevent this automatic priming effect – the fact that the conscious mind can prevent this priming effect demonstrates its power to inhibit pre-potent automatic reactions (in this example, a priming effect; other empirical data on this effect are discussed below).

This result points to something important about conscious awareness: *somehow*, the generation of conscious processing (in this example, by supra-threshold prime-word presentation) enables the inhibition of pre-potent (automatic) responses. This is a fundamental role for consciousness: in unfamiliar or unpredictable environments, being *unable* to stop the running of automatic (on-line) routines would be a severe disadvantage – instead of being the successful predator with a hearty meal as a result, one might be the meal of a predator.

A Model of Behavioural Control

We have now reached the stage of sketching a general model of behavioural control, sufficient to explicate the role of individual differences in cognition. As we saw above, defensive systems of FFFS and BIS may be differentiated, to some extent, in terms of on-line and off-line processes, respectively – although, as noted, there are gradations of off-line processing at higher levels of the FFFS defensive hierarchy (see Fig. 1.3) – this distinction accords with Rothbart's negative affective system (~FFFS) and effortful control (~BIS) (see above).

In a review of the literature, Toates (1998) draws attention to the fact that both on-line (S-R) and off-line (cognitive) processes are observed in human and non-human animals, and that consideration of these reflexive and reflective systems, respectively, help us to better understand normal and abnormal behaviour in general, and consciousness in particular. To these two applications, we can now add individual differences in cognition.

Toates' (1998) model comprises the following elements. A stimulus has a given strength of tendency to produce a response; that is, a stimulus has a response-eliciting potential, which varies from zero to some maximum value (this strength depends upon innate factors and learning). "Cognition" in this context refers to those processes that encode knowledge about the world in a form not tied to particular behaviours (but, as shown below, they influence such behaviours). Where there is uncertainty, novelty or a mismatch of actual against expected outcomes, behavioural control shifts from the on-line processing to off-line processing.

This model contends that some actions that can be organised at the reflexive on-line level (e.g. fleeing from a predator) can nonetheless be affected by reflective off-line processes. For example, a fear state that is experienced consciously has the capacity to sensitise the whole defensive system and, thereby, affect *subsequent* fast, automatic responses. Thus, Toates' model emphasises the cybernetic weights attached to motor programs, off-line processes modify the weights of on-line responses.

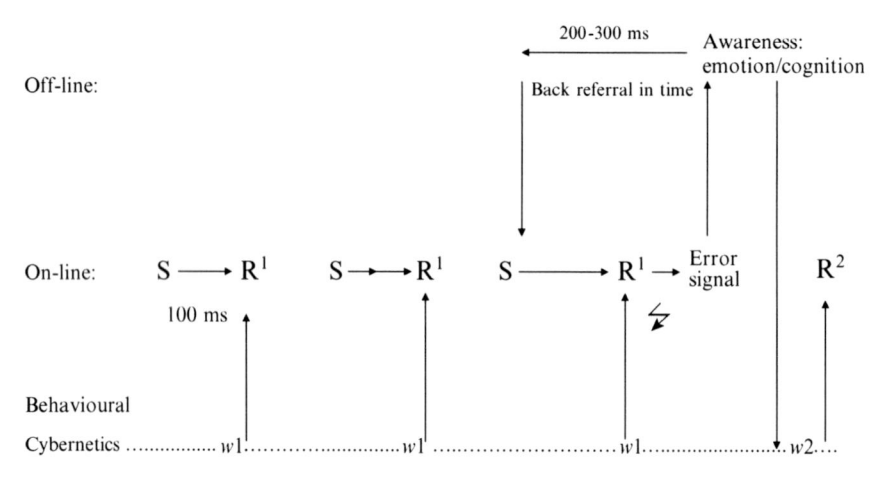

Fig. 1.4 Late error detection model of the function of consciousness. Off-line (reflective) processes monitor the success of on-line (reflexive) processes, and when "everything is going to plan", on-line processes are not interrupted. When an error signal (⚡) is detected (i.e. mismatch between *expected* and *actual* state of the world), the salient stimuli features of internal (e.g. memory) and external (both perceptual in terms of imagery, etc.; and affective, in terms of emotion) worlds are taken off-line, represented and displayed in a medium that is experienced as conscious awareness, where they are subject to fine-grained analysis – all of this can happen within hundreds of milliseconds. Although off-line conscious experience lags behind on-line processes, crucially, off-line processing can alter the cybernetic weights (e.g. $w2$) of on-line processes and, thereby exert a causal influence on *subsequent* on-line processes (R^2) when the same (or similar) stimuli/worlds are encountered. Subjectively, this process is seamless, and importantly, the lag in causal effect is obscured by "back referral in time", which provides the illusion that the experience is occurring at the same moment as the stimuli that it represents

The relevance of on-line and off-line systems can now be seen. According to this model, on-line (nonconscious) processes are modified by off-line (conscious) processes; in Toates' terminology, the weights attached to response propensities in on-line processes are adjusted on the basis of the fine-grained off-line processes. Gray (2004) also uses the terminology of cybernetics with behavioural weights attached to specific stimuli (see Corr, 2006).

Off-line processes have a causal effect on *subsequent* on-line processes; in other words, our behaviour is modified by experience: we *learn*. (Before our discussion slides blindly into a dualistic mode of thinking, it needs to be emphasised that both on-line and off-line processes are products of the brain, and that off-line processes are also prepared and executed non-consciously; however, the two levels of processing have different functions) Specifically, they differ: (a) in their temporal characteristics; (b) their level of analysis; and (c) their representation in conscious awareness (see Fig. 1.4). Thus, on-line behaviour, which *always* comes before the generation of conscious awareness, can be modified by off-line processing that brings to the fore salient features (e.g. novelty and mismatch) that attracts attention and is subject to further analysis, the outcome of which is changed cybernetic weights of the on-line system.

What-If Simulations

Consistent with the general form of Gray's (2004) model is the additional idea that consciousness allows "what-if" simulations of future behaviour, produced off-line in a virtual reality environment (e.g. imagination) that represents the important features of the real physical environment. Indeed, this function seems highly important to human beings: much of our time is spent *imagining* the likely consequences of our behaviour and making plans for the future. Such behaviours require complex computational processes, specifically involving inferences concerning the likely behaviour of other people, based on a "theory of mind". It is obvious that personality in particular relates to such simulations, and, it may be speculated that much of the "energy" for neurotic disorders comes from these off-line cognitive processes. In this regard, it is probable that variance in neuroticism will require an explanation to incorporate longer-term, off-line cognitive processes that decouple these processes from actual stimuli: thus, we can have "free-floating" anxiety and "worry about worry" – but once again, they can exert their effects only by influencing on-line processing routines.

Emotions present a special problem, because they are generated after the behaviour that is designed to deal with the emotion-provoking stimulus has been initiated – they come too late to affect the *immediate* on-line processes to which they refer (e.g. subjective sensation of pain after you have withdrawn your hand from the hot stove). This very fact might give a clue to their function, namely, hedonically to bathe off-line *re*presentations so as to simulate their significance in terms of their real world importance (e.g. the fear of a snake, the worry of the job interview, the jealousy of a sexual partner) – the distinction between motivation and emotion, which is relevant to this debate is discussed in detail elsewhere (McNaughton & Corr, 2009). According to this theoretical position, the experience of what we term "emotion" does not affect immediate on-line brain–behavioural processes to which it refers, but it can alter the cybernetic weights of on-line processes and, thereby, affect subsequent behaviour. In passing, it may be noted that this general theoretical position goes a long way to dissolving the differences between the James–Lange (behaviour → emotion) and cognitive appraisal (cognition → emotion → behaviour) positions concerning the causal role of emotion: both positions may be seen to be correct, but they operate differentially at on-line (reflexive) and off-line (reflective) processes.

Implications of Reflexive and Reflective Processes for Individual Differences in Cognition

We are now in a position to summarise the main points of the discussion.

1. Many of the variables falling under the rubric of "cognition" (especially those available to conscious awareness and involving concepts of the self) come too late in the causal chain of events to affect the behaviour they *re*present.
2. Cognition need not involve conscious awareness, but then this form of "cognition" (e.g. priming) does not differ in fundamental respects from "on-line" reflexive behaviour (it may still be relatively complex, e.g. language comprehension) – in this way, pre/non-conscious cognition does not pose a problem for the model presented here of individual differences in cognition (but it must be stripped of any "late" concepts involving consciousness).
3. In relation to point 2, we may ask:
   (a) To what extent are beliefs, values, intentions, etc. on-line and to the extent that they are off-line.
   (b) If such beliefs, values and intentions are, indeed, on-line and reflexive, then how can they differ, in fundamental terms, from on-line reflexive "biological" processes (e.g. basic defensive reactions, as discussed above?). At this point of synthesis, "biological" and "cognitive" levels collapse to a single on-line process; and as such, our only problem remains to show how *conscious* cognition (off-line) relates to on-line processes.
4. *All* behaviour, at the moment of preparation and execution, is the result of on-line reflexive processes, but *future instances* of these behaviours may be modified by off-line reflective (cognitive conscious) processes by changes in on-line cybernetic weights.
5. According to this model, reflexive and reflective processes serve very different functions, are compatible, and need to be integrated into a unified general theory of behavioural control.

Some Implications

Some interesting conclusions, with practical applications, flow from a serious consideration of the separate and joint roles of reflexive and reflective processes.

First, we could have all the "will" (i.e. conscious desire) in the world to behave in a certain way (e.g. dieting), but this "will" can only translate into actual behaviour if it interfaces with on-line systems that are responsible for priming effects of by hunger, desire, etc.

Secondly, in the case of emotional engagement and expression, we may see a dysfunction of regulation in mood disorders, where on-line defensive reactions are difficult to stop or inhibit (e.g. violent rage) – drugs may directly inhibit these on-line processes, but off-line talk therapy (e.g. cognitive–behavioural therapy, which usually has an on-line behaviour component) would have the power to modify the cybernetic weights of the on-line system. This process distinction is consistent with the commonly found gap between counter-productive behaviour and the conscious desire not to engage in such behaviour.

Thirdly, there may be an insufficient lack of representation in off-line processes, leading to hard-to-stop counter-productive behaviour. For example, smoking may be difficult to stop because there is more representation in on-line processes than off-line ones; and the same would be true for most forms of drug dependence.

Fourthly, in psychiatry, we often witness the breakdown in the normal regulation of on-line and off-line systems, with material prematurely entering off-line consciousness where it may be experienced (i.e. qualia are produced) as delusions and hallucinations, as seen in the case of schizophrenia. This example points to the aberrations seen when on-line material, inappropriately, is taken off line for conscious processing. We also see this aberrant process in the many varieties of neurotic disorder.

Empirical Evidence

There has been a paucity of evidence directly addressing individual differences in how on-line and off-line processes interface. One intriguing finding, from the clinical literature, was reported by Jermann, Van der Linden, Adam, Ceschi, and Perroud (2005). These authors noted that memory deficits linked to depression are well-established, including impairments in situations that require conscious recollection of an (explicit) episode, whereas implicit memory task performance is, relatively, spared. This distinction suggests that depressed patients are impaired in their ability to use effortful (conscious) processing (both encoding and retrieval) – their automatic processes are intact. Using the Process Dissociation Procedure (PDP; Jacoby, Toth, & Yonelinas, 1993) – which enables a distinction to be made between automatic (via familiarity judgments) and controlled (via recollection data) processing (all stimuli presented above perceptual threshold) – this study employed inclusion instructions (i.e. complete the word-stem with the prime-word) and exclusion instructions (i.e. do not complete the word-stem with the prime-word). In the exclusion condition, controlled and automatic processes work in opposite directions, creating interference. Jermann et al. (2005) reported that clinically depressed patients, compared with normal controls, had lower estimates of controlled processing, but their automatic processes were intact. This automatic-controlled distinction may account for the impaired ability of depressed patients to inhibit, by off-line system activation, their pre-potent ruminative thoughts that, themselves, are mediated by the on-line and automatic defensive system, as discussed above in terms of RST. In passing, it is interesting to note that one of the most effective psychological treatments for depression, namely Cognitive Behavioural Therapy (CBT), is aimed at addressing the controlled level of cognitions (albeit, with an on-line, practical, components as well).

In relation to individual differences measures, several studies have addressed the automatic-controlled processing distinction. Corr (2003) reported that both the traits of psychoticism and neuroticism impaired automatic processing (i.e. the procedural learning of the sequence of stimuli) in the presence of controlled (attentional) dual-task processing, but only when the controlled task was difficult (i.e. mental arithmetic). When the controlled dual task was relatively easy (i.e. counting of nonsense syllables), only (high) psychoticism was related to impaired procedural learning. These results suggest that psychoticism, and to a lesser extent neuroticism, impairs procedural learning in the context of conscious processing, a finding which may point to why this dysfunctional automatic-controlled interface leads to the cognitive dysfunctions seen in psychoticism (e.g. impaired learning of stimulus irrelevance, as shown by latent inhibition) and neuroticism (e.g. impaired processing of stimulus regularities, which may underlie the inability to resolve cognitive conflicts, hence producing the rumination, threat-perception, and worry that accompanies high neuroticism). These data seem to show that major factors of personality are related to individual differences in the interplay of automatic and controlled processes.

A similar study by Szymura, Śmigasiewicz and Corr (2007) lends support to the above findings. Using a divided attention task, they reported that psychoticism was related to the degree of attentional flexibility, specifically, low psychoticism individuals performed best with a regular selection rule that was predictable, whereas high psychoticism individuals performed best with a random selection rule where the presentation of stimuli was irregular. The interpretation of these data is that, with the change in the random selection rule, individuals had to detect signals that previously served as distractors and that poor cognitive inhibition provided high psychoticism individuals with a relative performance advantage (a similar performance advantage is seen in latent inhibition, where a failure to inhibit the irrelevant stimulus in phase one of the task leads to faster associative learning of the pre-exposed, irrelevant stimulus, now serving as the CS in phase two, and the US). These data show that the personality trait of psychoticism does not necessarily impair attentional performance; indeed, in this study, high psychoticism individuals performed well especially in attentional efficiency tasks that required small demands of attentional control, in dual-task conditions (at least, with slow stimulus presentation times), and where inhibition of previously presented material is a disadvantage to subsequent performance. These results are intriguing when psychoticism is seen in the light of schizophrenia research, where attentional dysfunctions loom large and where is a profound disruption of the smooth interplay of controlled and automatic processes.

The involvement of psychoticism in controlled processing is also demonstrated by Smillie, Cooper, Tharp, and Pelling (2009), who showed that psychoticism, but not extraversion or neuroticism, had involvement in the switching of an explicit rule (i.e. extra-dimensional rule shifting), as measured using an analogue of the Wisconsin Card Sorting Task (WCST), as well as in reversal of a reinforcement-contingency (i.e. reversal learning), as measured by a modified version of the Iowa Gambling Task (IGT). Specifically, high psychoticism is related to poorer rule updating in response to unannounced extra-dimensional shifts on the WCST; and, unlike low psychoticism individuals, those scoring high on this personality measure failed to show performance improvement on reversal learning on the IGT. Although, in this study, no attempt was made to contrast automatic and controlled processes, in such tasks as the WCST and IGT, automatic processes would be involved – a similar point is made by Jacoby et al. (1993) in relation to explicit and implicit memory tasks.

Clearly, further research is needed to clarify the precise role played by psychoticism in the automatic and controlled distinction, and this may prove especially informative in relation to how psychoticism relates to the schizophrenia spectrum (e.g. the impaired inhibitory processes seen in both high psychoticism subjects and patients diagnosed as having schizophrenia; see Corr, 2003). Adding a measure of cognitive consciousness to such studies, along with explicit error signals, would enable the test of the model proposed here in more rigorous terms.

Conclusions

I have highlighted what I perceive to be some fundamental problems raised by a consideration of individual differences in cognition, and proposed a, albeit tentative, solution. It was first noted that unification of psychology still has not been achieved. It is concluded that this unsatisfactory state of affairs is partly the result of these fundamental problems not being acknowledged and appreciated. Next, I defined cognition, and then related it to the plethora of dual-process models that populate the psychological literature. Discussion of these matters was in the form of scene setting. The lateness of conscious awareness was then described, and its implications outlined. Then, the implications of seeing this topic from the Martian point of view was noted; and, perhaps more convincingly, theoretical insights from clinical neuropsychology of phantoms of the mind, discussed in relation to zombie processes, pointed to two fundamental levels of processing. Jeffrey Gray's model of the functions of conscious awareness was next delineated. This model emphasised the inhibition of on-line (reflexive) pre-potent behaviours, which was illustrated in relation to basic defensive systems of personality. Lastly, a model of behavioural control was sketched, and implications of the model proffered.

The focus of this chapter has been on conscious awareness and basic defensive systems. However, it is evident that there are many individual difference variables that play important roles in the control and regulation of behaviour (e.g. intelligence), and that there are many cognitive mechanisms that play similarly important roles (e.g. working memory). In the attempt to provide a tentative solution to the major problem of how reflective (off-line consciousness) and reflexive (on-line automatic routines) interface together – or, as stated above, at least, an indication of the general form such a solution may take – I have chosen to focus on only a small number of major processes for two main reasons: the first was to show how the problem of the reflexive–reflective interface may be addressed; and the second was to take, as examples, pervasive processes of wide-ranging influence. In further development of the model here presented, it will be necessary to include additional individual differences and cognitive factors.

I started this chapter with the aim of scratching a theoretical itch, which has now been satisfied. I doubt that the many assumptions and inferences drawn in this chapter will find universal consent; however, I do hope that they provoke critical thinking, of both theoretical and empirical issues, of the complexity of relating individual differences in cognition, especially those that are represented in conscious awareness. Whether these ideas are themselves examples of off-line aberrations of thought must await further scrutiny and research.

References

Baars, B. (1997). *In the theater of consciousness: the workspace of the Mind.* New York: Oxford University Press.
Baddeley, A. (1986). *Working memory.* Oxford: Clarendon Press.
Blackmore, S. (2003). *Consciousness: an introduction.* London: Hodder and Stoughton.
Carver, C. S. (2005). Impulse and constraint: perspectives from personality psychology, convergence with theory in other areas, and potential for integration. *Personality and Social Psychology Review, 9,* 312–333.
Chalmers, D. J. (1995). Facing up to the problem of consciousness. *Journal of Consciousness Studies, 2,* 200–219.
Corr, P. J. (2003). Personality and dual-task processing: disruption of procedural learning by declarative processing. *Personality and Individual Differences, 33,* 1–25.
Corr, P. J. (2006). *Understanding biological psychology.* Oxford: Blackwell.
Corr, P. J. (2007). Personality and psychology: Hans Eysenck's unifying themes. *The Psychologist, 20,* 666–669.
Corr, P. J. (Ed.). (2008). *The reinforcement sensitivity theory of personality.* Cambridge: Cambridge University Press.
Cronbach, L. (1957). The two disciplines of scientific psychology. *American Psychologist, 12,* 671–684.
Debner, J. A., & Jacoby, L. L. (1994). Unconscious perception: attention, awareness and control. *Journal of Experimental Psychology: Learning, Memory, and Cognition, 20,* 304–317.

Dennett, D. C. (1991). *Consciousness explained*. Boston, MA: Little Brown.
Eisenberg, N. (2002). Emotion-related regulation and its relation to quality of social functioning. In W. W. Hartup & R. A. Weinberg (Eds.), *Child psychology in retrospect and prospect: the Minnesota Symposium on Child Psychology* (Vol. 32, pp. 133–171). Mahwah, NJ: Lawrence Erlbaum Associates.
Epstein, S. (1973). The self-concept revisited: or a theory of a theory. *American Psychologist, 28*, 404–416.
Epstein, S. (1994). Integration of the cognitive and psychodynamic unconscious. *American Psychologist, 49*, 709–724.
Evans, J. St B. T. (2003). In two minds: dual-process accounts of reasoning. *Trends in Cognitive Sciences, 7*, 454–459.
Eysenck, H. J. (1965). *Fact and fiction in psychology*. Middlesex: Penguin.
Eysenck, H. J. (1997). Personality and experimental psychology: the unification of psychology and the possibility of a paradigm. *Journal of Personality and Social Psychology, 73*, 1224–1237.
Goodale, M. A., & Milner, A. D. (2006). Sight unseen: two visual systems, one brain. *The Psychologist, 19*, 660–663.
Gray, J. A. (1982). *The neuropsychology of anxiety: an enquiry into the functions of the septo-hippocampal system*. Oxford: Oxford University Press.
Gray, J. A. (2004). *Consciousness: creeping up on the hard problem*. Oxford: Oxford University Press.
Gray, J. A., & McNaughton, N. (2000). *The neuropsychology of anxiety: an enquiry into the functions of the septo-hippocampal system* (2nd ed.). Oxford: Oxford University Press.
Harnish, R. M. (2002). *Minds, brains, computers: an historical introduction to the foundations of cognitive science*. Oxford: Blackwell.
Hirsh, R. (1974). The hippocampus and contextual retrieval of information from memory. *Behavioural Biology, 12*, 421–444.
Jackendorff, R. (1987). *Consciousness and the computational mind*. Cambridge, MA: MIT Press.
Jacoby, L. L. Toth, J. P. & Yonelinas, A. P. (1993). Separating conscious and unconscious influences of memory: measuring recollection. *Journal of Experimental Psychology: General, 122*, 139–154.
Jermann, F. Van der Linden, M., Adam, S., Ceschi, G., & Perroud, A. (2005). Controlled and automatic uses of memory in depressed patients: effect of retention interval lengths. *Behaviour Research and Therapy, 43*, 681–690.
Libet, B. (1982). Brain stimulation in the study of neuronal functions for conscious sensory experiences. *Human Neurobiology, 1*, 235–242.
Libet, B. (1985). Unconscious cerebral initiative and the role of conscious will in voluntary action. *Behavioral and Brain Sciences, 8*, 529–566.
Libet, B. (2003). Timing of conscious experience: reply to the 2002 commentaries on Libet's findings. *Consciousness and Cognition, 12*, 321–331.
Libet, B. (2004). *Mind time: the temporal factor in consciousness*. Cambridge, MA: Harvard University Press.
Lieberman, M. D., Gaunt, R. Gilbert, D. T., & Trope, Y. (2002). Reflection and reflexion: a social cognitive neuroscience approach to attributional inference. In M. Zanna (Ed.), *Advances in experimental social psychology* (pp. 199–249). San Diego, CA: Academic.
Matthews, G. (2008). Reinforcement sensitivity theory: a critique from cognitive science. In P. J. Corr (Ed.), *The reinforcement sensitivity theory of personality* (pp. 482–507). Cambridge: Cambridge University Press.
McNaughton, N., & Corr, P. J. (2004). A two-dimensional view of defensive systems: defensive distance and fear/anxiety. *Neuroscience and Biobehavioural Reviews, 28*, 285–305.
McNaughton, N., & Corr, P. J. (2008a). Animal cognition and human personality. In P. J. Corr (Ed.), *The reinforcement sensitivity theory of personality* (pp. 95–119). Cambridge: Cambridge University Press.
McNaughton, N., & Corr, P. J. (2008b). The neuropsychology of fear and anxiety: a foundation for Reinforcement Sensitivity Theory. In P. J. Corr (Ed.), *The reinforcement sensitivity theory of personality*. Cambridge: Cambridge University Press.
McNaughton, N., & Corr, P. J. (2009). Central theories of motivation and emotion. In G. G. Berntson & J. T. Cacioppo (Eds.), *Handbook of neuroscience for the behavioural sciences* (pp. 710–773). London: Wiley.
Metcalfe, J., & Mischel, W. (1999). A hot/cool system analysis of delay of gratification: dynamics of willpower. *Psychological Review, 106*, 3–19.
Newell, A. (1982). The knowledge level. *Artificial Intelligence, 18*, 87–127.
Ortony, A. Norman, D. A., & Revelle, W. (2005). Affect and proto-affect in effective functioning. In J. M. Fellous & M. A. Arbib (Eds.), *Who needs emotions? The brain meets the machine* (pp. 95–199). New York: Oxford University Press.
Pylyshyn, Z. W. (1999). What's in your mind? In E. Lepore & Z. W. Pylyshyn (Eds.), *What is cognitive science?* Malden, MA: Blackwell.
Ramachandran, V. S. (2003). *The emerging mind*. London: Profile Books.
Ramachandran, V. S. (2005). *Phantoms in the brain*. London: Harper Collins.

Revelle, W., & Oehlberg, K. (2008). Integrating experimental and observational personality research: the contributions of Hans Eysenck. *Journal of Research in Personality, 76*, 1387–1414.

Rolls, E. T. (1999). *The brain and emotion*. Oxford: Oxford University Press.

Rothbart, M. K., & Bates, J. E. (2006). Temperament in children's development. In W. Damon, R. Lerner, & N. Eisenberg (Eds.), *Handbook of child psychology: Vol. 3, Social, emotional, and personality development* (6th ed., pp. 99–166). New York: Wiley.

Smillie, L. D., Cooper, A. J., Tharp, I. J., & Pelling, E. L. (2009). Individual differences in cognitive control: the role of psychoticism and working memory in set-shifting. *British Journal of Psychology, 100*, 629–643.

Szymura, B., Smigasiewicz, K., & Corr, P. (2007). Psychoticism and attentional flexibility. *Personality and Individual Differences, 43*, 2033–2046.

Toates, F. (1998). The interaction of cognitive and stimulus-response processes in the control of behaviour. *Neuroscience and Biobehavioral Reviews, 22*, 59–83.

Toates, F. (2006). A model of the hierarchy of behaviour, cognition, and consciousness. *Consciousness and Cognition, 15*, 75–118.

Velmans, M. (1991). Is human information processing conscious? *Behavioural and Brain Sciences, 14*, 651–726.

Velmans, M. (2000). *Understanding consciousness*. London: Routledge.

Weiskrantz, L. (1986). *Blindsight: a case study and implications*. Oxford: Oxford University Press.

Zhu, J. (2003). Reclaiming volition: an alternative interpretation of Libet's experiment. *Journal of Consciousness Studies, 10*, 61–77.

Chapter 2
Individual Differences in Cognition: New Methods for Examining the Personality-Cognition Link

William Revelle, Joshua Wilt, and Allen Rosenthal

Overview

Understanding how all people are the same, some are the same, and yet none are the same is a fundamental challenge to personality and individual differences theorists in particular and psychologists in general (Kluckhohn & Murray, 1953; Revelle, 1995). Unfortunately, there is little work that actually addresses the challenge of Kluckhohn and Murray. As is true for the rest of psychology, there is a strong trend toward fragmentation of the field of individual differences. Particularly in the United States, there is a tendency in personality and individual differences toward the lack of integration of theories of (non-cognitive) personality dimensions with individual differences in cognition. The chapters of this book are partly meant to rectify this shortcoming. We will do our part by reviewing some of the prior research on the effects of non-cognitive variables upon cognition and then introduce a new procedure, "Synthetic Aperture Personality Assessment" (SAPA) as a tool for exploring cognitive and non-cognitive aspects of personality.

Although most of the current taxonomic research in personality emphasizes three (giant) to five (big) dimensions of personality, an alternative framework is to organize personality in terms of the four fundamental aspects of human nature that have long been subjects of psychological theory. Sources and descriptions of differences in Affect, Cognition, and Desire have been studied as predictors and explanations of Behavior (the ACDs of B or, more simply, the ABCDs) since Plato at least. How people differ in what they feel, what they think, and what they want largely determines what they do. But to study the ABCDs requires studying them together rather than in isolation. The central theme of this book is the integration of individual differences in cognition with non-cognitive dimensions of personality. This is a beginning, but a full-fledged integration will require a better understanding of all aspects of the ABCDs.

The ABCDs of Personality

Personality is an abstraction used to explain consistency and coherency in an individual's pattern of Affects, Cognitions, Desires, and Behaviors. What one feels, thinks, wants, and does changes from moment to moment and from situation to situation but shows a patterning across situations and over time that may be used to recognize, describe, and even to understand a person. The task of the personality

---

W. Revelle (✉), J. Wilt, and A. Rosenthal
Department of Psychology, Northwestern University, 633 Clark Street, Evanston, IL, 60208, USA
e-mail: revelle@northwestern.edu

researcher is to identify the consistencies and differences within and between individuals (what one feels, thinks, wants, and does) and eventually to try to explain them in terms of a set of testable hypotheses (why one feels, thinks, wants, and does; Revelle, 2007).

Early Greek philosophers explained the distinction between thoughts, feelings, and desires as representing the activity of the brain, the heart, and the liver. Although this biological model is now seen as a curiosity, the triology of mind (Hilgard, 1980) still drives current psychological theory (Ortony, Norman, & Revelle, 2005). Indeed, entire subfields of psychology have organized around what we feel (consider the journal of *Emotion* and the International Society for Research on Emotion), what we think (e.g., the journal *Cognition*, the International Society for Intelligence Research and publications on cognitive science and cognitive neuroscience), and what we want (e.g., the journal *Motivation*, and the recently created Society for the Study of Motivation) as explanations of what we do. The International Society for the Study of Individual Differences includes members who study all four of the ABCDs and many who try to integrate pairs or triplets of these aspects.

In an analysis of the role of emotions in man and machine that emphasized the role of emotions in effective functioning, Ortony et al. (2005) argued that it is necessary to consider the interaction of the ABCDs at three broad levels of functioning: the *reactive*, the *routine*, and the *reflective*. Environmental cues at the *reactive* level evoke fixed action patterns, while at the *routine* level they evoke action tendencies, which in turn elicit actions. In a negative feedback loop, these actions, in turn, reduce the action tendencies that evoked them (Atkinson & Birch, 1970; Revelle & Michaels, 1976; Revelle, 1986). The *reflective* layer is a control layer for the two lower ones that monitors and steers the performance of the reactive and routine levels. This multilevel control model of the ABCDs owes much, of course, to the prior work of Broadbent (1971), MacLean and Kral (1973), Sloman, Chrisley, and Scheutz (2005) and had been proposed in a less complete form earlier (Revelle, 1993).

The ABCDs may be used as a conceptual framework for the study of a particular personality dimension, (e.g., extraversion (Wilt & Revelle, 2009) – see Table 2.1), or as a framework for integrating

Table 2.1 Using the ABCD approach to organize personality studies: the example of extraversion. Representative studies have been chosen for each of the four basic components and the six "edges" of extraversion

Component	Study	Finding
A	Lucas and Fujita (2000)	A meta-analysis of 35 studies revealed an average correlation close to .40 between extraversion and positive affect
B	Paunonen (2003)	Extraversion was positively related to alcohol consumption, parties attended, dating variety, and exercise
C	Uziel (2006)	Extraversion was related to cognitive evaluations of hypothetical events as more positive but not less negative
D	Roberts and Robins (2000)	Extraversion was related to endorsing more economic, political, and hedonistic goals
Edge	Study	Finding
A–B	Fleeson, Malanos, and Achille (2002)	Regardless of an individual's trait level of extraversion, instructions to "act extraverted" in a group discussion increased concurrent positive affect
A–C	Robinson, Meier, and Vargas (2005)	Among individuals scoring low on extraversion, quickness to categorize threatening stimuli as threatening related to experiencing negative affect in daily life
A–D	Elliot and Thrash (2002)	Scales measuring extraversion, positive affect, and approach motivation loaded together on a higher-order factor termed "approach temperament"
B–C	Lucas and Diener (2001)	Extraversion related to the cognitive interpretation of social behavior as highly rewarding under pleasant conditions
B–D	Heller, Komar, and Lee (2007)	Goals categorized as approaching positive outcomes were related to extraverted behavioral content
C–D	Lieberman and Rosenthal (2001)	Extraversion related to higher performance on the cognitive task of nonverbal decoding when individuals held conversation–maintenance goals

research across disparate fields. The four fundamental components can be analyzed separately, or as six pairwise "edges" (e.g., Affect×Cognition, Affect×Behavior, etc.), four "facets" of triples (e.g., Affect×Behavior×Cognition, etc.) or a complete integration of all four. Examples of "edge" studies that include the cognitive aspect include the effect of affective biases in cognitive appraisal (Rogers & Revelle, 1998; Weiler, 1992), the effect of cognitive representations upon behavioral variability (Klirs & Revelle, 1986), the effect of the trait of obsessiveness upon cognitive biases (Yovel, Revelle, & Mineka, 2005), and the effect of affective states upon categorization (Gasper & Clore, 2002).

Examples of Lab-Based Studies of the ABCD "Edges"

Affective Biases in Cognitive Processing

Experimental personality research as well as experimental psychopathology has long been interested in the effect of short-term (state) and long-term (trait) differences in affect on cognitive processing (Mineka & Gilboa, 1998). Indeed, a classic theory of depression associates trait/state depression with a cognitive bias toward remembering negative events (Beck & Weishaar, 1989). Many studies of anxiety use the "dot probe" task (using choice reaction time measures to a dot presented following positive, negative, or neutral cues). Using this paradigm, it is possible to show attentional biases toward or away from threat that vary as a function of state and trait anxiety (MacLeod, Rutherford, Campbell, Ebsworthy, & Holker, 2002). Trait anxiety affects the speed at which threatening faces "pop-out" of a crowd (Gilboa-Schechtman, Ben-Artzi, Jeczemien, Marom, & Hermesh, 2004) and the likelihood of categorizing faces as threatening versus neutral after exposure to punishment (Yoon & Zinbarg, 2007). The speed at which people recover from an emotional induction can be assessed by the persistence of impaired reaction times to naming the color of emotionally valenced words (Williams, Mathews, & MacLeod, 1996) following an emotion induction (Gilboa & Revelle, 1994; Gilboa-Schechtman, Revelle, & Gotlib, 2000).

Affective Versus Cognitive Processing

Many words include both semantic and affective content. Consider which phrase in the following triplet does not belong (or is least similar to the other two): drown, fall down, or swim? Drown and fall down both have a negative valence, but drown and swim are semantic associates. On a more positive note, consider hug, smile, and face. Hug and smile share positive valence, but face and smile are semantic associates. Based upon the interpretation of Gray's original Reinforcement Sensitivity Theory (Gray, 1987), Weiler (1992) showed how individual differences in sensitivity to pleasant (SPS) versus sensitivity to unpleasant stimuli (SUPS) were independent of each other (Table 2.2) and related to the tendency to classify words based upon their positive affect (sensitivity to pleasant) or negative affect (sensitivity to unpleasant). As would be expected, SPS was associated with Extraversion, Sociability, and Surgency while SUPS was related to Neuroticism (Weiler, 1992).

State and Trait Effects on Affective Versus Cognitive Processing

In a follow up of Weiler's study (Weiler, 1992), Rogers & Revelle (1998) examined the effect of mood state and personality trait on similarity in judgments of words differing on affective and semantic content. Trait extraversion and trait neuroticism interacted in judging word pairs differing

Table 2.2 Representative items from Weiler's sensitivity to pleasant and unpleasant stimuli scale. Factor loadings for the first two factors are shown

SPS	SUPS	Item
−0.56	0.02	The beauty of sunsets is greatly over-rated
−0.55	−0.06	I prefer to take my bath or shower as quickly as possible just to get it over with
−0.51	0.09	The warmth of an open fireplace does not especially sooth or calm me
0.51	0.11	When I pass by a bakery, I just love the smell of fresh baked breads and pastries
0.50	−0.04	Beautiful scenery can touch something deep and strong inside me
0.47	−0.22	I have been fascinated with the dancing of flames in a fire place
−0.45	0.12	I don't find anything exhilarating about a thunderstorm
0.44	0.05	Having my back massaged feels wonderful to me
0.18	0.52	I am always adjusting the thermostat, or wishing I could
0.15	0.49	It is very annoying to me when a radio isn't tuned quite right
0.15	0.49	I find body odor extremely offensive
0.15	0.48	I find it very disappointing when something doesn't taste as good as I thought it would
−0.05	−0.47	Bad odors have seldom bothered me
0.12	0.46	Even the smallest piece of gravel in my shoe just drives me crazy until I can get it out
−0.09	0.44	I have terrible feelings when I am not sure that I will succeed
0.31	0.42	It is important to me to get the water temperature just right when I take a bath or shower

in affective content. High levels of neuroticism were associated with judging affectively negative word pairs as more similar than affectively positive pairs, but only for high levels of extraversion. More extraverted participants judged positive word pairs as more similar than negative pairs, but only if they were low on neuroticism. State Negative Affect was associated with faster response times in categorizing negative words than positive words, even when trait extraversion and neuroticism were controlled statistically.

But stimuli need not be valenced or threatening to be affected by affective state. When judging the similarity of objects, one can use global or local characteristics to make the judgments. Induced positive affect increases the use of global cues while induced negative affect increases the use of local cues (Gasper & Clore, 2002).

Individual Differences in Cognitive Representation and Behavioral Variability

A fundamental finding from cognitive psychology is that behavior is a function not of the objective environment, but of the environment as perceived and cognitively structured. How individuals organize their views about their world (their life space) determines their behaviors in the actual world (Lewin, Adams, & Zener, 1935). As an elegant example of this concept, Wish, Deutsch and Biener (1970) found that individuals categorized nations along several independent dimensions: e.g., developed–less developed, communist–noncommunist, northern–southern. Using a program for scaling individual differences in multidimensional scaling, INDSCAL (Carroll & Arabie, 1980; Carroll & Chang, 1970), Wish et al. (1970) found that individual differences in how much these dimensions were weighted predicted attitudes toward the Viet Nam War. Those who weighted the developed–undeveloped dimension more were much more in favor of withdrawing from Viet Nam, while those who weighted the communist–non communist dimension more were in favor of continued hostilities.

At a more individual level, an INDSCAL analysis of stressful situations showed that college students reported greater consistency of behaviors between situations that they thought of as similar (based upon their personally weighted multidimensional space) rather than situations judged as similar by the entire group (Klirs & Revelle, 1986). Individual differences in breadth of cognitive processing are related to obsessive compulsive behaviors (Yovel et al., 2005). Highly obsessive individuals (as judged by self report) are much more hindered by details when asked to do a speeded classification task of large letters made up of conflicting smaller letters using the "forest-trees" task of Navon (1977).

These studies of the "edges" of the ABCDs are merely examples of the ways in which individual differences in affect, cognition, and desires affect behavior. They are all examples of what can be done in lab-based studies and are thus limited in sample size as well as generalizability. In the rest of this chapter, we consider a new technology for studying individual differences in the ABCDs that does not have this limitation.

Synthetic Aperture Personality Assessment: Using the Web for Data Collection

Studies of individual differences in cognitive and non-cognitive aspects of personality are frequently limited by the sample sizes available in the typical university research setting. Small but stable relationships are difficult to detect when one is limited to 50–100 subjects, and detecting complex relationships between multiple measures is difficult when participants are limited to short 1 or 2-h studies. Alternative procedures might involve large research groups collecting data across many research sites (e.g., the Programme for International Student Assessment – PISA), but these can be costly and time consuming to conduct. A relatively new procedure is to use web-based data collection techniques to increase the sample size both numerically as well as in breadth with little loss of validity (Fraley, 2004; Gosling, Vazire, Srivastava, & John, 2004; Skitka & Sargis, 2006). Although some very large samples are available this way (e.g., the >300,000 reported by Gosling et al.), the studies are typically limited to short questionnaires or basic cognitive tasks (Greenwald, Nosek, & Banaji, 2003).

A variation of standard web-based assessment methods is to borrow by analogy a technique used in radio and optical astronomy: Synthetic Aperture Measurement. The resolution of a telescope is limited by its diameter which may be functionally increased a great deal by combining input from multiple, linked sites into one coherent image. Effectively, a very large telescope is created by synthesizing the input of many smaller ones. A classic example in radio astronomy is the Very Large Array in Socorro, New Mexico where 27 relatively small (≈25 m) radio telescopes are spread out in a Y-shaped configuration to simulate the resolution of a 36 km telescope. The configuration is adjustable so that the telescope can either emphasize resolution (by maximizing the distance covered) or sensitivity (by concentrating the telescopes close to each other). Similar techniques are used in optical inferometry at the Keck Observatory in Hawaii with "outriggers" to supplement the main telescope.

These techniques are available for psychologists taking advantage of the internet and web browsers. Rather than combining signals from the same source using different telescopes as is done in astronomy, the structure of personality can be studied by combining the responses of many people across more items than any one person is willing to take.[1] This, not actually a new procedure for the Educational Testing Service, has long used the very large samples available when students take the SAT or GRE

---

[1] The analogy is not perfect, for in astronomy the synthetic aperture technique provides a clearer image of one object, but when done by synthesizing covariance matrices, the higher resolution is applied to the structure of the measures, rather than to any individual.

to develop new items by randomly giving small subsets of items to much smaller (but still quite large, e.g., $N \approx 1{,}000$) subsamples of students. Now, by using open source and public domain software, this procedure is available to all of us.

The basic procedure is very simple. From a large set of personality and ability items ($P > 400$), a smaller subset of items ($n \approx 60\text{--}75$) are presented to any one subject. With random sampling of the items, all possible pairs of $P*(P-1)/2$ are eventually presented. As the number of subjects grows (currently $N > 84{,}000$), each item has been given to $N*(n/P)^2$ subjects, and each pair of items has been given to subjects.

The SAPA Methodology

Item Pool

During the past century, the measurement of personality and ability has tended to be fragmented by separate groups of individuals using proprietary sets of measures. Indeed, the proprietary nature is partly seen in the choice of names for these inventories and tests: the Minnesota Multiphasic Personality Inventory, the California Personality Inventory, the Eysenck Personality Inventory/Questionnaire/Profiler, the Freiburg Personality Inventory, Guilford-Zimmerman Temperament Survey, the Hogan Personality Inventory, the Jackson Personality Research Form, the Meyers-Briggs Type Inventory, the Stanford-Binet, the Wechsler Adult Intelligence Scale, the Wechsler Intelligence Scale for Children, etc. Each of these tests was carefully developed by researcher groups, and each is protected by copyright. Although some groups allow non-profit use of the measures for minimal cost, this is the exception. Many of these inventories have similar sounding scales, but given the expense, there are a limited number of studies directly comparing the inventories (Grucza & Goldberg, 2007).

A welcome alternative to the proprietary nature of personality measurement is the International Personality Item Pool (IPIP) developed by Lewis Goldberg (1999). Including more than 2,400 items in the form of sentence stems, the IPIP collaboratory has at least 269 scales targeted at everything from achievement striving to vitality/zest and includes particular scales designed to provide public domain scales meant to be parallel to those found in at least 17 commonly used personality inventories. All of the IPIP items and the common personality inventories have been given to the same community sample in Eugene/Springfield, Oregon, and item statistics are freely available from Goldberg and his associates. Some have questioned the open and free use of the IPIP items with respect to the possibility of the public learning to fake personality tests used in employment settings. Others have worried about whether the freedom to select items will lead to fragmentation of constructs rather than the hoped-for integration (Goldberg et al., 2006).

Even more proprietary than non-cognitive personality scales and items are measures of intellectual ability. Items and scales are either under copyright or completely idiosyncratic to particular labs and usually not openly published. Finding open source measures of ability is very difficult. Thus, to create a set of open source, public domain ability items, it is necessary to develop and validate our own. The hope is that this endeavor will inspire others to add items to the basic pool. As of now, 56 ability items have been constructed by writing items to measure vocabulary, verbal and mathematical reasoning, and abstract reasoning using geometric analogies. The analogies were constructed following the principles discussed by Mulholland, Pellegrino, and Glaser (1980) and involved the varying levels of memory load by varying the number of transformations between elements of the analogy (Leon & Revelle, 1985). The geometric analogy items appear somewhat similar to items from a Raven's progressive matrix (Raven, 1989). Plans are to develop more items and add them to the total pool. Here, we report an initial validation of these items against themselves as well as against self-reported measures of scholastic ability.

Subjects

The Personality Project (http://personality-project.org) is part of an effort to increase the scientific literacy and understanding of personality theory of the general population. *The Personality Project*, and its affiliated site, *Great Ideas in Personality* which was developed lovingly by G. Scott Acton until he died, provide information about personality theory and research for the interested web surfer. The roughly 1–3,000 daily visitors to these two sites see a small notice about a web-based personality test that offers personal feedback. On the *Personality Project* this is just a single line on the first page, on the *Great Ideas* site, this is one of many tests listed in a section on personality tests.

From these 1–3,000 visitors, as well as those who come from the results of online search engines, about 100 per day visit the site http://test.personality-project.org. That is, about 36,000 people per year flow through the SAPA procedure. As discussed in reviews of web-based research (Fraley, 2004; Gosling et al., 2004; Skitka & Sargis, 2006), the participants are demographically diverse but not a representative sample of anybody other than those who want to take web-based surveys. They are 70% female, with a median age of 23 (Table 2.3). However, they are probably more diverse than participants available through any means other than an international random survey. Roughly 1/3 of the participants have completed less than 14 years of schooling, 1/3 are attending college, and 1/3 have finished college. 1/6 have completed a graduate or professional degree (Table 2.3). Although roughly 4/5 of the participants are from North America, 16 countries (representing almost 92% of the total) have more than 250 participants each (Table 2.4).

Software and Hardware

The testing site, as well as the *Personality Project* and *Great Ideas* sites, is maintained on two Apple Macintosh G4 desktop computers[2] running an open source web server application, Apache. The code for the test is written in two open source languages, PHP and HTML and makes use of a powerful

Table 2.3 Age and education statistics of the first 80,471 subjects

	All participants	Males	Females
Age			
Minimum	10	10	10
First quartile	19	19	19
Median	23	23	24
Third quartile	34	34	34
Maximum	99	99	99
Mean	27.56	27.37	27.65
10% trimmed mean	25.91	25.61	26.06
Education			
Less than 12 years	13	15	12
High school graduate	8	9	7
Some college, did not graduate	10	10	10
Currently attending college	34	32	36
College graduate	17	16	18
Graduate or professional degree	17	18	17
N	80,471	25,476	55,045

---

[2] These machines are not particularly powerful and as of this writing are three generations older than what is currently available. That is, the SAPA procedure is not computationally intensive.

Table 2.4 Although 80% of the participants are from North America, substantial numbers of participants report coming from other countries. Of the 207 countries represented, 92% of the participants come from those 16 countries with 250 or more respondents. There are 38 countries with more than 100 respondents

Country	Count	Cumulative	Percent	Cumulative %
USA	59,792	59,792	74.30	74.30
Canada	4,180	63,972	5.19	79.50
UK	2,731	66,703	3.39	82.89
Australia	2,305	69,008	2.86	85.76
India	1,169	70,177	1.45	87.21
Philippines	505	70,682	0.63	87.84
Malaysia	412	71,094	0.51	88.35
China	411	71,505	0.51	88.86
Mexico	394	71,899	0.49	89.35
Sweden	389	72,288	0.48	89.83
Germany	370	72,658	0.46	90.29
Singapore	369	73,027	0.46	90.75
Poland	289	73,316	0.36	91.11

(and also open source and free) database program, mySQL. All analyses reported are done using the open source and publicly available statistics and data analysis language R (R Development Core Team, 2007). All of the code for this project is available from the senior author.

Procedure

When a participant arrives at the first page of the SAPA personality inventory, they are given a brief welcome screen, and then asked to agree to a consent form. The next page asks some basic demographic information (age, sex, education, and country of residence). If they are from the United States, they are then asked about their ethnic identity and if they have taken either or both of the SAT and the ACT. If so, they are asked to report their SAT Verbal and Quantitative scores, and their ACT total score.[3]

Following the demographic pages, participants are given 60 personality items with a six point response format ranging from "very inaccurate" to "very accurate." For Study 3 (see below), this was then followed by 12 music preference items. For studies 3–6 and ongoing, they are then given 14 ability items.

When participants finish all of the above items, they are then given feedback on their personality scores. This feedback is adapted from that given by John Johnson on an alternative (and longer) web-based Big 5 inventory (Johnson, 2005). Scores are reported as means (on the 1–6 scale for the items) as well as percentile equivalents (estimated from earlier data). The results are presented numerically, graphically, and in paragraph form. The paragraphs distinguish between high, medium, and low scores. Participants are given a personalized URL with their scores that they are encouraged to put into their own personal web page or blog (which then entices more participants to the site).

The personality items used in the SAPA project so far mainly represent a subset of the 2,400 International Personality Item Pool (IPIP) items made available by Goldberg (1999), with a particular emphasis on those used to assess "Big 5" dimensions as well as detailed studies focusing on particular content domains. Although the ideal case would sample items at random from the entire set, it was necessary to be somewhat systematic in order to recruit participants. Each set of items includes 50

---

[3]For the first year, the questions about SAT and ACT were not given. For the first part of the second year, just total SAT was requested, but since January, 2006, all participants were asked for their SAT V and SAT Q scores.

items (sampled from 100) that were developed as markers of five personality dimensions, "the Big 5" (Goldberg, 1990; Goldberg et al., 2006), and an additional 10–20 exploratory items sampled from 300 to 400 items of current interest. Scores on the "Big 5" items are reported using paragraph descriptors developed by John Johnson at Pennsylvania State University for another web-based survey and using norms developed locally.

Analytical Techniques for SAPA Data

As is obvious from the description of the data collection, there are no participants with complete data. Thus, descriptive statistics, correlation matrices, factor analyses, cluster analyses, and regressions are based upon pairwise rather than casewise deletion of subjects with missing data. Given the sampling design, some pairs of items have far more observations than do other pairs. All structural analyses (factor analysis and regression analysis) were done on the pairwise deleted correlation matrix. Intercorrelations between scales were calculated by synthetically forming the within and between scale correlation matrices from the composites of the raw item correlation matrices. Functions were developed for the R computing environment (R Development Core Team, 2007) to do these operations on the synthetically combined data matrices. Many of these functions are available to the R user in the psych package (Revelle, 2008), available from the Comprehensive R Archive Network (CRAN) http://cran.r-project.org website. This website serves as a repository for more than 1,300 packages that have been contributed to R.

The multidimensional structure of the personality and ability items was investigated using both factor analysis and cluster analysis technique of the composite matrices. Principal Axis factor analysis was done using the factor.pa function and cluster analysis was done using the ICLUST function. The ICLUST algorithm (Revelle, 1979) has been adapted to R and is included as part of the psych package. Originally, it was developed with the specific goal of dimensional reduction of "messy" matrices such as those found with personality or ability items. The algorithm is similar to most hierarchical clustering algorithms in that it:

1. Forms a matrix of proximities (correlations).
2. Finds the most similar pair.
3. Combines this pair if the pair would be better (in terms of alpha and beta) than each part.
4. Repeats steps 2 and 3 until no pairs meet the criterion.

ICLUST differs from many clustering algorithm in that it stops clustering when the internal consistency estimates (either the α or β coefficients) fail to increase. α is an estimate of internal consistency based upon the average inter-item correlation as well as the number of items (Cronbach, 1951), β is an estimate of the worst split half reliability of a test and is an estimate of the general factor saturation of the test (Revelle, 1979). Zinbarg, Revelle, Yovel, and Li (2005) compare these two estimates with yet another estimate of the general factor saturation, ω_h (McDonald, 1999), and conclude that ω_h is superior in most cases, although β is useful as a criterion in clustering applications. Revelle & Zinbarg (2009) consider these and eight other estimates of reliability as well.

Data Cleaning

A typical problem in web-based surveys is to distinguish legitimate unique responders from people who are trying the test multiple times. Because of concerns about confidentiality, some identifying information (e.g., MAC numbers of the computer or TCP/IP numbers for the network connection) are not collected. Participants are asked if they have taken the test before, and if so, are excluded from the subsequent analysis. To detect multiple responses from the same user over a brief period of time, a random identification number is generated and stored for the duration of the connection. Only the first record of information with this unique number is processed. In addition, screening is done for similar patterns of responses across all the items (Johnson, 2005). Given the random nature of the items presented, it is unlikely that two people will get the exact same patterns of items and, if they do, even less likely that they will agree in almost all their responses. However, participants who respond to the questions, get their feedback, and then see what will happen if they change a few items that are detected this way and are excluded. Finally, participants with reported ages less than 10 or more than 100 are considered to have been deceptive and are rejected.

Personality and Ability as Assessed by the SAPA Methodology

The use of the SAPA procedure is an ongoing project of the Personality, Motivation, and Cognition Laboratory at Northwestern University. Here, we briefly outline results from seven different studies that have been conducted so far. The first four studies are relatively smaller demonstrations of the power of the SAPA technique to quickly focus on a particular target construct and will be summarized briefly. We spend considerably more time discussing the power of SAPA as shown in the last three studies.

SAPA Can Provide High Resolution of Particular Traits

Study 1: Proof of Concept: Right Wing Authoritarianism[4]

The study of the Authoritarian personality (Adorno, 1950) was particularly active immediately following World War II but fell out of favor in the 1960s and 1970s. More recently, the concept has become a topic of study in terms of Right Wing Authoritarianism–RWA, (Altemeyer, 1988) which is seen as a tendency to be hierarchical, conventional, and intolerant (Butler, 2000). Prior work has shown systematic (negative) correlations with openness and positive correlations with social dominance. As a demonstration and proof of concept of the SAPA technique, we examined whether the findings from these prior studies could be replicated in a web-based study. The answer was a clear "yes." For the first ≈2,500 participants sampled, the items of the Big 5 allowed for a recovery of five dimensions, and the pattern of correlations with RWA matched that of prior studies. RWA correlated .23 with Conscientiousness and −.33 with Openness (Revelle & Laun, 2004).

Study 2: Personality, Music Preference and Cognition[5]

The second study used the SAPA method to examine the relationship of personality dimensions with music preferences, and introduced the study of cognitive ability into the SAPA procedure. Prior work (Rentfrow & Gosling, 2003) had shown systematic differences in preferences for various musical genres. In terms of interpersonal behavior, musical preferences are one of first things people discover about each other in social interactions (Rentfrow & Gosling, 2006). Measuring musical preferences seemed to be a very logical extension of the SAPA procedure.

---

[4]Conducted as part of an honors thesis by Gregory Laun.
[5]Participants numbering 2,557 were collected as part of an honors thesis by Melissa Liebert, subsequent data have been collected as a continuing part of the SAPA project.

Sixty musical preference items were presented, representing the 14 genres included in the Short Test of Music Preferences (STOMP) developed by Rentfrow & Gosling (2003) and incorporating additional items adapted from Litle & Zuckerman (1986). 52,065 subjects responded to 12 item samples of the 60 music items. Because there were large gender differences in endorsement frequencies for some genres (e.g., women particularly liked Broadway musicals and TV soundtracks; men particularly liked heavy metal) factor and cluster analysis were done for males and females separately. As is true for all correlation or covariance matrices, determining the optimal dimensionality is more art than science. Cluster analysis solutions using ICLUST showed a single cluster for men and four clusters for women. Using the Very Simple Structure criterion (which compares goodness of fit of solutions of progressively more complex structure (Revelle & Rocklin, 1979)), it was clear that music preferences were not simple structured and that the best solution was one of complexity two for six factors. (Complexity reflects the number of non-zero loadings per item. Thus, a complexity one solution attempts to recreate the correlation matrix from a simple structure factor matrix where all except the largest loadings are set to 0. A complexity two solution sets all but the largest two to zero.) Considering complexity one solutions, only three broad factors showed substantial factor congruence across gender. These factors then broke down into more complicated solutions within gender. The three broad factors could be interpreted as representing (1) classical, folk, and jazz, (2) rock, and (3) popular/easy listening.

These three music factors were then correlated with the personality and demographic data. The classical, folk, and jazz items were most related to openness (.34), age (.30), agreeableness (.25), and education (.25). Preference for the rock items were negatively correlated with age (−.25) and positively with openness (.15). Preferences for popular and easy listening music was correlated with agreeableness (.33), gender (females preferred it more, $r=.26$), conscientiousness, (.19) and extraversion (.17). At the item level, of the 323 IPIP, ability, and music items, the single item most correlated with gender was a preference for Broadway musicals ($r=.28$).

Study 3: Measurement of Trust and Trustworthiness[6]

Trust and trustworthiness are essential elements of social interaction. It is difficult to conceive of daily life without exhibiting trust in others. The detection of cheating is important for humans as well as fish (Bshary & Grutter, 2002, 2006). To what extent are these two essential concepts represented in standard measures of personality? In a two-part study, Evans & Revelle (2007) examined the factorial structure and correlations with Big 5 measures using SAPA technology, and then validated their scales using an experimental procedure known as the Investment Game (Berg, Dickhaut, & McCabe, 1995; Bohnet & Croson, 2004). With $N=8,183$, Trust and Trustworthiness correlated highly with each other (.50) but did show differential patterns of correlations with Big 5 scales: Trust correlated positively with Agreeableness (.65), and Extraversion (.58), and negatively with Neuroticism (−.61). Trustworthiness correlated positively with Conscientiousness (.60) and Agreeableness (.62). Multiple regression showed that trust was best predicted by agreeableness and negative neuroticism while trustworthiness was predicted by agreeableness and conscientiousness.

Study 4: Measurement of Machiavellianism[7]

In a follow up study, examining the basis of trusting behavior in the Investment Game setting, the trust items from Study 3 were supplemented with items taken from Machiavellianism (Mach) scales, which are intended to measure a person's willingness to manipulate others (Paulhus & Williams, 2002).

---

[6]Conducted as part of an honors thesis by Anthony Evans.
[7]Conducted as part of an honors thesis by Samantha Holland.

With $N > 16,000$ participants, Mach items were shown to have a two dimensional structure. Factor 1 was related to the traditional definition of Mach, the tendency to manipulate and deceive others for personal gain. Factor 2 was related to the belief that the true nature of other people is basically self-serving and unethical. These factors were labeled "Inner Mach" and "Outer Mach," respectively, in order to capture the contrast between the first factor's emphasis on the self and the second factor's emphasis on others.

SAPA Can Resolve Broader Traits

The following three studies will be presented in more detail in order to illustrate how the SAPA technique can be applied in a variety of ways. The first study shows how the synthetic "telescope" can be focused to address questions pertaining purely to personality theory, while the second generalizes the technique to answer questions about cognitive ability. The last study reviews the findings concerning the overall structure of Big 5 scales as they relate to each other, to ability, and to various demographic characteristics.

Study 5: Measurement of Extraversion Facets

The higher-order trait dimension of extraversion has been identified as one of the fundamental dimensions of personality through biological and taxometric approaches (Costa & McCrae, 1992; Digman, 1990; Eysenck & Himmelweit, 1947; Eysenck, 1970, 1973; Goldberg, 1990; Norman, 1963). However, disagreements about how to best characterize the core of extraversion and its facets remain prominent in the personality psychology literature (Ashton, Lee, & Paunonen, 2002; Costa & McCrae, 1998; DeYoung, Quilty, & Peterson, 2007; Hofstee, Raad, & Goldberg, 1992; Lucas, Diener, Grob, Suh, & Shao, 2000; Watson & Clark, 1997; Wilt & Revelle, in press). One possible reason that consensus definitions for the core and facets of extraversion have not been achieved is that most items used to measure extraversion comprise a mixture of affective and behavioral components (Pytlik Zillig, Hemenover, & Dienstbier, 2002) that fail to delineate extraversion into conceptually distinct facets reflecting purely positive affect, behavioral activity, and the desire for social attention. Study 5 is an illustration of how to use SAPA methodology to construct and evaluate personality facet scales measuring positive affect, behavioral activity, and desire for social attention. We selected items that seemed to be pure measures of each distinct facet by searching through the items used to measure extraversion in the IPIP (Goldberg, 1999), which contains items targeted to measure the most commonly used extraversion scales such as the NEO instruments (Costa & McCrae, 1992), the Abridged Big-Five Circumplex (AB5C) (Hofstee et al., 1992), and the newly developed Big-Five Aspect Scale (DeYoung et al., 2007). Items used to measure each facet are shown in Table 2.5. As of this writing, over 16,000 subjects have taken these facet scales. From the synthetic correlation matrix, we evaluated the properties of the new facet scales. The facets were highly correlated with each other and each facet had high internal consistency (Table 2.5). The general factor saturation of the items was estimated by an ω_h of 0.55, indicating that a common latent variable (hypothesized as extraversion in this case) accounted for a 55% of the variance of the items (Revelle & Zinbarg, 2009; Zinbarg et al., 2005). ω_h is found by extracting a general, second order factor from the obliquely rotated first order factors, and then through a Schmid–Leiman transformation, finding the amount of item variance accounted for by that general factor. The lower order factors that emerged closely resemble the hypothesized structure of the facet scales, as items in each scale generally had their highest loading on the appropriate factor (see Table 2.5).

Table 2.5 Items measuring positive affect, behavioral activity, and desire for social attention facets and their factor loadings on three oblique factors

Facets and Items	Factor 1	Factor 2	Factor 3
Positive affect			
Laugh a lot	.80	−.11	.01
Have a lot of fun	.78	−.02	.06
Express childlike joy	.66	−.16	.17
Radiate joy	.62	.10	.21
Laugh my way through life	.60	−.06	.16
Feel that I have a lot of inner strength	.54	.26	−.21
Feel healthy and vibrant most of the time	.47	.25	.09
Have great stamina	.16	.47	−.10
Behavioral activity			
Try to lead others	−.10	.86	.13
See myself as a good leader	−.05	.84	−.05
Have leadership abilities	−.07	.78	.08
Automatically take charge	.08	.69	−.04
Can easily push myself forward	.27	.55	−.24
Have a strong personality	.03	.48	.26
Maintain high energy throughout the day	.35	.41	−.10
Am usually active and full of energy	.55	.40	−.01
Wait for my turn (R)	.34	.01	−.55
Desire for social attention			
Like to attract attention	.05	.08	.78
Demand to be the center of interest	−.02	−.08	.71
Enjoy being part of a loud crowd	.21	−.06	.71
Can't do without the company of others	.08	−.07	.55
Love large parties	.17	.23	.54
Usually like to spend my free time with people	.14	.12	.49
Boast about my virtues	−.25	.11	.43
Rarely enjoy being with people (R)	.22	.28	.39
Don't like crowded events (R)	.27	.16	.36
Am afraid to draw attention to myself (R)	.11	.29	.32
Would not enjoy a job that involves social interaction (R)	.24	.26	.26
Like to amuse others	.34	.07	.15
Act comfortably with others	.31	.32	.08

To examine the convergent and discriminant validity of the facets, we found the correlations between each facet and each Big 5 domain scale. Table 2.6 shows that the social attention facet had very high convergent and discriminant validity, as indicated by high correlations with the extraversion scale but not the other Big 5 scales. The positive affect and behavioral activity facets also had high convergent and discriminant validity, as both of these facets correlated more strongly with the extraversion domain scale than any other Big 5 domain. These results could be interpreted as meaning that the social attention facet was a better marker of extraversion than the positive affect and behavioral activity facets. However, the pattern of correlations between the extraversion facets and the Big 5 domains may be unique to the item pool used to measure extraversion facets in this study. If items were drawn from extraversion scales emphasizing affective content, such as the Multidimensional Personality Questionnaire (Tellegen, 1982) or behavioral content, such as the Eysenck Personality Inventory (Eysenck & Eysenck, 1968), it is possible that the positive affect or

Table 2.6 Extraversion facet scales and Big 5 domain scales. Number of items in each scale, scale reliabilities, and correlations between extraversion facet scales and Big 5 domain scales are shown

Scale	N	Cronbach's α	Positive affect	Behavioral activity	Desire for social attention
Positive affect	8	.84	–	–	–
Behavioral activity	9	.83	.56	–	–
Desire for social attention	13	.85	.56	.55	–
Extraversion	20	.93	.62	.72	.83
Agreeableness	20	.90	.48	.30	.35
Conscientiousness	20	.92	.22	.32	−.03
Emotional stability	20	.93	.37	.28	.08
Openness	20	.83	.30	.42	.15

behavioral activity facets would have emerged as the better markers of extraversion than the social attention facet. Summing across analyses, the new facet scales seem to be a generally good but not optimal way to measure extraversion and its distinct components. Future efforts to improve the scales should focus on raising the discriminant validity of the positive affect and behavioral activity facets and determining whether additional facets (such as a cognitive facet) should be added to the scales. The SAPA technique provides another advantage pertinent to improving scales, as it is "easy" to add and subtract items from the active item pool using PHP, allowing for increased flexibility and adaptation in scale construction.

Study 6: Public Domain Assessment of Ability

Although originally developed as an open source procedure for studying non-cognitive aspects of personality, the SAPA procedure has been applied to studying individual differences in cognitive ability. Starting in 2005, each participant was given 14 items thought to measure cognitive ability. These items were sampled in two sets of seven from a total pool of 56 items developed by Liebert (2006). The items were written to test alphanumeric pattern recognition, general knowledge, vocabulary, logical reasoning, and spatial reasoning. Example items from this set are in Table 2.5 and Fig. 2.1. In addition to these 14 items, any participant from the United States was asked if he/she had taken either the SAT or ACT exam, and if so, to report her/his scores. The hope was to be able to validate the new items against each other as well as against the (self-reported) standardized tests. Prior work has shown that self-reported SAT scores are highly correlated with actual scores, although self-reports are somewhat inflated (Kuncel, Crede, & Thomas, 2005; Mayer et al., 2007). Basic descriptive statistics for these standardized tests (Table 2.7) are remarkably similar to actual scores for college undergraduates (Mayer et al.).

For the SAPA procedure to be useful in assessing ability online, the items need to show basic psychometric properties. They need to span the difficulty range, need to correlate with each other and to correlate with known markers of ability. The results so far suggest that we were successful in all of these objectives. Item difficulties (percent correct) ranged from .15 to .96 with a mean of .58, a median of .62, and the first and third quartiles of .40 and .77. The average intercorrelation of all 56 items was .08. The average correlations with SAT, SATV, SATQ, and ACT were .12, .10, .12, and .12. All of these values are for unselected items. The results are much more promising when basic item analysis is done. Because exploratory work suggested that 1 parameter (Rasch) or 2 parameter Item Response Theory estimates (Embretson & Reise, 2000) were not particularly better than simple sum scores, we report the sum scores analysis.

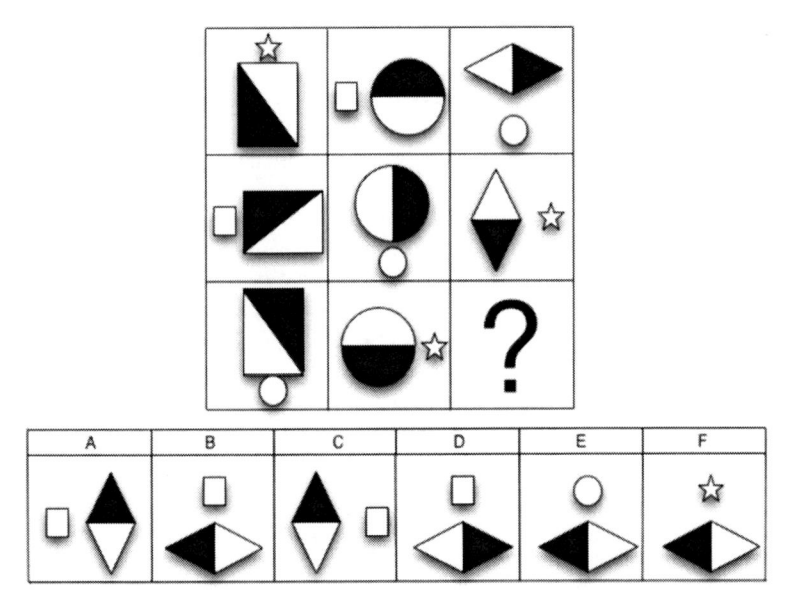

Fig. 2.1 An example of a geometric reasoning problem. Each problem differs in the number of elements and number of transformations per element. The participant is to choose the response that replaces the ?

Table 2.7 Descriptive statistics for the self-reported SAT, SATV, SATQ, and ACT

	N	Mean	Sd	Median
All participants				
SAT	3,378	1,194	215	1,200
SATV	10,987	613	110	620
SATQ	10,852	606	112	610
ACT	16,020	25.6	5.0	26
Males				
SAT	1,357	1,214	223	1,210
SATV	4,285	613	111	620
SATQ	4,248	622	114	640
ACT	4,845	25.9	5.4	26
Females				
SAT	2,021	1,180	208	1,190
SATV	6,702	614	110	620
SATQ	6,604	595	109	600
ACT	11,175	25.5	4.9	26

There are a number of ways to analyze these scales. Each participant took two 7-item scales. All possible pairs of scales (i.e., 14 items each) were then given across participants. Although each person took 14 ability items, the intercorrelations of these scales cannot be found directly from the data or can be calculated synthetically. The analysis can be done at the scale level (7 or 14 items per scale) or the overall covariance structure level (56 items). For both analyses, it is possible to validate the scales or overall factor structure by using the SAT/ACT scores.

Given the exploratory status of the 56 items (see Table 2.8 for example items), we examined the structure of the entire (synthetic) correlation matrix. From prior work on the structure of ability, we expected a hierarchical structure with several correlated primaries and a higher order g factor. This structure was confirmed by using the Very Simple Structure (Revelle & Rocklin, 1979)

Table 2.8 Example ability items with the number of items presented and an estimate of internal consistency (all items were multiple choice)

Type	N	α	Example item stem
General knowledge	7	.46	Tycho Brahe was a famous:
Classification	7	.28	Please mark the word that does not match the other words
Pattern	7	.58	In the following alphanumeric series, what letter comes next?
Math reasoning	7	.63	Adam and Melissa went fly-fishing and caught a total of 32 salmon Melissa caught three times as many salmon as Adam. How many salmon did Adam catch?
Vocabulary	6	.35	The opposite of an "ambiguous" situation is a/an (blank) situation
Verbal analogy	8	.28	CLOCK is to TIME as SCALE is to?
Geometric analogy	14	.64	See Fig. 2.1

Table 2.9 The correlations of self-reported ability measures and unit weighted factor estimates. After the first ≈5,000 participants, total SAT was replaced by the two subtests (SATV and SATQ), and thus there are no cross correlations between these measures. α reliabilities are reported on the diagonal for the factor estimates. Combined reflects unit weighted scores of the best 36 items, reasoning, spatial, and verbal are unit weighted scores of the salient items on the corresponding oblique factors. The correlations between the combined score and the three factors are inflated due to item overlap. Correlations above the diagonal are corrected for attenuation. There is no correction for the reliabilities of education, age, or the SAT and ACT scores. Gender was coded 1 for M, 2 for F

	M/F	Edu	Age	SAT	SATV	SATQ	ACT	Reas	Spat	Verb	Comb
Gender	1.00	0.03	0.01	−0.08	0.01	−0.12	−0.04	−0.15	−0.09	0.16	−0.09
Education	0.03	1.00	0.45	0.02	0.11	0.09	0.12	0.35	0.25	0.03	0.23
Age	0.01	0.45	1.00	−0.04	0.04	0.01	0.12	0.24	0.09	0.03	0.09
SAT	−0.08	0.02	−0.04	1.00	NA	NA	0.65	0.48	0.32	0.13	0.31
SATV	0.01	0.11	0.04	NA	1.00	0.62	0.54	0.50	0.25	0.12	0.25
SATQ	−0.12	0.09	0.01	NA	0.62	1.00	0.57	0.50	0.38	0.10	0.36
ACT	−0.04	0.12	0.12	0.65	0.54	0.57	1.00	0.55	0.35	0.13	0.34
Reasoning	−0.13	0.30	0.21	0.41	0.43	0.43	0.47	0.73	0.75	0.43	0.77
Spatial	−0.08	0.22	0.08	0.28	0.22	0.33	0.30	0.56	0.77	0.38	1.25
Verbal	0.10	0.02	0.02	0.08	0.08	0.06	0.08	0.24	0.22	0.42	0.92
Combined	−0.08	0.27	0.15	0.37	0.34	0.40	0.41	0.84	0.88	0.45	0.83

criterion which showed a clear one factor solution for complexity one, and a three factor solution for complexity two. The ω_h value when three lower order factors were extracted was .64. The alpha value for the entire 56 items was .88, and the ω_t was .89. See Revelle & Zinbarg (2009) for the meaning of these three and other estimates of reliability. The 14 salient items on the first factor were a mix of reasoning and vocabulary items, the 18 salients on the second factor were seven alphanumeric series questions and 11 spatial analogies, and the six salients on the third factor were verbal logic items. The salient items on the g factor as extracted using either omega (38 items) or ICLUST (37 items) were chiefly a mix of items from the first two factors.

Internal structure is not enough to show the utility of these factors. Unit weighted scales were used to predict real world criteria such as education and age as well as the self-reported test scores (Table 2.9). The independent contribution of the three oblique ability factors for predicting the criteria may be seen in a set of multiple regressions (Table 2.10). It is clear that for research purposes, we can use short online ability measures to predict level of education or standardized ability measures. It is interesting that the short reasoning factor (assessed with just 14 items and an α of

2 Individual Differences in Cognition: New Methods for Examining the Personality-Cognition Link 43

Table 2.10 Regressions predicting demographic and test performance from the SAPA ability factors. Values are standardized beta weights and multiple Rs

	Gender	Education	Age	SAT	SATV	SATQ	ACT
Reasoning	−0.15	0.28	0.25	0.39	0.47	0.38	0.45
Spatial	−0.03	0.08	−0.04	0.08	−0.04	0.13	0.07
Verbal	0.14	−0.05	−0.03	−0.05	−0.02	−0.06	−0.03
Multiple R	0.19	0.32	0.22	0.43	0.44	0.46	0.48

Fig. 2.2 Using a Schmid Leiman transformation, the structure of the self reported ability tests and the web based assessment can be revealed with a common general factor as well as two orthogonal residual factors

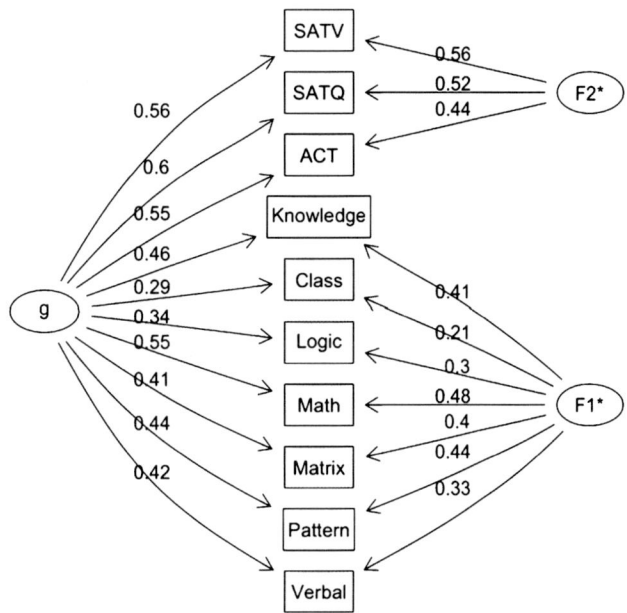

Schmid Leiman solution of ability measures

just .73), is such a good measure. The Spatial factor, although not the best predictor of any of the standardized tests, is clearly assessing a component of ability not tapped by the reasoning factor.

The hierarchical structure of the self-reported ability measures and the online ability measures can be seen graphically by plotting the results of a Schmid–Leiman transformation (Schmid & Leiman, 1957) to extract a general factor and two orthogonal residual factors (Fig. 2.2). The residual factors clearly represent method: one being self-reported ability, the second being our online (and shorter and thus less reliable) measures.

The relationships can be examined in more detail in two ways: (1) what is the effect of the demographic and ability measures on Big 5 scales (Table 2.13) and (2) what is the effect of the Big 5 on demographic and ability measures (Table 2.14). In two sets of hierarchical regressions, it is clear that the Big 5 scales are systematically related to Gender (Stability and Agreeableness), to age and education (Conscientiousness), and to intellectual ability, assessed either by our new procedures, or conventional standardized tests (Openness). But these relations go both ways, for gender, education, age, and the ability scales all could be meaningfully predicted by the Big 5 measures (Table 2.13).

Table 2.11 Hierarchical regression predicting SAPA ability factors from self-reported standardized tests. Values are standardized beta weights and multiple Rs

	Combined	Reasoning	Spatial	Verbal
Step 1				
SATV	0.12	0.27	0.00	0.07
SATQ	0.34	0.27	0.33	0.02
Multiple R	0.42	0.49	0.33	0.08
Step 2				
SATV	0.04	0.18	−0.06	0.05
SATQ	0.24	0.16	0.25	−0.01
ACT	0.25	0.29	0.20	0.07
Multiple R	0.46	0.54	0.36	0.10

Table 2.12 Correlations between the Big 5 measures, demographics, and ability measures. Reliabilities for the Big 5 are shown in the appropriate diagonal

	Extra	Stability	Cons	Agree	Open
Gender	0.07	−0.20	0.13	0.25	−0.10
Education	0.00	0.05	0.18	0.10	0.16
Age	−0.01	0.09	0.20	0.10	0.13
SAT	−0.11	0.02	−0.08	−0.14	0.25
SATV	−0.07	0.02	−0.08	−0.05	0.33
SATQ	−0.05	0.09	−0.02	−0.08	0.23
ACT	−0.05	0.04	−0.01	−0.06	0.30
Combined	−0.08	0.10	0.00	0.00	0.28
Reasoning	−0.08	0.09	−0.02	−0.03	0.30
Spatial	−0.07	0.09	0.01	0.00	0.20
Verbal	0.04	0.02	0.08	0.12	0.10
Extraversion	0.93	0.28	0.14	0.41	0.30
Stability	0.28	0.93	0.17	0.17	0.17
Conscientiousness	0.14	0.17	0.92	0.25	0.13
Agreeableness	0.41	0.17	0.25	0.90	0.21
Openness	0.30	0.17	0.13	0.21	0.83

Study 7: Integrating Cognitive and Non-cognitive Measures of Personality: The "Big 5" Meet IQ

To examine the relationship of "non-cognitive" and "cognitive" aspects of personality we correlated the Big 5 composite scores with the ability scores discussed in Study 6. We did this for the >66,000 participants with Big 5 and IQ items. Each of the Big 5 composite scales was estimated by using 20 composite items. The IQ factors were estimated by unit weighted composites of the salient items. In addition to these measures, we also examined the relationships with the demographic variables of age, gender, and education (Table 2.12). These zero order correlations show that gender (male=1, female=2) was positively correlated with Agreeableness (.25) and negatively correlated with Emotional Stability (−.20). Older and more educated participants were more Conscientious (.18 and .20) and more Open (.13 and .16). Of the Big 5, Openness was most related to the ability measures ($.23 < r < .33$). The correlation of ability with openness partly reflects the emphasis on "intellect" in the choice of the openness scales from the IPIP (Tables 2.13 and 2.14).

Table 2.13 Hierarchical regressions predicting Big 5 measures from demographic and ability measures. Values are standardized beta weights and multiple Rs

	Extra	Stability	Cons	Agree	Open
Step 1					
Gender	0.07	−0.20	0.12	0.25	−0.11
Education	0.00	0.02	0.11	0.05	0.13
Age	−0.01	0.08	0.15	0.07	0.07
Multiple R	0.07	0.22	0.26	0.27	0.20
Step 2					
Gender	0.05	−0.20	0.10	0.23	−0.08
Education	0.03	0.01	0.13	0.07	0.06
Age	−0.01	0.08	0.16	0.08	0.05
Reasoning	−0.07	0.01	−0.11	−0.07	0.23
Spatial	−0.05	0.06	0.02	0.01	0.04
Verbal	0.06	0.03	0.08	0.11	0.04
Multiple R	0.12	0.23	0.28	0.29	0.32
Step 3					
Gender	0.05	−0.19	0.11	0.23	−0.10
Education	0.03	0.01	0.13	0.07	0.07
Age	−0.01	0.08	0.16	0.08	0.05
Reasoning	−0.05	0.00	−0.09	−0.03	0.08
Spatial	−0.06	0.05	0.00	0.01	0.05
Verbal	0.06	0.03	0.09	0.10	0.05
SATV	−0.06	−0.04	−0.13	−0.02	0.24
SATQ	0.03	0.08	0.09	−0.02	−0.07
ACT	0.00	−0.02	0.02	−0.05	0.13
Multiple R	0.13	0.24	0.30	0.30	0.41

Table 2.14 Hierarchical regression predicting demographic and ability measures from the Big 5 measures. Values are standardized beta weights and multiple Rs. Note that the Giant 2 of Extraversion and Emotional Stability have the weakest effects in predicting demographic or ability measures

	Gender	Edu	Age	SAT	SATV	SATQ	ACT
Step 1							
Extraversion	0.14	−0.02	−0.04	−0.13	−0.08	−0.08	−0.07
Stability	−0.24	0.05	0.10	0.06	0.04	0.11	0.06
Multiple R	0.24	0.05	0.10	0.12	0.08	0.12	0.08
Step 2							
Extraversion	0.12	−0.03	−0.06	−0.12	−0.07	−0.08	−0.07
Stability	−0.26	0.03	0.07	0.07	0.05	0.12	0.06
Conscientiousness	0.16	0.18	0.20	−0.07	−0.08	−0.03	−0.03
Multiple R	0.28	0.18	0.22	0.14	0.11	0.12	0.08
Step 3							
Extraversion	0.06	−0.10	−0.11	−0.15	−0.16	−0.11	−0.13
Stability	−0.26	0.01	0.06	0.04	0.02	0.10	0.03
Conscientiousness	0.12	0.15	0.17	−0.07	−0.10	−0.03	−0.02
Agreeableness	0.27	0.07	0.07	−0.13	−0.05	−0.10	−0.08
Openness	−0.15	0.15	0.12	0.33	0.40	0.27	0.35
Multiple R	0.39	0.24	0.25	0.35	0.39	0.29	0.34

Summary and Conclusions

The proper study of personality integrates affect, behavior, cognition, and desires. But to study all of these aspects at the same time would seem to require large samples of participants taking many different instruments. We have an introduced an alternative procedure, Synthetic Aperture Personality Assessment, which allows us to combine data from many different individuals taking overlapping but non-identical surveys. These techniques have been used to explore structural questions about cognitive and non-cognitive aspects of personality as well as to explore the link between these two aspects of an individual. Although some of the results are merely demonstrations of the technique, others provide greater insight into the structure of cognitive ability and non-cognitive sensitivities. The goal of the SAPA project is to allow others to take advantage of these open source procedures and to proceed to build a greater understanding of personality structure and processes.

References

Adorno, T. W. (1950). *The authoritarian personality* (1st ed.). New York: Harper.
Altemeyer, B. (1988). *Enemies of freedom: understanding right-wing authoritarianism* (1st ed.). San Francisco: Jossey-Bass Publishers.
Ashton, M. C., Lee, K., & Paunonen, S. V. (2002). What is the central feature of extraversion?: social attention versus reward sensitivity. *Journal of Personality and Social Psychology, 83*(1), 245–251.
Atkinson, J. W., & Birch, D. (1970). *The dynamics of action*. New York, NY: Wiley.
Beck, A. T., & Weishaar, M. E. (1989). Cognitive therapy. In A. Freeman, K. M. Simon, L. E. Beutler, & H. Arkowitz (Eds.), *Comprehensive handbook of cognitive therapy* (pp. 21–36). New York, NY: Plenum.
Berg, J., Dickhaut, J., & McCabe, K. (1995). Trust, reciprocity, and social history. *Games and Economic Behavior, 10*(1), 122–142.
Bohnet, I., & Croson, R. (2004). Trust and trustworthiness. *Journal of Economic Behavior & Organization, 55*(4), 443–445.
Broadbent, D. (1971). *Decision and stress*. London: Academic.
Bshary, R., & Grutter, A. S. (2002). Asymmetric cheating opportunities and partner control in a cleaner fish mutualism. *Animal Behaviour, 63*(3), 547–555.
Bshary, R., & Grutter, A. S. (2006). Image scoring and cooperation in a cleaner fish mutualism. *Nature, 441*(7096), 975–978.
Butler, J. C. (2000). Personality and emotional correlates of right-wing authoritarianism. *Social Behavior and Personality, 28*(1), 1–14.
Carroll, J. D., & Arabie, P. (1980). Multidimensional scaling. *Annual Review of Psychology, 31*, 607–649.
Carroll, J. D., & Chang, J. J. (1970). Reanalysis of some color data of Helm's by INDSCAL procedure for individual differences multidimensional scaling. *Proceedings of the Annual Convention of the American Psychological Association, 5*(Pt. 1), 137–138.
Costa, P. T., & McCrae, R. R. (1992). Four ways five factors are basic. *Personality and Individual Differences, 13*(6), 653–665.
Costa, P. T., & McCrae, R. R. (1998). Six approaches to the explication of facet-level traits: examples from conscientiousness. *European Journal of Personality, 12*(2), 117–134.
Cronbach, L. J. (1951). Coefficient alpha and the internal structure of tests. *Psychometrika, 16*, 297–334.
DeYoung, C. G., Quilty, L. C., & Peterson, J. B. (2007). Between facets and domains: 10 aspects of the big five. *Journal of Personality and Social Psychology, 93*(5), 880–896.
Digman, J. M. (1990). Personality structure: emergence of the five-factor model. *Annual Review of Psychology, 41*, 417–440.
Elliot, A. J., & Thrash, T. M. (2002). Approach-avoidance motivation in personality: approach-avoidance temperaments and goals. *Journal of Personality and Social Psychology, 82*, 804–818.
Embretson, S. E., & Reise, S. P. (2000). *Item response theory for psychologists*. Mahwah, N.J.: Lawrence Erlbaum Associates.
Evans, A. M., & Revelle, W. (2007). *Survey and behavioral measurements of interpersonal trust* (unpublished).
Eysenck, H. J. (1970). *Readings in extraversion-introversion*. London: Staples Press.
Eysenck, H. J. (1973). *Eysenck on extraversion*. New York, NY: Wiley.

Eysenck, H. J., & Eysenck, S. B. G. (1968). *Manual for the eysenck personality inventory*. San Diego, CA: Educational and Industrial Testing Service.

Eysenck, H. J., & Himmelweit, H. T. (1947). *Dimensions of personality; a record of research carried out in collaboration with H.T. Himmelweit [and others]*. London: K. Paul, Trench.

Fleeson, W., Malanos, A. B., & Achille, N. M. (2002). An intraindividual process approach to the relationship between extraversion and positive affect: is acting extraverted as "good" as being extraverted? *Journal of Personality and Social Psychology, 83*(6), 1409–1422.

Fraley, R. C. (2004). *How to conduct behavioral research over the internet: a beginner's guide to HTML and CGI/Perl*. New York: Guilford Press.

Gasper, K., & Clore, G. L. (2002). Attending to the big picture: mood and global versus local processing of visual information. *Psychological Science, 13*(1), 34–40.

Gilboa, E., & Revelle, W. (1994). Personality and the structure of affective responses. In S. H. M. van Goozen, N. E. Van de Poll, & J. A. Sergeant (Eds.), *Emotions: essays on emotion theory* (pp. 135–159). Hillsdale, NJ: Lawrence Erlbaum Associates.

Gilboa-Schechtman, E., Ben-Artzi, E., Jeczemien, P., Marom, S., & Hermesh, H. (2004). Depression impairs the ability to ignore the emotional aspects of facial expressions: evidence from the garner task. *Cognition and Emotion, 18*(2), 209–231.

Gilboa-Schechtman, E., Revelle, W., & Gotlib, I. H. (2000). Stroop interference following mood induction: emotionality, mood congruence and concern relevance. *Cognitive Therapy and Research, 24*(5), 491–502.

Goldberg, L. R. (1990). An alternative "description of personality": the big-five factor structure. *Journal of Personality and Social Psychology, 59*(6), 1216–1229.

Goldberg, L. R. (1999). A broad-bandwidth, public domain, personality inventory measuring the lower-level facets of several five-factor models. In I. Mervielde, I. Deary, F. De Fruyt, & F. Ostendorf (Eds.), *Personality psychology in Europe* (Vol. 7, pp. 7–28). Tilburg, the Netherlands: Tilburg University Press.

Goldberg, L. R., Johnson, J. A., Eber, H. W., Hogan, R., Ashton, M. C., & Cloninger, C. R. (2006). The international personality item pool and the future of public-domain personality measures. *Journal of Research in Personality, 40*(1), 84–96.

Gosling, S. D., Vazire, S., Srivastava, S., & John, O. P. (2004). Should we trust web-based studies? A comparative analysis of six preconceptions about internet questionnaires. *American Psychologist, 59*(2), 93–104.

Gray, J. A. (1987). Perspectives on anxiety and impulsivity: a commentary. *Journal of Research in Personality, 21*(4), 493–509.

Greenwald, A. G., Nosek, B. A., & Banaji, M. R. (2003). Understanding and using the implicit association test: I. An improved scoring algorithm. *Journal of Personality and Social Psychology, 85*(2), 197–216.

Grucza, R. A., & Goldberg, L. R. (2007). The comparative validity of 11 modern personality inventories: predictions of behavioral acts, informant reports, and clinical indicators. *Journal of Personality Assessment, 89*(2), 167–187.

Heller, D., Komar, J., & Lee, W. B. (2007). The dynamics of personality states, goals, and well-being. *Personality and Social Psychology Bulletin, 33*(6), 898–910.

Hilgard, E. R. (1980). The trilogy of mind: cognition, affection, and conation. *Journal of the History of the Behavioral Sciences, 16*, 107–117.

Hofstee, W. K., de Raad, B., & Goldberg, L. R. (1992). Integration of the big five and circumplex approaches to trait structure. *Journal of Personality and Social Psychology, 63*(1), 146–163.

Johnson, J. A. (2005). Ascertaining the validity of individual protocols from web-based personality inventories. *Journal of Research in Personality, 39*(1), 103–129.

Klirs, E. G., & Revelle, W. (1986). Predicting variability from perceived situational similarity. *Journal of Research in Personality, 20*(1), 34–50.

Kluckhohn, C., & Murray, H. A. (1953). Personality formation: the determinants. In C. Kluckhohn, H. A. Murray, & D. M. Schneider (Eds.), *Personality in nature, society, and culture* (pp. 53–67). New York: Alfred A. Knopf.

Kuncel, N. R., Crede, M., & Thomas, L. L. (2005). The validity of self-reported grade point averages, class ranks, and test scores: a meta-analysis and review of the literature. *Review of Educational Research, 75*(1), 63–82.

Leon, M. R., & Revelle, W. (1985). Effects of anxiety on analogical reasoning: a test of three theoretical models. *Journal of Personality and Social Psychology, 49*(5), 1302–1315.

Lewin, K., Adams, D. K., & Zener, K. E. (1935). *A dynamic theory of personality* (1st ed.). New York: McGraw-Hill.

Lieberman, M. D., & Rosenthal, R. (2001). Why introverts can't always tell who likes them: multitasking and nonverbal decoding. *Journal of Personality and Social Psychology, 80*(2), 294–310.

Liebert, M. (2006). *A Public-Domain Assessment of Music Preferences as a Function of Personality and General Intelligence*. Honors Thesis. Department of Psychology, Northwestern University.

Litle, P., & Zuckerman, M. (1986). Sensation seeking and music preferences. *Personality and Individual Differences, 7*(4), 575–577.

Lucas, R. E., & Diener, E. (2001). Understanding extraverts' enjoyment of social situations: the importance of pleasantness. *Journal of Personality and Social Psychology, 81*(2), 343–356.

Lucas, R. E., Diener, E., Grob, A., Suh, E. M., & Shao, L. (2000). Cross-cultural evidence for the fundamental features of extraversion. *Journal of Personality and Social Psychology, 79*(3), 452–468.

Lucas, R. E., & Fujita, F. (2000). Factors influencing the relation between extraversion and pleasant affect. *Journal of Personality and Social Psychology, 79*(6), 1039–1056.

MacLean, P. D., & Kral, V. A. (1973). *A triune concept of the brain and behaviour*. Toronto: University of Toronto Press.

MacLeod, C., Rutherford, E., Campbell, L., Ebsworthy, G., & Holker, L. (2002). Selective attention and emotional vulnerability: assessing the causal basis of their association through the experimental manipulation of attentional bias. *Journal of Abnormal Psychology, 111*(1), 107–123.

Mayer, R. E., Stull, A. T., Campbell, J., Almeroth, K., Bimber, B., & Chun, D. (2007). Overestimation bias in self-reported SAT scores. *Educational Psychology Review, 19*(4), 443–454.

McDonald, R. P. (1999). *Test theory: a unified treatment*. Mahwah, NJ: Lawrence Erlbaum Associates.

Mineka, S., & Gilboa, E. (1998). Cognitive biases in anxiety and depression. In W. F. Flack & J. D. Laird (Eds.), *Emotions in psychopathology: theory and research* (pp. 216–228). New York, NY: Oxford University Press.

Mulholland, T. M., Pellegrino, J. W., & Glaser, R. (1980). Components of geometric analogy solution. *Cognitive Psychology, 12*(2), 252–284.

Navon, D. (1977). Forest before trees: the precedence of global features in visual perception. *Cognitive Psychology, 9*(3), 353–383.

Norman, W. T. (1963). Toward an adequate taxonomy of personality attributes: replicated factors structure in peer nomination personality ratings. *Journal of Abnormal and Social Psychology, 66*(6), 574–583.

Ortony, A., Norman, D. A., & Revelle, W. (2005). Effective functioning: a three level model of affect, motivation, cognition, and behavior. In J. Fellous & M. Arbib (Eds.), *Who needs emotions? The brain meets the machine* (pp. 173–202). New York: Oxford University Press.

Paulhus, D. L., & Williams, K. M. (2002). The dark triad of personality: narcissism, machiavellianism and psychopathy. *Journal of Research in Personality, 36*(6), 556–653.

Paunonen, S. V. (2003). Big five factors of personality and replicated predictions of behavior. *Journal of Personality and Social Psychology, 84*(2), 411–422.

Pytlik Zillig, L. M., Hemenover, S. H., & Dienstbier, R. A. (2002). What do we assess when we assess a big 5 trait? A content analysis of the affective, behavioral and cognitive processes represented in the big 5 personality inventories. *Personality and Social Psychology Bulletin, 28*(6), 847–858.

Raven, J. (1989). The Raven Progressive Matrices: a review of national norming studies and ethnic and socioeconomic variation within the united states. *Journal of Educational Measurement, 26*(1), 1–16.

R Development Core Team. (2007). *R: A language and environment for statistical computing*. Vienna, Austria: R Foundation for Statistical Computing.

Rentfrow, P. J., & Gosling, S. D. (2003). The do re mi's of everyday life: the structure and personality correlates of music preferences. *Journal of Personality and Social Psychology, 84*(6), 1236–1256.

Rentfrow, P. J., & Gosling, S. D. (2006). Message in a ballad: the role of music preferences in interpersonal perception. *Psychological Science, 17*(3), 236–242.

Revelle, W. (1979). Hierarchical cluster-analysis and the internal structure of tests. *Multivariate Behavioral Research, 14*(1), 57–74.

Revelle, W. (1986). Motivation and efficiency of cognitive performance. In D. R. Brown & J. Veroff (Eds.), *Frontiers of motivational psychology: essays in honor of J. W. Atkinson* (pp. 105–131). New York: Springer.

Revelle, W. (1993). Individual differences in personality and motivation: 'non-cognitive' determinants of cognitive performance. In A. Baddeley & L. Weiskrantz (Eds.), *Attention: selection, awareness, and control: a tribute to Donald Broadbent* (pp. 346–373). New York, NY: Clarendon Press/Oxford University Press.

Revelle, W. (1995). Personality processes. *Annual Review of Psychology, 46*, 295–328.

Revelle, W. (2007). Experimental approaches to the study of personality. In R. Robins, R. C. Fraley, & R. F. Krueger (Eds.), *Handbook of research methods in personality psychology* (pp. 37–61). New York: Guilford.

Revelle, W. (2008). *psych: procedures for personality and psychological research* (R package version 1.0-43).

Revelle, W., & Laun, G. (2004). *Synthetic aperture personality assessment: a progress report and a proposal*. Presented at the annual meeting of the Society of Multivariate Experimental Psychology.

Revelle, W., & Michaels, E. J. (1976). Theory of achievement-motivation revisited – implications of inertial tendencies. *Psychological Review, 83*(5), 394–404.

Revelle, W., & Rocklin, T. (1979). Very simple structure – alternative procedure for estimating the optimal number of interpretable factors. *Multivariate Behavioral Research, 14*(4), 403–414.

Revelle, W., & Zinbarg, R. E. (2009). Coefficients alpha, beta, omega and the glb: comments on Sijtsma. *Psychometika, 74*(1), 145–154.

Roberts, B. W., & Robins, R. W. (2000). Broad dispositions, broad aspirations: the intersection of personality traits and major life goals. *Personality and Social Psychology Bulletin, 26*(10), 1284–1296.

Robinson, M. D., Meier, B. P., & Vargas, P. T. (2005). Extraversion, threat categorizations, and negative affect: a reaction time approach to avoidance motivation. *Journal of Personality, 73*(5), 1397–1436.

Rogers, G. M., & Revelle, W. (1998). Personality, mood, and the evaluation of affective and neutral word pairs. *Journal of Personality and Social Psychology, 74*(6), 1592–1605.

Schmid, J. J., & Leiman, J. M. (1957). The development of hierarchical factor solutions. *Psychometrika, 22*(1), 83–90.

Skitka, L. J., & Sargis, E. G. (2006). The internet as psychological laboratory. *Annual Review of Psychology, 57*, 529–555.

Sloman, A., Chrisley, R., & Scheutz, M. (2005). The architectural basis of affective states and processes. In J. M. Fellous & M. A. Arbib (Eds.), *Who needs emotions? The brain meets the machine* (pp. 203–244). New York, NY: Oxford University Press.

Tellegen, A. (1982). *Brief manual for the differential personality questionnaire.* University of Minnesota.

Uziel, L. (2006). The extraverted and the neurotic glasses are of different colors. *Personality and Individual Differences, 41*(4), 745–754.

Watson, D., & Clark, L. A. (1997). Extraversion and its positive emotional core. In R. Hogan, J. Johnson, & S. Briggs (Eds.), *Handbook of personality psychology* (pp. 767–793). San Diego, CA: Academic.

Weiler, M. A. (1992). *Sensitivity to affectively valenced stimuli.* Unpublished doctoral dissertation, Northwestern University.

Williams, J. M. G., Mathews, A., & MacLeod, C. (1996). The emotional Stroop task and psychopathology. *Psychological Bulletin, 120*(1), 3–24.

Wilt, J. and Revelle W. (2009). Extraversion In M. Leary and R. H. Hoyle, (Eds.), *Handbook of Individual Dierences in Social Behavior*, chapter 3, New York, NY; Guilford Press 27–45.

Wish, M., Deutsch, M., & Biener, L. (1970). Differences in conceptual structures of nations: an exploratory study. *Journal of Personality and Social Psychology, 16*(3), 361–373.

Yoon, K. L., & Zinbarg, R. E. (2007). Threat is in the eye of the beholder: social anxiety and the interpretation of ambiguous facial expressions. *Behaviour Research and Therapy, 45*(4), 839–847.

Yovel, I., Revelle, W., & Mineka, S. (2005). Who sees trees before forest? The obsessive-compulsive style of visual attention. *Psychological Science, 16*(2), 123–129.

Zinbarg, R. E., Revelle, W., Yovel, I., & Li, W. (2005). Cronbach's alpha, Revelle's beta, and McDonald's (omega h): Their relations with each other and two alternative conceptualizations of reliability. *Psychometrika, 70*(1), 123–133.

Chapter 3
The Relationship Between Intelligence and Pavlovian Temperament Traits: The Role of Gender and Level of Intelligence

Magdalena Kaczmarek, Jan Strelau, and Agnieszka Miklewska

Introduction

From the very beginning of scientific research in psychology, the question about the relationship between intelligence and personality has been attracting attention. Chamorro-Premuzic and Furnham (2006) mentioned seven reasons that justify the interest of both these aspects of human characteristics at the same time. Both intelligence and personality traits are latent psychological constructs, which are manifested in individual differences in human behavior that can be systematically measured and observed. Individual differences in intelligence as well as in personality traits are quite stable along a life span, and to a given extent genetically determined; thus, in regard to both of them, the predictive role in educational and occupational setting is revealed. Moreover, both aspects – intelligence and personality – play a central role in the history of individual differences studies. As mentioned in our previous publications (Miklewska, Kaczmarek, & Strelau, 2006; Miklewska, Strelau, & Kaczmarek, 2004), many personality researchers, such as Thurstone, Guilford, Eysenck, and Cattell, showed interest in both intelligence and personality.

Ackerman and Heggestad (1997) indicated that Cronbach's idea of categorizing ability tests was according to measures of *maximum* performance, whereas personality tests measured *typical* performance. This crucial distinction is fundamental for separating these two characteristics in analyses. The authors drew a conclusion that focusing on maximum performance leads to underestimation of the relationships with personality as well as involves lower predictive value of intelligence understood and measured in such a way. According to Ackerman and Heggestad (1997), the solution is turning interest toward new concepts, such as typical intellectual engagement or self-assessed intelligence (Furnham & Dissou, 2007). Ackerman and Heggested claim that measure of typical intelligence enables to link intelligence with personality as well as to enhance the predictive value of intelligence both in scholastic and occupational settings. However, such ideas, including concepts of new faces of intelligence, like emotional, social or practical intelligence, meet with critical voices. For instance,

---

M. Kaczmarek
Interdisciplinary Center for Behavior-Genetic Research, University of Warsaw
Stawki 5/7, 00-183 Warsaw, Poland

J. Strelau (✉)
Faculty of Psychology, Warsaw School of Social Sciences and Humanities,
Chodakowska 19/31, 03-815, Warsaw, Poland
e-mail: jan.strelau@swps.edu.pl

A. Miklewska
Jan Długosz Academy, Częstochowa, Poland

Snow (1992) proves that intelligence as a maximum performance holds true as a predictor of the level of performance, and it has been still worth taking into account in personality research.

Although intelligence and personality traits seem to be relatively orthogonal aspects describing differences in human behavior, there is a vast body of research revealing some systematic relationships between intelligence and personality. Especially, distinction between intelligence and temperament as a part of personality can be formulated: intelligence is concerned with the content, the efficacy of behavior, whereas temperament describes the formal aspects of behavior and answers the question "how it was done".

Chamorro-Premuzic and Furnham (2006) established a theoretical framework for studying such relationships which includes two levels of description making a distinction between intelligence as performance ("measured" intelligence) and intelligence as actual cognitive ability ("actual" intelligence). The first level consists of describing relationships between personality and "measured" intelligence. Among personality variables such traits as neuroticism and extraversion are recognized. Neuroticism derived from Eysenck's PEN theory as well as from the Big Five factor model of personality seems to be related to intelligence mostly because of the overlap with test anxiety, which provides underestimation in intelligence tests. The correlations between intelligence and neuroticism in studies taken into consideration by Ackerman and Heggestad (1997) were negative and weak, and meta-analysis attributed a score of −15 for general intelligence. However, the relationship with neuroticism is still not clear. If neuroticism is related to intelligence because of this role of moderator of arousal, the relationship between neuroticism and intelligence may vary according to other factors. Such variables as age and gender may modify the perception of measurement of intelligence as a stressful situation and change the pattern of relationship between neuroticism and intelligence understood as performance. On the other hand, extraversion, which is composed of impulsivity, among others, and whose relationship with intelligence is less consistent, seems to be mostly related to the speed of reactions, including mental processes. In Ackerman and Heggestad's meta-analysis, the relationship resulted in 0.08 for general intelligence. The second level of theoretically based relationships between intelligence and personality consists of correlations of personality traits with so-called "actual" intelligence. In this case, traits that may influence the development of intelligence are conscientiousness and openness (to experience) derived from the Big Five model of personality. As Chamorro-Premuzic and Furnham (2006) argue, openness to experiences which leads to higher curiosity can stimulate the development of intelligence, whereas conscientiousness can play a compensational role toward intelligence.

Although the majority of researchers take the Big Five personality traits into account, some other traits of personality rouse interest as well (cf. Chamorro-Premuzic, Furnham, & Petrides, 2006). In our previous publications, we discussed the theoretical framework for studying relationships between intelligence and temperamental traits (Miklewska et al., 2004, 2006; Strelau, Zawadzki, & Piotrowska, 2001).

Temperament is defined as personality traits which are present since early childhood that can be observed not only in human behavior but also in animals, and refers rather to formal aspects of behavior (Strelau, 1998). Formal characteristics of behavior can be considered in terms of energetic and temporal patterns. Temperamental traits, being more or less unspecific, penetrate all kinds of behavior, whatever the content or direction of this behavior.

Summing up the discussion on the relationship between intelligence and temperament; we consider three different points of view that justify the expectation of correlations between temperament and intelligence:

1. the idea of common ground;
2. the idea of temperamental traits as factors playing a role in the development of intelligence;
3. the idea of temperamental traits as factors influencing the measurement of intelligence.

Developing the idea of common ground, we concentrated our attention on two potential bases – speed of behavior (reaction time) and chronic level of arousal. Reaction time (RT) can be treated as the component joining these two areas of investigation. In the context of the Pavlovian theory of temperament, mobility of the nervous system (MO) is a temperament trait expressed in the temporal aspects of behavior. On the other hand, there is empirical support showing that the *g* factor and the Intelligence Quotient (IQ) are negatively related to RT (Deary, 2000; Jensen, 1993). In fact, there are results showing that mobility of the nervous system is positively related to measures of intelligence (cf. Brebner & Stough, 1995; Strelau et al., 2001). For instance, in our research, MO correlates with scores in Raven's Progressive Matrices on the level of 0.13 (Miklewska et al., 2004).

The second linkage between temperament and intelligence may be explained by referring to the concepts of arousal and arousability. Individual differences in the chronic level of arousal (i.e., arousability) to which such traits as neuroticism or strength of excitation (SE) refer are expressed in the need for stimulation and ability to process stimulation. On the other hand, the level of arousal influences the efficacy of learning. Furthermore, there are some concepts of intelligence that describe this phenomenon in terms of arousal (Robinson & Behbehani, 1996). Such concepts of intelligence which refer to resource of attention and working memory draw the conclusion that ability to process stimulation may moderate, through the level of arousal, the strength of such resources (cf. Nęcka, 1997).

The idea of overlapping temperament and intelligence (hypothesis of "common ground" of existence) leads to expectations that such relationships should be universe, and refer rather to the fluid aspect of intelligence and could not be gender- or age-specific. On the other hand, if the point of departure is that ability to process information is related to the need for stimulation, some age-, gender- and level-of-intelligence-specific expectations can be formulated. The process of the development of intelligence is under the influence of the environment and depends, among other things, on individual activity. Thus, such personal characteristics which moderate the intensity and kinds of activity and moderate the environmental impact may influence this process. The influence on the development of intelligence of such temperament trait as strength of excitation can be different in different stages of age, depending on gender and can also be related to the level of potential intelligence. For instance, people with higher intelligence level can prefer more intellectual tasks, and these tasks may be main sources of stimulation to them. From this point of view, it may be expected that in individuals with higher intelligence, the correlation between level of intelligence and such temperamental trait as strength of excitation may be stronger. Such correlation should be also higher when changes in intelligence occur – during childhood and adolescence. Such expectations were generally revealed in our previous analyses, in which we focused on cross-sectional comparisons in successive age groups (Miklewska et al., 2004, 2006). The question arises if gender is another factor that can modify the pattern of relationships.

It is worth mentioning that both intelligence and temperament develop and change in ontogenesis. Intelligence changes across the life span quantitatively and qualitatively. Also temperamental traits develop, however these traits are relatively stable and are observed from very early stages of life. From this point of view, it may be expected that temperament can be treated as the condition under which the development of intelligence occurs. However, this reasoning can be turned away: intelligence may impact on temperamental traits development as well.

Finally, temperament as the moderator of human behavior under stress, such as, for example, a situation of intelligence assessment, may influence the behavior during test performance. From this point of view, the relationship between temperamental traits and intelligence can also depend on other factors like age, gender, and level of intelligence. Such expectations are in line with the knowledge of self development. In children test anxiety can be less salient than in adolescents or adults. The modificatory role of test anxiety may also depend on the level of intelligence: subjects who have lower level of intelligence have to confront with many tasks which are unsolvable for them.

In our previous papers, we focused on differences in patterns of relationships between Pavlovian temperament traits and fluid as well as crystallized aspects of intelligence in respect to age. The aim of these analyses is to verify our expectations about gender and level of intelligence as factors that also may modify the pattern of the temperament–intelligence relationship.

Method

Participants

Eight hundred and thirty-one subjects participated in this project. The range of age was 4 to 88 years ($M = 22.71$; $SD = 19.13$). They were divided into seven age groups representing successive stages in human development. Details regarding their demographic characteristics are given in Table 3.1.

Measures

To measure temperament traits, the Pavlovian Temperament Survey (PTS) was applied, and for assessing intelligence Raven's Progressive Matrices (RPM) and the Army General Classification Test (AGCT) were administered to subjects.

The Pavlovian temperament survey. The Pavlovian Temperament Survey (PTS; Strelau, Angleitner, & Newberry, 1999; Strelau & Zawadzki, 1998) is composed of three following scales: strength of excitation (SE), strength of inhibition (SI), and mobility of the central nervous system (MO) which refer to temperament traits as understood by Pavlov (1928). The PTS includes 57 items (19 per scale). The original version was developed as a self-rating questionnaire for adolescents and adults.

For assessing temperament in children (two youngest groups aged 4 to 9), Miklewska (2001) adapted the adult version of PTS as a parent-rating inventory administered to mothers (PTS-C). PTS-C also consists of 57 items comprising three scales analogous to PTS.

Following Pavlov the authors of the PTS inventory described SE as the trait expressed in endurance under highly and/or long-lasting stimulation and in efficiency of behavior when the individual is confronted with difficult (stressful) situations. SI reveals itself in behavioral control, for example, in the ability to refrain from some forbidden or adverse behavior. In turn, MO shows itself in the speed of reactions and the speed of changing behavior adequately to environmental changes. Cross-cultural studies conducted on over a dozen of PTS language versions show satisfactory reliability and validity measures (Strelau et al., 1999).

Raven's progressive matrices. For the young children, the Colored Progressive Matrices in Classic form (CPM) was applied and for the rest of the groups of participants – the Standard Progressive Matrices also in Classic form (SPM). Both tests measure general intellectual ability (Spearman's g factor) known as fluid intelligence (g_f) when referring to Cattel's theory of intelligence (Cattell, 1971; Deary, 2000). The psychometric properties of RPM are comparable to its original versions (Jaworowska & Szustrowa, 2000; Raven, Raven, & Court, 1998).

Table 3.1 Characteristics of subjects divided into seven age groups

Number of group	Age characteristics	Number of participants	Percent shared in the total sample	Gender Females	Males
1	Preschoolers: 4–5 years	112	13.5	62	50
2	School-age children: 8–9 years	129	15.5	63	66
3	Younger adolescents: 13–14 years	117	14.1	60	57
4	Older adolescents: 16–17 years	141	17.0	73	68
5	Younger adults: 20–25 years	128	15.4	71	57
6	Middle-aged adults: 35–40 years	100	12.0	54	46
7	Older adults: 60–80 years	104	12.5	60	44
Total		831	100	443	388

Polish adaptation of the army general classification test. Additionally, the Polish adaptation of the civilian version of the AGCT (Barnette, 1955; Science Research Associates, 1948) conducted by Choynowski (1980) was administered. The AGCT, which refers to three of the seven primary mental abilities distinguished by Thurstone (1948) – verbal ability, numerical ability, and spatial ability – requires operating acquired knowledge and skills. According to Cattell's (1971) model of intelligence, this test refers mainly to crystallized intelligence (g_c). The AGCT consists of three scales (50 tasks per scale): verbal ability, numerical ability, and spatial ability. The scales are highly correlated with each other, so they can be summed up to a general score (AGCT-GS). In further analyses, only the general score was included. The AGCT was administered only to adolescents and adults.

The disadvantage of this test is that it was adapted over 20 years before being applied in this study, so its psychometric properties may be questionable. But when our study was conducted, competitive tests measuring g_c with no time limit that could be administered to groups had not been available in Poland.

Procedure

Participants and the parents of participants (in case of children) were asked to take part in the study and if they agreed, they were informed about the aim of this project. The measures were administered as follows: in groups of children, mothers rated temperament of their children on the PTS-C scales, and after this stage the children were asked to solve the CPM test. The remaining groups of participants started from the AGCT, then they solved the SPM, and after this stage the PTS was administered. The study was conducted in the presence of at least one psychologist under standardized instructions. Some measures were collected during group sessions, and some – in individual sessions. There was no time limit.

Results

The analyses of descriptive statistics of the included variables revealed significant differences especially in SPM and AGCT-GS scores between the age groups (cf. Table 3.2). Such differences were expected and justified by the developmental changes in intelligence across life-span (Horn, 1967). In order to control these effects, all measures were standardized in the successive age groups and totaled to one score and further analyses were carried out on standardized variables.

In our previous studies (Miklewska et al., 2004, 2006), the relationships between intelligence and temperament traits were analyzed, taking into account the whole group of participants, as well as seven successive age groups (cf. Table 3.1). Summing up, we obtained the following results:

1. Analyses conducted on the whole group revealed that there are some small but significant relationships between temperament and intelligence: both measures of intelligence are positively, although weakly, related to MO (RPM – $r=0.13$; $p<0.01$; AGCT-GS – $r=0.15$; $p<0.01$).
2. The pattern of relationships between temperament traits and general ability is not stable through the successive age groups.
3. MO is positively related to SPM (measure of g_f) in the middle-aged adults (group 6; $r=0.20$; $p<0.01$) and also to AGCT-GS (measure of g_c) in both groups: younger adults (group 5; $r=0.23$; $p<0.01$) and middle-aged adults (group 6; $r=0.21$; $p<0.01$).
4. In school-age children (group 2), there is a significant relationship between temperament and g_f: the score of the SPM test is positively related to SE ($r=0.24$; $p<0.01$).

Table 3.2 Means, medians, and standard deviations for all variables measured in all groups

Variable	Group 1 M	Me	SD	Group 2 M	Me	SD	Group 3 M	Me	SD	Group 4 M	Me	SD	Group 5 M	Me	SD	Group 6 M	Me	SD	Group 7 M	Me	SD
CPM/SPM	16.2	16.0	4.5	32.5	34.0	10.4	42.1	43.0	7.7	43.3	45.0	7.4	47.3	48.00	7.1	51.7	53.0	6.3	39.5	42.0	12.4
AGCT-GS	–	–	–	–	–	–	76.8	78.0	17.9	88.1	87.0	19.5	100.4	100.0	19.8	111.3	114.5	23.0	85.6	86.5	26.4
SE	46.1	46.0	6.6	44.1	44.0	6.9	45.8	46.0	6.0	46.5	46.0	7.5	47.1	47.0	7.1	46.8	46.0	8.5	42.9	42.5	7.1
SI	41.9	42.0	7.8	45.3	45.0	6.4	48.9	49.0	6.0	48.3	48.0	6.5	49.1	49.0	5.6	51.2	52.0	7.0	50.5	52.0	7.2
MO	57.0	57.0	7.4	55.0	55.0	7.4	51.9	51.0	7.6	51.7	52.0	7.1	54.0	54.0	7.0	52.1	53.0	8.0	48.4	49.0	8.6

Note: *CPM/SPM* colored progressive matrices/standard progressive matrices, *AGCT-GS* army general classification test (civilian version) – General Score, *SE* strength of excitation, *SI* strength of inhibition, *MO* mobility of nervous processes

Table 3.3 Coefficients of correlation between temperament traits and general intelligence (fluid and crystallized) in groups of different level of intelligence

	Low g_f CPM/SPM All	F	M	Average g_f CPM/SPM All	F	M	AGCT-GS All	F	M	High g_f CPM/SPM All	F	M	AGCT-GS All	F	M
PTS scales															
SE	0.02	−0.02	0.10	−0.02	0.01	−0.04	0.08	−0.04	0.16	0.08	0.09	0.04	0.15*	0.12	0.16
SI	0.08	0.08	0.13	0.07	−0.01	0.15	0.02	−0.02	0.05	0.02	−0.08	0.17*	0.14	0.20	0.04
MO	0.02	−0.05	0.10	0.01	0.01	0.01	0.05	0.05	0.04	−0.02	−0.01	−0.02	0.20**	0.21*	0.22*

	Low g_c SPM All	F	M	Average g_c SPM All	F	M	AGCT-GS All	F	M	High g_c SPM All	F	M	AGCT-GS All	F	M
PTS scales															
SE	−0.05	−0.11	0.01	−0.05	−0.04	−0.06	0.04	0.08	−0.01	03	−0.01	0.05	16*	0.15	0.14
SI	−0.02	−0.14	0.18	−0.05	−0.10	0.06	−0.08	−0.12	−0.02	09	0.10	0.09	0.10	0.15	0.05
MO	0.11	0.12	0.06	0.08	0.18	−0.07	0.15	0.14	0.19	0.16*	0.20*	0.11	0.10	0.20*	0.01

Note: *CPM/SPM* colored progressive matrices/standard progressive matrices, *AGCT-GS* army general classification test (civilian version) – general score, *SE* strength of excitation, *SI* strength of inhibition, *MO* mobility of nervous processes, *F* females, *M* males
*$p < 0.05$

Trying to find other potential factors which can modify the pattern of correlation between temperamental traits and intelligence, we split the data into three levels of intelligence, and accordingly, distinguished three groups of subjects, separately for SPM and ACCT-GS scores: (1) 33% of lower scores in SPM (L-g_f group) and in AGCT-GS (L-g_c group), (2) 33% of average scores in SPM (A-g_f group) and in AGCT-GS (A-g_c group), and (3) 33% of higher scores in SPM (H-g_f group) and in AGCT-GS (H-g_c group). Correlational analyses were conducted within these groups. In Table 3.3, the coefficients of correlation are displayed for the three groups separately, including gender-specific subgroups.

Findings from Table 3.3 suggest that the level of intelligence modifies the pattern of correlation between the Pavlovian temperamental traits and the score of intelligence. In respect to the H-g_f group, there are some significant correlations: AGCT-GS is positively related to strength of excitation (SE) as well as to mobility of nervous system (MO). The relationship with MO holds true in both gender subgroups; however, the relationship with SE is valid only for the whole group. Moreover, in the H-g_f group, SPM scores are positively related to strength of inhibition (SI) but only among boys and men. It is worth to adding that in case of the H-g_f group, intelligence is more homogeneous, so the significant level of correlation is less likely. In respect to L-g_f and A-g_f groups, no correlations occurred between intelligence (g_f and g_c) and temperamental traits.

To some extent, the pattern of correlation between intelligence and temperament changed when the g_c groups were taken into account. In respect to the L-g_c group, SI correlates with AGCT-GS scores in the whole sample as well as in the male subsample. Considering the H-g_c group, most of the correlations refer to the MO – intelligence relationship. Here, MO correlates positively with SPM scores in the whole group, and with both – SPM and AGCT-GS – scores in the female subsamples. Additionally, the AGCT-GS scores correlate positively with SE but only for the whole group. No correlation between intelligence and temperament occurred when the A-fc group was taken into account.

Although all coefficients of correlation between intelligence and temperament are weak (none exceeds 0.27), the general pattern which shows that in groups of higher level of intelligence correlations with some temperamental traits occur more often as compared to groups with lower level is consistent with the literature (Harris, Vernon, & Jang, 2004). Moreover, findings show that the pattern of correlation can change when gender subgroups are taken into account.

Searching for other factors that can modify the correlation between temperament and intelligence, age was taken into account. For this purpose, the subjects were divided into three groups: children (1 and 2 age group), adolescents (3 and 4 age group), and adults (5, 6, and 7 age groups). The results of replicated analyses of correlation in these samples are shown in Table 3.4.

The findings from Table 3.4 may lead to the following observations:

1. In the H-g_f group, SE is positively related to the AGCT-GS scores but only in adolescents, also MO is positively related to AGCT-GS scores but only in adults.
2. In the A-g_f group, SI is positively related to SPM scores but only in adolescents.
3. In the H-g_c group, only in adolescents the SPM scores are positively related to MO.
4. In the A-g_c group, SE is negatively related to SPM only in adolescents, whereas MO is positively related to AGCT-GS but only in adults.
5. In the L-g_c group, AGCT-SG scores are positively related to SI in adolescents, and MO but in adults.

Conclusion drawn from these results says that the pattern of correlations between Pavlovian temperament traits and measures of both fluid and crystallized intelligence is inconsistent along the samples of higher intelligence (H-g_f and H-g_c), gender, and age. Mostly, it is the mobility of nervous system that is related to intelligence. This trait which measures the speed of reactions and the speed of changing behavior adequately to environmental changes, correlates moderate and positively with both aspects of intelligence, but these correlations are stronger in adolescents and adults as well as in higher intelligence groups (especially in group H-g_f). Generally, gender does not change these

Table 3.4 Coefficients of correlation between temperament traits and general intelligence (fluid and crystallized) in successive age groups (children, adolescence, adults) – separately for groups differing in level of intelligence

PTS scales	Low g_f SPM A	B	C	AGCT-GS B	C	Average g_f SPM A	B	C	AGCT-GS B	C	High g_f SPM A	B	C	AGCT-GS B	C
SE	0.13	−0.01	0.01	−0.14	−0.07	0.06	−0.09	−0.01	0.19	−0.01	0.08	0.13	−0.03	0.24*	0.08
SI	0.16	0.09	0.05	0.02	0.03	0.07	0.23*	−0.08	0.02	−0.01	0.12	−0.10	−0.02	0.10	0.16
MO	−0.14	0.09	0.07	0.02	0.08	0.07	−0.03	0.01	0.01	0.07	−0.14	0.17	−0.06	0.18	0.20*

PTS scales	Low g_c SPM B	C	AGCT-GS B	C	Average g_c SPM B	C	AGCT-GS B	C	High g_c SPM B	C	AGCT-GS B	C
SE	−0.10	−0.03	−0.07	0.08	−0.23*	0.06	0.04	0.05	0.03	0.04	0.21	0.12
SI	0.07	−0.02	0.25*	0.16	−0.02	−0.08	−0.12	−0.05	0.08	0.10	0.12	0.08
MO	0.16	−0.06	0.02	0.20*	−0.03	0.14	0.08	0.20*	0.22*	0.12	0.11	0.08

Note: *CPM/SPM* colored progressive matrices/standard progressive matrices, *AGCT-GS* army general classification test (civilian version) – general score, *SE* strength of excitation, *SI* strength of inhibition, *MO* mobility of nervous processes, *A* children, *B* adolescents, *C* adults
*$p < 0.05$

Table 3.5 Means and differences in intelligence level between groups of different level of temperamental traits

	Temperament groups				
	Low SE	Average SE	High SE		
Intelligence tests	M (SD)	M (SD)	M (SD)	F	Tukey's HSD test
CPM/SPM	−0.03 (0.99)	−0.06 (1.04)	0.12 (0.95)	2.24	Ns
AGCT-GS	−0.05 (0.88)	−0.03 (1.06)	0.03 (1.01)	0.28	Ns
Intelligence tests	Low SI	Average SI	High SI		
	M (SD)	M (SD)	M (SD)		
CPM/SPM	−0.04 (1.05)	−0.04 (0.96)	0.15 (0.90)	3.55*	Low-high*Average-high*
AGCT-GS	−0.02 (1.06)	−0.06 (0.95)	0.11 (0.95)	1.63	Ns
Intelligence tests	Low MO	Average MO	High MO		
	M (SD)	M (SD)	M (SD)		
CPM/SPM	−0.20 (1.06)	0.10 (0.94)	0.13 (0.92)	8.75**	Low-high**Low-average**
AGCT-GS	−0.20 (1.03)	0.01 (0.98)	0.23 (0.92)	8.16**	Low-high*Low-average# Average-high#

Note: *CPM/SPM* colored progressive matrices/standard progressive matrices, *AGCT-GS* army general classification test (civilian version) – general score, *SE* strength of excitation, *SI* strength of inhibition, *MO* mobility of nervous processes
#$p<0.10$; *$p<0.05$; **$p<0.01$

relationships. Strength of excitation seems to be the second important trait correlated with the level of intelligence. However, SE, expressed in endurance under highly and/or long-lasting stimulation and in efficiency of behavior when the individual is confronted with difficult (stressful) situations, is related to intelligence in the H-g_f and H-g_c groups and mostly in adolescents. In adolescents, the relationship between intelligence and SE can be askew-linear: there is positive correlation with AGCT-GS scores in the H-g_f group, whereas in the A-g_c group the correlation with SPM is negative. Strength of inhibition, which reveals itself in behavioral control, is related to intelligence very slightly: there are some positive correlations but with one exception in groups of lower and average intelligence. The role of SI is mostly specific for adolescents and males.

Trying to find the role of different levels of temperament traits in relation to intelligence, the means in CPM/SPM and AGCT-GS scores were related to three levels of intensity of temperamental traits: low, average, and high. The temperament groups (low, average, high) were derived always as 1/3 of scores. The results are shown in Table 3.5.

The levels of intensity of mobility of nervous system differ both in CPM/SPM and AGCT-GS. In case of CPM/SPM scores, post hoc analyses show that low level of MO influences in more considerable degree the level of intelligence than average and high level of MO. Also F was significant for the comparison of means on CPM/SPM for high strength of inhibition. In this case, post hoc analysis shows that SI is more strongly related to higher level of CPM/SPM comparing to low and average level of SI. There are no relationships between intelligence and different levels of strength of excitation.

Conclusions

In our previous studies, it was revealed that there are some weak but significant relationships between Pavlovian temperament traits and intelligence. The trait mostly related to intelligence is mobility of nervous system, expressed in the speed of reactions and the speed of changing behavior adequately to environmental changes. The role of this trait is the most salient in the adolescent and adult groups as opposite to the group of children. Age-specificity is occurring also in case of strength of excitation. Although it is positively related with intelligence in children, it tends to be negatively related after childhood.

Results, in which gender and level of intelligence specificity were taken into consideration, show that the pattern of correlations between temperament and intelligence may be under influence of these two factors as well.

Generally, correlation between temperament and intelligence tends to be higher in the higher intelligence group. It refers mostly to mobility of the nervous system and – on level of the whole group not divided into age groups – to strength of excitations. On the contrary, strength of inhibition is significantly related to g_c but only in the lower g_c group, and this relationship is specific to males. This relationship may indicate on some compensational gender-specific role of this trait. According to concepts of intelligence which put stress on the role of cognitive control as the process of underlying psychometric intelligence differences (Embretson, 1995), correlation between the SI and intelligence may be expected. However, our results showing weak relationship between strength of inhibition and intelligence, suggest that the concept of control is heterogeneous and cognitive control is weakly predicted by temperament.

The explanation of such patterns of relationship is difficult. On the one hand, it may be expected that in more homogeneous groups (limited range of intelligence) correlations may vanish. On the other hand, there are some data showing, that in the group of higher intelligence the relationships with personality are stronger (Harris et al., 2004). For example, Baker and Bichsel (2006) revealed that although correlations between intelligence and the Big Five personality traits are weaker and insignificant during old adulthood in comparison with young adulthood, only in the former group of cognitively superior, there were significant correlations with agreeableness.

The correlations between temperamental traits and both aspects of intelligence among lower, average, and superior intelligent subjects changes with age. Generally, the mentioned relationships are the strongest in adolescents. Interestingly, in this group the role of strength of excitation seems to be the most complex. While, in the group of superior g_f SE is positively related to g_c, in the group of moderate scores in g_c there is negative relationship between SE and g_f. Such findings suggest that, as expected, the role of strength of excitation and possible of other traits referring to the ability of process stimulation may depend on the level of intelligence. In more intelligent subjects undertaking intellectual tasks may be an important source of seeking stimulations, whereas in case of lower intelligent ones searching for stimulation, for example, in physical tasks may not influence the development of intelligence or even may restrain this development.

Relationship between intelligence and temperament depends on the level of intelligence and may be modified by gender and age. Also the level of temperamental traits may have an impact.

However, correlations between temperament and intelligence are generally weak and changeable along age and gender, studying these relationships seems to be valid. It helps understanding the functional role of both personality and intelligence and, as a consequence, it may contribute to the predictive role of both individual characteristics of behavior.

Acknowledgments The study was partly supported by Subsidy for Scientists granted to Professor Jan Strelau by the Polish Foundation of Sciences.

References

Ackerman, P. L., & Heggestad, E. D. (1997). Intelligence, personality, and interests: evidence for overlapping traits. *Psychological Bulletin, 121*, 219–245.

Baker, T. J., & Bichsel, J. (2006). Personality predictors of intelligence: differences between young and cognitively healthy older adults. *Personality and Individual Differences, 41*, 861–871.

Barnette, W. L. (1955). Diagnostic features of the AGCT. *The Journal of Social Psychology, 42*, 241–247.
Brebner, J., & Stough, C. (1995). Theoretical and empirical relationships between personality and intelligence. In: Saklofske DH. & Zeidner M (eds) International handbook of personality and intelligence. Plenum Press, New York, pp 321–347.
Cattell, R. B. (1971). Abilities: their structure, growth, and action. Houghton Mifflin, New York.
Chamorro-Premuzic, T., & Furnham, A. (2006). Intellectual competence and intelligent personality: a third way in differential psychology. *Review of General Psychology, 10*, 251–267.
Chamorro-Premuzic, T., Furnham, A., & Petrides, K. (2006). Personality and intelligence. The relationship of Eysenck's giant three with verbal and numeric ability. *Journal of Individual Differences, 27*, 147–150.
Choynowski, M. (1980). Testy Psychologiczne w Poradnictwie Wychowawczo-Zawodowym [Psychological tests in educational and professional assessment]. Panstwowe Wydawnictwo Naukowe, Warszawa.
Deary, I. J. (2000). Looking down on human intelligence: from psychometrics to the brain. Oxford University Press, Oxford.
Embretson, S. E. (1995). The role of working memory capacity and general control processes in intelligence. *Intelligence, 20*, 169–189.
Furnham, A., & Dissou, G. (2007). The relationship between self-estimated and test-derived scores of personality and intelligence. *Journal of Individual Differences, 28*, 37–44.
Harris, J. A., Vernon, P. A., & Jang, K. L. (2004). *Personality variance differences by intelligence.* Oral presentation in 12th European Conference on Personality, 18–22 July, 2004, Groningen, The Netherlands.
Horn, J. L. (1967). Intelligence – why it growths, why it declines. *Trans Action, 5*, 23–31.
Jaworowska, A., & Szustrowa, T. (2000). *Test Matryc Ravena w Wersji Standard. Formy: Klasyczna, Równoległa, Plus. Polska Standaryzacja. Podręcznik* [Polish adaptation of Raven's Progressive Matrices test. Classic, Parallel and Plus Versions. Manual]. Pracownia Testów Psychologicznych (PTP), Warszawa.
Jensen, A. R. (1993). Why is reaction time correlated with psychometric g? *Current Directions in Psychological Science, 7*, 53–56.
Miklewska, A. (2001). *Temperament a Inteligencja – Studium Rozwojowe* [Temperament and intelligence: developmental approach]. Unpublished doctoral dissertation, Instytut Psychologii Uniwersytetu Śląskiego, Katowice.
Miklewska, A., Strelau, J., & Kaczmarek, M. (2004). Związek cech temperamentu w ujęciu Pawłowa z inteligencją płynną, skrystalizowaną i z wykształceniem w różnych okresach życia człowieka [Relationship between the Pavlovian temperamental traits and fluid and crystallized intelligence as well as education in succesive developmental stages]. *Studia Psychologiczne, 42*, 53–65.
Miklewska, A., Kaczmarek, M., & Strelau, J. (2006). The relationship between temperament and intelligence: cross-sectional study in successive age groups. *Personality and Individual Differences, 40*, 643–654.
Necka, E. (1997). Attention, working memmory, and arousal: concepts apt to account for the "process of intelligence". In: Matthews G (ed) Cognitive science perspectives on personality and emotion. Elsevier Science, Amsterdam, pp 503–554.
Pavlov, I. P. (1928). Lectures on conditioned reflexes: twenty-five years of objective study of the higher nervous activity (behaviour) of animals. Liveright Publishing Corporation, New York.
Raven, J., Raven, J. C., & Court, J. H. (1998). Raven manual: Section 3. Standard progressive matrices. Edition 1998 introducing the parallel and plus versions. Oxford Psychological Press, Oxford.
Robinson, D. L., & Behbehani, J. (1996). Intelligence differences: neural transmission errors or cerebral arousability? *Kybernetes, 26*, 407–424.
Science Research Associates (1948). Examiner manual for the first civilian edition of the army general classification test revised. Author, Chicago.
Snow, R. (1992). Aptitude theory: yesterday, today, and tomorrow. *Educational Psychologist, 27*, 5–32.
Strelau, J. (1998). Temperament: a psychological perspective. Plenum, New York.
Strelau, J., & Zawadzki, B. (1998). *Kwestionariusz Temperamentu PTS. Podręcznik* [PTS. Polish version. Manual]. Pracownia Testów Psychologicznych (PTP), Warszawa.
Strelau, J., Angleitner, A., & Newberry, B.H. (1999). The Pavlovian temperament survey (PTS): an international handbook. Hogrefe & Huber, Göttingen, Germany.
Strelau, J., Zawadzki, B., & Piotrowska, A. (2001). Temperament and intelligence: a psychometric approach to the links between both phenomena. In: Collis JM, Messick S (eds) Intelligence and personality: bridging the gap in theory and measurement. Erlbaum, Mahawah, NJ, pp 61–78.
Thurstone, L. L. (1948). Primary mental abilities. The University of Chicago Press, Chicago.

Chapter 4
General Models of Individual Differences in Cognition: The Commentaries

Philip Corr, William Revelle, Joshua Wilt, and Allen Rosenthal

1. Which brain systems are critical for understanding systematic individual differences in cognition?

Philip Corr

The answer to this question depends upon one's theoretical orientation. I favour a broad-brush approach in the tradition promulgated by Hans Eysenck and others which lays stress on thinking of personality not as yet another separate faculty of mind but rather as the outcome of the functioning of crucial brain–behavioural processes/systems, with individual differences in the operating parameters of these processes/systems giving rise to what we call "personality" – the grand learning theorist, Hull, made essentially the same point many years ago (his approach stimulated Eysenck to develop his first causal theory of personality in 1957). This perspective sees "personality" as the flip-side of the brain–behavioural coin, including its cognitive components. Which brain–behavioural systems are crucial to individual differences in cognition? According to Corr (2007), crucial systems for personality show the following characteristics: (1) they exert pervasive and significant influences on psychological functions; and (2) they serve to differentiate people in terms of habitual forms of behaviour. In addition, the systems involved in systematic variations in behaviour, emotion and cognition that correspond to crucial underlying brain–behavioural systems must also show: (1) significant polymorphic variation in the population; and (2) stability over time.

As so many systems are now suspected of having a polygenic basis, the door is left wide open for many brain–behavioural systems to contribute to systematic variation in personality; however, there are some major systems that should attract our attention when trying to construct the foundation for a comprehensive causal model of personality, including its cognitive parts. A good example of this approach is seen in the postulation of three neuropsychological systems, related to emotion, motivation and learning, namely, Jeffrey Gray's reinforcement sensitivity theory (RST), which argues that it is individual differences in the operating parameters of these basic and necessary systems that gives rise to the foundations of personality, both human and non-human, healthy and abnormal (Corr, 2008). At this level of analysis, appraisal (primary and secondary) processes of motivationally significant stimuli are crucial, as seen in the effectiveness of cognitive behavioural therapy to restructure interpretation of events. Built upon this basic cognitive–behavioural architecture is the panoply of related cognitive processes involved in decision-making, categorisation, semantic processing, inhibitory processing, etc., as well as the cognitive processes involved in the generation and processing of the contents of consciousness.

The above answer points not just to specific cognitive systems – which, in the normal course of events, will only ever be exposed fully by careful research – but to where such research should be focused. This theoretical disposition helps render viable the possibility of unifying the two major schools of psychology, showing that the experimental approach and the differential approach are mutually compatible and, indeed, complementary ways of viewing the flip side of the same brain–behavioural processes/systems, including the full array of cognitive components involved in personality and individual differences.

William Revelle, Joshua Wilt and Allen Rosenthal

Although we prefer to leave this discussion to others, it is worth mentioning the important data of Aljoscha Neubauer (this volume, see also Neubauer & Fink, 2009) and others who have shown that levels of brain activation should not necessarily be considered direct measures of cognitive functioning, as high ability is associated with *less* activation of specific cortical regions than is lower ability. In addition, the broad pattern of activation seen when doing complex cognitive tasks thought to involve working memory might be associated with the increased effort involved, rather than specific increases in the functioning of memory systems.

2. What is the proper direction of causation: do individual differences in traits (personality and ability) influence cognitive processes or do variations in cognition determine traits?
and
3. To what extent can cognition (as a common ground) constitute a missing link between temperamental and abilities facets of "personality" as broadly understood?

Philip Corr

The framing of this question encourages a form of perspective bias, and begs the question as to what is meant by "personality", especially the meaning of a personality *trait* and the implication that a trait may be separated from cognition in some meaningful way. Framed thus, this may not be the most helpful way to try to understand the relationship between personality (or ability) and cognition.

Systematic individual differences in important brain–behavioural systems, including those of the "cognitive" variety, most likely reflect a complex hierarchical arrangement, with basic defensive and approach systems at the bottom, and more cognitive systems towards the top. The distinction between automatic and controlled processes may be especially significant here. Assuming that we have solved the problem of how off-line (controlled) and on-line (automatic) processes interface – and this assumption might be no more than a promissory note written on a bank with an empty safe – it is probable that environmental factors determine whether traits influence cognitive processes or cognition influence traits. To answer this question properly would require the formulation of a model of personality–cognition–behaviour, and then fair and adequate tests of it. I doubt whether once we have achieved this level of theoretical sophistication, we would continue to ask questions about how "individual differences in traits (personality and ability) influence cognitive processes?" – for how do we know that cognitive processes are not part and parcel of these traits – or how "variations in cognition determine traits?" We might, instead, want to talk about how fundamental brain–behavioural systems interact in the production of specific forms of emotion, cognition and behaviour under specific ecological conditions (e.g., dealing with an aggressive predator vs. playing chess). Seeing nomothetic processes/systems and individual differences as flip sides of the same coin negates this question – at least, in the specific form it is expressed – and may point to the true nature of traits and cognition as one integrated psychological package (see McNaughton & Corr, 2008a, b).

William Revelle, Joshua Wilt and Allen Rosenthal

The direction of causation is between the basal (trait) level and the momentary state. A useful distinction to make is between traits (characteristics of individuals over time) and states (characteristics of individuals at a particular moment). Traits may be conceived: (1) as rates of change in states as a function of situations; or (2) as probabilities of being in a particular state in a particular situation. State levels vary from moment to moment and from situation to situation and are positively correlated with trait level. For example, the trait of anxiety is seen in a rapid increase in state anxiety when in a threatening situation; the trait of cognitive ability is a rapid movement through a problem space when confronted with a cognitive task; the trait of extraversion reflects a more rapid attainment of a sociable state when presented with social cues. Cognitive processes are not uniform but rather vary as a function of the current level, availability, and allocation of cognitive resources. That is to say, they are state variables. Pure measures of latent ability are impossible to attain for the observed output reflects ability as well as resource availability and allocation which in turn reflect individual differences in cognitive ability as well as such non-cognitive personality variables as impulsivity or anxiety. For instance, although chiefly a function of cognitive ability, complex cognitive performance on tasks similar to Graduate Record Exams show systematic and replicable patterns of interactions between trait levels of impulsivity, time of day, and levels of caffeine induced arousal (Revelle, 1993; Revelle, Amaral, & Turriff, 1976; Revelle, Humphreys, Simon, & Gilliland, 1980). Trait anxiety interacts with time pressure and task components (affecting both attentional and memory load) to affect problem solving on complex geometric analogies (Leon & Revelle, 1985). Cognitive resources may be depleted through sleep deprivation (Broadbent, 1971), time of day (Revelle et al., 1980), or through social interaction (Richeson & Trawalter, 2005). Our model of how energetic and directional components of motivation affect short term memory and sustained information transfer (attentional) aspects of cognitive processing (Humphreys & Revelle, 1984, Revelle, 1993), although complex, probably underestimates the complexity of the personality–motivation–cognition relationship.

Traits and their corresponding states are encompassed in our definition of personality writ large. In our chapter and elsewhere (Ortony, Norman, & Revelle, 2005; Revelle, 2007; Wilt & Revelle, 2009); we define personality as the coherent patterning of affect, behaviour, cognition and desire (ABCDs) over time and space. Both temperamental (e.g., extraversion) and ability (e.g., intelligence) traits are thus conceptualised as being composed of different ABCD components – the example of extraversion's ABCD components is elaborated in our chapter. From this view, it is possible that shared cognitive components – in addition to affective, behavioural, or motivational components – account for the overlap and thereby forge a common ground between temperamental and ability traits. Unfortunately, theoretical and empirical scrutiny of the cognitive processes included in non-cognitive traits is uncommon. We are thus heartened by the efforts of Kaczmarek, Strelau, & Miklewska (this volume) to discuss how temperament and ability traits relate to cognitive processes. We are especially intrigued by the idea that the overlap among temperament and ability traits may be accounted for by shared cognitive processes. This theoretical position may be especially helpful in unpacking the relationship between the personality trait of openness (or intellect) and the ability trait of general intelligence (Revelle, Wilt, & Rosenthal, this volume). Borrowing from Kaczmarek and colleagues' reasoning about why the Pavlovian trait of mobility should be related to intelligence, we hypothesize that openness/intellect and intelligence are both related to speed of processing as well as working memory capacity. Open and intellectual individuals' enjoyment of complex cognitive tasks (Costa & McCrae, 1992; Goldberg, 1990) suggests that openness may comprise superior cognitive resources. We encourage further investigations into this hypothesis specifically, and we also call for the more general application of Kaczmarek and colleagues' framework for thinking about traits and cognitive processes.

4. How do individual differences in trait variables compare with individual differences in state variables as predictors of cognitive performance?

Philip Corr

Traits typically refer to the distal *potential* for activation and behavioural output (e.g., emotion, cognition or behaviour); in contrast states typically refer to proximal *output*, reflecting the interplay of trait potential and environmental demands, as well as being influenced by the moment-by-moment temporary fluctuations of the neuroendocrine system. It would be tempting to say that traits refer to more basic (relatively automatic) reactions, while states reflect the complexity of trait x situation interactions, and they may well be some value in making this distinction. However, traits reflect operations at all levels of the brain–behavioural control hierarchy, from basic automatic reflexes to controlled and conscious processes. In complex, unfamiliar, or otherwise problematic environments, flexibility, deliberation and control of behaviour is necessary and here we see the evocation of higher-level cognition, which in its grandest form is experienced in the medium of conscious awareness. In terms of this perspective, states relate to outputs, where simple or complex, singularly or multifactorially determined.

There is a potential problem with the definition and operationalism of state *measures*, which are found often to relate best to cognitive processes and performance, and, arguably, often for a rather trivial reason: the proximal (theoretical and temporal) association of the two sets of variables (state predictors and performance outcomes). For example, a close association of states and cognitive performance is seen when state measures are specifically designed to measure the very cognitive processes they purport to "predict". For example, it should come as little surprise that state measures of worry "predict" interference in cognitive processing, or that negative self-schema "predict" cognitive performance on a semantic decision task with self-referential words. State measures can be useful in delineating and describing the component processes involved in cognitive performance, but often their causal status is confused, or at least ambiguous.

The primary function of personality is to predict future behaviour (and its related components) on the basis of variation in major brain–behavioural systems; the more pervasive the power of prediction, the more impressive the system (or "trait") – when these traits (e.g., anxiety) predict, and help to explain, the genesis of major psychological phenomena (e.g., clinical anxiety) then the trait may, with sufficient justification, may be awarded a rare status. Importantly, it is necessary for theory to state *how* and *why* the trait leads to the psychological outcome – the RST of personality (Corr, 2008), is one example of this desideratum.

Trait variables are usually, indeed, intentionally so, more broad-based than state measures – this latter feature reflects their temporal and theoretical proximity to target performances indicators – designed to predict a wider range of behaviour. However, the price paid for this wide-frame angle is less specificity and more statistical error. The empirical trick is to achieve a balance between trait generality and state specificity, not losing sight of the requirement that traits predict behaviour in ways that go beyond mere proximal homology. Trait theory also needs to show how trait *potential* is expressed in *state* activation; that is, a theory of *process*.

William Revelle, Joshua Wilt and Allen Rosenthal

Strong prediction marries the breadth of the predictor with the breadth of the criterion. The broader the criterion measure, the broader the predictor variable needs to be (Wittmann, 1990). Trait variables are distal predictors while state variables are proximal. That is, even the most able person, when sleep deprived or distracted by emotionally salient cues, will show decrements in cognitive functioning. To predict cognitive performance in a particular situation (say a brief cognitive task in a lab), we need to know the trait levels of ability (e.g., working memory capacity, the content of procedural and semantic memories), impulsivity and anxiety, but more importantly, state levels of energetic and tense arousal, task engagement, and potential distractors. As we predict broader performance (e.g., class room performance in physics over the year), the state variables become less important and higher level ability factors (spatial reasoning, working memory capacity) become more important. But to predict the cumulative performance over several years, we also need to know the non-cognitive variables of consciousness and typical intellectual engagement as well as openness (Ackerman & Heggestad, 1997; Revelle, 1987; Roberts, Kuncel, Shiner, Caspi, & Goldberg, 2007).

5. Should the models of individual differences in cognition differ for conscious and unconscious information processing?

Philip Corr

Information processing models of cognition have tended to eliminate consciousness by ignoring the subjective nature of much of psychological phenomena. In one sense, this has had a major benefit, namely, the formulation of formal models that have not get lost in the theoretical fog surrounding issues of consciousness. In another sense, this widespread disinterest in conscious awareness and experience has resulted in cognitive models that do not tally well with the psychological phenomena of conscious experience that simply no one would deny are important in their own life! (Often, though, these same people consider that it is not terribly important in the lives of their experimental subjects, at least as it pertains to the theoretical models they are testing.)

The gulf between models that lay different emphasis upon the importance of conscious experience is seen in two, hitherto separate, cognitive domains: cognitive psychology and cognitive therapy. Cognitive psychology tends to focus on processes, often described in some form of boxology or consciousness-free zone of associative networks; in contrast, cognitive therapy focuses on the subjective nature of depression, anxiety, etc., specifically its meaning to patients, and the underlying cognitive processes that are, at least in principle, amenable to conscious processing and self-report. (Recent years has seen a productive rapprochement of these two approaches.)

The fact that the *output* of conscious processing is open to introspection and self-report is itself first-person datum; this datum is of a very different quality to the third-person datum of standard cognitive processing models. However, underlying conscious and unconsciousness information processing may not be different, and we should expect that it uses the same neural "code". The problem is how do we index the two systems, something which is not so easily achieved in the case of unconscious processing – although the latter may be indexed by consciously performed tasks (e.g., the Jacoby exclusion task). One major obstacle to the construction of information processing models is the ever-presence of rarifying consciousness, by giving it privileged status beyond its causal importance. As seen in the Corr chapter, what we experience consciously (i.e., contents of consciousness) is only one part of ongoing processing, and then only a partially accurate representation of prior (~100 ms) neural activation (different neural activation is, of course necessary to instantiate the medium of conscious awareness in the first place). Specifically, all conscious processing is prepared and initiated entirely unconsciously – including that involved in generating conscious awareness itself – so what we experience in the medium of conscious awareness is not veridical of the world (but there is usually a good enough physical–psychological correspondence for this discrepancy not to matter too much for everyday concerns – although this illusion is of great import to the scientist).

When constructing causal models of brain–cognitive processes, the lateness and partiality of conscious awareness needs to be fully respected and incorporated into any model that purports to capture the essential features of conscious experience on which so much of personality data rests. However, it should be doubted whether the nature of information processing is fundamentally different in unconscious and conscious processing – at least this is a sensible starting point. (However, it has to be freely admitted that our ignorance of the neural and cognitive processes involved in the generation of conscious awareness is so great that we should be at liberty to entertain other accounts of conscious information processing, including more exotic accounts such as those related to quantum physics; see Gray, 2004.) No theoretical doors need to be closed; and certainly none securely bolted.

A useful way to start to approach the problem of conscious vs. unconscious processing is to think in terms of a hierarchically arranged set of brain–behavioural modules, that takes into account both the first-person (experienced and self-reportable) and third-person (experimental data) perspectives in ways that achieve some harmony between these respective accounts. In a fundamental sense, the *process* of cognition (both unconscious and conscious), and individual differences therein, must be separate from the *output-content* of cognition which contains the *qualia* of experience divorced from the necessary prior processing; and, furthermore, this differentiation needs to be separated from the cognitive processing involved in the generation of the medium of conscious awareness itself.

Although it is not possible at this stage to state, with any degree of confidence, the nature of unconscious vs. conscious information processing, it is time to take seriously the data we also have in our possession concerning the lateness of conscious experience and other issues surround the experience of consciousness. Only once we have a firm grasp on the problems at hand will we be in a position to start providing psychologically valid models of information processing.

William Revelle, Joshua Wilt and Allen Rosenthal

Corr's theory of the functional relationships between unconscious and conscious processing (this volume) may be useful in clearing up the current debate over whether and when individual differences in unconscious and conscious processes are related to each other (Fazio & Olson, 2003). Corr draws from Jeffrey Gray (1982) in proposing that unconscious or on-line processes govern information processing until a comparator detects a discrepancy between actual stimuli encountered in the world and expected stimuli. The comparator registers the discrepancy as an error and engages conscious processes, which subsequently work to modify the error and thus adjust on-line processing. As such, this model predicts that unconscious and conscious information processing should be more closely related in particular domains in which conscious processes are frequently engaged and thus have had more opportunities to modify unconscious processes. This prediction fits well with empirical evidence suggesting that (a) implicit and explicit attitudes are more closely aligned when individuals have more experience with targets of evaluation (Nosek, 2005), and (b) implicit and explicit anxiety biases are more closely related in more anxious individuals (Bar-Haim, Lamy, Pergamin, Bakermans-Kranenburg, & van Ijzendoorn, 2007).

Corr goes on to offer the example of how neurobehavioral systems related to RST might work in concert to bring about conscious processing as just one of the many possible ways that conscious and unconscious processes interact. We offer a more general metaphor for such interactions by considering the graphical user interface (GUI, e.g., desktop screen) of a computer as akin to conscious information processing and the software running on the computer as unconscious information processing. The GUI represents the applications that are currently available for direct usage in a similar way to how people represent stimuli that are currently available to consciousness. The processes of the computer software cannot be perceived by interacting with the GUI and continue uninterrupted until an error is detected. At this point, the error may be displayed on the GUI, similar to how an error-detection mechanism engages consciousness.

References

Ackerman, P. L., & Heggestad, E. D. (1997). Intelligence, personality, and interests: evidence for overlapping traits. *Psychological Bulletin, 121*, 219–245.
Bar-Haim, Y., Lamy, D., Pergamin, L., Bakermans-Kranenburg, M. J., & van Ijzendoorn, M. H. (2007). Threat-related attentional bias in anxious and nonanxious individuals: a meta-analytic study. *Psychological Bulletin, 133*, 1–24.
Broadbent, D. (1971). Decision and stress. Academic Press, London.
Corr, P. J. (2007). Personality and psychology: Hans Eysenck's unifying themes. *The Psychologist, 20*, 666–669.
Corr, P. J. (2008). Reinforcement sensitivity theory (RST): introduction. In: Corr PJ (ed) The reinforcement sensitivity theory of personality. Cambridge University Press, Cambridge.
Costa, P. T., & McCrae, R. R. (1992). NEO PI-R professional manual. Psychological Assessment Resources, Inc., Odessa, FL.
Eysenck, H. J. (1957). The dynamics of anxiety and hysteria. Preger, New York.
Fazio, R. H., & Olson, M. A. (2003). Implicit measures in social cognition research: their meaning and uses. *Annual Review of Psychology, 54*, 297–327.
Goldberg, L. R. (1990). An alternative "description of personality": the big-five factor structure. *Journal of Personality and Social Psychology, 59*, 1216–1229.
Gray, J. A. (1982). Neuropsychological theory of anxiety: an investigation of the septal-hippocampal system. Cambridge University Press, Cambridge.
Gray, J. A. (2004). Consciousness: creeping up on the hard problem. Oxford University Press, Oxford.
Humphreys, M. S., & Revelle, W. (1984). Personality, motivation, and performance: a theory of the relationship between individual differences and information processing. *Psychological Review, 91*, 153–184.
Leon, M. R., & Revelle, W. (1985). Effects of anxiety on analogical reasoning: A test of three theoretical models. *Journal of Personality and Social Psychology, 49*(5), 1302–1315.
McNaughton, N., & Corr, P. J. (2008a). The neuropsychology of fear and anxiety: a foundation for reinforcement sensitivity theory. In: Corr, P. J. (ed) The reinforcement sensitivity theory of personality. Cambridge University Press, Cambridge.
McNaughton, N., & Corr, P. J. (2008b). Animal cognition and human personality. In: Corr PJ (ed) The reinforcement sensitivity theory of personality. Cambridge University Press, Cambridge.
Neubauer, A. C., & Fink, A. (2009). Intelligence and neural efficiency: measures of brain activation versus measures of functional connectivity in the brain. *Intelligence, 37*(2), 223–229.
Nosek, B. A. (2005). Moderators of the relationship between implicit and explicit evaluation. Journal of Experimental Psychology: *General, 134*, 565–584.
Ortony, A., Norman, D. A., & Revelle, W. (2005). Effective functioning: a three level model of affect, motivation, cognition, and behavior. In: Fellous JM, Arbib MA (eds) Who needs emotions? The brain meets the machine. Oxford University Press, New York, pp 173–202.
Revelle, W., Amaral, P., & Turriff, S. (1976). Introversion-extraversion, time stress, and caffeine: the effect on verbal performance. *Science, 192*, 149–150.
Revelle, W., Humphreys, M. S., Simon, L., & Gilliland, K. (1980). Interactive effect of personality, time of day, and caffeine – test of the arousal model. Journal of Experimental Psychology: *General, 109*(1), 1–31.
Revelle, W. (1987). Personality and motivation: sources of inefficiency in cognitive performance. *Journal of Research in Personality, 21*, 436–452.
Revelle, W. (1993). Individual differences in personality and motivation: 'non-cognitive' determinants of cognitive performance. In A. Baddeley and L. Weiskrantz, editors, Attention: Selection, awareness, and control: A tribute to Donald Broadbent. Clarendon Press/Oxford University Press, New York, NY, pp 346–373.
Revelle, W. (2007). Experimental approaches to the study of personality. In: Robins B, Fraley C, Krueger R (eds) Handbook of research methods in personality psychology. Guilford Press, New York, pp 37–61.

Richeson, J. A., & Trawalter, S, (2005). Why do interracial interactions impair executive function? A resource depletion account. *Journal of Personality and Social Psychology, 88*, 934–947.

Roberts, B.W., Kuncel, N.R., Shiner, R., Caspi, A., & Goldberg, L.R. (2007). The power of personality: the comparative validity of personality traits, socioeconomic status, and cognitive ability for predicting important life outcomes. *Perspectives on Psychological Science, 2*, 313–345.

Wilt, J., & Revelle, W. (2009). Extraversion. In: Leary M (ed) Handbook of individual differences in social behavior. Guilford, New York.

Wittmann, W.W. (1990), Brunswik-symmetry and the five-data-box conceptualization: a framework for comprehensive evaluation research. *Zeitschrift fur Padagogische Psychologie, 4*, 241–251.

Part II
Individual Differences in Cognition from a Neurophysiological Perspective

Chapter 5
Neuroscientific Approaches to the Study of Individual Differences in Cognition and Personality

Aljoscha C. Neubauer and Andreas Fink

Neurophysiology of Intelligence: The Neural Efficiency Hypothesis

In the particular field of the psychology of individual differences, the one that deals with cognitive performance probably has the longest and maybe the most comprehensive research tradition. Individual differences in cognitive ability, viz. intelligence, now span more than 100 years of research tradition, if we start from Francis Galton's (1883) notion of intelligence as an inherited feature of an efficiently functioning central nervous system (CNS). While it is mostly known that his approach to measure CNS efficiency by using simple sensory and motor tasks (that he correlated with indices of success and accomplishment) was not particularly successful, later on his approach received extensive attention. Basically starting with Erwin Roth's (1964) study on "Die Geschwindigkeit der Informationsverarbeitung und ihr Zusammenhang mit Intelligenz" (The relationship of speed of information processing to intelligence), considerable evidence on the relationship between basic information processing characteristics of individuals and their measured cognitive ability (now using psychometric intelligence tests) has been collected. Some of the most highly visible intelligence researchers who deal with this line of research, recently provided excellent reviews (Deary, 2000; Jensen, 2006) showing that there is an overwhelming evidence for a positive relationship between speed of information processing and psychometric intelligence. Proponents of this line of research often refer to the basic quality of such elementary cognitive tasks (ECTs), assuming that they measure relatively close to fundamental processes of the brain. Recently, a second important elementary cognitive approach to human intelligence has collected a considerable body of evidence for a relationship of working memory and central executive functioning with psychometric intelligence (e.g., Collette & van der Linden, 2002; Conway, Cowen, Bunting, Therriault, & Minkoff, 2002; Engle, Tuholski, Laughlin, & Conway, 1999; Smith & Jonides, 2003).

At almost the same time as Erwin Roth's study, the nativity of neuroscientific approaches to human psychometric intelligence could be dated; although the term neuroscience was not coined at that time the first neurophysiological approach to human intelligence was published by Ertl and Schafer (1969). They measured the latencies of the evoked potential (EP) and, by finding negative relationships with intelligence, they neurophysiologically confirmed Roth's behavioral findings of a quicker information processing in brighter brains. With the advent of modern neuroscientific methods, viz. brain imaging techniques like Positron Emission Tomography (PET) and (functional) Magnetic Resonance Imaging ((f)MRI), as well as the availability of multichannel electroencephalographic (EEG) and magnetoencephalographic (MEG) recording systems with up to 64 or even

A.C. Neubauer (✉) and A. Fink
Institute of Psychology, Karl-Franzens-University Graz, Maiffredygasse 12b, A-8010, Graz, Austria
e-mail: aljoscha.neubauer@uni-graz.at

128 channels, the focus in the field of neurosciences and particularly in the neuroscientific study of intelligence has changed.

In 1988, the influential PET study by Richard Haier and colleagues marked the starting point of the brain imaging approach to intelligence. In a small sample of $N=8$ participants they observed an inverse relationship between brain glucose metabolism during performance of a well-known intelligence test (Raven's Advanced Progressive Matrices) and the score in this test: Participants with higher cognitive ability devised less energy consumption of the brain, leading Haier and colleagues to formulate what has meanwhile become a well-known notion, viz. the neural efficiency hypothesis (NEH) of intelligence. In the following, we will focus on evidence of brain activation correlates of intelligence. However, in this particular context, it is worthy to note that there have also been some attempts to relate parameters of the peripheral nervous system to psychometrically determined intelligence (e.g., Vernon & Mori, 1992; Wickett & Vernon, 1994). Given that the main concern of this chapter is the investigation of *brain* activity in relation to intelligence, this research line is not discussed any further here. A meta-analytic review of studies on the relationship between intelligence and activity of the peripheral nervous system can be found in Vernon, Wickett, Bazana, and Stelmack (2000).

The readers' attention should also be drawn to a second strand of research which has provided a body of evidence on structural correlates of human intelligence. This body of evidence has recently been synthesized by Jung and Haier (2007) in the form of their so-called "parieto-frontal integration" (P-FIT) of intelligence. In reviewing 37 neuroimaging studies, mostly on structural correlates of intelligence, they tried to answer the question of how the anatomical aspects of gray matter and white matter relate topographically to intelligence. Furthermore, they showed that some frontal as well as some parietal areas of the cortex are related to intelligence. Individuals with more gray matter (neurons, synapses, dendrites) and more white matter (myelinated axons) in these areas usually display higher psychometric intelligence scores, constituting what could be considered the "brain hardware" for human intelligence.

In this chapter, we focus on the other aspect, i.e., functional brain activation in relation to intelligence. Based on a later confirmation of his finding, Haier introduced the fundamental concept of *neural efficiency* for explaining individual differences in human cognitive ability: "Intelligence is not a function of how hard the brain works but rather how efficiently it works. ... This efficiency may derive from the disuse of many brain areas irrelevant for good task performance as well as the more focused use of specific task-relevant areas" (Haier, Siegel, Tang, Abel, & Buchsbaum, 1992, pp. 415–416).

In the sequel, a larger number of studies using various measures of dynamic brain activation or energy consumption have corroborated the NEH (see Neubauer & Fink, submitted). These studies include measurements of PET (Andreasen et al., 1995), Single Photon Emission Computer Tomography (SPECT, Charlot, Tzourio, Zilbovicius, Mazoyer, & Denis, 1992), fMRI (Ruff, Knauff, Fangmeier, & Spreer, 2003), as well as electroencephalographic studies involving different EEG parameters (Event-related Desynchronization: Neubauer, Grabner, Fink, & Neuper, 2005; Slow Potential Topography: Vitouch et al., 1997; complexity of EEG dynamics: Jaušovec, 1998). Basically, all these studies have revealed evidence that brighter (as compared to less intelligent) individuals display lower and topographically more focused brain activation during cognitive task performance. However, though there are numerous studies in support of the NEH, there have also been some modifications and a few refutations. The modifications mainly concern four aspects:

1. *Sex as a moderator variable*: Those few studies that compared brain activity–ability correlations between female and male participants support the NEH more prominently in men (Grabner, Fink, Stipacek, Neuper, & Neubauer, 2004; Haier & Benbow, 1995; Jaušovec & Jaušovec, 2005; Neubauer & Fink, 2003).

2. *Interactions with sex and task content*: In two studies of our laboratory, we additionally found participants' sex to interact with task content and/or the ability domain. By employing verbal, numerical, and figural–spatial elementary cognitive tasks (Posner's classic letter matching task: Posner & Mitchell, 1967), we observed that the neural efficiency pattern emerged for males predominantly in the figural–spatial task condition, and for females only in the verbal matching task (Neubauer, Fink, & Schrausser, 2002, see Neubauer et al., 2005, for a replication and extension).
3. *Interactions with task complexity and task difficulty*: Some studies have tested the influence of task complexity on the relationship between intelligence and brain activation. Studies that have employed rather easy elementary cognitive tasks have found that a certain level of task complexity is required for the neural efficiency phenomenon to emerge (Neubauer, Sange, & Pfurtscheller, 1999; but see also Neubauer & Fink, 2003). Studies employing fairly complex tasks during the measurement of brain activation (e.g., intelligence test items) have, on the contrary, shown that the relationship might disappear or even reverse when the tasks get too complex (Doppelmayr, Klimesch, Hödlmoser, Sauseng, & Gruber, 2005, in using Raven items). This is a remarkable finding as it might suggest that the processing capacity of more intelligent individuals is not taxed so strongly by easier tasks, allowing them to "save energy," which they can then devote to the processing of the difficult tasks (where some of the less intelligent might already have "capitulated").
4. *Neural efficiency for frontal but not for parietal brain areas*: While earlier studies dealt with neural efficiency without emphasizing or dealing with topographical aspects, some recent studies have taken a closer look at this and reported a topographically more differentiated picture. In two EEG studies (Gevins & Smith, 2000; Jaušovec & Jaušovec, 2004) as well as in two fMRI studies (Lee et al., 2006; Rypma et al., 2006), more able individuals displayed less (pre-)frontal but more parietal cortical activation. Interestingly, two of these studies employed working memory tasks (Gevins, Jaušovec) and (Lee) a reasoning task, which – on the basis of the well-known close association of reasoning ability with working memory capacity (cf. Kyllonen & Christal, 1990) – makes sense. The only exception to this is the study by Rypma et al. (2006) who employed a simple speeded processing task (digit–symbol task) that possibly could also be solved with the help of the working memory.

Concluding this section, it should be remarked that some studies reported evidence of higher brain activation in brighter individuals (e.g., Gray, Chabris, & Braver, 2003). Similar findings have been reported by the working group around Wolfgang Klimesch. He mostly employed tasks that tax (semantic) long-term memory and/or episodic memory, and, in these tasks, good performers consistently exhibited greater brain activation (mostly event-related desynchronization in the EEG; Klimesch, Doppelmayr, Pachinger, & Russegger, 1997, 1999, 2006; Klimesch et al., 1996). A possible explanation of this discrepancy could be seen in the fact that the employed tasks involve long-term memory, while in most of the studies confirming NEH the employed tasks do not draw on long-term memory demands (see also Doppelmayr et al., 2005). Hence, the involvement of long-term memory processing demands might also constitute a relevant moderator variable in the relationship between brain activity and intelligence. Future research should address this important issue by systematically contrasting tasks requiring long-term memory processes with tasks that do not involve such demands. In this particular context, the influence of other important individual differences variables, such as participants' sex or age (which has not yet been analyzed in relation to NEH), should be also investigated.

In fact, the issue is not settled yet, which is why we currently can only conclude with a quote that nicely describes the current status of knowledge regarding the NEH: [Neural efficiency] "is an intriguing hypothesis, although other studies have sometimes found the opposite relationship, or have qualified the relationship. … Such complexity is to be expected, given the topic" (Gray & Thompson, 2004).

Neurophysiological Correlates of Creative Thinking

Research into the neurophysiology of intelligence has shown that brighter individuals are more efficient than less intelligent individuals during the performance of a broad range of cognitive tasks (e.g., elementary cognitive information processing, during reasoning or during the performance of working memory tasks; cf. Neubauer & Fink, submitted). Highly talented or gifted individuals may not only be proficient in rather intelligence-related ability domains but may display superior performance in other types of thinking as well. In this context, individual differences in the ability to think creatively have been identified as another main source of individual differences in the complex mental ability domain.

Creativity is needed in science, pedagogy, or education just as in the industrial or economic domain. However, despite its crucial role in almost all areas of our everyday life, no conclusive definition of this mental ability construct has been achieved yet. Prominent researchers agree that creativity is the ability to produce work that is novel (original, unique), useful, and generative (e.g., Sternberg & Lubart, 1996). In a similar way, creativity is seen in the production of a novel work that is accepted as tenable, useful or satisfying by a specific group (Stein, 1953). Scientific research on creativity has been influenced by J. P. Guilford's (1967) well-known concept of divergent (as opposed to convergent) thinking. While in convergent thinking the only correct answer to a given problem has to be discovered (as it is the case in conventional intelligence test tasks), in divergent thinking a given problem might be solved and tackled in many different ways. Highly creative individuals are believed to be more capable of producing a broader range of different associations to a given stimulus. In a psychometrical sense, as originally suggested by Guilford (1950), divergent thinking can be measured by a number of variables such as ideational fluency (i.e., number of ideas), degree of novelty (or uniqueness/originality) of ideas, the ability to think flexibly (i.e., the ability to produce different types of ideas), or the ability to elaborate on an idea. While convergent thinking involves rather intelligence-related demands (i.e., requiring the production of the one and only *correct* solution), divergent thinking is more free-associative and, thus, may be viewed as a useful estimate of creative thought (Runco, 1999).

Research into possible neural bases of creativity has been stimulated by Kris' (1952) supposition of primary process cognition, Mendelsohn's (1976) hypothesis of defocused attention, and Mednick's (1962) assumption of individual differences in associative hierarchies. According to these psychological theories, creative individuals are assumed to be more capable of shifting between secondary and primary modes of thinking, or to "regress" to primary process cognition that is needed in the generation of novel, original ideas. While secondary processes are abstract and logic-analytical, primary process cognition refers to states such as dreaming or reverie. Creative individuals are also believed to display "flat" (i.e., more and broader associations to a given stimulus) instead of "steep" associational hierarchies (just a few, common associations to a given stimulus). Moreover, they are thought to be able to attend to more things at the same time (i.e., defocused attention) instead of just narrowly attending to a single task or event. Martindale (1999) suggests that primary process cognition, defocused attention, and flat associational hierarchies are more likely to occur if an individual is in a state of low cortical arousal. Martindale's so-called low arousal theory of creativity has been empirically tested in some studies using the electroencephalogram (EEG). In Martindale and Hines (1975), highly creative individuals exhibited higher alpha wave activity (which was interpreted as lower cortical arousal) while performing a well-known creativity task, i.e., the Alternate Uses Test. Similarly, in Martindale and Hasenfus (1978), highly creative individuals showed higher levels of alpha activity than less creative subjects during an inspirational phase (i.e., thinking of a story) but not during an elaboration phase.

Valuable insights into possible brain correlates of creative thinking have been revealed by recent EEG studies, which contrasted brain activity patterns during convergent versus divergent modes of thinking. For example, when participants were required to name as many unusual uses of a common, everyday object or to think of as many consequences as possible of a given hypothetical situation, they display a different pattern of electrophysiological brain activity than during the performance of more intelligence-related tasks (e.g., mental arithmetic). Mölle, Marshall, Wolf, Fehm, and Born (1999) reported higher EEG complexity during the performance of more "free-associative" types of tasks, which could be the result of a larger number of independently oscillating neural assemblies during this type of thinking. Similarly, Jaušovec and Jaušovec (2000) as well as Razoumnikova (2000) reported findings which also indicate that convergent and divergent thinking are accompanied by different activity patterns in the EEG (see also Jaušovec, 2000). In line with this, we recently also observed evidence that performance of more "free associative" tasks of creative thinking (e.g., generating unusual uses of conventional objects or responding creatively to utopian situations) were associated with stronger EEG alpha activity than tasks involving less creativity-related demands (e.g., completing German suffixes in an original way; Fink, Benedek, Grabner, Staudt, & Neubauer, 2007).

Another promising approach in the neuroscientific study of creative thinking is to investigate brain activity patterns that are associated with the production of highly creative (as opposed to less creative) ideas. This exciting research question has been stimulated by Jung-Beeman et al. (2004) who investigated brain correlates underlying the subjective experience of "AHA!" The authors had their participants work on remote associate problems (finding a compound to three given stimulus words) and compared brain activity during solutions that were accompanied by subjective experience of "AHA!" with those that were solved without insight. Stimulated by Jung-Beeman et al.'s approach, Fink and Neubauer (2006) have also investigated how brain states during the production of highly original ideas might be differentiated from those observed during the production of less original ideas. Participants were required to generate original ideas to verbal problems that are in need of explanation (e.g., "*A light in the darkness*") and to hypothetical situations that will actually never happen (e.g., "*Imagine, there were a creeping plant rising up to the sky. What would await you at the end of this plant?*"). In order to obtain a measure of originality of the responses given during the performance of experimental tasks, we applied an external rating procedure similar to Amabile's (1982) consensual agreement technique that has frequently been employed in this field of research. To this end, three female and three male raters were requested to evaluate the responses of the participants given during the experiment with respect to their originality on a five-point rating scale (ranging from 1, "highly original," to 5, "not original at all"). Subsequently, the ratings were averaged over all raters (who displayed satisfying internal consistency in their ratings) so that one originality score was available for each single response.

During performance of the creative idea generation tasks, participants were required to press the "IDEA-button" whenever an idea related to the problem presented on screen came into their mind. Upon button press, a message appeared on screen prompting the participants to vocalize their idea (which was recorded by the experimenter) and to confirm it by pressing the ENTER-button whereupon the stimulus reappeared on screen. Thereby, the time-point of idea production is self-directed by the participants, EEG movement artifacts caused by typing or free-hand writing can be avoided, and the IDEA-button responses provide triggers for analyzing critical EEG time intervals (e.g., directly before the production of an original idea). Accordingly, on the basis of the responses a participant gave in a task, we obtained a high-original and a low-original list of trials by means of a median split within each single task and participant.

Analyses revealed that creative problem solving was generally accompanied by relatively strong increases in EEG alpha power relative to the pre-stimulus reference condition (referred to as "task-" or "event-related" synchronization of alpha activity). In addition to this, more original (as opposed to less original) ideas were accompanied by a stronger synchronization of alpha activity in centroparietal regions of the cortex. This finding is not only in agreement with Jung-Beeman et al.'s (2004) "alpha" effect observed during subjective experience of "AHA!" (viz. an increase in alpha activity in insight as compared to noninsight solutions) but also fits into previous research reports which found parietal brain regions being critically involved in divergent or creative thinking tasks too (e.g., Bechtereva et al., 2004; Razoumnikova, 2004).

Motivated by the finding of the Neubauer et al. (2005) study, which indicates that females and males of varying verbal ability show different patterns of brain activity when engaged in the performance of verbal tasks, we have also investigated sex- and intelligence-related effects on brain activity in the context of creative idea generation (as the production or generation of ideas also falls into the verbal stimulus domain). As reported in Fink and Neubauer (2006), we observed evidence that brain activity during creative idea generation appears to be moderated by individual differences in verbal intelligence and participants' sex. In responding creatively to hypothetical (e.g., "*A light in the darkness*") and utopian situations (e.g., "*What would happen if suddenly an ice-age broke in*"), males and females of varying verbal intelligence level exhibited different patterns of alpha synchronization, particularly apparent in frontal regions of the cortex. While verbally proficient females (in contrast to those of average verbal intelligence) displayed a stronger synchronization of alpha activity during the production of original ideas, the opposite result pattern was observed in males: The production of original ideas in verbally intelligent males was accompanied by a lower synchronization of alpha activity than in the group of average verbal ability. The finding that females and males of varying verbal ability showed different patterns of alpha synchronization during the generation of creative ideas appears to be particularly exciting inasmuch as it resembles the result pattern that we have tentatively also observed on the behavioral level. Analyses of performance data yielded a higher ideational fluency (viewed as a prerequisite of high originality; Guilford, 1950) in verbally intelligent females than in females with average verbal ability, whereas in the male sample exactly the opposite was found, viz. a higher fluency in the group of average than in the group of verbally more intelligent individuals (cf. Fink & Neubauer, 2006).

Both during the performance of intelligence-related tasks (verbal and visuospatial task employed in Neubauer et al., 2005) and during creative idea generation (Fink & Neubauer, 2006), we observed intelligence and sex-related effects on EEG alpha activity. As has been revealed by the Neubauer et al. (2005) study, during the performance of the verbal matching task only in females verbal intelligence and ERD were negatively correlated (i.e., neural efficiency). In contrast, when males were engaged in the performance of the verbal task, verbally more intelligent males displayed more brain activation than lower intelligent males. With respect to creative idea generation, males and females again displayed a contrary neurophysiological result pattern as it was evident by different patterns of alpha synchronization in women and men. Though these latter findings certainly await replication in larger samples, they could, along with the Neubauer et al. (2005) findings, point to some interesting sex differences in the processing of verbal stimulus material. Presumably due to their higher proficiency in this domain, females seem to process verbal information more efficiently than males. In terms of the alpha inhibition hypothesis (Klimesch et al., 2007), our findings would be compatible with the interpretation that females are more capable of maintaining top-down control on internal information processing by inhibiting interference from external (task-irrelevant) input. However, irrespective of the possible functional meaning of the observed sex differences, the Fink and Neubauer (2006) study also provides evidence of an interaction between intelligence and creativity on the neurophysiological level (cf. also Jaušovec, 2000). The finding that (in both sexes) intelligence-related effects of brain activity were more evident when participants produced more original as opposed to less original ideas strongly suggests that creative idea generation is moderated by individual differences in verbal intellectual ability.

Taken together, neuroscientific studies on creativity have yielded some valuable insights into potential brain correlates underlying creative thinking. In this particular context EEG activity in the alpha frequency band (approximately in the frequency range between 8 and 12 Hz) has proven to be particularly sensitive to creativity-related task demands (e.g., Fink et al., 2007; Jaušovec, 2000; Jung-Beeman et al., 2004; Martindale, 1999; Razoumnikova, 2007). More specifically, EEG studies reveal evidence that the generation of original ideas is associated with alpha synchronization in frontal brain regions and with a diffuse and widespread pattern of alpha synchronization over posterior parietal cortical regions (e.g., Fink et al., 2009). This diffuse und widespread pattern of alpha synchronization in posterior brain regions may – in agreement with recent models of creativity (Dietrich, 2004) – facilitate the (re-)combination of already stored semantic information that is normally distantly related. The observed alpha synchronization in frontal brain regions could suggest that during the generation of novel, original ideas frontal brain regions are in a state of heightened internal information processing or attention, less likely to be disturbed by interfering cognitive processes or external input. Hence, these findings also indicate that creativity is not localized in a specific brain area (in terms of activation or deactivation of a certain brain area). Neuroscientific findings rather suggest that creative thinking is the result of the coordinated interplay between different, especially frontal and posterior parietal cortical areas.

Personality and Ability

Research into the neurophysiology of human intelligence differences has also attended to the research question as to how efficient brain functioning is influenced by individual differences in classic personality traits. This particularly applies to the personality dimension extraversion–introversion, which has been linked to biological systems as well. According to H. J. Eysenck's (1967) well-known arousal theory, individual differences in extraversion are related to activity differences in the ascending reticular activation system, a loop connecting the reticular formation with the cortex. This neural circuit is thought to mediate cortical arousal induced by incoming external input and the level of extraversion is proposed to be inversely related to cortical arousal. According to this, extraverts are assumed to show relatively low cortical arousal, resulting in a need to seek external stimulation in order to increase their (suboptimal) arousal level. Introverted individuals, in contrast, are believed to display comparatively high levels of cortical arousal and, hence, tend to avoid additional external stimulation.

Motivated by Eysenck's theory, the personality dimension extraversion–introversion has been related to different measures of cortical arousal derived from the human EEG (for a comprehensive review see Matthews & Gilliland, 1999). In the vast majority of these studies, EEG alpha wave activity (i.e., EEG activity roughly between 7 and 13 Hz) has been used as an index of cortical arousal. Empirical studies, however, yielded inconsistent findings. While some studies found evidence in favor of Eysenck's hypothesis of a weaker cortical arousal in extraverted as compared to introverted individuals (e.g., Gale et al., 2001; Tran et al., 2001), other studies failed to find such a relationship (e.g., Hagemann et al., 1999; Schmidtke & Heller, 2004; cf. also Gale, 1983). This might, at least partly, be due to the possibility that more or less arousal-inducing test conditions might be better or worse suited to allow for activation (i.e., arousal) differences between intro- and extraverts (Gale, 1983). In light of Gale's argumentation, so-called "moderate" arousal-inducing conditions, e.g., when individuals are asked to alternately open and close their eyes, are more likely to confirm Eysenck's (1967) predictions as compared to low arousal-inducing ("boring") conditions, where individuals are instructed to do nothing but simply lie down (where extraverts are assumed to stimulate themselves by cogitation), or – in a high arousal-inducing condition – to perform an effortful, cognitively demanding task, where the "over-aroused" introverts are presumed to adopt self-relaxation strategies in order to induce a state of calmness (cf. Gale, 1983).

Another critical point that might account for inconsistencies in this field of research could be the specific alpha frequency range to which extraversion has been related to. Most of the studies dealing with the extraversion–activation relationship analyzed cortical activity within the traditional alpha frequency band, i.e., in the frequency band ranging between 7 and 13 Hz. However, as outlined by Klimesch (1999), broad band analyses of electrophysiological brain activity should be treated with caution, since they may obscure possible frequency specific effects. As will be shown below, the studies conducted in our laboratory yielded evidence that EEG activity in the lower alpha frequency range (approx. in the range between 6 and 8 Hz) is most sensitive to extraversion-related effects, while brain oscillations in the faster EEG alpha frequency ranges (e.g., between 10 and 12 Hz) were more likely to reflect intelligence-related effects. Hence, a possible reason for failing to detect extraversion-related effects on cortical activation patterns could also be the fact that in the majority of studies extraversion has been analyzed in the broad alpha frequency band.

Extraversion and Brain Activity During Cognitive Task Performance

There are numerous research reports which emphasize the role of extraversion as being particularly sensitive in accounting for individual differences in brain reactivity to emotional stimuli (Canli, 2004). Besides these studies, extraversion-related effects on brain activity have also been investigated in response to more classic cognitive task demands. For instance, Kumari, Ffytche, Williams, and Gray (2004) and Chavanon, Wacker, Leue, and Stemmler (2007) recently reported extraversion effects on brain activity during the performance of a working memory task. Similarly, Gray et al. (2005) investigated the effects of affective personality traits (behavioral inhibition and behavioral approach sensitivity) on brain activity (by means of fMRI) during working memory processing. The authors report evidence that the efficient processing of information appears to be modulated by individual differences in personality.

We have also analyzed the influence of the personality dimension extraversion on brain activity during cognitive processing employing a wide range of different cognitive tasks. In a first study (Fink, Schrausser, & Neubauer, 2002), we analyzed the event-related desynchronization (ERD) of alpha activity during the performance of Posner's classic letter matching test (Posner & Mitchell, 1967), in which participants had to judge the semantic identity of two simultaneously presented verbal stimuli. We observed an interaction between individuals' intelligence and extraversion levels in the lower alpha frequency range (approx. between 6 and 8 Hz): The pattern of this interaction suggests that only extraverted individuals exhibited the expected inverse brain–IQ relationship while in introverted individuals an opposite result pattern was found. In another study (Fink & Neubauer, 2004), we measured ERD during the performance of a reasoning task (i.e., Stankov's Triplet numbers test; Stankov, 2000) which consists of five test conditions with increasing complexity. This study yields evidence that the extraversion–activation relationship might be moderated by the task demands: more complex or more "arousing" conditions were more likely to produce the inverse extraversion–activation relationship, while in easier (i.e., low arousal-inducing) conditions of the test introverted individuals were cortically less aroused than extraverts (see also M. W. Eysenck, 1982). Again, this effect could only be observed in the lower alpha band (~6–8 Hz). Extraversion effects were not only restricted to elementary cognitive or reasoning tasks, but we found extraversion-related effects on brain activity (with less brain activation in extraverted than in introverted individuals) during the performance of working memory tasks as well (Fink, Grabner, Neuper, & Neubauer, 2005) – most prominent in right-hemispheric frontal–parietal regions, i.e., regions that are known to be involved in attention and working memory (e.g., Coull, 1998; Posner & Petersen, 1990).

Individual differences in EEG alpha activity were not only observed to be associated with the personality dimension extraversion–introversion but they may constitute a possible biological basis of creative thinking as well (Fink et al., 2009; Jaušovec, 2000; Jung-Beeman et al., 2004). In a recent study of our laboratory (Fink & Neubauer, 2008), we investigated cortical activity in the EEG alpha band while extraverted and introverted individuals were confronted with different creative idea generation tasks. On the basis of the originality of responses given during the experiment, participants were divided into a lower and a higher originality group. Interestingly, we observed an interaction between extraversion and originality on the neurophysiological level: Those extraverted individuals who produced original responses during creative idea generation exhibited the largest amount of alpha power, whereas in less original introverts the lowest level of alpha power was observed.

In extending the design used in our former studies, where we analyzed the role of extraversion as a possible moderator variable in "classic" cognitive task performance (i.e., performance of mental speed, reasoning, working memory, or creative thinking tasks), we investigated the extraversion–activation relationship also in the context of emotional information processing (Fink, 2005). Specifically, we used the ERD method in order to test whether individual differences in extraversion were correlated with cortical activity during performance of an emotional face processing task requiring participants to judge the equivalence of two simultaneously presented facial emotions. In addition to this, the ERD during performance of a verbal (judging the semantic identity of words) as well as a figural (judging the identity of arrows) task was measured in order to assess whether cortical activity during emotional face processing might be differentiated from that observed during performance of "classic" cognitive tasks. Generally, the findings of that study suggest that extraversion is differently involved when a different kind of information processing is required. While extraversion effects during cognitive information processing largely match those found in our previous studies – particularly with respect to its restriction to lower EEG alpha frequency ranges – extraversion effects during emotional information processing were reflected in different parameters of the EEG (i.e., only found in the more task-specific upper alpha band). Analyses reveal that when participants' task was to judge whether the presented facial emotions were equivalent or not (emotion task), extraverted individuals were more likely to display a lower cortical activation (lower ERD) than introverts, primarily in the left hemisphere. In contrast, when the presented facial stimuli had to be judged with respect to the identity of their sex (control task), no obvious differences were found between both groups. Subsequent analyses conducted separately for the emotion task suggest that extraversion effects during emotional information processing were localized in cortical areas that are known to be active during processing of speech (left-hemispheric frontocentral and centroparietal regions) – with less brain activation in (the more communicative and talkative) extraverts (on the particular role of left-hemispheric cortices in the perception of emotion conveyed through meaningful speech see Kucharska-Pietura, Phillips, Gernand, & David, 2003). Interestingly, this effect was only observed in the upper alpha band, viz. roughly in the frequency range between 9.6 and 11.6 Hz.

At first sight, the existence of extraversion effects in the upper alpha frequency band appears to run counter to our previous work, revealing extraversion-related effects primarily in the lower EEG alpha bands. However, as has been repeatedly demonstrated by Klimesch and colleagues (for a review see Klimesch, 1999), the upper alpha band selectively responds to specific task demands (such as semantic memory processes), while activity in the lower alpha bands is believed to reflect more general task demands, such as expectancy or alertness. In line with this, we observed intelligence-related (i.e., more task-related) effects more prominently in the upper alpha rather than the lower alpha bands (Grabner et al., 2004; Neubauer et al., 2002, 2005). Hence, we could then assume that individual differences in extraversion are more directly or specifically involved in emotional than in cognitive information processing and, as a consequence, more likely to be reflected in the (task-specific) upper alpha band. Thus, the findings of the Fink (2005) study do not only suggest a different use of the cortex in introverted vs. extraverted individuals when engaged in emotional face processing; the more distinct association of extraversion effects with either the lower alpha or the upper alpha bands depending on the kind of information processed (cognitive vs. emotional, respectively) also hints at possible (functionally) different facets of the personality dimension extraversion.

Conclusion

In this chapter, we started with the well-established finding in the neuroscientific study of human intelligence that brighter individuals use their brains more efficiently when engaged in the performance of cognitively demanding tasks than less intelligent people do. This has been confirmed in a variety of studies employing a broad range of different cognitive task demands (see Neubauer & Fink, submitted). However, recent studies in this field of research reveal evidence that neurally efficient brain functioning appears to be moderated by task content and individuals' sex (Neubauer et al., 2002, 2005). Both females and males show neural efficiency primarily in that domain in which they usually perform better: females in the verbal domain, and males in the visuospatial ability domain. Moreover, it has also been observed that neural efficiency varies with the intelligence component. For instance, in Neubauer and Fink (2003), neural efficiency (i.e., inverse relationship between brain activation and intelligence) during reasoning was much more pronounced when fluid intelligence instead of crystallized or general mental ability was taken as a measure of intellectual ability (see also Grabner et al., 2004). Furthermore, in the Neubauer et al. (2005) study, in the female sample, neural efficiency was only apparent when performance during the verbal task was specifically related to verbal intelligence, while in males the inverse intelligence-activation relationship was more likely observed when performance in the visuospatial task was specifically related to figural intelligence.

In this chapter, we have also briefly addressed the research question as to how brain efficiency is influenced by individual differences in classic personality traits such as extraversion/introversion. In this context, we focused on our studies on the extraversion–brain activity relationship, which yield strong empirical evidence that individual differences in extraversion account for variability in brain activity during the performance of a wide range of cognitive tasks (e.g., mental speed: Fink et al., 2002; reasoning: Fink & Neubauer, 2004; or working memory: Fink et al., 2005, see also Chavanon et al., 2007). One important issue in this context is that ability (i.e., intelligence) and personality (i.e., extraversion) appear to be reflected in different parameters of the human EEG: We found brain activity in the lower EEG alpha bands (roughly in the frequency range between 6 and 10 Hz) primarily reflecting personality (i.e., extraversion) related effects, while effects related to cognitive ability (i.e., intelligence) were predominantly observed in the upper alpha frequency band (~10–12 Hz; see Grabner et al., 2004; Neubauer & Fink, 2003; Neubauer et al., 2002, 2005).

But what could be the functional meaning of the association of extraversion with EEG activity in the lower alpha bands? ERD in the lower alpha band can be observed in response to almost all types of cognitive tasks and might thus reflect unspecific task demands such as basic alertness or arousal (Klimesch, 1999). Eysenck (1967) claimed that extraverted individuals are low in cortical arousal, as opposed to introverts who chronically show a stronger cortical arousal. The personality dimension extraversion could, thus, as our findings indicate, play a particular role in mediating unspecific task demands such as basic alertness, vigilance, or arousal, which are necessary to perform successfully on a given cognitive task. Interestingly, extraversion-related effects on cortical activity appear to be strongest exactly in those cortical regions that are actually needed to perform successfully on the task. This was, for instance, evident during working memory processing (see Fink et al., 2005), where extraverted (as compared to introverted) individuals showed a lower cortical activity in right-hemispheric frontal–parietal regions – regions that are known to be involved in attention and working memory. In a broader sense, the finding that individual differences in the personality dimension extraversion account for variability in brain responses to a variety of cognitive demands also supports the idea of personality (extraversion) and ability as interplaying rather than independent domains. At first sight, this appears to be counterintuitive insofar as none of our studies revealed a significant correlation between personality (i.e., extraversion) and ability indices (e.g., intelligence, working memory performance, reaction times etc.) at a purely behavioral level.

However, similar to Gray et al.'s (2005) argumentation, personality and ability appear to be interrelated in subtle ways, since they may modulate cortical activity in overlapping cortical areas that are needed to perform successfully on a given cognitive task.

References

Amabile, T. M. (1982). Social psychology of creativity: A consensual assessment technique. *Journal of Personality and Social Psychology, 43*, 997–1013.
Andreasen, N. C., O'Leary, D. S., Arndt, S., Cizadlo, T., Rezai, K., Watkins, G. L., et al. (1995). PET Studies of memory: Novel and practiced free recall of complex narratives. *NeuroImage, 2*, 284–295.
Bechtereva, N. P., Korotkov, A. D., Pakhomov, S. V., Roudas, M. S., Starchenko, M. G., & Medvedev, S. V. (2004). PET study of brain maintenance of verbal creative activity. *International Journal of Psychophysiology, 53*, 11–20.
Canli, T. (2004). Functional brain mapping of extraversion and neuroticism: Learning from individual differences in emotion processing. *Journal of Personality, 72*, 1105–1132.
Charlot, V., Tzourio, N., Zilbovicius, M., Mazoyer, B., & Denis, M. (1992). Different mental imagery abilities result in different regional cerebral blood flow activation patterns during cognitive tasks. *Neuropsychologia, 30*, 565–580.
Chavanon, M.-L., Wacker, J., Leue, A., & Stemmler, G. (2007). Evidence for a dopaminergic link between working memory and agentic extraversion: An analysis for load-related changes in EEG alpha 1 activity. *Biological Psychology, 74*, 46–59.
Collette, F., & Van der Linden, M. (2002). Brain imaging of the central executive component of working memory. *Neuroscience and Biobehavioral Reviews, 26*, 105–125.
Conway, A. R. A., Cowen, N., Bunting, M. F., Therriault, D. J., & Minkoff, S. R. B. (2002). A latent variable analysis of working memory capacity, short-term memory capacity, processing speed, and general fluid intelligence. *Intelligence, 30*, 163–183.
Coull, J. T. (1998). Neural correlates of attention and arousal: Insights from electrophysiology, functional neuroimaging and psychopharmacology. *Progress in Neurobiology, 55*, 343–361.
Deary, I. J. (2000). *Looking down on human intelligence: From psychometrics to the brain.* Oxford, NY: Oxford University Press.
Dietrich, A. (2004). The cognitive neuroscience of creativity. *Psychonomic Bulletin & Review, 11*, 1011–1026.
Doppelmayr, M., Klimesch, W., Hödlmoser, K., Sauseng, P., & Gruber, W. (2005). Intelligence related upper alpha desynchronization in a semantic memory task. *Brain Research Bulletin, 66*, 171–177.
Engle, R. W., Tuholski, S. W., Laughlin, J. E., & Conway, A. R. A. (1999). Working memory, short-term memory, and general fluid intelligence: A latent-variable approach. *Journal of Experimental Psychology: General, 128*, 309–331.
Ertl, J., & Schafer, E. (1969). Brain response correlates of psychometric intelligence. *Nature, 223*, 421–422.
Eysenck, H. J. (1967). *The biological basis of personality.* Springfield, IL: Charles C. Thomas.
Eysenck, M. W. (1982). *Attention and arousal.* New York: Springer.
Fink, A. (2005). Event-related desynchronization in the EEG during emotional and cognitive information processing: Differential effects of extraversion. *Biological Psychology, 70*, 152–160.
Fink, A., Benedek, M., Grabner, R. H., Staudt, B., & Neubauer, A. C. (2007). Creativity meets neuroscience: Experimental tasks for the neuroscientific study of creative thinking. *Methods, 42*, 68–76.
Fink, A., Grabner, R. H., Benedek, M., Reishofer, G., Hauswirth, V., Fally, M., et al. (2009). The creative brain: Investigation of brain activity during creative problem solving by means of EEG and fMRI. *Human Brain Mapping, 30*(3), 734–748.
Fink, A., Grabner, R. H., Neuper, C., & Neubauer, A. C. (2005). Extraversion and cortical activation during memory performance. *International Journal of Psychophysiology, 56*, 129–141.
Fink, A., & Neubauer, A. C. (2004). Extraversion and cortical activation: Effects of task complexity. *Personality and Individual Differences, 36*, 333–347.
Fink, A., & Neubauer, A. C. (2006). EEG alpha oscillations during the performance of verbal creativity tasks: Differential effects of sex and verbal intelligence. *International Journal of Psychophysiology, 62*, 46–53.
Fink, A., & Neubauer, A. C. (2008). Eysenck meets Martindale: The relationship between extraversion and creativity from a neuroscientific perspective. *Personality and Individual Differences, 44*, 299–310.
Fink, A., Schrausser, D. G., & Neubauer, A. C. (2002). The moderating influence of extraversion on the relationship between IQ and cortical activation. *Personality and Individual Differences, 33*, 311–326.
Gale, A. (1983). Electroencephalographic studies of extraversion-introversion: A case study in the psychophysiology of individual differences. *Personality and Individual Differences, 4*, 371–380.
Gale, A., Edwards, J., Morris, P., Moore, R., & Forrester, D. (2001). Extraversion-introversion, neuroticism-stability, and EEG indicators of positive and negative emphatic mood. *Personality and Individual Differences, 30*, 449–461.

Galton, F. (1883). *Inquiries into human faculty and its development*. London: Macmillan.
Gevins, A., & Smith, M. E. (2000). Neurophysiological measures of working memory and individual differences in cognitive ability and cognitive style. *Cerebral Cortex, 10,* 829–839.
Grabner, R. H., Fink, A., Stipacek, A., Neuper, C., & Neubauer, A. C. (2004). Intelligence and working memory systems: Evidence of neural efficiency in alpha band ERD. *Cognitive Brain Research, 20,* 212–225.
Gray, J. R., Burgess, G. C., Schaefer, A., Yarkoni, T., Larsen, R. J., & Braver, T. S. (2005). Affective personality differences in neural processing efficiency confirmed using fMRI. *Cognitive, Affective & Behavioral Neuroscience, 5,* 182–190.
Gray, J. R., Chabris, C. F., & Braver, T. S. (2003). Neural mechanisms of general fluid intelligence. *Nature Neuroscience, 6,* 316–322.
Gray, J. R., & Thompson, P. M. (2004). Neurobiology of intelligence: Science and ethics. *Nature Reviews Neuroscience, 5,* 471–482.
Guilford, J. P. (1950). Creativity. *The American Psychologist, 5,* 444–454.
Guilford, J. P. (1967). *The nature of human intelligence*. New York: McGraw-Hill.
Hagemann, D., Naumann, E., Lurken, A., Becker, G., Maier, S., & Bartussek, D. (1999). EEG asymmetry, dispositional mood and personality. *Personality and Individual Differences, 27,* 541–568.
Haier, R., & Benbow, C. P. (1995). Sex differences and lateralization in temporal lobe glucose metabolism during mathematical reasoning. *Developmental Neuropsychology, 11,* 405–414.
Haier, R. J., Siegel, B. V., Nuechterlein, K. H., Hazlett, E., Wu, J. C., Paek, J., et al. (1988). Cortical glucose metabolic rate correlates of abstract reasoning and attention studied with positron emission tomography. *Intelligence, 12,* 199–217.
Haier, R. J., Siegel, B., Tang, C., Abel, L., & Buchsbaum, M. S. (1992). Intelligence and changes in regional cerebral glucose metabolic rate following learning. *Intelligence, 16,* 415–426.
Jaušovec, N. (1998). Are gifted individuals less chaotic thinkers? *Personality and Individual Differences, 25,* 253–267.
Jaušovec, N. (2000). Differences in cognitive processes between gifted, intelligent, creative, and average individuals while solving complex problems: An EEG study. *Intelligence, 28,* 213–237.
Jaušovec, N., & Jaušovec, K. (2000). EEG activity during the performance of complex mental problems. *International Journal of Psychophysiology, 36,* 73–88.
Jaušovec, N., & Jaušovec, K. (2004). Differences in induced brain activity during the performance of learning and working-memory tasks related to intelligence. *Brain and Cognition, 54,* 65–74.
Jaušovec, N., & Jaušovec, K. (2005). Differences in induced gamma and upper alpha oscillations in the human brain related to verbal/performance and emotional intelligence. *International Journal of Psychophysiology, 56,* 223–235.
Jensen, A. R. (2006). *Clocking the mind: Mental chronometry and individual differences*. Oxford: Elsevier.
Jung, R. E., & Haier, R. J. (2007). The parieto-frontal integration theory (P-FIT) of intelligence: Converging neuroimaging evidence. *Behavioral and Brain Sciences, 30,* 135–154.
Jung-Beeman, M., Bowden, E. M., Haberman, J., Frymiare, J. L., Arambel-Liu, S., Greenblatt, R., et al. (2004). Neural activity when people solve verbal problems with insight. *PLoS Biology, 2,* 500–510.
Klimesch, W. (1999). EEG alpha and theta oscillations reflect cognitive and memory performance: A review and analysis. *Brain Research Reviews, 29,* 169–195.
Klimesch, W., Doppelmayr, M., & Hanslmayr, S. (2006). Upper alpha ERD and absolute power: Their meaning for memory performance. In C. Neuper & W. Klimesch (Eds.), *Progress in brain research: Vol. 159 Event-related dynamics of brain oscillations* (pp. 151–165). Amsterdam: Elsevier.
Klimesch, W., Doppelmayr, M., Pachinger, T., & Russegger, H. (1997). Event-related desynchronization in the alpha band and the processing of semantic information. *Cognitive Brain Research, 6,* 83–94.
Klimesch, W., Doppelmayr, M., Schwaiger, J., Auinger, P., & Winkler, T. (1999). "Paradoxical" alpha synchronization in a memory task. *Cognitive Brain Research, 7,* 493–501.
Klimesch, W., Sauseng, P., & Hanslmayr, S. (2007). EEG alpha oscillations: The inhibition timing hypothesis. *Brain Research Reviews, 53,* 63–88.
Klimesch, W., Schimke, H., Doppelmayr, M., Ripper, B., Schwaiger, J., & Pfurtscheller, G. (1996). Event-related desynchronization (ERD) and the Dm-effect: Does alpha desynchronization during encoding predict later recall performance? *International Journal of Psychophysiology, 24,* 47–60.
Kris, E. (1952). *Psychoanalytic explorations in art*. New York: International Universities Press.
Kucharska-Pietura, K., Phillips, M. L., Gernand, W., & David, A. S. (2003). Perception of emotions from faces and voices following unilateral brain damage. *Neuropsychologia, 41,* 1082–1090.
Kumari, V., Ffytche, D. H., Williams, S. C., & Gray, J. A. (2004). Personality predicts brain responses to cognitive demands. *Journal of Neuroscience, 24,* 10636–10641.
Kyllonen, P. C., & Christal, R. E. (1990). Reasoning ability is (little more than) working memory capacity?! *Intelligence, 14,* 389–433.
Lee, K. H., Choi, Y. Y., Gray, J. R., Cho, S. H., Chae, J.-H., Lee, S., et al. (2006). Neural correlates of superior intelligence: Stronger recruitment of posterior parietal cortex. *NeuroImage, 29,* 578–586.
Martindale, C. (1999). Biological bases of creativity. In R. Sternberg (Ed.), *Handbook of creativity* (pp. 137–152). Cambridge, UK: Cambridge University Press.

Martindale, C., & Hasenfus, N. (1978). EEG differences as a function of creativity, stage of the creative process, and effort to be original. *Biological Psychology, 6*, 157–167.

Martindale, C., & Hines, D. (1975). Creativity and cortical activation during creative, intellectual, and EEG feedback tasks. *Biological Psychology, 3*, 71–80.

Matthews, G., & Gilliland, K. (1999). The personality theories of H. J. Eysenck and J. A. Gray: A comparative review. *Personality and Individual Differences, 26*, 583–626.

Mednick, S. A. (1962). The associative basis of the creative process. *Psychological Review, 69*, 220–232.

Mendelsohn, G. A. (1976). Associative and attentional processes in creative performance. *Journal of Personality, 44*, 341–369.

Mölle, M., Marshall, L., Wolf, B., Fehm, H. L., & Born, J. (1999). EEG complexity and performance measures of creative thinking. *Psychophysiology, 36*, 95–104.

Neubauer, A. C., & Fink, A. (2003). Fluid intelligence and neural efficiency: Effects of task complexity and sex. *Personality and Individual Differences, 35*, 811–827.

Neubauer, A. C., & Fink, A. (2009). Intelligence and Neural efficiency. *Neuroscience & Biobehavioral Reviews, 33*, 1004–1023.

Neubauer, A. C., Fink, A., & Schrausser, D. G. (2002). Intelligence and neural efficiency: The influence of task content and sex on the brain-IQ relationship. *Intelligence, 30*, 515–536.

Neubauer, A. C., Grabner, R. H., Fink, A., & Neuper, C. (2005). Intelligence and neural efficiency: Further evidence of the influence of task content and sex on the brain-IQ relationship. *Cognitive Brain Research, 25*, 217–225.

Neubauer, A. C., Sange, G., & Pfurtscheller, G. (1999). Psychometric intelligence and event-related desynchronisation during performance of a letter matching task. In G. Pfurtscheller & F. H. Lopes da Silva (Eds.), *Event-Related Desynchronization (ERD) and Related Oscillatory EEG-phenomena of the awake brain* (pp. 219–231). Amsterdam: Elsevier.

Posner, M. I., & Mitchell, R. F. (1967). Chronometric analysis of classification. *Psychological Review, 74*, 392–409.

Posner, M. I., & Petersen, S. E. (1990). The attention system of the human brain. *Annual Review of Neuroscience, 13*, 25–42.

Razoumnikova, O. M. (2000). Functional organization of different brain areas during convergent and divergent thinking: An EEG investigation. *Cognitive Brain Research, 10*, 11–18.

Razoumnikova, O. M. (2004). Gender differences in hemispheric organization during divergent thinking: An EEG investigation in human subjects. *Neuroscience Letters, 362*, 193–195.

Razoumnikova, O. M. (2007). Creativity related cortex activity in the remote associates task. *Brain Research Bulletin, 73*, 96–102.

Roth, E. (1964). Die Geschwindigkeit der Verarbeitung von Information und ihr Zusammenhang mit Intelligenz [The relationship of speed of information processing to intelligence]. *Zeitschrift für Experimentelle und Angewandte Psychologie, 11*, 616–622.

Ruff, C. C., Knauff, M., Fangmeier, T., & Spreer, J. (2003). Reasoning and working memory: Common and distinct neural processes. *Neuropsychologia, 41*, 1241–1253.

Runco, M. A. (1999). Divergent thinking. In M. A. Runco & S. R. Pritzker (Eds.), *Encyclopedia of creativity* (pp. 577–582). San Diego, CA: Academic Press.

Rypma, B., Berger, J. S., Prabhakaran, V., Bly, B. M., Kimberg, D. Y., Biswal, B. B., et al. (2006). Neural correlates of cognitive efficiency. *NeuroImage, 33*, 969–979.

Schmidtke, J. I., & Heller, W. (2004). Personality, affect and EEG: Predicting patterns of regional brain activity related to extraversion and neuroticism. *Personality and Individual Differences, 36*, 717–732.

Smith, E. E., & Jonides, J. (2003). Executive control and thought. In L. Squire (Ed.), *Fundamentals of neuroscience* (pp. 1377–1394). New York: Academic Press.

Stankov, L. (2000). Complexity, metacognition, and intelligence. *Intelligence, 28*, 121–143.

Stein, M. I. (1953). Creativity and culture. *Journal of Psychology, 36*, 311–322.

Sternberg, R. J., & Lubart, T. (1996). Investing in creativity. *The American Psychologist, 51*(7), 677–688.

Tran, Y., Craig, A., & McIsaac, P. (2001). Extraversion-introversion and 8–13 Hz waves in frontal cortical regions. *Personality and Individual Differences, 30*, 205–215.

Vernon, P. A., & Mori, M. (1992). Intelligence, reaction times, and peripheral nerve conduction velocity. *Intelligence, 16*, 273–288.

Vernon, P. A., Wickett, J. C., Bazana, P. G., & Stelmack, R. M. (2000). The neuropsychology and psychophysiology of human intelligence. In R. J. Sternberg (Ed.), *Handbook of intelligence* (pp. 245–264). New York: Cambridge University Press.

Vitouch, O., Bauer, H., Gittler, G., Leodolter, M., & Leodolter, U. (1997). Cortical activity of good and poor spatial test performers during spatial and verbal processing studied with slow potential topography. *International Journal of Psychophysiology, 27*, 183–199.

Wickett, J. C., & Vernon, P. A. (1994). Peripheral nerve conduction velocity, reaction time, and intelligence: An attempt to replicate Vernon and Mori (1992). *Intelligence, 18*, 127–131.

Chapter 6
Cognitive Neuroscience Approaches to Individual Differences in Working Memory and Executive Control: Conceptual and Methodological Issues

Tal Yarkoni and Todd S. Braver

Analyses of individual differences play an important role in cognitive neuroscience studies of working memory and executive control (WM/EC). Many studies examining the neural substrates of working memory have relied upon correlations between brain activity and either task performance measures or trait measures of cognitive ability. However, there are important conceptual and methodological issues that surround the use of individual difference measures to explain brain activation patterns. These issues make the interpretation of correlations a more complex endeavor than is typically appreciated.

In this chapter, we review several issues that have been of long-standing concern in behavioral research on individual differences and that are equally relevant to cognitive neuroscience studies of executive control and working memory. The chapter is structured into three parts. In the first part, we provide a selective review of the literature in this domain, highlighting the most common individual difference approaches, as well as emerging trends. The scope of the review is restricted to human neuroimaging studies using fMRI methods, since this is the domain in which most of the relevant work has been conducted. However, we expect that many of the issues and relevant findings will apply equally well to other cognitive neuroscience methods (e.g., PET, ERP, TMS, etc).

The second part discusses the conceptual relationship between within-subject and individual differences analyses, focusing particular attention on situations in which within-subject and individual differences analyses produce seemingly discrepant results. Finally, in the third part, we selectively review a number of statistical and methodological concerns that arise when conducting individual differences analyses of fMRI data, including the relative lack of statistical power, the absence of data concerning the reliability of individual differences in the BOLD signal, and the deleterious effects of outliers.

An Overview of Individual Differences Approaches

Because of the high cost of conducting fMRI research and the importance of using large samples in individual differences research (see "Methodological and Statistical Considerations"), individual differences analyses in fMRI studies of WM/EC are typically conducted as an opportunistic complement to within-subject analyses and are rarely the primary focus of a study. As such, most individual differences analyses of fMRI data are subject to many or all of the following constraints:

T. Yarkoni and T.S. Braver (✉)
Departments of Psychology & Radiology, Washington University, Campus Box 1125, St. Louis, MO 63130, USA
e-mail: tbraver@wustl.edu

1. Relatively small sample sizes (the current norm appears to be between 15 and 20 participants);
2. Systematic exclusion of participants with certain characteristics in order to ensure relatively homogeneous samples (e.g., screening participants based on age, gender, or WM capacity);
3. Use of experimental manipulations that are chosen in part because they are known to produce consistent changes in behavior across participants;
4. Titration of task difficulty to ensure that all participants' performance levels fall within bounds amenable to within-subject analyses (e.g., a minimum cutoff of 80% accuracy);
5. Little or no measurement of preexisting differences in participants' cognitive abilities and/or personalities (e.g., as might be assessed using batteries of psychometric measures).

All of these constraints have a deleterious effect on the probability of detecting individual differences effects and/or generalizing significant effects to the broader population. While practical considerations make it difficult to overcome many of these limitations (e.g., collecting data from much larger samples is often not viable, from a financial perspective), a number of different approaches have been used to increase detection power and/or support stronger inferences when analyzing individual differences. We selectively highlight a number of fMRI studies that have used such approaches.

Continuous vs. Extreme Groups Designs

While participant samples in most fMRI studies are randomly sampled (subject to general constraints on demographic variables such as age and gender), some studies have attempted to maximize power to detect individual differences effects by using *extreme groups* (EG) designs in which participants are stratified into two or more groups based on their scores on some variable of interest (e.g., WM capacity or fluid intelligence; Larson, Haier, LaCasse, & Hazen, 1995; Lee et al., 2006; Mecklinger, Weber, Gunter, & Engle, 2003; Osaka et al., 2003). This approach increases the power to detect effects by reducing the variance between participant groups relative to the variance within groups, thereby inflating effect sizes and making them easier to detect.[1] For example, Lee and colleagues selected participants into two groups based on their scores on the Raven's Advanced Progressive Matrices (RAPM; Raven, Raven, & Court, 1998), a putative measure of *g*, or general intelligence (Lee et al., 2006). Both groups showed increased activation in frontal and parietal regions when performing a high *g*-loaded task relative to a low *g*-loaded cognitive task; however, the increase was substantially greater for the high-*g* group than the low-*g* group. The effect sizes observed (with peak correlations of about 0.8 between RAPM scores and brain activation) would almost certainly have been smaller if a random sample of participants had been recruited.

The increase in power obtained using EG designs is not without its costs (for review, see Preacher et al., 2005). Inflated effect sizes produced by EG designs may lead researchers to overestimate the importance of the effects in the general population (one simple solution to this problem is to pay less attention to effect sizes that result from EG studies). Moreover, an EG design will preclude identification of nonlinear effects (e.g., a curvilinear relationship between brain activation and task performance) that require examination of a full distribution of scores. Nevertheless, in cases where researchers are interested in a specific dimension of individual differences, have limited data collection resources, and detection power is more important than accurate characterization of effect size, EG samples may be preferable to random samples.

---

[1] It should be noted that extreme groups designs are *not* equivalent to post-hoc dichotomization of participants based on a median split of scores on some variable of interest. The latter approach substantially *reduces* power and is almost never justified (Cohen, 1983; MacCallum, Zhang, Preacher, & Rucker, 2002; Preacher, Rucker, MacCallum, & Nicewander, 2005). The same is true for subsampling extreme groups from a larger sample (e.g., performing a *t*-test comparing the lowest-scoring ten participants to the highest-scoring ten participants drawn from a full sample of 60 participants).

Behavioral Approaches

As noted above, the variables used to predict individual differences in brain activation are selected opportunistically in most fMRI studies of WM/EC. Most commonly, they include simple performance measures of in-scanner behavioral performance such as response accuracy (Callicott et al., 1999; Gray, Chabris, & Braver, 2003; Yarkoni, Gray, & Braver, submitted) or reaction time (Rypma, Berger, & D'Esposito, 2002; Rypma & D'Esposito, 1999; Schaefer et al., 2006; Wager, Sylvester, et al., 2005). This approach is straightforward to implement (typically requiring no special consideration when designing an experiment) and can provide valuable insights into the relationship between task performance and activation increases or decreases. On the other hand, it does not allow researchers to differentiate *state* effects (some participants may perform better or worse during a given session for relatively uninteresting reasons) from *trait* effects (some participants consistently perform better than others). Moreover, the source of a particular brain–behavior correlation may be relatively unclear (e.g., is a positive relationship between dorsolateral prefrontal cortex (DLPFC) and verbal WM performance evidence of increased WM capacity (a trait effect) or of greater effort expenditure (a state effect)?).

To overcome such limitations, a small number of studies have related brain activation not only to in-scanner behavioral tasks but also to tasks or measures administered outside of the scanner. These include both standard ability-based measures of WM span or fluid intelligence (e.g., Geake & Hansen, 2005; Gray et al., 2003; Haier, White, & Alkire, 2003; Lee et al., 2006) and questionnaire-based personality measures of dimensions such as extraversion and neuroticism (Gray & Braver, 2002; Gray et al., 2005; Kumari, Ffytche, Williams, & Gray, 2004). For example, Yarkoni and colleagues recently used multiple psychometric measures of cognitive ability to demonstrate that activation in a region of medial posterior parietal cortex (PPC) during a 3-back WM task correlated significantly with fluid and spatial abilities but not with crystallized or verbal abilities (Yarkoni, Gray, et al., submitted). This finding suggested that individuals who recruited mPPC activation more extensively (and performed more accurately) may have implicitly relied on a spatial strategy, despite the fact that the task itself had no overt spatial element. Such an inference would not be possible solely on the basis of correlations between brain activation and in-scanner performance, and requires the use of additional behavioral measures.

Another compelling illustration of the utility of behavioral measures is found in studies investigating the relationship between behaviorally measured WM capacity and the influence of dopaminergic drugs on in-scanner task performance and brain activation (S. E. Gibbs & D'Esposito, 2005; S. E. B. Gibbs & D'Esposito, 2006; Kimberg, Aguirre, Lease, & D'Esposito, 2001; Mattay et al., 2000; Mehta et al., 2000). At the group level, such studies have produced somewhat mixed results: administration of a dopamine-enhancing agent may improve WM performance and/or decrease cortical activation (Kimberg et al., 2001; Mehta et al., 2000), produce no main effect (S. E. Gibbs & D'Esposito, 2005), or even *impair* performance (S. E. B. Gibbs & D'Esposito, 2006). Importantly, however, these mixed effects are moderated by individual differences in baseline WM capacity. Across several studies, low-capacity individuals consistently benefit more from dopaminergic drugs than high-capacity individuals (S. E. Gibbs & D'Esposito, 2005; Kimberg, D'Esposito, & Farah, 1997; Mattay et al., 2000; Mehta et al., 2000), a finding that sheds considerable light on what would otherwise be a murky literature, and may have important practical implications for the use of such drugs.

Statistical Approaches

Most individual differences analyses in fMRI studies consist of basic parametric or nonparametric correlation tests (e.g., Pearson's and Spearman's correlation coefficients, respectively). However, some studies have gone beyond simple correlational analyses and have applied more sophisticated analytical procedures common in psychometric studies of WM/EC to fMRI data. One such approach is statistical mediation analysis, which indicates whether a set of correlations between variables A, B, and C is consistent with a causal model postulating that the effect of variable A on variable C is at least partly explained through the mediating role of variable B (MacKinnon, Lockwood, Hoffman, West, & Sheets, 2002). Several fMRI studies have used mediation analyses to identify brain regions that significantly mediate the relationship between two behavioral variables (e.g., Richeson et al., 2003; Tom, Fox, Trepel, & Poldrack, 2007; Yarkoni, Braver, Gray, & Green, 2005), though the number of applications to the domain of WM/EC remains limited. One study notable for its use of mediation analysis in a relatively large sample ($n = 50$) was reported by Gray and colleagues (Gray et al., 2003). They conducted an fMRI experiment in which participants completed a standard measure of fluid intelligence (RAPM) and subsequently performed a challenging 3-back WM task in the scanner. The study's design enabled the authors to identify a region in the left lateral prefrontal cortex (PFC) that statistically *mediated* the correlation between fluid intelligence and 3-back response accuracy – a stronger inference than would be afforded simply by observing a correlation between brain activation and task performance.

Another statistical technique widely used in psychometric WM/EC research is structural equation modeling (SEM; Bollen, 1989; Kline, 1998), which enables researchers to estimate, evaluate, and develop causal models of the relationships between variables (Friedman & Miyake, 2004; Kane et al., 2004). To date, cognitive neuroscientists interested in WM/EC have used SEM primarily to model interactions between different brain regions and/or WM task conditions (for review, see Schlösser, Wagner, & Sauer, 2006), and only secondarily to relate individual differences measures of WM to brain activation (but see, e.g., Glabus et al., 2003; Kondo et al., 2004). However, in principle, a unified SEM framework could integrate both behavioral and neural data – e.g., by mapping latent variables derived from behavioral measures onto distinct brain networks (Kim, Zhu, Chang, Bentler, & Ernst, 2007). Of course, such efforts are likely to be hampered by considerable practical obstacles – e.g., the need for large sample sizes, multiple in-scanner sessions, etc. – so SEM approaches on the scale of existing behavioral analyses (Conway, Cowan, Bunting, Therriault, & Minkoff, 2002; Engle, Tuholski, Laughlin, & Conway, 1999; Kane et al., 2004) may not be viable.

An alternative multivariate technique used in a number of WM/EC studies involving individual differences (e.g., Caplan, McIntosh, & De Rosa, 2007; Della-Maggiore et al., 2000; Grady et al., 1998) is Partial Least Squares (PLS; McIntosh, Bookstein, Haxby, & Grady, 1996; McIntosh & Lobaugh, 2004). Like SEM, PLS focuses on network-level activation rather than individual voxels or brain regions; however, unlike other multivariate approaches, PLS seeks to identify patterns of brain activation that covary maximally with a reference set of variables (e.g., an experimental design matrix or a set of individual difference variables). For example, Caplan and colleagues recently used PLS to identify two distributed brain networks that independently predicted individual differences in the successful resolution of proactive interference (Caplan et al., 2007). The use of a multivariate approach allowed the authors to model brain activation at the level of functional networks rather than isolated regions, an approach that would not have been possible using conventional univariate methods. However, PLS remains susceptible to many of the limitations of SEM (e.g., the fundamental need for a large sample size when focusing primarily on individual differences).

The Relationship Between Within-Subject and Individual Differences Analyses

How are individual differences analyses conceptually related to more common within-subject analyses (e.g., paired *t*-tests)? One common intuition is that the results of the two types of analyses should tend to converge. That is, regions in which an experimental manipulation elicits greater activation on a within-subject level should also show reliable between-subjects variation, such that activation is greater in individuals who capably perform the task than in individuals who do not. There is some empirical support for this idea; for example, DLPFC activation reliably increases as a function of WM load (Braver et al., 1997; Callicott et al., 1999), and several studies have found a positive correlation between DLPFC activation and higher WM capacity or greater fluid intelligence (Gray et al., 2003; Lee et al., 2006). On the other hand, there are arguably more instances in the literature of within-subject and between-subjects analyses producing effects in conceptually *opposing* directions. For example, older adults often show greater prefrontal activation than younger adults when performing effortful cognitive tasks despite exhibiting a poorer level of behavioral performance (Cabeza, Anderson, Locantore, & McIntosh, 2002; Reuter-Lorenz, 2002). In young adults, many studies have similarly found greater activation in regions such as lateral PFC and anterior cingulate cortex (ACC) in participants who perform poorly than those who perform well. The ACC is thought to be involved in monitoring for conflict, and in several studies, individuals who perform more poorly on tasks involving cognitive conflict have shown greater ACC activation (Bunge, Ochsner, Desmond, Glover, & Gabrieli, 2001; Hester, Fassbender, & Garavan, 2004; MacDonald, Cohen, Stenger, & Carter, 2000; Wager, Sylvester, et al., 2005). Left ventrolateral PFC (VLPFC) is thought to be involved in resolving proactive interference (Jonides & Nee, 2006), yet individuals who are good at overcoming proactive interference show *less* VLPFC activation than individuals who are not (Nee, Jonides, & Berman, 2007).

There is often a plausible explanation for the opposing directions of within-subject and individual differences effects. For example, the observation that susceptibility to interference during cognitive conflict-inducing tasks correlates positively with ACC activation might be attributed to the fact that the ACC tracks the amount of *input* conflict rather than the degree to which its resolution is successful (e.g., Wager, Sylvester, et al., 2005). More generally, frontoparietal hyperactivations in older adults and poorly performing young adults are often attributed to compensatory processing or differences in *neural efficiency* (Gray et al., 2005; Haier et al., 1992; Larson et al., 1995; Rypma et al., 2006). That is, older adults and inefficient young adults are thought to require greater effort expenditure to achieve the same level of performance as highly performing young adults, leading to relative increases in frontoparietal activation. This interpretation affords easy reconciliation of the apparent contradiction between individual differences and within-subject effects. However, the explanatory power of this perspective is limited, as it provides no indication as to *why* individuals might vary considerably in cognitive efficiency, or why correlations between frontoparietal activation and cognitive performance are positive in some studies but negative in others.

An additional consideration is that correlations between mean reaction time (RT), a primary measure of behavioral performance, and brain activation may simply reflect basic properties of the blood oxygen level dependent (BOLD) signal detected by fMRI. In a recent multistudy analysis, we demonstrated that trial-by-trial differences in reaction time correlate positively with lateral PFC and MFC activation in a task-independent manner (Yarkoni, Barch, Gray, Conturo, & Braver, submitted). The explanation accorded to this finding was that frontal increases on slower trials reflect linear summation of the hemodynamic response over time (cf. Burock, Buckner, Woldorff, Rosen, & Dale, 1998; Dale & Buckner, 1997). While we did not report individual differences analyses of RT, a temporal summation account should hold both within and across individuals. That is, individuals who sustain attention to task-relevant information for a longer period of time may show a greater summation of the BOLD signal in frontal regions, irrespective of whether that time is used efficiently or not. Given this possibility, caution should probably be exercised when using individual differences in RT as a predictor of brain activity. A preferable approach is to rely on response accuracy as a measure of performance while statistically controlling for individual differences in RT. Unfortunately, this approach is not viable for many tasks in which RT is the primary measure of performance. Nevertheless, given that it is possible to include RT as a trial-by-trial covariate in fMRI analyses, effectively controlling for this source of variance, it might be useful in such studies to test how the inclusion of an RT covariate influences individual difference effects.

Spatial Dissociations

Discrepancies between within-subject and individual differences analyses need not manifest as conceptually opposing effects within the same brain regions. Often, individual differences analyses simply fail to reveal *any* significant effects in regions that show a robust within-subject effect. In such cases, lack of statistical power, which we discuss at length in the next section, is a likely culprit, because individual differences analyses almost invariably have considerably lower power than within-subject effects. Alternatively, individual differences analyses and within-subject analyses may both reveal significant effects but in spatially dissociable regions (Bunge et al., 2001; Locke & Braver, 2008; Yarkoni, Gray, et al., submitted). For example, in a recent large-sample ($n=94$) fMRI study using a 3-back WM task, we found a dissociation between frontoparietal regions canonically implicated in cognitive control and a region of medial posterior parietal cortex (mPPC) not usually implicated in WM/EC (Yarkoni, Gray, et al., submitted). Frontoparietal regions showed strong within-subject effects of trial difficulty but inconsistent associations with response accuracy either within or across individuals. In contrast, mPPC activation showed relatively weak effects of trial difficulty but robust associations with response accuracy both within and across subjects.

How should spatial dissociations between within-subject and individual differences effects be interpreted? On the one hand, such findings may seem counterintuitive, because regions that do not appear to be recruited *on average* during performance of a task may seem like unlikely candidates for individual differences effects. Indeed, some evidence suggests that the BOLD signal tends to be more reliable across individuals in regions that show strong within-subject effects than in those that do not (Aron, Gluck, & Poldrack, 2006; Specht, Willmes, Shah, & Jaencke, 2003). On the other hand, there is no logical necessity for within-subject and between-subject sources of variance to produce converging results. Indeed, from a statistical standpoint, within-subject and between-subject effects are in tension, because between-subjects variance counts as error in within-subject analyses, and vice versa. This observation raises concerns that one of the most common individual differences approaches in fMRI studies – namely identifying regions-of-interest (ROIs) on the basis of within-subject analyses and subsequently testing them for correlational effects – may actually *reduce* the probability of detecting significant effects. Omura and colleagues recently advocated precisely the opposite approach, suggesting that researchers interested in correlational effects should focus their search on regions in which between-subjects variance is largest relative to within-subject variance (Omura, Aron, & Canli, 2005). However, the viability of the latter approach depends on the assumption that the signal in regions with a high BS/WS variance ratio is reliable. If, as the studies cited above suggest, reliability tends to be highest in regions that show the strongest *within*-subject effects, there would be little utility in such an approach. Additional empirical studies are needed in order clarify the issue.

Integrative Interpretation of Within-Subject and Individual Differences Results

Although directional or spatial dissociations between within-subject and individual differences analyses may be difficult to interpret, they can potentially also serve as a powerful tool for characterizing the functional role of different brain regions. Within-subject and individual differences analyses reflect independent sources of variance, are sensitive to different kinds of processes, and afford qualitatively different conclusions. We focus here on two kinds of inferences afforded when combining the two forms of analysis. First, within-subject analyses are, by definition, most sensitive to processes that are consistent across all participants, including those that are *necessary* for performing a task. For example, the fact that the "task-positive" frontoparietal network (Fox et al., 2005) is activated during virtually all tasks involving cognitive effort (Buchsbaum, Greer, Chang, & Berman, 2005; Duncan & Owen, 2000; Owen, McMillan, Laird, & Bullmore, 2005; Wager, Jonides, & Reading, 2004) likely indicates that an intact frontoparietal network is necessary in order to maintain a minimal level of goal-directed attention; however, this network may play little or no role in supporting many of the task-specific processes that distinguish one effortful cognitive task from another. In contrast, variability in performance across individuals is most likely to reflect those processes that can be recruited in varying degrees to produce incremental gains in performance. These include both processes that can vary quantitatively in strength (e.g., the amount of effort one exerts during the task) as well as qualitatively different strategies that may vary across individuals (e.g., in an *N*-back task, participants may use either familiarity-based or proactive strategies; Braver, Gray, & Burgess, 2007; Kane, Conway, Miura, & Colflesh, 2007).

A second and related point is that combining standard subtractive contrasts of different experimental conditions with correlational analyses of individual differences can help distinguish neural processes that are causally involved in modulating overt behavior from those that are epiphenomenal with respect to overt behavior and may even *result* from behavioral changes. A common strategy in fMRI studies is to demonstrate that an experimental manipulation elicits changes in both overt behavior and brain activation, and to then causally attribute the former to the latter. For example, the view that the left inferior frontal gyrus plays a role in resisting cognitive interference during goal-directed processing is based largely on observations that activation in left IFG increases in proportion to the amount of proactive interference present in the environment (for review, see Jonides & Nee, 2006). Such evidence cannot conclusively rule out the possibility that left IFG activation tracks some epiphenomenal cognitive process that covaries with the amount of interference present on a trial but does not itself influence the behavioral response (e.g., familiarity of the interfering stimulus). The causal inference is more strongly supported if it can be shown that changes in IFG activation correlate in meaningful ways with individual differences in resistance to proactive interference (e.g., Gray et al., 2003; Nee et al., 2007).

Of course, brain–behavior relationships can be investigated not only at the level of individual differences, but also within-subject, using trial-by-trial differences in behavior to predict corresponding changes in brain activation. For example, if left IFG is involved in resolving proactive interference, it should presumably show greater activation on trials when participants successfully resist interference than on trials on which they succumb to interference. Integrative approaches that model brain–behavior relationships both within and across subjects should be encouraged, because they can provide even more sophisticated inferences. For example, significant correlations with performance across subjects but not within subjects may indicate that individuals are using qualitatively different strategies that are relatively stable within-session. In a recent fMRI study of decision-making under uncertainty in which participants repeatedly chose between high-probability small rewards and low-probability large rewards (e.g., 90% of 100 points vs. 25% chance of 400 points), we found that activation in PPC correlated strongly with "rational" choice (i.e., selection of the higher expected value) across individuals but not on a trial-by-trial basis (Yarkoni & Braver, 2008). This finding likely reflects the fact that participants who explicitly computed the expected value of each reward – an ability that depends on mental arithmetic operations supported by PPC (Dehaene, Piazza, Pinel, & Cohen, 2005) – were likely to make very few suboptimal choices, whereas those who used heuristic strategies (e.g., selecting the higher-probability reward) did not compute expected value and hence did not activate PPC. The interpretation would have been very different had the PPC covaried with rational choice within subjects but *not* across subjects. In the latter case, a more plausible interpretation would be that participants tended to all use similar computational strategies, and that decision-making performance was largely a function of trial-specific variables (e.g., the difficulty of the trial, random fluctuations in internal noise levels, etc.).

In sum, the relationship between within-subject and individual differences analyses is complex, and the two kinds of analyses should not be viewed simply as two sides of the same coin. Individual differences analyses offer researchers more than just a second shot at detecting a hypothesized effect. An integrative approach that complements standard experimental contrasts with individual differences analyses as well as trial-by-trial correlations with behavior can potentially provide researchers with sophisticated and powerful insights into brain–behavior relationships that would be difficult to achieve by other means.

Methodological and Statistical Considerations

Power and Sample Size

A paramount consideration when conducting virtually any kind of psychological experiment is statistical power, or the probability that a statistical test will produce a significant result in cases where the tested effect is indeed present in the population. Power is a direct function of three parameters: effect size, statistical threshold, and the sensitivity of the data, which in turn depends on measurement reliability and sample size. Measurement reliability is discussed in greater detail in the next section; for present purposes, we focus on the role of sample size as it is the parameter most easily manipulated by investigators, and arguably the one that presents neuroimaging investigators with the greatest problems.

fMRI studies of individual differences are consistently underpowered. The importance of ensuring that a study has adequate statistical power should be readily apparent. If power is simply the ability to detect the effect one is looking for, why bother conducting a study that has little chance of producing significant results? Yet failures to consider power prior to conducting experimental investigations are surprisingly common in the psychological sciences, as a result of which power levels are often dismally low (for recent discussion, see Maxwell, 2004).

To date, relatively few studies have explored issues related to statistical power in functional neuroimaging studies. The majority of such studies have focused on power-related issues in the context of fMRI design choices – e.g., the trade-off between the ability to *detect* a specific hemodynamic response function and the ability to successfully *estimate* the shape of that response (e.g., Friston, Holmes, Poline, Price, & Frith, 1996; Liu, Frank, Wong, & Buxton, 2001). Only a handful of studies have attempted to determine the number of subjects required in order to ensure an adequate level of power in mixed-model fMRI analyses (Desmond & Glover, 2002; Mumford & Nichols, 2008; Murphy & Garavan, 2004; Thirion et al., 2007), and these studies have focused exclusively on within-subject analyses (e.g., paired t-tests contrasting activation in two experimental conditions). No study we know of has attempted to generate power estimates for individual differences analyses in fMRI studies. This absence is problematic, because individual differences analyses have lower power to detect effects than within-subject analyses (assuming that effect size, statistical threshold, and sample size are held constant), and one cannot simply generalize recommendations made specifically for within-subject analyses to the domain of individual differences.

To provide estimates of the sample sizes needed to ensure adequate statistical power in individual differences fMRI analyses, we generated power curves for a standard correlation test (Pearson's r) using parameters that are realistic for fMRI studies (Fig. 6.1). For comparison purposes, equivalent curves are presented for a paired t-test analysis. Table 6.1 provides point estimates of power level for these two statistical tests at several different effect sizes, sample sizes, and statistical significance thresholds. The figure and table support two main conclusions. First, correlational analyses have substantially lower power to detect effects than one-sample t-tests under realistic circumstances. For example, a one-sample t-test has 92% power to detect a "large" effect size of $d=0.8$ in a sample

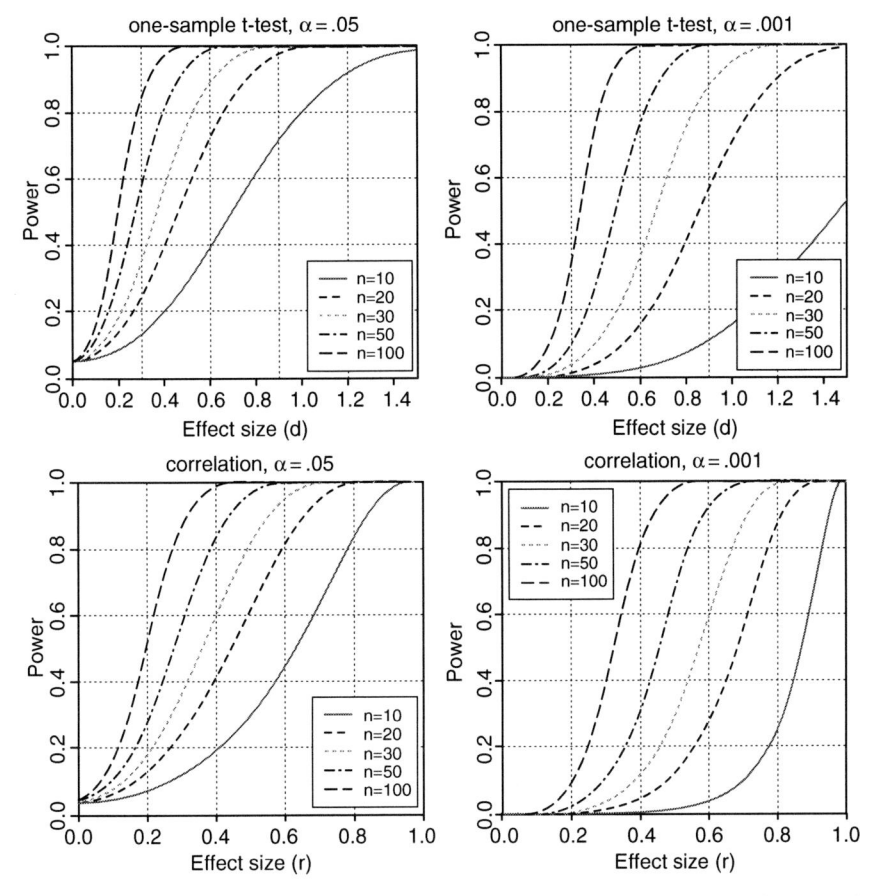

Fig. 6.1 Statistical power as a function of test type (*top* = one-sample *t*-test, *bottom* = Pearson's *r*), sample size, and effect size

of 20 subjects at $p < 0.05$. Yet a d of 0.8 is equivalent to an r of approximately 0.37,[2] and power to detect a correlation of this size at $p < 0.05$ in the same sample is only 35%. Achieving a conventionally adequate power level of 0.8 for this correlational test would require a sample size of 55 – more than double that recommended by power studies that have focused on within-subject analyses (typically about $n = 25$; Desmond & Glover, 2002; Murphy & Garavan, 2004; Thirion et al., 2007).

These analyses make clear that the majority of fMRI analyses of individual differences have very little power to detect all but the most powerful correlational effects. A cursory review of fMRI studies of individual differences in WM and executive control suggests that sample sizes of approximately 15–20 are the norm in previous research. While some studies have used much larger samples (Gray et al., 2003; Hester et al., 2004; Schaefer et al., 2006; Yarkoni, Gray, et al., submitted), others have reported results based on samples as small as 6–9 individuals (Callicott et al., 1999; Fiebach, Rissman, & D'Esposito, 2006; Mattay et al., 2000; Rypma & D'Esposito, 1999). Moreover, many studies that employed individual differences analyses have relied at least in part on whole-brain analyses, necessitating conservative statistical thresholds on the order of $p < 0.001$ or less. When one considers that a correlation test has only 12% power to detect even a "large" correlation of 0.5 at

---

[2]Cohen's (1988, p. 23) formula provides $r \approx d / \sqrt{d^2 + 4}$.

Table 6.1 Statistical power for correlation and one-sample *t*-test

n	Effect size measure r	d	Correlation power	One-sample *t*-test power	Relative decrease (%)
α = 0.05					
10	0.1	0.2	0.05	0.09	44.4
	0.3	0.63	0.12	0.43	72.1
	0.5	1.15	0.3	0.9	66.7
	0.7	1.96	0.63	1	37.0
20	0.1	0.2	0.06	0.13	53.8
	0.3	0.63	0.24	0.76	68.4
	0.5	1.15	0.62	1	38.0
	0.7	1.96	0.95	1	5.0
30	0.1	0.2	0.08	0.19	57.9
	0.3	0.63	0.36	0.91	60.4
	0.5	1.15	0.82	1	18.0
	0.7	1.96	0.99	1	1.0
50	0.1	0.2	0.1	0.28	64.3
	0.3	0.63	0.56	0.99	43.4
	0.5	1.15	0.97	1	3.0
	0.7	1.96	1	1	0.0
α = 0.001					
10	0.1	0.2	0	0	–
	0.3	0.63	0	0.03	100.0
	0.5	1.15	0.02	0.25	92.0
	0.7	1.96	0.1	0.85	88.2
20	0.1	0.2	0	0.01	100.0
	0.3	0.63	0.01	0.2	95.0
	0.5	1.15	0.12	0.87	86.2
	0.7	1.96	0.57	1	43.0
30	0.1	0.2	0	0.01	100.0
	0.3	0.63	0.04	0.44	90.9
	0.5	1.15	0.3	0.99	69.7
	0.7	1.96	0.88	1	12.0
50	0.1	0.2	0	0.03	100.0
	0.3	0.63	0.11	0.82	86.6
	0.5	1.15	0.67	1	33.0
	0.7	1.96	1	1	0.0

$p < 0.001$ in a sample size of $n = 20$, it becomes clear that the typical fMRI study of individual differences in WM has little hope of detecting many, if not most, meaningful effects.[3] Thus, there are strong incentives for researchers to use larger samples and theoretically driven analyses that allow ROI-level hypotheses to be tested at more liberal thresholds.

Small samples and effect size inflation. An underappreciated but important consequence of using small sample sizes is that the effect size of significant results may be grossly inflated (Bradley, Smith, & Stoica, 2002; Muncer, Craigie, & Holmes, 2003). When sample sizes are small enough and/or population effects weak enough, the critical value for a statistical test may be much higher than the actual population effect size, so the only way to detect a significant effect is to capitalize

---

[3]Note that values of $r \geq 0.5$ are extremely rare in most areas of psychology; see Meyer et al. (2001) for a review indicating that most effects across broad domains of psychology and medicine are in the range of 0.1–0.3.

on chance. Failure to consider the possibility of such inflation can then have a number of deleterious effects. First, researchers may grossly overestimate the importance of their findings. Second, the combination of inflated effect sizes and low statistical power may lead researchers to erroneously conclude not only that observed effects are very strong but also that they are highly *selective*. Suppose for example that performance on a WM task shows a uniform correlation of 0.3 with activation across the entire brain in the general population. In a sample of 20 subjects, power to detect a significant correlation for any given observation is only 1.4% at a whole-brain α-level of 0.001. Thus, in a brain comprised of 100,000 voxels, a whole-brain analysis will detect only ~1,400 significant voxels on average – and the mean significant r value in these voxels will be highly inflated, at approximately 0.73.[4] An uncritical researcher examining the threshold output from a statistical test could then easily conclude that task performance is very strongly correlated with activation in highly selective brain regions, when in fact the actual population effect is much weaker and shows no spatial selectivity whatsoever.

Finally, inflated effect sizes may lead to misallocation of considerable resources as replications and extensions of a reported "large" effect are unsuccessfully attempted. As studies accumulate, the literature addressing a given research question may come to appear full of "mixed results," with some studies detecting an effect and others failing to, or detecting effects of very different sizes. If one allows that initial reports of correlational effects sometimes grossly overestimate the size of the effect, it should not be surprising if subsequent studies with similar or even larger sample sizes often fail to replicate the original effect, or successfully replicate the effect with a much smaller effect size. Consider, for example, two recent studies by Gray and colleagues (Gray & Braver, 2002; Gray et al., 2005). In a first study, the authors identified strong correlations (0.63–0.84) between participants' BAS scores (measures of behavioral approach tendencies, respectively) and caudal ACC activation in several WM conditions (Gray & Braver, 2002). Yet, in a follow-up study (Gray et al., 2005), with a much larger sample size ($N > 50$), the same correlations were at a much lower level (0.28–0.37). Had a smaller sample size been used in the follow-up study, even a partial replication would have been exceedingly unlikely, and the authors might then have concluded that the initial set of findings were false positives, or reflected some unknown experimental difference. Yet, the seeming discrepancy is easily explained by noting that effect sizes in the first experiment were likely inflated due to small sample size ($n = 14$). In fact, the correlation achieved in the follow-up study was well within the confidence intervals of the effect in the original study but led to a qualitatively different assessment regarding the importance of the personality effect.

In sum, a realistic assessment of power in fMRI studies of individual differences can help researchers avoid undue excitement about the strength and selectivity of observed effects, can provide a realistic assessment of the likelihood of replicating previous effects, and may help explain away many instances of seemingly conflicting findings.

Data peeking and Type I error inflation. A final issue related to the use of small samples in fMRI studies concerns the tendency of fMRI researchers to "peek" at the data – that is, to periodically reanalyze the data every time one or more subjects are added to the sample. Because fMRI data collection and processing is laborious and extremely expensive, the practice of data peeking may seem to make good practical sense. If a targeted effect is already present in a small sample, why bother increasing the sample size at great expense?

While the act of inspecting the data is not harmful in and of itself, the decision to *terminate* data collection as soon as significant results are obtained is rarely if ever defensible. Early termination can lead to substantial inflation of Type I error, because a researcher may erroneously accept a spurious effect that would have gone away if data collection had continued (for discussion of this issue, see Armitage, McPherson, & Rowe, 1969; Pocock, 2006; Strube, 2006; Wagenmakers, 2007).

---

[4]For the sake of simplicity, this example assumes that each voxel represents an independent observation.

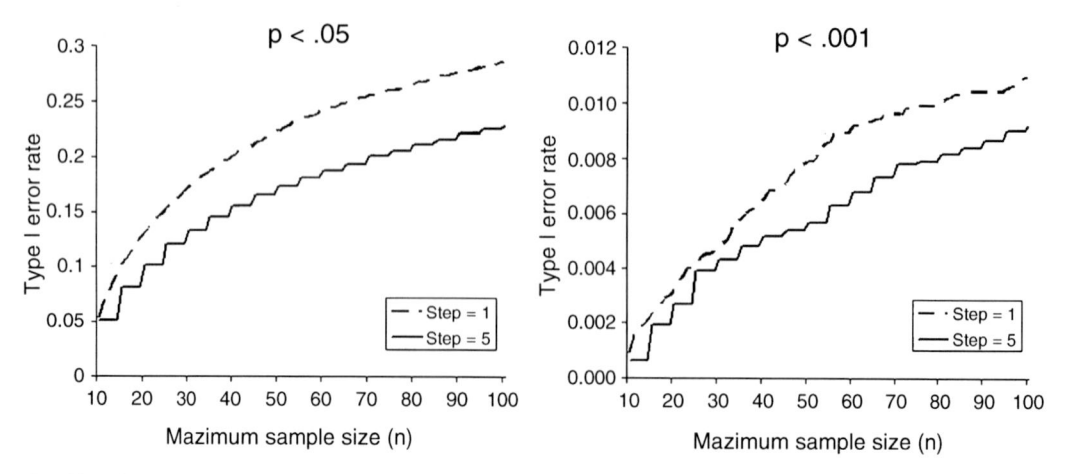

Fig. 6.2 Effects of data peeking on Type I error rate as a function of statistical threshold, sample size, and peeking interval (1 vs. 5). Peeking is assumed to begin after ten participants; beginning earlier would further inflate false positives

Figure 6.2 plots the Type I error rate associated with data peeking for common sample sizes and statistical thresholds (cf. Strube, 2006). Inflation of Type I error is considerable in virtually all cases. For example, given a maximum sample size of 30 and an α-level of 0.05, the probability of falsely detecting a significant effect is over 17% if peeking begins after ten subjects, the correlation is computed every time a subject is added to the sample, and one assumes that the study terminates as soon as a significant effect is found. At a conventional whole-brain threshold of $p<0.001$, the corresponding Type I error rate for the same sample is approximately 0.5% – still low in absolute terms, but a fivefold increase over the nominal rate. If data peeking occurs at less frequent intervals, the inflation factor decreases; however, it remains unacceptably high even at a peeking interval of five subjects (Type I error rate = ~13.4% at $p<0.05$ and ~0.4% at $p<0.001$).

Practical recommendations. Practically speaking, what can researchers do to address the above power-related concerns? We make six recommendations:

1. *Use larger samples.* Whenever possible, the simplest and best cure for a lack of power is to increase the sample size. Use of small samples is often justified anecdotally by noting that effect sizes in fMRI research are very large, making their detection relatively easy. However, as the power curves and Monte Carlo simulations presented above show, there is reason to doubt such assertions. The fact that small-sample studies routinely obtain correlations of 0.7–0.9 almost certainly reflects massive effect size inflation rather than unusually large brain–behavior correlations in the population. Simply put, researchers who are serious about investigating individual differences with fMRI must be willing to collect larger samples. Based on the results presented here, we would suggest $n=40$ as a reasonable lower limit for a study focused *primarily* on individual differences analyses. This sample size is still suboptimal from a power standpoint but may represent an acceptable trade-off between the need to ensure adequate power while limiting data collection costs. However, this generalization should be taken with a grain of salt, and is no substitute for study-specific power calculations.
2. *Perform (and report) power calculations.* There is little reason not to conduct power calculations prior to beginning fMRI data collection. Many power analysis tools are freely available either as stand-alone applications or as add-ons to popular statistics packages,[5] and several websites

---

[5] We used *R* and the add-on *pwr* library to perform all of the calculations and simulations reported in this chapter.

provide instantaneous power calculations for various statistical procedures. The time investment required to perform a series of power calculations is negligible and the potential pitfalls of failing to do so are enormous. There is no good reason we can see for failing to report power calculations whenever individual differences analyses are reported in fMRI studies. Reviewers and editors should similarly be encouraged to request or require authors to report power calculations when none are provided.
3. *Test a priori hypotheses whenever possible.* While whole-brain analyses are an important complement to any set of focused regional analyses, the use of ROI-level tests allows correlations to be tested at much more liberal statistical thresholds (e.g., $p<0.05$ instead of $p<0.001$). Of course, testing too many hypotheses at a regional level can introduce its own multiple-comparisons problem, and the privileged status of theoretical hypotheses should not be abused by testing several dozen regions without further controlling the Type I error rate.
4. *Do not base sample size decisions on inspection of provisional data.* While some amount of data peeking for quality assurance purposes may be inevitable in fMRI studies, researchers should peek only to ensure to adequacy of the fMRI signal itself, and not the adequacy of the results in relation to the hypothesis. Researchers should not cease collecting fMRI data once sufficiently interesting results are obtained, nor should they chase a marginal correlation with additional subjects until it becomes significant. The recommended approach is to select a sample size based on a priori power calculations and stick to it. Deviating from the chosen sample size based on preliminary results will result in considerable inflation of Type I error.
5. *Avoid attributing null results or replication failures to experimental factors without good cause.* It is often tempting to attribute a replication failure to some minute difference between the original and present studies. However, unless sample size is very large and/or the expected effects are extremely strong, by far the most plausible explanations for a null result in an individual differences fMRI analysis are that (a) the present null result represents a Type II error or (b) the original result represented a Type I error.
6. *Pay little attention to the apparent strength or spatial selectivity of correlational effects.* Small sample sizes may dramatically inflate the size of significant effects, and low power tends to induce an illusion of spatial selectivity. Consequently, a good deal of skepticism should be applied when interpreting small-sample size correlational results that appear to be very strong and highly selective.

Reliability

Reliability refers to the ability of an instrument or measure to produce consistent results when tested under similar conditions. Measurement reliability is a paramount concern in virtually all empirical investigations because the reliability of a measure sets an upper bound on the extent to which its variance is available to correlate with other measures (Cohen, West, Aiken, & Cohen, 2002). The detectable correlation between the *observed* scores of two variables is formally equivalent to the square root of the product of the two reliabilities multiplied by the true population correlation. Attenuation of effects due to measurement unreliability may have few practical consequences in cases where effects and/or sample sizes are very large because, so long as an effect is detectable and estimates of measurement reliability are available, it is always possible to correct for unreliability and estimate the true population effect size. However, as the above discussion of power should make clear, fMRI studies rarely occupy this privileged niche. Given the small sample sizes typical of fMRI studies, a difference between population-level and sample-level effect sizes could easily amount to the difference between a significant effect and a null result. Thus, the viability of individual differences analyses in fMRI studies depends critically on ensuring that the measures used – whether of behavior or brain function – are sufficiently reliable.

Behavioral measures. By convention, reliability coefficients of 0.8 are considered adequate in most domains of psychological research, and coefficients of 0.9 or more are generally considered high. Given that most fMRI analyses of individual differences in WM and executive control use behavioral measures (e.g., task performance or cognitive ability measures) to predict brain activity, one might expect a similar convention to hold in the fMRI literature. Unfortunately, reliability coefficients for behavioral measures are rarely reported in fMRI studies. This absence is of little concern in studies that use standard measures that have been psychometrically validated – e.g., the RAPM or Engle and colleagues' version of the Operation Span task (Unsworth, Heitz, Schrock, & Engle, 2005) – because it is unlikely that the reliability of such measures will depart radically from published norms for any given study. However, many fMRI studies use nonstandard individual differences measures as predictors of brain activation, e.g., measures of RT or response accuracy derived from idiosyncratically implemented or entirely novel cognitive tasks. In the latter case, it is important to supplement any reported correlational results with an estimate of the reliability of the measures involved. Given that reliability can be easily estimated in a variety of ways (e.g., virtually all major statistical packages can easily compute Cronbach's α, the most common measure of internal consistency), researchers should be encouraged to report a coefficient of reliability for all individual differences measures used to predict brain activity – a step only a few fMRI studies have taken (e.g., Gillath, Bunge, Shaver, Wendelken, & Mikulincer, 2005; Heinz et al., 2004).

Neuroimaging measures. In contrast to behavioral measures, it is not quite as straightforward for researchers to estimate the reliability of the BOLD signal. Subjects are typically tested on only one occasion in most studies, and measurements at different voxels or scanning frames cannot be thought of as items of a measure in the same sense as questions on a questionnaire. The most viable route to determining reliability given such constraints is to compute some form of split-half reliability coefficient, e.g., by comparing activation across different runs within the same session, or by randomly coding events of a single type using two different variables. While this approach is admittedly time-consuming, and produces results that may be difficult to interpret and report because reliability coefficients may vary considerably from voxel to voxel and experimental condition to experimental condition, we believe the potential benefits are sufficiently great to warrant wider adoption.

General estimates of the reliability of fMRI data can be gleaned from a number of studies that have explicitly sought to quantify the reliability of the BOLD signal.[6] Overall, such studies provide a mixed picture. On the positive side, several studies that assessed test–retest reliability at varying intervals reported adequate or even high reliability coefficients across a range of experimental tasks (e.g., Aron et al., 2006; Fernandez et al., 2003; Specht et al., 2003). For example, Aron et al. (2006) scanned eight participants who performed a classification learning task on two separate occasions 1 year apart and found intraclass correlation coefficients (ICCs) greater than 0.8 in many voxels that were activated at the group level. Such results clearly demonstrate that it is *possible* to measure brain activation reliably with fMRI; however, there is no guarantee that this conclusion will generalize across different samples, designs, scanners, and experimental contrasts.

---

[6] Note that the term *reliability* is used here to refer specifically to the stability of the rank order of BOLD activation across subjects. That is, the BOLD signal can be considered reliable if individuals who show high levels of activation when scanned on one occasion also show high levels of activation when scanned on another occasion under the same conditions. The term reliability is also often used to refer to the *replicability* or *reproducibility* of fMRI results at the group level – e.g., deeming the BOLD signal reliable if approximately the same pattern of group-level activation can be replicated across different samples, scanners, institutions, task variants, etc. Although these two senses of reliability are interrelated, they are not equivalent. We focus here only on the former sense, as it is the one relevant for individual differences analyses.

Indeed, other studies have provided decidedly less optimistic results (Johnstone et al., 2005; Manoach et al., 2001; Manuck, Brown, Forbes, & Hariri, 2007). For example, Johnstone et al. 2005 investigated the test–retest reliability of amygdala reactivity to neutral and fearful faces across three testing occasions spanning 8 weeks. ICCs peaked around 0.8 in the left amygdala, but were near zero in the right amygdala for several contrasts. Manuck et al. 2007 conducted a similar study but with a longer (1 year) test–retest interval. In contrast to Johnstone et al.'s results, Manuck et al. found moderate stability in the right amygdala ($r=0.59$) but no stability in the left amygdala ($r=-0.08$). Note that low test–retest reliability does not necessarily imply low reliability in general as test–retest reliability estimates can differ considerably from estimates of internal consistency. That is, it is possible for regional brain activation to show adequate reliability on one occasion yet fail to show consistency over time due to the systematic influence of other factors (e.g., participants' mood). Nonetheless, the complete absence of temporal consistency in some analyses is cause for concern and raises the worrisome possibility that correlational effects may be impossible to detect in some regions and experiments.[7] Moreover, even in studies that have identified highly reliable activations, the locus of reliable signal tends to be circumscribed to those regions that show significant group-level involvement in the task (Aron et al., 2006; Specht et al., 2003), potentially limiting the scope of individual differences analyses even further.

Increasing reliability. Considerable work remains to be done in order to better understand the conditions that affect the reliability of individual differences in the BOLD signal. In the interim, several steps can be taken in the hopes of increasing reliability. First, researchers should take care to use reliable behavioral measures as predictors of brain activity and should report reliability coefficients for such measures whenever possible. Second, in cases where the process is not too laborious, researchers can obtain rough estimates of BOLD signal reliability by conducting split-half analyses as noted above. Third, reliability can be increased by employing data reduction or latent variable techniques such as principal components analysis (PCA) or SEM that "triangulate" on reliable variance. For example, factor analytic techniques can be used to extract a small number of latent activation variables from a large number of ROIs or behavioral variables (Badre, Poldrack, Paré-Blagoev, Insler, & Wagner, 2005; Peterson et al., 1999; Wager, Sylvester, et al., 2005; Yarkoni, Gray, et al., submitted) or from a single ROI across different contrasts (Yarkoni, Gray, et al., submitted). Such factors, which reflect only common (and therefore, reliable) variance, are more likely to correlate with behavioral variables, other things being equal. (A secondary benefit of such an approach is the reduction in the number of statistical comparisons tested.)

Finally, researchers who are specifically interested in individual differences and are willing to sacrifice some power to detect within-subject effects may be able to increase the reliability of brain activation measures by deliberately selecting experimental tasks that produce highly variable performance across individuals. For example, if one's goal is to investigate the neural correlates of individual differences in WM capacity, maximal reliability is likely to be attained when the experimental task used in the scanner is relatively difficult, and a wide range of performance levels is observed. Conversely, when a task is relatively easy and performance is near ceiling levels for most participants, as is common in many fMRI studies of WM, activation in regions associated with task performance may be relatively unreliable because the amount of effort a participant invests may have little influence on their performance level (i.e., one could invest a little effort or a lot, and the behavioral data would not reflect this variability).

---

[7]It may also be that these low test-retest correlations reflect a genuine lack of stable individual differences. However, the strong hemispheric asymmetry and conflicting findings across studies seem to weigh against such a conclusion, as does the fact that numerous studies have detected individual differences effects in the amygdala using similar contrasts (Canli, Sivers, Whitfield, Gotlib, & Gabrieli, 2002; Canli et al., 2001).

Outliers

One of the most important topics in statistical research methodology concerns how researchers should identify and deal with outliers – extreme observations that fall outside the expected bounds of a distribution. In addition to standard reasons for worrying about outliers – that they skew the distribution, inflate the variance, and can bias results – there are at least three additional reasons why outliers may present particular cause for concern in the domain of neuroimaging. First, neuroimaging sample sizes are heavily constrained by the high cost of data collection. Thus, the most general strategy for reducing outlier influence – increasing sample size – is often not viable. Second, neuroimaging datasets are highly susceptible to various forms of artifact, potentially resulting in a disproportionate number of outliers (Ojemann et al., 1997; Wager, Keller, Lacey, & Jonides, 2005). Third, the large number of statistical comparisons performed in typical neuroimaging analyses can easily result in a failure to detect outliers, since it is not possible to visually inspect a scatter plot for each comparison of interest as behavioral researchers commonly do. When reporting significant correlations in specific brain regions, researchers often display the corresponding scatter plots and explicitly discuss the potential role of outliers if they are present. This approach works well for voxels or regions that a statistical test or prior hypothesis have indicated are worth examining, but it is of no help in cases where a real correlation exists but is obscured by an outlier that biases the regression coefficient *away* from significance and consequently *fails* to be detected. The need to preemptively identify and control for the influence of outliers therefore calls for the use of procedures other than the standard parametric tests.

Identifying outliers. Numerous methods exist for visually or quantitatively identifying outliers (for review, see Barnett & Lewis, 1994; Iglewicz & Hoaglin, 1993). In practice, the most common approaches are to either label observations as outliers based on a semiarbitrary prespecified criterion (e.g., falling more than N standard deviations from the mean) or to employ the boxplot method, which identifies as outliers any observations that fall a certain distance outside the interquartile range (McGill, Tukey, & Larsen, 1978; Tukey, 1977). These methods are easy to apply but are relatively unprincipled and do not provide guidance concerning how to deal with outliers once they have been identified. A common approach in many areas of psychology (e.g., analyses of RT in cognitive psychology; for review, see Ratcliff, 1993) is to simply remove all observations labeled as outliers from analysis. However, this approach may be inadvisable for individual differences analyses in neuroimaging studies where sample sizes are small and power is already low to begin with; moreover, dropping outliers arbitrarily is liable to bias resulting in regression coefficients (often in ways that, intentionally or not, favor the hypothesis). An alternative is to apply a mathematical transformation to the data (e.g., taking the natural logarithm) so as to alter the shape of the distribution and minimize outlier influence. A disadvantage of the latter approach is that it complicates interpretation of results, since the conceptualization of the transformed variable is often unclear. Whereas a value given in percent change in the BOLD signal is readily interpretable, a log-transformed BOLD change value may not be. Moreover, there is rarely a principled reason to apply a particular mathematical transformation to the data, potentially resulting in a series of post-hoc transformations that can lead to capitalization on chance if researchers are not careful.

Accommodating outliers. A potentially preferable alternative to manipulating the data itself is the use of statistical procedures that can accommodate outliers by reducing their influence. One class of such techniques includes nonparametric tests which make no assumptions about the distributions of the variables being tested. For example, Pearson's correlation coefficient can be replaced with a number of alternatives such as Spearman's rho, Kendall's tau, or bootstrapped correlation coefficients (for reviews, see Chen & Popovich, 2002; Efron & Tibshirani, 1993; Nichols & Holmes, 2002; Siegel & Castellan, 1988). These tests are appropriate in cases where assumptions of normality are violated (as they may be in the presence of outliers); however, they trade off decreased susceptibility to outliers and distribution violations against lower power to detect correlations when the assumption of normality is met (Siegel & Castellan, 1988). Of course, given the central limit theorem, such normality assumptions are going to be more likely to be violated when the sample size is small ($N<30$), so this issue may be especially important for neuroimaging studies. Nonparametric statistical approaches have been discussed previously in the neuroimaging literature, in terms of these tradeoffs (for a review and discussion of available software tools, see Nichols & Holmes, 2002).

An alternative class of methods, termed *robust* estimation methods, reduce outlier influence by downweighting extreme scores in various ways (Cleveland, 1979; Rousseeuw & Leroy, 1987; Wager, Keller, et al., 2005). In contrast to most nonparametric methods, simulation studies suggest that many robust estimation methods retain nearly the same level of power as parametric methods under conditions of normality while providing the expected increase in power in the presence of outliers. Wager and colleagues recently used both simulated and empirical data to demonstrate that robust estimation techniques can provide substantial power increases in neuroimaging analyses affected by outliers without affecting the false positive rate (Wager, Keller, et al., 2005). Importantly, they show that there is virtually no penalty associated with the use of robust estimation when the data contain *no* outliers. Given appropriate software implementation, widespread use of robust estimation in neuroimaging analysis could therefore provide a relatively principled approach to minimizing the influence of outliers without requiring any special attention or expertise on the part of researchers. The primary limitation of such methods is that they are somewhat more computationally intensive than ordinary least-squares regression.

Conclusions

Individual differences approaches have found their way into the toolkits of an ever-increasing number of cognitive neuroscientists studying WM/EC. Such approaches have the potential to greatly further understanding of WM/EC; however, their use should ideally be guided by an appreciation of their limitations. A number of specific methodological issues should be carefully considered when planning, conducting, or analyzing a study involving individual differences analyses. This chapter considered a number of such issues, including statistical power limitations, effect size inflation, measurement reliability, and treatment of outliers. An overarching theme is that these issues overlap only partially with those that apply to standard within-subject analyses based on experimental contrasts. Likewise, we feel it is important that researchers treat individual differences and within-subject analysis approaches as complementary tools that are differentially sensitive to specific kinds of mechanisms, and not simply as two different ways to test for convergent effects. Although we focused primarily on fMRI studies in the present chapter, the issues we discuss are widely applicable to other cognitive neuroscience methods such as PET, TMS, and EEG/ERP. Our hope is that other researchers will find these considerations useful and take them into account in future when designing studies involving analyses of individual differences, and interpreting their results.

References

Armitage, P., McPherson, C. K., & Rowe, B. C. (1969). Repeated significance tests on accumulating data. *Journal of the Royal Statistical Society, Series A, 132*, 235–244.

Aron, A. R., Gluck, M. A., & Poldrack, R. A. (2006). Long-term test–retest reliability of functional MRI in a classification learning task. *NeuroImage, 29*, 1000–1006.

Badre, D., Poldrack, R. A., Paré-Blagoev, E. J., Insler, R. Z., & Wagner, A. D. (2005). Dissociable controlled retrieval and generalized selection mechanisms in ventrolateral prefrontal cortex. *Neuron, 47*(6), 907–918.

Barnett, V., & Lewis, T. (1994). *Outliers in statistical data*. Chichester: Wiley.

Bollen, K. A. (1989). *Structural equations with latent variables.* New York: Wiley.
Bradley, M. T., Smith, D., & Stoica, G. (2002). A Monte-Carlo estimation of effect size distortion due to significance testing. *Perceptual and Motor Skills, 95*(3), 837–842.
Braver, T. S., Cohen, J. D., Nystrom, L. E., Jonides, J., Smith, E. E., & Noll, D. C. (1997). A parametric study of prefrontal cortex involvement in human working memory. *NeuroImage, 5*(1), 49–62.
Braver, T. S., Gray, J. R., & Burgess, G. C. (2007). Explaining the many varieties of working memory variation: Dual mechanisms of cognitive control. In A. R. A. Conway, C. Jarrold, M. J. Kane, A. Miyake, & J. N. Towse (Eds.), *Variation in working memory.* Oxford: Oxford University Press.
Buchsbaum, B. R., Greer, S., Chang, W. L., & Berman, K. F. (2005). Meta-analysis of neuroimaging studies of the Wisconsin card-sorting task and component processes. *Human Brain Mapping, 25*(1), 35–45.
Bunge, S. A., Ochsner, K. N., Desmond, J. E., Glover, G. H., & Gabrieli, J. D. E. (2001). Prefrontal regions involved in keeping information in and out of mind. *Brain, 124*(10), 2074.
Burock, M. A., Buckner, R. L., Woldorff, M. G., Rosen, B. R., & Dale, A. M. (1998). Randomized event-related experimental designs allow for extremely rapid presentation rates using functional MRI. *Neuroreport, 9*(16), 3735–3739.
Cabeza, R., Anderson, N. D., Locantore, J. K., & McIntosh, A. R. (2002). Aging gracefully: Compensatory brain activity in high-performing older adults. *NeuroImage, 17*(3), 1394–1402.
Callicott, J. H., Mattay, V. S., Bertolino, A., Finn, K., Coppola, R., Frank, J. A., et al. (1999). Physiological characteristics of capacity constraints in working memory as revealed by functional MRI. *Cerebral Cortex, 9*(1), 20–26.
Canli, T., Sivers, H., Whitfield, S. L., Gotlib, I. H., & Gabrieli, J. D. (2002). Amygdala response to happy faces as a function of extraversion. *Science, 296*(5576), 2191.
Canli, T., Zhao, Z., Desmond, J. E., Kang, E., Gross, J., & Gabrieli, J. D. (2001). An fMRI study of personality influences on brain reactivity to emotional stimuli. *Behavioral Neuroscience, 115*(1), 33–42.
Caplan, J. B., McIntosh, A. R., & De Rosa, E. (2007). Two distinct functional networks for successful resolution of proactive interference. *Cerebral Cortex, 17*(7), 1650.
Chen, P. Y., & Popovich, P. M. (2002). *Correlation: Parametric and nonparametric measures.* Thousand Oaks, CA: Sage.
Cleveland, W. S. (1979). Robust locally weighted regression and smoothing scatterplots. *Journal of the American Statistical Association, 74*(368), 829–836.
Cohen, J. (1983). The cost of dichotomization. *Applied Psychological Measurement, 7*(3), 249.
Cohen, J. (1988). Statistical power analysis for the behavioral sciences (2nd Ed.), Lawrence Erlbaum, Hillsdale, NJ.
Cohen, J., West, S. G., Aiken, L., & Cohen, P. (2002). *Applied multiple regression/correlation analysis for the behavioral sciences.* Mahwah, NJ: Lawrence Erlbaum Associates.
Conway, A. R. A., Cowan, N., Bunting, M. F., Therriault, D. J., & Minkoff, S. R. B. (2002). A latent variable analysis of working memory capacity, short-term memory capacity, processing speed, and general fluid intelligence. *Intelligence, 30*(2), 163–183.
Dale, A. M., & Buckner, R. L. (1997). Selective averaging of rapidly presented individual trials using fMRI. *Human Brain Mapping, 5*(5), 329–340.
Dehaene, S., Piazza, M., Pinel, P., & Cohen, L. (2005). Three parietal circuits for number processing. In J. I. D. Campbell (Ed.), *Handbook of mathematical cognition* (pp. 433–455). New York: Psychology Press.
Della-Maggiore, V., Sekuler, A. B., Grady, C. L., Bennett, P. J., Sekuler, R., & McIntosh, A. R. (2000). Corticolimbic interactions associated with performance on a short-term memory task are modified by age. *Journal of Neuroscience, 20*(22), 8410.
Desmond, J. E., & Glover, G. H. (2002). Estimating sample size in functional MRI (fMRI) neuroimaging studies: Statistical power analyses. *Journal of Neuroscience Methods, 118*(2), 115–128.
Duncan, J., & Owen, A. M. (2000). Common regions of the human frontal lobe recruited by diverse cognitive demands. *Trends in Neurosciences, 23*(10), 475–483.
Efron, B., & Tibshirani, R. (1993). *An introduction to the bootstrap.* Boca Raton, FL: Chapman & Hall/CRC.
Engle, R. W., Tuholski, S. W., Laughlin, J. E., & Conway, A. R. (1999). Working memory, short-term memory, and general fluid intelligence: A latent-variable approach. *Journal of Experimental Psychology: General, 128*(3), 309–331.
Fernandez, G., Specht, K., Weis, S., Tendolkar, I., Reuber, M., Fell, J., et al. (2003). Intrasubject reproducibility of presurgical language lateralization and mapping using fMRI. *Neurology, 60*(6), 969–975.
Fiebach, C. J., Rissman, J., & D'Esposito, M. (2006). Modulation of inferotemporal cortex activation during verbal working memory maintenance. *Neuron, 51*(2), 251–261.
Fox, M. D., Snyder, A. Z., Vincent, J. L., Corbetta, M., Van Essen, D. C., & Raichle, M. E. (2005). The human brain is intrinsically organized into dynamic, anticorrelated functional networks. *Proceedings of the National Academy of Sciences, 102*(27), 9673–9678.
Friedman, N. P., & Miyake, A. (2004). The relations among inhibition and interference control functions: A latent-variable analysis. *Journal of Experimental Psychology: General, 133*(1), 101–135.

Friston, K. J., Holmes, A., Poline, J. B., Price, C. J., & Frith, C. D. (1996). Detecting activations in PET and fMRI: Levels of inference and power. *NeuroImage, 4*(3), 223–235.

Geake, J. G., & Hansen, P. C. (2005). Neural correlates of intelligence as revealed by fMRI of fluid analogies. *NeuroImage, 26*(2), 555–564.

Gibbs, S. E., & D'Esposito, M. (2005). Individual capacity differences predict working memory performance and prefrontal activity following dopamine receptor stimulation. *Cognitive, Affective & Behavioral Neuroscience, 5*(2), 212–221.

Gibbs, S. E. B., & D'Esposito, M. (2006). A functional magnetic resonance imaging study of the effects of pergolide, a dopamine receptor agonist, on component processes of working memory. *Neuroscience, 139*(1), 359–371.

Gillath, O., Bunge, S. A., Shaver, P. R., Wendelken, C., & Mikulincer, M. (2005). Attachment-style differences in the ability to suppress negative thoughts: Exploring the neural correlates. *NeuroImage, 28*, 835–847.

Glabus, M. F., Horwitz, B., Holt, J. L., Kohn, P. D., Gerton, B. K., Callicott, J. H., et al. (2003). Interindividual differences in functional interactions among prefrontal, parietal and parahippocampal regions during working memory. *Cerebral Cortex, 13*(12), 1352–1361.

Grady, C. L., McIntosh, A. R., Bookstein, F., Horwitz, B., Rapoport, S. I., & Haxby, J. V. (1998). Age-related changes in regional cerebral blood flow during working memory for faces. *NeuroImage, 8*(4), 409–425.

Gray, J. R., & Braver, T. S. (2002). Personality predicts working-memory-related activation in the caudal anterior cingulate cortex. *Cognitive, Affective & Behavioral Neuroscience, 2*(1), 64–75.

Gray, J. R., Burgess, G. C., Schaefer, A., Yarkoni, T., Larsen, R. J., & Braver, T. S. (2005). Affective personality differences in neural processing efficiency confirmed using fMRI. *Cognitive, Affective & Behavioral Neuroscience, 5*, 182–190.

Gray, J. R., Chabris, C. F., & Braver, T. S. (2003). Neural mechanisms of general fluid intelligence. *Nature Neuroscience, 6*(3), 316–322.

Haier, R. J., Siegel, B. V., Jr., MacLachlan, A., Soderling, E., Lottenberg, S., & Buchsbaum, M. S. (1992). Regional glucose metabolic changes after learning a complex visuospatial/motor task: A positron emission tomographic study. *Brain Research, 570*(1–2), 134–143.

Haier, R. J., White, N. S., & Alkire, M. T. (2003). Individual differences in general intelligence correlate with brain function during nonreasoning tasks. *Intelligence, 31*(5), 429–441.

Heinz, A., Siessmeier, T., Wrase, J., Hermann, D., Klein, S., Grusser-Sinopoli, S. M., et al. (2004). Correlation between dopamine D2 receptors in the ventral striatum and central processing of alcohol cues and craving. *American Journal of Psychiatry, 161*(10), 1783–1789.

Hester, R., Fassbender, C., & Garavan, H. (2004). Individual differences in error processing: A review and reanalysis of three event-related fMRI studies using the GO/NOGO task. *Cerebral Cortex, 14*(9), 986–994.

Iglewicz, B., & Hoaglin, D. C. (1993). *How to detect and handle outliers.* Milwaukee, WI: ASQ Quality Press.

Johnstone, T., Somerville, L. H., Alexander, A. L., Oakes, T. R., Davidson, R. J., Kalin, N. H., et al. (2005). Stability of amygdala BOLD response to fearful faces over multiple scan sessions. *NeuroImage, 25*, 1112–1123.

Jonides, J., & Nee, D. E. (2006). Brain mechanisms of proactive interference in working memory. *Neuroscience, 139*(1), 181–193.

Kane, M. J., Conway, A. R., Miura, T. K., & Colflesh, G. J. (2007). Working memory, attention control, and the n-back task: A question of construct validity. *Journal of Experimental Psychology: Learning, Memory, and Cognition, 33*(3), 615–622.

Kane, M. J., Hambrick, D. Z., Tuholski, S. W., Wilhelm, O., Payne, T. W., & Engle, R. W. (2004). The generality of working memory capacity: A latent-variable approach to verbal and visuospatial memory span and reasoning. *Journal of Experimental Psychology: General, 133*(2), 189–21728.

Kim, J., Zhu, W., Chang, L., Bentler, P. M., & Ernst, T. (2007). Unified structural equation modeling approach for the analysis of multisubject, multivariate functional MRI data. *Human Brain Mapping, 28*(2), 85–93.

Kimberg, D. Y., Aguirre, G. K., Lease, J., & D'Esposito, M. (2001). Cortical effects of bromocriptine, a D-2 dopamine receptor agonist, in human subjects, revealed by fMRI. *Human Brain Mapping, 12*(4), 246–257.

Kimberg, D. Y., D'Esposito, M., & Farah, M. J. (1997). Effects of bromocriptine on human subjects depend on working memory capacity. *Neuroreport, 8*(16), 3581.

Kline, R. B. (1998). *Principles and practice of structural equation modeling.* New York: Guilford.

Kondo, H., Morishita, M., Osaka, N., Osaka, M., Fukuyama, H., & Shibasaki, H. (2004). Functional roles of the cingulo-frontal network in performance on working memory. *NeuroImage, 21*(1), 2–14.

Kumari, V., Ffytche, D. H., Williams, S. C., & Gray, J. A. (2004). Personality predicts brain responses to cognitive demands. *Journal of Neuroscience, 24*(47), 10636.

Larson, G. E., Haier, R. J., LaCasse, L., & Hazen, K. (1995). Evaluation of a "mental effort" hypothesis for correlations between cortical metabolism and intelligence. *Intelligence, 21*(3), 267–278.

Lee, K. H., Choi, Y. Y., Gray, J. R., Cho, S. H., Chae, J. H., Lee, S., et al. (2006). Neural correlates of superior intelligence: Stronger recruitment of posterior parietal cortex. *NeuroImage, 29*(2), 578–586.

Liu, T. T., Frank, L. R., Wong, E. C., & Buxton, R. B. (2001). Detection power, estimation efficiency, and predictability in event-related fMRI. *NeuroImage, 13*(4), 759–773.

Locke, H. S., & Braver, T. S. (2008). Motivational influences on cognitive control: Behavior, brain activation, and individual differences. *Cognitive, Affective & Behavioral Neuroscience, 8*(1), 99–112.

MacCallum, R. C., Zhang, S., Preacher, K. J., & Rucker, D. D. (2002). On the practice of dichotomization of quantitative variables. *Psychological Methods, 7*(1), 19–40.

MacDonald, A. W., Cohen, J. D., Stenger, V. A., & Carter, C. S. (2000). Dissociating the role of the dorsolateral prefrontal and anterior cingulate cortex in cognitive control. *Science, 288*(5472), 1835.

MacKinnon, D. P., Lockwood, C. M., Hoffman, J. M., West, S. G., & Sheets, V. (2002). A comparison of methods to test mediation and other intervening variable effects. *Psychological Methods, 7*(1), 83–104.

Manoach, D. S., Halpern, E. F., Kramer, T. S., Chang, Y., Goff, D. C., Rauch, S. L., et al. (2001). Test-retest reliability of a functional MRI working memory paradigm in normal and schizophrenic subjects. *American Journal of Psychiatry, 158*(6), 955–958.

Manuck, S. B., Brown, S. M., Forbes, E. E., & Hariri, A. R. (2007). Temporal stability of individual differences in amygdala reactivity. *American Journal of Psychiatry, 164*(10), 1613.

Mattay, V. S., Callicott, J. H., Bertolino, A., Heaton, I., Frank, J. A., Coppola, R., et al. (2000). Effects of dextroamphetamine on cognitive performance and cortical activation. *NeuroImage, 12*(3), 268–275.

Maxwell, S. E. (2004). The persistence of underpowered studies in psychological research: Causes, consequences, and remedies. *Psychological Methods, 9*(2), 147–163.

McGill, R., Tukey, J. W., & Larsen, W. A. (1978). Variations of box plots. *The American Statistician, 32*(1), 12–16.

McIntosh, A. R., Bookstein, F. L., Haxby, J. V., & Grady, C. L. (1996). Spatial pattern analysis of functional brain images using Partial Least Squares. *NeuroImage, 3*(3), 143–157.

McIntosh, A. R., & Lobaugh, N. J. (2004). Partial least squares analysis of neuroimaging data: Applications and advances. *NeuroImage, 23*, 250–263.

Mecklinger, A., Weber, K., Gunter, T. C., & Engle, R. W. (2003). Dissociable brain mechanisms for inhibitory control: Effects of interference content and working memory capacity. *Cognitive Brain Research, 18*(1), 26–38.

Mehta, M. A., Owen, A. M., Sahakian, B. J., Mavaddat, N., Pickard, J. D., & Robbins, T. W. (2000). Methylphenidate enhances working memory by modulating discrete frontal and parietal lobe regions in the human brain. *Journal of Neuroscience, 20*(6), RC65.

Meyer, G. J., Finn, S. E., Eyde, L. D., Kay, G. G., Moreland, K. L., Dies, R. R., et al. (2001). Psychological testing and psychological assessment: A review of evidence and issues. *American Psychologist, 56*(2), 128–165.

Mumford, J. A., & Nichols, T. E. (2008). Power calculation for group fMRI studies accounting for arbitrary design and temporal autocorrelation. *NeuroImage, 39*(1), 261–268.

Muncer, S. J., Craigie, M., & Holmes, J. (2003). Meta-analysis and power: Some suggestions for the use of power in research synthesis. *Understanding Statistics, 2*(1), 1–12.

Murphy, K., & Garavan, H. (2004). An empirical investigation into the number of subjects required for an event-related fMRI study. *NeuroImage, 22*(2), 879–885.

Nee, D. E., Jonides, J., & Berman, M. G. (2007). Neural mechanisms of proactive interference-resolution. *NeuroImage, 38*(4), 740–751.

Nichols, T. E., & Holmes, A. P. (2002). Nonparametric permutation tests for functional neuroimaging: A primer with examples. *Human Brain Mapping, 15*(1), 1–25.

Ojemann, J. G., Akbudak, E., Snyder, A. Z., McKinstry, R. C., Raichle, M. E., & Conturo, T. E. (1997). Anatomic localization and quantitative analysis of gradient refocused echo-planar fMRI susceptibility artifacts. *NeuroImage, 6*(3), 156–167.

Omura, K., Aron, A., & Canli, T. (2005). Variance maps as a novel tool for localizing regions of interest in imaging studies of individual differences. *Cognitive, Affective & Behavioral Neuroscience, 5*(2), 252–261.

Osaka, M., Osaka, N., Kondo, H., Morishita, M., Fukuyama, H., Aso, T., et al. (2003). The neural basis of individual differences in working memory capacity: An fMRI study. *NeuroImage, 18*(3), 789–797.

Owen, A. M., McMillan, K. M., Laird, A. R., & Bullmore, E. (2005). N-back working memory paradigm: A meta-analysis of normative functional neuroimaging studies. *Human Brain Mapping, 25*(1), 46–59.

Peterson, B. S., Skudlarski, P., Gatenby, J. C., Zhang, H., Anderson, A. W., & Gore, J. C. (1999). An fMRI study of stroop word-color interference: Evidence for cingulate subregions subserving multiple distributed attentional systems. *Biological Psychiatry, 45*(10), 1237–1258.

Pocock, S. J. (2006). Current controversies in data monitoring for clinical trials. *Clinical Trials, 3*(6), 513.

Preacher, K. J., Rucker, D. D., MacCallum, R. C., & Nicewander, W. A. (2005). Use of the extreme groups approach: A critical reexamination and new recommendations. *Psychological Methods, 10*, 178–192.

Ratcliff, R. (1993). Methods for dealing with reaction time outliers. *Psychological Bulletin, 114*(3), 510–532.

Raven, J., Raven, J. C., & Court, J. H. (1998). *Manual for Raven's progressive matrices and vocabulary scales*. Oxford, UK: Oxford Psychologists Press.

Reuter-Lorenz, P. A. (2002). New visions of the aging mind and brain. *Trends in Cognitive Sciences, 6*(9), 394–400.

Richeson, J. A., Baird, A. A., Gordon, H. L., Heatherton, T. F., Wyland, C. L., Trawalter, S., et al. (2003). An fMRI investigation of the impact of interracial contact on executive function. *Nature Neuroscience, 6*(12), 1323–1328.

Rousseeuw, P. J., & Leroy, A. M. (1987). *Robust regression and outlier detection.* New York: Wiley.

Rypma, B., Berger, J. S., & D'Esposito, M. (2002). The influence of working-memory demand and subject performance on prefrontal cortical activity. *Journal of Cognitive Neuroscience, 14*(5), 721–731.

Rypma, B., Berger, J. S., Prabhakaran, V., Martin Bly, B., Kimberg, D. Y., Biswal, B. B., et al. (2006). Neural correlates of cognitive efficiency. *NeuroImage, 33*(3), 969–979.

Rypma, B., & D'Esposito, M. (1999). The roles of prefrontal brain regions in components of working memory: Effects of memory load and individual differences. *Proceedings of the National Academy of Sciences, 96*(11), 6558–6563.

Schaefer, A., Braver, T. S., Reynolds, J. R., Burgess, G. C., Yarkoni, T., & Gray, J. R. (2006). Individual differences in amygdala activity predict response speed during working memory. *Journal of Neuroscience, 26*(40), 10120–10128.

Schlösser, R. G. M., Wagner, G., & Sauer, H. (2006). Assessing the working memory network: Studies with functional magnetic resonance imaging and structural equation modeling. *Neuroscience, 139*(1), 91–103.

Siegel, S., & Castellan, N. J. (1988). *Nonparametric statistics for the behavioral sciences.* New York: McGraw-Hill.

Specht, K., Willmes, K., Shah, N. J., & Jaencke, L. (2003). Assessment of reliability in functional imaging studies. *Journal of Magnetic Resonance Imaging, 17*(4), 463–471.

Strube, M. J. (2006). SNOOP: A program for demonstrating the consequences of premature and repeated null hypothesis testing. *Behavior Research Methods, 38*(1), 24–27.

Thirion, B., Pinel, P., Mériaux, S., Roche, A., Dehaene, S., & Poline, J. B. (2007). Analysis of a large fMRI cohort: Statistical and methodological issues for group analyses. *NeuroImage, 35*(1), 105–120.

Tom, S. M., Fox, C. R., Trepel, C., & Poldrack, R. A. (2007). The neural basis of loss aversion in decision-making under risk. *Science, 315*(5811), 515.

Tukey, J. W. (1977). *Exploratory data analysis.* Reading, MA: Addison-Wesley.

Unsworth, N., Heitz, R. P., Schrock, J. C., & Engle, R. W. (2005). An automated version of the operation span task. *Behavior Research Methods, 37*(3), 498–505.

Wagenmakers, E. J. (2007). A practical solution to the pervasive problems of p values. *Psychonomic Bulletin & Review, 14*(5), 779–804.

Wager, T. D., Jonides, J., & Reading, S. (2004). Neuroimaging studies of shifting attention: A meta-analysis. *NeuroImage, 22*(4), 1679–1693.

Wager, T. D., Keller, M. C., Lacey, S. C., & Jonides, J. (2005). Increased sensitivity in neuroimaging analyses using robust regression. *NeuroImage, 26*(1), 99–113.

Wager, T. D., Sylvester, C. Y. C., Lacey, S. C., Nee, D. E., Franklin, M., & Jonides, J. (2005). Common and unique components of response inhibition revealed by fMRI. *NeuroImage, 27*(2), 323–340.

Yarkoni, T., Barch, D. M., Gray, J. A., Conturo, T., & Braver, T. S. (2009). BOLD correlates of trial-by-trial reaction time variability in gray and white matter: a multi-study fMRI analysis. *PLoS ONE, 4*, e4527.

Yarkoni, T., & Braver, T. S. (2008). *Dissociable influences of probability, magnitude, and expected value on decision-making.* Paper presented at the Cognitive Neuroscience Society, San Francisco, CA.

Yarkoni, T., Braver, T. S., Gray, J. R., & Green, L. (2005). Prefrontal brain activity predicts temporally extended decision-making behavior. *Journal of the Experimental Analysis of Behavior, 84*(3), 537–554.

Yarkoni, T., Gray, J. R., & Braver, T. S. (submitted). Medial posterior parietal cortex activation predicts working memory performance within and across subjects.

Chapter 7
Emotional Intelligence and Gender: A Neurophysiological Perspective

Norbert Jaušovec and Ksenija Jaušovec

The focus of the present chapter is on neuropsychological underpinnings of gender differences in mental abilities, in general, and emotional intelligence (EI). As stressed by Nyborg (1994), it is a topic which is a minefield of methodological and theoretical problems. It is also a sensitive area packed with ideology and concern over "political correctness." For example, test constructors have calibrated their instruments to conform to dogmas of equality between genders. Certain test items were removed, so that the test no longer showed a gender difference in overall intelligence (Vogel, 1990; Wechsler, 1981). Some recent findings, indicating that males outscore females by about 3.8 IQ points (Jackson & Rushton, 2006; Lynn & Irwing, 2004), are therefore puzzling and difficult to explain. Is the difference even greater? Have the test constructors done a bad job? Nyborg (2005, p. 507) concluded that "[p]roper methodology identifies a male advantage in g that increases exponentially at higher levels, relates to brain size, and explains, at least in part, the universal male dominance in society." The central thesis of this chapter is that gender should be a major variable in studying the relation between individual differences in ability and brain activity.

The chapter is divided into two parts. The first part provides a brief overview of gender differences in general and EI. The second part focuses on neurophysiological research relating brain activity with the level of ability and gender. Presented is also a recent study which examined the influence that gender has on brain responses to emotional stimuli.

Behavioral Findings

Emotional Intelligence

Intelligence represents the individual's overall level of intellectual ability. It serves as a general concept that includes several groups of mental abilities. One of the most influential divisions of intelligence splits it into verbal, performance and social intelligence (Thorndike, 1920). Social intelligence has been described as the ability to understand and manage people, and to act wisely in social situations (Thorndike & Stein, 1937). More recently, Cantor and Kihlstrom (1985, 1987) proposed social intelligence as a construct referring to a central personality process that underpins social behavior. Over the last decade, the concept of EI has received much attention in the popular and scientific literature. There exist different definitions and operationalizations of EI. Bar-On (2000) is of the opinion that

---

N. Jaušovec (✉) and K. Jaušovec
Faculty of Philosophy, University of Maribor, Koroška 160, 2000 Maribor, Slovenia
e-mail: norbert.jausovec@uni-mb.si

EMOTIONAL INTELLIGENCE

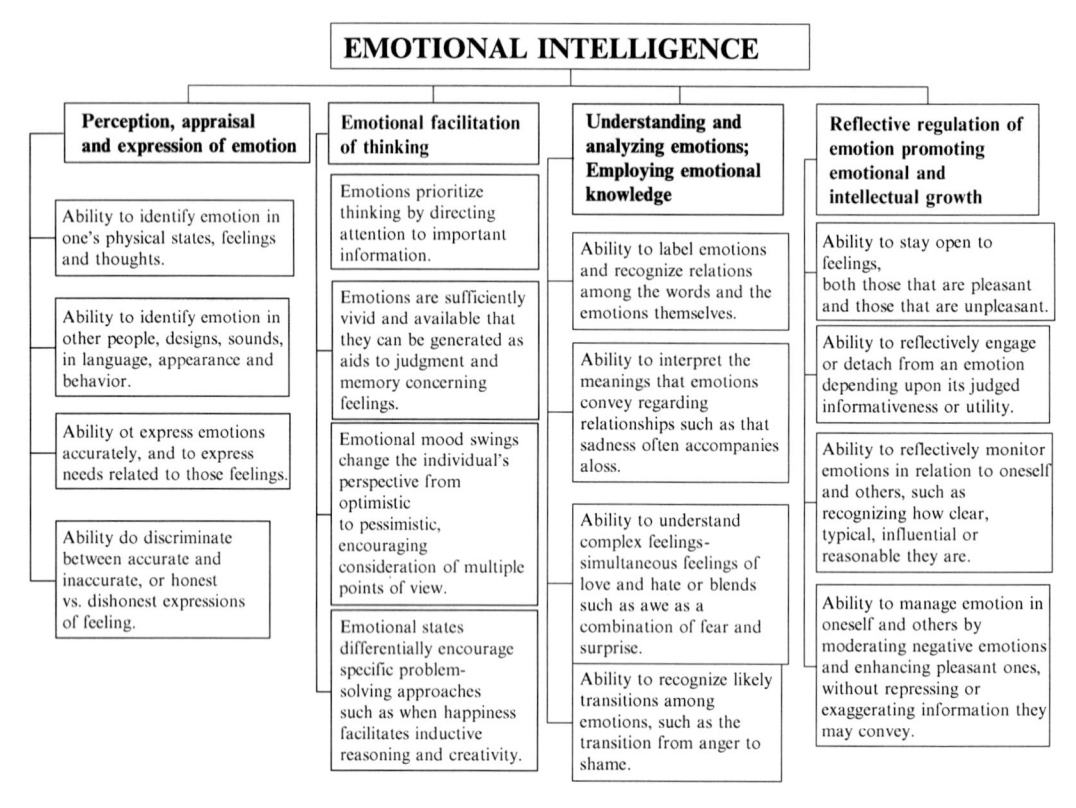

Perception, appraisal and expression of emotion	Emotional facilitation of thinking	Understanding and analyzing emotions; Employing emotional knowledge	Reflective regulation of emotion promoting emotional and intellectual growth
Ability to identify emotion in one's physical states, feelings and thoughts.	Emotions prioritize thinking by directing attention to important information.	Ability to label emotions and recognize relations among the words and the emotions themselves.	Ability to stay open to feelings, both those that are pleasant and those that are unpleasant.
Ability to identify emotion in other people, designs, sounds, in language, appearance and behavior.	Emotions are sufficiently vivid and available that they can be generated as aids to judgment and memory concerning feelings.	Ability to interpret the meanings that emotions convey regarding relationships such as that sadness often accompanies a loss.	Ability to reflectively engage or detach from an emotion depending upon its judged informativeness or utility.
Ability ot express emotions accurately, and to express needs related to those feelings.	Emotional mood swings change the individual's perspective from optimistic to pessimistic, encouraging consideration of multiple points of view.	Ability to understand complex feelings-simultaneous feelings of love and hate or blends such as awe as a combination of fear and surprise.	Ability to reflectively monitor emotions in relation to oneself and others, such as recognizing how clear, typical, influential or reasonable they are.
Ability do discriminate between accurate and inaccurate, or honest vs. dishonest expressions of feeling.	Emotional states differentially encourage specific problem-solving approaches such as when happiness facilitates inductive reasoning and creativity.	Ability to recognize likely transitions among emotions, such as the transition from anger to shame.	Ability to manage emotion in oneself and others by moderating negative emotions and enhancing pleasant ones, without repressing or exaggerating information they may convey.

Fig. 7.1 The main components of emotional intelligence

EI is a composite of different facets compromising cognitive, motivational, and affective constructs. On the other hand, Mayer, Caruso, and Salovey (2000) underline the ability character of EI. They define it as the ability to recognize emotion, reason with emotion and emotion-related information, and process emotional information as part of general problem-solving (see Fig. 7.1). This conception of EI to some extent corresponds to social intelligence. It further suggests some equally general indications of personality traits and general intelligence that it may embody. A concern that was raised by several researchers (e.g., De Raad, 2005; Schulte, Ree, & Carretta, 2004) was that one could question the usefulness of EI for enhancing the understanding of the determinants of human performance. This concern was supported by some recent studies – Schulte et al. (2004) reported a corrected multiple, $R=0.806$, between EI and other well-known constructs: the Big Five personality dimensions, and g. A similar finding was reported by De Raad (2005). In the study, 42% of EI items were accommodated by the Big Five personality factor Emotional Stability.

Given that our research interest is on differences in ability, we conceptualize EI as an ability and classify it as an intelligence.

Gender Differences

Probably one of the first written accounts for female superiority in verbal ability is found in an ancient Sanskrit book, suggesting that nine shares of speech were given to women and one to men (Nyborg, 1994). However, more recent systematic analyses suggest that females surpass males in some, but not necessarily all, areas of verbal ability (Garai & Scheinfeld, 1968; Halpern, 2004;

Jensen, 1998). Specifically, females seem to have an advantage in episodic memory tasks where verbal processing is required or can be used, as well as in verbal fluency (Herlitz, Nilsson, & Backman, 1997; Maitland, Herlitz, Nyberg, Backman, & Nilsson, 2004).

The most robust and pronounced gender difference is seen in spatial abilities. A meta-analysis of studies published before 1973 found an average difference of about half of a standard deviation in favor of males on tests of visuo-spatial ability (Hyde, 1981). Factor analytic studies have shown that spatial ability is not a unitary process and can be divided into three categories: spatial perception, mental rotation, and spatial visualization (Linn & Peterson, 1985). Most pronounced gender differences of nearly one standard deviation have been mainly reported for mental rotation tasks (Mackintosh & Bennett, 2005; Masters & Sanders, 1993; Voyer, Voyer, & Bryden, 1995). In contrast, the empirical performance data support the overall conclusion that there is at most a small gender difference in general ability (Colom & Lynn, 2004; Lynn & Irwing, 2004).

It was further found that females surpass males on tests of EI (Amelang & Steinmayr, 2006; Extremera, Fernandez-Berrocal, & Salovey, 2006; Mayer, Salovey, & Caruso, 2002; Mayer et al., 2000; Rooy, Alonso, & Viswesvaran, 2005), as well as emotional awareness (Boden & Berenbaum, 2007; Ciarrochi, Hynes, & Crittenden, 2005; Lindholm, Lehtinen, Hyyppa, & Puukka, 1990; Parker, Taylor, & Bagby, 1989, 2003; Salminen, Saarijarvi, Aarela, Toikka, & Kauhanen, 1999).

Emotional awareness (EA) is an individual differences construct – similar to EI – that consists of two dimensions (Coffey, Berenbaum, & Kerns, 2003; Gohm & Clore, 2000, 2002):

1. Attention to emotions is the extent to which a person attends to his/her emotional experience and uses this information; and
2. Clarity of emotions is the extent to which a person can identify, discriminate between (e.g., anger versus anxiety), and understand what they are feeling and why.

Gender-related differences in EI have been observed in samples drawn from different cultures; hence the phenomenon that female students score higher in self-report and ability measures of EI seems to be a cross-cultural phenomenon. It was further observed that males and females also differ in self-estimated and measured EI (Petrides & Furnham, 2000). They found a significant difference in the "social skills" factor of the EI questionnaire, with females scoring higher than males. This was in the opposite direction from the difference in self-estimated EI, where males' self-estimates were higher than the females'.

It seems further that women are superior to men at recognizing facial expressions of emotions, which is a component of EI (for a review of studies see Hall, 1978, 1984; McClure, 2000). Explanations for the gender difference range from sexual inequalities in power and social status (e.g., see Hall, 1984; Henley, 1977; Weitz, 1974) to evolutionary perspectives based on women's near-universal responsibility for child-rearing (e.g., Babchuk, Hames, & Thompson, 1985). The primary caretaker hypothesis proposed by Babchuk et al. (1985) contends that females, as a result of their evolutionary role as primary caretakers, will display evolved adaptations that enhance the probability of survival of their offspring. In humans, these adaptations are hypothesized to include the fast and accurate decoding of facial affect, an important means of communication, especially in preverbal infants.

Neurophysiological Findings

Verbal and Performance Components of Intelligence

Neurophysiological research has been mainly interested in the verbal and performance components of intelligence (Anokhin, Lutzenberger, & Birbaumer, 1999; Haier & Benbow, 1995; Haier et al., 1988; Haier, Siegel, Tang, Abel, & Buchsbaum, 1992; Jaušovec, 1996, 1998, 2000; Jaušovec & Jaušovec,

2000a, 2000b; Jaušovec & Jaušovec, 2001; Lutzenberger, Birbaumer, Flor, Rockstroh, & Elbert, 1992; Neubauer, Freudenthaler, & Pfurtscheller, 1995; Neubauer & Fink, 2003; Neubauer, Fink, & Schrausser, 2002; Neubauer, Sange, & Pfurtscheller, 1999; O'Boyle, Benbow, & Alexander, 1995; – for a detailed overview see Table 7.1). Most of these studies have demonstrated a negative correlation between brain

Table 7.1 Overview of studies investigating the relationship between brain activity and intelligence

Author	Method	Tasks used	NET[a]
Anokhin et al. (1999)	EEG coherence and dimensional complexity. Broad band: theta, alpha and beta	Verbal (naming of categories); and visuo-spatial (mental rotation) tasks	Y
Doppelmayr et al. (2002)	Log-transformed EEG power values, in three narrow alpha frequency bands	resting (correlation with different intelligence tasks – LGT-3 and IST-70)	N
Gevins and Smith (2000)	ERP, EEG power values, theta, lower alpha band	Working memory tasks ("n-back")	Y/N
Haier et al. (1988)	PET – fluor-2-deoxyglucose	Raven's Advanced progressive matrices	Y
Haier et al. (1992)	PET – fluor-2-deoxyglucose	Computer game "Tetris"	Y
Haier and Benbow (1995)	PET – deoxyglucose	Mathematical reasoning	Y
Haier et al. (2003)	PET – fluor-2-deoxyglucose	Raven's Advanced progressive matrices, viewing emotional video tapes	Y
Jaušovec (1996)	EEG spectral power. Broad alpha band	Resting, solving of closed and open problems, free-recall tasks	Y
Jaušovec (1998)	EEG spectral power and entropy measures. Broad alpha band	Resting, Stroop tasks, reasoning tasks, numerical tasks	Y
Jaušovec (2000)	EEG spectral power and coherence. Lower (7.9–10.0 Hz) and upper alpha band (10.1–12.9 Hz)	Solving of closed and open problems	Y
Jaušovec and Jaušovec (2000a)	ERP – approximated entropy measures	Visual and auditory oddball tasks	Y
Jaušovec and Jaušovec (2000b)	Induced and event-related ERD, theta (4–7 Hz) and upper alpha (10–13)	Auditory oddball task	Y
Jaušovec and Jaušovec (2001)	EEG current density – LORETA	Auditory oddball task	Y
Jaušovec et al. (2001)	Induced and event-related ERD, theta (4.4–6.4 Hz), lower-2 alpha (8.4–10.4 Hz), upper alpha (10.4–12.4)	Emotional intelligence tasks	Y
Jaušovec and Jaušovec (2003)	EEG current density – LORETA	Raven's Advanced progressive matrices, Emotional intelligence tasks	Y
Jaušovec and Jaušovec (2004a)	EEG current density – LORETA, induced ERD, theta (4.4–6.3 Hz), lower-1 alpha (6.4–8.3) lower-2 alpha (8.4–10.3 Hz), upper alpha (10.4–12.3)	Memory tasks	N
Jaušovec and Jaušovec (2004b)	Induced ERD, theta (4.17–6.16 Hz), lower-1 alpha (6.17–8.16) lower-2 alpha (8.17–10.16 Hz), upper alpha (10.17–12.16)	Working memory and learning tasks	Y/N
Jaušovec and Jaušovec (2005a)	Induced ERD and upper alpha (10.17–12.16 Hz) and gamma (31–49 Hz)	Raven's Advanced progressive matrices, identifying emotions in pictures	Y/N

(continued)

Table 7.1 (continued)

Author	Method	Tasks used	NET[a]
Klimesch (1999)	ERD, theta, upper alpha band	semantic and episodic memory tasks	N
Klimesch and Doppelmayr (2001)	Log-transformed EEG power values, in three narrow alpha frequency bands	resting (correlation with different intelligence tasks – LGT-3 and IST-70)	N
Lutzenberger et al. (1992)	EEG dimensional complexity. Broad band: 2–35 Hz	Resting, emotional imagery	N
Neubauer et al. (1995)	ERD, upper alpha	sentence verification test	Y
Neubauer et al. (1999)	ERD, narrow alpha bands (8–10 Hz, 10–12 Hz)	Posner's letter matching task	Y
Neubauer et al. (2002)	ERD, upper alpha (10.70–12.69 Hz)	Posner's matching tasks (verbal, numerical, figural)	Y
Neubauer and Fink (2003)	ERD, upper alpha (10.10–12.09 Hz)	Stankov's Triplet Number test	Y
O'Boyle et al. (1995)	EEG spectral power. Broad alpha band	Chimerical face processing, word processing	Y

[a]*NET* neural efficiency theory (*Y* = supporting NET; *N* = not supporting NET)

activity under cognitive load and intelligence. The explanation of these findings was an efficiency theory. This efficiency may derive from the nonuse of many brain areas irrelevant for good task performance as well as the more focused use of specific task-relevant areas in high intelligent individuals. It was even suggested that high and low intelligent individuals preferentially activate different neural circuits even though no reasoning or problem solving was required (Haier, White, & Alkire, 2003; Jaušovec & Jaušovec, 2003).

Studies which have used memory and learning tasks requiring encoding of information have produced some inconsistent results, opposite to what would be predicted by the neural efficiency hypothesis (Doppelmayr, Klimesch, Stadler, Pöllhuber, & Heine, 2002; Jaušovec & Jaušovec, 2004a; Klimesch, 1999; Klimesch & Doppelmayr, 2001). Some studies have shown a specific topographic pattern of differences related to the level of intelligence. High-ability subjects made relatively greater use of parietal regions, whereas low-ability subjects relied more exclusively on frontal regions (Gevins & Smith, 2000; Jaušovec & Jaušovec, 2004a). More generally, these results suggest that higher-ability subjects tend to better identify strategies needed for the solution of the task at hand. It was further reported that high intelligent subjects displayed more brain activity in the early stages of task performance, while average individuals showed a reverse pattern. This temporal distribution of brain activity suggests that cognitive processes in high intelligent individuals are faster than in average intelligent individuals (Jaušovec & Jaušovec, 2004b).

A second characteristic of the reported studies employing the EEG methodology was that they have almost exclusively based their findings on analyzing the alpha (7–12 Hz) and theta (4–6 Hz) bands, probably because the relationship of activity in these bands with mental effort is well documented. Alpha amplitude tends to decrease (desynchronization) with increases in mental effort, while theta band amplitude tends to increase (synchronization) (Klimesch, 1996, 1997, 1999; Nunez, Wingeier, & Silberstein, 2001). Recent research has revealed that the gamma band (>30 Hz) may be of particular relevance to cognition – e.g., attention and arousal, basic acoustic and visual perception, perception of gestalt and language, music perception (for a review, see Başar, Başar-Eroglu, Karakaş, & Schürmann, 2001; Bhattacharya, Petsche, & Pereda, 2001; Pulvermüller, Birbaumer, Lutzenberger, & Mohr, 1997; Tallon-Baudry & Bertrand, 1999). Of special relevance for high level cognitive processes is the induced gamma band activity. In contrast to evoked gamma responses which are strictly phase-locked, induced gamma activity consists of oscillatory bursts whose latency jitters from trial to trial, and its temporal relationship with stimulus onset is fairly loose (Tallon-Baudry & Bertrand, 1999). It has been suggested that induced gamma activity reflects a binding mechanism which is enhanced when a coherent percept is created in response to a given stimulus. Neuronal activity is expressed in spatially separate areas of the cortex, which requires processes for linking the separate nodes of activity, thereby allowing identification of the object as a whole. The linking mechanism is provided by the oscillations in the gamma-band (Singer & Gray, 1995). To our knowledge, there are only few studies relating gamma-band activity to the level of intelligence. Some indirect conclusions on the relationship between gamma band oscillations and intelligence can be made based on the research of Strüber (Strüber, Basar-Eroglu, Hoff, & Stadler, 2000), and Bhattacharya (Bhattacharya et al., 2001). Using visual motion tasks, Strüber showed that better task performance was associated with higher gamma band activity. Bhattacharya showed that while listening to music, degrees of the gamma band synchrony over distributed cortical areas were found to be significantly higher in musicians than nonmusicians. In a recent study (Jaušovec & Jaušovec, 2005a), students, who could be clustered as high-average verbal/performance intelligent were performing Raven's advanced progressive matrices, and identifying emotions in pictures. Significant differences in event-related desynchronization/synchronization (ERD/ERS) related to verbal/performance intelligence were only observed while respondents solved the matrices. The high and average intelligent groups displayed temporal and spatial differently induced gamma band activity. The temporal distribution of ERD/ERS in the gamma band suggests that the integration of visual information in high intelligent individuals was faster than in average ones. A second characteristic of brain activity in high intelligent individuals was that induced gamma band synchronization and coherence were more intense over the parietooccipital brain areas, while in average intelligent individuals they were more intense over frontal brain areas. Several PET and fMRI studies have shown that parietooccipital brain areas play a central role in spatial encoding and retrieval, as well as spatial perception and imagery, while frontal areas are more involved in monitoring and manipulating information held in the working memory (Cabeza & Nyberg, 2000). From this viewpoint, the greater involvement of the parieto-occipital brain areas in more intelligent individuals could point to a more adequate strategy use which to a greater extent focused on the figural information provided by the Raven's matrices.

Another approach to studying salient brain areas involved in intelligence is to examine how individual differences in intelligence among subjects correlate with brain functioning while subjects are at rest. However, the comparison between studies is difficult because different measures were used to investigate brain activity. In general, two categories of EEG variables are correlated with IQ and neuropsychological performance:

1. Power or amplitude measures and,
2. Network connection measures such as coherence, phase delays and nonlinear dynamical models of network complexity.

It is assumed that the amplitude of the EEG is mainly influenced by the number of synchronous synaptic generators and much less by asynchronous generators, or the total number of generators. EEG coherence is a somewhat different measure than EEG synchrony. It is a measure of phase angle consistency or phase "variability" between pairs of signals in each frequency band. Thus, it provides an estimate of functional interactions between oscillating systems and may yield information about network formation and brain binding – coupling/decoupling of brain areas. Local and/or distant cortico-cortical projections have been described in the central nervous system and are thought to be involved in tasks requiring the recruitment of multiple cognitive subsystems (Nunez et al., 2001). Coherence could thus be an indicator of information flow along these interconnecting pathways. The relation between EEG coherence and synchrony is rather complex. Sources that are synchronous will also tend to be coherent; however, the converse need not be true. For example, desynchronization is associated with amplitude reduction, but may still be coherent if the sources are 180° out of phase, so their individual contributions to EEG amplitude tend to cancel out. The measure of dimensional complexity reflects the complexity of neural generators – the relative number of concurrently oscillating neuronal assemblies and degrees of freedom in the competitive interaction between them. It appears to be relatively independent of EEG spectral power, and inversely related to coherence (Anokhin et al., 1999).

It was suggested that a faster oscillating brain reflects rapid information processing associated with high intelligence (Anokhin & Vogel, 1996; Klimesch, 1997). Support for this theory is provided by the studies of Giannitrapani (1969), who reported a significant correlation between IQ and the average EEG frequency in a group of 18 adults; of Anokhin and Vogel (1996) who obtained a correlation of 0.35 between alpha peak frequency and verbal abilities; and of Klimesch (1997), who found that the alpha peak frequency of good working memory performers lies about 1 Hz higher than that of poor working memory performers. Further, a study by Lehtovirta et al. (1996), comparing Alzheimer's patients with controls, found that the alpha peak frequency of Alzheimer's patients was significantly lower than that of controls. All these studies suggested that high intelligence is associated with a faster oscillating brain; however, some recent large-scale studies could not replicate these findings (Jaušovec & Jaušovec, 2000c; Posthuma, Neale, Boomsma, & de Geus, 2000).

Using a nonlinear dynamical analysis of the multichannel EEG, Lutzenberger et al. (1992) showed that during resting conditions, subjects with high IQs demonstrated higher dimensional complexity in the EEG pattern than subjects with low IQs. Yet, in a follow up study (Anokhin et al., 1999), a negative correlation between the level of IQ and dimensional complexity was obtained. In yet another study (Jaušovec, 1998), no correlation between the complexity of oscillations in the resting brain and IQ could be observed.

Similarly inconsistent are the findings using EEG power measures. Several studies by Jaušovec have shown positive (Jaušovec, 1996), negative (Jaušovec, 1997), and no significant correlations (Jaušovec, 1998; Jaušovec & Jaušovec, 2000a), between resting alpha power and IQ. Contradictory are also the findings of other researchers. Doppelmayr et al. (2002) reported significant positive correlations between resting power measures in three individually determined narrow alpha frequency bands and scores on two German intelligence tests measuring semantic memory and the ability to learn new material. By contrast, Razoumnikova (2003) reported a negative correlation between lower-alpha power and intelligence. Razoumnikova further showed that high intelligent individuals displayed higher coherence (coupling of brain areas) than did low intelligent individuals. A similar finding was also reported by Jaušovec and Jaušovec (2000c), but only for the eyes-open relaxed state, whereas for the eyes-closed resting condition no significant correlations were obtained. The explanation for the diversity of results was usually ascribed to methodological differences. However, in our opinion, the main reason for the diversity is that most of the studies neglected gender related differences in abilities.

Gender Differences

Despite the fact that robust gender differences on the behavioral level in spatial (McGee, 1979), and verbal abilities (Garai & Scheinfeld, 1968) have been observed, many of the above reported studies generalized the relationship between intelligence and brain activity on only male samples (Anokhin & Vogel, 1996; Lutzenberger et al., 1992; Razoumnikova, 2003), or on predominantly female samples (Doppelmayr et al., 2002; Jaušovec, 1996, 1997, 1998; Jaušovec & Jaušovec, 2000a). Some recent EEG studies relating intelligence with brain activity under cognitive load have shown that males while solving numerical and figural tasks are more likely to produce cortical activation patterns which are in line with the neural efficiency hypothesis (i.e., less activation in brighter individuals), whereas in females for the same tasks no significant differences could be observed (Fink & Neubauer, 2006; Jaušovec & Jaušovec, 2008; Neubauer & Fink, 2003; Neubauer et al., 2002). Differences between males and females related to IQ were also observed in resting EEG

(Jaušovec & Jaušovec, 2005b). Brain activity of males decreased with the level of general intelligence, whereas an opposite pattern of brain activity was observed in females. This difference was most pronounced in the upper-alpha band, which is related to semantic memory processes (Klimesch, 1999). It was further found that highly intelligent males displayed greater decoupling of frontal brain areas, whereas highly intelligent females showed more coupling between frontal and parietal/ occipital brain areas. Further, a positive correlation between peak frequency and intelligence ($r=0.39$), and verbal intelligence ($r=0.41$) was observed only for male respondents.

Gender related differences were also observed in EEG coherence and global field power studies. The results of Corsi-Cabrera, Arce, Ramos, and Guevara (1997) and Rescher and Rappelsberger (1999) indicate different intra- and interhemispheric correlations of EEG activity in males and females, a finding commonly related to gender differences in certain brain structures (e.g., the posterior corpus callosum). Skrandies, Reik, and Kunze (1999) found a consistently larger global field power in females, suggesting that during visual information processing, different neural assemblies are activated in males and females. Empirical evidence favoring gender differences in physiological parameters of cortical activation comes also from PET, fMRI, and brain nerve conduction velocity studies. It was found that for figural tasks males show significantly stronger parietal activation, while females show significantly greater frontal activation (Weiss et al., 2003). A similar greater left frontal brain activation in females was also observed in relation to verbal intelligence scores Pfleiderer et al. (2004). Nyberg, Habib, and Herlitz (2000) observed gender differences in brain activation during memory retrieval, while Haier and Benbow (1995) reported a positive relationship in glucose metabolic rate in temporal lobe regions and mathematical reasoning ability only in men. A similar finding was also reported by Mansour, Haier, and Buchsbaum (1996). In a recent study by Reed, Vernon, and Johnson (2004) brain nerve conduction velocity, the speed at which impulses travel along nerves, was compared in the visual nerve pathway of males and females. It was found that the mean brain nerve conduction velocity of males was about 4% faster than in females.

Summarizing these findings suggests that gender related differences in intelligence can be observed in relation to the type of task (verbal/figural), and activated brain regions (frontal versus temporal-occipital and parieto-occipital areas). A tentative conceptual framework for the differences observed could be provided by age changes in white matter in the brain. It is now established that during childhood and adolescence the volume of white matter (WM: nerve axons, myelin around the axons, and glial cells) in the brain steadily increases. In males this volume probably increases faster than in females (De Bellis et al., 2001). This would also explain the finding that, among adults, males have an advantage of approximately 4 IQ points (Colom & Lynn, 2004). The increase in WM could be due to increased myelination, increased axon size, glial proliferation, or a combination of these (De Bellis et al., 2001).

Such sexual dimorphism in the neuroanatomic correlates of intelligence could also be the result of women possessing more neuronal processes but fewer neurons compared to men (De Courten-Myers, 1999). There exists a greater association in women between white matter properties and IQ, whereas in men there is a higher correlation between grey matter density and IQ (Gur et al., 1999; Haier, Jung, Yeo, Head, & Alkire, 2005). Further support for this hypothesis comes from some recent developmental studies (Schmithorst & Holland, 2007; Schmithorst, Holland, & Plante, 2006) indicating an increasing reliance on inter-hemispheric connectivity in girls with age.

Emotional Intelligence

Only recently has neurophysiological research has paid some attention to EI. In our lab, we have conducted several studies mainly investigating individual differences in brain functioning related to the level of EI. In a second line of research, we started to investigate differences in brain functioning between males and females while processing information with emotional content. In all our studies, we measured EI with the experimental version of MSCEIT (Mayer et al., 2002).

In our first two studies (Jaušovec & Jaušovec, 2005a; Jaušovec, Jaušovec, & Gerlič, 2001), we compared high and average to below average emotionally intelligent students while they were solving items from an EI test – the respondents had to mentally determine how much each feeling (happiness, sadness, fear, surprise, etc.) is expressed by the presented face or picture. In both studies, respondents in the alpha band displayed brain activity patterns which were in line with the neural efficiency theory. Similar findings were also reported by Freudenthaler, Fink, and Neubauer (2006). On the other hand, the pattern of ERD/ERS in the induced gamma band (second study), was contrary to what would be predicted by the neural efficiency theory – the high emotional intelligent group displayed induced gamma band ERS, while the average intelligent group displayed induced gamma band ERD. The difference increased from stimulus onset till 4,000 ms. A possible explanation for the findings could be that the high emotional intelligent individuals identified emotions in faces by relying more on figural and less on semantic information provided by the displayed pictures. This would explain the increased ERS in the induced gamma band and the decreased ERD in the induced upper alpha band shown by the high emotional intelligent group. A reverse strategy – more semantically and less figural oriented – could be hypothesized for the average emotional intelligent group of individuals.

In a recent study (Jaušovec & Jaušovec, 2005b), the relationship between resting EEG and EI was investigated. The general finding was that males and females differed in resting brain activity related to their level of EI; however, this difference was much less pronounced than for the verbal and performance components of intelligence. In males, the correlations between log-transformed alpha power and experiential EI had a reverse pattern to that of the correlations with IQ, whereas strategic EI correlated negatively with log-transformed alpha power similarly as did IQ. The same pattern of correlations between coherence in the parieto-occipital areas and experiential EI area score could be also observed in the lower-1 alpha band. For females significant correlations between strategic EI and decoupling in frontal brain areas and between experiential EI and the parieto-occipital coupling of brain areas were obtained. The reverse tendency in correlations for the area scores experiential and strategic EI is expected, because experiential EI refers to more intuitive components of EI, whereas strategic EI is more "logical," indicating the respondents ability to understand and manage emotions.

In yet another study (Jaušovec & Jaušovec, 2008), in three experiments, gender and ability (performance and EI) related differences in brain activity while respondents were solving spatial rotation tasks and identifying emotions in faces were investigated. The most robust gender related difference in brain activity was observed in the lower-2 alpha band. Males and females displayed an inverse IQ–activation relationship in just that domain in which they usually perform better: females in the EI domain, and males in the visuo-spatial ability domain. A similar pattern of brain activity could also be observed for the male/female respondents with different levels of performance and emotional IQ. It was suggested that high ability representatives of both genders to some extent compensate for their inferior skills in solving specific tasks (males in emotional tasks and females in spatial rotation tasks) by increasing their level of attention.

Study

The aim of the study was to further examine the influence that gender has on brain responses to emotional stimuli. First, we endeavored to investigate neuroelectric responses of respondents to a distinct content category ("erotic"), as well as to the more general dimensions of emotional valence (positive, negative, and neutral). Second, we distinguished between more exogenous neuroelectric components – which mainly depend on the physical properties of sensory stimuli and are not influenced by cognitive manipulations – and endogenous components which depend on the nature of the subjects' interaction with the stimulus. We focused on the P3 and P1 ERP components. The P3 is emitted after stimulus evaluation, whereas the P1 is related to selective attention. Also investigated were differences in evoked and induced gamma band response (GBA). Finally, the discrimination of picture categories occurred during passive viewing and was internally driven – the respondents were not asked to make any judgments or motor responses. Since to our knowledge there are no former studies related to this topic we consider the research endeavor to be mostly of an explorative nature. Our general expectation was that males and females would differ in their neuroelectric responses in relation to the four picture categories.

The 28 male and 30 female students participating in the experiment were equalized with respect to verbal and performance intelligence (WAIS-R), EI (experimental version of MSCEIT, Mayer et al., 2002), and the personality factors of Extraversion and Neuroticism (BFQ, Caprara, Barbaranelli, Borgogni, Bucik, & Boben, 2002). This equalization was done because a great body of research (see previous sections of this chapter) indicated that differences in intelligence (e.g., Haier et al., 1988; Jaušovec, 1998), EI (Jaušovec & Jaušovec, 2005a, 2005b), and personality factors (Eysenck & Eysenck, 1985), are reflected in brain activity. Stimuli were 60 color slides selected from the International Affective Pictures System (IAPS) (Lang, Bradley, & Cuthbert, 2005) according to the valence dimension. Subjects were told that a series of emotional slides would be presented and that they should attend to each picture for the entire time it appeared on the screen.

The ERP averaging was performed for each group of pictures (neutral, positive, negative, erotic). Mean amplitudes were measured using the following time windows: P1 (40–120) and P3 (250–500 ms). The induced GBA for each group of pictures was determined using the method of complex demodulation with a simultaneous signal envelope computation (Thatcher, Toro, Pflieger, & Hallet, 1994). The quantification of induced gamma was done using the intertrial variance method (Pfurtscheller, 1999). The evoked gamma response was determined using the digital filtering method (Karakaş & Başar, 1998). The EEG data, prior to ERP averaging, were digital bandpass filtered (31–49 Hz). For each group of pictures, peak-to-baseline amplitudes were determined in the 0–150 ms time window.

A three-way general linear model (GLM) for repeated measures was used to analyze the data obtained. Used was a subset of electrodes (F3, Fz, F4, C3, Cz, C4, P3, Pz, P4), and tested for the factors "type" (four categories of pictures); "anterior–posterior" (three levels), and "laterality" (three levels) as within-subjects factors and gender as between-subject factor. As can be seen in Table 7.2, significant differences related to the type of picture were present in the two ERP (P1 and P3), and GBA (evoked and induced gamma) measures.

Table 7.2 Effects of picture category, scalp location, gender on selected ERP measures and pairwise comparison for the factor type for erotic (E), negative (N), positive (P) and neutral (Nu) pictures

Factors	df (factor, error)	F	P<	Pairwise comparison
P1 (40–120 ms)				
Type	3,149.8	3.87	0.01	E**>P, Nu
P3 (250–500 ms)				
Type	3,136.0	40.67	0.000	E**, N**>P, Nu
Type × laterality	6,128.2	2.98	0.047	
Type × anterior-posterior	6,250.4	2.45	0.040	
Gender × laterality	2,112.0	5.78	0.004	
Evoked gamma (0–150 ms)				
Type	3,168.2	57.91	0.000	E**, N**, P**>Nu
Type × laterality	6,259.9	2.67	0.026	
Gender	1,56	18.70	0.000	Female>Male
Induced gamma (200–400 ms)				
Type	3,158.7	3.62	0.016	E*, N*>Nu

*$P<0.05$; **$P<0.01$

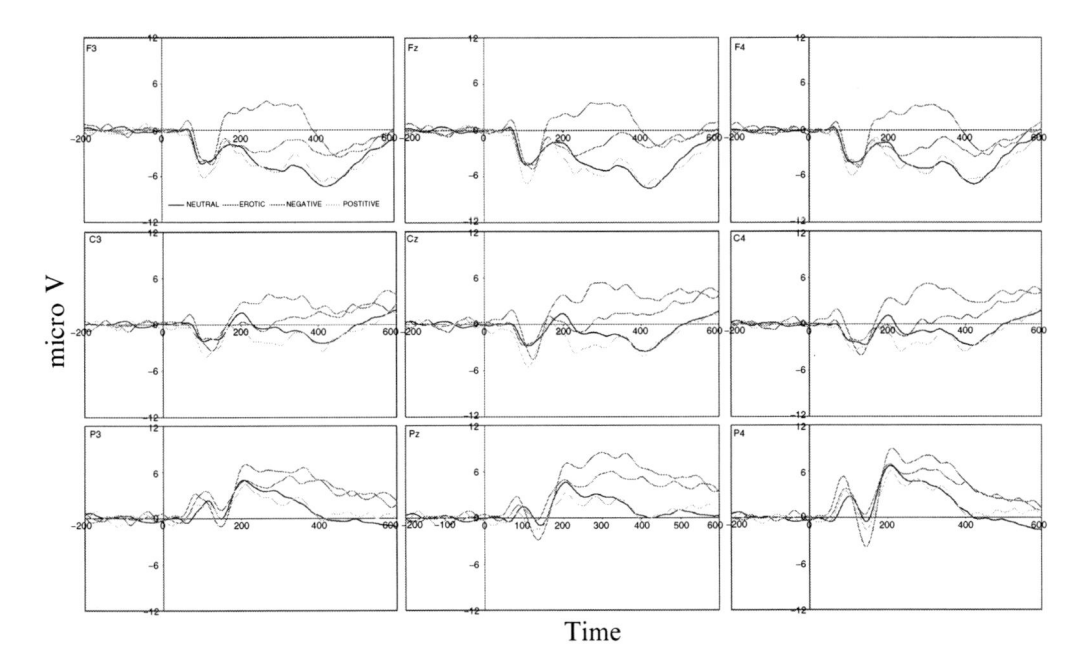

Fig. 7.2 Grand averages (digitally filtered at 30 Hz) across all male participants for neutral, erotic, positive and negative groups of pictures

The highest P1 and P3 amplitudes were observed for the pictures with erotic content as compared with the positive and neutral ones. Also high was the P3 amplitude for the pictures with a negative emotional content (see Figs. 7.2 and 7.3).

For the P3 response, the GLM also revealed a significant type by laterality as well as type by anterior–posterior effect. The P3 amplitudes of the neutral, positive and negative pictures displayed a similar pattern, being higher in the left and right hemispheres as compared with the vertex electrode locations. On the other hand, the amplitudes of the erotic figures were higher in the vertex and right hemisphere electrode locations as compared with the left hemisphere. The P3 amplitudes of the negative and erotic pictures differed more in the frontal and central locations than in the posterior locations, whereas the positive and neutral figures showed almost identical amplitude levels in the anterior and posterior locations.

The P3 amplitudes revealed also a significant gender by laterality effect. The P3 amplitudes of females were higher in the left and right hemispheres and lower in the vertex electrode locations compared with males' P3 amplitudes. The differences in P3 amplitudes between males and females were most pronounced in the right hemisphere.

The evoked gamma response showed a significant effect of the factor type and an interaction effect between the factor type and laterality. All pictures with an emotional content (positive, negative and erotic) evoked a higher amplitude than did the neutral pictures (see Fig. 7.4). In the left hemisphere, the amplitudes of the erotic and negative pictures were higher than the amplitudes of the positive pictures.

Also significant was the main effect of the gender factor. Females displayed a higher amplitude of the evoked gamma response than did males (see Fig. 7.5).

The amplitudes of the induced gamma response showed only a main effect of the factor type. The erotic and negative pictures induced a higher amplitude than did the neutral pictures. No gender related differences were observed.

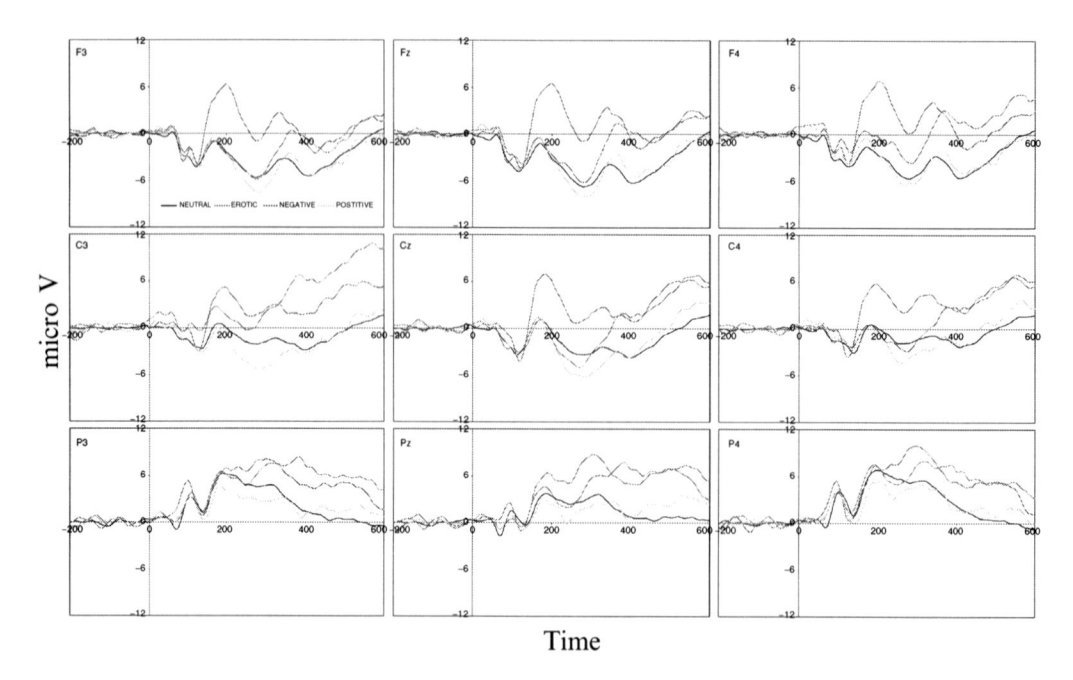

Fig. 7.3 Grand averages (digitally filtered at 30 Hz) across all female participants for neutral, erotic, positive and negative groups of pictures

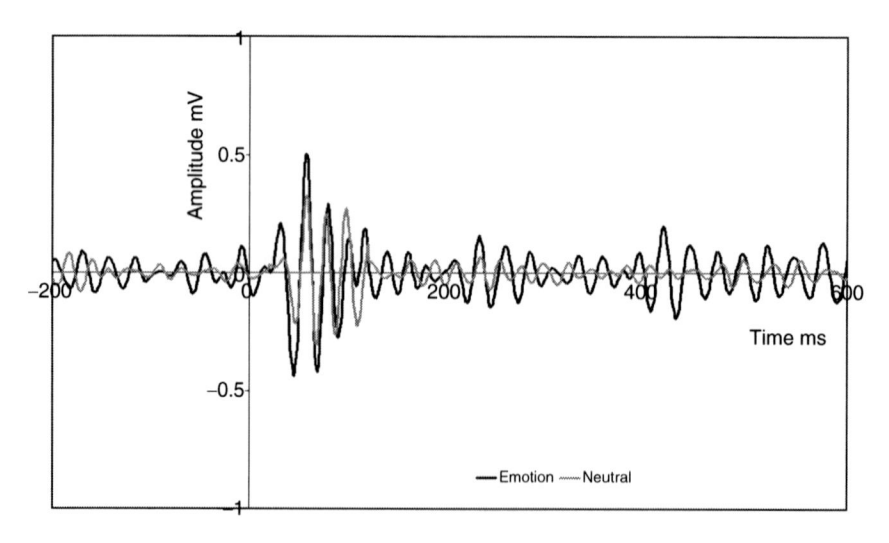

Fig. 7.4 Grand averages bandpass filtered between 31 and 49 Hz across all participants, electrode locations for neutral, and pictures with emotional content averaged across erotic, positive and negative pictures

The quantification of the induced gamma response partly depends on the power in the reference interval. This complicates the comparisons of values between different groups, since group differences might be due not only to cortical activity during task performance but also to differences in resting conditions. For this reason, the reference power was analyzed. A GLM for repeated measures showed a significant main effect of the factor gender (F (1,56)=5.80; $p<0.019$). Females displayed higher amplitudes of the resting induced gamma than did males.

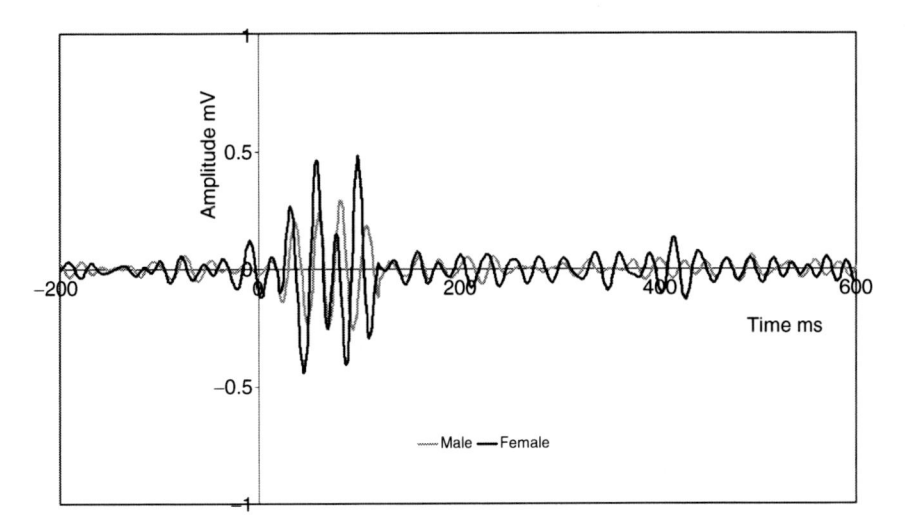

Fig. 7.5 Grand averages bandpass filtered between 31 and 49 Hz across all stimuli and electrode locations for male and female participants

Erotic pictures evoked the most robust neuroelectric responses in both males and females. This discrimination was present in the early time window of the P1 component of the ERP – a proximal index of attention allocation – and even more pronounced in the later endogenous component of the P3 – functionally considered response-related (decision-making). The findings are in line with previous research (Radilovà, Figar, & Radil, 1984; Anokhin et al., 2006), suggesting that the human brain is able to discriminate rapidly between specific contents of visual settings. Also in line with previous research (Bernat et al., 2001; Ito, Cacioppo, & Lang, 1998; Smith, Cacioppo, Larsen & Chatrand, 2003) is the finding that negative pictures elicited a more positive amplitude than positive and neutral ones. This difference was also present in the induced gamma associated with perception of coherent visual stimuli (Tallon-Baudry & Bertrand, 1999).

A different pattern of discrimination was observed for the evoked gamma response. A higher gamma amplitude was observed for all three groups of pictures with emotional content as compared with the neutral ones. A possible explanation for this may be the sensory origin of the early gamma response, thus being a phenomenon of the sensory register (Karakaş & Başar, 1998). One could further speculate that amplitude modulations of this early time-locked response reflect amplified processing of stimulus features characterizing stimuli with any emotional content, whereas the P1 component is only sensitive to stimuli with an erotic content. This would further suggest that the evoked gamma does not co-occur with the P1 response. A similar finding was reported by Keil et al. (2001). In their study, the early gamma was only sensitive to aversive stimuli.

With respect to the central question of the study, namely if gender has an influence on the neuroelectric brain responses to emotional stimuli, the data were less conclusive. The main finding is that females displayed much higher early gamma amplitude than did males. Together with the finding that females displayed higher induced gamma amplitudes in the resting period prior to stimulus onset, as well as findings of other studies indicating higher amplitudes of alpha beta and gamma oscillations in females (Aurlien et al., 2004; Jaušovec & Jaušovec, 2007) this could suggest that the differences may be due to subtle differences in brain structure and related metabolism (Cahill, 2003; Pfleiderer et al., 2004), and to the effects of estrogens and progestins on the neuronal dynamics (McEwen, Alves, Bulloch, & Weiland, 1997), and are not related to differences in emotional processing between males and females. It can be speculated that males and females differ in their early stages of information processing that include visual sensory and perceptual operations, with no regard to the emotional content of the stimuli. This may be only true for visual stimuli, as for auditory stimuli no gender related differences in the evoked gamma response were observed (Karakaş et al., 2006). This finding is in concordance with findings on the behavioral level indicating a female superiority in perceptual speed, the ability to rapidly absorb the details of a visual stimulus, which has been recognized since the 1940s (e.g., Harshman, Hampson, & Berenbaum, 1983; Kim & Petrakis, 1998; Tyler, 1965; Wesman, 1949) and generalizes to many types of visual stimuli.

A second gender related difference was observed for the P3 amplitudes – females displayed higher P3 amplitudes in the right and left hemispheres than did males. Again, these differences were not related to the emotional content of the presented stimuli.

The results do suggest that evolutionary processes have shaped neural mechanisms for efficient discrimination of stimuli directly relevant to reproduction and survival. It can be further speculated that males and females differ only in the way in which they process visual stimuli in general but not in relation to their emotional content. It seems that males and females are equally efficient in discriminating erotic and negative settings from those with no reproduction relevance or physical threat.

Conclusion

The few studies which have been conducted to explore the relationship between brain activity and EI do not allow for a firm conclusion, but just for a tentative one, expressing the opinion of the researchers in our lab. The following points summarize this opinion:

1. Verbal/performance, and EI represent distinct components of the cognitive architecture. Support for this assumption provided two studies conducted in our lab (Jaušovec & Jaušovec, 2005a; Jaušovec et al., 2001).
2. The neural efficiency phenomenon is not restricted to the cognitive ability domain but might also play an important role in the emotional ability domain. Several studies have shown that respondents especially in the alpha band displayed brain activity patterns which were in line with the neural efficiency theory (Freudenthaler et al., 2006; Jaušovec & Jaušovec, 2005a, 2008; Jaušovec et al., 2001).
3. Males and females, having different levels of EI, differ in their brain activity while performing EI tasks. This difference, which was predominantly observed in the gamma band, can be partly the result of a female superiority in perceptual speed in the visual domain and the mainly visual tasks used.

References

Amelang, M., & Steinmayr, R. (2006). Is there a validity increment for tests of emotional intelligence in explaining the variance of performance criteria? *Intelligence, 34*, 459–468.

Anokhin, A. P., Golosheykin, S., Sirevaag, E., Kristjansson, S., Rohrbaugh, J. W., & Heath, A. C. (2006). Rapid discrimination of visual scene content in the human brain. *Brain Research, 1093*, 167–177.

Anokhin, A. P., Lutzenberger, W., & Birbaumer, N. (1999). Spatiotemporal organization of brain dynamics and intelligence: An EEG study in adolescents. *International Journal of Psychophysiology, 33*, 259–273.

Anokhin, A., & Vogel, F. (1996). EEG alpha rhythm frequency and intelligence in normal adults. *Intelligence, 23*, 1–14.

Aurlien, H., Gjerde, O. I., Aarseth, J. H., Eldøen, G., Karlsen, B., Skeidsvoll, H., et al. (2004). EEG background activity described by a large computerized database. *Clinical Neurophysiology, 115*, 665–673.

Babchuk, W. A., Hames, R. B., & Thompson, R. A. (1985). Sex differences in the recognition of infant facial expressions of emotion: The primary caretaker hypothesis. *Ethology and Sociobiology, 6*, 89–101.

Bar-On, R. (2000). Emotional and social intelligence: Insights from the emotional quotient inventory. In R. Bar-On & J. D. A. Parker (Eds.), *The handbook of emotional intelligence* (pp. 363–388). San Francisco: Jossey-Bass.

Başar, E., Başar-Eroglu, C., Krakaş, S., & Schürmann, M. (2001). Gamma, alpha delta, and theta oscillations govern cognitive processes. *International Journal of Psychophysiology, 39*, 241–248.

Bernat, E., Bunce, S., & Shevrin, H. (2001). Event-related brain potentials differentiate positive and negative mood adjectives during both supraliminal and subliminal visual processing. *International Journal of Psychophysiology, 42*, 11–34.

Bhattacharya, J., Petsche, H., & Pereda, E. (2001). Long-range synchrony in the γ band: Role in music perception. *The Journal of Neuroscience, 21*, 6329–6337.

Boden, M. T., & Berenbaum, H. (2007). Emotional awareness, gender, and suspiciousness. *Cognition and Emotion, 21*, 268–280.

Cabeza, R., & Nyberg, L. (2000). Imaging cognition II: An empirical review of 275 PET and fMRI studies. *Journal of Cognitive Neuroscience, 12*, 1–47.

Cahill, L. (2003). Sex-related influences on the neurobiology of emotional influenced memory. *Annals of the New York Academy of Science, 985*, 163–173.

Cantor, N., & Kihlstrom, J. F. (1985). Social intelligence: The cognitive basis of personality. In P. Shaver (Ed.), *Review of personality and social psychology* (Vol. 6, pp. 15–33). Beverly Hills, CA: Sage.

Cantor, N., & Kihlstrom, J. F. (1987). *Personality and social intelligence*. Englewood Cliffs, NJ: Prentice-Hall.

Caprara, G. V., Barbaranelli, C., Borgogni, L., Bucik, V., & Boben, D. (2002). *Model "velikih pet" Priro nik za merjenje strukture osebnosti*. Ljubljana: Center za psihodiagnostična sredstva.

Ciarrochi, J., Hynes, K., & Crittenden, N. (2005). Can men do better if they try harder: Sex and motivational effects on emotional awareness. *Cognition and Emotion, 19*, 133–141.

Coffey, E., Berenbaum, H., & Kerns, J. K. (2003). The dimensions of emotional intelligence, alexithymia, and mood awareness: Associations with personality and performance on an emotional Stroop task. *Cognition and Emotion, 17*, 671–679.

Colom, R., & Lynn, R. (2004). Testing the developmental theory of sex differences in intelligence on 12–18 year olds. *Personality and Individual Differences, 36*, 75–82.

Corsi-Cabrera, M., Arce, C., Ramos, J., & Guevara, M. A. (1997). Effect of spatial ability and sex on inter- and intrahemispheric correlation of EEG activity. *Electroencephalography and Clinical Neurophysiology, 102*, 5–11.

De Bellis, M. D., Keshavan, M. S., Beers, S. R., Hall, J., Frustaci, K., Masalehdan, A., et al. (2001). Sex differences in brain maturation during childhood and adolescence. *Cerebral Cortex, 11*, 552–557.

De Courten-Myers, G. M. (1999). The human cerebral cortex: Gender differences in structure and function. *Journal of Neuropathology and Experimental Neurology, 58*, 217–226.

De Raad, B. (2005). The trait-coverage of emotional intelligence. *Personality and Individual Differences, 38*, 673–687.

Doppelmayr, M., Klimesch, W., Stadler, W., Pöllhuber, D., & Heine, C. (2002). EEG alpha power and intelligence. *Intelligence, 30*, 289–302.

Extremera, N., Fernandez-Berrocal, P., & Salovey, P. (2006). Spanish version of the Mayer-Salovey-Caruso emotional intelligence test (MSCEIT). Version 2.0: Reliabilities, age and gender differences. *Psicothema, 18*, 42–48.

Eysenck, H. J., & Eysenck, M. W. (1985). *Personality and individual differences*. New York: Plenum.

Fink, A., & Neubauer, A. C. (2006). EEG alpha oscillations during the performance of verbal creativity tasks: Differential effects of sex and verbal intelligence. *International Journal of Psychophysiology, 62*, 46–53.

Freudenthaler, H. H., Fink, A., & Neubauer, A. C. (2006). Emotional abilities and cortical activation during emotional information processing. *Personality and Individual Differences, 41*, 685–695.

Garai, J., & Scheinfeld, A. (1968). Sex differences in mental and behavioral traits. *Genetic Psychology Monographs, 77*, 169–299.

Gevins, A., & Smith, M. E. (2000). Neurophysiological measures of working memory and individual differences in cognitive ability and cognitive style. *Cerebral Cortex, 10*, 830–839.

Giannitrapani, D. (1969). EEG average frequency and intelligence. *Electroencephalography and Clinical Neurophysiology, 27*, 480–486.

Gohm, C. L., & Clore, G. L. (2000). Individual differences in emotional experience: Mapping available scales to processes. *Personality and Social Psychology Bulletin, 26*, 679–697.

Gohm, C. L., & Clore, G. L. (2002). Four latent traits of emotional experience and their involvement in well-being, coping, and their attributional style. *Cognition and Emotion, 16*, 495–518.

Gur, R. C., Turetsky, B. I., Matsui, M., Yan, M., Bilker, W., Hughett, P., et al. (1999). Sex differences in brain gray and white matter in healthy young adults: Correlations with cognitive performance. *Journal of Neuroscience, 19*, 4065–4072.

Haier, R. J., & Benbow, C. P. (1995). Sex differences and lateralization in temporal lobe glucose metabolism during mathematical reasoning. *Developmental Neuropsychology, 4*, 405–414.

Haier, R. J., Jung, R. E., Yeo, R. A., Head, K., & Alkire, M. T. (2005). The neuroanatomy of general intelligence: Sex matters. *Neuroimage, 25*, 320–327.

Haier, R. J., Neuchterlein, K. H., Hazlett, E., Wu, J. C., Paek, J., Browning, H. L., et al. (1988). Cortical glucose metabolic rate correlates of abstract reasoning and attention studied with positron emission tomography. *Intelligence, 12*, 199–217.

Haier, R. J., Siegel, B., Tang, C., Abel, L., & Buchsbaum, M. S. (1992). Intelligence and changes in regional cerebral glucose metabolic rate following learning. *Intelligence, 16*, 415–426.

Haier, R. J., White, N. S., & Alkire, M. T. (2003). Individual differences in general intelligence correlate with brain function during nonreasoning tasks. *Intelligence, 31*, 429–441.

Hall, J. A. (1978). Gender effects in decoding nonverbal cues. *Psychological Bulletin, 85*, 845–857.

Hall, J. A. (1984). *Nonverbal sex differences: Communication accuracy and expressive style.* Baltimore: Johns Hopkins University Press.

Halpern, D. F. (2004). A cognitive-process taxonomy for sex differences in cognitive abilities. *Current Directions in Psychological Science, 13*, 135–139.

Harshman, R. A., Hampson, E., & Berenbaum, S. A. (1983). Individual differences in cognitive abilities and brain organization: Part I. Sex and handedness differences in ability. *Canadian Journal of Psychology, 37*, 144–192.

Henley, N. M. (1977). *Body politics: Power, sex and nonverbal communication.* Englewood Cliffs, NJ: Prentice-Hall.

Herlitz, A., Nilsson, L. G., & Backman, L. (1997). Gender differences in episodic memory. *Memory and Cognition, 25*, 801–811.

Hyde, J. S. (1981). How large are cognitive gender differences? *American Psychologist, 36*, 892–901.

Ito, T. A., Cacioppo, J. T., & Lang, P. J. (1998). Eliciting affect using the International Affective Picture System: trajectories through evaluative space. *Personality and Social Psychology Bulletin, 24*, 855–879.

Jackson, N. D., & Rushton, J. P. (2006). Males have greater g: Sex differences in general mental ability from 100,000 17- to 18-year-olds on the scholastic assessment test. *Intelligence, 34*, 479–486.

Jaušovec, N. (1996). Differences in EEG alpha activity related to giftedness. *Intelligence, 23*, 159–173.

Jaušovec, N. (1997). Differences in EEG alpha activity between gifted and non-identified individuals: Insights into problem solving. *Gifted Child Quarterly, 41*, 26–32.

Jaušovec, N. (1998). Are gifted individuals less chaotic thinkers? *Personality and Individual Differences, 25*, 253–267.

Jaušovec, N. (2000). Differences in cognitive processes between gifted, intelligent, creative and average individuals while solving complex problems: An EEG study. *Intelligence, 28*, 213–237.

Jaušovec, N., & Jaušovec, K. (2000a). Correlations between ERP parameters and intelligence: A reconsideration. *Biological Psychology, 50*, 137–154.

Jaušovec, N., & Jaušovec, K. (2000b). Differences in event-related and induced brain oscillations in the theta and alpha frequency bands related to human intelligence. *Neuroscience Letters, 293*, 191–194.

Jaušovec, N., & Jaušovec, K. (2000c). Differences in resting EEG related to ability. *Brain Topography, 12*, 229–240.

Jaušovec, N., & Jaušovec, K. (2001). Differences in EEG current density related to intelligence. *Cognitive Brain Research, 12*, 55–60.

Jaušovec, N., & Jaušovec, K. (2003). Spatiotemporal brain activity related to intelligence: A low resolution brain electromagnetic tomography study. *Cognitive Brain Research, 16*, 267–272.

Jaušovec, N., & Jaušovec, K. (2004a). Intelligence related differences in induced brain activity during the performance of memory tasks. *Personality and Individual Differences, 36*, 597–612.

Jaušovec, N., & Jaušovec, K. (2004b). Differences in induced brain activity during the performance of learning and working-memory tasks related to intelligence. *Brain and Cognition, 54*, 65–74.

Jaušovec, N., & Jaušovec, K. (2005a). Differences in induced gamma and upper alpha oscillations in the human brain related to verbal/performance and emotional intelligence. *International Journal of Psychophysiology, 56*, 223–235.

Jaušovec, N., & Jaušovec, K. (2005b). Sex differences in brain activity related to general and emotional intelligence. *Brain and Cognition, 59*, 277–286.

Jaušovec, N., & Jaušovec, K. (2007). Personality, gender and brain oscillations. *International Journal of Psychophysiology, 66*(2007), 215–224.

Jaušovec, N., & Jaušovec, K. (2008). Spatial-rotation and recognizing emotions: Gender related differences in brain activity. *Intelligence, 36*, 383–393.

Jaušovec, N., Jaušovec, K., & Gerlič, I. (2001). Differences in event related and induced EEG patterns in the theta and alpha frequency bands related to human emotional intelligence. *Neuroscience Letters, 311*, 93–96.

Jensen, A. (1998). *The g factor.* Westport, CN: Praeger.

Karakaş, S., & Başar, E. (1998). Early gamma response is sensory in origin: A conclusion based on cross-comparison of results from multiple experimental paradigms. *International Journal of Psychophysiology, 31*, 13–31.

Karakaş, S., Tüfekçi, İ., Bekçi, B., Çakmak, E. D., Doğutepe, E., Erzengin, Ö. U., et al. (2006). Early time-locked gamma response and gender specificity. *International Journal of Psychophysiology, 60*, 225–239.

Keil, A., Müller, M. M., Gruber, T., Weinbruch, C., Stolarova, M., & Elbert, T. (2001). Effects of emotional arousal in the cerebral hemispheres: A study of oscillatory brain activity and event-related potentials. *Clinical Neurophysiology, 112*, 2057–2068.

Kim, H. S., & Petrakis, E. (1998). Visuoperceptual speed of karate practitioners at three levels of skill. *Perceptual and Motor Skills, 87*, 96–98.

Klimesch, W. (1996). Memory processes, brain oscillations and EEG synchronization. *International Journal of Psychophysiology, 24*, 61–100.

Klimesch, W. (1997). EEG-alpha rhythms and memory processes. *International Journal of Psychophysiology, 26,* 319–340.

Klimesch, W. (1999). EEG alpha and theta oscillations reflect cognitive and memory performance: A review and analysis. *Brain Research Reviews, 29,* 169–195.

Klimesch, W., & Doppelmayr, M. (2001). *High frequency alpha and intelligence.* Paper presented at the 10th biennial meeting of ISSID, Edinburgh.

Lang, P. J., Bradley, M. M., & Cuthbert, B. N. (2005). *International affective picture system (IAPS): Affective ratings of pictures and instructional manual. Technical report A-6.* Bainesville, FL: University of Florida.

Lehtovirta, M., Partanen, J., Kononen, M., Soininen, H., Helisalmi, S., Mannermaa, A., et al. (1996). Spectral analysis of EEG in Alzheimer's disease: Relation to apolipoprotein E polymorphism. *Neurobiology of Aging, 17,* 523–526.

Lindholm, T., Lehtinen, V., Hyyppa, M. T., & Puukka, P. (1990). Alexithymic features in relation to the dexamethasone suppression test in a Finnish population sample. *American Journal of Psychiatry, 147,* 1216–1219.

Linn, M. C., & Peterson, A. C. (1985). Emergence and characterization of sex differences in spatial ability: A meta-analysis. *Child Development, 56,* 1479–1498.

Lutzenberger, W., Birbaumer, N., Flor, H., Rockstroh, B., & Elbert, T. (1992). Dimensional analysis of the human EEG and intelligence. *Neuroscience Letters, 143,* 10–14.

Lynn, R., & Irwing, P. (2004). Sex differences on the progressive matrices: A meta-analysis. *Intelligence, 32,* 481–498.

Mackintosh, N. J., & Bennett, E. S. (2005). What do Raven's matrices measure? An analysis in terms of sex differences. *Intelligence, 33,* 663–664.

Maitland, S. B., Herlitz, A., Nyberg, L., Backman, L., & Nilsson, L. G. (2004). Selective sex differences in declarative memory. *Memory and Cognition, 32,* 1160–1169.

Mansour, C. S., Haier, R. J., & Buchsbaum, M. S. (1996). Gender comparison of cerebral glucose metabolic rate in healthy adults during a cognitive task. *Personality and Individual Differences, 20,* 183–191.

Masters, M. S., & Sanders, B. (1993). Is the gender difference in mental rotation disappearing? *Behavior Genetics, 23,* 337–341.

Mayer, J. D., Caruso, D. R., & Salovey, P. (2000). Emotional intelligence meets traditional standards for an intelligence. *Intelligence, 27,* 267–298.

Mayer, J. D., Salovey, P., & Caruso, D. R. (2002). *Mayer-Salovey-Caruso emotional intelligence test (MSCEIT).* Toronto: MHS.

McClure, E. B. (2000). A meta-analytic review of sex differences in facial expression processing and their development in infants, children, and adolescents. *Psychological Bulletin, 126,* 424–453.

McEwen, B. S., Alves, S. E., Bulloch, K., & Weiland, N. G. (1997). Ovarian steroids and the brain: Implication for cognition and aging. *Neurology, 48,* 8–15.

McGee, M. (1979). Human spatial abilities: Psychometric studies and environmental, generic, hormonal, and neurological influences. *Psychological Bulletin, 86,* 889–917.

Neubauer, A. C., & Fink, A. (2003). Fluid intelligence and neural efficiency: Effects of task complexity and sex. *Personality and Individual Differences, 35,* 811–827.

Neubauer, A. C., Fink, A., & Schrausser, D. G. (2002). Intelligence and neural efficiency: The influence of task content and sex on the brain – IQ relationship. *Intelligence, 30,* 515–536.

Neubauer, V., Freudenthaler, H. H., & Pfurtscheller, G. (1995). Intelligence and spatiotemporal patterns of event-related desynchronization. *Intelligence, 3,* 249–266.

Neubauer, A. C., Sange, G., & Pfurtscheller, G. (1999). Psychometric intelligence and event-related desynchronization during performance of a letter matching task. In G. Pfurtscheller & F. H. da Silva Lopes (Eds.), *Handbook of electroencephalography and clinical neuropsychology. Event-related desynchronization* (Vol. 6, pp. 219–232). Amsterdam: Elsevier.

Nunez, P. L., Wingeier, B. M., & Silberstein, R. B. (2001). Spatial-temporal structures of human alpha rhythms: Theory, microcurrent sources, multiscale measurements, and global binding of local networks. *Human Brain Mapping, 13,* 125–164.

Nyberg, L., Habib, R., & Herlitz, A. (2000). Brain activation during episodic memory retrieval: Sex differences. *Acta Psychologica, 105,* 181–194.

Nyborg, H. (1994). The neuropsychology of sex-related differences in brain and specific abilities: Hormones, developmental dynamics and new paradigm. In P. A. Vernon (Ed.), *The neuropsychology of individual differences* (pp. 59–113). London: Academic Press INC.

Nyborg, H. (2005). Sex-related differences in general intelligence g, brain size, and social status. *Personality and Individual Differences, 39,* 497–509.

O'Boyle, M. W., Benbow, C. P., & Alexander, J. E. (1995). Sex differences, hemispheric laterality, and associated brain activity in the intellectually gifted. *Developmental Neuropsychology, 4,* 415–443.

Parker, J. D. A., Taylor, G. J., & Bagby, R. M. (1989). The alexithymia construct: Relationship with sociodemographic variables and intelligence. *Comparative Psychiatry, 30,* 434–441.

Parker, J. D. A., Taylor, G. J., & Bagby, R. M. (2003). The 20-item Toronto alexithymia scale III. Reliability and factorial validity in a community population. *Journal of Psychosomatic Research, 55*, 269–275.

Petrides, K. V., & Furnham, A. (2000). Gender differences in measured and self-estimated trait emotional intelligence. *Sex Roles, 42*, 449–461.

Pfleiderer, B., Ohrmann, A. P., Suslow, B. T., Wolgast, B. M., Gerlach, B. A. L., Heindela, C. W., et al. (2004). N-acetylaspartate levels of left frontal cortex are associated with verbal intelligence in women but not in men: A proton magnetic resonance spectroscopy study. *Neuroscience, 123*, 1053–1058.

Pfurtscheller, G. (1999). Quantification of ERD and ERS in the time domain. In G. Pfurtscheller & F. H. da Silva Lopes (Eds.), *Handbook of electroencephalography and clinical neuropsychology, event-related desynchronization* (Vol. 6, pp. 89–105). Elsevier: Amsterdam.

Posthuma, D., Neale, M. C., Boomsma, D. I., & de Geus, E. J. C. (2000). Are smarter brains running faster? Heritability of alpha peak frequency, IQ, and their interrelation. *Behavior Genetics, 3*, 567–579.

Pulvermüller, F., Birbaumer, N., Lutzenberger, W., & Mohr, B. (1997). High frequency brain activity: Its possible role in attention, perception and language processing. *Progress in Neurobiology, 52*, 427–445.

Radilovà, J., Figar, S., & Radil, T. (1984). Emotional states influence the visual evoked-potentials. *Activitas Nervosa Superior, 26*, 159–160.

Razoumnikova, O. (2003). Interaction of personality and intelligence factors in cortex activity modulation. *Personality and Individual Differences, 35*, 135–162.

Reed, T. E., Vernon, P. A., & Johnson, A. M. (2004). Sex difference in brain nerve conduction velocity in normal humans. *Neuropsychologia, 42*, 1709–1714.

Rescher, B., & Rappelsberger, P. (1999). Gender dependent EEG-changes during a mental rotation task. *International Journal of Psychophysiology, 33*, 209–222.

Rooy, D. L., Alonso, A., & Viswesvaran, C. (2005). Group differences in emotional intelligence scores: Theoretical and practical implications. *Personality and Individual Differences, 38*, 689–700.

Salminen, J. K., Saarijarvi, S., Aarela, E., Toikka, T., & Kauhanen, J. (1999). Prevalence of alexithymia and its association with sociodemographic variables in the general population of Finland. *Journal of Psychosomatic Research, 46*, 75–82.

Schmithorst, V. J., & Holland, S. K. (2007). Sex differences in the development of neuroanatomical functional connectivity underlying intelligence found using Bayesian connectivity analysis. *NeuroImage, 35*, 406–419.

Schmithorst, V. J., Holland, S. K., & Plante, E. (2006). Cognitive modules utilized for narrative comprehension in children: A functional magnetic resonance imaging study. *NeuroImage, 29*, 254–266.

Schulte, M. J., Ree, M. J., & Carretta, T. R. (2004). Emotional intelligence: Not much more than g and personality. *Personality and Individual Differences, 37*, 1059–1068.

Singer, W., & Gray, C. M. (1995). Visual feature integration and the temporal correlation hypothesis. *Annual Review of Neuroscience, 18*, 555–586.

Skrandies, W., Reik, P., & Kunze, Ch. (1999). Topography of evoked brain activity during mental arithmetic and language tasks: Sex differences. *Neuropsychologia, 37*, 421–430.

Smith, N. K., Cacioppo, J. T., Larsen, J. T., & Chatrand, T. L. (2003). May I have your attention, please: Electrocortical responses to positive and negative stimuli. *Neuropsychologia, 41*, 171–183.

Strüber, D., Basar-Eroglu, C., Hoff, E., & Stadler, M. (2000). Reversal-rate dependent differences in the EEG gamma-band during multistable visual perception. *International Journal of Psychophysiology, 38*, 243–252.

Tallon-Baudry, C., & Bertrand, O. (1999). Oscillatory γ activity in humans and its role in object representation. *Trends in Neurosciences, 19*, 151–162.

Thatcher, R. W., Toro, C., Pflieger, M. E., & Hallet, M. (1994). Human neural network dynamics using multimodal registration of EEG, PET and MRI. In R. W. Thatcher, M. Hallet, & T. Zeffiro (Eds.), *Functional neuroimaging: Technical foundations* (pp. 259–267). Orlando FL: Academic Press.

Thorndike, E. L. (1920). Intelligence and its use. *Harper's Magazine, 140*, 227–235.

Thorndike, R. L., & Stein, S. (1937). An evaluation of the attempts to measure social intelligence. *Psychological Bulletin, 34*, 275–285.

Tyler, L. E. (1965). *The psychology of human differences* (3rd ed.). New York: Appleton-Century-Crofts.

Vogel, S. (1990). Gender differences in intelligence, language, visuo-motor abilities and academic achievement in students with learning disabilities: A review of the literature. *Journal of Learning Disability, 23*, 44–52.

Voyer, D., Voyer, S., & Bryden, M. P. (1995). Magnitude of sex differences in spatial ability: A meta-analysis and consideration of critical variables. *Psychological Bulletin, 117*, 250–270.

Wechsler, D. (1981). *WAIS-R manual: Wechsler adult intelligence scale-revised*. New York: Psychological Corporation.

Weiss, E., Siedentopf, C. M., Hofer, A., Deisenhammer, E. A., Hoptman, M. J., Kremser, C., et al. (2003). Sex differences in brain activation pattern during a visuospatial cognitive task: A functional magnetic resonance imaging study in healthy volunteers. *Neuroscience Letters, 344*, 169–172.

Weitz, S. (1974). *Nonverbal communication: Readings with commentary*. New York: Oxford University Press.

Wesman, A. G. (1949). Separation of sex groups in test reporting. *Journal of Educational Psychology, 40*, 223–229.

Chapter 8
Learned Irrelevance Revisited: Pathology-Based Individual Differences, Normal Variation and Neural Correlates

Aleksandra Gruszka, Adam Hampshire, and Adrian M. Owen

Introduction

The function of the human executive system can broadly be described as the seeking out and processing of those signals and memories that are of the greatest relevance when guiding deliberate and adaptive behaviours. This task is not easy, however, since it requires almost constant shifting of attention in response to irregular alterations in the contingencies relating stimuli, responses, and environmental feedback. An individual's current belief regarding these contingencies guides response within a given context, and the representation of this belief and its consequent behaviour is often referred to as an "attentional set". Consequently, attentional set-shifting is an important executive function responsible for altering a behavioural response in reaction to the changing contingencies (Cools, Barker, Sahakian, & Robbins, 2001; Gotham, Brown, & Marsden, 1986). Such flexibility underlies a wide range of behaviours: the better the set-shifting capacity, the more flexible the person is at adapting to change. At the other end of this continuum are many psychiatric groups, neurodegenerative groups and even healthy elderly and young subjects that have been shown repeatedly to be impaired in attentional set-shifting performance. One specific form of these impairments lies in an inability to attend to, or to learn about, information which has previously been shown to be irrelevant. This phenomenon called learned irrelevance (LI) (Mackintosh, 1973) is very mysterious, because unlike other aspects of attentional set-shifting, it appears to be neither dependent on the frontal lobe (e.g. Owen et al., 1993) nor affected by dopamine (Owen et al., 1993; Słabosz et al., 2006), and, therefore, may not be coded for in the parts of the brain that are typically considered "executive" at all.

The aim of this chapter is to discuss recent advances in the area of LI in humans and to show how the latest trends in executive-function research can be applied to the study of LI. The first trend is the application of experimental paradigms that provide measures of putative cognitive functions much more precisely than the measures that have been offered by "classical" neuropsychological methods (Aron, 2008). One such paradigm is the ID/ED visual discrimination learning paradigm (e.g. Downes et al., 1989; Owen et al., 1992) modelled after the most prominent neuropsychological tool for studying attentional set-shifting deficits, namely Wisconsin Card Sorting Task (WCST; Grant & Berg, 1948). The ID/ED paradigm allows the operationalization of the dependent variables in a much more reliable way. It makes them much more sensitive to the effects of brain damage or

---

A. Gruszka (✉)
Institute of Psychology, Jagiellonian University, Al. Mickiewicza 3, 31-120 Cracow, Poland
e-mail: rusalka@apple.phils.uj.edu.pl

A. Hampshire and A.M. Owen
MRC Cognition and Brain Sciences Unit, 15 Chaucer Road, Cambridge, CB2 7EF, UK

pathophysiology. In the first section of this chapter, we review studies that have utilised the ID/ED paradigm to investigate normal and pathology-based individual differences in LI. The utility of such analyses is motivated by the fact that dissociable patterns of LI deficits were observed in patients with circumscribed frontal-lobe removals, and both medicated and non-medicated patients with Parkinson's disease (PD). An understanding of these patterns may lead us to unravel the distinctive roles played by different frontal striatal circuits (Alexander, Delong, & Strick, 1986), or the different roles played by the cortical and striatal portions of those circuits.

The second trend in executive-function research is the implementation of advanced neuroscience techniques, such as brain imaging (Aron, 2008). In the second section of the present chapter, we describe our study that aimed to investigate the neural mechanisms underlying dissociable components of attentional set-shifting, including LI. Taken together, the combined approach based on the two trends enables a finer delineation of executive functions than was possible with classical paradigms. In our opinion, the combined approach will ultimately allow us to answer the question of how the LI effect is rooted in actual neural systems. One may say that this chapter exemplifies a situation where individual differences are less important as such; rather, the dissociable patterns of results obtained for various neuropsychological groups and the normal population are more significant, since these dissociable patterns may help us understand the neural and neurochemical mechanisms underlying the investigated phenomena.

Learned Irrelevance and a Visual Learning Paradigm

Studies of human executive functions first began when several tests of behavioural flexibility, now considered classic, were administered to patients with frontal lobe lesions. Among these tests, the WCST was given a particularly prominent place in standard neuropsychological testing of attentional set-shifting ability. The WCST requires participants to sort a deck of cards according to a number of dimensions. Each card varies in three dimensions – number, colour and shape – and as each card is presented, the subject is required to match it according to a specified dimension. After a certain number of correct "sorts", the rule is changed and the subject is required to start sorting according to an alternative dimension. In order to comply with the new task requirements, subjects have to override a tendency to stick to a previously relevant rule. It has been shown repeatedly that damage to various regions of the frontal lobe produces behavioural impairment on the WCST, particularly for conditions in which the subject had to overcome a prepotent response tendency. However, the results indicating that impaired performance on the WCST is linked to frontal-lobe dysfunction have often been inconsistent. In separate studies, dorsolateral (Demakis, 2003), orbitofrontal (Dias, Robbins, & Roberts, 1997) and medial (Drewe, 1974) brain areas have been implicated in various aspects of WCST performance. In fact, it has been argued that there is no clear support for the role of the WCST as a diagnostic tool of frontal lobe damage (Mountain & Snow, 1993; Reitan & Wolfson, 1994), since diffuse brain injury (Fork et al., 2005) as well as localised damage to specific non-frontal regions (Anderson, Bigler, & Blatter, 1995; Canavan et al., 1989; Hermann, Wyler, & Richey, 1988; Horner, Flashman, Freides, Epstein, & Bakay, 1996) can produce similar cognitive impairments. In addition, several cases have been reported in which there was a lack of an impairment in spite of frontal-lobe pathology (Anderson, Damasio, Jones, & Tranel, 1991; Eslinger & Damasio, 1985).

Some of the inconsistency is probably related to the low psychological resolution of the WCST. Completing the test involves the recruitment of a number of different executive functions (e.g. performance monitoring, integration of feedback, rule-induction, set-shifting, and suppression of previous sorting rules), and these may be coded in discrete circuits – some of which may not be within the frontal lobes. The WCST requires subjects to shift attentional set away from the previously relevant dimension. The term "set", used in this context, refers to a predisposition to attend selectively to a particular stimulus dimension (such as "colour" or "shape"), established on the basis of reinforcing feedback (i.e. "correct" or "incorrect" cues). However, there are many forms of shifting implicit in the WCST. For example, a new rule may require that subjects shift attentional-set either to the other so-far "incorrect" *exemplar* of the same dimension (e.g. from *red* to *blue*) or to shift their attention to the other so-far "incorrect" *dimension* (e.g. from *shape* to *colour*). Studies with humans and experimental primates have suggested that these two forms of shifting – extra-dimensional (ED) shifting and reversal shifting, respectively – are subserved by dissociable regions within the frontal cortex. While EDS shifting is hampered by damage to the dorsolateral prefrontal cortex (DLPFC), reversal shifting is impaired by lesions to the OFC or ventromedial frontal cortex (and not the DLPFC) (Dias, Robbins, & Roberts, 1996; Fellows & Farah, 2003; Jones & Mishkin, 1972). As a result, using the WCST it has not been possible to define a specific area within the frontal cortex that is critically involved in attentional set-shifting and several recent studies (Downes et al., 1989; Owen et al., 1992; Roberts, Robbins, & Everitt, 1988) have argued that pure "set-shifting ability" may be more accurately assessed using the intra- and extra-dimensional shifting paradigm described frequently in the animal learning literature (Mackintosh, 1983). An "intradimensional shift" (IDS) occurs when a subject is required to cease responding to one exemplar of a particular stimulus dimension (e.g. "*blue*" from the dimension "*colour*") and must begin responding to a new exemplar of that same dimension (e.g. "*red*"). As mentioned above, an "extradimensional shift" (EDS) occurs when a subject is required to switch responding to a novel exemplar of a previously irrelevant dimension (e.g. from "*blue*" to "*squares*" from the dimension "*shape*"). In discrimination learning tasks, impairments in neuropsychological or neurological populations are observed mainly when an EDS shift is required, rather than when an IDS shift is required (Downes et al., 1989; Roberts et al., 1988). In one study, a group of neurosurgical patients with frontal-lobe lesions were shown to be specifically impaired in their ability to shift response set to the previously irrelevant stimulus dimension (i.e. at the EDS stage of learning) but *not* to shift attention to new exemplars of a previously relevant dimension (i.e. at the IDS stage of learning) (Owen, Roberts, Polkey, Sahakian, & Robbins, 1991). By comparison, patients with medial temporal-lobe excisions were not impaired in their ability to perform either shift.

Furthermore, EDS deficits in attentional set-shifting have been dissected further into two separate contributing mechanisms. It has been suggested that these deficits may reflect either an impairment in the ability to shift attention from a perceptual dimension that has been previously relevant (i.e. "perseveration"), or in the ability to shift to an alternative perceptual dimension that has been previously perceived as irrelevant (i.e. "learned irrelevance") (Owen et al., 1993). This distinction plays an important role in the context of neuropathology (Owen et al., 1993), since separate cognitive and possibly neurochemical mechanisms of perseveration and LI have been suggested (Maes, Damen, & Eling, 2004; Owen et al., 1993).

The phenomenon of perseveration seems much better understood, both in terms of the underlying cognitive operations and the neuroanatomical structures, despite the fact that existing studies imply a predominance of the LI over perseveration mechanism in the normal population (Maes, Vich, & Eling, 2006; Maes et al., 2004). Perseverative behaviour on WCST-like tasks may result from several types of endogenous adaptive control errors, i.e. failures in rule induction (i.e. forming hypotheses concerning the new rule), inability to shift attentional set (the configuration of appropriate task sets to test these hypotheses and the suppression of no-longer-relevant task sets), or deficient monitoring of performance (Ridderinkhof, Span, & van der Molen, 2002). As for the neural correlates of perseverative behaviour, it appears to be a general consensus in clinical studies, experimental neuropsychology and cognitive neuroimaging that perseverative behaviour mainly reflects inefficient prefrontal function (see Barcelo, Sanz, Molina, & Rubia, 1997 for a review). Brenda Milner (1963) was the first author to link poor WCTS performance with circumscribed DLPFC lesions rather than OFC or more posterior lesions. In addition, she concluded that patients with frontal-lobe lesions were more susceptible to "perseverative errors", i.e. persisting responding according to the previously relevant rule despite continued negative feedback. Since Milner's report (1963) the specific relationship between perseverative behaviour and deficiencies in frontal cortex functioning has been confirmed many times (e.g. Barcelo et al., 1997; Barcelo & Santome-Calleja, 2000; Drewe, 1974; Stuss & Benson, 1984). Recent neuroimaging studies also suggest that overcoming perseverative tendencies correlates with activity in prefrontal regions (Nagahama, Okina, Suzuki, Nabatame, & Matsuda, 2005).

In contrast, the paucity of reports on LI in humans makes it poorly understood, both in terms of cognitive processes and neural/neurochemical mechanisms that underlie it. In cognitive terms, the phenomenon is clearly related to latent inhibition. However, whereas LI refers to impaired learning of an association between a conditioned stimulus and an unconditioned stimulus because of their uncorrelated presentations (Mackintosh, 1983), latent inhibition refers to disrupted learning following unreinforced presentations of the conditioned stimulus alone (Lubow, 1973; see Lubow, this volume). Several theories of latent inhibition can be used to account for LI (Gluck & Myers, 1993; Lubow, 1989; Weiner & Feldon, 1997). According to some authors, LI may be a special case of latent inhibition, occurring as a result of pre-exposure of the unconditioned stimulus and conditioned stimulus (Bonardi & Hall, 1996). According to others, however, LI is inexplicable as a simple summation of the two pre-exposure effects and cannot always be reduced to latent inhibition (Baker & Mackintosh, 1979; Bennett, Wills, Oakeshott, & Mackintosh, 2000; Matzel, Schachtman, & Miller, 1988). Instead, it is argued that explicit learning occurs about the absence of a correlation between the conditioned stimulus and the unconditioned stimulus. The outcome of this process then interferes with further learning about a subsequent positive correlation.

Because the relationship between LI and latent inhibition is so unclear, we decided to limit our analyses to those cases of LI described in the literature, that come from research based on a visual learning paradigm. In other words, in this way we operationalize our understanding of LI, to avoid comparing these two concepts and paradigms any further. Hoping that this approach may offer new understanding of individual differences in executive functioning, we will now review the evidence for individual differences in LI in various clinical populations, with particular emphasis on PD as the most extensively studied neuropsychological population in this context, and individual differences in LI as a function of age.

Pathology-Based Individual Differences in Learned Irrelevance

Parkinson's Disease

Idiopathic Parkinson's disease (PD) is a neurodegenerative disorder, which is clinically defined on the basis of a triad of motor symptoms: bradykinesia, rigidity and resting tremor. Nevertheless, cognitive impairments are a common characteristic of the condition and strong predictors of quality of life in such patients. Some of these impairments closely resemble frontal lobe deficits, including problems in shifting attentional set in both cognitive and motor domains (Cools, van den Bercken, Horstink, van Spaendonck, & Berger, 1984; Downes et al., 1989; Owen et al., 1992; van Spaendonck, Berger, Horstink, Buytenhuijs, & Cools, 1996). Numerous studies from the cognitive domain have shown that attentional set-shifting is impaired in the early stages of PD (e.g. Downes et al., 1989; Owen et al., 1992) and furthermore, it has been suggested that attentional set shifting is moderately selective to PD (e.g. deficits are not seen in early Alzheimer's disease; see Sahakian et al., 1990).

Attentional set-shifting performance in the patients with PD has been studied most extensively with the tests of visual discrimination learning described in the previous section (e.g. Downes et al., 1989; Owen et al., 1992). Using such tests, a number of studies have shown that PD patients are more impaired when a shift of attention is required between two different perceptual dimensions, i.e. EDS, than when a shift is required between two different values of the same dimension, i.e. IDS (Downes et al., 1989). However, no consensus has been reached regarding the mechanisms underlying the poor performance of PD patients. To account for these deficits, various cognitive mechanisms have been suggested, including impairments in set-shifting (e.g. Taylor, Saint-Cyr, & Lang, 1986), maintaining set (Flowers & Robertson, 1985; Taylor et al., 1986) or concept formation (Cooper, Sagar, Jordan, Harvey, & Sullivan, 1991).

As for LI, both medicated and non-medicated patients with PD (Downes et al., 1989) with mild or severe motor symptoms related to different stages of the condition (Owen et al., 1992) have been shown to be impaired on a test requiring shifting of attentional set. In a further study by Owen et al. (1993), the performance of medicated and non-medicated patients with PD was compared to that of patients with frontal-lobe lesions whilst undertaking a test that independently manipulated the perseveration and LI aspects of ED shifting. In the perseveration condition, patients were presented at the EDS with one dimension that was already familiar and had always been relevant to the task rule during previous stages of learning and with a second dimension that was novel. They were required to shift response set to the novel dimension, ignoring the previously relevant dimension (i.e. attempt to overcome the tendency to perseverate). In the LI condition, patients were presented at the EDS with one dimension that was already familiar but had been irrelevant during all previous stages of learning and with a second dimension that was novel. They were required to shift response set to the familiar (but previously irrelevant) dimension, ignoring the novel dimension (i.e. attempting to overcome LI).

In the study by Owen et al. (1993), the patients with frontal lobe excisions committed the highest number of errors in the perseveration condition out of the groups participating in the study (i.e. the control group and the two PD groups – medicated and non-medicated). At the same time, the frontal-lobe group performance on LI was comparable to the performance of the healthy control group in this condition. In contrast, non-medicated patients with PD exhibited problems in both the perseveration condition and the LI condition, while medicated patients with PD were impaired only at the LI condition. These results have several major implications for understanding the nature of attentional set-shifting deficits both in PD and as an executive function in general. First, they suggest that the major set-shifting deficits reported in both patients with PD and frontal lobe patients may involve fundamentally different, though related cognitive processes, with both perseveration and LI contributing to the cognitive impairments observed in PD, and perseveration, but not LI, contributing to set-shifting impairments in frontal-lobe patients. Second, perseveration, but not LI, responds to L-dopa therapy, suggesting that the former, but not the latter, is related to the central dopaminergic deficit in PD.

However, various aspects of the LI hypothesis as a mechanism accounting for attentional set-shifting deficits in PD remained controversial. Van Spaendonck et al. (1995) were not able to reproduce reliable LI impairments in patients with PD with a classical card sorting design, and hence, they have attributed attentional set-shifting deficits in PD to problems with self-generation of problem solving strategies. Similarly, Gauntlett-Gilbert, Roberts, and Brown (1999) failed to show that the performance of the patients with PD (vs. controls) was preferentially improved under the circumstances where strong LI acquired during a pre-shifting stage of a visual discrimination learning task should actually facilitate the performance at the subsequent shifting phase.

Recently, in an attempt to better define the cognitive and neural basis of the learnt irrelevance phenomena, we have developed a novel visual discrimination learning test, which allowed for a finer delineation of factors responsible for LI by avoiding the introduction of a novel dimension at the EDS stage of the test (Słabosz et al., 2006). This manipulation prevented the possibly confounding effect of novelty on the LI measure.

Instead of introducing a novel dimension, the authors varied the extent to which a target dimension was irrelevant prior to the EDS, and the participants were required to shift attentional set to a dimension that had been either fully irrelevant or partly reinforced (see Fig. 8.1). Prior to the EDS stage of the test, the stimuli were characterised by three dimensions: colour, shape and number of items; and up to the EDS stage only one of the three dimensions (colour) was relevant to the discrimination rule and consistently reinforced. At the same time, the level of task irrelevance of the other two dimensions was varied, with one dimension (either shape or number) being fully irrelevant, and the other dimension being partly reinforced. In the case of the fully irrelevant dimension, any given value of this dimension (e.g. square or circle) randomly co-occurred with the reinforced

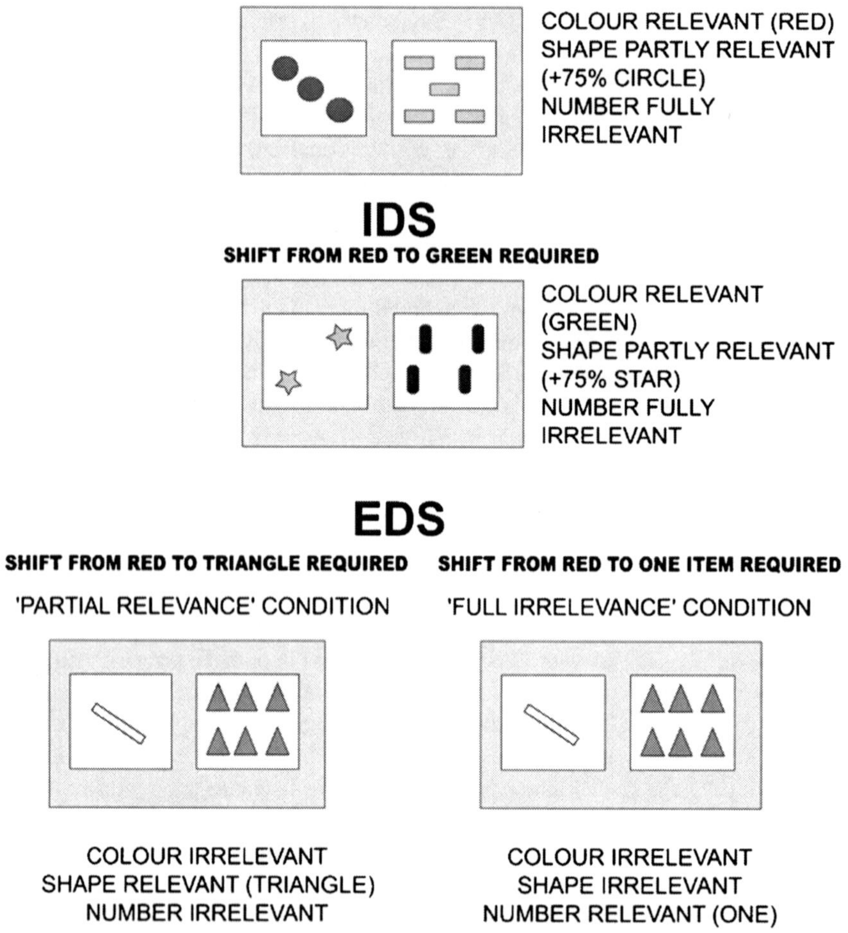

IDS
SHIFT FROM RED TO GREEN REQUIRED

COLOUR RELEVANT (RED)
SHAPE PARTLY RELEVANT
(+75% CIRCLE)
NUMBER FULLY
IRRELEVANT

COLOUR RELEVANT
(GREEN)
SHAPE PARTLY RELEVANT
(+75% STAR)
NUMBER FULLY
IRRELEVANT

EDS

SHIFT FROM RED TO TRIANGLE REQUIRED   **SHIFT FROM RED TO ONE ITEM REQUIRED**
'PARTIAL RELEVANCE' CONDITION   'FULL IRRELEVANCE' CONDITION

COLOUR IRRELEVANT
SHAPE RELEVANT (TRIANGLE)
NUMBER IRRELEVANT

COLOUR IRRELEVANT
SHAPE IRRELEVANT
NUMBER RELEVANT (ONE)

Fig. 8.1 Learned irrelevance: summary of the procedure for the IDS and EDS stages of the learned irrelevance task. Stimuli shown are only examples (from Słabosz et al., 2006)

value of the currently relevant dimension (i.e. blue or red). In other words, the fully irrelevant dimension was reinforced randomly and in this sense was equivalent to the irrelevant dimension of the original CANTAB ID/ED task. In contrast, in the case of the partially relevant dimension, one exemplar co-occurred with the reinforced value of the currently relevant dimension on 75% of trials preceding the EDS. As a result, the partially relevant dimension predicted the reinforcement at a level that was greater than chance. At the EDS stage of the task, the participants were required to shift their attention either to the previously irrelevant dimension (the full irrelevance condition) or to the dimension that had previously been partially reinforced (the partial relevance condition). The results revealed that patients with PD made more errors than control participants in the fully irrelevant condition but not in the partially relevant condition (see Fig. 8.2). Moreover, L-dopa had no effect on the patients' task performance, despite improving their working memory – as shown in a separate control task. These results confirm that LI is a significant factor accounting for attentional set-shifting deficits in patients with PD, although unlike other executive impairments in this group, the phenomenon appears to be unrelated to their central dopaminergic deficit.

These findings (Słabosz et al., 2006) have advanced our understanding of LI in two important ways. First, in previous studies of LI (Gauntlett-Gilbert et al., 1999; Owen et al., 1993), a significant confound has been the possible effects of stimulus novelty on EDS performance. That is to say,

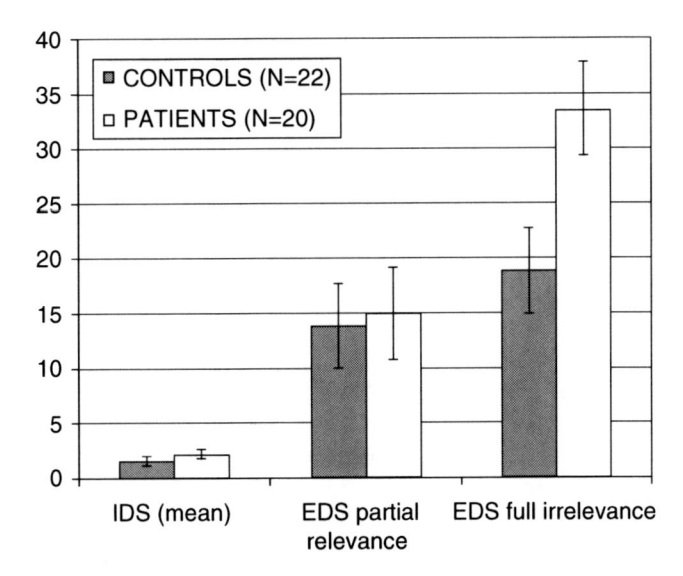

Fig. 8.2 Learned irrelevance: effect of PD pathology on error rate. The mean number of errors for the healthy volunteers over their two testing sessions and the patients with PD recorded "on" and "off" L-dopa medication are shown for both the IDS and EDS. Bars represent standard error of the mean (from Słabosz et al., 2006)

shifts to a previously irrelevant dimension were compared with shifts to a novel dimension, to make inferences about LI. This is important because deficits in novelty pop-out effects have been reported previously in patients with PD (Lubow, Dressler, & Kaplan, 1999; Tsuchiya, Yamaguchi, & Kobayashi, 2000). In our recent study (Słabosz et al., 2006), no such confound existed, as inferences about LI were based on comparisons between full and partial irrelevance conditions, neither of which involved the introduction of a novel dimension. Second and more importantly, the research by Słabosz et al. (2006) and related studies have suggested that LI appears to be neither dependent on the frontal lobe (e.g. Owen et al., 1993) nor affected by dopamine and therefore, may not be executive at all. Thus, the question that remains is whether a plausible neural and/or neurochemical account can be formulated for the phenomenon of LI.

Pathologies Other Than PD

Unfortunately, relevant data from other clinical groups is sparse, although the fact that patients with circumscribed excisions of the frontal cortex are unaffected on LI tasks implicates mechanisms other than those that are traditionally considered to be executive. Although patients with schizophrenia have recently been reported as showing abnormal performance during a test of LI, the pattern of impairments suggests a reduced rather than an enhanced effect (Gal et al., 2005). Thus, among first-episode schizophrenic patients, cue–target associations to (irrelevant) pre-exposed cues were as fast as those to novel cues (see also Gal et al., 2005), exactly the opposite pattern to that which would be predicted in PD on the basis of the previous findings (Owen et al., 1993; Słabosz et al., 2006). Although such evidence may suggest a role for dopamine in LI, the direct manipulation of dopamine levels through medication conducted in the study by Słabosz et al. (2006) more strongly suggests otherwise. In fact, the lack of effect of L-dopa and of frontal-lobe damage (Owen et al., 1993) on LI in patients with PD suggests that neither the dopaminergic mechanisms of the striatum nor the prefrontal cortex mediate this process. In monkeys, prefrontal dopamine depletion impairs spatial working memory but has no significant effect on extradimensional set-shifting performance (Roberts et al., 1994), a result that is broadly consistent with those of the study by Słabosz et al. (2006). Although pathologies affecting neurotransmitters other than dopamine in PD have been proposed, including noradrenergic, serotoninergic and cholinergic deafferentation of the cortex (Agid, Javoy Agid, & Ruberg, 1987), the dopamine hypothesis remains a leading factor in understanding PD.

Normal Variation in Learned Irrelevance

Age-Related Variation in Learned Irrelevance

Unfortunately, not much is known about the modulatory role of age on susceptibility to LI, since to our knowledge only one study has examined this issue directly. Słabosz et al. (2006) compared the performance of elderly and young volunteers on the LI task described above. The mean ages of the two groups were 35.9 years and 68.5 years, respectively. This comparison revealed no significant differences for the cross-group comparisons. Thus, aging did not seem to influence LI performance. However, this conclusion needs to be treated with caution and has yet to be confirmed. Moreover, this observation contrasts markedly with the well-recognised result that aging enhances susceptibility to perseveration (Foldi, Helm-Estabrooks, Redfield, & Nickel, 2003). Bearing in mind that frontal lobe deficiencies are considered to be the main age-related neural pathology (Hampshire, Gruszka, Fallon, & Owen, 2008), this result suggests again that the mechanisms of LI may not be frontal at all.

To sum up, a differential pattern of susceptibility to LI has been observed in the frontal-lobe patients, patients with PD who are "on" dopaminergic medication, and PD patients who are "off" medication. While the frontal-lobe patients seem to be able to overcome LI, both groups of patients with PD are comparably susceptible to it. Similarly, aging does not seem to affect susceptibility to LI. This all suggests that mechanisms other than those that are dependent on the frontal cortex and those that are related to the dopaminergic system are responsible for LI. This coherent picture is somehow blurred by the recent findings revealing that patients with schizophrenia exhibit a reduced LI effect (Young et al., 2005). Although this pattern of results would suggest a dopaminergic basis for LI (given the known dopaminergic pathology in schizophrenia), the study by Słabosz et al. (2006) designed specifically to test this hypothesis strongly suggests otherwise. Thus, on the basis of clinical data alone, it has not been possible to define specific neural or neurochemical mechanisms that are critically involved in LI.

Neural Correlates of Learned Irrelevance

A variety of neuroimaging and neuropsychological studies have led to the view that the neural circuitry responsible for co-ordinating attentional set-shifting consists of many parts, including the dorsolateral and ventrolateral prefrontal cortices, the anterior cingulate, and the posterior parietal cortex. Whilst the existence of this network is no longer a matter of debate, the contributions made by these anatomically distinct components are, as yet, poorly defined. Much of the current confusion regarding the precise nature of frontoparietal organisation results from the use of complex and cognitively heterogeneous task manipulations when attempting to functionally dissociate frontoparietal influences (see Hampshire & Owen, 2006, for discussion) – reflecting the confusion in the behavioural research on attentional set-shifting as discussed above.

Studying LI poses even more problems for neuroimaging because LI is usually demonstrated as a one-off, between-groups difference in trials involving learning to perform an EDS. In other words, the LI paradigms that to date have been used to examine behavioural effects are unsuitable for the repeated measurements that are a prerequisite for fMRI analysis (Owen et al., 1993; Słabosz et al., 2006) due to the fact that the dependent measure is the percentage of subjects who passed to the next (e.g. EDS) stage of the task (e.g. Owen et al., 1992) or completed the number of trials needed to learn the EDS (e.g. Słabosz et al., 2006). An additional limitation to these conventional LI paradigms is that they use a between-subject design (e.g. Owen et al., 1993) and, as a result, an LI effect can be determined only by group comparisons. Thus, to our knowledge, only one study has investigated neural correlates of LI directly (Young et al., 2005), having demonstrated involvement in LI of various components of the hippocampal formation, in agreement with studies on latent inhibition. Studies with experimental animals have also shown a key role played by limbic structures in mediating latent inhibition (Gray et al., 1995, 1997). Dopaminergic function in the mesolimbic pathway, terminating in the nucleus accumbens, appears to be critical (Joseph et al., 2000), as does activity in the hippocampal formation and entorhinal cortex (Honey & Good, 1993). However, Young et al. (2005) have used a different paradigm (i.e. cue-target association learning) to the visual learning paradigm discussed here and their findings derive from a relatively small sample, which needs replication.

The above mentioned limitations of imaging studies of shifting attentional set were addressed by a recent fMRI study by Hampshire and Owen (2006). In this study, a novel approach was used: the responses of the volunteer dictated the order and pace of experimental events. In this way, it was not the experimental design but the focus of attention that defined the events that were used in the fMRI model (e.g. attentional shifts). The chosen decision-making strategies and attentional shifts were thus functionally and behaviourally examined independently of the will of the experimenter. The study used many stimulus sets each containing stimuli of two distinct types (faces and buildings) and modelled switches of attention between stimuli of the same type (IDS) and between stimuli of different types (EDS). Hampshire and Owen (2006) intermixed these transient attentional control functions that could therefore be contrasted at the event level in the current trial and error situation. Accordingly, EDS and IDS were compared directly, effectively isolating the extra-dimensional component of shifting from other switch-related processes, such as inhibition of the previously relevant response (Nakahara, Hayashi, Konishi, & Miyashita, 2002). Switch and feedback events were modelled separately thanks to the use of the novel partial feedback paradigm that allowed regions involved in abstract reward processing and/or the implementation of attentional control to be modelled separately.

The behavioural data showed that moving attention between stimulus dimensions caused more errors, and took longer, than moving attention between stimuli of the same type. This difference must reflect the typical strategy employed by the volunteers to solve the task since both extra- and intra-dimensional target changes could logically be solved within the same number of trials. The main query for the imaging data, therefore, was whether this component of attentional control (EDS) would be associated with any specific neural substrate. Accordingly, when shifts in the focus of attention between stimulus types (EDS) were directly compared with shifts within stimulus type (IDS), significant activation was seen only in the VLPFC and the preSMA. Based on these findings, the authors suggested that the commonly observed increase in reaction time for extradimensional shifting reflects the time taken for the ventrolateral frontal cortex to bias attentional processing between competing stimulus dimensions (Hampshire & Owen, 2006). Such attentional biasing, or "tuning", while relevant to many components of set-shifting, is probably maximal when a complete reconfiguration of the attentional set is required, as is the case during a shift from one dimension to another (competing) dimension.

Recently, the paradigm developed by Hampshire and Owen (2006) has been adapted to include LI and perseveration aspects of EDS performance (Gruszka, Hampshire and Owen, in prep.). The procedure of the current task differed from the original design (Hampshire & Owen, 2006) in several important ways in order to resemble the LI/perseveration paradigm proposed by Owen et al. (1993) more closely. First of all, there were several abstract dimensions introduced in a course of the task (i.e. shape, colour, number, spatial location of the pattern, texture, instead of faces and buildings) and subjects were required to switch between these dimensions in a pseudo-random manner. Hence, when the stimulus set was changed after a criterion number of continuous correct selections was achieved, one novel dimension was introduced (i.e. absent before this change), and

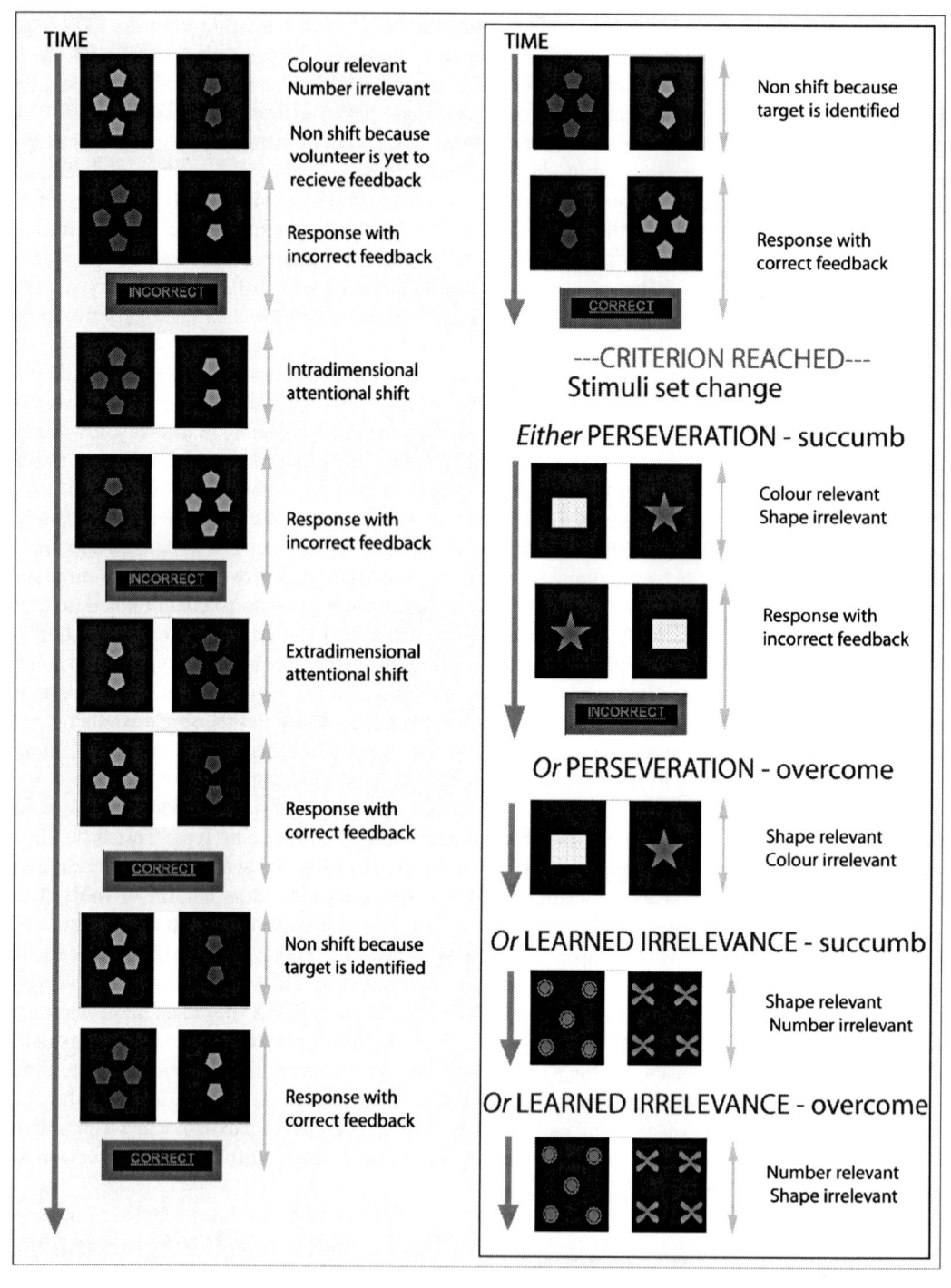

Fig. 8.3 Learned irrelevance and perseveration: illustration of a typical series of trials. Stimuli shown are for example only (from Gruszka et al., in prep.)

one previously present dimension remained (either previously relevant or previously irrelevant dimension; see Fig. 8.3). This resulted in four main task conditions that were defined by the dimension that the selected exemplar belonged to when a new set of stimuli was presented. These were: (1) LI succumbing condition (i.e. choosing the novel dimension when the previously irrelevant dimension and the novel dimension were present), (2) LI overcoming condition (i.e. choosing the previously irrelevant dimension when the previously irrelevant dimension and the novel dimension were present), (3) PE succumbing condition (i.e. choosing the previously relevant dimension when the previously relevant dimension and the novel dimension were present), and finally (4) PE overcoming condition (i.e. choosing the novel dimension when the previously relevant dimension and the novel dimension were present). This allowed events related to LI and PE to be contrasted directly. The behavioural data showed that in agreement with expectations, shifts of attention under both LI and PE "succumbing" conditions were easier for the subject than those requiring overcoming LI or PE, respectively (Fig. 8.4).

Overall, the imaging results of the pilot study reported here confirmed the results obtained by Hampshire and Owen (2006) with a broad activation of the fronto-parietal network when comparing working out versus knowing the target (see Fig. 8.5). This suggests that in general, the paradigm is suitable for studying more complex attentional set-shifting activities than the simple two-dimensional task used by Hampshire and Owen (2006). However, the results of the EDS-IDS contrast differ substantially from those obtained by Hampshire and Owen (see Fig. 8.6), with a greater proportion of the frontoparietal network recruited when switching attention between stimulus dimensions. Note that this activation included a significant DLPFC component. Previously, in a block-design positron emission tomography (PET) study, Rogers, Andrews, Grasby, Brooks, and Robbins (2000) have shown increased activity in DLPFC, but not VLPFC, during EDS when compared to IDS. However, unlike to the study by Hampshire and Owen (2006), it is likely that in both Rogers et al. (2000) and the current study, the activation observed could well have been due to the additional

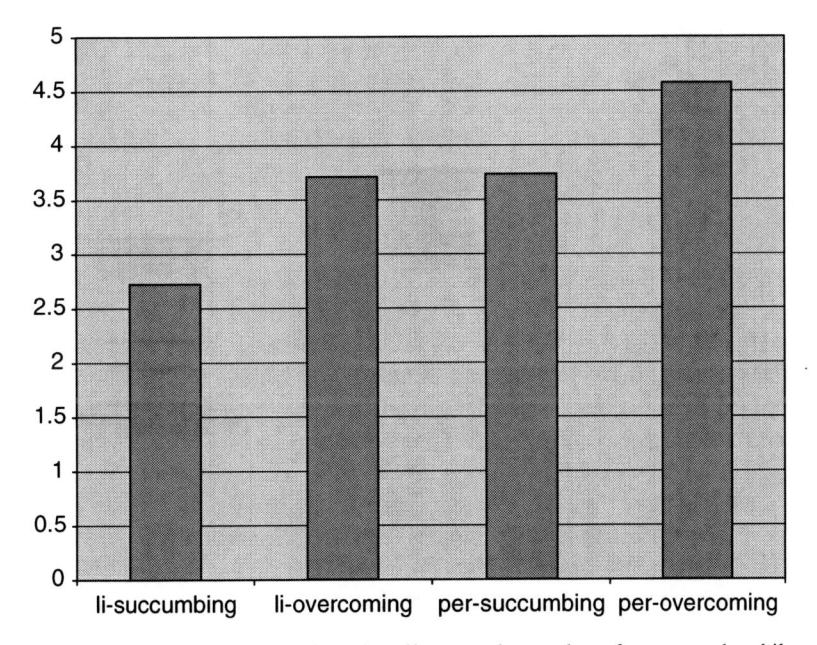

Fig. 8.4 Learned irrelevance and perseveration: the effects on the number of errors made while searching for the target under learned irrelevance and perseveration overcoming/succumbing conditions (from Gruszka et al., in prep.)

Hampshire & Owen 2006

Gruszka et al in prep

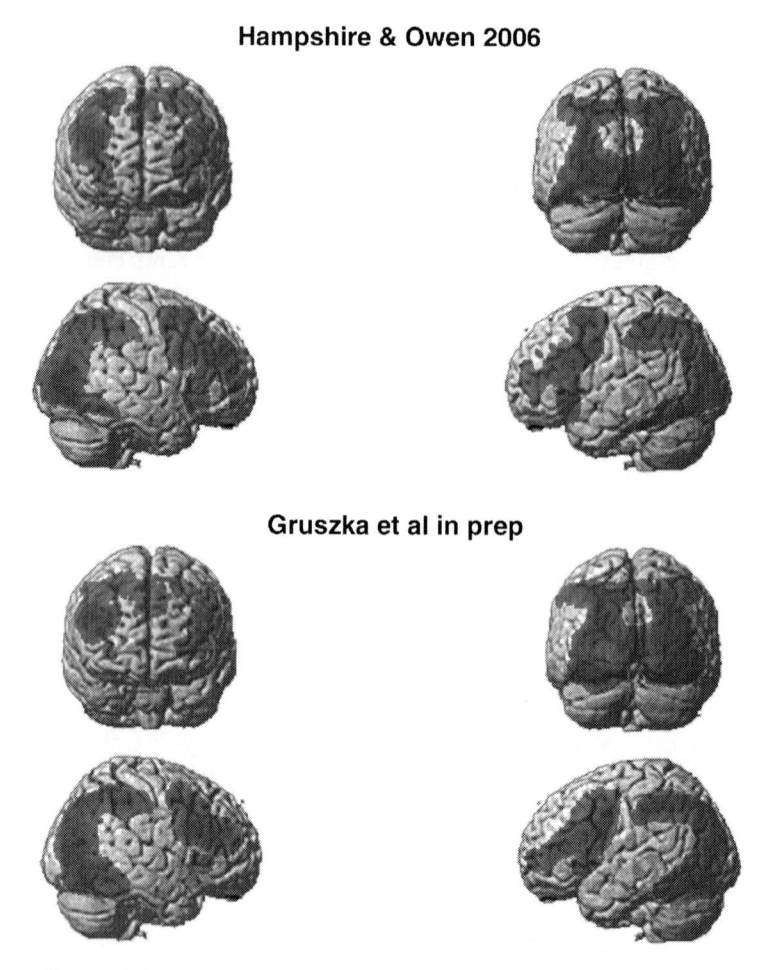

Fig. 8.5 Contrast of events during the period of time when the volunteer was working out the target minus those when the target was known compared across study by Hampshire and Owen (2006) and study Gruszka et al., (in prep.)

demands of actively working out which dimensions were relevant to the task, rather than the more specific shift of attention between dimensions. This result highlights a possible dissociation between the VLPFC and the DLPFC, with the former involved in routine switches of attention within a well defined attentional set and the latter involved in identifying which rules and dimensions are most relevant for forming that attentional set.

As to LI and PE components of the task, there were two main contrasts of interests. The first was the comparison of the two LI conditions: overcoming vs. succumbing at the moment of set change (i.e. choosing the previously irrelevant dimension when the previously irrelevant dimension and the novel were present minus choosing the novel dimension when the previously irrelevant dimension and the novel dimension were present). The second contrast was the comparison of both LI conditions (overcoming and succumbing) minus both PE conditions (overcoming and succumbing) at the moment of set change (i.e. taking the new set when the previously irrelevant dimension and the novel were present minus when the previously relevant dimension and the

Hampshire & Owen 2006

Gruszka et al in prep

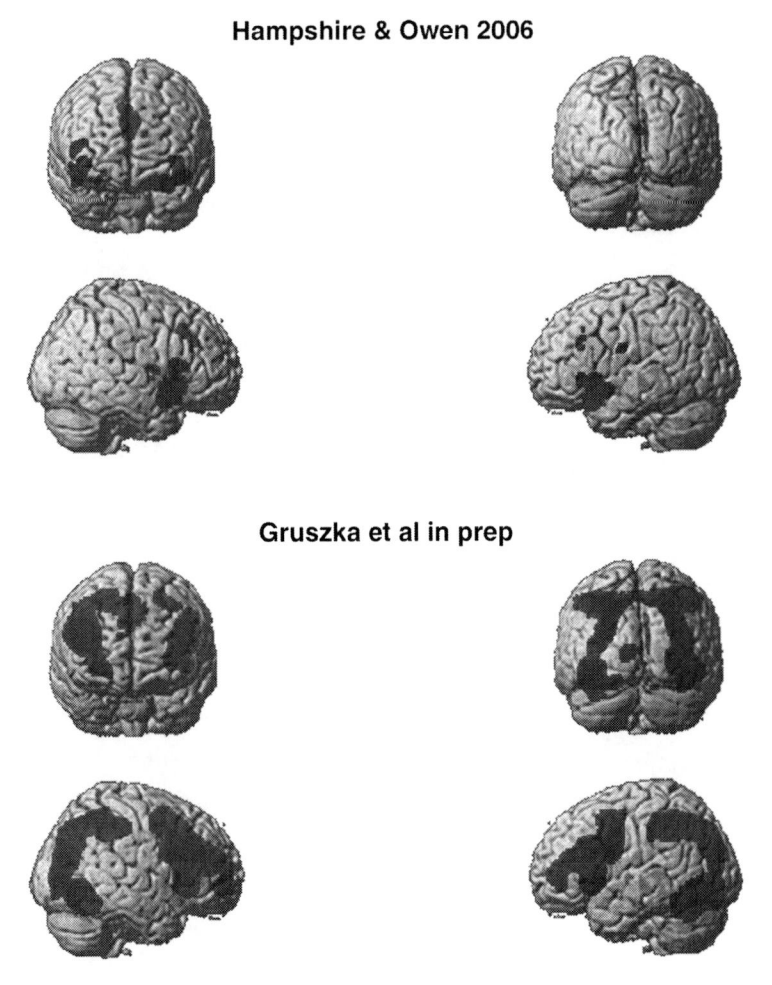

Fig. 8.6 Learned irrelevance and perseveration: contrast of EDS events minus IDS events compared across study by Hampshire and Owen (2006) and study Gruszka et al., (in prep.)

novel dimension were present). At this preliminary stage, the data were examined with both the exploratory ROIs analyses using a set of anatomical ROIs from the AAL set (Tzourio-Mazoyer, 2002) from MarsBar and the whole brain analysis. In the ROI analysis, the caudate nucleus appeared significantly more active when overcoming LI than when succumbing to LI in the left hemisphere, and just below threshold in the right hemisphere. The anterior cingulate cortex (ACC) showed a significant main effect of LI conditions minus PE conditions bilaterally, and a sub threshold trend ($p=0.06$ 1 tailed) towards increased activity for overcoming LI compared with succumbing to LI (see: Fig. 8.7). This latter result was also found using a whole brain analysis, although it did not stand up to correction. However, Fig. 8.8 shows the contrast of the two LI conditions at $p=0.005$ uncorrected with a voxel extent threshold of 50 with the main cluster centred near the ACC. Unfortunately, no other significant activations were observed for any contrasts involving the LI and PE task comparisons, even though behaviourally the test was

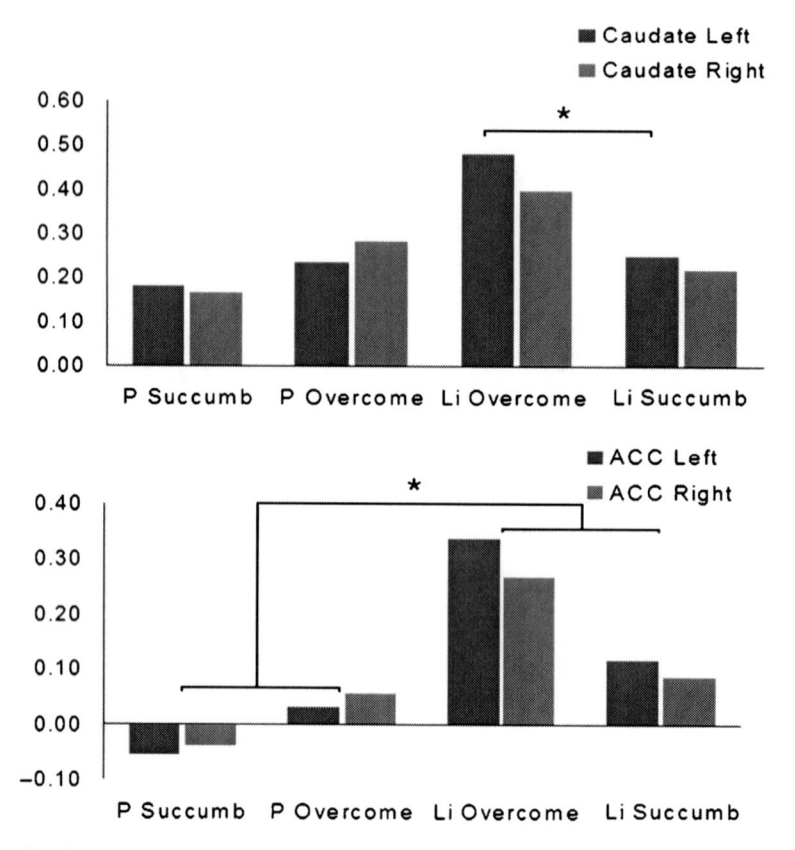

Fig. 8.7 Learned irrelevance and perseveration: contrasting learned irrelevance overcoming vs. succumbing conditions at the moment of set change and contrasting learned irrelevance and perseveration at the moment of set change (from Gruszka et al., in prep.)

sensitive enough to reveal differences between these conditions at the behavioural level. This lack of significant results paralleled by significant behavioural differences suggests that the task was probably underpowered because of the noisy nature of fMRI, and the experiment needs to be repeated with a higher number of events. Moreover, given the limits of spatial resolution of fMRI with human subjects, one can assume that these results are broadly consistent with those from the animal literature that have demonstrated the involvement in LI of various components of the hippocampal formation (Gray et al., 1995, 1997; Weiner & Feldon, 1997).

The pattern of results obtained by Gruszka, Hampshire and Owen (in prep.) appears to indicate that the ACC and caudate may play roles in dealing with/overcoming LI and not PE. The role of ACC and caudate in executive control is well established, also the effect of PD on these areas is known. However, the result is unexpected given previous findings and given the lack of DA modulation on LI. Further research is required to confirm the relationship of this very preliminary result to previous behavioural studies of LI. More specifically, in order to determine if the repeated overcoming of LI recruits the ACC and caudate, the reliability of the result needs to be confirmed in a follow up study that has greater statistical power. Furthermore, the questions must be answered as to whether LI is still impaired in PD over multiple repeated trials and if such an impairment is still evident, whether that impairment is still insensitive to dopaminergic medication.

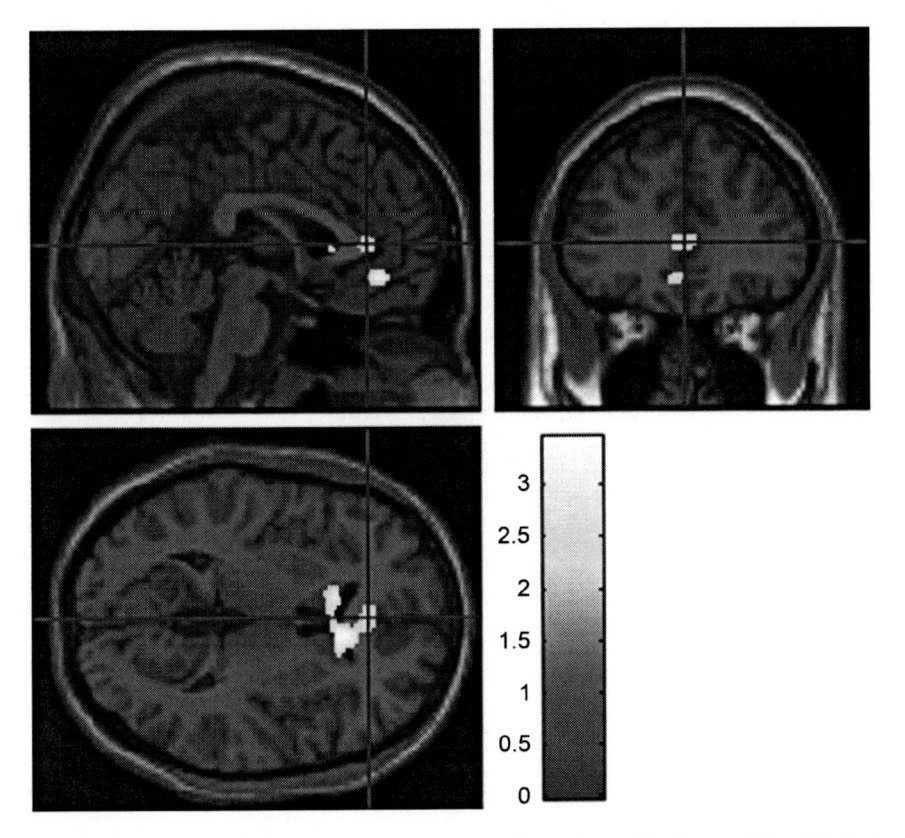

Fig. 8.8 Learned irrelevance: contrasting overcoming vs. succumbing to learned irrelevance. The whole brain analysis at $p=0.005$ uncorrected level but with a voxel extent threshold of 50 (from Gruszka et al., in prep.)

References

Agid, Y., Javoy Agid, F., & Ruberg, M. (1987). Biochemistry of neurotransmitters in Parkinson's disease. In C. D. Marsden & S. Fahn (Eds.), *Movement disorders* (Vol. 2, pp. 166–230). London: Butterworth.

Alexander, G. E., Delong, M. R., & Strick, P. L. (1986). Parallel organization of functionally segregated circuits linking basal ganglia and cortex. *Annual Review of Neuroscience, 9*, 357–381.

Anderson, C. V., Bigler, E. D., & Blatter, D. D. (1995). Frontal lobe lesions, diffuse damage, and neuropsychological functioning in traumatic brain-injured patients. *Journal of Clinical and Experimental Neuropsychology, 17*(6), 900–908.

Anderson, S. V., Damasio, H., Jones, R. D., & Tranel, D. (1991). Wisconsin card sorting test performance as a measure of frontal lobe damage. *Journal of Clinical and Experimental Neuropsychology, 13*(6), 909–922.

Aron, A. R. (2008). Progress in executive-function research. From tasks to functions to regions to networks. *Current Directions in Psychological Science, 17*(2), 124–129.

Baker, A. G., & Mackintosh, N. J. (1979). Preexposure to the CS alone, US alone, or CS and US uncorrelated: Latent inhibition, blocking by context or learned irrelevance? *Learning and Motivation, 10*(3), 278–294.

Barcelo, F., & Santome-Calleja, A. (2000). A critical review of the specificity of the Wisconsin card sorting test for the assessment of prefrontal function. *Revista de Neurologia, 30*, 855–864.

Barcelo, F., Sanz, M., Molina, V., & Rubia, J. F. (1997). The Wisconsin card sorting test and the assessment of frontal function: A validation study with event-related potentials. *Neuropsychologia, 35*, 399–408.

Bennett, C. H., Wills, S. J., Oakeshott, S. M., & Mackintosh, N. J. (2000). Is the context specificity of latent inhibition a sufficient explanation of learned irrelevance? *The Quarterly Journal of Experimental Psychology. B, Comparative and Physiological Psychology, 53*(3), 239–253.

Bonardi, C., & Hall, G. (1996). Learned irrelevance: No more than the sum of CS and US preexposure effects? *Journal of Experimental Psychology: Animal Behavior Processes, 22*(2), 183–191.

Canavan, A. G. M., Passingham, R. E., Marsden, C. D., Quinn, N., Wyke, M., & Polkey, C. E. (1989). The performance on learning tasks of patients in the early stages of Parkinson's disease. *Neuropsychologia, 27*, 141–156.

Cools, R., Barker, R. A., Sahakian, B. J., & Robbins, T. W. (2001). Mechanisms of cognitive set flexibility in Parkinson's disease. *Brain, 124*, 2503–2512.

Cools, A. R., van den Bercken, J. H., Horstink, M. W., van Spaendonck, K. P., & Berger, H. J. (1984). Cognitive and motor shifting aptitude disorder in Parkinson's disease. *Journal of Neurology, Neurosurgery, and Psychiatry, 47*(5), 443–453.

Cooper, J. A., Sagar, H. J., Jordan, N., Harvey, N. S., & Sullivan, E. V. (1991). Cognitive impairment in early, untreated Parkinson's disease and its relationship to motor disability. *Brain, 114*, 2095–2122.

Demakis, G. J. (2003). A meta-analytic review of the sensitivity of the Wisconsin card sorting test to frontal and lateralized frontal brain damage. *Neuropsychology, 17*(2), 255–264.

Dias, R., Robbins, T. W., & Roberts, A. C. (1996). Dissociation in prefrontal cortex of affective and attentional shifts. *Nature, 380*, 69–72.

Dias, R., Robbins, T. W., & Roberts, A. C. (1997). Dissociable forms of inhibitory control within prefrontal cortex with an analog of the Wisconsin card sort test: Restriction to novel situations and independence from 'on-line' processing. *Journal of Neuroscience, 17*(23), 9285–9297.

Downes, J. J., Roberts, A. C., Sahakian, B. J., Evenden, J. L., Morris, R. G., & Robbins, T. W. (1989). Impaired extra-dimensional shift performance in medicated and unmedicated Parkinson's disease: Evidence for a specific attentional dysfunction. *Neuropsychologia, 27*(11–12), 1329–1343.

Drewe, E. A. (1974). The effect of type and area of brain lesion on Wisconsin card sorting test performance. *Cortex, 10*(2), 159–170.

Eslinger, P. J., & Damasio, A. R. (1985). Severe disturbance of higher cognition after bilateral frontal lobe ablation patient EVR. *Neurology, 35*, 1731–1741.

Fellows, L. K., & Farah, M. J. (2003). Ventromedial frontal cortex mediates affective shifting in humans: Evidence from a reversal learning paradigm. *Brain, 126*, 1830–1837.

Flowers, K. A., & Robertson, C. (1985). The effect of Parkinson's disease on the ability to maintain a mental set. *Journal of Neurology, Neurosurgery, and Psychiatry, 48*, 517–529.

Foldi, N. S., Helm-Estabrooks, N., Redfield, J., & Nickel, D. G. (2003). Perseveration in normal aging: A comparison of perseveration rates on design fluency and verbal generative tasks. *Aging, Neuropsychology, and Cognition, 10*(4), 268–280.

Fork, M., Bartels, C., Ebert, A. D., Grubich, C., Synowitz, H., & Wallesch, C. W. (2005). Neuropsychological sequelae of diffuse traumatic brain injury. *Brain Injury, 19*(2), 101–108.

Gal, G., Mendlovic, S., Bloch, Y., Beitler, G., Levkovitz, Y., Young, A. M. J., et al. (2005). Learned irrelevance is disrupted in first-episode but not chronic schizophrenia patients. *Behavioural Brain Research, 159*(2), 267–275.

Gauntlett-Gilbert, J., Roberts, R. C., & Brown, V. J. (1999). Mechanisms underlying attentional set-shifting in Parkinson's disease. *Neuropsychologia, 37*(5), 605–616.

Gluck, M., & Myers, C. (1993). Hippocampal mediation of stimulus representation: A computational theory. *Hippocampus, 3*, 491–516.

Gotham, A.-M., Brown, R. G., & Marsden, C. D. (1986). Levodopa treatment may benefit or impair frontal function in Parkinson's disease. *The Lancet, 328*(8513), 970–971.

Grant, D. A., & Berg, E. A. (1948). A behavioral analysis of degree of reinforcement and ease of shifting to new responses in a Weigl-type card-sorting problem. *Journal of Experimental Psychology, 38*, 404–411.

Gray, J. A., Joseph, M. H., Hemsley, D. R., Young, A. M. J., Warburton, E. C., Boulenguez, P., et al. (1995). The role of mesolimbic dopaminergic and retrohippocampal afferents to the nucleus accumbens in latent inhibition: implications for schizophrenia. *Behavioural Brain Research, 71*, 19–31.

Gray, J. A., Moran, P. M., Grigoryan, G. A., Peters, S. L., Young, A. M. J., & Joseph, M. H. (1997). Latent inhibition: The nucleus accumbens connection revisited. *Behavioural Brain Research, 88*, 27–34.

Gruszka, A., Hampshire, A., & Owen, A. M. (in prep.). Contrasting cortical and subcortical activations produced by learned irrelevance and perseveration.

Hampshire, A., Gruszka, A., Fallon, S. J., & Owen, A. M. (2008). Inefficiency in self-organised attentional switching in the normal ageing population is associated with decreased activity in the ventrolateral prefrontal cortex. *Journal of Cognitive Neuroscience, 20*, 1670–1686.

Hampshire, A., & Owen, A. M. (2006). Fractionating attentional control using event-related fMRI. *Cerebral Cortex, 16*(12), 1679–1689.

Hermann, B. P., Wyler, A. R., & Richey, E. T. (1988). Wisconsin card sorting test performance in patients with complex partial seizures of temporal-lobe origin. *Journal of Clinical and Experimental Neuropsychology, 10*(4), 467–476.

Honey, R. C., & Good, M. (1993). Selective hippocampal lesions abolish the contextual specificity of latent inhibition and conditioning. *Behavioral Neuroscience, 107*, 23–33.

Horner, M. D., Flashman, L. A., Freides, D., Epstein, C. M., & Bakay, R. A. (1996). Temporal lobe epilepsy and performance on the Wisconsin card sorting test. *Journal of Clinical and Experimental Neuropsychology, 18*(2), 310–313.

Jones, B., & Mishkin, M. (1972). Limbic lesions and the problem of stimulus-reinforcement associations. *Experimental Neurology, 36*, 362–377.

Joseph, M. H., Peters, S. L., Moran, P. M., Grigoryan, G. A., Young, A. M. J., & Gray, J. A. (2000). Modulation of latent inhibition in the rat by altered dopamine transmission in the nucleus accumbens at the time of conditioning. *Neuroscience, 101*, 921–930.

Lubow, R. E. (1973). Latent inhibition. *Psychological Bulletin, 79*(6), 398–407.

Lubow, R. E. (1989). *Latent inhibition and conditioned attention theory*. New York: Cambridge Uniersity Press.

Lubow, R. E., Dressler, R., & Kaplan, O. (1999). The effects of target and distractor familiarity on visual search in de novo Parkinson's disease patients: Latent inhibition and novel pop-out. *Neuropsychology, 13*(3), 415–423.

Mackintosh, N. J. (1973). Stimulus selection: Learning to ignore stimuli that predict no change in reinforcement. In R. A. Hinde & J. S. Hinde (Eds.), *Constraints on learning* (pp. 75–96). London: Academic Press.

Mackintosh, N. J. (1983). *Conditioning and associative learning*. Oxford: The Clarenden Press.

Maes, J. H. R., Damen, M. D. C., & Eling, P. A. T. M. (2004). More learned irrelevance than perseveration errors in rule shifting in healthy subjects. *Brain and Cognition, 54*, 201–211.

Maes, J. H. R., Vich, J., & Eling, P. A. (2006). Learned irrelevance and perseveration in a total change dimensional shift task. *Brain and Cognition, 62*(1), 74–79.

Matzel, L. D., Schachtman, T. R., & Miller, R. R. (1988). Learned irrelevance exceeds the sum of CS-Preexposure and US-Preexposure deficits. *Journal of Experimental Psychology: Animal Behavior Processes, 14*(3), 311–319.

Milner, B. (1963). Effects of different brain lesions on card sorting. *Archives of Neurology, 9*, 90–100.

Mountain, M. A., & Snow, W. G. (1993). Wisconsin card sorting test as a measure of frontal pathology: A review. *Clinical Neuropsychology, 7*, 108–118.

Nagahama, Y., Okina, T., Suzuki, N., Nabatame, H., & Matsuda, M. (2005). The cerebral correlates of different types of perseveration in the Wisconsin card sorting test. *Journal of Neurology, Neurosurgery and Psychiatry, 76*, 169–175.

Nakahara, K., Hayashi, T., Konishi, S., & Miyashita, Y. (2002). Functional MRI of macaque monkeys performing a cognitive set-shifting task. *Science, 295*, 1532–1536.

Owen, A. M., James, M., Leigh, P. N., Summers, B. A., Marsden, C. D., Quinn, N. P., et al. (1992). Fronto-striatal cognitive deficits at different stages of Parkinson's disease. *Brain: A Journal of Neurology, 115*(6), 1727–1751.

Owen, A. M., Roberts, A. C., Hodges, J. R., Summers, B. A., Polkey, C. E., & Robbins, T. W. (1993). Contrasting mechanisms of impaired attentional set-shifting in patients with frontal lobe damage or Parkinson's disease. *Brain: A Journal of Neurology, 116*(5), 1159–1175.

Owen, A. M., Roberts, A. C., Polkey, C. E., Sahakian, B. J., & Robbins, T. W. (1991). Extra-dimensional versus intra-dimensional set shifting performance following frontal lobe excisions, temporal lobe excisions or amygdalo-hippocampectomy in Man. *Neuropsychologia, 29*, 993–1006.

Reitan, R. M., & Wolfson, D. (1994). A selective and critical review of neuropsychological deficits and the frontal lobes. *Neuropsychology Review, 4*, 161–198.

Ridderinkhof, K. R., Span, M. M., & van der Molen, M. W. (2002). Perseverative behavior and adaptive control in older adults: Performance monitoring, rule induction, and set shifting. *Brain and Cognition, 49*, 382–401.

Roberts, A. C., De Salvia, M. A., Wilkinson, L. S., Collins, P., Muir, J. L., Everitt, B. J., et al. (1994). 6-Hydroxydopamine lesions of the prefrontal cortex in monkeys enhance performance on an analog of the Wisconsin card sort test: Possible interactions with subcortical dopamine. *The Journal of Neuroscience: The Official Journal of the Society for Neuroscience, 14*(5, Part 1), 2531–2544.

Roberts, A. C., Robbins, T. W., & Everitt, B. J. (1988). The effects of intradimensional and extradimensional shifts on visual discrimination learning in humans and non-human primates. *Quarterly Journal of Experimental Psychology, 40B*, 321–341.

Rogers, R. D., Andrews, T. C., Grasby, P. M., Brooks, D. J., & Robbins, T. W. (2000). Contrasting cortical and subcortical activations produced by attentional-set shifting and reversal learning in humans. *Journal of Cognitive Neuroscience, 12*, 142–162.

Sahakian, B. J., Downes, J. J., Eagger, S., & Evenden, J. L., et al. (1990). Sparing of attentional relative to mnemonic function in a subgroup of patients with dementia of the Alzheimer type. *Neuropsychologia, 28*(11), 1197–1213.

Słabosz, A., Lewis, S. J. G., migasiewicz, K., Szymura, B., Barker, R. A., & Owen, A. M. (2006). The role of learned irrelevance in attentional set-shifting impairments in Parkinson's disease. *Neuropsychology, 20*(5), 578–588.

Stuss, D. T., & Benson, D. F. (1984). Neuropsychological studies of the frontal lobes. *Psychological Bulletin, 95*(1), 3–28.

Taylor, A. E., Saint-Cyr, J. A., & Lang, A. E. (1986). Frontal lobe disfunction in Parkinson's disease. *Brain, 109*, 845–883.

Tsuchiya, H., Yamaguchi, S., & Kobayashi, S. (2000). Impaired novelty detection and frontal lobe dysfunction in Parkinson's disease. *Neuropsychologia, 38*(5), 645–654.

Tzourio-Mazoyer, N., Landeau, B., Papathanassiou, D., Crivello, F., Etard, O., Delcroix, N., Mazoyer, B., & Joliot, M. (2002). Automated anatomical labeling of activations in SPM using a macroscopic anatomical parcellation of the MNI MRI single-subject brain. *Neuroimage, 15*(1), 273–89.

van Spaendonck, K. P. M., Berger, H. J. C., Horstink, M. W. I. M., Borm, G. F., & Cools, A. R. (1995). Card sorting performance in Parkinson's disease: A comparison between acquisition and shifting performance. *Journal of Clinical and Experimental Neuropsychology, 17*(6), 918–925.

van Spaendonck, K. P. M., Berger, H. J. C., Horstink, M. W. I. M., Buytenhuijs, E. L., & Cools, A. R. (1996). Executive functions and disease characteristics in Parkinson's disease. *Neuropsychologia, 34*(7), 617–626.

Weiner, I., & Feldon, J. (1997). The switching model of latent inhibition: An update of neural substrates. *Behavioural Brain Research, 88*, 11–25.

Young, A. M. J., Kumari, V., Mehrotra, R., Hemsley, D. R., Andrew, C., Sharma, T., Williams, S. C. R., & Gray, J. A., (2005). Disruption of learned irrelevance in acute schizophrenia in a novel continuous within-subject paradigm suitable for fMRI. *Behavioural Brain Research, 156*(2), 277–288.

Chapter 9
Post-Soviet Psychology and Individual Differences in Cognition: A Psychophysiological Perspective

Almira Kustubayeva

Introduction

In spite of propaganda promoting collectivism and human equality in Soviet times, the study of individual differences was developed due to Pavlov's great contributions to understanding the physiological basis of individual differences. Pavlov made a priority of studying the properties of the higher nervous system, leading to the development of psychophysiological approaches to individual differences by his followers. A key idea developed by Pavlov and his followers was that individual differences in conditioning reflexes support different styles of behavioral regulation and temperament. This insight has led to a distinctive Soviet perspective on individual differences in executive control. Therefore, before going to the main topic of this chapter, I would like to introduce the most important psychophysiological contributions that have influenced the development of the psychology of individual differences.

The Most Important Contributions That Have Influenced the Development of the Psychology of Individual Differences

> "It seems, that for psychologists... our research should have great importance, because they have to constitute the main fundament of psychological knowledge...fundamental laws, over which all this high complexity... of human inner life...can be viewed. The physiologists will find these fundamental laws, and not in the far future" (Pavlov, 1951, pp. 105–106).

Pavlov's far-seeing expression underlines the significance of physiological contributions in the development of psychology, especially in the field of differential psychology. Pavlov undoubtedly laid the basis on which this field was later established in Russia. Certainly, to understand post-Soviet research in the area of the biological basis for individual differences, it is necessary to go back to examine important historical contributions in physiology and psychophysiology.

To begin with, we have the well-known Reflex Theory that was described first in Setchenov's book *Reflexi golovnogo mozga* [Reflexes of the brain] (1863) and later expanded by I.P. Pavlov as an experimental physiology of the higher nervous system. The discovery of the inhibition that is now called Setchenov's inhibition was truly a great contribution for understanding nervous processes.

A. Kustubayeva (✉)
Department of Psychology, Al-Farabi Kazakh National University, Almaty, Al-Farabi 71, Kazakhstan 480078
e-mail: kustubayeva@yahoo.com

I.M. Setchenov proposed "involuntary and voluntary" reflex mechanisms of brain activity and concluded that psychology in isolation from physiology is not science. Later, Pavlov developed the reflex theory that was based on 3 principles: causality – there are no processes without cause; structure – there are no processes without brain structure, all brain processes are confined to structure; analysis and synthesis – all processes involve the analysis and synthesis of the stimulus. Ivan Michaelovich Setchenov was called the "father of physiology" whereas Ivan Petrovich Pavlov is "acknowledged as one of the founding fathers of modern experimental psychology" (Corr & Perkins, 2006). In fact, Pavlov's ingenious discovery starts with a pure physiological experiment about regulation of the digestive system and concludes by bringing about an absolutely new branch of physiology of the higher nervous system. He proved Setchenov's idea experimentally by showing the potential to study the psyche by physiological methods. The perspicacious observation of the individual differences in conditioning reflex was explained by the distinction between excitatory and inhibitory processes, their strength, balance, and mobility. Pavlov's four general types of nervous system correspond with Hippocrates's temperament classifications: (1) strong nervous processes, unbalanced – choleric; (2) strong, balanced, mobile – sanguine; (3) strong, balanced, inert – phlegmatic; (4) weak – melancholic. Later, Pavlov suggested specific types of higher nervous systems based on the development of first and second signal systems: (1) "khudozhestvennii" (artistic) with the prevalence of the first signal system; (2) "mislitelnii" (intellectual) – the prevalence of the second signal system; (3) "smeshannii" (middle, or mixed) – balanced first and second systems. The first signal system is a system for response to immediate objects. The second signal system is a system that depends on the mediation of a "signal of signals" through language.

Pavlov's experimental methods for studying conditioned reflexes were used by many followers, especially in terms of individual differences in conditioning reflex and peculiarities of the nervous system processes (Ivanov-Smolensky, 1952; Nebilitcyn, 1976; Teplov, 1955a, 1955b; and many others).

The second influential theory is the well-known structural-functional model of brain integrative work (theory of three functional blocks theory, 1970) suggested by Alexander Romanovich Luria (1902–1977), who is referred to as the "Beethoven of Psychology" (Smekal, 1995), "father of neurophysiology and psychophysiology." The first bloc, which includes the brainstem, reticular formation, mediobasal cortex, and limbic system, regulates nonspecific activation (it keeps appropriate tonus of normal work conditions for higher cortical areas). The second bloc consists of the posterior cortex – occipital, temporal, parietal areas, and is responsible for perception. The third bloc (anterior cortex) – the programming bloc – regulates collation and comparison of the acting effects with initial expectations (Luria, 1966, 1970). Luria and his colleagues studied perception, thinking, and decision making of people from different central Asian countries and Siberia that resulted in the publication of the book on *Historic Development of cognitive Processes* which has influenced many cultural psychologists (Luria, 1974). He was the first researcher who suggested the principles to plan and control behavior by the use of language that was later called NeuroLinguistic Programming. Luria's investigation of cross-cultural speech differences revealed that they correspond to differences in cognition.

He established a new single-subject monographic research method in the psychology of personality by describing the seemingly limitless memory of Mr Shereshevski in his book *Malenkaya knizhka o bolshoi pamayti* [Small Book about Big Memory] (Luria, 1968).

The third physiological theory that is important for differential psychophysiology was the Functional System Theory developed by Petr Kuzmich Anokhin (Anokhin, 1975; Anokhin, 1974; Anokhin, 1984). This theory suggests a description of behavior as a hierarchy of functional systems. The centre of this systemic approach to a behavioral act is the decision making that follows a perceptual process of afferential synthesis, guided by memory and the person's dominant motivation. Decision making includes both generation of an Action Program, and what Anokhin terms the Action Program and Acceptor of the action results (Fig. 9.1). By this he meant an expectancy of the outcome of the Action Program. Following execution of the action, comparison of the final results of the action with the anticipated result generates a "system-creating factor," which determines the

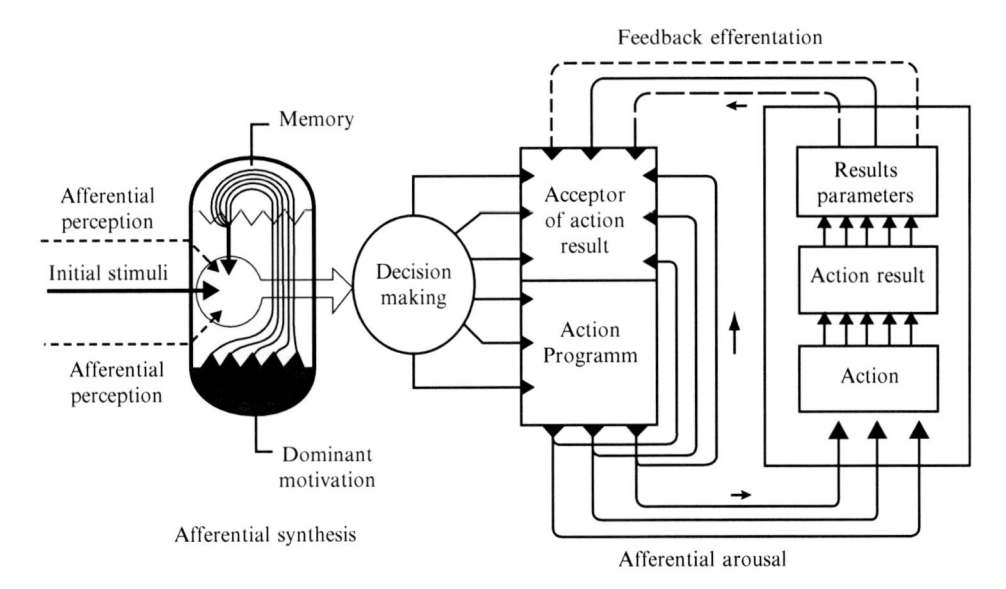

Fig. 9.1 Functional system (Anokhin, 1968) from Anokhin, P.K. Phynkcionalnaya systema, kak metodologicheskii princip biologicheskogo i physiologicheskogo issledovaniya. [Functional system as the methodological principle of biological and physiological research]. In book "Sistemnaya organizacia phisiologicheskie funkcii". [Systematical organization of the physiological function]

fate of the functional system. If they correspond to each other, we will have a positive emotion; in the opposite case, we will feel a negative emotion. The positive emotion reinforces the functional system, whereas the negative emotion destroys the functional system and increases the behavioral activity for the creation of a new functional system starting from afferent stimulation and creating new decisions until the adaptive result will satisfy expectations.

This system effectively manages to form a unique conjunction of psychology and physiology. Anokhin also proposed the systemogenesis theory, together with heterogenesis principles. Systemogenesis is the irregular maturing of the hierarchical regulation development of functional systems in ontogenesis. First of all, there are the most important parts for survival of the functional system mature. The development of behavioral acts is accompanied by maturation of different parts of a functional system at different times of ontogenesis. The functional system theory influenced development of numerous theories of individual differences. Examples are seen in Rusalov's theory of formal-dynamic properties of the individuality, Soroko's theory of the types of plasticity, and Shadrikov's ability theory.

The fourth theory is the theory of organisation of the thinking process as a system of flexible and rigid units suggested and verified in numerous studies by Natalie Petrovna Bekhtereva. Long-term study of brain neuron activity revealed that mental activity provided by working brain area complexes is composed of "flexible" and "rigid" units (Bekhtereva, 2007; Bekhtereva, 1978; Bekhtereva, 2004). Those brain regions that are activated stably and constantly during cognitive performance are called the "rigid units." Additional brain regions fire simultaneously depending on a variety of different conditions and are called "flexible units." This theory was verified by numerous positron emission tomography (PET) studies carried on at the Human Brain Institute, established by Natalie Petrovna (Bekhtereva, 2007; Bekhtereva, 2004; Bekhtereva, Danko, Starchenko, Pakhomov, & Medvedev, 2001). Other discoveries made by her were no less important: the error detector, and the participation of subcortical neurons in speech comprehension, hence, in mental activity (Bekhtereva & Gretchin, 1968; Bekhtereva, Kropotov, Ponomarev, & Etlinger, 1990; Bekhtereva et al., 1978; Bekhtereva and Nagornova, 2007). At Human Brain Institute, they developed two main scientific directions: (1) brain organization of thinking, emotional processes, and consciousness; and (2) diagnostic optimization of the treatment brain and nervous system diseases (Bekhtereva, 2004; Bekhtereva, 2007).

There are a numerous other theories and discoveries that have not been mentioned here and they are no less worth our attention but, going back to our main goal, we will stop here and start to follow the history of individual differences, particularly in cognitive ability and cognition.

Soviet Period: Differential Psychophysiology and Individual Differences in Cognitive Ability and Cognition

The School of Teplov and Nebilitcyn of Differential Psychophysiology

> "The application of psychological principles should always be based on knowledge of individual differences. In the absence of that, all psychological principles became so abstract that their practical value seems doubtful" (Teplov, 2003, p. 261)

This point of view defined the long-term research program in individual differences and a new branch "differential psychology" has emerged here. An adherent to the Pavlov's conception of the individual differences in Higher nervous system, B.M. Teplov asserted the necessity of the extension of research in this direction by using new methods and techniques. His report: "The Theory of Types of Higher Nervous system activity and Psychology" at the International Congress of Psychology (Teplov, 1955a, 1955b) became an important step from physiology to psychology of individual differences. He improved the research methods that studied the parameters of the higher nervous system and allowed new principles to be proposed. B.M. Teplov suggested the idea that the strength of the nervous system should be combined with sensitivity in a single property and called reactivity. He proved that the strength of the nervous system has a negative correlation with the sensitivity. The combination of the weak type of nervous system with higher sensitivity, detected in numerous studies, refuted the wrong view about inferiority of the weak type of nervous system. He said: "For all types it is possible to develop all social personal traits. However, to develop these traits it must be based on specific ways that essentially depend intrinsically on the type of nervous system." This idea defined the mutual relations of the psychological and physiological components in differential science.

The important step for development of differential psychophysiology was the inculcation of the electrophysiological method (EEG-electroencephalography). V.D. Nebilitcyn, who was a talented disciple of Teplov's, provided EEG research on parameters of the nervous system during different reflex conditioning (conditioned reflex, orienting reflex and their extinction, differentiating inhibition and delayed inhibition). In brief, his EEG studies showed: (1) the extinction rates of conditioned reflex, orienting reflex are objective indexes of the balance of nervous processes, but differentiating inhibition is less informative, and that delayed inhibition is not an informative parameter; (2) significant correlation between the strength of nervous system (measured by EEG) and sensitiveness (measured by absolute hearing threshold); (3) the lack of correlation of the strength of nervous system and EEG parameters; (4) significant correlation between alpha-index and the balance of the nervous system (Nebilitcyn, 1976).

The Teplov–Nebilitcyn school established the principles for the development of differential psychophysiology: only the involuntary reaction methods should be used for study of nervous system properties; each nervous system property forms the aggregates of indexes, which are correlated with each other where the one of the indexes becomes main and referent; trinomial principle of the organization of the nervous system properties – index of properties in excitation, similar index of inhibition, and derived index of the balance of these properties. Teplov and Nebilitcyn (Nebilitcyn 1976) suggested new independent parameters of the nervous system: "lability" as a

Properties of higher nervous system

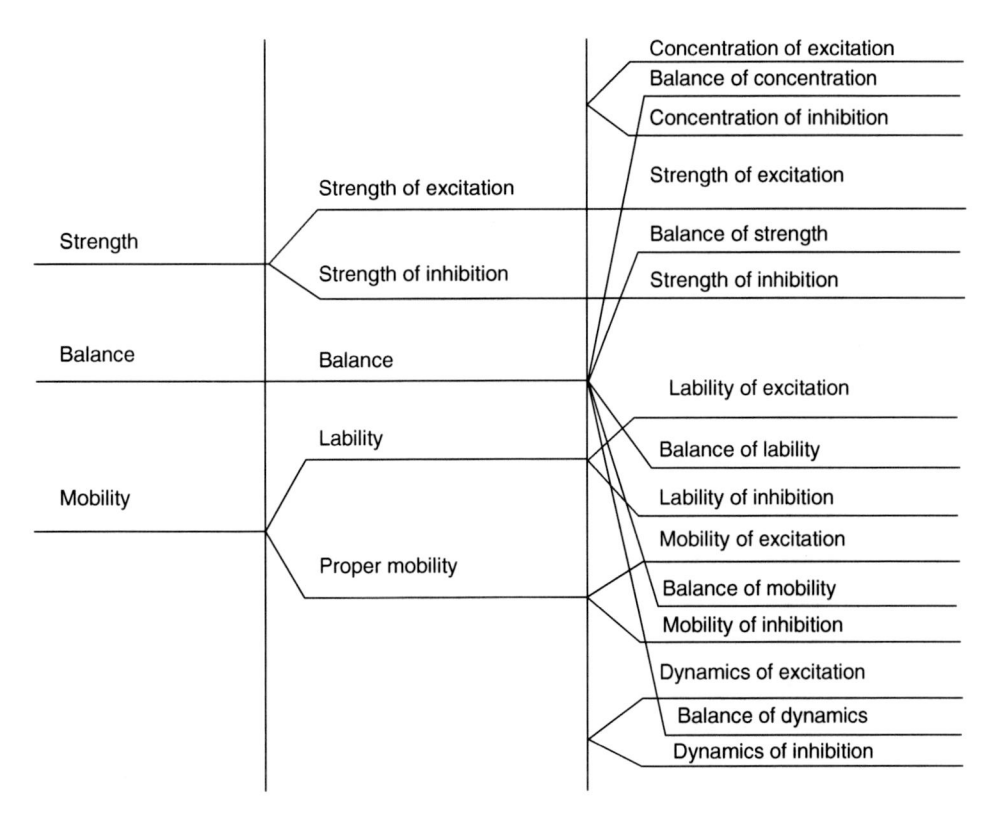

Level 1	Level 2	Level 3
Strength	Strength of excitation	Concentration of excitation
		Balance of concentration
		Concentration of inhibition
		Strength of excitation
	Strength of inhibition	Balance of strength
		Strength of inhibition
Balance	Balance	
Mobility	Lability	Lability of excitation
		Balance of lability
		Lability of inhibition
	Proper mobility	Mobility of excitation
		Balance of mobility
		Mobility of inhibition
		Dynamics of excitation
		Balance of dynamics
		Dynamics of inhibition

Fig. 9.2 Properties of higher nervous system (Rusalov, 1979). Reprinted and translated from Rusalov, V. M. (1979). *Biologicheskie Osnovi Individualno-Psihologicheskih Razlichii [Biological basis of individual psychological differences]*. Moscow: Nauka. Reproduced with permission from the publisher

characteristic of the excitation and inhibition rate, and "dynamics" as an excitation dynamic and inhibition dynamic. Dynamics was demonstrated by Nebilitcyn's EEG study that proposed the neurological substance of excitations (based on reticular formation) and inhibitions (based on frontal cortex) dynamics. The lability was studied more precisely later by E.A. Golubeva using EEG reactions to different frequency photo- and phonostimulations (Golubeva, 1980, 1989). The numerous studies of Teplov and Nebilitcyn determined 12 distinct properties of the higher nervous system that supported the three fundamental Pavlovian properties (see Fig. 9.2). Additionally, M.N. Borisova suggested the "concentration" of the inhibition and excitation, and Golubeva the general "activation" as further properties (Rusalov, 1979).

The study of the traditional nervous system characteristics (strength, mobility, and balance) in different sensory systems revealed lack of correspondence to each other. Nebilitcyn (1972, 1976) called these characteristics *specific properties* because they reflect only the specific function of the local anatomic–morphological brain structure. He suggested that the *general properties*, governed by regulatory function of frontal lobes with the reticular formation and limbic system, are the biological roots of the individual differences. Therefore, differences in emotionality, based on frontal-limbic system function, and differences in activity, based on frontal-reticular system function, are basic personal characteristics.

According to Nebilitcyn's position, individual differences in human mental activity are moderated by variety in the general properties of the nervous system provided by frontal-reticular system. To clarify this proposal, Nebilitcyn and his colleagues did EEG research on motor and mental activity. They found the motor characteristics (such as individual tempo, the tendency for action variability, and necessity in action) and the mental activity characteristics (the tendency for variability of mental activity, seeking novelty, and mental effort) positively correlate with beta oscillations in frontal lobes. Nebilitcyn (1976) concluded that differences in motor and mental activity fundamentally depend on the differences in excitation/inhibition in frontal lobes.

Teplov's Ability Concept and EEG Studies in Cognitive Abilities and Cognitive Functions

A natural extension of studying individual differences in human activity is the attempt to learn how to explain individual differences in human abilities, pioneered by Teplov. His doctoral thesis was devoted to psychology of musical abilities (1940). Teplov defined the concept of ability that was based on the *general* and *special* abilities as properties of the higher nervous system. He proposed analytical methods to study abilities and inclinations. Teplov's ability concept is based on his understanding of the biological and social roots in personality. The abilities are an integral complex of psychophysiological, psychological, and social characteristics. Therefore, integrative approaches were used by followers in studies of correlation between abilities and properties of the nervous system (Golubeva, 1980, 1989). The first level is defined by nervous system properties as the general index; the other two, functional asymmetry and the sensory systems characteristics, are sources of specific properties. Correlation were seen between the communicative (language, pedagogical, musical), cognitive abilities (memory, verbal, nonverbal, mathematical) and properties of the nervous system. For instance, language abilities that were studied with students during intensive foreign language courses and communicative abilities (the ability to understand emotional state of others, connectivity, and tenderness – currently close in meaning to the term emotional intelligence) were correlated with weakness and lability of the nervous system (Kabardov & Matova, 1988; Kabardov, 1989). Nonverbal ability corresponds with lability and activity and the opposing verbal ability corresponds with inertness, inactivity, and weakness of the nervous system (Golubeva, 1989; Pechenkov, 1989). Mathematical ability was positively associated with strength of nervous system (Guseva et al., 1989).

A long-term study of memory as the basic cognitive function influenced by individual differences in nervous system properties measured by EEG was conducted by Golubeva (1980). The summary of research results: (1) Subjects who have the strong nervous system, measured by reaction of rhythm transformation under photostimulation by low frequency, have more productive memory. Only in semantic memory is there an advantage for a weak nervous system; (2) The lability index provided by high-frequency photostimulation positively correlated with productivity of involuntary memory and, on the other hand, inertness – with voluntary memory; (3) The balance of nervous system, measured by stimulations in theta bands, was also an informative parameter: the subjects with higher excitation processes (more activated) have more productive verbal memory. In contrast, nonverbal memory positively correlated with inhibition prevalence; (4) The individual differences in memory were measured to estimate ability for success in academic work and the correlation was high. These results underlined that the differences in regulation of inhibition and excitation processes (as bases of higher nervous system properties) are important for individual differences in memory.

It is necessary to mention that Pavlov's ideas about the Higher Nervous system, and its importance for psychology were preceded by Boiko (1976) who divided physiology into two processes – pure physiology and "mental physiology." To continue the view of two type of brain processes, E.N. Sokolov differentiated the "consciousness neurons." E.N. Sokolov and his colleagues elaborated the coding information in the brain structure in the form of vectors of multidimensional space of signs. He developed "vector" psychophysiology as the direction of neurophysiology and psychophysiology framed by geometrical models of cognitive processes (Sokolov, 1994). He studied physiological mechanisms of memory by using extra- and introneuronal registration of reactions to stimulus and discovered the pacemaker (endogenous oscillation) mechanism; he found the neuronal mechanism of predictive reflection (Sokolov, 1969). Further attempts to describe the psychological processes in terms of neuronal mechanisms and brain electrical activity were undertaken in Livanov's laboratory. Livanov (1982) noticed that under a simple stimulus (like ordinary light), the reaction times of a subject differed according to the subject's state of higher excitation or lower excitation. But when the simple light stimulus is changed to number stimulus, this difference in reaction time disappeared and spatial synchronization (long-range, long-distance) of cortical areas oscillations increased. Moreover, the verbal task induced higher synchronization in frontal lobes, and arithmetic task induced double the intensive synchronization in parietal–occipital areas.

Inspired that such interesting results could be obtained by measuring mental activity with EEG, Livanov and Sviderskaya (1984) extended this research to find out differences in EEG synchronization depending on personal characteristics, emotional state, state of mood, and activity in healthy participants and patients with schizophrenia. Individual variability in EEG changes under cognitive tasks was connected with emotional state and personal characteristics. In reality, the level of nonspecific synchronization between different brain areas corresponds with the level of the task difficulty, but it is the level of specific local synchronization between different brain areas which corresponds to criteria for productive activity (effectiveness of task performance). Also, Krupnov (1984) revealed the negative correlation between alpha rhythm and mental activity. At the same time, Kiroi and Petrosova (1983) showed the decrease of the level of spatial synchronization of EEG biopotentials. Later, they worked out in detail that the increase of spatial synchronization under cognitive tasks occurs predominantly only in low frequency bands. The decrease in alpha and beta waves corresponds with the level of emotional tension (Kiroi, 1987; Kiroi, Mamin, & Khachaturyan, 1988).

The use of EEG methods along with EP (evoked potential) became popular for studying individual differences and cognitive functions (Bodunov, 1985; Danilova, 1982; Guseva & Shlyahta, 1974; Rusalov, 1979; Ribalko, Lukomskaia, & Svyatogor, 1985; Soroko, Bekshaev, & Sidorov, 1990 and many others).

Other Popular Theories in Psychology of Individual Differences and Their Contributions in Understanding Individual Differences in Cognition

Rusalov's concept of temperament is one of the more popular theories and his Structure of Temperament Questionnaire (STQ, Rusalov, 1989) has been widely used in post-Soviet area. Rusalov's (1989) idea was to describe the intellectual behavior in probabilistic environments by using terms of Anokhin's functional system. The long term study of neurodynamical and psychodynamical constitutions (nervous system properties and their EEG indexes, different mental activity, sensitivity, self-regulation, plasticity, intelligence, general abilities and others) in different conditions (determinate and probabilistic) brought the new concept of *the 12-dimensional structure of human temperament* that he first began to describe in his book "Biological basic of the individual-psychological differences" (1979). This structure consists of 4 properties (ergonicity, plasticity, individual tempo, and emotionality) in 3 spheres (psychomotor, intellectual, social). The 4 properties are based on four-stages of the functional system structure (Anokhin, 1968, 1974, 1975; see Fig. 9.1): ergonicity – on afferental synthesis; plasticity – on decision-making; individual tempo – on implementation of the action program; and emotional sensitivity – on feedback to the acceptor of the action result. Also, 3 spheres of human behavior – psychomotor, intellectual, and social – may describe as functional systems, so each of them is characterized by 4 properties. Equally important were the results of the correlation between general nervous system properties, measured by integral EEG parameters, and general abilities. For example, the EEG spatial–temporal coherence negatively correlates with plasticity of self-regulation, and beta-2 correlates with sensitivity to probabilistic environments and plasticity, parameters of slow waves – with variability in speed of creation of a prognosis (Rusalov, 1979). Some Western psychologists have also investigated an English translation of Rusalov's questionnaire and established some limited overlap between some of its scales and extraversion and neuroticism (Brebner & Stough, 1993).

V.S. Merlin's theory is an attempt to integrate two branches: psychophysiological (Teplov, Nebitlicin) and psychological (Leontiev). Merlin (1986) suggested a comprehensive whole of human properties as an integration of hierarchical levels of personality correlated with each other in many different ways. V.S. Merlin summarized the long-term studies of mutual relations between all systems and subsystems discovered by his laboratory in the book "Ocherk integralnogo issledovaniya individualnosti" [Studies of integral research of individuality] (1986).

Merlin investigated personality empirically by measuring various nervous system properties in samples of factory workers. These studies supported an extension of integral individuality theory that included concepts of individual style of activity and individual style of communication. Individual activity style is an organized system of interrelated actions aimed to achieve a certain goal. The individuality in different levels and uncertainty of activity in different levels (neuromorphological, neurophysiological, etc.) provides for the individual activity style. The compensating function of individual style is, for example, when subjects with different nervous system properties have the same result in an activity because of appropriate style adjusted to receive the same results in that activity. Merlin called the compensating function of individual style as a system created factor (according to Anokhin's theory).

An important place in Soviet psychology belongs to B.G. Ananiev who created a synthetic personology theory. In his book *Chelovek kak predmet poznania/Man as a Subject of Study* (1969), a person is depicted as: (1) "an organism, (2) an individual who develops and has one's own life trajectory, (3) a unique personality enmeshed in social relationships, and (4) a subject of cognition and creation relating by one's products to the realm of values." He with colleagues conducted research aimed at learning about mutual relations between neurodynamical characteristics, temperament (extraversion–introversion), intelligence (verbal and nonverbal), attention, different psychomotor, vegetative, and biochemical function. They found intelligence to be the first factor (as a result of factor analysis). Ananiev (1969) noticed that intelligence theories do not consider personality characteristics, and, on the other hand, the personality theories do not consider intelligence. Dvorayashkina (1969) drew attention to fact that the intellectual factor negatively correlated with basal metabolism rate. So, higher level of intelligence was defined by lower level of expenditure of energy, and higher level of attention and productivity of mental activity. At the same time, Palei (1971) noticed that the low intelligence also correlated with lower metabolic rate. To explain this controversy, he suggested idea about informational – energetic relations in neuropsychic activity. Ananiev (1969) reviewed age- and sex-specificity in neurodynamical properties that influenced perception, cognition, and behavior (in children and old people). B.G. Ananiev's theory of intelligence (1969) is based on numerous empirical studies of cognitive functions (attention, memory, thinking) as components of the intellectual system. The intelligence structure was described as both introfunctional relations (relations between the properties of one cognitive function, for example, between volume and selectivity of attention) and extrafunctional relations (relations between different cognitive functions, for example, between memory and attention) in ontogenetic dynamics: differentiation and integration of cognitive functions. He concluded that intelligence has regulative functions with regard to levels of individuality – psychophysiological and psychological. B.G. Ananiev inferred that regulation of excitation and inhibition is the main factor of age-specificity. Along with hierarchical (vertical – from brainstem to cortex) regulation, he paid attention to bilateral (horizontal – between hemispheres) regulation. The bilateral regulation is characterized by an increase of interhemispheric relations in ontogenesis. Ananiev suggested that vertical regulations descend with age and horizontal regulation extends with age. Thus, over the life-span, intelligence development occurs in both regressive and progressive ways. These different developmental processes are consistent with Anokhin's heterochronic principle, which states that different parts of a functional system develop over different timespans. To judge from observations of Kholodnaya (2007), the increase in bilateral regulation connects with level of conceptual experience and activity of conceptual thinking.

Post-Soviet Period: Differential "Cognitology." EEG-Research of Individual Differences in Cognitive Ability and Cognitive Function

As seen from the review described above, an individual difference in cognition was one of the most interesting items for scientists in the field of differential psychology. All studies were related in some form to this item. Individuality theories tried to prove their reliability through study of various mental activity and research about differences in cognitive abilities. At the same time, cognitive studies were increasingly directed to various to questions about individual differences. So, this gap between these two branches is diminishing and they are consolidating in the area of "differential cognitology" (Libin, 2006).

Individual Differences in Cognitive Abilities and Cognitive Styles

According to E.A. Golubeva, activation and self-regulation are preconditions of abilities, and the properties of nervous system are natural preconditions for different styles of self-regulation and activation. E.A. Golubeva (2005) integrated long-term complex research results of differential psychology and psychophysiology in her book *Sposobnosti. Lichnost. Individualnost* (Abilities. Personality. Individuality). This book includes the electrophysiological studies of nervous system properties and their relations with individual psychological differences in special abilities (musical, mathematical, etc.) and common abilities (memory, intellect). The functional asymmetry (horizontal regulation) was an important component of individual differences in linguistic abilities (Kabardov, 2004; Ahutina, Yablokova, & Polonskaya, 2000 and others). M.K. Kabardov and his colleagues, in experimental studies of dichotomy "language-speech," revealed the individual configuration of the physiological, psychological/psycholinguistic behavioral levels. He further suggested the typology: "communicative-speech," "cognitive-linguistic," and "mixed" types and described their differences in cognitive function.

Kabardov and Arcishevskaya (1997) developed the understanding of communicative ability. Teplov's approach to personality and ability study were extended by Guseva (1997) in musical abilities, S.A. Izumova (1993, 1995) in literary, mathematical and mnemonic abilities, A.M. Matushkin (2003) in creativity ("alloy of cognitive and personal components" and others.

Leites (1997, 2003) developed the age-specific approach to ability investigations. He noticed, that individuality and age interrelated and overlapped in specific periods of ability development, and age-specific regulation modify individual differences. He suggested that the "individual-natural" and "natural-age-specific" components of ability should be separated. For example, some properties of nervous system become apparent only at specific ages, and age specificity could conceal the individual characteristics.

Shadrikov (1997) described the intellectual abilities as a psychical functional system property that defined the productivity and individual intensity of this functional system and regulated by feedback principle. He elucidated the structure of abilities in terms of Anokhin's functional systems (1975). From this point of view, the psychometrical intelligence, creativity, learning ability, and cognitive styles are the properties of the psychical functional system.

The individual style is one of the popular items for investigations among differential psychologists (Merlin, 1986; Ilin, 2004 – activity style; Morosanova, 2002 – self-regulation style; Kholodnaya & Kostrikina, 2002 – cognitive style and many others). Underlining the meaning of each of the styles (cognitive, activity, and others) and individuality components (the peculiarities of higher nervous system, temperament, character) in empirical studies, A. Libin suggested the "unified concept of human style" as a hierarchical functional structure of frames. "A human individual can be viewed as a complex interactive developing system analyzed in the context of cognitive and emotional processes, personality and behavior styles, and group differences such as gender, age, race, and culture" (Libin, 2006, p. 542).

Kholodnaya (2002, 2007) considered the cognitive style and cognitive abilities as prerequisites of intellectual competency in scientific and technological activity. Her research has focused on cognitive styles that include impulsivity/reflectivity and rigidity/flexibility. Although typically thought of as bipolar dimensions, Kholodnaya's empirical studies suggest that each cognitive style may be split into four separate poles, described as a "quadra polar dimension" (Kholodnaya, 2002). For example, impulsivity may be split into both fast-accurate and fast-inaccurate styles. She proposed that the basis of "splitting" of cognitive style poles is a unique cognitive mechanism, primarily as factor of intellectual control. According to Kholodnaya (1997, 2002), intelligence is a special form of organization of mental experience, presented as a composite mental structure generated from the mental area of reflection and the mental representations of existence. Mental structures are cognitive experience, metacognitive experience, intentional experience, and intellectual abilities. Kholodnaya's laboratory of ability psychology (Institute of Psychology of Russian Academy of Sciences) conducts studies devoted to intelligence from different perspectives. A.N. Voronin and N. Gabrielyan (1999) studied the relation of intelligence and personality in group interaction; S. Safonceva and A.N. Voronin (2000) – the relation of creativity and intelligence in age-specific groups; S.D. Birukov (2001) – genetic and environment determinants of individuality and intelligence; N.B. Gorunova and V.N. Druzhinin (2001) – the relations of intelligence and productivity of different activity, resource model of intelligence (Kholodnaya, 2002).

Druzhinin (2001) proposed the phenomenon of "intellectual threshold" (minimal level of intellect necessary for success in concrete activity) and model of "intellectual range." In an experimental study, he showed individual differences in intelligence levels associated with differences in cognitive resource components: the volume of short-term and sensory memory, reaction time on making choices, parameters of productivity of the selection of notions. Although "resources" are notoriously to define, V.N. Druzhinin noticed that cognitive resources are possible to describe in terms of M.A. Kholodnaya's "mental area" theory and A.N. Lebedev's psychophysiological theory.

Based on Bernstein's theory of movement construction levels, B.M. Velichkovskii suggested the Grand Design model of intelligence (1986b, 2006) – the levels of cognitive organization and behavior regulation: Paleokinetic regulation (A), Synergy (B), Spatial field (C), Object perception (D), Conceptual structure (E), and Metacognitive coordination (F). The vertical integration from spinal cord to prefrontal cortex provide from elementary (tonus regulation) to complex functions (self-regulation, self-control) (Velichkovsky, 2006).

Thus, post-Soviet research has addressed individual differences in range of cognitive constructs, including various specific cognitive abilities, dimensions of cognitive style, and general intelligence.

EEG Studies on Individual Differences in Cognition and Regulation

The EEG method is one of the prospective approaches that allow the integration of differential and cognitive psychology since it is broadly used in both dimensions of psychophysiology. Lebedev (1997) hypothesized that refractory period and alpha rhythms are individual characteristics of information processing based on Livanov's studies listed earlier. Therefore, EEG parameters are highly informative in measuring attention capacity, memory capacity, and personal traits. The numerous experimental studies (Lebedev, 1985; Lebedev, 1997; Lebedev, 2002; Lebedev et al., 1997; Lebedev & Luckii, 1972; Markina et al., 1995) resulted in a proposed formula to measure the capacity for memory and attention. The study of learning success among students and EEG parameters offered a prediction based on regression analysis, where a learning success index was defined by the following EEG parameters: P56-synchronization index in O1–O2 (%), A5or-alpha5 (12 Hz) PSD in O1, A4or-alpha4 (11 Hz) PSD (power spectral density) in O2, and P23 – synchronization index on F4–C3 (%) (Lebedev, 2002).

The mathematical analysis of the relations between EEG parameters and individual differences measured by Rusalov's STQ and MMPI supports personality description by using only EEG method (Lebedev et al., 2002). For example, the next equation is prognostic for communicational emotionality (i.e., as measured by the questionnaires): Pro=56,417+0,145*DIO+0.0702*P56-0,369*A2T (where Procommunicational emotionality; DIO-fractal dimension multiplied by 100 and correlation coefficient between O1 and O2; A2T-alpha2 (9 Hz) PSD in O1). So, Lebedev proposed that this optimistic view of the future of EEG methods for explaining cognitive functions and their individuality will help to find the laws of cognitive psychology (Lebedev, 2000; Lebedev, 2001).

In recent years, EEG research has become increasingly important as a method for distinguishing different regulative mechanisms that may vary across individuals.

Razoumnikova (2003) hypothesized that the personality and intelligence "modulate each other via a common neural basis in the cortex and subcortical structures," and "the stable predominance of one or another brain system (frontal-thalamic, limbic, brain-stem) can be associated, on the one hand, with systematic differences in cognitive processes and, on the other hand, with behavioral organization, classified in accordance with personality typology and mediating a rigid and stable (or "hard") style of behavior." Her study of the interaction of personality, intelligence factors and the baseline EEG parameters supported this idea. The subjects with high IQ revealed the greater long-distance coherence between anterior and posterior cortex (differently in verbal and numerical intelligence), and also greater desynchronization of the theta1-alpha2 rhythms and the greater power beta-2 with right dominance, and characterized by high and low personality scores. The personality traits displayed the specific profiles of the coherence and spectral power of EEG (for example, extraversion negatively correlates with interhemispheric coherence in the alpha-2 band). She concluded that high-intelligence subjects have stable neuronal cooperation associated with personality differences in excitatory–inhibitory processes of separate brain systems: cortical-brain-stem system in introversion/extraversion, cortical–limbic system in neuroticism/high emotional stability, and thalamic–cortical system in sensation/intuition. Furthermore, Razoumnikova (2000, 2007), investigated the differences in the functional brain activity during convergent and divergent thinking. The results showed the decreases in spectral power in theta (associated with attention increases) and alpha-1 bands (associated with activation increases) under convergent task in female and male groups. The gender differences were observed in mechanisms of activation during successfully completed divergent task: male group showed significant growth in beta-2 and lower desynchronization in alpha-1 and, conversely, female group revealed lower beta-2 and higher desynchronization in alpha-1. The author said these reciprocal relations were explained by differences in cortical–subcortical regulations voluntary, involuntary, and "differential" attention. Higher creativity was associated with higher coherence in the central–parietal areas of both hemispheres, and greater ipsilateral connections in the right cortex. Volf and Razumnikova (2004) expanded the study of creativity in relation to attention, motivation, and gender differences.

Anokhin et al. (1999) found that long distance coherence (between frontal and parietal–occipital areas) in theta band (associated with attention) positively correlated with cognitive abilities. Moreover, they measured EEG dimension as indexes of complexity and unpredictability of neural oscillatory dynamics underlying the EEG time series. The EEG dimension and coherence showed inverse relationships. A.P. Anokhin suggested that biological factors of individual differences in cognitive abilities are possible to measure by ratio of order to chaos in task-related brain dynamics. Probably, this ratio could refer to regulation specificity. The entropy of EEG rhythms reflects the chaos of brain activity as well. It was shown that the decrease of entropy during cognitive tasks is associated with the increase of brain system regulation (Byasheva & Shvecova, 1993). The age specificity of EEG related to vertical regulation maturation (increase in alpha "moda" (dominant frequency), increase the stability of alpha, decrease theta, etc.) and corresponds with cognitive function and emotion development in ontogenesis (Anokhin et al., 1999; Byasheva & Shvecova, 1993; Dubrovinskaya & Farber, 1993; Farber et al., 1994; Bogomolova & Farber, 1995 and others).

Large numbers of EEG-studies were devoted to the cognitive functions (Bezrukikh & Khryanin, 2003; Chernigovskaya et al., 2005, 2007; Gorev, 2007; Farber et al., 2004; Dubrovinskaya & Machinskaya, 2002, and others), cognitive abilities (Ahutina et al., 2000; Biyasheva, 1998; Kabardov & Matova, 1988) and emotion (Rusalova & Kostunina, 1999) provided by interhemispheric asymmetry (horizontal regulation). The differences in strategy of integration of the brain activity (measured by EEG components – spectral power density and coherence) were found during attention processes and visual–spatial task in children regardless of handedness (Bezrukikh & Khryanin, 2003).

According to Knyazev and Slobodskaya (Knyazev & Slobodskaya, 2003, 2006; Knyazev, G.G., 2006), to understand EEG oscillations function in behavior regulation it is necessary to consider evolution. Based on T.H. Bullock's comparative studies of EEG brain activity in animals and P.D. MacLean's triune brain concept, authors suggested three systems based on three oscillations: delta, theta, and alpha that correspond to three hierarchical phylogenetic brain systems – brainstem, limbic, and cortical–thalamic. These three systems (reciprocally related to each other) regulate behavior: delta regulates the biological needs; theta – emotions and contextual memory; alpha – perception, recognition, and semantic memory. The evolutionary new systems control the older systems. The individual differences in three systems relations define individual differences in behavior. The authors in their empirical research found that reciprocal relations of alpha–delta in adults and theta–delta in children correlate with anxiety. They explained these facts by the prevalence of cognitive regulation of anxiety in adults, and emotional regulation – in children (Knyazev & Slobodskaya, 2006).

The cognitive effectiveness was correlated positively with alpha and negatively with theta (Markina et al., 2000). The higher volume of short-term memory corresponds to a higher level of temperamental activity (measured by Rusalov's QST) and higher spectral power of alpha, whereas lower volume of short-term memory correlated with emotional sensitivity and higher spectral power of theta. As authors noticed, such reciprocal relation between alpha and theta were observed by L.A. Yurlin as well. These results agree with N.N. Danilova's observations are that subjects with regular and higher alpha in EEG show higher spontaneous activity, more accuracy in work, even under stress, and better short term-memory than subjects with lower alpha. The alpha rhythm as cortical–thalamic rhythm associated with informational channel. Rusalov (1979) showed that external emotional signal corresponds with alpha desynchronization as a result of attention increase, contrary to the internal emotion induction accompanied by the synchronization of alpha. According to Simonov's informational theory of emotion (1981), the theta rhythm is not only an index of limbic system activation but it is also an index of memory processes related to hippocampus. Aftanas et al. (Aftanas et al., 2001; Aftanas et al., 2004) revealed the increases in evoked synchronization in delta, theta, beta, and gamma correlated with emotional impact of stimuli from the International Affective Picture System and synchronization and desynchronization in the alpha-2 band. Authors confirmed that lower theta rhythms in posterior areas are evidence of earlier extraction emotional signals (at 0–400 ms), whereas in higher theta, alpha-2, and gamma, this process delayed (to 600–1,000 ms).

Nevertheless, the EEG study of positive and negative emotion induction revealed the increase of SPM in all frequency bands that authors explained by changes in a cortical–thalamic regulation system (Danko et al., 2003; Danko, 2006).

Psychophysiologists have placed special emphasis on gamma rhythms as a cognitive rhythm (Danilova et al., 2005; Danko, 2006; Danko et al., 2005; Nagornova, 2007). According to Danilova and colleagues, the evoked and induced gamma rhythm participated in sensory encoding. They used the combination of the 3D dipole tracing methods with structural MRI in order to prove discrete pattern of gamma oscillations in cognitive functions. Gamma oscillations play an important role in selective attention, learning, and memory as the modulator of cortical synchronization for mutual cortical–cortical interactions among neuronal populations (Kaiser & Lutzenberger, 2003; Munk, 2001). Therefore, the gamma rhythms are informative parameters for investigations cognitive regulation.

Besides the EEG methods, new technologies such as PET and fMRI were used for study of cognitive functions. For example, Bekhtereva et al. (2001) studied brain organization of creativity by PET and EEG. Creative performance (the composition of stories with the given words belonging to the same or different semantic fields) was compared to a noncreative/control task (the reconstruction of correct grammatical forms in a presented text and memorizing of a set of words). Depending on the strategy of subjects, the two areas in frontal lobes that were mainly activated during the creative task were Brodmann's areas (BA) 39 (first type) and 40 (second type). Additionally, specific interhemispheric interaction measured by EEG coherence was demonstrated in relation to creativity (Bekhtereva et al., 2001). So, combination of EEG and PET, fMRI research will make clear the mechanisms of individuality in cognitive functions.

Integration of Cognitive and Emotional Control

Some of the studies of the EEG previously discussed (e.g., Aftanas et al., 2004; Danko et al., 2003) raise the issues of the interrelationship and integration of cognitive and emotional regulation systems. Another perspective has been provided by one of Luria's students and followers, B. Velichkovsky. According to Velichkovsky's (2006) opinion, the lack of "hot cognition" studies and investigation of only "cold cognition" is one of the main problems in cognitive science. He included a chapter on "Cognitive-affective science" in his book *Kognitivnaya nauka: osnovi psihologii poznaniay* [Cognitive Science: Foundations of Epistemic Psychology] (2006). In this chapter, Velichkovsky considered the issue about the regulation of cognition and emotion performed by a separate executive system and discussed it from the perspective of hierarchical levels of regulation. Velichkovsky suggested that emotions also (as intelligence structure In Grand Design model) observe the levels structure and that, at higher levels of cognitive organization, it is more difficult to separate the emotion and cognition processes. Already Luria (1966) described two types of frontal syndrome ("disexecutive syndrome"): difficulties in goal changes and difficulties on concentration. Velichkovsky (2006) tried to explain these different effects in terms of emotional influences discovered by C.S. Carver: positive emotion increases dopamine that creates the impression of a successful result and readiness to change goal, and negative emotion (insufficient dopamine) inversely relates to impression of lack of success that keeps on the one goal for a long time. Velichkovsky discussed Western studies that separate executive control in emotion and cognition, and views from opposite side, how emotion influences cognition and suggests that this position will clarify individual differences in future. He thinks that "it is an absurd idea about two separate evolutions – one for affective and further cognitive mechanisms" (Velichkovsky, 2006, p. 367). Furthermore, emotion was considered as a lower level of unified systemic organization of behavior in Aleksandrov's theory of consciousness that is based on Anokhin's Functional system (Aleksandrov & Sams, 2005). Yu.I. Aleksandrov criticized the separate mechanisms of emotion and consciousness. Soviet psychology has generally seen emotion and cognition as highly integrated so that we cannot say that emotion regulates cognition, or cognition regulates emotion.

The integration tendency was notably supported not only by differential psychologists focusing on cognition but also cognitive psychologists who observed individual differences in their experiments on cognition. Remarkable theoretical and empirical contributions in cognitive and individuality development were made by E.A. Sergienko. Her recent book *Rannee kognitivnoe razvitie* [Early cognitive development] (2006) resulted from studies of anticipation and mental representativeness and the ability to regulate behavior in early childhood. By analyzing empirical studies of children's cognitive function in a modern theoretical frame, she proposed important ideas for understanding children's cognition and proper cognition mechanisms development in integrative processes. Sergienko (2006, 2007) suggested that the corner stone of individuality is the individual differences in control that are based on these positions: (1) "Cognitive, emotional and operational components of psychic organization are in indissoluble unity," (2) "Subject as the bearer of psyche realizes the integrative relations of all components," (3) "The organization of three components of behavior control will possess its own specificity (that creates the individual pattern of self-regulation) ... Originality in organization of behavior control components combine with the universal regularities of subject formation." These hypotheses were examined in different studies in Cognitive laboratory of Institute of Psychology (U.V. Kovaleva, G.A. Ryazanceva, D.K. Golovanova, O.V. Mozjuhina, G.A. Vilenskaya and others) (Sergienko, 2006, 2007). The control as an integrative factor in individuality and cognition permeates through all processes.

The concept of the individual's self-regulation style was proposed by Morosanova (2002). This concept was based on O.A. Konopkin's structural-functional model of self-regulation (1995). V.I. Morosanova created the questionnaire SSP-98 – "stilevie osobennosti samoregulyacii povedeniya" [Style peculiarities of behavior self-regulation] that consists of 6 scales: goal planning, modelling of the conditions to achieve this goal, action programming, estimation and correction of results, flexibility, and self-dependency. A series of empirical studies on connections with extraversion and neuroticism, cognitive styles, accentuated personality, and motivations showed that the styles of self-regulation have their own specific definition.

The post-Soviet period of differential psychology development was characterized by integration processes: the integration between different fields and schools, the integration with international tradition. The book *Differentcialnaya psihologia: na peresechenii Rossisckih, Evropeiskih, e Americanskih tradicii* [Differential psychology on the Crossroad of European, Russian and American Traditions] written by Libin (2006) is the evidence of realization the necessity of integration of science. He included one small chapter under the topic: "Differential cognitology: differences in cognition processes." So, the integration will bring the new branches, such as "differential cognitology," and "affective cognitology."

Soroko's Brain Plasticity Theory and Prospects for Development

The study of the brain plasticity was conducted by large number of scientists, mostly on a neuronal level, or by the EP method. EEG has been less used, although, brain plasticity can be determined by well known EEG components (an attenuated measure of the extracellular current flow from summated activity of many neurons). Soroko et al. (1990) created a new approach to EEG analyses by viewing the whole brain as a dynamic system that is subordinated by Anokhin's functional system principles and Behtereva's principles of 'hard' or 'flexible' coupling of neuronal assembles. The EEG components reflect the mechanism of central relationships and these relations are not casual, rather they have some interdependence. Brain plasticity, intended as a pattern of functional and structural changes in responses to environmental events, is underlined by several mechanisms. Besides cortical changes such as changes at the neuronal level representational patterns, morphologic and functional changes at the neuronal level have been hypothesized. EEG methods allow description of the temporal dynamics of cortical activation and their inhibitory or excitatory functional significance. Soroko created a new approach to EEG analysis that considered the whole brain by taking into account every EEG oscillation function (beta, alpha, theta and delta).

The premises of the theory are: (1) EEG rhythms reflect the mechanisms of interrelation regulation; (2) The relations between EEG components must have definite interdependence; (3) Methods of the transition probability matrix from one EEG wave to another reflects the interdependence of different EEG waves; (4) Brain plasticity is determined by the probabilities of transitions between EEG rhythms; (5) Brain plasticity is related to self-regulation ability, which, in turn, characterizes adaptability.

Soroko's study results showed three types of cortical self-regulation organization. The first type is characterized by a higher probability of transitions in alpha waves which Soroko called

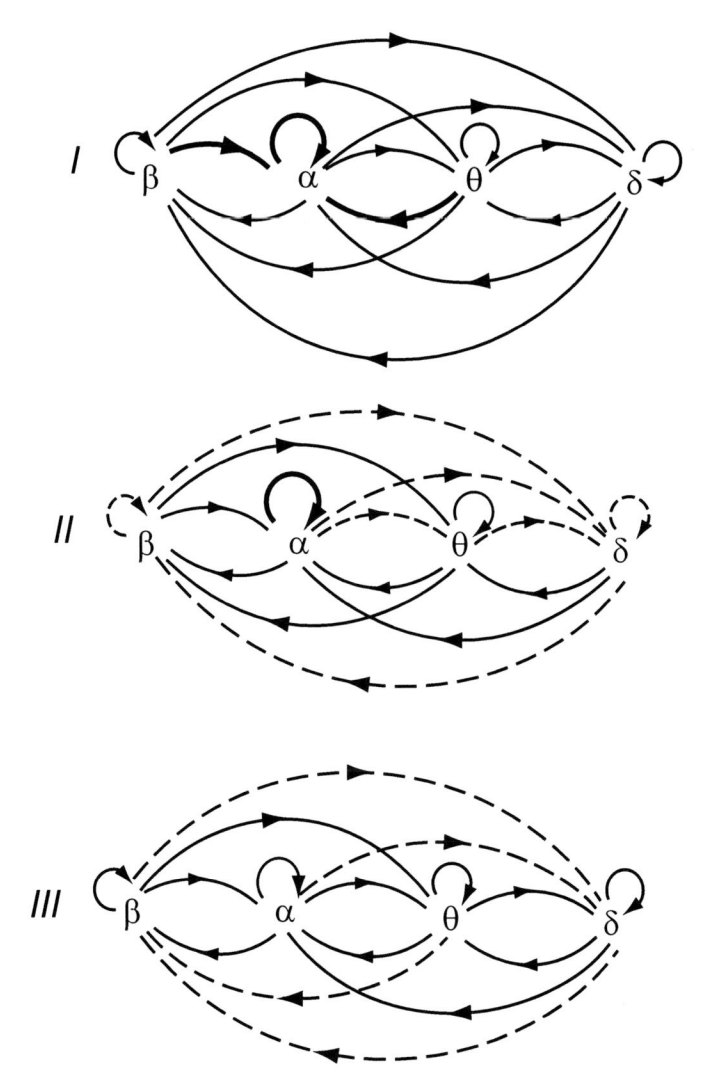

Fig. 9.3 Individual-typological structure of the statical relationships between EEG components Reprinted with permission from Soroko, S. I., Bekshaev, S. S., & Sidorov, Y. A. (1990). Osnovnie tipi mekhanizmov samoregulaycii mozga.//The principal types of brain self-regulation mechanisms. L., Nauka

Type I:
- with higher probability of transitions to and from alpha-waves ("alpha functional nucleus")
- adjusts to new environments faster and more efficiently than the II and III types dominant cortical regulation

Type II:
- two "functional nucleuses": alpha (leading) and theta (subordinate)
- higher rate of conjunction between alpha and theta waves
- cortical–limbic regulation

Type III:
- no "functional nucleus," equal transitions different waves
- limbic–brainstem regulation

"alpha functional nucleus." It's well known that Alpha oscillations play an important role in a resting functional state. Long-term studies revealed that subjects who have the first type of brain plasticity adjust to new environments (Antarctic environment, mountain hypoxia) faster and more efficiently than the II and III types (Fig. 9.3) (Soroko et al., 2002). Soroko suggested that the first type of plasticity subjects have dominant cortical regulation. The subjects with the second type are characterized by two functional centralization systems ("two functional nuclei") with leading alpha and subordinating theta, higher rate of conjunction between alpha and theta waves, and cortical–limbic regulation. The third type subjects are without any specific centralization in EEG oscillations – no "functional nucleus," that means equal-probability transitions between different waves. Also, Soroko stated that the third type subjects had limbic-brainstem regulation type.

To support the theory Soroko and his colleagues carried out further research:

1. The study of entropy of the EEG parameters has shown that individuals with Type I and II have stable EEG component interrelations, whereas type III has unstable type of interrelations.
2. The long-term study of adjustment to a new environment revealed more effective physiological system adaptation and higher workload tolerance in individuals with I type of plasticity.
3. The EEG studies of biofeedback self-regulation: biofeedback training was performed in healthy participants during adjustment to new environment (Antarctica), mountain hypoxia, and in patients with neuroses, manic-depressive disorder. Alpha biofeedback training was more effective for the first type of plasticity; beta-biofeedback was more effective on subjects with the second type of plasticity.
4. The study of the individual differences (personality factors such as extraversion, measured with R.B. Cattell's questionnaire) related to types of plasticity. That is, extraversion related positively to Type I plasticity (Soroko et al., 1990).

Soroko's theory is one of the first attempts at the classification of individual differences based on physiological understanding of the brain plasticity in humans. Taking into account that his work was based on long studies started more than 20 years ago and that the improvement of new statistical methods and the increased development of the understanding of EEG (for example, gamma in cognitive function), we must try to develop this theory for a better understanding of the nature of brain plasticity. Obviously, the idea of measuring the probability of the transitions of different oscillations from one to another in order to find the specific analytical information about the relations between EEG rhythms to estimate brain plasticity is undoubtedly of scientific importance. As we have seen from review above, the style of regulation was always central to the classification of individual differences in differential psychology. As Sergienko proposed, the corner stone of individuality is control of behavior on three levels – cognitive, emotional, and operational/activity. Review of EEG studies allows us to conclude that EEG method is informative and integrative method to study cognition, individual differences, and emotion, and may reflect regulations laws in adjustment processes.

Our preliminary investigation was devoted to the Soroko's brain plasticity theory and individual differences in cognitive abilities and temperament (Kustubayeva et al., 2008). We supported the results obtained by Soroko that the first type of plasticity is associated with extraversion. Additionally, our empirical study has shown higher general ability level was demonstrated by subjects with the third type of plasticity, whereas the higher numerical ability correlated with the second type of plasticity. Significant differences between the types were observed in reaction time on a simple visual–motor task. There is no difference between the three groups of plasticity in reaction time on vigilance task and coping strategy. Additionally, the subjects with first type of plasticity revealed the higher score in "motor tempo" (faster motor activity) and "motor ergonicity" (higher motor endurance) and lower score in "plasticity in communication" (more flexible communication) measured by Rusalov's STQ. "Plasticity in communication" correlated positively with beta probability and neurodynamical balance. The results tell us that the plasticity types related with individual differences in temperament and cognitive abilities and they promote the next steps for our investigations: (1) To find the classification of types plasticity in comparison baseline level with functional load – physiological, cognitive, and emotional. (2) As a physiological load, we started to use vasoactive stress reactions (hyperventilation and breath holding) of brain activity. Hyperventilation involves the hypocapnia, vasoconstriction, reduce in cerebral blood flow, and shifts the cortical integration level on the diencephalic level (alpha decrease and delta increase observe in EEG), which changes the state of consciousness. Therefore, to measure brain plasticity in such physiological reactions will bring clarification in cortical-subcortical regulation. (3) As cognitive load we plan to use "intellectual plasticity tasks" (Rusalov, 1979) to see whether physiological plasticity type relates to cognitive plasticity. (4) As an emotional load we started to use emotion induction tasks and emotion regulation tasks. The preliminary study has shown that the fear induction elicited increases in theta, whereas the reappraisal instruction involved alpha desynchronization and gamma synchronization, probably, as a result of cognitive activation during emotional regulation (Tolegenova et al., 2008). (5) Additional to probability measuring, we will consider the spectral power and coherence analyses, not only alpha, beta, theta, and delta but gamma as well, which is recognized now as a cognitive rhythm.

So, Soroko's brain plasticity theory is the first attempt to classify brain plasticity, and it is also one of the first attempts in classification of individual differences in brain rhythms transitions measured by EEG. EEG methods are widely known and used in investigations of Individual differences, cognitive function, emotional, and functional state. This appears the right way to classify individual differences in brain plasticity with functional load (physiological, cognitive and emotional) by using EEG. We expect that the plasticity type will reflect the general laws in regulation of the brain functions.

Conclusion

In my chapter, I have tried to describe chronologically the most popular theories during Soviet times and recent years that were devoted to individual differences in cognitive abilities and cognition. In a short chapter, it is not possible to review the whole of differential psychophysiology or cognitive psychophysiology. Hence, special attention was paid to regulation as the central question in individual differences. Indeed, the study on regulation of digestive systems brought Pavlov to individual differences in properties of higher nervous system. Due to high popularity of Pavlov's ideas, the physiological approach to regulation has been widely extended by physiologists (Anokhin, 1974, 1975; Bernstein, 1967; Luria, 1966, 1970) and psychologists (Ananiev, 1969; Nebilitcyn, 1976), raising the issue of the interrelationship between physiological and mental regulation. Which regulation is dominant: neural or psychological? Is mental activity controlled by neural dynamics, or does the mind regulate physiological reflexes? Before we can answer these questions, it is necessary to define more precisely what is meant by psychological regulation, mental activity, or mind. If Pavlov suggested that reflexes are bases of higher nervous system activity (that may include mental activity), Sokolov (1969, 1977) suggested "consciousness neurons" as bases of psychological processes and, therefore, that mental activity is the complex integrative activity of specific neurons. So, these questions are transformed into how integrative system relates to their parts, and where and how integrations of parts become the mind. The integrative system of the hierarchical control mechanisms and self-regulation based on feedback mechanisms are general principles of regulation, whether psychological or physiological. The functioning of the hierarchical system was variously described in terms of reflex theory (Pavlov, 1951; Setchenov, 1866), functional system theory (Anokhin, 1974, 1984), theory of three functional blocs system (Luria, 1966, 1970), theory of levels of movement construction (Bernstein, 1967), horizontal and vertical system theory (Ananiev, 1969), or Grand Design model of intelligence (Velichkovsky, 2006). In particular, different styles of regulation were the key in individual differences. Individual differences in the properties of higher nervous system are based on regulation of both excitation and inhibition processes. The differences in frontal–limbic system (as relations inhibitory–excitation processes) provide different pattern of emotional regulation and differences in frontal–reticular system define different pattern of mental activity regulation (Nebilitcyn, 1976). The types of plasticity are based on specific regulative mechanisms – cortical, cortical–limbic, limbic–brainstem (Soroko et al., 1990).

It is worth comparing these perspectives on individual differences with Western concepts based on cognitive theories of executive control. There are several key areas of similarity. Indeed, Luria's work on the dysexecutive syndrome was instrumental in differentiating executive function from other aspects of cognition. Both Eastern European and Western approaches to regulatory control are based on the idea of a hierarchy of levels, with a cognitive level at the top. For example, Luria identified the top level of control with anterior cortex. A further similarity is the role of feedback in guiding self-regulation, as discussed in most depth by P.K. Anokhin. However, there are also some points on which there are differences in emphasis between East and West (but not necessarily fundamental differences). Historically, Pavlov and Setchenev aimed to generalize principles of regulation of physiological systems to psychological functioning, and post-Soviet psychology maintains an interest in parallels between physiological and psychological regulatory systems. Evolutionary themes have also frequently been highlighted in differentiating mechanisms ontogenetically or phylogenetically. Ananiev's concept of horizontal regulation suggests possible differentiation of control mechanisms within the same level of the hierarchy, such as intrahemispheric mechanisms whose relationship may change ontogenetically. Another possible instance of horizontal regulation might seem to be the separation of cognition and emotion as distinct but interacting control systems, as developed in some Western theories of emotion. However, Velichkovsky has criticized the idea of a sharp distinction between cognitive and emotional regulative systems (Velichkovsky, 2006).

These similarities and contrasts between Eastern European and Western theories of regulatory control have counterparts in relation to models of individual differences. For example, Rusalov's model of personality is based on several properties of Anokhin's functional systems, arriving at a dimensional structure distinct from Western personality models (although there may be correspondences at an empirical level). The basis for Soroko's three self-regulation types in different organizations of functional nuclei is quite different from any Western theory of individual differences in self-regulation. Several post-Soviet researchers have provided distinctive theoretical perspectives on individual difference constructs prominent in Western accounts, including cognitive style (Kholodnaya, 1997, 2002). An important idea is that individual difference factors may relate to different levels within a vertical control hierarchy. For example, theorists including Soroko, Razoumnikova, and Knyazev relate individual differences to the phylogenetic structuring of the brain into brainstem, limbic, and corticothalamic circuits, and to the interactions between these levels of control. An important methodological facet of this research is the use of the EEG to differentiate different modes of control, as exemplified by the work of the three researchers just mentioned. Empirical studies using EEG measures of spectral power density and coherence have added to understanding of individual differences in personality, intelligence and self-regulation, as well as the interrelationships of different domains of individual differences (e.g., personality and ability).

In conclusion, post-Soviet psychology has tended to include executive control within broader models of self-regulation. It is emphasized that regulation is still a central problem in differential, cognitive, and emotional psychophysiology. The process of integrating different branches of psychology, and integrating the Western and Eastern traditions, will bring productive results to clarify the most difficult questions in understanding individual differences in regulation processes. This review paper aimed to give a brief introduction to Soviet/post-Soviet traditions in differential psychophysiology in order to improve the integration process.

Acknowledgments I would like to thank Professor Gerald Matthews, who was my supervisor during my JFDP (Junior Faculty Development Program) Fellowship, for encouraging me to write this paper, and for his useful comments throughout its preparation. JFDP is a United States Government Program sponsored by the Bureau of Educational and Cultural Affairs of the U.S. Department of State and administered by American Councils for International Education. I am also grateful to Russell H. Ragsdale for his help.

References

Aftanas, L. I., Reva, N. V., Varlamov, A. A., Pavlov, S. V., & Makhnev, V. P. (2004). Analysis of evoked EEG synchronization and desynchronization in conditions of emotional activation in humans: temporal and topographic characteristics. *Neuroscience and Behavioral Physiology, 34*(8), 859–867.

Aftanas, L. I., Varlamov, A. A., Pavlov, S. V., Makhney, V. P., & Reva, N. V. (2001). Affective picture processing: Event-related synchronization within individuality defined human theta band is modulates by valence dimension. *Neuroscience Letter, 303*(2), 115–118.

Ahutina, T. V., Yablokova, L. V., & Polonskaya, N. N. (2000). Neiropsihologicheskii analiz individual'nyh razlichii u detei [Neuropsychological analyses of individual differences in children: Parameters of estimation]. In E. D. Khomskaya & V. A. Moskvina (Eds.), *Neiropsihologiya i Psihofiziologiya Individual'nyh Razlichii [Neuropsychology and psychophysiology of individual differences]* (pp. 132–152). Moscow-Orenburg: OOIPKRO.

Aleksandrov, U. I., & Sams, M. E. (2005). Emotion and consciousness: Ends of a continuum. *Cognitive Brain Research, 25*(2), 387–405.

Ananiev, B. G. (1969). Chelovek kak predmet poznania [Man as a Subject of Study]. Leningrad.

Anokhin, P. K. (1968). Phynkcionalnaya systema, kak metodologicheskii princip biologicheskogo i physiologicheskogo issledovaniya. [Functional system as the methodological principle of biological and physiological research]. In book "Sistemnaya organizacia phisiological function". [Systematical organization of the physiological function].

Anokhin, P. K. (1974). The functional system as a basis of the physiological architecture of the behavioural act. In P. K. Anokhin (Ed.), *Biology and neurophysiology of the conditioned reflex and its role in adaptive behaviour* (pp. 190–254). New York: Pergamon Press.

Anokhin, P. K. (1975). *Ocherki po Phisiologii Functionalnih System [The study of physiology of functional system]*. Moscow: Medicina.

Anokhin, P. K. (1984). Idei e facti v razrabotke teorii functionlnih system [The ideas and facts in functional system theory development]. *Psihologicheskii Jurnal, 5*(2), 107–118.

Anokhin, A. P., Lutzenberger, W., & Birbaumer, N. (1999). Spatiotemporal organization of brain dynamics and intelligence: An EEG study in adolescents. *International Journal of Psychophysiology, 33*(3), 259–273.

Bekhtereva, N. P. (1978). *The neurophysiological aspects of human mental activity* (2nd ed.). New York: Oxford University Press. Revised and Completed.

Bekhtereva, N. P. (2004). O nauchnoi shkole [On the Scientific School]. *Fiziologiya Cheloveka, 30*(4), 5–18.

Bekhtereva, N. P. (2007). *Magya Mozga i Labirinti Jizni [Brain magic and life labyrinths]*. Moscow: ACT.

Bekhtereva, N. P., & Gretchin, V. B. (1968). Physiological foundation of mental activity. *International Review of Neurobiology, 11*, 239–246.

Bekhtereva, N. P., Kropotov, J. D., Ponomarev, V. A., & Etlinger, S. C. (1990). In search of cerebral error detectors. *International Journal of Psychophysiology, 8*, 261–273.

Bekhtereva, N. P., & Nagornova, Z. V. (2007). Dinamica kogerentnosti EEG pri vipolnenii zadanii na neverbalnyu (obraznyu) creativnost [Changes in EEG Coherence during Tests for Nonverbal (Figurative) Creativity]. *Fiziologiya Cheloveka, 33*(5), 5–13.

Bekhtereva, N. P., Danko, S. G., Starchenko, M. G., Pakhomov, S. V., & Medvedev, S. V. (2001). Issledovanie mozgovoi organizacii tvorchestva. Soobshenie III. Aktivacia mozga po dannim analiza lokalnogo mozgovogo krovotoka e EEG [Study of the Brain Organization of Creativity: III. Brain Activation Assessed by the Local Cerebral Blood Flow and EEG]. Fiziologiya Cheloveka, 27(4), 6–14.

Bernstein, N. B. (1967). *The coordination and regulation of movements*. Oxford, England: Pergamon Press.

Bezrukikh, M. M., & Khryanin, A. V. (2003). Osobennosti functionalnoi organizacii mozga y pravorukih e levorukih detei 6-7 let pri vipolnenii zritelno-prostranstvennih zadanii raznogo yrovnya slojnosti. SoobshenieI. Sravnitelnii analiz parametrov EEG pri zritelno-prostranstvennoi deatelnosti nizkogo yrovnya slojnosti [Features of the Brain Functional Organization in Right- and Left-handed 6- to 7-Year-Old Children during Visuospatial Performance of Different Complexity: I. Comparative Analysis of EEG Parameters during Simple Visuospatial Performance]. *Fiziologiya Cheloveka, 29*(3), 33–40.

Birukov, S. D. (2001). Psihologiya individualnih razlichii [Psychology of individual differences]. *Psyhologiya, Piter*.

Bodunov, M. V. (1985). Sootnoshenie nestacionarnih svoistv EEG s vremennime characteristikami povedenia cheloveka [The corresponding of unstationary properties of EEG with temporal characteristics of human behaviour]. *Psikhologicheskii Zhurnal, 6*(6), 125–133.

Bogomolova, I. V., & Farber, D. A. (1995). Electrophysiologichekii analiz zritelnoi perceptivnoi pamyati. Soobschnie 1 [Electrophysiologic analysis of the visual perceptive memory. Report1]. *Fiziologiya Cheloveka, 21*(4), 13–22.

Boiko, E. I. (1976). Mechanizmi umstvennoi deyatelnosti [Mechanisms of mental activity], Moscow: Pedagogika.

Brebner, J., & Stough, C. (1993). The relationship between the structure of temperament and extraversion and neuroticism. *Personality and Individual Differences, 14*(4), 623–626.

Byasheva, Z. G., & Shvecova, E. V. (1993). Informacionnii podhod k analizy vozrastnoi dinamici EEG malchikov e podrostkov 7–18 let pri reshenii v yme arifmeticheskih zadach [The informational approach to EEG analyses of age specific dynamics in boys 7–18 years old during arithmetic tasks]. *Fiziologiya Cheloveka, 19*(5), 5–11.

Biyasheva, Z. G. (1998). EEG-issledovanie formirovaniya verbalnoi funkcii v ontogeneze shkolnikiv 17-18 let. [EEG study of the verbal function ontogenetic development in students 17-18 years old]. *Izvestiya MN-AN RK*, Biological series, *1*, 48–52.

Chernigovskaya, T. V. (2007). The mirror brain, concepts, and language: The price for anthropogenesis. *Neuroscience and Behavioural Physiology, 37*(3), 293–302.

Chernigovskaya, T. V., Gavrilova, T. A., Voinov, A. V., & Strelnikov, K. N. (2005). Sensomotornii i cognitivnii lateralnii profil [Sensorimotor and cognitive laterality profiles]. *Fiziologiya Cheloveka, 31*(2), 24–33.

Corr, Ph J, & Perkins, A. M. (2006). The role of theory in the psychophysiology of personality: From Ivan Pavlov to Jeffrey Gray. *International Journal of Psychophysiology, 62*(3), 367–376.

Danilova, N. N. (1982). The activation dynamics in the learning process and its reflection. In R. Sinz & M. R. Rosenzweig (Eds.), *Psychophysiology* (pp. 407–412). Jena (GDR) and Amsterdam (Netherlands): VEB Gustav Fischer Verlag and Elsevier Biomedial Press.

Danilova, N. N., Bikov, N. B., Pirogov, Y. A., & Sokolov, E. N. (2005). Issledovanie chastotnoi specifichnosti oscillyatorov gamma-ritma metodami dipolnogo analiza e anatomicheskoi magnitno-resonansnoi tomographii [The study of the gamma rhythms frequency specificity by dipoles analyses and anatomical MRT]. *Biomedicinskie Tehnologii e Radioelectronika, 4–5*, 89–97.

Danko, S. G. (2006). Ob otrajenii razlichnih aspectov aktivacii mozga v electroencephalogramme: Chto pokazivaet kolichesvennaya characteristica sostoyanii pokoya s otkritimi i zakritimi glazami [The Reflection of Different Aspects of Brain Activation in the Electroencephalogram: Quantitative Electroencephalography of the States of Rest with the Eyes Open and Closed]. *Fiziologiya Cheloveka, 32*(4), 5–17.

Danko, S. G., Bekhtereva, N. P., Kachalova, L. M., Shemyakina, N. V., & Antonova, L. V. (2003). Electrophisiologicheskie correlyati mislennogog perejivaniya emotionalnih lichnih i scenicheskih situacii. Report II. Characteristiki prostanstvennoi sinhronizacii [Electroencephalographic correlates of mental performance of emotional autobiographic and scenic situations: II. Characteristics of spatial synchronization]. *Fiziologiya Cheloveka, 29*(6) 31–40.

Danko, S. G., Bekhtereva, N. P., Kachalova, L. M., Shemyakina, N. V., & Startchenko, M. G. (2005). Electrophisiological correlyati sostoyanii mozga pri verbalnom obuchenii. Soobshenie: II. Characteristiki prostanstvennoi sinhronizaii EEG [Electroencephalographic correlates of brain states during verbal learning: II. Characteristics of EEG spatial synchronization]. *Fiziologiya Cheloveka, 31*(6), 5–12.

Druzhinin, V. N. (2001). *Cognitivnie sposobnosti. Structure. Diagnostika. Razvitie* [Cognitive abilities. Structure. Diagnostics. Development]. Moscow, St. Peterburg: Imaton-M.

Dubrovinskaya, N. V., & Farber, D. A. (1993). Emocii e ih rol v kognitivnih processah na raznih etapah ontogeneza [Emotion and role in cognitive processes on different levels of ontogenesis]. *Fiziologiya Cheloveka, 19*(3), 16.

Dubrovinskaya, N. V., & Machinskaya, R. I. (2002). Reactivnost θ i α diapasonov EEG pri proizvolnom vnimanii u detei mladshego shkolnogo vozrasta [Reactivity of and EEG Frequency Bands in Voluntary Attention in Junior Schoolchildren]. *Fiziologiya Cheloveka, 28*(5), 15–20.

Dvorayashkina, M. D. (1969). Opit komplexnogo e psyhophysiologicheskogo isychenia structuri lichnosti [Complex and psychophysiological study of personality structure]. In B. G. Ananiev, *Chelovek e obshestvo* (pp. 138–144). St. Petersburg: Leningrad State University, IV.

Farber, D. A., Beteleva, T. G., & Ignat'eva, I. S. (2004). Fynctionalnaya organizacia mozga v processe realizacii rabochei pamyati [Functional organization of the brain during the operation of working memory]. *Fiziologiya Cheloveka, 30*(2), 5–12.

Farber, D. A., Dubrovinskaya, N. V., Knyazeva, M. G., & Machinskaya, R. I. (1994). Formirovanie bipolusharnih strategii kognitivnoi deatelnosti v ontogeneze [The bypolar strategy of cognitive activity in ontogenesis]. *Uspehi Phisiologicheskih Nauk, 25*, 99.

Golubeva, E. A. (1980). *Individualnie osobennosti pamyati cheloveka [Individual peculiarities of human memory]*. Moscow: Pedagogika.

Golubeva, E. A. (1989). Differencialnii podhod k sposobnostiam i sklonnostiam [Differential approach to abilities and gifts]. *Psikhologicheskii Zhurnal, 10*(4), 75–87.

Golubeva, E. A. (2005). Sposobnosti. Lichnost. Individualnost. [The abilities. Personality. Individuality], Dubna: Phenix.

Gorev, A. S. (2007). Vliyanie proizvolnoi regulaycii functionalnogo sostoaynia na organizaciuy korkovih processov pri mnesticheskoi deaytelnosti u shkolnokov 9–10 let [Effects of voluntary control of the functional state on the organization of cortical processes during mnemonic activity in schoolchildren aged nine to ten years]. *Fiziologiya Cheloveka, 33*(2), 35–41.

Gorunova, N. B., & Druzhinin, V. N. (2001). Operacionnie desriptori kognitivnogo resursa e productivnoste resheniaya testovih zadach e zadach-golovolomok [The operational descriptors of the cognitive resource and productivity of test solving tasks and puzzles solving tasks]. *Psikhologicheskii Zhurnal, 4*, 21–29.

Guseva, E. P. (1997). Psihophisiologicheskoe izuchenie myzikalnih sposobnostei [Psychophysiological study of musical abilities]. In E. A. Golubeva (Ed.), *Sposobnosti: k 100-letiu so dnya rojdenia B.M. Teplova* (pp. 231–258). Dubna: Phenix.

Guseva, E. P., & Levochkina, I. A. (1989). Psihophisiologicheskie osobennosti shkolnikov s virazhennimi matematicheskimi e musicalnimi sposobnostyami [Psychophysiological peculiarities in schoolchildren with expressed mathematical and musical abilities]. The conference proceeding *Defectologia. Psihofiziologia. Differencialnaya psyhofiziologia*. Moscow, 90–91.

Guseva, E. P., & Shlyahta, N. F. (1974). Nekotorie osobennosti pokazatelei bioelectricheskoi activnosti mozga u podrostkov [The peculiarities of bioelectrical brain activity in adolescents]. In *Problemi Differencialnoi Psyhophisiologi* (pp. 199–214). Moscow, Nauka

Ilin, E. P. (2004). *Psihologia Individualnih Razlichii* [Psychology of individual differences]. Saint-Petersburg, Piter.

Ivanov-Smolensky, A. G. (1952). *Ocherki Patofiziologii Visshei Nervnoi Deyatelnosti [The studies of psychophysiology of higher nervous activity]*. Moscow: Medgiz.

Izumova, S. A. (1993). Individualno-tipicheskie osobennosti shkolnikov s literaturnimi e matematicheskimi sposobnostyami [Individual-typological peculiarities in pupils with literature and mathematical abilities]. *Psikhologicheskii Zhurnal, 14*, 137–146.

Izumova, S. A. (1995). *Priroda Mnemicheskih Sposobnostei e Differenciacia Obuchenia [The nature of mnemic abilities and differential learning]*. Moscow, Nauka.

Kabardov, M. K. (1989). Communicaivno-rechevie i cognitivno-lingisticheskie sposobnosti [Communicative-speech and cognitive-linguistic abilities]. In E.A. Golubeva (Ed.), Sposobnosti i sklonnosti. 103–128.

Kabardov, M. K. (2004). K istorii stanovlenia differencialnoi psyhophisiologii v psihologicheskom institute [The history of differential psychophysiology in Psychological Institute]. *Voprosi Psihologii, 2*, 81–92.

Kabardov, M. K., & Arcishevskaya, E. V. (1997). Tipologia yazikovih sposobnostei [Typology of language abilities]. In *Sposobnosti. K 100-letiu so dnay rojdenia B.M. Teplova [The abilities. B.M. Teplov's 100-anniversary]* (pp. 259–288). Dubna: Phenix.

Kabardov, M. K., & Matova, M. A. (1988). Mejpolusharnaya assimetria e vrbalnie e neverbalnie komponenti poznavaelnih sposobnostei [Interhemispheric asymmetry and verbal and nonverbal components of cognitive abilities in pupils]. *Voprosi Psihologii, 6*, 106–115.

Kaiser, J., & Lutzenberger, W. (2003). Induced gamma-band activity and human brain function. *Neuroscientist, 9*(6), 475–484.

Kholodnaya, M. A. (1997). *Psyhologia Intellecta: Paradoxi Issledovania [Psychology of intelligence: Research paradoxes]*. Moscow: Tomsk.

Kholodnaya, M. A. (2002). Osnovnie napravlenia izuchenia psihologii sposobnostei v institute psihologii RAN [The main directions of the studies in psychology of the abilities at the Institute of Psychology of Russian Academy of Sciences]. *Psikhologicheskii Zhurnal, 23*(3), 13–22.

Kholodnaya, M. A. (2007). Theoria intellecta B.G. Ananieva: retrospectivnii i perspectivnii aspecti. [B.G. Ananiev's theory of intelligence: retrospective and perspective aspects]. *Psikhologicheskii zhurnal, 28*(5), 49–60.

Kholodnaya, M. A., & Kostrikina, I. S. (2002). Osobennosti cognitivnih stilei "impulsivnost/reflectivnost" i "rigidnost/gibkost poznavatelnogo contrlay" u lic s visokimi i sverhporogovimi znacheniyami IQ [Peculiarities of "impulsivity/reflectivity" and "rigidity/flexibility of cognitive control" styles in subjects with high and exceptionally high IQ score]. *Psikhologicheskii Zhurnal, 23*(6), 72–82.

Kiroi, V. N. (1987). Prostranstvenno-vremennaya organizacia electricheskoi activnosti mozga cheloveka v sostoyanii spokoinogo bodrstvovaniya i pri reshenii mislitelnih zadach [The spatial-temporal organization of human brain electrical activity in baseline level and under mental task solving]. *Zhurnal Vysshiei Nervnoi Deyatel'nosti im I. P. Pavlova, 37*(6), 1025.

Kiroi, V. N., Mamin, R. A., & Khachaturyan, E. V. (1988). Issledovanie prostranstvennoi sinhronizacii korkovih pri intelletualnom napryajenii [The study of spatial synchronization of cortical potentials under intellectual tension]. *Psikhologicheskii Zhurnal, 9*(1), 75–83.

Kiroi, V. N., & Petrosova, T. A. (1983). Prostranstvennaya organizacia biopotencialov neocortexa cheloveka i ee informacionnii analis [The spatial organization of human neocortex biopotentials and its informational analyses]. *Psikhologicheskii Zhurnal, 4*(5), 142–147.

Knyazev, G. G. (2006). EEG correlates of personality types. *The Netherlands Journal of Psychology, 62*(2), 82–90.

Knyazev, G. G., & Slobodskaya, H. R. (2003). Personality trait of behavioral inhibition is associated with oscillatory systems reciprocal relationships. *International Journal of Psychophysiology, 48*, 247–261.

Knyazev, G. G., & Slobodskaya, H. R. (2006). Personality types and behavioural activation and inhibition in adolescents. *Personality and Individual Differences, 41*(8), 1385–1395.

Konopkin, O. A. (1995). Psihicheskaya samoreguliacia proizvolnoi aktivnosti cheloveka (structurno–functionalnii aspect) [Psychological selfregulation of human voluntary activity (structural–functional aspects)]. *Voprosi Psihologii, 1*, 5–12.

Krupnov, A. I. (1984). Psihologicheskie problemi issledovaniya aktivnosti cheloveka. [Psychological problems of the human activity research]. *Voprosi Psihologii, 3,* 25–32.

Kustubayeva, A. M., Muitunova, A., & Turebekov, B. (2008). Temperament e tipi plastichnosti [The temperament and types of plasticity]. *Poisk, 1,* 61–67.

Lebedev, A. N. (1985). Edinici pamyati I svyazannie s nimi osobennosti rechi [Memory units and related with them speech peculiarities]. In T. N. Ushakova (Ed.), *Psihophisiologicheskie i Psihologicheskie Issledovaniaya Rechi [Psychological and psychophysiological studies of speech]* (pp. 26–44). Moscow: Nauka.

Lebedev, A. N. (1997). Constanta M. N. Livanova v kolichestvennom opisanii psyhologicheskih yavlenii [M. N. Livanov's constant in quantitative description of psychological events]. *Psikhologicheskii Zhurnal, 6,* 96–105.

Lebedev, A. N. (2000). The way from Weber's constant to laws of cognitive psychology. *Synergie, Syntropie, Nichtlineare Systeme. Verlag im Wissenschaftzentrum, 6,* 323–344

Lebedev, A. N. (2001). The oscillatory mechanisms of memory. *Cognitive Processing, 2,* 57–66.

Lebedev, A. N. (2002). Cognitivnaya psyhophisiologia na rubeje stoletii [Cognitive psychophysiology at the turn of the century]. *Psikhologicheskii Zhurnal, 23*(1), 93–100.

Lebedev, A. N., Artemenko, O. I., & Belehov, Y. N. (1997). Diagnostika intellektualnoi odarennosti po electroencephalogramme [The diagnostic of intellectual gifts by electroencephalogram]. *Psyhologichskoe Obozrenie, 1*(4), 34–38.

Lebedev, A. N., & Luckii, V. A. (1972). Raschet zakonomernostei zritelnogo vospriyatiay po chastotnim characeritikam electroencephalogrammi [The calculation of visual perception law by characteristics of electroencephalogram]. *Ergonomica, 4,* 95–134.

Lebedev, A. N., Mishkin, I. Y., & Bovin, B. G. (2002). Ocenka psihologicheskih parametov lichnosti po elctroencephalogramme [Estimation of psychological parameters of personality by electroencephalogram]. *Psikhologicheskii Zhurnal, 23*(3), 96–104.

Leites, N. S. (1997). *Vozrastnaya Odarennost e Individualnie Razlichia [Age endowments and individual differences].* Moscow: Nauka.

Leites, N. S. (2003). O priznakah detskoi odarennosti [Children endowments]. *Voprosi Psihologii, 4,* 13–19.

Libin, A. (2006). *Differencialnaya Psyhologia: Na Peresechenii Rossiskih, Europeiskih, e Americanskih Tradicii [Differential psychology on the Crossroad of European, Russian and American Traditions].* Moscow: Eksmo.

Livanov, M. N. (1982). Electroencephalogramma e mishlenie [Electroencephalogram and thinking]. *Psikhologicheskii Zhurnal, 3*(2), 127–137.

Livanov, M. N., & Sviderskaya, N. E. (1984). Psihologicheskie aspecti phenomena prostranstvennoi sinhronizacii potencialov [Psychological aspects of spatial synchronization phenomena]. *Psikhologicheskii Zhurnal, 5*(5), 71–83.

Luria, A. R. (1966). *Higher cortical functions in man.* New York: Basic Books.

Luria, A. R. (1968). *Malenkaya Knizhka o Bjlshoi Pamyati [Small Book about Big Memory].* Moscow: Moscow State University (MGU).

Luria, A. R. (1970). *Mozg Cheloveka i Psihicheskie Processi [Human brain and mental processes].* Moscow: Pedagogika.

Luria, A. R. (1974). *Ob Istoricheskom Razvitii Poznavatelnih Processov [On Historic Development of cognitive Processes].* Moscow: Moscow State University (MGU).

Markina, A. V., Malceva, I. V., & Lebedev, A. N. (1995). Svyaz parametrov alfa-ritma s obiemom kratkovremennoi pamyati [The relation of alpha rhythms parameters with short-term memory volume]. *Psikhologicheskii Zhurnal, 2,* 128–132.

Markina, A. V., Pashina, A Kh, & Rumanova, N. B. (2000). Svyaz ritmov electroencephalogrammi s cognitivno-lichnostnimi osobennostyami cheloveka [The relation of the electroencephalograms rhythms with cognitive-personal human peculiarities]. *Psikhologicheskii Zhurnal, 5,* 48–55.

Matushkin, A. M. (2003). *Mishlenie, Obychenie, Tvorchestvo [Thinking, learning, and creativity].* Voronezh: NPO Modek.

Merlin, V. S. (1986). *Ocherk Integralnogo Issledovaniay Individualnosti [Studies of integral research of individuality].* Moscow: Pedagogika.

Morosanova, V. I. (2002). Lichnostnie aspecti samoregulyacii proizvolnoi aktivnosti cheloveka [Personal aspects of self-regulation human voluntary activity]. *Psikhologicheskii Zhurnal, 23*(6), 5–17.

Munk, M. H. J. (2001). Role of gamma oscillations for information processing and memory formation in the neocortex. In C. Holscher (Ed.), *Neuronal mechanisms of memory formation* (pp. 167–191). Cambridge: Cambridge University Press

Nagornova, Z. V. (2007). Dinamica moshnosti EEG pri vipolnenii zadanii na neverbalnuy (obraznuy) kreativnost [Changes in the EEG Power during Tests for Nonverbal (Figurative) Creativity]. *Fiziologiya Cheloveka, 33*(3), 26–34.

Nebilitcyn, V. D. (1972). *Fundamental properties of the human nervous system* (G. L. Mangan, Trans.). New York: Plenum.

Nebilitcyn, V. D. (1976). *Psyhophysiologicheskie Issledovaniay Individualnih Razlichii [Psychophysiological research of individual differences]*. Moscow: Nauka.

Palei, I. M. (1971). K psihophisiologicheskomy issledovaniu structuri individualno-tipologicheskih osobennostei cheloveka v svazi s "iformacionno-energeticheskimi sootnosheniyami v nervno-psihicheskoi deatelnosti" [Psychophisiological investigation of structure of human individual-typological peculiarities in relation with "informational-energetic relationships in nervous-psychic activity"]. In A. S. Pashkova (Ed.), *Chelovek e obshestvo* (pp. 150–154). St. Petersburg: Leningrad State University (LGU).

Pavlov, I. P. (1951). *Polnoe Sobranie Sochinenii [Collected works]*. Moscow: Academia Nauk SSSR.

Pechenkov, V. V. (1989). Problema sootnosheniya obshih i specialno chelovecheskih tipov visshei nervnoi deyatelnosti i ih psihologicheskih proyavlenii [The problem of the relationship of common and specific types of the high nervous system activity and their psychological meaning] In book Sposbnosti i sklonnosti: komplexnie issledovaniya [Abilities and gifts: complex research]. Moscow.

Razoumnikova, O. M. (2000). Functional organization of different brain areas during convergent and divergent thinking: An EEG investigation. *Cognitive Brain Research, 10*(1–2), 11–18.

Razoumnikova, O. M. (2007). Functionalnoe znachenie biopotencialov α_2-diapasona pri konvergentnom i divergentnom verbalnom mishlenii [The functional significance of α_2 frequency range for convergent and divergent verbal thinking]. *Fiziologiya Cheloveka, 33*(2), 23–34.

Razoumnikova, O. M. (2003). Interaction of personality and intelligence factors in cortex activity modulation. *Personality and Individual Differences, 35*, 135–162.

Ribalko, E. F., Lukomskaia, S. A., & Svyatogor, I. A. (1985). Svyaz pokazatelei vnimania e electrophisiologicheskih characterisitic mozga [The relation of attentions parameters and electrophysiological characteristics of brain]. *Psikhologicheskii Zhurnal, 6*(6), 135–141.

Rusalov, V. M. (1979). *Biologicheskie Osnovi Individualno-Psihologicheskih Razlichii [Biological basis of individual psychological differences]*. Moscow: Nauka.

Rusalov, V. M. (1989). Object-related and communicative aspects of human temperament: A new questionnaire of the structure of temperament. *Personality and Individual Differences, 10*(8), 817–827.

Rusalova, M. N., & Kostunina, M. B. (1999). Chastotno-amplitudnaya characteristiki levogo e pravogo polushariipri mislennom vosproizvedenii emotionalno okrashennih obrazov [Frequency and Amplitude Characteristics of the Left and Right Hemispheres in Subjects Experiencing Imaginary Emotions]. *Fiziologiya Cheloveka, 25*(5), 50.

Safonceva, S. V., & Voronin, A. N. (2000). Vliyanie extrversii-introversii na vzaimosvyaz intellecta i cretivnosti [The influence of extroversion-introversion on relationship of intellect and creativity]. *Psikhologicheskii Zhurnal, 5*, 56–64.

Sergienko, E. A. (2006). *Rannee Kognitivnoe Razvitie. Novii Vzglyad [Early cognitive development. New approach]*. Moscow: Institute Psychologii RAN

Sergienko, E. A. (2007). Stanovlenie kontrolya povedenia kak proyavlenie individualnosti e ego rol v processe adaptacii [The behaviour control as individuality and its role in adjustment]. In L. G. Dikaya & A. L. M. Jouravlev (Eds.), *Psihologia Adaptacii e Socialnaya Sreda: Sovremennie Podhodi, Problemi, Perspectivi. Part 3. Lichnostnie Determinanti Adaptacii* (pp. 251–276). Moscow: Institute Psychologii RAN.

Setchenov, I. M. (1866, 2007). *Reflexi Golovnogo Mozga [Reflexes of the brain]*. A. Golovachev's typography.

Shadrikov, V. D. (1997). *Sposobnosti Cheloveka [Human abilities]*. Voronej: NPO Modek.

Smekal, V. (1995). Psychology in East Europe. Plenary paper at First British and East European Psychology Group Conference, Banska Bystrica, Slovakia. http://www.beepg.org.uk>Books>Banks Bystrica

Sokolov, E. N. (1969). *Mekhanizmi Pamyati 2-d, Seriya: Iz nasledyia mirovoi psihologii [Series: From the heritage of world psychology. [Mechanizms of memory]*. Moscow: Moscow State University (MGU).

Sokolov, E. N. (1977). Brain functions: Neuronal mechanisms of learning and memory. *Annual Review of Psychology, 28*, 85–112.

Sokolov, E. N. (1994). Vector coding in neuronal nets: Color vision Origins. In K. H. Pribram (Ed.), *Brain and self organization* (pp. 463–473). Hillsdale: Lawrence Erlbaum Associates.

Soroko, S. I., Bekshaev, S. S., & Sidorov, Y. A. (1990). *Osnovnie Tipi Mekhanizmov Samoregulaycii Mozga [The principal types of brain selfregulation mechanisms]*. Leningrad, Nauka.

Soroko, S. I., Kurmashev, R. A., & Dzhunusova, G. S. (2002). Rearrangements of the algorithms of interaction between wave components of EEGs in subjects with different mechanisms of brain self-regulation during adaptation to high altitudes. *Fiziologiya Cheloveka, 28*(6), 647–656.

Teplov, B. M. (1955a). Uchenie o tipah visshei nervnoi deyatelnosti e psyhologya [The study of the Higher Nervous system activity and psychology]. *Voprosi Psyhologii, 1*, 36–41.

Teplov, B. M. (1955b). O ponyatiyah slabosti i inertnosti nervnoi sistemi [About the weakness and inertness of nervous system]. *Voprosi psihologii, 6*, 3–15.

Teplov, B. M. (2003). *Psyhologia i psyhophysiologia individualnih razlichii: izbrannie psyhologicheskie trudi* [Psychology and psychophysiology of individual differences: selected psychological works]. Under red. M.G. Yaroshevskogo. Voronej: NPO Modek.

Tolegenova, A., Jakupov, S., Kustubayeva, A., Matthews, G., & Bakieva, D. (2008). EEG study of emotion-regulation. Second Biennial Symposium on Personality and Social Psychology, Warsaw, Poland.

Velichkovsky, B. M. (2006). *Kognitivnaya Nauka. Osnovi Psihologii Poznania* [Cognitive Science: Foundations of Epistemic Psychology]. Moscow: Smisl Academia.

Volf, N. V., & Razoumnikova, O. M. (2004). Polovie razlichiaya polusharnih prostranstvenno-vremennih patternov EEG pri vosproizvedenii verbalnoi informacii [Gender Differences in Hemispheric Spatiotemporal EEG Patterns upon Reproduction of Verbal Information]. *Fiziologiya Cheloveka, 30*(3), 27–34.

Voronin, A. N., & Gabrielyan, N. (1999). Intellect kak moderator proyavleniya lichostnih osobennostei v situaciayh gruppovogo vzaimodeistviya [Intelligence as modertor of personal pecularities in situation of interactions in the group]. In *Intellect i tvorchestv [Intelligence and creativity]* (pp. 49–59). Moscow: Institute Psychologii RAN.

Chapter 10
Individual Differences in Cognition from a Neurophysiological Perspective: The Commentaries

Todd S. Braver, Tal Yarkoni, Aleksandra Gruszka, Adam Hampshire,
Adrian M. Owen, Norbert Jaušovec, Ksenija Jaušovec,
Almira Kustubayeva, Aljoscha C. Neubauer, and Andreas Fink

1. Does the concept of general arousal have a central place in modern neuroscience theory?

Todd Braver and Tal Yarkoni

We think this is an open empirical question. A good analogy is the concept of general intelligence, which has been the focus of many recent neuroscience studies. It is ultimately an empirical question as to whether intelligence is best described as a single monolithic construct or in terms of narrower lower-order abilities (e.g., visuospatial ability, verbal intelligence, etc.). Some studies have found important brain structural and functional correlates of general intelligence, when treated as a monolithic construct (e.g., Thompson). However, other work has led potential to refinement or revision of the construct (e.g., placing focus on lower-level processes, such as interference control). The concept of arousal has received less attention in cognitive neuroscience research, but the situation may nevertheless be similar. Is there a monolithic arousal system in the brain? Perhaps not, just as few people would argue that there is a single "intelligence system"; on the other hand, we suspect that when arousal is operationalized in relatively general ways – e.g., in terms of individuals' propensity to respond to emotional stimuli, their basal activity level, etc. – there will be identifiable neural correlates. Moreover, it may turn out that the construct of general arousal has little utility when compared to narrower conceptions of arousal, much as some would argue that notions of general intelligence are ill-founded. In this regard, the recent work on the locus coeruleus/norepinephrine (LC–NE) system is instructive (Aston-Jones & Cohen, 2005). Although the LC–NE system has long been linked to arousal, current theorizing suggests a more nuanced functional account that can still explain relevant arousal phenomena (i.e., the Yerkes-Dodson U-shaped relationship to performance), but also provides a narrower and more constrained interpretation of relevant functional mechanisms (e.g., attentional effects of tonic vs. phasic LC–NE activity). Thus, like much of cognitive neuroscience research, it is important not only to search for neural correlates of classic psychological constructs, but also to utilize new data to revise, refine and reshape such constructs.

Aleksandra Gruszka, Adam Hampshire and Adrian M. Owen

At the moment, the answer to this question is "No". Currently, the concept of "general arousal" – as a subject of an ongoing psychological debate whether it is a valid construct at all – does not play an important role in neuroscience, unless more specific uses of the term arousal (i.e., as wakefulness in a context of a role of noradrenergic locus coeruleus in circadian regulation of arousal or as vigilance in a context of attentional performance) are considered. In a way, the status of "general arousal" is similar to the status of "attentional resources". Both these terms are very broad and ill-defined and have been extensively criticized. At the same time, both constructs are surprisingly vivacious as they are often used to account for a wide variety of behavioral observations in the absence of more suitable hypothetical constructs. Perhaps a less obvious yet exciting possibility would be to use behavior–brain based associations to gain empirical constraints that help to parse "general arousal" into more valid psychological constructs to account for individual differences in a set of dispositions described jointly as "general arousal". This promise, however, is still an open question.

Norbert Jaušovec and Ksenija Jaušovec

No, but this is just an opinion, and I have no arguments to support or refute the answer. It is mainly based on my recall of articles I read when preparing my research.

Almira Kustubayeva

Since G. Moruzzi and H.W. Magoun discovered the "arousal reaction", the concept of general arousal has influenced understanding of neurophysiological mechanisms of behavior. Arousal has been represented in different theories such as extraversion theory, optimal arousal theory of motivation, cognitive arousal theory of emotion, etc. A vast number of neurophysiological studies have provided mixed evidence, sometimes supporting and sometimes contradicting the various theories. To what extent the arousal concept has a central place in modern neuroscience is an arguable question. Modern neuroscience has been basically oriented to assume localization of cognitive functions in specific brain areas ever since Broca and others found relationships between specific brain areas and cognitive functions such as speech, movement, and other functions. So far, we have a large number of neuroimaging studies that have shown activation of different brain networks under different cognitive tasks performed in experimentally controlled conditions. Nevertheless, generalization vs. localization remains a main issue in cognitive neuroscience. All higher cortical functions such as working memory, learning, and problem solving are involved in multiple areas of brain activity. Luria's hierarchical systems approach has been valuable for exploring basic principles of cognitive function (Kustubayeva, this volume). The first bloc, which includes the brainstem, reticular formation, mediobasal cortex and limbic system, regulates nonspecific activation and modulates appropriate tonus of normal work conditions for higher cortical areas. In my opinion, the operation of this bloc supports the significance and topicality of arousal theory. Hierarchical models of cognition have inspired the modern neuroscience of complex brain mechanisms. Basar's theory of whole-brain-work explains oscillatory dynamics of the brain during cognitive function, which supports an idea about "constant reciprocal activation within the subprocesses of attention, perception, learning, and remembering" (APLR alliance; Basar, 2006). Friston's "Free energy theory" (Friston & Stephan, 2007) concerns brain functions as a part of an entire system.

In terms of physiological understanding, arousal is related to the regulation of function, and regulation of balance of excitatory and inhibitory processes. In particular, Pavlov's idea of higher nervous system properties comes from the study of digestive regulation. Inhibitory processes shape excitation of specific brain areas during regulation of the nervous system. Indeed, the concept of inhibitory control is one of the central ones in understanding mechanisms of executive control, and development of self-regulation (Fernandez-Duque, Baird, & Posner, 2000).

2. What advances in methods may be critical for future individual differences research?

Todd S. Braver and Tal Yarkoni

As we note in our chapter, the current Achilles heel of individual differences research, at least in the cognitive neuroscience literature, is insufficient power due to the use of small sample sizes. For researchers who rely primarily on psychophysiological techniques that are (relatively) cost-effective, there is a simple solution that requires no methodological advances: collect more data! But fMRI and PET scanners have considerable maintenance and operating costs, and it is unlikely that the cost of using these techniques will fall dramatically any time soon. As such, we would suggest that a stronger push is needed toward the development of novel multivariate statistical techniques that may indirectly compensate for insufficient power, e.g., by increasing measurement reliability, decreasing the number of statistical comparisons conducted, and so on. Ultimately, of course, we want what everyone else wants: a neuroimaging technique that has the spatial resolution of fMRI, the temporal resolution of EEG, and the cost of a behavioral study.

Aleksandra Gruszka, Adam Hampshire and Adrian M. Owen

The chapter by Yarkoni and Braver makes an excellent contribution to the answer to this question and, indeed, it is difficult to add up at the moment. In the ideal world, psychologists would wish to have a kind of litmus paper that would serve as an indicator of various perfectly theoretically valid constructs (e.g., a level of extraversion, neuroticism or intelligence) with least possible effort from our participants. In a more realistic fashion, we would all wish to replace our imperfect questionnaires with a set of theoretically driven, perfectly validated tasks critical for neurotics, extraverts and so on, that would be decomposed into cognitive components perfectly localized to discrete brain regions and thus suitable for neuroimaging. The outcomes of studies utilizing such perfectly validated paradigms then could be linked to molecular and behavior genetics. Such genomic imaging strategy will eventually bridge the gaps between psychological theory, biological mechanism and genome and help us progress from the question of *how* people differ from each other to *why* they differ from each other in the first place. Although methodological and practical difficulties are substantial, some preliminary findings suggest proof-of concept. So in the future, we will see what advances in methods will be critical for future individual differences research. Perhaps the more intriguing answer which needs to be foreseen now is, however, what we will do with such detailed knowledge.

Norbert Jaušovec and Ksenija Jaušovec

A central problem in brain research is the amount of collected data. The situation is to some extent bizarre: on the one hand, we are trying to increase the amount of data by increasing sampling rates, the number of channels, etc., while on the other, we are trying to reduce the collected data by down sampling, averaging, and similar procedures. This second step is necessary because of technical reasons (e.g., computing time), but also to make the data comprehensible and applicable to the brain or cognitive model we are using. For this second step, beside linear methods, there are not many other options which would meet the complex relationship between cognition and brain activity. Recently, dynamic causal modeling (DCM) has been introduced into EEG/MEG research (David, Harrison, & Friston, 2005; Friston, 2003). In DCM, one views the brain as a dynamic network of interacting sources that produces observable responses. DCM is not an exploratory technique; it does not explore all possible models: DCM tests specific models of connectivity and, through model selection, can provide evidence in favor of one model relative to others. In my opinion, a promising approach which could be also relevant for future individual differences research.

Almira Kustubayeva

As mentioned earlier, more complex and sophisticated approaches to the study of brain functions will be critical for understanding individual differences. Each modern neuroscience method (fMRI, PET, MEG, EEG and others) has its own advantages and disadvantages. The combination of different methods could help understand brain function as a complex system. Improvements of statistical analysis in demonstrating the synthesis of interrelations between brain areas, and spatial and temporal integration have advantages for this approach. Such techniques include component analysis in fMRI, nonlinear dynamics, and analysis of coherence in the EEG.

Aljoscha C. Neubauer and Andreas Fink

The advancement as well as the technical/methodical refinement of modern neuroimaging techniques (such as fMRI, PET or EEG) facilitates the investigation of brain activity patterns during the performance of a broad range of different cognitive tasks. So far neuroscientific studies have yielded valuable insights into possible brain correlates underlying different personality and ability variables. For instance, neuroimaging studies in the field of intelligence research have produced evidence of structural (Jung & Haier, 2007) or functional (Neubauer, Fink, & Grabner, 2006) brain correlates of (individual differences) in intelligence. Moreover, neuroscientific research has contributed to demystifying insight (Bowden, Jung-Beeman, Fleck, & Kounios, 2005) or creative thinking (Fink, Benedek, Grabner, Staudt, & Neubauer, 2007) that has long been grounded solely on anectodical reports.

Each of the available neuroscientific measurement methods has its pros and cons regarding the particular context of the study of different facets of cognitive thinking. The primary advantage of fMRI lies in its high spatial accuracy, but it does not allow for the study of cognition with high temporal resolution (as opposed to EEG techniques). The observed changes in brain activity (e.g., from a pre-stimulus reference condition to an activation interval) occur rather slowly, thereby complicating the analysis of time-related brain activity patterns during the process of cognitive thinking. EEG techniques, in contrast, allow for a fine-grained temporal analysis of brain activation that is observed in response to a particular cognitive event (e.g., immediately prior to the production of an original idea). Furthermore, in analyzing the functional cooperation (or functional coupling, respectively) between different cortical areas, EEG techniques have turned out to be a valuable tool in the study of cognition. Hence, future neuroscientific studies in the field of personality and cognition will benefit from a combined use of different measurement methods.

Another critical point in the neuroscientific study of cognition is that most of the experimental tasks are comparatively simple or basic types of tasks that have to be modified (or simplified, respectively) in order to be reasonably applicable in neurophysiological measurements. Thus, the employed tasks can only be indicative of basic or elementary aspects of cognitive thinking and performance in these tasks might not be generalizable to "real-life" creative or intellectual achievements. The investigation of cognitive processes in the neuroscientific laboratory is additionally complicated by the fact that participants (unlike to their natural environment) are required to respond to stimuli while they are mounted with an electrode cap sitting in a shielded EEG cabin or lying supine in the fMRI scanner. These situations bear some important restrictions like rather high noise levels in the scanner or the necessity to avoid gross movements, especially eye movements which restrict the collection of additional potentially important behavioral information like, e.g., the analysis of eye movement or gaze behavior. Thus, future research in this field is challenged by the investigation of brain activity in response to more complex cognitive tasks, combined with other methods like eye-tracking.

In addition, neuroscientific research would gain in importance if the functional meaning of brain activation as measured by means of different methods like EEG, fMRI or NIRS is more carefully understood. Currently, it is not well understood how different indicators of brain function like some EEG parameters, the hemodynamic response in NIRS and the BOLD signal in fMRT are related to one another. Sometimes even conflicting interpretations exist, e.g., regarding the interpretation of event-related alpha synchronization in the EEG (e.g., Klimesch, Sauseng, & Hanslmayr, 2007). This concerns the validity of physiological activation parameters, but another important issue is the reliability and the long-term stability of the diverse parameters. Neurophysiological brain activation parameters, in our view, can be regarded as useful individual differences variable if and only if they display some stability over shorter (weeks) and longer (months) time-intervals. In our knowledge, such data have been collected rarely, mostly for EEG parameters (e.g., Neuper, Grabner, Fink, & Neubauer, 2005).

That way neuroscientific measurement methods can – along with behavioral or psychometric research methods – be a valuable and powerful tool in the study of cognition in as much as they could contribute to a deeper and much more fine-grained scientific understanding of different psychological or cognitive processes.

3. Can ability and personality be assigned to separate brain systems?

Todd S. Braver and Tal Yarkoni

Yes and No. We do agree with the general sense that *specific* abilities or personality dimensions appear to segregate spatially. To some extent, one might argue that many of the major dimensions of personality (e.g., extraversion and neuroticism) appear to primarily reflect variability in subcortical or systems-level structure and function (e.g., differential distribution or density of neurotransmitter receptors, differences in amygdala volume, etc.), whereas differences in cognitive ability are more likely to reflect variability in the structure and function of cortical structures such as the prefrontal cortex. But we disagree with the notion that a *general* distinction between ability and personality can be made. For example, Openness to Experience is generally thought of as a personality dimension, yet it predicts a wide range of cognitive abilities moderately well (DeYoung, Peterson, & Higgins, 2005). We see no a priori reason to suppose that individual differences in ability and personality should have qualitatively different neural substrates.

Norbert Jaušovec and Ksenija Jaušovec

Personality, intelligence, emotions etc., are models, psychologists have designed to enable the study of the human psyche. I would be surprised that nature and evolution has followed the same schema in developing the human brain. From a psychometric perspective, ability is the most well defined psychological construct and there is little question as to the validity of IQ tests. For instance, in a survey of more than 10,000 investigations, Ghiselli (1966) showed that the single best predictor of any job was an intelligence test. Thus, one would expect that we could easily observe differences also on the level of brain activity. However, as was shown in this book section, the reality is more complex, and we can only say that those who are brighter while solving problems show less brain activity than those who are of average ability. In the field of personality matters are different. Until the past few years, there was little consensus concerning the structure of personality, there is still some uncertainty concerning how personality should be measured. Most often, personality is measured using questionnaires, and there has been a growing acceptance of a five-factor model of personality. The diverse and sometimes contradicting findings of research into the biological bases of personality traits make a generalization rather difficult. It is possible that the biological theories may be improved through discriminating multiple systems underpinning traits, or in analyzing brain activity of persons with different personality and ability structures – different configuration of traits within the individual.

In a recent study conducted in our lab (Jaušovec & Jaušovec, 2007), it was found that the highest contribution to the observed differences between personality subtypes was provided by female overcontrolled neurotics. Based on these findings, one could hypothesize that differences in brain activity between personality subtypes are only observed in relation to a specific configuration of some traits and gender. In females, a low level of emotional intelligence in combination with neuroticism and hostility seem to be a prominent candidate for study. Further research should therefore focus on comparing brain activity of individuals of opposite sexes with a similar structure of personality traits having the highest impact on individual differences (e.g., emotional intelligence, neuroticism, agreeableness), while equalizing the other dimensions (including also the level of verbal and performance intelligence). Such an approach would mean a combination between the dimensional, or variable-centered, approach and the typological, or person-centered, approach to personality, and in our opinion could provide additional insight into the brain-activity–personality relation.

Almira Kustubayeva

As mentioned in chapter 9, according to B. Teplov, the abilities are an integral complex of psychophysiological, psychological, and social characteristics. V. D. Shadrikov described the intellectual abilities in terms of Anokhin's functional systems. From this point of view, psychometric intelligence, creativity, learning ability, and cognitive styles are the properties of the psychical functional system that is regulated by the feedback principle. B. M. Velichkovskii suggested the Grand Design model of intelligence – the levels of cognitive organization and behavior regulation are based on Bernstein's theory of movement construction levels. Ability and personality are two psychological dimensions that have shown correlations in numerous studies with psychometric measurements. Individual differences of properties of higher nervous system have been correlated with cognitive abilities. Assuming that ability and personality belong to common regulation brain systems, or executive control systems, they are supported by overlapping nonspecific brain systems, as well as some differences in specific functional brain areas. According to Posner et al. (1997), different cognitive skills may have common activation of the relevant brain areas during task performance through attention.

4. Does research in neuroscience clearly discriminate mechanisms for attention from mechanisms for executive control of attention?

Todd S. Braver and Tal Yarkoni

We do not think so. There remains a good deal of confusion and debate as to where attention ends and executive control begins. For example, many attention researchers distinguish between ventral and dorsal attentional brain networks, ignoring the marked degree of overlap of these networks with putative executive control networks; conversely, many working memory and executive control researchers (unfortunately, including ourselves) often speak of *the* cognitive control network as if it was a monolithic system with a single function. When researchers ascribe functional roles to more circumscribed chunks of brain tissue, confusion also often arises; for example, is the dorsolateral prefrontal cortex better characterized as a region that supports top-down control over attention, manipulation of information actively maintained in working memory, or inhibition of interference (or even some other function, such as action planning)? To some degree, these conceptions overlap (Postle, 2006), and in any case, it is not clear which, if any, is *the* fundamental operation the region supports. A second issue, that often gets glossed over, is the distinction between the source and the site (or target) of attentional effects. We do believe there is something to the general notion that posterior perceptually-oriented cortical (and subcortical) regions are likely to serve as the site of top-down attentional effects.

Furthermore, a cognitive system as complex as our own must have some way of representing and manipulating goal-relevant information independently of moment-by-moment changes in visuospatial attention. It is plausible to suppose that something like a rostral-caudal gradient exists, so that long-term and medium-term goals are maintained in relatively anterior cortical regions (e.g., anterior portions of lateral prefrontal and parietal cortex), while more posterior regions of these same networks might be engaged by the execution of shorter-term action plans consistent with these goals. One component of this shorter-term action plan may be the direction of frontoparietal attentional systems to focus on specific aspects of the world as needed. We just do not think that this kind of story is sufficiently well worked out at present.

Almira Kustubayeva

Luria discriminated mechanisms of involuntary attention that children developed in earlier childhood and voluntary attentional processes that developed later. A. Uhtomskii suggested "dominance theory". The dominant area of excitatory processes subordinates a surrounding inhibitory area so as to govern and execute our behavior. I. P. Pavlov described the mechanism of the orienting reflex as involuntary attention and called it the "What is it?" reflex. The orienting reflex is easy to observe as a large spreading alpha desynchronization in EEG. Sokolov explained the desynchronization effect by a special form activation of neurons, which has been called "novelty neurons". The combination of "Novelty detectors/neurons" and "neurons of identity" determines enhancement of orienting reflex (OR). Sokolov, Lyytinen, Sponks, and Näätänen (2002) brought in the term of "conditioned OR" – referring to a voluntary form of OR to a significant stimulus. Unconditioned and conditioned OR (corresponding with involuntary/voluntary attention) may both contribute to the Mismatch Negativity (negative potential evoked by a deviant stimulus) mechanism. Näätänen & Michie (1979) proposed two components of MMN: sensory-specific (automatic) and frontal generator (attention switch, voluntary control). The interaction of voluntary vs. involuntary attention involves prefrontal cortex activity functioning as control system. Behterev, Orbeli, Anohkin, and Kropotov have described attention as a multilevel organization in which nonspecific activation influences on tonus of attention and frontal area regulate the direction of attention. Kropotov (2008) revealed the role of inhibition in developmental impairments in ADHD children (children were shown to exhibit lower amplitudes of GO and NOGO P300 components in comparison to normal groups).

Prefrontal cortex has been implicated in executive function by many authors. Three areas – the ventromedial (VMPFC)-orbitofrontal cortex (OFC), dorsolateral prefrontal (DLPFC), and the anterior cingulate cortex (ACC) – were identified: VMPFC and OFC as emotional processing, reward and inhibition processes, and decision-making; DLPFC as attentional, selective and sustained attention, novelty processing, choice, working memory, and language function; ACC as division of attention, and both cognitive and emotional regulation (Banfield and Vohs, 2004). fMRI studies (Fan, McCandliss, Fossella, Flombaum, & Posner, 2005) described attentional networks for alerting, orienting and executive attention based on a different anatomy. Alerting attention is sensitivity to incoming stimuli provided by activation of locus coeruleus, right frontal, and parietal cortex. Orienting attention (selection of information) is associated with superior parietal cortex, temporal parietal junction, frontal eye fields, and superior colliculus. Executive attention is "supervisory" in that it guides our thoughts, emotion, and behavior, via the anterior cingulate, lateral ventral, prefrontal cortex, and basal ganglia (Posner & Rothbart, 2007). Neuroscience models provide the distinction between executive attention and other attentional systems.

5. How does work on brain motivation systems contribute to understanding individual differences in executive control?

Todd S. Braver and Tal Yarkoni

If one conceptualizes executive control not only as the *capacity* to exert control over one's own thought and action but also as the *prioritization* of such goals, then it follows that motivation and executive control are intimately linked. For example, most people's performance at most cognitive tasks can be at least transiently enhanced by offering an incentive for good performance (e.g., money). Likewise, some studies, including our own, have found that such manipulations can enhance activation in brain cognitive control systems (Locke & Braver, 2008). Furthermore, from a neuroanatomical perspective, there is already strong evidence to suggest a high degree of overlap in components of brain motivation and cognitive control systems (e.g., the midbrain dopamine system).

In an ecological context, one of the central questions any complex organism faces is how to regulate the rate at which it expends energy on cognitively demanding activities. For reasons that are not presently understood, the deployment of executive control appears to have important cognitive (and potentially, energetic) costs associated with it. Thus, the extent to which such processes are engaged may crucially depend upon a cost–benefit analysis. Affective-motivational signals (e.g., the presence of reward or punishment cues) may provide the necessary signal to elicit increased engaged of control, based on a higher estimate of utility or value for such processes. From an individual differences standpoint, this sets up a number of very interesting research questions: Why are some people seemingly indefatigable, and able to maintain a high level of control over extended periods, and without exogenous feedback regarding performance success (or other types of reward/punishment signals). Conversely, why do some people, even those who may have the *capacity* for a high level of performance, tend not to reach such levels under low-motivation conditions? Why are some people more highly motivated by the presence of exogenous reward cues than others? The study of such questions using cognitive neuroscience techniques is still in its infancy, but we view this as one of the most promising areas of research to open up in recent years.

Almira Kustubayeva

A brain motivation system and its role in individual differences were described by P. V. Simonov in the classic book "Motivated Brain" and by Simonov, Ershov, and Bastow (1991) in a chapter on "Motivational nucleus of personality". Assuming 3 types of needs – biological, social, and intellectual – Simonov provided examples of how different types of brain damage can influence a hierarchy of needs. Some EEG studies also relate motivation and personality. Knyazev and Slobodskaya

(2003) suggested that alpha oscillations reflect inhibitory control (attention). Alpha is reciprocally related to slow oscillations, including delta (as motivational system activity) and theta (as emotional system). Fast and slow rhythms play different roles in BAS and BIS systems. fMRI studies showed increasing activity in brain areas responsible for executive control–dorsolateral prefrontal cortex (DLPFC) – during a reward condition (Pochon et al., 2002; Taylor et al., 2004). Locke and Braver (2008) found that a reward-incentive condition, compared with penalty-incentive and baseline conditions, activated the participant's cognitive strategy, which was associated with primarily right posterior and prefrontal cortex (RLPFC). Reward expectancy and sensitivity to reward were correlated with activity in reward-related regions, including the subcallosal gyrus, the OFC, and the caudate nucleus. BAS was also correlated with sustained activity in the right frontopolar cortex. So, motivation is a complex construct that is related to brain functional state, together with emotion influences on executive control.

References

Aston-Jones, G., & Cohen, J. D. (2005). An integrative theory of locus coeruleus–norepinephrine function: adaptive gain and optimal performance. *Annual Review of Neuroscience, 28*, 403–450.

Banfield, R. F., & Vohs, K. D. (2004). Handbook of self-regulation: research, theory, and applications. Guilford, New York

Basar, E. (2006). The theory of the whole-brain-work. International Journal of Psychophysiology 60(2):133–138

Bowden, E. M., Jung-Beeman, M., Fleck. J., & Kounios, J. (2005). New approaches to demystifying insight. *Trends in Cognitive Sciences, 9*, 322–328.

David, O., Harrison, L., & Friston, K. J. (2005). Modelling event-related responses in the brain. *NeuroImage, 25*:756–770

DeYoung, C. G., Peterson, J. B., & Higgins, D. M. (2005). Sources of openness/intellect: cognitive and neuropsychological correlates of the fifth factor of personality. *Journal of Personality, 73*, 825–858.

Fan, J., McCandliss, B. D., Fossella, J., Flombaum, J. I., & Posner, M. I. (2005). The activation of attentional networks. *NeuroImage, 26*, 471–479.

Fernandez-Duque, D., Baird, J. A., & Posner, M. I. (2000). Executive attention and metacognitive regulation. Consciousness and Cognition *9*, 288–307.

Fink, A., Benedek, M., Grabner, R. H., Staudt, B., & Neubauer, A. C. (2007). Creativity meets neuroscience: experimental tasks for the neuroscientific study of creative thinking. *Methods, 42*, 68–76.

Friston, K. (2003). Learning and inference in the brain. *Neural Networks, 16*, 1325–1352.

Friston, K, & Stephan, K. E. (2007). Free energy and the brain. *Synthese, 159*, 417–458.

Ghiselli, E. E. (1966). The validity of occupational aptitude tests. Wiley, New York

Jaušovec, N., Jaušovec, K. (2007). Personality, gender and brain oscillations. *International Journal of Psychophysiology, 66*, 214–225.

Jung, R. E., & Haier, R. J. (2007). The parieto-frontal integration theory (P-FIT) of intelligence: converging neuroimaging evidence. *Behavioral and Brain Sciences, 30*, 135–154.

Klimesch, W., Sauseng, & P., Hanslmayr, S. (2007). EEG alpha oscillations: the inhibition-timing hypothesis. *Brain Research Reviews, 53*, 63–88.

Knyazev, G. G., & Slobodskaya, H. R. (2003). Personality trait of behavioral inhibition is associated with oscillatory systems reciprocal relationships. *International Journal of Psychophysiology, 48*, 247–261.

Kropotov, J. (2008). Quantitative EEG, event-related potentials and neurotherapy. Academic, San Diego, CA.

Locke, H. S., & Braver, T. S. (2008). Motivational influences on cognitive control: behavior, brain activation, and individual differences. Cognitive, Affective and Behavioral Neuroscience, *8*(1), 99–112.

Neubauer, A. C., Fink, A., & Grabner, R.H. (2006). Sensitivity of alpha band ERD/ERS to individual differences in cognition. In: Neuper, C., Klimesch, W. (eds) Event-related dynamics of brain oscillations – Progress in brain research, vol 159. Elsevier, Amsterdam, pp 167–178.

Näätänen, R., & Michie, P.T. (1979). Early selective-attention effects on the evoked potential: a critical review and reinterpretation. *Biological Psychology, 8*(2), 81–136.

Neuper, C., Grabner, R. H., Fink, A., & Neubauer, A. C. (2005). Long-term stability and consistency of EEG event-related (de-)synchronization across different cognitive tasks. *Clinical Neurophysiology, 116*, 1681–1694.

Pochon, J. B., Levy, R., Fossati, P., Lehéricy, S., Poline, J. -B., & Pillon, B. et al. (2002). The neural system that bridges reward and cognition in humans: an fMRI study. *Proceedings of the National Academy of Sciences, 99*, 5669–5674.

Posner, M. I., & Rothlart, M. K. (2007). Research on attention networks as a model for the integration of psychological science. *Annual Review of Psychology, 58*, 1–23.

Posner, M. I., DiGirolamo, G. J., & Fernandez-Duque, D. (1997). Brain mechanisms of cognitive skills. *Consciousness and Cognition, 6*(2–3), 267–90.

Postle, B. R. (2006). Working memory as an emergent property of the mind and brain. *Neuroscience, 139*, 23–38.

Simonov, P. V., Ershov, P. M., & Bastow, A. (1991). Temperament, character and personality: biobehavioral concepts in science, art, and social psychology. Taylor & Francis, New York.

Sokolov, E. N., Lyytinen, H., Spinks, J. A., & Näätänen, R. (2002). The orienting response in information processing. Lawrence Erlbaum, NJ.

Taylor, S. F., Welsh, R. C., Wager, T. D., Phan, K. L., Fitzgerald, K. D., & Gehring, W. J. (2004). A functional neuroimaging study of motivation and executive function. *NeuroImage, 21*, 1045–1054.

Part III
Individual Differences in Attentional Mechanisms

Chapter 11
Psychopathology and Individual Differences in Latent Inhibition: Schizophrenia and Schizotypality

R.E. Lubow and Oren Kaplan

Introduction

When a stimulus is repeatedly presented in such a manner that it is not attended (i.e., it is not followed by a consequence), it subsequently becomes deficient in its ability to enter into or express new associations. This phenomenon, latent inhibition (LI), has been widely explored in animal and humans with a variety of learning tasks (for a review, see Lubow, 1989). Functionally, LI appears to protect the organism from information overload by attenuating the processing of previously irrelevant stimuli.

The first demonstration of the LI effect occurred 50 years ago (Lubow & Moore, 1959). In the following 20 years, LI studies focused mainly on establishing the generality of the phenomenon, and then on attempts to integrate it with extant learning theories, mostly by appealing to a loss of stimulus salience and, in relation to that, to the conditioning of inattention. The publication of an early review article (Lubow, 1973) and several papers that related LI deficits to schizophrenia (e.g., Baruch, Hemsley, & Gray, 1988a; Gray, Hemsley, & Gray, 1992; for a review, see Lubow, 2005) led to an accelerated expansion of research. The rationale for such LI studies was based on the conjunction of two premises: (1) LI reflects the operation of the normal ability to ignore irrelevant stimuli; and (2) schizophrenic patients (at least acute patients with positive symptoms) are highly distractible, displaying an inability to focus attention on task-relevant information (e.g., Barch, Carter, Hachten, Usher, & Cohen, 1999; McGhie & Chapman, 1961; Ohman, Nordby, & d'Elia, 1986).

There are many different procedures for producing LI in humans, ranging from classical conditioning to visual search, but the most common of them is associative rule-learning (for reviews, see Lubow, 1989; Lubow & Gewirtz, 1995; Lubow & Kaplan, 2005). Irrespective of the particular paradigm, they all contain a stimulus preexposure phase followed by a phase that requires the learning of a new association and then a test phase. Very often, the acquisition and test phases are combined. In preexposure, a stimulus that is not followed by any consequence (CS-0) is presented a number of times, anywhere between 1 and 100, depending on the preparation. In animals and in young children, this condition results in an interference with the subsequent acquisition or expression of any new association with that stimulus. However, there is considerable evidence to indicate that LI in adult humans requires a "masking task" in the preexposure phase, the purpose of which is to divert attention from the critical to-be-tested preexposed stimulus (PE). This issue, which impacts on LI theories, will be addressed later in this paper.

R.E. Lubow (✉)
Department of Psychology, Tel Aviv University, Ramat Aviv 69978, Israel
e-mail: lubow@freud.tau.ac.il

O. Kaplan
The College of Management, Rishon Lezion, Israel

In a typical example of a masked LI experiment, Zalstein-Orda and Lubow (1995) preexposed the same meaningless shape (to-be-CS) over a series of many trials. Each trial was accompanied by a different trigram from a finite set that repeated itself several times. This masking task, designed to divert attention from the PE stimulus, required the subject to determine the number of repetitions of the set. In the test, the masking stimuli continued to be present on each trial, but on any given trial either the preexposed shape or a novel shape might appear. The subject had to learn that a change in the numerical value of a counter was associated with the presence of the previously irrelevant PE stimulus. The PE group reached the learning criterion more slowly than the NPE group, thereby demonstrating the LI effect (for similar results with between-group designs, see e.g., Burch, Hemsley, & Joseph, 2004; Gray, Fernandez, Williams, Ruddle, & Snowden, 2002; and with within-subject designs, e.g., De La Casa & Lubow, 2001; Gray, Snowden, Peoples, Hemsley, & Gray, 2003; Swerdlow et al., 2003).

Pathology-Based Individual Differences

There are four categories of human LI studies that have examined individual differences that relate to pathology. The first three concern LI and schizophrenia and include groups of schizophrenia patients, healthy subjects who score high on schizotypal questionnaires and healthy subjects who have been administered drugs known to attenuate or provoke symptoms of schizophrenia. The fourth category contains a heterogeneous grouping of LI experiments with participants suffering from a variety of *apparently* unrelated pathologies.

Latent Inhibition and Schizophrenia

Much knowledge has been accumulated regarding LI and schizophrenia, particularly in regard to the involvement of dopaminergic systems (for reviews, see e.g., Lubow, 2005; Weiner, 2003). In the first LI-schizophrenia study, Lubow, Weiner, Schlossberg, and Baruch (1987) investigated LI effects in paranoid and nonparanoid patients. Based on the animal literature, they expected to find attenuated LI in the two patient groups compared to healthy controls. However, both groups had intact LI, arguably because they were under a medication regimen that at least partially restored normal attentional functions. Subsequent research in this area has concentrated on two subpopulations of schizophrenic patients, acute and chronic. The first group is characterized by either being free of antipsychotic drugs and/or at the beginning of treatment. Many studies have indicated that this latter group is deficient in LI (Baruch et al., 1988a; Gray, Hemsley, et al., 1992; Gray, Pilowsky, Gray, & Kerwin, 1995; Lubow, Kaplan, Abramovich, Rudnick, & Laor, 2000a; Rascle et al., 2001; Vaitl et al., 2002; Williams et al., 1998; Young, Moran, & Joseph, 2005; for an exception, see Swerdlow et al., 2005).

As opposed to acute nonmedicated patients, chronic medicated schizophrenics exhibit intact LI (Baruch et al., 1988a; Gray, Hemsley, et al., 1992; Leumann, Feldon, Vollenweider, & Ludewig, 2002; Lubow et al., 1987). However, a recent study by Cohen et al. (2004) suggests that the LI effect in schizophrenia is even more complex. Based on Weiner (2003), they expected patients with negative symptoms and patients with positive symptoms to exhibit different patterns of LI. Indeed, schizophrenic patients who simultaneously displayed high levels of negative symptoms and low levels of positive symptoms had *potentiated* LI. Schizophrenic groups with other combinations of positive and negative symptoms did not differ from controls. These findings may explain some of the contradictory results in the literature, and together with Weiner's (2003) "two-headed" model of schizophrenia, based on animal studies, may have important implications for treatment and drug development.

Latent Inhibition and Schizotypy

If one accepts the assumption that psychotic tendencies exist on a continuum (e.g., Chapman, Edell, & Chapman, 1980; Claridge & Broks, 1984; Eysenck & Eysenck, 1976), with one extreme being the well-adapted normal, and the other a hospitalized patient group, then *healthy* subjects who are differentiated on the basis of high symptom-related scores should exhibit behavioral/cognitive effects that parallel those that occur in the pathological state. The concept of schizotypy, or psychotic-proneness, is based on this assumption, and it receives support from family studies that indicate that the genetic vulnerability to schizophrenia may be manifested in nonpsychotic individuals as a schizophrenia-like personality (e.g., Nuechterlein et al., 2002). Investigating cognitive dysfunctions in these otherwise healthy groups has the advantage of isolating the predisposition to schizophrenia from possible confounding factors, such as symptoms that interfere with testing, hospitalization, medication, and social stigma (Mednick & McNeil, 1973).

In general, the schizotypal personality includes four components: aberrant perceptions and beliefs (unusual experiences), cognitive disorganization, introvertive anhedonia, and asocial behavior. It can be assessed with self-report instruments such as the Schizotypal Personality Questionnaire (SPQ; Raine, 1991), which draws on the nine features of schizotypal personality disorder as defined by DSM-III-R (American Psychiatric Association, 2000). Six of the subscales relate to positive symptoms of schizotypy (ideas of reference, odd beliefs/magical thinking, unusual perceptual experiences, eccentric/odd behavior and appearance, odd speech, and suspicious/paranoid ideation). Two subscales relate to negative symptoms (no close friends and constricted affect).The ninth subscale, social anxiety, is related to affective symptoms of schizotypy.

Given the above rationale, the study of the relationship between LI and schizophrenia has been extended to healthy populations that are differentiated on the basis of schizotypy scores, usually by median-split (e.g., Baruch, Hemsley, & Gray, 1988b; Braunstein-Bercovitz & Lubow, 1998) but sometimes also by subscale scores (e.g., Burch et al., 2004; Gray et al., 2002).

As would be expected from the results with schizophrenic patients, healthy subjects who score high on schizotypal personality questionnaires exhibit reduced LI compared to low psychotic-prone subjects (e.g., Baruch et al., 1988b; Braunstein-Bercovitz & Lubow, 1998; Gray et al., 2002; Lubow, Ingberg-Sachs, Zalstein-Orda, & Gewirtz, 1992; for an exception, see Wuthrich & Bates, 2001; for a review, see Braunstein-Bercovitz, Rammsayer, Gibbons, & Lubow, 2002). In a study that raised questions in regard to the continuity hypothesis, Serra, Jones, Toone, and Gray (2001, Exp. 2) examined LI in three groups: chronic schizophrenic patients, their symptom-free first-degree relatives who were divided into schizotypal and nonschizotypal groups, and, for comparison, an unrelated healthy group from Experiment 1. All three groups from Experiment 2 showed reduced LI compared to the control group. However, the differences in LI were primarily a result of very rapid learning by the NPE control group.

In the meantime, the overwhelming majority of experiments show that nonsymptomatic high-schizotypal normals exhibit attenuated LI compared to low-schizotypals, as do acute nonmedicated schizophrenic patients compared to healthy controls. Furthermore, the attenuated LI appears to be associated with the positive symptoms that characterize the acute, unmedicated state of patients and with the schizotypal questionnaire subscale scores that also reflect positive type symptoms. In regard to this latter point, Evans, Gray, and Snowden (2007) found that attenuated LI in high-schizotypal normals was limited to those subjects who scored high on the dimension of Unusual Experiences. Such data would seem to support the continuity model as do the parallel effects of antipsychotic and psychosis-producing drugs on LI in patient and healthy control groups (see below).

Latent Inhibition in Healthy Groups that Receive Dopaminergic-Related Drugs

The predictive validity for the animal-LI model of schizophrenia is reinforced by results from pharmacological studies (for reviews, see e.g., Moser, Hitchcock, Lister, & Moran, 2000; Tzschentke, 2001; Weiner, 2003). Thus, amphetamine, an indirect dopamine agonist, which by itself produces positive symptoms of schizophrenia in normal subjects (e.g., Ellinwood, 1967; Zahn, Rappaport, & Thompson, 1981) and exacerbates such symptoms in schizophrenics (e.g., Angrist, Rotrosen, & Gershon, 1980; Sato, Numachi, & Hamamura, 1992), attenuates LI in rats (e.g., Weiner, Lubow, & Feldon, 1984, 1988) and humans (e.g., Gray, Pickering, Hemsley, Dawling, & Gray, 1992b; Kumari et al., 1999). On the other hand, nonselective dopamine-receptor antagonists, such as chlorpromazine and haloperidol, effective neuroleptics, reverse this attenuation and produce a super-LI effect, again both in rats (e.g., Peters & Joseph, 1993; Weiner & Feldon, 1987) and humans (e.g., McCartan et al., 2001; Williams et al., 1996, 1997).

Atypical antipsychotic drugs also produce the expected potentiation of LI. Thus, clozapine (e.g., Moran, Fischer, Hitchcock, & Moser, 1996; Shadach, Feldon, & Weiner, 1999), olanzapine (e.g., Gosselin, Oberling, & Di Scala, 1996), remoxipride (Nadal, 2001; Trimble, Bell, & King, 1997), and rispiridone (e.g., Alves, Delucia, & Silva, 2002; Alves & Silva, 2001) enhance LI or reverse the LI-reducing effects of the indirect dopamine agents. In general, the effective dosages of most clinically effective neuroleptics are similar to those dosages that enhance LI (Dunn, Atwater, & Kilts, 1993).

Latent Inhibition and Pathologies Other than Schizophrenia

In addition to the schizophrenia-related experiments, LI has been studied in a number of other pathologies, including Parkinson's Disease, Tourette's Disorder, Anxiety, Attention Deficit Hyperactivity Disorder, and Obsessive Compulsive Disorder.

Anxiety. There is considerable evidence in the cognitive literature that anxiety interferes with the ability to ignore irrelevant stimuli (for review, see Eysenck, Derakshan, Santos, & Calvo, 2007). On this basis, plus the fact that anxiety, in addition to having serotonergic involvement, is also related to elevated dopaminergic activity (e.g., Nutt, Bell, & Malizia, 1998), one might expect that LI would be attenuated by high levels of anxiety. In support of this possibility, Braunstein-Bercovitz (2000) factor analyzed SPQ scores and found significant components for anxiety and perceptual-disorganization. Furthermore, there was a significant correlation between the first factor and trait-anxiety as measured by the State and Trait Anxiety Inventory (Spielberger, Gorsuch, & Lushene, 1970). Perceptual disorganization was also significantly correlated with trait-anxiety, but it was significantly lower than that with anxiety. These findings suggest that low LI in schizotypal and schizophrenic subjects may be due to anxiety and not necessarily to the positive symptoms themselves (Braunstein-Bercovitz et al., 2002). Indeed, the positive symptoms may serve to increase anxiety (see below).

Since subjects characterized as Type-A personalities are considered to have a highly stressful life style, and stress is related to anxiety, one also would expect Type-As to exhibit less LI than Type-Bs. Indeed, this was demonstrated in the only study that examined this prediction (De la Casa, 1994).

Braunstein-Bercovitz, Dimentman-Ashkenazi, and Lubow (2001) tested the anxiety hypothesis by manipulating stress in two rule-learning experiments, one in the laboratory and one in the field. In both cases, adult subjects in the low-stress but not high-stress condition exhibited LI. However, Lubow, Toren, Laor, and Kaplan (2000b), using the visual search paradigm with clinically diagnosed anxious children found no difference in LI between these children and healthy controls.

Obsessive–compulsive disorder (OCD). A rule-learning study by Swerdlow, Hartston, and Hartman (1999) found potentiated LI in a group of OCD adults. Such an effect was absent in an earlier study (Swerdlow, Braff, Hartston, Perry, & Geyer, 1996a), perhaps due to a ceiling effect imposed by task difficulty. Indeed, Kaplan et al. (2006) replicated the super-LI effect in OCD patients using the relatively simple visual search LI task. Although OCD and Tourette's syndrome have high rates of bidirectional comorbidity, Swerdlow, Magulac, Filion, and Zinner (1996b) reported that children and adults with TS showed normal LI effects compared to healthy controls.

The super-LI effect in OCD patients poses an apparent paradox. Since OCD belongs to the category of DSM-IV TR anxiety disorders (American Psychiatric Association, 2000), one might expect such patients to show attenuated LI (see above). However, the difficulty that OCD individuals have in *switching* between cognitive sets (e.g., Head, Bolton, & Hymas, 1989) may also interfere with their ability to learn that the previously irrelevant stimulus has become relevant in the test, and thus may generate a super-LI effect. That OCD patients display a super-LI effect suggests that, for them, "rigidity" is stronger than "anxiety," at least within the stimulus preexposure paradigm.

Attention deficit hyperactivity disorder (ADHD). The pharmacological treatment for ADHD creates yet another paradox for LI theory. On the one hand, methylphenidate (a dopamine agonist) should reduce LI. On the other hand, the improvement of attention caused by this drug should enhance LI.

Two studies have looked at LI in ADHD children. Lubow and Josman (1993), using a rule-learning procedure, reported no LI in ADHD children, although LI was present in healthy controls. With the visual search procedure, Lubow et al. (2005) found that nonmedicated ADHD children had less LI for left-side targets than right-side targets. This effect was absent in the normal control and the medicated ADHD groups, suggesting that methylphenidate may have normalized a lateralized attentional deficit in ADHD. Such an effect would be congruent with the claim that ADHD is related to right frontal striate dysfunction (for a review, see Stefanatos & Wasserstein, 2001).

Parkinson's disease (PD). PD patients suffer from a deficiency of dopamine and they typically are treated with a dopamine agonist (L-dopa). Therefore, it was expected that de novo, unmedicated patients would exhibit potentiated LI. Lubow, Dressler, and Kaplan (1999), using the visual search procedure, found potentiated LI, but only in female PD patients with right-side motor symptoms compared to normal controls and to female PD patients with left-side symptoms. Male patients with right-side symptoms did not exhibit LI. Thus, as with the ADHD children, the LI abnormalities in PD patients appear to have a lateralized component.

Theoretical Issues for Latent Inhibition and Their Implications for Schizophrenia

Although there have been many explanations of the LI effect in the animal literature (for reviews, see Hall, 1991; Lubow, 1989), current theories reside within two major categories, attentional/association deficit (A-theories), and retrieval-competition (R-theories). A-theories, of which there are several versions (e.g., Lubow, 1989; Mackintosh, 1975; Pearce & Hall, 1980), assume that irrelevant stimulus preexposure degrades attention to that stimulus (salience reduction). As a consequence, future associability of the stimulus is decreased and new learning is made more difficult. In contrast, R-theories, tested in three-stage experimental paradigms consisting of separate preexposure, acquisition, and test stages, claim that there is no impairment of preexposed stimulus associability. Instead, the PE and NPE groups enter the acquisition phase with the same capacity to form new associations with the test stimulus, i.e., the associative strength that accrues to the conditioned stimulus in the acquisition phase is the same for both groups. According to R-theory, in the stage-three test, the association that was formed during the preexposure phase (CS-0) competes with the CS-US association that was formed in the acquisition phase (e.g., Bouton, 1993; Miller, Kasprow, & Schachtman, 1986). Thus, the NPE group performs better than the PE group because there is only the second association to be retrieved, whereas the PE group retrieves both associations, ones that are in conflict with each other.

Although A- and R-theories may disagree as to whether the source of the LI effect is in the preexposure or in the test stage, both accounts accept that something is learned during preexposure. Whether that association is CS-0, CS-context, context-0, or a higher order conditional association whereby the context becomes an occasion-setter for the expression of a CS-0 is, as yet, unresolved. Nor is it evident, which if any of these possibilities is uniquely compatible with an A- or R-interpretation of LI.

Since most human-LI studies were designed on the background of their implications for schizophrenia, they were significantly influenced by the attentional component of A-theories. Nevertheless, it has become increasingly clear that a comprehensive theory of LI has to incorporate attentional processes in preexposure *and* retrieval processes in test. Furthermore, it would seem to be important to relate this distinction between learning and performance factors to the schizophrenia-modulated LI data.

To begin with, the consensus opinion that schizophrenia represents a disorder of attention (e.g., Anscombe, 1987; Braff, 1993; Mirsky & Duncan, 1986; Nuechterlein & Dawson, 1984) requires a confirmation that LI, at least in part, is indeed governed by such processes. This position gains support from experiments that demonstrate that generating LI in adult humans requires a masking task in the preexposure stage, and that LI is modulated by the difficulty (load) of the masking task.

The Role of the Masking Task

With the exception of several electrodermal conditioning studies (see below), the vast majority of experiments that have successfully elicited LI in adults have preexposed the to-be-target stimulus while the subject was occupied with a masking task (e.g., Gray, Hemsley, et al., 1992; Gray, Pickering, et al., 1992; Lubow et al., 1992; Pineno, De la Casa, Lubow, & Miller, 2006; for an exception, Escobar, Arcediano, & Miller, 2003). Furthermore, numerous experiments with nonmasked stimulus preexposures have failed to produce an LI effect (e.g., Graham & McLaren, 1998; for a review, see Lubow, 2005). Most importantly, studies that have *explicitly* compared masked and nonmasked conditions have obtained LI with the former but not with the latter (Braunstein-Bercovitz & Lubow, 1998; De la Casa & Lubow, 2001; Ginton, Urca, & Lubow, 1975; Graham & McLaren, 1998; Lubow, Caspy, & Schnur, 1982). Notably, in all of these experiments, the masking task response was qualitatively *different* from the test task response. In fact, the cluster of electrodermal conditioning studies that have obtained LI without masking (e.g., Lipp, Siddle, & Vaitl, 1992; Lipp & Vaitl, 1992) invariably elicit the *same* response in the preexposure and conditioning/test stages, a condition that allows for simple interference effects.

That the masking task is a necessary condition for the production of LI can be accounted for by accepting the assumption that it diverts attention or processing resources from the preexposed stimulus. Additional compelling evidence for the role of attention in LI was provided by Braunstein-Bercovitz, Hen, and Lubow (2004) and Braunstein-Bercovitz and Lubow (1998). Both papers reported that LI was not only a function of masking task load but that there was significant interaction between load and schizotypy level. With a low-load masking task, low schizotypals exhibited normal LI. However, LI was abolished in high-schizotypals. With a high-load masking task, the effects were reversed; low-schizotypals did not exhibit LI, and high schizotypals demonstrated intact LI. Similar results have been reported by Della Casa, Hoefer, Weiner, and Feldon (1999) and Hoefer, Della Casa, and Feldon (1998).

Although these studies clearly indicate that LI is modulated by a stage-1 attentional process, they do not negate the possibility that LI also is affected by stage-2 and/or stage-3 retrieval factors. Indeed, this option is supported by LI experiments that have examined the effects of context-change and retention interval.

The Roles of Context and Retention Interval

Normally, LI experiments make a point of using the same context in the preexposure and acquisition/test stages. However, if the contexts are different from each other, then LI, even in humans, is disrupted (e.g., Gray et al., 2001; Nelson & Sanjuan, 2006; Zalstein-Orda & Lubow, 1995; for review of animal literature, see Lubow, 1989, pp. 74–82). These results are critical for R-theories because in the preexposure phase the subject has no knowledge of the forthcoming acquisition-test conditions, context or otherwise. Therefore, during the preexposure stage, the context-same and the context-different groups must process the PE stimulus and context information in an *identical* manner, and any difference in performance between the two groups in the test must be attributed to a process occurring *after* preexposure.

A retrieval-failure account of LI also gains support from animal experiments that have manipulated the time between the stage-2 acquisition and stage-3 test stages. Most of these studies have found that LI decreases as a function of the retention interval (e.g., for a review, see Lubow & De la Casa, 2005). Recall that R-theory proposes that, following stimulus preexposure, the acquisition of the new association to the old stimulus proceeds normally. However, in the test stage, when the subject again encounters the stimulus that was preexposed and then conditioned, two competing associations are retrieved, representing the opposing associations previously learned in the prior phases. However, if one varies the time between acquisition and test, and LI is found after a short but not long delay, this is evidence that with the short-delay the CS-US association was acquired but not manifest, and that something occurred during the longer delay that allowed the *normal* association that was encoded in the acquisition phase to be retrieved.[1]

Integrating and Expanding A- and R-Theories of Latent Inhibition

In summary, although the acquisition of normal LI may be explained primarily by A-theory processes operating in the stimulus preexposure stage, the modulation of LI by post-preexposure variables requires explanatory constructs from R-theory. In other words, an inclusive theory of LI must not only incorporate postulates that allow for *different* preexposure conditions (e.g., PE and NPE) to produce differential effects but also ones that allows for the *same* stimulus preexposure conditions to produce different test-dependent condition effects. The two sets of variables correspond to those that are manipulated *during* the preexposure phase (e.g., number and duration of stimulus preexposures, masking task load) and modulate the acquisition of LI, and those that are manipulated *after* the preexposure stage and frequently correspond to retrieval processes that produce a "release" from LI (e.g., context change, delay of testing).

---

[1] Several recent studies have failed to find a diminution of LI after a long acquisition-test interval. Quite the opposite, when the long retention interval was spent in a context that was different from the contexts of the other stages, a super-LI effect was obtained (for a review, see Lubow & De la Casa, 2005).

However, in addition to accepting the *general* premises of A- and R-theories, there are other potentially important considerations that should be recognized. For one, it is necessary to differentiate between two processes operating in stage-1, stimulus-property encoding (e.g., shape, color), and stimulus-relationship encoding (e.g., CS-0; CS-context, CS-US), and to acknowledge that the former precedes the latter (Lubow, 2005). This latter point follows from the fact that LI is stimulus-specific (i.e., preexposure to stimulus A does not affect performance to stimulus B; for review, see Lubow, 1989, pp. 58–59). If LI is stimulus-specific, then relationships with that stimulus cannot be acquired without first encoding the qualitative aspects of the stimulus itself. As a consequence, a *small* number of stimulus preexposures should produce facilitation of subsequent learning as compared to no preexposure or to extensive preexposures. This should occur because during the first few stimulus preexposures, some of the stimulus properties were encoded *before* the critical association, CS-0 and/or CS-context, could be acquired. Thus, a subject with very few stimulus preexposures has an advantage in the acquisition of the subsequent CS-US association because that association also depends on stimulus-property encoding. With an increase in the number of stimulus preexposures, relationship-encoding proceeds, and the initial positive transfer eventually becomes negative (LI), at least if the context remains constant across stages. The evidence that relatively few stimulus preexposures facilitate subsequent learning, even when contexts are constant, comes primarily from animal studies (e.g., Bennett, Tremain, & Mackintosh, 1996; Hoffmann & Spear, 1989; Prados, 2000). However, one experiment suggests a similar effect for humans (Burch et al., 2004).

Implications for Schizophrenia

The above analyses indicate that the apparently simple LI effect is, in fact, quite complex. This point needs no further emphasis than that of noting that explanations of LI have invoked such different general processes as those found in A- and R-theories. The complexity becomes even more compelling when one tries to relate the LI abnormalities in schizophrenia to specific underlying cognitive mechanisms. In doing so, one can appeal to stimulus encoding deficits for either stimulus properties or stimulus relationships; and, if stimulus properties, then one can ask whether it is unique to punctate stimuli that are not followed by consequences, or to the stimuli that compose the context; and, if stimulus relationships, which ones- CS-0, CS-context, or some higher order occasion setting function? And, of course, it must be determined whether the same answers apply equally to patients with different symptoms, as for example, positive and negative.

In short, knowing that schizophrenic patients and high-schizotypal normals exhibit aberrant LI data does not, *by itself*, provide critical information in regard to understanding the pathologies of schizophrenia. Nevertheless, the LI anomalies in schizophrenia patients and high schizotypal normals may clarify some of the experiential aspects of the disease. For example, if attenuated LI reflects the patient's inability to ignore objectively meaningless irrelevant stimuli (e.g., Lubow, 1989, 2005), then this suggests some accompanying phenomenological effects. On the one hand, experiencing the "mad" rush of relatively unfiltered stimuli can be a symptom of the underlying pathology. At the same time, this can be a *cause* of further disorientation and confusion that, in turn, would increase anxiety and exacerbate the original problem. Within this framework, positive symptoms such as delusions and hallucinations can be viewed as adaptive responses. The imposition of some apparent order on an otherwise chaotic experiential array of stimuli can reduce anxiety and thereby suspend a devastating iterative process. Alternatively, escape from the maelstrom of meaningless events can be achieved by summoning up negative symptoms, such as apathy and withdrawal. In brief, schizophrenia can be seen as a defense against a system breakdown that would otherwise result in conscious experience being inundated with phenomenally novel, meaningless stimuli. Frith (1979) has described the end product of this collapse in similar terms, referring to the inability of schizophrenics to limit the contents of consciousness. Abnormal LI effects in schizophrenia patients appear to reflect this state, with attenuated LI being associated with positive symptoms, and potentiated LI with negative symptoms. For the subject with positive symptoms, LI may be decreased because *attention* to the preexposed irrelevant stimulus is maintained, a condition that can affect either subsequent associability directly, as originally proposed by A-theories, or subsequent retrieval of the one or more associations acquired during the preexposure stage. For the subject with negative symptoms, LI may be increased because the preexposed stimulus is relatively unattended in the first place. As a consequence, CS-0 and/or CS-context associations may be acquired more effectively than for normals, thereby facilitating subsequent retrievability of those associations.

Although the above accounts combine the major themes of A- and R-theories, the specific descriptions of their operations remain quite speculative, perhaps because of the scarcity of data regarding stimulus property and stimulus relationship encoding. Clearly, given the number of different processes that may underlie the apparently simple LI effect, one can generate a variety of alternative explanations for the relationship between schizophrenia symptom types and the effects of irrelevant stimulus preexposures. It is equally clear that we have reached a point where we now know the direction that future research has to take in order to provide more definitive explanations.

References

Alves, C. R. R., Delucia, R., & Silva, M. T. A. (2002). Effects of fencamfamine on latent inhibition. *Progress in Neuro-Psychopharmacology and Biological Psychiatry, 26,* 1089–1093.
Alves, C. R. R., & Silva, M. T. (2001). Facilitation of latent inhibition by the atypical antipsychotic risperidone. *Pharmacology Biochemistry and Behavior, 68,* 503–506.
American Psychiatric Association. (2000). *Diagnostic and statistical manual of mental disorders DSM-IV-TR.* Washington, DC: American Psychiatric Association.
Angrist, B., Rotrosen, J., & Gershon, S. (1980). Differential effects of amphetamine and neuroleptics on negative vs positive symptoms in schizophrenia. *Psychopharmacology, 72,* 17–19.
Anscombe, R. (1987). The disorder of consciousness in schizophrenia. *Schizophrenia Bulletin, 13,* 241–260.
Barch, D. M., Carter, C. S., Hachten, P. C., Usher, M., & Cohen, J. D. (1999). The "benefits" of distractibility: Mechanisms underlying increased Stroop effects in schizophrenia. *Schizophrenia Bulletin, 25,* 749–762.
Baruch, I., Hemsley, D. R., & Gray, J. A. (1988a). Differential performance of acute and chronic schizophrenics in a latent inhibition task. *Journal of Nervous and Mental Disease, 176,* 598–606.
Baruch, I., Hemsley, D. R., & Gray, J. A. (1988b). Latent inhibition and 'psychotic proneness' in normal subjects. *Personality and Individual Differences, 9,* 777–784.
Bennett, C. H., Tremain, M., & Mackintosh, N. J. (1996). Facilitation and retardation of flavor conditioning following prior exposure to the CS. *Quarterly Journal of Experimental Psychology, 49B,* 220–230.
Bouton, M. E. (1993). Context, time, and memory retrieval in the interference paradigms of Pavlovian learning. *Psychological Bulletin, 114,* 80–99.
Braff, D. L. (1993). Information processing and attention dysfunctions in schizophrenia. *Schizophrenia Bulletin, 19,* 233–259.
Braunstein-Bercovitz, H. (2000). Is the attentional dysfunction in schizotypy related to anxiety? *Schizophrenia Research, 46,* 255–267.
Braunstein-Bercovitz, H., Dimentman-Ashkenazi, I., & Lubow, R. E. (2001). Stress affects the selection of relevant from irrelevant stimuli. *Emotion, 1,* 182–192.
Braunstein-Bercovitz, H., Hen, I., & Lubow, R. E. (2004). Masking task load modulates latent inhibition: support for a distraction model of irrelevant information processing by high schizotypal participants. *Cognition and Emotion, 18,* 1135–1144.
Braunstein-Bercovitz, H., & Lubow, R. E. (1998). Are high schizotypal normals distractible or limited in attentional resources? A study of latent inhibition as a function of masking task load and schizotypy. *Journal of Abnormal Psychology, 107,* 659–670.
Braunstein-Bercovitz, H., Rammsayer, T., Gibbons, H., & Lubow, R. E. (2002). Latent inhibition deficits in high schizotypal normals: symptom-specific or anxiety-related? A review. *Schizophrenia Research, 53,* 109–121.
Burch, G. S. J., Hemsley, D. R., & Joseph, M. H. (2004). Trials-to-criterion latent inhibition in humans as a function of stimulus pre-exposure and positive schizotypy. *British Journal of Psychology, 95,* 179–196.

Chapman, L. J., Edell, W. S., & Chapman, J. P. (1980). Physical anhedonia, perceptual aberration, and psychosis proneness. *Schizophrenia Bulletin, 6*, 639–653.

Claridge, G. S., & Broks, P. (1984). Schizotypy and hemisphere function-I: theoretical considerations and the measurement of schizotypy. *Personality and Individual Differences, 5*, 633–648.

Cohen, E., Sereni, N., Kaplan, O., Weizman, A., Kikinzon, L., Weiner, I., et al. (2004). The relation between latent inhibition and symptom-types in young schizophrenics. *Behavioural Brain Research, 149*, 113–122.

De la Casa, L. G. (1994). Latent inhibition and recall of irrelevant stimuli in type-A and type-B subjects. *Revista de Psicologia General y Aplicada, 47*, 289–300.

De la Casa, G., & Lubow, R. E. (2001). Latent inhibition with a response time measure from a within-subject design: effects of number of preexposures, masking task, context change, and delay. *Neuropsychology, 15*, 244–253.

Della Casa, V., Hoefer, I., Weiner, I., & Feldon, J. (1999). Effects of smoking status and schizotypy on latent inhibition. *Journal of Psychopharmacology, 13*, 362–368.

Dunn, L. A., Atwater, G., & Kilts, C. (1993). Effects of antipsychotic drugs on latent inhibition: sensitivity and specificity of an animal behavioral model of clinical drug action. *Psychopharmacology, 112*, 315–323.

Ellinwood, E. H. J. (1967). Amphetamine psychosis: I. Description of the individuals and process. *Journal of Nervous and Mental Disease, 144*, 273–283.

Escobar, M., Arcediano, F., & Miller, R. R. (2003). Latent inhibition in human adults without masking. *Journal of Experimental Psychology: Learning, Memory, and Cognition, 29*, 1028–1040.

Evans, L. H., Gray, N. S., & Snowden, R. J. (2007). A new continuous within-participants latent inhibition task: examining associations with schizotypy dimensions, smoking status and gender. *Biological Psychology, 74*, 365–373.

Eysenck, M. W., Derakshan, N., Santos, R., & Calvo, M. G. (2007). Anxiety and cognitive performance: attentional control theory. *Emotion, 7*, 336–353.

Eysenck, H. J., & Eysenck, S. B. G. (1976). *Psychoticism as a dimension of personality*. London: Hodder and Stoughton.

Frith, C. D. (1979). Consciousness, information processing and schizophrenia. *The British Journal of Psychiatry, 134*, 225–235.

Ginton, A., Urca, G., & Lubow, R. E. (1975). The effects of preexposure to a nonattended stimulus on subsequent learning: latent inhibition in adults. *Bulletin of the Psychonomic Society, 5*, 5–8.

Gosselin, G., Oberling, P., & Di Scala, G. (1996). Antagonism of amphetamine-induced disruption of latent inhibition by the atypical antipsychotic olanzapine in rats. *Behavioural Pharmacology, 7*, 820–826.

Graham, S., & Mclaren, I. P. L. (1998). Retardation in human discrimination learning as a consequence of preexposure: latent inhibition or negative priming? *Quarterly Journal of Experimental Psychology, 51B*, 155–172.

Gray, N. S., Fernandez, M., Williams, J., Ruddle, R. A., & Snowden, R. J. (2002). Which schizotypal dimensions abolish latent inhibition? *British Journal of Clinical Psychology, 41*, 271–284.

Gray, N. S., Hemsley, D. R., & Gray, J. A. (1992). Abolition of latent inhibition in acute, but not chronic, schizophrenics. *Neurology, Psychiatry, and Brain Research, 1*, 83–89.

Gray, N. S., Pickering, A. D., Hemsley, D. R., Dawling, S., & Gray, J. A. (1992). Abolition of latent inhibition by a single 5 mg dose of d-amphetamine in man. *Psychopharmacology, 107*, 425–430.

Gray, N. S., Pilowsky, L. S., Gray, J. A., & Kerwin, R. W. (1995). Latent inhibition in drug naive schizophrenics: relationship to duration of illness and dopamine D2 binding using SPET. *Schizophrenia Research, 17*, 95–107.

Gray, N. S., Snowden, R. J., Peoples, M., Hemsley, D. R., & Gray, J. A. (2003). A demonstration of within-subjects latent inhibition in the human: limitations and advantages. *Behavioural Brain Research, 138*, 1–8.

Gray, N. S., Williams, J., Fernandez, M., Ruddle, R. A., Good, M. A., & Snowden, R. J. (2001). Context dependent latent inhibition in adult humans. *Quarterly Journal of Experimental Psychology, 54B*, 233–245.

Hall, G. (1991). *Perceptual and associative learning*. Oxford, England: Clarendon.

Head, D., Bolton, D., & Hymas, N. (1989). Deficit in cognitive shifting ability in patients with obsessive-compulsive disorder. *Biological Psychiatry, 25*, 929–937.

Hoefer, I., Della Casa, V., & Feldon, J. (1998). The interaction between schizotypy and latent inhibition: modulation by experimental parameters. *Personality and Individual Differences, 26*, 1075–1088.

Hoffmann, H., & Spear, N. E. (1989). Facilitation and impairment of conditioning in the preweanling rat after prior exposure to the conditioned stimulus. *Animal Learning and Behavior, 17*, 63–69.

Kaplan, O., Dar, R., Rosenthal, L., Hermesh, H., Fux, M., & Lubow, R. E. (2006). Obsessive-compulsive disorder patients display enhanced latent inhibition on a visual search task. *Behavior Research and Therapy, 44*, 1137–1145.

Kumari, V., Cotter, P. A., Mulligen, O. F., Checkley, S. A., Gray, N. S., Hemsley, D. R., et al. (1999). Effects of d-amphetamine and haloperidol on latent inhibition in healthy male volunteers. *Journal of Psychopharmacology, 13*, 398–405.

Leumann, L., Feldon, J., Vollenweider, F. X., & Ludewig, K. (2002). Effects of typical and atypical antipsychotics on prepulse inhibition and latent inhibition in chronic schizophrenia. *Biological Psychiatry, 52*, 729–739.

Lipp, O. V., Siddle, D. A. T., & Vaitl, D. (1992). Latent inhibition in humans: single cue conditioning revisited. *Journal of Experimental Psychology: Animal Behavior Processes, 18*, 115–125.

Lipp, O. V., & Vaitl, D. (1992). Latent inhibition in human Pavlovian differential conditioning: effects of additional stimulation after preexposure and relation to schizotypal traits. *Personality and Individual Differences, 13*, 1003–1012.

Lubow, R. E. (1973). Latent inhibition. *Psychological Bulletin, 79*, 398–407.

Lubow, R. E. (1989). *Latent inhibition and conditioned attention theory*. New-York: Cambridge University Press.

Lubow, R. E. (2005). Construct validity of the animal latent inhibition model of selective attention deficits in schizophrenia. *Schizophrenia Bulletin, 31*, 139–153.

Lubow, R. E., Braunstein-Bercovitz, H., Blumenthal, O., Kaplan, O., & Toren, P. (2005). Latent inhibition and asymmetrical visualspatial attention in children with ADHD. *Child Neuropsychology, 11*, 445–457.

Lubow, R. E., Caspy, T., & Schnur, P. (1982). Latent inhibition and learned helplessness in children: similarities and differences. *Journal of Experimental Child Psychology, 34*, 231–256.

Lubow, R. E., & De la Casa, L. G. (2005). There is a time and a place for everything: bidirectional modulations of latent inhibition by time-induced context differentiation. *Psychonomic Bulletin and Review, 12*, 806–821.

Lubow, R. E., Dressler, R., & Kaplan, O. (1999). Visual search and latent inhibition in de novo Parkinson patients. *Neuropsychology, 13*, 415–423.

Lubow, R. E., & Gewirtz, J. C. (1995). Latent inhibition in humans: data, theory, and implications for Schizophrenia. *Psychological Bulletin, 117*, 87–103.

Lubow, R. E., Ingberg-Sachs, Y., Zalstein-Orda, N., & Gewirtz, J. C. (1992). Disruption of latent inhibition in high psychotic-prone normal subjects. *Personality and Individual Differences, 13*, 563–572.

Lubow, R. E., & Josman, Z. E. (1993). Latent inhibition deficits in hyperactive children. *Journal of Child Psychology and Psychiatry, 84*, 859–875.

Lubow, R. E., & Kaplan, O. (2005). The visual search analog of latent inhibition: implications for theories of irrelevant stimulus processing in normal and schizophrenic groups. *Psychonomic Bulletin and Review, 12*, 224–243.

Lubow, R. E., Kaplan, O., Abramovich, P., Rudnick, A., & Laor, N. (2000). Visual search in schizophrenia: latent inhibition and novel popout effects. *Schizophrenia Research, 45*, 145–156.

Lubow, R. E., & Moore, A. U. (1959). Latent inhibition: the effect of non-reinforced pre-exposure to conditional stimulus. *Journal of Comparative and Physiological Psychology, 52*, 416–419.

Lubow, R. E., Toren, P., Laor, N., & Kaplan, O. (2000). The effects of target and distractor familiarity on visual search in anxious children: latent inhibition and novel pop-out. *Journal of Anxiety Disorders, 14*, 41–56.

Lubow, R. E., Weiner, I., Schlossberg, A., & Baruch, I. (1987). Latent inhibition and schizophrenia. *Bulletin of the Psychonomic Society, 25*, 464–467.

Mackintosh, N. J. (1975). A theory of attention: variations in the associability of stimuli with reinforcement. *Psychological Review, 82*, 276–284.

McCartan, D., Bell, R., Green, J. F., Campbell, C., Trimble, K., Pickering, A., et al. (2001). The differential effects of chlorpromazine and haloperidol on latent inhibition in healthy volunteers. *Journal of Psychopharmacology, 15*, 96–104.

McGhie, A., & Chapman, J. (1961). Disorders of attention and perception in early schizophrenia. *British Journal of Medical Psychology, 34*, 103–116.

Mednick, S. A., & McNeil, T. F. (1973). Current methodology in research on the etiology of schizophrenia: serious difficulties which suggest the use of the high-risk-group method. *Psychological Bulletin, 70*, 681–693.

Miller, R. R., Kasprow, W. J., & Schachtman, T. R. (1986). Retrieval variability: sources and consequences. *American Journal of Psychology, 99*, 145–218.

Mirsky, A. F., & Duncan, C. C. (1986). Etiology and expression of schizophrenia: neurobiological and social factors. *Annual Review of Psychology, 37*, 291–319.

Moran, P. M., Fischer, T. R., Hitchcock, J. M., & Moser, P. C. (1996). Effects of clozapine on latent inhibition in the rat. *Behavioural Pharmacology, 7*, 42–48.

Moser, P. C., Hitchcock, J. M., Lister, S., & Moran, P. M. (2000). The pharmacology of latent inhibition as an animal model of schizophrenia. *Brain Research Reviews, 33*, 275–307.

Nadal, R. (2001). Pharmacology of the atypical antipsychotic remoxipride, a dopamine D2 receptor antagonist. *CNS Drug Reviews, 7*, 265–282.

Nelson, J. B., & Sanjuan, M. D. C. (2006). A context-specific latent inhibition effect in a human conditioned suppression task. *Quarterly Journal of Experimental Psychology, 59*, 1003–1020.

Nuechterlein, K. H., Asarnow, R. F., Subotnik, K. L., Foelson, D. L., Payne, D. L., Kendler, K. S., et al. (2002). The structure of schizotypy: relationships between neurocognitve and personality disorder features in relatives of schizophrenic patients in the UCLA Family Study. *Schizophrenia Research, 54*, 1211–130.

Nuechterlein, K. H., & Dawson, M. E. (1984). Information processing and attentional functioning in the developmental course of schizophrenic disorders. *Schizophrenia Bulletin, 10*, 160–203.

Nutt, D. J., Bell, C. J., & Malizia, A. L. (1998). Brain mechanisms of social anxiety disorder. *Journal of Clinical Psychiatry, 12*, 31–38.

Ohman, A., Nordby, H., & d'Elia, G. (1986). Orienting and schizophrenia: stimulus significance, attention, and distraction in a signaled reaction time task. *Journal of Abnormal Psychology, 95*, 326–334.

Pearce, J. M., & Hall, G. (1980). A model of Pavlovian learning: variations in the effectiveness of conditioned but not of unconditioned stimuli. *Psychological Review, 87*, 532–553.

Peters, S. L., & Joseph, M. (1993). Haloperidol potentiation of latent inhibition in rats: evidence for a critical role at conditioning rather than pre-exposure. *Behavioural Pharmacology, 4*, 183–186.

Pineno, O., De la Casa, L. G., Lubow, R. E., & Miller, R. R. (2006). Some determinants of latent inhibition in human predictive learning. *Learning and Motivation, 37*, 42–65.

Prados, J. (2000). Effects of varying the amounts of preexposure to spatial cues on a subsequent navigational task. *Quarterly Journal of Experimental Psychology, 53B*, 139–148.

Raine, A. (1991). The SPQ: a scale for the assessment of schizotypal personality based on DSM-III-R criteria. *Schizophrenia Bulletin, 17*, 555–564.

Rascle, C., Mazas, O., Vaiva, G., Tournant, M., Raybois, O., Goudemond, N., et al. (2001). Clinical features of latent inhibition in schizophrenia. *Schizophrenia Research, 51*, 149–161.

Sato, M., Numachi, Y., & Hamamura, T. (1992). Relapse of paranoid psychotic state in methamphetamine model of schizophrenia. *Schizophrenia Bulletin, 18*, 115–122.

Serra, A. M., Jones, S. H., Toone, B., & Gray, J. A. (2001). Impaired associative learning in chronic schizophrenics and their first-degree relatives: a study of latent inhibition and the Kamin blocking effect. *Schizophrenia Research, 48*, 273–289.

Shadach, E., Feldon, J., & Weiner, I. (1999). Clozapineinduced potentiation of latent inhibition is due to its action in the conditioning stage: implications for the mechanism of action of antipsychotic drugs. *International Journal of Neuropsychopharmacology, 2*, 283–291.

Spielberger, C. D., Gorsuch, R. L., & Lushene, R. E. (1970). *Manual for the state-trait anxiety inventory (self-evaluation questionnaire)*. Palo Alto, CA: Consulting Psychologists Press.

Stefanatos, G. A., & Wasserstein, J. (2001). Attention/deficit hyperactivity disorder as a right hemisphere syndrome. *Annals of the New York Academy of Sciences, 931*, 172–195.

Swerdlow, N. R., Braff, D. L., Hartston, H., Perry, W., & Geyer, M. A. (1996). Latent inhibition in schizophrenia. *Schizophrenia Research, 20*, 91–103.

Swerdlow, N. R., Hartston, H. J., & Hartman, P. L. (1999). Enhanced visual latent inhibition in obsessive-compulsive disorder. *Biological Psychiatry, 45*, 482–488.

Swerdlow, N. R., Magulac, M., Filion, D., & Zinner, S. (1996). Visuospatial priming and latent inhibition in children and adults with Tourette's disorder. *Neuropsychology, 10*, 485–494.

Swerdlow, N. R., Stephany, N., Wasserman, L. C., Talledo, J., Sharp, R., & Auerbach, P. P. (2003). Dopamine agonists disrupt visual latent inhibition in normal males using a within-subject paradigm. *Psychopharmacology, 169*, 314–320.

Swerdlow, N. R., Stephany, N., Wasserman, L. C., Talledo, J., Sharp, R., Minassian, A., et al. (2005). Intact visual latent inhibition in schizophrenia patients in a within-subject paradigm. *Schizophrenia Research, 72*, 169–183.

Trimble, K. M., Bell, R., & King, D. J. (1997). Enhancement of latent inhibition in the rat by the atypical antipsychotic agent remoxipride. *Pharmacology, Biochemistry, and Behavior, 56*, 809–816.

Tzschentke, T. M. (2001). Pharmacology and behavioral pharmacology of the mesocortical dopamine system. *Progress in Neurobiology, 63*, 241–320.

Vaitl, D., Lipp, O., Bauer, U., Schuler, G., Stark, R., Zimmermann, M., et al. (2002). Latent inhibition and schizophrenia: Pavlovian conditioning of autonomic responses. *Schizophrenia Research, 55*, 147–158.

Weiner, I. (2003). The "two-headed" latent inhibition model of schizophrenia: modeling positive and negative symptoms and their treatment. *Psychopharmacology, 169*, 257–297.

Weiner, I., & Feldon, J. (1987). Facilitation of latent inhibition by haloperidol. *Psychopharmacology, 91*, 248–253.

Weiner, I., Lubow, R. E., & Feldon, J. (1984). Abolition of the expression but not the acquisition of latent inhibition by chronic amphetamine in rats. *Psychopharmacology, 83*, 194–199.

Weiner, I., Lubow, R. E., & Feldon, J. (1988). Disruption of latent inhibition by acute administration of low doses of amphetamine. *Pharmacology, Biochemistry and Behavior, 30*, 871–878.

Williams, J. H., Wellman, N. A., Geaney, D. P., Cowan, P. J., Feldon, J., & Rawlins, J. N. P. (1996). Anti-psychotic drug effects in a model of schizophrenic attentional disorder: a randomized controlled trial of the effects of haloperidol on latent inhibition in healthy people. *Biological Psychiatry, 40*, 1135–1143.

Williams, J. H., Wellman, N. A., Geaney, D. P., Cowen, P. J., Feldon, J., & Rawlins, J. N. P. (1998). Reduced latent inhibition in people with schizophrenia: an effect of psychosis or of its treatment. *British Journal of Psychiatry, 172*, 243–249.

Williams, J. H., Wellman, N. A., Geaney, D. P., Feldon, J., Cowen, P. J., & Rawlins, J. N. P. (1997). Haloperidol enhances latent inhibition in visual tasks in healthy people. *Psychopharmacology, 133*, 262–268.

Wuthrich, V., & Bates, T. C. (2001). Schizotypy and latent inhibition: non-linear linkage between psychometric and cognitive markers. *Personality and Individual Differences, 30*, 783–798.

Young, A. M. J., Moran, P. M., & Joseph, M. H. (2005). The role of dopamine in conditioning and latent inhibition: what, when, where and how? *Neuroscience and Biobehavioral Reviews, 29*, 963–976.

Zahn, T., Rappaport, J. L., & Thompson, C. L. (1981). Autonomic effects of dextroamphetamine in normal men: implications for hyperactivity and schizophrenia. *Psychiatry Research, 4*, 39–47.

Zalstein-Orda, N., & Lubow, R. E. (1995). Context control of negative transfer induced by preexposure to irrelevant stimuli: latent inhibition in humans. *Learning and Motivation, 26*, 11–28.

Chapter 12
Attentional Control Theory of Anxiety: Recent Developments

Michael W. Eysenck

Introduction

There have been relatively few attempts to understand the effects of anxiety (whether regarded as a personality dimension or as a mood state) on task performance directly from the perspective of cognitive psychology. However, attentional control theory (Eysenck, Derakshan, Santos, & Calvo, 2007) is an attempt to do precisely that. As is discussed in this chapter, it is assumed that there is an important distinction between positive attentional control and negative attentional control. It is also assumed that anxiety impairs the efficiency of both forms of attentional control. However, the adverse effects of such impaired efficiency on performance can be reduced or eliminated when anxious individuals utilise additional resources or effort. Research that provides general support for these assumptions is discussed, and implications for future research are discussed.

Previous Theorising of Anxiety Effects on Performance

There have been various attempts theoretically to try to explain the effects of anxiety on the performance of various tasks of a cognitive nature, but most of these theories were not framed within the context of cognitive psychology. It is important to note at the outset that anxiety can be regarded either as a personality dimension (i.e. trait anxiety as assessed, for example, by Spielberger's State-Trait Anxiety Inventory (STAI): Spielberger, Gorsuch, Lushene, Vagg, & Jacobs, 1983) or as a mood state (state anxiety, which can also be assessed by the STAI) that varies between individuals. In practice, most research in this area has focused on trait anxiety. However, it should be emphasised that trait anxiety and state anxiety typically correlate moderately positively with each other. The precise magnitude of the correlation varies from study to study but is typically about +0.5 (Eysenck, 1982). As a consequence, it has proved difficult in practice to disentangle their effects on performance. This ambiguity in much of the evidence should be borne in mind in the following section.

M.W. Eysenck (✉)
Department of Psychology, Royal Holloway University of London, Egham, Surrey, TW20 0EX, UK
e-mail: m.eysenck@rhul.ac.uk

Cognitive Interference Theory

In principle, there are several different parts of the cognitive system (e.g. basic perceptual processes; long-term memory) that could be affected by anxiety when individuals are instructed to perform complex tasks involving neutral stimuli. However, there is a reasonable consensus that the most consequential effects of anxiety are on the attentional system rather than on other information-processing systems. Historically, one of the most influential approaches was the cognitive interference theory put forward by Sarason (e.g. 1988). According to Sarason (1988, p. 5), "Proneness to self-preoccupation and, most specifically, to worry over evaluation is a powerful component of what is referred to as test anxiety". The implication of this theory in more contemporary terminology is that anxiety impairs attentional control with respect to task-irrelevant internal stimuli (e.g. self-relevant worries).

There are various predictions that follow from the hypothesis that anxiety leads to self-preoccupation and worry over evaluation. First, it is predicted that the effects of anxiety on performance will typically be adverse given that task-irrelevant processing reduces the attentional resources available for the processing of task-relevant stimuli. Second, it is predicted that the adverse effects of anxiety on performance should be greater when evaluative instructions are used than when non-evaluative instructions are used, because the former instructions are more likely to activate task-irrelevant worries. Third, it is predicted that the adverse effects of anxiety on performance should be greater when the task in question is complex and highly attentionally demanding than when it is not. The argument here is that any loss of attentional resources will have a greater effect on attentionally demanding tasks (originally suggested by Kahneman, 1973).

In broad terms, there is support for all three of the main predictions of cognitive interference theory (see Eysenck, 1992, for a review). For example, Morris, Davis, and Hutchings (1981) reviewed research on test anxiety and task performance. They pointed out that test anxiety consists of two major components, namely, worry and emotionality. The research consistently indicates that the negative effects of anxiety on performance are due almost entirely to worry rather than to emotionality.

In spite of the fact that there is compelling evidence that Sarason's emphasis on the role of the attentional system in mediating the effects of anxiety on performance, his approach possesses several limitations. First, it was assumed within cognitive interference theory that the direction of causality is from worry and self-preoccupation to task processing. However, there is some evidence suggesting that the causality can also proceed in the opposite direction. Rapee (1993) compared the effects of several tasks on worry-related thoughts. He found that random-letter generation (a demanding task that places high demands on attentional processes) reduced the incidence of worry-related thoughts. In contrast, tasks that placed minimal demands on the attentional system (word repetition; fixed-order key presses) did not reduce worry-related thoughts.

Second, cognitive interference theory exaggerates the role played by worry and self-preoccupation. According to the theory, anxious individuals should perform worse than non-anxious ones when they experience more task-irrelevant thoughts. However, there are several studies in which that was not the case. For example, Blankstein, Toner, and Flett (1989) and Blankstein, Flett, Boase, and Toner (1990) compared the performance of low and high test-anxious groups on an anagram task. They found that there was no group difference in anagram performance in spite of the fact that the anxious group reported substantially more negative task-irrelevant thoughts.

Third, and of direct relevance to the central theme of this book, Sarason failed to specify precisely how anxiety affects the attentional system. As a consequence, it is often difficult to make specific predictions from the theory. In addition, studies designed to test cognitive interference theory provide only indirect support for the theory. For example, the finding that anxiety impairs performance with evaluative instructions but not with non-evaluative instructions is entirely consistent with the hypothesis that anxiety reduces the availability of attentional resources, but this interpretation is by no means the only possible one.

Processing Efficiency Theory

The first systematic attempt to specify more clearly the effects of anxiety on the cognitive system was contained within processing efficiency theory (Eysenck & Calvo, 1992). One of the main starting points of processing efficiency theory was the assumption that the effects of anxiety should be considered within the context of Baddeley's (1986) working memory system. According to Baddeley, this system consists of three main components (recently increased to four: Baddeley, 2001), which are arranged hierarchically. The central executive (an attention-like, domain-free system) is at the top of the hierarchy, and is believed to be much involved in functions such as planning, strategy selection, and attentional control. There are two other components: (1) the phonological loop, which is involved in the rehearsal of verbal material; and (2) the visuo-spatial sketchpad, which is involved in the processing and transient storage of visual and spatial information.

The key prediction following from the above assumptions was that most of the adverse effects of anxiety on cognitive processing involve the central executive component of the working memory system. Baddeley (1986) assumed that the central executive was a unitary system, and so it was assumed within processing efficiency theory that anxiety impaired the functioning of this unitary system. However, it is important to distinguish between *performance effectiveness* (the quality of performance as assessed by conventional behavioural measures) and *processing efficiency* (the relationship between performance effectiveness and use of resources or effort). In essence, anxious individuals often exert more effort than nonanxious ones. As a consequence, there are generally greater adverse effects of anxiety on processing efficiency than on performance effectiveness.

There is considerable empirical support for processing efficiency theory (see Eysenck & Calvo, 1992, and Eysenck et al., 2007, for reviews). Some of the strongest supporting evidence was reported by Eysenck, Payne, and Derakshan (2005). Participants low and high in trait anxiety performed a complex visuo-spatial task (the Corsi task) as their main or primary task. At the same time, they performed a less important secondary task that required the use of the central executive, the phonological loop, or the visuo-spatial sketchpad. The key finding was that performance on the Corsi task was only significantly worse in the high-anxious group than in the low-anxious group when the secondary task required use of the central executive. This pattern of findings suggests that anxiety utilises some of the resources of the central executive (presumably through task-irrelevant thoughts) but has little or no effect on processing within the phonological loop or the visuo-spatial sketchpad.

Executive Functions of Attentional Control

Processing efficiency theory represented a clear advance on cognitive interference theory. It pinpointed the working memory system as being importantly implicated in the effects of anxiety on the cognitive system, it drew a fundamental distinction between processing efficiency and performance effectiveness, and it established a more precise framework within which to study the cognitive processes affected and unaffected by anxiety. However, processing efficiency theory was limited because it did not specify in any detail how anxiety affects the various functions of the central executive. An important reason for this was that in the early 1990s little was known about the number or nature of the main attentional or other functions involving the central executive. Indeed, it remains the case that there is uncertainty and controversy on this issue.

One of the most influential attempts to identify the major functions of the central executive system was that of Smith and Jonides (1999). They produced a list of five functions. First, there is switching between tasks. Second, there is planning sub-tasks in order to reach some pre-determined goal. Third, there is selective attention combined with inhibition. Fourth, there is updating and checking the information that is contained within working memory. Fifth, there is a function concerned with coding representations in working memory based on information about when and where the stimuli relating to the representations were encountered.

The most obvious limitation of the approach taken by Smith and Jonides (1999) is that it was not based directly on empirical evidence. Instead, it represented a reasonable attempt to make sense of a diverse set of findings. In contrast, Miyake et al. (2000) and Friedman and Miyake (2004) did not make any a priori assumptions about the number or nature of executive functions. Instead, they administered many tasks that are generally assumed to involve the central executive, and then submitted the resultant data to latent variable analysis. This empirically based approach led to the identification of three major functions: the *inhibition function*; the *shifting function*; and the *updating function*. These functions are largely independent. However, there are positive inter-correlations among them, which suggests that they may depend at least in part on some common processing resources.

Inhibition

The inhibition function is basically involved to resist performance disruption from task-irrelevant stimuli or responses. According to Miyake et al. (2000, p. 57), inhibition can be defined as, "one's ability to deliberately inhibit dominant, automatic, or prepotent responses when necessary". Friedman and Miyake (2004) extended the scope of the inhibition function to include inhibiting attention to task-irrelevant stimuli. It is important to note that numerous kinds of inhibition have been identified. For example, Nigg (2000) argued that there are eight forms of inhibition including interference control, cognitive inhibition, behavioural inhibition, and automatic inhibition of attention.

Shifting

The shifting function is involved in permitting flexible shifting of attention either within or between tasks to preserve focus on the most task-relevant stimuli. According to Miyake et al. (2000, p. 55), the shifting function involves, "shifting back and forth between multiple tasks, operations, or mental sets".

Information Updating

The updating function is mostly concerned with the transient storage of information. According to Miyake et al. (2000, p. 56), the updating function involves "updating and monitoring of working memory representations". It can appropriately be regarded as a measure of basic attentional or short-term memory capacity. It is encouraging that there is a reasonable overlap between these three functions and those identified by Smith and Jonides (1999). The inhibition function resembles the third function (selective attention and inhibition) identified by Smith and Jonides (1999). The shifting function is similar to Smith and Jonides' first function (switching between tasks). The updating function is similar to Smith and Jonides' fourth function, namely, updating and checking.

Attentional Control Theory of Anxiety Effects on Performance

Eysenck et al.'s (2007) attentional control theory used the tripartite division of the central executive proposed by Miyake et al. (2000) as the basis for some of their main theoretical assumptions. According to the theory, anxiety impairs the efficiency of two rather separate kinds of attentional control. First, there is negative attentional control. This involves the inhibition function and is used to prevent task-irrelevant stimuli (whether internal or external) from distracting attention away from task-relevant stimuli (Friedman & Miyake, 2004). In addition, it is assumed that the inhibition function also includes inhibiting prepotent responses, and that anxiety also impairs the inhibition function under those circumstances.

Second, there is positive attentional control, which is used to ensure that attention is deployed flexibly in response to changing task demands or requirements. In other words, anxiety impairs the efficiency of the inhibition function (negative attentional control) and of the shifting function (positive attentional control).

What about the effects of anxiety on the updating function? According to attentional control theory, this function is not directly affected by anxiety. Friedman et al. (2006) argued that this function (which seems to involve some basic short-term memory capacity) differs in an important way from the inhibition and shifting functions. More specifically, they found that performance on tasks involving the updating function correlated highly with measures of fluid and of crystallised intelligence. In contrast, performance on tasks involving the inhibition or shifting function failed to correlate significantly with either fluid or crystallised intelligence. The implication is that the updating function assesses some basic cognitive capacity related to intelligence rather than to anxiety.

Attentional control theory focuses on the effects on efficiency and on performance of individual differences in anxiety. Individuals differ in both trait anxiety (anxiety as a personality dimension) and state anxiety (anxiety as the current experience of anxiety). The available evidence suggests that both trait anxiety and state anxiety contribute to impaired attentional control. However, their respective contributions remain elusive for three reasons. First, trait anxiety and state anxiety typically correlate moderately highly with each other, which makes it difficult to discriminate between effects due to trait anxiety and those due to state anxiety. Second, the great majority of studies have focused on trait anxiety (or test anxiety) and have produced equivocal findings in which it is unclear whether the group differences reflect trait anxiety, state anxiety, or some combination of both. Third, there are remarkably few studies in which state anxiety has been experimentally manipulated, but this is perhaps the only method of disentangling properly the effects of trait and state anxiety on performance.

Research Findings

Eysenck et al. (2007) provide a review of the evidence relating to attentional control theory. Most of this research provides reasonable support for the theory. We will start by considering research focusing on the crucial distinction between processing efficiency and performance effectiveness, which is as important within attentional control theory as within processing efficiency theory. After that, we will consider recent unpublished research on the inhibition and shifting functions. It is worth pointing out that there is a very large discrepancy in the amount of anxiety research focusing on the inhibition function and on the shifting function. There have been approximately 30 studies on anxiety and the inhibition function, but practically none on anxiety and the shifting function. Accordingly, we will focus mainly on recent research on the shifting function.

One of the major predictions of attentional control theory is that anxiety impairs processing efficiency to a greater extent than performance effectiveness. Much of the evidence discussed by Eysenck et al. (2007) is consistent with that prediction. However, one of the issues that has proved difficult to address adequately is that of assessing processing efficiency with precision. Performance effectiveness can be assessed by conventional behavioural measures of performance, but efficiency also involves some assessment of the use of resources or effort during task processing. Recent research by Santos, Wall, and Eysenck (submitted) used functional magnetic resonance imaging (fMRI) to provide a more direct assessment of processing efficiency than any used hitherto in relation to the shifting function identified within attentional control theory. However, promising findings had been obtained previously, and will be discussed here.

One appropriate way of assessing processing efficiency is based on the *probe technique* (e.g. Johnston, 1972). In essence, use of this technique involves participants performing a main or primary task under two conditions. In one condition, this task is performed on its own. In the second condition, there is also a secondary task that needs to be performed occasionally and at unpredictable times. This secondary task is typically very easy (e.g. responding as fast as possible to an auditory probe). Of importance, participants are instructed in this latter condition to perform the main or primary task as well as possible and only to use spare processing capacity to perform the secondary task. The key assumption is that performance on the secondary or probe task provides an estimate of processing efficiency: individuals who are inefficient will allocate nearly all their processing resources to the primary task, and so will perform slowly on the secondary task.

Eysenck and Payne (in preparation) used the probe technique in two experiments. In the first experiment, the primary task involved letter transformation. Four letters were presented, and participants had to transform all four letters by working through the alphabet the requisite distance before responding. For example, "CHFR+4" would have "GLJV" as the correct answer. This task becomes progressively harder as participants work through it, and the auditory probe could be presented at any point. There were two main findings. One was that the high-anxious participants responded more slowly to the auditory probe on average than the low-anxious ones. The other main finding was that the adverse effects of anxiety on speed of responding to the probe were greater as the demands of the main task increased.

In their second experiment, Eysenck and Payne (in preparation) used a different main or primary task. This time, participants had to perform four simple mathematical operations before producing the answer. The findings from this experiment replicated those of the first experiment. That is, high-anxious participants responded more slowly than low-anxious ones to the auditory probe, and this was especially the case when the demands of the primary task were great.

Research by other investigators using the probe technique has produced similar findings. For example, Williams, Vickers, and Rodrigues (2002) compared the performance of low-anxious and high-anxious individuals on their main task (involving table tennis). The high-anxious individuals also had significantly slower probe reaction times using auditory probe stimuli than the low-anxious ones, indicating that they had poor processing efficiency. Murray and Janelle (2003) had low-anxious and high-anxious participants perform a simulated driving task as their primary task. The key finding was that high-anxious participants had slower probe reaction times also using auditory probe stimuli than low-anxious ones, and this effect was greatest under competitive conditions.

We turn now to studies concerned with the effects of anxiety on the inhibition function. Published research in this area has predominantly reported that anxious individuals are more susceptible to distraction, thus supporting the notion that anxiety impairs the inhibition function (see Eysenck et al., 2007, for a review). However, there is an important limitation that applies to most of this research. The typical paradigm has involved comparing performance in distraction and no-distraction conditions or in high- and low-distraction conditions. What has usually been found is that the performance of high-anxious individuals is more adversely affected by distractors than is that of low-anxious ones. This is entirely consistent with the notion that anxiety impairs negative attentional control. However, the failure to assess attentional processes means that their role in mediating the behavioural findings has not been established.

In recent research, Derakshan, Ansari, Hansard, Shoker and Eysenck (2009) used the *antisaccade task* as a way of testing the notion that anxiety impairs the efficiency of the inhibition function more directly than has been achieved hitherto. Participants performing the antisaccade task are presented with a peripheral cue to one side of a central fixation point. They are explicitly instructed to avoid looking at the cue but are instead to direct their gaze as rapidly as possible to the other side of the fixation point. The main dependent variable is the latency of the first correct saccade (i.e. an eye movement towards the side opposite to the side on which the cue is presented). As Hutton and Ettinger (2006) argued in their review, it is reasonable to assume that part of what is involved on the antisaccade task is use of the inhibition function to prevent reflexive saccades to the cue. That justifies use of the antisaccade task as a way to assess the inhibition function. Its use is also justified by Miyake et al.'s (2000) finding that the antisaccade task loaded more highly than any other task on the inhibition function. We also used a control condition (the prosaccade task), in which participants were instructed to gaze at the cue when it appeared. In this condition, the inhibition function is not required.

In their first experiment, Derakshan et al. (2009) obtained the predicted significant interaction between anxiety and task (antisaccade task vs. prosaccade task). There was no effect of anxiety on the prosaccade task, which did not involve the inhibition function. However, as predicted, the high-anxious participants took significantly longer than the low-anxious ones to make the first correct saccade on the antisaccade task. While it is accepted that eye movements do not provide a direct assessment of attentional processes, it nevertheless seems reasonable to regard them as less indirect than most behavioural measures (e.g. percentage correct).

In their second experiment, Derakshan et al. (2009) also used the antisaccade and prosaccade tasks. The main difference between this experiment and the first one was that three different cues were used. More specifically, angry, happy, and neutral facial expressions were presented as cues on different trials. The rationale for this was the common finding that the increased susceptibility of high-anxious individuals to distracting stimuli is greater for threat-related stimuli than for non-threat-related ones (see Eysenck et al., 2007, for a review). There was a highly significant three-way interaction on latency of the first correct saccade based on the factors of task (antisaccade vs. prosaccade), valence (angry, happy, or neutral), and group (high-anxious vs. low-anxious). The pattern of this interaction was as predicted by attentional control theory. The adverse effects of anxiety on latency were found on the antisaccade task but not on the prosaccade task, and within the antisaccade task the effects of anxiety were greatest when the cue was threat-related.

The findings obtained by Derakshan et al. (2009) indicated clearly that there were significant adverse effects of anxiety when the inhibition is required but no effects at all when the inhibition function was not required. That means that the costs of inhibition are greater for high-anxious than for low-anxious individuals, although the data have not specifically been analysed in terms of inhibition costs.

We turn now to research on anxiety and the shifting function. Derakshan, Smyth, and Eysenck (in preparation) carried out the most thorough study to date. The optimal method for studying the shifting function is to make use of task-switching paradigms (see Monsell, 2003, for a review). What is of fundamental importance in task-switching paradigms is to have two conditions in which all participants in both conditions perform exactly the same two tasks. The only consequential difference between the two conditions concerns the pattern of trials on the two tasks. In the switching condition, participants alternate rapidly between the two tasks either in a predictable (e.g. task A on odd-numbered trials, task B on even-numbered trials) or unpredictable fashion (e.g. there is a 30% chance of task alternation on each trial). In contrast, in the non-switching condition, there is a solid block of trials all of which involve the same task, followed by another solid block of trials all of which involve the other task. Since the tasks are the same in both conditions, the crucial difference is that the shifting function is needed repeatedly in the switching condition but not in the non-switching condition. Thus, the prediction is that anxiety will impair processing efficiency (and perhaps also performance effectiveness) more in the switching condition than in the non-switching condition.

Derakshan et al. (in preparation) used several conditions. In one pair of conditions, the two tasks were multiplication and division problems. In the other pair of conditions, the two tasks were addition and subtraction problems. The switching condition involved alternation of tasks on every single trial. What happened was that two numbers were presented on each trial. A cue specifying the arithmetical process to be performed was either present or absent.

What did Derakshan et al. (in preparation) find? The most important finding theoretically was that there was a highly significant interaction between anxiety and task switching, and the pattern of the interaction was precisely as predicted. More specifically, high-anxious participants performed much more slowly under task-switching conditions requiring use of the shifting function than under non-switching conditions. In contrast, low-anxious participants performed comparably in the task-switching and non-switching conditions. In addition, the high-anxious group only performed significantly worse than the low-anxious group under task-switching conditions. These findings indicate that anxiety increases shifting costs although no direct measure of such costs was taken.

In the study by Derakshan et al. (in preparation), there was another important finding relating to the comparison between cueing and non-cueing conditions. Theoretically, it was assumed that the presence of a cue specifying the arithmetical process required on that trial would reduce the demands on attentional control compared to the condition in which there was no cue. As a result of that, it was predicted that the adverse effects of anxiety on performance should be greater in the cue-absent condition than in the cue-present condition. As predicted, there was a significant interaction between anxiety and cueing. The slower performance of the high-anxious participants than of the low-anxious participants was much more pronounced in the cue-absent condition than in the cue-present condition.

Santos et al. (submitted) also considered the effects of anxiety on the shifting function. In their study, participants were exposed to three conditions varying in the amount of task switching that was involved. The high-switching condition involved a task change three times in six trials, the low-switching condition involved a task change once in six trials, and the no-switching condition involved solid blocks of one task. There were three tasks altogether, all of which had to be performed on single digits presented on a computer screen. All of the tasks were simple, which explains why there were no effects of anxiety on task performance. However, an important aspect of the study was that fMRI was used to assess patterns of brain activation in all three conditions.

What predictions concerning the fMRI findings follow from attentional control theory? In essence, it was assumed that the increase in brain activation in the high-switching and low-switching conditions compared to the no-switching condition reflected the increase in use of cognitive processing resources when the shifting function was required. As a consequence, inefficient use of the shifting function by anxious individuals compared to non-anxious ones should be associated with a greater increase in brain activation for the former group.

There is another prediction that can be made. Wager, Jonides, and Reading (2004) reviewed studies that have focused on identifying those areas of the brain activated when individuals are engaged on tasks that involve the shifting function. Several different brain areas are involved, but various areas within the prefrontal cortex and associated areas seem to be of particular importance. If anxious individuals exhibit inefficient use of the shifting function, then it can be predicted that switching conditions should produce a greater increase in brain activation within those areas (especially BA9/46 and the anterior cingulated) for high-anxious than for low-anxious individuals.

What did Santos et al. (submitted) find? In essence, both of the major theoretical predictions were supported. First, high-anxious individuals showed a greater increase in brain activation than low-anxious ones when dealing with task switching (low-switching or high-switching). This finding coupled with the lack of effect of anxiety on task performance indicates that anxiety impaired processing efficiency when the shifting function was used. Second, a part of the prefrontal cortex (BA9/46) involved in the shifting function and attentional control showed a greater increase in the high-switch condition than the no-switch condition in high-anxious individuals. In addition, the anterior cingulate showed a greater increase in the low-switch condition than in the no-switch condition in high-anxious individuals. However, there were differential effects of anxiety on various other brain areas, so more research is needed to clarify the precise effects of anxiety on the shifting function.

Conclusions and Future Research

Evidence relating to three of the major assumptions of attentional control theory has been discussed. The focus of much recent research has been to test these assumptions more directly than has been done previously. Thus, for example, the probe technique and fMRI have been applied to the assessment of processing efficiency, and attentional processes under distraction conditions have been assessed by using an eye tracker. It is encouraging that the theoretically predicted findings continue to be obtained under these more stringent conditions. In addition, the novel prediction that anxiety should impair the efficient usage of the shifting function is starting to receive strong empirical research. In ongoing research, the finding that anxiety slows the latency of the first correct saccade on the antisaccade task has been replicated twice more (Derakshan et al., in preparation). Thus, it appears that attentional control theory provides a valuable theoretical framework within which to study the effects of anxiety on performance.

Implications for the Cognitive System Theory

In this section, I briefly speculate on the possible implications of the theoretical and empirical approach taken here for theories of attention and executive function. The starting point is the assumption that no single line of evidence is likely to provide decisive support for any theory within cognitive psychology. Instead, what is needed is converging evidence for any given theory based on different kinds of research (e.g. behavioural; neuroimaging). Consider, for example, Miyake et al.'s (2000) theory (developed by Friedman & Miyake, 2004), according to which there are three major executive functions, namely, the inhibition, shifting, and updating functions. They provided support for their theory via the use of latent-variable analyses based on the data from many executive tasks. However, while these analyses were consistent with the notion of three executive functions, they provided only limited support. First, there were positive inter-correlations among the three functions, so there is some doubt about their discriminability. Second, patterns of inter-correlations are intrinsically limited in terms of what they can tell us about executive functions.

Miyake et al.'s (2000) empirical approach was based upon assessing individual differences in performance on several executive tasks. However, they did not identify the key dimensions of individual differences responsible for differing levels of performance on each function. Real progress would be made if it were possible to find dimensions of individual differences relating in different ways to different functions. Precisely this was done by Friedman et al. (2006). As we have seen, they found that individual differences in intelligence predicted performance on tasks requiring the updating function but not on those requiring the inhibition or shifting function. That is important evidence, because it strengthens the argument that the updating function is separate from the other two functions in its demands on the cognitive system. Note, however, that Nęcka (1999) found that intelligence was significantly related to strength of attentional inhibition.

We have found evidence that individual differences in anxiety predict performance on tasks involving the inhibition or shifting functions but not on those involving the updating function. Such evidence provides additional support for Miyake et al.'s (2000) assumption that the updating function is distinctively different from the other two functions.

In sum, individual-difference approaches offer the prospect of assisting in the task of specifying more clearly the number and nature of executive functions. It is encouraging that such approaches are becoming much more common, as is shown by several other chapters in this volume.

Acknowledgements The research discussed here was supported by a research grant from the Economic and Social Research Council awarded jointly to Michael W. Eysenck and to Nazanin Derakshan. We are extremely grateful for this support.

References

Baddeley, A. D. (1986). *Working memory*. Oxford: Clarendon Press.
Baddeley, A. D. (2001). Is working memory still working? *American Psychologist, 56*, 851–864.
Blankstein, K. R., Flett, G. L., Boase, P., & Toner, B. B. (1990). Thought listing and endorsement measures of self-referential thinking in test anxiety. *Anxiety Research, 2*, 103–111.

Blankstein, K. R., Toner, B. B., & Flett, G. L. (1989). Test anxiety and the contents of consciousness: Thought-listing and endorsement measures. *Journal of Research in Personality, 23,* 269–286.

Derakshan, N., Eysenck, M. W., & Ansari, T. L. (in preparation). Testing attentional control theory

Derakshan, N., Ansari, T. L., Hansard, M., Shoker, L., & Eysenck, M. W. (2009). Anxiety, inhibition, efficiency, and effectiveness: An investigation using the antisaccade task. *Experimental Psychology, 56,* 48–55.

Eysenck, M. W. (1982). *Attention and arousal: Cognition and performance.* Berlin: Springer Verlag.

Eysenck, M. W. (1992). *Anxiety: The cognitive perspective.* Hove, UK: Lawrence Erlbaum Associates.

Eysenck, M. W., & Calvo, M. G. (1992). Anxiety and performance: The processing efficiency theory. *Cognition and Emotion, 6,* 409–434.

Eysenck, M. W., & Payne, S. (in preparation). Anxiety and processing efficiency assessed by a measure of spare processing capacity.

Eysenck, M. W., Derakshan, N., Santos, R., & Calvo, M. G. (2007). Anxiety and cognitive performance: Attentional control theory. *Emotion, 7,* 409–434.

Eysenck, M. W., Payne, S., & Derakshan, N. (2005). Trait anxiety, visuo-spatial processing, and working memory. *Cognition and Emotion, 19,* 1214–1228.

Friedman, N. P., & Miyake, A. (2004). The relations among inhibition and interference control functions: A latent-variable analysis. *Journal of Experimental Psychology: General, 133,* 101–135.

Friedman, N. P., Miyake, A., Corley, R. P., Young, S. E., DeFries, J. C., & Hewitt, J. K. (2006). Not all executive functions are related to intelligence. *Psychological Science, 17,* 172–179.

Hutton, S. B., & Ettinger, U. (2006). The antisaccade task as a research tool in psychopathology: A critical review. *Psychophysiology, 43,* 302–313.

Johnston, W. A. (1972). Processing capacity consumed in memory tasks. *Psychonomic Science, 29,* 272–274.

Kahneman, D. (1973). *Attention and effort.* Englewood Cliffs: Prentice Hall.

Miyake, A., Friedman, N. P., Emerson, M. J., Witzki, A. H., Howerter, A., & Wager, T. D. (2000). The unity and diversity of executive functions and their contributions to complex 'frontal lobe' tasks: A latent variable analysis. *Cognitive Psychology, 41,* 49–100.

Monsell, S. (2003). Task switching. *Trends in Cognitive Sciences, 7,* 134–140.

Morris, L. W., Davis, M. A., & Hutchings, C. H. (1981). Cognitive and emotional components of anxiety: Literature review and a revised worry-emotionality scale. *Journal of Educational Psychology, 73,* 541–555.

Murray, N. P., & Janelle, C. M. (2003). Anxiety and performance: A visual search examination of the processing efficiency theory. *Journal of Sport and Exercise Psychology, 25,* 171–187.

Nęcka, E. (1999). Learning, automaticity, and attention: An individual differences approach. In P. L. Ackerman, P. C. Kyllonen, & R. D. Roberts (Eds.), *Learning and individual differences: Process, trait and content determinants.* Washington, DC: American Psychological Association.

Nigg, J. T. (2000). On inhibition/disinhibition in developmental psychopathology: Views from cognitive and personality psychology and a working inhibition taxonomy. *Psychological Bulletin, 126,* 220–246.

Rapee, R. M. (1993). The utilisation of working memory by worry. *Behaviour Research and Therapy, 31,* 617–620.

Santos, R., Wall, M. B., & Eysenck, M. W. (submitted). Anxiety and processing efficiency: fMRI evidence.

Sarason, I. G. (1988). Anxiety, self-preoccupation and attention. *Anxiety Research, 1,* 3–7.

Smith, E. E., & Jonides, J. (1999). Storage and executive processes in the frontal lobes. *Science, 283,* 1657–1661.

Spielberger, C. D., Gorsuch, R. L., Lushene, R., Vagg, P. R., & Jacobs, G. A. (1983). *Manual for the state-trait anxiety inventory.* Palo Alto, CA: Consulting Psychologists Press.

Wager, T. D., Jonides, J., & Reading, S. (2004). Neuroimaging studies of shifting attention: A meta-analysis. *NeuroImage, 22,* 1679–1693.

Williams, A. M., Vickers, J., & Rodrigues, S. (2002). The effects of anxiety on visual search, movement kinematics, and performance in table tennis: A test of Eysenck and Calvo's processing efficiency theory. *Journal of Sport and Exercise Psychology, 24,* 438–455.

Chapter 13
Task Engagement, Attention, and Executive Control

Gerald Matthews, Joel S. Warm, Lauren E. Reinerman, Lisa K. Langheim, and Dyani J. Saxby

Introduction

There is a conventional tale of stress, attention, and performance that goes as follows. External stressors, such as noise and threat, elevate the general arousal of the cerebral cortex, which in turn impacts the efficiency of information-processing and performance. According to the inverted-U principle, both the excessive arousal evoked by stimulating agents and the under-arousal associated with fatigue and sleep loss lead to impairment of attention. Unfortunately, this simple story is untrue. At the heart of the problem is the complexity of both arousal and attention. In this chapter, we will review the more subtle narrative that is emerging from studies of individual differences in subjective arousal.

That arousal has something to do with attention is neither new nor controversial. A simple demonstration is provided by Norman Mackworth's classic studies of vigilance. Sustained monitoring for target stimuli is both attentionally demanding and de-arousing in relation to typical central and autonomic arousal indices (Davies & Parasuraman, 1982). Mackworth (1948) demonstrated progressive loss of performance (vigilance decrement) on both simulations of military tasks including monitoring radar screens, and laboratory analogue tasks. However, vigilance decrement was much reduced when operators were given the stimulant drug amphetamine, implying that loss of cortical arousal might be a causal influence on attention.

Other arousing stressors, such as noise and heat, do not typically improve vigilance and other demanding attentional tasks, and may even produce performance impairments (Matthews, Davies, Westerman, & Stammers, 2000; Matthews, Schwean, Campbell, Saklofske, & Mohamed, 2000). Such observations revived the Yerkes–Dodson law originally suggested by animal learning data as a general principle for human performance (Broadhurst, 1957). Amphetamine prevents vigilance

G. Matthews (✉)
Department of Psychology, University of Cincinnati, Cincinnati, OH, 45221, USA
e-mail: gerald.matthews@uc.edu

J.S. Warm
Senior Scientist (ST), Warfighter Interface Division, Air Force Research Laboratory, Wright-Patterson AFB, Ohio, USA

L.E. Reinerman
Applied Cognition and Training Immersive Virtual Environments Lab (ACTIVE), University of Central Florida, 3100 Technology Parkway, Orlando, FL 32826, USA

L.K. Langheim
Department of Psychology, University of Cincinnati, Cincinnati, OH 45221, USA

D.J. Saxby
Department of Psychology, University of Cincinnati, Cincinnati, OH 45221, USA

decrement because the monotony of vigilance lowers arousal. The drug brings arousal back towards the optimal, middle part of its range. By contrast, noise and heat tend to over-arouse the person, leading to loss of performance. Eysenck's (1967) arousal theory of personality brought these notions into differential psychology; introverts may be prone to over-arousal, extraverts to under-arousal. Arousal theory can then be used as the basic for predicting performance correlates of extraversion. For example, extraverts should perform poorly on under-stimulating tasks such as vigilance, although such predictions have met with mixed success (Koelega, 1992).

The deficiencies of the inverted-U model are well-known, and need little repetition here (see Hancock & Ganey, 2003; Matthews, Davies et al., 2000; Matthews, Schwean et al., 2000). In brief, they are as follows. First, multiple brain systems control both cortical arousal and attention; it is unlikely that there is any general relationship between the two constructs. Second, any given stressor typically produces multiple changes in psychological and physiological functioning, so that any concomitant performance change may have nothing to do with arousal (e.g., noise is distracting). Third, most apparent demonstrations of the Yerkes–Dodson Law rely on a post hoc fit of data to the inverted-U. Fourth, although the traditional arousal indices of psychophysiology may predict performance in specific circumstances, there is little empirical evidence for any general arousal – performance association (Matthews & Amelang, 1993). Fifth, tests of the arousal theory of personality (Eysenck, 1967) have also often failed in relation to effects of extraversion and neuroticism on performance (Matthews, 1992; Matthews & Gilliland, 1999).

The disintegration of the Yerkes–Dodson Law as a general principle for stress research coincided with the development of alternative, cognitive-psychological perspectives (Eysenck, 1982). If observed performance is the outcome of many separate component processes, corresponding to different brain systems, stressors may have different effects on tasks drawing on different processes. Furthermore, if arousal is itself multidimensional, there may be multiple mappings between components of arousal and components of processing. In this new multipolar spirit, the influential theory proposed by Humphreys and Revelle (1984) suggested that multiple energetic constructs (arousal and effort) mapped onto multiple information-processing resources (corresponding to attention and short term memory). Differentiation of multiple mechanisms is the paradigm for contemporary research on stress and performance. Any given stressor may elicit a constellation of changes in basic neural functioning, "virtual" information-processing, and choice and regulation of task strategy (Matthews, 2001). Whether these changes in processing influence observed performance depends on the specific processes controlling performance of the task concerned. Careful experimental research is needed to identify specific pathways mediating stressor effects on performance.

Effects of stressors on performance operate within a larger self-regulative process described by the transactional model of stress and emotion (Lazarus, 1999; Szalma, 2008). The person's evaluation of their own mental functioning contributes to appraisals of stress and well-being, and may drive corrective coping efforts. For example, anxious individuals may apply compensatory effort to mitigate loss of processing efficiency resulting from worry (Eysenck & Calvo, 1992). Fatigued drivers may take rest breaks or attempt to raise their own arousal (Matthews, Saxby, Funke, Emo, & Desmond, in press). Performance change must be understood in the wider context of the dynamic interaction between operator and task environment (Matthews, 2001).

This chapter is concerned less with general perspectives on stress and performance (see Hancock & Szalma, 2008; Matthews, 2001) than with the specific problem of individual differences in arousal and attention. In a post-Yerkes–Dodson world, how can we find meaningful arousal and attention constructs that relate meaningfully to individual differences? The research described in this chapter owes much to the pivotal work of Robert Thayer (1978, 1989, 1996) on self-report arousal. Thayer's arousal theory has three critical features that set it apart from earlier arousal theories. First, it is explicitly multidimensional in discriminating energetic arousal (e.g., vigor, pleasurable excitement) from tense arousal (e.g., nervousness, anxiety). Energy and tension constitute distinct dimensions that have different antecedents and consequences for behavior.

Second, both forms of arousal express complex biopsychological states that are distributed across multiple physiological and mental components. Self-reports provide a more valid index of integrated system activity than any single psychophysiological index. Third, the systems are functional in supporting the organism's readiness to adapt to specific external demands. Energetic arousal prepares the organism for vigorous, goal-directed motor activity; tense arousal anticipates fight or flight. In classical arousal theory, detrimental effects of stressors appear almost as an accidental byproduct of an over-heated cortex. Thayer's analysis suggests that performance outcomes may be related more closely to the functional purposes of arousal states.

In this chapter, we first review research that identifies energetic arousal ("energy") as a marker for the availability of attentional resources. Next, we will locate energy as one of several facets of a broader feature of subjective state labeled "task engagement," that also includes task motivation and concentration. This state factor represents a mode of adaptation to task demands signaling a commitment to investment of effort in task performance (Matthews et al., 2002). Recent empirical studies show that task engagement is reciprocally linked to self-regulative processes, including appraisal of challenge and use of task-focused coping. Like energy, task engagement correlates with performance on demanding attentional tasks. Research suggests several possible mechanisms. As well as providing a marker for a virtual "resource," task engagement may also signal neurophysiological readiness for intensive attention, and task-directed effortful control of attention. We will outline a cognitive architecture for regulation and control of attention that may interact with subjective engagement. We will conclude that individual differences in task engagement are critical for attention, but multi-leveled explanations of engagement are needed.

Energetic Arousal and Attentional Efficiency

Arousal and Resource Availability

Early studies of self-report arousal (Thayer, 1978) established that energy correlated with performance of tasks including reaction time, verbal learning, and retrieval from semantic memory, whereas tense arousal did not. Following up these initial findings, Matthews, Davies, and Lees (1990) investigated how individual differences in energy were related to vigilance. There are several reasons for focusing on vigilance as a test-bed for studies of arousal. First, as already mentioned, Mackworth (1948) established the beneficial effects of amphetamine on vigilance, a finding replicated with other stimulant drugs such as caffeine (Temple et al., 2000). Second, although monitoring tasks are sometimes seen as rather undemanding, there is accumulating evidence that sustaining attention during vigilance in fact imposes high mental demands and a high workload as indicated by standard metrics (Warm & Dember, 1998). Third, vigilance tasks may be configured to show rapid decrement over intervals as short as 5–10 min (Nuechterlein, Parasuraman, & Jiang, 1983), affording ease of experimentation. Fourth, studies of both short and longer-duration vigilance tasks support an attentional resource model of vigilance. Sustained monitoring drains the availability of resources, leading to performance decrement (Warm, Matthews, & Finomore, 2008).

Arousal is also linked to attentional enhancement within the general performance theory of Humphreys and Revelle (1984). These authors distinguished two separate resource pools, one for sustained information transfer (SIT: focused attention) and one for short-term memory (STM). Two energetic constructs mapped onto these resources. Arousal increased availability of SIT resources but decreased STM resources. The second energetic construct, effort, related to enhanced SIT resources and mediated harmful effects of anxiety, which diverts effort off-task. Sustained attention requires primarily SIT resources, so that the theory successfully predicts the facilitative effects of stimulants on vigilance. The theory is also compatible with the resource model of vigilance just described (Warm, Matthews, & Finomore, 2008). It also addresses personality factors, but this part of the theory is beyond the scope of this chapter (cf., Nęcka, 1997).

A limitation of the Humphreys and Revelle (1984) theory is that it treated arousal as a unitary construct, whereas Thayer (1989) and others (e.g., Robbins, Milstein, & Dalley, 2004) viewed it as multi-dimensional. Given Thayer's (1978) findings on arousal and performance, it is more likely that energetic arousal would predict superior vigilance than tense arousal. Matthews, Davies, and Lees (1990) assessed both arousal dimensions, prior to performance of a version of the Nuechterlein, Parasuraman, and Jiang (1983) short vigilance task. This task requires subjects to detect a single-digit target in a stream of consecutive digits, presented briefly (40 ms) at a high event rate of 1 stimulus/s. The task may be made more demanding by degrading stimulus quality. Matthews, Davies, and Lees (1990) employed both an undegraded version and a version in which stimuli were degraded with a pattern mask.

The design allows opposite predictions to be derived from the Yerkes-Dodson Law and the Humphreys and Revelle (1984) resource theory. In traditional arousal theory, the optimal level of arousal is lower for more difficult tasks. The theory predicts that high arousal should have a relatively more beneficial effect on the undegraded compared with the degraded task version. By contrast, more demanding task versions require more investment of resources, so that the resource theory predicts that arousal should have a stronger facilitative effect on the degraded task version, relative to the undegraded task version.

In fact, the resource theory prediction was supported (Matthews, Davies, & Lees 1990). The study replicated Nuechterlein et al. (1983) finding of greater perceptual sensitivity decrement with the degraded version, attributed to progressive resource depletion over time. Consistent with Thayer's (1978) findings, energy but not tension was related to performance. Energetic arousal was related to higher perceptual sensitivity on the more demanding, degraded task version but was unrelated to performance on the easier, undegraded version. Plausibly, energy indicates individual differences in the size of the resource pool (resource availability).

Generalization of Findings

A weakness of resource theory is that it is often uncertain that performance is limited by a general resource, as opposed to overload of some specific component process (Pashler, 1998). For example, the facilitative effect of energetic arousal obtained by Matthews, Davies, and Lees (1990) might be attributed to individual differences in the perceptual process of encoding masked visual stimuli, rather than to some more general resource. There are two solutions to the dilemma. The first is to establish generalization of the effect across tasks making qualitatively different demands on information-processing. The second is to conduct a formal test for resource allocation using dual-task paradigms.

Matthews, Davies, and Lees (1990) demonstrated facilitative effects of energy across a range of tasks, including a self-paced visual vigilance task in which stimuli were undegraded and a letter transformation task employing auditory stimuli. They also tested for associations between arousal and speed of visual search, using the Shiffrin and Schneider (1977) paradigm, which differentiates controlled and automatic search. Only controlled search requires substantial resource investment, so the Humphreys and Revelle (1984) theory predicts that high arousal should facilitate controlled but not automatic search. This prediction was confirmed (Matthews, Davies, & Lees 1990).

Matthews, Davies, and Holley (1990) tested for associations between energy and perceptual sensitivity across a range of demanding, high event-rate vigilance tasks. Two task parameters that are often used to differentiate different classes of vigilance task (See, Howe, Warm, & Dember, 1995) were manipulated. First, tasks may require either a sensory discrimination (e.g., identifying a masked digit) or a cognitive/symbolic discrimination (e.g., discriminating odd from even digits). Second, tasks may require either a simultaneous or a successive discrimination. In simultaneous tasks, each stimulus provides sufficient information to discriminate a critical or target stimulus, whereas on successive tasks information must be integrated across trials to discriminate the target. Successive tasks thus require more working memory and may be more strongly resource-limited (Davies & Parasuraman, 1982). In fact, Matthews, Davies, and Holley (1990) found that the facilitative effect of energy generalized across all task types. Consistent with resource theory, energy was related to performance only of those task versions that showed a perceptual sensitivity decrement. Energy was uncorrelated with tasks that appeared to be data-limited, either through being too easy or too hard to be sensitive to resource allocation.

Studies of dual-task performance also proved compatible with the Humphreys and Revelle (1984) resource theory. Matthews and Davies (1998) compared both single- and dual-task vigilance, as well as simultaneous and successive task versions. Energetic arousal was most facilitative in the task condition presumed to be most demanding of resources: a successive task performed in a dual-task condition. Matthews and Margetts (1991) performed a formal test of the relationship between energy and resource allocation by constructing Performance Operating Characteristics (POCs: Wickens & Hollands, 1999) for subject groups high and low in energy. The POC is constructed by varying the priorities given to two paired tasks and evaluating whether there is a smooth tradeoff function in performance levels, indicative of graded reallocation of resources. Matthews and Margetts (1991) varied the priorities assigned to each of two semantic search tasks. Plotting POCs verified that resource availability was higher in high energy than in low energy individuals. However, the relationship between energy and search speed was also moderated by priority, with the facilitative effect of energy increasing for higher priority task components. High-energy individuals may strategically allocate their additional resources to the task components, which need them most. A similar tendency for energy to facilitate high- but not low-priority task elements has been reported for vigilance (Matthews & Davies, 2001) and for simulated vehicle driving (Funke, Matthews, Warm, & Emo, 2007).

Further Issues

The findings reviewed so far suggest strong support for the facilitative effect of arousal on attention specified by the Humphreys and Revelle (1984) theory, provided that "arousal" is identified with Thayer's energetic arousal construct. Evidence primarily came from studies of sustained and controlled search. Other task paradigms provided a more nuanced picture. Associations between energy and short-term memory were inconsistent across studies. Whereas Matthews, Davies, and Lees (1990) found no effect of energy on controlled memory search, Matthews and Westerman (1994) did find a facilitative effect on this task, using a larger memory set; 6 as opposed to 4 characters. However, energy also interacted with tension, such that working memory was best for high energy/low tension individuals. Dickman (2002) obtained a complex set of relationships between his own energy scale and reading comprehension; either linear or curvilinear associations were found between energy and accuracy of reading, depending on time of day. Effects of energy on relatively complex verbal tasks require further exploration.

Nęcka (1997) performed several studies using both a divided attention task ("DIVA") requiring search for letter targets in conjunction with a simple psychomotor task and a short term memory scanning task. These studies addressed several issues relating to resource models of intelligence and personality, but we will focus here on self-report arousal data. By contrast with the research previously described, Nęcka (1997) took separate measures of high energy (activation) and low energy (drowsiness or deactivation). Consistent with the findings reviewed above, Nęcka reported that high energy related to shorter reaction time and better control of the secondary task in the dual-task condition of the DIVA paradigm. However, subjects low in deactivation committed more false positive errors in the dual-task condition, contrary to expectation. The energy scales also showed inconsistent associations with errors on the memory scanning task, varying across positive and negative trials.

Task Engagement and Self-Regulation

The studies reviewed so far suggest that energetic arousal is a marker for attentional resource availability. Next, we look in more depth at the relationship of energy and executive control processes. There are two inter-related roles that energy might play. First, variation in energy may itself be an *outcome* of executive processing. Appraisal theories (e.g., Lazarus, 1999) link positive emotion to appraisals such as intrinsic pleasantness and expectations of progress toward a valued goal. Typically, though, such theories are concerned with happiness, which is not the same as energetic arousal (Matthews, Jones, & Chamberlain, 1990). Carver and Scheier (2005) relate engagement, in the sense of orientation towards task goals, to appraising oneself as competent at the task.

Choice and regulation of coping strategy may also serve to raise or lower energy; use of problem-focused coping and positive reframing of the situation may support continued engagement (Carver & Scheier, 2005). Studies of fatigue in performance settings suggest that tiredness in part results from choosing to employ avoidance coping rather than task-focused coping (Matthews & Desmond, 2002). Second, resource allocation is itself an executive process (Norman & Shallice, 1986). High energy individuals seem to funnel resources toward higher-priority task components (Matthews & Davies, 2001; Matthews & Margetts, 1991), but the impact of energy on the executive processes that control resource allocation remains unclear.

Recent work on the new state construct of task engagement (Matthews et al., 2002) may help to clarify the relationship between energetic arousal and individual differences in executive processing. Task engagement binds together energy, concentration, and motivation as a broad subjective state that facilitates certain forms of attention. In this section, we will describe the psychometric basis for task engagement, followed by studies that investigate the roles of appraisal and coping in changes in engagement during task performance. The next section revisits performance issues in the light of recent studies of engagement and attention.

Psychometrics of Task Engagement

Factor Structure of Subjective States

Most studies of the subjective stress of task performance have focused on mood responses such as anxiety and arousal. However, the perspective of the traditional "trilogy of mind" suggests that demanding tasks may elicit changes not just in affect, but also in motivation and cognition. Matthews et al. (1999, 2002) set out to sample subjective states experienced in performance settings in all three domains of experience. Item sets to represent key state constructs were compiled from various existing state instruments, such as Sarason et al. (1995) Cognitive Interference Questionnaire. Items were written for some additional constructs.

The new questionnaire, the Dundee Stress State Questionnaire (DSSQ), was administered to 1,061 participants who performed various demanding tasks. Factor analysis identified 10 factors: three mood factors (replicating Matthews, Jones, & Chamberlain, 1990), six cognitive factors, and a single motivation factor. A later study (Matthews, Campbell, & Falconer, 2001) used factor analysis to separate two distinct motivation dimensions. The first-order factors were themselves correlated, so a second-order factor analysis of the scales was conducted (Matthews et al., 2002). Three

Table 13.1 Correspondences between second-order factors and first-order scales on the Dundee Stress State Questionnaire (Matthews, Warm et al., 2001; Matthews et al., 2002)

Factor	Scale	Items	Example item	Scale α
Task engagement	Energetic arousal	8	I feel... Vigorous	80
	Task interest	7	The content of the task is interesting	75
	Success motivation	7	I want to perform better than most people do	87
	Concentration	7	My mind is wandering a great deal (–ve)	85
Distress	Tension	8	I feel... Nervous	82
	Hedonic tone (low)	8	I feel... Contented	86
	Confidence-control (low)	6	I feel confident about my abilities	80
Worry	Self-focus	8	I am reflecting about myself	85
	Self-esteem	7	I am worrying about looking foolish (–ve)	87
	CI (task-relevant)	8	I have thoughts of... How much time I have left	78
	CI (task-irrelevant)	8	I have thoughts of... Personal worries	86

Note: CI, cognitive interference

higher-order factors were extracted and labeled *task engagement*, *distress,* and *worry*. Similar factor solutions were found in pre-task, post-task, and change score data, suggesting a robust dimensional structure. The modified set of 11 first-order factors is illustrated in Table 13.1, together with the second-order factors to which they correspond. The table does not show additional minor loadings of first-order scales on factors.

Task engagement brings together constructs from all three domains of experience. It was defined by loadings on energetic arousal (affect), task motivation, and concentration (cognition). Although these first-order factors were only moderately correlated (range of rs: 0.40–0.48), the higher-order engagement factor explained from 71 to 89% of the reliable variance in these scales (Matthews et al., 2002). Thus, energetic arousal is quite closely aligned with task engagement, although the latter is a more broadly-based factor. Both of the motivation factors extracted by Matthews, Warm, Dember, Mizoguchi, and Smith (2001) – striving for success and intrinsic task interest – also proved to load on task engagement. The second higher-order factor, distress, was defined by the mood variables of tense arousal and poor hedonic tone and the cognitive dimension of low confidence and control. The third factor, worry, was exclusively cognitive, bringing together self-focused attention, low self-esteem and cognitive interference (intrusive thoughts) relating to both the task and personal concerns.

Validation

Extensive work on validating the DSSQ scales was conducted (e.g., Matthews & Falconer, 2002; Matthews et al., 1999, 2002, 2006). In this section, we provide a brief overview of the validation effort before looking at the cognitive bases of task engagement in more depth. One of the main lines of evidence came from studies of task-induced stress. Administering the DSSQ before and after task performance allows quantification of the pattern of state change induced by task performance. Change scores may be expressed as standard scores (z-scores), scaled against the normative sample data compiled by Matthews et al. (1999).

Qualitatively different tasks elicit different patterns of state change. For example, Fig. 13.1 compares the profiles of change for four tasks (data from Matthews et al., 2002). An undemanding control task (reading magazines) showed little change in engagement or distress, together with a decline in worry as attention is refocused from the self to the task. By contrast, visual vigilance lowered task engagement, and a time-pressured working memory task elicited high distress. A simulation of a customer service task produced moderate distress with only small changes on the

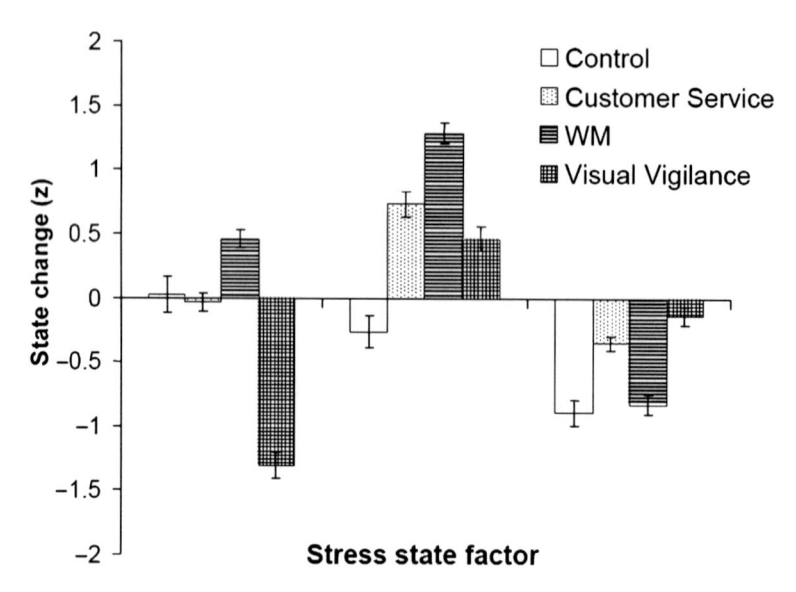

Fig. 13.1 Change scores for DSSQ state factors in four task conditions. Error bars indicate standard errors. WM = Working Memory

other factors. The figure shows state change patterns for the three second-order factors of the DSSQ, but more fine-grained evaluations of state change can be obtained from the primary factors. Profiles of state change may also be obtained from field studies of tasks such as car driving and long-haul vehicle operation in order to investigate real-life issues such as driver fatigue (Matthews, 2002).

Stress states are meaningfully related to personality traits. From the perspective of the Five Factor Model (McCrae & Costa, 2008), neuroticism typically correlates with distress and worry, whereas conscientiousness and agreeableness are the most reliable predictors of task engagement (e.g., Matthews et al., 1999). Although extraversion is frequently linked to positive mood, our data show only a weak tendency for this trait to correlate with task engagement. For example, Matthews et al. (2002) reported a correlation of 0.23 ($P<0.01$, $N=328$) with extraversion in pre-task data and a non-significant correlation of 0.10 in post-task data. Correlation magnitudes for even the more reliable trait-state associations are typically modest (0.2–0.4), indicating that, at least in the performance context, much of the variance in states is unrelated to the major traits. Matthews and Campbell (1999) showed that trait-state correlations remain moderate even when data are aggregated across multiple occasions.

Individual Differences in Self-Regulation

What determines the individual's level of task engagement in a given performance context? Probably, multiple factors exert an influence on subjective state, and these include biological factors, as evidenced by studies showing the sensitivity of energetic arousal to drugs, endogenous biological rhythms and motor activity (Thayer, 1989). As further discussed below, engagement can plausibly be related to a neural Behavioral Activation System (BAS: Corr, 2008) controlling approach behavior and response to reward stimuli. The extent to which subjective states are isomorphic with activity levels in neural systems is open to debate (cf., Corr, 2008; Matthews, 2000, 2008) and beyond the scope of this chapter. The assumption here (cf., Lazarus, 1999) is that task engagement is supported by symbolic, cognitive processes as well as neural activations; indeed states may serve to integrate a variety of cues

Table 13.2 Summary of four studies assessing task engagement and cognitive stress processes during performance of demanding tasks

Study	N	Task(s)
1. Langheim et al. (2007)	210	Brief visual vigilance task ("simultaneous" or "successive" version)
2. Matthews and Campbell (in press)	144	Rapid information processing task (two event rates)
3. Matthews et al. (2006)	200	One of four tasks (vigilance, working memory, impossible anagrams, reading magazines)
4. Fellner et al. (2007)	129	Visual search for facial emotion, recognition of emotional "micro-expressions"

to adaptive status and goal satisfaction. Matthews et al. (2002), building on Lazarus's (1999) emotion theory, suggested that the broad state dimensions measured by the DSSQ correspond to transactional relationships between the performer and the task environment. Thus, the states are essentially psychological in nature, although they interact with underlying neural processes.

Empirical Studies of Engagement, Appraisal and Coping

The transactional perspective implies that the cognitive processes that support adaptation to task demands will influence task engagement. Table 13.2 summarizes the designs of four studies that investigated the interplay between cognition and subjective state in controlled laboratory settings. Studies 1 and 2 investigated high-workload signal detection tasks; task parameters were manipulated on a between-subjects basis. Study 3 employed three stressful tasks, together with a non-stressful condition (reading magazines); task type was manipulated between-subjects. In Study 4, all subjects performed two tasks requiring processing of emotional stimuli. Tasks employed in these studies typically lowered performance and elevated distress, with some variation across different tasks and conditions.

In each study, the person first completed a pre-task assessment of their subjective state (DSSQ). Following task performance, the participant completed a post-task DSSQ, the NASA-TLX workload scale (Hart & Staveland, 1988), plus two questionnaires for cognitive stress processes. The Appraisal of Life Events Scale (ALE: Ferguson, Matthews, & Cox, 1999) measures primary appraisal dimensions specified by Lazarus (1999); an additional scale for perceived controllability as an element of secondary appraisal was included in these studies. The Coping Inventory for Task Stress (CITS: Matthews & Campbell, 1998) measures three fundamental dimensions of coping – task-focus, emotion-focus and avoidance – using items relevant to the performance context.

Across studies, four of the cognitive process variables were reliably associated with task engagement – challenge, controllability, task-focused coping and avoidance coping. Other elements of cognition, including threat appraisal and emotion-focused coping were associated with distress and worry, but discussion here is limited to task engagement. Table 13.3 shows selected correlations between engagement measured prior to the task and subsequent appraisal and coping. Pre-task engagement appeared to bias subsequent cognitive processes. More engaged participants were more likely to appraise the task as challenging and controllable, more likely to use task-focused coping and less likely to use avoidance coping. The Table also shows the equivalent set of correlations between stress cognitions and post-task engagement. Because participants rated their cognitions and state during task performance, these represent concurrent correlations. The same pattern was evident as in the pre-task data, but correlation magnitudes were higher. Correlations between task engagement and overall NASA-TLX workload were generally close to zero in these studies. However, as shown in the last two rows of the table, pre- and post-task engagement correlated with the effort rating scale on the NASA-TLX. The data suggest a bidirectional relationship, such that higher engagement

Table 13.3 Correlations between appraisal, coping and effort scales and task engagement, assessed pre- and post-performance, in four studies

		Study			
		SVT	RIP	Stress	Facial
Challenge	Pre	0.259**	0.328**	0.209**	0.261**
	Post	0.534**	0.636**	0.642**	0.554**
Controllability	Pre	0.187**	0.269**	0.131	0.231**
	Post	0.279**	0.369**	0.278**	0.267**
Task-focus	Pre	0.452**	0.314**	0.268**	0.190*
	Post	0.649**	0.644**	0.455**	0.542**
Avoidance	Pre	−0.374**	−0.414**	−0.176*	−0.401**
	Post	−0.534**	−0.651**	−0.602**	−0.496**
Effort	Pre	0.241**	0.267**	0.121	0.184*
	Post	0.397**	0.599**	0.368**	0.383**

SVT, short vigilance task; *RIP*, rapid information processing; Stress, stressful task set; Facial, facial processing
*$P < 0.05$
**$P < 0.01$

Table 13.4 The prediction of post-task task engagement: Summary of regression statistics from four studies

		Study			
Step		SVT	RIP	Stress	Facial
Control variables	ΔR^2	0.281	0.324	0.263	0.252
	df	2,207	2,141	4,195	1,127
	F	40.40**	33.79**	17.36**	42.70**
Appraisal	ΔR^2	0.201	0.239	0.303	0.236
	df	3,204	3,138	3,192	3,124
	F	27.61**	25.09**	44.59**	18.98**
Coping	ΔR^2	0.116	0.111	0.110	0.097
	df	3,201	3,135	3,189	3,121
	F	19.65**	15.38**	21.35**	9.43**
Final equation	R	0.777**	0.821**	0.822**	0.764**
βs in final equation	Pre-task state	0.228**	0.243**	0.186**	0.283**
	Challenge	0.222**	0.294**	0.391**	0.335**
	Controllability	0.083	0.058	0.173**	0.138*
	Task-focus	0.343**	0.270**	0.179**	0.304**
	Avoidance	−0.187**	0.265**	−0.305**	−0.079

SVT, Short vigilance task; *RIP*, rapid information processing; Stress, stressful task set; Facial, facial processing
Statistics are given for three steps in a hierarchical regression model, together with Rs and regression coefficients (βs) for key predictors in the final regression equation
*$P < 0.05$
**$P < 0.01$

initially promotes more constructive cognitions of the task, which, in turn, feed back to maintain the state of engagement.

Table 13.4 summarizes multiple regression statistics. In each case, the dependent variable was post-task engagement. The first step was to enter control variables, including pre-task state engagement, to control for the carry-over of initial state into the performance phase. Task factors were also entered at this step, where task was manipulated between-subjects. The three appraisal scales from the modified ALE were entered at the second step, followed by the three CITS coping variables at the third step. Thirty to forty percent of the variance in task engagement induced by the task could

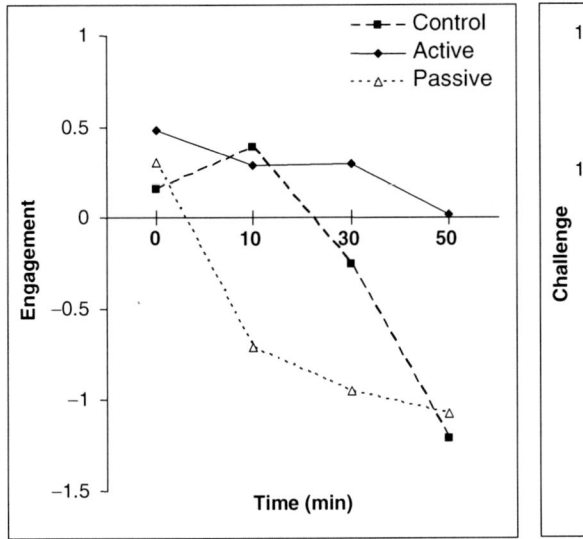

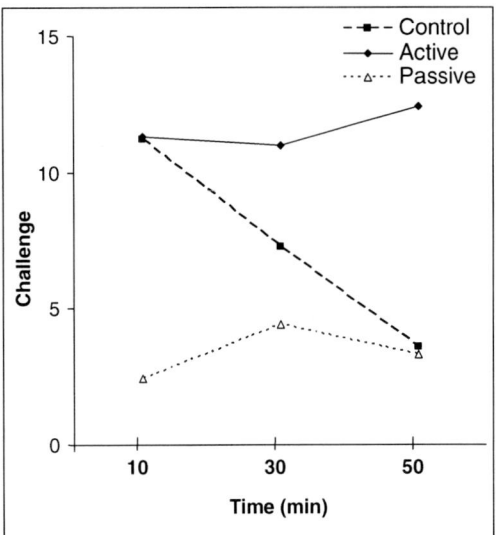

Fig. 13.2 Effects of active and passive fatigue manipulations during drives of differing durations on task engagement (*left panel*) and challenge appraisal (*right panel*)

be attributed to individual differences in appraisal and coping. In addition, the regression coefficients for the predictors in the final equation suggest that challenge and controllability appraisal, task-focused coping, and low avoidance coping were generally independently predictive of change in engagement. Similar findings have been obtained in a field setting, in which customer service operators performed a simulation of work activities (Matthews & Falconer, 2002). Thus, changes in task engagement are not tied to any single cognitive process, but relate to an integration of multiple processes that jointly support sustained commitment of effort to the task (Matthews et al., 2002).

Fatigue, Challenge, and Perceived Control

One application of self-regulative theory is in understanding fatigue states. Desmond and Hancock (2001) differentiated active fatigue, induced by high workloads (e.g., driving on a busy freeway) and passive fatigue, related to monotony and boredom (e.g., driving long-distance on a traffic-free highway). Saxby, Matthews, and Hitchcock (2007) used a driving simulator to induce these two different types of fatigue state, across drives differing in duration. As shown in Fig. 13.2 (left panel), task engagement was maintained better during active fatigue (workload induced by frequent wind gusts) than during passive fatigue (driving an automated vehicle). Further analyses (not reported by Saxby, Matthews, & Hitchcock, 2007) showed that effects of the fatigue inductions on challenge appraisal corresponded to those on engagement (Fig. 13.2 – right panel). Challenge was uniformly high during active fatigue, low during passive fatigue, and declined over time in the control condition. Indeed, declines in challenge in the last two conditions appeared to precede loss of engagement. By contrast, although task-focused coping was higher in the active fatigue condition than in the other two conditions, changes over time in task-focus did not correspond closely to changes in task-engagement.

Two studies of workload transition (Helton et al., 2004, 2008) also suggest that challenge plays a pivotal role in maintaining task engagement. These studies used vigilance tasks in which workload could be manipulated by varying signal salience. Observers who were shifted from low to high workload (decreasing salience) showed elevated task engagement relative to non-shifted control subjects. Conversely, high-to-low workload shift tended to reduce task engagement. The effect of increasing workload appears to be a mobilization of task engagement to meet the cognitive challenge (Helton et al., 2008).

Other research suggests a key role for the extent to which the task affords personal control and task-focus. Szalma, Hancock, Dember, and Warm (2006) found that providing knowledge of results (KR) during a vigilance task enhanced task engagement; KR may increase participants' attention to their own responses. Parsons, Warm, Nelson, Riley, and Matthews (2007) investigated performance on a task representing the military operation of detecting hostile units. In the control condition, participants were required only to detect stimuli representing enemy units, as in standard vigilance. In another condition, participants were able to use the mouse to acquire and destroy the enemy following detection. The additional scope for action had the effect of elevating task engagement and objective signal detection rates, relative to the control condition.

The data reviewed identify task engagement as a concomitant of self-regulation (Matthews & Zeidner, 2004). Broadly, engagement is a concomitant of choosing effortful, task-focused strategies for managing the demands of performance environments, supported by multiple appraisal and coping processes, as suggested by the regression data (Table 13.4). Engagement and task-focus may feed off one another in a virtuous cycle. Conversely, fatigue leads to use of avoidance in place of task-focus and progressive loss of task engagement (Matthews & Desmond, 2002). People may also voluntarily seek to raise engagement as a mood-regulation strategy to enhance performance. Thayer (1996, Chap. 9) lists various strategies that people use to enhance energy, including a variety of mentally and physically stimulating activities, such as exercise, as well as resting. Thus, in line with adaptive accounts of emotion (Ketelaar & Clore, 1997), task engagement may function both to provide the performer with information about their readiness to commit effort to the task, and with the motivation to work to maintain engagement.

Task Engagement and Performance

The preceding section addressed cognitive influences on task engagement responses to demanding tasks. Next, we revisit the issue of how subjective state relates to objective performance in the light of recent studies of engagement. First, we review studies that show that the facilitative effects of energetic arousal on demanding tasks replicate for the broader-based construct of task engagement. These studies include experiments showing that task engagement may mediate effects of external stressors on performance. Finally, we turn to mechanisms for beneficial effects of engagement and present evidence that both neural and cognitive-strategic mechanisms may be implicated.

Task Engagement Facilitates Attention

As part of the initial research to validate the DSSQ, Matthews et al. (1999) had 229 participants perform short sensory vigilance tasks similar to those used in previous research on energetic arousal (Matthews, Davies, & Holley 1990). The subject's task was to view pairs of lines and respond to a target stimulus in which one or both lines was longer than the standard length. Line length varied randomly around the mean for the stimulus during the 300 ms presentation time, making the discrimination more demanding. Significant performance decrements were found over a 12 min task duration. Task engagement was significantly correlated with perceptual sensitivity on both a simultaneous task version (one line of the pair is longer; $r=0.17$, $P<0.05$) and a successive version (both lines of the pair is longer, $r=0.22$, $P<0.01$). Correlations of similar magnitude were found for energetic arousal.

Two recent studies (Helton et al., 2008; Langheim et al., 2007) employed a brief vigilance task designed to be an analogue of longer sustained monitoring tasks. Participants were required to discriminate pairs of characters briefly presented (40 ms) against the background of a visual mask pattern. Temple et al. (2000) demonstrated that the vigilance decrement on this task was reduced by caffeine. Similarly, both Helton et al. (2008) and Langheim et al. (2007) found that task engagement measured prior to performance was modestly but significantly correlated with subsequent vigilance, with rs in the 0.2–0.3 range.

These studies confirm that task engagement is a consistent predictor of vigilance. Other studies have tested whether the state factor also relates to other attentionally demanding tasks, with generally positive results. Fellner et al. (2007) investigated individual differences in processing emotional stimuli, using two paradigms. One was a visual search paradigm requiring controlled search for emotional targets (facial expressions) and non-emotional targets (categories of nut). The second task required participants to identify brief (200 ms) "micro-expressions" of emotion (Ekman, 2003), at three intervals during a video training procedure. Results showed that task engagement correlated with speed of search for both emotional and non-emotional targets. Engagement also correlated with more accurate identification of micro-expressions following training. Fellner et al. (2006) also found some evidence for higher engagement relating to discrimination learning on a task using facial stimuli, depending on task parameters. Engagement also relates to superior working memory (Matthews & Campbell, 1999). Significant correlations between engagement and the various performance indices in these studies were in the 0.2–0.04 range.

Funke, Matthews, Warm, and Emo (2007) found that high engagement was associated with superior control of the position of the vehicle on the road, in a study of simulated driving. Other driving studies conducted in our lab have typically not shown any association between engagement and driver performance. The key feature of the Funke et al. (2007) study may be its use of a concurrent attentional task; drivers were required to respond to pedestrian hazard stimuli. However, similar to earlier studies of energy (Matthews & Margetts, 1991), it was the primary task of driving (accuracy of steering) that was sensitive to engagement, not the secondary attentional task.

Two studies using the Temple et al. (2000) task tested whether changes in task engagement may mediate the impact of energizing and de-energizing stressors on vigilance. Matthews, Warm et al. (2001) investigated the effects of cold infection. Two hundred and four participants were tested in a healthy state. Those who subsequently contracted a cold ($N=96$) were re-tested in that condition, while the remaining 108 served as healthy controls. Cold infection had the effects of both lowering task engagement (by c. 0.7 SD, relative to norms) and impairing performance. Furthermore, task engagement correlated at 0.29 ($P<0.01$) with detection rate on the vigilance task. A regression analysis suggested that the effect of cold infection was entirely mediated by task engagement, so that the subjective state factor provides an effective marker for the neurocognitive impairment produced by the viral infection.

Helton, Warm, Matthews, and Corcoran (2002) exposed participants to loud, stereo jet engine noise during performance of the Temple et al. (2000) brief vigilance task. Maximum amplitude of the noise was 95 dBA. The noise stimulus actually raised task engagement, by about 0.4 SD, and also improved vigilance, relative to control subjects who performed in quiet conditions. Task engagement correlated at 0.37 ($P<0.01$) with detection rate. Again, multivariate analyses suggested a mediating role for task engagement. Figure 13.3 shows the structural model fitted to the data by Helton et al. It defines both task engagement and vigilance as latent factors. Causal paths connect noise to engagement, and engagement to vigilance. (The model also includes the effect of a signal salience manipulation, which was independent of engagement).

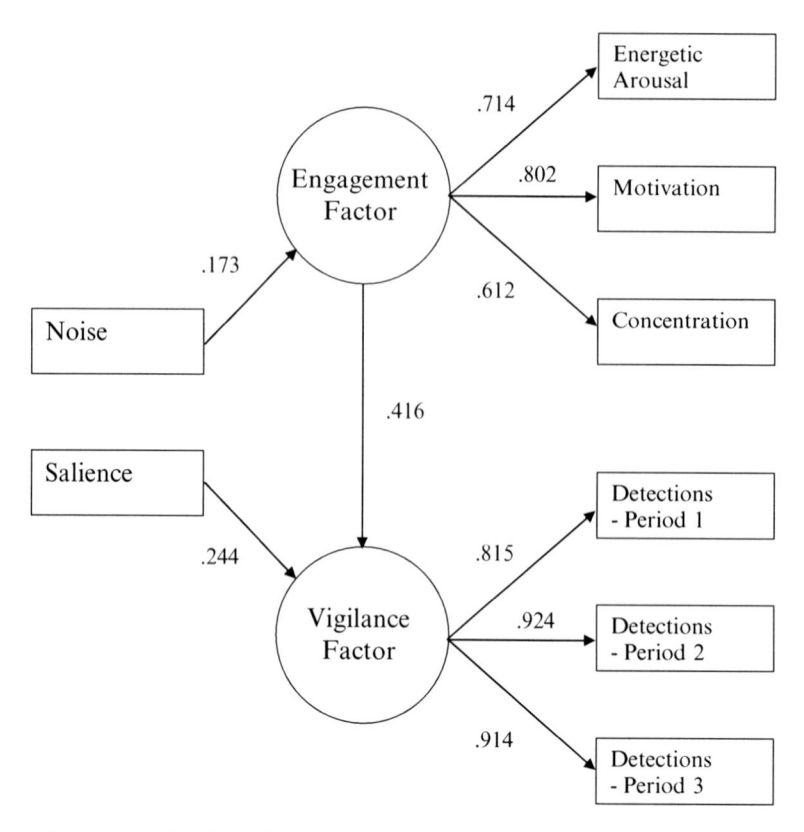

Fig. 13.3 Latent factor model for effect of task engagement on vigilance

Cerebral Bloodflow as a Marker for Resources

The studies of task engagement and attention just reviewed fortify the conclusion of earlier studies (Matthews & Davies, 1998) that energy and allied subjective states provide a marker for individual differences in resource availability, consistent with the Humphreys and Revelle (1984) resource theory. However, the studies reviewed did not address in any detail mechanisms for attentional facilitation in states of high task engagement. One potential route towards elucidating the facilitation effect is to explore the neurological underpinnings of the engagement state. Engagement has been shown to relate to various autonomic arousal indices (Fairclough & Venables, 2006), including reduced alpha in the EEG, reduced cardiac sinus arrhythmia and higher respiration rate. However, its neurological bases largely remain to be explored, although, as mentioned, it may plausibly be linked to a dopaminergic reward or approach system.

In recent work, we have explored a novel psychophysiological technique for evaluating competence for performing vigilance tasks (Matthews, Warm, & Washburn, 2007; Reinerman, Matthews, Warm, & Langheim, 2007; Reinerman et al., 2006). The velocity of bloodflow in the medial cerebral arteries may be measured using transcranial Doppler sonography (TCD: Aaslid, 1986). A transceiver that emits pulses of ultrasound is placed over the zygomatic arch of the skull. The blood corpuscles moving in the medial artery reflect the ultrasound, producing a Doppler shift in its frequency. The transceiver records the reflected ultrasound and analysis of the Doppler shift allows the velocity of the blood cells to be measured. The velocity measure may be interpreted as an index of metabolic activity.

Several subsequent studies in our laboratory (e.g., Hitchcock et al., 2002) have shown that the vigilance decrement in performance was paralleled by a corresponding decline in cerebral blood flow velocity (CBFV). Task factors that control vigilance decrement (e.g., simultaneous vs. successive discrimination) also control CBFV decline in the right hemisphere. The lateralization of task effects corresponds to evidence from fMRI and other sources that suggest sustained attention is controlled by a network of right hemisphere structures (Parasuraman, Warm, & See, 1998). Importantly, the experimental studies (e.g., Hitchcock et al., 2002) included control conditions in which subjects viewed the task stimuli passively, for the same duration as the actual task, with no requirement to respond to critical signals. In the absence of a performance imperative, CBFV remains constant in both hemispheres. Thus, the effect is directly tied to the mental workload of performing the task, and cannot be attributed to loss of arousal or boredom.

Matthews et al. (2007; see also Reinerman et al., 2006, 2007) conducted two studies that investigated the inter-relationships of TCD, vigilance and subjective measures. The aim was to test whether measurements of TCD might be used to predict subsequent individual differences in vigilance. The design involved two phases of performance testing. First, participants were exposed to a "cognitive challenge" in the form of a battery of three short, high workload tasks (working memory, tracking, signal detection). Previous studies have shown that short tasks elicit increases in CBFV (Stroobant & Vingerhoets, 2000), which may index increased resource mobilization. If so, individual differences in the phasic CBFV response may provide a measure of availability of resources for subsequent attentional tasks. In the second phase of the study, participants performed a 36-min vigilance task. It was predicted that the phasic CBFV measure would predict perceptual sensitivity on this task. In addition, the DSSQ was administered before and after each performance phase, and the CITS measure of coping was given after the short task battery and following completion of the vigilance task. It was expected that the task engagement response to the task battery would predict vigilance performance.

Predictions were tested in two studies. In the first (Reinerman et al., 2006; $N=187$), a sensory vigilance task was employed; subjects were required to detect critical signals in a display resembling an air traffic control task. In the second study (Reinerman et al., 2007; $N=107$), a cognitive vigilance task was used. Subjects were required to decode letter sequences in order to detect targets, requiring use of working memory. Manipulation checks verified that subjects responded to task demands as expected. Performing the short task battery increased CBFV, relative to initial baseline, whereas bloodflow declined during performance of the vigilance tasks. Both tasks showed declines in detection rates (i.e., vigilance decrement). Turning to individual differences, Reinerman et al. (2006) found that initial task engagement (measured prior to the short battery) correlated with right-hemisphere phasic CBFV (0.25, $P<0.01$). Engagement and CITS task-focused coping measured following performance of the battery also correlated with this CBFV index ($rs=0.26$, 0.23, respectively, both $Ps<0.01$). The second study (Reinerman et al., 2007), which used a smaller sample, failed to replicate these findings, perhaps because of a lack of statistical power.

Table 13.5 shows correlates of perceptual sensitivity on the vigilance task in the two studies. Left and right-hemisphere CBFV measures were both predictive of subsequent vigilance. The pre-vigil measures of task engagement and task-focused coping refer to the subject's ratings of the

Table 13.5 Predictors of perceptual sensitivity (A′) in two studies employing transcranial Doppler sonography (TCD)

Task	CBFV Left H	CBFV Right H	States (DSSQ) Engagement (pre-vigil)	States (DSSQ) Engagement (post-vigil)	Coping (CITS) Task-focus (pre-vigil)	Coping (CITS) Task-focus (post-vigil)
Sensory vigilance	0.176*	0.240**	0.319**	0.219**	0.254**	0.311**
Cognitive vigilance	0.306**	0.389**	0.294**	0.199**	0.174	0.388**

CBFV, Cerebral bloodflow velocity; *DSSQ*, Dundee Stress State Questionnaire; *CITS*, Coping Inventory for Task Situations; *H*, hemisphere
*$P<0.05$
**$P<0.01$

short task battery and thus preceded the vigilance task in time. The post-vigil measures evaluated experience during the vigilance task. Both sets of correlations suggested that task engagement and task-focused coping are consistently related to vigilance. Multiple regressions showed that subjective state added to the variance explained by CBFV in both studies (Reinerman et al., 2006, 2007); use of multiple subjective and physiological indices may optimize prediction of individual differences in sustained attention.

We may be able to index individual differences in resource availability physiologically, via TCD. Additional features of the data support the resource hypothesis. Reinerman et al. (2006, 2007) compared averaged measures of left- and right-hemisphere CBFV with responses to the specific tasks comprising the short battery. An alternative explanation to resource theory is that the CBFV response reflects recruitment of specific component processes required for each individual task, rather than some more general resource. In this case, correlations between specific task CBFV responses and subsequent vigilance performance should vary with the degree of match in processing between the specific tasks and the vigilance task. It would be predicted that CBFV response to the line length discrimination task would be the strongest predictor of the sensory vigilance task employed by Reinerman et al. (2006), whereas the working memory task would predict cognitive vigilance most strongly (Reinerman et al., 2007). In fact, these predictions were not confirmed; there was no systematic difference between the component tasks of the short battery as CBFV-based predictors of vigilance, consistent with a resource model.

Another finding suggestive of a general resource is that right- and left-hemisphere CBFV responses were positively correlated and were similarly related to vigilance. A multiple resource model might predict that right-hemisphere CBFV would predict sensory vigilance more strongly, whereas left-hemisphere CBFV would relate to cognitive vigilance, but these predictions were not supported. There may be a common executive system that sustains a variety of qualitatively different processing operations (cf., Norman & Shallice, 1986).

Other features of the data indicate the difficulties of finding a single valid index of individual differences in resources. Across the two studies, subjective task engagement and CBFV were only weakly correlated. Individually, both types of index have validity, but it is difficult to link them both to a common latent resource factor. A further issue is that CBFV measured *concurrently* with vigilance did not relate reliably to either performance or subjective state. Although declines in CBFV observed during vigilance are diagnostic of attentional impairment in group data, the magnitude of the decline does not seem to indicate individual attentional function. Increases and decreases in CBFV may be diagnostic of rather different processes.

To summarize, task-evoked increases in bloodflow may provide an index of individual differences in resource availability, supporting a neuroscience approach to individual differences in sustained attention. However, localizing the neural systems responsible remains challenging. So too, is the development of a more elaborated resource model that integrates the physiological and subjective concomitants of resource availability.

Cognitive Stress Processes

An alternative explanation for task engagement effects refers to the self-regulative processes that manage stressful encounters, as described in transactional stress theory (Lazarus, 1999). Szalma (2008) has highlighted the impact of individual differences in coping on stress and performance outcomes. As described above, allowing the operator enhanced control over the task environment appears to raise both task engagement and sustained attention (Parsons et al., 2007).

The Reinerman et al. (2006, 2007) studies also demonstrated that coping predicts both sensory and cognitive vigilance (see Table 13.5). A further study (Matthews & Campbell, in press) investigated both appraisal and coping as correlates of vigilance, using the ALE (Ferguson et al., 1999) and an additional controllability scale to assess appraisal. They aimed specifically to investigate sustained performance in a stressful environment characterized by overload of attention. Participants were required to detect sequences of three odd or three even digits in a sequence of single digits, as in a typical cognitive vigilance task. However, stimulus presentation rates were set to be so high as to preclude successful performance. DSSQ data confirmed that the task induced both task disengagement and high levels of distress. Task engagement was significantly correlated with detection rate on the task ($r=0.33$, $P<0.01$). Correlations of similar magnitude with vigilance performance were found with task-focused coping, appraisals of challenge and controllability and (low) avoidance coping. Regression analyses failed to suggest any precedence among these predictors, suggesting that it is the complex of cognitive processes and the task engagement state that support superior attention.

A Note on Personality

This section has focused on associations between three types of variable: subjective states, cognitive stress process and objective indices of attention. A fourth class of variable – stable personality traits – may also influence individual differences in self-regulation (Robinson & Sedikides, in press). Prior research would suggest that extraversion should be especially important, given previous studies linking this trait to positive, excited affect, to challenge and task-focused coping and to vigilance (Matthews, Davies et al., 2000; Matthews, Deary, & Whiteman, 2003; Matthews, Schwean et al., 2000). Extraversion has also been linked to the Behavioral Activation System (Corr, 2008) that may contribute to task engagement, as further discussed in the next section. However, while extravert-introvert differences may play a role in task engagement, there are reasons to de-emphasize the trait in the context of attentional performance. First, in the studies reviewed above (see Table 13.2), extraversion was a rather weak predictor of engagement, challenge and task-focus. Second, the positive correlation between extraversion and energy would suggest that extraverts should perform relatively well on vigilance tasks; in fact, introverts typically do better. It appears that effects of extraversion on vigilance are not directly mediated by individual differences in arousal (Matthews, Davies, & Holley 1990; Matthews, Davies, & Lees 1990).

Third, the most reliable effects of extraversion on attention are interactive in nature. Extraverts typically perform better under high arousal, as evidenced in studies using arousal manipulations such as caffeine (Humphreys & Revelle, 1984), studies measuring arousal psychophysiologically (Matthews & Amelang, 1993) and studies measuring arousal through subjective scales (Matthews & Harley, 1993). The effect may reverse in the evening (Humphreys & Revelle, 1984). Information-processing analyses suggest that extraversion x arousal interactions are supported by low-level activation processes rather than resources under executive control (Matthews & Harley, 1993). Thus, these effects are distinct from the facilitative effects of energy and task engagement under discussion here.

Other personality traits may, in fact, be more relevant to individual differences in task engagement than extraversion, including, potentially, dedicated scales for the BAS (e.g., Carver & Scheier, 2005). A series of studies by Szalma (e.g., Szalma et al., 2006) and Helton (e.g., Helton et al., 1999) have implicated optimism-pessimism as an influence on engagement. Our research has found that Conscientiousness and Agreeableness are modestly, but fairly consistently, correlated with engagement in performance settings (Matthews et al., 1999).

The study of the brief vigilance task listed in Table 13.2 (Langheim et al., 2007) found that a variety of traits including cognitive failures, schizotypy and impulsivity correlated with (lower) task engagement, with the Big Five traits statistically controlled. In practical settings, traits linked to a specific context, such as driver fatigue proneness, have also proved predictive of task-induced changes in task engagement (Matthews & Desmond, 1998).

Theoretical Integration

Studies of task engagement and attention are compatible with resource models of arousal (Humphreys & Revelle, 1984; Matthews & Davies, 1998), in showing that, like energy, task engagement correlates with resource availability. However, the studies reviewed in the previous section suggest both some extensions and challenges to resource theory. A theory should accommodate the following key observations:

1. Task engagement and performance are reciprocally related. Not only does engagement predict performance, but performance of demanding but monotonous tasks depresses engagement. Theory should specify the mechanisms mediating the dynamic process of interaction between operator and task environment.
2. Task engagement may, in part, index fundamental changes in processing efficiency. Theory should specify how task engagement influences operating parameters of the neural and/or cognitive architectures.
3. Task engagement also relates to self-regulative processes, such as choice of coping strategy. Theory should specify how engagement is linked to voluntary strategic processes for managing task demands.

Matthews (2001) outlined a general framework for research on stress factors and performance that provides a starting point for elaborating resource theory. He pointed out that most stressors, such as noise and heat, exert multiple effects on neurocognitive functioning. For example, noise raises nonspecific arousal, narrows attention and changes high-level cognitions of the task. The multifaceted nature of stressor effects on performance may be understood within the "classical theory" of cognitive science developed by Pylyshyn (1984) and others. Three levels of interaction may be differentiated. First, some stressor effects result from biophysical processes controlling neural functioning. Second, virtual cognitive processes operating on symbolic representations can be abstracted from the neural substrate. Third, strategic processes are governed by high-level personal beliefs that do not directly correspond to specific information-processing components. Applying this analysis to task engagement might implicate (1) dopaminergic reward systems of the brain, (2) resource availability treated as a virtual cognitive construct, and (3) challenge appraisals and a preference for task-focused coping.

Biological Bases for Task Engagement

Caution is needed in any attempt to map task engagement onto specific brain structures. Neuroimaging studies of positive affect have produced rather inconsistent results (Barrett & Wager, 2006), although these authors identify some evidence for greater medial prefrontal cortex activation in states of approach-related affect, especially in the left hemisphere. Contemporary neuroscience (e.g., Burgdorf & Panksepp, 2006; Kringelbach, 2005) typically links positive affect to multiple brain structures including both subcortical areas (e.g., ventral striatum) and frontal cortical sites (e.g., orbitofrontal cortex). Burgdorf and Panksepp (2006) suggest that there may be separate circuits supporting appetitive energization and consummatory pleasure, a distinction that roughly corresponds to the psychometric distinction between energetic arousal and hedonic tone as elements of mood (Matthews, Jones, & Chamberlain, 1990). They describe ventral striatal dopamine systems as important for the appetitive system; consummatory pleasure is supported by opiate and GABA systems rather than dopamine. On the other hand, Berridge and Kringelbach (2008) assign a motivational but not a hedonic function to the subcortical dopaminergic circuits. Given that task engagement has both motivational and hedonic elements (as well as an attentional component), the subjective state may correspond, at least loosely, to the orbitofrontal (and related prefrontal) sites to which Berridge and Kringelbach (2008) assign the function of integrating information from sensory and motivational pathways to generate pleasure.

In personality research, the circuitry for approach and appetitive behavior is conceptualized as a Behavioral Activation System (BAS) within the larger Reinforcement Sensitivity Theory (RST) advanced by Corr (2008). Pickering and Smillie (2008) claim that ascending dopaminergic projections to structures including striatum and prefrontal cortex play a major role in the BAS. The parallels between the neural systems described by RST and the psychological bases for self-regulation have been widely noted (e.g., Carver & Scheier, 2005). Thus, it is again reasonable to suggest that task engagement correlates with activity in these pathways, although the magnitude of the correlation is unclear. It is also plausible that the subjective experience of being engaged relates to multiple brain structures within a distributed system. It would also be reasonable to relate task engagement to the executive system described by Posner (e.g., Posner et al., 2007), localized in the anterior cingulate cortex and other areas, which supports attention to demanding tasks, and self-regulation of cognition and emotion. In this account, we focus on psychological theory, but integrating this theory with neuropsychological accounts of affective regulation of behavior is an important task for the future. However, there may be limits on how precisely subjective task engagement may be localized in the brain.

A Cognitive Architecture for Self-Regulation

Self-regulative aspects of task engagement are centered on approach motivations. How does the person regulate their goals for successful performance and their strategies for attaining those goals? Here, we can only sketch out some suggestions as to how the problem should be tackled. In brief, there are three requirements for a self-regulative model of this domain. First, we need to specify the self-regulative machinery that controls effortful striving towards success in the performance context. There are various approaches described in the literature on performance motivation, but here we will focus on the cybernetic theory developed by researchers including Carver and Scheier (2005). Second, we need to specify relationships between self-regulative processes and affect (which may be bidirectional). Third, we need to specify relationships between self-regulative processes and the attentional processes that govern observed performance (also bidirectional).

Wells and Matthews (1994) proposed a cognitive architecture of self-regulation in the context of negative affect. Discrepancies between preferred and actual status (e.g., an overt threat) initiated Self-Referent Executive (S-REF) processing which initiated compensatory coping intended to reduce the discrepancy (e.g., threat avoidance). In addition to the executive system (the S-REF), the architecture also included a network of lower-level processing units, and a repository of declarative and procedural self-knowledge in long-term memory. Functioning of the SREF interacted with both lower-level processing and self-knowledge. Following Norman and Shallice (1986), top-down control of lower-level modules is limited by a general resource for supervisory control.

By analogy with the concept of Self-Referent Executive Processing (S-REF: Wells & Matthews, 1994), we propose that the executive system may also function in a mode of Task-Referent Executive Processing (T-REF). Broadly, T-REF processing is initiated by signals that effort is needed to maintain progress towards a valued task goal, and is sustained until the goal is attained, or until the goal is reappraised as unattainable or of insufficient priority to justify continued effort.

Figure 13.4 shows an outline model of executive function and coping. As in a standard closed-loop cybernetic system (e.g., Carver & Scheier, in press), executive processing is initiated by a discrepancy between a target state or goal (i.e., achieving some performance standard) and appraisal of current performance. Discrepancy may elicit various forms of coping. The S-REF model (Wells & Matthews, 1994) delineates some of the multiple factors that may influence discrepancy processing,

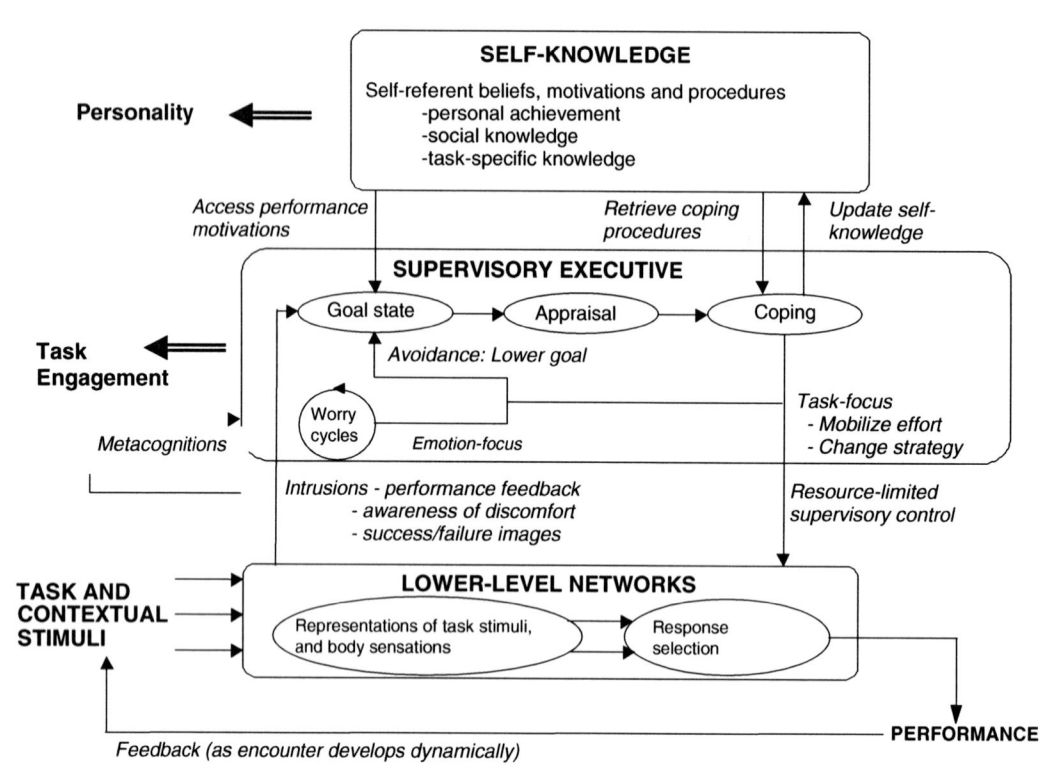

Fig. 13.4 An architecture for task-referent self-regulation

which may also apply to task-related executive functioning. These include intrusions from lower-level processing; in this case, perhaps a thought or image of success which reinforces performance goals. The S-REF model also emphasizes the use of schema-like self-knowledge in interpreting input to the executive system (e.g., pessimistic self-appraisal). Indeed, self-knowledge may contribute to individual differences in stable personality traits (Matthews, Davies et al., 2000; Matthews, Schwean et al., 2000; Robinson & Sedikides, in press).

As in the S-REF model, the operator's retrieval of performance-related beliefs and motivations from self-knowledge will influence initiation of executive processing. Thayer (1989) suggested that cognitions of self-efficacy (Bandura, 1989) might promote energy. More broadly, a variety of self-beliefs, including self-concept, self-efficacy and positive outcome expectancies have been linked to academic motivation and performance settings (Schunk & Pajares, 2005). In related work, Dweck (1999) has explored how self-beliefs influence effort and goals in academic setting and differentiated learning or mastery goals from performance goals. Broadly, much social-cognitive theory converges on the importance of self-related cognitions in approach motivation. Operators who believe they lack competence may fail to engage task-directed executive processing.

Appraisals of challenge will tend to initiate task-focused coping strategies such as increasing effort (as well as other, task-specific strategies). In this "T-REF" mode, resources will be allocated to enhancing lower-level processing, especially higher-priority components (Matthews & Davies, 2001), even if sustaining effort induces discomfort. Less adaptive strategies include avoidance (reducing effort) and emotion-focus (reflecting on the task and its personal significance). Feedback signals indicative of the outcome of task-focused coping will influence whether task-directed effort is sustained (cf., Szalma et al., 2006); for example, if coping is unsuccessful in maintaining progress towards task goals, task-focus may be replaced by avoidance.

Task Engagement and Self-Regulation

How does the operation of the feedback system influence subjective state, and how does state influence its operation? In general, we suppose that task engagement reflects the overall status of the system as functioning to maintain task-directed effort and commitment (Matthews et al., 2002). Consistent with this assumption, social-cognitive theories of self-regulation typically link positive affect to approach goals (e.g., Pekrun, Elliot, & Maier, 2006). The regression data reviewed above (see Table 13.4) suggest that engagement reflects an integration of cognitive self-regulative processes rather than any individual process. Thus, engagement is an output of the system as a whole. Carver and Scheier (2005) make the interesting suggestion that high levels of positive affect correspond to making faster progress towards goals than expected, so that the happy person may tend to "coast" and reduce effort somewhat. The data summarized in Table 13.3 represent monotonic associations between task engagement and task-focused coping/effort, showing that task engagement should be distinguished from positive affect. Indeed, the factor analytic data show only a secondary loading for hedonic tone (positive mood) on the task engagement factor (Matthews et al., 2002).

Task engagement may also reciprocally influence self-regulation. The S-REF model (Wells, 2000; Wells & Matthews, 1994) emphasized the role of metacognition in negative affect. For example, worry about one's own worry ("meta-worry") may serve to maintain anxiety and emotional distress. Metacognitions that one's own engagement is desirable and productive may bias self-regulation towards task-focused coping and effort. Conversely, metacognitive beliefs that fatigue and bodily discomfort are undesirable may motivate the person towards lowering task goals and prioritizing comfort and rest (Fairclough, 2001). As Thayer (1989, Chap. 5) discusses, it is likely that the person continually monitors energy and allots resources to activities in relation to awareness of energy. Such metacognitive processes may explain why pre-task engagement predicts future appraisal and coping as shown in Table 13.3. There is also a further, indirect path through which task engagement may influence self-regulation. If high engagement does indeed lead to better objective performance, then the person will tend to receive more positive feedback, which is likely to sustain engagement. Conversely, fatigue may potentially lead to performance failure and disengagement from the task.

Engagement and Performance Revisited

Locating the feedback system within the S-REF architecture (Wells & Matthews, 1994) helps us to understand how task engagement may relate to performance, just as the original S-REF model clarified relationships between anxiety and attention. To use an automotive metaphor, Humphreys and Revelle (1984) separated the gas pedal (arousal) from steering (effort). The present account emphasizes that increased energetic arousal and task-directed effort typically work together as part of the same over-arching task engagement response. Nevertheless, there may be multiple pathways between engagement and objective performance, consistent with the cognitive science framework for stress effects (Matthews, 2001).

First, engagement signals the state of the underlying neurocognitive architecture, expressed most simply as the availability of attentional resources, perhaps supported by the dopaminergic circuits of the BAS (Corr, 2008). Increased CBFV may be one concomitant of this system (Reinerman et al., 2006, 2007). Importantly, the neural substrate for resources may be influenced by psychological processes such as scope for exerting active control over the task environment (Parsons et al., 2007), and processing of performance feedback (Szalma et al., 2006). As in Thayer's (1989, 1996) original conception of energetic arousal, the subjective state may reflect an integration of biological and cognitive influences.

Second, engagement signals a cognitive-adaptive process (Matthews, 2001), as the person seeks to mobilize and direct resources to the task most effectively. Linking engagement to voluntary control of task performance raises the difficult question of how resources and effort should be distinguished (cf., Humphreys & Revelle, 1984). A two-level control hierarchy (e.g., Norman & Shallice, 1986), might relate effort to the initiation of control operations, whereas resources constrain the influence of those operations on lower-level processing. We might distinguish subjective effort as the discomfort attaching to executive operations from resources as the strength of intervention necessary to influence lower-level processing. Like doing household chores, some mental operations may be attentionally undemanding but require effortful and discomforting activation of task goals.

States of fatigue may support a contrary adaptation of attempting to conserve energy and resources, by seeking to maintain some minimal competence (lowered performance goals) rather than striving for performance excellence (Matthews & Desmond, 2002). A more elaborated account of the process would accommodate the social-cognitive theory of achievement and approach motivations briefly introduced above (e.g., Dweck, 1999).

Finally, as in the case of the S-REF, we note the likelihood of dynamic processes that serve to sustain or to discourage T-REF processing and subjective task engagement. During performance, both virtuous and vicious cycles may develop. Investments of effort in the task that pay off in performance enhancements may serve to sustain task engagement. Indeed, operators may set themselves progressively more challenging task goals. Conversely, as elaborated in studies of fatigue (Fairclough, 2001; Matthews & Desmond, 2002), performance failure and task monotony may perpetuate a vicious cycle of ever-decreasing engagement and use of avoidance coping. In this case, the T-REF may be activated only episodically to prevent complete performance breakdown.

Over longer periods of time, operation of the T-REF may influence the content of self-knowledge. As described by social cognitive theories (e.g., Bandura, 1989), successful task mastery is likely to build contextual self-efficacy and skills for implementing task-focused coping, whereas failure experiences encourage procedures for avoidance. The ability of contextualized traits, such as driver fatigue-proneness (Matthews & Desmond, 1998), to predict engagement may result from self-knowledge linked to specific activities, such as driving. Vehicle drivers – as well as individuals in other specialized contexts – may acquire a self-concept that represents themes of boredom, lack of personal efficacy and fatigue-proneness.

Conclusions

We began this chapter by advancing the simple proposition that individual differences in energetic arousal provide a marker for attentional resource availability, consistent with the Humphreys and Revelle (1984) performance theory. Recent research allows this hypothesis to be elaborated in several respects. First, energy is one facet of a broader subjective state factor of task engagement that binds elevated mood to performance motivations and concentration. Second, the relationship between subjective task engagement and information processing is bi-directional, and both paths are regulated by executive processing. Changes in engagement reflect self-regulative processes including appraisal and coping, consistent with existing cognitive theories of affect (e.g., Carver & Scheier, in press). Conversely, individual differences in engagement influence executive control over attention. Like energy, high engagement functions as a marker for resource availability, but its effects may also be mediated by task-focused coping and effort. Third, theoretical accounts of the interplay between engagement and attention require multi-leveled explanations in line with a cognitive science understanding of stress (Matthews, 2000, 2001). The account here acknowledges the importance of the neurological architecture for attention and approach motivation, but focused primarily on self-regulative processes. We have proposed that executive systems include a "task-relevant" mode that interacts with self-knowledge and lower-level processing networks in maintaining task-directed effort and commitment. Subjective engagement signals the intervention of executive processing in maintaining progress toward personally-important task goals.

Acknowledgements Some of this work was supported by the U.S. Army Medical Research and Materiel Command under Contract No. DAMD17-04-C-0002. The views, opinions, and/or findings contained in this report are those of the author(s) and should not be construed as an official Department of the Army position, policy or decision unless so designated by other documentation. In the conduct of research where humans are the subjects, the investigator(s) adhered to the policies regarding the protection of human subjects as prescribed by 45 CFR 46 and 32 CFR 219 (Protection of Human Subjects).

References

Aaslid, R. (1986). Transcranial Doppler examination techniques. In R. Aaslid (Ed.), *Transcranial Doppler sonography* (pp. 39–59). New York: Springer.
Bandura, A. (1989). Human agency in social cognitive theory. *American Psychologist, 44*, 1175–1184.
Barrett, L. F., & Wager, D. (2006). The structure of emotion: Evidence from neuroimaging studies. *Current Directions in Psychological Science, 15*, 79–83.
Berridge, K. C., & Kringelbach, L. (2008). Affective neuroscience of pleasure: Reward in humans and animals. *Psychopharmacology, 199*, 457–480.
Broadhurst, P. L. (1957). Emotionality and the Yerkes-Dodson Law. *Journal of Experimental Psychology, 54*, 345–352.
Burgdorf, J., & Panksepp, J. (2006). The neurobiology of positive emotions. *Neuroscience and Biobehavioral Reviews, 30*, 173–187.
Carver, C. S., & Scheier, M. F. (2005). Engagement, disengagement, coping, and catastrophe. In A. J. Elliot & C. S. Dweck (Eds.), *Handbook of competence and motivation* (pp. 527–547). New York: Guilford Press.
Carver, C. S., & Scheier, M. F. (2009). Self-regulation and control in personality functioning. In P. J. Corr & G. Matthews (Eds.), *Cambridge handbook of personality* (pp. 427–440). Cambridge: Cambridge University Press.
Corr, P. J. (2008). Reinforcement sensitivity theory (RST): Introduction. In P. L. Corr (Ed.), *The reinforcement sensitivity theory of personality* (pp. 1–43). Cambridge: Cambridge University Press.
Davies, D. R., & Parasuraman, R. (1982). *The psychology of vigilance*. London: Academic.
Desmond, P. A., & Hancock, P. A. (2001). Active and passive fatigue states. In P. A. Hancock & P. A. Desmond (Eds.), *Stress, workload and fatigue* (pp. 455–465). Mahwah, NJ: Lawrence Erlbaum.
Dickman, S. J. (2002). Dimensions of arousal: Wakefulness and vigor. *Human Factors, 44*, 429–442.
Dweck, C. S. (1999). *Self-theories: Their role in motivation, personality and development*. New York: Psychology Press.
Ekman, P. (2003). *METT. Micro expression training tool*. CD-Rom. Available from http://www.emotionsrevealed.com
Eysenck, H. J. (1967). *The biological basis of personality*. Springfield, IL: Thomas.
Eysenck, M. W. (1982). *Attention and arousal: Cognition and performance*. New York: Springer.
Eysenck, M. W., & Calvo, M. G. (1992). Anxiety and performance: The processing efficiency theory. *Cognition and Emotion, 6*, 409–434.
Fairclough, S. H. (2001). Mental effort regulation and the functional impairment of the driver. In P. A. Hancock & P. A. Desmond (Eds.), *Stress, workload and fatigue* (pp. 479–502). Mahwah, NJ: Erlbaum.
Fairclough, S. H., & Venables, L. (2006). Prediction of subjective states from psychophysiology: A multivariate approach. *Biological Psychology, 71*, 100–110.
Fellner, A., Matthews, G., Warm, J.S., Zeidner, M., & Roberts, R.D. (2006). Learning to discriminate terrorists: The effects of emotional intelligence and emotive cues. *Proceedings of the Human Factors and Ergonomics Society, 50*, 1619–1623.
Fellner, A., Matthews, G., Funke, G. J., Emo, A. K., Zeidner, M., Pérez-González, J. C., et al. (2007). The effects of emotional intelligence on visual search of emotional stimuli and emotion identification. *Proceedings of the Human Factors and Ergonomics Society, 51*, 845–849.
Ferguson, E., Matthews, G., & Cox, T. (1999). The appraisal of life events (ALE) scale: Reliability and validity. *British Journal of Health Psychology, 4*, 97–116.
Funke, G. J., Matthews, G., Warm, J. S., & Emo, A. (2007). Vehicle automation: A remedy for driver stress? *Ergonomics, 50*, 1302–1323.
Hancock, P. A., & Ganey, N. (2003). From the inverted-U to the extended-U: The evolution of a law of psychology. *Journal of Human Performance in Extreme Environments, 7*, 5–14.

Hancock, P. A., & Szalma, J. L. (2008). Stress and performance. In P. A. Hancock & J. L. Szalma (Eds.), *Performance under stress* (pp. 1–18). Aldershot, UK: Ashgate Publishing.

Hart, S. G., & Staveland, L. E. (1988). Development of NASA-TLX (task load index): Results of empirical and theoretical research. In P. A. Hancock & N. Meshkati (Eds.), *Human mental workload* (pp. 139–183). Oxford, UK: North-Holland.

Helton, W. S., Dember, W. N., Warm, J. S., & Matthews, G. (1999). Optimism-pessimism and false failure feedback: Effects on vigilance performance. *Current Psychology: Research and Review, 18*, 311–325.

Helton, W. S., Shaw, T. H., Warm, J. S., Matthews, G., Dember, W. N., & Hancock, P. A. (2004). Demand transitions in vigilance: Effects on performance efficiency and stress. In D. A. Vincenzi, M. Mouloua, & P. A. Hancock (Eds.), *Human performance, situation awareness and automation: Current research and trends, HPSAAII* (Vol. 1, pp. 258–262). Mahwah, NJ: Erlbaum.

Helton, W. S., Shaw, T. H., Warm, J. S., Matthews, G., Dember, W. N., & Hancock, P. A. (2008). Effects of warned and unwarned demand transitions on vigilance performance and stress. *Anxiety, Stress and Coping, 21*, 173–184.

Helton, W. S., Warm, J. S., Matthews, G., & Corcoran, K. J. (2002). Further tests of an abbreviated vigilance task: Effects of signal salience and jet aircraft noise on performance efficiency and stress. *Proceedings of the Human Factors and Ergonomics Society, 46*, 1546–1550.

Hitchcock, E. M., Warm, J. S., Matthews, G., Dember, W. N., Shear, P. K., Mayeben, D. W., et al. (2002). Automation cueing modulates cerebral blood flow and vigilance in a simulated air traffic control task. *Theoretical Issues in Ergonomics Science, 4*, 89–112.

Humphreys, M. S., & Revelle, W. (1984). Personality, motivation and performance: A theory of the relationship between individual differences and information processing. *Psychological Review, 91*, 153–184.

Ketelaar, T., & Clore, G. L. (1997). Emotion and reason: The proximate effects and ultimate functions of emotion. In G. Matthews (Ed.), *Cognitive science perspectives on personality and emotion* (pp. 355–396). Amsterdam: Elsevier.

Koelega, H. S. (1992). Extraversion and vigilance performance: 30 years of inconsistencies. *Psychological Bulletin, 112*, 239–258.

Kringelbach, M. L. (2005). The human orbitofrontal cortex: Linking reward to hedonic experience. *Nature Reviews Neuroscience, 6*, 691–702.

Langheim, L., Matthews, G., Warm, J. S., Reinerman, L. E., Shaw, T. H., Finomore, V. S., et al. (2007). *The long pursuit: in search of predictors of individual differences in vigilance.* Paper presented at the Thirteenth Meeting of the International Society for the Study of Individual Differences, Giessen, Germany, July 2007.

Lazarus, R. S. (1999). *Stress and emotion: A new synthesis.* New York: Springer.

Mackworth, N. H. (1948). The breakdown of vigilance during prolonged visual search. *Quarterly Journal of Experimental Psychology, 1*, 6–21.

Matthews, G. (1992). Extraversion. In A. P. Smith & D. M. Jones (Eds.), *Handbook of human performance. Vol. 3: State and trait* (pp. 95–126). London: Academic

Matthews, G. (2000). A cognitive science critique of biological theories of personality traits. *History and Philosophy of Psychology, 2*, 1–17.

Matthews, G. (2001). Levels of transaction: A cognitive sciences framework for operator stress. In P. A. Hancock & P. A. Desmond (Eds.), *Stress, workload and fatigue* (pp. 5–33). Mahwah, NJ: Erlbaum.

Matthews, G. (2002). Towards a transactional ergonomics for driver stress and fatigue. *Theoretical Issues in Ergonomics Science, 3*, 195–211.

Matthews, G. (2008). Reinforcement sensitivity theory: A critique from cognitive science. In P. L. Corr (Ed.), *The reinforcement sensitivity theory of personality* (pp. 482–527). Cambridge: Cambridge University Press.

Matthews, G., & Amelang, M. (1993). Extraversion, arousal theory and performance: A study of individual differences in the EEG. *Personality and Individual Differences, 14*, 347–364.

Matthews, G., & Campbell, S. E. (1998). Task-induced stress and individual differences in coping. *Proceedings of the Human Factors and Ergonomics Society, 42*, 821–825.

Matthews, G., & Campbell, S. E. (1999). Individual differences in stress response and working memory. *Proceedings of the Human Factors and Ergonomics Society, 43*, 634–638.

Matthews, G., & Campbell, S. E. (2009). Sustained performance under overload: Personality and individual differences in stress and coping. *Theoretical Issues in Ergonomics Science, 10*, 417–442.

Matthews, G., Campbell, S., Falconer, S. (2001). Assessment of motivational states in performance environments. *Proceedings of the Human Factors and Ergonomics Society, 45*, 906–910.

Matthews, G., Campbell, S. E., Falconer, S., Joyner, L., Huggins, J., Gilliland, K., et al. (2002). Fundamental dimensions of subjective state in performance settings: Task engagement, distress and worry. *Emotion, 2*, 315–340.

Matthews, G., & Davies, D. R. (1998). Arousal and vigilance: The role of task demands. In R. R. Hoffman, M. F. Sherrick, & J. S. Warm (Eds.), *Viewing psychology as a whole: The integrative science of William N. Dember* (pp. 113–144). Washington, DC: American Psychological Association.

Matthews, G., & Davies, D. R. (2001). Individual differences in energetic arousal and sustained attention: A dual-task study. *Personality and Individual Differences, 31*, 575–589.

Matthews, G., Davies, D. R., & Holley, P. J. (1990). Extraversion, arousal and visual sustained attention: The role of resource availability. *Personality and Individual Differences, 11*, 1159–1173.

Matthews, G., Davies, D. R., & Lees, J. L. (1990). Arousal, extraversion, and individual differences in resource availability. *Journal of Personality and Social Psychology, 59*, 150–168.

Matthews, G., Davies, D. R., Westerman, S. J., & Stammers, R. B. (2000). *Human performance: Cognition, stress and individual differences*. Hove, UK: Psychology Press.

Matthews, G., Deary, I. J., & Whiteman, M. C. (2003). *Personality traits* (2nd ed.). Cambridge: Cambridge University Press.

Matthews, G., & Desmond, P. A. (1998). Personality and multiple dimensions of task-induced fatigue: A study of simulated driving. *Personality and Individual Differences, 25*, 443–458.

Matthews, G., & Desmond, P. A. (2002). Task-induced fatigue states and simulated driving performance. *Quarterly Journal of Experimental Psychology, 55A*, 659–686.

Matthews, G., Emo, A. K., Funke, G., Zeidner, M., Roberts, R. D., Costa, P. T., Jr., et al. (2006). Emotional intelligence, personality, and task-induced stress. *Journal of Experimental Psychology: Applied, 12*, 96–107.

Matthews, G., & Falconer, S. (2002). Personality, coping and task-induced stress in customer service personnel. *Proceedings of the Human Factors and Ergonomics Society, 46*, 963–967.

Matthews, G., & Gilliland, K. (1999). The personality theories of H. J. Eysenck and J. A. Gray: A comparative review. *Personality and Individual Differences, 26*, 583–626.

Matthews, G., & Harley, T. A. (1993). Effects of extraversion and self-report arousal on semantic priming: A connectionist approach. *Journal of Personality and Social Psychology, 65*, 735–756.

Matthews, G., Jones, D. M., & Chamberlain, A. G. (1990). Refining the measurement of mood: The UWIST mood adjective checklist. *British Journal of Psychology, 81*, 17–42.

Matthews, G., Joyner, L., Gilliland, K., Campbell, S. E., Falconer, S., & Huggins, J. (1999). Validation of a comprehensive stress state questionnaire: Towards a state "Big Three." In I. Mervielde, I. J. Dreary, F. DeFruyt, & F. Ostendorf (Eds.), *Personality psychology in Europe* (Vol. 7, pp. 335–350). Tilburg, Netherlands: Tilburg University Press.

Matthews, G., & Margetts, I. (1991). Self-report arousal and divided attention: A study of performance operating characteristics. *Human Performance, 4*, 107–125.

Matthews, G., Saxby, D. J., Funke, G. J., Emo, A. K., & Desmond, P. A. (in press). Driving in states of fatigue or stress. In D. Fisher, M. Rizzo, J. Caird, & J. Lee (Eds.), *Handbook of driving simulation for engineering, medicine and psychology*. Boca Raton, FL: Taylor and Francis

Matthews, G., Schwean, V. L., Campbell, S. E., Saklofske, D. H., & Mohamed, A. A. R. (2000). Personality, self-regulation and adaptation: A cognitive-social framework. In M. Boekarts, P. R. Pintrich, & M. Zeidner (Eds.), *Handbook of self-regulation* (pp. 171–207). New York: Academic.

Matthews, G., Warm, J. S., Dember, W. N., Mizoguchi, H., & Smith, A. P. (2001). The common cold impairs visual attention, psychomotor performance, and task engagement. *Proceedings of the Human Factors and Ergonomics Society, 45*, 1377–1381.

Matthews, G., Warm, J. S., & Washburn, D. (2007). *Diagnostic methods for predicting performance impairment associated with combat stress*. Report for U.S. Army Medical Research and Materiel Command, contract # W23RYX-3106-N605

Matthews, G., & Westerman, S. J. (1994). Energy and tension as predictors of controlled visual and memory search. *Personality and Individual Differences, 17*, 617–626.

Matthews, G., & Zeidner, M. (2004). Traits, states and the trilogy of mind: An adaptive perspective on intellectual functioning. In D. Dai & R. J. Sternberg (Eds.), *Motivation, emotion, and cognition: Integrative perspectives on intellectual functioning and development* (pp. 143–174). Mahwah, NJ: Lawrence Erlbaum.

McCrae, R. R., & Costa, P. T., Jr. (2008). Empirical and theoretical status of the Five-Factor Model of personality traits. In G. J. Boyle, G. Matthews, & D. H. Saklofske (Eds.), *Handbook of personality theory and assessment: Volume 1: Personality theories and models*. Thousand Oaks, CA: Sage.

Nęcka, E. (1997). Attention, working memory and arousal: Concepts apt to account for the "process of intelligence". In G. Matthews (Ed.), *Cognitive science perspectives on personality and emotion* (pp. 503–554). Amsterdam: Elsevier.

Norman, D. A., & Shallice, T. (1986). Attention to action: willed and automatic control of behaviour. In R. J. Davidson, G. E. Schwartz & D. Shapiro (Eds.), *Consciousness and self-regulation: Advances in research* (Vol. 4, pp. 1–18). New York: Plenum

Nuechterlein, K. H., Parasuraman, R., & Jiang, Q. (1983). Visual sustained attention: Image degradation produces rapid sensitivity decrement over time. *Science, 220*, 327–329.

Parasuraman, R., Warm, J. S., & See, J. E. (1998). Brain systems of vigilance. In R. Parasuraman (Ed.), *The attentive brain* (pp. 221–256). Cambridge, MA: MIT Press.

Parsons, K. S., Warm, J. S., Nelson, W. T., Riley, M., & Matthews, G. (2007). Detection-action linkage in vigilance: effects on workload and stress. *Proceedings of the Human Factors and Ergonomics Society, 51*, 1291–1295.

Pashler, H. E. (1998). *The psychology of attention*. Cambridge, MA: MIT Press.

Pekrun, R., Elliot, A. J., & Maier, M. A. (2006). Achievement goals and discrete achievement emotions: A theoretical model and prospective test. *Journal of Educational Psychology, 98*, 583–597.

Pickering, A. D., & Smillie, L. D. (2008). The behavioural activation system: Challenges and opportunities. In P. L. Corr (Ed.), *The reinforcement sensitivity theory of personality* (pp. 120–154). Cambridge: Cambridge University Press.

Posner, M. I., Rothbart, M. K., Sheese, B. E., & Tang, Y. (2007). The anterior cingulate gyrus and the mechanism of self-regulation. *Cognitive, Affective and Behavioral Neuroscience, 7*, 391–395.

Pylyshyn, Z. W. (1984). *Computation and cognition: Toward a foundation for cognitive science*. Cambridge, MA: MIT Press.

Reinerman, L., Matthews, G., Warm, J. S., & Langheim, L. (2007). Predicting cognitive vigilance performance from cerebral blood flow velocity and task engagement. *Proceedings of the Human Factors and Ergonomics Society, 51*, 850–854.

Reinerman, L. E., Matthews, G., Warm, J. S., Langheim, L. K., Parsons, K., Proctor, C. A., et al. (2006). Cerebral blood flow velocity and task engagement as predictors of vigilance performance. *Proceedings of the Human Factors and Ergonomics Society, 50*, 1254–1258.

Robbins, T. W., Milstein, J. A., & Dalley, J. W. (2004). Neuropharmacology of attention. In M. I. Posner (Ed.), *Cognitive neuroscience of attention* (pp. 283–293). New York: Guilford Press.

Robinson, M. D., & Sedikides, C. (2009). Traits and the self: Toward an integration. In P. J. Corr & G. Matthews (Eds.), *Cambridge handbook of personality* (pp. 457–472). Cambridge: Cambridge University Press.

Sarason, I. G., Sarason, B. R., & Pierce, G. R. (1995). Cognitive interference: At the intelligence-personality crossroads. In D. Saklofske & M. Zeidner (Eds.), *International handbook of personality and intelligence* (pp. 285–296). New York: Plenum.

Saxby, D. J., Matthews, G., & Hitchcock, T. (2007). Fatigue states are multidimensional: Evidence from studies of simulated driving. In *Proceedings of the driving simulation conference – North America 2007*. Iowa City, IA: University of Iowa.

Schunk, D. H., & Pajares, F. (2005). Competence perceptions and academic functioning. In A. J. Elliot & C. S. Dweck (Eds.), *Handbook of competence and motivation* (pp. 85–104). New York: Guilford Press.

See, J. E., Howe, S. R., Warm, J. S., & Dember, W. N. (1995). Meta-analysis of the sensitivity decrement in vigilance. *Psychological Bulletin, 117*, 230–249.

Shiffrin, R. M., & Schneider, W. (1977). Controlled and automatic human information processing: II. Perceptual learning, automatic attending and a general theory. *Psychological Review, 84*, 127–190.

Stroobant, N., & Vingerhoets, G. (2000). Transcranial Doppler ultrasonography monitoring of cerebral hemodynamics during performance of cognitive tasks: A review. *Neuropsychology Review, 10*, 213–231.

Szalma, J. L. (2008). Individual differences in stress reaction. In P. A. Hancock & J. L. Szalma (Eds.), *Performance under stress* (pp. 323–357). Aldershot, UK: Ashgate Publishing.

Szalma, J. L., Hancock, P. A., Dember, W. N., & Warm, J. S. (2006). Training for vigilance: The effect of knowledge of results format and dispositional optimism and pessimism on performance and stress. *British Journal of Psychology, 97*, 115–135.

Temple, J. G., Warm, J. S., Dember, W. N., Jones, K. S., LaGrange, C. M., & Matthews, G. (2000). The effects of signal salience and caffeine on performance, workload, and stress in an abbreviated vigilance task. *Human Factors, 42*, 183–194.

Thayer, R. E. (1978). Toward a psychological theory of multidimensional activation (arousal). *Motivation and Emotion, 2*, 1–34.

Thayer, R. E. (1989). *The biopsychology of mood and arousal*. Oxford: Oxford University Press.

Thayer, R. E. (1996). *The origin of everyday moods*. New York: Oxford University Press.

Warm, J. S., & Dember, W. N. (1998). Tests of a vigilance taxonomy. In R. R. Hoffman, M. F. Sherrick & J. S. Warm (Eds.), *Viewing psychology as a whole: The integrative science of William N. Dember* (pp. 87–112). Washington, DC: American Psychological Association.

Warm, J. S., Matthews, G., & Finomore, V. S. (2008). Workload and stress in sustained attention. In P. A. Hancock & J. L. Szalma (Eds.), *Performance under stress* (pp. 115–141). Aldershot, UK: Ashgate Publishing.

Wells, A. (2000). *Emotional disorders and metacognition: Innovative cognitive therapy*. New York: Wiley.

Wells, A., & Matthews, G. (1994). *Attention and emotion: A clinical perspective*. Hove: Erlbaum.

Wickens, C. D., & Hollands, J. G. (1999). *Engineering psychology and human performance* (3rd ed.). Upper Saddle River, NJ: Prentice-Hall.

Chapter 14
Individual Differences in Resource Allocation Policy

Błażej Szymura

Introduction

Apart from many other things, people differ in the way they allocate their attentional resources to the tasks they are engaged in. Individual differences in attentional resources management seem interesting as correlates of temperament/personality and intellectual traits (Eysenck, 1982; Nęcka, 1997). Although the differences in the effectiveness of attentional resources management with regard to individual difference variables are not very salient (these variables usually explain no more than 10–15% of variance in attentional task performance), it still seems worth asking whether people characterized by different levels of intelligence or creativity, a different necessity of extraversion, neuroticism or psychoticism trait also differ in the specificity of attentional functioning – the major strategy by which the cognitive system protects its limited capacity against overload (Broadbent, 1982). Knowledge of such relationships should increase our understanding of the cognitive mechanisms of human temperament/personality and intelligence. It should also be helpful in the creation of an integrated model of cognitive performance, which also takes into account inter-individual variability.

Firstly, in this chapter, the capacity theory of attention (Kahneman, 1973) will be described in brief. Besides many other statements, this theory establishes the link between attentional resources and the level of arousal, as displayed by the nervous system. There are a variety of theories of attentional resources or capacity, of which Kahneman's is just one (e.g., Hasher & Zacks, 1979; Hirst & Kalmar, 1987; Navon, 1984; Wickens, 1984), but only Kahneman's theory directly makes quantity of available resources and quality of strategies for resources allocation conditional on the arousal level. On the contrary, Malleable Attentional Resource Theory (MART in its "strongest" form; Young & Stanton, 2002, p. 367) even states that "the size of attentional resources pools ... is independent in variations of arousal and effort" and it is "relying purely on task demands."

However, the basic assumptions of many theories of individual differences in cognitive performance refer to the relationship between resources and arousal and thus directly to Kahneman's theory (e.g., Eysenck, 1982; Humphreys & Revelle, 1984; Nęcka, 1997). It seems that Kahneman's theory of attention is still worth deliberation, at least from the perspective of individual differences. That is why Kahneman's theory has been chosen as a starter for further consideration presented here. However, one should notice that this theory is not completely free from failure. For example, on the basis of its statements it is still difficult to decide whether attentional performance reflects either quantity of

B. Szymura (✉)
Jagiellonian University, Cracow, Poland

available resources or quality of strategies for resources allocation (Nęcka, 2000). Also Matthews and Desmond (2002) found that sometimes (if the primary task is easy) adding a second task (that causes resource investment) may even improve primary task performance, a process that may be attributed to effort regulation rather than resources management.

Secondly, the biological theories of some selected temperament/personality (Eysenck, 1967) and intellectual (Martindale, 1999; Nęcka, 1997) traits will be briefly presented. These theories revealed the relationship between individual difference characteristics and the arousal level of the whole or different parts of the nervous system. These considerations will allow the formulation of predictions concerning the arousal links between temperament/personality/intellectual variables and the effectiveness of attentional resources allocation policy.

In the following section, these predictions will be validated on the basis of empirical material obtained in several studies conducted in our own research group with the use of a specially developed test of attentional performance (Divided Attention Test – DIVA; Nęcka, 1997; brief description in upcoming section). Finally, some conclusions concerning the existing theories of human attentional performance and the relationship between individual difference traits and attention will be drawn.

The Capacity Theory of Attention

According to the capacity theory of attention (Kahneman, 1973), information processing limitations can be explained by assuming that there is general limit to the capacity to perform mental work. This limited capacity can be distributed between concurrent activities. According to Kahneman (1973), the construct of "pay attention" refers to the terms "invest attentional capacity" and "exert mental effort."[1]

Different mental activities impose different demands on the limited capacity. An easy task requires little effort, whereas a difficult task requires a lot of it. According to Kahneman (1973), the mobilization of mental effort is controlled not by the task performer's intention but by the demands of the task. When the supply of attentional resources does not meet the task demands, performance decreases or even fails completely. The investment of "mental fuel" usually increases with the task's demands. However, this increase is typically insufficient to fully compensate for increased task complexity. Some mental effort is exerted even when there is no demand from the performed task. The process of stimuli monitoring still requires some attentional capacity, even in the most relaxed state. This capacity is known as spare capacity. It decreases as the mental effort invested in the task increases. Then attention is withdrawn from perceptual monitoring, and attentional resources are allocated to the performed task.

The limited capacity system and the physiological arousal system are closely related. More capacity is available when arousal is moderately high than when it is low (Kahneman, 1973). However, the arousal level varies continuously when a subject is engaged in mental activity, depending on the mental load imposed by the task performed. Attention is limited, but the capacity limit varies from moment to moment. Tasks at different levels of complexity create different degrees of arousal. The level of arousal is controlled by the demands imposed by the activities in which the

---

[1] Note, however, that some modern theories distinguish effort from resources. For example, Humphreys and Revelle (1984, p. 158) defined effort "as the motivational state commonly understood to mean trying hard or being involved in a task". They also made clear distinction between the subjective feeling of trying hard and on-task effort, defined in terms of resources allocation.

cognitive system engages (Kahneman, 1973) as well as by miscellaneous determinants, such as intensity of stimulation or any physiological effects of substance intake (e.g., caffeine, alcohol, drugs; Anderson & Revelle, 1983) and drive state (Humphreys & Revelle, 1984). Thus, a state of high arousal may reflect both invested mental effort and what is happening to the subject (e.g., the stress to which he or she is exposed).

Variations in the task demands cause corresponding variation of arousal, but variations of arousal states also affect the resources allocation policy. The Yerkes–Dodson law states that the task performance quality is an inverted U-shaped function of arousal. The range of performance improvement with increasing arousal also varies with the task complexity (Yerkes & Dodson, 1908). The capacity theory of attention explains the detrimental effects of low and high arousal states. The task performance failure of the underaroused subject is easily explained by assuming that the mental effort exerted in the task is insufficient. However, the detrimental effects of the overarousal state must be explained in other terms. According to Easterbrook (1959), an increase of arousal causes a restriction of a range of cues that the cognitive system uses as guides to action. This restriction eventually causes the relevant cues to be ignored. Although high arousal causes an increased tendency to focus on a few relevant cues, the selection of these cues involves a discrimination between them and others that may also be relevant. Thus, a state of high arousal impairs such discriminations, with a reduced ability to focus on all relevant cues.

The range of usable cues is narrower for simple than for complex tasks. Thus, the optimal level of arousal should be relatively high in a simple task. It also implies that chronically overaroused subjects should perform poorly in complex tasks and relatively better in simple tasks (Kahneman, 1973). However, a state of high arousal is associated not only with the process of attentional narrowing but also with increased attentional lability: difficulties in controlling attention by fine discriminations and strategy changes in various tasks (e.g., a matter that the speed-accuracy trade off is solved). Instead, the state of low arousal is associated with failure to adopt the task set or to evaluate the quality of performance.

Attention is divisible (Kahneman, 1973). The allocation of limited capacity is a matter of degree – attention is divisible only at low levels of mental effort (i.e., in a low arousal state) and more unitary at high levels (i.e., in a high arousal state). Thus, interference between simultaneously performed tasks occurs due to the insufficient response of the attentional system to the task's demand. The amount of interference is an increasing function of mental load: high mental load leads to attention narrowing when effort is high. Thus, the concept of limited capacity is helpful in understanding the quality of dual task performance. If the mental effort that can be exerted at any time is limited, any two tasks whose joint demands exceed the limits must be mutually interfering. Consequently, one of the mental activities typically draws most of the attention, leaving little left for the other. There would therefore seem to be no single-channel bottleneck (Broadbent, 1971) in the perceptual system – monitoring several channels is possible (Allport, Antonis, & Reynolds, 1972), but less effective than monitoring a single channel (Ninio & Kahneman, 1974). The negative correlation between responses to simultaneous stimuli is reduced when the responses are made less demanding.

In sum, Kahneman (1973) stated that attention is either selective or divisible, but always controllable. It can be directly allocated to facilitate the processing of selected perceptual units and/or the execution of selected units of performance. However, in some attentional conditions (e.g., in a state of low arousal), it can also be allocated to facilitate the processing of multiple, simultaneous units of performance. It should be noted that multitasking is also possible in high arousal states, however the high-aroused subjects are at risk of underprioritizing secondary task components. The most important matter for further consideration seems to be Kahneman's claim that the policy of attentional allocation depends on arousal level and reflects the performer's permanent dispositions. This statement allows a prediction to be formulated regarding the existence of stable individual differences in attentional resources management.

Individual Differences in the Arousal State

Physiologically, arousal is a complex syndrome of excitation of certain parts of the central and autonomous nervous system. Early conceptions of arousal assumed its homogeneity; these models treated arousal as a unidimensional phenomenon from coma to intensive excitation (Duffy, 1962). Eysenck (1967) also claimed arousal as the unidimensional continuum of activation states. He distinguished arousal from autonomic activation. The first refers to brain cortex activation, whereas the second refers to the activation of the autonomic nervous system, which occurs in emotional states. In contrast, Thayer (1989) proposed the division of unidimensional arousal into dimensions of energetic and tense arousal. The first is responsible for the amount of mental effort invested by the cognitive system in the activities in which it engages, whereas the second is responsible for immediate reactions to threatening events. Thayer's energetic arousal reflects H. J. Eysenck's general arousal, whereas tense arousal is comparable to autonomic activation.

According to the PEN biological theory of personality (Psychoticism – Extraversion – Neuroticism; Eysenck, 1967), the extraversion dimension is identified with differences in levels of activity in the ascending reticular activating system (ARAS). ARAS is the part of the central nervous system that is responsible for the excitation of numerous sites in the cerebral cortex (Moruzzi & Magoun, 1949). Extraverts are characterized by lower levels of ARAS activity than introverts. Thus, introverts are chronically more cortically aroused than extraverts. Unfortunately, Zuckerman (1997), reviewing literature on E, reported that introverts and extraverts do not differ on general arousal levels in normal basal conditions. He also noticed that measures of skin conductance, heart rate, and cortical activation indicate introverts to be more arousable than extraverts to stimuli of moderate intensity and extraverts to be more arousable than introverts to high intense stimuli.[2] Thus, it seems reasonable to conclude that introverts in a normal condition show a greater responsiveness to stimulation (Eysenck & Eysenck, 1985) and that individual differences in nervous system activation between extraverts and introverts depend more upon arousability than general arousal level (Eysenck, 1994). However, arousability is still related to general arousal level due to "stimulus hunger" (Gale, 1969) and the tendency to reach "optimal level of arousal" (Eysenck, 1982). Extraverts show a tendency to seek intense stimuli, whereas introverts show a need to augment upcoming stimulation (Geen, 1984).

Individual differences in neuroticism depend upon the functioning of autonomic activation (Eysenck, 1967). People high in neuroticism produce activity in the visceral brain (VB) more readily than emotionally stable people. Both arousal systems – the visceral brain and corticoreticular loop – are only partially independent of each other (Eysenck & Eysenck, 1985). Cortical arousal can also be produced through activity in the VB system and its collaterals with the ARAS system. Thus, people high in neuroticism tend to be chronically more cortically aroused, but only when subjected to emotional stimuli or placed in a stressful condition, as the visceral brain appears to be largely concerned with emotion. According to Thayer (1989), the differences between extraverts and introverts should be visible in the level of energetic arousal, whereas the differences between people high and low in neuroticism should be visible in the level of tense arousal.

The data concerning the biological basis of neuroticism is even more contradictory than the results obtained in extraversion-arousal studies. Stelmack (1981), reviewing literature on N, indicated that the relation between neuroticism and psychophysiological responsiveness has not been reported with sufficient consistency to prove H. J. Eysenck's prediction on the biological determinants of N trait. However, Eysenck (1967) postulated that neuroticism is related to individual differences in excitability

---

[2] Note, however, that Matthews and Gilliland (1999) found solid empirical support for Eysenck's claim on the biological basis of extraversion restricted only to data obtained in the studies on phasic electrodermal response and eyelid conditioning.

and emotional responsiveness. Thus, the differences in autonomic activation should occur only under relatively stressful conditions. In an attempt to save his hypothesis on physiological correlates of neuroticism, the author of PEN theory claimed that his prediction had not yet been put to an adequate test (Eysenck & Eysenck, 1985). When the test was adequate (i.e., the presented stimuli possess a strong emotional character), subjects high in neuroticism indeed usually showed greater arousal levels than emotionally stable ones (e.g., Mangan, 1974; erotic pictures).

Psychoticism is not identified with any particular differences in the arousal level of any part of the nervous system. The biological basis of P trait is rather unclear (Eysenck, 1992). The results of some studies suggest that psychoticism can be identified with the differences in the level of energetic arousal in the similar way as extraversion is. People high in psychoticism often show reduced cortical and autonomous arousal (Beh & Harrod, 1998; Kaiser, Beauvale, & Bener, 1997; Matthews & Amelang, 1993). However, such people also demonstrate difficulties with an effective regulation of the "optimal level of arousal." Their arousability does not match with their actual energetic arousal level. According to Claridge (1987), psychoticism can be connected with difficulties in the proper regulation of the arousal level, due to a functional dissociation between several mechanisms that sustain or regulate activation levels in different arousal systems.

PEN traits are not the only individual difference variables related to the arousal level. According to FTI theory (Formal Theory of Intelligence; Nęcka, 1997), intelligence is simply a process of oscillation between the cognitive, structural limitations imposed by the arousal states. Attentional resources capacity and working memory capacity both depend upon the level of arousal. Fewer attentional resources are available when arousal is low and less working memory capacity is available when arousal is high. According to Nęcka (1997), the Yerkes–Dodson law (1908) should be explained in terms of cognitive, structural limitations imposed by either low or high arousal state. The optimal level of arousal usually guarantees the best performance level, due to the sufficient capacities of both the attentional and memory cognitive subsystems. Task performance failure in the low arousal state can be easily explained by assuming that the amount of attentional resources exerted in the task is insufficient, whereas task performance failure in the high arousal state may be explained by assuming an insufficiency of working memory capacity.

Highly intelligent people are characterized by a greater amount of attentional resources (Stankov, 1983, 2005) and a greater working memory capacity (Ackerman, Beier, & Boyle, 2005; Kyllonen & Christal, 1990). According to FTI theory, they lose relatively less than people of low intelligence if their level of arousal drops or climbs too high, with respect to current mental activities, task requirements, and external circumstances. Thus, being "intelligent" means less sensitivity to change in arousal level and less dependency on transient states of arousal. In the series of experimental studies, Nęcka (1997, 2000) partially confirmed his theoretical claims. Although arousal level was measured only with the use of self-report Thayer's Adjective Check List (ACL) questionnaire, the obtained results clearly revealed that people of high IQ showed smaller variations in ACL scores and a narrower range of ACL scores during the performance of attentional and short-term memory tasks. Highly intelligent subjects performed better in all cognitive tasks. Moreover, the differences between people of high and low intelligence were especially visible in more demanding experimental conditions that caused corresponding larger variations of arousal states.

Creativity as a trait can also be identified with differences in arousal level. While intelligence can be related to a reduced variance in arousal level, creativity seems to be inversely related to arousal. Martindale (1999), reviewing literature on the relationship between creativity and arousal, suggested that highly creative people are characterized by a stronger psychophysiological responsiveness to stimuli of moderate intensity (Martindale, Anderson, Moore, & West, 1996), a wider variation in arousability and a more adequate automatic adaptation of the momentary arousal state to task demands. Divergent thinking tests (e.g., Guilford's tasks) are usually better performed in the state of low arousal, with convergent thinking tasks (e.g., RAPM intelligence test) better performed in a high arousal state (Jaušovec, 1997). Creative people often show low cortical arousal while solving divergent thinking tasks and high cortical arousal when performing intelligence tests (Martindale & Hines, 1975).

Different stages of creative thinking (e.g., inspiration, verification) may benefit from different momentary levels of arousal (Martindale, 1999). The overall variance in the arousal level is usually less pronounced in less creative subjects.

In summary, it is reasonable to conclude that the differences in the necessity for some basic personality/temperamental traits (extraversion, neuroticism, psychoticism) and the differences in the level of some general intellectual abilities (intelligence, creativity) are reflected on the physiological level by the differences in the arousal level of the whole, or some parts of the nervous system. Extraverts seem to be chronically underaroused, with introverts and neurotics chronically overaroused – albeit the latter in emotionally stressful conditions only. Psychotics show difficulties with arousal modulation to reach "optimal level of arousal." Conversely, intelligent people show less dependency on arousal state, while more creative people adapt better to arousal state requirements imposed by actual mental activities. These observations allow the formulation of clear predictions regarding individual differences in attentional resource allocation policy with regard to temperamental and intellectual traits.

Hypothetical Individual Differences in Resource Allocation Policy

On the basis of the capacity theory of attention (Kahneman, 1973), the biological theory of personality (Eysenck, 1967), the Formal Theory of Intelligence (Nęcka, 1997), and the model of creativity–arousal relationship (Martindale, 1999) predictions on attentional performance with regard to concerned individual difference variables can be formulated.

These differences should be clearly visible especially in the dual task condition. The dual task design permits the comparison of the performance of different tasks in common units. This is achieved by the subsidiary-task method, in which the subject is instructed to perform a primary task and to devote only remaining capacity to a secondary task. The quality of the performance of the subsidiary task provides a measure of the load imposed by the primary task (Hunt & Lansman, 1982; Kahneman, 1973). While performing the single task, the amount of mental effort required as well as the corresponding momentary change in arousal level are sufficient enough to reveal individual differences in resources allocation policy (Szymura & Nęcka, 2005).

Extroverts should show better attentional task performance in the dual task condition due to chronically low energetic arousal level, whereas introverts and neurotics should perform worse in such conditions due to chronically high arousal levels (M. W. Eysenck, 1982). The latter group will perform worse only in a relatively stressful condition (Eysenck & Eysenck, 1985). This stressful attentional condition can be easily created either by presenting strong distractors or by imposing time-pressure (Snodgrass, Luce, & Galanter, 1967). According to Kahneman (1973), time-pressure is an important determinant of mental effort. Indeed, Liao and Moray (1993) found that participants invest more effort with higher time pressure. A task that imposes a heavy load on working memory or speeds up a required reaction necessarily imposes severe time-pressure.

Intelligent people should show better attentional task performance in any circumstance, but especially in the dual task condition (Stankov, 1983), due to a lower dependency on transient states of arousal (Nęcka, 1997). Highly creative people should outperform less creative people due to a better process of arousal state adaptation to the requirements imposed by the attentional test, especially in conditions where such an adaptation due to the task rules exchange is required. Conversely,[3] psychotics who show difficulties in the momentary arousal regulation process should perform attentional dual tasks much worse in any conditions.

---

[3] According to Eysenck (1992), cognitive correlates of creativity and psychoticism are similar (the weakness of inhibition hypothesis). However, further consideration on arousal–creativity and arousal–psychoticims relationships suggest different effectiveness of dual task performance of highly creative subjects and subjects scoring high on P scale.

The DIVA Test for the Effectiveness of Resource Allocation Policy

The computerized task called Divided Attention (DIVA) was developed by Nęcka, Wolski, & Szymura (Nęcka, 1997; Szymura, 1999). A computer screen shows a panel consisting of a target letter inside a small frame, and several probe letters outside the frame (see Fig. 14.1). There are signals, noises, and distractors among probe letters that should be compared to the target letter. The first part of the task utilizes only the central panel and consists of detecting signals while ignoring noises and distractors. Subjects are required to detect every occurrence of the probe, which fulfils the selection criterion. The right-hand mouse key should be pressed quickly to confirm detection. A lack of response is registered as a miss. Three versions of the DIVA test regarding selection task difficulty have been already developed. They differ in selection criterion.

In the *EASY-DIVA* test, the signal that should be detected is exactly the same as the target letter (e.g., <R, R>; see Fig. 14.1). Invalid letters ("noise") are different from the target (e.g., <R,C>). Also, a category of distracting letters is introduced: the distractors are semantically identical with the target but differ in case (e.g., <R,r>). The subjects are instructed to ignore noise and distractor letters. Pressing the response key during the occurrence of these letters is taken as a false alarm.

In the *DIFF-DIVA* test, the signal is semantically the same as the target but differs in case (e.g., <R,r>, see Fig. 14.2). Noise letters are even more different from the target (e.g., <R,c>). However, the distraction becomes stronger as distracting letters are identical with the target both semantically and in case (e.g., <R,R>).

The *SUPERDIFF-DIVA* test consists of two selectivity tasks with different selection rules. Information about the selection rule is provided by the color of the display. An easy task (easy selection criterion as used in the EASY-DIVA test; E) is shown in green, with difficult tasks (difficult selection criterion as used in the DIFF-DIVA test; D) shown in red. There are two versions of the SUPERDIFF-DIVA task, with either a regular (i.e., EEDDEEDDEEDD...) or random (e.g., EDEEDEDDDEED...) task arrangement. The later version is more difficult than the former one, because it is impossible to predict the random alternation of selection rules whereas it is easy to

Fig. 14.1 The computer display of the selection task of the EASY-DIVA test. <R, R> – a pair of letters which should be detected; R central – target; R peripheral – signal; r peripheral – distractor; C, D – noise

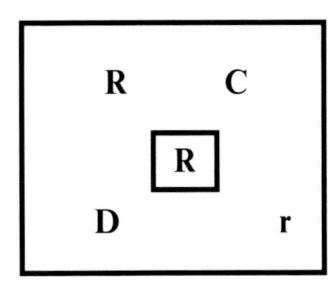

Fig 14.2 The computer display of the selection task of the DIFF-DIVA test. <R, r> – a pair of letters which should be detected; R central – target; R peripheral – distractor; r peripheral – signal; c, d – noise

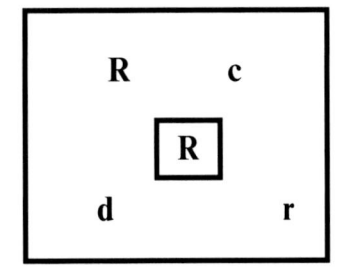

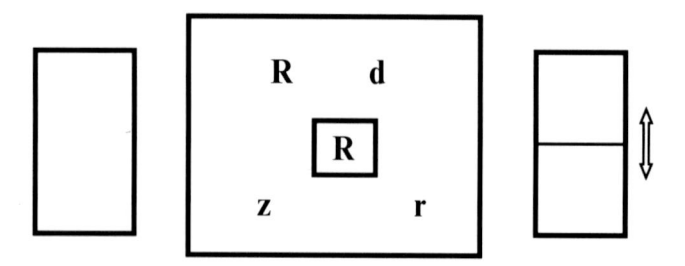

Fig. 14.3 The computer display of both tasks of the DIVA test

know which rule is the following one in regular alternation of selection rules. Subjects are not informed about task arrangements.

Every second, one probe letter disappears with another replacing it. The location of new probe letters, as well as their sequence, is randomized. The central target changes every 20 s, also in an unpredictable way. To analyze the effect of time pressure, the DIFF-DIVA version of the test has been modified. The difference is the speed of stimuli presentation. In the *TURBO-DIVA* test, it equals 1 probe per 650 ms.

The second part of the DIVA test consists of the simultaneous performance of two tasks (see Fig. 14.3). The main selectivity task remains the same as in the single task condition. However, concurrently with the main selectivity task, subjects have to control the position of a "moving bar," being displayed on one of two additional panels. The subjects' task is to keep the bar in the middle of the panel. The left-hand mouse key has to be pressed quickly, in order to lift the bar, and avoid to allow its dropping. Each panel includes "quiet zone" indicated by the markers. When the bar moves out of the quiet zone, the computer generates an unpleasant noise. Subjects are told to avoid the noise by keeping the bar in the middle position.

There are three basic independent variables manipulated in each version of the DIVA test: (1) distraction - i.e., the presence or absence of distracting letters; (2) set size - i.e., the number [3, 4 or 5] of letters appearing at the same time inside the main panel; (3) single versus dual task - i.e., either only detection (the first part of the test) or detection with manipulation of the "moving bar" control (the second part). Two further variables are manipulated, but not in each version of the DIVA test. The influence on attentional performance of series variable i.e., the same sequence of experimental conditions repeated three times in each part of the attention test, is checked in all developed versions except the SUPERDIFF-DIVA test. The influence of the break variable between selectivity tasks (the break is included in each moment of the central target letter change) is tested only in the SUPERDIFF-DIVA test.

Three measures of task performance are registered: (1) reaction time; (2) the number of false alarms (unnecessary "detection"); (3) the number of misses (lack of detection). In the statistical analyses, the following dependent variables are usually used: reaction times of accurate responses and overall number of errors.

The DIVA test seems differentiated in difficulty. Its difficulty is rooted, first of all, in the necessity of efficiently controlling two simultaneous actions, each of which is not very easy in itself. The selectivity task is a dynamic modification of a well-known letter-categorization task (Posner & Michell, 1967). The dual task condition has been developed on the basis of the "easy to hard" paradigm (Hunt, 1980; Hunt & Lansman, 1982). Theoretically, such tasks probably demand that a large amount of attentional resources be allocated to the competing actions, which is hardly possible, due to the limited capacity of the resources themselves (Kahneman, 1973).

The DIVA test has proved to be an appropriate tool to assess various aspects of attention: selectivity, divided attention, and attentional shifting (Nęcka, 1997; Szymura, 1999; Szymura & Nęcka, 1998; Szymura, Śmigasiewicz, & Corr, 2007; Szymura & Wodniecka, 2003). The dual task interference effect is usually obtained with the use of the DIVA test regardless of its version. However, in agreement with experimental manipulations, the extent of interference varies with the difficulty of the DIVA task – the cost of simultaneous task performance is the greatest in the SUPER-DIFF DIVA test, and the smallest in the EASY-DIVA test. Thus, the models referring to differential effects with regard to resources management could be verified with the use of the DIVA test.

Individual Differences in DIVA Test Performance

Ten experiments have already been conducted using different versions of the DIVA test. Over 800 subjects have voluntarily participated, mainly undergraduate students. Individual differences in resources allocation policy with regard to personality/temperamental traits have been tested, using all developed versions of the test. So far the relationship between intelligence and attentional performance has been investigated using the EASY-DIVA and the DIFF-DIVA versions of the test, whereas links between attentional resources allocation and creativity have already been established using the SUPERDIFF-DIVA version only. Instead of describing the results of each separate experiment, only the general pattern of results will be presented.

The differences between extraverts and introverts were obtained only by the use of the EASY-DIVA and the DIFF-DIVA test. They were observed with respect to the overall number of errors dependent variable. There was practically no difference between subjects scoring low and high in the E scale of the EPQ-R questionnaire in the single task condition of both the EASY and the DIFF versions of the DIVA test. However, in the dual task condition of the DIFF-DIVA test, extraverts committed significantly fewer errors, but only when the set size was 4 or 5 (see Fig. 14.4). In the easier variation of the selectivity task (set size equal 3), the groups concerned did not differ. This finding is consistent with the prediction based on the capacity theory of attention and the arousal model of extraversion, which assumes that extraverts deal better with the selectivity task in more demanding conditions (competing tasks plus increased set size).

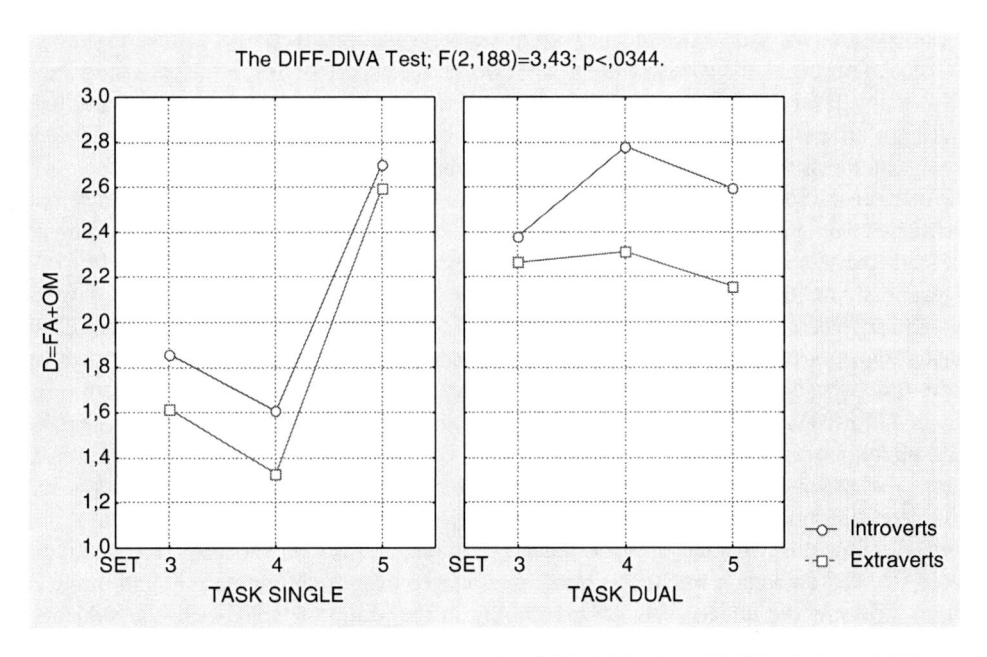

Fig. 14.4 Extraversion, dual task, set size and error rate, The DIFF-DIVA Test; $F(2,188)=3,43$; $p<0.0344$

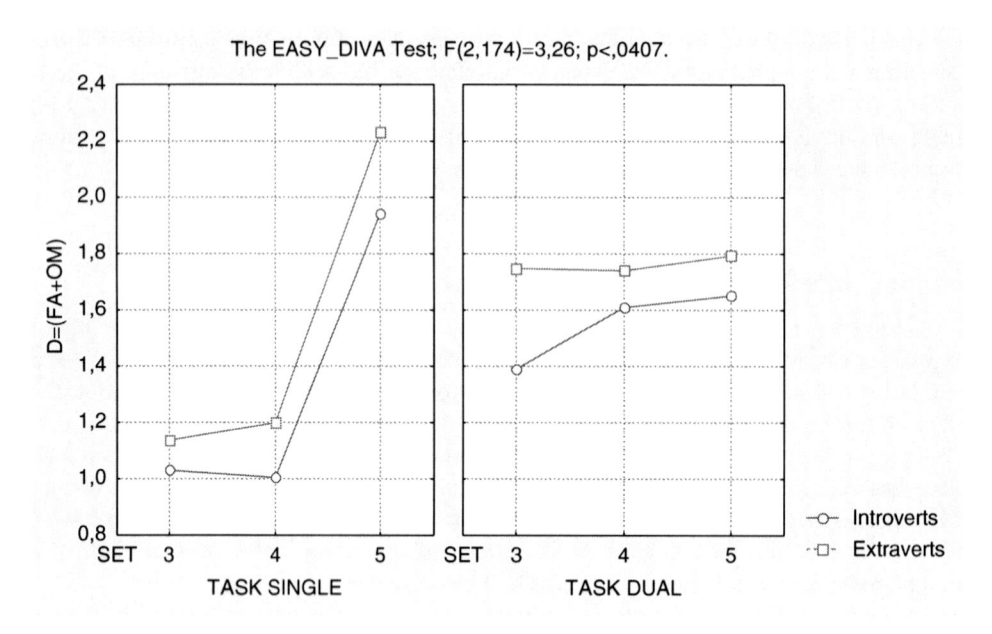

Fig. 14.5 Extraversion, dual task, set size and error rate. The EASY_DIVA Test; $F(2,174)=3,26$; $p<0.0407$

On the other hand, introverts outperformed extraverts when performing the EASY-DIVA test. Again, the E-I dimension appeared significant in a three-way interaction with the single versus dual task and set size variables (see Fig. 14.5). Introverts performed slightly better in all test conditions (except the single task condition, where no differences with regard to extraversion were observed), but their superiority was particularly noticeable in the dual task condition, when the set size equaled 3. This finding is again consistent with the prediction based on the arousal model of extraversion, which assumes that introverts should deal better with monotonous but relatively less demanding tasks. The EASY-DIVA test seems to meet these criteria. However, the superiority of introverts cannot be interpreted as being in favor of the capacity theory of attention, which assumes strong dual task interference in high arousal state. More results concerning extraversion-attentional performance links as observed with the use of the DIVA test are described elsewhere (Szymura & Nęcka, 1998).

The differences between subjects scoring high and low in N scale of the EPQ-R questionnaire were obtained only with the use of the TURBO-DIVA test. Subjects characterized by a strong necessity of neuroticism scored more misses, especially in the dual task condition (see Fig. 14.6). There were practically no differences between subjects scoring high and low in the N scale in the single task condition, whereas in the dual task condition, neurotics detected fewer signals than did stable subjects. People scoring high in neuroticism seem to show the same level of performance on the attention task as stable subjects do (lack of neuroticism-attentional performance interactions with the use of DIFF-DIVA test with slow stimuli presentation ratio), unless the stimuli presentation is speeded up and therefore going beyond the subjects' control. The quicker the stimuli presentation, the worse the neurotics' performance and also the more pronounced the differences between high and low neuroticism scorers in response accuracy. In the versions of TURBO-DIVA used, test speed of stimuli presentation equaled 1 probe letter per either 650 ms or 850 ms. This manipulation appeared stressful enough to impair the attentional mechanism of neurotics, although in the easier condition (850 ms) the effects were observed only in the group of highly neurotic subjects (top quartile). This finding is consistent with the prediction based on the arousal model of neuroticism,

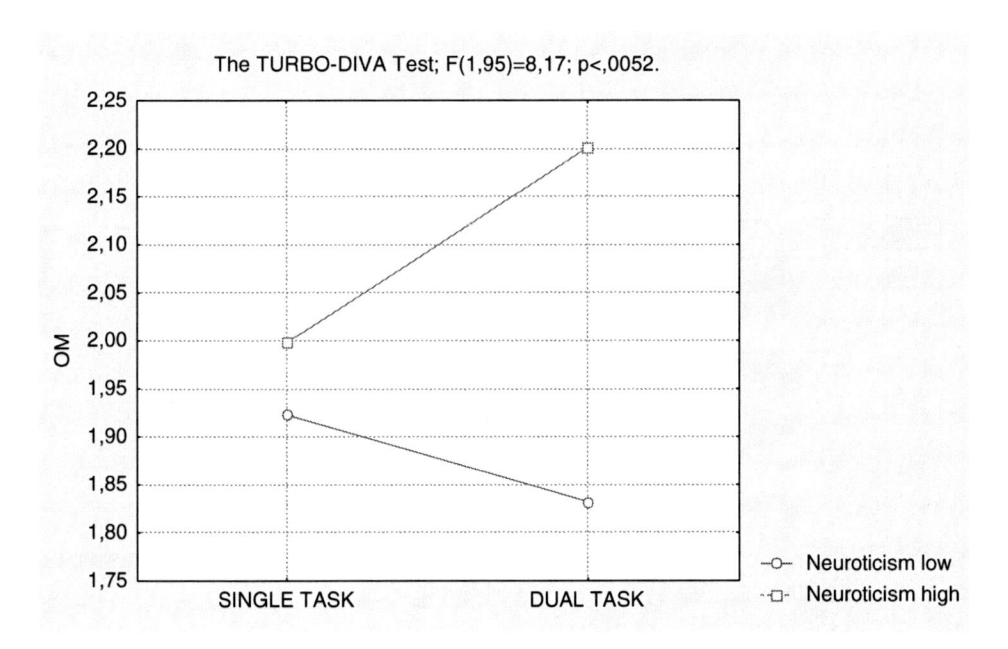

Fig. 14.6 Neuroticism, dual task and error rate. The TURBO_DIVA Test; $F(1,95) = 8,17$; $p < 0.0052$

which postulates the existence of an attention narrowing mechanism in high N scorers in the stressful condition. The obtained results also confirmed the prediction based on the capacity theory of attention, which assumes that time-pressure is an important determinant of mental effort. More results concerning neuroticism-attentional performance links as observed with the use of the TURBO-DIVA test is described elsewhere (Szymura & Wodniecka, 2003).

The differences between subjects scoring high and low in the P scale of EPQ-R questionnaire were obtained only with the use of the SUPERDIFF-DIVA test. High psychoticism scorers performed better in the random task arrangement in comparison to the regular task arrangement; they committed fewer false alarms than subjects scoring low in P scale. Surprisingly, in the dual task condition of the random task arrangement SUPERDIFF-DIVA test, high psychoticism subjects performed more accurately than did those of low psychoticism, but only in the lack of the breaks condition (see Fig. 14.7). The secondary task of this version of the DIVA test seems to be effective mainly for low P scorers. However, these subjects committed fewer false alarms than ones scoring high in the P scale in the regular task arrangement condition.

These results are not in the favor of the arousal model of psychoticism, which assumes that when facing difficulties with arousal regulation, high P scorers will always control their attentional processes much worse than low P scorers. However, they are fully understandable, if the SUPERDIFF-DIVA test is recognized as a negative priming task. With the change of the selection rule, subjects have to detect signals that previously served as distractors. Poor cognitive inhibition thus provides high P scorers with a selective advantage (Bullen & Himsley, 1984; Gruszka, 1999; Stavridou & Furnham, 1996). More results concerning psychoticism–attention relationship as observed with the use of the DIVA test are further described elsewhere (Szymura et al., 2007).

People of high IQ (as measured by RAPM test) outperformed subjects of low intelligence in almost every condition of the EASY-DIVA and the DIFF-DIVA tests. High RAPM scorers detected the signals faster and committed fewer errors (either false alarms or omissions) than low Raven test scorers, especially in the dual task condition (see Fig. 14.8). The differences between people of high and low intelligence increased with the set size increase and when distraction letters were presented.

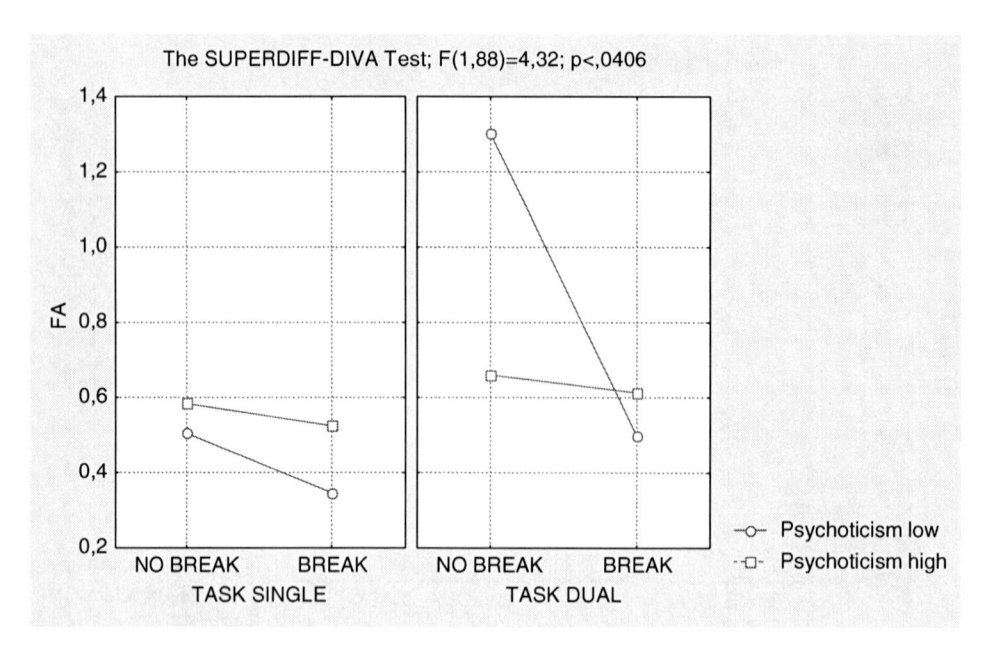

Fig. 14.7 Psychoticism, dual task, break and error rate. The SUPERDIFF_DIVA Test; $F(1,88)=4,32$; $p<0.0406$

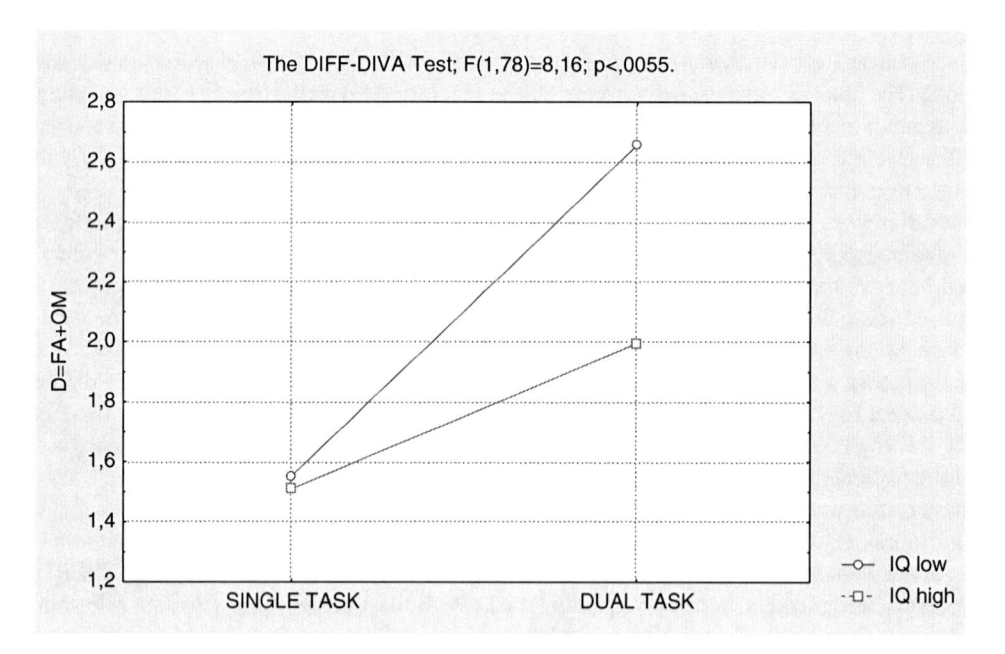

Fig. 14.8 Intelligence, dual task and error rate. The DIFF_DIVA Test; $F(1,78)=8,16$; $p<0.0055$

Moreover, people of high IQ also performed the secondary task significantly better: the length of incorrect task performance (i.e., the length of the unpleasant noise generated by the DIVA procedure) was shorter for them in comparison to low IQ subjects. Thus, intelligent people performed both tasks of the DIVA test better, which proves that the influence of general intellectual traits on the attentional resource allocation process is much stronger than personality/temperament properties. These results favor the Formal Theory of Intelligence, which assumes that intelligence is positively related to the amount of attentional resources (better performance of the DIVA test regardless of the task's condition) and negatively related to variance of momentary arousal as imposed by the task's demands (less dependency on an increase of the DIVA test complexity). More results concerning intelligence–attention relationship as observed with the use of the DIVA test are available elsewhere (Szymura & Nęcka, in prep.).

Highly creative people (as measured by the Urban-Jellen test) showed an increased accuracy in comparison to poorly creative subjects in the SUPERDIFF-DIVA test. The first produced fewer omissions regardless of test conditions and fewer false alarms at the beginning of the attentional task (series 1) in comparison to low scorers in the Urban-Jellen test. However, superiority of the highly creative subjects seemed to be independent of the amount of mental effort imposed by the task – no interactions with the dual task variable were observed this time. These results are congruent with the hypothesis of the positive relationship between creativity and effectiveness of attentional control (Groborz & Nęcka, 2003).[4]

Conclusions

Kahneman (1973) claimed that the policy of attentional allocation depends on the arousal level of the nervous system. More specifically, he suggested that attentional resources management depends on a momentary and changeable arousal state, imposed by task conditions and demands, substance intake, time of the day, etc. This hypothesis has been well proved by Revelle and his colleagues (Anderson & Revelle, 1983; Humphreys & Revelle, 1984; Revelle & Loftus, 1990). On the basis of the aforementioned results, a slightly different statement can be made. Attentional allocation policy also depends on the level of constitutional arousal that reflects the necessity of some temperamental/personality variables, such as extraversion and neuroticism. This statement is an addition to the original capacity theory of attention (Eysenck, 1982). Although Kahneman (1973) suggested that resources management and exerted "mental effort" reflect the performer's permanent dispositions, nowhere did he specify what those dispositions are.

However, attentional allocation policy does not rely solely on the level of constitutional arousal as reflected by temperament/personality traits. This relationship is further modified by the task demands (Eysenck, 1982) that cause momentary changes in the arousal state (Nęcka, 1997). According to the capacity theory of attention, chronically low-aroused extraverts should always perform the DIVA test in the dual task conditions better. However, this is not the case: chronically high-aroused introverts can outperform extraverts even in the dual task condition of attentional test, unless overall task demands are very arousable. It seems reasonable to conclude that relationships between some temperamental/personality traits and attention may be even epiphenomenal to the interactive effects of these variables and momentary arousal on performance (Matthews, 1987, 1992; Matthews & Deary, 2002).

Szymura and Nęcka (2005) formulated hypotheses concerning the relationships between temperament/personality and attention based on two assumptions. They assumed that (1) individual differences

---

[4] Groborz and Nęcka (2003) defined attentional control as mechanism that reduces chaos in the output of the information processing system (reduction of possible albeit unnecessary response tendencies) and measured its effectiveness with the use of Stroop and Navon tasks. High creative subjects showed better interference control. The reduction of unnecessary response tendencies due to selectivity rules alternation is also strongly demanded in selectivity task of the SUPER-DIFF DIVA test. Thus, high creative subjects perform this test generally better. However, dual task coordination is not one of the aspects of so defined attentional control. What is more, Nęcka (1999) found that high creative subjects perform the DIVA test in the dual task condition even worse than low creative ones.

turn out to be visible only when the attentional task is demanding enough and that (2) what is demanding for one person may be at all not demanding for another. They postulated the existence of specific attentional deficits displayed by people characterized by different scores on the dimensions of extraversion/introversion, neuroticism, and psychoticism, as imposed by specific task demands. The results presented above support these claims. Firstly, individual differences with regard to temperament/personality traits were negligible when the attentional tasks were easy (e.g., in the single task condition of the DIVA test). Secondly, the demanding conditions that impaired the attentional performance of extraverts, introverts, neurotics, and psychotics seemed to be completely different. Time-pressure decreased the attentional efficiency of neurotics while having no impact on the attentional performance of extraverts or high P scorers. Selection rules alternation appeared demanding enough to reveal the deficits of people scoring low and high in the psychoticism scale. This DIVA test manipulation did not serve to show any differences with regard to either extraversion or neuroticism. Finally, the richness of stimulation and the level of information processing during stimuli analysis and selection both influenced the attentional performance of extraverts and introverts, but showed no impact on effectiveness of the attentional mechanisms of either neurotics or psychotics.

Intelligent people performed the DIVA test better in any circumstances, but especially in the dual task condition. The task conditions that required many resources more clearly revealed the advantage of people scoring high in intelligence test – mostly as far as performance correctness is concerned. These results favor Stankov's (1983, 1988, 2005) and Hunt's (1980; Hunt & Lansman, 1982) theory of intelligence. However, highly intelligent people also performed faster than low intelligent people and this difference was all the more visible when test conditions were easier. These results are in agreement with the "chronometry of intelligence" theory of Jensen (1982, 2005). Thus, the highly intelligent people display a more effective attentional allocation policy – as far as correctness is concerned – when the task requires many resources and also for performance speed when the task is less demanding (Schweizer, 1996a, 1996b).

Highly creative people and high P scorers performed better in the SUPERDIFF-DIVA test, which requires a changeable amount of resources during the course of the test, due to permanent selection criterion change in the selection task. The former probably adapt better to the continuously changing task demands than to the novel task situation – their superiority is independent of task demands. Thus, creativity seems to go some way beyond intelligence (Sternberg, 2001). High P scorers showed better attentional resource management only in special conditions of the DIVA test where the weakness of inhibition mechanisms was of great importance. The similarity of attentional resources policy of highly creative people and high P scorers in such circumstances is in agreement with Eysenck's (1992, 1994) weakness of inhibition hypothesis as an explanation of the psychoticism–creativity link. However, creativity seems to go also some way beyond psychoticism – the advantage of highly creative people in attentional control is visible regardless of the version of the SUPERDIFF-DIVA test. These results are also supporting evidence for the hypothesis of a positive relationship between creativity and the effectiveness of attentional control (Groborz & Nęcka, 2003).

The above-presented results with regard to intelligence and creativity suggest another addition to the capacity theory of attention. Attentional resources management depends not only on both a momentary arousal state, imposed by task conditions and demands, as well as a constitutional level of arousal, biologically determined (extraversion, neuroticism, psychoticism), but also on sensitivity to changes in the arousal state (intelligence) and an ability to adapt to the arousal state fluctuation (creativity).

References

Ackerman, P. L., Beier, M. E., & Boyle, M. O. (2005). Working memory and intelligence: The same or different constructs. *Psychological Bulletin, 131*, 30–60.

Allport, A., Antonis, B., & Reynolds, P. (1972). On the division of attention: A disproof of the single channel hypothesis. *Quarterly Journal of Experimental Psychology, 24*, 225–235.

Anderson, K. J., & Revelle, W. (1983). The interactive effects of caffeine, impulsivity, and task demands on a visual search task. *Personality and Individual Differences, 4*, 127–134.
Beh, H. C., & Harrod, M.-E. (1998). Physiological responses in high-P subjects during active and passive coping. *International Journal of Psychophysiology, 28*, 291–300.
Broadbent, D. E. (1971). *Decision and Stress*. London: Academic.
Broadbent, D. E. (1982). Task combination and selective intake of information. *Acta Psychologica, 50*, 253–290.
Bullen, J. G., & Himsley, D. R. (1984). Psychoticism and visual recognition threshold. *Personality and Individual Differences, 5*, 633–648.
Claridge, G. S. (1987). Psychoticism and arousal. In J. Strelau & H. J. Eysenck (Eds.), *Personality dimensions and arousal* (pp. 133–150). New York: Plenum.
Duffy, E. (1962). *Activation and behavior*. New York: Wiley.
Easterbrook, J. A. (1959). The effect of emotion on cue utilisation and the organisation of behaviour. *Psychological Review, 66*, 183–201.
Eysenck, H. J. (1967). *The biological basis of personality*. Springfield: CC Thomas.
Eysenck, M. W. (1982). *Attention and arousal*. Berlin: Springer.
Eysenck, H. J. (1992). The definition and measurement of psychoticism. *Personality and Individual Differences, 13*, 757–785.
Eysenck, H. J. (1994). Personality: Biological foundations. In P. A. Vernon (Ed.), *The neuropsychology of individual differences* (pp. 151–256). San Diego: Academic.
Eysenck, H. J., & Eysenck, M. W. (1985). *Personality and individual differences: A natural science approach*. New York: Plenum.
Gale, A. (1969). "Stimulus hunger": Individual differences in operant strategy in a button-pressing task. *Behaviour Research and Therapy, 7*, 265–274.
Geen, R. G. (1984). Preffered stimulations levels in introverts and extraverts: Effect on arousal and performance. *Journal of Personality and Social Psychology, 46*, 1303–1312.
Groborz, M., & Nęcka, E. (2003). Creativity and cognitive control: Exploration of generation and evaluation skills. *Creativity Research Journal, 15*, 183–197.
Gruszka, A. (1999). Relationship between basic personality dimensions and the attentional mechanism of cognitive inhibition. *Polish Psychological Bulletin, 30*, 129–142.
Hasher, L., & Zacks, R. T. (1979). Automatic and effortful processes in memory. *Journal of Experimental Psychology: General, 108*, 356–388.
Hirst, W., & Kalmar, D. (1987). Characterizing attentional resources. *Journal of Experimental Psychology: General, 116*, 68–81.
Humphreys, M. S., & Revelle, W. (1984). Personality, motivation, and performance: A theory of the relationship between individual differences and information processing. *Psychological Review, 91*, 153–184.
Hunt, E. (1980). Intelligence as an information processing concept. *British Journal of Psychology, 71*, 449–474.
Hunt, E., & Lansman, M. (1982). Individual differences in attention. In R. J. Sternberg (Ed.), *Advances in the psychology of human intelligence* (pp. 207–254). Hillsdale, NJ: LEA.
Jaušovec, N. (1997). Differences in EEG activity during the solution of closed and open problems. *Creativity Research Journal, 10*, 317–324.
Jensen, A. R. (1982). The chronometry of intelligence. In R. J. Sternberg (Ed.), *Advances in the psychology of human intelligence* (pp. 255–311). Hillsdale, NJ: LEA.
Jensen, A. R. (2005). Mental chronometry and the unification of differential psychology. In R. J. Sternberg & J. E. Pretz (Eds.), *Cognition and intelligence* (pp. 26–50). Cambridge: Cambridge University Press.
Kahneman, D. (1973). *Attention and effort*. New Jersey: Prentice Hall.
Kaiser, J., Beauvale, A., & Bener, J. (1997). Evoked cardiac response as a function of cognitive load differs between subjects separated on the main personality dimensions. *Personality and Individual Differences, 22*, 241–248.
Kyllonen, P., & Christal, R. (1990). Reasoning ability is (little more than) working memory capacity? *Intelligence, 14*, 389–433.
Liao, I., & Moray, N. (1993). A simulation study of human performance deterioration and mental workload. *Le Travail Humain, 6*, 321–344.
Mangan, G. L. (1974). Personality and conditioning: Some personality, cognitive and psychophysiological parameters of classical appetitive (sexual) GSR conditioning. *Pavlovian Journal of Biological Science, 9*, 125–135.
Martindale, C. (1999). Biological bases of creativity. In R. J. Sternberg (Ed.), *Handbook of creativity* (pp. 137–152). Cambridge: Cambridge University Press.
Martindale, C., Anderson, K., Moore, K., & West, A. N. (1996). Creativity, oversensitivity, and rate of habituation. *Personality and Individual Differences, 20*, 423–427.
Martindale, C., & Hines, D. (1975). Creativity and cortical activation during creative, intellectual, and EEG feedback tasks. *Biological Psychology, 3*, 71–80.
Matthews, G. (1987). Personality and multidimensional arousal: A study of two dimensions of extraversion. *Personality and Individual Differences, 8*, 9–16.

Matthews, G. (1992). Extraversion. In A. P. Smith & D. M. Jones (Eds.), *Handbook of human performance* (pp. 96–193). London: Academic.
Matthews, G., & Amelang, M. (1993). Extraversion, arousal theory and performance: A study of individual differences in the EEG. *Personality and Individual Differences, 14,* 347–363.
Matthews, G., & Deary, I. J. (2002). *Personality traits.* Cambridge: Cambridge University Press.
Matthews, G., & Desmond, P. A. (2002). Task-induced fatigue states and simulated driving performance. *Quarterly Journal of Experimental Psychology, 55A,* 659–686.
Matthews, G., & Gilliland, K. (1999). The personality theories of H. J. Eysenck and J. A. Gray: a comparative review. *Personality and Individual Differences, 26,* 583–626.
Moruzzi, G., & Magoun, H. W. (1949). Brain stem reticular formation and activation of the EEG. *Electroencephalography and Clinical Neurophysiology, 1,* 455–473.
Navon, D. (1984). Resources – a theoretical soup stone? *Psychological Review, 91,* 216–234.
Nęcka, E. (1997). Attention, working memory and arousal: Concepts apt to account for "the process of intelligence". In G. Matthews (Ed.), *Cognitive science perspectives on personality end emotion* (pp. 503–554). Amsterdam: Elsevier Science.
Nęcka, E. (1999). Creativity and attention. *Polish Psychological Bulletin, 30,* 85–97.
Nęcka, E. (2000). *Pobudzenie Intelektu. Zarys Formalnej Teorii Inteligencji.* [The Formal Theory of Intelligence]. Cracow: Universitas.
Ninio, A., & Kahneman, D. (1974). Reaction time in focused and in divided attention. *Journal of Experimental Psychology, 103,* 393–399.
Revelle, W., & Loftus, D. A. (1990). Individual differences and arousal: Implications for the study of mood and memory. *Cognition and Emotion, 4,* 209–237.
Schweizer, K. (1996a). Level of encoding, preattentive processing and working memory capacity as sources of cognitive ability. *Personality and Individual Differences, 21,* 759–766.
Schweizer, K. (1996b). The speed-accuracy transition due to task complexity. *Intelligence, 22,* 115–128.
Snodgrass, J. G., Luce, R. D., & Galanter, E. (1967). Some experiments on simple and choice reaction time. *Journal of Experimental Psychology, 75,* 1–17.
Stankov, L. (1983). Attention and intelligence. *Journal of Educational Psychology, 75,* 471–490.
Stankov, L. (1988). Attention and intelligence. *Psychology of Aging, 3,* 59–74.
Stankov, L. (2005). Reductionism versus charting: Ways of examining the role o lower-order cognitive processes in intelligence. In R. J. Sternberg & J. E. Pretz (Eds.), *Cognition and intelligence* (pp. 51–67). Cambridge: Cambridge University Press.
Stavridou, A., & Furnham, A. (1996). The relationship between psychoticism, trait creativity and the attentional mechanism of cognitive inhibition. *Personality and Individual Differences, 21,* 143–153.
Stelmack, R. M. (1981). The psychophysiology of extraversion and neuroticism. In H. J. Eysenck (Ed.), *A model of personality* (pp. 38–64). Berlin: Springer.
Sternberg, R. (2001). What is the common thread of creativity? *American Psychologist, 56,* 360–362.
Szymura, B. (1999). On the organization of the processes of selective attention. *Polish Psychological Bulletin, 30,* 69–84.
Szymura, B., & Nęcka, E. (1998). Visual selective attention and personality: An experimental verification of three models of extroversion. *Personality and Individual Differences, 24,* 713–729.
Szymura, B., & Nęcka, E. (2005). Three superfactors of personality and three aspects of attention. In A. Eliasz, S. E. Hampson, & B. de Raad (Eds.), *Advances in personality psychology* (pp. 75–90). Hove: Psychology Press.
Szymura, B., & Nęcka, E. (in prep.). *Attention and intelligence.* Manuscript in preparation.
Szymura, B., Śmigasiewicz, K., & Corr, P. J. J. (2007). Psychoticism and flexibility of attention. *Personality and Individual Differences, 43,* 2033–2046.
Szymura, B., & Wodniecka, Z. (2003). What really bothers neurotics? In search for factors impairing attentional performance. *Personality and Individual Differences, 34,* 109–126.
Thayer, R. E. (1989). *The biopsychology of mood and arousal.* New York: Oxford University Press.
Wickens, C. D. (1984). Processing resources in attention. In R. Parasuraman & R. Davies (Eds.), *Varieties of attention* (pp. 63–101). New York: Academic.
Yerkes, R. M., & Dodson, J. D. (1908). The relation of strength of stimuli to rapidity of habit-information. *Journal of Comparative Neurology and Psychology, 18,* 459–482.
Zuckerman, M. (1997). The psychobiological basis of personality. In H. Nyborg (Ed.), *The scientific study of human nature: Tribute to Hans J. Eysenck at eighty* (pp. 3–16). Amsterdam: Elsevier.

Chapter 15
The Relationship of Attention and Intelligence

Karl Schweizer

The relationship between attention and intelligence is usually considered as the relationship between a basic ability and a complex ability in the sense that attention is a source, determinant or constituent of intelligence. In this chapter, the term constituent is preferred since it represents the idea of an assembly of basic abilities giving rise to a complex ability especially well. The assembly of basic abilities is usually addressed as the cognitive basis of intelligence (Schweizer, 2005). Although at first view attention may appear as a natural member of the assembly of basic abilities, the close consideration of the complexity of the concept may lead to doubts in the trueness of the assumed membership. This complexity is the result of the research efforts of a large number of experimental researchers who have created a variety of facets, types, dimensions and measures of attention (Pashler, 1998), and it provides a number of perspectives for considering the relationship between attention and intelligence. Such a number of different perspectives, however, are not really an advantage since the perspectives are a source of inconsistency and even controversy. Therefore, in this field of research, it is necessary to evaluate the empirical evidence concerning the relationship between attention and intelligence especially carefully and to concentrate on attempts of integrating the various perspectives.

Historical Ambiguity Due to Conceptual Variety

Spearman (1927) has already discussed this relationship at length in the book titled *The Ability of Man*, and in doing so given special weight to the idea of attention as a major constituent of intelligence. He even considered "the view that *g* measures attention" (p. 344). However, despite Spearman's arguments, the reputation of attention as constituent has not been at its best since the appearance of the book. This is obvious from a large survey on expert opinion on intelligence and aptitude testing of psychologists and educational specialists (Snyderman & Rothman, 1987). The experts had to evaluate the importance of elements of intelligence (e.g. abstract thinking and reasoning, problem-solving ability, memory, mental speed). Furthermore, they were asked to add important elements that were not included in the original list. The report of the results of this survey ended up with an ordered list of important elements and percentages of respondents checking an element as important. Attention was *not* included in this list. The disregard of attention was a rather interesting observation in the light of the

---

K. Schweizer (✉)
Department of Psychology, Goethe University Frankfurt, Mertonstr. 17, 60054 Frankfurt a. M., Germany
e-mail: k.schweizer@psych.uni-frankfurt.de

previously published review of findings concerning the relationship of attention and intelligence by Stankov (1983). This review provided some evidence in favour of the assumed relationship between attention and intelligence. Interestingly, after completing another study that did not provide the expected endorsement of the assumed relationship between attention and intelligence even Stankov (1989) considered attention as "a disappearing link". A subsequent screening of the research works published between 1985 and 2000 revealed positive and negative findings concerning the relationship between attention and intelligence (Schweizer, Zimmermann, & Koch, 2000). Approximately one half of the findings supported the assumption of such a relationship (e.g. Crawford, 1991; De Jong & Das-Small, 1995; Nęcka, 1996; Roberts, Beh, Spilsbury, & Stankov, 1991; Roberts, Beh, & Stankov, 1988; Stankov, Roberts, & Spilsbury, 1994), whereas the other half did not (e.g. Fogarty & Stankov, 1988; Lansman & Hunt, 1982; Lansman, Poltrock, & Hunt, 1983; Neubauer, Bauer, & Hoeller, 1992 [Study 1]; Rockstroh & Schweizer, 2001; Schweizer & Moosbrugger, 1999). Only recently, the balance seems to have changed in favour of the assumed relationship.

It is worthwhile to consider the reasons for calling the assumed relationship into question in some detail since this endeavour can lead to a better understanding of the nature of the relationship. Prominent reasons are the special role of attention in information processing, methodological issues and the experimental psychologists' tendency to concentrate on very specific aspects of information processing unrelated to the issue of interest. First, it must be pointed out that the role of attention in information processing is complicated since it cannot be associated with a specific result. There is the fact that attention is a kind of addendum to information processing. To some degree, information processing can occur independent of attention, as in the case of preattentive processing that happens below the level of consciousness (Velmans, 1991) and also in the case of automatic processing (Logan, 1992). Attention cannot be considered equivalent to a transformation process or even a cognitive operation. When Jensen (1982) investigated the relevance of the processes stimulated by the choice reaction time task, attention did not enter the list of essential processes. The perceptual process included in this list can occur independent of attention although the assignment of attention can speed it up considerably (Posner & Snyder, 1975; Schweizer, 1994). The necessity of forming alliances with cognitive processes is especially obvious from the two modes of processing proposed by Schneider and Shiffrin (1977; Shiffrin & Schneider, 1977). The two modes can be considered as two ways of information processing with considerably differing properties: controlled and automatic processing. Controlled processing is processing under the guidance and supervision of attention, whereas automatic processing occurs almost completely independent of attention. Interestingly, the latter mode is considered as faster than the former mode. In sum, it is the role of attention as addendum to another process that casts doubts on the status of attention as a member of the assembly of basic abilities, and that gives rise to the question as to whether it is attention or the transformation process that is the true constituent of intelligence.

Second, there have been methodological issues or better methodological complications that may have prevented the establishment of a firm conceptual association of attention and intelligence. It is an obvious fact that attention and intelligence are associated with two different methodological approaches which Cronbach (1957) considered as the two disciplines of psychology. While the conceptual elaboration of attention mainly occurred within the experimental approach, the research on intelligence was mainly conducted according to the guidelines of the differential approach. Major aims of these approaches were the design of complex models for predicting performance on the one hand and the identification of quite specific demands giving rise to experimental effects on the other hand. The complications resulting from the differences between these approaches are obvious: (1) there is the concentration on the prediction of a large amount of variance in the differential approach and the concentration on the isolation of very specific effects in the experimental approach. As a consequence, a concept that appears promising in the experimental approach may fail in combination with the differential approach because it accounts for too small an amount of variance. (2) The size and composition of samples is another critical issue. Differential research demands large samples. In a recent debate concerning a currently preferred method of differential research, structural equation modelling, it was stated that the minimum sample size should be 200 (Barrett, 2007). This is a considerable sample size in the light of the average sample of experimental research that is usually a fraction of 200. Furthermore, a lot of experimental research is conducted with selected samples (e.g. diagnostic groups). Therefore, the generality of the results is rather restricted. (3) Another issue of importance are the measures. The measures of differential research are expected to show an appropriate quality. Foremost, they must prove to be valid and reliable in empirical investigations. Inappropriate measures give reason for calling the results of research into question. In contrast, many of the measures applied in experimental research are not the result of a rigorous construction process and, therefore, show impurity in measurement (Schweizer, 2007). So-called content validity is usually considered sufficient for experimental measures. The problems resulting from the interaction of the two methodological approaches can be exemplary studied in the transfer of the concept of divided attention from the experimental approach to the differential approach. Dual tasks have been constructed for providing data that enable an empirical investigation of this concept. In such tasks, different treatment levels pose different demands to information processing. Increasing demands are expected to be associated with either increasing reaction time or decreasing accuracy. All the differential researchers adopting this concept and corresponding measures succeeded in reproducing this effect. In contrast, the results concerning the correlation with intelligence were not unequivocal. Some researchers were able to show that the change in demand is associated with a corresponding change of the relationship between reaction time respectively accuracy and the measure of intelligence (Hunt, 1980; Roberts et al., 1988, 1991; Stankov, 1988; Szymura & Nęcka, 1998), whereas others were unable to provide results demonstrating the expected modification of the relationship between attention and intelligence (Lansman, 1978; Lansman & Hunt, 1982; Lansman et al., 1983; Myors, Stankov, & Oliphant, 1989). There is reason for assuming that the measures were not well enough prepared for the demonstration of a stable and substantial increase respectively decreases in correlation.

Third, the experimental psychologists' tendency to concentrate on very specific aspects of information processing needs to be taken into consideration. Progress in experimental research to a considerable degree means the concentration on subprocesses restricted to individual stages in information processing by performing micro analytic studies. These subprocesses are usually associated with characteristic demands, and some of them have given rise to metaphors of attention (Fernandez-Duque & Johnson, 1999, 2002). Several metaphors have been proposed in combination with theories of attention, such as the spotlight metaphor that is to be considered an allusion to the effect of a flashlight on perception (Hernández-Peón according to Wachtel, 1967). Other metaphors are attention as limited resource, attention as information filter, attention as competition and attention as time-sharing mechanism. It is a typical property of such metaphors that they allude to characteristics of information processing machines. Some of these metaphors ostensibly provide arguments in favour of a relationship between attention and intelligence, as it is the case with attention as limited resource and attention as time-sharing mechanism. Furthermore, the concentration on very specific aspects of information processing has given rise to a number of different ideas concerning structure and function of attention. As a consequence, attention is no longer considered a unitary concept. In 1969, Moray listed five different concepts of attention. The length of this list of concepts has increased since that time considerably (see Mirsky, Anthony, Duncan, Ahearn, & Kellam, 1991; Moosbrugger, Goldhammer, & Schweizer, 2006). A comparison of concepts can reveal that these concepts refer to quite different stages of information processing and show different characteristics, so that it is reasonable to address them as different types of attention. In considering the various metaphors and types of attention with respect to intelligence, it becomes obvious that an unambiguous position is not possible. Some types of attention seem to be important with respect to intelligence, whereas others appear to be negligible since they refer to a peripheral or petty part of information processing. Furthermore, the metaphors are to be perceived as ideas instead as proofs in favour of a substantial relationship.

Towards a Conceptual Clarification Due to a Structural Framework

William James' position, who stated that "everybody knows what attention is" (1890/1950, p. 261), provides the basis for communicating the contents of the previous section. However, this is a debatable position in the light of the variety of metaphors and types of attention. Therefore, it is not really a surprise that a completely contrary position is taken by Pashler (1998) who even argues that "[no] one knows what attention is, and there may even not be an 'it' there to be known about" (p. 1).

In either case, it is useful to have a working definition in order to provide a better basis for the communication in the following sections. This definition is expected to include generally accepted ideas with respect to attention. A definition provided by Coull (1998) is quite well suited for this purpose. This definition reads: "Attention ... may be thought of in the simplest terms as the appropriate allocation of processing resources to relevant stimuli" (p. 344). This definition integrates a number of ideas concerning the functioning of attention, as for example "attentional capacity", "shared allocation of attention", "focal allocation of attention", "attention switching", "divided attention". A disadvantage of this definition is the apparent bias in the direction of perception that is characteristic of attention research in general. Early attention research mainly concentrated on perception (e. g. Broadbent, 1958), and even today it is possible to meet colleagues who associate attention with perception. The shift in the direction of higher mental processing requires the integration of the idea of control that is considered essential in performing successfully according to demanding tasks (Norman & Shallice, 1980; Shallice & Burgess, 1993). The large number of possible processing routes provides ample opportunity for deviations from a complex processing plan. This shift is closely associated with the emergence of the concept of working memory (e.g. Baddeley, 1986). Therefore, a slight modification of Coull's definition is necessary. The working definition for this chapter must combine the aspects of allocation (of resources) and of control. However, this working definition may still be considered deficient since it includes the concept of resources that was called "a theoretical soup stone" (Navon, 1984). For avoiding this kind of deficiency, the reader is advised to consider "resources" as umbrella term that applies to all kinds of cognitive processes, in particular transformation and storage processes. In one of the following sections, I even select a non-cognitive perspective and describe the assignment of resources as the recruitment of neurons. In sum, it is reasonable to consider attention at the core as the allocation and control of limited processing resources in stimulus-driven and data-driven mental information processing.

First-Order Attention and Its Relationship to Intelligence

As already indicated, the literature on attention does not suggest a unitary concept. The variety of task demands and the complications at the various stages of information processing suggest the consideration of specific characteristics of processing in addition to the aforementioned general characteristics. As a consequence, a number of different "attentions" are available which may be considered as types of attention. The list of types discussed in this section is probably not complete. First, there is Moray's list published in 1969. It includes mental concentration, search, selective and divided attention and vigilance. *Mental concentration* denotes the type of attention characterized by considerable mental effort that is continuously applied (Heitz, Unsworth, & Engle, 2005; Kinchla, 1992; Stankov, 1983). The label of this type of attention has changed since Moray's days from mental concentration to *sustained attention*. A review of the studies investigating the relationship between this type of attention and intelligence yielded a correlation of moderate size ($r=0.31$) (Schmidt-Atzert & Bühner, 2000). A corresponding result was achieved in an investigation restricted to measures of mental concentration according to the original concept (Schmidt-Atzert, Bühner, &

Enders, 2006). *Search* denotes the type of attention that is required for screening long lists for the presence of letters, numbers or simple figures, where the distracters are also letters, numbers or simple figures. The measures are usually constructed according to the Bourdon (1902) principle. Because of the tasks typically applied for the assessment of search, a close association between this type of attention and the clerical-perceptual speed factor of the factor models of intelligence can be assumed (Stankov, 1983). Stankov et al. (1994) report a correlation of −0.20 of search and fluid intelligence. *Selective attention* that is closely linked to *focused attention* and frequently addressed as *selective/focused attention* comes close to the meaning of "ordinary" attention. It is especially favourable for stimulus discrimination since it cares for the allocation of the processing resources to a specific type of stimulus respectively to the stimulus appearing in the focus of vision. There is reason for assuming an association of this type of attention and intelligence since discrimination time substantially correlates with intelligence. The reported results suggest a correlation of approximately −0.30 (Deary, 2000; Schweizer & Koch, 2003). *Divided attention* has for some time been considered the most promising candidate with respect to the relationship between attention and intelligence since divided attention focuses on the effect of capacity limitations. It denotes the ability to divide the attentional resources according to the demands of different processing tasks. In assuming that the limitations characterizing attention also limit information processing in general this type of attention was considered as being especially important with respect to intelligence (Hunt, 1980). In the case of divided attention, a correlation alone is insufficient evidence since an increase in correlation is predicted. As already indicated, the results achieved for this type of attention are not unequivocal. Finally, *vigilance* denotes a type of attention that is measured by tasks requiring the detection of infrequent stimuli over a prolonged period of time. Another label that is frequently used is *alertness*. The emphasis is on the prolonged period of time in combination with the infrequency of the stimulus. Therefore, it can be characterized as the ability to attend to specific stimuli for a very long time although the rate of appearance is very low. This type of attention has so far not given rise to convincing correlations with intelligence. In a recent study, the correlations was about −0.15 (Schweizer, Moosbrugger, & Goldhammer, 2005). More recent compilations of types of attention (Coull, 1998; Van Zomeren & Brouwer, 1994) additionally list attention switching and spatial attention. *Attention switching* denotes the ability to shift the focus of attention quickly between different task requirements. The corresponding tasks usually demand the shift from one location to another location where the final location is not previously known but indicated by a cue. In a way, attention switching reflects cognitive flexibility. A correlation of −0.18 of attention switching and intelligence was observed (Schweizer et al. 2005). A somewhat different ability is addressed by *spatial attention*. It denotes the ability to locate a target appearing in an unexpected location in contrast to an expected location. The cue that is always directed to the expected location is correct in the majority of trials, so that in the remaining trials an incorrect expectation handicaps performance. This measure of attention correlated with intelligence (−0.20) (Schweizer et al. 2005). Neither one of the latter types of attention has so far stimulated a bulk of research works concerning the relationship of attention and intelligence (for an exception see Schweizer et al. 2005).

The majority of the aforementioned types of attention refer to perception. During the last decades, the emerging interest in working memory has gradually extended the concept of attention to higher mental processing. Baddeley and Hitch (1974) questioned the unity of short-term memory and, thus, contributed to the development of the concept of working memory (Baddeley, 1986) with a differentiated structure as alternative. It includes two slave systems (articulatory or phonological loop, and visuospatial sketch-pad) and the central executive. The central executive is shaped according to the supervisory attentional system which assures controlled information processing (Norman & Shallice, 1980; Shallice & Burgess, 1993). The further elaboration of the supervisory attentional system ended up with the concept of *controlled attention* respectively *executive attention* as domain-general capacity (Engle & Kane, 2004; Heitz et al., 2005; Kane & Engle, 2003). Attention also plays a major role in an alternative concept of working memory that suggests the emergence of working memory as the result of assigning attention to items of information stored in memory (Cowan, 1988, 1995). There is some work elaborating on the arguments suggesting a relationship between controlled attention respectively executive attention and intelligence (Heitz et al.). Furthermore, there are several studies suggesting a substantial relationship of *controlled attention* respectively *executive attention* on one hand and intelligence on the other hand starting with the study by de Jong and Das-Small's (1995). Their Star Counting Test as measure of *controlled attention* respectively *executive attention* has repeatedly been demonstrated as contributing to the prediction of intelligence (e.g. Schweizer & Koch, 2003). There is also the possibility to consider *controlled attention* respectively *executive attention* as a latent variable based on a number of appropriate indicators. Kane et al. (2004) demonstrated that this latent variable considerably contributes to the prediction of fluid intelligence. The meta-analytic study by Ackerman, Beier, and Boyle (2005) suggests a (raw) correlation of 0.32 between working memory and intelligence. Although this correlation applies to working memory as a whole, there is reason to assume that the results for the components are more or less the same.

Furthermore, there are components of the action-oriented approach to attention by Neumann (1992, 1996) that mainly concentrates on higher mental processing. Although these components refer to very specific aspects of information processing that are not obviously associated with specific task demands, they are considered as types of attention in this chapter since they have given rise to corresponding measures (Heyden, 1999; Heyden & Moosbrugger, 1997). These are the types of behavioural inhibition, selection-for-action, action planning, skill-based interference, and arousal/activation/effort. *Behavioural inhibition* denotes the capability of suppressing secondary demands in favour of primary demands in completing dual tasks. *Selection-for-action* denotes the capability of making use of cues in spatial tasks. *Action planning* denotes the capability of establishing interlinked plans and performing according to such plans. *Skill-based interference* denotes the capability of dealing with conflicting demands to the same processing skill. Finally, the remaining arousal/activation/effort component is a background variable but not a type and, therefore, not given further consideration. Since the measures associated with these types of attention have only recently become available, there is not yet a bulk of results concerning the relationship of attention and intelligence (for an exception see Schweizer et al., 2005).

The majority of tasks constructed for representing one of the abovementioned types are quite easy tasks. The few more difficult tasks represent the attention component of working memory. Most of the attention tasks tap processing speed either directly or indirectly. In contrast, the efficiency of working memory is usually assessed in considering accuracy or the number of errors. These characteristics are more or less in agreement with the findings of research into the effect of complexity (difficulty) on the relationship between processing time and error score on one hand and intelligence on the other hand (Schweizer, 1996a, 1996b). According to the findings of this research, substantial correlations with intelligence can be expected for reaction time, respectively processing speed, when the task is easy, and for accuracy, respectively the numbers of errors, when the task is difficult.

Attention as Hierarchical Structure

The variety of types of attention gives rise to the questions whether these types have something in common and whether it is possible to integrate them into an overall structure. So far, some formal models of attention (e.g. Kahneman & Treisman, 1984; Posner & Rafal, 1987; Pribram & McGuinnes, 1974) that, however, show a rather limited capability for integrating all the types have been proposed. Furthermore, there are a very few empirical investigations of the structure of attention, that integrate a considerable share of the aforementioned types. In this section, these investigations are reported in some detail. There are a few studies where exploratory factor analysis is applied and one study with confirmatory factor analysis.

One investigation of the structure of attention was conducted by Mirsky et al. (1991). This investigation was inspired by work on the attention deficits in schizophrenia. An attempt to classify these deficits led to three so-called elements of attention: focus, sustain and shift (Zubin, 1975). The authors of the investigation modified this set of elements of attention by changing one element and including a further element. The modified set included focus-execute, shift, sustain and encode as elements. Starting from these elements of attention 13 attention performance scores provided the basis for the structural investigation. The sample of the investigation showed a considerable size. However, approximately two-thirds of the sample stemmed from clinical groups showing various kinds of disorders, whereas the remaining third was composed of normal volunteers. Exploratory factor analysis of the data led to four factors. These factors were characterized as perceptual-motor speed, flexibility, vigilance and numerical-mnemonic and showed to be related to the modified set of elements of attention. Pogge, Stokes, and Harvey (1994) provided support for Mirsky's model by means of an independent investigation with psychiatric patients. However, despite the replication, the validity of the results is somewhat impaired because of the lack of representativeness: the representativeness of the investigation is limited with respect to sample and to the types of attention. It can be suspected that the presence of groups of patients with specific deficits may have caused structural peculiarities.

Schmidt, Trueblood, Merwin and Durham (1994) questioned the appropriateness of the measures applied in the previous studies and, as a consequence, conducted another study. Their approach was characterized by a systematic and methodologically rigorous procedure: they cared for a broad collection of clinical tests that were often cited as attentional measures. Furthermore, they checked and eventually transformed the data in such a way that they finally corresponded to the procedural assumptions. The 12 attentional measures of the study were investigated by exploratory factor analysis. The sample consisted of 120 outpatients. Most of them showed neuropsychological impairments. The authors of the study discussed one- and two-factor solutions as the outcome of this study. The one-factor solution is an argument in favour of the existence of general attention. The factors of the two-factor solution were characterized as visuo-motor scanning and visual/auditory spanning. An inspection of the loadings reveals that the measures associated with the first factor are mainly demanding to perception and the measures associated with the second factor demanding to higher mental processing. Despite the authors' endeavour to present a methodological sound study, it is not clear whether it is representative with respect to the types of attention and the non-clinical population.

A confirmatory approach to the investigation of the structure of attention was selected by Moosbrugger et al. (2006). Eleven different types of attention were considered (alertness, selective/focused attention, attentional switching, spatial attention, supervisory attention, sustained attention, attention according to the concentration tradition, attention as inhibition, attention as planning, divided attention, attention as interference). These types were taken from Posner's research tradition (Posner & Boise, 1971; Posner & Petersen, 1990; Posner & Rafal, 1987), the working memory-based tradition (Baddeley, 1986; Engle, Tuholski, Laughlin, & Conway, 1999; Norman & Shallice, 1980) and the action-orientation in research (Neumann, 1992, 1996). Each one of the different types of attention was represented by an established measure with the exception of attention according to the concentration tradition. This type was represented by several measures. The sample included 232 normal participants between 19 and 40 years of age. The participants were university students who were paid for participation, so that an unselected and age-homogeneous sample from the upper half of the intelligence distribution resulted. The main aim of this investigation was to find out whether the diversity of types of attention could be integrated into a model with upper-level general attention respectively whether two upper-level attention factors are necessary for integrating the types of attention. Upper-level general attention was suggested by the unity of information processing and the relatedness of the various types of attention. In contrast, two upper-level attention factors were in line with the various distinctions made in the field of attention research. There was the distinction of active and passive attention that was also characterized as goal-directed control of attention and stimulus-driven control of attention (Egeth & Yantis, 1997). Furthermore, there was the distinction of sensory attention and executive attention that emphasized the different locations of attentional control in information processing (Fuster, 2005). A special degree of homogeneity of attentional control with respect to perception was also a major characteristic of Bundesen's (1990) the theory of visual attention. The coordination of attentional control with respect to executive processes was emphasized by Logan and Gordon (2001). Their theory of executive control suggests executive control over the subordinate processes including the process of stimulus selection. The theoretical work led to several formal models that were constructed and investigated. However, at the core, there are only three different models: (1) the general attention model, (2) the two-factor model with non-nested factors, and (3) the two-factor model with nested factors.

Figure 15.1 gives illustrations of the three models. The general attention model includes one latent variable respectively factor that relates to all the manifest variables that are measures representing types. The difference between the two two-factor models is obvious. In the two-factor model with non-nested factors, each manifest variable is related to one latent variable only. In contrast, in the two-factor model with nested factors, there are some manifest variables that relate to two latent variables. It needs to be added that in the two-factor model with non-nested factors, the latent variables respectively the factors were allowed to correlate among each other, whereas they were prevented from correlating with each other in the two-factor model with nested factors. The fit statistics obtained for the three models were clearly in favour of the two-factor model with nested factors although the other two-factor model also showed an acceptable to good degree of model-data fit (Moosbrugger et al., 2006). In contrast, the general attention model showed to be inappropriate. The two factors of the two-factor model with nested factors could be interpreted as perceptual attention (Bundesen, 1990) and executive attention (Logan & Gordon, 2001).

The two-factor model with non-nested and correlated factors seems to suggest an additional upper-level factor, so that finally a hierarchical model is achieved. If the correlation of the first-order factors is sufficiently high, it actually gives rise to an upper-level factor that may be interpreted as general attention factor. It is interesting to find that the two-factor model with nested factors also includes a general attention factor. However, it is a first-order general attention factor since it is restricted to the lower level of factors. So there are two options. The results of the study by

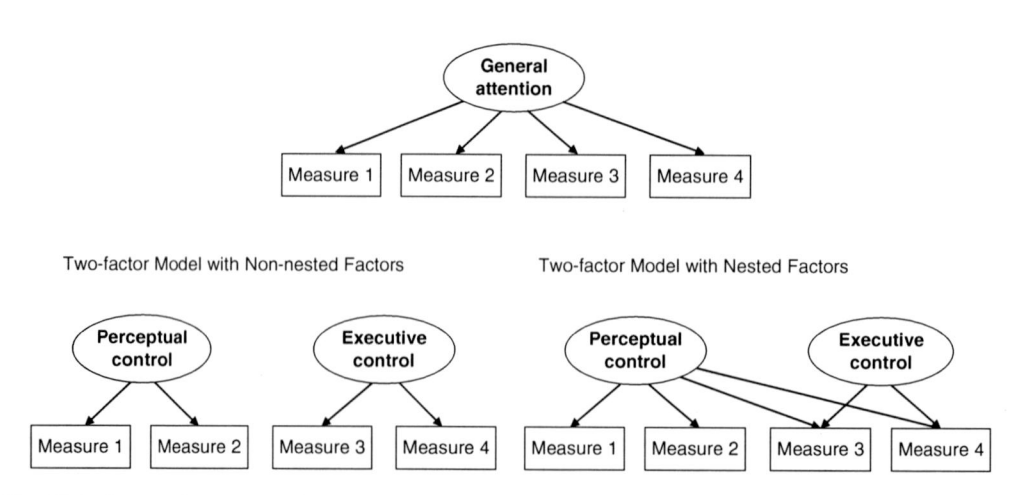

Fig. 15.1 Structural models considered for representing attention

Moosbrugger et al. (2006) suggest that the general attention factor should be represented at the lower latent level instead of the upper latent level.

There is some degree of agreement between the result of the latter study and the two-factor solution by Schmidt et al. (1994) since in each case one factor refers to perception and the other one to higher mental processing. Furthermore, these studies show a better degree of representativeness than the other studies that seem to reflect types as results in the first place and, therefore, are not really appropriate for the purpose of integration. Consequently, the two-factor model seems to be the preferable one.

Arguments for an Upper-Level Relationship

Because of the evidence in favour of a hierarchical structure of attention, the investigation of the relationship between attention and intelligence can be concentrated on upper-level attention. It is no more of primary importance to demonstrate such a relationship for each type of attention.

Taking Coull's (1998) modified definition of attention at the outset, the question arises as to what is the meaning of attention as the allocation of resources at the upper level. Since there is the possibility of preattentive processing, it is reasonable to perceive the allocation of resources as the recruitment of additional neurons of the brain for improving performance in encoding a stimulus or in processing according to a specific task demand. Recruitment means the establishment of coordinated activity of neurons. In a way, coordinated activity is a deviation away from the "normal" state of brain functioning that is characterized by a mixture of rhythmic and transient activity. Since self-regulatory systems tend to return to the "normal" state, it can be expected that sooner or later the usual mixture of rhythmic and transient activity replaces coordinated activity. Preventing the brain from returning to the "normal" state requires control. In the case of perception, it is perceptual control as postulated by Bundesen (1990) that is expected to prevent the allocation of resources to other stimuli. In higher mental processing, the emphasis is on the control of the course of processing in the light of the multitude of alternative courses resulting from the establishment of many specific and general skills. The multitude of courses provides many opportunities for deviating from the given processing plan. Executive control as proposed by Logan and Gordon (2001) is necessary for avoiding such deviations. If there is control according to complex data-driven processing plans, we have the phenomenological experience of considerable mental effort that needs to be exerted. This experience is especially apparent in situations requiring sustained attention (see Heitz et al., 2005; Kinchla, 1992; Stankov, 1983).

Attention as perceptual control pertains to perception. The allocation of resources in perception can be expected to cause an acceleration of perceptual processing. The recruitment of additional neurons should speed up the process of encoding information. Therefore, it is rather likely that processing time respectively mental speed is influenced by attention as proposed by Heitz et al. (2005). An effect of attention on processing time in completing perceptual tasks instead of on accuracy is rather likely since the likelihood of errors is very low in perceptual tasks. Consequently, there is a kind of parallelism between the discussion concerning the relationship between attention and intelligence on one hand and the discussion concentrating on the relationship between mental speed and intelligence on the other hand. Mechanisms relating the occurrence of errors in completing intelligence test tasks to the trade-off between processing speed and information decay were proposed as account for the relationship between mental speed and intelligence (Jensen, 1982; Salthouse, 1996; Schweizer, 2001).

The problem with this account is that it applies equally well to both biology-based speed and speed resulting from the allocation of resources in combination with perceptual control which is addressed as attention-paced speed in this paragraph. The observation of an inhomogeneity of processing speed

(Kranzler & Jensen, 1991; Roberts & Stankov, 1999) presumably provides the solution to this problem. Whereas biology-based speed can be assumed to be independent of the type of mental activity, attention-paced speed is likely to vary since the possible improvement due to attention depends on the type of mental activity. Two frequently investigated activities are signal detection and stimulus discrimination that may serve as examples. Since stimulus discrimination is a complex process including feature analysis, it can be expected to profit more from attention than signal detection, so that speed of stimulus discrimination should be to a higher degree due to attention than the speed of signal detection. Interestingly, the correlation of inspection time, that is mainly stimulus discrimination, with intelligence is significantly higher than the correlation of choice reaction time, that requires signal detection only, with intelligence (compare the metaanalytic results by Jensen, 1987, and Grudnik & Kranzler, 2001). This observation is confirmed by an investigation that applies similar measurement procedures for signal detection and stimulus discrimination (Schweizer & Koch, 2003). Consequently, there is reason for assuming that attention-paced speed is a major source of the correlation between processing speed respectively mental speed and intelligence.

Attention as executive control is restricted to higher mental processing that is a special type of processing associated with working memory (Kane & Engle, 2003) and frequently characterized as controlled processing (Schneider & Shiffrin, 1977). Interestingly, increasing the efficiency of higher mental processing usually means transforming controlled into automatic processing. The increased efficiency is due to the establishment of some kind of tracks respectively specific courses of processing, as indicated in the previous paragraph. The tracks result from priming or long-term associations of micro-processes. However, the benefits of tracks are not available without complications. If task demands require a deviation from established tracks that can be perceived as automatic response tendencies (Unsworth & Engle, 2007), special effort is necessary. Therefore, in higher mental processing, Coull's attention as allocation of processing resources must be accompanied by the prevention of alternative courses of action along the established old tracks. Engle and Kane's (2004) theory of executive control gives a more detailed account of the functional necessities. There must be "one factor of control to be the maintenance of the task goals in active memory" (pp. 185–186) and a second factor that cares for "the resolution of response competition or conflict, particularly when proponent or habitual behaviours conflict with behaviours appropriate to the current task goal" (p. 186). Therefore, attentional efficiency in higher mental processing means correct processing and, consequently, accuracy in the first place.

It is reasonable to consider the relationship between executive attention and intelligence from the perspective of intelligence test tasks that are especially good markers of intelligence. Such makers are characterized by a high degree of complexity (Stankov, 2000). The demands of such tasks are usually complex and require to operate according to a complex processing plan (Halford, Wilson, & Phillips, 1998). Usually, a sequence of different operations needs to be performed in order to complete such a task. Furthermore, there is an obvious relationship between the number of operations and the number of established tracks that need to be avoided. The degree of complexity normally determines the likelihood of an error. In this situation, the efficiency of executive attention is very important for success. Consequently, there is reason for assuming a substantial relationship between executive attention and intelligence.

Evidence Suggesting an Upper-Level Relationship of Attention and Intelligence

Attention can be assumed to be especially closely related to fluid intelligence since this type of intelligence reflects basic properties of information processing. According to presently preferred hierarchical models of intelligence, as for example Carroll's (1993) Three Stratum

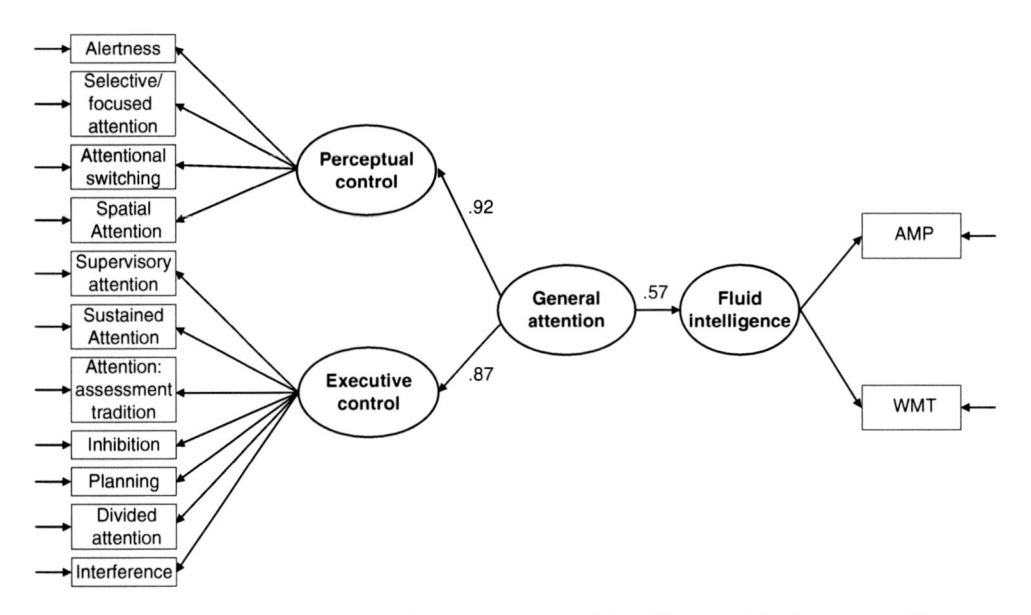

Fig. 15.2 Model for predicting fluid intelligence based on a hierarchical model of attention with parameter estimates

Model of Intelligence and its extension, the CHC Model (Alfonso, Flanagan, & Radwan, 2005; McGrew, 2005) fluid intelligence is a second-stratum ability. Furthermore, fluid intelligence was shown to be especially closely related to general intelligence (Gustafsson, 1984).

Both the two two-factor models of attention were considered in investigating the relationship between upper-level attention and intelligence since they represent different approaches in investigating structure. The two-factor model with non-nested factors represents the hierarchical approach, whereas the two-factor model with nested factors is associated with the non-hierarchical approach. Since the latent variables respectively factors of the two-factor model with non-nested factors show a high correlation among each other, it is necessary to add a second-order latent variable to this model.

The corresponding hierarchical model of attention provides the left-hand part of Fig. 15.2. The right-hand part includes the measurement model of fluid intelligence, which serves as criterion. In this model, only the second-order latent variable of attention is related to fluid intelligence that is a first-order latent variable in this investigation. This model shows an acceptable degree of fit (Schweizer et al., 2005). General attention predicts 32% of the variance of intelligence.

The attention part of Fig. 15.2 implicitly suggests a three-level hierarchy. The additional level is necessary in order to optimize prediction. Considered in more detail, if the general latent variable of attention is removed from the model, only one of the two links relating the first-order latent variables of attention to the first-order latent variable of intelligence reaches the level of significance. However, if these links are investigated individually, each one reaches the level of significance: attention as perceptual control (0.56) and attention as executive control (0.54). Consequently, staying with the first-order latent variables of attention yields a misleading result since the contribution of one of the two sources of intelligence is concealed.

The two-factor model with nested factors was also transformed into a complete structural equation model by adding intelligence as criterion. Figure 15.3 provides an illustration of this model.

This model includes two uncorrelated first-order latent variable of attention and one first-order latent variable of fluid intelligence. Since there is a breakdown of variance into components, it can be assumed that there is no overlap in predicting fluid intelligence. This model

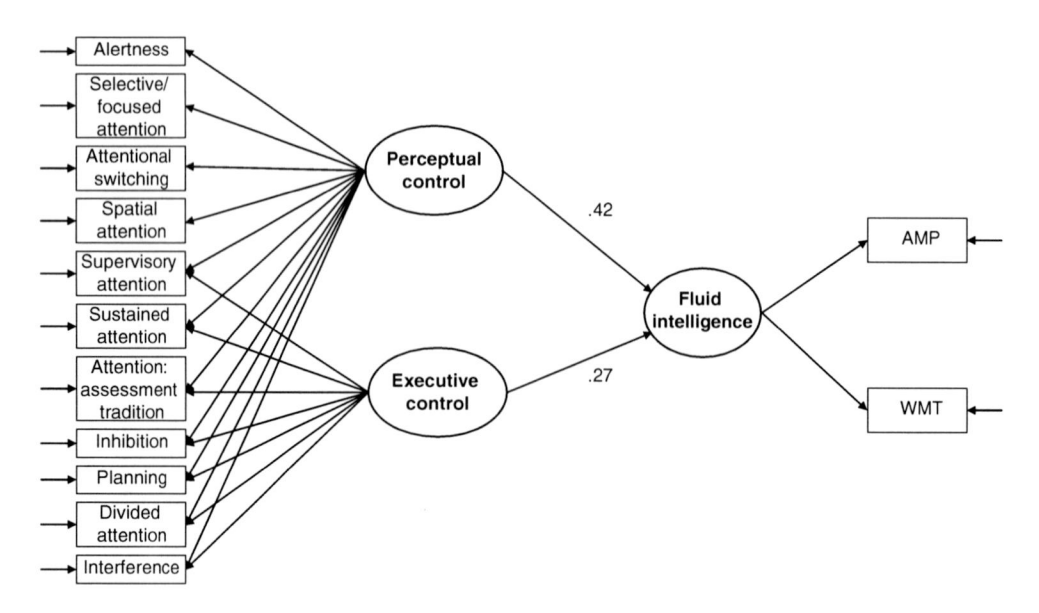

Fig. 15.3 Model for predicting fluid intelligence based on a non-hierarchical model of attention including overlapping latent variables with parameter estimates

shows a good degree of model-data fit. Each one of the latent predictor variables contributes to the prediction of fluid intelligence (perceptual control: 0.42; executive control: 0.27). Apparently, when the latent variable representing attention as executive control is stripped of the contribution of attention as perceptual control, it is still a predictor of the latent variable representing fluid intelligence although the contribution is smaller in this model than in the previous model. All in all, the results achieved for a large sample indicate that higher-order attention is related to fluid intelligence.

Furthermore, the study by Kane et al. (2004) provides evidence for an upper-level relationship between attention as executive control and intelligence. This study needs to be mentioned since attention as executive control is conceptualized as a latent variable that relates to a large set of span measures included in the study. The sample shows a good size, and the investigation of the relationship between attention as executive control and intelligence occurs at the latent level. This investigation yielded a correlation of 0.51. The size of this correlation is rather similar to the size of the correlations observed in the previous study.

Two other studies that indirectly investigated the relationship between attention as executive control and intelligence were published by Buehner, Krumm, Ziegler, and Pluecken (2006) and Buehner, Krumm, and Pick (2005). These studies included a latent variable denoted coordination that can be considered as a component of attention as executive control and that is based on several measures. The results of these studies are also in favour of the assumption of a substantial relationship between attention and intelligence (restricted to reasoning) (Buehner et al., 2006: 0.60 at latent level; Buehner et al., 2005: 0.40 at latent level).

Conclusion

The status of attention as constituent of intelligence has for a long time been undecided for a number of reasons. For some time, there has been the alleged restriction of attention to perception that excluded it from playing a major role in higher mental processing. Furthermore, there is the necessity to form an association with another process causing insecurity concerning the ascription of an effect. Moreover, there is the variety of types of attention with somewhat differing properties that led to contradictory results concerning the relationship between attention and intelligence. In sum, there has been a lot of confusion concerning the nature of attention. The situation has changed recently because of structural investigations that bestow a structure upon the diversity of types of attention. The structure provides the opportunity to accept a variety of types of attention at the lower level and to merge these types into a few structural units at the upper level. The advantage of the available structure is that it concentrates the search for the relationship between attention and intelligence to the upper level. There is reason for assuming that there are two upper-level units of attention referring to perceptual and higher mental processing. Furthermore, there is cortical substrate that appears to be closely associated with the corresponding functions (Fuster, 2005): the lateral prefrontal cortex with attention associated with perceptual processing and the anterior cingulate area of the prefrontal cortex with attention associated with effortful higher mental processing. As expected, the upper-level units of attention show to be correlated with intelligence. A substantial proportion of intelligence is predicted by attention, and this is a reasonable proportion that is well founded in current theory of cognition. A cautionary note needs to be added with respect to the validity of attention measures. Attention as addendum requires that special care is given to constructing measures. The fact that similar measures are used for the assessment of mental speed, perceptual efficiency and attention stresses the importance of this cautionary note. Accordingly, mental speed has been suggested to be mediated by a number of higher-order processes (Neubauer, 1997). Attention is probably the most reasonable mediator.

References

Ackerman, P. L., Beier, M. E., & Boyle, M. O. (2005). Working memory and intelligence: The same or different constructs? *Psychological Bulletin, 131*, 30–60.

Alfonso, V. C., Flanagan, D. P., & Radwan, S. (2005). The impact of the Cattell-Horn-Carroll theory on test development and interpretation of cognitive and academic abilities. In D. P. Flanagan & P. Harrison (Eds.), *Contemporary intellectual assessment: Theories, tests, and issues* (pp. 185–202). New York: Guilford.

Baddeley, A. D., & Hitch, G. J. (1974). Working memory. In G. H. Bower (Ed.), *The psychology of learning and motivation: Advances in research and theory* (Vol. 8, pp. 47–89). New York, NY: Academic Press.

Baddeley, A. D. (1986). *Working memory*. Oxford: Clarendon.

Barrett, P. (2007). Structural equation modeling: Adjusting model fit. *Personality and Individual Differences, 42*, 815–824.

Bourdon, B. (1902). Recherches sur l'habitude. *Année Psychologique, 8*, 327–385.

Broadbent, D. (1958). *Perception and communication*. New York: Pergamon.

Buehner, M., Krumm, S., & Pick, M. (2005). Reasoning = working memory ≠ attention. *Intelligence, 33*, 251–272.

Buehner, M., Krumm, S., Ziegler, M., & Pluecken, T. (2006). Cognitive abilities and their interplay: Reasoning, crystallized intelligence, working memory components, and sustained attention. *Journal of Individual Differences, 27*, 57–72.

Bundesen, C. (1990). A theory of visual attention. *Psychological Review, 97*, 523–547.

Carroll, J. B. (1993). *Human cognitive abilities*. New York: Cambridge University Press.

Coull, J. T. (1998). Neural correlates of attention and arousal: Insights from electrophysiology, functional neuroimaging and psychopharmacology. *Progress in Neurobiology, 55*, 343–361.

Cowan, N. (1988). Evolving concepts of memory storage, selective attention, and their mutual constraints within the human information processing system. *Psychological Bulletin, 104*, 163–191.

Cowan, N. (1995). *Attention and memory: An integrated framework*. Oxford, England: Oxford University Press.

Crawford, J. D. (1991). The relationship between tests of sustained attention and fluid intelligence. *Personality and Individual Differences, 12*, 599–611.

Cronbach, L. J. (1957). The two disciplines of scientific psychology. *American Psychologist, 30*, 116–127.

De Jong, P. F., & Das-Small, A. (1995). Attention and intelligence: The validity of the Star Counting Test. *Journal of Educational Psychology, 87*, 80–92.

Deary, I. (2000). Simple information processing and intelligence. In R. J. Sternberg (Ed.), *Handbook of intelligence* (pp. 267–284). New York: Cambridge University Press.

Egeth, H. E., & Yantis, S. (1997). Visual attention: Control, representation, and time control. *Annual Review of Psychology, 48*, 269–297.

Engle, R. W., & Kane, M. J. (2004). Executive attention, working memory capacity, and a two-factor theory of cognitive control. In B. H. Ross (Ed.), *The psychology of learning and motivation: Advances in research and theory* (Vol. 44, pp. 145–199). New York: Elsevier Science.

Engle, R. W., Tuholski, S. W., Laughlin, J. E., & Conway, A. R. A. (1999). Working memory, short-term memory, and general fluid intelligence: A latent-variable approach. *Journal of Experimental Psychology: General, 128*, 309–331.

Fernandez-Duque, D., & Johnson, M. L. (1999). Attention metaphors: How metaphors guide the cognitive psychology of attention. *Cognitive Science, 23*, 83–116.

Fernandez-Duque, D., & Johnson, M. L. (2002). Cause and effect theories of attention: The role of conceptual metaphors. *Review of General Psychology, 6*, 153–165.

Fogarty, G., & Stankov, L. (1988). Abilities involved in performance on competing tasks. *Personality and Individual Differences, 9*, 35–49.

Fuster, J. M. (2005). The cortical substrate of general intelligence. *Cortex, 41*, 228–229.

Grudnik, J. L., & Kranzler, J. H. (2001). Meta-analysis of the relationship between intelligence and inspection time. *Intelligence, 29*, 523–535.

Gustafsson, J. E. (1984). A unifying model for the structure of intellectual abilities. *Intelligence, 8*, 179–203.

Halford, G. S., Wilson, W. H., & Phillips, S. (1998). Processing capacity defined by relational complexity: Implications for comparative, developmental, and cognitive psychology. *Behavioral and Brain Sciences, 21*, 803–864.

Heitz, R. P., Unsworth, N., & Engle, R. W. (2005). Working memory capacity, attention control, and fluid intelligence. In O. Wilhelm & R. W. Engle (Eds.), *Handbook of understanding and measuring intelligence* (pp. 61–77). Thousand Oaks, CA: Sage.

Heyden, M. (1999). *Entwicklung und Erprobung einer multidimensionalen Aufmerksamkeits-Testbatterie* [Development and validation of a multidimensional attention test battery]. Unpublished Doctorial Dissertation, Senckenbergische Bibliothek, Frankfurt a. M.

Heyden, M., & Moosbrugger, H. (1997). *Die Entwicklung einer computerbasierten Testbatterie zur Erfassung der fünf Aufmerksamkeitskomponenten nach Neumann* [The development of a computerized test battery for assessing the five attention components according to Neumann]. Frankfurt a. M.: Arbeiten aus dem Institut für Psychologie der J. W. Goethe-Universität, Issue 2, 1997.

Hunt, E. (1980). Intelligence as an information-processing concept. *British Journal of Psychology, 71*, 449–474.

James, W. (1950). *The principles of psychology*. New York: Dover. (Original work published in 1890)

Jensen, A. R. (1982). The chronometry of intelligence. In R. J. Sternberg (Ed.), *Advances in research on intelligence* (Vol. 1). Hillsdale, NJ: Erlbaum.

Jensen, A. R. (1987). Individual differences in the Hick paradigm. In P. A. Vernon (Ed.), *Speed of information processing and intelligence*. Norwood, NJ: Ablex.

Kahneman, D., & Treisman, A. (1984). Changing views of attention and automaticity. In R. Parasuraman & D. R. Davies (Eds.), *Varieties of attention* (pp. 29–61). New York: Academic.

Kane, M. J., & Engle, R. W. (2003). Working memory capacity and the control of attention: The contributions of goal neglect, response competition, and task set to Stroop interference. *Journal of Experimental Psychology: General, 132*, 47–70.

Kane, M. J., Hambrick, D. Z., Tuholski, S. W., Wilhelm, O., Payne, T. W., & Engle, R. W. (2004). The generality of working memory capacity: A latent-variable approach to verbal and visuospatial memory span and reasoning. *Journal of Experimental Psychology: General, 133*, 189–217.

Kinchla, R. A. (1992). Attention. *Annual Review of Psychology, 43*, 711–742.

Kranzler, J. H., & Jensen, A. R. (1991). The nature of psychometric g: Unitary proces or a number of independent process? *Intelligence, 15*, 397–422.

Lansman, M. (1978). *An attentional approach to individual differences in immediate memory*. Technical Report, Department of Psychology, University of Washington, Seattle, WA.

Lansman, M., & Hunt, E. (1982). Individual differences in secondary task performance. *Memory and Cognition, 10*, 10–24.

Lansman, M., Poltrock, S., & Hunt, E. (1983). Individual differences in the ability to focus and divide attention. *Intelligence, 7*, 299–312.

Logan, G. D. (1992). Attention and preattention in theories of automaticity. *American Journal of Psychology, 105*, 317–339.

Logan, G. D., & Gordon, R. D. (2001). Executive control of visual attention in dual-task situations. *Psychological Review, 108*, 393–434.

McGrew, K. S. (2005). The Cattell-Horn-Carroll theory of cognitive abilities: Past, present, and future. In D. P. Flanagan & P. L. Harrison (Eds.), *Contemporary intellectual assessment: Theories, tests, and issues* (pp. 136–181). New York: Guilford.

Mirsky, A. F., Anthony, B. J., Duncan, C. C., Ahearn, M. B., & Kellam, S. G. (1991). Analysis of elements of attention: A neuropsychological approach. *Neuropsychology Review, 2*, 109–145.

Moosbrugger, H., Goldhammer, F., & Schweizer, K. (2006). Latent factors underlying individual differences in attention measures: Perceptive attention and executive control. *European Journal of Psychological Assessment, 22*, 177–188.

Myors, B., Stankov, L., & Oliphant, G. (1989). Competing tasks, working memory, and intelligence. *Australian Journal of Psychology, 41*, 1–16.

Navon, D. (1984). Resources – a theoretical soup stone? *Psychological Review, 91*, 216–234.

Nęcka, E. (1996). The attentive mind: Intelligence in relation to selective attention, sustained attention and dual task performance. *Polish Psychological Bulletin, 27*, 3–24.

Neubauer, A. C. (1997). The mental speed approach to the assessment of intelligence. *Advances in Cognition and Educational Practice, 4*, 149–173.

Neubauer, A. C., Bauer, C., & Hoeller, G. (1992). Intelligence attention, motivation and speed-accuracy trade-off in the HICK paradigm. *Personality and Individual Differences, 13*, 1325–1332.

Neumann, O. (1992). Theorien der Aufmerksamkeit: Von Metaphern zu Mechanismen [Theories of attention: from metaphors to mechanisms]. *Psychologische Rundschau, 43*, 83–101.

Neumann, O. (1996). Theories of attention. In O. Neumann & A. F. Sanders (Eds.), *Handbook of perception and action* (pp. 389–446). San Diego: Academic Press.

Norman, D. A., & Shallice, T. (1980). *Attention to action: Willed and automatic control of behavior* (CHIP Report no. 99). San Diego, CA: University of California, Center of Human Information Processing.

Pashler, H. E. (1998). *The Psychology of attention*. Cambridge, MA: MIT Press.

Pogge, D. L., Stokes, J. M., & Harvey, P. D. (1994). Empirical evaluation of the factorial structure of attention in adolescent psychiatric patients. *Journal of Clinical and Experimental Neuropsychology, 16*, 344–353.

Posner, M. I., & Boise, S. J. (1971). Components of attention. *Psychological Review, 78*, 391–408.

Posner, M. I., & Petersen, S. E. (1990). The attention system of the human brain. *Annual Review of Neuroscience, 13*, 25–41.

Posner, M. I., & Rafal, R. D. (1987). Cognitive theories of attention and the rehabilitation of attention deficits. In M. Meier, A. Benton, & L. Diller (Eds.), *Neuropsychological rehabilitation* (pp. 182–201). New York: Guilford.

Posner, M. I., & Snyder, C. R. R. (1975). Facilitation and inhibition in the processing of signals. In P. M. A. Rabbitt & S. Dornic (Eds.), *Attention and performance V* (pp. 655–668). New York: Academic.

Pribram, K. H., & McGuinnes, D. (1974). Arousal, activation, and effort in the control of attention. *Psychological Review, 82*, 116–149.

Roberts, R. D., Beh, H. C., Spilsbury, G., & Stankov, L. (1991). Evidence for an attentional model of human intelligence using the competing task paradigm. *Personality and Individual Differences, 12*, 445–455.

Roberts, R. D., Beh, H. C., & Stankov, L. (1988). Hick's Law, competing tasks, and intelligence. *Intelligence, 12*, 101–120.

Roberts, R. D., & Stankov, L. (1999). Individual differences in speed of mental processing and human cognitive abilities: Toward a taxonomic model. *Learning and Individual Differences, 11*, 1–120.

Rockstroh, S., & Schweizer, K. (2001). The contributions of memory and attention processes to cognitive abilities. *The Journal of General Psychology, 128*, 30–42.

Salthouse, T. A. (1996). The processing-speed theory of adult age differences in cognition. *Psychological Review, 103*, 403–428.

Schmidt, M., Trueblood, W., Merwin, M., & Durham, R.L. (1994). How much do "attention" tests tell us? *Archives of Clinical Neuropsychology, 9*, 383–394.

Schmidt-Atzert, L., & Bühner, M. (2000). Aufmerksamkeit und Intelligenz [Attention and intelligence]. In K. Schweizer (Ed.), *Intelligenz und Kognition* (pp. 125–151). Landau: Verlag Empirische Pädagogik.

Schmidt-Atzert, L., Bühner, M., & Enders, P. (2006). Do concentration tests assess concentration? Analyzing components of concentration test performance. *Diagnostica, 52*, 33–44.

Schneider, W., & Shiffrin, R. M. (1977). Controlled and automatic human information processing: I. Detection, search, and attention. *Psychological Review, 84*, 1–55.

Schweizer, K. (1994). Focal-attentive and preattentive processes in letter- and figure-search tasks. *Perceptual and Motor Skills, 79*, 1347–1354.

Schweizer, K. (1996a). The speed-accuracy transition due to task complexity. *Intelligence, 22*, 115–128.

Schweizer, K. (1996b). Level of encoding, preattentive processing, and working-memory capacity as sources of cognitive ability. *Personality and Individual Differences, 21*, 759–766.

Schweizer, K. (2001). On the role of mechanisms when the processing complexity is high. *European Psychologist, 6*, 133–143.

Schweizer, K. (2005). An overview of research into the cognitive basis of intelligence. *Journal of Differential Psychology, 26*, 43–51.

Schweizer, K. (2007). Investigating the relationship of working memory tasks and fluid intelligence tests by means of the fixed-links model in considering the impurity problem. *Intelligence, 35*, 591–604.

Schweizer, K., & Koch, W. (2003). Perceptual processes and cognitive ability. *Intelligence, 31*, 211–235.

Schweizer, K., & Moosbrugger, H. (1999). Aufmerksamkeit, Intelligenz und Verarbeitungsgeschwindigkeit als Komponenten der mentalen Leistungsfähigkeit [Attention, intelligence and processing speed as components of mental ability]. *Zeitschrift für Differentielle und Diagnostische Psychologie, 20*, 126–132.

Schweizer, K., Moosbrugger, H., & Goldhammer, F. (2005). The structure of the relationship between attention and intelligence. *Intelligence, 33*, 589–611.

Schweizer, K., Zimmermann, P., & Koch, W. (2000). Sustained attention, intelligence and the crucial role of perceptual processes. *Learning and Individual Differences, 12*, 271–286.

Shallice, T., & Burgess, P. (1993). Supervisory control of action and thought selection. In A. D. Baddeley & L. Weiskrantz (Eds.), *Attention: Selection, awareness and control: A tribute to donald broadbent* (pp. 171–187). Oxford: Clarendon.

Shiffrin, R. M., & Schneider, W. (1977). Controlled and automatic human information processing: II. Perceptual learning, automatic attending, and a general theory. *Psychological Review, 84*, 127–190.

Snyderman, M., & Rothman, S. (1987). Survey of expert opinion on intelligence and attitude testing. *American Psychologist, 42*, 137–144.

Spearman, C. (1927). *The ability of man.* London: McMillan.

Stankov, L. (1983). Attention and intelligence. *Journal of Educational Psychology, 72*, 21–44.

Stankov, L. (1988). Single tests, competing tasks and their relationship to the broad factors of intelligence. *Personality and Individual Differences, 9*, 25–33.

Stankov, L. (2000). Complexity, metacognition and fluid intelligence. *Intelligence, 28*, 121–143.

Stankov, L. (1989). Attentional resources and intelligence. A disappearing link. *Personality and Individual Differences, 10*, 957–968.

Stankov, L., Roberts, R., & Spilsbury, G. (1994). Attention and speed of test-taking in intelligence and aging. *Personality and Individual Differences, 17*, 273–284.

Szymura, B., & Nęcka, E. (1998). Visual selective attention and personality: An experimental verification of three models of extraversion. *Personality and Individual Differences, 24*, 713–729.

Unsworth, N., & Engle, R. W. (2007). The nature of individual differences in working memory capacity: Active maintenance in prime memory and controlled search form secondary memory. *Psychological Review, 114*, 104–132.

Van Zomeren, A. H., & Brouwer, W. H. (1994). *Clinical neuropsychology of attention.* New York: Oxford University Press.

Velmans, M. (1991). Is human information processing conscious? *Behavioral and Brain Sciences, 14*, 651–726.

Wachtel, P. L. (1967). Consequences of broad and narrow attention. *Psychological Bulletin, 68*, 417–429.

Zubin, J. (1975). Problem of attention in schizophrenia. In M. L. Kietzman, S. Sutton, & J. Zubin (Eds.), *Experimental approaches to psychopathology* (pp. 139–166). New York: Academic.

Chapter 16
Intelligence and Cognitive Control

Adam Chuderski and Edward Nęcka

Introduction

The concept of "intelligence" has evolved in order to account for two facts, namely, intraindividual stability and interindividual variability of human intellectual performance. On one hand, people who outperform others in one class of tasks that involve reasoning, abstracting, or learning, will most probably excel in any other class of such tasks. On the other hand, within any class of cognitive tasks, one can find people who perform in an outstanding way as well as ones who fail. Early studies on the structure of intelligence examined if there is one general ability factor that manifests itself in all cognitive activities (g factor; Spearman, 1927) or maybe more domain-specific factors (e.g., linguistic, mathematical, etc., Thurstone, 1938) exist. These studies have converged to the widely accepted proposal (Caroll, 1993) of the three-layer hierarchy of factors, with general ability (g) on its highest level, several subordinate group factors (loading groups of tasks like mnemonic or perceptual tasks) on the middle level, and many low-level specific factors for particular tasks (e.g., one for perceptual speed). The most important middle-level factor is general fluid intelligence (Gf; Cattell, 1971), which represents human ability to adapt to the novelty and complexity by means of discovery of abstract relations in the environment and by their efficient goal-oriented application. In this respect, Gf differs from crystallized intelligence (Gc factor; ibidem), which consists in the application of one's existing knowledge to the requirements of a situation.

The research on intelligence has switched to the identification of biological and cognitive mechanisms determining the level of g and, more often, of Gf factor. In the domain of cognition (for a review of neurobiological studies we refer the reader to: Neubauer and Fink, this volume), numerous studies reported significant correlations between intelligence test scores and performance on single elementary cognitive tasks (e.g., Nęcka, 1994; Turner & Engle, 1989). High correlations are usually observed when aggregated variables, representing common variance extracted from different measures of the same theoretical construct, are used. For instance, Kyllonen and Cristal (1990), who adopted the factor analytical approach, found that the reasoning factor (i.e., general intelligence)

A. Chuderski (✉)
Institute of Psychology, Jagiellonian University, Al. Mickiewicza 3, 31-120 Krakow, Poland
e-mail: adam.chuderski@gmail.com

E. Nęcka
The Warsaw School of Social Sciences and Humanities, Warsaw, Poland

correlated with the factor extracted from a large battery of short term memory (STM) and working memory (WM) tasks at the 0.80 level. This finding made the authors conclude that the reasoning ability was "little more than" working memory capacity (WMC). However, their understanding of WMC was close to the STM research tradition, where capacity is viewed as a specific number of items possible to store for a short time. Contemporary studies of this kind define capacity of working memory as the mechanism responsible for active maintenance of information during cognitive processing. Moreover, such studies usually adopt the structural equation modeling approach. For example, in the study by Colom, Rebollo, Palacios, Juan-Espinosa, and Kyllonen (2004), WMC variable, calculated from more than 20 different cognitive tasks, explained on average (across three studies) 92% of variance in intelligence. Other studies reported much smaller, but still substantial, amount of common variability between WM measures and g or Gf factors (e.g., 57% in the study by Süß, Oberauer, Wittmann, Wilhelm, & Schulze, 2002). It seems to us that such discrepancies between empirical findings result from diversity of WM tasks, on one hand, and diversity of intelligence measures, on the other hand. Some WM tasks are strongly implicated in the processes of cognitive control, attention, or various forms of active processing, whereas others remain mostly "mnemonic" in nature: the more active processing a given task requires, the stronger its correlation with g or Gf (compare: Ackerman, Beier, & Boyle, 2005; Oberauer, Schulze, Wilhelm, & Süß, 2005). It is also possible that some tests of general intelligence (like Raven's matrices) engage working memory and attention, whereas others first of all require attentional processes (Schweizer & Moosbrugger, 2004).

Anyway, correlational studies solely cannot decide whether intelligence (e.g., seen as a biological feature) causes efficient cognition (Ackerman et al., 2005; Colom et al., 2004) or maybe basic cognitive processes are fundamental to g and Gf (Kane, 2005; Nęcka, 1994). Moreover, such studies seem unlikely to identify a cognitive mechanism that basic cognitive processing and intelligence may have in common. Latent variables, like WMC, are derived from scores on many relatively complex tasks, so they are no more than statistical constructs similar to g or Gf. One may even argue that one mystery (g) is being explained by another mystery (WMC). This results in correlational methods often being supported by experimental and formal methods that aim at identifying basic cognitive mechanisms and parameters, which determine individual effectiveness in tests or situations involving general intelligence.

On the grounds of such an approach, four main (and several minor) theories have been proposed so far to explain cognitive basis of intelligence. One feature of human cognitive architecture hypothesized to underlie general intelligence is the speed of information processing (Jensen, 2005). On the contrary, some suggested that what determines the level of Gf is the capacity or scope of the most active and directly accessible working memory structure called either primary memory (Unsworth & Engle, 2006) or the focus of attention (Cowan, 2001) that results in the number of arbitrary bindings (Oberauer, Süβ, Wilhelm, & Sander, 2007) or dimensions of relations (Halford, Wilson, & Phillips, 1998) that can be processed simultaneously. Another candidate for a cognitive basis of intelligence is the efficiency of certain functions of attention (Nęcka, 1994, 1996; Schweizer, this volume). The most influential hypothesis postulates that it is neither a feature of working memory nor attention by itself that matters but the efficiency of control processes, which operate upon these structures and determine the level of intelligence (Engle & Kane, 2004). These control processes allow for active maintenance of information relevant to the current goal, even in the face of interference; at the same time, they inhibit information irrelevant to that goal.

In this chapter, we aim to support the idea that intelligent people are characterized by more efficient control they can exert over information processing. Firstly, we precisely define the construct of cognitive control and aim to identify its main attributes and functions. Then, we review existing data on the role of cognitive control in general (especially, fluid) intelligence; we also present our new findings concerning this issue. Finally, some future directions for research on cognitive control and intelligence will be proposed.

Cognitive Control

Cognitive control, often also referred to as executive control (e.g., Yarkoni & Braver, this volume), may be defined as set of processes that instead of representing mental states directly, influence and organize such states according to some internal goals of the cognitive system. Due to control processes the human mind is able to momentarily bind any stimulus with any response, even when no inborn or learned associations between the former and the latter exist (Goschke, 2000). So, control is especially needed in novel or difficult situations that involve weakly learned or arbitrary sequences of responses, when great amount of planning is required, when errors are likely (and must be quickly corrected), and when dominant but not relevant tendencies to think or behave have to be overcome (Norman & Shallice, 1986).

Control processes can be classified according to some dimensions. First of all, control exerted from inside of an organism without any external influence (endogenous control) may be opposed to exogenous control initiated by stimuli coming from the environment (Rogers & Monsell, 1995). In most cases, cognitive control is a mixture of both types of processes.

We propose to categorize control processes according to another dimension, namely, the strength of influence they can exert (Chuderski, 2006). Full control consists in the ability of the controlling process to cause any change into the controlled process in a so-called open-loop. Directing our visual attention to arbitrary sequence of locations may serve as a good example of the full control. Regulation is a weaker form of control because thanks to it an organism can only react to some feedback signal from the regulated process in order to cause changes that bring it closer to (in a negative closed-loop) or farther from (in a positive closed-loop) a given goal, standard, or reference value. For instance, a negative feedback may focus our attention in response to increasing distance between our eyes and a fixation point. Another form of control is self-constraining, which consists in setting the boundary conditions that the control or regulation processes cannot exceed. Keeping the focus of attention within a visual field that should be searched through is a good example of such a control. Monitoring is the weakest form of control because it is not able to influence any process in an active way, but it can detect its states and initiate some other control or regulation processes, if necessary.

How many controlling functions are there within human cognition is a disputable question. For instance, four types of executive control processes were investigated by Miyake, Friedman, Emerson, Witzki, and Howerter (2000). These authors introduced the following taxonomy: updating of working memory, inhibition of prepotent responses, mental set shifting,[1] and dual task coordination. Updating consists in continuous "refreshment" of the contents of working memory, and it is measured with methods such as n-back (McErlee, 2001), running memory (Mayes, 1988), or memory counters (Larson, Merritt, & Williams, 1988) tasks. The common feature of all these tasks is that, in order to perform them accurately, people have to continuously insert some stimuli to active memory while deleting others, because what in one moment is a noise or a distracter, quickly becomes a target (or otherwise). Inhibition deals with volitional stopping of dominant but task-irrelevant thought or response tendency, which, if emitted without control, would cause errors. Inhibition is measured with such paradigms as stop-signal (Logan & Cowan, 1984), go/no-go (Eimer, 1993), antisaccade tasks (Roberts, Hager, & Heron, 1994), or interference tasks like Stroop (MacLeod, 1991) or Navon (1977) tasks. Mental set shifting (Rogers & Monsell, 1995) involves frequent alternating substitution of task-sets (goals and rules associated with tasks) in working memory.

---

[1] The term "shifting" is sometimes confused with "switching". In line with the position held by Miyake et al. (2000), we suggest that the former should refer to mental functions and the latter – to experimental paradigms (switching of attention, switching between tasks).

Dual tasking requires simultaneous coordination of two mental or motor activities (Pashler, 1998). Using confirmatory factor analysis, Miyake et al. (2000) estimated that the three former functions are independent, though moderately correlated (r=between 0.42 and 0.63). The function of dual tasking could not be reduced to any combination of these constructs and it was classified by the authors as a complex cognitive activity. Therefore, they concluded with the taxonomy of three executive functions: updating, inhibition, and shifting.

Yet, brain imaging studies (e.g., Collette & Van der Linden, 2002) suggest that dual tasking is "wired" by separate neural networks and thus should be regarded as a distinct control function. According to Smith and Jonides (1999), who also applied the brain imaging approach, there are at least five executive functions, but different from those proposed by Miyake et al. (2000), namely, (1) focusing attention on relevant stimulation, (2) appropriate scheduling of sequences of responses that constitute complex actions (cf. Norman & Shallice, 1986), (3) planning goal-oriented actions, (4) working memory updating, and (5) operations performed on data stored in working memory ("coding" these data for time and place of appearance). The authors claim that all these functions can be separated on the basis of impairments observed in patients suffering from prefrontal brain damages.

One can argue that Miyake et al.'s, Collette and Van der Linden's, or Smith and Jonides' taxonomies do not reveal really different control functions, but they just capture different task-specific requirements fulfilled by the same set of control mechanisms. Engle and Kane (2004) proposed two general control functions: active maintenance of task goals and resolution of response conflicts. In such a perspective, updating is simply active holding of targets and to-be-targets while resolving conflicts caused by interfering distracters. Task switching consists in activating proper task-set and efficiently resolving its conflict with competitive task-set. In more neurobiologically oriented proposal, Braver, Gray, and Burgess (2007) postulated that these two distinct functions differ in operating modes of cognitive control: the former carries out proactive control (future oriented, early selecting, preparatory, global, strongly related to a current goal) and the latter consists in reactive control (past-oriented, late correction, interference resolution, and item-specific). They showed that both control modes have different computational characteristics and become efficient in different situations, so they both serve independent but mutually complementary functions emerging from dynamic interactions of several brain structures. As an evidence for computational realizability of this idea, Smoleń and Chuderski (in press) have implemented mechanisms of dual control in a computational architecture and showed that it can simulate human behavior in numerous situations involving executive control with one set of general control processes.

Cognitive control in general can thus be understood (Goschke, 2000) as a resolution of cognitive trade-offs (e.g., to activate or to deactivate certain goal, process, or response tendency). An example of such a general cognitive trade-off concerns decision how to allocate limited resources to concurrent processes in the optimal way (Kahneman, 1973). Another example refers to decisions either to carry on the exploration of a situation, which is an expensive process that brings new data increasing probability of apt decision, or to start exploitation of the data already gathered (Holland, 1975).

Efficient control over cognitive processes implies behavioral control exerted over one's own body and important elements of the environment. Thus, it allows personal control over the state of the whole organism (its beliefs, goals, long-term plans) that can be autonomously changed. The importance of cognitive control for personal control is best seen in cases of control deficits due to neurobiological disorders. In such cases, people continuously skip important elements of behavioral sequences, emit improper responses triggered by strongly associated stimuli, persevere even if an original goal has already been reached, and are unable to use feedback information (Smith & Jonides, 1999; Wilson, Evans, Alderman, Burgess, & Emslie, 1997). But even for healthy people personal control is both effortful and resourceful, and its failures (e.g., addictions, aggressive behavior, or helplessness) happen quite commonly (Baumeister & Vohs, 2004). Vast evidence exists that such dysfunctions result from inefficient cognitive control (e.g., problem drinking appears to be related to weak prepotent response inhibition; Whitney, Hinson, and Jameson, 2006).

Research on cognitive and personal control helps us to understand control without appealing to any homuncular concepts like "will" or "self" (Monsell & Driver, 2000). Cognitive psychology is currently advancing these research in order to be able to distinguish control processes from regular ones and to measure cognitive control aptly.

Intelligence and Cognitive Control

Motivated by the fact that many definitions of intelligence include control or metacognition as its crucial definiens (e.g., Sternberg, 1985), some researchers investigated formal characteristics of intelligence tests in order to identify the role of control processes. The classical study (Carpenter, Just, & Shell, 1990) in this line of research deals with computational modeling of Raven's Progressive Matrices test, which is a standard measure of general fluid intelligence. The authors constructed two models of Raven's PM solver that qualitatively differed in regard to control ability to activate and manage subgoals generated during reasoning process and to cope with conflicts among multiple goals. Simpler version of the model, FAIRRAVEN, was able to reach performance of an average intelligent human being. The model used three groups of processes (perceptual analysis of a matrix, rule induction and generalization, and rule application to possible solutions of this matrix), which are believed necessary for solving easy and medium Raven's problems. It fired all applicable productions in parallel but failed to solve correctly 11 out of 34 problems it was given (two remaining Raven's test items could not be translated into model's input code so they were not simulated with the model). A BETTERRAVEN version of the model had two additional characteristics. First, it included additional rules that allowed the model for the greater level of abstraction. However, as a result, in the case of the most complex problems, parallel operation of the model evoked too many alternative rules to handle with efficiency. The crucial difference between the two models was a fourth class of productions for goal management and for resolving conflicts among alternative goals. Due to improved control, the BETTERRAVEN model applied rules serially and it was able to backtrack from unpromising moves. The model solved all 34 input problems, thus simulating the results of highly intelligent humans. Although extra WMC improved processing a bit, it was not able to fully substitute increased cognitive control.

Inspired by Carpenter et al.'s (1990) work, Susan Embretson (1995) aimed to test empirically the assumption that WMC and effectiveness of general control processes determine performance in Gf tests. She viewed control as a factor responsible for appropriate and efficient utilization of capacity provided by working memory. When control processes work well, even limited memory store may be sufficient if exploited efficiently. Embretson designed 130 items of her new Abstract Reasoning Test. The items differed in the number of relations needed to be kept in mind simultaneously in order to obtain correct solution. In other words, the items differed in relational complexity (Halford et al., 1998). Increasing demand for working memory was expected to decrease accuracy and such a manipulation, according to Embretson, should reveal the influence of WMC on performance on Gf test. Moreover, the author assumed that differences in accuracy among people for items on the same level of complexity probably result from differences in effectiveness of control processes. So, Embretson was able to estimate both the extent to which interindividual differences in general intellectual ability may be explained by variation in WMC and the extent to which they may be explained by the quality of control processes. The former factor explained 48% of variance in total score on Abstract Reasoning Test, the latter accounted for 71% of this variance, and both factors were jointly able to explain 92% of variance in test score. So, control had the strongest impact on reasoning performance though it was significantly supported by WMC.

Unsworth and Engle (2005) backed up Embretson's conclusions in reference to the original Raven's PM test. They divided test items into four groups according to load imposed by these items on working memory (from low to high load estimated on the basis of three factors: item's difficulty, the number of its governing rules, and the type of these rules). The correlations between participants' WMC (estimated with the operation span task, see Turner and Engle, 1989) and their scores in first three groups of items were high but did not differ significantly from one another ($r = 0.324$, 0.294, and 0.331, $p < 0.001$, for the first, second, and third quartile, respectively); in the case of the most complex items the correlation was not significant due to the floor effect. If some kind of capacity had determined the correlation between Gf test and WMC, these correlations should appear stronger and stronger with increasing load on working memory, as high-WMC participants should have exhibited the largest advantage over low-WMC subjects in the case of the most memory-demanding items. The results contradicted this hypothesis and supported the view that control processes rather than some memory capacity form the basis for performance on both WM tasks and Raven's PM test.

Some psychometric studies examined relations between latent variables reflecting control processes and Gf with the use of structural equation models. Engle, Tuholski, Laughlin, and Conway (1999; see also Conway, Cowan, Bunting, Therriault, & Minkoff, 2002) estimated efficiency of control processes utilizing three WM span tasks and three STM tasks. They assumed that the portion of variance common to WM and STM tasks would reflect memory capacity and that the residual variance in relatively more complex WM tasks would reflect influence of control processes. When the common variance was statistically eliminated, residual latent variable still significantly correlated with Gf ($r = 0.49$), while STM-Gf path coefficient appeared insignificant. In a similar study, Kane et al. (2004) modified Engle et al.'s (1999) technique. They used a nested model in which a common variance from scores in six WM tasks (with verbal, numerical, or figural stimuli) formed one latent variable (WM capacity), a common variance from scores in six STM tasks (using similar stimuli) formed another variable (STM capacity), and a common variance from scores in all twelve tasks formed variable reflecting executive control. The authors believed that due to Gf unrestricted sample and to the use of nonverbal stimuli, which are more difficult to process, all WM and STM tasks involved cognitive control. After partialing out variance representing memory capacities, the variance common for all the tasks, which was expected to reflect cognitive control, significantly correlated with the Gf variable ($r = 0.52$).

However, the problem with interpretation of above cited studies results from the fact that they used indirect indices of cognitive control calculated on the basis of disputable assumption that either the residual variance in WM tasks scores (e.g., Engle et al., 1999) or the variance common to WM and STM tasks (e.g., Kane et al., 2004) represents controlled processing. In our recent study (Paulewicz, Chuderski, & Nęcka, 2007) we tested directly how performance on five computerized tasks, three directly engaging cognitive control functions postulated by Miyake et al. (2000) plus one dual tasking test (Pashler, 1998) and one goal monitoring and activation task (Duncan, Emslie, Williams, Johnson, & Freer, 1996), was related to Gf latent variable. We used n-back task with two-digit numbers as stimuli to estimate updating function. Two-part test of inhibition required categorization of digits into odd or even, but in 15% of trials well-learned responses had to be inhibited: in the first part of the test responses were to be withheld for digits one and two, in its second part opposite response keys were to be pressed when the digit was surrounded by a border. Cued task-switching test was used in two conditions. In a predictable one, every three trials a task changed from categorizing letters onto vowels or consonants to categorizing them as having angles (i.e., A, E, K, N) or not (i.e., C, O, S, U), or vice versa. In unpredictable switching, tasks consisting on categorizing digits according to parity or magnitude (i.e., higher or lower than 5) changed randomly. In both conditions, a cue presented 500 ms before each stimulus indicated the proper task. For dual tasking, we used a test that required speeded left-hand response if both presented digits were odd and, immediately after, right-hand response if two presented letters were identical. Although this solution differs from the paradigm introduced by Kahneman (1973), it is based on the notion of psychological refractory period (PRP) (Pashler, 1998): a response that is supposed to be performed as the second in line needs more time to be executed compared to the single task condition because it must "wait" for its turn. The magnitude of such time costs is interpreted as an index of efficiency of dual tasking (Byrne & Anderson, 2001; Logan & Gordon, 2001; see also "Rationale and general method" section). The fifth task involved categorizing one of the two presented streams of figures onto triangles and quadrangles. Stimuli were presented randomly, but figures in both streams were always opposite (i.e., one triangle and one quadrangle) at the same time. Direct (arrows pointing at proper string) or indirect ("+" symbol for switching the stream or "=" symbol for staying with the same stream) cues indicated the stream of stimuli to be categorized. Participants had to monitor and interpret cues and activate goals if switching was necessary. We observed the goal neglect effect originally reported by Duncan et al. (1996): low-Gf participants committed significantly more errors only in indirect cue condition, when most probably a new task goal had to be activated from episodic memory according to indirect cues and the focus of attention had to be endogenously shifted to relevant stimuli. Although it has not been resolved whether the task taps some new control function related to organization of task rules and goals (Duncan et al., 2008), or rather it is related to WM updating or shifting, this task seems to impose high general load on control mechanisms and it makes both low-Gf participants (ibidem) and frontal lobe patients (Duncan et al., 1996) show impaired performance.

From accuracy scores in task conditions involving control (e.g., the error difference between switch and repeat trials in switching test or the accuracy in indirect cue trials in goal activation test), we calculated the latent variable interpreted as reflecting interindividually varied efficiency of cognitive control. In a structural equation model (including also latent variables for Gf and for the efficiency of insight problem solving) that had a very good fit to the observed data, the highly significant (equalled to 0.76) standardized path coefficient between cognitive control variable and Gf was observed. As far as we know, our study was the first one that directly related the latent measure of cognitive control derived from a few executive control tasks and the Gf latent measure and proved that they shared the substantial part (58%) of common variance. This SEM study provided also the evidence for the crucial role of Gf in higher mental processes by showing that Gf accounted for three fourth of the variance in insight problem solving.

Aside from latent variable analyses of general executive ability and Gf, also research that relates single measures of particular cognitive control functions supports the existence of strong links between control and intelligence. For example, several studies on memory updating show its relation to measures of general fluid intelligence. Cowan et al. (2005) reported significant correlations (rs = 0.35 – 0.51) between scores in running memory task and scores on scholastic as well as general ability tests in both children and adult samples (however, the authors interpret these relations in terms of capacity rather than control of attention). Gray, Chabris, and Braver (2003) found significant correlation ($r = 0.36$) between score on Raven's PM and accuracy of detection of repeated letters in n-back task, as well as similar correlation in case of rejection of lure foils within this task. In our own study (Chuderska & Chuderski, 2009), a figural analogy test (correlating highly with Raven's PM) correlated moderately with accuracy in n-back task ($r = 0.42$).

With respect to the function of inhibition, there is some evidence for its significant link to Gf. Dempster and Corkill (1999) reviewed several studies on manifestations of perceptual and response conflict resolution (they named them resistance to interference). Generally, results showed moderate correlations between most of reviewed indices and Gf, but one of the correlations between index of performance on incongruent condition in Stroop test and Gf factor (loading Raven's PM and a math problems test) appeared high ($r = 0.46$), indicating advantage of intelligent people in dealing with interference. Such a result has also been observed in our lab (Nęcka, 1999) with the use of a version of Navon task. The task consisted in categorizing large letters built out of smaller letters, which could be identical to the large letter (e.g., T built out of ts; congruent condition) or different from it

(T built out of ws; incongruent condition). The difference in latencies between incongruent and congruent conditions, which probably indicated efficiency of inhibiting conflicting responses, correlated significantly ($r=0.29$, averaged in four experimental sessions) with scores in Raven's PM. In our above cited study (Chuderska & Chuderski, 2009), figural analogy test score considered as a fluid intelligence measure correlated significantly with distracter inhibition costs in Eriksen and Eriksen's (1974) flankers task, but this correlation was rather weak ($r=0.23$).

The results of studies on task switching and dual tasking are much more ambiguous. Some researchers reported moderate correlations between intelligence and both task switching (Salthouse, Fristoe, McGuthry, & Hambrick, 1998) and dual tasking (Ben-Shakhar & Sheffer, 2001), but other studies provided no support for relations between these constructs and Gf. For example, Süβ et al. (2002) found very weak correlation (path coefficient of only 0.24) between reasoning and task switching latent variables when the latter had been correlated with WMC. Stankov (1989) summarized results of studies on relation between dual tasking and intelligence as a "disappearing link." Some (e.g., Oberauer et al., 2007) interpret such a weak relation between Gf and both task switching and dual tasking costs as the evidence that cognitive control does not underlie fluid intelligence. Instead, these authors propose that the number of elements or relations that can be actively maintained or bound in working memory determines the level of mental ability (see also Halford et al., 1998). Others (e.g., Kane, Conway, Hambrick, & Engle, 2007) explain this status quo as a result of the fact that most of task switching tests exploit explicit cueing of tasks and so do not impose high demands on control. What the participants have only to do in such tests is to match the incoming cue-stimulus pair with a well-learned proper response. No volitional control processes may be involved in explicit task cueing procedure (Logan & Bundesen, 2003). Moreover, one of us criticized the methodology of Stankov's dual tasking studies – when latency costs are properly calculated their relation to Gf measures appears significant (Nęcka, 1994, 1996, 1997). One can also argue that it is the complexity of an attentional task that modifies the relationship of shifted or divided attention with intelligence. Schweizer (1996) showed that intelligence test scores correlated with speed rather than accuracy if the task was simple, but they started to correlate with accuracy rather than speed if the task was more complex or difficult. So, if the task is at the moderate level of difficulty, one should expect relatively strong relationship with intelligence. Relevant findings can be found in Nęcka (1994, 1996, 1997); see also the chapter by Szymura in this volume.

Below we report two recent experiments clarifying the ambiguous issue of the relation between general mental ability and both accuracy and latency indices of dual tasking. Our goal is to provide the evidence that such a relation exists but the extent to which cognitive control is involved in dual tasking is very susceptible to aspects of experimental conditions involving the demand on cognitive control. Small procedural changes related to these aspects may make the Gf-dual tasking link disappear.

Experiments on Dual Tasking

Rationale and General Method

In general, we adopted a so-called quasiexperimental or microanalytic approach (Hambrick, Kane, & Engle, 2005). In this approach, the correlation between a measure of an elementary cognitive function and a measure of efficacy of higher-order cognition (or an analogous difference between means in basic performance for people performing high vs. low in high-level tasks) is treated as a dependent variable. The goal is to use appropriate experimental manipulations influencing elementary functions in order to make this correlation (or a respective difference) appear and disappear. If we are able to influence a correlational link in this way, we may assume that the crucial aspect of such a manipulation is also crucial for the relation between investigated low- and high-level constructs.

Specifically, we designed a test of dual task coordination in order to avoid supposed disadvantages of both task switching and dual tasking methods used in most of the previous studies. In case of explicit cueing and long intervals between subsequent trials in task switching tests, the amount of control needed to perform the tests is probably relatively low. There is no consensus whether switching cost represents the index of cognitive control at all and some researchers provided strong evidence that it may result from some kind of automatic processing (e.g., Allport & Wylie, 2000; Logan & Bundesen, 2003). On the other hand, dual tests that involve continuous performance in two concurrent tasks, most often used in research on Gf-divided attention link (e.g., Nęcka, 1994; Stankov, 1989), do not allow for controlling the order of mental operations, as participants can use various attention allocation strategies while dealing with both tasks. Thus these tests measure only some global costs of dual tasking, which cannot be precisely interpreted in mechanistical terms (Pashler, 1998, pp. 265–271). So, in designing our task, we utilized a method that lays halfway in between task switching and continuous dual tasking, namely the PRP paradigm. PRP tasks consist in concurrent or almost concurrent presentation of two stimuli, while people are supposed to categorize them as fast as possible and to emit two accurate responses in an instructed order. As consecutive PRP trials are separated by proper breaks, the experimental situation is more controllable than in the continuous dual task paradigm. Within cognitive psychology PRP tasks are widely believed to be simple but still apt measures of the interference resulting from control over dual task performance (e.g., Byrne & Anderson, 2001; Logan & Gordon, 2001; Pashler, 1998). In the present research, we adopt the idea that coordination of two closely following simple mental operations imposes high demand on cognitive control and we will be looking for subtle changes in experimental situations increasing or decreasing control demands that will cause Gf-dual tasking correlation (and respective differences in dual tasking indices between high- and low-Gf participants) to appear and disappear, in order to support the hypothesis that fluid intelligence may be related to dual task performance, but only when a dual tasking situation imposes the considerable load on cognitive control processes.

Finally, we assume that control consisting in coordination of two motor responses may be different from "pure" control consisting in coordination of two cognitive processes, such as loading to and deleting from working memory. We expect that this pure control will impose enough demand for cognitive system for correlation with Gf to appear. Additional demand for motor control may result in an increase of this correlation, but is not necessary for the correlation to appear. To isolate cognitive control without need to coordinate two responses we merged PRP and go/no-go paradigms and introduced trials that required two distinct mental processes but just one motor response.

The method amounted to presentation of numerous dual task trials separated with 500 ms breaks. In each trial, four stimuli (each 0.8 × 1.0 cm in size, black on light grey background) were presented on random in the center of the computer screen, for a few seconds apiece, and were composed in 2 × 2 matrix (2.5 × 3.0 cm in size) with two digits on one random diagonal and two letters on the opposite one. The task was to compare the parity of digits (semantic criterion) and to compare the identity of letters (physical criterion). If the digits were odd then the left response button should be pressed with the left hand. If the two letters were identical, the right response button should be pressed with the right hand. In each session of the task, 40 matrices were presented. Some matrices included pairs of both odd digits and identical letters and thus required two responses. Some matrices included two odd digits but different letters, or they included identical letters but one or two even digits, and thus required two mental operations but only one response. Some matrices did not include any target pair of stimuli. Before experimental sessions, participants were always trained on each of two tasks separately and subsequently they were trained in dual task condition. Participants were expected to perform mentally two tasks in the order stated in an appropriate instruction (the main task parameter manipulated in experiments). Other task parameters that varied between experiments and conditions were matrix presentation time and the relative proportion of the trials requiring one response and trials requiring two responses in one session.

Experiment 1

In this experiment, we used time-pressure to assure high demand for cognitive control in dual categorization task combined with go/no-go responses, the manipulation supported by previous empirical and simulation results (Jones, Cho, Nystrom, Cohen, & Braver, 2002). We expected that an important source of difficulty for less intelligent people would be the need for fully internal, endogeonous activation of the proper task, when no external cue indicated which task was to be done (analogically to goal neglect phenomenon). We expected that when a more direct cue is introduced, highly intelligent people would lose their advantage and the correlation between task performance and Gf would disappear. We also expected that pure cognitive control and response coordination are two distinct sources of demand for executive system separately contributing to variance in Gf, so additional need for motor control in PRP task would bring significant influence on performance and would make correlation between Gf and dual task performance (as well as the respective difference in means) increase.

Participants. 139 students from several colleges in Lodz, Poland, participated in the study (53 females, mean age 22.1 years, age ranged from 18 to 31 years). They were paid ~5 euro for 3-h participation. Seventy and 69 participants were assigned to two groups according to the order they registered for the experiment.

Design and procedure. The task described above was used. Each matrix was presented only for 2 s, each session consisted of 10 trials with two responses required, 10 trials with only digit target pair (left hand response required), 10 trials with only letter target pair (right hand response required), and 10 trials with no target pair. There were five experimental sessions separated by short breaks. Instructions presented before the test indicated the order in which the tasks should be done: first digit comparison and then letter comparison. In two-response trials, if a participant responded in a wrong order, sound beep indicated an error.

In one ("no-cue") group, digits and letters appeared simultaneously on the computer screen. In the other ("cue") group, letters appeared with stimulus onset asynchrony (SOA), 500 ms after digits. We expected that in the cue group, the order of stimuli appearance would make activation of the proper task easier. In the no-cue group, participants had to remember and activate tasks in the expected order without any external help.

One single task session for each task and two dual task sessions were administered for training before experimental sessions. Before the computerized task, participants were tested with Raven's Advanced Progressive Matrices for maximum of 45 min. Total number of correctly solved items was taken as estimate of individual general fluid intelligence level.

Independent variables were (1) cue/no-cue group (SOA=500 or 0 ms, respectively), (2) the number of responses required (1 or 2), and (3) the Gf level according to Raven's score median split (low- or high-Gf). Mean accuracy was calculated from 100 possible responses in each experimental condition and was taken as dependent variable.

Results. Results in Raven's PM (36 items) were as follows: scores ranged from 7 to 34, $M = 21.61$, $SD = 6.37$. Cue and no-cue groups did not differ significantly in Raven test scores (21.95 vs. 21.27, respectively).

As expected, due to short stimuli matrix presentation time in PRP task, RT distribution was trimmed and long responses resulted in errors. In consequence, no differential effects concerning latencies were observed.

Unfortunately, in Experiment 1, we did not collect accuracy data in single-task training sessions, so we were not able to calculate dual tasking accuracy costs (i.e., difference in mean accuracy between dual task and single task sessions). However, experimenters reported high accuracy in obviously very easy single task training sessions. Mean proportions of errors in these training sessions in Experiment 2 (when we corrected the methodological fault and recorded baseline single task performance) that were conducted before experimental sessions (i.e., the ones administered in the same way as in Experiment 1) equaled to 5.81% in case of letter task and to 7.82% in case of digit task, while mean proportions of errors in experimental sessions averaged over both cue groups in the present experiment were almost doubled in case of analogous one-response dual task condition ($M = 11.25$ and 12.69%, for letter and digit task, respectively). So, strong premises exist that substantial proportion of errors reported below most probably was dual task specific, especially when huge time pressure applied in Experiment 1 is taken into account.

The accuracy correlated with Raven's score in the no-cue group both for one- ($r = 0.380$, $p < 0.001$) and two-response ($r = 0.526$, $p < 0.001$) conditions (rs difference insignificant, one-tailed test), but no significant correlation was observed in the cue group ($r = 0.203$, $r = 0.081$, respectively). The difference in correlation values between no-cue and cue groups in case of one-response condition did not reach statistical significance ($p = 0.13$, one-tailed test), but it was highly significant in case of two-response condition ($p < 0.02$, one-tailed test).

We performed $2 \times 2 \times 2$ (cue/no-cue group × Raven's group × number of responses) between-within subjects ANOVA on accuracy data (presented in Table 16.1). The analysis yielded three significant main effects: accuracy was lower in the no-cue than in the cue group ($F[1,135] = 36.11$; $p < 0.001$), it was also lower in Gf-low than in Gf-high group ($F[1,135] = 13.11$; $p < 0.001$), and it was lower when two responses were required ($F[1,135] = 11.64$; $p < 0.001$). Both group factors entered a significant two-way interaction ($F[1,135] = 4.61$; $p = 0.033$): the difference between Gf groups was significant ($F[1,68] = 13.36$; $p < 0.001$) in the no-cue group, but insignificant ($F[1,67] = 1.46$; ns) in the cue group. The factors entered a significant ($F[1,135] = 15.56$; $p < 0.001$) three-way interaction with the number of responses: the difference between Gf groups in no-cue condition was larger if two responses were required than when only one response had to be emitted. In both one- and two-response conditions, the difference in difference in mean performance of Gf-high versus Gf-low groups was significantly (ps < 0.001, one-tailed t test) higher in no-cue condition.

Discussion. The results confirm both hypotheses. Significant correlations between accuracy of dual task coordination and general fluid intelligence, as well as significant differences in mean accuracy between Gf-low and Gf-high groups, were observed in the no-cue condition, when stimuli were presented simultaneously and carried no information on the proper order of mental operations, but these correlations and differences were no longer significant in cue condition, when participants could overpass the demand for control over the order of stimuli comparisons with observing temporal succession of item pairs. The Gf – dual task performance correlation was stronger in case of cue condition in comparison to no-cue one, though this difference was significant only for two-response trials. Analogous differences in differences between high- and low-Gf participants were significantly larger for both response conditions. We interpret these effects as a result of the difference between both cue conditions concerning the amount of endogenous control needed to do the task. Lack of external cueing appeared much harder for less intelligent participants than for more intelligent ones because the former could not compensate for the absence of cueing with their own cognitive control resources, whereas the latter could do that.

Clear links between intelligence and dual tasking were observed even if only mental operations had to be coordinated, that is, when just one response was to be emitted. Additional requirement to control response selection made Gf-accuracy correlation in the no-cue group slightly higher

Table 16.1 Mean accuracy in % (and standard deviations) for low-Gf and high-Gf groups and differences between means in all experimental conditions (significant differences in bold) of Experiment 1

Condition	No cue – one response	No cue – two responses	Cue – one response	Cue – two responses
Low-Gf	80.71 (2.07)	71.88 (2.41)	90.57 (1.47)	91.42 (1.50)
High-Gf	86.72 (2.02)	86.66 (2.34)	94.72 (1.73)	92.57 (1.76)
Difference	**6.01**	**14.78**	4.15	1.15

(unfortunately, insignificantly, probably due to too small sample); moreover, it significantly increased the difference in accuracy between Gf groups ($\Delta=8.68\%$, $p<0.001$). This finding indicates that goal activation and response coordination or response conflict resolution are two control processes independently differentiating more intelligent people from less intelligent ones, what seems to support dual theories of control that relate separately both these mechanisms to intelligence (e.g., Engle & Kane, 2004; Braver et al., 2007). However, the results of Experiment 1 need replication and extension due to some methodological weak points of this study, mostly regarding too short "response window," trimming the observed latencies, and the lack of measures of baseline performance, which did not allow for precise calculation of specific dual tasking costs.

Experiment 2

This experiment was aimed to extend the findings from Experiment 1 concerning no-cue condition (we no longer tested participants in cued trials) with enhanced methodology. Firstly, we gave our participants more time for responding in order to test if correlations with Gf would be revealed for not trimmed response latencies. Moreover, we wanted to observe if the specific dual tasking error costs, which in Experiment 2 would rarely result from imposed time pressure as enough time was allowed, still correlated with fluid intelligence. This time we were able to calculate precisely both error and latency costs with measuring performance in single task sessions and subtracting it from dual task performance. In order to further investigate factors that determine relations between dual task coordination and intelligence, apart from the use of condition that required specified order of mental operations as administered in Experiment 1 (so-called "order" condition), we introduced another (i.e., "no-order") condition, in which both stimuli pairs were also presented simultaneously but an order in which tasks should be performed was not specified (in fact, participants were encouraged to do both tasks in parallel). We wanted to test an alternative (to the endogenous control hypothesis) explanation of the observation that dual tasking in the no-cue condition was so difficult for low-Gf participants. This explanation refers to the working memory overload: concurrent representation of two tasks may be so demanding for working memory that greater total WM capacity or the capacity of its specific part (see Oberauer et al., 2007) may possibly differentiate high-Gf from low-Gf people in PRP task. When in the cue condition of Experiment 1 two tasks were separated in time, less intelligent participants might have loaded just one task representation at a time, so differences in WMC ceased to matter. Surely, in no-order condition of Experiment 2, for the correct performance it is required to keep both tasks active in WM at the same time, so if it is WMC that matters, correlation between a dependent variable and Gf should stay significant. On contrary, if the ability to control the sequence of cognitive operations (and not greater WM capacity) makes more intelligent people do better in dual tasking test (and this is a hypothesis we wanted to support), releasing the constraint on the order of operations should make this correlation disappear.

Another change between Experiment 1 and 2 was that we did not investigate two-response condition anymore. Small number of trials with both digits and letters forming target pairs was introduced, but only to keep participants vigilant for proper order of mental operations (in the order condition), and we did not analyze data from these trials. Instead, we tested effects of task type (digits vs. letters) to examine precisely whether the participants do or do not follow our instructions on the order of tasks. In the order group, dual task latencies for the latter task should be longer than latencies for the former task, as the latter task would have to "wait" for the former one to be completed, while in the no-order group these latencies should not differ significantly as both tasks should be executed simultaneously or on random.

Participants. 171 students from several colleges in Lodz and in Cracow, Poland, as well as young men recruited with newspaper ads in Lodz participated in the study (97 females, mean age 23.6

years, age ranged from 17 to 36 years). They were paid ~5 euro for 4-h participation. 99 participants were assigned to the order group, 72 ones were included into the no-order group, according to the order they registered for the experiment.

Design and procedure. The task described in the general method section was used. Digits and letters appeared simultaneously in each matrix for 4 s. Each session consisted of only four trials with two responses required, 16 trials with only digit target pair (left hand response required), 16 trials with only letter target pair (right hand response required), and four trials with no target pair. Three experimental sessions were administered in the order group, while six sessions were included into the no-order group (as we expected no significant Gf differences here, we aimed to increase the reliability of the measurement). The instructions presented before the test indicated the order in which tasks should be performed: first letter comparison, and then digit comparison in the order group (note that order was reversed relative to Experiment 1) or "compare both pairs of stimuli in any order, try to do it in parallel" in the no-order group. In two-response trials, if a participant responded in a wrong order, sound beep indicated an error.

Two single task (one for each task, stimuli presentation time equaled to 2 s) and one dual task training session (4 s presentation time) were administered. To measure baseline performance, two single task experimental sessions for each task, one before and one after dual task experimental sessions, were administered. Introduction of postexperimental single task sessions was aimed to test if the effects of categorization speed-up during the relatively long task affected performance in dual task sessions.

Before the computerized task, participants were tested with Raven's Progressive Matrices Advanced for maximum of 60 min and with Figural Analogy Test (TAO), designed in our lab (Orzechowski & Chuderski, unpublished manuscript), that involved solving of figural analogies in the form: "A is to B as C is to X," where one X was to be chosen from four alternatives, for another 60 min. The factor calculated from total number of correctly solved items in both tests was taken as the estimate of individual Gf level.

Independent variables were (1) the group (order or no-order), (2) the task (letters or digits), (3) the Gf level according to Gf factor median split (low- or high-Gf). Accuracy dual tasking cost was calculated by subtracting mean proportion of correct responses in 48 trials in each task in the order condition and in 96 trials in each task in the no-order condition from mean proportion of correct responses in 32 trials in single task sessions for each task. Dual tasking latency cost for each task and condition was calculated as a difference between mean latency of corrects responses in dual task sessions and mean latency in single task sessions. These costs were taken as dependent variables. Calculation of dual tasking cost allowed for not accounting for individual differences in both accuracy and speed of basic information processing and motor responding, which laid out of the focus of our study.

Results. Results in Raven's PM (36 items) were as follows: scores ranged from 2 to 35, $M = 18.22$, SD = 7.20. TAO test (36 items) scores ranged from 3 to 36, $M = 20.65$, SD = 7.76. Both groups did not differ significantly in Raven nor TAO test scores ($F < 1$). Gf factor calculated from both scores explained 92.6% of their variance (Eigenvalue = 1.85).

Low-Gf subjects committed more errors than high-Gf ones in both single task (9.30% vs. 4.58%, respectively, $F[1,167] = 10.23$; $p = 0.002$) and dual task condition (17.64% vs. 10.77%, respectively, $F[1,167] = 8.24$; $p = 0.005$) independently of order and task conditions. As intended, releasing the time pressure significantly decreased proportion of errors in order condition of Experiment 2 in comparison to no-cue condition of Experiment 1 (9.18% vs. 16.20%, $p < 0.001$, t test, one-tailed), namely in two conditions of these experiments that apart from stimuli presentation time and order of digit and letter tasks were administered in the same way, and thus the performance in these tasks can be directly compared. Respective response latencies increased in Experiment 2, but as a direct result of enlarging time allowed for participants to deliver the response (i.e., enlarged from 2 to 4 s).

In 2×2×2 (order group × Gf group × task) between-within subjects ANOVA on dual-tasking accuracy costs, only the order factor appeared significant ($F[1,167] = 27.25$; $p < 0.001$): more errors were committed when no order was specified than when subjects performed tasks in the specified order (12.37% vs. 3.56%, respectively). No significant effects for Gf group factor were observed. Most interestingly, no significant correlations with Gf factor for accuracy costs in any experimental condition were observed. Thus, we turned to analysis of dual tasking latency costs.

Latencies in both single task sessions (i.e., before vs. after dual task sessions) did not differed significantly, so using mean baseline latencies in both single task sessions for calculation of latency costs seemed validated. These baseline RTs correlated with Gf factor in case of letter task ($r=-0.309$, $p<0.001$) but not in case of digit task ($r=-0.126$, ns). Analysis of dual tasking latency costs gave interesting results. These costs (presented in Table 16.2) in the order condition correlated significantly ($r=-0.249$; $p=0.013$) with Gf factor for the latter task (digits) but not for the former one ($r=-0.128$, $p>0.2$). Both correlations in the no-order condition were insignificant ($r=0.170$, $p>0.15$; $r=-0.109$, $p>0.3$, for letter and digit tasks, respectively). Between condition (i.e., order vs. no-order) difference in r values was significant in case of letter task but, unfortunately, not in case of digit task ($p=0.03$ and $p>0.17$, respectively, one-tailed test). When aggregated over tasks, Gf-dual tasking latency cost correlation was significant only for order condition ($r=-0.225$, $p=0.025$), and not for no-order condition ($r=0.034$, $p>0.7$), and the significance of difference between respective r values ($p=0.055$, one-tailed test) almost reached the adopted alpha level (0.05).

ANOVA of latency costs revealed one significant ($F[1,167]=152.26$; $p<0.001$) main effect of order group: mean latency costs were much higher in the order group than in the no-order group (532 vs. 180 ms). Order × task two-way interaction was significant ($F[1,167]=31.35$; $p<0.001$): the difference (206 ms) between costs in letter and digit tasks in the order condition was highly significant ($F[1,167]=97.17$; $p<0.001$), while the difference between costs (35 ms) of these two tasks in the no-order condition was insignificant. Significant effects were observed for Gf group factor, which entered two-way interaction ($F[1,167]=7.07$; $p=0.009$) with order condition: the Gf groups differed significantly only in the order condition and did not differ in no-order condition.

Discussion. Due to removal of time pressure or, alternatively but equally possible, due to some other experimental changes imposed in Experiment 2, this time the differences in accuracy between low- and high-Gf participants most probably reflected advantage of the latter in general processing, as they were less error-prone in both single- and dual task conditions. No significant correlations between Gf and specific dual tasking accuracy costs were found. Thus, the differences between low- and high-Gf people in accuracy in dual task situation observed in Experiment 1 most probably were not the result of immanent inability of Gf-low participants to perform correctly in such situations. Gf-low people could perform dual tasking correctly, but as the below discussed results indicate, it took them more time to coordinate two mental operations when such a coordination was required.

Differential effects in dual tasking were revealed in case of latency costs. Analysis of these costs showed that manipulation with tasks order instruction was successful. Participants paid much larger latency costs when they had to preserve the appropriate order of mental operations (order group) than when they could perform both operations in any order (no-order group). In the order group, we observed standard PRP effect of costs for digit task much higher than costs for letter tasks indicating that digit task had to "wait" for the letter task to be completed. This effect proved that order group participants did follow the task order instructions, while insignificant respective difference in no-order group suggests that these participants did not impose any preference or priority for any particular task.

Table 16.2 Mean dual tasking latency costs in ms (and standard deviations) for low-Gf and high-Gf groups and differences between means in all experimental conditions (significant differences in bold) of Experiment 2

Condition	Order – letter task	Order – digit task	No order – letter task	No order – digit task
Low-Gf	467 (25)	706 (32)	123 (36)	195 (37)
High-Gf	390 (25)	563 (32)	201 (36)	200 (37)
Difference	**77**	**143**	78	5

We observed Gf differential effects in the condition with specified order of tasks and only for the second task to be performed. This indicates that performance in dual tasking is not related to Gf in a general way; rather, it is only controlled sequential scheduling of mental operations that seems critical for intelligence. The chance that this scheduling failed was especially high in case of subsequent process (i.e., the digit task following the letter task) that had to be endogenously shifted to. This was the very case when Gf-low participants performance was especially impaired. The correlation between Gf and dual tasking latency costs was (almost) significantly higher in order condition than in no-order one. We claim that our results implicate that the ordered condition of dual tasking test involved the huge amount of cognitive control and therefore it effectively differentiated low- and high-Gf participants. In the no-order condition, when no scheduling of cognitive processes was needed, less control was involved and thus no significant correlations with Gf were observed. This conclusion seems to be supported by the analysis of errors: additional control in the order condition highly decreased proportion of errors. When cognitive processing was "set free" in the no-order condition and probably less control was devoted to accurate categorization in dual task situation, observed error costs were four times larger than in order condition.

In our opinion, a hypothesis which assumes that WMC (defined as the number of distinct chunks or bindings that can be maintained in the active part of WM) is critical for intelligence did not gain enough support in our data. The no-order condition demanded the same (if not greater, due to concurrent processing) amount of WMC, but it did not make low- and high-Gf subjects differ in dual tasking costs. When equal WMC but higher need for the coordination of tasks was needed in the order condition, significant individual differences effects and higher Gf-costs correlations were observed. Positive results in favor of control hypothesis strongly support this explanation of the link between fluid intelligence and dual tasking as measured by the PRP paradigm.

Summary and Conclusions

Regarding the first of the three pivotal questions of the present volume, in the domain of cognitive basis of individual differences in general intelligence, four leading theories have been proposed. Postulated factors responsible for intelligence level are: processing speed, characteristics of attention, capacity of active part of working memory, and efficiency of cognitive control. The most comprehensive empirical and computational support has been obtained for two of them: WM capacity theory and cognitive control theory.

In this chapter, we precisely defined the concept of cognitive control and subsequently we reviewed the existing evidence for the important role of cognitive control for fluid intelligence. We relied on both formal studies of abstract relational reasoning involved in Gf tests and empirical studies relating Gf tests scores with measures of cognitive control. The data are the most univocal in reference to control functions of inhibition and working memory updating. Less clear results concern control functions of task switching and of dual tasking.

In our own research (Paulewicz et al., 2007), we used structural equation modeling to explore the relations between cognitive control and intelligence. Analysis of latent variables explaining variability in a few potentially distinct control functions revealed that control and intelligence share almost two third of a common variance. These conclusions were supported by another recent psychometric research of ours (Chuderska & Chuderski, 2009), which allowed us to relate efficacy of WM updating and inhibition to Gf. Our two most recent quasiexperiments presented in this chapter showed that cognitive control in dual tasking is required only in very specific conditions, namely when precise coordination and scheduling of mental operations is needed, but when the control is exerted then it assures high accuracy of processing, especially in the case of highly intelligent people. The study indicated that when cognitive control is involved to a lesser extent, dual tasking situation did not differentiated between low- and high-Gf participants. Thus, we see cognitive control as one of the most important faculties of human mind allowing it for integration and coordination of many different cognitive processes and modules, as well as for exhibiting coherent and goal-oriented behavior. We believe that the construct of cognitive control, once precisely defined, is the most promising candidate for the explanation of the cognitive mechanisms of general intelligence. However, although the hypothesis on WMC-Gf link was not supported in the present study, both theories of control and working memory (or its specific subsystem) capacity need not be mutually exclusive, and as Carpenter et al.'s (1990) and Embretson's (1995) seminal studies as well as the recent study by Cowan, Fristoe, Elliott, Brunner, and Saults (2006) showed, both constructs may contribute for distinct (though partially overlapping) sources of variance in general mental ability.

Our results support Kane et al.'s (2007) view that insignificant correlations between indices of task switching or concurrent processing and intelligence are usually being observed due to weak involvement of cognitive control in such tasks. In two studies, we showed that manifestation of cognitive control in the experimental situation that lays in between task switching and dual tasking paradigms, when it is properly measured, is strongly related to general fluid mental ability. As we successfully influenced correlation between Gf and dual task performance (i.e., we successfully applied the quasiexperimental method), obtaining high and significant r values in some dual tasking situations while reporting low and insignificant r values in others, we believe that previous inconclusive results on Gf-dual tasking and Gf-task switching links should be reanalyzed in regard to the amount of control that was required by particular tests.

Finally, we want to propose some directions for the methods of further research on cognitive basis of intelligence. Firstly, we believe that the quasiexperimental approach we and others (Hambrick et al., 2005) advocate is crucial for the effective examination of relations between indices of cognitive processing and intellectual ability. It does not suffice to find a significant correlation between an elementary cognitive task and an intelligence test score or to relate latent variables reflecting intelligence and some low-level cognitive construct in order to successfully explain the mechanisms of common variability. One has to treat the Gf and low-level mechanism correlation as a dependent variable and to modify its strength (including its elimination) in order to identify the factors responsible for individual level of intelligence.

Secondly, efforts for obtaining direct experimental test of influence of the efficiency of cognitive control on intelligence should be carried out. For example, several studies indicated that executive control can be effectively trained due to variable-priority learning in dual tasking (Gopher, 1993) or due to proper cognitive feedback in random interval generation (Stettner & Nęcka, 2003). Moreover, a study by Jaeggi, Buschkuehl, Jonides, and Perrig (2008) suggested that extensive training on a WM updating task can cause significant gain in young adults Gf retest score, comparing to a respective control group. The increase in Gf appeared to be a linear function of training time and started to be effective after 12 days of training (however, this result has recently been undermined; Moody, 2009). Therefore, if participants' general control ability can be improved in an experimental group, by comparison of scores in pre- and postexperimental intelligence testing, we should be able to check directly some causal effects of increasing the efficiency of control (or some other elementary cognitive process) on general mental ability.

Thirdly, as numerous successful computational models of abstract relational reasoning central to general fluid intelligence have recently been proposed (Doumas, Hummel, & Sandhofer, 2008; Hummel & Holyoak, 2003; Wilson, Halford, Gray, & Phillips, 2001), computer simulations of differences in control efficiency during reasoning performed within these models may shed much light on the information-processing mechanisms that make some so intellectually gifted while others so cognitively limited. As within cognitive science the method of computational modeling proved to be very successful in explaining domains such as problem solving, learning, language production and comprehension, and reasoning, maybe it is time now to introduce the cognitive science of individual differences, which would merge experimental and computational methods in the endeavor of explaining the nature of interindividual differences in the general mental ability (see Chuderski, Stettner, & Orzechowski, 2007; Lewandowsky & Heit, 2006).

Acknowledgements This work was supported by grant no. N106 2155 33 ("Cognitive control in attention and working memory functioning") sponsored to Edward Nęcka by Polish Ministry of Science and Higher Education (years 2007–2010). We would like to thank Jarosław Kwiatkowski for programming the experimental task, and Marcin Wasiak, Zbigniew Stettner, Radek Wujcik, and Dariusz Asanowicz for conducting the experiments.

References

Ackerman, P. L., Beier, M. E., & Boyle, M. O. (2005). Working memory and intelligence: The same or different constructs? *Psychological Bulletin, 131*, 30–60.

Allport, A., & Wylie, G. (2000). Task switching, stimulus response binding, and negative training. In J. Driver & S. Monsell (Eds.), *Control of cognitive processes, attention and performance XVIII* (pp. 35–70). Cambridge, MA: MIT.

Baumeister, R. F., & Vohs, K. D. (2004). *Handbook of Self-regulation*. New York: Guilford.

Ben-Shakhar, G., & Sheffer, L. (2001). The relationship between the ability to divide attention and standard measures of general cognitive abilities. *Intelligence, 29*, 293–306.

Braver, T. S., Gray, J. R., & Burgess, G. C. (2007). Explaining the many varieties of working memory variation: Dual mechanisms of cognitive control. In A. R. A. Conway, C. Jarrold, M. J. Kane, A. Miyake & J. N. Towse (Eds.), *Variation in Working Memory* (pp. 76–108). Oxford: Oxford University Press.

Byrne, M. D., & Anderson, J. R. (2001). Serial modules in parallel: The psychological refractory period and perfect time-sharing. *Psychological Review, 108*, 847–869.

Caroll, J. B. (1993). *Human cognitive abilities: A survey of factor-analytic studies*. Cambridge: Cambridge University Press.

Carpenter, P. A., Just, M. A., & Shell, P. (1990). What one intelligence test measures: A theoretical account of the processing in the Raven Progressive Matrices test. *Psychological Review, 97*, 404–431.

Cattell, R. B. (1971). *Abilities: Their structure, growth and action*. Boston: Houghton Mifflin.

Chuderska, A., & Chuderski, A. (2009). Executive control in analogical reasoning: Beyond interference resolution. In N. Taatgen, H. van Rijn, J. Nerbonne, & L. Schomaker (Eds.), *Proceedings of the 31st Annual Conference of the Cognitive Science Society* (pp. 1758–1763). Austin, TX: Cognitive Science Society.

Chuderski, A. (2006). *Kontrola Poznawcza w Przełączaniu Pomiędzy Zadaniami: Model Obliczeniowy [Cognitive control in task switching: A computational model]*. Unpublished doctoral dissertation, Jagiellonian University, Cracow

Chuderski, A., Stettner, Z., & Orzechowski, J. (2007). Computational modeling of individual differences in short term memory search. *Cognitive Systems Research, 8*, 161–173.

Collette, F., & Van der Linden, M. (2002). Brain imaging of the central executive component of working memory. *Neuroscience and Biobehavioral Reviews, 26*, 105–125.

Colom, R., Rebollo, I., Palacios, A., Juan-Espinosa, M., & Kyllonen, P. C. (2004). Working memory is (almost) perfectly predicted by g. *Intelligence, 32*, 277–296.

Conway, A. R. A., Cowan, N., Bunting, M. F., Therriault, D. J., & Minkoff, S. R. (2002). A latent variable analysis of working memory capacity, short-term memory capacity, processing speed, and general fluid intelligence. *Intelligence, 30*, 163–183.

Cowan, N. (2001). The magical number 4 in short-term memory: A reconsideration of mental storage capacity. *Behavioral and Brain Sciences, 24*, 87–185.

Cowan, N., Elliott, E. M., Saults, J. S., Morey, C. C., Mattox, S., Hismjatullina, A., et al. (2005). On the capacity of attention: Its estimation and its role in working memory and cognitive aptitudes. *Cognitive Psychology, 51*, 42–100.

Cowan, N., Fristoe, N. M., Elliott, E. M., Brunner, R. P., & Saults, J. S. (2006). Scope of attention, control of attention, and intelligence in children and adults. *Memory and Cognition, 34*, 1754–1768.

Dempster, F. N., & Corkill, A. J. (1999). Individual differences in susceptibility to interference and general cognitive ability. *Acta Psychologica, 101*, 395–416.

Doumas, L. A. A., Hummel, J. E., & Sandhofer, C. M. (2008). A theory of the discovery and predication of relational concepts. *Psychological Review, 115*, 1–43.

Duncan, J., Emslie, H., Williams, P., Johnson, R., & Freer, C. (1996). Intelligence and the frontal lobe: The organization of goal-directed behavior. *Cognitive Psychology, 30*, 257–303.

Duncan, J., Parr, A., Woolgar, A., Thompson, R., Bright, P., Cox, S., et al. (2008). Goal neglect and Spearman's *g*: Competing parts of a complex task. *Journal of Experimental Psychology: General, 137*, 131–148.

Eimer, M. (1993). ERPs elicited by Go and Nogo stimuli: Effects of attention and stimulus probability. *Biological Psychology, 35*, 123–138.

Embretson, S. E. (1995). The role of working memory capacity and general control processes in intelligence. *Intelligence, 20*, 169–189.

Engle, R. W., & Kane, M. J. (2004). Executive attention, working memory capacity, and a two-factor theory of cognitive control. In B. Ross (Ed.), *The psychology of learning and motivation* (Vol. 44, pp. 145–199). New York: Elsevier.

Engle, R. W., Tuholski, S. W., Laughlin, J. E., & Conway, A. R. A. (1999). Working memory, short-term memory, and general fluid intelligence: A latent-variable approach. *Journal of Experimental Psychology: General, 128*, 309–331.

Eriksen, B. A., & Eriksen, C. W. (1974). The importance of being first: A tachostoscopic study of the contribution of each letter to the recognition of four letter words. *Perception and Psychophysics, 15*, 66–72.

Gopher, D. (1993). The skill of attention control: Acquisition and execution of attention strategies. In D. Meyer & S. Kornblum (Eds.), *Attention and Performance XIV: Synergies in Experimental Psychology, Artificial Intelligence, and Cognitive Neuroscience - A Silver Jubilee*. Cambridge, MA: MIT Press.

Goschke, T. (2000). Intentional reconfiguration and involuntary persistence in task set switching. In J. Driver & S. Monsell (Eds.), *Attention and performance, XVIII* (pp. 331–355). Cambridge, MA: MIT.

Gray, J. R., Chabris, C. F., & Braver, T. S. (2003). Neural mechanisms of general fluid intelligence. *Nature Neuroscience, 6*, 316–322.

Halford, G. S., Wilson, W. H., & Phillips, S. (1998). Processing capacity defined by relational complexity: Implications for comparative, developmental, and cognitive psychology. *Behavioral and Brain Sciences, 21*, 803–864.

Hambrick, D. Z., Engle, R. W., & Kane, M. J. (2005). The role of working memory in higher-level cognition: Domain-specific vs. domain-general perspectives. In R. J. Sternberg & J. Pretz (Eds.), *Intelligence and cognition* (pp. 104–121). New York: Cambridge University Press.

Holland, J. J. (1975). *Adaptation in natural and artificial systems*. Ann Arbor, MI: University of Michigan Press.

Hummel, J. E., & Holyoak, K. J. (2003). A symbolic-connectionist theory of relational inference and generalization. *Psychological Review, 110*, 220–264.

Jaeggi, S. M., Buschkuehl, M., Jonides, J., & Perrig, W. J. (2008). Improving fluid intelligence with training on working memory. *Proceedings of the National Academy of Sciences, 105*, 6829–6833.

Jensen, A. (2005). Mental chronometry and the unification of differential psychology. In R. J. Sternberg & J. E. Pretz (Eds.), *Cognition and intelligence: Identifying the mechanisms of the mind* (pp. 26–50). Cambridge: Cambridge University Press.

Jones, A. D., Cho, R. Y., Nystrom, L. E., Cohen, J. D., & Braver, T. S. (2002). A computational model of anterior cingulate function in speeded response tasks: Effects of frequency, sequence, and conflict. *Cognitive, Affective and Behavioral Neuroscience, 2*, 300–317.

Kahneman, D. (1973). *Attention and effort*. New York: Prentice Hall.

Kane, M. J. (2005). Full frontal fluidity? Looking in on the neuroimaging of reasoning and intelligence. In O. Wilhelm & R. W. Engle (Eds.), *Handbook of understanding and measuring intelligence* (pp. 141–164). Thousand Oaks, CA: Sage.

Kane, M. J., Conway, A. R. A., Hambrick, D. Z., & Engle, R. W. (2007). Variation in working memory capacity as variation in executive attention and control. In A. R. A. Conway, C. Jarrold, M. J. Kane, A. Miyake, & J. N. Towse (Eds.), *Variation in working memory* (pp. 21–48). Oxford: Oxford University Press.

Kane, M. J., Hambrick, D. Z., Tuholski, S. W., Wilhelm, O., Payne, T. W., & Engle, R. W. (2004). The generality of working memory capacity: A latent variable approach to verbal and visuo-spatial memory span and reasoning. *Journal of Experimental Psychology: General, 133*, 189–217.

Kyllonen, P. C., & Cristal, R. E. (1990). Reasoning ability is (little more than) working memory capacity. *Intelligence, 14*, 389–433.

Larson, G. E., Merritt, C. R., & Williams, S. E. (1988). Information processing and intelligence: Some implications of task complexity. *Intelligence, 1*, 131–147.

Lewandowsky, S., & Heit, E. (2006). Some targets for memory models. *Journal of Memory and Language, 55*, 441–446.

Logan, G. D., & Bundesen, C. (2003). Clever homunculus: Is there an endogenous act of control in the explicit task-cuing procedure? *Journal of Experimental Psychology: Human Perception and Performance, 29*, 575–599.

Logan, G. D., & Cowan, W. B. (1984). On the ability to inhibit thought and action: A theory of an act of control. *Psychological Review, 91*, 295–327.

Logan, G. D., & Gordon, R. D. (2001). Executive control of visual attention in dual-task situations. *Psychological Review, 108*, 393–434.

MacLeod, C. (1991). Half a century of research on the Stroop effect: An integrative review. *Psychological Bulletin, 109*, 163–203.

Mayes, J. T. (1988). On the nature of echoic persistence: Experiments with running memory. *Journal of Experimental Psychology: Learning, Memory & Cognition, 14*, 278–288.

McErlee, B. (2001). Working memory and focal attention. *Journal of Experimental Psychology: Learning, Memory, and Cognition, 27*, 817–835.

Miyake, A., Friedman, N. P., Emerson, M. J., Witzki, A. H., & Howerter, A. (2000). The unity and diversity of executive functions and their contributions to complex "frontal lobe" tasks: A latent variable analysis. *Cognitive Psychology, 41*, 49–100.

Moody, D. E. (2009). Can intelligence be increased by training on a task of working memory? *Intelligence, 37*, 327–328.

Monsell, S., & Driver, J. (2000). Banishing the control homunculus. In J. Driver & S. Monsell (Eds.), *Control of cognitive processes, attention and performance XVIII* (pp. 3–31). Cambridge, MA: MIT.

Navon, D. (1977). Forests before trees: The precedence of global features in visual perception. *Cognitive Psychology, 9*, 353–383.

Nęcka, E. (1994). *Inteligencja i Procesy Poznawcze*. [Intelligence and cognitive processing]. Cracow: Impuls.

Nęcka, E. (1996). The attentive mind: Intelligence in relation to selective attention, sustained attention, and dual task performance. *Polish Psychological Bulletin, 27*, 3–24.

Nęcka, E. (1997). Attention, working memory, and arousal: Concepts apt to account for the "process of intelligence". In G. Matthews (Ed.), *Cognitive science perspectives on personality and emotion* (pp. 503–554). Amsterdam: Elsevier Science.

Nęcka, E. (1999). Learning, automaticity, and attention: An individual differences approach. In P. L. Ackerman, P. C. Kyllonen, & R. D. Roberts (Eds.), *Learning and individual differences: Process, trait, and content determinants* (pp. 161–181). Washington, DC: American Psychological Association.

Norman, D. A., & Shallice, T. (1986). Attention and action: Willed and automatic control of behavior. In R. J. Davidson, G. E. Schwartz, & D. Shapiro (Eds.), *Consciousness and self-regulation: Advances in research and theory* (Vol. 4, pp. 1–18). New York: Plenum.

Oberauer, K., Schulze, R., Wilhelm, O., & Süß, H.-M. (2005). Working memory and intelligence – their correlation and their relation: Comment on Ackerman, Beier, and Boyle (2005). *Psychological Bulletin, 131*, 61–65.

Oberauer, K., Süß, H. M., Wilhelm, O., & Sander, N. (2007). Individual differences in working memory capacity and reasoning ability. In A. R. A. Conway, C. Jarrold, M. J. Kane, A. Miyake, & J. N. Towse (Eds.), *Variation in working memory* (pp. 49–75). Oxford: Oxford University Press.

Orzechowski, J., & Chuderski, A. (unpublished). *TAO figural analogy test: Test & manual*. Cracow: Institute of Psychology, Jagiellonian University.

Pashler, H. (1998). *The psychology of attention*. Cambridge, MA: MIT.

Paulewicz, B., Chuderski, A., & Nęcka, E. (2007). Insight problem solving, fluid intelligence, and executive control: A structural equation modeling approach. In S. Vosniadou, D. Kayser, & A. Protopapas (Eds.), *Proceedings of the 2nd European cognitive science conference* (pp. 586–591). Hove: Laurence Erlbaum.

Roberts, R. J., Hager, L. D., & Heron, C. (1994). Prefrontal cognitive processes: Working memory and inhibition in the antisaccade task. *Journal of Experimental Psychology: General, 123*, 374–393.

Rogers, R. D., & Monsell, S. (1995). Costs of a predictable switch between simple cognitive tasks. *Journal of Experimental Psychology: General, 124*, 207–231.

Salthouse, T., Fristoe, N., McGuthry, K. E., & Hambrick, D. Z. (1998). Relation of task switching to speed, age, and fluid intelligence. *Psychology and Aging, 13*, 445–461.

Schweizer, K. (1996). The speed-ability transition due to task complexity. *Intelligence, 22*, 115–128.

Schweizer, K., & Moosbrugger, H. (2004). Attention and working memory as predictors of intelligence. *Intelligence, 32*, 329–347.

Smith, E. E., & Jonides, J. (1999). Storage and executive processes in the frontal lobe. *Science, 283*, 1657–1661.

Smoleń, T., & Chuderski, A. (in press). Modeling adaptive strategies in Stroop with a new architecture of executive control. In S. Ohlsson & R. Catrambone (eds.). *Proceedings of the 32nd Annual Conference of Cognitive Science Society*. Austin, TX: Cognitive Science Society.

Spearman, C. (1927). *The abilities of man*. London: Macmillan.

Stankov, L. (1989). Attentional resources and intelligence: A disappearing link. *Personality and Individual Differences, 10*, 957–968.

Sternberg, R. J. (1985). *Beyond IQ: A triarchic theory of human intelligence*. Cambridge: Cambridge University Press.

Stettner, Z., & Nęcka, E. (2003). Pozytywny wpływ informacji zwrotnej na generowanie losowych interwałów czasowych [Positive influence of feedback on random interval generation]. *Studia Psychologiczne, 41*, 131–148.

Süß, H. M., Oberauer, K., Wittmann, W. W., Wilhelm, O., & Schulze, R. (2002). Working memory capacity explains reasoning ability – and a little bit more. *Intelligence, 30*, 261–288.

Thurstone, L. L. (1938). *Primary mental abilities*. Chicago: University of Chicago Press.

Turner, M. L., & Engle, R. W. (1989). Working memory capacity: An individual differences approach. *Journal of Memory and Language, 28*, 127–154.

Unsworth, N., & Engle, R. W. (2005). Working memory capacity and fluid abilities: Examining the correlation between Operation Span and Raven. *Intelligence, 33*, 67–81.

Unsworth, N., & Engle, R. W. (2006). The nature of individual differences in working memory capacity: Active maintenance in primary memory and controlled search from secondary memory. *Psychological Review, 114*, 104–132.

Whitney, P., Hinson, J. N., & Jameson, T. L. (2006). From executive control to self-control: Predicting problem drinking among college students. *Applied Cognitive Psychology, 20*, 823–835.

Wilson, B. A., Evans, J. J., Alderman, N., Burges, P. W., & Emslie, H. (1997). Behavioural assessment of the dysexecutive syndrome. In P. Rabbitt (Ed.), *Methodology of frontal and executive function* (pp. 239–250). Hove, UK: Psychology Press.

Wilson, W. H., Halford, G. S., Gray, B., & Phillips, S. (2001). The STAR-2 Model for mapping hierarchically structured analogs. In D. Gentner, K. J. Holyoak, & B. Kokinov (Eds.), *The analogical mind: Perspectives from cognitive science* (pp. 125–159). Cambridge, MA: MIT.

Chapter 17
Individual Differences in Attention: The Commentaries

Michael W. Eysenck, Gerald Matthews, Edward Nęcka, Adam Chuderski,
Karl Schweizer, and Błażej Szymura

Michael W. Eysenck

In this commentary, I will focus on a few key issues and priorities for future research on individual differences in attention. More specifically, I will consider the following: (a) the kinds of tasks that are most relevant for assessing attentional and executive processes; (b) attentional biases and cognitive performance; and (c) the most relevant dimensions of individual differences.

Tasks to Assess Attentional and Executive Processes

Even a rapid consideration of the burgeoning literature on attentional and executive processes indicates that researchers have used a bewildering number of different tasks to assess those processes. The situation is not dissimilar at a more theoretical level, where the number and nature of postulated executive processes vary considerably from one theorist to another. In my opinion, we can learn something from the field of psychometrics. It is acknowledged within psychometrics that it is crucially important at an early stage of research to establish an appropriate *taxonomy* in which major categories and their interrelationships are established. Thus, for example, factor analysis and other statistical methods have been used to demonstrate that five approximately orthogonal dimensions can account for much (or most) of the variation in personality across individuals. For reasons that are not entirely clear to me, cognitive psychology has only rarely adopted an analogous approach. However, I will briefly consider one relevant line of research.

As emphasized in my chapter in this book, Miyake et al. (2000) have attempted to provide a solid empirical basis for identifying major executive functions. In essence, they applied latent variable analysis to several tasks in order to establish which ones clustered together. This led them to identify three executive functions: the inhibition function; the shifting function; and the updating function. This approach has much to recommend and would be very desirable for future research to build on the foundation established by Miyake et al. (2000). However, Miyake et al.'s approach has three significant limitations. First, it is difficult to decide which tasks should be selected, and the outcome clearly depends importantly on those initial decisions. Second, close inspection of the patterns of the raw intertask correlations obtained by Miyake et al. indicates that even tasks allegedly involving the same underlying executive function typically correlated only moderately (+0.3 to +0.4) with each other. Third, the three executive functions all correlated positively with each other, suggesting that there may be a very general executive function as well as more specific ones.

What is the take-home message for future research? It would be desirable to have access to "process-pure" tasks that involved a single attentional or executive process. However, that does not seem to be possible. What may be the optimal approach is to carry out research along the lines adopted by Miyake et al. (2000), but using many more tasks under a greater variety of conditions.

Suppose we discovered that tasks x, y, and z all involve the same attentional or executive function. We could then administer all three tasks to groups varying along the individual differences dimension (e.g., trait anxiety). If consistent and theoretically predicted patterns of individual differences were found across all three tasks, this would provide reasonable evidence that the dimension of individual differences being studied has a significant impact on the attentional/executive function of interest. At the very least, this approach would be an improvement on the common approach of using a single task that is assumed (on very limited evidence) to assess a given function.

Attentional Biases and Cognitive Performance

Most research that has considered anxiety and attention falls into one of two categories. On the one hand, there is a considerable amount of research focusing on anxiety and attentional biases, in which the emphasis is on the impact of threat-related stimuli on patterns of attentional allocation. On the other hand, there is much research concerned with the notion that some of the effects of anxiety on cognitive performance are mediated by attentional processes. In such research, all of the task stimuli are typically neutral in terms of emotional valence.

One of the key assumptions underlying attentional control theory (Eysenck, Derakshan, Santos, & Calvo, 2007) is that we need a theoretical and empirical synthesis of these two contrasting approaches. More specifically, there should be more research on anxiety and cognitive performance that includes threat-related and neutral stimuli and in which attentional biases are assessed. For example, it is assumed within attentional control theory that anxious individuals are more distractible than nonanxious ones, and that this enhanced distractibility (and thus negative impact on performance) is greater when distracting stimuli are threat-related.

Dimensions of Individual Differences

The theoretical approach adopted by Williams, Watts, MacLeod, and Mathews (1997) has deservedly been very influential. However, there is increasing evidence that their key theoretical assumptions are oversimplified. In spite of that, the overarching notions that memory biases are more associated with depression than with anxiety whereas attentional biases are more associated with anxiety than with depression are of lasting value. Of relevance, Eysenck, Payne, and Santos (2006) found that anxiety tended to be associated with future-oriented threatening events whereas depression was associated with past-oriented threatening events.

What is the relevance of the above ideas to future research on individual differences in attentional processes? In essence, the nontask stimuli attended to by anxious and depressed individuals should differ in predictable ways. Depressed individuals often disengage from current environmental stimuli to focus on negative long-term memories. In contrast, anxious individuals are more engaged in attentional scanning of the environment and their internal focus tends to be on future worries and threats. It seems reasonable to conclude that a detailed analysis of the effects of anxiety and depression on attentional processes will form an important part of any comprehensive understanding of the effects of these emotional states on the cognitive system.

Gerald Matthews

Understanding individual differences in attention poses a number of challenges. Not the least of these are the well-known difficulties in conceptualizing and measuring both attention and individual differences as multidimensional constructs. Thus, the question of *how multiple dimensions of individual differences can be mapped onto multiple executive control functions of attention* is critical. Latent factor models of individual differences in the domains of ability and personality are much better developed than those for attention. Schweizer discusses the application of multistratum models of intelligence, for example, and personality models such as the Five Factor Model need little introduction. It remains unclear whether it is preferable to work with higher levels of these models (e.g., general intelligence, extraversion) or with more narrow, lower-level facets that may be more closely related to attention.

Research on the dimensionality of attention has been much less extensive, in part because of difficulties in sampling the universe of possible attentional tasks systematically. In addition, specific issues have proved problematic, such as whether a multitasking factor can be differentiated from dimensions defined by single-task performance. Fortunately, researchers (see Chuderski & Nęcka, Schweizer) are beginning to make more use of modern multivariate statistics in developing models of dimensions of attention as latent constructs. Another approach (see Eysenck) is to use neuropsychological accounts of multiple attentional circuits to inform individual difference research. Following the work of Akira Miyake, Eysenck differentiates inhibition, shifting and updating as separable executive functions that may map onto different aspects of individual differences.

The contributions to this section of the book show how theoretical and psychometric clarity assist in identifying the key mappings between constructs. I will note two unresolved issues. First, there seem to be disagreement among researchers on the optimal latent factor structure of attention. For example, by contrast with Eysenck, Schweizer argues for a single executive control factor – which does not include the shifting function described by Miyake. Second, there remains a tension between the view of attention emerging from cognitive neuroscience as a set of highly localized circuits and more integrative psychological models framed in relation to broad – but potentially elusive – constructs such as working memory and attentional resources (see Matthews et al.). As Schweizer discusses, hierarchical models may resolve this tension.

Better understanding of the latent factors that shape observed individual differences in attention naturally informs choice of *the optimal attentional tasks for investigating individual differences in attention*. The wide array of tasks used in past research, sometimes chosen on an ad hoc basis, has impeded progress. Even within a relatively narrowly defined area of inquiry, such as vigilance, findings may differ radically depending on the exact choice of task. In the case of selective attention, tasks such as the emotional Stroop and dot-probe task may have assumed a preeminent position for historical reasons, irrespective of whether they correspond well to latent constructs. It is premature to list a set of definitive tasks that do represent single latent constructs effectively, but the chapters in this section provide a number of illustrations of good practice in the area. The challenge that remains is to develop a test battery for a systematic evaluation of dimensions of attention. Progress requires the thorough validation and evaluation process described by Schlegel and Gilliland (2007).

Accordingly, improvements in measurement of attention should help to answer the long-standing question of whether *intelligence influences attentional performance more strongly in simple attentional tasks (according to Jensen) or rather in difficult ones (according to Stankov)*. Ideally, we could distinguish latent factors corresponding to the prototypical simple tasks (inspection time, choice reaction) and complex tasks (multitasking) used in this research. Schweizer's chapter provides one such resolution to the problem. Fluid intelligence relates to both perceptual control ("simple") and, independently, to executive control ("complex"). Chuderski & Nęcka offer a more fine-grained account of the executive control element. They reject the notion that intelligence relates to dual-tasking or working memory in any general sense. Rather, intelligence is specifically linked to inhibition and updating, specifically the controlled sequential scheduling of mental operations. Such analyses also help to move us beyond the simplistic notion of simplicity as a feature of tasks. Eysenck notes additional evidence that intelligence relates to updating, although not to inhibition. A general difficulty here is whether null results reflect the specific choice of tasks – do some but not all inhibition tasks relate to intelligence?

Moving from intelligence to personality, much research has addressed the issue of *how individual difference traits for emotionality (e.g., neuroticism, anxiety, depression) are connected with qualitative individual differences in attention, such as narrowing or broadening attentional focus*. Such research moves beyond the issue of how emotional factors may impact the overall efficiency of attention (e.g., Matthews et al.). In an earlier account of anxiety, Eysenck (1992) discussed the hypervigilance of anxious individuals. Initially, attentional focus is wide as the person monitors for threat, but narrows done following threat detection. Effects of this kind may be accommodated, at least to some degree within theories of executive functioning (Eysenck et al., 2007). Wells and Matthews (2006) argued that understanding qualitative attentional differences requires consideration of the *content* of attention and cognition. Top-down control of attention in part reflects the activation of schemas that guide search and prioritization of information. Although biasing effects of anxiety likely reflect both bottom-up and top-down mechanisms (Eysenck et al., 2007), theory in this area has yet to fully engage with the role of self-knowledge in actively directing attentional focusing. Wells and Matthews also discussed the key role of metacognition in regulating emotional experience and attention. Lubow and Kaplan make the interesting point that the hallucinations and delusions associated with schizophrenia may represent an adaptive attempt to impose order on the rush of stimuli admitted into consciousness by defective filtering. Again, we might expect the content of these experiences to correspond to personal concerns and self-knowledge.

The final, and related, issue is *the extent to which abnormality in attentional functioning explains individual differences in traits related to psychopathology*. As Lubow & Kaplan discuss, in the context of schizophrenia, correlations between pathological traits and attention are open to differing interpretations. The typical experimental study encourages a view of the (stable) trait as an influence on the (unstable) attentional function. For example, schizotypy may impair latent inhibition (Lubow and Kaplan) and trait anxiety may impair aspects of executive control (Eysenck). In addition, there is the intriguing possibility that abnormality in attention may actually be a cause of psychopathology. As Lubow and Kaplan discuss, failure to inhibit irrelevant or bizarre thoughts and ideation may be a source of vulnerability to schizophrenia. Recent experimental work (Wilson, MacLeod, Mathews, & Rutherford, 2006) has also suggested that attentional and interpretive biases towards threat may be causal influences on anxiety. Further progress may require the dynamic approach advocated by Wells and Matthews (2006). There may be a bidirectional relationship between anxiety and attention that develops and changes over time as abnormality in attention comes to influence the person's self-schema (e.g., overattention to threat leads to unrealistic negative self-beliefs). Similarly, Lubow and Kaplan state that the individual's attempt to cope with the breakdown of inhibition may shape the nature of their symptomatology.

In conclusion, the chapters in this section illustrate how integrating recent advances in cognitive theory, neuroscience, and psychometrics is providing us with better specification of the multiple relationships between individual difference constructs and attention. Causal modeling of these associations remains a major challenge and may require more attention to dynamic self-regulative processes.

1. How can multiple dimensions of individual differences be mapped onto multiple executive control functions of attention?

Edward Nęcka and Adam Chuderski

Controlled, or executive, attention seems to be related first of all to general fluid intelligence. In our opinion, intelligence is largely accounted for by efficiency of cognitive control. The data showing strong links between intelligence and working memory also suggest that it is the controlling aspect of working memory that counts as a correlate of general fluid intelligence, although there are various interpretations of this relationship. One possibility is that both effectiveness of executive control and some storage or attentional capacity independently influence the level of fluid intelligence.

Another question is, which aspects of cognitive control, also known as executive functions, are more or less important as correlates of intelligence. For instance, task switching does not do quite well in this "job," maybe due to the fact that many task switching tasks require automatic rather than controlled performance. On the other hand, working memory updating or goal monitoring appears to be much more important for general fluid intelligence. Our own work suggests that executive control over coordination of multiple cognitive processes, often referred to as divided attention, contributes significantly to fluid ability.

Błażej Szymura

M. W. Eysenck's (see this volume) future research suggestion – to find dimensions of individual differences relating in different ways to different executive control functions of attention – seems very promising. This kind of research should help in assessing the number and in describing the nature of executive functions as related to different individual difference traits. However, this kind of experimental studies should be – in my opinion – restricted rather to personality area. General abilities (e.g., intelligence, creativity) are related positively to almost each already detected executive function of attention. Indeed, there is some existing evidence that individual differences in intelligence do not allow to predict the performance on the tasks requiring inhibition or shifting functions (e.g., Friedman et al., 2006). However, Nęcka (1999) found intelligence significantly related to strength of inhibition in Navon interference task. Also, creativity correlated with strength of inhibition in Stroop task (Groborz & Nęcka, 2003) and effectiveness of shifting (Szymura, Śmigasiewicz, & Corr, 2007). Instead, the groups of personality traits seem related to different executive control functions in different ways. It is predicted here that anxiety (see M. W. Eysenck, this volume), neuroticism (as strongly related to anxiety), and psychoticism (weakness of inhibition hypothesis; H. J. Eysenck, 1992) should be related to inhibition and shifting, whereas impulsivity and extraversion (see the outcomes of some STM studies) – to updating. The confirmation of such hypothesis will suggest that updating function can be differentiated on the base of different individual differences correlates from shifting and inhibition functions (the same individual differences correlates).

2. Does intelligence influence attentional performance more strongly in simple attentional tasks (according to Jensen) or rather in difficult ones (according to Stankov)?

Edward Nęcka and Adam Chuderski

First of all, we are not convinced that intelligence "influences" attentional performance because it is quite possible that intelligence is influenced itself by attention. According to the top-down mode of explanation, intelligence – understood as general cognitive ability – accounts for basic cognitive skills, including attentional skills. However, one must not ignore another possibility, namely, that intelligence – being a rather complex skill – needs to be accounted for by quite simple and well operationalized factors, like cognitive speed, attention, or working memory. The second possibility is based on the top-down mode of explanation. Which of these positions will be adopted by a theoretician is a question of his/her preferences rather than of "hard" scientific data. It is obvious that correlational approach, including the regression model, allows for both lines of theorizing.

So, let us redefine the question: is intelligence connected more strongly with attentional parameters in simple or difficult tasks? In our opinion, the relationship of intelligence with attention occurs in both situations, although different indices of attentional performance will appear significant as correlates of intelligence. If a task is relatively simple, the general mental ability appears to correlate with chronometric indices (e.g., speed of selection), whereas if a task is relatively complex, intelligence tends to correlate with accuracy. There are some empirical results supporting this position (e.g., Schweizer, Nęcka).

There are two problems with complex task, though. Firstly, such a task may be quite difficult to interpret in terms of specific attentional processes that are necessary to deal with it. In other words, we do not know what such a test tests. Secondly, such a task is bound to correlate with general intelligence because, by definition, general intellectual ability is necessary to deal with any cognitive task of some difficulty. So, it seems to us that using complex cognitive tasks may be quite risky unless one intends to investigate some specific issues, such as strategies of dealing with complex tasks.

Karl Schweizer

In the eyes of many of my colleagues and in my own eyes, the question is a bit misleading. It suggests that intelligence is something that is different from cognitive and biological structures and units where cognitive and biological denote two different perspectives of basically the same things. These colleagues and I would prefer the reformulation of the question into "Do the cognitive and biological sources of intelligence including relevant attention components influence performance in completing simple attentional tasks (according to Jensen) more strongly than in completing difficult ones (according to Stankov)?"

After reading all the chapter of this section, the reader remains with the impression that the executive functions are likely to generate individual differences in performance that correlate with performance in completing measures of intelligence. The importance of executive functions is highlighted in the chapters by Chuderski and Nęcka, Eysenck, Matthews, Warm, Reinerman, Langheim and Saxby, and in my own chapter. Furthermore, in a more indirect way, Szymura also stresses the importance of the executive function. Therefore, the first attempt of answering the question must be made from the perspective of executive functions.

Since executive functions are associated with working memory, it can be assumed that they preferably contribute to completing working memory tasks. Most working memory tasks are quite difficult or complex, which is the characterization preferred by Stankov. Differences in performance according to working memory tasks are usually differences in accuracy whereas processing time is not a good indicator of efficiency. The problem is that complex tasks allow for various processing plans so that the variability in processing time is partly due to differences between the processing plans. Therefore, the answer to the question must be in favor of the difficult option, as it is proposed by Stankov.

But nevertheless, the answer concerning the easy option must be considered carefully. As I indicated in my chapter, attention is not a unitary concept. Therefore, the emphasis in the chapters of this section on attention as executive functions does not exclude the possibility that there are other components or types of attention being relevant with respect to attention and that these components of types substantially influence performance in completing simple attentional tasks.

Błażej Szymura

Intelligence is related to each type of attention and influences performance in all attentional tasks (Schweizer, Moosbrugger, & Goldhammer, 2005). However, intelligence can improve both or only one of the performance indexes: correctness and speed of attentional processing. In easy tasks, usually no differences in performance correctness are observed. Low and high intelligent people can differ then only in speed of their reactions. In difficult tasks, only small differences in the speed of solution finding are observed. Low and high intelligent people use similar amount of time to prepare their reactions but differ in their correctness. That is why Jensen (2005) – using simple RT tasks – obtained the same strong relationship (0.3–0.6) between intelligence and speed of attentional processing as Stankov (2005) revealed between intelligence and correctness of attentional processing in complex dual tasks. Schweizer (1996a, 1996b) confirmed that the correlation between intelligence and speed of attentional processing could drop from 0.5 to 0.2 and the correlation between intelligence and correctness of attentional processing could rise from 0.2 to 0.5 with increment of the task complexity. Thus, intelligence influences attentional performance with similar power in simple and difficult attentional tasks, but its impact differs in quality.

3. To what extent does abnormality in attentional functioning explain individual differences in traits related to psychopathology?

Edward Nęcka and Adam Chuderski

Some behavioral disorders, like ADHD, are rooted in attentional deficits by definition. There is also plenty of data suggesting the existence of links between attentional bias and anxiety. Anxious people may be sensitive to signals of threat; therefore, they need less time to detect a stimulus that is a symptom of potential danger. Such people are also unable to ignore stimuli that are somehow associated, even symbolically, with danger, risk, or threat. This phenomenon is best exemplified by specific experimental methods, such as clinical version of the Stroop task. A person is confronted with negative words (e.g., "loss" or "accident") that are made with different colors. The task is to ignore the meaning of words in order to concentrate on their color. It is usually easier to ignore the meaning of neutral words than the meaning of negative words, which is a phenomenon called attentional bias. This effect is relatively more salient in the case of anxious or neurotic people. Michael W. Eysenck argues that anxiety may be accounted for by hypersensitivity to threatening stimuli: the more one's attention is biased toward negative events, the higher level of one's anxiety, and the higher level of anxiety, the more one's attention is biased. This theory may be useful to understand trait anxiety at least in some cases but it seems quite possible that another group of anxious people show the opposite patterns, namely, the tendency to ignore signals of threat. Regardless of an individual strategy of coping with threat, the phenomenon of trait anxiety seems to be closely connected with some kind of attentional bias.

Another line of research deals with links between deficits in controlled attention and behavioral and social anomalies. For example, some data show that people who have problems with response inhibition in simple tasks more easily fall into addiction (e.g., problem drinking). Other data show that children with genetic disorders resulting in impaired social skills perform badly also in executive tests. These results are supported by neuroimaging research, which shows decreased activity in brain structures associated with controlled processing (like anterior cingulate cortex) in people often undertaking risky, dangerous behavior. Numerous behavioral anomalies, such as addictions, eating disorders (e.g., bulimia or anorexia), abnormal purchase, poorly controlled sexuality, or criminal acts, seem to be related to disturbed self-control (for a comprehensive review, see Baumeister & Vohs, 2004). However, strong empirical support for these accounts, which explains directly how attentional and executive deficits result in high-level traits related to social pathologies, is still very scarce.

4. How are individual difference traits for emotionality (e.g., neuroticism, anxiety, depression) connected with qualitative individual differences in attention, such as narrowing or broadening attentional focus?

Edward Nęcka and Adam Chuderski

First of all, we doubt whether it is advisable to postulate the existence of "qualitative" differences in attention. Broadening or narrowing one's attentional focus can be accounted for in terms of quantitative differences. If some trait is a bipolar dimension, every person can be described as occupying a specific point on the continuum rather than representing one out of several "qualitative" categories. Researchers often divide their samples into two, three, or four "qualitative" subgroups according to an arbitrary criterion (e.g., median point or quartiles) but this procedure does not allow claiming that any qualitatively separate modes of attentional functioning do really exist. Moreover, the broadening/narrowing dimension seems to refer to intraindividual differences better than to differences between individuals. Everyone can make his/her attention more or less broad or narrow according to the context or task demands. It does not imply that some of us may feel (or perform) better in one of these states of attention. Some of us may therefore prefer one of these states, and such preferences may be correlated with other dimensions of individual differences. It seems that the broadening/narrowing dimension is relevant for creativity, understood both as latent disposition and actual achievement. It is well established that creative individuals tend to be more susceptible to distraction, as if their attentional filter was "leaking."

5. What are the optimal attentional tasks for investigating individual differences in attention?

Edward Nęcka and Adam Chuderski

In general, individual differences are best investigated with tasks that generate a great deal of variance. If there were no variability in human cognitive performance, there would be no room for studying individual differences. Such a possibility is purely hypothetical. However, it is fairly possible that some individual differences, although actually in existence, are severely restricted in range. If a cognitive skill is relatively basic, simple, and "old" from the evolutionary point of view, its range of intraindividual variability may be severely narrowed. Which skills of this kind belong to the broad category of attentional phenomena is a further question, but undoubtedly, the more automatic a function is, the less variability may be observed concerning its level of individual performance. For instance, the parameters of Posner's orienting subsystem of attention seem to be less dependent on the general rule of individual differences than the parameters of the executive subsystem. It would be quite interesting to know what the range of individual differences in the case of such phenomena as inhibition of return or detection of movement in the visual field is, but it seems that their variance must be rather restricted. It does not mean that individual differences in such processes are impossible, or inadvisable, to study. On the contrary, we need to know which attentional skills are relatively more or less susceptible to vary across individuals. However, if we are not interested in individual differences in attention itself but look for attentional correlates of higher-level traits, such as intelligence or personality, we must take into account the risk of not finding anything interesting. Restriction of range inevitably leads to lowering of correlation coefficients, even to the nil value, due to the well-known statistical rule that if almost everybody do at the almost top level of performance, a measured skill cannot correlate with anything.

Błażej Szymura

The answer depends primarily on accepted definition of attention. If selection (detecting signals while ignoring noises and distractors) is the main or even the only one attentional function (Broadbent, 1971), the optimal attention tasks should be relatively easy and performance on these tasks should not rely on resources management. Flanker Test (Eriksen & Eriksen, 1974) and Letter Categorization Task (Posner & Mitchel, 1967) seem good examples of experimental tasks on selection as the main attentional function. Indeed, there are some evidence that performance on easy selection tasks is individually differentiated (e.g., Matthews & Dorn, 1989, showed that searching for signal characterized by nondistinctive feature is differentiated with regard to intelligence).

However, if attention is a multidimensional, unitary concept (Johnston & Heinz, 1978; Nęcka, 1997), studying the only one chosen attentional function (e.g., selection) means ignoring the other valid aspects of attention (e.g., division of attention and attentional resources management, shifting attention between the tasks, broadening and narrowing attention, sustained attention, etc.). The complex and difficult tests (e.g., DIVA, Nęcka, 1997; see Szymura this volume) that allow to measure various aspects of attention at the same time seem therefore the best task to investigate more fully attentional functions. They seem also better for investigating individual differences in attention due to its complexity and difficulty, because usually (except general abilities, see answer to question 1) individual differences in attentional processing turn out to be visible only when the attentional task is demanding enough (Szymura & Nęcka, 2005). Thus, in the future studies, the use of the demanding tests based on the unitary, multidimensional concept of attention, rather than use simple attentional tasks will allow mapping multiple dimensions of temperament and personality onto multiple aspects or functions of attention.

References

Baumeister, R. F., & Vohs, K. D. (Eds.). (2004). *Handbook of self-regulation*. New York: Guilford.
Broadbent, D. E. (1971). *Decision and stress*. London: Academic.
Eriksen, B. A., & Eriksen, C. W. (1974). Effects of noise letters upon the identification of a target letter in a nonsearch task. *Perception and Psychophysics, 16*, 143–149.
Eysenck, M. W. (1992). *Anxiety: The cognitive perspective*. Hove, UK: Lawrence Erlbaum Associates.
Eysenck, M. W. (this volume). *Attentional control theory of anxiety: Recent developments*.
Eysenck, M. W., Derakshan, N., Santos, R., & Calvo, M. G. (2007). Anxiety and cognitive performance: Attentional control theory. *Emotion, 7*, 336–353.
Eysenck, M. W., Payne, S., & Santos, R. (2006). Anxiety and depression: Past, present, and future events. *Cognition and Emotion, 20*, 274–294.
Friedman, N. P., Miyake, A., Corley, R. P., Young, S. E., Defries, J. C., & Hewitt, J. K. (2002). Not all executive functions are related to intelligence. *Psychological Science, 17*(2), 172–179.
Groborz, M., & Nęcka, E. (2003). Creativity and cognitive control: Exploration of generation and evaluation skills. *Creativity Research Journal, 15*, 183–197.
Jensen, A. R. (2005). Mental chronometry and the unification of differential psychology. In R. J. Sternberg & J. E. Pretz (Eds.), *Cognition and intelligence* (pp. 26–50). Cambridge: Cambridge University Press.
Johnston, W. A., & Heinz, S. P. (1978). Flexibility and capacity demands of attention. *Journal of Experimental Psychology: General, 107*, 420–435.
Matthews, G., & Dorn, L. (1989). IQ and choice reaction time: An information processing analysis. *Intelligence, 13*, 299–317.
Miyake, A., Friedman, N. P., Emerson, M. J., Wizki, A. H., Howerter, A., & Wager, T. D. (2000). The unity and diversity of executive functions and their contributions to complex "frontal lobe" tasks: A latent variable analysis. *Cognitive Psychology, 41*, 49–100.
Nęcka, E. (1997). Attention, working memory and arousal: concepts apt to account for "the process of intelligence". In G. Matthews (Ed.), *Cognitive science perspectives on personality end emotion* (pp. 503–554). Amsterdam: Elsevier Science.
Nęcka, E. (1999). Creativity and attention. *Polish Psychological Bulletin, 30*, 85–97.

Posner, M. I., & Mitchel, R. F. (1967). Chronometric analysis of classification. *Psychological Review, 74*, 392–409.

Schlegel, R. E., & Gilliland, K. (2007). Development and quality assurance of computer-based assessment batteries. *Archives of Clinical Neuropsychology, 22*(1), S49–S61.

Schweizer, K. (1996a). Level of encoding, preattentive processing and working memory capacity as sources of cognitive ability. *Personality and Individual Differences, 21*, 759–766.

Schweizer, K. (1996b). The speed-accuracy transition due to task complexity. *Intelligence, 22*, 115–128.

Schweizer, K., Moosbrugger, H., & Goldhammer, F. (2005). The structure of the relationship between attention and intelligence. *Intelligence, 33*, 589–611.

Stankov, L. (2005). Reductionism versus charting: Ways of examining the role o lower-order cognitive processes in intelligence. In R. J. Sternberg & J. E. Pretz (Eds.), *Cognition and intelligence* (pp. 51–67). Cambridge: Cambridge University Press.

Szymura, B., & Nęcka, E. (2005). Three superfactors of personality and three aspects of attention. In A. Eliasz, S. E. Hampson, & B. de Raad (Eds.), *Advances in personality psychology* (pp. 75–90). Hove: Psychology Press.

Szymura, B., Śmigasiewicz, K., & Corr, P. J. J. (2007). Psychoticism and flexibility of attention. *Personality and Individual Differences, 43*, 2033–2046.

Wells, A., & Matthews, G. (2006). Cognitive vulnerability to anxiety disorders: An integration. In L. B. Alloy & J. H. Riskind (Eds.), *Cognitive vulnerability to emotional disorders* (pp. 303–325). Hillsdale, NJ: Lawrence Erlbaum.

Williams, J. M. G., Watts, F. N., MacLeod, C., & Mathews, A. (1997). *Cognitive psychology and emotional disorders* (2nd ed.). Chichester, UK: Wiley.

Wilson, E. J., MacLeod, C., Mathews, A., & Rutherford, E. M. (2006). The causal role of interpretive bias in anxiety reactivity. *Journal of Abnormal Psychology, 115*, 103–111.

Part IV
Individual Differences in Working Memory Functioning and Higher-Order Processing

Chapter 18
Trait and State Differences in Working Memory Capacity

Małgorzata Ilkowska and Randall W. Engle

Trait and State Differences in Working Memory Capacity

Everyday, we use the limited resources of working memory (WM) across situations. For example, we use them as we drive to work attempting to create and maintain a list of tasks and meetings for the day. In this situation, imagine that an unexpected phone call informs us that two meetings have been rescheduled: a first one for a different time today and a second one for tomorrow. After receiving this message, we attempt to update our newly created task list within WM to incorporate the new meeting times. At the same time, we resist interference from the new information we have received from the recent phone call and from other thoughts that this call has brought to mind. Bear in mind that all this happens while we are driving a car, a task that is entirely different from creating, maintaining, and updating our schedule for the day. Some of us manage these tasks simultaneously without much effort, whereas some of us cannot perform this sequence successfully, forgetting half of today's tasks or making the wrong turn. To complicate this picture, individual differences in managing information in WM partly stem from temporary states of mind that influence a successful management of the task at hand. Let us imagine that the driver had to prepare a talk for one of today's meetings and spent the whole night preparing. In addition, she might have had an argument with her spouse in the morning. Thus, she might have experienced sleep deprivation, stress, anxiety, and fatigue, which are additional factors that often worsen our ability to utilize WM.

As the example above shows, the ability to effectively use and share the resources of WM is influenced by both stable and variable characteristics. In the complex WM system, different representations are temporarily stored in various formats, where attention control processes also interact to maintain and update temporarily active information. In our example, the driver's daily schedule is the maintained information, and the rescheduling is updating the existing information to the new situation. Additionally, this example includes other information, such as thoughts unrelated to either driving or the daily schedule, extraneous information treated as irrelevant to the task. Such information usually accompanies the current goal and most of the time has to be suppressed or inhibited.

Our chapter reviews research that examines individual differences in working memory capacity (WMC) across variety of tasks. We argue that these individual differences may reflect both a person's abiding traits as well as factors related to momentary fluctuations in a person's behavior and thoughts. We also look at possible implications in normal individuals as well as those suffering from psychopathology.

M. Ilkowska (✉) and R.W. Engle
School of Psychology, Georgia Institute of Technology, 654 Cherry Street, Atlanta, GA 30332-0710, USA
e-mail: ilkowska@gatech.edu

Processes Important in Working Memory

In our example, we have named only a subset of processes crucial for proper functioning of a complex WM system. WM comprises not only the processes needed for exerting proper memory strategies in order to complete a specific goal, such as encoding, maintenance, and retrieval, but also controlled attention. Controlled attention allows focusing on the relevant information. WM differs from short-term memory by the presence of this attention component. Attentional control influences performance on complex executive tasks differently at subsequent stages of processing, from encoding, maintenance, shifting, updating, and making decisions to responding.

Maintenance and updating are crucial components of WM. The maintenance of a current goal involves keeping information active for temporary processing and using that information for completing the task. Updating, on the other hand, allows focusing attention on new information, so that we can change our strategies or ways to approach the goal state. Furthermore, updating allows new information to become the focus of attention. Thus, information focused previously is either overwritten or allowed to decay. Therefore, the ability to successfully maintain and update information is pivotal in utilizing WM resources, especially in the face of distractors and other irrelevant material usually accompanying the relevant information. Later in processing, using the maintained information to guide selection of the appropriate response becomes especially important when an alternative option is prepotent but contextually inappropriate. In our example, the driver may need to stop to get coffee after having such a rough night. However, she must turn right at an intersection where she normally turns left to get to work. If she is temporarily distracted, she may fall into the habit of getting in the left lane before realizing she had intended to pick up her coffee.

In sum, WM differently influences performance on complex executive tasks whether we keep goals active in memory, update, or manipulate its content by inhibiting prepotent responses or switching between tasks. Inhibiting irrelevant information usually interleaves with maintaining relevant information and with updating the content in order to accommodate a new situation. How to study such a complex net of interrelated processes?

Researchers choose an array of approaches to examine WM processes and its relation to cognitive functioning. Some researchers focus on examining distinct subsets of processes important in successful functioning of WM. For example, Nigg (2000; Nigg, Carr, Martel, & Henderson, 2007) focuses on one specific process of inhibitory control to examine functioning of WM in healthy and in attention-deficit hyperactivity disorder (ADHD) patient population. He discusses a related process of disinhibition to denote it as one of the major impairments of executive control in ADHD. Other researchers attempt to reconcile all the processes important in WM in a more general framework of executive functioning and treat this general frame as a starting point in disentangling the most important processes in higher-order cognitive functioning (Barkley, 2001; Friedman & Miyake, 2004; Miyake, Friedman, Emerson, Witzki, & Howerter, 2000; Shimamura, 2000). For example, Miyake and colleagues (2000) proposed three processes important in executive control: inhibiting prepotent responses, updating WM, and shifting between tasks. Schmeichel (2007), on the other hand, contrasts inhibition and updating with maintenance claiming that attention control as well as response inhibition and exaggeration have similar effects on executive control and on subsequent task performance. Finally, Oberauer, Süß, Wilhelm, and Wittman (2003) distinguish three processes important in WM: simultaneous storage and processing, supervision important in task switching, and coordination of different task elements important in process monitoring.

Working Memory Models

A common feature of numerous working memory models (cf. Miyake & Shah, 1999) is the presence of a central control unit that controls types and levels of processing, disposing commands executed by subordinate components. Probably the most influential amongst a variety of WM models is the model proposed by Baddeley and Hitch (1974). This model assumes that WM is a multicomponent system important for variety of cognitive tasks. Comprising storage and processing, the model has three components: the central executive and two slave systems. The slave systems are responsible for processing of verbal, speech-based information (articulatory loop) and visual-spatial information (visual-spatial sketchpad). The central executive, on the other hand, flexibly allocates the processing and storage components of the WM system. Norman and Shallice (1986) introduced similar conceptualization of the executive component, based on the concept of spreading activation, which they labeled the supervisory attentional system (SAS; see also Shallice & Burgess, 1993). In this model, automatic activation of schemas driven by goals and contextual information provides the base for information intended for different levels and spreading activation. This results in higher activation of some schemas and inhibition of others. In some situations, the limited capacity SAS intervenes by redirecting and giving schemas appropriate priorities, inhibiting those incompatible with a current goal. Finally, Cowan's model (1988, 1997) introduces the central executive and a limited capacity focus of attention that controls processes and levels of activation of various memory representations within long-term memory.

Not all models, however, implicate the presence of a central control unit. For example, Schneider and Detweiler (1987) proposed a model based on parallel distributed processing that differentiates between automatic and controlled processes (see also Posner & Snyder, 1975; Feldman Barrett, Tugade, & Engle, 2004; Shiffrin & Schneider, 1984). In this model, controlled processes have replaced the central control unit. These processes distributed across modules of a specific modality and context decide what information to transmit and in what order. Recent conceptualizations refer to the mutual existence of controlled and automatic processes and the most recent model incorporates a control network at the neural level comprising multiple brain areas that play a crucial role in controlling a range of cognitive operations (Chein & Schneider, 2005; Schneider & Chein, 2003).

Working Memory Capacity

WMC as a Control of Attention

Top-down control is important for executive attention as well as for processing and storing information, especially under interference. Our view of WM as control of attention in an online fashion ties together two cognitive processes, attention control and memory (Engle, 2001; Engle, Tuholski, Laughlin, & Conway, 1999; Engle & Kane, 2004; Kane, Bleckley, Conway, & Engle, 2001; Kane & Engle, 2002). Attention control mechanism is alike the concept of limited-capacity central executive in the three WM models described earlier: Baddeley and Hitch's (1974), Norman & Shallice's SAS as well as the control network (Schneider & Chein, 2003).

According to Unsworth and Engle (2007), individual differences in WMC stem mainly from fluctuations in the ability to maintain information active in primary memory and from efficient search and retrieval of information stored in the secondary memory. The authors suggest that individuals low in WMC are poorer in executing these two processes and, as in our example, they may take the wrong turn while simultaneously driving and updating the daily schedule. Thus, both primary memory and secondary memory play a vital role in active maintenance and retrieval of goal-related information.

Trait and State WMC

WMC is important across different domains, contexts, and perspectives, including cognitive, social, and emotional information processing (Redick, Heitz, & Engle, 2007; Unsworth, Heitz, & Engle, 2005). Thus, we deploy resources reserved for WM and attention across numerous situations.

If we presume that WM is crucial in situations where controlled processing must take the precedence upon automatic processing, we thus assume that controlled processes are executed while maintaining and retrieving relevant information. Execution of control processes allows discarding irrelevant representations and resisting temptation to respond in a prepotent way (Conway & Engle, 1994; Rosen & Engle, 1997). Attention control prevents opting for prepotent responses inappropriate to the current task, facilitating selection of responses of a low strength when needed (Kane & Engle, 2003). However, the same resources used in cognitive control are most likely influenced by a variety of situational factors. As our example shows, at the same time we inhibit task-unrelated thoughts and resolve conflict between the priorities of driving a car and updating the daily schedule.

Given the conceptualization of WMC as the ability to control attention involved in active information processing in primary memory and retrieval from secondary memory, we introduce further differentiation of the processes important in conceptualization of WMC as a state and trait. Next, we discuss how the execution of effortful control influences the resources used for temporary states and those determined by biological factors. We describe WMC as a trait and state looking at genetic, neurotransmitters, and brain structures important in higher-order cognition, as well as biological and personality situational factors influencing cognitive abilities in a temporary fashion.

Measures of WMC: Revealing Trait Underpinnings of Individual Differences in WMC

Individual differences in the ability to control attention are especially pronounced while attempting to resist a prepotent response when not desired, resist interference of irrelevant information, or when WM demands are high. Tasks measuring individual differences in WMC attempt to mimic these exact situations. Studies examining this phenomenon divide the sample into groups based on the performance on complex tasks, such as operation span, reading span, and symmetry span, using serial recall as a measure of how much person can hold in memory while also performing a secondary task. Then, high and low WMC individuals are compared on a target task examining processes important in WM functioning. People high in WMC usually outperform those low in WMC on a wide array of cognitive tasks. Specifically, when under cognitive or emotional load, people low in WMC are worse in inhibiting irrelevant information, or in other words, are worse in keeping just relevant information active in memory, whether it is updating or maintaining a goal defined by the task.

The pioneering research started from Daneman and Carpenter's (1980) investigation of the relationship between reading comprehension and scores from the Scholastic Aptitude Test (SAT). High correlations between scores on WMC task and performance on the verbal SAT showed by Daneman and Carpenter (1980) prompted researchers to investigate the relationship between WMC and cognitive performance across different tasks and domains. The studies overall agree that the WMC construct is domain general as shown by similar relationships holding across domains and for simple and complex tasks (Conway, Cowan, Bunting, Therriault, & Minkoff, 2002; Conway & Engle, 1996; Engle, Kane, & Tuholski, 1999; Engle, Tuholski, et al., 1999; Feldman Barrett et al., 2004; Kane et al., 2004). Similarly, as Schneider and Chein (2003) proposed, cognitive control mechanisms are domain general, too.

Complex span tasks are dual tasks engaging both processing and storage components. In Daneman and Carpenter's (1980) reading span task (RSPAN), participants read sentences and recall the last word from each sentence in sets from two to seven. In another complex span task, the operation span task (OSPAN; Turner & Engle, 1989; see also Conway et al., 2005), participants solve math problems and remember words placed after each equation in the set, as in the following example: "Is $8/2+5=6$? (yes/no), TREE". At the end of each set, participant recalls all words from the set in a correct serial order.

Again, individual differences in WMC are observed in situations requiring controlled attention, such as when deciding between conflicting responses involving automatic versus controlled mode of responding and when the circumstances require dealing with interference between relevant and to-be-ignored information. If we assume that low WMC individuals are more likely to use automatic way of responding, they should be hurt more when pushed to respond in a less habitual manner. On the other hand, high WMC individuals should perform better in such situations due to their better ability to inhibit prepotent response in favor of a more controlled choice when a situation requires it. Indeed, the results of various studies examining individual differences in WMC show this pattern of performance differences between extreme WMC groups across different tasks and domains. Next, we turn to the more detailed discussion aimed at investigating individual differences in WMC as controlled attention.

Auditory domain. The amazing feature of a human auditory system is the ability to attend selectively to relevant information by quickly directing attention to important information and filtering out all irrelevant information treated as a noise. Individuals vary in the ability to detect an important stimulus in the presence of a noise, but we do not always know when or where this critical information will appear. For example, in one situation a person may need to attend selectively to one stimulus instead of another, whereas another situation requires the person to divide attention between two stimuli of an equal importance. In some situations, being suddenly captured by a salient stimulus from the environment is advantageous, as when somebody is calling your name and you are able to direct your attention to the person that have just called you. This effect of noticing your own name among the host of the surrounding sounds defines the famous "cocktail party effect" (Cherry, 1953). The nature of the dichotic listening task that acts upon this effect is to have participants repeat aloud words heard in one ear while attempting to ignore information fed into the other ear (Moray, 1959). At one point in the experiment, the participant's own name is fed to the to-be-ignored auditory channel. Studies indicate that the number of those reporting hearing their name differs for high and low WMC spans. Specifically, in one version of the task just outlined, Conway, Cowan, and Bunting (2001) found that high spans report hearing their name less frequently than low spans (20 and 65%, respectively). Thus, low WMC individuals show poorer ability to block distracting, task-irrelevant information. Interestingly, in a follow-up study, Colflesh and Conway (2007) observed an opposite pattern, showing that 67% of high spans and 35% of low spans reported hearing their name during a dichotic listening task. However, in this version, participants were told in advance to listen for their own name to appear at some point during the experiment.

Thus, when comparing the results of these two studies, in the shadowing task that requires recruiting selective attention to one channel, WMC is thought to be important in focusing on the shadowed channel and blocking signal processing of the ignored channel. As was shown, low spans are more likely to report hearing their name, likely because they are less able to sustain focused attention to the appropriate auditory input. Interestingly, the only shadowing errors that low spans exhibited were around the time their name was presented in the to-be-ignored channel. Therefore, not all distractors impair performance of low spans but only those of a particular salience, such as their own name. In contrast, successful performance on the divided attention task requires simultaneous monitoring of multiple sensory inputs. High spans reported hearing their name more often, suggesting that they used the advanced instruction to change their method of processing for the competing auditory information. Thus, although the pattern of results changed across the two experiments, the findings make sense when one considers that in both cases high spans utilized attention in a flexible manner to achieve the task goal successfully.

Visual domain. Focusing towards a new stimulus in the environment is a natural response that can be elicited even in newborns. Similarly, an attempt to search efficiently and quickly for a particular feature among various other stimuli may be a matter of life and death in a natural environment. Researchers investigating individual differences in WMC in visual selective attention tasks report similar patterns of results as in auditory selective attention. If high WMC spans have better ability to focus on relevant information or, in other words, are better at filtering out the irrelevant information, they should be less distracted by stimuli that are incompatible with the correct response. This hypothesis has been investigated in the flanker task (Eriksen & Eriksen, 1974). In the flanker task, participants are instructed to identify a central target letter surrounded by distractor letters. Distractor letters are either the same (compatible) or differ from the neighboring letters (incompatible). Heitz and Engle (2007) demonstrated that, given sufficient amount of time, high and low spans were both able to achieve high accuracy, even on incompatible trials. However, when instructions encouraged faster processing, high spans achieved ceiling performance on incompatible trials much faster than low spans did. Heitz & Engle interpreted their results as indicating the importance of WMC in selective attending to targets, as the group differences were only obtained with the interfering incompatible distractors.

Assuming that WMC describes the ability to control attention, comprising elements of memory and attention, the simpler explanation that high spans just learn faster due to more resources used seems not likely (see discussion in Heitz & Engle, 2007; Engle & Kane, 2004; Conway et al., 2002; Kane et al., 2001; but see Norman & Bobrow, 1975). As noted earlier, individual differences in WMC emerge for conflicting trials, for example, on incompatible trials bearing high interference. It might well be that high spans simply are able to better utilize and allocate resources to fight interference, not differing in the amount of resources available. Thus, considering faster learning, if high spans were simply faster, the differences between the span groups would have been seen across trial types, for example both incompatible and compatible trial types. In another words, span differences are seen in situations requiring effortful control, such as the ability to overcome habitual response or suppress irrelevant information. Note that span differences dissipate in compatible trials where no conflict is involved and response that is more automatic is facilitated.

Another characteristic that differentiates high and low spans is the ability to suppress a prepotent response when a task requires it. In the antisaccade task (Hallett, 1978), a visual stimulus is presented that indicates where the participant is going to direct attention. The direction of looking differs across trials being towards (prosaccade) or away (antisaccade) from the flickering cue. The natural reaction is to look at novel and changing stimuli in the environment, and, as such, the antisaccade condition defines a situation where one must prevent being captured by the prepotent response (Kane et al., 2001; Unsworth, Schrock, & Engle, 2004).

In Kane et al. (2001), participants saw a flickering cue to either side of a fixation point. Next, they saw a letter at the same location as the cue shown previously (prosaccade condition) or at the location on the other side of the screen (antisaccade condition). As predicted, low spans were less accurate only in the antisaccade condition, suggesting that they had more difficulty than high spans suppressing the automatic response of orienting toward the cue. Instead, they surrendered to the attention-capturing stimulus. The performance difference between high and low spans disappeared for prosaccade trials, a condition not introducing response conflict.

Interestingly, if participants performed a prosaccade block after a few antisaccade blocks, low spans were slower to identify the correct letter in the prosaccade condition and to change the strategy after accommodating and establishing a new automatic way of responding. That indicates further that low spans are impaired not only when selecting the contextually appropriate response in the presence of a competing habitual response, as their worse performance in the antisaccade trials shows, but also in updating instructions, as shown by their worse performance in a prosaccade block following a number of antisaccade trials. More direct evidence that low spans are prone to orient attention toward the cue instead of away from it as in the antisaccade condition was obtained by a follow-up study (Unsworth et al., 2004). Participants did not have to discriminate letters; instead, while their eye movements were recorded, they were instructed to simply look towards or away from the peripheral cue. Even in this simpler task version, low WMC spans made more errors and were slower in the antisaccade condition than high spans.

We should note, however, that high-span superiority is not universal. In the flanker and antisaccade tasks, the span groups performed equivalently when the "natural" response was correct, namely, in the compatible trials in the flanker task and the prosaccade trials in the antisaccade task. In addition, span-group equivalence has been obtained in visual search tasks, task switching, or involving switch costs (see Unsworth & Engle, 2007, for review).

Verbal domain. The Stroop task (Stroop, 1935) is a classic interference paradigm that requires active maintenance of a goal inconsistent with a more natural response. Thus, instead of naming or reading the word (congruent trial), the correct response is to name the color of the ink in which a word is printed (incongruent trial representing conflict). One variation of the Stroop task differentiating between high and low spans manipulates the proportion of congruent and incongruent trials (Kane & Engle, 2003; Logan & Zbrodoff, 1979). When the majority of trials are congruent, participant has to exert the strongest overt control over the more habitual response of word reading. Thus, infrequent change of the response type requires more effortful control than exertion of automatic responding, unlike when presented with an equal number of congruent and incongruent trials or with only one trial type. Indeed, experimental results confirmed that a condition involving infrequent number of incongruent trials appeared the most difficult for low spans. They made twice as many errors as high spans and were faster in responding to congruent trials, indicating that low spans, indeed, prefer responding automatically (Kane & Engle, 2003).

As we mentioned earlier, interference from a similar material or situations encountered previously often prompts errors and poorer performance. When we park our car each day in the same parking lot, it gets harder each time to remember the specific location where the vehicle was parked. Here, the familiar context that recently or repeatedly occurs does not allow discriminating well between new and old information. This effect is called proactive interference (PI). In one version of the PI task, participants attended to a three-letter stimulus and counted backward during the delay periods from 0 to 18 s, making the task to remember the letters more difficult (Brown, 1958; Peterson & Peterson, 1959). This secondary counting task caused a significant decrease in remembering the letters after just a few seconds of the delay, and nearly a complete forgetting at longer delays. Kane and Engle (2000) examined the effects of the PI on WMC, determined by the performance on the OSPAN task, in recalling word lists task intermixed with another, unrelated task preventing rehearsal of the to-be-remembered material. The argument behind the task was that similar material occurring consecutively, for example, by introducing two lists of words belonging to the same semantic category, will cause the most interference, especially when participants are told to remember the words for further recall. The more similar lists, the greater the drop in performance most likely caused by the interference from similar previous lists (Keppel & Underwood, 1962). Kane & Engle introduced the PI buildup by presenting three lists of semantically related words, in succession. After the PI had built up by interference between semantically related words from the lists, a new, semantically unrelated list was presented. The last list served as the release from PI since semantically unrelated words do not induce interference to the previously presented material. If high spans use controlled attention that can be used to fight the effects of PI, they should be better from the low spans in exhibiting superior recall rates. However, when introduced to additional load that prevents from using controlled attention, there should be drop in the performance level of the high spans. On the other hand, if low spans use automatic processing more often, additional load should not affect them further (see also Rosen & Engle, 1997). Indeed, low spans experienced more PI progressing through the experiment than high spans did. This implies that, indeed, they do not use the controlled attention to fight with the effects of the PI. Low spans produced a steeper decline in the number of remembered words. They also experienced more dual-task costs even before the increase of interference from a similar material built up by the PI. On the other hand, when introduced to an unrelated secondary task, both groups performed similarly. Interestingly, high spans recalled even less information than previously and their performance decreased to the level of low spans. Similar results report studies examining sensitivity to PI in young and older adults. Here, older adults experienced greater susceptibility to PI (Lustig, May, & Hasher, 2001; May, Hasher, & Kane, 1999).

In short, the likely explanation of the effects of PI on WMC is that, because low spans do not allocate attention to relieve the effects of interference, they experience stronger PI buildup than high spans do. In contrast, high spans are negatively affected by the secondary task because they use attentional resources additionally to diminish the adverse effects of PI (Kane & Engle, 2000; Engle, 2002; see also Bunting, 2006). Interesting implication of the PI buildup studies is that since PI disappears under no interference, such as with no secondary task or when remembering unrelated memory lists, to-be-recalled information is not lost over the delay period. Thus, rehearsing material, changing context or differentiating stimulus type may serve as possible mechanisms releasing from the PI leading to better remembering (Bunting, 2006).

Finally, aggregation of interference or its increase over a recall period is another example that introduces the PI buildup that makes retrieval of information more difficult. This situation was examined in a verbal fluency task. In the verbal fluency task, participants generate animal names during a specified period of time (Rosen & Engle, 1997). This kind of task requires incorporating strategic search from secondary memory to prevent repetition of already recalled words. More importantly, the words recalled first are usually the most frequently used exemplars from a given category. Thus, as the time passes, participants search for less frequently used words. In Rosen and Engle (1997) study, high spans produced more names since they had sufficient resources to control for names already chosen and still were able to use cues allowing them to produce more exemplars. However, the situation changed under divided attention condition. High and low spans performed similarly, because the load from additional task reduced temporarily the fluency capability of the high span group.

In sum, the results presented in this section suggest that low spans most of the time perform worse than high spans in situations involving interference. Specifically, in various situations that require responding in a less habitual way, high spans utilize controlled attention more successfully and engage more efficiently in the search process from the secondary memory. Researchers have tested numerous other theories aimed to explain individual differences in WMC including differences due to cognitive factors, such as processing speed, mental effort, rehearsal, word knowledge, motivational and strategic factors, task difficulty, or task-specific components.[1]

Trait WMC: The Brain Structures, Genetic Underpinnings, and Neurotransmitters

As we have already pointed out, individual differences in WMC are most pronounced when choosing among competing responses, overriding habitual responses under situational factors, such as anxiety, or when under a high cognitive load as when performing a dual task (cf. Ashcraft & Kirk, 2001; Steele & Josephs, 1990; Bishop, Duncan, Brett, & Lawrence, 2004). In the following section, we consider how genetic and neural factors may shape the capacity of WM. We also show that individual differences in cognitive and neural mechanisms relate to the differences in temperament and personality. However, the scope precludes us from inclusion of more detailed description of all the situational factors that may influence WMC as a trait or state. This includes additionally external and internal factors influencing the experiment outcome, even as trivial a state variable as sitting in an uncomfortable chair in the experiment room, or factors pertaining to mind wandering (see McVay & Kane, this volume). Thus, the next section briefly discusses the specific brain structures that may

---

[1] For extended discussion concerning alternative hypotheses of what might cause individual differences in WMC, see Engle and Kane (2004) and Engle et al. (1992).

relate to the performance differences between high and low WMC individuals. The section that will follow demonstrates that these biological factors are only a subset of factors influencing WMC task performance in the laboratory and in everyday situations requiring utilization of the scarce and fragile WM resources.

Brain Structures

The prefrontal cortex (PFC), anterior cingulate (ACC), and basal ganglia (BG) have been identified as the most important brain structures for functioning of the executive attention component of WM (Kane & Engle, 2002; Miller, 2000; Shallice & Burgess, 1993; Bush et al., 1998; Smith & Jonides, 1998; 1999; McNab & Klingberg, 2008; but see Reitan & Wolfson, 1994). The PFC is important in WM functioning, as its activity in various WM tasks shows (Goldman-Rakic, 1987; Kane & Engle, 2002; Shimamura, 2000). An example task widely used in imaging studies of WM is the n-back task (Jonides et al., 1997). Participant sees string of stimuli (verbal, nonverbal, spatial) consecutively appearing on the screen. The task is to report for each consecutive stimulus, whether the stimulus on screen is identical to the item n-stimuli back.

In addition, the PFC plays a role in various other cognitive processes including goal-directed behavior, practice, automaticity and rewards (Miller, 2000; Miller & Cohen, 2001). Furthermore, the PFC dysfunction especially has been implicated in development of neurodegenerative diseases, multiple sclerosis (Albin, Young, & Penney, 1989; D'Esposito et al., 1996; Nebel et al., 2007), psychopathology (e.g., schizophrenia; Perlstein, Dixit, Carter, Noll, & Cohen, 2003; Barch, 2005; 2006), and has been linked to age-related cognitive decline (Hasher & Zacks, 1988).

Dorsolateral PFC (DLPFC) is especially important for the processes related to control and executive attention. DLPFC regulates goals and guards cognitive control processes, such as action, planning, reasoning, decision-making, dynamic filtering of information, as well as segregation and integration of information related to emotional functioning (De Pisapia, Slomski, & Braver, 2007; Dolcos & McCarthy, 2006; Kerns et al., 2004; Shimamura, 2000). Furthermore, it guides various processes important in WMC reviewed earlier, such as resisting interference, maintaining the goal despite distractions, inhibiting irrelevant information, resolving conflict, or interference caused by the PI (left inferior frontal cortex in particular, Jonides & Nee, 2006; Kane & Engle, 2002; Mecklinger, Weber, Gunter, & Engle, 2003; Baddeley, 1996; Shallice & Burgess, 1993; Perlstein, Elbert, & Stenger, 2002; Botvinick, Braver, Barch, Carter, & Cohen, 2001). An increase in DLPFC activation is also present in dual tasks, observed during increasing task loads, and sometimes explained as an increase in mental effort (Jaeggi et al., 2003). Interestingly, Jaeggi et al. (2007) observed the apparent change in the DLPFC activation especially for low-performing participants, while high-performing participants did not show such substantial changes in activation. The authors attributed these smaller changes to more efficient processing utilized by high spans. Mecklinger et al. (2003) demonstrated that high spans are less prone to interference than low spans in a letter and object memory task. Participants decided if a probe belonged to the set of stimuli presented earlier. Overall, high spans were less prone to interference, whereas low spans showed substantial interference costs in the letter task. Interestingly, high spans made more errors than low spans in object interference trials. In this study, the PFC activation in the high span group was observed for both interference and control trials in the letter task, whereas in the low span group, it was true *only* during the interference trials, suggesting that high WMC spans are able to allocate attention in a controllable way across situations.

The ACC, another important brain structure here, is responsible for monitoring and resolution of conflict followed by error corrections (Braver, Barch, & Gray, 2001; Weissman, Giesbrecht, Song, Mangun, & Woldorff, 2003). The ACC is important as well in response selection across modalities

(Braver et al., 2001; Bush et al., 1998). In social contexts, the ACC has been implicated in conflict resolution involving emotional stimuli, especially when reacting to conflict from emotionally salient, irrelevant distractors (Bishop et al., 2004). Similarly, suppression of unwanted thoughts or inhibition of threat-related distractors involves the ACC activation as well (Mitchell et al., 2007).

According to dual-system models of cognitive control, the ACC and PFC usually show simultaneous activation during task processing, where the ACC represents conflict monitoring or error-detection system and the PFC acts as a regulatory system suppressing incompatible responses (Kerns et al., 2004). Furthermore, Michell et al. (2007) argue that whereas the ACC is responsible for transient processes during cognitive control, for example, during thought suppression, the PFC is responsible for sustained processes involving cognitive control. Following this approach, the ACC is a secondary control process enabling successful suppression of unwanted thoughts. It is worth noting, however, that activity observed in both areas has been inversely related. For example, in the emotional valence task, Perlstein et al. (2002, 2003) showed that more activation in the PFC accompanied less activation in the ACC.

Finally, the basal ganglia (BG) controls access to WM. The BG is activated in planning and set shifting, and contributes to a selective gating mechanism that chooses relevant information for attention biased encoding. Additionally, this selective gating mechanism has been shown to be regulated by dopaminergic system (Albin et al., 1989; McNab & Klingberg, 2008). Importantly, McNab and Klingberg (2008) argue that activity in the BG is important in the ability to exert control during encoding and guarantees that only relevant information is processed. Indeed, researchers observe joint activity in the PFC and BG during WM encoding, just before filtering out irrelevant stimuli.

This short section barely touches the complicated matter of how exactly our brain processes information related to various aspects of WM. Still, many questions exist in the neurocognitive area to determine the relations and the involvement of specific brain areas or neural net activation patterns in particular WM processes. For example, it is still an ongoing debate whether the nature of activation of particular brain areas proceeds in terms of different WM processes as proposed by Petrides (1996) in two levels of mnemonic executive processing with ventrolateral frontal cortex for active retrieval and middorsolateral frontal cortex for WM monitoring, or by the type of information, for example, verbal or visuospatial, as suggested by Goldman-Rakic (1995).[2] Another interesting issue refers to whether the superiority of performance on WM and fluid reasoning tasks stems from the volume of active brain areas or the functional activation of the specific networks (e.g., Lee et al., 2006; Chein & Schneider, 2005).

Influence of Genetics and Neurotransmitters

Recently developed methods allow targeting specific neurotransmitters and linking their functioning to particular cognitive processes. Although still in its early stages, the research establishes clear paths as to which neurotransmitters and genes play a role in cognitive functioning, including WM and intelligence (Ando, Ono, & Wright, 2001; Cools, Gibbs, Miyakawa, Jagust, & D'Esposito, 2008; Luciano et al., 2001; Toga & Thompson, 2005).

Dopamine (DA) is a key neurotransmitter regulating a variety of cognitive functions comprising WM, cognitive flexibility, abstract reasoning, temporal analysis of information, and action planning, to name a few (Fossella et al., 2002; Glatt & Freimer, 2002; Johnson, 2007; Mehta & Riedel, 2006; Previc, 1999; Savitz, Solms, & Ramesar, 2006). DA also mediates cognitive functioning and the PFC activity. However, the relationship between DA and cognition is complex. One illustration

---

[2] We thank the editors to point that out.

is that, as commonly observed, for example, in schizophrenia, ADHD, depression and aging, either too low or too high levels of DA may disrupt cognitive functioning (Kellendonk et al., 2006; Manor et al., 2002; but see Swainson, Oosterlaan, et al., 2000; DiMaio, Grizenko, & Joober, 2003; Hartlage, Alloy, Vazquez, & Dykman, 1993; Suhara et al., 1991). The inverted "U" shape function explanation of DA influence on cognitive functioning allows understanding different relationship between cognitive task performance and DA. For example, impaired cognitive flexibility might stem from too little DA levels (e.g., Nolan, Bilder, Lachman, & Volavka, 2004; Swainson, Oosterlaan, et al., 2000; Swainson, Rogers, et al., 2000). This relationship depends among others on the task characteristic and cognitive demands and can be manipulated pharmacologically (Cools, Barker, Sahakian, & Robbins, 2001; Goldman-Rakic, Muly III, & Williams, 2000; Swainson, Rogers, et al., 2000).

Research examining the role of DA in WM concentrates on DA agonists as targeted in older adults' cognitive functioning. Among the five kinds of DA receptors, there are two distinct groups characterized by excitatory (D1-like) or inhibitory (D2-like) effects (cf. Savitz et al., 2006; Mehta & Riedel, 2006; Gibbs & D'Esposito, 2005). D1 receptor has been linked to a control gating mechanism in the PFC at the encoding stage of WM processing. D2 concentrates on a reward-based information and plays a role in WM updating. However, the crucial aspect appears to be the ratio of D1 to D2 that keeps the amount of DA in a state of equilibrium. Surely, DA is not the only neurotransmitter related to cognitive function. For example, glutamate has been involved jointly with DA in cognitive functioning as well (Kodama, Hikosaka, & Watanabe, 2002) and serotonin with memory and amnesia (cf. Meneses & Perez-Garcia, 2007).

Catechol-*O*-methyl transferase (COMT) is one of the enzymes important in cognitive functioning that regulates levels and transmission of DA within the PFC. Two variants of the COMT gene have been examined in relation to WM. These are *val* allele and *met* allele; the *val* allele is associated with lower synaptic levels of DA (Savitz et al., 2006) and represents a high activity, whereas *met* is a low activity genotype. Most studies have found that the *met* allele (*met/met*) is associated with better performance on WM tasks (for an extended review see Savitz et al., 2006; Fossella et al., 2002), whereas the *val* (*val/val*) allele is often associated with worse performance on WM tasks. *Val/val* has also been associated with a greater number of perseverative errors across different WM tasks that implement high attention control (Blasi et al., 2005; de Frias et al., 2005; MacDonald, Carter, Flory, Ferrell, & Manuck, 2007). However, Williams-Gray and colleagues (2008) in an attentional control task showed that the early PD patients with *met/met* genotype had difficulty with forming an attentional set, which was revealed additionally in the diminished activation in frontoparietal brain areas. Similarly, *met/met* patients executed longer times for planning, related to lowered activation across the frontoparietal network (Williams-Gray, Hampshire, Robbins, et al., 2007). Interestingly, Nolan and colleagues (2004) suggested that the disparate results of cognitive performance of *met/met* and *val/val* genotypes might stem from the observation that the *met* allele participants might perform better on tasks characterized by cognitive stability (akin to WM maintenance), whereas they perform worse on tasks requiring switching, requiring cognitive flexibility. Thus, both dopaminergic drugs and the type of the COMT genotype likely influence both the brain activation and WM-related behaviors. As such, the influence of DA levels on cognitive task performance and a disparate influence of L-dopa on the activity of frontal brain regions in Parkinson's disease is a promising research on the nature of processes influencing cognitive performance (Owen, 2004; Swainson, Oosterlaan, et al., 2000; Swainson, Rogers, et al., 2000; Williams-Gray, Hampshire, Barker, et al., 2008).

Finally, monoamine oxidase A (MAOA) is another enzyme that, together with dopamine receptor D4 (DRD4), influences error and conflict monitoring associated with the ACC functioning. For example, Fan, Fossella, Sommer, Wu, and Posner (2003) showed that the amount of activation in the ACC during an executive attention task differed depending on the DRD4 and MAOA gene polymorphisms and with better performance associated with higher ACC activity.

State WMC as Transient Changes from the Baseline Trait WMC

Various temporary factors may affect the level of performance on WMC tasks, such as transient changes in mood states, but they do not affect the overall correlation between these tasks and higher order cognition (Engle & Kane, 2004; Schmeichel, 2007; Wegner, Erber, & Zanakos, 1993; Turley-Ames & Whitfield, 2003; but see Beilock & DeCaro, 2007).

Different biological, personality, and cognitive factors can induce state-related changes in WMC. Biological factors relate to fatigue, sleep deprivation, or physiological effects of threat-related changes in the organism. Personality factors relate to a person's characteristic pertaining to reactions to the effects caused by induction of anxiety, stress, or affect, as well as the person's characteristic way of processing those states. Finally, cognitive temporal factors are performance-related factors pertaining to high cognitive load or to cognitive effects induced by a task in internal states, such as dealing with negative thoughts, ruminations, or compulsions. Next, we briefly describe these various factors and discuss how they influence WMC.

Biological Factors: Sleep Deprivation, Fatigue, Physiological Effects of Threat and Anxiety

Sleep deprivation has been linked to overall impairments in decision-making, judgment, and finally, to worse cognitive performance on achievement tests. Meanwhile, sleep deprivation impairs WMC-related processing that involves the PFC, especially maintaining and updating information relevant to the task (Harrison & Horne, 2000; Killgore, Balkin, & Wesensten, 2006; Smith, McEvoy, & Gevins, 2002). Likewise, we can relate WM impairments due to sleep deprivation to situations when a person attempts to exert control, but in addition to maintaining the goal to do well and retrieving needed information, the person needs to allocate extra resources simply to stay awake. The importance of these effects as causing cognitive impairments has been stressed further in sleep disorders and evaluated especially in the assessment of alertness and cognitive performance impairments that sleep disorders likely cause (Smith et al., 2002).

Researchers observe significant changes in cognitive performance even after only a moderate sleep loss beyond changes related to a general slowing due to prolonged sleep deprivation. For example, performance and judgment problems may occur after just one or two nights of sleep deprivation. Interestingly, after one night of sleep deprivation, researchers report loss related to impairments in encoding and even in forming memories (Chee & Choo, 2004). Furthermore, the effects of practice of WM task over time are simply not seen for individuals with less number of hours of sleep during a few consecutive days as compared with people sleeping 8 h a night (Casement, Broussard, Mullington, & Press, 2006). Interestingly, the impairment patterns are similar to patterns seen in prefrontal patients (Yoo, Hu, Gujar, Jolesz, & Walker, 2007) and those observed in older adults (Chee & Choo, 2004; Harrison, Horne, & Rothwell, 2000). However, we should note that the changes and patterns of brain activation after just 24 h of sleep deprivation are quite complex. They involve different behaviors as shown in the PFC and ACC activation patterns and depend on the time, task, age, and exact period of sleep deprivation. In psychopathology, additional impairments may include dissociative symptoms, such as elevated or strengthened symptoms in the dissociative identity disorder (Giesbrecht, Smeets, Leppink, Jelicic, & Merckelbach, 2007; Killgore et al., 2006).

Another temporary factor influencing WM is mental (cognitive) fatigue. Its effects also include temporal impairment in WM functioning. Mental fatigue describes cognitive effects of a long and sustained exposure to a cognitively demanding task (Lorist, Boksem, & Ridderinkhof, 2005).

For example, Persson, Welsh, Jonides, and Reuter-Lorenz (2007) demonstrated these compromised effects in tasks involving resolving conflict or resisting interference. Mental fatigue may also act as a resource depletion that impairs WM functioning in a similar fashion to depletion effects observed in a stereotype threat situations or in a self-regulatory failure (Richeson et al., 2003; Vohs & Heatherton, 2000). Additionally, as in sleep deprivation, temporal impairment related to mental fatigue has been linked to different activation levels in the ACC, leading to less error detections and corrections, and higher overall error rate. For example, similar pattern has been observed in individuals with mental fatigue and with chronic fatigue syndrome (Caseras et al., 2006; Lorist et al., 2005). Finally, Lorist et al. (2005) linked mental fatigue with DA functioning, explaining problems related to mental fatigue by fluctuations of the DA levels with too high or too low levels of DA impairing cognitive control and the ACC activity, resulting in more errors.

Threat is another biological factor, the effects of which may relate to difficulties in WM performance, and is associated mostly with physiological changes in arousal levels caused by threatening situations. Research demonstrates that threat, similarly to stress, narrows the focus of attention and acts on WMC depending on the task demands and task goals. For example, in addition to cognitive impairments under threatening conditions, threat elevates anxiety levels and an overall physiological arousal (Osborne, 2007). This, in addition, can be related further to how a person can overcome the adverse effects of these biological factors on WM functioning, that is, by looking at the influence of personality factors.

Personality-Related Factors: Threat, Anxiety, Stress, "Choking" Under Pressure, and Affect

When we consider a threat from a personality perspective, we take into account social and cognitive effects of threat-related anxiety ascribed to specific threatening situations. The literature agrees that a stereotype threat makes salient the fear if a person believes in a particular stereotype (behavior or idea) and eventually leads to diminishing of available resources for successful utilization of WMC and attention. For example, anxiety and threat-evoked anxiety have been implicated as having disruptive performance effects on spatial WM tasks (Lavric, Rippon, & Gray, 2003; Shackman et al., 2006). Other examples include stereotype threat induced during cognitive or skilled performance, or during interracial interactions (Beilock, Jellison, Rydell, McConnell, & Carr, 2006; Beilock, Rydell, & McConnell, 2007; Quinn & Spencer, 2001; Richeson & Shelton, 2003; Schmader & Johns, 2003; Trawalter & Richeson, 2006).

However, when distracted away from thoughts and actions that induce and maintain the threatening stereotype threat state, its negative effects are substantially reduced and its activation weakens. On the other hand, focusing on particular situational factors or a purpose for performing a task that activates a stereotype may impair performance on a cognitive task. In one study, participants performed Ravens Progressive Matrices test under two different conditions (Croizet et al., 2004). The authors induced stereotype threat situation by implementing different instructions pertaining to the purpose of taking the test. Participants who received information that the test measures their cognitive ability had performed at a similar level as controls. However, the performance significantly dropped for participants who were told that the test measures their reputation of lower ability. Croizet et al. (2004) indicated that additional mental load that disrupts performance in the reputation condition is a possible mechanism responsible for group differences in this study.

Similar effects arise when examining the relationship between stress and WM task performance. For example, Klein and Boals (2001) reasoned that more life event stress causes worse performance on WM task. Similar explanatory mechanisms implementing stress as an additional load may act with respect to stressful events. In another example, Beilock et al. (2007) showed that elevated stress lead high span individuals to perform worse, at a similar level as the low span group. However, when stress was taken off the task, high spans improved their performance, whereas low spans remained at the same level as under stress.

The characteristic pattern of impaired performance of high spans under specific circumstances is referred to as a "choking under pressure" (Beilock & Carr, 2001; 2005; Beilock, Kulp, Holt, & Carr, 2004). The authors argued that this phenomenon might stem from different strategies implemented by high and low WM span individuals. In fact, they noticed that low spans use simple strategies irrespectively of the presence or absence of a stressful stimulus, whereas high spans perform better under low-stress condition simply because they implement strategies that are more efficient. Conversely, high spans cannot implement these strategies under high-pressure situations that force them to use simpler strategies, which do not always result in a correct solution (Beilock et al., 2007). Beilock et al. (2004) argued that one possible way out from that conundrum is to practice problems. When participants practiced their problems, they were able to reduce the negative effects of "choking under pressure". This is in line with emerging research on WM training (e.g., Jaeggi, Buschkuehl, Jonides, & Perrig, 2008; Jaeggi et al., 2007; Klingberg, Forssberg, & Westerberg, 2002; Klingberg et al., 2005; Thorell, Lindqvist, Bergman, Bohlin, & Klingberg, 2009).

Affect and regulating emotions also induce temporal changes in WMC. For example, high cognitive control can diminish resources available for a subsequent task and impair the ability to update, ignore distractors, or ability to inhibit predominant writing tendencies (Schmeichel, 2007). However, Klein and Boals (2001) showed that the mutual influence of emotion and cognition is not straightforward. Thus, task goals and the nature of the processes also influence this relationship since different emotional processes depend differently on a task context (Gross & Levenson, 1997; Kensinger & Corkin, 2003; Richards & Gross, 2000).

Cognitive Factors: Cognitive Control Under Load, WMC Improvement

As reviewed earlier, Kane and Engle (2000) and Rosen and Engle (1997) have demonstrated that load diminishes scarce WM resources. As the load increases, even high spans experience performance decrease when required to divide their attention between two tasks. Thus, it might be implied that when WM load increases, the executive control of attention decreases (Hester & Garavan, 2005). This causes temporary impairment in the ability to fight distraction, resist interference, or inhibit irrelevant information. Furthermore, similar adverse effects on WMC should be seen across verbal and nonverbal task, as the inhibitory mechanisms sensitive to high load are domain free (Conway et al., 1999).

Applying this way of reasoning to unsuccessful suppression of ruminations often observed in depression and other mood disorders, ruminations and other extraneous thoughts may serve as an additional cognitive load as well. A decreased ability to inhibit irrelevant or unwanted thoughts results in fewer available resources for maintaining important goals or for resisting interference from irrelevant distractors. Intrusive thoughts and ruminations in depression can be activated by extraneous cues relevant to these ruminations picked up from the environment, the mechanism also observed in drug addictions (Brewin & Beaton, 2002; Brewin & Smart, 2005; Hester & Garavan, 2005). Since these ruminations are not relevant to the task, the result is worse task performance (cf. Dalgleish et al., 2007). Finally, depressive individuals also exhibit impairments in effortful processing. Instead, they often implement more automatic cognitions in their thought processes. Therefore, their performance decreases; firstly due to lower utilization of effortful processing and secondly, resulting from diminished ability to fight interference. Again, these processes may be mediated by DA functioning (Hartlage et al., 1993).

WMC Improvement

WMC can be temporarily increased as the effect of extensive training and practice, mimicked by practice-related changes in brain activation (Jaeggi et al., 2007; 2008; Olesen, Westerberg, & Klingberg, 2003). These practice effects can even transfer to nontrained tasks as Klingberg et al. (2002; 2005; see also Thorell et al., 2009) showed in children and young adults with ADHD. In addition, other studies claim to observe effects of training in expanding focus of attention (Verhaeghen, Cerella, & Basak, 2004; but see Oberauer, 2006).

WM tasks show good reliability and stability at the test–retest sessions 6-weeks apart (e.g., Klein & Fiss, 1999; Waters & Caplan, 2003). They also show practice effects, which might be applied to deliberate WM training important in improving rehabilitation outcomes or cognitive performance in environments highly relying on WM processes. In this fast-emerging literature, example studies examine learning difficulties in neurodevelopmental disorders (Gathercole & Alloway, 2006), the influence of L-dopa on learning by repetitive training (Knecht et al., 2004), or applied as a part of a rehabilitation in stroke (Westernberg et al., 2007) and traumatic brain injury patients (Serino et al., 2007). Training usually lasts about 5 weeks. The studies not only report training-related improvements in behavioral results lasting a number of months in comparison to control groups but also related changes in cortical activity (Dahlin, Stigsdotter Nelly, Larsson, Bäckman, & Nyberg, 2008; Westerberg & Klingberg, 2007). Moreover, the transfer effects are observed for tasks engaging similar processes, for example, other WM, attention, reasoning tasks (Dahlin et al., 2008; Westerberg & Klingberg, 2007; Westernberg et al., 2007), or ability to resist interference (Persson & Reuter-Lorenz, 2008). Some of the positive effects of such training sessions include reduced symptoms (Klingberg et al., 2005; Serino et al., 2007; Westernberg et al., 2007) or even improvements of patients' everyday life functioning (Serino et al., 2007).

Various studies have examined the effects of cognitive performance on different executive attention tasks by looking at the effects of administration of DA drugs. DA antagonists, such as pergolide and bromocriptine (Mehta & Riedel, 2006, for a review) and L-dopa (Knecht et al., 2004) are often used for treatment of Parkinson's disease. Yet, the results so far are mixed and the reports of higher WMC improvements differ across tasks, groups, or even in whether high or low WMC span improvements are reported (high; Kimberg & D'Esposito, 1997; 2003; or low spans; Gibbs & D'Esposito, 2005). Additional caution in interpretation of the results of the training studies is concern over a low number of participants reported in majority of the studies, which also might be a reason of inconsistent results.

Implications

Discovering and assessing the sources of any cognitive impairment considering WM and its capacity is especially important in diagnosis of illness or even a mild impairment, as well as in achievement tests. Differentiating between state and trait WMC may be beneficial in looking at the ways of approaching and recognizing cognitive problems that either stem from temporary factors, such as anxiety, or biological factors, such as disruptions in neurotransmitter functioning.

Trait WMC: Neurodegenerative Disorders and Psychopathology

Assessing the severity of WM impairments is crucial in a variety of brain-related diseases, such as traumatic brain injuries and other instances where patients experience problems with maintaining goal directed behavior in WM and attention. The assessment of the severity of impairment is of extreme relevance since problems related to inhibition, attention control, and suppression of unwanted thoughts occur across various mental and neurodegenerative disorders. Examples include Alzheimer's disease (AD), Parkinson's disease (PD), Mild Cognitive Impairment (MCI), traumatic brain injury (TBI), schizophrenia, depression, ADHD, Obsessive-Compulsive Disorder (OCD), or autism (Diamond, 2005; Pennington & Ozonoff, 1996).

Most psychopathology is characterized by impairments related to inhibitory mechanisms. For example, mood disorders and depression are concerned with inhibiting ruminations (Wenzlaff, Wegner, & Roper, 1988). Often, these ruminations are subject to perseveration and are signs of attentional inflexibility. However, due to their different influence mechanisms on attentional control, variety of forms of ruminations may represent different cognitive mechanisms. For example, inhibitory problems are associated with depressive ruminations, whereas angry ruminations relate to problems with task switching (Whitmer & Banich, 2007).

Another example of a mental disorder where researchers observe impaired inhibition and attention control is OCD. The OCD inhibitory impairments may be explained by a mechanism related to attentional bias (Muller & Roberts, 2004). Attentional bias primes threatening information related to compulsions and obsessions, the main symptoms of OCD, causing problems with inhibiting these threatening or negative thoughts. For example, Muller and Roberts (2004) found that the Stroop task interference correlates with the amount of OCD symptoms.

Neurodegenerative disorders include impairments in inhibitory control as well. In one study, Alzheimer's disease patients made more errors in the antisaccade condition due to problems with correcting errors and inhibiting a habitual response of not looking towards the cue (Crawford et al., 2005). Additionally, this impairment was positively correlated with cognitive measures of dementia. In another study, researchers compared performance of patients with AD and those with MCI (Belleville, Chertkow, & Gauthier, 2007). Whereas MCI patients exhibited impairments only in some WM tasks, AD patients had problems with all administered WM tasks. Thus, even patients with the MCI show some level of WM impairment such as poorer planning and executing goals (Altgassen, Phillips, Kopp, & Kliegel, 2007). This may imply existence of a continuum of progressive cognitive impairments. As the authors argued, by showing such a continuum of attentional control problems from the MCI to AD, WM tasks can be used to monitor and diagnose early stages of the disease and prompt clinical attention early enough to slow down its progress. Implications may also be important for rehabilitation programs. As described in a case study by Vallat et al. (2005), they can be used for attenuating the cognitive impairments caused by brain injuries or strokes and targeted specifically at improving WM. Finally, similarly to PD patients, TBI patients experience the biggest challenge with planning, formulation, and execution of goals. In one study, TBI patients were assigned to either "assigning specific goal" condition or "do your best" condition. Interestingly, when assigned to a specific goal, patients were able to improve their performance significantly in comparison to the less specific assignment to "do your best" (Gauggel & Billino, 2002).

State WMC: Achievement Tests and Stereotype Threat

How well one can perform on the tasks measuring WMC predicts performance on a variety of higher-order cognitive tasks. The common factor of these tasks aimed at capturing individual differences in WMC is the ability to draw inferences about numerous higher order cognitive functions. Examples include various processes important in learning and language processing, such as reading and listening comprehension (Daneman & Carpenter, 1980), vocabulary learning (Daneman & Green, 1986), language comprehension (King & Just, 1991) as well as complex learning (Kyllonen & Stephens, 1990), writing, and note-taking (Kiewra & Benton, 1988). Other situations include reasoning and fluid abilities (Kyllonen & Christal, 1990; Conway et al., 2002; Engle, Kane, & Tuholski, 1999; Engle, Tuholski, et al., 1999; for review see also Orzechowski, this volume), and various other skills (Engle, 2001; Engle & Kane, 2004).[3]

Achievement tests constitute one area of possible implications of state differences in WMC. Research has shown that test anxiety influences performance of some individuals to a greater extent than others. As Ashcraft and Kirk (2001) and other researchers demonstrate, high math anxiety negatively influences cognitive performance on a math test by impairing performance by temporarily shrinking WMC resources. The authors reason that worries consume WMC resources needed for solving math problems in a similar fashion as focusing attention on a threat impairs processing of nonthreat information (Borkovec & Inz, 1990; Borkovec, Lyonfields, Wiser, & Diehl, 1993; Lavric et al., 2003; Mathews & Mackintosh, 1998; Mathews, Mackintosh, & Fulcher, 1997). For example, such adverse effects may be seen in performance on math problems in high WMC individuals. As they are subjected to a high-pressure environment, their performance deteriorates to the level of performance of low spans (Beilock & Carr, 2005; Beilock et al., 2007; Osborne, 2007). These facts call for a need to take into account gender or ethnic group differing in the strength of influence caused by the relevant temporary threatening situation. Similarly, it should be taken into account in academic performance and test anxiety in order to diminish the negative outcomes not related to actual level of ability or knowledge of a subject.

Similar mechanisms that preclude successful performance are seen in intelligence tests of different ethnic groups and in women solving math tests. In such situations, stereotype threat associates the test with a specific stereotype making it salient at the time of the test (Schmader & Johns, 2003). Furthermore, in studies researching inferiority of women math performance when a stereotype was made salient, Krendl and colleagues (2008) observed less activation in prefrontal regions and other brain regions associated with math learning normally active during math performance. What they observed instead was a higher activation of the brain regions normally active during processing of social and emotional information, including ventral ACC (see also Richeson et al., 2003).

Another implication pertains to stereotype threat involving situations other than achievement tests, such as interracial stereotyping after interaction with a different race (Richeson & Shelton, 2003; Trawalter & Richeson, 2006) or similar mechanisms induced in situations of stress and test anxiety. These states distract through material irrelevant to the task, such as threat inducing intrusive thoughts or anxiety caused by inability to discard the threatening information. This, in turn, leaves less attentional resources available for the task (Keogh & French, 2001).

Overcoming Capacity Limits

As stated earlier, practice frees WM resources, especially under a high load (Beilock & DeCaro, 2007; Beilock, et al., 2007; Chein & Schneider, 2005). Practice reduces the load by making practiced problems more automatic, thus leaving more resources for complex processing. Studies show that merely introducing to a high load may lead to reduction in distractor interference due to narrowed focusing on a task (Forster & Lavie, 2007). Specifically, individuals that are more distractible in a daily life are usually more vulnerable to interference due to this distractibility. When under a high load, however, they focus their attention on the task. That leads to better performance due to reducing the interference normally present where there is no load. The opposite is true for individuals usually reporting low levels of interference. For them, the performance worsens in a similar fashion that high spans' in "choking under pressure" situations.

---

[3] Interested readers are directed to Wilhelm and Engle (2005; see also Shamosh et al., 2008; Wright et al., 2000).

Interestingly, under specific circumstances, moderate levels of stress lead to reconfiguration of strategies and adaptation to the depleted resources of WM (Steinhauser, Maier, & Hübner, 2007). In addition, focusing attention on task relevant information may also help to alleviate the negative effects of stress. In fact, research shows instances where focusing attention on relevant information due to narrowing attention under stress lead to less interference under high rather than low stress situations; that time, unlike in "choking under pressure" (Chajut & Algom, 2003; Hockey, 1997).

Finally, Wegner (1994) discusses various implications of the mechanisms of thought suppression. When WMC is low, a person-relevant instead of task-relevant thoughts take the precedence. Relaxation techniques that may lead to inverting such mechanism may as well positively influence other aspect of a daily life. These include mood control, increased concentration, pain control, sleep, and various social interactions. Lastly, it should be noted that before implementing different techniques that may overcome the negative effects of WMC depletion, we should remember that the level of improvement and the goals are tied both to motivation and to the realistic nature of the to-be-accomplished goal (Niemivirta, 1999).

Concluding Remarks

In this chapter, we attempted to review the literature relevant to WMC seen as a trait, a stable characteristic of an individual, as well as WMC as a state relating to various situational factors that temporarily influence WMC functioning. We have also shown that in some instances WMC can be improved. Finally, we have indicated some of the implications of looking at WMC as a state and trait construct that may be useful in monitoring performance in normal individuals and in psychopathology concerned with problems related to information processing and goal-related behaviors. Still to come is a fascinating journey of discovering the entire biological mechanism and the interplay between the brain, neurotransmitters, genes, and situational factors that influence WMC and cognitive control of behavior.

References

Albin, R. L., Young, A. B., & Penney, J. B. (1989). The functional anatomy of basal ganglia disorders. *Trends in Neuroscience, 12*, 366–375.

Altgassen, M., Phillips, L., Kopp, U., & Kliegel, M. (2007). Role of working memory components in planning performance of individuals with Parkinson's disease. *Neuropsychologia, 45*, 2393–2397.

Ando, J., Ono, Y., & Wright, M. J. (2001). Genetic structure of spatial and verbal working memory. *Behavior Genetics, 31*, 615–624.

Ashcraft, M. H., & Kirk, E. P. (2001). The relationships among working memory, math anxiety, and performance. *Journal of Experimental Psychology. General, 130*, 224–237.

Baddeley, A. D., & Hitch, G. (1974). Working memory. In G. A. Bower (Ed.), *The psychology of learning and motivation* (Vol. 8, pp. 47–89). New York: Academic.

Baddeley, A. D. (1996). Exploring the central executive. *The Quarterly Journal of Experimental Psychology, 49A*, 5–18.

Barch, D. M. (2005). The cognitive neuroscience of schizophrenia. *Annual Reviews of Clinical Psychology, 1*, 321–353.

Barch, D. M. (2006). What can research on schizophrenia tell us about the cognitive neuroscience of working memory? *Neuroscience, 139*, 73–84.

Barkley, R. A. (2001). The executive functions and self-regulation: an evolutionary neuropsychological perspective. *Neuropsychology Review, 11*, 1–29.

Beilock, S. L., & Carr, T. H. (2001). On the fragility of skilled performance: what governs choking under pressure? *Journal of Experimental Psychology. General, 130*, 701–725.

Beilock, S. L., & Carr, T. H. (2005). When high-powered people fail. Working memory and "choking under pressure" in math. *Psychological Science, 16*, 101–105.

Beilock, S. L., Kulp, C. A., Holt, L. E., & Carr, T. H. (2004). More on the fragility of performance: choking under pressure in mathematical problem solving. *Journal of Experimental Psychology. General, 133*, 584–600.

Beilock, S. L., & DeCaro, M. S. (2007). From poor performance to success under stress: working memory, strategy selection, and mathematical problem solving under pressure. *Journal of Experimental Psychology. Learning, Memory, & Cognition, 33*, 983–998.

Beilock, S. L., Jellison, W. A., Rydell, R. J., McConnell, A. R., & Carr, T. H. (2006). On the causal mechanisms of stereotype threat: can skills that don't rely heavily on working memory still be threatened? *Personality and Social Psychology Bulletin, 32*, 1059–1071.

Beilock, S. L., Rydell, R. J., & McConnell, A. R. (2007). Stereotype threat and working memory: mechanisms, alleviation, and spillover. *Journal of Experimental Psychology. General, 136*, 256–276.

Belleville, S., Chertkow, H., & Gauthier, S. (2007). Working memory and control of attention in persons with Alzheimer's disease and mild cognitive impairment. *Neuropsychology, 21*, 458–469.

Bishop, S., Duncan, J., Brett, M., & Lawrence, A. D. (2004). Prefrontal cortical function and anxiety: controlling attention to threat-related stimuli. *Nature Neuroscience, 7*, 184–188.

Blasi, G., Mattay, V. S., Bertolino, A., Elvevag, B., Callicott, J. H., Das, S., et al. (2005). Effect of Catchol-0-Methyltransferase $val^{158}met$ genotype on attentional control. *The Journal of Neuroscience, 25*, 5038–5045.

Borkovec, T. D., & Inz, I. (1990). The nature of worry in generalized anxiety disorder: a predominance of thought activity. *Behavior Research and Therapy, 28*, 153–158.

Borkovec, T. D., Lyonfields, J. D., Wiser, S. L., & Diehl, I. (1993). The role of worrisome thinking in the suppression of cardiovascular response to phobic imagery. *Behavior Research and Therapy, 31*, 321–324.

Botvinick, M. M., Braver, T. S., Barch, D. M., Carter, C. S., & Cohen, J. D. (2001). Conflict monitoring and cognitive control. *Psychological Review, 108*, 624–652.

Braver, T. S., Barch, D. M., & Gray, J. R. (2001). Anterior cingulate cortex and response conflict: effects of frequency, inhibition and errors. *Cerebral Cortex, 11*, 825–836.

Brewin, C. R., & Beaton, A. (2002). Thought suppression, intelligence, and working memory capacity. *Behaviour Research and Therapy, 40*, 923–930.

Brewin, C. R., & Smart, L. (2005). Working memory capacity and suppression of intrusive thoughts. *Journal of Behavior Therapy and Experimental Psychiatry, 36*, 61–68.

Brown, J. A. (1958). Some tests of the decay theory of immediate memory. *Quarterly Journal of Experimental Psychology, 10*, 12–21.

Bunting, M. (2006). Proactive interference and item similarity in working memory. *Journal of Experimental Psychology. Learning, Memory, & Cognition, 32*, 183–196.

Bush, G., Whalen, P. J., Rosen, B. P., Jenike, M. A., McInerney, S. C., & Rauch, S. L. (1998). The counting Stroop: an interference task specialized for functional neuroimaging – validation study with functional MRI. *Human Brain Mapping, 6*, 270–282.

Casement, M. D., Broussard, J. L., Mullington, J. M., & Press, D. Z. (2006). The contribution of sleep to improvement in working memory scanning speed: a study of prolonged sleep restriction. *Biological Psychology, 72*, 208–212.

Caseras, X., Mataix-Cols, D., Giampietro, V., Rimes, K. S., Ntsmmrt, M., Zelaya, F., et al. (2006). Probing the working memory system in chronic fatigue syndrome: a functional magnetic resonance imaging study using the n-back task. *Psychosomatic Medicine, 68*, 947–955.

Chajut, E., & Algom, D. (2003). Selective attention improves under stress: implications for theories of social cognition. *Journal of Personality and Social Psychology, 85*, 231–248.

Chee, M. W., & Choo, W. C. (2004). Functional imaging of working memory after 24h of sleep deprivation. *The Journal of Neuroscience, 24*, 4560–4567.

Chein, J. M., & Schneider, W. (2005). Neuroimaging studies of practice-related change: fMRI and meta-analytic evidence of a domain-general control network for learning. *Cognitive Brain Research, 25*, 607–623.

Cherry, E. C. (1953). Some experiments on the recognition of speech, with one and with two ears. *Journal of the Acoustical Society of America, 25*, 975–979.

Colflesh, G. J. H., & Conway, A. R. A. (2007). Individual differences in working memory capacity and divided attention in dichotic listening. *Psychonomic Bulletin and Review, 14*, 699–703.

Conway, A. R. A., & Engle, R. W. (1994). Working memory and retrieval: a resource-dependent inhibition model. *Journal of Experimental Psychology. General, 123*, 354–373.

Conway, A. R. A., & Engle, R. W. (1996). Individual differences in working memory capacity: more evidence for a general capacity theory. *Memory, 4*, 577–590.

Conway, A. R. A., Cowan, N., & Bunting, M. F. (2001). The cocktail party phenomenon revisited: the importance of working memory capacity. *Psychonomic Bulletin and Review, 8*, 331–335.

Conway, A. R. A., Cowan, N., Bunting, M. F., Therriault, D. J., & Minkoff, S. R. B. (2002). A latent variable analysis of working memory capacity, short-term memory capacity, processing speed, and general fluid intelligence. *Intelligence, 30*, 163–183.

Conway, A. R. A., Kane, M. J., Bunting, M. F., Hambrick, D. Z., Wilhelm, O., & Engle, R. E. (2005). Working memory span tasks: a methodological review and user's guide. *Psychonomic Bulletin and Review, 12*, 769–786.

Conway, A. R. A., Tuholski, S. W., Shisler, R. J., & Engle, R. W. (1999). The effect of memory load on negative priming: an individual differences investigation. *Memory and Cognition, 27*, 1042–1050.

Cools, R., Barker, R. A., Sahakian, B. J., & Robbins, T. W. (2001). Enhanced or impaired cognitive function in Parkinson's disease as a function of dopaminergic medication and task demands. *Cerebral Corex, 11*, 1136–1143.

Cools, R., Gibbs, S. E., Miyakawa, A., Jagust, W., & D'Esposito, M. (2008). Working memory capacity predicts dopamine synthesis capacity in the human striatum. *The Journal of Neuroscience, 28*, 1208–1212.

Cowan, N. (1988). Evolving concepts of memory storage, selective attention, and their mutual constraints within the human information processing system. *Psychological Bulletin, 104*, 103–191.

Cowan, N. (1997). *Attention and memory. An integrated framework* (Oxford Psychology Series 26). New York: Oxford University Press.

Crawford, T. J., Higham, S., Renvoize, T., Patel, J., Dale, M., Suriya, A., et al. (2005). Inhibitory control of saccadic eye movements and cognitive impairment in Alzheimer's disease. *Biological Psychiatry, 57*, 1052–1060.

Croizet, J. C., Despres, G., Gauzins, M. E., Huguet, P., Leyens, J. P., & Meot, A. (2004). Stereotype threat undermines intellectual performance by triggering a disruptive mental load. *Personality and Social Psychology Bulletin, 30*, 721–731.

D'Esposito, M., Onishi, K., Thompson, H., Robinson, K., Armstrong, C., & Grossman, M. (1996). Working memory impairments in multiple sclerosis: evidence from a dual-task paradigm. *Neuropsychology, 10*, 51–56.

Dahlin, E., Stigsdotter Nelly, A., Larsson, A., Bäckman, L., & Nyberg, L. (2008). Transfer of learning after updating training mediated by the striatum. *Science, 320*, 1510–1512.

Dalgleish, T., Williams, J. M. G., Golden, A. J., Perkins, N., Feldman Barrett, L., Barnard, P. J., et al. (2007). Reduced specificity of autobiographical memory and depression: the role of the executive control. *Journal of Experimental Psychology. General, 136*, 23–42.

Daneman, M., & Carpenter, P. A. (1980). Individual differences in working memory and reading. *Journal of Verbal Learning and Verbal Behavior, 19*, 459–466.

Daneman, M., & Green, I. (1986). Individual differences in comprehending and producing words in context. *Journal of Memory and Language, 25*, 1–8.

De Pisapia, N., Slomski, J. A., & Braver, T. S. (2007). Functional specializations in lateral prefrontal cortex associated with the integration and segregation of information in working memory. *Cerebral Cortex, 17*, 993–1006.

Diamond, A. (2005). Attention-deficit disorder (attention-deficit/hyperactivity disorder without hyperactivity): a neurobiologically and behaviorally distinct disorder from attention-deficit/hyperactivity disorder (with hyperactivity). *Development and Psychopathology, 17*, 807–825.

DiMaio, S., Grizenko, N., & Joober, R. (2003). Dopamine genes and attention-deficit hyperactivity disorder: a review. *Journal of Psychiatry Neuroscience, 28*, 27–38.

Dolcos, F., & McCarthy, G. (2006). Brain systems mediating cognitive interference by emotional distraction. *The Journal of Neuroscience, 26*, 2072–2079.

Engle, R. W. (2001). What is working-memory capacity? In H. L. Roediger III & J. S. Nairne (Eds.), *The nature of remembering: essays in honor of Robert G. Crowder* (pp. 297–314). Washington, DC: American Psychological Association.

Engle, R. W. (2002). Working memory capacity as executive attention. *Current Directions in Psychological Science, 11*, 19–23.

Engle, R. W., & Kane, M. J. (2004). Executive attention, working memory capacity, and a two-factor theory of cognitive control. In B. Ross (Ed.), *The Psychology of Learning and Motivation* (Vol. 44, pp. 145–199). New York: Elsevier.

Engle, R. W., Cantor, J., & Carullo, J. (1992). Individual differences in working memory and comprehension: a test of four hypotheses. *Journal of Experimental Psychology. Learning, Memory and Cognition, 18*, 972–992.

Engle, R. W., Kane, M. J., & Tuholski, S. W. (1999). Individual differences in working memory capacity and what they tell us about controlled attention, general fluid intelligence and functions of the prefrontal cortex. In A. Miyake & P. Shah (Eds.), *Models of working memory: mechanisms of active maintenance and executive control* (pp. 102–134). London: Cambridge Press.

Engle, R. W., Tuholski, S. W., Laughlin, J. E., & Conway, A. R. A. (1999). Working memory, short-term memory and general fluid intelligence: a latent variable approach. *Journal of Experimental Psychology. General, 128*, 309–331.

Eriksen, B. A., & Eriksen, C. W. (1974). Effects of noise letters upon the identification of a target letter in a nonsearch task. *Perception and Psychophysics, 16*, 143–149.

Fan, J., Fossella, J., Sommer, T., Wu, Y., & Posner, M. I. (2003). Mapping the genetic variation of executive attention onto brain activity. *Proc Natl Acad Sci USA, 100*, 7406–7411.

Feldman Barrett, L., Tugade, M. M., & Engle, R. W. (2004). Individual differences in working memory capacity and dual-process theories of mind. *Psychollogical Bulletin, 130*, 553–573.

Forster, S., & Lavie, N. (2007). High perceptual load makes everybody equal. *Psychological Science, 18*, 377–381.

Fossella, J., Sommer, T., Fan, J., Wu, Y., Swanson, J. M., Pfaff, D. W., et al. (2002). Assessing the molecular genetics of attention networks. *BMC Neuroscience, 3*, 14–25.

de Frias, C. M., Annerbrink, K., Westberg, L., Erikkson, E., Adolfsson, R., & Nilsson, G. (2005). Catchol-O-methyltransferase val158met polymorphism is associated with cognitive performance in nondemented adults. *Journal of Cognitive Neuroscience, 17*, 1018–1025.

Friedman, N. P., & Miyake, A. (2004). The relations among inhibition and interference control functions: a latent-variable analysis. *Journal of Experimental Psychology. General, 133*, 101–135.

Gathercole, S. E., & Alloway, T. P. (2006). Practitioner review: short-term and working memory impairments in neurodevelopmental disorders: diagnosis and remedial support. *Journal of Child Psychology and Psychiatry, 47*, 4–15.

Gauggel, S., & Billino, J. (2002). The effects of goal setting on the arithmetic performance of brain-damaged patients. *Archives of Clinical Neuropsychology, 17*, 283–294.

Gibbs, S. E. B., & D'Esposito, M. (2005). Individual capacity differences predict working memory performance and prefrontal activity following dopamine receptor stimulation. *Cognitive, Affective and Behavioral Neuroscience, 5*, 212–221.

Giesbrecht, T., Smeets, T., Leppink, J., Jelicic, M., & Merckelbach, H. (2007). Acute dissociation after 1 night of sleep loss. *Journal of Abnormal Psychology, 116*, 599–606.

Glatt, C. E., & Freimer, N. B. (2002). Association analysis of candidate genes for neuropsychiatric disease: the perpetual campaign. *Trends in Genetics, 18*, 307–312.

Goldman-Rakic, P. S. (1995). Architecture of the prefrontal cortex and the central executive. *Annals of the New York Academy of Sciences, 769*, 71–83.

Goldman-Rakic, P. S. (1987). Circuitry of primate prefrontal cortex and regulation of behavior by representational knowledge. In F. Plum & V. Mountcastle (Eds.), *Handbook of physiology* (Vol. 5, pp. 373–417). Bethesda, MD: APS.

Goldman-Rakic, P. S., Muly, E. C., III, & Williams, G. V. (2000). D(1) receptors in prefrontal cells and circuits. *Brain Research Reviews, 31*, 295–301.

Gross, J. J., & Levenson, R. W. (1997). Hiding feelings: the acute effects of inhibiting negative and positive emotion. *Journal of Abnormal Psychology, 106*, 95–103.

Hallett, P. E. (1978). Primary and secondary saccades to goals defined by instructions. *Vision Research, 18*, 1279–1296.

Harrison, Y., & Horne, J. A. (2000). The impact of sleep deprivation on decision making: a review. *Journal of Experimental Psychology. Applied, 6*, 236–249.

Harrison, Y., Horne, J. A., & Rothwell, A. (2000). Prefrontal neuropsychological effects of sleep deprivation in young adults – a model of healthy aging? *Sleep, 23*, 1067–1073.

Hartlage, S., Alloy, L. B., Vazquez, C., & Dykman, B. (1993). Automatic and effortful processing in depression. *Psychological Bulletin, 113*, 247–278.

Hasher, L., & Zacks, R. T. (1988). Working memory, comprehension, and aging: a review and a new view. In G. H. Bower (Ed.), *The psychology of learning and motivation* (Vol. 22, pp. 193–225). New York: Academic Press.

Heitz, R. P., & Engle, R. W. (2007). Focusing the spotlight: individual differences in visual attention control. *Journal of Experimental Psychology. General, 136*, 217–240.

Hester, R., & Garavan, H. (2005). Working memory and executive function: the influence of content and load on the control of attention. *Memory and Cognition, 33*, 221–233.

Hockey, G. R. (1997). Compensatory control in the regulation of human performance under stress and high workload: a cognitive-energetical framework. *Biological Psychology, 45*, 73–93.

Jaeggi, S. M., Buschkuehl, M., Etienne, A., Ozdoba, C., Perrig, W. J., & Nirkko, A. C. (2007). On how high performers keep cool brains in situations of cognitive overload. *Cognitive, Affective and Behavioral Neuroscience, 7*, 75–89.

Jaeggi, S. M., Buschkuehl, M., Jonides, J., & Perrig, W. J. (2008). Improving fluid intelligence with training on working memory. *Proc Natl Acad Sci USA, 105*, 6829–6833.

Jaeggi, S.M., Seewer, R., Nirkko, A.C., Eckstein D., Schroth, G., Groner, R., & Gutbrod, K. (2003). Does excessive memory load attenuate activation in the prefrontal cortex? Load-dependent processing in single and dual tasks: functional magnetic resonance imaging study. *Neuroimage, 19*, 210–225.

Johnson, W. (2007). Genetic and environmental influences on behavior: capturing all the interplay. *Psychological Review, 114*, 423–440.

Jonides, J., & Nee, D. E. (2006). Brain mechanisms of proactive interference in working memory. *Neuroscience, 139*, 181–193.

Jonides, J., Schumacher, E. G., Smith, E. E., Lauber, E., Awh, E., Minoshima, S., et al. (1997). Verbal working memory load affects regional brain activation as measured by PET. *Journal of Cognitive Neuroscience, 9*, 462–475.

Kane, M. J., & Engle, R. W. (2000). Working-memory capacity, proactive interference, and divided attention: limits on long-term memory retrieval. *Journal of Experimental Psychology. Learning, Memory and Cognition, 26*, 336–358.

Kane, M. J., & Engle, R. W. (2002). The role of prefrontal cortex in working-memory capacity, executive attention, and general fluid intelligence: an individual differences perspective. *Psychonomic Bulletin and Review, 9*, 637–671.

Kane, M. J., & Engle, R. W. (2003). Working memory capacity and the control of attention: the contributions of goal neglect, response competition, and task set to Stroop interference. *Journal of Experimental Psychology. General, 132*, 47–70.

Kane, M. J., Bleckley, K. M., Conway, A. R. A., & Engle, R. W. (2001). A controlled-attention view of working-memory capacity. *Journal of Experimental Psychology. General, 130*, 169–183.

Kane, M. J., Hambrick, D. Z., Tuholski, S. W., Wilhelm, O., Payne, T. W., & Engle, R. W. (2004). The generality of working memory capacity: a latent variable approach to verbal and visuospatial memory span and reasoning. *Journal of Experimental Psychology. General, 133*, 189–217.

Kellendonk, C., Simpson, E. H., Polan, H. J., Malleret, G., Vronskaya, S., Winiger, V., et al. (2006). Transient and selective overexpression of dopamine D2 receptors in the striatum causes persistent abnormalities in prefrontal cortex functioning. *Neuron, 49*, 603–615.

Kensinger, E. A., & Corkin, S. (2003). Effect of negative emotional content on working memory and long-term memory. *Emotion, 3*, 378–393.

Keogh, E., & French, C. C. (2001). Test anxiety, evaluative stress, and susceptibility to distraction from threat. *European Journal of Personality, 15*, 123–141.

Keppel, G., & Underwood, B. J. (1962). Proactive inhibition in short-term retention of single items. *Journal of Verbal Learning and Verbal Behavior, 1*, 153–161.

Kerns, J. G., Cohen, J. D., MacDonald, A. W., III, Cho, R. Y., Stenger, V. A., & Carter, C. S. (2004). Anterior cingulate, conflict monitoring, and adjustments in control. *Science, 303*, 1023–1026.

Kiewra, K. A., & Benton, S. L. (1988). The relationship between information-processing ability and notetaking. *Contemporary Educational Psychology, 13*, 33–44.

Killgore, W. D. S., Balkin, T. J., & Wesensten, N. J. (2006). Impaired decision making following 49h of sleep deprivation. *Journal of Sleep Research, 15*, 7–13.

Kimberg, D. Y., & D'Esposito, M. (1997). Effects of bromocriptine on human subjects depend on working memory capacity. *Cognitive Neuroreport, 8*, 3581–3585.

Kimberg, D. Y., & D'Esposito, M. (2003). Cognitive effects of the dopamine receptor agonist pergolide. *Neuropsychologia, 41*, 1020–1027.

King, J., & Just, M. A. (1991). Individual differences in syntactic processing: the role of working memory. *Journal of memory and Language, 30*, 580–602.

Klein, K., & Boals, A. (2001). The relationship of life event stress and working memory capacity. *Applied Cognitive Psychology, 15*, 565–579.

Klein, K., & Fiss, W. H. (1999). The reliability and stability of the Turner and Engle working memory task. *Behavior Research Methods, Instruments and Computers, 31*, 429–432.

Klingberg, T., Fernell, E., Olesen, P. J., Johnson, M., Gustafsson, P., Dahlström, K., et al. (2005). Computerized training of working memory in children with ADHD – a randomized, controlled trial. *Journal of the American Academy of Child and Adolescent Psychiatry, 44*, 177–186.

Klingberg, T., Forssberg, H., & Westerberg, H. (2002). Training of working memory in children with ADHD. *Journal of Clinical and Experimental Neuropsychology, 24*, 781–791.

Knecht, S., Breitenstein, C., Bushuven, S., Wailke, S., Kamping, S., Flöel, A., et al. (2004). Levodopa: faster and better word learning in normal humans. *Annals of Neurology, 56*, 20–26.

Kodama, T., Hikosaka, K., & Watanabe, M. (2002). Differential changes in glutamate concentration in the primate prefrontal cortex during spatial delayed alternation and sensory-guided tasks. *Experimental Brain Research, 145*, 133–141.

Krendl, A. C., Richeson, J. A., Kelley, W. M., & Heatherton, T. F. (2008). The negative consequences of threat – a functional magnetic resonance imaging investigation of the neural mechanisms underlying women's underperformance in math. *Psychological Science, 19*, 168–175.

Kyllonen, P. C., & Christal, R. E. (1990). Reasoning ability is (little more than) working memory capacity?! *Intelligence, 14*, 389–433.

Kyllonen, P. C., & Stephens, D. L. (1990). Cognitive abilities as determinants of success in acquiring logic skill. *Learning and Individual Differences, 2*, 129–160.

Lavric, A., Rippon, G., & Gray, J. R. (2003). Threat-evoked anxiety disrupts spatial working memory performance: an attentional account. *Cognitive Therapy and Research, 27*, 489–504.

Lee, K.H., Choi, Y.Y., Gray, J.R., Cho, S.H., Chae, J-H., Lee, S., & Kim, K. (2006). Neural correlates of superior intelligence: Stronger recruitment of posterior parietal cortex. *Neuroimage, 29*, 578–586.

Logan, G. D., & Zbrodoff, N. J. (1979). When it helps to be misled: facilitative effects of increasing the frequency of conflicting stimuli in a Stroop-like task. *Memory and Cognition, 7*, 166–174.

Lorist, M. M., Boksem, M. A. S., & Ridderinkhof, K. R. (2005). Impaired cognitive control and reduced cingulate activity during mental fatigue. *Cognitive Brain Research, 24*, 199–205.

Luciano, M., Wright, M. J., Smith, G. A., Geffen, G. M., Geffen, L. B., & Martin, N. G. (2001). Genetic covariance among measures of information processing speed, working memory, and IQ. *Behavior Genetics, 6,* 581–592.

Lustig, C., May, C. P., & Hasher, L. (2001). Working memory span and the role of proactive interference. *Journal of Experimental Psychology. General, 130,* 199–207.

MacDonald, A. W., III, Carter, C. S., Flory, J. D., Ferrell, R. E., & Manuck, S. B. (2007). COMT Val158Met and executive control: a test of the benefit of specific deficits to translational research. *Journal of Abnormal Psychology, 116,* 306–312.

Manor, I., Tyano, S., Eisenberg, J., Bachner-Melman, R., Kotler, M., & Ebstein, R. P. (2002). The short DRD4 repeats confer risk to attention deficit hyperactivity disorder in a family-based design and impair performance on a continuous performance test (TOVA). *Molecular Psychiatry, 7,* 790–794.

Mathews, A., & Mackintosh, B. (1998). A cognitive model of selective processing in anxiety. *Cognitive Therapy and Research, 122,* 539–560.

Mathews, A., Mackintosh, B., & Fulcher, E. P. (1997). Cognitive biases in anxiety and attention to threat. *Trends in Cognitive Sciences, 1,* 341–346.

May, C. P., Hasher, L., & Kane, M. J. (1999). The role of interference in memory span. *Memory and Cognition, 27,* 759–767.

McNab, F., & Klingberg, T. (2008). Prefrontal cortex and basal ganglia control access to working memory. *Nature Neuroscience, 11,* 103–107.

Mecklinger, A., Weber, K., Gunter, T. C., & Engle, R. W. (2003). Dissociable brain mechanisms for inhibitory control: effects of interference content and working memory capacity. *Cognitive Brain Research, 18,* 26–38.

Mehta, M. A., & Riedel, W. J. (2006). Dopaminergic enhancement of cognitive function. *Current Pharmaceutical Design, 12,* 2487–2500.

Meneses, A., & Perez-Garcia, G. (2007). 5-HT$_{1A}$ receptors and memory. *Neuroscience and Behavioral Reviews, 31,* 705–727.

Miller, E. K. (2000). The prefrontal cortex and cognitive control. *Nature Reviews. Neuroscience, 1,* 59–65.

Miller, E. K., & Cohen, J. D. (2001). An integrative theory of prefrontal cortex function. *Annual Reviews of Neuroscience, 24,* 167–202.

Mitchell, J. P., Heatherton, T. F., Kelley, W. M., Wyland, C. L., Wegner, D. M., & McCrae, C. N. (2007). Separating sustained from transient aspects of cognitive control during thought suppression. *Psychological Science, 18,* 292–297.

Miyake, A., & Shah, P. (1999). *Models of working memory: mechanisms of active maintenance and executive control.* New York: Cambridge University Press.

Miyake, A., Friedman, N. P., Emerson, M. J., Witzki, A. H., & Howerter, A. (2000). The unity and diversity of executive functions and their contributions to complex "frontal lobe" tasks: a latent variable analysis. *Cognitive Psychology, 41,* 49–100.

Moray, N. (1959). Attention in dichotic listening: affective cues and the influence of instructions. *The Quarterly Journal of Experimental Psychology, 11,* 59–60.

Muller, J., & Roberts, J. E. (2004). Memory and attention in obsessive-compulsive disorder: a review. *Anxiety Disorders, 19,* 1–28.

Nebel, K., Wiese, H., Seyfarth, J., Gizewski, E. R., Stude, P., Ciener, H.-C., et al. (2007). Activity of attention related structures in multiple sclerosis patients. *Brain Research, 1151,* 150–160.

Niemivirta, M. (1999). Motivational and cognitive predictors of goal setting and task performance. *International Journal of Educational Research, 31,* 499–513.

Nigg, J. T. (2000). On inhibition/disinhibition in developmental psychopathology: views from cognitive and personality psychology and a working inhibition taxonomy. *Psychological Bulletin, 126,* 220–246.

Nigg, J. T., Carr, L. A., Martel, M. M., & Henderson, J. M. (2007). Concepts of inhibition and developmental psychopathology. In C. MacCleod & D. Gorfein (Eds.), *Inhibition in cognition* (pp. 259–277). Washington, DC: American Psychological Association Press.

Nolan, K. A., Bilder, R. M., Lachman, H. M., & Volavka, J. (2004). Catechol O-methyltransferase val[158] met polymorphism in schizophrenia: differential effects of Val and Met alleles on cognitive stability and flexibilty. *American Journal of Psychiatry, 161,* 359–361.

Norman, D. A., & Bobrow, D. G. (1975). On data-limited and resource-limited processes. *Cognitive Psychology, 7,* 44–64.

Norman, D. A., & Shallice, T. (1986). Attention to action: willed and automatic control of behavior. In R. J. Davidson, G. E. Schwartz, & D. Shapiro (Eds.), *Consciousness and self-regulation: advances in research and theory* (Vol. 4, pp. 1–18). New York: Plenum.

Oberauer, K. (2006). Is the focus of attention in working memory expanded through practice? *Journal of Experimental Psychology. Learning, Memory and Cognition, 32,* 197–214.

Oberauer, K., Süß, K.-M., Wilhelm, O., & Wittman, W. W. (2003). The multiple faces of working memory: storage, processing, supervision, and coordination. *Intelligence, 31,* 167–193.

Olesen, P. J., Westerberg, H., & Klingberg, T. (2003). Increased prefrontal and parietal activity after training of working memory. *Nature Neuroscience, 7,* 75–79.

Osborne, J. W. (2007). Linking stereotype threat and anxiety. *Educational Psychology, 27*, 135–154.

Owen, A. M. (2004). Cognitive dysfunction in Parkinson's disease: the role of frontostriatal circuitry. *The Neuroscientist, 9*, 1–13.

Pennington, B. F., & Ozonoff, S. (1996). Executive functions and developmental psychopathology. *Journal of Child Psychology and Psychiatry, 37*, 51–87.

Perlstein, W. M., Dixit, N. K., Carter, C. S., Noll, D. C., & Cohen, J. D. (2003). Prefrontal cortex dysfunction mediates deficits in working memory and prepotent responding in schizophrenia. *Biological Psychiatry, 53*, 25–38.

Perlstein, W. M., Elbert, T., & Stenger, V. A. (2002). Dissociation in human prefrontal cortex of affective influences on working memory-related activity. *Proc Natl Acad Sci USA, 99*, 1736–1741.

Persson, J., & Reuter-Lorenz, P. A. (2008). Gaining control: training executive function and far transfer of the ability to resolve interference. *Psychological Science, 19*, 881–888.

Persson, J., Welsh, K. M., Jonides, J., & Reuter-Lorenz, P. A. (2007). Cognitive fatigue of executive processes: interaction between interference resolution tasks. *Neuropsychologia, 45*, 1571–1579.

Peterson, L. R., & Peterson, M. J. (1959). Short-term retention of individual verbal items. *Journal of Experimental Psychology, 58*, 193–198.

Petrides, M. (1996). Specialized systems for the processing of mnemonic information within the primate frontal cortex. *Philosophical Transactions of the Royal Society of London, 351*, 1455–1462.

Posner, M. I., & Snyder, Ch R R. (1975). Attention and cognitive control. In R. Solso (Ed.), *Information processing and cognition: the Loyola symposium*. Hillsdale, NJ: Lawrence Erlbaum Associates.

Previc, F. H. (1999). Dopamine and the origins of human intelligence. *Brain and Cognition, 41*, 299–350.

Quinn, D. M., & Spencer, S. J. (2001). The interference of stereotype threat with women's generation of mathematical problem-solving strategies. *Journal of Social Issues, 57*, 55–71.

Redick, T. S., Heitz, R. P., & Engle, R. W. (2007). Working memory capacity and inhibition: cognitive and social consequences. In D. S. Gorfein & C. M. MacLeod (Eds.), *Inhibition in cognition* (pp. 125–142). Washington, DC: American Psychological Association.

Reitan, R. M., & Wolfson, D. (1994). A selective and critical review of neuropsychological deficits and the frontal lobes. *Neuropsychology Review, 4*, 161–198.

Richards, J. M., & Gross, J. J. (2000). Emotion regulation and memory: the cognitive costs of keeping one's cool. *Journal of Personality and Social Psychology, 79*, 410–424.

Richeson, J. A., & Shelton, J. N. (2003). When prejudice does not pay: effects of interracial contact on executive function. *Psychological Science, 14*, 287–290.

Richeson, J. A., Baird, A. A., Gordon, H. L., Heatherton, T. F., Wyland, C. L., Trawalter, S., et al. (2003). An fMRI investigation of the impact of interracial contact on executive function. *Nature Neuroscience, 6*, 1323–1328.

Rosen, V. M., & Engle, R. W. (1997). Forward and backward serial recall. *Intelligence, 25*, 37–47.

Savitz, J., Solms, M., & Ramesar, R. (2006). The molecular genetics of cognition: dopamine, COMT and BDNF. *Genes, Brain and Behavior, 5*, 311–328.

Schmader, T., & Johns, M. (2003). Converging evidence that stereotype threat reduces working memory capacity. *Journal of Personality and Social Psychology, 85*, 440–452.

Schmeichel, B. J. (2007). Attention control, memory updating, and emotion regulation temporarily reduce the capacity for executive control. *Journal of Experimental Psychology. General, 136*, 241–255.

Schneider, W., & Chein, J. M. (2003). Controlled & automatic processing: behavior, theory, and biological mechanisms. *Cognitive Science, 27*, 525–559.

Schneider, W., & Detweiler, M. (1987). A connectionist/control architecture for working memory. In G. H. Bower (Ed.), *The psychology of learning and motivation* (Vol. 21, pp. 53–119). New York: Academic.

Serino, A., Ciaramelli, E., Di Santantonio, A., Malagu, S., Servadei, F., & Ladavas, E. (2007). A pilot study for rehabilitation of central executive deficits after traumatic brain injury. *Brain Injury, 21*, 11–19.

Shackman, A. J., Sarinopoulos, I., Maxwell, J. S., Pizzagalli, D. A., Lavric, A., & Davidson, R. J. (2006). Anxiety selectively disrupts visuospatial working memory. *Emotion, 6*, 40–61.

Shallice, T., & Burgess, P. W. (1993). Supervisory control of action and thought selection. In A. Baddeley & L. Weiskrantz (Eds.), *Attention: selection, awareness, and control: a tribute to donald broadbent* (pp. 171–187). Oxford, England: Clarendon.

Shamosh, N. A., DeYoung, C., Green, A. E., Reis, D. L., Johnson, M. R., Conway, A. R. A., et al. (2008). Individual differences in delay discounting. *Psychological Science, 19*, 904–911.

Shiffrin, R. M., & Schneider, W. (1984). Automatic and controlled processing revisited. *Psychological Review, 91*, 269–276.

Shimamura, A. P. (2000). Toward a cognitive neuroscience of metacognition. *Consciousness and Cognition, 9*, 313–323.

Smith, E. E., & Jonides, J. (1998). Neuroimaging analyses of human working memory. *Proc Natl Acad Sci USA, 95*, 12061–12068.

Smith, E. E., & Jonides, J. (1999). Storage and executive processes in the frontal lobes. *Science Review, Neuroscience, 283*, 1657–1661.

Smith, M. E., McEvoy, L. K., & Gevins, A. (2002). The impact of moderate sleep loss on neurophysiologic signals during working memory task performance. *Sleep, 25*, 784–794.

Steele, C. M., & Josephs, R. A. (1990). Alcohol myopia: its prized and dangerous effects. *American Psychologist, 45*, 921–933.

Steinhauser, M., Maier, M., & Hübner, R. (2007). Cognitive control under stress: how stress affects strategies of task-set reconfiguration. *Psychological Science, 18*, 540–545.

Stroop, J. R. (1935). Studies of interference in serial verbal reactions. *Journal of Experimental Psychology, 18*, 643–662.

Suhara, T., Fukuda, H., Inoue, O., Itoh, T., Suzuki, K., Yamasaki, T., et al. (1991). Age-related changes in human D1 dopamine receptors measured by positron emission tomography. *Psychopharmacology, 103*, 41–45.

Swainson, R., Rogers, R. D., Sahakian, B. J., Summers, B. A., Polkey, C. E., & Robbins, T. W. (2000). Probabilistic learning and reversal deficits in patients with Parkinson's disease or frontal or temporal lobe lesions: possible adverse effects of dopaminergic medication. *Neuropsychologia, 38*, 596–612.

Swainson, J., Oosterlaan, J., Murias, M., Schuck, S., Flodman, P., Spence, M. A., et al. (2000). Attention deficit/hyperactivity disorder children with a 7-repeat allele of the dopamine receptor D4 gene have extreme behavior but normal performance on critical neuropsychological tests of attention. *Proc Natl Acad Sci USA, 97*, 4754–4759.

Thorell, L. B., Lindqvist, S., Bergman, S., Bohlin, G., & Klingberg, T. (2009). Training and transfer effects of executive functions in preschool children. *Developmental Science, 11*, 969–976.

Toga, A. W., & Thompson, P. M. (2005). Genetics of brain structure and intelligence. *Annual Reviews of Neuroscience, 28*, 1–23.

Trawalter, S., & Richeson, J. A. (2006). Regulatory focus and executive function after interracial interactions. *Journal of Experimental Social Psychology, 42*, 406–412.

Turley-Ames, K. J., & Whitfield, M. M. (2003). Strategy training and working memory task performance. *Journal of Memory and Language, 49*, 446–468.

Turner, M. L., & Engle, R. W. (1989). Is working memory capacity task dependent? *Journal of Memory and Language, 28*, 127–154.

Unsworth, N., & Engle, R. W. (2007). The nature of individual differences in working memory capacity: active maintenance in primary memory and controlled search from secondary memory. *Psychological Review, 114*, 104–132.

Unsworth, N., Heitz, R. P., & Engle, R. W. (2005). Working memory capacity in hot and cold cognition. In R. W. Engle, G. S dek, U. Hecker, & D. N. McIntosh (Eds.), *Cognitive limitations in aging and psychopathology* (pp. 19–43). New York: Cambridge University Press.

Unsworth, N., Schrock, J. C., & Engle, R. W. (2004). Working memory capacity and the antisaccade task: individual differences in voluntary saccade control. *Journal of Experimental Psychology. Learning, Memory and Cognition, 30*, 1302–1321.

Vallat, C., Azouvi, P., Hardisson, H., Meffert, R., Tessier, C., & Pradat-Diehl, P. (2005). Rehabilitation of verbal working memory after left hemisphere stroke. *Brain Injury, 19*, 1157–1164.

Verhaeghen, P., Cerella, J., & Basak, C. (2004). A working memory workout: how to expand the focus of serial attention from one to four items in 10 hours or less. *Journal of Experimental Psychology. Learning, Memory and Cognition, 30*, 1322–1337.

Vohs, K. D., & Heatherton, T. F. (2000). Self-regulatory failure: a resource-depletion approach. *Psychological Science, 11*, 249–254.

Waters, G. S., & Caplan, D. (2003). The reliability and stability of verbal working memory measures. *Behavior Research Methods, Instruments and Computers, 35*, 550–564.

Wegner, D. M. (1994). Ironic processes of mental control. *Psychological Review, 101*, 34–52.

Wegner, D. M., Erber, R., & Zanakos, S. (1993). Ironic processes in the mental control of mood and mood-related thought. *Journal of Personality and Social Psychology, 65*, 1093–1104.

Weissman, D. H., Giesbrecht, B., Song, A. W., Mangun, G. R., & Woldorff, M. G. (2003). Conflict monitoring in the human anterior cingulate cortex during selective attention to global and local object features. *Neuroimage, 19*, 1361–1368.

Wenzlaff, R. M., Wegner, D. M., & Roper, D. W. (1988). Depression and mental control: the resurgence of unwanted negative thoughts. *Journal of Personality and Social Psychology, 55*, 882–892.

Westerberg, H., & Klingberg, T. (2007). Changes in cortical activity after training of working memory – a single-subject analysis. *Physiology and Behavior, 92*, 186–192.

Westernberg, H., Jacobaeus, H., Hirvikoski, T., Clevberger, P., Östensson, M.-L., Bartfai, A., et al. (2007). Computerized working memory training after stroke – a pilot study. *Brain Injury, 21*, 21–29.

Whitmer, A. J., & Banich, M. T. (2007). Inhibition versus switching deficits in different forms of rumination. *Psychological Science, 18*, 546–553.

Wilhelm, O., & Engle, R. W. (2005). *Handbook of understanding and measuring intelligence*. CA: SAGE.

Williams-Gray, C. H., Hampshire, A., Barker, R. A., & Owen, A. M. (2008). Attentional control in Parkinson's disease is dependent on COMT val[158]met genotype. *Brain, 131*, 397–408.

Williams-Gray, C. H., Hampshire, A., Robbins, T. W., Owen, A. M., & Barker, R. A. (2007). Catehol O-Methyltransferase val[158]met genotype influences frontoparietal activity during planning in patients with Parkinson's disease. *The Journal of Neuroscience, 27*, 4832–4838.

Wright, M., De Geus, E., Ando, J., Luciano, M., Posthuma, D., Ono, Y., et al. (2000). Genetics of cognition: outline of a collaborative twin study. *Twin Research, 4*, 48–56.

Yoo, S.-S., Hu, P. T., Gujar, N., Jolesz, F. A., & Walker, M. P. (2007). A deficit in the ability to form new human memories without sleep. *Nature Neuroscience, 10*, 385–392.

Chapter 19
Adrift in the Stream of Thought: The Effects of Mind Wandering on Executive Control and Working Memory Capacity

Jennifer C. McVay and Michael J. Kane

Our minds wander. Sometimes, that's good – we can ponder scientific questions, practice important conversations, or just plan daily events while we engage in routine or dull tasks. Sometimes, thought, that's bad – we may worry excessively, reexperience traumatic events repeatedly, or (most relevant to present purposes) simply become distracted by thoughts, images, or fantasies that interfere with our ongoing activities. Such interference is especially likely to become problematic during tasks that are cognitively demanding.

Despite its ubiquity in human mental life, and its frequently disruptive effects, mind wandering has garnered only scant attention from cognitive psychology (e.g., Giambra, 1995; Schooler, 2002; Smallwood & Schooler, 2006; Wegner, 1997). This is unfortunate but understandable. If one considers only the fantastical content of some mind-wandering episodes (those we might call "daydreams"), the phenomenon seems to be more central to the concerns of clinical or personality psychology if not the humanities (e.g., Bowling, 1950). Moreover, the covert mental processes that cognitive psychology regularly studies leave a behavioral residue that can be measured objectively, such as accuracy rate or response latency. The stream of thought, in contrast, leaves no overt behavior in its wake other than introspective self-reports, and our field has learned to be skeptical of these (Nisbett & Wilson, 1977).

We agree that a healthy skepticism is always warranted regarding people's reports of their own subjective experiences, including those about thought content (e.g., Schwitzgebel, 2008). At the same time, our chapter will argue (from robust empirical data) for the general validity of subjects' mind-wandering reports, at least under particular conditions. Moreover, we will contend that mind-wandering reports are useful as measures of failed executive control in the moment, and of normal variation in executive-control capabilities within and among healthy adults. Our research, and others', demonstrates that mind-wandering experiences tend to precede executive-control errors, and that people who experience more mind-wandering episodes also commit more performance errors. We will thus argue for a causal role for conscious thought in the willful control of action.

Our Approach to Executive Control: Variation in Working Memory Capacity

"Executive control" is a broad term that is used differently by different subfields in psychology and neuroscience and even by different investigators within these subfields. When we refer to executive control, we mean the collection of cognitive processes that allow for volitional, goal-directed behavior,

---

J.C. McVay and M.J. Kane (✉)
Department of Psychology, University of North Carolina at Greensboro, Greensboro, NC 27402-6170, USA
e-mail: mjkane@uncg.edu

particularly in contexts where that behavior is challenged by environmental or mental distractors, or by learned habitual responses that are currently inappropriate. Our research, which we will describe in more detail below, has illuminated several functions to be especially important to performing well in the face of distraction and response conflict: *goal maintenance* and *competition resolution* (for more thorough treatments, see Engle & Kane, 2004; Kane, Conway, Hambrick, & Engle, 2007; for a related view, see Braver, Gray, & Burgess, 2007). Goal maintenance refers to processes that actively sustain ready access to goal-relevant information, either within or outside conscious awareness, which proactively biases downstream information-processing in accordance with intentions. Competition resolution refers to mechanisms that, in the face of cognitive conflict (e.g., memory interference, stimulus-response incompatibility, elicited-but-incorrect responses), reactively facilitate goal-relevant memory representations or response tendencies, inhibit goal-irrelevant memory representations or response tendencies, or both.

Our general empirical strategy for studying these executive-control functions has been to assess individual differences in working memory capacity (WMC), via "complex span" tasks, and then to observe how these WM-related differences play themselves out in lower-level attention tasks that are thought to engage controlled processing (or not). In doing so, we follow Cronbach's (1957) recommendation of testing for individual-by-treatment interactions as a way of harnessing the combined strengths of experimental and correlational methods, here to learn more about the broad constructs we are interested in (e.g., WMC, executive control) and the specific tasks we use to measure those constructs (e.g., complex span, *Stroop* tasks). Like Cronbach (and like other contributors to this volume), we believe that the experimentalist's study of variation among treatments can be effectively combined with the psychometrician's study of variation among people, and this combination will result in a more complete view of human behavior, generally, and of executive control, in particular, than will either of these methods in isolation (Kane & Miyake, 2008).

We have focused our Cronbachian efforts on WMC because a large literature, based on a variety of tasks and subject populations, demonstrates complex-span measures to predict individual differences in a broad range of higher-order cognitive abilities, such as language comprehension, complex learning, and reasoning through novel problems (e.g., Daneman & Merikle, 1996; Engle, Tuholski, Laughlin, & Conway, 1999; Gathercole & Pickering, 2000; Kyllonen & Christal, 1990; Kyllonen & Stephens, 1990). WMC thus appears to be an important contributor to general fluid intelligence beyond any particular domain-specific skills or strategies that it may also be associated with. Moreover, at a theoretical level, WMC measures were developed to assess specifically the "central executive" functions of Baddeley's (1986, 2000, 2007) working memory model (Daneman & Carpenter, 1980). They do so by requiring subjects to keep items accessible in memory while also engaging in a demanding secondary processing task, and so they seem to require attentional along with memorial processes.

To be more concrete, complex span tasks present short lists of to-be-remembered items, such as individual words, letters, digits, or visuospatial patterns, interspersed with an unrelated processing task, such as judging sentences, verifying equations, or mentally rotating objects. Most researchers require serial-order recall of the item lists, which usually vary in length from a minimum of two items to a maximum of five or six items; although subjects must maintain some criterion level of accuracy in the processing task, scores typically reflect only the recall rates for the memory items (for a methodological review, see Conway et al., 2005). In our laboratory, we often create a composite score from at least three different complex span tasks that have been developed for fully automated testing (Unsworth, Heitz, Schrock, & Engle, 2005): (1) operation span (OSPAN), which tests memory for words or letters embedded within an equation-verification task (is the provided answer to each equation correct?) (2) reading span (RSPAN), which tests memory for words or letters embedded within a sentence-judgment task (is each sentence sensible or nonsensical?), and; (3) spatial span (SSPAN), which tests memory for spatial locations within a matrix in alternation with a symmetry-judgment task (is each novel pattern vertically symmetrical?). The key advantage to combining multiple WMC measures from the same subjects is that it reduces the impact of task-specific error variance that is unrelated to the latent WMC construct (e.g., arithmetic knowledge in OSPAN; mental-rotation skill in SSPAN). Individual differences in such a composite measure from complex span tasks are therefore more likely to reflect primarily individual differences in WMC rather than individual differences in some other skills or abilities.

Variation in Working Memory Capacity as Variation in Executive Attention

Our theoretical perspective, which we have described as a "controlled attention" or "executive attention" view of WMC, holds that the robust empirical association between measures of complex span and tests of higher-order cognitive abilities is due to their both drawing upon, in part, domain-general, attentional-control mechanisms (Engle & Kane, 2004; Kane, Hambrick, & Conway, 2005; Kane, Conway et al., 2007). Indirect evidence for this view comes from investigating the performance of complex-span tasks themselves. For example, recent work by Unsworth and Engle (2006, 2007; see Ilkowska & Engle, this volume) indicates that complex span – and its relation to complex cognition – is dually driven by mechanisms that actively maintain a limited number of representations in the focus of attention and, perhaps primarily, by cue-driven retrieval processes that recover inactive representations from long-term memory (LTM). In fact, traditional LTM-retrieval tasks, such as immediate free recall, appear to measure the WMC construct (and account for variation in higher-order cognition) just as well as complex span tasks do (Ilkowska & Engle, this volume). We do not yet know the extent to which executive-attention mechanisms are involved in such cue-driven retrieval. Previous research, however, indicates that LTM retrieval is attention demanding, at least in interference-rich contexts that characterize complex span tasks (e.g., Conway & Engle, 1996; Kane & Engle, 2000; Rosen & Engle, 1997).

More direct evidence for a link between WMC and executive attention comes from studies that examine WMC-related individual differences in the performance of attention-control tasks that make little or no demand on LTM-retrieval processes. Instead, these tasks seem to elicit WMC-related variation in the goal-maintenance and competition-resolution functions we described earlier. In the antisaccade task, for example, subjects are asked to move their eyes and attention away from salient visual-onset cues; if a cue flashes on the right, subjects should look to the left, and if a cue flashes on the left, they should look to the right. WMC predicts two aspects of antisaccade performance (Kane, Bleckley, Conway, & Engle, 2001; Unsworth, Schrock, & Engle, 2004). First, lower-WMC subjects make more eye-movement errors than do higher-WMC subjects, by looking at the cue rather than away from it. These overt action errors suggest that lower-WMC subjects fail more often than higher-WMC subjects to maintain sufficient access to task goals, in the moment, to control their behavior. We refer to such failures as "goal neglect" (see Duncan, 1995). Second, lower-WMC subjects are slower to initiate their accurately directed eye movements than are higher-WMC subjects. These slow responses suggest that lower-WMC subjects have particular difficulty resolving the competition between habitual and goal-appropriate responses on a trial-by-trial basis, even when the goal is sufficiently maintained to produce the desired action.

Our subsequent investigation of the Stroop task (Kane & Engle, 2003) replicated these basic findings while demonstrating more clearly the independence of goal-neglect and competition-resolution functions of executive control. Using a computerized color-word Stroop task in four experiments, we manipulated the proportion of congruent trials as a means to vary the importance of active goal maintenance to success. Low-congruent conditions presented color words that matched their hues on only 0–20% of trials (e.g., *RED* appearing in red), whereas high-congruent conditions presented word-hue matches on 75–80% of trials (see Logan & Zbrodoff, 1979). All conditions presented critical incongruent trials, where the words and hues were in conflict (*BLUE* appearing in red), and some conditions also presented occasional neutral stimuli (*JKM* in red). Our idea was that, in the low-congruent task, the color-naming goal is externally and repeatedly reinforced by the context because most trials present color-word conflict; control in low-congruent conditions is thus supported by the environment. In contrast, in the high-congruent task, the color-naming goal is not reinforced because most trials present color-word matches rather than mismatches; here, then, subjects must endogenously maintain goal activation throughout the task. If subjects lose access to the goal and begin to read words rather than name colors, accuracy will remain generally high (from the experimenter's perspective) because the colors and words require the same overt response. However, on the rare trials that present color-word conflict, goal neglect will be evident in erroneous word-reading responses.

Kane and Engle (2003) found that low-congruent conditions produced modest WMC-related differences in response time (RT) interference, but not in errors, with lower-WMC subjects naming colors on incongruent trials a bit more slowly than higher-WMC subjects. As in the antisaccade task, then, lower-WMC subjects had greater difficulty resolving competition between color and word dimensions, even when responding was goal directed. In contrast, high-congruent conditions elicited dramatic accuracy differences related to WMC. Lower-WMC subjects committed 50–100% more color-naming errors than did higher-WMC subjects, with most reflecting overt word reading. As well, lower-WMC subjects responded more quickly here to the *congruent* trials than did higher-WMC subjects, suggesting that lower-WMC subjects more often read the word aloud (a faster, more habitual response than color naming) than did higher-WMC subjects. Both high error rates and fast congruent responses are signatures of lower-WMC subjects failing to maintain adequate access to goal representations during the high-congruent Stroop task, and thus experiencing more frequent goal neglect.

Mind Wandering as an Executive-Control Failure

If competition-resolution and goal-maintenance mechanisms both contribute to successful executive control, then we must consider at least two sources of control failures. The source of the conflict that competition–resolution processes must contend with is often a shared cue to both a habitual (erroneous) and an intended (correct) response. For example, the color word in the Stroop task cues the dominant reading response; the visual flash in the antisaccade task cues the dominant orienting response. In both situations, even when the task goal is being maintained, the interference from competing responses may temporarily impede appropriate action. By analogy, we may also consider what competes with goal maintenance in contexts that tend to produce goal neglect. Why do people sometimes fail to maintain sufficient goal access to control behavior?

When goal maintenance fails, we observe the correct response being replaced by the dominant-but-inappropriate response. This may suggest that the dominant response goal (e.g., "*read the words*") actually replaces the intention (e.g., "*name the colors*") in working memory. Or, it may be that something else elicits the loss of goal activation that then causes the system to default to an automatic action schema. We propose that the latter is more likely. Specifically, we suggest that goal maintenance is often hijacked by task-unrelated thought (TUT), resulting in both the subjective experience of mind wandering and habit-based errors.

The experience of TUT, or mind wandering, represents a failure to maintain focal attention on the task at hand. It seems noteworthy, then, that mainstream cognitive research on attention largely ignores the contribution of on- versus off-task thoughts to performance, emphasizing instead the stimulus, context, and expectancy factors that contribute to attentional selection, set, and orienting. Our claim, in contrast, is that conscious thoughts actually matter. It bears reminding that human research subjects do not exist in the vacuum of the experimental laboratory, and that the extraexperimental goals, interests, and thoughts that subjects bring into the testing room may represent a tremendously important individual-difference and situational variable in the expression of attention-control capabilities. If we are right, it would seem irresponsible to ignore the potential contributions of off-task thoughts to executive functions and their variation. Goal-appropriate actions may depend, at least in part, on conscious thought being directed at those very actions.

The Measurement of Mind Wandering

A challenge arises, then, regarding the objective and reliable measurement of inherently subjective on- and off-task thoughts. Antrobus, Singer, and Greenberg (1966) introduced a measurement to address the challenge of assessing mind wandering during ongoing activities. During a vigilance task, they asked subject to indicate, at the end of each trial block, whether they had experienced any TUTs. This block-by-block assessment of mind wandering provided a new tool, the "thought probe," to the field. Many versions of thought probes are now used in the literature. Some experimenters ask their subjects to verbalize their thought content at various points during the task and subsequently code them for task-relatedness (e.g., Smallwood, Baracia, Lowe, & Obonsawin, 2003; Smallwood, Davies et al., 2004); others employ a rating scale indicating the frequency of off-task thinking during a given period (e.g., Antrobus et al.; McGuire, Paulesu, Frackowiak, & Frith, 1996). We argue that the best and most objective type of probe requires only a simple binary or categorical choice response (e.g., TUT vs. on-task thought) in order to minimize both the interruption to the task and the potential translation problems between an idiosyncratic thought or image and the language required to convey conscious states to the experimenter. Probes can also either be experimenter-scheduled or self-initiated. Self-initiated reports rely on meta-awareness of the mind wandering episode as it occurs and, therefore, are a less reliable measure of mind wandering as it relates to task performance (for a review, see Smallwood & Schooler, 2006).

A potential criticism of any particular thought-probe technique is that social desirability and thought monitoring might reactively change the frequency of mind-wandering episodes. For example, Filler and Giambra (1973) predicted that the expectation of thought probes would increase reports of mind wandering during a vigilance task. Instead of warning subjects before the experiment that they would have to report their thoughts, the authors waited until part of the task was complete to ask subjects about TUTs (i.e., after the first, second, or third block of the ongoing task). Contrary to predictions, Filler and Giambra found *fewer* TUTs when subjects knew earlier about the thought probes, suggesting that subjects' awareness of their mind wandering in the first block caused them to exert more control during the second. Expected thought probes may therefore underestimate TUTs.

Despite any potential biases inherent in probed thought reports, they have effectively established some basic, replicable characteristics of mind wandering. For example, its frequency decreases with task complexity (Grodsky & Giambra, 1990–1991; Teasdale et al., 1995), with task difficulty (Antrobus, Singer, Goldstein, & Fortgang, 1970; Filler & Giambra, 1973; Grodsky & Giambra, 1990–1991; McGuire et al., 1996; McKiernan, D'Angelo, Kaufman, & Binder, 2006; Smallwood, Obonsawin, & Reid, 2002–2003; Teasdale, Proctor, Lloyd, & Baddeley, 1993) and with heightened task motivation (Antrobus et al., 1966). Conversely, mind wandering increases with time on (boring) tasks (Antrobus, Coleman, & Singer, 1967; Antrobus et al., 1966; Smallwood, Davies et al., 2004; Smallwood, Heim, Riby, & Davies, 2006, Smallwood et al., 2002–2003; Teasdale et al., 1995) and with experimental manipulations designed to prime subjects' personal concerns unrelated to the ongoing task (Antrobus et al., 1966). We will say more about the validity of thought reports later (see also Smallwood & Schooler, 2006), but we note here that such systematic variation in TUT reports, along similar variables across different studies, provides supportive evidence for validity.

Also, individual differences in the propensity to experience TUTs appear stable over time and reliable across a variety of primary tasks. For example, Grodsky and Giambra (1990–1991) found that, while TUT rates were lower during a complex reading task than during a vigilance task, people with higher TUT rates in one task also had higher rates in the other ($r=0.51$). Giambra (1995) also demonstrated the test–retest reliability of the thought-probe procedure during vigilance tasks. Mind-wandering reports correlated at $r=0.77$ for tests conducted 1–14 days apart and $r=0.81$ for tests conducted 12 months apart. Furthermore, recent work from our lab finds that TUT rates during a laboratory go/no-go task predict probed TUT rates (via experience-sampling methodology) during daily life activities ($b=1.29$, $SE=0.607$, $t(68)=2.12$; McVay, Kane, & Kwapil, 2009). Whatever mechanisms are responsible for lapses of attention, then, they appear to be stable across people, tasks, contexts, and time. Moreover, variation in mind-wandering rates is predicted by other stable individual-difference variables, such as psychopathology: TUT rates are higher for people diagnosed with AD/HD than for controls (McVay et al., 2008; Shaw & Giambra, 1993) and higher for more, than for less, dysphoric subjects (Smallwood, O'Connor, & Heim, 2004–2005), while TUT rates are lower for clinically depressed people than for controls (Giambra, Grodsky, Belongie, & Rosenberg, 1994–1995) and lower for ruminators than for nonruminators (Smallwood et al., 2004–2005).

Brain Wandering and Goal Directed Behavior

Neuroimaging studies have now identified several regions of the brain, labeled the "default mode network" (Raichle et al., 2001), which consistently show deactivations in activity when subjects shift from a passive resting state (in which thoughts tend to drift) to an attention-demanding, or goal-driven, activity; they are considered "default" because they represent the spontaneous cognitive activity that people engage in when they have no particular goal, or task to complete. These brain regions (including medial frontal cortex, lateral and medial parietal cortex, and medial temporal cortex) have thus been implicated in mind-wandering experiences, which decrease during attention-demanding tasks (e.g., Antrobus et al., 1966). McGuire et al. (1996) first proposed the connection between mind-wandering and activation in specific regions of the brain. Using positron emission tomography (PET), they found that individual differences in TUT rates were significantly correlated with default network activation during rest and several cognitive tasks (in the latter case, such mind-wandering/default-activation should have interfered with task performance).

In an fMRI study, McKiernan et al. (2006) manipulated the difficulty of processing required by an auditory target-detection task, expecting to find both TUT-rate and default-network differences between difficulty conditions. Subjects first responded to unpredictable thought probes (for on-task vs. off-task thoughts) during the tone-detection task and during "rest" in a sham fMRI scanner; they subsequently performed tone detection in alternation with rest during neuroimaging. As predicted, as task difficulty increased, TUTs increased and task-induced deactivations (TIDs) decreased (i.e., the default network was less active as the task became more difficult). More importantly, the authors report an association between the average TUT frequency at each difficulty level and the average TID at the same difficulty level ($r=-0.90$) suggesting that the observed TID reflected reductions in off-task thinking. Mason et al. (2007) also demonstrated the relation between TUT rate (measured during the task) and changes in fMRI-assessed activity in the default-mode network ($rs>0.50$). TUT rates were lower, and default-mode deactivations were greater, during an unpracticed visuospatial WM task than during a practiced task, indicating that the (mind-wandering) processes occurring during rest continued to a greater degree during more automated tasks. As well, individual differences in these deactivations correlated with a retrospective questionnaire about mind-wandering experiences, the Imaginal Processes Inventory ($rs \approx 0.60$).

Mind Wandering and Goal Neglect

We conceive ongoing conscious cognition as reflecting a balance between task-related and task-unrelated images and thoughts (or between default-network and task-network brain regions). There are times in life when it is not necessary to devote attention to the immediate external environment, such as on a long bus ride or when one's current task is largely automatic. These occasions provide the opportunity for a person to willfully turn attention toward TUTs. For example, during a bus ride, you might write a mental grocery list or consider a recent interaction with a colleague. In these situations, TUTs are not likely to interfere with the task goal (i.e., getting home) and, therefore, an appropriate balance is maintained. If, however, you are so engaged in thought that you miss your bus stop, the balance is off and TUTs have become detrimental. It is this situation – where off-task cognitions interfere with the ongoing task goals and produce goal-neglect errors – that is of primary interest to us.

Indirect evidence for a causal connection between off-task thoughts and performance errors comes from diary studies of action slips (e.g., Reason, 1990; Reason & Mycielska, 1982), where absent-minded mistakes (e.g., pouring coffee into a bowl of cereal instead of milk; driving home the normal route instead of stopping at the store) are frequently reported while subjects are preoccupied by TUTs. In the famous quote from James (1890), absent-minded people are known to go into their bedrooms to change clothes for dinner, only to subsequently find themselves in bed. During such complex, but erroneous, action sequences, a person's mind seems to be "elsewhere," apparently allowing a habitual, but inappropriate, action schema to control behavior. But does mind-wandering itself actually cause such action slips?

Unfortunately, most empirical mind-wandering studies have focused on vigilance tasks that elicit ceiling-level performance, and so these studies cannot help us evaluate an ostensible link between mind wandering and performance error. Fortunately, a few studies have used more complex, attention-demanding tasks, and these have shown clear evidence for mind wandering's disruptive effects. Schooler, Reichle, and Halpern (2004) assessed the impact of TUTs on reading by administering a comprehension test immediately after a TUT was reported; the test items addressed the portion of the text that had just been "read." When compared to midpassage tests given to control subjects who were not probed for TUTs, comprehension accuracy was worse on passages following a TUT report ($Ms = 78\%$ vs. 54%). Teasdale et al. (1995) also observed deficits in a more traditional executive-control task, random number generation, in trial blocks during which subjects reported a TUT. Subjects were asked to generate a series of random numbers, one per second for 100–120 s, and to report their thought contents at the end of a block (recorded verbatim and coded for task-relatedness). The digit series generated in blocks without TUT reports were significantly more random (and so, conforming to the demanding task goals) than those accompanied by a TUT report. We discuss further evidence for a causal role of conscious thought on performance, from our own laboratory, below.

Mind Wandering, Goal Neglect, and WMC

The executive-attention theory of WMC (e.g., Engle & Kane, 2004; Kane, Brown et al., 2007) argues that WMC tasks capture, in part, the goal-maintenance function of executive control and, therefore, they should predict individual differences in the subjective experience of mind wandering. We first demonstrated this relation in daily life using the experience-sampling method (Kane, Brown et al., 2007). One hundred and twenty-six subjects, having previously completed WMC screening, carried Palm Pilot PDAs, which beeped them randomly throughout the day for 7 days. At the beep, subjects completed an electronic questionnaire that first asked whether their mind had wandered to something other than what they were doing (whatever that was). Subjects then answered additional questions about their thought content, their perceived control over their thoughts, and about their current activity. We predicted that during cognitively demanding activities (as in laboratory tasks, such as Stroop and antisaccade), lower-WMC subjects would suffer more off-task thoughts than would higher-WMC subjects. However, during routine, everyday activities that required little in the way of cognitive control, we predicted little or no WMC-related variation; when there is little need to focus attention, there is little reason to expect WMC to matter.

Indeed, when averaged across all daily life contexts, many of which were not cognitively demanding, WMC had no effect on mind-wandering rates. Only cognitively demanding contexts discriminated the higher from lower-WMC subjects: During self-reported concentration attempts and high-effort/high-challenge tasks – where lapses should hurt performance – lower-WMC subjects mind-wandered more frequently than did higher-WMC subjects (as assessed via multilevel modeling; $b=0.022$, $SE=0.006$, $t(122)=3.98$). These findings provide powerful, ecologically valid evidence for our attentional view of WMC, and for the notion that some of the attentional difficulties demonstrated by lower-WMC subjects may be linked to off-task thinking.

At the same time, our experience-sampling protocol did not allow us to examine how (or whether) off-task thoughts affected our subjects' performance of their daily life activities. Although we intend to address this question in a future protocol, such a performance assessment will necessarily rely on subjects' monitoring their own behavior and such assessments may be error prone and subject to bias. We have therefore conducted a laboratory investigation of executive control and thought content, in which performance accuracy could be assessed objectively and subjects' thoughts could be probed at critical times (McVay & Kane, 2009). We expected WMC to predict both mind-wandering rates and performance errors. As well, we hypothesized that some (if not most) of the performance variance accounted for by WMC variation would be shared with mind-wandering rate. That is, task errors attributable to deficits in goal maintenance, which lower-WMC subjects commit more than do higher-WMC subjects, should largely be the result of mind wandering.

We conducted our study using the Sustained Attention to Response Task (SART; Manly, Robertson, Galloway, & Hawkins, 1999; Robertson, Manly, Andrade, Baddeley, & Yiend, 1997), a task that elicits high error rates and that was previously shown to correlate with global self-report measures of cognitive failures (Robertson et al., 1997) and end-of-block thought reports (Smallwood, Davies et al., 2004). The SART is a go/no-go task in which stimuli are presented rapidly (250 ms; 900 ms mask) and subjects respond to all stimuli expect infrequent (11%) targets. In the original SART, the stimuli were digits 1–9 and the target was "3"; we presented stimulus words that required a perceptual response (upper vs. lowercase letters) or a semantic response (animal vs. food exemplar) as a between-subjects processing-demand manipulation. Subjects responded to every instance of one category (e.g., animals) and withheld responding to the rare instances of the other category (e.g., foods). The processing-demand manipulation did not produce any important effects and so we will not discuss it further.

We administered numerous thought probes to assess mind wandering during the SART. After 60% of the no-go target trials, a screen appeared that asked subjects to indicate what they had been thinking in the moment before the probe. The probes presented seven categories of thought, determined through our pilot testing; subjects were trained on the categories prior to the start of the task.

1. The task – *Select this number if your thoughts were about the word you saw or its meaning or if you were thinking about pressing the space bar.*
2. Task performance – *Select this number if your thoughts were about how well you are doing on the task, how many you are getting right, or frustrations with the task.*
3. Everyday stuff – *Select this number if your thoughts were about what you did recently, what you are going to do later, or casual, everyday, routine things.*
4. Current state of being – *Select this number if you were thinking about being sleepy, hungry, bored, or any other current state.*

5. Personal worries – *Select this number if your thoughts were about life concerns such as a test coming up or a fight with a friend.*
6. Daydreams – *Select this number for fantasy or thoughts disconnected from reality.*
7. Other – *Select "other" ONLY if your thoughts do not fit into any of the other category options.*

Only the numbers and names of the categories appeared on the subsequent thought probes. We used categories here rather than asking subjects to report their thoughts aloud, in order to eliminate discomfort in verbalizing personal thoughts (Smallwood, Davies et al., 2004; Smallwood et al., 2002–2003; 2003; Teasdale et al., 1993; 1995) and to minimize the interruption to the ongoing task to collect thought reports (probe response time $M=2,300$ ms). The first two categories were coded as on-task thinking and as task-related interference (TRI; Smallwood et al., 2006), respectively. The rest were coded as TUTs. We inserted thought probes following target trials in order to directly connect reports of mind-wandering to errors.

Our findings indicated that mind-wandering contributes to goal neglect errors in the SART. Subjects had a lower accuracy rate on target trials where they reported off-task thinking ($M=0.42$) than when they were on-task ($M=0.66$) and their overall accuracy correlated negatively with TUT rate ($r=-0.37$). Moreover, intrasubject variation in RT to the frequent nontarget trials, which provides an index of general fluctuations in attention to the task, correlated significantly with TUT rate ($r=0.40$).

Of primary importance, we predicted a mediating role for mind wandering between WMC and goal neglect. WMC variation did significantly predict SART accuracy ($r=0.29$), RT variability ($r=-0.35$), and TUT rate ($r=-0.22$). Critically, hierarchical regression also indicated that TUT rate accounted for about half of WMC's shared variance with performance (accuracy and RT variability), indicating that TUT experiences mediated, in part, the relation between WMC and goal neglect.

Mind Wandering as Thought Interference: A Cause of Executive Control Failures

Colloquially, a person may claim to "have a lot on her mind" as an excuse for a mistake or express a need to "get her head in the game" when she feels she is inadequately focusing on the task at hand. These common phrases reflect the subjective experience of the relationship between off-task thinking and errors. Most people have experienced the less-than-optimal performance that accompanies interfering thoughts in stressful or worrisome situations. We reemphasize, here, that subjects' "real world" concerns do not disappear when they enter the artificial world of our laboratory to complete experiments. Rather, these extralaboratory concerns may have a significant impact on subjects' performance. That is, in the process of completing a task, TUTs about a worrisome situation, or about everyday things to do, may act as interference to the task goals in the same way that conflicting task stimuli interfere with attention to target stimuli. Klinger (1971, 1999) has defined the nature of this internal interference with his current concerns theory.

A *current concern* is a state of mind that is proposed to exist between the formation of an intention and its completion or abandonment. In other words, when someone forms an intention to achieve a goal sometime in the future, that intention exists as a current concern until the intention is satisfied or discarded. This language mirrors the definition of a prospective memory (Einstein & McDaniel, 2005; Smith, 2003; Smith & Bayen, 2004). Most of the time, however, prospective-memory researchers limit their focus to relatively simple intention–action associations that are, themselves, embedded in a simple ongoing task. For example, subjects may be asked to vocally indicate whenever a nonword appears in a sequence of words that they are categorizing as animate versus inanimate via key-press. A current concern, in contrast, is not limited to simple actions to be associated with event- or time-based cues. Although current concerns can be as simple as "buy milk at the store tonight," they can also be as complex and abstract as "improve my relationship with my mother." Likewise, "I must do well in school" may be a current concern that remains unsatisfied until graduation, even though many subgoals (which also exist as current concerns, such as "study for tomorrow's quiz") are completed along the way.

By Klinger's (1971, 1999) view, current concerns are activated by relevant environmental or mental events and when active they compete for attention with external stimuli. The likelihood of a current concern "winning" such competition against ongoing thought, and thus entering consciousness, depends on its importance and imminence. Current concerns that are self-rated as more important, and those that require some action in the near future, are more likely to gain entrance into awareness (Klinger, Barta, & Maxeiner, 1980). One way to explore empirically the consequences of current-concern activation on concurrent cognitive performance is thus to manipulate subjects' exposure to concern-related cues. Antrobus et al. (1966) pioneered this technique by introducing a concern prior to administration of a vigilance task with mind-wandering probes. College-student subjects sat briefly in a waiting room before the critical part of the experiment where, for half the subjects, a realistic mock radio broadcast reported an escalation of the Vietnam War. Subjects exposed to this broadcast reported substantially more mind wandering during the subsequent vigilance task than did controls. Presumably, the experimental subjects became preoccupied with thoughts of the war (and implications for the draft) and were less able to maintain their attention on the task at hand. In 1966, the potential personal impact of the Vietnam War was certainly a concern for most young Americans. By cuing this concern prior to testing the attention of their subjects, Antrobus et al. (1966) demonstrated the dramatic impact that extralaboratory concerns can have on laboratory performance.

In a more recent study, McVay and Kane (2007) embedded cues to subjects' personal concerns in the ongoing task. Our question was whether priming subjects' personal goals would trigger TUTs and subsequent executive-control errors. If so, we would have compelling evidence for the *causal* impact of off-task thoughts on behavior, whereas previous laboratory studies of mind-wandering have all relied on *correlations* of thought reports with performance under various task contexts.

Our subjects first reported some of their personal goals and concerns on the Personal Concerns Inventory (Cox & Klinger, 2004), which was completed along with several other surveys. We used subjects' ratings of importance and imminence to select two personal goals to cue in a separate session, 2 days later. These concerns were converted into word triplets designed to capture the idea of the goal while using as few of the subjects' own words as possible. These goal triplets were then presented periodically, in sequence, during a SART task. For example, the goal, *"pay my piano accompanist this week"* might be converted to the word triplet: *compensate–piano–helper*. In the SART, words were presented one at a time and subjects responded to nontargets (lowercase words) and withheld the response for target items (uppercase words). The concern-related word triplets were always presented as nontarget stimuli (lowercase words) and always appeared in the same order (always a few words before critical target trials and thought probes). Note that for successful task completion, subjects did not have to read any of the words for meaning but rather to make a simple perceptual judgment about them.

We compared subjects' performance and thought reports on personal-goal-cued trials to two kinds of control events that occurred with equal frequency: Yoked goal triplets from another subject that did not match any of the current subject's reported concerns, and nongoal-related word triplets that all subjects saw and that should not correspond to any subject's concerns (e.g., *close–wooden–doors*). Thus, throughout the SART, subjects saw nongoal triplet cues, their own personal goal cues, and another subject's goal cues, all followed soon after by target events and thought probes.

Based on current concerns theory and the Antrobus et al. (1966) study, we expected that subjects would report more mind wandering following cues to their own personal goals and concerns. Furthermore, we expected this interference to impair performance on the SART no-go targets. In fact, subjects reported significantly higher TUT rates and had significantly lower accuracy rates for targets following personal-goal cues (44% TUTs; 64% errors) than those following nongoal control cues (38% TUTs; 48% errors). And, as predicted, mind wandering and errors were also numerically higher following personal-goal cues versus other-subject goal cues (42% TUTs; 61% errors), but these differences were not statistically significant. We suspect that the lack of significance here reflects the limited range of goals and concerns across our undergraduate subjects. Although we attempted to use other subjects' cues that were unrelated to the personal goals and concerns reported by the subject, many of the academic, social, financial, and family-related concerns of our subjects were probably not unique. We are therefore encouraged by the raw pattern of data here, and for the next step in this line of research, we plan to better control the degree to which the control cues relate to each subject's current concerns.

For now, however, we suggest that thoughts about personal concerns and goals are automatically and continuously generated (perhaps by the default-mode network of the brain) and compete for attention with on-task thoughts. When the interference is too great for the person's executive-control system to block or inhibit (whether due to fatigue, stress, disorder/disease, or low WMC), these thoughts supplant task-related thoughts in conscious awareness. So, in some cases, it is the build-up of the interference from thoughts such as current concerns that overwhelm the control system and cause disruptions to conscious focus that may, in turn, cause performance failures. The finding that mind-wandering rates increase when current concerns are primed via pretask information (Antrobus et al., 1966) or via in-task cues (McVay & Kane, 2007) provides evidence that current concerns interfere with task-related thoughts. The in-the-moment connection between mind wandering and task performance suggests that thought-control failures may sometimes result in executive-control failures in performance.

Testing the Waters

Psychology has begun to wade, tentatively, back into the stream of thought flow in order to test important hypotheses about consciousness, attention, and executive control. After decades of standing on shore for fear of reviving historical controversies about introspective methods, we should ask whether today's methods of assessing subjects' subjective experience of off-task and on-task thought are generally valid and worthy of scientific consideration. We believe that the answer to this question is a provisional – but optimistic – "yes." As we already noted above, the empirical literature on mind wandering demonstrates that TUT experiences vary systematically with particular experimental manipulations, replicated across multiple subject samples in different laboratories. As well, a consistent brain-activity signature, found in separate samples across multiple research groups, distinguishes self-reported TUT states from task-oriented states (and people who TUT frequently from people who TUT infrequently).

We argue, moreover, that our research provides additional – and particularly compelling – evidence for the validity of mind-wandering self reports. First, our studies of mind wandering in the laboratory (McVay & Kane, 2009) and in daily life (Kane, Brown et al., 2007) both show that *subjective*, self-reported experiences of off-task thought are predicted by *objective* tests of WMC. Even though we assessed WMC and mind wandering in separate sessions (that actually appeared to subjects as completely separate studies), and even though our subjects had no basis on which to compare their own WMC to others', people with lower-WMC reported mind wandering more often than did people with higher-WMC during a laboratory test of executive control and during cognitively demanding daily life activities. Moreover, the mind-wandering rates we measured in the laboratory varied systematically, not only with performance measures that were obvious to subjects (which, therefore, could reactively influence their thought reports), such as target accuracy, but also with measures that were unlikely be detected or monitored by subjects, such as overall RT variability. Finally, we have primed our subjects' personal goals during executive-control tasks and found that these primes elicit increased TUT reports and increased error rates, despite the fact that our subjects reported no awareness (when queried at the end of the experiment) that any of the task stimuli were related to their goals or concerns. Together, we argue that these findings suggest strongly that subjects accurately report their subjective experiences of off-task thought when probed during ongoing activities, and that contextual and individual variation in off-task thought reports are meaningfully related to important cognitive constructs such as WMC, executive control, and goals.

Conclusions

A broad theme of our mind-wandering research, and its implications for individual differences work in psychology and neuroscience, is that human subjects bring with them to the lab a plethora of experiences, memories, plans, and ongoing thoughts that influence their performance on cognitive tasks. In trying to understand individual or group differences in cognitive functioning, these extralaboratory concerns are usually considered noise and thus they represent within-group error in our statistical analyses. However, just as Cronbach (1957) called on experimental psychologists to embrace the interindividual variation that they regarded as measurement error, we suggest that researchers who study attention, working memory, executive control, and individual differences therein should consider how subjects' extraexperimental goals and concerns might affect their stream of conscious experience during cognitive tasks, and how these experiences might lead systematically to particular varieties of attention and memory errors that are of theoretical and practical importance. Our findings suggest that at least some of the variance shared by WMC and executive-control tasks, for example, is explained by individual differences in propensity for mind-wandering. We therefore wonder about the extent to which other WMC- and attention-related findings, such as those discussed in the present volume, may also have mind wandering at their source.

References

Antrobus, J. S., Coleman, R., & Singer, J. L. (1967). Signal-detection performance by subjects differing in predisposition to daydreaming. *Journal of Consulting Psychology, 31*, 487–491.

Antrobus, J. S., Singer, J. L., Goldstein, S., & Fortgang, M. (1970). Mindwandering and cognitive structure. *Transactions of the New York Academy of sciences, 32*, 242–252.

Antrobus, J. S., Singer, J. L., & Greenberg, S. (1966). Studies in the stream of consciousness: Experimental suppression of spontaneous cognitive processes. *Perceptual and Motor Skills, 23*, 399–417.

Baddeley, A. D. (1986). *Working memory*. London/New York: Oxford University Press.

Baddeley, A. D. (2000). Short-term and working memory. In E. Tulving & F. I. M. Craik (Eds.), *The Oxford handbook of memory* (pp. 77–92). New York: Oxford University Press.

Baddeley, A. (2007). *Working memory, thought, and action*. New York, NY: Oxford University Press.

Bowling, L. E. (1950). What is the stream of consciousness technique? *Publications of the Modern Language Association of America, 65*(4), 333–335.

Braver, T. S., Gray, J. R., & Burgess, G. C. (2007). Explaining the many varieties of working memory variation: Dual mechanisms of cognitive control. In A. R. A. Conway, C. Jarrold, M. J. Kane, A. Miyake, & J. N. Towse (Eds.), *Variation in working memory* (pp. 76–106). Oxford: Oxford University Press.

Conway, A. R. A., & Engle, R. W. (1996). Individual differences in working memory capacity: More evidence for a general capacity theory. *Memory, 4*, 577–590.

Conway, A. R. A., Kane, M. J., Bunting, M. F., Hambrick, D. Z., Wilhelm, O., & Engle, R. W. (2005). Working memory span tasks: A methodological review and user's guide. *Psychonomic Bulletin & Review, 12*, 769–786.

Cox, W. M., & Klinger, E. (2004). *Handbook of motivational counseling: Concepts, approaches and assessment*. New York: Wiley.

Cronbach, L. J. (1957). The two disciplines of scientific psychology. *American Psychologist, 12*, 671–684.

Daneman, M., & Carpenter, P. A. (1980). Individual differences in working memory and reading. *Journal of Verbal Learning and Verbal Behavior, 19*, 450–466.

Daneman, M., & Merikle, P. M. (1996). Working memory and language comprehension: A meta-analysis. *Psychonomic Bulletin & Review, 3*, 422–433.

Duncan, J. (1995). Attention, intelligence, and the frontal lobes. In M. Gazzaniga (Ed.), *The cognitive neurosciences* (pp. 721–733). Cambridge, MA: MIT.

Einstein, G. O., & McDaniel, M. A. (2005). Prospective memory: Multiple retrieval processes. *Current Directions in Psychological Science, 14*, 286–290.

Engle, R. W., & Kane, M. J. (2004). Executive attention, working memory capacity, and a two-factor theory of cognitive control. In B. Ross (Ed.), *The psychology of learning and motivation* (pp. 145–199). New York: Academic.

Engle, R. W., Tuholski, S. W., Laughlin, J. E., & Conway, A. R. A. (1999). Working memory, short-term memory and general fluid intelligence: A latent variable approach. *Journal of Experimental Psychology: General, 128*, 309–331.

Filler, M. S., & Giambra, L. M. (1973). Daydreaming as a function of cueing and task difficulty. *Perceptual and Motor Skills, 37*, 503–509.

Gathercole, S. E., & Pickering, S. J. (2000). Working memory deficits in children with low achievements in the national curriculum at 7 years of age. *British Journal of Educational Psychology, 70*, 177–194.

Giambra, L. M. (1995). A laboratory method for investigating influences on switching attention to task-unrelated imagery and thought. *Consciousness and Cognition, 4*, 1–21.

Giambra, L. M, Grodsky, A., Belongie, C., & Rosenberg, E. H. (1994–1995). Depression and thought intrusions, relating thought frequency to activation and arousal. *Imagination, Cognition and Personality, 14*(1), 19–29.

Grodsky, A., & Giambra, L. M. (1990–1991). The consistency across vigilance and reading tasks of individual differences in the occurrence of task-unrelated and task-related images and thoughts. *Imagination, Cognition and Personality, 10,* 39–52.

James, W. (1890/1998). *The Principles of Psychology*. New York: H. Holt and Company.

Kane, M. J., Bleckley, M. K., Conway, A. R. A., & Engle, R. W. (2001). A controlled-attention view of working-memory capacity. *Journal of Experimental Psychology: General, 130*, 169–183.

Kane, M. J., Brown, L. H., Little, J. C., Silvia, P. J., Myin-Germeys, I., & Kwapil, T. R. (2007). For whom the mind wanders, and when: An experience-sampling study of working memory and executive control in daily life. *Psychological Science, 18*, 614–621.

Kane, M. J., Conway, A. R. A., Hambrick, D. Z., & Engle, R. W. (2007). Variation in working memory capacity as variation in executive attention and control. In A. R. A. Conway, C. Jarrold, M. J. Kane, A. Miyake, & J. N. Towse (Eds.), *Variations in working memory* (pp. 21–48). New York: Oxford University Press.

Kane, M. J., & Engle, R. W. (2000). Working memory capacity, proactive interference, and divided attention: Limits on long-term memory retrieval. *Journal of Experimental Psychology: Learning, Memory, and Cognition, 26*, 333–358.

Kane, M. J., & Engle, R. W. (2003). Working-memory capacity and the control of attention: The contributions of goal neglect, response competition, and task set to Stroop interference. *Journal of Experimental Psychology: General, 132*, 47–70.

Kane, M. J., Hambrick, D. Z., & Conway, A. R. A. (2005). Working memory capacity and fluid intelligence are strongly related constructs: Comment on Ackerman, Beier, and Boyle (2005). *Psychological Bulletin, 131*, 66–71.

Kane, M. J., & Miyake, T. M. (2008). Individual differences in episodic memory. In H. L. Roediger, III (Ed.), *Cognitive psychology of memory*. Vol. 2 of *Learning and memory: A comprehensive reference*, 4 vols. (J. Byrne, Editor). Oxford: Elsevier

Klinger, E. (1971). *Structure and functions of fantasy*. New York: Wiley.

Klinger, E. (1999). Thought flow: Properties and mechanisms underlying shifts in content. In J. A. Singer & P. Salovey (Eds.), *At play in the fields of consciousness: Essays in honor of Jerome L. Singer* (pp. 29–50). Mahwah, NJ: Lawrence Erlbaum Associates.

Klinger, E. C., Barta, S. G., & Maxeiner, M. E. (1980). Motivational correlates of thought, content, frequency and commitment. *Journal of Personality and Social Psychology, 39*, 1222–1237.

Kyllonen, P. C., & Christal, R. E. (1990). Reasoning ability is (little more than) working-memory capacity. *Intelligence, 14*, 389–433.

Kyllonen, P. C., & Stephens, D. L. (1990). Cognitive abilities as determinants of success in acquiring logic skill. *Learning and Individual Differences, 2*, 129–160.

Logan, G. D., & Zbrodoff, N. J. (1979). When it helps to be misled: Facilitative effects of increasing the frequency of conflicting stimuli in a Stroop-like task. *Memory & Cognition, 7*, 166–174.

Manly, T., Robertson, I. H., Galloway, M., & Hawkins, K. (1999). The absent mind: Further investigations of sustained attention to response. *Neuropsychologia, 37*, 661–670.

Mason, M. F., Norton, M. I., Van Horn, J. D., Wegner, D. M., Grafton, S. T., & Macrae, C. N. (2007). Wandering minds: The default network and stimulus-independent thought. *Science, 19,* 393–395.

McGuire, P. K., Paulesu, E., Frackowiak, R. S. J., & Frith, C. D. (1996). Brain activity during stimulus independent thought. *NeuroReport, 7,* 2095–2099.

McKiernan, K. A., D'Angelo, B. R., Kaufman, J. N., & Binder, J. R. (2006). Interrupting the stream of consciousness: An fMRI investigiation. *NeuroImage, 29,* 1185–1191.

McVay, J. C., & Kane, M. J. (2007). *Personal goals and mind wandering in a Sustained Attention to Response Task*. Poster presented at the annual meeting of North Carolina Cognition Group, Chapel Hill, NC.

McVay, J. C., & Kane, M. J. (2009). Conducting the train of thought: Working memory capacity, goal neglect, and mind-wandering in an executive-control task. *Journal of Experimental Psychology: Learning, Memory and Cognition, 35*, 196–204.

McVay, J. C., Kane, M. J., & Kwapil, T. R. (2009). Tracking the train of thought from the laboratory into everyday life: An experience-sampling study of mind-wandering across controlled and ecological contexts. *Psychonomic Bulletin & Review, 16*, 857–863.

McVay, J. C., Knouse, L., Mitchell, J., Brown, L., Kane, M. J., & Kwapil, T. R. (2008). *Impaired conductors in the train of thought? Mind wandering in attention deficit/hyperactivity disorder*. Poster presented at the annual meeting of Association for Psychological Science, Chicago, IL.

Nisbett, R. E., & Wilson, T. D. (1977). Telling more than we can know: Verbal reports on mental processes. *Psychological Review, 84*, 3.

Raichle, M. E., MacLeod, A. M., Snyder, A. Z., Powers, W. J., Gusnard, D. A., & Shulman, G. L. (2001). A default mode of brain function. *Proceedings of the National Academy of Sciences, 98*, 676–682.

Reason, J. T. (1990). *Human error*. Cambridge, England: Cambridge University Press.

Reason, J. T., & Mycielska, K. (1982). *Absent minded? The psychology of mental lapses and everyday errors*. Englewood Cliffs, NJ: Prentice Hall.

Robertson, I. H., Manly, T., Andrade, J., Baddeley, B. T., & Yiend, J. (1997). Oops: Performance correlates of everyday attentional failures in traumatic brain injured and normal subjects. *Neurospsychologia, 35*, 747–758.

Rosen, V. M., & Engle, R. W. (1997). The role of working memory capacity in retrieval. *Journal of Experimental Psychology: General, 126*, 211–227.

Schooler, J. W. (2002). Re-representing consciousness: Dissociations between experience and meta-consciousness. *Trends in Cognitive Sciences, 6*, 339–344.

Schooler, J. W., Reichle, E. D., & Halpern, D. V. (2004). Zoning out while reading: Evidence for dissociations between experience and metaconsciousness. In D. Levin (Ed.), *Thinking and seeing: Visual metacognition in adults and children* (pp. 203–226). Cambridge, MA: MIT.

Schwitzgebel, E. (2008). The unreliability of naïve introspection. *Philosophical Review, 117*(2), 245–273.

Shaw, G. A., & Giambra, L. M. (1993). Task unrelated thoughts of college students diagnosed as hyperactive in childhood. *Developmental Neuropsychology, 9*, 17–30.

Smallwood, J., Baraciaia, S. F., Lowe, M., & Obonsawin, M. C. (2003). Task-unrelated-thought whilst encoding information. *Consciousness and Cognition, 12*, 452–484.

Smallwood, J., Davies, J. B., Heim, D., Finnigan, F., Sudberry, M. V., O Connor, R. C., et al. (2004). Subjective experience and the attentional lapse. Task engagement and disengagement during sustained attention. *Consciousness and Cognition, 4*, 657–690.

Smallwood, J., Heim, D., Riby, L., & Davies, J. D. (2006). Encoding during the attentional lapse: Accuracy of encoding during the semantic SART. *Consciousness and Cognition, 15*, 218–231.

Smallwood, J., O'Connor, R. C., & Heim, D. (2004–2005). Rumination, dysphoria and subjective experience. *Imagination, Cognition and Personality, 24*, 355–367.

Smallwood, J., Obonsawin, M. C., & Reid, H. (2002–2003). The effects of block duration and task demands on the experience of task-unrelated-thought. *Imagination, cognition and Personality, 22*, 12–31.

Smallwood, J., & Schooler, J. W. (2006). The restless mind. *Psychological Bulletin, 132*, 946–958.

Smith, R. E. (2003). Conscious capacity and prospective memory: A new perspective. *Journal of Experimental Psychology: Learning, Memory, and Cognition, 29*, 347–361.

Smith, R. E., & Bayen, U. J. (2004). A multinomial model of event-based prospective memory. *Journal of Experimental Psychology: Learning, Memory, and Cognition, 30*, 756–777.

Teasdale, J. D., Dritschel, B. H., Taylor, M. J., Proctor, L., Lloyd, C. A., Nimmo-Smith, I., et al. (1995). Stimulus-independent thought depends on central executive resources. *Memory and Cognition, 23*, 551–559.

Teasdale, J. D., Proctor, L., Lloyd, C. A., & Baddeley, A. (1993). Working memory and stimulus-independent-thought: Effects of memory load and presentation rate. *European Journal of Psychology, 5*, 417–433.

Unsworth, N., & Engle, R. W. (2006). A temporal-contextual retrieval account of complex span: An analysis of errors. *Journal of Memory and Language, 54*, 346–362.

Unsworth, N., & Engle, R. W. (2007). On the division of short-term and working memory: An examination of simple and complex span and their relation to higher order abilities. *Psychological Bulletin, 133*, 1038–1066.

Unsworth, N., Heitz, R. C., Schrock, J. C., & Engle, R. W. (2005). An automated version of the operation span task. *Behavior Research Methods, 37*, 498–505.

Unsworth, N., Schrock, J. C., & Engle, R. W. (2004). Working memory capacity and the antisaccade task: Individual differences in voluntary saccade control. *Journal of Experimental Psychology: Learning, Memory, and Cognition, 30*, 1302–1321.

Wegner, D. M. (1997). Why the mind wanders. In J. D. Cohen & J. W. Schooler (Eds.), *Scientific approaches to consciousness* (pp. 295–315). Mahwah, NJ: Erlbaum.

Chapter 20
The Unique Cognitive Limitation in Subclinical Depression: The Impairment of Mental Model Construction

Grzegorz Sedek, Aneta Brzezicka, and Ulrich von Hecker

The notion of "depression" is frequently employed to describe a broader category of depressive symptoms, dysphoria, and the depression syndrome as such (Joormann, 2005). Numerous debates in the literature have addressed the issue of continuity, the question of whether moderate depression symptoms (called subclinical depression) differ quantitatively or qualitatively from severe clinical depression. Flett, Vredenburg, and Kramses (1997) drew up a summary indicating that the available data is generally consistent with the hypothesis of continuity. In this chapter, we review data from studies in which subclinical forms of depressive disorders were taken into account: those that are mild in terms of severity. Depression is then seen as an affective disorder characterized by persistent negative mood (without an elevated level of arousal) and specific deficits in cognitive functioning. These deficits include "ruminative" thinking, recurring ideas and thoughts with negative or self-devaluing content. Such deficits also involve individuals with depression experiencing difficulty in solving complex cognitive problems, and solving problems that require reasoning about deeper social relations.

There are a number of explanations for an impaired performance on complex tasks in depressed individuals; drawing on cognitive resources or memory limitations (Burt, Zembar, & Niederehe, 1995; Gotlib, Roberts, & Gilboa, 1996; Hasher & Zacks, 1979; Weingartner, 1986), impaired inhibition (Hertel 2004; Joormann, 2005), lowered efficiency of cognitive strategies (Hartlage, Alloy, Vazquez, & Dykman, 1993; Kofta & Sedek, 1998; Smith, Tracy, & Murray, 1993; von Hecker & Sedek, 1999), or lack of cognitive initiative (Hertel 1997; Hertel & Hardin, 1990) as explanatory concepts.

In this chapter, we review the results of our research program that examined the hypothesis that cognitive deficits in depression become especially evident in tasks that require the integration of piecemeal information into a more coherent mental representation, such as mental models (Johnson-Laird, 1983). In order to study integrative deficits in more detail, we have focused our research on the explanation of potential impairments of depressed participants in several paradigms (construction of social cliques, linear and classical syllogisms, situation models in text comprehension), that is, on complex and multistep tasks such as usually benefit from the on-line generation of mental models (Brewer, 1987; Greeno, 1989; Huttenlocher, 1968; Johnson-Laird, 1996). In this sense, we will tackle one of the most intriguing problems within the literature concerning depressive deficits in cognitive task performance, namely, its unique context-specificity. People who suffer from (subclinical or mild) depression perform quite normally on some cognitive tasks, whereas they show serious impairments in other, apparently similar tasks.

G. Sedek (✉) and A. Brzezicka
Interdisciplinary Center for Applied Cognitive Studies, Warsaw School of Social Psychology and Humanities, Chodakowska 19/31, 03-815, Warsaw, Poland
e-mail: gsedek@swps.edu.pl

U. von Hecker
School of Psychology, Cardiff University, Cardiff, Wales, UK

For example, Smith et al. (1993) found that ongoing dysphoric mood in college students' impaired category-learning performance on so-called criterial attribute tasks, which require flexible testing of candidate hypotheses, concentrating on new hypotheses while discarding old, disproven ones. Yet, depressed individuals performed normally on so-called family resemblance tasks, which allowed for a broader, more evenly spread attention across all feature dimensions on the basis of perceived overall similarity between stimuli. In the much more elaborated field of memory deficits in depression, Hertel and her collaborators (Hertel, 1997; Hertel & Hardin 1990; Hertel & Rude, 1991) found that depressed participants failed to initiate optional strategies but performed normally when the task itself engaged and directed their use. Related empirical evidence showed intriguing patterns of relations between the degree of structure within memory materials, and impairments under depression: Depressed people, in comparison to controls, demonstrated substantial impairments with moderately structured materials, but no memory deficits under conditions of high degree of structure in the materials (Channon, Baker, & Robertson, 1993; Watts & Cooper, 1989).

In the present chapter, we approach the issue of cognitive limitations in depression in terms of the cognitive exhaustion model (Kofta & Sedek, 1998; Sedek & Kofta, 1990; Sedek, Kofta, & Tyszka, 1993). The idea will be elaborated that many of these cognitive limitations (difficulties in systematic hypothesis testing, lack of more sophisticated processing strategies, insufficient cognitive structuring) might be due to serious deficits in generating comprehensive mental representations, such as mental models. We use the term mental model according to the Johnson-Laird theory (1983) that defines a mental model as a construction based on incoming data (such as premises in reasoning tasks), generated online during the process of solving the task. Mental models are representations of parts of the external world (or imaginary situations), which resemble or preserve some of their structural and functional properties.

Capacity Reduction Models

A number of researchers have argued that many cognitive deficits reported for depressive people are due to a reduction of cognitive capacity, and that these impairments cannot be explained simply by motivational deficits (Ellis, Ottaway, Varner, Becker, & Moore, 1997; Gotlib et al., 1996; Hartlage et al., 1993). According to Hasher and Zacks (1979), cognitive capacity is reduced in depressed individuals, resulting in insufficient free attentional resources for performing more effortful, demanding tasks. Similarly, Ellis and Ashbrook (1988) suggested that cognitive capacity is reduced in depression, and that depressed people primarily allocate the remaining attentional resources to focus on depression-relevant thoughts (depressive rumination) and irrelevant task processing (focusing on irrelevant features of the task). Both models predict that depressive impairments in cognitive task performance (e.g., in memory tasks) should be linearly related to the cognitive complexity of presented problems. This means that for simple tasks, no differences should be observed between depressed and nondepressed people. Pronounced differences should only be visible in more difficult tasks. On the other hand, even mild depression may interfere with cognitive performance if the task requires effortful or complex processing.

Initiative Deficits in Depression

The capacity reduction view has been questioned by Paula Hertel and her collaborators (Hertel, 2004; Hertel & Hardin 1990; Hertel & Rude 1991). They provided experimental evidence that the central deficit in depression does not necessarily consist in reduced capacity but rather in reduced initiation of certain processing strategies, that is, typically complex strategies that would most efficiently support task execution. Such strategies may not be explicitly required by instruction, or even be obvious from the task structure itself. Thus, the authors postulated that depressive impairments are likely to be revealed by tasks that do permit, but not necessitate the spontaneous use of complex strategies.

Where in the cognitive system does the central deficit in depression lie? As will be explained further in the next section, what the Cognitive Exhaustion Model sees as basic is a reduced ability to engage in more integrative steps of processing. Different from the "capacity" view, this model claims a qualitative rather than a quantitative shift in mental functioning. That is, while effortful processing and detailed scrutiny of incoming pieces of information might still be possible, such pieces might not be integrated to yield an overall picture. Different from the "lack of initiation" view, we suggest that even in the presence of initiative, the more integrative steps will often be unsuccessful in depressed subjects. Thus, they will be unable to construct clear and cohesive mental models of their memory contents.

Cognitive Exhaustion Model

The idea that cognitive dysfunctions in depressive states, as well as in states of induced helplessness, basically stem from impaired mental modeling is the central claim made by Kofta and Sedek (1998) in their formulation of the cognitive exhaustion model. This information-processing approach (Sedek & Kofta, 1990; Sedek et al., 1993) assumes that people are likely to engage in systematic mental activity when dealing with problem solving situations. They attempt to understand the meaning of task demands, they notice and pay attention to diagnostic pieces of information, detect regularities or inconsistencies, and so forth.

When the situation is controllable, these mental activities stimulate people to engage in more generative modes of thinking, i.e., in the construction of integrative memory representations, such as mental models. However, in uncontrollable surroundings (e.g., when attempting to solve an unsolvable problem), such activity remains futile because it cannot lead to real progress. By definition, in unsolvable situations, no reliable explanatory rules can be found for solving the problem. Therefore, although an individual might generate quite a few preliminary hypotheses, he or she would eventually not be able to differentiate between good and poor ideas in seeking a solution. As another important issue, under induced uncontrollability, the engagement in task solving leads to a heightened uncertainty which cannot be reduced despite trying (Kofta & Sedek, 1999).

It is hypothesized (see: Kofta & Sedek, 1998; Sedek & Kofta, 1990) that prolonged cognitive effort without "cognitive gain" results in an altered psychological state, which we term cognitive exhaustion. The essential quality of this transitory state is a generalized impairment of constructive and integrative mental processing. Therefore, after uncontrollable preexposure, an individual's ability to form new ideas and generate hypotheses is diminished. In terms of general adaptive functions, cognitive exhaustion states seem especially disruptive to more complex problem solving requiring nonroutine, flexible steps of processing in either achievement or interpersonal domains. The primacy of the cognitive underpinnings of this phenomenon is supported by data showing that these deficits emerge in conditions which minimize the likelihood of effort withdrawal as an ego-protective maneuver, i.e., in the absence of social performance feedback, as well as in situations when negative mood is statistically controlled for (Kofta & Sedek, 1989; Sedek & Kofta, 1990). In another study, just after people had been exposed to uncontrollable events, their pattern of predecisional information search was altered in a way indicating cognitive exhaustion: Participants tended to avoid effortful information-gathering strategies (Sedek et al., 1993; for similar findings with dysphoric subjects, see Conway & Giannopoulos, 1993). The cognitive exhaustion model has been used to account for generalized deficits such as impaired cognitive functioning in depression, and intellectual helplessness in school settings (Sedek & Kofta, 1990; Sedek & McIntosh, 1998).

It is important to note that a number of researchers found close parallels between some aspects of cognitive functioning in depression and the state resulting from preexposure to uncontrollability (Abramson, Seligman, & Teasdale, 1978; Kuhl, 1984; Pittman & D'Agostino, 1989; Seligman, 1975). In line with our own cognitive exhaustion model (Kofta & Sedek, 1998), we assume that some of the cognitive impairments observed in depression can be explained in terms of experienced uncontrollability (being confronted with an unsolvable situation which leads to uncertainty). This experience may stem from past, irreversible life events, from subsequent ruminating, or from counterfactual thinking (Davis, Wortman, Silver, & Thompson, 1995; Niedenthal, Tangney, & Gavanski, 1994). It is hypothesized that uncontrollability and, in particular, ruminating thoughts about uncontrollable conditions, lead to a depletion of those cognitive resources that support generative and flexible, constructive thinking. Constructive thinking may still be initiated by depressive individuals, at times even more vigorously than by nondepressives. Nevertheless, it might yield less success in terms of the quality of new, integrative constructions, such as mental models. On the other hand, depressed persons' performance is seldom impaired in tasks dealing with basic, immediate information sampling, accuracy, or simple decision making (for a review, Kofta & Sedek, 1998; McIntosh, Sedek, Fojas, Brzezicka, & Kofta, 2005).

At the most general level, our research hypothesis can be stated as follows. According to the cognitive exhaustion model, depression should especially impair the processing of tasks that require the generation of new ideas and flexible thinking. It should hinder the production of nonstandard solutions to cognitive or interpersonal problems. According to this view, such adverse consequences are likely to occur in tasks that are complex, cognitively demanding, and lacking redundancy. These are exactly the situations in which effective mental model construction would be most beneficial to a proper understanding of the respective task problem, or of the overall social situation. On the other hand, primary attempts to such processing, such as initial information sampling, memory retrieval, and selectivity towards diagnostic pieces of information should be relatively unimpaired in depression and induced control loss.

Depression and Mental Modeling in the Social Domain

Whereas our general argument is not necessarily tied to the social domain, in the present series of studies we tested it in a task involving the construction of social mental models. A growing research has documented that depression not only impairs performance in neutral cognitive tasks, but may also prove disruptive to social problem solving as well. For example, Marx, Williams, and Claridge (1992) demonstrated that depressed participants suffered from a deficit in different measures of social problem solving when compared with nondepressed and clinical control counterparts. Many other investigators, both in their theoretical contributions and empirical research, (e.g., Gotlib & Hammen, 1992) have stressed the observation of less socially skillful interpersonal behavior in depressed persons. We hypothesize that part of these difficulties in the social domain might be attributed to the depressives' general impairment in organizing interrelated input information into coherent mental representations.

In our research (von Hecker & Sedek, 1999), we employed a process tracing method in order to study the construction of social mental models. Basically, we focused on mental models about a set of perceived sentiment relations (Heider, 1958). There is experimental evidence showing that sets of sentiment relations like, e.g., "A and B like each other," resp., "A and C dislike each other," and so on, are simultaneously represented in memory by means of so-called mental cliques, i.e., mental models in which people perceived as liking each other are placed into one and the same clique, whereas people disliking each other are placed into different cliques. These structures, as can be shown, are constructed from piecemeal information, i.e., from individual relations, in a process

20 The Unique Cognitive Limitation in Subclinical Depression

Two cliques model		Three cliques model
Adrian + Brian		Adrian + Brian
Chris + Daniel		Chris + Daniel
Edward + Frank		Edward + Frank
Brian − Daniel		Brian − Daniel
Daniel − Frank		Daniel − Frank
Brian + Frank	Critical Relation	**Brian − Frank**

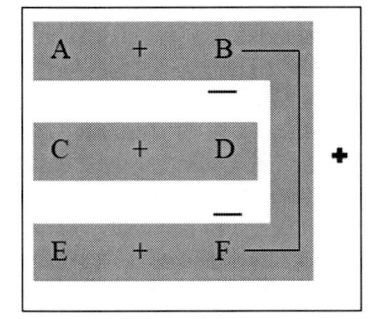

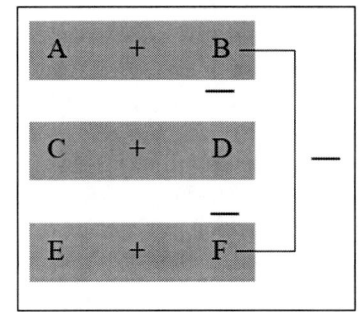

Fig. 20.1 Sequence of sentiment relations and the graphical form of the mental models of social cliques

guided by a step-by-step integration of more or less diagnostic information (Hummert, Crockett, & Kemper, 1990; von Hecker, 1997). For example, consider the simple sets of relations shown in Fig. 20.1 (the actual experimental material was more complex because it contained a mix of diagnostic and nondiagnostic information).

Let each pair of names (first letters of names in the diagram) represent one particular piecemeal sentiment relation, presented in isolation, whereby "+" and "−" stand for "like each other," and "dislike each other," respectively. It can be easily seen from the diagram that there is always exactly one relation, e.g., the one between persons B (e.g., "Brian") and F (e.g., "Frank"), which is most diagnostic, or critical concerning the kind of overall representation that would be possible to form about the whole set of sentiment relations. If and only if persons B and F like each other, it is possible to arrange the whole set of relations in this figure into exactly two cliques of people who mutually like each other. The first of these cliques would have persons A, B, E, and F as members, and the other one would have C and D as members. This holds for the leftmost part of Fig. 20.1. However, once the information about the sentiment between persons B and F is changed to a "dislike" between these two people, as it is done in part B of Fig. 20.1, the only clique arrangement possible is now one of exactly three cliques. The first of these is formed by persons A and B, the second comprises persons C and D, and the third has persons E and F as members. Our experimental procedure involves the step-by-step learning of relation sets of the kind just described. Participants are asked to study one single relation at a time on a computer screen, at a self-paced presentation rate.

In this and in the subsequent studies, college students were classified as subclinically depressed (scores ranging 10 and above) and nondepressed (scores ranging between 0 and 5), using the Beck Depression Inventory (BDI; Beck, 1967). They were tested on the BDI twice at an interval of 1 week. In order to participate in the study, participants' BDI scores at the second appointment had to fall within the same classification as the first appointment, to ensure reliability. The results of this research (von Hecker & Sedek, 1999) showed that depressed participants, like nondepressed, allocated more study time to diagnostic relations (between persons B and F), thereby recognizing the diagnostic value of such types of relations. However, unlike nondepressed participants, depressed participants did not use diagnostic relations adequately for the purpose of model construction. In subsequent tests, the quality of the constructed social mental models was found to be impaired by both control loss experience and depression (von Hecker & Sedek, 1999, Experiments 2 and 3). More specifically, both depressed participants and participants after uncontrollability training made more incorrect inferences in terms of the actual number of cliques. Moreover, their allocation of individual target persons to particular cliques was more imprecise in comparison to the control groups. Additionally, we observed that depression was associated with failure to disengage from undiagnostic pieces of information, after a diagnostic one had been processed (i.e., BF relation). Control participants, after processing the diagnostic relation, reduced study times for subsequent nondiagnostic ones, whereas depressed participants displayed relatively long study times even for undiagnostic information, after the diagnostic one had been processed. These findings are in line with the cognitive exhaustion model which assumes that both the experience of control loss and depression should primarily interfere with the solving of tasks that require generative forms of thinking, or tasks that are complex and cognitively demanding (cf. Kofta & Sedek, 1998; von Hecker, Sedek, & McIntosh, 2000). Our approach clearly concedes that processing effort as such, as well as processing quality in less generative, more top-down, or schema-guided tasks might be unimpaired or even enhanced under depression or control loss experience. Thus, participants in those states have been shown to meticulously process behavioral information in order to derive trait inferences from behavioral information (Gannon, Skowronski, & Betz, 1994; Weary, Marsh, Gleicher, & Edwards, 1993). Our point is however, that despite their exerted cognitive effort, due to their cognitive exhaustion state, depressives' performance will suffer particularly in those tasks that demand the deployment of integrative strategies in order to construct novel memory representations in a bottom-up way.

Depression and Linear Order Reasoning

The next series of studies (Sedek & von Hecker, 2004) provided a conceptual replication and an extension of these findings. Linear order construction (linear syllogisms) is another paradigm that may clearly exemplify our perspective on mental models as a process of integrating piecemeal information. The construction of linear orders from pairwise relational information that implies transitivity has received attention since the early days of cognitive psychology, as well as cognitive developmental psychology (Huttenlocher, 1968; Johnson-Laird, 1983; Piaget & Inhelder, 1974; Potts, 1972; Sternberg, 1980).

In this experimental procedure, participants were asked in each trial to study three pairs of relations, e.g., "A>B," "B>C," and "C>D," with "A"..."D" standing for first names, and ">" standing for a relational signifier such as "taller," "older," which was transitive by common-sense definition. An integrated mental model representation (Johnson-Laird, 1983) of such a set of pairs would always be a linear order "A>B>C>D." Immediately after presentation of the three pairs, participants were tested on all possible pairs within the order, i.e., AB, BC, CD (adjacent pairs, which had been learned), AC, BD (two-step relations), and AD (end point relation), by prompting participants with statements in either a correct (e.g., "A>D") or false format (e.g., "D>A"), and asking them for a speeded verification. The difficulty of integrating the three pairs was varied by administering sequences in which

Table 20.1 Two phases of linear order paradigm and the constructed mental array

Study phase (freely paced for participants)
   Brenda is smarter than Alice
   Alice is smarter than Doris
   Doris is smarter than Carol
Test phase (freely paced for participants)
   Carol smarter than Doris: True or *False*?   *(adjacent relation – memory test)*
   Alice smarter than Carol: *True* or False?   *(2-step relation – integrating 2 premises)*
   Brenda smarter than Carol: *True* or False?   *(endpoints relation – integrating 3 premises)*

Mental array: Brenda > Alice > Doris > Carol

Fig. 20.2 The proportion of correct answers as a function of group (depression) and pair distance (memory vs. reasoning). Errors bars represent standard errors of the mean

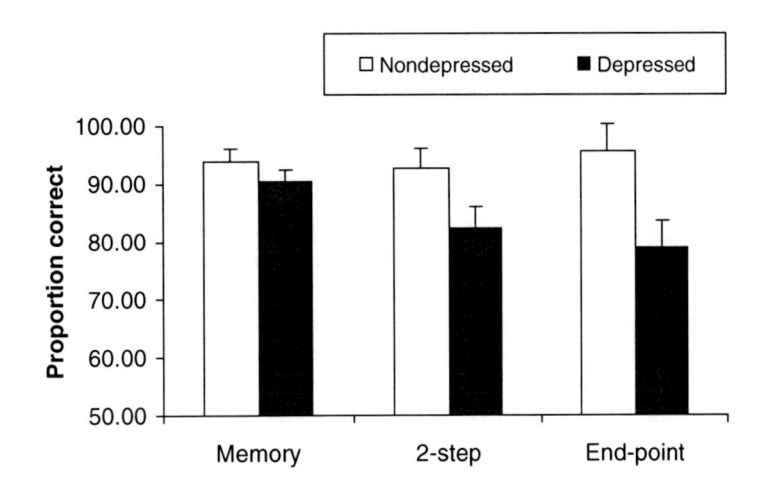

subsequent pairs always had an element in common by which the two could be linked (e.g., "B>C" being presented after "A>B"), versus other sequences in which the pairs were presented in a scrambled way such that there was less overlap of elements between subsequent pairs.

Table 20.1 exemplifies the procedure for the easiest type of linear orders. Study time was self-paced, thus allowing the assessment of participants' motivation and of their time allocation patterns. During the test phase, participants were asked about the just presented *adjacent* pair information (one-step relations; this was used as a measure of memory retrieval, and did not constitute a reasoning test per se). They were also asked two questions about to-be-inferred, but not presented, pair relations, which demanded generative reasoning. The questions about two-step relations (e.g., relations between Brenda and Doris or Alice and Carol) referred to relations between persons that spanned a distance of two steps on the hypothetical mental array, and demanded integration of information from two presented pairs. The questions about relations between end-point persons (e.g., Brenda and Carol) dealt with inferred pairs that spanned the maximum array distance of three steps and demanded integration of information from all three presented pairs.

To study the construction of mental models in subclinical depressed mood more systematically, the linear order construction paradigm as described above was used, in order to address transitive inference making as a basic mechanism of generative reasoning (for a detailed report, see Sedek & von Hecker, 2004, Experiment 1). The results of this experiment were clear (see Fig. 20.2). For the nondepressed group, there was a constant high level of accuracy across analyzed pair distances (adjacent – end point). This strongly suggests that in this group, participants tended to retrieve their answers from an integrated model, as queries on inferred end point relations (pair distance = 3) were answered with no less accuracy than explicitly learned, adjacent ones (pair distance = 1). On the other hand, in the depressed group, there was a substantial decrease of accuracy from explicitly learned to inferred relations. Following our reasoning outlined above, we concluded from this pattern that depressed individuals did not spontaneously integrate the pairs during learning, but retrieved the pairs at the time of the query to make transitive inferences at this later point in time. This interpretation is further supported by the analysis of response latencies for correct responses. We found that nondepressed participants responded with equal speed to inferred, more distant relations as they responded to adjacent relations. On the other hand, depressed participants showed an increase in latency for inferred, wider-distant pairs when compared to the pairs they had seen during learning.

It is of further interest to note that despite the apparent differences in terms of achieved mental model construction, both groups showed strikingly similar behavior during learning. Namely, overall study times were similar in both groups. As further analyses showed, it took both groups longer to study pairs from more difficult orders than pairs from easier orders, and for both groups this was particularly the case when studying any third pair in the sequence. The observation that both groups apparently exerted similar amounts of effort in their constructive attempts is consistent with previously discussed findings on social cliques' models (von Hecker & Sedek, 1999). According to those results, depressed participants, despite engaging in the type of mental activity that is necessary to construct a mental model, are actually not successful in doing so.

In the last study on linear orders (Sedek & von Hecker, 2004; Study 4), we compared depressives' performance in the linear order task with that of elderly participants, and we additionally used Operation Span (OSPAN; Turner & Engle, 1989) as a measure of working memory capacity. This measure captures simultaneous maintenance and processing and is assumed to share variance with executive control functions. Engle and coworkers argue that the reason why a working memory measure such as OSPAN correlates with higher order cognitive functions is not individual differences in the storage component, but individual differences in the central executive component, what they call a domain-unspecific executive attention component (Conway & Engle, 1996; Engle, Tuholski, Laughlin, & Conway, 1999; see also Ilkowska & Engle, this volume). In this study, both OSPAN and mental speed measures reliably mediated the relationship between age and linear order reasoning. However, depression was not correlated with those measures, and special attenuation analyses did not show any reduction of the relationship between depression and linear order reasoning when Operation Span was partialled out (Sedek & von Hecker, 2004). In this study, we did not analyze the potential role of OSPAN as a moderator of the relationship between depression and linear order reasoning. To examine this possibility, we reanalyzed the data, dividing the depressed sample by median split into high vs. low OSPAN participants, and carried out 2×2 (Depression by OSPAN) analysis of variance on end-point performance which can be seen as the purest measure for reasoning (end-point queries require the integration of all three premises). There were strong main effects (worse performance of depressed as compared to nondepressed, and much worse performance of those with low as compared to high OSPAN). Of special interest, this reanalysis also revealed a strong interaction effect (see Fig. 20.3), thus confirming the moderating role of OSPAN. There were

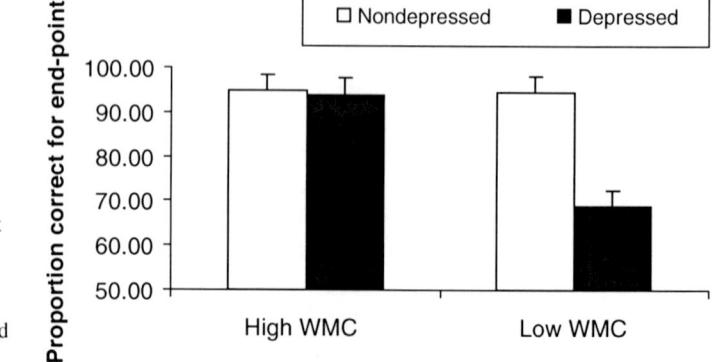

Fig. 20.3 The proportion of correct answers as a function of group (depression) and working memory capacity (high vs. low Operation Span). Errors bars represent standard errors of the mean

no differences between depressed and nondepressed participants when both groups possessed high levels of Operation Span. However, there was a dramatic impairment in the depressed as compared with the nondepressed group at low levels of working memory capacity. A simple effects analysis yielded analog results, that is, only in the low capacity group a significant difference was found between depressed and nondepressed participants. The results are not completely robust because a ceiling effect is possible. However, results of this reanalysis offer preliminary research evidence that although high levels of WMC might constitute a cognitive buffer that can help to overcome the negative impact of depression on higher order cognitive processes, still, on the other side, low levels of WMC might be seen as a risk factor that might be responsible for the exceptionally low level of cognitive functioning among depressed individuals.

Neural Correlates of Linear Order Reasoning in Depression

The neural correlates of various forms of mental model construction have been studied recently, using brain imaging techniques. The results indicate that the part of the brain most frequently activated when reasoning is the prefrontal cortex (PFC; Acuna, Eliassen, Donoghue, & Sanes, 2002; Kroger et al., 2002). During deductive reasoning, the PFC in the left hemisphere is most active, in addition to the left temporal lobe and the parietal and occipital lobes on both sides. When solving tasks where the relations between objects are analyzed (such as in the linear order learning procedure described above, see Sedek & von Hecker, 2004), the parietal–occipital–frontal network becomes active, suggesting the use of spatially organized mental models for solving tasks of this sort (Knauff, Mulack, Kassubek, Salih, & Greenlee, 2002).

In a recent study using functional magnetic resonance (fMRI) imaging, Hinton, von Hecker, Singh, and Wise (2008) examined the brains of 26 individuals as they carried out a linear order reasoning task as just described. Of the participants, 12 were identified as mildly depressed and 14 as nondepressed, as diagnosed by the Beck Depression Inventory. In this study, both depressed and nondepressed groups actually performed equally well in the task, which might reflect ceiling effects, having to do with heightened levels of arousal and attention as a result of being part of the scanning procedure. However, mildly depressed individuals evidenced a significantly different pattern of brain activation from the nondepressed. In particular, depressed individuals had higher levels of activation in parts of the parietal cortex than the nondepressed group when responding to query relations in the test stage, immediately after the three individual relations had been learned. Under the assumption that the linear mental model representing the rank order between the four people was less accessible or less activated in the depressed, this outcome would appear plausible. In other words, depressed individuals would still have to activate those parietal regions more than the nondepressed, that is, those regions that are known to be involved in processing spatial aspects of mental models (Acuna et al., 2002; Knauff et al., 2002), in order to arrive at the same level of performance. This interpretation is in line with our general hypothesis that depressed individuals, unlike the nondepressed, experience more difficulty when attempting to construct a linear mental model of a set of stimuli. As the postexperimental interview data from this study show, depressed individuals did engage in constructive efforts, that is, they did attempt to form a linear array model in their mind. However, much in the sense of the notion of "cognitive exertion without cognitive gain" (Sedek & Kofta, 1990), the models constructed by the depressed might have turned out less clear or accessible than in nondepressed individuals, which is why the former group needed more activation at test, to make the spatial aspects sufficiently salient to arrive at the same behavioral outcome (see Fangmeier, Knauff, Ruff, & Sloutsky, 2006, p. 328, for a similar line of argumentation). This interpretation means that the present neuroimaging data can substantiate earlier claims to the extent that in subclinical depression, integrated mental representations are less thoroughly, or less spontaneously constructed (Sedek & von Hecker, 2004; von Hecker & Sedek, 1999).

Depression, Syllogistic Reasoning and Operation Span of WM

In the next studies (Sedek, Oberauer, & von Hecker, 2008), we applied the classical paradigm using categorical syllogisms to examine the relationship between subclinical depression and integrative reasoning, aiming at gathering some additional evidence on the moderating role of Operation Span. A categorical syllogism, in the simpler evaluative form, consists of two premises (that are assumed to be true, independently of the content) and a conclusion that is to be evaluated as valid (when it follows logically from premises) or invalid (when it does not follow from the premises). For example, assuming that:

> Premise 1 – All things in the refrigerator can be eaten, and
> Premise 2 – Some light bulbs are in the refrigerator,
> it validly follows by logic:
> Conclusion – Some light bulbs can be eaten.

Johnson-Laird and his coworkers developed the most well-known model of syllogistic reasoning, based on mental modeling (Bucciarelli & Johnson-Laird, 1999; Johnson-Laird, 1983). According to this conception, during solving of a categorical syllogism, participants construct a mental model based on the terms and quantifiers in the premises. Such mental models simulate the possible options of relations between terms. The different mental models are compared to one another to contrast different solutions that might be possible, based on the premises. In line with this theory, participants go through three stages when solving syllogisms. In the first stage, an initial model is constructed based on the information from the first premise. In the second stage, information from second premise is added, and participants use this more comprehensive model to draw a conclusion. In the third stage, people examine this initial conclusion by constructing alternative mental models. According to this theory, syllogisms that support the construction of one single model are easier than those supporting two or three different mental models. Research evidence confirmed that working memory maintenance and capacity is related to the accuracy of syllogistic reasoning. For example, Copeland and Radvansky (2004) recently demonstrated a reliable relation between OSPAN and syllogistic reasoning performance. Another interesting aspect of concrete syllogisms that is relevant for the present research is the possibility of group differences in the so-called belief bias (Gilinski & Judd, 1994). Belief bias means that people's personal beliefs and factual knowledge may affect their ability to reason logically. Robust research evidence showed that participants, when presented with arguments to evaluate, tended to endorse conclusions they believed to be true, despite the instructions to base their judgments on logical reasoning alone. Research of Gilinski and Judd (1994) showed that the relationship between aging and syllogistic reasoning (accuracy and belief bias) is mediated by working memory span (composite of several span measures). The interesting question arises whether in the case of depression, OSPAN will again (as in the case of linear orders) be a moderator of the relationship between depression and performance on syllogisms.

In our recent research (Sedek et al., 2008) we used both the simplest versions of syllogisms (demanding the construction of only one single mental model) and more complex versions demanding the construction of two or three mental models (Table 20.2 presents some exemplars of those syllogisms). To stimulate the emergence of belief bias in the cover story, we informed the participants that they would read about some observations carried out in a normal garden (believable conclusions) versus in a garden with radical genetic transformations (unbelievable conclusions). The observations (premises) themselves were to be taken as valid; however, the task of participants was to decide whether the conclusions from them, made by the gardener, were logically correct (valid) or incorrect (invalid). As shown on exemplary cases in Table 20.2, some syllogisms were valid and believable, some valid and unbelievable, some were invalid and believable, and finally some of them were invalid and unbelievable. The participants were 111 high school students divided by median splits on the BDI depression scale and on the Operation Span measure.

20 The Unique Cognitive Limitation in Subclinical Depression

Table 20.2 The exemplars of valid and invalid syllogisms from with believable and unbelievable concussions

Validity	Abstract form	Believable (normal park)	Unbelievable (park with genetic engineering)
Valid 1 MM	All A are B All B are C →All A are C	All apple-trees have a red mark All trees with a red mark are leaved →All apple-trees are leaved	All apple-trees have a red mark All trees with a red mark are conifers →All apple-trees are conifers
Invalid 1 MM	All A are B All B are C →All C are A	All fruits are ripe All ripe fruits are apples →All apples are fruits	All fruits are ripe All ripe fruits are cubic eggs →All cubic eggs are fruits
Valid 3 MM	No A are B All B are C →Some C are not A	No roots are light All light things easily flying Some easily flying things are not roots	No roots are light All light things are trees Some trees have no roots
Invalid 3 MM	No A are B All B are C →Some A are not C	No maples are pine-trees All pine-trees in the park are protected →Some maples are not protected	No maples are pine-trees All pine-trees have leaves →Some maples have not leaves

Fig. 20.4 The proportion of correct answers as a function of logic (valid vs. invalid) and type of conclusions (believable vs. unbelievable). Errors bars represent standard errors of the mean

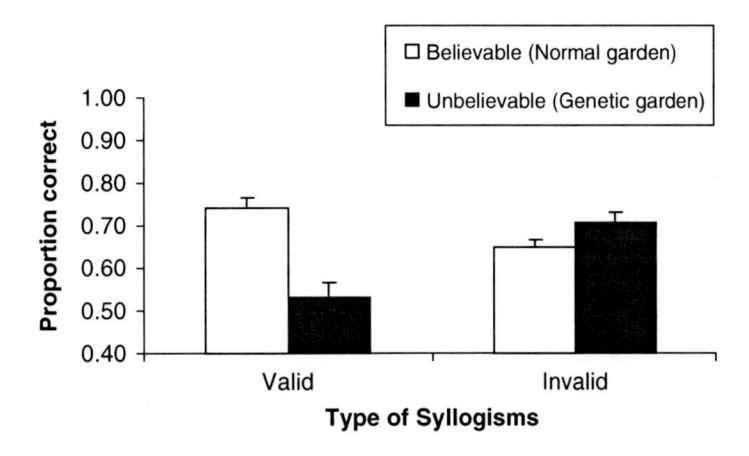

In line with predictions, there were main effects of depression and operation span on the accuracy of performance (worse performance in depressed group in comparison to nondepressed, and much worse performance in low as compared to high OSPAN participants). Also, there was a robust belief bias effect for the whole sample (see Fig. 20.4), that is, there was a reliable interaction effect between logic (valid vs. invalid) and belief (believable vs. unbelievable conclusions). Namely, among the valid syllogisms, accuracy was higher for believable than for unbelievable conclusions, whereas the opposite was true for invalid syllogisms. To elucidate the influence of depression and working memory span on belief bias in more detail, we constructed a single measure of this construct, based on the following formula that adds and subtracts accuracies for particular types of relevant syllogisms:

Belief Bias = (Acc. of valid & believable Acc. of valid & unbelievable) +
(Acc. of invalid & unbelievable -Acc. of invalid & believable)

Values around zero indicate a lack of belief bias in syllogisms performance, whereas higher positive values indicate more bias. The Depression×Operation Span ANOVA on this belief bias measure yielded two reliable main effects and, most interestingly, a strong interaction effect (see Fig. 20.5). As it is clearly visible, for participants with high levels of working memory capacity, the belief bias was virtually absent, even for those with high scores on the depression measure. A different pattern emerged for participants with low working memory span. In this group, depressed participants in comparison to nondepressed showed much higher levels of belief bias. Interestingly, the moderating effect of OSPAN that we had observed for the relation between depression and the construction of

Fig. 20.5 The mean value of belief bias as a function of group (depression) and working memory capacity (high vs. low Operation Span). Errors bars represent standard errors of the mean

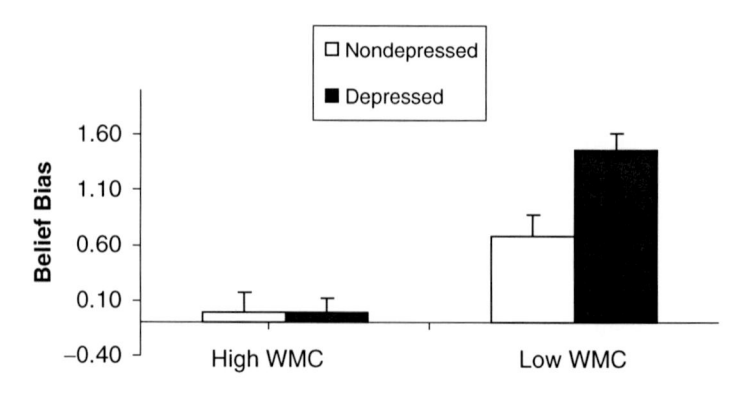

mental models was now replicated for syllogism resolution, albeit not in terms of the general accuracy score, but in terms of belief bias.

Depression and Situation Models of Text Comprehension

In another study, depressed and nondepressed participants were examined for their effectiveness to process and retrieve information from text. We focused on the construction of situation models relative to other forms of text comprehension (Sedek & Zientecka, 2008). According to recent theories of text comprehension, a written text might be represented in the three forms: the surface form, the textbase form, and the situation model (Johnson-Laird, 1983; Radvansky, Zwaan, Curiel, & Copeland, 2001; Schmalhofer & Glavanow, 1986). The surface level is an exact representation of the presented text. The textbase level contains some small modifications of the original text (e.g., paraphrases), but the specific sentence form is preserved. The situation model, finally, is not a detailed representation of the text, but contains the abstract meaning of the events described in the text, along with inferences from the text. According to the comprehension literature, the construction of a precise situation model is the main goal of comprehension, and such situation models create knowledge that might be useful at later times (Kintsch 1998). Radvansky and his coworkers (Radvansky & Copeland, 2004; Radvansky et al., 2001) noticed that the construction of situation models from the texts is a form of everyday logic that resembles the generation of mental models in syllogism tasks. However, there arose interesting differences when the text comprehension paradigm was applied in the aging research. Namely, older adults were much better than young adults in the construction of a situation model (the meaning of the text), although the elderly were much worse than the young in terms of surface and textbase knowledge (memory for the actual words and syntax). Additionally, the generation of situation models was not related to OSPAN (Radvansky & Copeland, 2004).

The intriguing research question was whether depression would also impair the generative form of comprehending a text, or rather, since text comprehension constitutes a well-overlearned, distinctive cognitive ability, it would be relatively preserved in depressed individuals, in a similar way as this ability appeared to be preserved in older age. If the first case were true, it would confirm that depression has a disruptive impact on a wide range of mental model construction processes, even on such as the construction of a situation model which is not directly related to formal logical reasoning. Were the second option true, it would mean that the impairing effects of depression are restricted to the mental model constructions that are based on logical reasoning.

In our research, we used an experimental paradigm (Radvansky et al., 2001; Schmalhofer & Glavanow, 1986) that allowed us to differentiate the influences of the surface form, textbase, and situation model representations in text memory. Namely, after reading a one-page, detailed text about some historical events, participants were given a memory recognition test. There were four types of

Table 20.3 Recognition test. Proportion of "Yes" responses

Proportion of "yes" responses

	Correct	Paraphrase	Inference	Wrong
Nondepressed	0.73	0.58	0.37	0.25
Depressed	0.74	0.69	0.33	0.35

Fig. 20.6 The proportion of correct answers as a function of group (depression) and text representation (surface, text base or situation model). Errors bars represent standard errors of the mean

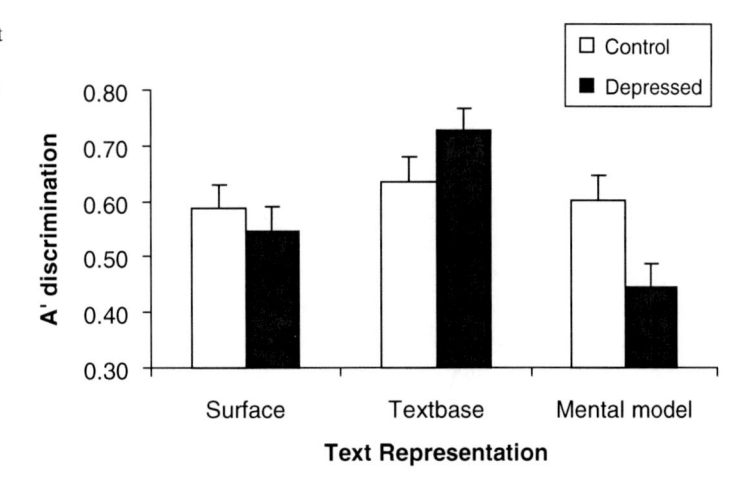

probes (in each case, the participants were asked to indicate if a given sentence was presented in the original text):

1. Verbatim probes – actual sentences from the text;
2. Paraphrase probes – sentences with slightly changed propositions;
3. Inference probes – sentences that were not mentioned but did contain inferences that were consistent with the text;
4. Wrong probes – sentences that were not mentioned and contained inferences that were inconsistent with the text.

The proportion of "yes" responses is presented in Table 20.3. The proportion of correct answers (the probe sentence was actually presented in the text) is shown in the first column. The other proportions of incorrect answers were used for calculating the appropriate level of text comprehension. The A' discrimination, a nonparametric signal detection measure (Snodgrass & Corwin, 1988) was used as measure to target any given form of representation, as follows. The ability to discriminate verbatim from paraphrase probes was used as an index of surface discrimination. For the surface representation measure, the proportion of verbatim "yes" responses were considered hits, and the proportion of "yes" responses to paraphrase items were considered false alarms. Similarly, the ability to differentiate between paraphrase and inference probes was used as an index of the textbase form of representation. For this purpose, "yes" responses to paraphrase items were considered hits, and "yes" responses to inference items were considered false alarms. Finally, the ability to differentiate between consistent and inconsistent inferences provided an index of an existing situation model. For the situation model representation, consistent inferences were considered hits, whereas inferences inconsistent with the text were considered false alarms.

A mixed $3 \times 2 \times 2$ ANOVA (Text Representation × Depression × Operation Span) yielded an interesting and reliable Depression × Text Representation interaction (see Fig. 20.6). Namely, depressed participants showed a significantly lower level of situation model representation in comparison to nondepressed students. However, the differences for surface and textbase forms were not significant.

This time, confirming the results of Radvansky and Copeland (2004), the OSPAN measure for working memory was not related to the representation level, and also the interaction between depression and operation span was not reliable. The results support the idea that a general limitation in integrative processes during the construction of mental models is associated with subclinical depression. Even when situation models did not demand the applying of logical rules, as in the previous paradigms (social cliques, linear orders, categorical syllogisms), the construction of meaning from the written text ("what was the text about?") was reduced in depressed states, while memory performance with regards to the actual text details was preserved pretty well.

Defocused Attention in Depression

Impairments in the construction of mental models, as outlined in the earlier sections of this chapter, may have part of their explanation in the way how depressed individuals allocate their attention. This idea is mainly driven by the consideration that the complex process of integrating piecemeal information into a coherent mental model will normally benefit from a focused mode of attention. Indeed, earlier research has already investigated attentional control as a cognitive mechanism likely to be affected by sad mood (Gotlib et al., 1996; Linville, 1996). Attentional control, that is, the focusing on task-relevant information as well as the not-attending to, potentially intruding, irrelevant information, appears to be difficult for depressed individuals (see also Hertel, 1997; Hertel & Rude, 1991). Thus, there is some evidence that would imply or suggest an association of a defocused mode of attention with the pattern of depressive deficits as discussed above. However, some of our research suggests addressing this discussion from still another angle. Instead of exclusively seeing the reported pattern of depressives' performance under a deficit point of view, it could prove fruitful to instead see it in terms of the possible adaptive functions of emotional states in general, and depressed mood in particular. Some classical theories of emotions and their ecological context suggest that emotions might have consequences on the general "attentional mode" that an individual is in at any given time. Oatley and Johnson-Laird (1987) proposed a functional theory of emotions, in which they define the adaptive value of emotional states as providing transitions within sequential action plans. For depressed mood, the typical transition may be initiated by a "failure of major plan or loss of active goal," and it would occur via the emotion of sadness. Sadness is associated with "do nothing and/or search for new plan" (p. 36). When finding itself in such a transition, an organism may well benefit from an open, unfocused, unselective, low-effort mode of attention that allows new stimuli to be perceived and registered for later use, although those stimuli could well appear irrelevant under the old, to-be-abandoned, plan (see Klinger, 1975).

If depressed mood is associated with a defocused mode of attention, which does not necessarily imply an "impairment" (see the results by Smith, Tracy, & Murray, 1993, as discussed above), then one should be able to elicit even superior cognitive performance in the depressives, as compared to the nondepressed, when the processing of irrelevant aspects of a stimulus is concerned. To examine this prediction with respect to memory performance, we used a source monitoring paradigm that allowed us to separate, at a parametric level, various components of memory performance, relating to relevant and irrelevant aspects of the materials learnt.

In our study (von Hecker & Meiser, 2005), 44 nondepressed and 30 depressed participants (BDI-selected) had to learn 64 individual nouns that were presented individually on a computer screen, each one on either the left or the right side of the screen, and each one surrounded by either a red or green frame. Participants were told that they later would be asked to recognize these 64 words as "old" when randomly presented among 64 distractors. They were also instructed to remember the location of each word for later identification. Color of frame was not mentioned. In the later test stage, however, participants were not only queried about old/new decisions for each presented test word, but if a participant responded "old," they were asked about the side on which that word had been presented on the screen, and, additionally, what the color of its frame had been. This way, for each word they had classified as "old," participants attempted to remember one source dimension that had been relevant (location), and one that had been irrelevant (frame color) at the time of encoding.

The results showed that nondepressed participants' memory for frame color was virtually nil; the pertinent parameter was statistically not different from zero. However, the same parameter was significantly larger and different from zero in the depressed group, showing that this group in fact displayed some memory for the irrelevant stimulus feature. Parameters did not differ between the two groups for old/new decisions or for location, which means that both groups performed at the same level in terms of the relevant task components. Since the overall memory performance, taken relevant and irrelevant aspects together, appears to be even superior in the depressed group as compared to the nondepressed group, these results are not consistent with a deficit model. Instead, they are consistent with the view that depression may be associated with a defocused mode of attention which might be a characteristic of the sad emotion in terms of its adaptive cognitive functions (Klinger, 1975; Oatley & Johnson-Laird, 1987). One might compare the defocused state of attention observed in depressed individuals to some observations from research on creativity (e.g., Martindale, 1977), from which it appears that defocused attention in the context of creativity constitutes a preliminary stage during the process of creative thinking. Whereas in a creativity process, defocused attention is followed by other stages, leading to positive and original outcomes, in depressed people defocused attention seems to have similarities with creative processing only during the very first, preparatory phase, which is primarily about the perceiving and gathering of piecemeal information. Concerning subsequent steps of information processing, there is much less similarity to creativity. We should also emphasize that the constraints of the source monitoring task we used are such that creativity as a mental state did not appear to be facilitated by this task or its context.

Summary and Conclusion

The reviewed research presented compelling evidence for the existence of a unique cognitive limitation in subclinical depression: The impairment of the construction of mental models. These specific limitations were found among depressed participants across various paradigms tapping into mental model construction: (a) mental models of interpersonal sentiment relations (social cliques' models); (b) linear order reasoning (mental arrays); (c) evaluation of categorical syllogisms (mental models of logical relations); (d) situation models (inferences about the meaning of written text). Research on mental models (Brewer, 1987; Garnham, 1997; Greeno, 1989; Holland, Holyoak, Nisbett, & Thagard, 1986; Johnson-Laird, 1996) has demonstrated that a successful on-line construction of global, holistic representations of any experienced situation during information input is of crucial importance. This holds especially for complex tasks and for social perception, because mental models simplify processing, promote understanding and prediction, and thereby improve control over the course of events. Our experiments confirmed the hypothesis that depression specifically impairs the integrative processes necessary for an on-line generation of these coherent and pragmatically useful mental representations.

These patterns of findings are highly distinctive from the research on cognitive limitations in aging (Engle, Sedek, von Hecker, & McIntosh, 2005), where processes of mental model generation were also vigorously studied. Older adults were either superior in comparison to young adults in terms of deriving meaning from written text – that is, in the generation of situation models (Radvansky et al., 2001), or the influence of aging on integrative forms of reasoning was nearly completely mediated by impairments in simpler cognitive processes, such as mental speed or working memory capacity (Gilinski & Judd, 1994; Salthouse, 2001; Sedek & von Hecker, 2004).

Our research teams in Warsaw and Cardiff have been intensively involved in interdisciplinary research applying modern neuroscientific methods (examining of fMRI and EEG) in order to obtain a deeper understanding of the brain mediators of the relationship between subclinical and clinical depression and these impairments in mental model generation. Work is also underway to obtain evidence of cognitive and neuroplasticity changes during different forms of clinical depression treatments. We believe that integrative research, linking cognitive approaches to the mechanisms of mental model building to methods of cognitive neuroscience might yield substantial progress in the understanding of the specificity of cognitive limitations in depression, and will enable us to obtain better insight in the nature of future effective treatments of severe depressed states.

Acknowledgments Preparation of this article was supported by MNiSW grants N N106040534 and N106 017 31/1344.

References

Abramson, L. Y., Seligman, M. E. P., & Teasdale, J. (1978). Learned helplessness in humans: Critique and reformulation. *Journal of Abnormal Psychology, 87,* 49–74.

Acuna, B. D., Eliassen, J. C., Donoghue, J. P., & Sanes, J. N. (2002). Frontal and parietal lobe activation during transitive inference in humans. *Cerebral Cortex, 12,* 1312–1321.

Beck, A. T. (1967). *Depression: Causes and treatment.* Philadelphia, PA: University of Pennsylvania Press.

Brewer, W. F. (1987). Schemas versus mental models in human memory. In P. Morris (Ed.), *Modelling cognition* (pp. 187–197). Chichester: Wiley.

Bucciarelli, M., & Johnson-Laird, P. N. (1999). Strategies in syllogistic reasoning. *Cognitive Science, 23,* 247–303.

Burt, D. B., Zembar, M. J., & Niederehe, G. (1995). Depression and memory impairment: A meta-analysis of the association, its pattern, and specificity. *Psychological Bulletin, 117,* 285–305.

Channon, S., Baker, J. E., & Robertson, M. M. (1993). Effects of structure and clustering on recall and recognition memory in clinical depression. *Journal of Abnormal Psychology, 102,* 323–326.

Conway, A. R. A., & Engle, R. W. (1996). Individual differences in working memory capacity: More evidence for a general capacity theory. *Memory, 4,* 577–590.

Conway, M., & Giannopoulos, C. (1993). Dysphoria and decision making: Limited information use for evaluation of multiattribute targets. *Journal of Personality and Social Psychology, 64,* 613–623.

Copeland, D. E., & Radvansky, G. A. (2004). Working memory and syllogistic reasoning. *The Quarterly Journal of Experimental Psychology, 57A,* 1437–1457.

Davis, C. G., Wortman, C. B., Silver, R. C., & Thompson, S. C. (1995). The undoing of traumatic life events. *Personality and Social Psychology Bulletin, 21,* 109–124.

Ellis, H. C., & Ashbrook, P. W. (1988). Resource allocation model of the effects of depressed mood states on memory. In K. Fiedler & J. Forgas (Eds.), *Affect, cognition and social behavior* (pp. 25–43). Toronto: Hogrefe.

Ellis, H. C., Ottaway, S. A., Varner, L. J., Becker, A. S., & Moore, B. A. (1997). Emotion, motivation, and text comprehension: The detection of contradictions in passages. *Journal of Experimental Psychology: General, 126,* 131–146.

Engle, R. W., Sedek, G., von Hecker, U., & McIntosh, D. N. (Eds.). (2005). *Cognitive limitations in aging and psychopathology.* New York: Cambridge University Press.

Engle, R. W., Tuholski, S. W., Laughlin, J. E., & Conway, A. R. A. (1999). Working memory, short-term memory and general fluid intelligence: A latent-variable approach. *Journal of Experimental Psychology: General, 128,* 309–331.

Fangmeier, T., Knauff, M., Ruff, C. C., & Sloutsky, V. (2006). fMRI evidence for a three-stage model of deductive reasoning. *Journal of Cognitive Neuroscience, 18,* 320–334.

Flett, G. L., Vredenburg, K., & Kramses, L. (1997). The continuity of depression in clinical and nonclinical samples. *Psychological Bulletin, 121,* 395–416.

Gannon, K. M., Skowronski, J. J., & Betz, A. L. (1994). Depressive diligence in social information processing: Implications for order effects in impressions and for social memory. *Social Cognition, 12,* 263–280.

Garnham, A. (1997). Representing information in mental models. In M. A. Conway (Ed.), *Cognitive models of memory* (pp. 149–172). Cambridge: MIT Press.

Gilinski, A., & Judd, B. B. (1994). Working memory bias in reasoning across the life span. *Psychology and Aging, 3,* 356–371.

Gotlib, I. H., & Hammen, C. (1992). *Psychological aspect of depression: Toward an interpersonal integration.* New York: Wiley.
Gotlib, I. H., Roberts, J. E., & Gilboa, E. (1996). Cognitive interference in depression. In I. G. Sarason, G. R. Pierce, & B. R. Sarason (Eds.), *Cognitive interference: Theories, methods and findings* (pp. 347–377). Mahwah, NJ: Lawrence Erlbaum Associates.
Greeno, J. G. (1989). Situations, mental models, and generative knowledge. In D. Klahr & K. Kotovsky (Eds.), *Complex information processing* (pp. 285–318). Hillsdale: Erlbaum.
Hartlage, S., Alloy, L. B., Vazquez, C., & Dykman, D. (1993). Automatic and effortful processing in depression. *Psychological Bulletin, 113*, 247–278.
Hasher, L., & Zacks, R. (1979). Automatic and effortful processes in memory. *Journal of Experimental Psychology: General, 108*, 356–388.
Heider, F. (1958). *The Psychology of interpersonal relations.* New York: Wiley.
Hertel, P. T. (1997). On the contributions of deficient cognitive control to memory impairments in depression. *Cognition and Emotion, 11*, 569–583.
Hertel, P. T. (2004). Memory for emotional and nonemotional events in depression: A question of habit? In D. Reisberg & P. Hertel (Eds.), *Memory and emotion.* New York: Oxford University Press.
Hertel, P. T., & Hardin, T. S. (1990). Remembering with and without awareness in depressed mood: Evidence of deficits in initiative. *Journal Experimental Psychology: General, 119*, 45–59.
Hertel, P. T., & Rude, S. S. (1991). Depressive deficits in memory: Focusing attention improves subsequent recall. *Journal Experimental Psychology: General, 120*, 301–309.
Hinton, E., von Hecker, U., Singh, K., & Wise, R. (2008). *Generative reasoning in subclinical depression: Exploring the neural basis.* Unpublished manuscript, Cardiff University.
Holland, J. H., Holyoak, K. J., Nisbett, R. E., & Thagard, P. R. (1986). *Induction: Processes of inference, learning and discovery.* Cambridge, MA: MIT Press.
Hummert, M. L., Crockett, W. H., & Kemper, S. (1990). Processing mechanisms underlying use of the balance schema. *Journal of Personality and Social Psychology, 58*, 5–21.
Huttenlocher, J. (1968). Constructing spatial images: A strategy in reasoning. *Psychological Review, 75*, 550–560.
Johnson-Laird, P. N. (1983). *Mental models: Towards a cognitive science of language, inference and consciousness.* Cambridge: Cambridge University Press.
Johnson-Laird, P. N. (1996). Images, models, and propositional representations. In M. de Vega, M. J. Intons-Peterson, P. N. Johnson-Laird, M. Denis, & M. Marschark (Eds.), *Models of visuospatial cognition* (pp. 90–127). Oxford: Oxford University Press.
Joormann, J. (2005). Inhibition, rumination, and mood regulation in depression. In R. W. Engle, G. Sedek, U. von Hecker, & D. N. McIntosh (Eds.), *Cognitive limitations in aging and psychopathology* (pp. 275–312). New York: Cambridge University Press.
Kintsch, W. (1998). *Comprehension: A paradigm for cognition.* Cambridge, UK: Cambridge University Press.
Klinger, E. (1975). Consequences of commitment to and disengagement from incentives. *Psychological Review, 82*, 1–25.
Knauff, M., Mulack, T., Kassubek, J., Salih, H. R., & Greenlee, M. W. (2002). Spatial imagery in deductive reasoning: A functional MRI study. *Cognitive Brain Research, 13*, 203–212.
Kofta, M., & Sedek, G. (1989). Repeated failure: A source of helplessness, or a factor irrelevant to its emergence? *Journal of Experimental Psychology: General, 118*, 3–12.
Kofta, M., & Sedek, G. (1998). Uncontrollability as a source of cognitive exhaustion: Implications for helplessness and depression. In M. Kofta, G. Weary, & G. Sedek (Eds.), *Personal control in action: Cognitive and motivational mechanisms* (pp. 391–418). New York: Plenum.
Kofta, M., & Sedek, G. (1999). Uncontrollability as irreducible uncertainty. *European Journal of Social Psychology, 29*, 577–590.
Kroger, J. K., Sabb, F. W., Fales, C. L., Bookheimer, S. Y., Cohen, M. S., & Holyoak, K. J. (2002). Recruitment of anterior dorsolateral prefrontal cortex in human reasoning: A parametric study of relational complexity. *Cerebral Cortex, 12*, 477–485.
Kuhl, J. (1984). Volitional aspects of achievement motivation and learned helplessness: Toward a comprehensive theory of action control. In B. Maher (Ed.), *Progress of experimental personality research* (Vol. 13, pp. 99–171). San Diego, CA: Academic.
Linville, P. (1996). Attention inhibition: Does it underlie ruminative thought? In R. S. Wyer (Ed.), *Advances in social cognition* (Vol. 9, pp. 121–133). Mahwah, NJ: Erlbaum.
Martindale, C. (1977). Creativity, consciousness, and cortical arousal. *Journal of Altered States of Consciousness, 3*, 69–87.
Marx, E. M., Williams, J. M. G., & Claridge, G. (1992). Depression and social problem solving. *Journal of Abnormal Psychology, 101*, 78–86.
McIntosh, D. N., Sedek, G., Fojas, S., Brzezicka-Rotkiewicz, A., & Kofta, M. (2005). Cognitive performance after preexposure to uncontrollability and in depressive state: Going with a simpler "Plan B". In R. W. Engle, G. Sedek, U.

von Hecker, & D. N. McIntosh (Eds.), *Cognitive limitations in aging and psychopathology* (pp. 219–246). New York: Cambridge University Press.

Niedenthal, P. M., Tangney, J. P., & Gavanski, I. (1994). "If I only weren't" versus "if only I hadn't": Distinguishing shame and guilt in counterfactual thinking. *Journal of Personality and Social Psychology, 67*, 585–595.

Oatley, K., & Johnson-Laird, P. N. (1987). Towards a cognitive theory of emotions. *Cognition and Emotion, 1*, 29–50.

Piaget, J., & Inhelder, B. (1974). *The child's construction of quantities: Conservation and atomism.* London: Routledge & Kegan Paul.

Pittman, T. S., & D'Agostino, P. R. (1989). Motivation and cognition: Control deprivation and the nature of subsequent information processing. *Journal of Experimental Social Psychology, 25*, 465–480.

Potts, G. R. (1972). Information processing strategies used in the encoding of linear orderings. *Journal of Verbal Learning and Verbal Behavior, 11*, 727–740.

Radvansky, G. A., & Copeland, D. E. (2004). Reasoning, integration, inference alteration, and text comprehension. *Canadian Journal of Experimental Psychology, 58*, 133–141.

Radvansky, G. A., Zwaan, R. A., Curiel, J. M., & Copeland, D. E. (2001). Situation models and aging. *Psychology and Aging, 16*, 145–160.

Salthouse, T. A. (2001). Attempted decomposition of age-related influences on two tests of reasoning. *Psychology and Aging, 16*, 251–263.

Schmalhofer, F., & Glavanow, D. (1986). Three components of understanding a programmer's manual: Verbatim, propositional, and situational representations. *Journal of Memory and Language, 25*, 279–294.

Sedek, G., & Kofta, M. (1990). When cognitive exertion does not yield cognitive gain: Toward an informational explanation of learned helplessness. *Journal of Personality and Social Psychology, 58*, 729–743.

Sedek, G., Kofta, M., & Tyszka, T. (1993). Effects of uncontrollability on subsequent decision making: Testing the cognitive exhaustion hypothesis. *Journal of Personality and Social Psychology, 65*, 1270–1281.

Sedek, G., & McIntosh, D. N. (1998). Intellectual helplessness: Domain specificity, teaching styles, and school achievement. In M. Kofta, G. Weary, & G. Sedek (Eds.), *Personal control in action: Cognitive and motivational mechanisms* (pp. 391–418). New York: Plenum.

Sedek, G., Oberauer, K., & von Hecker, U. (2008). *Influence of depression and working memory on belief bias and categorical reasoning.* Unpublished manuscript, Warsaw School of Social Psychology.

Sedek, G., & von Hecker, U. (2004). Effects of subclinical depression and aging on generative reasoning about linear orders: Same or different processing limitations? *Journal of Experimental Psychology: General, 133*, 237–260.

Sedek, G., & Zientecka (2008). *Situation models and depression.* Unpublished manuscript, Warsaw School of Social Psychology.

Seligman, M. E. P. (1975). *Helplessness: On depression, development and death.* San Francisco: W.H. Freeman.

Smith, J. D., Tracy, J. I., & Murray, M. J. (1993). Depression and category learning. *Journal of Experimental Psychology: General, 122*, 331–346.

Snodgrass, J., & Corwin, J. (1988). Pragmatics of measuring recognition memory: Applications to dementia and amnesia. *Journal of Experimental Psychology: General, 117*, 34–50.

Sternberg, R. J. (1980). Representation and process in linear syllogistic reasoning. *Journal of Experimental Psychology: General, 109*, 119–159.

Turner, M. L., & Engle, R. W. (1989). Is working memory capacity task dependent? *Journal of Memory and Language, 28*, 127–154.

von Hecker, U. (1997). How do logical inference rules help construct social mental models? *Journal of Experimental Social Psychology, 33*, 367–400.

von Hecker, U., & Meiser, T. (2005). Defocused attention in depressed mood: Evidence from source monitoring. *Emotion, 5*, 456–463.

von Hecker, U., & Sedek, G. (1999). Uncontrollability, depression, and the construction of mental models. *Journal of Personality and Social Psychology, 77*, 833–850.

von Hecker, U., Sedek, G., & McIntosh, D. N. (2000). Impaired systematic, higher order strategies in depression and helplessness: Testing implications of the cognitive exhaustion model. In U. von Hecker, S. Dutke, & G. Sedek (Eds.), *Generative mental processes and cognitive resources: Integrative research on adaptation and control* (pp. 245–276). Dordrecht: Kluwer.

Watts, F. N., & Cooper, Z. (1989). The effects of structural aspects of the recall of prose. *Journal of Abnormal Psychology, 98*, 150–153.

Weary, G., Marsh, K. L., Gleicher, F., & Edwards, J. A. (1993). Depression, control motivation, and the processing of information about others. In G. Weary, F. Gleicher, & K. L. Marsh (Eds.), *Control motivation and social cognition* (pp. 255–287). New York: Springer.

Weingartner, H. (1986). Automatic and effort demanding cognitive processes in depression. In L. W. Poon et al. (Eds.), *Handbook for clinical memory assessment of older adults* (pp. 218–225). Washington, DC: American Psychological Association.

Chapter 21
Working Memory Capacity and Individual Differences in Higher-Level Cognition

Jarosław Orzechowski

Introduction

Let's start with a riddle: what are the Authors referring to?

> "[It] is one of the greatest accomplishments of the human mind; it makes possible planning, reasoning, problem solving, reading, and abstraction." (Conway, Jarrold, Kane, Miyake, & Towse, 2007, p. 3)

> "This concept [of it] and its limits is a key part of human condition. [...] We need [it] to in language comprehension, [...]; in arithmetic, [...]; in reasoning, [...]; and in most other types of cognitive tasks." (Cowan, 2005a, p. 2)

If it was not for the names of the authors of the above quotes, which no doubt for majority of readers indicate unambiguously the context of "it," one could think that they are referring to terms like consciousness, abstract thinking, or the *g* factor. It is even more interesting that these quotes come from first pages of multipage books, where – in accordance with the rule "from the general to the particular" – one gives basic information about one's subject matter. However, as Nęcka (in print) felicitously says in a paper concerning this concept: "[...] *for some 2,500 years of psychology as a branch of philosophy, and then for almost 100 years of its independent development* [...], *it was not considered necessary to use* [this] *term*." Thus, it is a concept of equal importance in psychology as consciousness, thinking, and intelligence, but much younger.

It is truly interesting that psychology could do without the concept of working memory (WM) for such a long time; today, it would be unthinkable. But the idea of working memory is not as new as it seems. The concept of working memory was used for the first time fourteen years before the seminal article by Baddeley and Hitch (1974), in perhaps equally famous work by Miller, Galanter, and Pribram (1960).

Working Memory

Working memory has been recently defined as a *"temporary storage system under attentional control that underpins our capacity for complex thought"* (Baddeley, 2007, p. 1), or as the *"ability to mentally maintain information in active and readily accessible state, while concurrently and selectively processing new information"* or – more simply – as the *"ability to simultaneously maintain*

J. Orzechowski (✉)
Institute of Psychology, Jagiellonian University, Al. Mickiewicza 3, Cracow 31-120, Poland
e-mail: jarek@apple.phils.uj.edu.pl

and process goal-relevant information" (Conway et al., 2007, p. 3). An analysis of various definitions of WM shows that the differences among them are quite fundamental. Even in the above quoted descriptions, there is no agreement whether WM is a system, or an ability, or perhaps a process. Moreover, there is a serious fear that "*working memory is not memory system in itself, but a system for attention to memory [...]*" (Oberauer, Süß, Wilhelm, & Sander, 2007, p. 50). This fear comes from activation theories of WM (e.g., Cowan, 1988, 1995), where its function consists in making representations encoded in LTM available for intentional information processing. Diversity of WM definitions goes together with diversity of WM theories (see a review: Miyake & Shah, 1999). It seems, however, that WM researchers agree on at least several issues.

Firstly, almost everyone agrees that WM is a capacity-limited system,[1] although it is not clear how large this limitation is. Compared to the capacity of long-term memory, it is so huge, however, that WM capacity could be ignored in that context. But the problem is that if WM capacity was ignored by evolution, we would have probably lost our abilities to perform any complex cognitive tasks, or these abilities would have been seriously constrained. We can have some idea of possible effects of such omission from examining patients with frontal lobe pathology. These patients display deficits in execution of such tasks as Wisconsin Card Sorting test (Berman, Ostrem, Randolph, & Gold, 1995) or Tower of London test (Baker, Rogers, Owen, & Frith, 1996). These tasks are behavioral tests of frontal lobe damage, and at the same time are considered to be good measures of working memory, particularly of its executive functions.

So, WM is a system of a rather small capacity but of enormous importance for our minds. Unfortunately, WM researchers do not agree about the nature of the limitation of WM capacity. Initially, following the example of STM models, this limitation was understood more structurally as resulting from the capacity limitations within each of memory buffers (Baddeley & Hitch, 1974). At present, even Baddeley (2007) does not emphasize so strongly the structural separateness of WM subsystems. But only the activation theories allowed us to interpret the capacity limitations of WM in processual instead of structural terms, i.e., as the effect of individual differences in general executive abilities or attentional control (Conway & Engle, 1994; Engle, Kane, & Tuholski, 1999; Kyllonen & Christal, 1990). The factors limiting the amount of information that can be stored and processed in WM have been identified as the amount of available activation resources (Engle, Cantor, & Carullo, 1992), processing speed (Salthouse, 1996), resistance to interference (Oberauer et al., 2004), efficiency of inhibitory mechanism (Stoltzfus, Hasher, & Zacks, 1996), or time-related decay of information stored in working memory (Portrat, Barrouillet, & Camos, 2006). There are also some attempts to integrate the above (and other) mechanisms into one model. For instance, Barrouillet and his collaborators (Barrouillet, Bernardin, & Camos, 2004) define the capacity of WM in terms of the ability to allocate temporarily attentional resources to the pieces of information stored or being processed in WM. And thus, small capacity of WM is not resulting from any structural limitations but from the processual limitations of information processing speed with regard to allocating the limited resources. The more effective is the temporal allocation of resources; thanks to quick movement of focus of attention from one item to another, the more items are available for information processing. Another problem is the source of so radical limitation of WM capacity. But it is difficult to say whether this limitation results from the upper limit of nervous system capabilities (e.g., Miller, 1956), developmental limitations (Daneman & Merikle, 1996; Gathercole, Pickering, Ambridge, & Wearing, 2004), or optimal evolutionary adaptation to cope with particular problems (Elman, 1993; Mac Gregor, 1987).

---

[1] According to Cowan (2007), however, this is not a universal assumption. There are theories that do not share this view. As examples, one can point to the long-term working memory theory by Ericsson and Kintsh (1995), and to the theory of task conflict by Meyer and Kieras (1997a, 1997b).

Secondly, vast majority of WM models incorporate a control mechanism, usually an attentional one. But unfortunately, there is no agreement about a detailed list of control processes carried out by WM control system. Miyake and Shah (1999; see also Miyake et al., 2000), having analyzed research results and various theories of WM, distinguished three basic control functions of WM, i.e., inhibition, task-switching, and updating the content of working memory. However, the updating function does not correlate with other control functions; therefore, Oberauer (Oberauer et al., 2007) suggests that it should be excluded from the list, at least until new cognitive tasks are elaborated, because the existing tasks for updating (e.g., n-back task) engage simultaneously storage and processing, and that is why they are measures rather of capacity than pure updating. Moreover, accepted measures of cognitive control, such as switching of task-set, seem to be unrelated to WM capacity (Oberauer, Süß, Wilhelm, & Wittman, 2003), which shows immaturity of the concept of executive functions in WM models, because one can hardly expect functions of a single cognitive system not to be related to one another. Oberauer et al. (2003) named three a little bit different than Miyake and Shah executive functions: simultaneous storage and processing, supervision, and coordination. The first of these functions consists in simultaneous and short-term retention of information available in a given moment and in transformation or derivation of new information. The second function – supervision – involves continuous monitoring of current cognitive processes, in selective activation of representation and in suppression of irrelevant information in a given moment. And the third function – coordination – consists in integrating active elements in working memory into larger structures. Other researchers are inclined to assume the existence of many, sometimes very detailed, control functions (see Friedman & Miyake, 2004); so we do not have an unambiguous platform to analyze control functions.

Another problem concerning cognitive control within working memory is that behind this seemingly modern concept lies the problem of homunculus (see Conway et al., 2007; Miyake & Shah, 1999). All versions of the central executive, which is responsible for control (planning, monitoring) of processes going on in WM, seem to be burdened with a tacit assumption that there is "someone" in our mind, who is performing this control. WM researchers put a lot of effort trying to solve this problem; for instance, they treat this control as a property of a self-contained dynamic interactive network (Munakata, Morton, & O'Reilly, 2007). At this moment, however, the problem cannot be regarded as having been satisfactorily solved. There is also a purely theoretical problem of the relation between memory and attention, which eventually should be cleared, because at present the boundaries between the two concepts seem to be unclear. And it definitely should be resolved, because data gathered in research conducted with the use of neuroimagining technique seem to show that execution of some tasks for spatial memory and spatial attention engages the same parts of brain (Corbetta, Kincade, & Shulman, 2002). There are strong arguments that it is not a random coincidence, but there exists a common neural mechanism (see Awh, Vogel, & Oh, 2006). Perhaps, we will have to abandon one of these concepts, at least in the context of processes investigated by WM researchers. It is also important what is being controlled, because these are not only processes related to the short-term maintenance of data. The latter are important but only in the context of goal-directed processing. Many researchers (see Oberauer et al., 2007) clearly emphasize the distinction between primary cognitive processes, performed on representations currently stored in memory subsystems (e.g., Baddeley) or encompassed by the focus of attention (e.g., Cowan, Engle, McErlee, & Oberauer), and executive processes aiming to initiate and monitor the correctness of primary processes in the context of an overarching goal.

Thirdly, researchers seem to agree that working memory plays a key role for effective performance of higher-level cognition processes, such as reasoning, problem solving, decision making, and – more generally – abstract thinking. A list of issues that WM researchers could agree on is certainly longer, but the other issues would certainly be more difficult to agree on.

Despite the key and superior role of cognitive control for WM effectiveness and increasing interest in the relation between control functions and intelligence, the results of many studies show that working memory capacity (WMC) is the best single predictor of reasoning ability (Kyllonen & Christal, 1990; Süß, Oberauer, Wittmann, Wilhelm, & Schulze, 2002) and of – related to it – general fluid intelligence (Ackerman, Beier, & Boyle, 2002; Conway, Cowan, Bunting, Therriault, & Minkoff, 2002; Engle, Tuholski, Laughlin, & Conway, 1999). While the control mechanisms attributed to WM seem to be highly hypothetical, and their list is still under construction, the capacity of WM refers to the observable limitation of temporary storing and processing information. And although the foundation of this limitation is at least equally hypothetical as the control functions, this limitation is a fact.

This chapter contains a short review of the most recent hypotheses, research results, and theoretical discussions concerning the relation between WMC and higher-level cognition. The fundamental question posed by the researchers dealing with the subject is not whether this relation exists but what underpins it and how it extends our knowledge of both working memory and higher cognitive processes. The chapter deals mainly with one but an extensive area of research namely reasoning, both deductive and inductive. The data in this area come not just from papers dealing strictly with reasoning but also from research focused on fluid intelligence or fluid abilities, which are usually tested with the use of induction reasoning tasks.

Measurement of Working Memory Capacity

Group of memory span tasks are used to determine individual WM capacity by establishing its maximal load (see Conway et al., 2006). This kind of tasks was initially designed to determine the capacity of short-term memory (*simple span task*) or the general efficiency of information processing (*complex span task*). In studies dealing with working memory, these procedures were adapted and the subjects were required not only to store information but also to perform operations on the stored material. The most popular varieties of this task include reading span (Daneman & Carpenter, 1980), operation span (Turner & Engle, 1989), counting span (Case, Kurland, & Goldberg, 1982), verbal/math span task (Oberauer et al., 2003), and so on. For example, in the reading span task, subjects read aloud displayed sentences and at the same time they are asked to remember the last word from each sentence, and researchers can manipulate the number of displayed sentences and so the number of words to remember. A memory test is carried out after displaying several (usually 2–6) sentences. Sometimes, the subjects are additionally asked to verify the truth of each sentence after it has been presented (Turner & Engle, 1989) or to complete displayed sentences (e.g., George is clapping his …) and to remember the answers (Towse, Hitch, & Hutton, 2000). This forces them to simultaneously execute two tasks: processing the content of the sentence and remembering words. Other span tasks preserve the idea of a dual task but use another type of stimulus material. Subjects verify correctness of mathematical equations and simultaneously are trying to remember displayed words (operation span); they count a certain kind of stimuli, e.g., red circles displayed among other geometrical figures, and are asked to remember their sum total (counting span); or they are asked to remember words or numbers displayed between tests, which require making simple decisions (verbal/math span). The number and variety of such tasks, however, is much greater.

Apart from dual tasks, in the studies of WM functions, one uses also certain measures of working memory efficiency, which do not require subjects to store and process information simultaneously. As examples of this kind of tasks, one can distinguish n-back task (Gray, Chabris, & Braver, 2003) and running memory task (Mayes, 1988). The former requires subjects to detect a repetition in a series of stimuli (usually digits or letters) on exactly n-th (e.g., the third) position from the end of the series. The n-back task not only requires subjects to maintain in memory a set of presented stimuli but also requires them to update this set constantly. On the other hand, running memory task consists in presenting subjects with random-length strings of stimuli. The subjects are asked to recall the last several stimuli or state if a target appeared among the last several stimuli. Because the subjects cannot predict when the series will end, the task requires them to update actively their working memory, removing from it stimuli presented several steps back (and so no longer needed).

What is interesting is that recent studies show that the relation between WM and STM tasks is stronger and more complex than it was initially thought to be (see Colom, Abad, Rebollo, & Shih, 2005a). For instance, storing information in tasks requiring subjects to remember spatial information (e.g., layout of dots) or to recall nonspatial information according to some spatial rule (e.g., digits placed in particular way in a certain matrix) significantly engages control processes of working memory. Therefore, such tasks turn out to be good tests of working memory and highly correlate with other, more standard measures of WM, even if they do not include a secondary task (Oberauer, 2005). Even some verbal tasks, provided that silent repetition is limited and chunking pieces of information is obstructed or controlled, appear to be an accurate test of WM (Cowan et al., 2005).

Higher-Level Cognition

Higher-level cognitive processes can be understood as *"information processing phenomena in which the meta-cognitive factors of monitoring and control play a fundamental role"* (Nęcka & Orzechowski, 2005, p. 122). This term seems to be synonymous with complex cognition. It appears, however, that referring to meta-cognitive factors is not sufficiently distinctive, when we want to differentiate between low- and high-level cognition. The factors that could (individually or collectively) help to distinguish between them are: (1) number and/or complexity of mental models that represent a task, (2) number of factors influencing cognitive performance, (3) number of variables used to manipulate with the task's structure, and (4) time needed to complete a certain task (Nęcka & Orzechowski, 2005). Certainly, this list is not complete, and even if it was, the boundary between low and high level cognition would still be unclear, unless it was established arbitrarily. However, in psychology, it has become customary to classify phenomenon like reasoning, problem solving, and decision making as examples of higher-level cognition.

The most numerous and – it seems – most advanced studies are those focusing on the relation between WMC and individual differences in reasoning. Researchers were interested in these relations because they wanted to understand mechanisms of reasoning or intelligence. In Western culture, intelligence is sometimes defined (e.g., Terman) and operationalized as an ability to cope with problems that require abstract thinking. The most popular test of fluid intelligence: the Raven Progressive Matrices (Raven, Court, & Raven, 1983) comes down to the use of tasks requiring inductive reasoning on abstract material. Studies of reasoning by analogy (especially on nonverbal material) are also a source of interesting findings on the relations between WMC and individual differences as far as the effectiveness of inductive reasoning is concerned.

A separate and relatively new source of knowledge on the relation between WMC and higher-level cognition is provided by teams of researchers focusing on reasoning. Their work is valuable, because it supplements our understanding relations between working memory and those kinds of reasoning, which are rarely or never used in intelligence tests, e.g., syllogistic or conditional reasoning. Slightly smaller, but still substantial number of studies deals with the relations between WMC and problem solving as well as decision making. It is not surprising that results of such studies usually show positive correlations. That is why WM researchers are currently not so much interested if there is any relation between WMC and higher-level cognition, as in the mechanism of this relation. They also want to know how learning about this mechanism can enrich our knowledge about working memory and about the analyzed aspects of human complex cognition.

On the other hand, it does not mean that the relation between WMC and higher-level cognition is obvious and completely predictable. Kareev (1995) showed, for instance, that individual differences in working memory capacity are related to the ability to detect correlations. It turned out that subjects with smaller working memory capacity had advantage in the task that required them to detect correlations between two variables. Probably, smaller WM capacity favors simplification and seeing regularities, and that allows for more accurate assessment of the strength of correlation. From this and several similar studies, one can draw a conclusion that bigger working memory capacity does not always lead to greater effectiveness in performing complex cognitive tasks (Hertwig & Todd, 2003). But it is rather an exception than a rule.

Working Memory Capacity and Deductive Reasoning

Reasoning is the process of drawing conclusions from premises. Deductive reasoning consists in drawing conclusions from premises using formal rules of logic. Psychologists are interested in deductive reasoning because – at least at the beginning – research results clearly showed that thinking of formal logic, uneducated people differ from predictions of a normative theory, which most often encompasses basic laws of logic and principles of probability theory (see Evans, 2002). It turned out that, on the one hand, we make systematic logical errors, specific for various inference schemata; but on the other hand, the number of these errors is smaller if the content of deductive tasks is closer to everyday experience or individual competences (see Cosmides & Tooby, 1994; Griggs & Cox, 1982; Tooby & Cosmides, 1990). In all significant theories of deductive reasoning, i.e., the abstract-rule theory (1994b; Braine, Reiser, & Rumain, 1984, Rips, 1994a) and the mental models theory (Johnson-Laird, 1983, 1994; Johnson-Laird & Byrne, 1991), reasoning requires essential involvement of working memory, and the more difficult the task is, the higher this involvement must be. At this level of abstraction, predictions of both theories concerning working memory load do not differ substantially. The rule theory assumes however that reasoning consists in constructing "mental proofs," which connect premises and conclusions. Thus, the more mental steps must be made, the bigger is the working memory load, and consequently – the bigger probability of making errors. On the other hand, in the mental models theory, reasoning consists in creating mental simulations (models) in accordance with the data contained in the premises. The more complex representation of a problem situation is, the larger number of mental models must be created and/or the more complex are these models; consequently – the bigger are requirements for working memory and the greater is risk of error. These general predictions have been confirmed many times, and the researchers found positive correlations between WMC and the performance of the tasks requiring syllogistic reasoning (Kyllonen & Christal, 1990) as well as of the tasks requiring conditional reasoning (Barrouillet & Lecas, 1999; Toms, Morris, & Ward, 1993).

Research on the relation between WM and reasoning, conducted in recent years, has gone in various directions. Generally speaking, studies of the relation between reasoning and WM take into account various forms of reasoning and content of logical tasks as well as various WM functions. Thus, these studies deal with syllogistic and conditional reasoning as two basic kinds of reasoning (but also with e.g., conjunction, alternative) and the content of tasks understood in two ways: abstract vs. concrete, and verbal vs. spatial. Often, more and more WM researchers refer to particular functions of WM, using predictions about their relations with reasoning, especially those that differentiate the rule-theory and the mental models theory. Most often one can see references to Baddeley's multicomponent working memory model, but – mainly due to the research by Oberauer team – one can also find in the literature some attempts to combine particular executive functions with the effectiveness of reasoning.

Klauer, Stegmaier, and Meiser (1997) attempted to combine the effectiveness of particular WM structures, as understood by Baddeley, with certain tasks that required reasoning on nonimaginary content (propositions) and imagery content (spatial relations). The researchers used the dual task paradigm, selectively loading WM subsystems: phonological loop or visuospatial sketch-pad. They assumed that solving tasks that require spatial reasoning as well as simultaneous monitoring of the movement of figures on a computer screen will decrease the accuracy of conclusions. This follows from the involvement of the sketch-pad in both concurrent tasks. Similarly, if subjects are asked to perform a task on propositional content, and simultaneously they must repeat certain figures, the phonological loop will be involved in both tasks, and this will decrease accuracy of conclusions. The results only partly confirmed the above predictions: a decrease of conclusion accuracy was significantly higher in spatial tasks no matter what the kind of the secondary task was. A similar logic was used to verify executive functions involvement in reasoning. Again, the researchers used tasks that required reasoning on spatial material and in the form of propositions. But this time, the secondary task consisted in the procedure of random number generation. It turned out that the load of central executive has an influence on the correctness of conclusions drawn in both kinds of tasks requiring reasoning. Thus, the spatial tasks require bigger involvement of both WM subsystems than verbal tasks, but both kinds of tasks equally load the central executive.

There were many attempts to use the differences in predictions concerning WM involvement which follow from the abstract rule theory and the mental models theory, in order to resolve the dispute between supporters of both these theories. One such attempt was made by Garcia-Madruga and his collaborators (García-Madruga, Moreno, Carriedo, Gutiérrez, & Johnson-Laird, 2001). In their research, they used tasks containing conjunctions and alternatives.

It follows from the rule theory that both situations are comparable with respect to the number of rules that should be applied as well as to the number of mental steps that should be taken in order to solve the task correctly. Thus, there should be no differences in WM load in both conditions. Different predictions follow from the mental models theory. A conjunction is represented with the use of one mental model, while an alternative needs two or even three mental models. Thus, the working memory load will be different in these two conditions: it will be higher for an alternative than it is for a conjunction. Garcia-Madruga (García-Madruga et al., 2001) obtained results, which confirmed predictions coming from the mental models theory, but only when subjects were asked to draw conclusions themselves (in contrast to the condition in which they were asked to judge if a given conclusion is correct). On the other hand, Rips (2004a, 2004b) obtained results, which confirmed the predictions of the rule theory, when subjects were asked to judge the correctness of conclusions presented to them.

Markovits, Doyon, and Simoneau (2002) verified predictions of the mental models theory, based on a detailed analysis of relations between reasoning and individual differences in visual and verbal working memory. In the abstract rules theory, there is practically no need to refer to visual working memory (i.e., to involve visuospatial sketch-pad), even if a task's content is imaginary-spatial. Premises of the task are first of all translated into the abstract language of propositions. Further processing of these premises, requiring application of logical rules takes place only with the participation of verbal working memory (i.e., it involves phonological loop). Thus, the researchers assumed that it follows from the rule theory that the performance of the tasks requiring reasoning should correlate positively with the capacity of verbal working memory. Such correlation is not predicted in the case of visual working memory. The kind of material – abstract or concrete – does not matter for the load of various kinds of working memory, because in both cases the researchers used unified, prescriptive representations. On the other hand, the mental models theory assumes that there is a close relation between spatial abilities and reasoning (Johnson-Laird, 1983), as long as a quasi-analogue representation of a problem situation concerns a concrete material. Thus, in sentences with concrete content, there should be a positive relation between the effectiveness of reasoning and the capacity of visuospatial working memory. A similar relation would not take place in the case of tasks with abstract content. On the other hand, the capacity of verbal working memory would be important in the case of both concrete and abstract tasks, due to the semantic nature of inference processes. Markovits et al. (2002) used an approach quite common in the psychology of individual differences (and rare in the research on reasoning). First, they studied visual and verbal memory systems, testing individual efficiency of these systems, and then, they carried out a series of tasks requiring conditional reasoning based on concrete and abstract material. The results showed that in concrete tasks, the effectiveness depends on the capacity of both the phonological loop and the visuospatial sketch-pad, whereas in abstract tasks – it depends only on the capacity of phonological loop. Moreover, the researchers quote "hard" data from studies conducted with the use of a neuroimagining technique (fMRI), indicating that various brain structures are involved during reasoning on abstract and concrete material (e.g., Goel, Buchel, Frith, & Dolan, 2000), which seems to falsify the abstract rule theory, if one accepts the assumptions explained by the researchers.

Another interesting problem is the question what is domain-general and what is domain-specific in the involvement of working memory in various forms of reasoning. For instance, Capon, Handley, and Dennis (2003) analyzed the relation between particular components of working memory and the spatial and syllogistic reasoning. They tried to examine to what extent the performance of various tasks measuring WMC is related to the correctness of these two types of reasoning. They used simple and complex verbal and spatial WM measures (all in the form of WM span tasks). The obtained results indicate that both the effectiveness of reasoning in spatial tasks and in syllogisms is related to the capacity of visual working memory and the capacity of verbal working memory. The researchers manipulated the way the syllogisms and spatial tasks were presented. In both cases, the presentation was both verbal and visual. In the case of spatial tasks, a visual presentation of the task reduced the load of both WM subsystems, whereas the verbal presentation caused the involvement of both these subsystems. In the case of syllogisms, the form of presentation did not differentiate the level of involvement of both these subsystems, which was high in both the conditions of verbal and visual presentation. Thus, it seems that a visual presentation of a spatial task reduces the general WM load of the task rather than the load within a specific modality. In the case of syllogisms – the form of presentation does not seem to change the involvement of the general mechanism of WM. The researchers carried out a factor analysis and it confirmed the participation of central executive (general factor) in both types of reasoning.

The presented results seem to indicate – although it may be a somewhat premature conclusion – that the participation of WM subsystems differs depending on the type of reasoning and the material used. Thus, it seems that it is rather a domain-specific factor. However, in each of these cases, one can regularly detect the central executive involvement in reasoning, and it is a domain-general factor. This is, at least, the case in adults. On the other hand, studies of development of conditional reasoning conducted on children subjects by Barrouillet and Lecas (1998, 1999) seem to indicate a greater influence of WM capacity on the correctness of inference. It turned out that the differences between age groups of 8-year-olds, 11-year-olds, and 14-year-olds consists in the number of mental models constructed during conditional reasoning. In the youngest group, children used only one model of a given situation – the one which was directly described in the task (e.g., in the implication: "If you put on a white shirt, then you must put on green trousers" they did not consider other variants, i.e., what will be with the trousers, if they do not put on the white shirt, or what will be with the white shirt, if they do not put on green trousers). The researchers noticed that 11-year-olds used two models of the situation, and that 14-year-olds used three such models. The partial correlation between WMC and the correctness of inference (with the children's age controlled) was $r=0.65$. And when the children were divided into three groups according to the WM capacity, it turned out that in the group with the smallest WMC no one took into account all three models, while in the group with a middle WMC – 24% of the children used three models, and in the group with the greatest WMC as many as 67% did so.

The research on the relation between executive functions of WM and reasoning was undertaken by Oberauer and his collaborators (Oberauer et al., 2003). Oberauer attributes also a key role in reasoning to WMC, understood as the "*ability to provide direct access to several independent information elements (chunks) at the same time*" (Oberauer et al., 2007, p. 52). In reasoning, this ability is necessary for creating new relations between many elements representing a logical task, in order to integrate them into a new structural representation. The researchers assume that all kinds of tasks that require reasoning have a common property – construction of a new structural representation is needed in order to solve them. This kind of task involves all three functions distinguished by Oberauer, but it seems that the biggest role is played by derivation and coordination (Oberauer et al., 2003). However, the complexity of this new structural representation is limited by WM capacity. According to Oberauer, the so-called direct access area is of particular importance, because its capacity limits the number of elements, which can be simultaneously placed in the common cognitive coordination system. Thus, it limits the number of elements that can be taken into account in the process of integration and construction of a new structural representation. Oberauer et al. (2007) analyzed many different tasks that require deductive reasoning (syllogism, implications), inductive reasoning (series completion, matrices, analogies), as well as problem-solving tasks that require relational integration. They also presented evidence supporting the claim that there is a relation between the performance of these kinds of tasks and WMC. For instance, meta-analysis of own results (Süß et al., 2002) showed that the aggregated WMC factor (the means of z-transformed scores of all working memory measures) correlates with deductive reasoning (a reasoning factor from the Berlin Intelligence Structure Model) at the level of $r=0.76$–0.77, and with inductive reasoning (general intelligence factor) at the level of $r=0.69$–0.82. This means, according to Oberauer, that both constructs, i.e., working memory and reasoning are strongly related, but not the same. Oberauer concludes: *"Reasoning is, after all, a little bit more than working memory"* (Oberauer et al., 2007, p. 69). What makes the difference between them? A natural candidate would be the process of abstraction, present in vast majority of complex cognitive tasks, and this seems to be supported by research, including research using the techniques of neuroimagining (e.g., Green, Fugelsang, Kraemer, Shamosh, & Dunbar, 2006).

Independent experimental data that can partly support Oberauer's notion were presented by Buchner, Krumm, and Pick (2005). It turned out that two out of three control functions distinguished by Oberauer correlate with the accuracy of reasoning, namely: the storage and processing of information and the coordination. As an indicator of the accuracy of reasoning, the researchers used the score of an intelligence test; thus, one can assume that these data concern the effectiveness of inductive reasoning (analogy, similarity). Other results supporting Oberauer's notion were obtained by De Neys, Schaeken, and d'Ydewalle (2005), with regard to the process of constructing counter-examples, and by Vandierendonck, Dierckx, and De Vooghta (2004), with regard to a linear and relational syllogisms.

Working Memory Capacity and Inductive Reasoning

Inductive reasoning consists in deriving new claims or hypotheses from a finite number of cases, e.g., from observations. An analysis of particular premises leads – through induction – to detection and formulation of general regularities, expressed in a general statement. So the essence of inductive reasoning is making not fully justified generalizations, because they are derived from a limited number of observations. There is always a probability that the conclusion drawn on the basis of induction is wrong. On the other hand, induction is a way of inference which, as Holyoak and Nisbett (1988) put it, extends our knowledge in the face of uncertainty. Because most problems in real life are of inductive rather than deductive nature, tests of fluid intelligence (but not necessarily tests of crystallized intelligence) use inductive tasks, and in nonverbal form. For instance, in the Raven Progressive Matrices Test, subjects are required to find a relational rule, which governs the arrangement of simple graphic elements, and then to complete a missing element in each matrix. In this sense, it is a task requiring the subjects to perform analogical mapping. Other tests of fluid intelligence (e.g., Berlin Intelligence Structure Model) also use inductive tasks and require subjects to make mental transformations, which are an aspect of relational integration (see Oberauer et al., 2007). Because there are not many studies concerning the relation between WMC and other forms of inductive thinking, this section of the chapter will refer to data obtained in the research on fluid intelligence.

Like the research on the relations between WM and deductive reasoning, this research has also gone in various directions. It seems that the least interesting are studies aiming to find out the percentage of common variance between WMC and fluid intelligence (inductive reasoning, Gf – general fluid). The results of these studies, conducted with the use of a battery of WM and Gf tests, are inconclusive, although they unambiguously indicate that there is a relation between these two constructs. For example, Ackerman, Beier, and Boyle (2005) found in their meta-analysis of 86 studies conducted with the use of short-term or working memory tests as well as aptitude tests that the average strength of correlation between working memory and the g factor is relatively weak ($r=0.364$; $r=0.479$ after corrections adjusting to low reliability of methods). The authors questioned the thesis about vital influence of working memory on intellectual abilities, and suggested that the correlation of both measures results indirectly from the statistical nature of the g factor. Since it is assumed that the g factor fills to a certain extent all cognitive functions, then it manifests itself also in the effectiveness of executing tests of working memory. Meanwhile, Oberauer, Schulze, Wilhelm, and Süß (2005), when they assessed the strength of correlation between indices of WM efficiency and the level of IQ, found the correlation to be $r=0.85$ and presumed that WM efficiency is the most crucial predictor of intelligence, explaining 75% of its variance. The authors questioned some assumptions on which Ackerman et al. (2005) had based their meta-analysis. They suggested that this meta-analysis showed too low a correlation, because it had included some studies with inaccurate methods of measuring working memory and had not taken into account results acquired with Structural Equations Models.

Much more interesting are the attempts to establish a relation between working memory and fluid intelligence level. These studies also have their own special character. On the one hand, the researchers are, by and large, not interested in the variety of inductive reasoning forms (probably due to the fact that Gf test have very good psychometric parameters, which are practically in itself latent measures of fluid intelligence), unlike the researchers of deductive reasoning. On the other hand, various aspects of WM are examined far more thoroughly and operationalized in all possible varieties of STM and WM span tasks.

Currently, in studies of intelligence, the prevailing research methodology is Structural Equations Modelling. It consists in using at least two measurements (in practice there may be far more) of a given latent variable. This allows to reduce the variance of error and to extract from the measurement relatively pure measures of the examined constructs. However, this tool must be used carefully because in case of excessive aggregation of measured variables, one can obtain correlations close to one between the latent variables (e.g., Colom, Rebollo, Palacios, Juan-Espinosa, & Kyllonen, 2004; Kyllonen & Christal, 1990). The problem is that in some measures of intelligence, there are tasks that, to some extent, are loaded with the working memory factor, just like in some measures of WM, e.g., in complex span tasks, one can identify a load of fluid intelligence (inductive reasoning). Thus, it is not surprising to find such strong correlations between the latent measures of both constructs.

The basic problem concerning the relations between fluid abilities and WMC is participation of particular subsystems (verbal vs. spatial abilities) or executive functions in – as it is hypothetically assumed – determining individual differences with regard to inductive reasoning. One of the first such attempts was made by Shah and Miyake (1996) who wanted to find out whether the relation between WMC and Gf comes from general efficiency of working memory, or – on the contrary – whether the capacity of specific subsystems (verbal and visuospatial) is related to inductive reasoning on verbal and visuospatial material. The researchers used verbal and spatial memory tasks as well as verbal and spatial measures of intelligence. The result in a verbal span task was correlated

($r=0.45$) with the score in a verbal aptitude test, but it did not correlate significantly with the score in a spatial ability test. On the other hand, the result of a spatial span task was correlated with spatial abilities ($r=0.66$), but the researchers did not find a significant correlations with verbal abilities. Thus, it turned out that the relations between WMC and intellectual abilities are domain specific. Shah and Miyake checked also whether this specific relation between WMC and intellectual abilities is due to the memory aspect (type of material that was to remember) or the processing aspect (dual task) of working memory. It turned out that the result of a spatial task strongly correlated with spatial abilities, no matter if it was performed with a verbal or spatial secondary task. The result of a verbal span task strongly correlated with verbal abilities and also with both versions of the secondary task. Hence, it seems that it was the type of material used in a given task, and not the kind of operation, that was the cause of the observed relation.

Other logic was used by Engle et al. (1999). The researchers used two batteries of tasks, which tested separately functions of working memory and short-term memory. In the case of tasks that tested WM functions, they simultaneously measured storage of information and executive functions, whereas in the tasks for STM – they measured only the storage of information. Interestingly, it turned out that the latent measures of STM and WM are quite strongly correlated ($r=0.7$). However, after removing the common variance of both memory measures, it turned out that WMC significantly influenced the level of fluid intelligence, whereas the capacity of STM was not significantly related to Gf. Thus, the researchers assumed that the relation between working memory and Gf is due to the executive functions and not to the processes of information storage. Moreover, this relation was not modality-specific (verbal or spatial), because it appeared between a verbal measure of WM and a score in a reasoning test on figurative material. Similarly results obtained Conway, Cowan, Bunting, Therriault, and Minkoff (2002). They found a statistically significant correlation between verbal working memory and Gf measured by nonverbal tests ($r=0.60$), but correlations between Gf and indicators of STM capacity and processing speed turned out to be statistically insignificant.

The research quoted above does not answer the question what is the cause and what is the effect in the relation between working memory and fluid abilities. Even if we assume that the efficiency of working memory determines the ability to reason and solve problems, one should ask why this is the case. What properties of working memory decide that people perform the above mentioned mental activities more or less efficiently? If the relation between WM and general intelligence is due to a certain specific property of working memory, then what is this property? It seems that a natural candidate would be WMC that determines how many separate items a person is able to process simultaneously (Kane, Hambrick, & Conway, 2005; Süß et al., 2002). However, Cowan (2005b) in his adjustable-attention hypothesis assumes that it is the capacity of the focus of attention that is of key importance for the relation with intelligence. The focus of attention can include only one item – e.g., a goal representation under conditions of strong distraction and interference – but it can also actively encompass more, from 3 to 5 items. The researcher argues that the tasks requiring subjects to store and process information simultaneously are good predictors of intelligence (reasoning), because the secondary task prevents the subjects from chunking remembered pieces of information together or from repeating the pieces of information in the phonological loop. That is why these tasks measure accurately the capacity or scope of the focus of attention, without additional influence coming from automatic and more passive memory stores (i.e., the phonological loop). According to Cowan, the more items are included in the focus of attention, the more complex relations a person can discover among them, and the higher is his or her ability to perform abstract reasoning. In this respect, Cowan's view coincides with above described Oberauer's position, and, additionally, it confirms Oberauer's thesis about homogeneity of various forms of reasoning.

The nature of determination mentioned above is very interestingly explained by a model of relational reasoning (Halford, Wilson, & Phillips, 1998), which assumes that the greater the capacity of focus of attention, the more the dimensions of a relation (i.e., variables for a given predicate) that can be processed simultaneously. After all, finding hidden and – in most cases – multidimensional relations is a fundamental task in tests of reasoning and fluid intelligence.

Engle and his collaborators (e.g., Heitz, Unsworth, & Engle, 2005) suggest another explanation of the strong relation between working memory and Gf. Engle believes that the efficient control of attention determines how well a person is performing both memory tasks and aptitude tests. The key thing is to manage the content of the focus of attention in a way that activates pieces of information relevant for the current mental activity, especially under conditions of strong interference and conflict between competitive stimuli and processes, and which inhibits currently irrelevant pieces of information.

Unsworth and Engle (2005) carried out the analysis of the Raven Progressive Matrices Test focusing on the load imposed on working memory by each test item. The load was estimated on the basis of three independent indicators: a level of difficulty of each item, a number of rules needed to take into account to give a correct answer, and the kind of these rules. The results showed that the strength of relation between the efficiency of WM (measured by an operation span task) and the number of correctly solved test items in each of quartiles divided according to memory-consuming of particular items was similar. If the memory capacity was responsible for the correlation between the efficiency of WM and Gf, this correlation should increase in those parts of the test that have higher working memory demands, because mainly in these cases, persons with large memory capacity could reveal their advantage. Absence of this effect suggests, according to the researchers, that perhaps not the WMC but the control of attention is responsible for the relation between working memory and Gf, which is understood in terms of individual differences in efficiency of inductive reasoning.

Conclusions

Studies of relations between working memory and different kinds of reasoning are now at various points and stages. This is due to various research traditions, which imperfectly communicate with one another. It is visible even in the above review, which focused on deductive and inductive reasoning. Recently, however, there have been some attempts to identify a common mechanism of these kinds of reasoning. For instance, Oberauer suggests a relational integration mechanism, which is a *"parameter of cognitive system that affects a large number of different tasks, thereby explaining the common variance of many experimental working memory tasks, reasoning tasks from intelligence tests, and potentially complex cognitive achievements in everyday life"* (Oberauer et al. 2007, p. 52). Such attempts are not made for the first time (see Sternberg, 1985). However, Oberauer's thesis is supported by empirical data that show the absence of a separate factor for deductive and inductive reasoning (e.g., Wilhelm, 2005).

It seems, however, that each kind of reasoning has its own specific questions and research hypotheses. For instance, Stanovich and West (2000), in their studies of human rationality, proposed a hypothesis that there are two separate systems of reasoning. System 1 is primeval, evolutionary older, and is first initiated. Its activity is autonomous, does not require consciousness, and it is sufficient in many everyday situations. System 2 is complex, rational, conscious, and based on rules of logic. It is initiated mainly during formal education and during experiments on reasoning. The important thing is that effective operation of both systems requires working memory, but only in the case of System 1, a passive representation of data is sufficient for drawing conclusions, whereas initiating System 2 requires also initiating the mechanisms of information processing as well as executive functions in working memory. Thus, it seems that WM executive functions, rather than its capacity, will soon be in the focus of attention of researchers interested in reasoning. Hard neuropsychological data indicate that this is a promising line of research. For example, Prabhakaran and his colleagues (Prabhakaran, Smith, Desmond, Glover, & Gabrieli, 1997), using fMRI technique, analyzed execution of the Raven Progressive Matrices and other tasks requiring analytical and figural reasoning as well as – in control conditions – simple perceptualmotoric tasks. It turned out that analytic reasoning is correlated with activation of brain areas connected with verbal working memory as well as domain-independent associative and executive processes. Activity of frontal areas, connected with purposeful behavior, changes of strategy, and planning or executive control processes in working memory, also was found to be of vital importance. Figural reasoning turned out to be related to the activation of brain areas connected with spatial/object working memory. What is interesting, in the case of fluid reasoning during completing the Raven test, is that almost all cortexes were strongly activated, including areas identified with cognitive control.

In any event, if the hypothesis proposed by Stanovich and West was confirmed, the research on working memory would significantly contribute to the development of knowledge about basic mechanisms of reasoning. In studies of fluid intelligence, researchers have been for some time searching for the essence of relations between cognitive control and intelligence. However, we know very little about the nature of relations between these two constructs, especially that the mechanism of cognitive control still seems to be unclear and heterogeneous.

Thus, it seems that the concept of WM capacity is no longer the first choice when researchers look for a memory correlate of relational reasoning. Currently, they prefer the concept of cognitive control, which is rather of attentional nature. Hence, after clarifying relations between attention and working memory, the concept of WMC possibly will return to favor.

References

Ackerman, P. L., Beier, M. E., & Boyle, M. O. (2002). Individual differences in working memory within a nomological network of cognitive and perceptual speed abilities. *Journal of Experimental Psychology: General, 131*, 567–589.

Ackerman, P. L., Beier, M. E., & Boyle, M. O. (2005). Working memory and intelligence: The same or different constructs? *Psychological Bulletin, 131*, 30–60.

Awh, E., Vogel, E. K., & Oh, S. H. (2006). Interactions between attention and working memory. *Neuroscience, 139*(1), 201–208.

Baker, S. C., Rogers, R. D., Owen, A. M., Frith, C. D., Dolan, R. J., Frackowiak, R. S., & Robbins, T. W. (1996). Neural systems engaged by planning: a PET study of the Tower of London task. Neuropsychologia *34*(6), 515–526.

Baddeley, A. D. (2007). *Working memory, thought and action*. Oxford: Oxford University Press.

Baddeley, A. D., & Hitch, G. J. (1974). Working memory. In G. A. Bower (Ed.), *Recent advances in learning and motivation, 8* (pp. 47–90). New York: Academic.

Barrouillet, P., Bernardin, S., & Camos, V. (2004). Time constraints and resource sharing in adults' working memory spans. *Journal of Experimental Psychology: General, 133*, 83.

Barrouillet, P., & Lecas, J. F. (1998). How can mental models account for content effects in conditional reasoning: A developmental perspective. *Cognition, 67*, 209–253.

Barrouillet, P., & Lecas, J. F. (1999). Mental models in conditional reasoning and working memory. *Thinking and Reasoning, 5*, 289–302.

Berman, K. F., Ostrem, J. L., Randolph, C., & Gold, J. (1995). Physiological activation of a cortical network during performance of the Wisconsin Card Sorting test: A positron emission tomography study. *Neuropsychologia, 33*(8), 1027–1046.

Braine, M. D. S., Reiser, B. J., & Rumain, B. (1984). Some empirical justification for a theory of natural propositional logic. In G. H. Bower (Ed.), *The psychology of learning and motivation*. New York: Academic.

Buehner, M., Krumm, S., & Pick, M. (2005). Reasoning = working memory ≠ attention. Intelligence, *33*, 251–272.

Capon, A., Handley, S., & Dennis, I. (2003). Working memory and reasoning: An individual differences perspective. *Thinking and Reasoning, 9*, 203–244.

Case, R., Kurland, M., & Goldberg, J. (1982). Operational efficiency and the growth of short-term memory span. *Journal of Experimental Child Psychology, 33*, 386–404.

Colom, R., Abad, F., Rebollo, I., & Shih, P. C. (2005). Memory span and general intelligence: a latent-variable approach. Intelligence, *33*, 623–642.

Colom, R., Rebollo, I., Palacios, A., Juan-Espinosa, M., & Kyllonen, P. C. (2004). Working memory is (almost) perfectly predicted by g. *Intelligence, 32*, 277–296.

Conway, A. R. A., Cowan, N., Bunting, M. F., Therriault, D. J., & Minkoff, S. R. (2002). A latent variable analysis of working memory capacity, short-term memory capacity, processing speed, general fluid intelligence. *Intelligence, 30*, 163–183.

Conway, A. R. A., & Engle, R. W. (1994). Working memory and retrieval: A resource-dependent inhibition model. *Journal of Experimental Psychology: General, 123*, 354–373.

Conway, A. R. A., Jarrold, C., Kane, M. J., Miyake, A., & Towse, J. N. (2007). Variation in working memory: An introduction. In A. R. A. Conway, C. Jarrold, M. J. Kane, A. Miyake, & J. N. Towse (Eds.), *Variation in working memory* (pp. 3–17). Oxford: Oxford University Press.

Conway, A. R. A., Kane, M. J., Bunting, M. F., Hambrick, D. Z., Wilhelm, O., & Engle, R. W. (2006). Working memory span tasks: A methodological review and user's guide. *Psychonomic Bulletin and Review, 12*, 769–786.

Corbetta, M., Kincade, J. M., & Shulman, G. L. (2002). Neural systems for visual orienting and their relationships to spatial working memory. *Journal of Cognitive Neuroscience, 14*(3), 508–523.

Cosmides, L., & Tooby, J. (1994). Origins of domain specificity: The evolution of functional organization. In L. A. G. S. A. Hirschfeld (Ed.), *Mapping the mind: Domain specificity in cognition and culture* (pp. 85–116). New York: Cambridge University Press.

Cowan, N. (1988). Evolving conceptions of memory storage, selective attention, their mutual constraints within the human information processing system. *Psychological Bulletin, 104*, 163–191.

Cowan, N. (1995). *Attention and memory: An integrated framework*. Oxford Psychology Series, No. 26. New York: Oxford University Press

Cowan, N. (2005a). *Working memory capacity*. Hove, East Sussex: Psychology Press.

Cowan, N. (2005b). Understanding intelligence: A summary and an adjustable-attention hypothesis. In O. Wilhelm & R. W. Engle (Eds.), *Handbook of understanding and measuring intelligence* (pp. 469–488). Thousand Oaks: Sage Publications.

Cowan, N., Elliott, E. M., Saults, J. S., Morey, C. C., Mattox, S., Hismjatullina, A., et al. (2005). On the capacity of attention: Its estimation and its role in working memory and cognitive aptitudes. *Cognitive Psychology, 51*, 42–100.

Daneman, M., & Carpenter, P. A. (1980). Individual differences in working memory and reading. *Journal of Verbal Learning and Verbal Behavior, 19*, 450–466.

Daneman, M., & Merikle, P. M. (1996). Working memory and language comprehension: A meta-analysis. *Psychonomic Bulletin and Review, 3*, 422–433.

De Neys, W., Schaeken, W., & d'Ydewalle, D. (2005). Working memory and counterexample retrieval for causal conditionals. *Thinking and Reasoning, 11*, 123–150.

Elman, J. (1993). Learning and development in neural networks: The importance of starting small. *Cognition, 48*, 71–99.

Engle, R. W., Cantor, J., & Carullo, J. J. (1992). Individual differences in working memory and comprehension: A test of four hypotheses. *Journal of Experimental Psychology: Learning Memory and Cognition, 18*, 972–992.

Engle, R. W., Kane, M. J., & Tuholski, S. W. (1999). Individual differences in working memory capacity and what they tell us about controlled attention, general fluid intelligence and functions of the prefrontal cortex. In A. Miyake & P. Shah (Eds.), *Models of working memory: Mechanisms of active maintenance and executive control*. London: Cambridge Press.

Engle, R. W., Tuholski, S. W., Laughlin, J. E., & Conway, A. R. A. (1999). Working memory, short term memory and general fluid intelligence: A latent variable approach. *Journal of Experimental Psychology: General, 128*, 309–331.

Ericsson, K. A., & Kintsch, W. (1995). Long-term working memory. *Psychological Review, 102*, 211–245.

Evans, J.St.B.T. (2002). Logic and human reasoning: An assessment of the deduction paradigm. Psychological Bulletin, *128*, 978–996.

Friedman, N. P., & Miyake, A. (2004). The relations among inhibition and interference control functions: A latent-variable analysis. *Journal of Experimental Psychology: General, 133*, 101–135.

García-Madruga, J. A., Moreno, S., Carriedo, N., Gutiérrez, F., & Johnson-Laird, P. N. (2001). Are conjunctive inferences easier than disjunctive inferences? A comparison of rules and models. *Quarterly Journal of Experimental Psychology, 54A*, 613–632.

Gathercole, S. E., Pickering, S. J., Ambridge, B., & Wearing, H. (2004). The structure of working memory from 4 to 15 years of age. *Developmental Psychology, 40*, 177–190.

Goel, V., Buchel, C., Frith, C., & Dolan, R. J. (2000). Dissociation of mechanisms underlying syllogistic reasoning. *NeuroImage, 12*, 504–514.

Gray, J. R., Chabris, C. F., & Braver, T. S. (2003). Neural mechanisms of general fluid intelligence. *Nature Neuroscience, 6*, 316–322.

Green, A. E., Fugelsang, J. A., Kraemer, D. J., Shamosh, N. A., & Dunbar, K. N. (2006). Frontopolar cortex mediates abstract integration in analogy. *Brain Research, 1096*, 125–137.

Griggs, R. A., & Cox, J. R. (1982). The elusive thematic-materials effect in Wason's selection task. *British Journal of Psychology, 73*, 407–420.

Halford, G. S., Wilson, W. H., & Phillips, S. (1998). Processing capacity defined by relational complexity: Implications for comparative, developmental and cognitive psychology. *Behavioral and Brain Sciences, 21*, 803–831.

Heitz, R. P., Unsworth, N., & Engle, R. W. (2005). Working memory capacity, attention control, and fluid intelligence. In O. Wilhelm, R. W. Engle (Eds.), *Handbook of understanding and measuring intelligence* (pp. 61–78). Thousand Oaks: Sage Publications

Hertwig, R., & Todd, P. M. (2003). More is not always better: The benefits of cognitive limits. In L. Macchi & D. Hardman (Eds.), *The psychology of reasoning and decision making: A handbook*. Chichester: Wiley.

Holyoak, K. J., & Nisbett, R. E. (1988). Induction. In R. J. Sternberg & E. E. Smith (Eds.), *The psychology of thinking* (pp. 50–91). Cambridge: Cambridge University Press.

Johnson-Laird, P. N. (1983). *Mental models*. Cambridge: Cambridge University Press.

Johnson-Laird, P. N. (1994). Mental models and probabilistic thinking. *Cognition, 50*, 189–209.

Johnson-Laird, P. N., & Byrne, R. M. J. (1991). *Deduction*. Hove, Sussex: Erlbaum.

Kane, M. J., Hambrick, D. Z., & Conway, A. R. A. (2005). Working memory capacity and fluid intelligence are strongly related constructs: Comment on Ackerman, Beier, and Boyle (2005). *Psychological Bulletin, 131*, 66–71.

Kareev, Y. (1995). Through a narrow window: Working memory capacity and the detection of covariation. *Cognition, 56*, 263–269.

Klauer, K. C., Stegmaier, R., & Meiser, T. (1997). Working memory involvement in propositional and spatial reasoning. *Thinking and Reasoning, 3*, 9–47.

Kyllonen, P. C., & Christal, R. E. (1990). Reasoning ability is (little more than) working memory capacity? *Intelligence, 14*, 389–433.

Mac Gregor, J. N. (1987). Short-term memory capacity: Limitation or optimization? *Psychological Review, 94*(1), 107–108.

Markovits, H., Doyon, C., & Simoneau, M. (2002). Individual differences in working memory and conditional reasoning with concrete and abstract content. *Thinking and Reasoning, 8*, 97–107.

Mayes, J. T. (1988). On the nature of echoic persistence: Experiments with running memory. *Journal of Experimental Psychology: Learning, Memory and Cognition, 14*, 278–288.

Meyer, D. E., & Kieras, D. E. (1997a). A computational theory of executive control processes and human multiple-task performance: Part 1. Basic mechanisms. *Psychological Review, 104*, 3–65.

Meyer, D. E., & Kieras, D. E. (1997b). A computational theory of executive control processes and human multiple-task performance: Part 2. Accounts of psychological refractory-period phenomena. *Psychological Review, 104*, 749–791.

Miller, G. A. (1956). The magical number seven, plus or minus two: Some limits on our capacity for processing information. *Psychological Review, 63*, 81–97.

Miller, G. A., Galanter, E., & Pribram, K. H. (1960). *Plans and the structure of behavior*. New York: Holt. Rinehart and Winston.

Miyake, A., Friedman, N. P., Emerson, M. J., Witzki, A. H., Howerter, A., & Wager, T. D. (2000). The unity and diversity of executive functions and their contributions to complex "frontal lobe" tasks: A latent variable analysis. *Cognitive Psychology, 41*, 49–100.

Miyake, A., & Shah, P. (Eds.). (1999). *Models of working memory: Mechanisms of active maintenance and executive control*. London: Cambridge Press.

Munakata, Y., Morton, J. B., & O'Reilly, R. C. (2007). Computational and developmental approaches to variation in working memory. In R. A. Conway, C. Jarrold, M. Kane, A. Miyake, & J. Towse (Eds.), *Variation in working memory*. Oxford: Oxford University Press.

Nęcka, E., & Orzechowski, J. (2005). Higher-order cognition and intelligence. In R. Sternberg & J. Pretz (Eds.), *Cognition and intelligence: Identifying the mechanisms of the mind* (pp. 122–141). Cambridge: Cambridge University Press.

Oberauer, K. (2005). The measurement of working memory capacity. In O. Wilhelm & R. W. Engle (Eds.), *Handbook of understanding and measuring intelligence* (pp. 393–408). Thousand Oaks: Sage Publications.

Oberauer, K., Lange, E., & Engle, R. W. (2004). Working memory capacity and resistance to interference. Journal of Memory and Learning, *51*, 80–96.

Oberauer, K., Shulze, R., Wilhelm, O., & Süß, H. M. (2005). Working memory and intelligence – their correlation and their relation: Comment on Ackerman, Beier, and Boyle (2005). *Psychological Bulletin, 131*, 61–65.

Oberauer, K., Süß, H.-M., Wilhelm, O., & Sander, N. (2007). Individual differences in working memory capacity and reasoning ability. In A. R. A. Conway, C. Jarrold, M. J. Kane, A. Miyake, & J. N. Towse (Eds.), *Variation in working memory* (pp. 49–75). Oxford: Oxford University Press.

Oberauer, K., Süß, H. M., Wilhelm, O., & Wittman, W. W. (2003). The multiple facets of working memory: Storage, processing, supervision, and coordination. *Intelligence, 31*, 167–193.

Portrat, S., Barrouillet, P., & Camos, V. (2006). Time-related decay or interference-based forgetting in working memory? *Journal of Experimental Psychology: Learning Memory and Cognition, 34*(6), 1561–1564.

Prabhakaran, V., Smith, J. A. L., Desmond, J. E., Glover, G. H., & Gabrieli, J. D. E. (1997). Neuronal substrates of fluid reasoning: An fMRI study of neocortical activation during performance of the Raven's Progressive Matrices test. *Cognitive Psychology, 33*, 43–63.
Raven, J. C., Court, J. H., & Raven, J. (1983). *Manual for Raven's progressive matrices and vocabulary scales (section 4, advanced progressive matrices)*. London: H.K. Lewis.
Rips, L. J. (1994a). Deductive reasoning. In R. J. Sternberg (Ed.), *Handbook of perception and cognition: Thinking and problem solving* (pp. 149–178). New York: Cambridge University Press.
Rips, L. J. (1994b). *The psychology of proof: Deductive reasoning in human reasoning.* Cambridge: MIT Press.
Salthouse, T. A. (1996). The processing-speed theory of adult age differences in cognition. *Psychological Review, 103*, 403–428.
Shah, P., & Miyake, A. (1996). The separability of working memory resources for spatial thinking and language processing: An individual differences approach. *Journal of Experimental Psychology: General, 125*, 4–27.
Stanovich, K. E., & West, R. F. (2000). Individual differences in reasoning: Implications for the rationality debate? *Behavioral and Brain Sciences, 23*, 645–665.
Sternberg, R. J. (1985). *Beyond IQ: A triarchic theory of human intelligence.* New York: Cambridge University Press.
Stoltzfus, E. R., Hasher, L., & Zacks, R. T. (1996). Working memory and aging: Current status of the inhibitory view. In J. T. E. Richardson, R. W. Engle, L. Hasher, R. H. Logie, E. R. Stoltzfus, & R. T. Zacks (Eds.), *Counterpoints in cognition: Working memory and human cognition* (pp. 66–68). Oxford: Oxford University Press.
Süß, H. M., Oberauer, K., Wittmann, W. W., Wilhelm, O., & Schulze, R. (2002). Working memory capacity explains reasoning ability – and a little bit more. *Intelligence, 30*, 261–288.
Toms, M., Morris, N., & Ward, D. (1993). Working memory and conditional reasoning. *The Quarterly Journal of Experimental Psychology, 46A*, 679–699.
Tooby, J., & Cosmides, L. (1990). The past explains the present: Emotional adaptations and the structure of ancestral environments. *Ethnology and Sociobiology, 11*, 375–424.
Towse, J. N., Hitch, G. J., & Hutton, U. (2000). On the interpretation of working memory span in adults. *Memory and Cognition, 28*(3), 341–348.
Turner, M. L., & Engle, R. W. (1989). Working memory capacity: An individual differences approach. *Journal of Memory and Language, 28*, 127–154.
Unsworth, N., & Engle, R. W. (2005). Working memory capacity and fluid abilities: Examining the correlation between Operation Span and Raven. *Intelligence, 33*, 67–81.
Vandierendonck, A., Dierckx, V., & De Vooght, G. (2004). Mental model construction in linear reasoning: Evidence for the construction of initial annotated models. *The Quarterly Journal of Experimental Psychology, 57A*, 1369–1391.
Wilhelm, O. (2005). Measuring reasoning ability. In O. Wilhelm, & R. W. Engle (Eds.), *Understanding and measuring intelligence* (pp. 373–392). London: Sage.

Chapter 22
Motivation Towards Closure and Cognitive Resources: An Individual Differences Approach

Małgorzata Kossowska, Edward Orehek, and Arie W. Kruglanski

Introduction

Motivation and cognitive ability represent two basic determinants of information processing, influencing the ability to learn new knowledge and to carry out judgment and decision making tasks. However, cognitive and motivational influences on the results of information processing and performance are usually studied separately. On the one hand, numerous studies have investigated the role of cognitive-intellectual abilities in predicting individual differences in task performance. On the other hand, incentives, goal assignments, achievement motivation, expectancies, subjective valuation of outcomes, self-efficacy expectations, and a host of other motivational factors have been shown to influence goal choice, intended effort, task behavior, and mental performance. While the body of literature examining the role of cognitive ability and motivation in task performance is growing (e.g., Mitchell & Silver, 1990; Harris & Tetrick, 1993; Thompson, Roman, Moskowitz, Chaiken, & Bargh, 1994; Muraven & Slessareva, 2003), little research has been conducted on the cognitive processes involved in, and affected by, motivation (but see Kossowska, 2007a, b).

Therefore, this chapter aims to explore the relationship between epistemic motivation (need for cognitive closure) and cognitive ability (working memory processes[1]), as well as their influence on task performance. Need for (nonspecific) cognitive closure has been described by Kruglanski (1989; Kruglanski, Webster, & Klem, 1993; Webster & Kruglanski, 1994) as a dimension of individual differences in the striving for clear and certain knowledge, aimed at reducing the sense of cognitive uncertainty. During the last 20 years, the nature of the need for closure and its influence on both cognitive and social functioning has been extensively researched (e.g., Kruglanski et al., 1993; Webster & Kruglanski, 1994; Ford & Kruglanski, 1995; Dijksterhuis, van Knippenberg, Kruglanski, & Schaper, 1996). However, the cognitive processes contributing to (or related to) this motivation remain unknown. Based on considerations to be outlined shortly, we assumed that the need for

---

[1] We use the concept of working memory as it has been defined in the literature over the past two decades (for overview see: Feldman-Barrett, Tugade, & Engle, 2004). In fact, there is no universally agreed upon definition of WM. There are several aspects or components to working memory as resource allocation, buffer size, or processing capacity, and individual differences in working memory function could presumably result from each of them and from their interaction.

M. Kossowska (✉)
Institute of Psychology, Jagiellonian University, Al. Mickiewicza 3, 31-120, Cracow, Poland
e-mail: malgosia@apple.phils.uj.edu.pl

E. Orehek and A.W. Kruglanski
University of Maryland, College Park, MD, USA

closure may go hand in hand with certain cognitive limitations, related to working memory functioning. Moreover, it is expected that the relationship between need for closure and performance of judgment/decision tasks is mediated by a limitation in cognitive ability.

Individual Differences in Need for Cognitive Closure

According to the theory of lay epistemics, a person's epistemic motivations regulate the process of knowledge acquisition (Kruglanski, 1989). They are classified along a continuous dimension ranging from closure seeking to closure avoidance. The need for closure reflects the degree to which a person desires a definite answer to a question, any answer, as opposed to confusion or ambiguity (Kruglanski, 1989; Ford & Kruglanski, 1995). High levels of the need for cognitive closure favor a superficial analysis of incoming information, and motivate the search for information consistent with already existing knowledge structures. The resulting mental representation is often simplified; however, it ensures a sense of clarity, predictability, and order. High levels of the need to avoid closure are associated with a pronounced tolerance, and even a preference for, ambiguity, and uncertainty. When their need to avoid closure is high, individuals are inclined to avoid the formation of final judgments, leading to an openness to new information. Instead, knowers high on the need to avoid closure are motivated to perceive situations in a complex and nonstereotypical manner, to consider alternative interpretations, and to accommodate existing schemas to new information.

A considerable amount of research attests that people with the high degree of the need for closure make more stereotypical judgments (Dijksterhuis et al., 1996), rely on early information in impression formation (Kruglanski & Freund, 1983; Webster & Kruglanski, 1994), resist persuasion when firm knowledge is already held (Kruglanski et al., 1993), are less likely to assimilate new information to existing beliefs (Ford & Kruglanski, 1995), and exhibit a preference for conventional politics (Jost, Glaser, Kruglanski, & Sullaway, 2003; Kossowska & Van Hiel, 2003). Furthermore, the need for closure has been shown to lead to negative reactions to group deviates (Kruglanski & Webster, 1991), in-group favoritism (Shah, Kruglanski, & Thompson, 1998; Kruglanski, Shah, Pierro, & Mannetti, 2002), and to induce a task rather than a socio-emotional orientation to group activities and to foster conformity pressures during group discussions (De Grada, Kruglanski, Mannetti, & Pierro, 1999).

In general, the need for closure arises in contexts in which the benefits of closure, such as predictability and action, seem important or when an absence of closure seems costly. For example, time pressure implies the danger of missing an important deadline and therefore elevates the need for closure (e.g., Kruglanski & Freund, 1983). Another cost of lacking closure stems from the difficulty of further information processing. In instances in which processing seems effortful, laborious, or otherwise costly, need for closure is correspondingly heightened (e.g., Webster, Richter, & Kruglanski, 1995). Finally, need for closure is aroused when the task appears intrinsically dull and nonattractive (e.g., Webster, 1993). Under such circumstances, closure serves as a means of escaping an unpleasant (and, hence, subjectively costly) activity. As with the need for closure, the need to avoid closure is assumed to be based on the perceived costs of closure or cognitive commitment (e.g., envisioned penalties for an erroneous closure or perceived drawbacks of actions implied by closure), and/or the perceived benefits of suspending judgment (e.g., immunity from possible criticism of any closure) (Webster, 1993; Kruglanski, 1989). Intrinsic task interest may also represent a subjective benefit, because it instills the need to avoid closure and to prolong one's preoccupation with the task.

Thus, the foregoing findings suggest that the individual's motivation with respect to closure may vary as a function of the situation (see: Kruglanski, 2004). However, the need for closure is also conceptualized as a relatively stable individual difference dimension assessed via a questionnaire, including several facets: (1) a preference for order and predictability, (2) an intolerance of ambiguity, (3) decisiveness, and (4) a tendency toward closed mindedness (Kruglanski, DeGrada, Mannetti, Atash, & Webster, 1997; Mannetti, Pierro, Kruglanski, Taris, & Bezinovic, 2002; Kossowska, Van Hiel, Chun, & Kruglanski, 2002). Individuals with a high level of need for closure prefer order and predictability, are more decisive, more closed-minded, and uncomfortable with ambiguity. Such differences may spring from various sources, such as cultural norms, personal socialization histories that place the premium on confidence, "know how" and/or do not provide a comfortable environment to explore novel/uncertain stimuli. It is also likely that individual differences in elementary cognitive processes are important antecedents of individual differences in this need.

Thus, need for closure is claimed to be both a situationally induced motivation and a dimension of relatively stable individual differences, assumed to be functionally equivalent (i.e., the most effects of situational demands were replicated by means of individual differences measure of the need for closure, see for overview: Kruglanski & Webster, 1996). In the present work, we refer to the need for closure as assessed by an individual difference measure. The proposed line of studies is important because the previous research largely neglected to study this motivation as a stable individual characteristic in the relation to cognitive abilities. Thus, the results of the analysis seems to be important in the sense of extension our knowledge about cognitive-motivation interactions in general, as well as the cognitive nature of need for closure preference in specific.

Possible Cognitive Processes Contributing to the Need for Cognitive Closure

One possibility explored in what follows is that people with high degree of need for closure may strive for simplification, predictability, and stability in their views when the informational complexity in the environment exceeds their ability to manage it. If so, behaviors such as the reduction of information processing, as well as the structuring and simplification of information – typical of individuals high in the need for closure – could result from cognitive system limitations, which pose difficulties for the handling of complex information. Grounds for such expectations are provided by results of studies in which cognitive capacity reductions were induced via time pressure (Kruglanski & Freund, 1983), mental fatigue (Webster et al., 1995), environmental noise (Kruglanski et al., 1993), or alcohol ingestion (Webster, 1993). In varied experimental conditions, such manipulations "mimicked" or exerted the same effects as the need for closure measured as an individual difference variable. This raises the possibility that the need for closure as a relatively stable personality characteristic arises out of long standing "wired in" limitations in one's cognitive ability.[2]

But what may determine whether an individual's cognitive abilities are ample or limited? Salthouse (1988) noted that at least three different metaphors could be used to characterize the potential nature of processing ability and the associated effects of the level of performance. Cognitive ability might be thought of in terms of *speed* (how quickly information can be processed in working memory, e.g., Halford, Wilson, & Phillips, 1998), *space* (capacity available for storing information in working memory, e.g., Cowan, 2001), or *energy resources* available for initiating and supporting specific cognitive operation in working memory (e.g., Just & Carpenter, 1992). Recently, resource limitations have also been characterized in terms of *control mechanisms*, whereby indi-

---

[2] Note that need for closure is not an explicit index of cognitive resource usage, nor it is necessarily related to diminishing resources. As indicated by research involving this construct, however, high need for closure does appear to reflect a preference for relatively simple, routinized cognitive operations. Up to this point, there has been little work regarding factors responsible for determining one's need for closure. One potential way that such preference may be developed is through diminution of resources.

vidual differences in cognitive performance are tied to an individual's ability to maintain information in an active state ready to use in current processing or inhibit extraneous task information from entering working memory (e.g., Engle, Tuholski, Laughlin, & Conway, 1999; Kane, Bleckley, Conway, & Engle, 2001; Salthouse, Hambrick, & Lukas, 1996; Hess, 2002).

The series of studies presented here explored the possible relationships between need for closure understood as individual characteristic and these different conceptualizations of cognitive resource limitations (see also: Kossowska, 2007a, b).

Need for Cognitive Closure and the Rate of Processing Information

Most researchers define working memory as a system that holds certain mental contents in an active or accessible state (storage function), affording the performance of cognitive operations on these particular contents (executive function) (Salthouse, 1990; Baddeley, 1996; Oberauer, Suss, Wilhelm, & Wittmann, 2000). Storage components (called STM) is assumed to be limited and these limitations not only place restrictions on the performance of memory related tasks *as such*, but also of complex cognitive tasks such as problem solving, text analysis, or discourse comprehension (Miyake & Shah, 1999).

One way of overcoming this general limitation is tied to the *rate* of processing current information. Fast processing results in a better and more efficient handling of the complexity of the surrounding environment (Kyllonen & Christal, 1990; Miller & Vernon, 1992; Embretson, 1995). We can therefore deduce that individuals capable of a fast processing rate may be able to handle complex informational tasks with relative ease. On the contrary, individuals with a slow rate of processing may find complexity taxing and exhibit a tendency to structure and simplify reality. Thus, we assumed that need for closure should be characterized by a slow rate of information processing in storage buffer of working memory.

To test the rate of information processing, we used a computerized modification of Saul Sternberg's classic task (1969). This task has been used often in studies on the functioning of memory and intelligence (see Nęcka, 1992; 1997). The present version of the task involves a modification, namely a significant – almost threefold – increase of the rate of stimulus exposure. This alteration was intended to prevent participants from the use of mnemonic techniques. The procedure of the task was as follows: sets of digits between 0 and 9 appeared successively in the same location in the middle of a computer screen. The first digit was preceded by an asterisk (*) intended to attract the participants` attention and to fix their gaze on the middle of the screen immediately prior to the presentation of the stimulus series. The same asterisk appeared after the last digit in order to prevent storage of the last stimulus in sensory memory after the expiration of its presentation (Sperling & Speelman, 1970; Roediger, Marsh, & Lee, 2002; Berti & Schroger, 2003).

The digit sets presented to participants contained four, six, or eight digits. After the last digit in the presented set, a target digit appeared at the bottom of the screen. Participants' task was to press the right arrow on the keyboard (representing YES), when the digit was in a set presented earlier, or the left arrow (representing NO) when it was not. The computer recorded the reaction time and its correctness for all 144 trials.

To carry out this activity, participants need to hold the relevant cognitive content (i.e., the given digit set) in an accessible state and search it to decide whether it includes the target. The mean number of accurate responses is operationally defined as the participants` score and is treated as an indicator of storage-process efficiency. The reaction time of correct responses is considered an index of the rates of information search in working memory. Such search consists of successive comparisons of internal representations of the test stimulus to the appropriate symbols in memory, each comparison yielding either a match (a YES response) or a mismatch (a NO response).

The faster the reaction time, defined as the time from the onset of the stimulus to the occurrence of the response, the faster the processing of information in storage buffer. The more accurate the responses, the more elements from the presented set are assumed to be stored in the working memory.

Participants also responded to the Polish version of the Need for Closure Scale (Webster & Kruglanski, 1994; Kossowska, 2003). The scale consists of 42 items divided into five facet scales: (1) preference for order and structure in the environment, (2) predictability of future contexts, (3) decisiveness of judgments and choices, (4) affective discomfort occasioned by ambiguity, and (5) closed-mindedness. Prototypical items from each subscales of NFCS are as follows: "I think that having clear rules and order at work is essential for success" and "I believe that orderliness and organization are among the most important characteristics of a good student" (Preference for Order); "I do not like to be with people who are capable of unexpected actions" and "I do not like to go into a situation without knowing what I can expect from it" (Preference for Predictability); "I tend to put off making important decisions until the last possible moment" and "When I go shopping, I have difficulty deciding exactly what is that I want" (Decisiveness); "I do not like situations that are uncertain" and "I enjoy the uncertainty of going into a new situation without knowing what might happen" (Discomfort with Ambiguity); and "I always see many possible solutions to problems I face" and "When considering most conflict situations, I can usually see how both sides could be right" (Closed-mindedness). Participants answered on 6-points scales, with 1 = "strongly disagree" and 6 = "strongly agree." Each respondent's composite need for closure score was calculated by summing across all items (after reverse scoring the appropriate items).

The results indicated that individuals with high need for closure took significantly longer to react in both conditions of the task (YES as well as NO) as compared to individuals with low need for closure (see Fig. 22.1). This finding indicates that the rate of information search is slower in general for individuals with high (vs. low) need for closure. Note also that the slower reaction times of high versus low need for closure individuals were consistent across the three set sizes (see Fig. 22.2). This data supports the hypothesis that high need for closure individuals process information at a slower rate than individuals low on the need for closure.

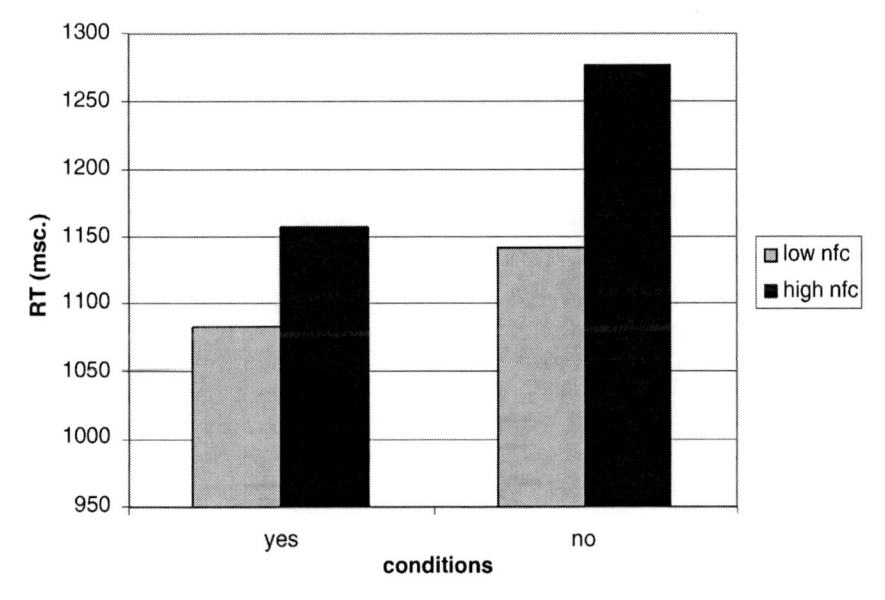

Fig. 22.1 Mean reaction times (in milliseconds) in search for information in working memory task under "yes" versus "no" conditions

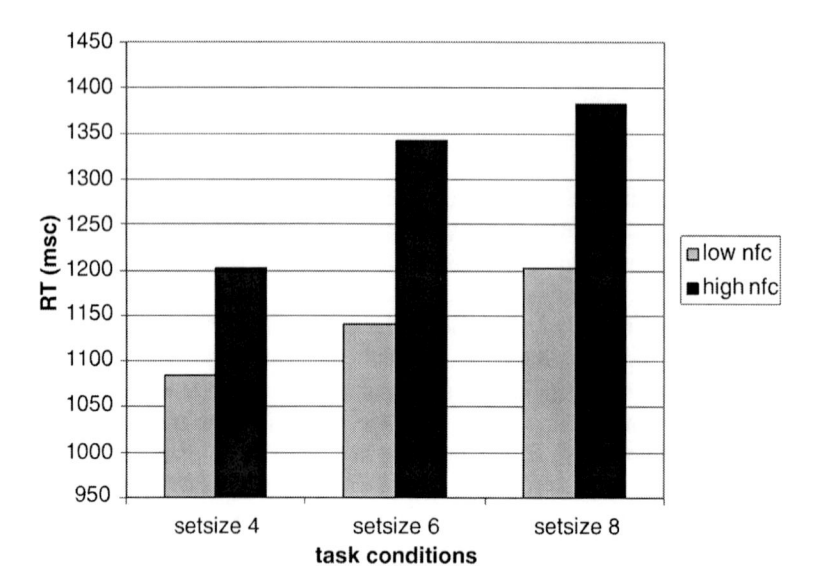

Fig. 22.2 Mean reaction times (in milliseconds) in search for information in working memory task regard to different set sizes

Finally, there was no significant difference between high versus low need for closure individuals in the accuracy of responses. This result suggests that high (vs. low) need for closure individuals are not less motivated to do well on the task, and reaction time differences between them reflect the limitations of their cognitive apparatus.

Might it be the case that high (vs. low) need for closure people are slower because they are more motivated to be accurate? This is unlikely in light of two considerations. First, no accuracy differences between high versus low need for closure individuals were found. Secondly, extensive prior evidence (Kruglanski & Webster, 1996; Kruglanski, 2004) suggests that need for closure is *inversely* related to accuracy concerns, and in fact a common way of situationally lowering the need for closure has been via accuracy instructions known to instill a "fear of invalidity" (Kruglanski & Freund, 1983; Kruglanski & Webster, 1996).

Need for Cognitive Closure and Working Memory Capacity

Working memory capacity, the construct typically measured by span tasks,[3] reflects the general capability to maintain information relevant to task goals, in a highly active state (e.g., Kane et al., 2001). Although the need for such active maintenance will be minimal in many contexts, it will be particularly important under conditions of interference. Interference slows and impairs memory retrieval and therefore puts a premium on keeping task-relevant information highly active and easily accessible. Individual differences in working memory capacity reflect the degree to which distracters capture attention away from actively maintaining goal-relevant information in working memory.

---

[3] Span task or operational span task – the task is to solve simple math equations while simultaneously remembering unrelated words.

Thus, content and goal oriented behavior in interference rich conditions requires both active maintenance of relevant information and the blocking or inhibiting of irrelevant information (De Jong, Berendsen, & Cools, 1999; Engle et al., 1999; Kane et al., 2001). We expected the need for closure to be associated with worse performance on the operation-span task. These results could be interpreted as smaller working memory capacity for high need for closure individuals.

Moreover, it is well established that social perceivers use normative judgment and decision rules only when sufficiently motivated (e.g., by "fear of invalidity") and when capacity for detailed processing is unconstrained (see: Chaiken, Liberman, & Eagly, 1989; Neuberg & Fiske, 1987; Tetlock, 1983; Kruglanski et al., 1993). The reduced cognitive and/or motivational capacity is more likely to lead to biased outcomes (e.g., Wang & Chen, 2006). Thus, assuming that working memory capacity is related to individual differences in need for cognitive closure, we expected that working memory capacity should mediate the relationship between need for closure and the well studied effects of information processing, as for example, the amount of prototypical information sought in a judgmental task.

It is well known that high need for closure affects the type of information sought, not merely its amount (e.g., Trope & Bassok, 1983; Mayseless & Kruglanski, 1987). Specifically, previous research has found that high need for closure individuals preferred prototypical information about the category, e.g., information on whether the individual possessed the prototypical features of an architect (interest in visual aesthetics, mathematical ability, creativity, elegant lifestyle), while attempting to test the focal hypothesis that she/he was an architect (Kruglanski & Mayseless, 1988). By contrast, individuals experiencing low need for closure preferred diagnostic information capable of discriminating among different possibilities regarding the target's professional affiliation (Trope & Bassok, 1983; Kruglanski, 2004). For example when testing the focal hypothesis that a target is an architect, individuals low on the need for closure generated the competing alternative that she/he might be a painter instead, and proceeded to seek diagnostic information with regard to the architect versus painter possibilities. Thus, low need for closure participants preferred information about mathematical ability and elegant lifestyle (presumed characteristics of architects but not painters), rather than information about creativity and interest in visual aesthetics (presumed common to both) (see Kruglanski & Mayseless, 1988).

We tested the expectations derived from previous study on restrictions of hypothesis generation under high need for closure in two studies (Legierski & Kossowska, 2008). In one of them, participants' working memory capacity was assessed using the operation-word span task (OSPAN), in which they solved series of simple mathematical operations while attempting to remember a list of unrelated words (La Pointe & Engle, 1990). Participants saw one operation-word string at a time, and each set of operation-word strings ranged from two to six items in length (e.g., $(5 \times 1) - 4 = 2$? beach). The OSPAN score was the sum of the recalled words for all sets recalled completely and in correct order. Additionally, we used exactly the same judgmental task as did Kruglanski and Mayseless (1988, Experiment 2). Participants were told that the experiment concerned people's ability to identify the occupations of others from evidence about their personalities. They were further told that their task would be to select interview questions they would use to determine whether an interviewee was a painter. A subtle mention of an alternate hypothesis was made by casually noting that "the interviewee could, of course, be a member of a different profession; for instance, he or she could be an architect." Participants were then handed a 32-item questionnaire (previously prepared and tested) including architect-characteristic values (high vs. low), painter-characteristic values (high vs. low), and architect versus painter diagnostic values (high vs. low). They were asked to select the 16 most useful questions for testing the target hypothesis. We computed a painter versus architect diagnostic ratio as an index of diagnostic information usage. They also completed the Polish version of the Need for Closure Scale (Kossowska, 2003).

First, as expected, the results of the study revealed that high need for closure participants performed less well on the OSPAN task than low need for closure participants. Moreover, high need for closure participants also obtained a lower indicator of the diagnostic information usage than low

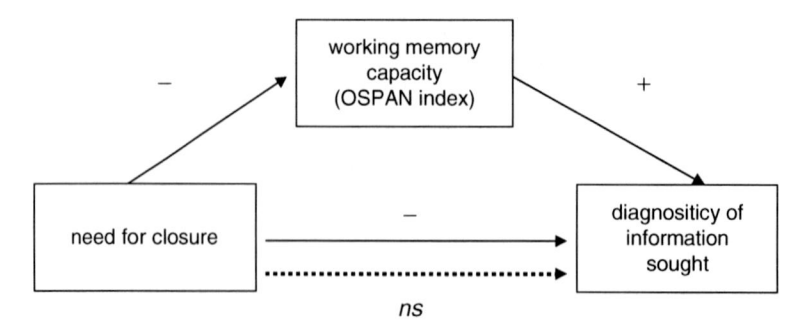

Fig. 22.3 Relationship between need for cognitive closure, working memory capacity, and the type of information sought

need for closure participants. As regards the mediation hypothesis, need for closure affected both the cognitive capacity variable as well as the type of information seeking variable (i.e., less diagnostic information). The working memory capacity variable affected the type of information sought. High (vs. low) working memory capacity participants searched more for diagnostic information. When the index of working memory capacity was controlled for, the relationship between need for closure and type of information sought dropped to nonsignificance, while the influence of working memory capacity remained significant. Thus, the results of this analysis confirm the assumptions that working memory capacity mediates the relationships between need for closure and type of information sought (see Fig. 22.3).

The results of the study described above supported the notion that variations in need for closure are related to variations in working memory capacity. Need for closure is related to limited working memory capacity measured by OSPAN task. Moreover, the results indicated that working memory capacity accounted for the relationship between need for closure and performance on a judgmental task. These findings provide evidence for our conceptual claim that need for closure is related to limited cognitive ability.

Need for Cognitive Closure and Ability to Controlled Processing

A basic assumptions underlying most research on cognitive functioning, including work in the social domain, is that executive cognitive functioning is governed in part by resources reflecting the cognitive system's ability to control cognitive activities and processes, particularly those performed simultaneously (Kahneman, 1973; Daneman & Carpenter, 1980; Hunt & Lansman, 1986; Stankov, 1988; Just & Carpenter, 1992). Older accounts viewed executive functions from a resource-sharing framework – the level of performance depends on the volume of resources, which can be flexible allocated, depending on the processing needs of the person, for a particular task, in particular context (Norman & Bobrow, 1975; Daneman & Merike, 1996; Engle, Kane, & Tuholski, 1999; Nęcka, 1999; Thompson et al., 1994; Hess, 2002). The greater the overall resource pool, the more resources individuals can allot to activities and tasks in which they are engaged. Furthermore, the larger the total volume of resources, the less are the negative effects of resource depletion caused by a number of activities carried out concomitantly, or by an excessive complexity of current cognitive activities (Stankov, 1988; Nęcka, 1999).

Currently, it is assumed that executive functions reflects individual differences in the ability to control attention associated with the central executive aspect of working memory (Engle et al., 1999). It can be thought of as an individual difference in the "source of goal-directed attention" that serves to activate, maintain or suppress memory representations. From the perspective of dual – process models of the mind, extremely popular in social cognition area (see Feldman-Barrett et al., 2004), individual differences in working memory functions likely influence the capability to engage in controlled processing, thereby determining persons' ability to control thoughts, feelings, and actions.

If it is assumed that individuals' need for closure is related to their limitations in executive functions, it follows that individuals with a high need for closure should be characterized by lesser cognitive ability, allocable to currently performed activities. Results of considerable studies (i.e., Baron, 1986; Dijksterhuis et al., 1996; Huguet, Galvaing, Monteil, & Dumas, 1999; Chajut & Algom, 2003) are consistent with such a possibility. This research attests that in conditions of cognitive load (and high need for closure) participants exhibit a tendency toward more schematic, stereotypical, and simplified judgments of reality. In the absence of cognitive load (and with low need for closure), participants perceive objects as more differentiated, complex, and less stereotypical. Under cognitive load, cognitive ability to controlled processing diminished relatively quickly for those who begin with smaller ability, and such individuals tend to take judgmental "shortcuts," using readily available cognitive patterns. They behave, thus, in a way typical of that exhibited by individuals with a high dispositional need for closure.

Accordingly, in the next set of studies (see: Kossowska, 2007a), we further investigated the hypothesized link between need for closure and limitation in control aspect of working memory. The results of the preceding studies are consistent with the notion that individuals with high (vs. low) need for closure have a cognitive deficit with regard to a processing of information in working memory (i.e., rate and capacity of information processing). If such deficits are due to limited cognitive control processes, participants with a high (vs. low) need for closure should show an impairment on a task particularly demanding to engage in controlled processing. Moreover, we expected that the relationship between need for closure and the range of information processing in a decision task would be mediated by a limitation in ability to controlled processing (an executive aspect of working memory).

In one of our studies, participants performed a task involving a random generation of intervals (known as the RIG task, Baddeley, Emslie, Kolodny, & Duncan, 1998), before performing the SciPic decision task (e.g., Payne, Bettman, & Johnson, 1993); participants subsequently completed the Polish version of the Need for Closure Scale (Kossowska, 2003).

The activity of generating random intervals is difficult, places significant load on the cognitive system and cannot be automatized (Wagenaar, 1970; Rapoport & Budescu, 1997). Therefore, researchers agree (e.g., Baddeley et al., 1998) on its particular capability of draining cognitive resources. This is so because the generation of random intervals requires the overcoming of strong automatisms, both learned (e.g., involved in the generation of letters or digits series) as well as inborn (e.g., a tendency to behave rhythmically) (Folkard & Monk, 1980). An increase in the predictability of the series (i.e., reduction in its requisite random nature) is thus taken to indicate an ability to controlled processing.

Participants' specific task of 5 min' duration is to strike the left mouse-key, using the dominant hand, in a completely arythmical manner. The ratio of random to rhythmical instances is recognized as an indicator of the ability to controlled processing allocated to this priority task. The calculation procedure for doing so was developed by Vandierendonck (2000). We expected that high (vs. low) need for closure would be negatively related to performance on this task.

The participants also completed SciPic – a computer-based information acquisition task (Payne et al., 1993; for detailed procedure see Kossowska, 2007b). The task was presented in the form of a 4×6 matrix, with four alternatives described by six cues (attributes) each. The task for the subject in each trial was to choose one of the four options presented in the table. Subjects could search the table by opening the covered cells with a mouse click. In order to open the next box, they had to close the previous one first. The final choice was also made by clicking the mouse on one of the four buttons on the screen. In this experiment, the subjects had to make 24 decisions. Two variables

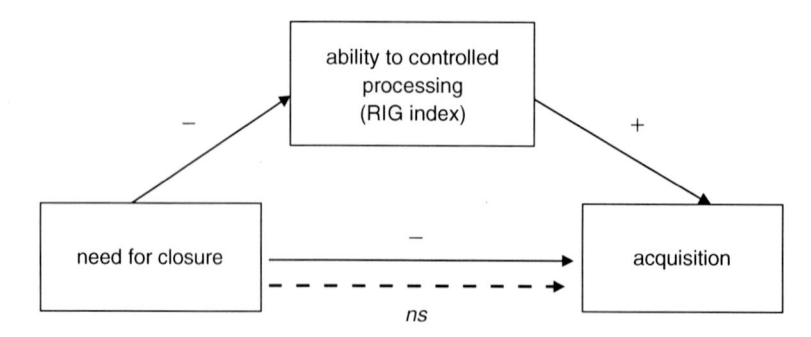

Fig. 22.4 Relationship between need for cognitive closure, ability to controlled processing, and the type of information sought in decision task

were used as indicators of information search: *decision time* – the average time participants spent while making the decision, and *acquisition* – the average number of information boxes opened.

As predicted, individuals with high (vs. low) need for closure generated significantly more rhythmical keystroke-sequences. These findings are consistent with the notion that high need for closure individuals exhibits a lesser ability to controlled processing than low need for closure individuals. In addition, the results showed that need for closure affected both the ability to controlled processing variable as well as the information search variable. Ability to controlled processing was also positively related to the acquisition of information. When controlling for the index of executive function of WM, the relationship between need for closure and the information search index turned nonsignificant, while the influence of ability to controlled processing remained significant. Thus, the results of this analysis confirmed the assumption that executive aspect of WM mediates the relationships between need for closure and information search (see Fig. 22.4).

The above analysis supported the notion that need for closure is related to limitations in ability to controlled processing measured by the random interval generated task. Moreover, the results indicated that a variable measuring an executive functions accounted for the relationship between the need for closure and performance in an information search task.

Motivation toward Closure and Cognitive Resources – Final Remarks

The purpose of this chapter was to summarize evidence supporting the notion that stable individual differences in the need for cognitive closure, tapped by the Need for Closure Scale (Webster & Kruglanski, 1994) are associated with identifiable individual differences in cognitive ability, specifically working memory functioning. We have considered the motivation toward closure because it represents a ubiquitous aspect of human functioning affecting all judgments and decision making in social and nonsocial contexts. Prior research has demonstrated that situational constraints on individuals' cognitive ability, such as time pressure, noise, mental fatigue, or alcoholic intoxication (for a review see Kruglanski, 2004) induce a momentary need for cognitive closure that significantly affects their manner of mental functioning (Kruglanski & Webster, 1996; Webster & Kruglanski, 1998). Accordingly, we have hypothesized increase in need for closure in conjunction with limitations that reflect diminishing resources, such as those having to do with basic cognitive skills. Although some researchers (e.g., Smith & DeCoster, 2000) suggested that motivation and capacity constraints have independent effects on information processing, from our standpoint (and in the light of the results of our studies), the two may not be completely independent.

The results of our studies consistently supported the above predictions. Specifically, the results of set of studies indicated that individuals characterized by a high (vs. low) need for cognitive closure exhibited a slower short – term memory search (set of Studies 1; Kossowska, 2005), lower working memory capacity (set of Studies 2; Legierski & Kossowska, 2008), and lower ability to controlled processing (set of Studies 3; Kossowska, 2007a). Moreover, we have provided evidence suggesting that limited processing ability mediates the relationship between need for closure and the type of information sought in a judgmental task (set of Studies 2) and the extent of information search in decision task (set of Studies 3).[4]

We have suggested that individual differences in need for closure are related to individual differences in cognitive capacity. Important question arises, however, due causality assumptions. On the one hand, it is possible that limitations of cognitive processes constitute need for closure. In support for the assumed causal direction in which cognitive resources induce a need for closure, the obtained results echo prior findings involving the situational inductions of the need for closure through various constraints imposed on participants' cognitive resources, namely time pressure, ambient noise, fatigue, or alcoholic intoxication (Kruglanski & Webster, 1996; Kruglanski, 2004). The three sets of studies provide multiple sources of evidence that are easy to explain according to a single principle stating that cognitive ability limitations is related to need for closure because of the need to simplify complex informational arrays. However, an alternative explanation of these findings would suggest that the need for closure contributed to the differences in cognitive ability measured in the studies. The mediation analysis reported in Sects. "Need for Cognitive Closure and Working Memory Capacity" and "Need for Cognitive Closure and Ability to Controlled Processing" of studies add slight support for this assumption. To argue for the reverse causal direction would require a different explanation for each cognitive ability task and the exclusion of the experimental research attesting to changes in need for closure as a result of cognitive load.

Finally, we are not presently proposing that cognitive capacity limitations constitute the sole source of individual differences in the need for cognitive closure. Other potential factors having to do with the individuals' family dynamics, cultural values, or personal history could well constitute additional sources of this motivation. Further research is needed to investigate these possibilities and also to determine whether these potentially diverse sources of the need for closure are functionally equivalent in shaping this important motivation.

Acknowledgments Research was supported by grant MNiSW PB 3557/32 (grant acknowledged to the first author).

References

Baddeley, A. (1996). Exploring the central executive. *Quarterly Journal of Experimental Psychology, 49A*, 5–28.
Baddeley, A., Emslie, H., Kolodny, J., & Duncan, J. (1998). Random generation and the executive control of working memory. *Quarterly Journal of Experimental Psychology. Human Experimental Psychology, 51A*, 819–852.
Baron, R. S. (1986). Distraction-conflict theory: progress and problems. In L. Berkowitz (Ed.), *Advances in Experimental Social Psychology* (Vol. 19, pp. 1–40). New York: Academic.
Berti, S., & Schroger, E. (2003). Die Bedeutung sensorischer Verarbeitung und Aufmerksamkeitssteuerung für Arbeitsgedächtnisfunktionen [Sensory memory and attentional control as a pre-requisite for working memory processes]. *Zeitschrift für Psychologie, 211*, 193–201.

---

[4] The question could arise if it might be a case that there is a 'third party' factor accounting for the results of our studies. The obvious candidate could be a level of intelligence. Individuals high in need for closure often limit their information processing activities. This may suggest a negative relationship between need for closure and intelligence. Empirically, the relationship between need for closure and intelligence is nonsignificant (see Webster & Kruglanski, 1994; Kossowska, 2003).

Chaiken, S., Liberman, A., & Eagly, A. (1989). Heuristic and systematic information processing within and beyond the persuasion context. In J. Uleman & J. Bargh (Eds.), *Unintended Thought* (pp. 212–252). New York: Guilford.

Chajut, E., & Algom, D. (2003). Selective attention improves under stress: implications for theories of social cognition. *Journal of Personality and Social Psychology, 85*, 231–248.

Cowan, N. (2001). The magical number 4 in short-term memory: a reconsideration of mental storage capacity. *Behavioral and Brain Sciences, 24*, 87–185.

Daneman, M., & Carpenter, P. (1980). Individual differences in working memory and reading. *Journal of Verbal Learning & Verbal Behavior, 19*, 450–466.

Daneman, M., & Merike, P. (1996). Working memory and language comprehension: a meta-analysis. *Psychonomic Bulletin and Review, 3*, 422–433.

De Grada, E., Kruglanski, A. W., Mannetti, L., & Pierro, A. (1999). Motivated cognition and group interaction: need for closure affects the contents and processes of collective negotiations. *Journal of Experimental Social Psychology, 35*, 346–365.

De Jong, R., Berendsen, E., & Cools, R. (1999). Goal neglect and inhibitory limitations: dissociable causes of interference effects in conflict situations. *Acta Psychologica, 101*, 379–394.

Dijksterhuis, A., van Knippenberg, A., Kruglanski, A. W., & Schaper, C. (1996). Motivated social cognition: need for closure effects on memory and judgment. *Journal of Experimental and Social Psychology, 32*, 254–270.

Embretson, S. E. (1995). The role of working memory capacity and general control processes in intelligence. *Intelligence, 20*, 169–189.

Engle, R., Kane, M., & Tuholski, S. (1999). Individual differences in working memory capacity and what they tell us about controlled attention, general fluid intelligence, and functions of the prefrontal cortex. In A. Miyake & P. Shah (Eds.), *Models of working memory: mechanisms of active maintenance and executive control* (pp. 102–134). New York: Cambridge University Press.

Engle, R., Tuholski, S., Laughlin, J., & Conway, N. (1999). Working memory, short-term memory, and general fluid intelligence: a latent-variable approach. *Journal of Experimental Psychology. General, 128*, 309–331.

Feldman-Barrett, L., Tugade, M., & Engle, R. (2004). Individual differences in working memory capacity and dual-processes theories of the mind. *Psychological Bulletin, 130*, 553–573.

Folkard, S., & Monk, T. (1980). Circadian rhythms in human memory. *British Journal of Psychology, 71*, 295–309.

Ford, T. E., & Kruglanski, A. W. (1995). Effects of epistemic motivations on the use of accessible constructs in social judgment. *Personality and Social Psychology Bulletin, 21*, 950–962.

Halford, G., Wilson, W., & Phillips, S. (1998). Processing capacity defined by relational complexity: implications for comparative, developmental, and cognitive psychology. *Behavioral and Brain Sciences, 21*, 803–864.

Harris, M., & Tetrick, L. (1993). Cognitive ability and motivational interventions: their effects on performance outcomes. *Current Psychology, 12*, 57–79.

Hess, T. (2002). Age-related constraints and adaptations in social information processing. In U. von Hecker, S. Dutke, & G. S dek (Eds.), *Generative mental processes and cognitive resources* (pp. 129–156). Dordrecht, The Netherlands: Kluwer Academic.

Huguet, P., Galvaing, M. P., Monteil, J. M., & Dumas, F. (1999). Social presence effects in the Stroop task: further evidence for an attentional view of social facilitation. *Journal of Personality and Social psychology, 77*, 1011–1025.

Hunt, E., & Lansman, M. (1986). Unified model of attention and problem solving. *Psychological Review, 93*, 446–461.

Jost, J., Glaser, J., Kruglanski, A., & Sullaway, F. (2003). Political conservatism as motivated social cognition. *Psychological Bulletin, 129*, 339–375.

Just, M., & Carpenter, P. (1992). A capacity theory of comprehension: individual differences in working memory. *Psychological Review, 99*, 122–149.

Kahneman, D. (1973). *Attention and effort*. Englewood Cliffs, NJ: Prentice Hall.

Kane, M., Bleckley, K., Conway, A., & Engle, R. (2001). A controlled-attention view of working-memory capacity. *Journal of Experimental Psychology. General, 130*, 169–183.

Kossowska, M. (2003). Różnice indywidualne w potrzebie poznawczego domknięcia. [Individual differences in need for cognitive closure]. *Przegląd Psychologiczny, 46*, 355–375.

Kossowska, M. (2005). *Umysł Niezmienny Poznawcze Mechanizmy Sztywności [Unchangeable mind Cognitive mechanisms of rigidity]*. Cracow: WUJ.

Kossowska, M. (2007a). Motivation toward closure and cognitive processes: an individual differences approach. *Personality and Individual Differences, 43*, 2149–2158.

Kossowska, M. (2007b). The role of cognitive inhibition in motivation toward closure. *Personality and Individual Differences, 42*, 1117–1126.

Kossowska, M., & Van Hiel, A. (2003). The relationship between need for closure and conservative beliefs in Western and Eastern Europe. *Political Psychology, 24*, 501–518.

Kossowska, M., Van Hiel, A., Chun, W. Y., & Kruglanski, A. W. (2002). The need for cognitive closure scale: structure, cross-cultural invariance, and comparison of mean ratings between European–American and East Asian samples. *Psychologica Belgica, 42,* 276–286.

Kruglanski, A. W. (1989). *Lay Epistemics and Human Knowledge.* New York: Plenum Press.

Kruglanski, A. W. (2004). *The psychology of closed mindedness.* New York: Psychology Press.

Kruglanski, A. W., DeGrada, E., Mannetti, L., Atash, M. N., & Webster, D. M. (1997). Psychological theory testing versus psychometric nay-saying: comment on Neuberg et al.'s (1997) critique of the Need for Closure Scale. *Journal of Personality and Social Psychology, 73,* 1005–1016.

Kruglanski, A. W., & Freund, T. (1983). The freezing and unfreezing of lay interferences: the effect of impressional primacy, ethnic stereotyping, and numerical anchoring. *Journal of Experimental Social Psychology, 19,* 448–468.

Kruglanski, A. W., & Mayseless, O. (1988). Contextual effects in hypothesis testing: the role of competing alternatives and epistemic motivations. *Social Cognition, 6,* 1–20.

Kruglanski, A. W., Shah, J., Pierro, A., & Mannetti, L. (2002). When similarity breeds content: need for closure and the allure of homogeneous and self-resembling groups. *Journal of Personality and Social Psychology, 83,* 648–662.

Kruglanski, A. W., & Webster, D. (1991). Group members reactions to opinion deviates and conformists at varying degrees of proximity to decision deadline and of environmental noise. *Journal of Personality and Social Psychology, 61,* 215–115.

Kruglanski, A. W., & Webster, D. M. (1996). Motivated closing of the mind: seizing and freezing. *Psychological Review, 103,* 263–283.

Kruglanski, A. W., Webster, D. M., & Klem, A. (1993). Motivated resistance and openness to persuasion in the presence or absence of prior information. *Journal of Personality and Social Psychology, 65,* 861–877.

Kyllonen, P., & Christal, R. (1990). The theory of comprehension: new frontiers of evidence and arguments. *Psychological Review, 103,* 389–433.

La Pointe, L., & Engle, R. (1990). Simple and complex word spans as measures of working memory capacity. *Journal of Experimental Psychology: Learning, Memory, and Cognition, 16,* 1118–1133.

Legierski, J., & Kossowska, M. (2008). Epistemic motivation, working memory and diagnostic information search. Unpublished manuscript.

Mannetti, L., Pierro, A., Kruglanski, A., Taris, T., & Bezinovic, P. (2002). A cross-cultural study in the need for cognitive closure scale: comparing its structure in Croatia, Italy, USA and the Netherlands. *The British Journal of Social Psychology, 41,* 139–156.

Mayseless, O. & Kruglanski, A. W. (1987). Accuracy of estimates in the social comparison of abilities. *Journal of Experimental Social Psychology, 23,* 217–229.

Miller, L. & Vernon, P. (1992). The general factor in short-term memory, intelligence, and reaction time. *Intelligence, 16,* 5–29.

Mitchell, T., & Silver, W. (1990). Individual and group goals when workers are interdependent: effects on task strategies and performance. *Journal of Applied Psychology, 75,* 185–193.

Miyake, A., & Shah, P. (1999). *Models of working memory. Mechanisms of active maintenance and executive control.* Cambridge: Cambridge University Press.

Muraven, M., & Slessareva, E. (2003). Mechanism of self-control failure: motivation and limited resources. *Personality and Social Psychology Bulletin, 29,* 894–906.

Necka, E. (1992). Cognitive analysis of intelligence: the significance of working memory processes. *Personality & Individual Differences, 13,* 1031–1046.

Necka, E. (1997). Attention, working memory and arousal: concept apt to account for "the process of intelligence". In G. Matthews (Ed.), *Cognitive science perspective on personality and emotion* (pp. 503–554). Amsterdam: Elsevier.

Necka, E. (1999). Learning, automaticity, and attention: an individual-differences approach. In P. L. Ackerman, P. C. Kyllonen, & R. D. Roberts (Eds.), *Learning and individual differences: process, trait, and content determinants* (pp. 161–184). Washington, DC: American Psychological Association.

Neuberg, S., & Fiske, S. (1987). Motivational influences on impression formation: outcome dependency, accuracy-driven attention, and individuating processes. *Journal of Personality and Social Psychology, 53,* 431–444.

Norman, D. A., & Bobrow, D. J. (1975). On data-limited and resources-limited processes. *Cognitive Psychology, 7,* 44–64.

Oberauer, K., Suss, H., Wilhelm, O., & Wittmann, W. (2000). Working memory capacity – facets of a cognitive ability construct. *Personality and Individual Differences, 29,* 1017–1046.

Payne, J., Bettman, J., & Johnson, E. (1993). The use of multiple strategies in judgment and choice. In N. J. Castellan Jr. (Ed.), *Individual and group decision making: current issues* (pp. 19–39). Hillsdale, NJ, England: Lawrence Erlbaum Associates.

Rapoport, A., & Budescu, D. (1997). Randomization in individual choice behavior. *Psychological Review, 104,* 603–617.

Roediger, H., Marsh, E., & Lee, S. (2002). Kinds of memory. In H. Pashler & D. Medin (Eds.), *Steven's handbook of experimental psychology (3rd ed.), Vol. 2: Memory and cognitive processes* (pp. 1–41). New York: Wiley.

Salthouse, T. A. (1988). The complexity of age × the complexity of functions: comment on Charness and Campbell (1988). *Journal of Experimental Psychology. General, 117*, 425–428.

Salthouse, T. A. (1990). Working memory as a processing resource in cognitive aging. *Developmental Review, 10*, 101–124.

Salthouse, T. A., Hambrick, D., & Lukas, K. (1996). Determinants of adult age differences on synthetic work performance. *Journal of Experimental Psychology. Applied, 2*, 305–329.

Shah, J., Kruglanski, A. W., & Thompson, E. (1998). Membership has its (epistemic) rewards: need for closure effects on in-group bias. *Journal of Personality and Social Psychology, 75*, 383–393.

Smith, E., & DeCoster, J. (2000). Dual-process models in social and cognitive psychology: conceptual integration and links to underlying memory systems. *Personality and Social Psychology Review, 4*, 108–132.

Sperling, G., & Speelman, R. (1970). Acoustic similarity and auditory short-term memory experiments and a model. In D. A. Norman (Ed.), *Models of human memory*. New York: Academic.

Stankov, L. (1988). Single tests, competing tasks, and their relationship to the broad factors of intelligence. *Personality and Individual Differences, 9*, 25–33.

Sternberg, S. (1969). The discovery of processing stages: extensions of Donders' method. *Acta Psychologica, 30*, 276–315.

Tetlock, P. (1983). Accountability and complexity of thought. *Journal of Personality and Social Psychology, 45*, 74–83.

Thompson, E., Roman, R., Moskowitz, G., Chaiken, S., & Bargh, J. (1994). Accuracy motivation attenuates covert priming: the systematic reprocessing of social information. *Journal of Personality and Social Psychology, 66*, 474–489.

Trope, Y., & Bassok, M. (1983). Information-gathering strategies in hypothesis-testing. *Journal of Experimental Social Psychology, 19*, 560–576.

Vandierendonck, A. (2000). Analyzing human random time generation behavior: a methodology and a computer program. *Behavior Research Methods, Instruments and Computers, 32*, 555–566.

Wagenaar, W. A. (1970). Subjective randomness and the capacity to generate information. *Acta Psychologica, 32*, 233–242.

Wang, M. & Chen Y. (2006). Age Differences in Attitude Change: Influences of Cognitive Resources and Motivation on Responses to Argument Quantity. *Psychology & Aging, 21*, 581–589.

Webster, D. M. (1993). Motivated augmentation and reduction of the overattribution bias. *Journal of Personality and Social Psychology, 65*, 261–271.

Webster, D. M., & Kruglanski, A. W. (1994). Individual differences in need for cognitive closure. *Journal of Personality and Social Psychology, 67*, 1049–1062.

Webster, D. & Kruglanski, A. W. (1998). Cognitive and social consequences of the need for cognitive closure. *European Review of Social Psychology, 8*, 133–173.

Webster, D., Richter, L., & Kruglanski, A. W. (1995). On leaping to conclusions when feeling tired: mental fatigue effects on impression primacy. *Journal of Experimental Social Psychology, 32*, 181–195.

Chapter 23
Mood as Information: The Regulatory Role of Personality

Magdalena Marszał-Wiśniewska and Dominika Zajusz

According to the mood-as-input model (Martin, 2001), moods operate much like any other piece of information. They serve as input in a configural processing system. Moods are processed in parallel with the target and contextual information in such a way that the meaning of the mood influences and is influenced by the meaning of other information. It is possible for either negative or positive feelings to convey either negative or positive evaluative and motivational implications, the nature of which depends on the context. Hence, the influence of mood on one's evaluations, motivations, and behaviors depends on the *interaction* of mood and situational conditions (which is the so-called *context-dependent effect of mood*), suggesting, for example, that the relation between the mood and the way of processing information (systematic vs. heuristic) differs depending on the interaction of mood and the context of the task.

Current research conducted in the frame of the mood-as-input model has generally ignored the modifying role of personality in the informative function of mood. The question: "Is the *context-dependent effect of mood* a general phenomenon or an interindividual diverse (i.e., depending on stable personality traits)?" still remains unanswered. This chapter aims, by referring to new research, to contribute an answer.

Basic Trends in the Study of Mood

Importance attached to the issue of mood, both as a subject for theoretical analysis and an object of psychological research, has been growing steadily since 1980s. On the one hand, theoretical considerations focus on the definition and the structure of affective phenomena (discussions center on models of the above mentioned phenomena), and on the other hand – empirical studies on mood, both correlational and experimental, are developing. The correlational approach entails the analysis of the relations between mood and personality traits (Watson, 2000), while the experimental approach tends to concentrate on the influence of mood on cognitive functioning: attention (e.g., Baumeister, Bratslavsky, Finkenauer, & Vohs, 2001; Bless, Clore, Golisano, Rabel, & Schwarz, 1996; Bless, Schwarz, & Wieland, 1996), creative thinking (e.g., Kaufmann & Vosburg, 1997, 2002), information processing, and evaluation (e.g., Martin & Clore, 2001; Schwarz & Clore, 1996).

M. Marszał-Wiśniewska (✉)
Institute of Psychology, Polish Academy of Sciences, ul. Chodakowska 19/31, 03-815, Warsaw, Poland
e-mail: marszal@psychpan.waw.pl

D. Zajusz
Warsaw School of Social Sciences and Humanities, Warsaw, Poland

Research of personality correlates of mood refers mainly to Eysenck's theory (1967, 1992), which states that introversion and neuroticism should correlate positively with a negative mood and tension, and extraversion – with a positive mood and energy. Research done by Matthews and his collaborators (Matthews, Deary, & Whiteman, 2003; Matthews, Jones, & Chamberlain, 1990), based on the three-dimensional model of mood (three correlated dimensions: hedonic tone, tense arousal and energetic arousal), has confirmed a positive correlation between neuroticism and tense arousal and a negative correlation between neuroticism and energetic arousal as well as hedonic tone. As for extraversion, its correlation with tense arousal was shown to be negligible; its correlation with energetic arousal and the hedonic tone was either positive (Matthews, Jones, et al., 1990), or nonsignificant (Matthews et al., 2003). Correlational research by Watson (2000), basing on the two-dimensional model of mood (two orthogonal dimensions: positive affect and negative affect) and making use of PANAS to asses mood and NEO-FFI to asses personality, also showed that negative mood has a strong positive correlation with neuroticism, but is not correlated with extraversion. Meanwhile, positive mood was found to have a strong positive correlation with extraversion and a weak negative correlation with neuroticism. Thus, research conducted to this date confirms the affective nature of neuroticism, and shows that this dimension reflects individual differences in experiencing negative moods. For extraversion, the results are not as clear-cut, although they do give evidence for a relation between this dimension of personality and positive affect. It should be stressed that although in general, these results support the relation between mood and primarily biologically determined personality traits, there is still little empirical data concerning the relation of mood with temperamental traits beyond extraversion and neuroticism. On the other hand, in research focusing on nontemperamental personality traits, there is a clear dominance of projects focusing on dimensions from the Big Five Model other than extraversion and neuroticism. These have shown that Openness is unrelated to mood experience, whereas Conscientiousness and Agreeableness have specific lower-order associations with mood (Allik & Realo, 1997; Watson, 2000). Conscientiousness is strongly related to Attentiveness (the subscale of basic positive affect, which contains descriptors such as "alert," "attentive," "determined"), whereas Agreeableness displays a consistent negative correlation with Hostility (the subscale of basic negative affect, which contains descriptors reflecting the emotions of anger, such as "irritable" and "angry").

Furthermore, theoretical considerations and research results alike demonstrate that apart from temperamental traits, relatively stable motivational tendencies of the subject also act as mood determinants. And so, for example, according to Watson's concept of Positive and Negative Affect (Watson, 2000; Watson, Clark, & Tellegen, 1988), the subject's motivational tendencies, related to the biobehavioral systems specified by Gray (1981), i.e., the Behavioral Activation System (BAS) and the Behavioral Inhibition System (BIS), play a crucial role in experiencing mood. The systems play an important adaptive function; they mediate approach – avoidance behaviors. The main function of the BAS is to direct the organism toward situations and experiences, which can potentially result in pleasure and reward. BIS, on the other hand, which Gray called the *stop, look, and listen system* (Gray, 1981), focuses attention on threatening stimuli and inhibits behavior that may result in displeasure and punishment. Most of the psychological research conducted to this date points at a moderate correlation between the BIS and a negative affect and a lack of correlation with positive affect, and at a positive correlation between the BAS and positive affect, with no correlation with negative affect (Carver & White, 1994; Heubeck, Wilkinson, & Cologen, 1998; Jorm et al., 1999). For example, research conducted by Carver and White (1994) has shown that the BIS, measured using BIS and BAS scales, correlates positively with the feeling of anxiety. No correlation has been observed between the BAS and the anxiety level. Research on emotional responses to day-to-day positive and negative events, by Gable and collaborators (Gable, Reis, & Elliot, 2000), demonstrates that in general, the BIS is a good predictor of negative emotional responses, and BAS – a good predictor of positive emotional responses. The fact that taking individual differences in motivational tendencies into account when analyzing the experienced mood is well-founded is confirmed by research based on Kuhl's Action Control Theory (1985, 1986, 1994). According to this theory, the difficulty of enactment of an intention (a goal) depends, among others, on volitional properties, i.e., individuals' disposition toward an action or a state orientation. Action orientation as a volitional property conduces to the efficiency of volitional control (will power), making an intention easier to realize, while state orientation reduces the efficiency of volitional control, making the intention more difficult to carry out. Until now, research has shown a statistically significant relation between state orientation and negative affect as measured on the PANAS scales and the experience of negative emotions in a task situation (Kanfer, Dugdale, & McDonald, 1994), as well as a negative mood, a low level of optimism and, in certain situations, a variability of mood (Marszał-Wiśniewska, 1999).

The second major trend in the study of moods is experimental research analyzing the role of mood in human functioning, especially its cognitive aspect. The idea that our moods can have a profound impact on our judgments and a variety of cognitive processes is not new. Interest in the mood–cognition relation increased noticeably after the publication of results showing mood-dependent recall (Bower, Montiero, & Gilligan, 1978) and mood-congruent evaluation, explained in term of mood-congruent memory (Isen, Shalker, Clark, & Karp, 1978). In the late 1980s and early 1990s, the fact that mood does not only influence the outcome of processing (e.g., memory, evaluation) but also the nature of processing, became obvious. It has been proved, for example, that a positive mood leads people to exert little effort in processing persuasive messages (Worth & Mackie, 1987) and that, in general, people in negative moods tend to use effortful, detailed-oriented, analytical processing strategies, whereas people in positive moods tend to use simple heuristics in processing information (Schwarz, 1990; Schwarz & Bless, 1991; Schwarz & Clore, 1988). More recent research (Martin & Clore, 2001) highlighted the greater complexity of mood–cognition relation. It showed, for instance, that the effects of mood on cognitive processing are dependent on a number of moderating variables (e.g., familiarity of target, task context, and attribution of source of mood). To account for these findings, various theoretical models have been developed (for a review, see Martin & Clore, 2001).

It should be stressed that these two basic trends in the study of mood are developing virtually independently from each other. The experimental trend analyzes the influence of mood on cognitive functioning while largely ignoring the existence of individual differences in the said functioning. While duly appreciating the importance of situational factors, authors of models explaining the relation between mood and cognition fail to take into account the significance of individual differences, treating them, at best, as a source of variance in measurement error. And conversely, researchers from the other, correlational trend, remain faithful to the tradition of research conducted within the framework of the psychology of individual differences, and concentrate mainly on identifying and describing differentiating properties (traits) relevant to the experienced mood. This type of research is characterized by the dispositional and differential approach typical for the "top-down" model. At the basis of this approach lies the assumption, that people have "naturally" different genetic equipment. Mechanisms that explain functioning are therefore to be found in biologically determined traits, which supposedly account for relatively stable differences between people's behaviors, emotions (including moods), and cognitive processes, regardless of the type of situation or environment in which they find themselves. These traits "deform" the perception of reality and a situation's meaning in a stable and specific manner.

Meanwhile, it would seem that research integrating the differential and cognitive paradigms could yield interesting results for theoretical conceptions from both fields of psychological knowledge. Finding individual differences in a person's mood-influenced cognitive functioning may, on one hand, make it possible to increase the precision of models regarding effects of affective states on cognition, by introducing personality-related variables and by uncovering interesting interactions between situational and individual factors. On the other hand, it could solve many problems for differential conceptions, concerning mostly the structural identity of traits coming from different taxonomies (e.g., neuroticism and anxiety as traits, or depressive tendencies and anxious tendencies).

It should be noted that the amount of data confirming the relevance of such an integrative approach is growing. To give an example, research conducted within the framework of *The Affect Infusion Model (AIM)* has revealed that people who score high on personality measures such as social desirability, Machiavellianism or trait anxiety are more likely to adopt a targeted, motivated processing strategy, and show significantly less affect infusion in their thoughts, plans or intergroup judgments (Ciarrochi & Forgas, 1999; Forgas, 1998). In contrast, those who score high on Openness to Feelings were found to show significantly greater affect infusion in consumer judgments than do low scores (Ciarrochi & Forgas, 2000).

Much of the research analyzing the influence of mood on cognitive functioning is based on two hypotheses: the mood-congruency hypothesis or trait-congruency hypothesis (Rusting, 1998). The first one predicts that individuals should better perceive, learn, and remember material consistent with their current mood state than material inconstant with their mood. Several studies showed that people in positive mood tend to notice and interpret event in an overly positive light, whereas people in negative mood tend to notice and interpret events negatively (e.g., Mayer, Gaschke, Braverman, & Evans, 1992; Mayer, McCormick, & Strong, 1995; Niedenthal & Setterlund, 1994; Wright & Bower, 1992). According to the second hypothesis, individual differences in emotional processing may also be caused by relatively stable personality traits that predispose certain individuals to process information that is congruent with those traits. In other words, individuals selectively attend to, retrieve, and reconstructed events so that they are consistent with their underlying personality traits, especially when those traits include an emotional component such as trait anger, trait anxiety, or depressive tendencies. Several studies showed that people with positively toned emotional traits are thought to notice and remember pleasant material, whereas those with negatively emotional traits are thought to notice and remember unpleasant material. (e.g., Bradley & Mogg, 1994; Burke & Mathews, 1992; Reed & Derryberry, 1995). Although conceptually related, the most of mood-congruency and trait –congruency studies have been done separately. Because the studies examining separate mood-congruency and trait-congruency effects have yielded some inconsistent findings (see Rusting, 1998, for a review), an interest in examining the combined effects of mood and traits have sparked.

In the widely published research concerning mood-congruent processing of affective stimuli, the evidence for the moderating influence of personality on mood –congruency is accumulating. It has been ascertained, for instance, that depressed individuals show trait-congruent attentional processing, but only in the presence of a negative mood state (Ingram, Bernet, & McLaughlin, 1994). The authors induced a negative or neutral mood, and had recovered-depressed and never-depressed individuals perform a dichotic listening task. They found that during a neutral mood state, the two groups performed equally well when shadowing positive and negative messages. However, during a negative mood, the depressed individuals made more errors in shadowing both positive and negative messages. This *mood x depression* interaction remained significant even when the authors reran the analyses controlling for individual differences in baseline performance, which suggests that the obtained effects were not simply the results of depressed individuals making more errors overall. Attentional studies of anxious individuals have also yielded some support for *personality x mood* interactions. In one study, Richards, French, Johnson, Naparstek, and Williams (1992) showed that, although induced anxious mood may influence attention to threatening cues for all individuals, those high in trait anxiety were less able than those low in trait anxiety to shift attention away from the threatening content of the anxiety-related words. The researchers induced anxious mood in individuals with high and low trait anxiety, and observed performance on the emotional Stroop task. The individuals high in trait anxiety were slower to name anxiety-related words when an anxious mood had been induced. This effect was stronger than for individuals low in trait anxiety.

Regarding the relation between affect and attention, Kolańczyk (2004) provided interesting data about the modifying role of individual differences concerning the type of mind (general cognitive preferences). In these studies conducted with affective priming paradigm, it was revealed that the conscious perception of the pictures of faces expressing different emotions (optimal priming stimuli) influences the subsequent evaluation of hexagrams (target stimuli) only in the condition of extensive attention (when individuals were instructed to visualize the free goal activity: a city tour in China) and in the condition of cognitive overload (when individuals were instructed to remember and keep in mind one five-digit number). In other words, affective priming effects (where the evaluations of affectively bland stimuli are congruent to priming affects) were observed only in the state of extensive attention (broad but shallow information processing) and in the state of overloaded attention (the limitation of cognitive resources). Moreover, the affective priming effects were revealed only for subjects with global-subjective type of mind, characterized by a tendency to global cognition, deductive reasoning, and by a tendency to use internal emotional criteria of cognition, based on subjective impressions, emotions and feelings. Thus, only persons whose mind operates as if conditions of extensive attention were engaged have a particular propensity to being guided by affect and they submit to its assimilative influences.

Smith and Petty (1995) provided some of the most direct evidence for the interactive effects of mood and personality on emotion-congruent judgment. In a series of studies, they examined how an induced negative mood state interacted with these personality traits to influence performance on a variety of cognitive tasks. Their results indicated that self-esteem moderated the relationship between negative mood and valence of stories written in response to an emotionally ambiguous pictorial cue. Following the negative mood induction, individuals low in self-esteem wrote more negatively toned stories, whereas individuals high in self-esteem wrote more positive stories. Other research has revealed that individual differences in other mood-regulative variables, such as tendency to ruminate or distract, may also moderate mood-congruency effects. Rumination is defined as thoughts and behaviors that focus the individual's attention on the negative mood, the causes and consequences of this mood, and self-evaluations related to the mood. Distraction is defined as thoughts and behaviors that focus attention away from the mood and its causes onto pleasant or neutral stimuli that are engaging enough to prevent the mind from wandering back to the source of negative affect (Nolen-Hoeksema, 1991; Tice & Baumeister, 1993). It turned out that for both sad (depressed) and angry moods, individuals who ruminate show mood-congruent judgment; those who distract do not show this effect (cf. Lyubomirsky & Nolen-Hoeksema, 1995; Rusting & Nolen-Hoeksema, 1998).

Studies using memory tasks to examine the influence of moods and traits on cognition, provide fairly consistent evidence supporting the idea that personality traits, including trait anxiety, neuroticism, trait anger/hostility, depression and self-esteem, moderate the mood-congruency effect in recall. High scores on these traits either amplify the mood-congruency effect or change the effect by producing mood-incongruent recall. It appeared, for example, that high-neuroticism individuals show a stronger mood-congruency effect in the recall of negative adjectives than low-neuroticism individuals (Rusting, 1998). The same pattern of findings has also been obtained in studies of the anger/hostility trait. Following a specific anger mood induction (a hostile social interaction), people high in hostility showed an increased recall of hostile adjectives (Allred & Smith, 1991).

There is also some evidence that traits related to mood-regulation may interact with mood to produce mood-incongruency effects. For instance, Smith and Petty (1995) found some evidence for mood-incongruency in their studies of self-esteem and negative mood regulation expectancies. They exposed participants to a series of newspaper headlines varying in positive, negative, and neutral emotional content, followed by a negative or neutral mood induction, and a recall test for the headlines. In addition to finding the typical trait-congruency effect (high self-esteem individuals remembered more positive headlines than low self-esteem individuals), they found an interaction between self-esteem and mood condition. Low self-esteem participants showed mood-congruent recall of headlines; they recalled more negative headlines in the negative mood condition, and more positive headlines in the positive mood condition. High self-esteem participants, however, recalled more positive headlines in the negative mood condition. Smith & Petty interpreted this mood-incongruent recall as an attempt by people high in self-esteem to regulate the negative mood state that had been induced by retrieving positive cues. The same pattern of findings has also been obtained in a study using autobiographical memory task (Smith & Petty, 1995). Low self-esteem participants showed mood-congruent memory; they retrieved more negative personal memories in the negative mood condition than in the neutral mood condition. High self-esteem participants, on the other hand, showed mood-incongruent recall. Following the negative mood induction, high self-esteem individuals retrieved more positive personal memories. The similar effect was found for subclinically depressed and nondepressed individuals (Josephson, Singer, & Salovey, 1996). Nondepressed people, such as high self-esteem individuals, appeared to regulate the negative mood that had been induced by retrieving positive memories.

The research results outlined above indicate that certain personality traits moderate the mood–cognition relation. They allow us to assume, among others, that traits related to mood regulation, such as self-esteem, lead to the regulation of induced negative moods and produce mood-incongruency effects. Other traits, including an emotional component, such as neuroticism and trait anger/hostility magnify negative mood-congruency effects. However, the studies examining personality–mood interactions give more consistent findings than those examining the effects of moods and traits separately (Rusting, 1998), more research exploring the nature of these interactions is needed. Such questions like "When are amplification versus incongruency effects obtained?", "Are interactions obtained for all emotional personality traits, or only for some?" are still open and wait for answers. One should note that although research providing evidence supporting the moderation approach, however infrequent, tends to be conducted in the field of cognition or social-cognition psychology, it remains in close relation to the increasingly popular trend of research in individual differences psychology. This trend strives to integrate "top-down" and "bottom-up" models by combining the dispositional and situational approaches as well as the process-oriented and differential approaches. The differential-dispositional approach seeks out mechanisms that explain human functioning as an interaction of genetically determined traits and environmental factors. It works on the assumption that genetically determined traits (e.g., temperamental traits) modify the significance of external factors (situations) and internal factors (the person's other traits). As a result, the same factors can have varying meanings, and different factors may be beneficial or detrimental for people with different level of a given trait. Moreover, the role of the same traits can vary depending on the situation – their influence may be seen only in certain circumstances, and could be entirely opposite in others. In the approach combining the differential and the process-oriented views, it is assumed that differences in traits (be they genetically determined or formed mainly under earlier influence of the environment) rely on the existence of distinct and discrete mechanisms (in addition to common ones) modifying cognitive and emotional processes as well as behavior. The same situations can trigger different processes, and the same processes may result in different behavior in people with different traits.

Mood as Input Model

A functioning person nearly always experiences an information deficit: we do not know everything; we cannot fully predict how events will develop or how other people will act, not even how we ourselves will act. Under these conditions, mood can play the role of an additional information source which may be used to fill in gaps. Generally speaking, a positive mood signals that no problems requiring the subject's reaction are present in the environment. In opposition, negative moods inform the subject that an intervention or a corrective action is in order. Consequently, experiencing a negative mood motivates a person to engage in systematic information processing, while experiencing a positive mood results in people not making a cognitive effort, relying on heuristics instead

(Bless, Mackie, & Schwarz, 1992; Bodenhausen, Kramer, & Susser, 1994; Schwarz & Bless, 1991; Schwarz & Clore, 1996). However, is that always the case? The *mood as input* model provides an interesting answer.

Martin's mood *as input* model (Martin, 2001; Martin, Abend, Sedikides, & Green, 1997; Martin & Davies, 1998; Martin & Stoner, 1996; Martin, Ward, Achee, & Wyer, 1993) is a variant of the informational approach, according to which moods serve as a source of information. Basing on the widely shared premise that the effects of mood on social judgment may reflect the use of one's feelings as a source of information, Schwarz and Clore developed an approach to mood effects on judgment that became known as the *mood as information* model (Schwarz & Clore, 1983, 1988). They later extended the model to feelings other than mood, and accordingly changed the label to *feelings as information*. (Clore, 1992; Schwarz, 1990). In the next extension, Schwarz suggested that the information provided by our feelings may trigger different processing strategies (Schwarz, 1990) and explored this hypothesis in collaboration with Bless and Bohner (Schwarz & Bless, 1991; Schwarz, Bless, & Bohner, 1991).

The *mood as input* model begins with the same basic assumption as the *mood as information* model (Clore, 1992; Clore et al., 2001; Schwarz, 2001; Schwarz & Bohner, 1996), namely that subjective experiences convey information. The models differ, however, in the mechanism by which this is assumed to occur.

According Schwarz and Clore's *mood (feelings) as information* model (Clore, 1992; Schwarz & Bohner, 1996; Schwarz & Clore, 1988), in the course of evaluating a target stimulus, people experience affective feedback. This feedback may include valenced thoughts and feelings that are not different in kind from the affective feedback that arises when one experiences a mood. Because of the close overlap between these two sources of feedback, people sometimes mistake aspects of their mood for the aspects of their appraisal of the target. One consequence of this confusion is a shift in people's target evaluation toward the valence of their moods (mood-congruent judgments). This process has been termed the "How do I feel about it" heuristic, and is the basic mechanism of the *mood as information* model. Rather than computing a complex judgment through systematic processing, people simple assess how they feel while evaluating the target and add this assessment into their evaluation. The result is mood-congruent judgment (more favorable evaluations under positive than negative mood). As long as people use the "How do I feel about it" heuristic, their evaluations will reflect mood congruence. In other words, with this heuristic, people use their moods as a bottom-line evaluation. According to *mood as information model*, only one effect of mood (e.g., mood-congruent judgment) is basic, whereas other effects (e.g., mood-incongruent judgment) are exceptions to basic rule.

The *mood as input* model, in contrast, rejects the above *basic/exception* explanation. The core assumption of the model is that the effects of mood on evaluation and motivation are context-dependent (Martin, 2001). According to the *mood as input* model, moods are not by themselves answers to evaluative questions and do not carry motivational implications. Positive moods do not tell us by themselves that everything is fine with the world, and neither do negative moods inform us, by themselves, that the world needs attending to. The evaluative and motivational implications conveyed by a given mood depend on the broader context, in which the mood is experienced. Martin assumes that moods operate like any other pieces of information (Martin, 2001; Martin & Stoner, 1997; Martin et al., 1993, 1996). They serve as input to a configural processing system, meaning that people do not consider each piece of information separately and then add (Clore, 1992) or average (Abele & Petzold, 1994) the pieces. Instead, they process information in parallel, and evaluate various pieces of information as a whole (Higgins & Rholes, 1976; Pusateri & Latane, 1982). The important consequence of the configural type of processing is that the implications of any given piece of information, including mood, can change with the context. For instance, a sad mood experienced at our own wedding or birthday party may result in attempts to improve the mood, thus triggering systematic processing in order to understand why we are sad in a situation that should normally make us happy.

The same motivations are less likely to be aroused when the sad mood is experienced in situations where sadness is socially expected (e.g., at a funeral). According to Martin's model (2001) people do not ask merely: "How do I feel about it?" They ask "What does it mean that I am feeling *this way in this context*?" In other words, people evaluate the targets by taking into consideration both their mood and some features of situation and doing this configurally. Moods are processed in parallel with contextual information in such a way that the meaning of the mood influences and is influenced by the meaning of other information. The meaning of a mood experience can change in different contexts, and therefore the evaluative and motivational implications of mood are mutable.

To sum up, the informational value of mood lies not so much in the moods themselves as in the interaction between mood and context. Moods provide input for evaluative, decisional and inference-making processes, and these processes determine the effects that one's mood will have on one's evaluations, motivations, and behaviors. This course of reasoning, known as the *context-dependent effect of mood*, implies that the influence of mood on one's evaluations, motivations, and behaviors depends on the *interaction* of mood and situational conditions.

In accordance with the *context-dependent effect of mood*, one's mood is not synonymous with one's evaluation. Whether a positive or negative mood leads to a favorable or unfavorable evaluation depends on the meaning of one's mood in that context. The question about the meaning of one's mood in different contexts is therefore a crucial one. In order to answer it, the *mood as input* model relies on the role-fulfillment process (Martin, 2001), also known as the "What would I feel if....?" process (Martin & Davies, 1998). This process can be characterized broadly as follows: when people make evaluations, they act as if they were asking themselves the question "What would I feel if....?" (For example, "what would I feel if the horror movie I just saw was a good horror movie?"). An evaluation is rendered subjectively when the person compares his/her current moods with the expected feelings. Favorable evaluations arise to the extent to which the person's moods (positive or negative) are congruent with what would be expected if the target had fulfilled a positive role. Unfavorable evaluations, in contrast, arise to the extent to which the person's moods are incongruent with what would be expected if the target had fulfilled a negative role. The role-fulfillment process described above is a variant of the process proposed by Higgins and Rholes (1976). The two researchers suggested a holistic-reference approach to explain impression formation. It posited that when people are given a verbal description comprising a role and a descriptor, (e.g., *caring mother*), they recall information about the target to which the description refers. Subsequently, they make use of this information to make two judgments. The first determines whether the target's role (i.e., *mother*) generally has a positive or negative social value. The other judgment tries to ascertain whether the descriptor (i.e., *caring*) lets the target fulfill its expected role (i.e., the role of a mother is to be caring rather than cruel). As a result, a caring mother is evaluated more favorably than a cruel mother, because it is the role of a mother to be caring. According to the *mood as input* model, moods fulfill the same function as descriptors. They inform about the extent to which the target fulfills its role. From this perspective, people can use their negative moods as information to make positive evaluations or use their positive moods as information to make negative evaluations.

To conclude the presentation of the *mood as input* model, we should note that because it presupposes context dependent evaluative and motivational implications of mood, it stresses the greater complexity of the informative function of mood. It becomes part of the increasingly popular tendency to criticize those theoretical conceptualizations, which oversimplify a person's functioning mechanism (e.g., by ignoring all effects other than mood congruent ones, or treating them as exceptions). It is also closely related to the transactional approach to psychological phenomena, which was developed mainly in the psychology of personality and individual differences (see for example Eliasz, 1990; Eliasz & Klonowicz, 2001; Pervin, 1976), and which states that an analysis of a person's functioning requires taking numerous codependencies, including person–situation relations.

Martin and his collaborators ran a series of experiments testing the context dependent implications of mood, focusing mainly on evaluative implications (making evaluations; Martin et al.,

1997), motivational implications (continuing or stopping activity, inducing systematic or heuristic information processing; Martin et al., 1993) and flexible and creative processing (Martin & Stoner, 1996). They showed generally that there are no inherent relations between the valence of one's mood and one's evaluations, motivations, and behaviors. Instead of that, the effect of any given mood depends on the context in which the mood is experienced.

A large part of the research on the *mood as input* model, while concentrating on intraindividual processes, fails to address the issue of the modifying role of personality in the informative function of mood. And yet, from individual differences perspective, it seems important to ask questions such as: "How do stable personality traits modify the influence of mood-situation interaction on a person's activity?", "Can personality traits strengthen or weaken the context-dependent implications of mood already seen in research, and if so, which traits can have that effect?", or "What are the limitations of the effects when one takes personality traits into account?" Answering them requires intensive research combining the differential and the process-oriented approaches. While we are far from the certainty that we will be able to answer all of these questions, we present below results which do not merely justify, but also encourage the investigation mood x situation x personality interactions.

Context-Dependent Motivational Effect of Mood: The Modifying Role of Personality

Let us begin with the brilliant explanation of the *mood as input* model as formulated by Martin and Davies (1998). From the configural view, "[…] any given mood experience is about as meaningful as the number 6. It conveys some context invariant information (i.e., a whole number between 5 and 7), but it has significance in a motivational or evaluative sense when it is placed in a context (e.g., 6 publications vs. 6 rejections)" (Martin & Davies, 1998, p. 47). Taking this reasoning further from the position of a psychologist of individual differences, one should add that both six publications and six rejections can have different meanings for people with different personality characteristics. Let us imagine, for example, a strongly neurotic person, who, in accordance with Gray's theory (1981) is highly sensitive to punishment and rewards, as opposed to an extravert, who is characterized by high sensitivity to rewards and low sensitivity to punishment. If we further assume that our sample neurotic person has low self-esteem, we can suppose that he or she will perceive both pieces of information (six publications and six rejections) as equally important, for instance – or even interpret "six publications" as proof of insufficient academic activity ("I could have done better and had more publications."). An extravert could, in turn, make light of the "six rejections," and if he or she happened to be a person with high self-esteem level, he or she could increase the meaning of "six publications." Consequently, the context-dependent effect of mood, i.e., the influence of the interaction between mood (number 6) and situation (publications vs. rejections) on various aspects of a person's functioning (including motivational aspects) can vary (e.g., strengthen or weaken an effect) depending on various personality traits and their internal relations.

In our own research, we decided to check how selected personality traits modify the context-dependent motivational implications of a mood. Our main goals were to confirm the *context-dependent motivational effect of mood* (as suggested by the *mood as input* model), and to analyze the influence of personality (temperamental and volitional traits) on this effect. Temperamental and volitional traits have been, so far, omitted in research on the *mood as input* model. Cognitively oriented researchers concentrated mainly on the role of the need for cognition as a personality trait (Martin et al., 1993). Furthermore, results concerning the influence of need for cognition on the motivational implications of mood were ambiguous. In one study (Martin et al., 1993) analyzing the influence of mood and different stop rules (*stop when you have enough information* versus *stop when you no longer enjoy the task*) on the course of activity, there were no significant effects associated with need for cognition. In other words, the authors obtained the same pattern of data for subjects with high and low need for cognition. In an analogous study (Martin et al., 1993; experiment 2) focused on memory-based processing task (generating a list of birds from memory), the results pattern was more complex. Apart from the main effect indicating that subjects high in need for cognition generated more birds than did subjects low in need for cognition, a three-way interaction (mood x stop rule x need for cognition) was also observed. This revealed that the predicted context-dependent effect of mood (two-way interaction between mood and stop rule) occurred only for subjects high in need for cognition, but not for subjects low in need for cognition. According to the researchers, this result makes it possible to infer that people who are low in need for cognition are reluctant to engage in effortful behavior, regardless of their mood.

Our research involved the measurement of temperamental and volitional traits (the first stage) and experimental study (the second stage). To assess temperamental traits, the Formal Characteristics of Behavior – Temperament Inventory (FCB-TI) was used (Strelau & Zawadzki, 1995). Volitional traits were measured with the Action Control Scale (ACS-90; Kuhl, 1994); Polish adaptation by Marszał-Wiśniewska (2002). The experimental study was the replication of the original experiment performed by Martin et al. (1993). The subjects (128 students) were randomly assigned to one of four between-groups conditions created by the factorial combination of valence of mood (positive vs. negative) and stop-rule (enough information vs. enjoy stop-rule).We placed subjects in positive or negative moods (induced experimentally), and then presented them with a stack of cards. On each card was a single behavior that a target person had ostensibly performed (there were 69 behaviors altogether). The subjects' task was to read the behaviors and form an impression of the target person. Half of the subjects were told to read the behaviors until they felt they had enough information (*enough information* stop-rule). Half were told to read the behaviors until they no longer enjoyed reading them (*enjoy* stop-rule). The amount of time subjects spent on the task and the number of cards the subjects read were analyzed. We should stress the fact that although our experiment was run in accordance with the procedure established by Martin et al. (1993; experiment 1), it made use of a different method of mood induction. To induce the appropriate moods, we used fragments of music (joyful and sad musical pieces) and stories (humorous and sad) read by subjects to background of joyful or sad music. In the original experiment by Martin et al. (1993), the moods were induced through film clips. This difference becomes especially important in the light of evidence indicating that the inconsistencies in the studies on mood effects may depend on the mood induction procedure (Rusting, 1998). The question whether using a different induction method would confirm the pattern of results obtained by Martin in his research is therefore relevant. It is worth noting that the efficiency of our mood induction procedure has been confirmed in the subjects' self-ratings of their current mood after induction. The participants completed the UWIST Mood Adjective Check List (Matthews, Jones, & Chamberlain, 1990); Polish adaptation by Goryńska (2005).

Temperamental and Volitional Traits

The relations between mood and biologically determined personality traits mentioned earlier in this chapter (e.g., Matthews, Jones, et al., 1990; Matthews et al., 2003) and the latter's influence on cognitive functioning (e.g., Matthews, Davies, & Holley, 1990; Rusting, 1998; Szymura & Nęcka, 2005) as well as relations between mood and volitional traits (Marszał-Wiśniewska, 1999) were the starting point for choosing temperamental and volitional traits. When it comes to temperamental traits, we based our research on the Regulative Theory of Temperament (RTT; Strelau, 1993, 1996, 1998). According to this theory, temperament is defined as basic, primarily biologically determined and relatively stable personality traits which apply to the formal, energetic, and temporal, characteristics of reactions and behavior. According to RTT assumptions (Strelau, 1996), temperament traits show interindividual differences in all forms of behavior and reactions (including affective ones). The RTT distinguishes six temperament traits: four in the energetic domain (endurance, emotional reactivity, activity and sensory sensitivity) and two in the temporal domain (briskness and perseveration); the relations of the traits that make up the energetic characteristics of behavior are assigned basic regulatory significance. Generally speaking, emotional reactivity and endurance reflect individual *stimulation processing capabilities* (SPC), while activity is responsible for the regulation of stimulation (ensuring the access of stimuli to the organism and satisfying the need for stimulation). The effectiveness of stimulation processing is a central theoretical construct in the RTT. This concept refers to the level of coherence between the amount of stimuli accessed and individual stimulation processing capabilities. According to the RTT, people with low stimulation processing capabilities (LSPC), i.e., those characterized by low endurance and high emotional reactivity, tend to avoid stimulation and perform best in low-stimulation conditions. Conversely, people with high capabilities (HSPC), i.e., those characterized by high endurance and low emotional reactivity, tend to seek stimulation, and perform best in high-stimulation conditions. Bearing in mind the fact that every situation has a certain stimulative value, and that according to the RTT the temperament fulfills an important regulatory function in all aspects of a person's functioning, the assumption that temperamental traits can modify the pattern of the context-dependent motivational effect of mood appears to be well-founded.

While analyzing the influence of mood on the course of activity, it seems justifiable to take into account those personality traits that facilitate or impede enacting of goals. We all know from everyday experience that the mere intention to stop smoking, for example, is not sufficient for the enactment. To be initiated and enacted, even simple activities require control processes (action control, volitional control) that help shield a selected action tendency against the continuous pressure of alternative action tendencies. According to Kuhl's Action Control Theory (Kuhl, 1985, 1986, 1994), the difficulty of enacting a goal (and consequently of interrupting or continuing the current goal-directed behavior) depends on volitional properties, i.e., individuals' disposition towards an action or a state-orientation. Individuals are action-oriented if their attention is focused on a fully developed action structure, and they can perform the intended action. A high degree of action orientation facilitates the enactment of goals. If the individual focuses his thoughts on the remaining elements without being able to initiate the intended action, he or she is state-oriented. Because state orientation involves repetitive and dysfunctional focusing on fixed aspects of situation, it impedes the achievement of goals (Kuhl, 1986). Depending on the element to which the individual directs his attention, various forms of state orientation may develop. Kuhl (1994) distinguished three different forms of action versus state orientation: (1) failure-related (disengagement vs. preoccupation), (2) decision-related (initiative vs. hesitation) and (3) performance-related (persistence vs. volatility). According to Kuhl's theory, there are relatively stable differences between individuals in the amount of action vs. state orientation (Kuhl, 1994). We can suppose that those differences, especially those in the decision-related action vs. state orientation form, can modify the influence of mood-situation interaction on the course of activity (e.g., by making the decision about continuing or interrupting a task easier or harder).

Results and Discussion

According to the hypothesis of context-dependent effect of mood (Martin et al., 1993), the influence of mood on the course of activity depends on the interaction of mood and situational conditions. The results we obtained confirm this hypothesis. Significant interaction between mood and situational

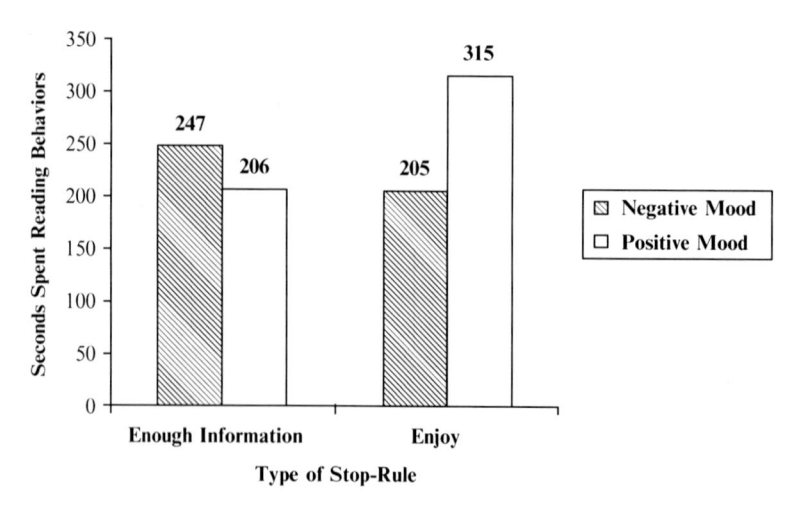

Fig. 23.1 Time spent reading behaviors as a function of mood and stop-rule

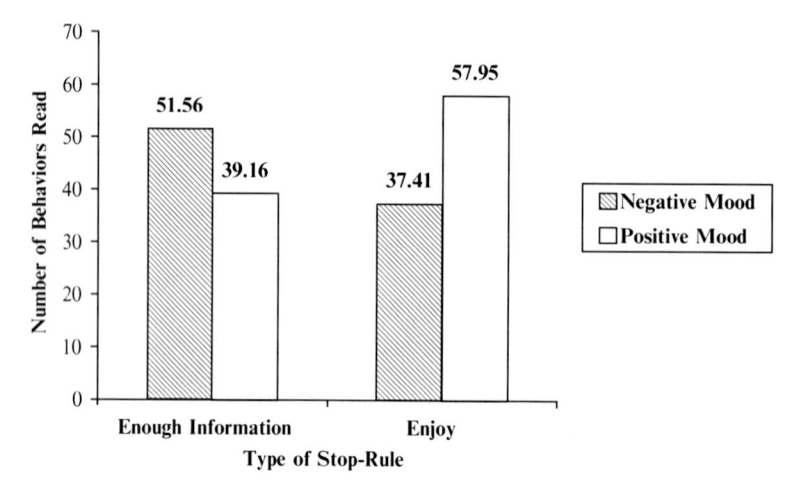

Fig. 23.2 Number of behaviors read as a function of mood and stop-rule

conditions (stop-rules) was revealed both in the case of the amount of time subjects spent on the task and in the number of cards the subjects read ($F(1,124) = 17.94$, $p < 0.001$ and $F(1,124) = 25.71$, $p < 0.001$, respectively). The amount of time subjects spent on the task differed as a function of their mood and their stop-rule (see Fig. 23.1). When given the sufficient (enough) information stop-rule, subjects in negative moods persisted longer than did those in positive mood. When given the enjoy stop-rule, subjects in positive moods persisted longer than did those in negative moods. Both of these pairwise comparisons were significant in planned contrasts ($p < 0.05$). The same pattern was obtained for the number of cards the subjects read (see Fig. 23.2). Subjects in positive moods took fewer cards than did subjects in negative moods when they were given the sufficient information stop-rule, while subjects in positive moods took more cards than did those in negative moods when given the joy stop-rule (the pairwise comparisons were significant in planned contrasts; $p < 0.05$). Thus, despite using a different mood induction procedure than the one employed by Martin et al. (1993),

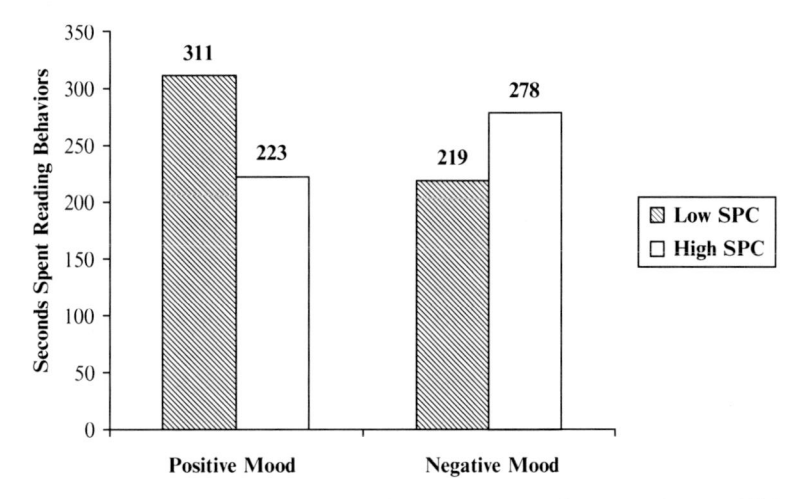

Fig. 23.3 Time spent reading behaviors as a function of mood and stimulation processing capabilities (SPC)

we replicated the pattern of results obtained in the original research. The results are consistent with the thesis that the context of the task changes the motivational implications of individual mood. Positive mood tells us to continue when it reflects our level of enjoyment but tells to stop when it reflects our level of goal attainment. Conversely, negative mood tells us to stop when it reflects our level of enjoyment but tells us to continue when it reflects our level of goal attainment. In addition, by referring the results to the way of information processing (systematic vs. heuristic), we can assume that more than a single type of information processing may be induced by a given mood.

On the assumption that the influence of moods on the course of activity depends not only on the situational conditions (stop-rules), but also on personality, temperamental and volitional traits were entered in our analyses. The results showed that time spent reading the behaviors is a function of mood and individual capabilities of stimulation processing ($F(1,80) = 7.45$, $p < 0.01$; see Fig. 23.3). The stimulation processing capabilities differentiate the amount of time subjects spent on the task in a positive mood. In a positive mood, subjects with low capabilities of stimulation processing, i.e., in accordance with the RTT, characterized by low endurance and high emotional reactivity, persisted longer than those with high capabilities of stimulation processing ($p < 0.05$). Moreover, the subjects with low capabilities of stimulation processing persisted longer in positive mood than in negative mood ($p < 0.05$). For the subjects with high capabilities of stimulation processing (i.e., characterized by high endurance and low emotional reactivity) no differences were found, whether their mood during the task was positive or negative. The same pattern was observed for the number of cards the subjects read ($F(1,80) = 8.85$, $p < 0.01$). Furthermore, it has been replicated in another study of ours, focusing on the motivational implications of mood, in which depressive tendencies were analyzed alongside temperamental traits. In addition, similar results were obtained in analyses that assessed emotional reactivity and endurance (the components of stimulation processing capabilities) separately. It turned out that mood only differentiates the number of behaviors the subjects read and the amount of time subjects spent on the task in the case of people with respectively high emotional reactivity and low endurance. To sum up, these results indicate that people with low stimulation processing capabilities are more dependent on their mood state than those with high stimulation processing capabilities. It seems especially interesting in the light of earlier research on the influence of mood and the need for cognition on a person's functioning (cf. Petty, Schumann, Richman, & Strathman, 1993), the findings of which suggest that moods may by more likely to influence the performance of low-need-for-cognition subjects when simple as opposed to effortful processing is involved. Bearing in mind the fact that the task performed by our subjects was not a cognitively demanding one (cf. Martin et al., 1993), and assuming a positive correlation between low need for cognition and low stimulation processing capabilities (according to RTT, low stimulation capabilities manifest themselves in the avoidance of stimulation, including cognitive stimulation relating to the fulfillment of one's need for cognition; cf. Strelau, 1996, 1998; Strelau & Zawadzki, 1995) our results seem to support the above suggestion. This allows us to presume that moods may be more likely to influence the performance of low-stimulation-processing subjects when they are engaged in a cognitively undemanding task (cf. Martin et al., 1993).

From the point of view of our research, a crucial question was whether temperamental and volitional traits change the result pattern typical for the context dependent effect of mood. Although no significant effects associated with the distinct temperamental or volitional traits were obtained (there were no significant three-way interactions among temperamental trait or volitional trait, valence of mood, and stop-rule), we did find that interaction between temperamental and volitional traits modifies the context-dependent motivational effect of mood. Our results showed that both the amount of time subjects spent on the task and the number of behaviors the subjects read are a function of mood, stop-rule, emotional reactivity (temperamental trait), and decision-related action vs. state orientation (volitional trait). In both cases, a significant four-way interaction ($F(1,112)=4.22$, $p<0.05$ and $F(1;112)=4.66$, $p<0.05$, respectively) was observed. Planned contrasts showed differences mainly in the "positive mood - enough information stop-rule" condition and the "negative mood and enjoy stop-rule" condition – in other words those that, in accordance with the general pattern of the context-dependent effect of mood, encourage heuristic information processing (Martin et al., 1993), i.e., shorten time spent reading behaviors and decrease the number of behaviors read. In the positive mood and enough information condition (and in the negative mood and enjoy condition, respectively), subjects with low emotional reactivity and state-orientation persisted longer and read more behaviors than subjects with low emotional reactivity and action-orientation ($p<0.05$), and than subjects with high emotional reactivity and state-orientation ($p<0.05$; see Fig. 23.4 for time spent reading behaviors). These findings may be interpreted in terms of internal "temperament-personality" coherence, i.e., the coherence between primarily biologically determined temperamental possibilities and other personality traits.

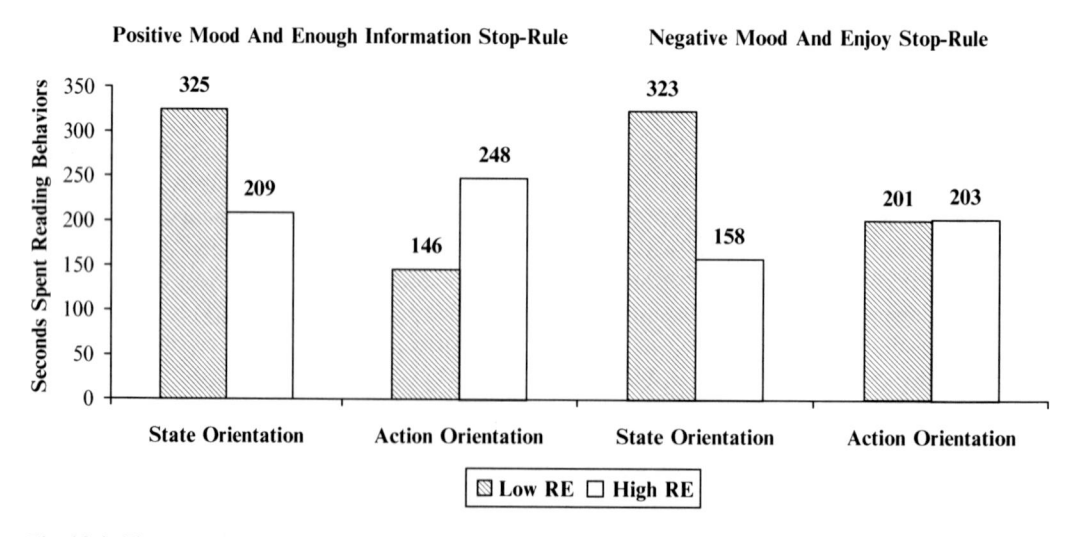

Fig. 23.4 Time spent reading behaviors as a function of mood, stop-rule, Emotional Reactivity (RE; temperamental trait) and Action vs. State Orientation (volitional trait)

To put it concisely: by "temperament-personality" coherence, we understand the consistency of temperamental traits relating to need for stimulation with other personality traits (such as, for example, volitional traits) relating to the fulfillment of one's need for stimulation, determined by the physiological mechanisms of temperament (Marszał-Wiśniewska, 1999, 2001). It is legitimate to use the term "internal coherence" both within the framework of the Transactional Model of Temperament (where temperament and personality are viewed as transactionally related components of a general stimulation regulation system; Eliasz, 1990; Eliasz & Klonowicz, 2001) and Strelau's (1996) RTT, according to which ineffective regulation of stimulation is partly caused by misfit between biologically determined temperamental possibilities and personality mechanisms as well as developed needs. We may therefore assume that the coexistence of low emotional reactivity (high need for stimulation) and action orientation or high emotional reactivity (low need for stimulation) and state orientation is a form of internal coherence. Correspondingly, one form of internal incoherence can be assumed to be a discrepancy between temperamental and volitional traits, i.e., low emotional reactivity (high need for stimulation) and state orientation or high emotional reactivity (low need for stimulation) and action orientation. Accordingly, the results we obtained allow us to infer that that the context-dependent effect of mood is weakened by intraindividual incoherence. In a positive mood, when given the *sufficient information* stop-rule, and in a negative mood when given *enjoy* stop-rule, incoherent subjects (i.e., low emotionally reactive and state orientated) persisted longer and read more behaviors than coherent subjects (i.e., low emotionally reactive and action oriented and high emotionally reactive and state oriented). In other words, in the above *mood-situation* conditions, incoherent subjects lengthen time spent reading behaviors and increase the number of behaviors read in contrast to coherent subjects. In fact, an interaction between valence of mood and stop-rule, consistent with "context-dependent effect of mood," was only reflected in the functioning of coherent subjects (for example, see Fig. 23.5). Although Fig. 23.5 only presents results concerning the amount of time subjects spent on the task, the same pattern was revealed for the number of behaviors subjects read. We obtained similar results in another study (Marszał-Wiśniewska & Zajusz, 2005), in which we focused on temperamental traits

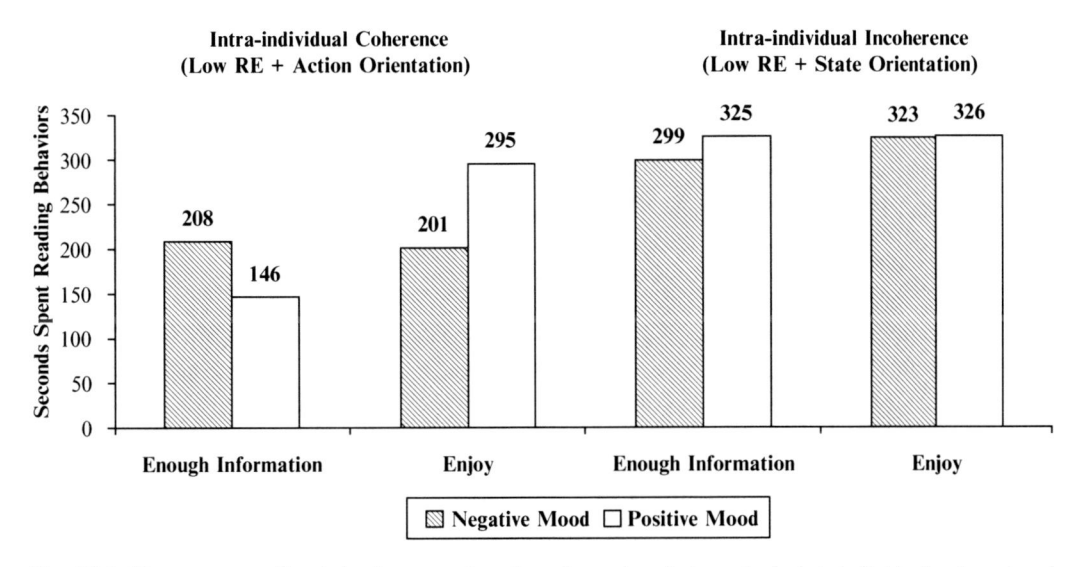

Fig. 23.5 Time spent reading behaviors as a function of mood and stop-rule in intraindividual coherent and incoherent subjects

and depressive tendencies. The predicted context-dependent motivational effects of mood occurred only for intracoherent subjects (low emotionally reactive and nondepressive), but not for incoherent subjects (low emotionally reactive and depressive). Bearing in mind the proven empirical relation between depression and state orientation (e.g., Kammer, 1994), these results are consistent with the ones discussed earlier.

According to *mood as input* model, moods are processed in an analogous holistic way. Individuals consider not only their moods but also some context information, and they do all of this concurrently. The obtained results seem to indicate that incoherent subjects experience greater difficulty with configural processing. Although according to Martin (2001) people can do it quickly and relatively effortlessly, we cannot exclude the possibility that the effectiveness of configural processing can be decreased by intraindividual incoherence of certain individual properties. This assumption is justified by results revealing the efficiency-reducing effects of discrepancy between temperamental and volitional traits (cf. Marszał-Wiśniewska, 1999, 2001). It has been shown, for example, that internal "temperament-volition" incoherence weakens the actualization of motivational control protecting a person from discouragement (e.g., by thinking about profits or advantages resulting from the execution of a goal; Marszał-Wiśniewska, 2001).

Summary and Closing Comments

Our research has confirmed the context-dependent motivational effect of mood. Despite the differences in our experimental procedure (different mood induction method), we have replicated the results achieved by Martin et al. (1993). The motivational implications of moods are mutable. Either positive or negative moods may be able to cause people to continue or stop cognitive processing. Positive moods tell people to continue in conditions that encourage striving for pleasure but tell people to stop in conditions stressing goal attainment. Negative moods tell people to stop in conditions that encourage striving for pleasure but tell people to continue in conditions stressing goal attainment.

What is more, it was shown that the influence of moods on the course of activity depends on temperamental and volitional traits. From among the temperamental traits, only those indicating individual stimulation processing capabilities, i.e., emotional reactivity and endurance, can differentiate the course of activity depending on the mood. Our research has demonstrated that persons with low stimulation processing capabilities are dependent on their mood state. Taking into account the fact that people with high stimulation processing capabilities are resistant to strong stimulation, including emotional stimulation, these results are not surprising. Is it, however, true both for cognitively easy and cognitively challenging tasks? Our research does not answer that question. The character of the experimental task leads to the more cautious conclusion that moods may be more likely to influence the performance of people with low stimulation processing capabilities when they are engaged in a cognitively undemanding task.

Interestingly, the research has revealed that the context-dependent motivational implications of mood are modified not so much by temperamental or volitional traits but more by their mutual relations. It emerged that the context-dependent effect of mood is weakened by internal "temperament-volition" incoherence (the inconsistency of temperamental traits relating to need for stimulation determined by the physiological mechanisms of temperament with volitional traits relating to the fulfillment of one's need for stimulation), and is strengthened by internal "temperament-volition" coherence (the consistency on the dimension: temperamental determined need for stimulation - volitional traits relating to the fulfillment of this need for stimulation). If, according to the *mood as input* model, the mood provides certain information in a given set of situational circumstances, our findings suggest that this information can vary depending on individual sets of temperamental and volitional traits.

Let us consider the following example: if a man is to finish his task when it stops being enjoyable, a negative mood tells him to do it ("I am experiencing a negative mood, which means I do not like this activity"). Such a course of reasoning, fully consistent with the general pattern of the context-dependent effect of mood, is, in the light of our results, true mostly for coherent people (low emotionally reactive and action oriented). However, it is not necessarily true for incoherent people (low emotionally reactive and state oriented). Our findings have revealed that incoherent participants interrupted their task later than coherent people. Perhaps for them, the negative mood can be interpreted differently (e.g., "I am experiencing a negative mood – this must mean that I am not sufficiently involved in my task, and I am going about it too carelessly. The pleasure will surely come later. It's worth the wait"). This assumption seems to make sense. Indeed, indecisiveness and hesitation can be construed to be the very essence of state orientation (especially decision-related state orientation). In this example, we referred to differences in the meaning of information. We cannot exclude the possibility that differences between internally coherent and incoherent people are connected with differing levels of configural processing efficiency, which we have already mentioned above. The hypothesis that the effectiveness of configural processing (i.e., processing target, context and mood information in an analogous holistic way, not separately; Martin, 2001) can be decreased by intraindividual incoherence of certain individual properties, is justified by findings showing the efficiency-reducing effects in the functioning people (including emotional and motivational functioning) with mismatched mechanisms of temperament and personality (e.g., Eliasz & Klonowicz, 2001; Marszał-Wiśniewska, 2001). Although more research will be necessary to confirm these assumptions, our results support the usefulness of the transactional approach for the analysis of individual differences pertaining to the informative function of mood. This approach encourages viewing psychological phenomena in terms of mutual codependencies between a person's various properties (personality traits, cognitive traits), various elements of the environment (situation), as well as mutual transactions between individual properties and situational aspects (e.g., Eliasz, 1990; Eliasz & Klonowicz, 2001; Matthews et al., 2003; Pervin, 1976). It also fits well with the current trend toward integrating "top-down" and "bottom-up" models by combining the dispositional approach with the situational one, as well as the differential approach with the process-oriented one. This type of research and analysis make it possible to showcase the limitations of general dependencies or regularities by demonstrating that some of them are only true for people with certain individual properties.

Convinced as we are that issue of the modifying role of personality in informative function of mood is a complex one, we believe that research in this area should continue. The results we have presented are certainly encouraging. When developing the *mood as input* model, Martin proposed that researchers assume that people process mood information in more complex, context-dependent way, rather than believe they do so in primitive way. We suggest that a further assumption should be made, one that is often overlooked by researchers analyzing the influence of mood on a person's functioning, yet obvious from the point of view of a psychologist of individual differences: the influence of moods on a person's functioning is interindividually diverse. It depends not only on the situation, but also on personality.

References

Abele, A., & Petzold, P. (1994). How does mood operate in an impression formation task? An information integration approach. *European Journal of Social Psychology, 24*, 173–187.

Allik, J., & Realo, A. (1997). Emotional experience and its relation to five-factor model in Estonian. *Journal of Personality, 65*, 625–647.

Allred, K. D., & Smith, T. W. (1991). Social cognition in cynical hostility. *Cognitive Therapy and Research, 15*, 399–412.

Baumeister, R. F., Bratslavsky, E., Finkenauer, C., & Vohs, K. D. (2001). Bad is stronger than good. *Review of General Psychology, 5*(4), 323–370.

Bless, H., Clore, G. L., Golisano, V., Rabel, C., & Schwarz, N. (1996). Mood and the use of scripts: Do happy moods really make people mindless? *Journal of Personality and Social Psychology, 71*, 665–678.

Bless, H., Mackie, D., & Schwarz, N. (1992). Mood effects on encoding and judgmental processes in persuasion. *Journal of Personality and Social Psychology, 63*, 585–595.

Bless, H., Schwarz, N., & Wieland, R. (1996). Mood and the impact of category membership and individuating information. *European Journal of Social Psychology, 26*, 935–959.

Bodenhausen, G., Kramer, G., & Susser, K. (1994). Happiness and stereotypic thinking in social judgment. *Journal of Personality and Social Psychology, 66*, 621–632.

Bower, G. H., Montiero, K. P., & Gilligan, S. G. (1978). Emotional mood as a context for learning and recall. *Journal of Verbal Learning and Verbal Behavior, 17*, 573–585.

Bradley, B. P., & Mogg, K. (1994). Mood and personality in recall of positive and negative information. *Behavior Research and Therapy, 31*, 137–141.

Burke, M., & Mathews, A. (1992). Autobiographical memory and clinical anxiety. *Cognition and Emotion, 6*, 23–35.

Carver, C. S., & White, T. L. (1994). Behavioral inhibition, behavioral activation, and affective responses to impending reward and punishment: The BIS/BAS scales. *Journal of Personality and Social Psychology, 67*, 319–333.

Ciarrochi, J. V., & Forgas, J. P. (1999). On being tense yet tolerant: The paradoxical effects of trait anxiety and aversive mood on intergroup judgments. *Group Dynamics: Theory, Research and Practice, 3*, 227–238.

Ciarrochi, J. V., & Forgas, J. P. (2000). The pleasure of possessions: Affective influences and personality in the evaluation of consumer items. *European Journal of Social Psychology, 30*, 631–649.

Clore, G. L. (1992). Cognitive phenomenology: Feelings and the construction of judgment. In L. L. Martin & A. Tesser (Eds.), *The construction of social judgments* (pp. 133–163). Hillsdale, NJ: Erlbaum.

Clore, G. L., Wyer, R. S., Dienes, B., Gasper, K., Gohm, C., & Isbell, L. (2001). Affective feelings as feedback: Some cognitive consequences. In L. L. Martin & G. L. Clore (Eds.), *Theories of mood and cognition* (pp. 27–62). Mahwah, NJ: Erlbaum.

Eliasz, A. (1990). Broadening the concept of temperament: From disposition to hypothetical construct. *European Journal of Personality, 4*, 287–302.

Eliasz, A., & Klonowicz, T. (2001). Top-down and bottom-up approaches to personality and their application to temperament. In A. Eliasz & A. Angleitner (Eds.), *Advances in research on temperament* (pp. 14–42). Lengerich: Pabst.

Eysenck, H. J. (1967). *The biological basis of personality*. Springfield, IL: Thomas.

Eysenck, M. W. (1992). *Anxiety: The cognitive perspective*. Hillsdale, NJ: Erlbaum.

Forgas, J. P. (1998). On being happy and mistaken: Mood effects on the fundamental attribution error. *Journal of Personality and Social Psychology, 75*, 318–331.

Gable, S. L., Reis, H. T., & Elliot, A. J. (2000). Behavioral activation and inhibition in everyday life. *Journal of Personality and Social Psychology, 78*, 1135–1149.

Goryńska, E. (2005). *Przymiotnikowa Skala Nastroju UMACL Geralda Matthewsa, A. Grahama Chamberlaina, Dylana M. Jonesa. Podręcznik* [Gerald Matthews', A. Graham Chamberlain's, Dylan M. Jones' mood adjective check list UMACL manual]. Warsaw: Pracownia Testów Psychologicznych Polskiego Towarzystwa Psychologicznego.

Gray, J. A. (1981). A critique of Eysenck's theory of personality. In H. J. Eysenck (Ed.), *A model for personality* (pp. 246–276). New York: Springer-Verlag.

Heubeck, B. G., Wilkinson, R. B., & Cologen, J. (1998). A second look at Carver and White's (1994) BIS/BAS scales. *Personality and Individual Differences, 25*, 785–800.

Higgins, E. T., & Rholes, W. S. (1976). Impression formation and role fulfillment: A "holistic reference" approach. *Journal of Experimental Social Psychology, 12*, 422–435.

Ingram, R. E., Bernet, C. Z., & McLaughlin, S. C. (1994). Attentional allocation processes in individuals at risk for depression. *Cognitive Therapy and Research, 4*, 317–332.

Isen, A. M., Shalker, T. E., Clark, M., & Karp, L. (1978). Affect, accessibility of material in memory and behavior: A cognitive loop? *Journal of Personality and Social Psychology, 36*, 1–12.

Jorm, A. F., Christensen, H., Henderson, A. S., Jacomb, P. A., Korten, A. E., & Rodgers, B. (1999). Using the BIS/BAS scales to measure behavioral inhibition and behavioral activation: Factor structure, validity and norms in a large community sample. *Personality and Individual Differences, 26*, 49–58.

Josephson, B. R., Singer, J. A., & Salovey, P. (1996). Mood regulation and memory: Repairing sad moods with happy memories. *Cognition and Emotion, 10*, 437–444.

Kammer, D. (1994). On depression and state orientation: A few empirical and theoretical remarks. In J. Kuhl & J. Beckmann (Eds.), *Volition and personality: Action versus state orientation* (pp. 351–362). Göttingen/Seattle: Hogrefe & Huber.

Kanfer, R., Dugdale, B., & McDonald, B. (1994). Empirical findings on the Action Control Scale in the context of complex skill acquisition. In J. Kuhl & J. Beckmann (Eds.), *Volition and personality: Action versus state orientation* (pp. 61–77). Göttingen, Germany: Hogrefe & Huber.

Kaufmann, G., & Vosburg, S. K. (1997). Paradoxial mood effects on creative problem solving. *Cognition and Emotion, 11*, 151–170.

Kaufmann, G., & Vosburg, S. K. (2002). Effects of mood on early and late idea production. *Creativity Research Journal, 14*, 317–330.

Kolańczyk, A. (2004). Stany uwagi sprzyjające wpływom afektu na ocenianie [States of attention fostering influences of affect on judgments]. *Studia Psychologiczne, 42*(1), 93–109.

Kuhl, J. (1985). Volitional mediators of cognitive-behavior consistency: Self-regulatory process and action versus state orientation. In J. Kuhl & J. Beckmann (Eds.), *Action control: From cognition to behavior* (pp. 101–128). New York: Springer-Verlag.

Kuhl, J. (1986). Motivation and information processing: A new look at decision making, dynamic change, and action control. In R. M. Sorrentino & E. T. Higgins (Eds.), *Handbook of motivation metacognition, foundations of social behavior* (pp. 404–434). New York: Guilford.

Kuhl, J. (1994). A theory of action and state orientations. In J. Kuhl & J. Beckmann (Eds.), *Volition and personality: Action versus state orientation* (pp. 9–46). Seattle, WA: Hogrefe & Huber.

Lyubomirsky, S., & Nolen-Hoeksema, S. (1995). Effects of self-focused rumination on negative thinking and interpersonal problem-solving. *Journal of Personality and Social Psychology, 69*, 176–190.

Marszał-Wiśniewska, M. (1999). *Siła Woli a Temperament [Will power and temperament]*. Warsaw: Wydawnictwo Instytutu Psychologii PAN.

Marszał-Wiśniewska, M. (2001). Self-regulatory abilities, temperament, and volition in everyday life situations. In H. Brandstätter & A. Eliasz (Eds.), *Persons, situations, and emotions: An ecological approach* (pp. 74–94). New York: Oxford University Press.

Marszał-Wiśniewska, M. (2002). Adaptacja Skali Kontroli Działania J. Kuhla (ACS-90) [Adaptation of action control scale by J. Kuhl]. *Studia Psychologiczne, 40*(2), 77–106.

Marszał-Wiśniewska, M., & Zajusz, D. (2005). *The informative function of mood: The modifying role of depressive tendencies and temperament.* Warsaw School of Social Psychology: unpublished data.

Martin, L. L. (2001). Mood as input: A configural view of mood effect. In J. P. Forgast (Ed.), *Feeling and thinking: The role of affect in social cognition* (pp. 135–157). New York: Cambridge University Press.

Martin, L. L., Abend, T., Sedikides, C., & Green, J. D. (1997). How would I feel if ...? Mood as input to a role fulfillment evaluation process. *Journal of Personality and Social Psychology, 73*, 242–253.

Martin, L. L., & Clore, G. L. (2001). *Theories of mood and cognition. A user's guidebook.* Mahwah, NJ: Lawrence Erlbaum Associates.

Martin, L. L., & Davies, B. (1998). Beyond hedonism and associationism: A configural view of the role of affect in self-regulation. *Motivation and Emotion, 22*, 33–51.

Martin, L. L., & Stoner, P. (1996). Mood as input: What we think about how we feel determines how we think. In L. L. Martin & A. Tesser (Eds.), *Striving and feeling: Interactions among goals, affect and self-regulation* (pp. 279–301). Hillsdale, NJ: Erlbaum.

Martin, L. L., Ward, D. W., Achee, J. W., & Wyer, R. S. (1993). Mood as input: People have to interpret the motivational implications of their moods. *Journal of Personality and Social Psychology, 64*, 317–326.

Matthews, G., Davies, D. R., & Holley, P. J. (1990). Extraversion, arousal, and visual sustained attention: The role of resource availability. *Personality and Individual Differences, 11*, 1159–1173.

Matthews, G., Deary, I. J., & Whiteman, M. C. (2003). *Personality traits.* Cambridge: Cambridge University Press.

Matthews, G., Jones, D. M., & Chamberlain, A. G. (1990). Refining the measurement of mood: The UWIST mood adjective checklist. *British Journal of Psychology, 81*, 17–42.

Mayer, J. D., Gaschke, Y. N., Braverman, D. L., & Evans, T. W. (1992). Mood-congruent judgment is a general effect. *Journal of Personality and Social Psychology, 63*, 119–132.

Mayer, J. D., McCormick, L. J., & Strong, S. E. (1995). Mood-congruent memory and natural mood: New evidence. *Personality and Social Psychology Bulletin, 21*, 736–746.

Niedenthal, P. A., & Setterlund, M. B. (1994). Emotion congruence in perception. *Personality and Social Psychology Bulletin, 20*, 401–411.

Nolen-Hoeksema, S. (1991). Responses to depression and their effects on the duration of depressive episodes. *Journal of Abnormal Psychology, 100*, 569–582.

Pervin, L. A. (1976). A free-response description approach to the analysis of person-situation interaction. *Journal of Personality and Social Psychology, 34*, 465–474.

Petty, R. E., Schumann, D. W., Richman, S. A., & Strathman, A. (1993). Positive mood and persuasion: Different roles for affect under high and low elaboration conditions. *Journal of Personality and Social Psychology, 64*, 5–20.

Pusateri, T. P., & Latane, B. (1982). Respect and admiration: Evidence for configural information integration of achieved and ascribed characteristics. *Personality and Social Psychology Bulletin, 8*, 87–93.

Reed, M. A., & Derryberry, D. (1995). Temperament and attention to positive and negative trait information. *Personality and Individual Differences, 18*, 135–147.

Richards, A., French, C. C., Johnson, W., Naparstek, J., & Williams, J. (1992). Effects of mood manipulation and anxiety on performance of an emotional Stroop task. *British Journal of Psychology, 83*, 479–491.

Rusting, C. L. (1998). Personality, mood, and cognitive processing of emotional information: Three conceptual frameworks. *Psychological Bulletin, 124*, 165–196.

Rusting, C. L., & Nolen-Hoeksema, S. (1998). Regulating responses to anger: Effects of rumination and distraction on angry mood. *Journal of Personality and Social Psychology, 74*, 790–803.

Schwarz, N. (1990). Feelings as information: Informational and motivational functions of affective states. In R. M. Sorrentino & E. T. Higgins (Eds.), *Handbook of motivation and cognition: Foundations of social behavior* (Vol. 2, pp. 527–561). New York: Guilford.

Schwarz, N. (2001). Feelings as information: Implications for affective influences on information processing. In L. L. Martin & G. L. Clore (Eds.), *Theories of mood and cognition: A user's handbook* (pp. 159–176). Mahwah, NJ: Erlbaum.

Schwarz, N., & Bless, B. (1991). Happy and mindless, but sad and smart? The impact of afective states on analytic reasoning. In J. P. Forgas (Ed.), *Emotion and social judgments* (pp. 55–71). London: Pergamon.

Schwarz, N., Bless, H., & Bohner, G. (1991). Mood and persuasion: Affective states influence the processing of persuasive communications. *Advances in Experimental Social Psychology, 24*, 161–199.

Schwarz, N., & Bohner, G. (1996). Feelings and their motivational implications: Moods and the action sequence. In P. M. Gollwitzer & J. A. Bargh (Eds.), *The psychology of action: Linking cognition and motivation to behavior* (pp. 119–145). New York: Guilford.

Schwarz, N., & Clore, G. L. (1983). Mood, misattribution, and judgments of well-being: Informative and directive functions of affective states. *Journal of Personality and Social Psychology, 45*, 513–523.

Schwarz, N., & Clore, G. L. (1988). How do I feel about it? The informative function of mood. In K. Fiedler & J. Forgas (Eds.), *Affect, cognition, and social behavior* (pp. 44–62). Toronto: C. J. Hogrefe.

Schwarz, N., & Clore, G. L. (1996). Feelings and phenomenal experiences. In E. T. Higgins & A. W. Kruglanski (Eds.), *Social psychology: A handbook of basic principles* (pp. 443–465). New York: Guilford.

Smith, S. M., & Petty, R. E. (1995). Personality moderators of mood congruency effects on cognition: The role of self-esteem and negative mood regulation. *Journal of Personality and Social Psychology, 68*, 1092–1107.

Strelau, J. (1993). The location of the regulative theory of temperament (RTT) among other temperament theories. In J. Hettema & I. J. Deary (Eds.), *Foundations of personality* (pp. 113–132). Dordrecht: Kluver.

Strelau, J. (1996). The regulative theory of temperament: Current status. *Personality and Individual Differences, 20*, 131–142.

Strelau, J. (1998). *Temperament: A psychological perspective*. New York: Plenum.

Strelau, J., & Zawadzki, B. (1995). The formal characteristics of behaviour – Temperament inventory (FCB – TI): validity studies. *European Journal of Personality, 9*, 207–229.

Szymura, B., & N cka, E. (2005). Three superfactors of personality and three aspects of attention. In A. Eliasz, S. E. Hampson, & B. de Raad (Eds.), *Advances in personality psychology* (pp. 75–90). Hove: Psychology Press.

Tice, D. M., & Baumeister, R. F. (1993). Controlling anger: Self-induced emotion change. In D. M. Wegner & J. W. Pennebaker (Eds.), *Handbook of mental control* (pp. 393–409). Englewood Cliffs, NJ: Prentice Hall.

Watson, D. (2000). *Mood and temperament*. New York: Guilford.

Watson, D., Clark, L., & Tellegen, A. (1988). Development and validation of brief measures of positive and negative affect. The PANAS scales. *Journal of Personality and Social Psychology, 54*, 1063–1070.

Worth, L. T., & Mackie, D. M. (1987). Cognitive mediation of positive affect in persuasion. *Social Cognition, 5*, 76–94.

Wright, W. F., & Bower, G. H. (1992). Mood effects on subjective probability assessment. *Organizational Behavior and Human Decision Processes, 52*, 276–291.

Chapter 24
Autobiographical Memory: Individual Differences and Developmental Course

Mary L. Courage and Mark L. Howe

The fate of our earliest autobiographical memories has been a matter of intense speculation for over a century (e.g., Freud, 1905/1953; Henri & Henri, 1895). The enduring interest in this topic has become stronger over the past few decades as important mental health and forensic questions on the accuracy and durability of adults' memories of childhood experiences have required answers. Coincident with (and partly as a consequence of) these questions, researchers have examined the fate of early memories in normally developing children and adults (for a review, see Howe, 2000). With this research direction, the emphasis shifted from the offset of infantile amnesia to its converse – the onset and development of autobiographical memory. We (e.g., Howe & Courage, 1993, 1997; Howe, Courage, & Edison, 2003; Howe, Courage, & Rooksby, 2009) have maintained that the necessary though not sufficient foundation for this achievement is the emergence of the cognitive self. The cognitive self refers to that objective aspect of the self that embodies the unique and recognizable features and characteristics that constitute one's self concept, or "me." This sense of the self contrasts with a different but related facet of the self that comprises the more subjective aspects of the self as a thinker, knower, and causal agent, or "I" (for a review see Courage & Howe, 2002). The cognitive self becomes stable at about 2 years of age and serves as a new organizer around which events can be encoded, stored, and retrieved as personal; that is, rather than being a memory for something that has happened, it is a memory of something that happened to "me." Subsequent developments in basic memory processes (e.g., encoding, storage, and retrieval) as well as language and other aspects of social cognition serve to elaborate and refine characteristics of the self and help to shape the nature and durability of autobiographical recall.

Much of this research has focused on the factors that underlie changes in autobiographical memory with age, although age alone is not necessarily the best predictor of what is recalled. More recent research indicates that a multiplicity of interactive individual and group differences in cognitive (e.g., self-concept, knowledge), biological (e.g., stress reactivity, gender), emotional (e.g., traumatic vs. nontraumatic; attachment status), linguistic (e.g., narrative skill), social (e.g., parent–child interaction styles) and cultural (e.g., self vs. community focus) factors also contribute to the recollection and reporting of personally experienced events. In this chapter we first provide some background on autobiographical memory research followed by a brief overview of the literature on the emergence of autobiographical memory in infants and young children. After that, we review

---

M.L. Courage
Memorial University, St. John's, NF, Canada

M.L. Howe (✉)
Department of Psychology, Lancaster University, Lancaster LA1 4YF, UK
e-mail: mark.howe@lancaster.ac.uk

some of the individual difference factors that affect the onset, durability, content, and fluency of autobiographical memory for routine and emotional events that are apparent in the recollections of older children and adults. We conclude with an integration of the two theoretical perspectives that have dominated the recent debate on the origin and development of autobiographical memory – the emergence of self versus the nature of sociolinguistic interactions between the child and others.

Some Background: Autobiographical Memory and Its Relationship to the Self

Autobiographical memory has been defined as memory for the events of one's life (Conway & Rubin, 1993). Such memories involve the who, what, where, when, and how of the personalized events that we experience as well as our emotional reactions to those events and our reflections on them. Autobiographical memory forms the personal life history that helps define the core of who we are. Although autobiographical memory can be considered a special case of event memory, it differs in the sense of personal involvement or ownership of the constituent events that it entails. Autobiographical memories are about specific events that happened to "me" at a particular time and in a particular place (e.g., one's first day at school) rather than generalized pieces of semantic knowledge about events related to the self (e.g., that one attended a particular school). The loss of this important self-memory relationship that occurs in amnesic conditions has devastating consequences for the individuals affected (e.g., Conway & Fthenaki, 2000), something that is most poignant in Alzheimer's disease.

Research on the durability and accuracy of autobiographical memories over time reveals both remarkable robustness and significant fragility (for a discussion see Bauer, 2007; White, 2002). In general, central components of events that are distinctive, emotionally charged (positively or negatively) (see Paz-Alonzo, Larson, Castelli, Alley, & Goodman, 2009), and that occurred within the age range of 10–30 years (or very recently) are recalled the best (i.e., the reminiscence bump) (see Rubin, Rahhal, & Poon, 1998). Those that are peripheral, routine, or that occurred before the age of 2 years (i.e., during infantile amnesia; for a review, see Howe, 2008) are recalled most poorly (e.g., Brewer, 1988; Usher & Neisser, 1993).

The importance of the relationship between autobiographical memory and the sense of self has long been recognized in the adult literature, and the theoretical perspectives on the nature of the relationship between them are diverse (e.g., for reviews see Beike, Lampien, & Behrand, 2004; Conway, 1996, 2005; Conway & Pleydell-Price, 2000; McAdams, 2001; Skowronski, 2004). Although a detailed review is beyond the scope of this chapter, suffice it to say that some have argued that autobiographical memory plays a central role in constituting the sense of self as an entity that is developed, expressed, and adapted through narrative construction and reconstruction of the past (e.g., McAdams, 1988; Singer & Salovy, 1993). As such, autobiographical memories contribute directly to the development and maintenance of a viable and stable self-concept through conversational exchanges with others about personally experienced past events. Alternatively, others contend that it is the self that directs the ways in which autobiographical memories are encoded, stored, and retrieved such that relevant autobiographical knowledge structures remain consistent with one's current self concept or "working self" goals (e.g., Conway & Pleydell-Price, 2000; Ross & Wilson, 2000). What both views express in common is that the relationship between the self and autobiographical memory is dynamic and interactive such that the self will construct (and reconstruct) the past and the past will construct (and reconstruct) the self. These diverging views on the primacy of the self in autobiographical memory are also reflected in the developmental literature on the onset and subsequent course of autobiographical memory (Howe et al., 2009).

Regardless of which view one prefers, a number of studies have shown that the best retained memories over the lifespan are those pertaining to the self, especially the self in times of transition (e.g., Conway, 1996). In particular, as the self goes through changes and stabilizes, events associated with those change points are well remembered (e.g., Csikszentmihalkyi & Beatie, 1979; Rubin et al., 1998). Although such findings highlight the importance of changes in the self in autobiographical memories, such transitions also represent unique occurrences in one's life, an idea that is consistent with other findings showing that the uniqueness of an event is one of the best overall predictors of recall generally (e.g., Howe, 2006a, 2006b; Howe, Courage, Vernescu, & Hunt, 2000) and autobiographical recall specifically (Betz & Skowronski, 1997; Brewer, 1988; Linton, 1979). Thus, it is clear that events about the self, particularly those that are personally consequential, transition defining, or otherwise distinctive, are best remembered autobiographically.

Although there is a large literature on the form and function of autobiographical memory in adults and older children (for reviews, see Conway, 2005; Conway & Rubin, 1993; Fivush & Haden, 2003; Rubin, 1996), there is far less empirical research on its early development. This is due in no small part to the circularity of how some researchers operationalize autobiographical memory, namely, that what constitutes a confirmation of an event memory as autobiographical depends on its verbal report as such by the individual. As infants and very young children are immature in both language production and in narrative skill, such confirmation is not possible and must, therefore, be inferred from their nonverbal behavior (e.g., reenactment of previously experienced events). Indeed, a number of researchers have shown that young children's nonverbal behaviors do provide a reliable and valid index of their autobiographical memory (see Howe et al., 2003). Once children become proficient language users and story tellers, their autobiographical memories become consistent with the verbal requirements in the definition of autobiographical memory above and can be assessed in more traditional ways. In what follows, we provide a brief overview of theories concerning the beginnings of autobiographical memory, ones that set the stage for interpreting and understanding the nature of individual differences in this all important memory system.

The Origin and Early Development of Autobiographical Memory

We contend that the necessary (though not sufficient) condition for the onset of autobiographical memory is the emergence of the cognitive self late in the second year of life (e.g., Howe & Courage, 1997; Howe et al., 2003). This achievement sets the lower limit on the age at which memories can be encoded, stored, and retrieved as personal. This fledgling cognitive self enables a new knowledge structure, whereby information and experience can be organized as autobiographical. Prior to the articulation of the self, infants learn and remember, but their experiences will not be recognized as specific events that happened to "me." After the onset of the cognitive self, adults' recollection of childhood events become more numerous and as with advances in memory more generally, are due to increases in storage maintenance and to strategic retrieval processes. Importantly, the onset of the cognitive self coincides roughly with the point at which studies have dated the onset of adults' earliest memories for significant life events (e.g., Eacott & Crawley, 1998; Usher & Neisser, 1993).

Research and theory on the nature and early development of the cognitive self have a long history (e.g., see Courage & Howe, 2002; Howe & Courage, 1993, 1997; Howe et al., 2003). Here, we provide a brief overview of the emergence of the objective, categorical (i.e., cognitive) aspect of the self described by William James (1890/1961) as the "me" component of the self and the one that we contend forms the cornerstone of autobiographical memory. Empirically, the first unambiguous sign of the emergent cognitive self occurs when the child recognizes that his or her mirror image is "me." This is assessed with a mirror self-recognition (MSR) test during which a dot of face paint is surreptitiously placed on the child's nose. The child who recognizes the marked image as "me" will touch his or her own nose as opposed to other mirror-directed reactions. Coincident with the onset of MSR, infants begin to show other signs of self-awareness such as embarrassment when confronted with their images and subsequently, at about 22 months of age, will provide a correct verbal label of the image (see Courage, Edison, & Howe, 2004). Although there is evidence from research with photo and video materials that infants can discriminate their facial and other body features from those of another infant from about 4 or 5 months (Bahrick, Moss, & Fadil, 1996; Legerstee, Anderson, & Schaffer, 1998; Rochat & Striano, 2002; Schmuckler, 1995), the level of self-knowledge inherent in these discriminations is unclear (but see Nielson, Suddendorf, & Slaughter, 2006).

However, visual self-recognition is only one facet of the self concept, one that can be readily operationalized for research with preverbal children. The self concept (and self-awareness) implies more than recognition of one's physical features and is a fundamental aspect of social cognitive development that has roots in the early weeks of life and continues to evolve throughout childhood and adolescence (for reviews see Butterworth, 1990; Cicchetti & Beeghly, 1990; Damon & Hart, 1988; Lewis, 1995; Neisser, 1993, 1995; Rochat, 1995, 2001). For example, Povinelli and his colleagues (Povinelli, Landau, & Perilloux, 1996; Povinelli, Landry, Theall, Clarke, & Castillo, 1999; Povinelli & Simon, 1998) have shown that MSR may be only the first step toward the recognition of the objective self as "temporally extended" and continuing to exist over time. They reported that 2-year-old children who were able to recognize themselves on-line, failed to do so after a brief delay and the provision of noncontingent feedback of themselves. It was not until about 5 years of age that children fully understood the relationship between the present self vis-a-vis the recent and more distant pasts. Regardless, most authors agree that the achievement of MSR is an important developmental milestone (Asendorpf & Baudonniere, 1993; Butterworth, 1990; Kagan, 1981; Lewis, 1994; Meltzoff, 1990; Neisser, 1993) and that a critical step is reached when children are able to represent themselves as an object of knowledge and imagination.

The key point to note from this is that at about the age of 2 years the cognitive self, a new organizer of information and experience, becomes available and facilitates the grouping and personalization of memories for events into what will become autobiographical memory. That childhood memories become more numerous after the onset of the self is expected given that (a) features associated with the self grow and expand, providing a larger base which encoding processes can reference, (b) improvements in the basic processes that drive memory (encoding, storage, and retrieval) that occur across development (attention, strategy use, knowledge, and metamemory) facilitate memory functioning in general (see Bjorklund, Dukes, & Brown, 2009), and (c) certain neurocognitive developments (e.g., prefrontal cortex) relevant to this expanding knowledge base (see Bauer, 2009) about the self occur in this time frame.

Alternative views of the onset and development of autobiographical memory set a different time course for this achievement. For example, Nelson, Fivush, and their colleagues (e.g., Fivush, 1997, 2009; Fivush, Haden, & Reese, 1996; Fivush & Reese, 1992; Nelson, 1996; Nelson & Fivush, 2004) adopting a sociolinguistic perspective contend that autobiographical memory follows from the child's ability to establish a "personal life story" in memory. This achievement occurs largely through conversations with adults and significant others with whom personal events and experiences are shared. As young children learn to talk about the past with adults, they begin to organize these events autobiographically in memory. Thus, the primary function of autobiographical memory is to develop a life history in time and to do that by telling others what one is like through narrating the events of the past. In this way, children learn both the form of reporting about past events and the social functions that talking about the past performs. However, this view of the emergence of autobiographical memory presupposes linguistic and narrative competence that is immature until the preschool years thus ruling out the infant and toddler periods (see also Pillemer & White, 1989). A related position has been taken by Perner and Ruffman (1995) who tied the emergence of autobiographical memory to general advances in metacognition, specifically to children's emerging theory of mind. They argue that event memory in very young children is based on "noetic" awareness or "knowing" something happened rather than on "autonoetic" awareness or "remembering" something happened (see Tulving, 1984). The transition from one to the other at about the age of four marks the beginning of autobiographical memory. Consistent with the sociolinguistic perspective, they believe that children's conversations with others (mothers in particular) serve as an important source of data for the development of their theory of the mind, in turn promoting the establishment of autobiographical memory.

Individual Differences in Autobiographical Memory

Research generated by these two disparate (but not mutually exclusive) theoretical perspectives on the substrates of autobiographical memory indicates that this achievement involves a complex and extended interaction between the individual, his or her developing perceptual and cognitive systems, and forces in the social (e.g., familial, institutional, cultural) environment in which he or she is growing up. Moreover, it has been the identification and examination of individual and group differences in these factors in relation to the early development of autobiographical memory that has informed the broader debate about its origin and subsequent course. Here, we focus primarily on the individual differences in autobiographical recollection that have emerged as a function of individual differences in the self, in sociolinguistic interactions between the child and significant others, and in their conjoint effects. We will also provide a brief review of what is known about individual differences in autobiographical memory for stressful events. Although such differences might logically be predicted from a host of biological (e.g., stress reactivity) cognitive (e.g., attention), and affective (e.g., attachment status) factors, they have remained elusive.

The Self

In the developmental literature, there have been few systematic studies of individual differences in the onset of the self or of the functional implications of early versus late self-recognition for autobiographical memory. Although cross-sectional studies indicate that there is a marked increase in children's success on the classic rouge task after about 18 months of age (e.g., Amsterdam, 1972; Asendorpf, Warkentin, & Baudonniere, 1996; Bullock & Lutkenhaus, 1990; Lewis & Brooks-Gunn, 1979; Lewis, Brooks-Gunn, & Jaskir, 1985) these studies also reveal substantial individual differences in the age of onset (i.e., from 15 to 24 months) (e.g., see Brooks-Gunn & Lewis, 1984). The origins of these individual differences have not been established conclusively. Although the onset of MSR has been related to mental age, attentiveness, and stress reactivity (e.g., Lewis & Brooks-Gunn, 1979; Lewis & Ramsay, 1997; Mans, Cicchetti, & Sroufe, 1978), a number of other factors (e.g., socioeconomic status, maternal education, gender, birth order, number of siblings) have been ruled out and others (e.g., attachment status, temperament, general cognitive ability) have provided inconclusive evidence (Brooks-Gunn & Lewis, 1984; DiBiase & Lewis, 1997; Lewis & Ramsay, 1997; Lewis, Sullivan, Stanger, & Weiss, 1989; Lewis et al., 1985; Schneider-Rosen & Cicchetti, 1991).

More recently, we (Courage et al., 2004; Howe et al., 2003) used a microgenetic approach to assess the development of the cognitive self in toddlers from 15 to 23 months of age. Data taken from cross-sectional samples showed the typical abrupt onset of MSR at about 18 months with a range from 15 to 23 months. The longitudinal data were generally consistent with this, but also indicated that within individual children, MSR emerged more gradually and showed wide variability in expression prior to becoming stable, a finding masked in the cross-sectional data. Moreover, regardless of age, infants who had achieved stable MSR performed better on a unique event memory task than did infants who had not achieved MSR. Consistent with these findings, Prudhomme (2005) found that the cognitive self was essential for early declarative, autobiographical memory and that children with an established cognitive self were not only better than those without a cognitive self on an elicited memory task, but they were also much more flexible when retrieving information. However, in a longitudinal study on this early self-memory relationship, Harley and Reese (1999) found that although individual differences in self-recognition skill (early vs. late MSR) at 19 months of age predicted toddler's independent memory for autobiographical events at 2.5 years, so too did parent–child interactional style during reminiscing about past events. In a subsequent follow-up study, Reese (2002) found that once children became language users, parent conversational style (i.e., high vs. low elaborative) and the child's language skill became increasingly important predictors of verbal memory reports. Collectively, these studies provide evidence that an early and stable self identity provides the foundation that facilitates the development of the autobiographical memory system which becomes elaborated with advances in language and narrative skill.

Sociolinguistic Interactions

As noted earlier, the sociolinguistic perspective on the onset of autobiographical memory sets a later beginning for this achievement and a developmental course rooted in language and social cognition. One of these perspectives has focused on the role of social interaction in the emergence of the autobiographical memory system, in particular, the sharing of experiences with others linguistically (Fivush, 2009; Fivush & Nelson, 2004; Fivush & Reese, 1992; Fivush et al., 1996; Hudson, 1990; Nelson, 1993). It is important to note however, that the functional aspects of memory should not be identified with its representational structure. Although autobiographical memories are typically reported verbally in a narrative format, their representation does not depend on language facility per se, but includes all of the encoding, storage, and retrieval processes that are integral to the formation of memories more generally (e.g., see Damasio, 1999; Howe, 1998b).

Research on the emergence of linguistic communication indicates that at about 2.5 years, most children begin to talk about specific events but that these early conversations are heavily "scaffolded" by adults (e.g., Hudson, 1990). By about 3 years, children assume more responsibility for talking about past events and begin to use the story or narrative form in these conversational interactions. However, although some of these advances begin to occur as early as 3–4 years of age, Nelson (1993) has maintained that "true" autobiographical memory is quite late to develop and may only be complete near the end of the preschool years. According to this sociolinguistic view, then, autobiographical memory is predicated on the development of rather sophisticated language-based representational skills, ones that do not emerge until children are about 5 or 6 years old. Once these skills are established, memories can be retained and organized around a life history, one that extends in time.

Because this sociolinguistic perspective places major importance on children's conversations about the past, particularly with their parents (and especially mothers), it is important to see what empirical support exists for the role of these conversations in children's autobiographical memory. Research conducted within this framework reveals that individual differences in the way that parents talk to their children about the past leads to individual differences in children's reporting of their own past experiences. In particular, two different parent conversational styles of talking with children have been identified. Parents who are "high-elaborative" provide a large amount of detailed information about past events. They elaborate and expand on the child's partial recall, ask further questions to enhance event detail, and correct the child's memory if necessary. In contrast, "low-elaborative" parents tend to repeat their questions over and over in an attempt to get a specific answer from the child, switch topics more frequently, and do not seek elaborative detail from the child's report. The high-elaborative style is associated with children's provision of more elaborative narratives, both concurrently and longitudinally (Haden, Hayne, & Fivush, 1997; Reese, Haden, & Fivush, 1993). There is evidence that adults' conversational styles do facilitate the richness and narrative organization of children's memory talk and in so doing plays an important role in children's developing ability to report autobiographical memories. However, it does not necessarily determine the content or accuracy of children's memory reports (see Fivush, 1994; Goodman, Quas, Batterman-Faunce, Riddlesberger, & Kuhn, 1994). In fact, reconstruction of events through conversations with others can lead to systematic distortions of memory details, ones that are congruent with the current beliefs and expectations of both conversational partners (e.g., Ross & Wilson, 2000). Thus, consistent with the memory literature more generally, the strategy of verbal rehearsal (elaborative or otherwise) can serve not only to reinforce and reinstate memories, but can also lead to errors in recall.

The Self, Sociolinguistic Interactions, and Culture

Although the origin of the cognitive sense of self (i.e., the "me" component) appears to be rooted primarily in cognitive development, its subsequent evolution into a mature self concept occurs in the context of family, society, and culture. As these contexts vary in their perspectives on the nature and importance of selfhood, their impact on the way that the self is apparent in the process of remembering and in what is remembered will also be expected to vary (e.g., Mullen, 1994; Wang, 2001). For example, in many Western cultures, a strong emphasis is placed on individuality and personal achievement that promotes the development and expression of an autonomous and independent self, one whose personal beliefs, attitudes, and goals are primary. In contrast, many Asian cultures place a greater emphasis on interpersonal connectedness, group solidarity, and achievement that promotes the development of a relational or a communal self. Such individuals tend to define themselves in terms of their social roles, duties, and responsibilities, and these come to comprise the critical features of one's sense of self. These different cultural self-constructs have a profound effect on individuals' perceptions and emotions during an ongoing event and consequently, the way that the event is encoded and subsequently remembered and recounted. Predictably, these different self-constructs will also affect caregivers' interactions with infants and children, such that they foster culturally appropriate self-systems that focus on autonomy or community as appropriate (e.g., see Wang & Conway, 2006).

Research on the onset, form, and content of autobiographical memories as a function of cultural differences in self construct indicate that there is a marked difference in the age at which adults in certain Eastern versus Western cultures can retrieve their earliest autobiographical memories. Typically, Americans and Europeans can date their earliest childhood memory from about 6 months earlier than do Asians and also show a greater age-linked increase in memory fluency (e.g., MacDonald, Uesiliana, & Hayne, 2000; Mullen, 1994; Wang, 2001; Wang, Conway, & Hou, 2004). These cultural differences suggest that the early appearance of an autonomous self-construct (as seen in Western cultures) might facilitate the formation of a unique and detailed personal history that contributes to the formation and organization of early events as having happened to "me." Moreover, the way in which the self is structured might further influence how autobiographical memory is represented, evaluated, and reconstructed over time (e.g., see Conway & Pleydell-Price, 2000). Individuals from cultures in which the focus is on an autonomous self might be more likely to encode and retrieve information that is related to the self than those from cultures who view the self as part of a community of selves who in turn may be attuned to information that forms collective or group-centred autobiographical memories. Indeed, research by Wang and colleagues (e.g., Wang, 2001; Wang, Leichtman, & White, 1998) has confirmed this. Compared to Chinese college students, American college students reported not only an earlier age of first memory but also reported more self-focused, specific, and emotionally elaborate content of those memories. Chinese students tended to provide briefer reports of general and routine collective events that were also emotionally neutral. Similar cultural differences in the content of autobiographical memories have been observed in preschool children (e.g., Han, Leichtman, & Wang, 1998; Wang, 2004; Wang & Leichtman, 2000). Interestingly, culture appears to affect not only the linguistic expression and content of event memories but also the perspective from which events that are encoded. In a recent study with Asian and American adults, Cohen and Gunz (2002) found that the contents of their memories of events were colored by their phenomenological experiences as members of these two cultures, with Asians being more likely than Americans to experience the self in memory from the perspective of the generalized other (e.g., to have more third person memories).

In the developmental literature, recent research shows that like the individual differences in children's conversational styles and their memory reports that correlate with parent talk, children in other cultures exposed to different conversational styles also differ in memory reporting. For example, some research shows that American mothers talk to their 3-year-olds about past events three times as often as do Korean mothers. Further, American children talk about past events more than do Korean children and as reported above, American adults report earlier autobiographical memories than do Korean adults (Han et al., 1998; Mullen, 1994; Mullen & Yi, 1995). Similar relationships were found between age of earliest memory, culture, and conversational interactions in a comparison group of Maori, Pakeha, and Asian adults living in New Zealand (MacDonald et al., 2000; Reese, Hayne, & MacDonald, 2008).

Interestingly, the different autobiographical memory profiles that have been related to cultural differences in self construct and sociolinguistic interaction are parallel to differences in autobiographical memory reports that have been observed as a function of gender. A consistent finding in the literature is that women have earlier first-memories than do men, although these differences are often small (e.g., Dudycha & Dudycha, 1941; Mullen 1994; Rubin, 2000). Moreover, women's autobiographical memory reports contain longer, more detailed, and more vivid accounts of their childhood experiences than do men's reports (e.g., see Bauer, 2007; Bauer, Stennes, & Haight, 2003; Fivush, 2009). Women and men also express different emotional content in their memory reports with anger, shame, guilt, and attachment issues common themes among women and concerns about competence, performance, achievement, and identity more commonly expressed by men (Cowan & Davidson, 1984; Dudycha & Dudycha, 1941). The origins of these individual differences between women and men in their reports of autobiographical events have typically been interpreted in a sociocultural framework. Particular emphasis has been placed on the different ways that boys and girls are socialized to talk about the past. Parents talk to their daughters more frequently and at greater length about the past than they do with their sons. They also place more emphasis on interpersonal and emotional aspects of experiences in conversation with their daughters when compared to the individual, emotionally neutral aspects that they emphasize with sons (for discussions see Bauer, 2007; Buckner & Fivush, 1998; Fivush, 1998). It is interesting to note that, in general, very few differences in nonverbal recall of events as a function of gender have been reported in studies with infants and preverbal children. This indicates that the gender differences that are apparent in later childhood and adulthood are not a function of memory processes per se but rather of the socialization of reminiscence that children learn through the particular characteristic narrative interactions that they experience in their familial and cultural environments.

Individual Differences in Autobiographical Memory for Emotional and Stressful Events

It is well known that stressful events lead to the release of adrenal stress hormones (e.g., catecholamines, glucocorticoids) and that these have been associated with alterations in memory and other cognitive processes (e.g., Cahill, 2000; Cahill & McGaugh, 1998). Although catecholamines and glucocorticoids have differential effects on the neural and neuroendocrine systems, they share an inverted-U shaped dose–response relationship such that small amounts have little effect on memory, moderate amounts can enhance memory, and large amounts can impair memory. What this means is that the psychobiology of stress is not straightforward and predicting whether memory in (or for) any particular stressful situation is enhanced or diminished depends on a host of factors such as the chronicity of the stress, its intensity, as well as on individual differences in reactivity to stress itself (see Howe, 1998a; Howe, Cicchetti, & Toth, 2006; Quas, Bauer, & Boyce, 2004).

Over a decade of research has failed to elucidate the nature of the relationship between stress and memory although a number of theories have been proposed, evaluated, and received mixed support. For example, Christianson (1992) suggested that during highly stressful events, memory for the central features of the event are strengthened whereas memory for the peripherals details is impaired. Alternatively, Deffenbacher, Bornstein, Penrod, and McGorty (2004) concluded from a meta-analysis of the stress and eyewitness memory literature that memory is best for moderately arousing stimuli and becomes poorer when high stress activates defensive processes. What is known is that both stress-induced catecholamines and glucocorticoids as well as the associated change in the delivery of oxygen to the brain that they precipitate, can modulate what gets stored in memory by altering (for better or worse) processes involved in encoding and consolidation of information and in the effectiveness of its retrieval (see Cahill & McGaugh, 1998; Howe, 1997, 1998a; Howe, Cicchetti et al., 2006; McGaugh, 2000). Further, there is evidence from nonhuman animal research that prolonged exposure to severe stress can precipitate damage to the developing brain (e.g., dendritic atrophy, neuronal death, hippocampal atrophy) in a variety of mammalian species and suggestive evidence of parallel effects in human adults and children (see Howe, Gicchetti et al., 2006; Nelson, 2007).

In part, the difficulty in establishing the relationship between stress and memory in humans is due to the fact that the results of the standard behavioral, self-report, physiological, and autonomic measures commonly used to measure stress rarely converge, especially in children (see Howe, Cicchetti et al., 2006). An additional and arguably larger difficulty is that a multitude of individual differences in cognitive (e.g., knowledge), temperamental (e.g., reactivity), social (parent–child interactions), emotional (attachment), and situational (interviewer support) factors will moderate the effects of the cascade of neuroendocrine reactions to the stressful situation (for reviews see Deffenbacher et al., 2004; Chae, Ogle, & Goodman, 2009; Christianson, 1992; Cordon, Pipe, Sayfan, Melinder, & Goodman, 2004).

As this issue has significant theoretical and practical implications, a large body of literature has evolved and some important facts have been established. Some of the strongest research has been done on children's memory for naturally occurring stressful events such as medical experiences (e.g., inoculations, voiding cystourethrogram fluoroscopy or VCUG), natural disasters (e.g., hurricanes, earthquakes), and sexual abuse and maltreatment (see chapters in Howe, Goodman, & Cicchetti, 2008). Interestingly, there is growing evidence from these studies that children's memory for stressful events operates in much the same way as memory for nonstressful events. Across the wide range methods, measures, situations, and ages employed in this research, it is generally the case that children's recall of the stressful events is quite accurate even after extended delays (but see Goodman, Batterman-Faunce, Schaff, & Kenney, 2002), though accuracy is compromised to some extent by the same reconstructive processes that affect memory more generally. For example, if an event (emotional or nonemotional) is personally distinctive or salient to the child, it will be better recalled than an event that is less so (e.g., Howe, 2006a, 2006b; Howe et al., 2000). In general, emotional or stressful events are distinctive, though ironically, cases of repeated maltreatment may lose their salience and appear to be recalled more poorly (see Howe, Cicchetti et al., 2006). Events that are personally experienced (e.g., venipuncture) generally leads to better recall than simple observation of the event (e.g., Gobbo, Mega, & Pipe, 2002). Finally, as noted above, a variety of parent–child interaction variables affect children's recall of emotional or stressful events in much the same way as they do for memory of nonstressful events. Parents who are highly elaborative in their conversational styles are likely to have children who provide more information in their reports of both stressful and nonstressful events (Fivush & Reese, 2002; McGuigan & Salmon, 2004). These parent–child exchanges not only provide an opportunity for rehearsal of the event but teach children how, what, and when to communicate their emotions and experiences to others.

It is interesting to note that high-elaborative parents are also more likely to have secure attachment relationships with their children than are low-elaborative parents (see Alexander, Quas, & Goodman, 2002; Fivush & Reese, 2002). Consistent with these parenting characteristics, children of parents who provided physical comfort after a stressful experience and who discussed the event with them before and after it occurred provided more accurate recall of the event than children whose parents did not (e.g., Goodman et al., 1994). Recently, the quality of the attachment between parent and child has emerged as an important intervening variable that moderates the child's response to a stressful situation and in so doing provides an insight into some of the contradictory findings about the role of stress and memory (e.g., see Alexander et al.; Chae et al., 2009).

According to Bowlby's (1969) theory of attachment, infants form internal working models about themselves and their caregivers through the routine, dynamic interactions that occur between them early in life. These stable representations of self and caregiver are used to interpret the intentions and actions of others, to form expectations of others' behavior in relation to them, and to regulate their own responses. Infants who experience secure attachment relationships as a result of sensitive, responsive, and consistent caretaking form internal working models that are coherent, organized, and facilitate the emerging sense of self. Those who develop insecure attachments develop internal working models that are disorganized and disruptive to a coherent sense of self. Secure and insecure (avoidant, anxious, disorganized) attachments in infancy and their associated internal working models are still evident in adulthood and continue to characterize their affective relationships with others and also their own parenting behavior (e.g., see Fraley, Garner, & Shaver, 2000; Simpson & Rholes, 1998). There is evidence that children and adults who are the product of secure attachments have better access to autobiographical memories (especially those with negative emotional content) and are less suggestible to misinformation than those with insecure attachments (e.g., see Alexander et al., 2002; Chae et al., 2009). Children with secure attachments also rate these memories as more positive and more vivid (Main, 1990; Wang & Conway, 2006). The mechanisms that might mediate the attachment-memory relationship are a focus of current research and include general factors such as the emerging sense of a secure self and the role that sociolinguistic interactions in secure and insecure dyads might play as well as more specific factors such as strategies that might facilitate (e.g., attentional focus) or interfere with (e.g., defensive exclusion) the encoding of emotional information and the presence of social support at the time of retrieval (for reviews see Chae et al., 2009; Paz-Alonzo et al., 2009).

Conclusion

To conclude, we have provided an overview of the empirical literature on the onset and developmental course of autobiographical memory and related it to two theoretical perspectives that have been prominent in trying to explain this achievement over the past few decades. One of these perspectives has focused on the emergence of the cognitive sense of self (e.g., see Howe et al., 2003) and the other has focused on sociolinguistic interactions that occur when children share their personal memories with others (e.g., see Fivush & Nelson, 2004). However, it may be that the debate over the importance of the cognitive self versus sociolinguistic factors in the development of autobiographical memory is more apparent than real. We continue to maintain that it is the emergence of the cognitive self late in the second year of life that launches autobiographical memory and that the coincident developments in language and social cognition that occur in the same time frame do not directly affect its onset. This time frame is consistent with the empirical literature on adults' recollection of childhood experiences, one that clearly shows that early memories are available from late in the second year of life.

Subsequent to the advent of the cognitive self, developmental advances in memory (e.g., encoding, storage, and retrieval processes; knowledge acquisition and reorganization), language, and social cognition assume increased importance as they provide for more stable memory representations as well as an expressive outlet for those recollections. As autobiographical memory continues to mature across childhood, what sociolinguistic theories make clear is that the language environment of the child, whether familial or cultural, serves to teach children that reporting memories is important, that such reports have a particular narrative structure and content, and a particular social and cognitive function. In that capacity, conversational exchanges not only provide a narrative structure for reporting events, but also serve to preserve (e.g., through rehearsal, reinstatement) or potentially alter (e.g., through reconstruction) memory records of personally experienced events.

We have also reviewed some of the individual differences in autobiographical memory and found that many of these were directly or indirectly related to individual differences in aspects of the self (e.g., early self-recognition, working self, cultural self) as well as to aspects of social cognition and socialization (e.g., parent conversational style, internal working models). These empirical findings have confirmed that autobiographical memory emerges first from an early sense of self that begins to appear in early infancy and becomes stabilized during the second postnatal year. Only at this time will familial, social, and cultural factors begin to affect the way in which the child perceives, thinks, and talks about him or herself and in so doing, further shapes the maturing self-concept and its expression in autobiographical memory.

References

Alexander, K. W., Quas, J. A., & Goodman, G. S. (2002). Theoretical advances in understanding children's memory for distressing events: The role of attachment. *Developmental Review, 22*, 490–519.
Amsterdam, B. (1972). Mirror self-image reactions before the age of two. *Developmental Psychobiology, 5*, 297–305.
Asendorpf, J., & Baudonniere, P.-M. (1993). Self-awareness and other awareness: Mirror self-recognition and synchronic imitation among unfamiliar peers. *Developmental Psychology, 29*, 88–95.
Asendorpf, J., Warkentin, V., & Baudonniere, P.-M. (1996). Self-awareness and other awareness II: Mirror self-recognition, social contingency awareness, and synchronic imitation. *Developmental Psychology, 32*, 313–321.
Bahrick, L., Moss, L., & Fadil, C. (1996). The development of visual self-recognition in infancy. *Ecological Psychology, 8*, 189–208.
Bauer, P. J. (2007). *Remembering the times of our lives: Memory in infancy and beyond*. Mahwah, NJ: Erlbaum.
Bauer, P. J. (2009). The cognitive neuroscience of the development of memory. In M. L. Courage & N. Cowan (Eds.), *The development of memory in infancy and childhood* (pp. 115–144). Hove, UK: Psychology Press.
Bauer, P. J., Stennes, L., & Haight, J. C. (2003). Representation of the inner self in autobiography: Women's and men's use of internal states language in personal narratives. *Memory, 11*, 27–42.
Beike, D. R., Lampien, J. M., & Behrend, D. A. (Eds.). (2004). *The self and memory*. New York: Psychology Press.
Betz, A. L., & Skowronski, J. J. (1997). Self-events and other-events: Temporal dating and event memory. *Memory and Cognition, 25*, 701–714.
Bjorklund, D. F., Dukes, C., & Brown, R. D. (2009). The development of memory strategies. In M. L. Courage & N. Cowan (Eds.), *The development of memory in infancy and childhood* (pp. 145–175). Hove, UK: Psychology Press.
Bowlby, J. (1969). *Attachment and loss* (Vol. 1). New York: Basic Books.
Brewer, W. F. (1988). Memory for randomly sampled autobiographical events. In U. Neisser & E. Winograd (Eds.), *Remembering reconsidered: Ecological and traditional approaches to the study of memory* (pp. 21–90). New York: Cambridge University Press.
Brooks-Gunn, J., & Lewis, M. (1984). The development of early self-recognition. *Developmental Review, 4*, 215–239.
Buckner, J. P., & Fivush, R. (1998). Gender and self in children's autobiographical narratives. *Applied Cognitive Psychology, 12*, 407–429.

Bullock, M., & Lutkenhaus, P. (1990). Who am I? Self-understanding in toddlers. *Merrill-Palmer Quarterly, 36*, 217–238.

Butterworth, G. E. (1990). Self-perception in infancy. In D. Cicchetti & M. Beeghly (Eds.), *The self in transition: Infancy to childhood* (pp. 119–137). Chicago: University of Chicago Press.

Cahill, L. (2000). Modulation of long-term memory storage in humans by emotional arousal: Adrenergic activation and the amygdale. In J. P. Aggleton (Ed.), *The amygdala: A functional analysis* (pp. 425–445). Oxford: Oxford University Press.

Cahill, L., & McGaugh, J. L. (1998). Mechanisms of emotional arousal and lasting declarative memory. *Trends in Neuroscience, 21*, 294–299.

Chae, Y., Ogle, C. M., & Goodman, G. S. (2009). Remembering traumatic childhood experiences: An attachment theory perspective. In J. A. Quas & R. Fivush (Eds.), *Emotion and memory in development: Biological, cognitive, and social considerations* (pp. 3-27). New York: Oxford University Press.

Christianson, S.-A. (1992). Emotional stress and eyewitness memory: A critical overview. *Psychological Bulletin, 112*, 284–309.

Cicchetti, D., & Beeghly, M. (Eds.). (1990). *The self in transition: Infancy to childhood*. Chicago: University of Chicago Press.

Cohen, D., & Gunz, A. (2002). As seen by the other ...: Perspectives on the self in the memories and emotional perceptions of easterners and westerners. *Psychological Science, 13*, 55–59.

Conway, M. A. (1996). Autobiographical knowledge and autobiographical memories. In D. Rubin (Ed.), *Remembering our past: Studies in autobiographical memory* (pp. 67–93). New York: Cambridge University Press.

Conway, M. A. (2005). Memory and the Self. *Journal of Memory and Language, 53*, 594–628.

Conway, M. A., & Fthenaki, A. (2000). Disruption and loss of autobiographical memory. In L. S. Cermak (Ed.), *Handbook of neuropsychology (2nd edition): Memory and its disorders* (pp. 281–312). Amsterdam: Elsevier.

Conway, M. A., & Pleydell-Price, C. W. (2000). The construction of autobiographical memories in the self-memory system. *Psychological Review, 107*, 261–288.

Conway, M. A., & Rubin, D. C. (1993). The structure of autobiographical memory. In A. F. Collins, S. E. Gathercole, M. A. Conway, & P. E. Morris (Eds.), *Theories of memory* (pp. 103–137). Hillsdale, NJ: Erlbaum.

Cordon, I. M., Pipe, M.-E., Sayfan, L., Melinder, A., & Goodman, G. S. (2004). Memory for traumatic experiences in early childhood. *Developmental Review, 24*, 101–132.

Courage, M. L., Edison, S., & Howe, M. L. (2004). Variability in the early development of visual self-recognition. *Infant Behavior and Development, 27*, 509–532.

Courage, M. L., & Howe, M. L. (2002). From infant to child: The dynamics of cognitive change in the second year of life. *Psychological Bulletin, 128*, 250–277.

Cowan, N., & Davidson, G. (1984). Salient childhood memories. *The Journal of Genetic Psychology, 145*, 101–107.

Csikszentmihalkyi, M., & Beatie, O. (1979). Life themes: A theoretical and empirical exploration of their origins and effects. *Journal of Humanistic Psychology, 19*, 45–63.

Damasio, A. (1999). *The feeling of what happens: Body and emotion in the making of consciousness*. New York: Harcourt Brace & Company.

Damon, W., & Hart, D. (1988). *Self-understanding in childhood and adolescence*. Cambridge, England: Cambridge University Press.

Deffenbacher, K. A., Bornstein, B. H., Penrod, S. D., & McGorty, E. K. (2004). A meta-analytic review of the effects of high stress on eyewitness memory. *Law and Human Behavior, 28*, 687–706.

DiBiase, R., & Lewis, M. (1997). The relation between temperament and embarrassment. *Cognition and Emotion, 11*, 259–271.

Dudycha, G. L., & Dudycha, M. M. (1941). Childhood memories: A review of the literature. *Psychological Bulletin, 36*, 668–682.

Eacott, M. J., & Crawley, R. A. (1998). The offset of childhood amnesia: Memory for events that occurred before age 3. *Journal of Experimental Psychology: General, 127*, 22–33.

Fivush, R. (1994). Young children's event recall: Are memories constructed through discourse? *Consciousness and Cognition, 3*, 356–373.

Fivush, R. (1997). Event memory in early childhood. In N. Cowan (Ed.), *The development of memory in childhood* (pp. 139–161). Hove, England: Psychology Press.

Fivush, R. (1998). Gender narratives: Elaboration, structure and emotion in parent-child reminiscing across the preschool years. In C. Thompson, D. Herrmann, D. Bruce, J. D. Payme, & M. Toglia (Eds.), *Autobiographical memory: Theoretical and applied perspectives* (pp. 79–103). Mahwah, NJ: Erlbaum.

Fivush, R. (2009). Sociocultural perspectives on autobiographical memory. In M. L. Courage & N. Cowan (Eds.), *The development of memory in infancy and childhood* (pp. 283–301). Hove, UK: Psychology Press.

Fivush, R., & Haden, C. A. (2003). *Autobiographical memory and the construction of a narrative self*. Mahwah, NJ: Erlbaum.

Fivush, R., Haden, C. A., & Reese, E. (1996). Remembering, recounting, and reminiscing: The development of autobiographical memory in social context. In D. Rubin (Ed.), *Remembering our past: Studies in autobiographical memory* (pp. 341–359). Cambridge, MA: Cambridge University Press.

Fivush, R., & Nelson, K. (2004). Culture and language in the emergence of autobiographical memory. *Psychological Science, 15*, 573–577.

Fivush, R., & Reese, E. (1992). The social construction of autobiographical memory. In M. A. Conway, D. C. Rubin, H. Spinnler, & W. A. Wagenaar (Eds.), *Theoretical perspectives on autobiographical memory* (pp. 115–132). Dordrecht, The Netherlands: Kluwer.

Fivush, R., & Reese, E. (2002). Reminiscing and relating: The development of parent-child talk about the past. In J. D. Webster & B. K. Haight (Eds.), *Critical advances in reminiscence work* (pp. 109–122). New York: Springer.

Fraley, R. C., Garner, J. P., & Shaver, P. R. (2000). Adult attachment and the defensive regulation of attention and memory: Examining the role of preemptive and postemptive defensive processes. *Journal of Personality and Social Psychology, 79*, 816–826.

Freud, S. (1905/1953). Three essays on the theory of sexuality. In J. Strachey (Ed.), *The standard edition of the complete psychological works of Sigmund Freud* (Vol. 7, pp. 135–243). London: Hogarth Press. (Original work published 1905)

Gobbo, C., Mega, C., & Pipe, M.-E. (2002). Does the nature of the experience influence children's suggestibility? A study of children's event memory. *Journal of Experimental Child Psychology, 81*, 502–530.

Goodman, G. S., Batterman-Faunce, J. M., Schaaf, J. M., & Kenney, R. (2002). Nearly 4 years after an event: Children's eyewitness memory and adults' perceptions of children's accuracy. *Child Abuse and Neglect, 26*, 849–884.

Goodman, G. S., Quas, J. A., Batterman-Faunce, J. M., Riddlesberger, M. M., & Kuhn, J. (1994). Predictors of accurate and inaccurate memories of traumatic events experienced in childhood. *Consciousness and Cognition, 3*, 269–294.

Haden, C. A., Haine, R. A., & Fivush, R. (1997). Developing narrative structure in parent-child reminiscing across the preschool years. *Developmental Psychology, 33*, 295–307.

Han, J. J., Leitchman, M. D., & Wang, Q. (1998). Autobiographical memory in Korean, Chinese, and American Children. *Developmental Psychology, 34*, 701–713.

Harley, K., & Reese, E. (1999). Origins of autobiographical memory. *Developmental Psychology, 35*, 1338–1348.

Henri, V., & Henri, C. (1895). On earliest recollections of childhood. *Psychological Review, 2*, 215–216.

Howe, M. L. (1997). Children's memory for traumatic experiences. *Learning and Individual Differences, 9*, 153–174.

Howe, M. L. (1998a). Individual differences in factors that modulate storage and retrieval of traumatic memories. *Development and Psychopathology, 10*, 681–698.

Howe, M. L. (1998b). Language is never enough: Memories are more than words reveal. *Applied Cognitive Psychology, 12*, 475–481.

Howe, M. L. (2000). *The fate of early memories: Developmental science and the retention of childhood experiences*. Washington, DC: American Psychological Association.

Howe, M. L. (2006a). Developmental invariance in distinctiveness effects in memory. *Developmental Psychology, 42*, 1193–1205.

Howe, M. L. (2006b). Distinctiveness effects in children's memory. In R. R. Hunt & J. Worthen (Eds.), *Distinctiveness and memory* (pp. 237–257). New York: Oxford University Press.

Howe, M. L. (2008). The nature of infantile amnesia. In J. H. Byrne (Ed.), *Learning and memory: a comprehensive reference. Volume 1: Learning theory and behavior* (pp. 287–297). London, UK: Elsevier.

Howe, M. L., Cicchetti, D., & Toth, S. L. (2006). Children's basic memory processes, stress, and maltreatment. *Development and Psychopathology, 18*, 759–769.

Howe, M. L., & Courage, M. L. (1993). On resolving the enigma of infantile amnesia. *Psychological Bulletin, 113*, 305–326.

Howe, M. L., & Courage, M. L. (1997). The emergence and early development of autobiographical memory. *Psychological Review, 104*, 499–523.

Howe, M. L., Courage, M. L., & Edison, S. E. (2003). When autobiographical memory begins. *Developmental Review, 23*, 471–494.

Howe, M. L., Courage, M. L., & Rooksby, M. (2009). The genesis and development of autobiographical memory. In M. L. Courage & N. Cowan (Eds.), *The development of memory in infancy and childhood* (pp. 177–196). Hove, UK: Psychology Press.

Howe, M. L., Courage, M. L., Vernescu, R., & Hunt, M. (2000). Distinctiveness effects in children's long-term retention. *Developmental Psychology, 36*, 778–792.

Howe, M. L., Goodman, G. S., & Cicchetti, D. (Eds.). (2008). *Stress, trauma and children's memory development: Neurobiological, cognitive, clinical and legal perspectives*. New York: Oxford University Press.

Howe, M. L., Toth, S., & Cicchetti, D. (2006). Memory and developmental psychopathology. In D. Cicchetti & D. Cohen (Eds.), *Developmental psychopathology: Developmental neuroscience* (2nd ed., Vol. 2. pp. 629–655). New York: Wiley.

Hudson, J. A. (1990). Constructive processing in children's event memory. *Developmental Psychology, 26*, 180–187.

James, W. (1890/1961). *The principles of psychology*. New York: Henry Holt.

Kagan, J. (1981). *The second year: The emergence of self awareness*. Cambridge, MA: Harvard University Press.

Legerstee, M., Anderson, D., & Schaffer, A. (1998). Five- and eight-month-old infants recognize their faces and voices as familiar and social stimuli. *Child Development, 69*, 37–50.

Lewis, M. (1994). Myself and me. In S. Parker, R. Mitchell, & M. Boccia (Eds.), *Self awareness in animals and humans: Developmental perspectives* (pp. 20–34). Cambridge, MA: Cambridge University Press.

Lewis, M. (1995). Aspects of the self: From systems to ideas. In P. Rochat (Ed.), *The self in infancy: Theory and research* (pp. 95–115). Amsterdam: Elsevier.

Lewis, M., & Brooks-Gunn, J. (1979). *Social cognition and the acquisition of self*. New York: Plenum.

Lewis, M., Brooks-Gunn, J., & Jaskir, J. (1985). Individual differences in early visual self-recognition. *Developmental Psychology, 21*, 1181–1187.

Lewis, M., & Ramsay, D. S. (1997). Stress reactivity and self-recognition. *Child Development, 68*(4), 621–629.

Lewis, M., Sullivan, M., Stanger, C., & Weiss, M. (1989). Self-development and self conscious emotions. *Child Development, 60*, 146–156.

Linton, M. (1979). Real-world memory after six years: An in vivo study of very long-term memory. In M. M. Gruneberg, P. E. Morris, & R. N. Sykes (Eds.), *Practical aspects of memory* (pp. 69–76). New York: Academic.

MacDonald, S., Uesiliana, K., & Haynes, H. (2000). Cross-cultural and gender differences in childhood amnesia. *Memory, 8*, 365–376.

Main, M. (1990). Cultural studies of attachment organization: Recent studies, changing methodologies, and the concept of conditional strategies. *Human Development, 33*, 48–61.

Mans, L., Cicchetti, D., & Sroufe, L. A. (1978). Mirror reaction of Down's syndrome infants and toddlers: Cognitive underpinnings of self-recognition. *Child Development, 49*, 1247–1250.

McAdams, D. P. (1988). *Power, intimacy, and the life story: Personological inquiries into identity*. New York: Guilford.

McAdams, D. P. (2001). The psychology of life stories. *Review of General Psychology, 5*, 100–122.

McGaugh, J. L. (2000). Memory: A century of consolidation. *Science, 287*, 248–251.

McGuigan, F., & Salmon, K. (2004). Time to talk: The influence of the timing of child-adult talk on children's event memory. *Child Development, 75*, 669–686.

Meltzoff, A. N. (1990). Toward a developmental cognitive science: The implications of cross-modal matching and imitation for the development of representation and memory in infants. In A. Diamond (Ed.), *The development and neural basis of higher cognitive functions* (Vol. 608, pp. 1–29). New York: New York Academy of Sciences.

Mullen, M. K. (1994). Earliest recollections of childhood: A demographic analysis. *Cognition, 52*, 55–79.

Mullen, M. K., & Yi, S. (1995). The cultural context of talk about the past: Implications for the development of autobiographical memory. *Cognitive Development, 10*, 407–419.

Neisser, U. (Ed.). (1993). *The perceived self*. New York: Cambridge University Press.

Neisser, U. (1995). Criteria for an ecological self. In P. Rochat (Ed.), *The self in infancy: Theory and research* (pp. 17–33). Amsterdam: Elsevier.

Nelson, C. A. (2007). A neurobiological perspective on early human deprivation. *Child Development Perspectives 1*, 13–18.

Nelson, K. (1993). The psychological and social origins of autobiographical memory. *Psychological Science, 4*, 7–14.

Nelson, K. (1996). *Language in cognitive development: The emergence of the mediated mind*. New York: Cambridge University Press.

Nelson, K., & Fivush, R. (2004). The emergence of autobiographical memory: A social cultural developmental theory. *Psychological Review, 111*, 486–511.

Nielson, M., Suddendorf, T., & Slaughter, V. (2006). Mirror self-recognition beyond the face. *Child Development, 77*, 1176–1185.

Paz-Alonzo, P. M., Larson, R. P., Castelli, P., Alley, D., & Goodman, G. S. (2009). Memory development: Emotion, stress, and trauma. In M. L. Courage & N. Cowan (Eds.), *The development of memory in infancy and childhood* (pp. 197–239). Hove, UK: Psychology Press.

Perner, J., & Ruffman, T. (1995). Episodic memory and autonoetic consciousness: Developmental evidence and a theory of childhood amnesia. *Journal of Experimental Child Psychology, 59*, 516–548.

Pillemer, D. B., & White, S. H. (1989). Childhood events recalled by children and adults. In H. W. Reese (Ed.), *Advances in child development and behavior* (Vol. 21, pp. 297–340). San Diego, CA: Academic.

Povinelli, D. J., Landau, K. R., & Perilloux, H. K. (1996). Self-recognition in young children using delayed versus live feedback: Evidence of a developmental asynchrony. *Child Development, 67*, 1540–1554.

Povinelli, D., Landry, A. M., Theall, L. A., Clarke, B. R., & Castile, C. M. (1999). Development of young children's understanding that the recent past is causally bound to the present. *Developmental Psychology, 35*, 1426–1439.

Povinelli, D. J., & Simon, B. B. (1998). Young children's understanding of briefly versus extremely delayed images of the self: Emergence of the autobiographical stance. *Developmental Psychology, 34*, 188–194.

Prudhomme, N. (2005). Early declarative memory and self-concept. *Infant Behavior and Development, 28*, 132–144.

Quas, J. A., Bauer, A., & Boyce, W. T. (2004). Physiological reactivity, social support, and memory in early childhood. *Child Development, 75*, 797–814.

Reese, E. (2002). A model of the origins of autobiographical memory. In J. Fagen & H. Hayne (Eds.), *Progress in infancy research* (Vol. 2, pp. 124–142). Mahwah, NJ: Erlbaum.

Reese, E., Haden, C. A., & Fivush, R. (1993). Mother-child conversations about the past: Relationships of style and memory over time. *Cognitive Development, 8*, 403–430.

Reese, E., Hayne, H., & MacDonald, S. (2008). Looking back to the future: Maori and Pakeha mother-child birth stories. *Child Development, 79*, 114–125.

Rochat, P. (1995). Early objectification of the self. In P. Rochat (Ed.), *The self in infancy: Theory and research* (pp. 53–71). Amsterdam: Elsevier.

Rochat, P. (2001). Origins of self-concept. In J. G. Bremner & A. Fogel (Eds.), *Blackwell handbook of infant development* (pp. 125–140). Oxford: Basil Blackwell.

Rochat, P., & Striano, T. (2002). Who is in the mirror? Self-other discrimination in specular images by four- and nine-month-old infants. *Child Development, 73*, 35–46.

Ross, M., & Wilson, A. E. (2000). Constructing and appraising past selves. In D. L. Schacter & E. Scarry (Eds.), *Memory, brain, and belief* (pp. 231–259). Cambridge, MA: Harvard University Press.

Rubin, D. C. (Ed.). (1996). *Remembering our past: Studies in autobiographical memory*. Cambridge: Cambridge University Press.

Rubin, D. C. (2000). The distribution of early childhood memories. *Memory, 8*, 265–269.

Rubin, D. C., Rahhal, T. A., & Poon, L. W. (1998). Things learned in early adulthood are remembered best. *Memory and Cognition, 26*, 3–19.

Schmuckler, M. A. (1995). Self-knowledge of body position: Integration of perceptual and action system information. In P. Rochat (Ed.), *The self in infancy: Theory and research* (pp. 221–242). Amsterdam: North Holland-Elsevier.

Schneider-Rosen, K., & Cicchetti, D. (1991). Early self-knowledge and emotional development: Visual self-recognition and affective reactions to mirror self-images in maltreated and non-maltreated toddlers. *Developmental Psychology, 27*, 471–478.

Simpson, J. A., & Rholes, W. S. (1998). *Attachment theory and close relationships*. New York: Guilford.

Singer, J. A., & Salovy, P. (1993). *The remembered self: Emotion and memory in personality*. New York: The Free.

Skowronski, J. J. (2004). Giving sight and voice to the blind mutes: An overview of theoretical ideas in autobiographical memory. *Social Cognition, 22*, 451–459.

Suddendorf, T. (1999). Children's understanding of the relation between delayed video representation and current reality: A test for self-awareness? *Journal of Experimental Child Psychology, 72*, 157–176.

Tulving, E. (1984). Precis of elements of episodic memory. *Behavioral and Brain Sciences, 7*, 223–238.

Usher, J. A., & Neisser, U. (1993). Childhood amnesia and the beginnings of memory for four early life events. *Journal of Experimental Psychology: General, 122*, 155–165.

Wang, Q. (2001). Cultural effects on adults' earliest childhood recollection and self-description: Implications for the relation between memory and self. *Journal of Personality and Social Psychology, 81*, 220–233.

Wang, Q. (2004). The emergence of cultural self construct: Autobiographical memory and self-description in American and Chinese children. *Developmental Psychology, 40*, 3–15.

Wang, Q., & Conway, M. A. (2006). Autobiographical memory, self, and culture. In L.-G. Nilsson & N. Ohta (Eds.), *Memory and society: Psychological perspectives* (pp. 9–27). Hove, UK: Psychology Press.

Wang, Q., Conway, M. A., & Hou, Y. (2004). Infantile amnesia: A cross-cultural investigation. *Cognitive Sciences, 1*, 123–135.

Wang, Q., & Leichtman, M. D. (2000). Same beginnings, different stories: A comparison of American and Chinese children's narratives. *Child Development, 71*, 1329–1346.

Wang, Q., Leichtman, M. D., & White, S. H. (1998). Childhood memory and self description in young Chinese adults: The impact of growing up an only child. *Cognition, 69*, 73–103.

White, R. (2002). Memory for events after twenty years. *Applied Cognitive Psychology, 16*, 603–612.

Chapter 25
Individual Differences in Working Memory and Higher-Ordered Processing: The Commentaries

Mary L. Courage, Mark L. Howe, Małgorzata Ilkowska, Randall W. Engle,
Małgorzata Kossowska, Edward Orehek, Arie W. Kruglanski,
Jennifer C. McVay, Michael J. Kane, Magdalena Marszał-Wiśniewska,
Dominika Zajusz, Jarosław Orzechowski, Grzegorz Sedek, and Aneta Brzezicka

Mary L. Courage and Mark L. Howe

Executive functions (EF) are those higher-level cognitive activities that include the monitoring and self-regulation of attention, thought, and action, and the ability to plan behavior and to inhibit inappropriate responses. These cognitive control processes are voluntary and effortful and have been described as providing a system for overriding routine or reflexive behavior in favor of more situationally appropriate and adaptive behavior (Shallice, 1988). As such, these processes are integrally tied to the functioning and development of working memory (WM) (see Cowan & Alloway, 2009). The significance of EF is evident in developmental conditions such as attention deficit hyperactivity disorder, autism, and fetal alcoholism spectrum disorder that are characterized by poor executive functioning across a variety of behavioral domains. Executive functioning activities are immature in infancy and toddlerhood but develop slowly over the preschool years and continue to be fine-tuned into adolescence. For example, research shows that 2-, 3-, and most 4-year-olds consistently perform poorly on a variety of tasks that require the ability to inhibit a prepotent but inappropriate response in a conflict task (e.g., dimensional switching), to demonstrate the theory of mind reasoning (e.g., false belief task), to mentally represent an object in two different ways simultaneously (e.g., the appearance-reality distinction task), or to execute a plan (e.g., motor sequencing tasks). In contrast, 5- and 6-year-olds succeed on these tasks, although some of the more sophisticated iterations of these will not be successfully performed until later childhood or adolescence (for a discussion see Goswami, 2007).

It is in this context of metacognitive development that a number of researchers have framed their arguments that the onset of the development of autobiographical memory does not begin to emerge until the late preschool years (Nelson, 1993; Perner & Ruffman, 1995; Pillemer & White, 1989; Povinelli & Simon, 1998). As noted in our chapter in this volume, this view originates somewhat in two different theoretical perspectives. Critical to these is the assumption that there is a fundamental distinction between event memory and autobiographical memory, one that rests on the child's acquisition of sophisticated representational skills which permit him or her to "... use the verbal representation of another person to set up a representation in one's own mental representation system, thus recognizing the verbal account as a reinstatement of one's prior experience" (Nelson, 1993, p. 12), or to possess autonoetic (i.e., self-knowing) consciousness such that "To remember something as experienced requires there to be a mental representation of the fact that the event is known because it has been experienced" (Perner & Ruffman, 1995, p. 543). Thus, in the former (sociolinguistic) model, autobiographical memory evolves from conversational interactions between the child and significant others, especially elaborative mothers. As a result, the child acquires narrative skills, which provide an outlet for the reporting of personal experiences and also serves to structure how these experiences are represented in memory. In the latter (autonoetic) model, autobiographical memory becomes possible only following achievements in metacognition, whereby children are able to have recollective experiences of remembering (as opposed to simply knowing about) past events. According to Perner and Ruffman (1995), such recollective experiences are unlikely before the age of 3–5 years, because before that age children do not understand the relationship between informational access (e.g., seeing) and knowledge. Although Perner and Ruffman do not specify the mechanism(s) that might underlie this metacognitive advance, they suggest that the social interaction model in general, and mother's elaborated talk about past episodes in particular, might play a significant role in the evolution of autonoetic consciousness, autobiographical memory, and in children's developing theory of the mind (see Perner & Lang, 1999). In both of these views, autobiographical memory requires cognitive skills that are well beyond those needed for the recollection of an event that may or may not have been personally experienced. The stringent criteria for an autobiographical memory espoused by these views clearly preclude its existence in toddlers.

Although EF do mature slowly across the childhood years, precursor signs of cognitive control are evident much earlier (Colombo, 2001; Posner & Rothbart, 2007). The alerting and orienting networks that guide the direction of the young infant's attention and selection of targets are present at birth in nascent form and mature rapidly over the first 6 months. During the second half of the first year, the rudiments of an executive attention system, one in which the infant begins to acquire a system of higher-level, endogenous or voluntary controls over the allocation and deployment of cognitive resources, begins to emerge. This capacity is evident in a wide range of behaviors. For example, infants' look duration to simple objects continues to decline, whereas their look duration to complex objects increases (Courage, Reynolds, & Richards, 2006). They also look more to their caregivers in situations that call for social referencing (Vaish & Striano, 2004) and joint attention (Carpenter, Nagell, & Tomasello, 1998) ,and they begin to show the beginnings of behavioral inhibition on the A-not-B task (Diamond, 1985). Further evidence of emerging intentionality is evident in improvements in deferred imitation (Hayne & Simcock, 2009), means-end problem solving (Willatts, 1990), and recall memory (Bauer, 2007) that occur late in the first year of life. By about 18 months of age, this endogenous control of attention acquires an increasingly executive function as toddlers also evaluate behavior progress and direct activity with goals and plans. These developments in executive attention and functioning are closely related to brain activity, in particular to the PFC, anterior cingulate, and frontal eye fields (see Posner & Rothbart, 2007). These changes in attention and their neural substrates enable (and may be enabled by) coincident changes in language (e.g., comprehension), cognition (e.g., representation), and self-regulation (e.g., behavioral inhibition) that begin in this time frame and continue to advance across the preschool years.

In contrast to the views of autobiographical memory as a late developing achievement, we contend that given the evidence for (a) infants' and toddlers' remarkable memory for the events that they experience, and (b) the precursor signs of executive functioning that are evident at the end of the second year of life, that autobiographical memory likely emerges much earlier in development. Specifically, we maintain that the fundamental condition for the onset of autobiographical memory is the emergence of the cognitive self that is evident late in the second year of life but, like executive functioning, likely has its roots earlier in infancy. Importantly, the onset of the cognitive self late in the second year of life coincides roughly with the point at which studies have dated the onset of adults' earliest memories for significant life events (e.g., Eacott & Crawley, 1998; Usher & Neisser, 1993). After the onset of the cognitive self, adults' recollection of childhood events become more numerous and as with advances in memory more generally, are due to increases in storage maintenance, to strategic encoding and retrieval processes, and to cognitive and linguistic development more generally.

Małgorzata Ilkowska and Randall W. Engle

Working memory is capacity limited, important in everyday situations related to goal directed behavior, prospective events or planning, associations between intention and action, situations involving goal neglect, as well as in short-term decisions involving choice among alternatives. To understand individual differences in WM functioning, we should take into account various factors. Obviously, the critical trait factors concern the brain mechanisms and structures, especially the PFC, the anterior cingulate (ACC), and the basal ganglia (BG), to name the most important ones. If working memory capacity (WMC) is a trait, and we believe it is, then understanding the genetics of WM and how those genes are implemented into behavior is essential. It is likely that individual genes have small effects and that various alleles interact. Thus, genetic studies must be large sample and focus on both additive and interactive effects of the various genes. It is likely that genetic effects are implemented in neurotransmitters, for example, dopamine, the most widely recognized neurotransmitter influencing WM. The emerging body of research, indeed, shows the existence of individual differences in WM functioning related to both genetic underpinnings and neurotransmitter functioning (Fossella et al., 2002; de Frias et al., 2005). However, another crucial aspect of future research on this problem must be a greater sample of tasks than has been used in the past. Much of the literature on genetics of WMC has used the N back task. This task is very useful for research using fMRI, but it has low reliability and mixed estimates of validity as a construct measure. Further, we must understand that any single measure of WMC is influenced by a wide array of variables beyond a true-score WMC. The only way to get a more complete picture of WMC as a construct is to use multiple measures that load on the construct (Engle, Tuholski, Laughlin, & Conway, 1999; Kane et al., 2004). Another part of the story is that individual differences in WM functioning might also stem from state-like factors including various situational or contextual parameters. In that instance, performance related fluctuations in WM functioning are short-term or temporary. The state factors may include diverse areas and different perspectives. Examples include the effects related to sleep deprivation, mental or physical fatigue, mood, anxiety, ruminations, or high cognitive load. Another area of state factors influencing WM functioning include various social situations, e.g., stereotype threat, achievement test situations, "mind wandering," or stress. Research also suggests that affect, negative and positive alike (probably a state and trait), influences functioning of WM and memory in general, for better or for worse.

Both state and trait factors influencing WM by either impairing or improving it temporarily or for a lifetime, influence different processes important for WM functioning to various extend. These processes include inhibition, maintenance, shifting and updating information, and instances involving focusing on relevant information, or resisting prepotent responses in situations requiring cognitive control when response conflict arises. Although we know a lot of pieces of the puzzle considering the functioning of various aspects of WM functioning across situations and from the individual differences perspective, there are still an ample number of questions of how to connect all the various findings across cognitive, biological, physiological, and neuroscience research areas concerned with WM.

Certainly, we know a lot about distinct functions and WM processes, in which the brain regions are involved with, as the research in these areas progresses. Researchers propose various theories related to the brain structures and mechanisms involved in WM and higher-order cognition. Those include the net of brain structures that allow for various cognitive control processes related to maintaining, updating, resisting interference, and filtering out irrelevant information. Particular examples include propositions of existence of a net of interrelated brain structures important in cognitive control (Chein & Schneider, 2005) or searching for a default mode of brain functioning (Raichle et al., 2001). Similarly, researchers stress importance of the interplay between the PFC responsible for actively maintaining representations (especially dorsolateral PFC), the ACC related to conflict resolution and correcting errors (Botvinick, Braver, Barch, Carter, & Cohen, 2001; Braver, Barch, & Gray, 2001; Bush, Luu, & Posner, 2000; Kane & Engle, 2002) as well as interplay between the PFC and BG (e.g., McNab & Klingberg, 2008). Furthermore, the ACC plays an important role in both cognitive and emotional information processing.

Can we separate individual difference factors influencing WM and those influencing attention? That is an excellent question for which we do not have a definite answer. Both WM and attention are defined by multiple subprocesses. Furthermore, attention seems to be tied closely with WM processes, although not all attention components (e.g., directing, orienting, alerting; Posner & Petersen, 1990) are similarly important in this relationship. For example, Redick and Engle (2006) showed that differences in WMC only corresponded to attention control, not orienting or alerting. Moreover, various researchers define WM itself differently, assigning the role of attention in WM processes a different weight and importance. At least in WM defined as executive attention (Engle, 2002) or involving focus of attention (Cowan, 1997), attention component seems to play an important role in WM functioning. However, the attention component is probably less important for retrieval from long-term memory, which is cue or context-driven process.

Although not familiar with particular research considering personality and different types of long-term memory (autobiographical, semantic, episodic), certain personality traits have been extensively studied in relation to memory and attention functioning. Extraversion/introversion and Neuroticism/stability, as well as related to them impulsivity and anxiety, respectively, have been the most widely studied personality traits in relation to cognitive processing (e.g., Mathews & Mackintosh, 1998; Revelle, 1993). Openness/Intellect is another one (e.g., DeYoung, Peterson, & Higgins, 2005). Since the research results concerning personality and memory factors (as well as attentional tasks) are mixed, additional investigations are needed to further establish whether certain personality characteristics influence (and how, if they are) various types of memory. On the other hand, the research shows that ability factors might influence memory processes, especially related to fluid abilities (fluid intelligence), but not likely influencing crystallized intelligence.

Development in genetics research and utilizing it together with behavioral studies, studies utilizing multitrait–multimethod (MTMM), structural equation modeling (SEM) methods, and finally, studies using combined methods in individual differences research are most likely the routes in the WM area research that could project in the near future. There is still a lot to know about WM and higher order cognitive functioning, to make more precise statements related to the involvement of different WM subprocesses, and further examine, for example, how these factors differentiate individuals high and low in WMC. Furthermore, since we know a lot about the mechanisms under which WM functions, under what situations WM is impaired by either trait or state factors, one route of the future research is to examine how and under what circumstances we can improve our memory, e.g., WM functioning. Is it possible to improve it substantially and whether the results are long-lasting or stable across long periods of time and whether these improved states obey the same laws and manipulation outcomes as before training? Those are only a sample of intriguing questions yet waiting for answers.

Grzegorz Sedek and Aneta Brzezicka

These comments will underscore the mutual relationships between individual differences in depression, WM, and higher-order processing. We will briefly review recent methodological developments in the relevant domain of clinical neuroscience and next attempt to show that the research reviewed in some other chapters might foster innovative and interdisciplinary research. To this end, we have paraphrased somewhat the initial questions posed by the Editors so as to better adapt them to our line of research, which does not consist in basic research on WM but rather concerns the role of WM as an important moderator/mediator of the relationship between emotional disorders and limitations in reasoning and text comprehension.

Neuroimaging of Depression, WM, and Reasoning Processes: Major Recent Methodological Developments with Implications for Depression Therapy

Existing research on functional neuroimaging in the diagnosis and treatment of clinical depression is fairly preliminary. The deviation noted most frequently in the literature on neuroimaging in depression is a reduced metabolism in the PFC, especially in its ventromedial area and in the anterior cingulate (Davidson, 2004). Another frequently identified deviation is a heightened metabolism in the structures of the limbic system, chiefly in the vicinity of the amygdale, more rarely in the hippocampus and BG (cf. Mayberg et al., 2002). All these structures are involved in emotion processing and are closely related to another area of PFC – the dorsolateral PFC, which is primarily involved in various cognitive processes and is particularly associated with WM and cognitive control. Some studies have also reported lower activity of the dorsolateral PFC in depressed participants, so malfunctions of each of the PFC areas mentioned above could lead to the expression of depressive symptoms, as well as to disturbed cognitive processes (see Koenigs et al., 2008). Our own ongoing research (Brzezicka, 2009), applying sequential EEG and fMRI measurements during the solving of memory and reasoning tasks, aims particularly to track changes in a group of depressed (as contrasted to control) individuals, in those lower-activity brain regions that are key to the effective functioning of WM and to reasoning processes. In this field, in particular, a range of well-replicated studies using EEG and fMRI have been performed, making it possible to pinpoint the cortical regions involved in WM and reasoning tasks. These results have shown that the regions particularly active when solving WM tasks are mainly the prefrontal areas of the brain (e.g., Onton, Delorme, & Makeig, 2005). Research reports on the brain structures linked to WM frequently mention the prefrontal areas of the brain and the anterior cingulate, a region linked to active control of attention and motor functions, mentioned as being key to the process of suppressing inadequate reactions (see Ilkowska & Engle, this volume, for a detailed review).

Moreover, the neuronal correlates of various forms of reasoning have repeatedly been studied using modern brain imaging techniques, with results indicating that the part of the brain most frequently activated when performing tasks requiring reasoning is the prefrontal and parietal cortex (PFC, Fangmeier, Knauff, Ruff, & Sloutsky, 2006). When solving tasks where the relations between objects are analyzed (such as in the procedure of linear orders described in our chapter, see Sedek et al., this volume) the parietal–occipital–frontal network becomes active, suggesting the use of spatially organized mental models for solving tasks of this sort (Knauff, Mulack, Kassubek, Salih, & Greenlee, 2002). Particularly intriguingly, these are parts of the brain that exhibit diminished activity during depression episodes and return to normal after successful therapy (Hugdahl et al., 2007).

The Role of WM Functions, Mind-Wandering, and Need for Cognitive Closure as Potential Moderators or Mediators of the Relationship Between Emotional Disorders and Higher-Order Processing

What mechanisms underpin depressive participants' limitations in mental model construction? We interpret the current findings on such limitations in terms of the cognitive exhaustion model (see Sedek et al., this volume). As outlined here, this model assumes that depressed individuals' cognition is characterized by less complex strategies as a result of ongoing ineffective mental effort. Recent attempts to provide more comprehensive measurement models for WM functions come from studies using latent variable analysis (see Orzechowski, this volume, for detailed and critical review). These approaches distinguish between EF in WM such as "shifting," "inhibition," "updating," and "coordination." We suggest that a functional framework of this kind may benefit from the consideration of an additional "integration" function (Sedek & von Hecker, 2004). Hence, integrating piecemeal information into a more coherent mental representation might be seen as a fundamental executive function of WM when it comes to generating a mental model of logical relations or situational model of written text (for similar arguments, see Waltz, 2005).

Our research has shown WM capacity to be a moderator of the impact of subclinical depression on reasoning, yet questions arise about methodologically more important mediating variable(s) of this relationship. An intriguing review of research concerning the effects of mind wandering on cognitive function performance (see McVay & Kane, this volume) points to one potentially fruitful avenue for seeking such mediating processes. Participants with low WM capacity (low WMC) are more prone to disruptive effects of mind wandering during complex task performance, whereas in our series of studies only depressives with low WMC demonstrated impairments in reasoning tasks demanding mental model generation. Furthermore, recent research (Smallwood, O'Connor, Sudbery, & Obonsawin, 2007) has more directly shown mind wandering to have detrimental effects on cognitive task performance among subclinically depressed participants.

Another potentially important mediator of the relationship between emotional disorders and higher order cognitions is the need for cognitive closure (see Kossowska, Orehek, & Kruglanski, this volume). These authors consider various constraints (e.g., fatigue, noise) that might evoke the tendency to simplify the cognitive complexity of generated reactions. Interestingly, exactly the same tendency of "avoiding cognitive effort" is assumed in our cognitive exhaustion model of depression and helplessness. Thus, incorporating measures of momentary need for cognitive closure might potentially shed some light on the mechanisms underpinning depressives' limitations in mental model construction.

The Role of Executive Functions in the Relationship Between Depression and Limitations in Autobiographic Memory

Our final comment concerns recent research on interesting relationships between depression, impairments of autobiographical memory, and EF (for a review of the origins of autobiographic memory, see Courage & Howe, this volume). Namely, recent research by Tim Dalgleish, Mark Williams and their associates (Dalgleish et al., 2007; Williams et al., 2007) demonstrated reduced specificity of autobiographical memory in emotional disorders, especially in depression. Of special interest for this section, underscoring the mutual relationships between WM functions and higher order cognitions, is that depressives showed several forms of diminished executive control (e.g., overly general memory search, inefficient inhibition) during their performance of an autobiographical memory test.

Finally and as a general concluding remark, let us note that it often seems quite difficult to integrate findings on WM and other cognitive functions across various emotional disorders' populations in view of the multiplicity of definitions, methodologies, and measures employed by various authors. Although the general picture is of cognitive deficits among people with depression, anxiety, or posttraumatic stress symptoms, the wide variety of methods used make comparisons and theoretical integration difficult. We hope that the interdisciplinary character of this volume will yield opportunities to design considerably better coordinated projects, stretching across different populations, based on the same, precisely defined methodologies of cognitive functions.

1. What kind of brain mechanisms determine the various constraints on WM and short-term recall (e.g., limited capacity, limited time of maintenance, etc.)?

Jennifer C. McVay and Michael J. Kane

WMC tasks are complex and multiply determined (and limited) by a host of mental processes, including domain-specific representational systems, rehearsal processes, strategies, and knowledge, and domain-general executive processes involved in active maintenance, interference control, retrieval, and memory search. Our view (e.g., Engle & Kane, 2004; Kane, Conway, Hambrick, & Engle, 2007) is that the covariation between WMC and varied complex cognitive abilities, however (including comprehension, visualization, and reasoning), is due largely to the domain-general, "executive" contributors to performance.

Magdalena Marszał-Wiśniewska and Dominika Zajusz

Giving a clear-cut answer to this question is not easy, since understanding the brain mechanisms that determine the functioning of WM is an interdisciplinary task requiring the integration of several scientific fields: cognitive psychology, functional anatomy of the nervous system, neurophysiology. Each of these disciplines is characterized by another way of explaining behavior and other analytical methods (Henson, 2005). Despite the fact that nowadays researchers have access to many promising tools, such as functional magnetic resonance imaging (fMRI), positron emission tomography (PET), electroencephalogram (EEG), or magnetoencephalogram (MEG), the integration of the experience from the above-mentioned disciplines has yet to be done. One of the obstacles on the way is the unsolved psychophysical problem, which is the set of philosophical issues around the relation between mental and neural events. For these reasons, the above-mentioned fields of research are currently rather complementary, although they inevitably tend to intensively influence each other, which leads to the emergence of a new scientific discipline – *cognitive neuroscience*.

Obviously, significant progress in understanding the cerebral basis of WM has been achieved thanks to techniques of functional brain imaging. On the one hand, the use of these very techniques have allowed to determine which structures are activated during the performance of tasks involving WM. Functional brain imaging studies of WM have found consistent activation in similar brain regions, including the dorsolateral PFC (i.e., middle frontal gyrus), ventrolateral PFC (i.e., inferior frontal gyrus), and posterior parietal cortex (e.g., Fletcher & Henson, 2001; Smith & Jonides, 1999). On the other hand, despite this significant progress, many questions regarding the relations and the involvement of specific brain areas or neural net activation in particular WM processes remain yet unanswered. For example, the role of the PFC is still unclear as to maintenance (i.e., the process of keeping information in mind in the absence of an external stimulus, including active rehearsal and storage), and for executive processes that involve reordering and updating of the information maintained (Narayanan et al., 2005; Rypma, Berger, & D'Esposito, 2002). Also unclear is the role of parietal structures which activate themselves both during the performance of tasks on spatial WM, selective attention, as during the performance of tasks involving executive attention (Awh, Vogel, & Oh, 2006; Owen, McMillan, Laird, & Bullmore, 2005). Although the resolution of these issues is certainly important, it is still necessary to go beyond interpretation in terms of correlates and try to describe the mechanism, that is to explain in what way the described cerebral structures influence and modify (limit) various aspects of WM. This requires further studies and an integrating analysis across levels in which research is guided by.

Jarosław Orzechowski

The constructs of WM and short-term memory (STM), treated in textbooks as fundamental cognitive processes, are the most complex concepts in this category. This is particularly well "visible" in neuroimaging, and not surprisingly, as there are many functions attributed to these processes (especially WM), and tasks used to examine them are very diverse and multi-faceted (the functions of processing and storing information). Classical STM tasks seem to be less complex, but they also can engage both above-mentioned WM functions (Colom, Abad, Rebollo, & Shih, 2005).

Research usually indicates that WM functions are localized in frontal and parietal cortical regions. For instance, a meta-analysis of n-back task (Owen et al., 2005) allowed to distinguish brain areas most often activated when the task is being performed, irrespective of the kind of stimuli and the level of memory loading. These are dorsolateral and ventrolateral PFC, lateral premotor cortex, dorsal cingulate and medial premotor cortex, frontal poles, and medial and lateral posterior parietal cortex. However, the problem with prefrontal cortical regions is that they are activated while performing quite different cognitive tasks (Duncan & Owen, 2000). So it is difficult to find a common ground for activity of this brain structure. Similar problems are with the parietal cortical regions. Even so, for me as a researcher in the field of individual differences and cognitive psychology, contemporary research on brain mechanisms of WM have brought some solid findings (although not as many as there are controversies). These include:

1. Various kinds of material generally engages different brain mechanisms, and these differences are based not only on the distinction between verbal and nonverbal information, because there is more and more evidence that visual and spatial aspects (traditionally combined) may in fact be separate.
    (a) In verbal tasks, a manipulation of delaying recall activates Broca's area, premotor cortex, left inferior and superior parietal cortex, supplementary motor area, anterior cingulate cortex, and cerebellum. A manipulation of memory loading activates similar regions, except for Broca's area and premotor cortex (Awh et al., 1996; Paulesu, Frith, & Frackowiak, 1993).
    (b) In visual and spatial tasks, it is sometimes found that there are separate brain activations characteristic for each type of these tasks. Smith et al. (1995) in visual tasks observed activation mainly in the left hemisphere, whereas in a version of these tasks which activates spatial memory – in the right hemisphere. But when the level of difficulty was similar in spatial memory tasks and in visual memory tasks, no difference was observed in the PFC (Postle, Stern, Rosen, & Corkin, 2000; Stern et al., 2000). It seems, however, that in the parietal cortex, there are different activations related to different type of material (Postle & D'Esposito, 1999).
2. In the process of storing various kinds of information, there are passive (maintaining) and active (repeating) brain mechanisms that are separately engaged. It was found that the relation between the level of WM loading and the activity of dorsolateral PFC is most clearly visible in the phase of information coding (when material is being organized). In the phase of delaying, researchers observed activity in the left-hemisphere inferior parietal cortex, which suggests that it is a brain localization of the basis of phonological store (Rypma & D'Esposito, 1999).

2. Which trait and state factors are critical for understanding individual differences in WM functioning?

Małgorzata Kossowska, Edward Orehek and Arie W. Kruglanski

Our conceptualization of the factors that influence WM function is variable-centered. By this, we mean that most psychological factors can be considered both state and trait variables. We assume that cognitive capacities and motivations fluctuate from moment to moment, as we use energy, consume food, become distracted, become fatigued, take naps, and gain or lose confidence. In addition, there exist general differences between individuals in their personalities, capacities, and motivations. For example, although each person's arousal level and memory functioning change throughout the course of a day, some people are typically more aroused and have superior memory capacity than others. When a variable-centered approach is adopted, the level of a given factor (e.g., the need for closure) can be estimated by obtaining a trait measure, or a state measure; it can also be manipulated via situational inducement. The program of research reported in our chapter on the relationship between cognitive capacity functioning and the need for closure provides a good example of this.

In our chapter, we first review the evidence for the influence of situationally induced cognitive capacity constraints on the need for cognitive closure. For example, time pressure (Kruglanski &

Freund, 1983), mental fatigue (Webster, Richter, & Kruglanski, 1995), ambient noise (Kruglanski, Webster, & Klem, 1993), and alcohol consumption (Webster, 1993) have all been shown to lead to an increased need for closure. The aim of the chapter was then to review the more recent evidence suggesting that chronic individual differences in cognitive capacity may lead to individual differences in the need for closure. In short, the data from the studies on using the trait operations conceptually replicated the pattern of findings using the state approach (Kossowska, 2007; Legierski & Kossowska, 2008). Therefore, our data in these research programs point to the potential motivational outcomes and consequences of WM capacities and constraints.

Jennifer C. McVay and Michael J. Kane

We view WMC as a relatively stable cognitive characteristic of adults, although it quite clearly declines with advanced age (e.g., Bopp & Verhaeghen, 2005), and it may be amenable to intervention (e.g., Klingberg et al., 2005) and susceptible to anxiety (e.g., Beilock & Carr, 2005). To the extent that we are correct, that mind-wandering susceptibility covaries with WMC and is partly responsible for WMC's covariation with complex cognition, and then other personality-, motivation-, and emotion-related trait variables that are related to off-task thinking might be usefully explored in connection to WMC. Examples include propensity for rumination and worry (e.g., Nolen-Hoeksema, Wisco, & Lyubomirsky, 2008; Watkins, 2008) and action versus state orientation (e.g., Kuhl & Beckmann, 1994). As well, state variables such as the number and urgency of subjects' personal concerns, and the extent to which the present context cues those concerns (e.g., Klinger, Barta, & Maxeiner, 1980) will affect mind-wandering rates and may thus covary with WMC.

Magdalena Marszał-Wiśniewska and Dominika Zajusz

The notion of arousal is an especially interesting issue in a whole range of questions regarding individual differences in WM. The effectiveness of WM depends on the amount of arousal (e.g., Anderson, Revelle, & Lynch, 1989; Revelle & Loftus, 1990), so it is natural to expect a relation between the functioning of WM and biologically determined personality traits that are related to individual differences in arousability (cortical, autonomic, behavioral; Strelau, 1994), such as extroversion–introversion, neuroticism or anxiety traits. Unfortunately, predictions of the momentary level of arousal based on the intensity of the above-mentioned traits turn out to be imprecise. The correlation between momentary arousal and arousability is small, even sometimes negligible, since many different situational factors can completely change the level of momentary arousal in people with a given intensity of these traits (Matthews & Deary, 2002). Moreover, the same state of momentary arousal can have varying consequences for cognitive functioning in people with different intensity of personality traits. For instance, it has been thus shown that during morning hours, a high level of momentary arousal reduced the capacity of STM in introverts and increased it in extroverts. During evening hours though, the same high level of momentary arousal induced memory deficiencies in introverts, while having no effect whatsoever on extroverts (Matthews, Jones, & Chamberlain, 1989). The picture of the *personality trait – momentary arousal – situation* dependency additionally complicates the fact that the level of momentary arousal permanently fluctuates because of the currently performed activities and cognitive tasks. Therefore, besides its inter-individual variability, its intra-individual variability has a great significance for cognitive functioning, including the effectiveness of WM. It seems interesting to ask whether this intra-individual variability is a relatively stable attribute of persons with given individual properties (personality, temperamental, cognitive) or simply reflects external influences, e.g., effect of environmental stress, fatigue or sleep deprivation. Research results have up to now not given a clear-cut answer (Lecerf, Ghisletta, & Jouffray, 2004). Still both studies aimed at the simultaneous analysis of the influence of momentary arousal, personality traits, and situational factors on the effectiveness of WM, and those aimed at the analysis of intra-individual variability of arousal, are a rarity – pursuing them seems inevitable for the understanding of individual differences in the functioning of WM.

Among the factors that influence the functioning of WM, affective states play an important role. The results of studies on the influence of mood suggest that mood can modify the effectiveness of the performance of tasks that involve EF of WM, by both increasing and decreasing the effectiveness of information processing. The facilitating influence of mood is particularly visible when it is related to the task material, and this both in the case of negative (e.g., Mitchell & Phillips, 2007) and positive mood (e.g., Ashby, Isen, & Turken, 1999; Isen, 1999). The restraining influence of mood (regardless of its valence) can be observed mostly in situations in which the mood alone is strong enough to lead to the use of cognitive resources and cause less effective processing of information not related to the mood, but being part of the matter of the cognitive task alone (e.g., Eysenck & Calvo, 1992).

Research on the influence of affectively laden stimuli show that the emotional content of a stimulus can direct attention. However, there are differences, depending on the study procedure, in the observed influence of emotional content of the stimulus on its processing. Emotionally laden stimuli can ease processing (e.g., Reimann & McNelly, 1995), but also impair it (Williams, Matthews, & McLeod, 1996). Moreover, it can depend on the stimulus value (Williams et al., 1996). Therefore, the influence of affective states (mood, emotions) on WM begs for further research that take into account both the value and intensity of analyzed affective states, and their specific influence on various functions of WM (such as maintenance or retrieval). In order for research to give conclusive results, it is essential to unify the methodological and experimental standards.

Jarosław Orzechowski

I think it is very important to correlate precisely inter-individual differences in the constitutional activation as well as intra-individual differences in the fluctuation of momentary activation with WM efficiency. The first task, if completed, might enable us to describe the relation between WM and temperamental features as well as personality traits, for which constitutional activation is critical. The successful completion of the second task could lead to our understanding of the relation between WM and performing of complex cognitive tasks, because it is still a mystery why, for instance, "WM is (almost) perfectly predicted by g", but does not seem to be related with the level of creative abilities. In the case of the relation between WM and g factor, some researchers suspect that the ability to regulate momentary activation influences this relation (Nęcka, 2000). Since an increase of activation generally reduces the availability of WM capacity, the ability to regulate the former is essential for copying with tasks which may excessively increase this activation, because, for instance, they are very difficult or are being performed under great stress. In the case of creative tasks, the ability to regulate the momentary activation may have an important influence on selective attention – modulating the strength of inhibitive processes according to momentary requirements of a task, for example, decreasing it in the phase of problem exploration or ideas generation, and increasing it in the phase of solutions assessment. As a result, these changes may lead to changes of WM efficiency, limiting the scope and complexity of available mental operations.

3. Are there any individual difference factors that affect WM but do not affect attention, and vice versa?

Małgorzata Kossowska, Edward Orehek and Arie W. Kruglanski

Baddeley and Hitch (1974) proposed a tripartite model of WM as composed of two slave storage systems (the phonological loop and the visuo-spatial sketch pad) and a coordinating master system, the *central executive*. Even though there is no general agreement on definition of the central executive to date (e.g., Baddeley, 2003; Miyake & Shah, 1999), most researchers have regarded it as a mental faculty that has evolved in the capacity to control attention. They demonstrate that it is responsible for the ability to engage in effortful, attentive processing, particularly in circumstances in which there is interference or distraction, and then it should be related to a host of activation, maintenance, and suppression effects in a range of complex cognitive tasks. This ability has been referred to as WMC (or executive attention; e.g., Engle, 2002). Contrary to what its name may suggest, WMC is not so much about memory capacity in terms of storage volume per se but rather about the ability to control attention to maintain information in an active, quickly retrievable state. Thus, it is difficult to make theoretical distinction between WM and attention: while talking about WM, in fact we talk about attention.

Moreover, individuals differ in this ability (Barrett, Tugade, & Engle, 2004), and these individual differences can be reliably assessed with complex span tasks (for a review, see Conway et al., 2005). These tasks engage the EF of WM because participants are required to keep some information active and quickly retrievable while periodically shifting their attention to some other processing task (Baddeley & Hitch, 1974). Although capacity is measured as the maximum number of target items (e.g., words, digits, spatial orientations) that can be recalled without error, our assumption is that the underlying construct is not a buffer, limited to some discrete number of bins or slots; instead, the construct is more continuous, ranging from those individuals who have more attentional resources (or who can regulate their attentional focus well) to those who have fewer resources (or who regulate less well) (see for the review Conway et al., 2005). Again, measuring EF of WM at the same time attentional functions are measured.

Taking into account the definition of WM and also the way of measuring WM functions, the constructs of WM and attention seems to be very closely related. More, attention is usually treated as a part of WM. Thus, it is hard to indicate individual factors that affect WM but not attention or vice versa.

Jennifer C. McVay and Michael J. Kane

Although we have not identified them in our research, there are surely factors that selectively and separately impact aspects of WMC and attention. Our research has demonstrated that performance of some attentional tasks, even quite difficult ones, does not covary with WMC. In the domain of visual attention, for example, we find that some visual-search tasks, while involving considerable top-down control, are uncorrelated with WMC (Kane, Poole, Tuholski, & Engle, 2006; Poole & Kane, 2009), while other search tasks involving control are significantly predicted by WMC variation (Poole & Kane, 2009; Sobel, Gerrie, Poole, & Kane, 2007). More research is necessary to pin down the reasons for these discrepant results, but they are quite consistent with the idea that WMC and attention (each of which is a complex, multifaceted construct) are not isomorphic, and so any number of individual-differences variables might affect one and not the other.

Magdalena Marszał-Wiśniewska and Dominika Zajusz

WM and attention are closely related to one another, so it is difficult to single out individual differences factors that are specific to each construct. Despite the apparent close interrelationship between WM and attention, most studies draw some distinctions between them or propose a subset or overlapping relation (e.g., Baars, 1997; Cowan, 1988). Although most studies have extended in exciting new ways the accounts of the relationship between WM and attention, there is still no general point of agreement (for a review, see Miyake & Shah, 1999).

Today, a promising direction of research is the development of a comprehensive account of how WM and attention interact. Particularly interesting explanations in this field have been lately given by studies in the paradigm of the load theory of attention (in which distractor rejection depends on the level and type of load involved in current processing; Lavie, 1995, 2005). It is known that WM maintains mental representations of a stimulus after the stimulus is gone and this process of maintenance can influence concurrent perception and cognition (Baddeley & Hitch, 1974; Courtney, Ungerleider, Keil, & Haxby, 1997; Downing, 2000). The load theory of attention predicts that concurrent WM load decreases selective attention as it consumes the cognitive resources needed to actively maintain stimulus processing priorities, which results in increased distractor interference in selective attention tasks, thus making people slower to respond to targets (de Fockert, Rees, Frith, & Lavie, 2001; Lavie, Hirst, de Fockert, & Viding, 2004). Meanwhile latest discoveries by Park, Kim, & Chun (2007) present new evidence that the *type* of concurrent WM load determines whether load benefits or impairs selective attention. When the WM items share the same limited-capacity processing with *targets* in a selective attention task, the load induces a loss of control that results in increased distractor interference (in conformity with Lavie's load theory; Lavie et al., 2004). However, when the WM items share limited-capacity processing with *distractors*, the load can actually attenuate distractor interference, facilitating target selection. In other words, WM load can either impair or benefit selective processing depending on how concurrent load overlaps with primary task. Thus, for a complete understanding of how attention and WM interact, it is necessary to carefully analyze both general and specific load effects in the executive control of task performance.

Jarosław Orzechowski

In my view, the answer to this question lies not as much (or not only) in the results of empirical studies, as in the theoretical and methodological assumptions connected with the measurement of both these constructs. It seems obvious that if we attribute control functions (traditionally understood attentionally) to WM, and if we use similar research paradigms (e.g., dual task) in both cases, then the individual factors influencing WM and attention will be similar. This sort of "unification" seems to be justified, as long as it limits the number of potential mechanisms explaining human behavior. In other words, we may soon need to change our thinking about human cognitive architecture and assume that control functions are common and superior to – more specific – processes of attention and WM. Such possibility is suggested by some researchers. Interestingly, in studies using neuroimagining, it was found that there is some overlapping of activations observed in the tasks for spatial WM and for spatial selective attention (Awh & Jonides, 2001). This supports the hypothesis proposed by Smyth and Scholey (1994) that processes of storing in the spatial WM are being realized by covert shifts of attention, and that is why we can speak here – by analogy to subvocal rehearsal in phonological loop – about spatial rehearsal. Therefore, it seems that the answer to the posed question depends on theoretical assumptions, and in order to give a binding opinion, one would need to clarify theoretical and methodological relations between both these constructs.

4. What are the most important recent methodological developments in the field of WM research and how they can be applied to study individual differences in WM?

Jennifer C. McVay and Michael J. Kane

Statistical tools, such as multivariate latent-variable techniques, and neuroimaging tools, such as ERP, PET, and fMRI, have had an enormous and positive impact on the last decade of WM research and, of course, they are already widely applied to the study of WMC-related individual differences.

Recent excitement regarding the apparent effectiveness of WMC-training procedures (e.g., Jaeggi, Buschkuehl, Jonides, & Perrig, 2008; Klingberg et al., 2005), and rapid developments regarding the genetic contributions to intelligence and EF (e.g., Friedman et al., 2008; Harlaar et al., 2005) are also likely to exert substantial influence of future work. As well, we immodestly hope that our contribution to this volume will prompt others to consider that the thought-probe technique may also prove to be of some use, at least, to investigators of WMC and executive control.

Magdalena Marszał-Wiśniewska and Dominika Zajusz

Among exciting new developmental fields, there is a research on the role of long-term knowledge and skills in performing working-memory tasks (Guida & Tardieu, 2005). This role became more obvious as more studies were conducted to examine people's performance of temporary memory for tasks more familiar and more meaningful to them (see experiments with chess positions, Chase & Simon, 1973; and restaurant orders, Ericsson & Polson, 1988). In this regard, the classical task in STM research, viz. the serial recall of digit sequences is not an exception: individuals can be trained to use their existing long-term knowledge to strategically encode the digit sequence to enhance later retrieval (Chase & Ericsson, 1981). Moreover, the strong impact of content knowledge on temporary memory is highlighted by developmental studies, which show that knowledgeable children can outperform less knowledgeable adults in the children's domains of expertise, such as chess (Chi, 1978) and soccer (Schneider, Körkel, & Wienert, 1989) (for more details, see Ericsson & Kintsch, 1995).

Thus, the existing question is about the implications of the effects of long-term knowledge and skills on the WM. The notion of "long-term WM" (LT-WM) was proposed by Ericsson and Kintsch (1995), who argued that long-term knowledge can be used to supplement the capacity of "short-term working memory" (ST-WM), which by itself is severely limited. Furthermore, they even claim that in fact long-term knowledge and skills could be able to provide a complete account of individual differences in the performance of WM, without any assumption about systematic differences in the capacity of ST-WM itself (e.g., the total amount of activation available, as put forth by Just and Carpenter (1992)). Although this provocative claim has yet to be supported by more evidence, it opens a new interesting direction (theoretical and methodological) in current research.

Jarosław Orzechowski

It seems to me that the most important methodological discoveries in the area of WM are not related with behavioral methods as such (although it must be acknowledged that researchers do more and more ingenious experimental manipulations). In recent years, the so-called SEM methods have become quite popular. They brought a new quality into the analysis of empirical data, allowing to track the direction of dependence between variables. In psychology of individual differences, in which direction of dependence is not obvious, this was a true breakthrough. Indirectly, SEM contributed to substantial improvement of the quality of gathered data, because it forced researchers to assess latent variables on the basis of measurements conducted with the help of various methods.

Because of the inevitable descent of analysis – also in the psychology of individual differences – to the neural level, the techniques of transcranial magnetic stimulation (TSM) may prove to be very useful. These methods allow us to determine causal contribution of brain structures in the processes of WM. Thanks to the possibility of inducing reversible and temporary disturbances of brain functions, we can find out which of these regions are necessary to perform a given task (Henson, 2005). It seems that we will see even more fundamental level of analysis. Recently, new techniques of functional analysis of neurochemical changes in the brain emerged, e.g., through registering the shifts in neurotransmitters' activity by PET (Aalto, Brück, Laine, Någren, & Rinne, 2005). Perhaps not straight away, but it seems possible that these methods can be applied both in basic research and in differential studies.

References

Aalto, S., Brück, A., Laine, M., Någren, K., & Rinne, J. O. (2005). Frontal and temporal dopamine release during working memory and attention tasks in healthy humans: A positron emission tomography study using the high-affinity dopamine D2 receptor ligand [11C]FLB 457. *Journal of Neuroscience, 25*(10), 2471–2477.

Anderson, K. J., Revelle, W., & Lynch, M. J. (1989). Caffeine, impulsivity, and memory scanning: A comparison of two explanations for the Yerkes and Dodson effect. *Motivation and Emotion, 13*, 1–20.

Ashby, F. G., Isen, A. M., & Turken, A. U. (1999). A neuropsychological theory of positive affect and its influence on cognition. *Psychological Review, 106*, 529–550.

Awh, E., & Jonides, J. (2001). Overlapping mechanisms of attention and spatial working memory. *Trends in Cognitive Sciences, 5*(3), 119–126.

Awh, E., Jonides, J., Smith, E. E., Schumacher, E. H., Koeppe, R. A., & Katz, S. (1996). Dissociation of storage and rehearsal in verbal working memory: Evidence from positron emission tomography. *Psychological Science, 7*(1), 25–31.

Awh, E., Vogel, E. K., & Oh, S. H. (2006). Interaction between attention and working memory. *Neuroscience, 139*(1), 201–208.

Baars, B. J. (1997). Some essential differences between consciousness and attention, perception, and working memory. *Consciousness and Cognition, 6*, 363–371.

Baddeley, A. D. (2003). Working memory: Looking back and looping forward. *Nature Reviews Neuroscience, 4*, 829–839.

Baddeley, A. D., & Hitch, G. J. (1974). Working memory. In G. A. Bower (Ed.), *The psychology of learning and motivation* (Vol. 8, pp. 47–90). New York: Academic Press.

Barrett, L., Tugade, M., & Engle, R. (2004). Individual differences in working memory capacity and dual-processes theories of the mind. *Psychological Bulletin, 130*, 553–573.

Bauer, P. J. (2007). *Remembering the times of our lives: Memory in infancy and beyond.* Hove, UK: The Psychology Press.

Beilock, S. L., & Carr, T. H. (2005). When high-powered people fail: Working memory and "choking under pressure" in math. *Psychological Science, 16*, 101–105.

Bopp, K. L., & Verhaeghen, P. (2005). Aging and verbal memory span: A meta-analysis. *Journal of Gerontology: Psychological Sciences, 60B*, 223–233.

Botvinick, M. M., Braver, T. S., Barch, D. M., Carter, C. S., & Cohen, J. D. (2001). Conflict monitoring and cognitive control. *Psychological Review, 108*, 624–652.

Braver, T. S., Barch, D. M., & Gray, J. R. (2001). Anterior cingulate cortex and response conflict: Effects of frequency, inhibition and errors. *Cerebral Cortex, 11*, 825–836.

Brzezicka, A. (2009). *The influence of dysphoric mood and helplessness training on memory and reasoning processes: The role of working memory and psychophysiological correlates of cognitive processes.* Unpublished research data.

Bush, G., Luu, P., & Posner, M. I. (2000). Cognitive and emotional influences in anterior cingulate cortex. *Trends in Cognitive Science, 4*, 215–222.

Carpenter, M., Nagell, K., & Tomasello, M. (1998). Social cognition, joint attention, and communicative competence from 9 to 15 months of age. *Monographs of the Society for Research in Child Development, 63*(4), 1–143. Serial no. 255.

Chase, W. G., & Ericsson, K. A. (1981). Skilled memory. In J. R. Anderson (Ed.), *Cognitive skills and their acquisition* (pp. 141–189). Hillsdale, NJ: Erlbaum.

Chase, W. G., & Simon, H. A. (1973). The mind's eye in chess. In W. G. Chase (Ed.), *Visual information processing.* New York: Academic Press.

Chein, J. M., & Schneider, W. (2005). Neuroimaging studies of practice-related change: fMRI and meta-analytic evidence of a domain-general control network for learning. *Cognitive Brain Research, 25*, 607–623.

Chi, M. T. H. (1978). Knowledge structures and memory development. In R. S. Seigler (Ed.), *Children's thinking: What develops?* (pp. 76–93). Hillsdale, NJ: Erlbaum.

Colom, R., Abad, F. J., Rebollo, I., & Shih, P. C. (2005). Memory span and general intelligence: A latent variable approach. *Intelligence, 33*, 623–642.

Colombo, J. (2001). The development of visual attention in infancy. *Annual Review of Psychology, 52*, 337–367.

Conway, A. R., Kane, M. J., Bunting, M. F., Hambrick, D. Z., Wilhelm, O., & Engle, R. W. (2005). Working memory span tasks: A methodological review and user's guide. *Psychonomic Bulletin and Review, 12*, 769–786.

Courage, M. L., Reynolds, G., & Richards, J. E. (2006). Infants' attention to patterned stimuli: Developmental change from 3 to 12 months of age. *Child Development, 77*, 680–695.

Courtney, S. M., Ungerleider, L. G., Keil, K., & Haxby, J. V. (1997). Transient and sustained activity in a distributed neural system for human working memory. *Nature, 386*, 608–611.

Cowan, N. (1988). Evolving conceptions of memory storage, selective attention, and their mutual constraints within the human information processing system. *Psychological Bulletin, 104*, 163–191.

Cowan, N. (1997). *Attention and Memory. An Integrated Framework* (Oxford Psychology Series 26). New York: Oxford University Press.

Cowan, N., & Alloway, T. (2009). The development of working memory in childhood. In M. Courage & N. Cowan (Eds.), *The development of memory in infancy and childhood* (pp. 303–342). Hove, UK: The Psychology Press.

Dalgleish, T., Williams, J. M. G., Golden, A. J., Perkins, R., Barrett, L. F., Barnard, P. J., et al. (2007). Reduced specificity of autobiographical memory and depression: The role of executive control. *Journal of Experimental Psychology. General, 136*, 23–42.

Davidson, R. J. (2004). What does the prefrontal cortex "do" in affect: Perspectives on frontal EEG asymmetry research. *Biological Psychology, 67*, 219–233.

de Fockert, J. W., Rees, G., Frith, C. D., & Lavie, N. (2001). The role of working memory in visual selective attention. *Science, 291*, 1803–1806.

de Frias, C. M., Annerbrink, K., Westberg, L., Erikkson, E., Adolfsson, R., & Nilsson, G. (2005). Catechol-O-Methyltransferase $val^{158}met$ polymorphism is associated with cognitive performance in nondemented adults. *Journal of Cognitive Neuroscience, 17*, 1018–1025.

DeYoung, C. G., Peterson, J. B., & Higgins, D. M. (2005). Sources of openness/intellect: Cognitive and neuropsychological correlates of the fifth factor of personality. *Journal of Personality, 73*, 825–858.

Diamond, A. (1985). The development of the ability to use recall to guide action, as indicated by infants' performance on the A-not-B task. *Child Development, 56*, 868–883.

Downing, P. E. (2000). Interactions between visual working memory and selective attention. *Psychological Science, 11*, 467–473.

Duncan, J., & Owen, A. M. (2000). Common regions of the human frontal lobe recruited by diverse cognitive demands. *Trends in Neurosciences, 23*(10), 475–483.

Eacott, M. J., & Crawley, R. A. (1998). The offset of childhood amnesia: Memory for events that occurred before age 3. *Journal of Experimental Psychology. General, 127*, 22–33.

Engle, R. W. (2002). Working memory capacity as executive attention. *Current Directions in Psychological Science, 11*, 19–23.

Engle, R. W., & Kane, M. J. (2004). Executive attention, working memory capacity, and a two-factor theory of cognitive control. In B. Ross (Ed.), *The psychology of learning and motivation* (pp. 145–199). New York: Academic Press.

Engle, R. W., Tuholski, S. W., Laughlin, J. E., & Conway, A. R. A. (1999). Working memory, short-term memory and general fluid intelligence: A latent variable approach. *Journal of Experimental Psychology. General, 128*, 309–331.

Ericsson, K. A., & Kintsch, W. (1995). Long-term working memory. *Psychological Review, 102*, 211–245.

Ericsson, K. A., & Polson, P. G. (1988). Memory for restaurant orders. In M. Chi, R. Glaser, & M. Farr (Eds.), *The nature of expertise* (pp. 23–70). Hillsdale, New York: Erlbaum.

Eysenck, M. W., & Calvo, M. (1992). Anxiety and performance: The processing theory. *Cognition and Emotion, 6*, 409–434.

Fangmeier, T., Knauff, M., Ruff, C. C., & Sloutsky, V. (2006). fMRI Evidence for a three-stage model of deductive reasoning. *Journal of Cognitive Neuroscience, 18*, 320–334.

Fletcher. P. C., & Henson, R. N. (2001). Frontal lobe and human memory: Insight from functional imaging. *Brain, 124*, 849–881.

Fossella, J., Sommer, T., Fan, J., Wu, Y., Swanson, J. M., Pfaff, D. W., et al. (2002). Assessing the molecular genetics of attention networks. *BMC Neuroscience, 3*, 14–25.

Friedman, N. P., Miyake, A., Young, S. E., DeFries, J. C., Corley, R. P., & Hewitt, J. K. (2008). Individual differences in executive functions are almost entirely genetic in origin. *Journal of Experimental Psychology. General, 137*, 201–225.

Goswami, U. (2007). *Cognitive development: The learning brain*. Hove, UK: The Psychology Press.

Guida, A., & Tardieu, H. (2005, on line). Is personalization a way to operationalise long-term working memory? *Current Psychological Letters. Behaviour, Brain and Cognition, 15*(1). Retrieved from http://cpl.revues.org/index439.html.

Harlaar, N., Butcher, L. M., Meaburn, E., Sham, P., Craig, I. W., & Plomin, R. (2005). A behavioural genomic analysis of DNA markers associated with general cognitive ability in 7-year-olds. *Journal of Child Psychology and Psychiatry, 46*, 1097–1107.

Hayne, H., & Simcock, G. (2009). Memory development in toddlers. In M. Courage & N. Cowan (Eds.), *The development of memory in infancy and childhood* (pp. 43–68). Hove, UK: The Psychology Press.

Henson, R. N. (2005). What can functional neuroimaging tell the experimental psychologist? *Quarterly Journal of Experimental Psychology Section A: Human Experimental Psychology, 58*(2), 193–233.

Hugdahl, K., Specht, K., Biringer, E., Weis, S., Elliott, R., Hammar, A., et al. (2007). Increased parietal and frontal activation after remission from recurrent major depression: A repeated fMRI study. *Cognitive Therapy and Research, 31*, 147–160.

Isen, A. M. (1999). Positive affect. In T. Dalgleish & M. Powers (Eds.), *The handbook of cognition and emotions* (pp. 75–94). Hillsdale, NJ: Erlbaum.

Jaeggi, S. M., Buschkuehl, M., Jonides, J., & Perrig, W. J. (2008). Improving fluid intelligence with training in working memory. *Proceedings of the National Academy of Sciences, 105*, 6829–6833.

Just, M. A., & Carpenter, P. A. (1992). A capacity theory of comprehension. *Psychological Review, 99*, 122–149.

Kane, M. J., Conway, A. R. A., Hambrick, D. Z., & Engle, R. W. (2007). Variation in working memory as variation in executive attention and control. In A. R. A. Conway, C. Jarrold, M. J. Kane, A. Miyake, & J. N. Towse (Eds.), *Variation in working memory* (pp. 21–48). New York: Oxford University Press.

Kane, M. J., & Engle, R. W. (2002). The role of prefrontal cortex in working-memory capacity, executive attention, and general fluid intelligence: An individual differences perspective. *Psychonomic Bulletin and Review, 9*, 637–671.

Kane, M. J., Hambrick, D. Z., Tuholski, S. W., Wilhelm, O., Payne, T. W., & Engle, R. W. (2004). The generality of working memory capacity: A latent variable approach to verbal and visuospatial memory span and reasoning. *Journal of Experimental Psychology. General, 133*, 189–217.

Kane, M. J., Poole, B. J., Tuholski, S. W., & Engle, R. W. (2006). Working memory capacity and the top-down control of visual search: Exploring the boundaries of "executive attention". *Journal of Experimental Psychology: Learning, Memory, and Cognition, 32*, 749–777.

Klingberg, T., Fernell, E., Olesen, P. J., Johnson, M., Gustafsson, P., Dahlström, K., et al. (2005). Computerized training of working memory in children with ADHD: A randomized, controlled trial. *Journal of the American Academy of Child and Adolescent Psychiatry, 44*, 177–186.

Klinger, E., Barta, S. G., & Maxeiner, M. E. (1980). Motivational correlates of thought content frequency and commitment. *Journal of Personality and Social Psychology, 39*, 1222–1237.

Knauff, M., Mulack, T., Kassubek, J., Salih, H. R., & Greenlee, M. W. (2002). Spatial imagery in deductive reasoning: A functional MRI study. *Cognitive Brain Research, 13*, 203–212.

Koenigs, M., Huey, E. D., Calamia, M., Raymont, V., Tranel, D., & Grafman, D. (2008). Distinct regions of prefrontal cortex mediate resistance and vulnerability to depression. *The Journal of Neuroscience, 28*(47), 12341–12348.

Kossowska, M. (2007). Motivation toward closure and cognitive processes: An individual differences approach. *Personality and Individual Differences, 43*, 2149–2158.

Kruglanski, A. W., & Freund, T. (1983). The freezing and unfreezing of lay interferences: The effect of impressional primacy, ethnic stereotyping, and numerical anchoring. *Journal of Experimental Social Psychology, 19*, 448–468.

Kruglanski, A. W., Webster, D. M., & Klem, A. (1993). Motivated resistance and openness to persuasion in the presence or absence of prior information. *Journal of Personality and Social Psychology, 65*, 861–877.

Kuhl, J., & Beckmann, J. (1994). *Volition and personality: Action versus state orientation*. Göttingen/Seattle: Hogrefe.

Lavie, N. (1995). Perceptual load as a necessary condition for selective attention. *Journal of Experimental Psychology: Human Perception and Performance, 21*, 451–468.

Lavie, N. (2005). Distracted and confused? Selective attention under load. *Trends in Cognitive Sciences, 9*, 75–82.

Lavie, N., Hirst, A., de Fockert, J. W., & Viding, E. (2004). Load theory of selective attention and cognitive control. *Journal of Experimental Psychology. General, 133*, 339–354.

Lecerf, T., Ghisletta, P., & Jouffray, C. (2004). Intraindividual variability and level of performance in four-visuospatial working memory tasks. *Swiss Journal of Psychology, 63*, 261–272.

Legierski, J., & Kossowska, M. (2008). *Epistemic motivation, working memory and diagnostic information search*. Unpublished manuscript.

Mathews, A., & Mackintosh, B. (1998). A cognitive-motivational analysis of anxiety. *Cognitive Therapy and Research, 122*, 539–560.

Matthews, G., & Deary, I. J. (2002). *Personality traits*. Cambridge: University Press.

Matthews, G., Jones, D. M., & Chamberlain, A. G. (1989). Interactive effects of extraversion and arousal on attentional task performance: Multiple resources or encoding processes? *Journal of Personality and Social Sciences, 56*, 629–639.

Mayberg, H. S., Silva, J. A., Brannan, S. K., Tekell, J. L., Mahurin, R. K., McGinnis, S., et al. (2002). The functional neuroanatomy of the placebo effect. *American Journal of Psychiatry, 159*, 728–737.

McNab, F., & Klingberg, T. (2008). Prefrontal cortex and basal ganglia control access to working memory. *Nature Neuroscience, 11*, 103–107.

Mitchell, R. L. C., & Phillips, L. H. (2007). The psychological, neurochemical and functional neuroanatomical mediators of the effects of positive and negative mood on executive functions. *Neuropsychologia, 45*, 617–629.

Miyake, A., & Shah, P. (1999). *Models of working memory: Mechanisms of active maintenance and executive control.* New York: Cambridge University Press.

Narayanan, N. S., Prabhakaran, V., Bunge, S. A., Christoff, K., Fine, E. M., & Gabrieli, J. D. E. (2005). The role of the prefrontal cortex in the maintenance of verbal working memory: An event related fMRI analysis. *Neuropsychology, 19*(2), 223–232.

Nęcka, E. (2000). *Pobudzenie Intelektu. Zarys Formalnej Teorii Inteligencji* (Arousal of the Intellect. Outline of a Formal Theory of Intelligence). Cracow: Universitas.

Nelson, K. (1993). The psychological and social origins of autobiographical memory. *Psychological Science, 4*, 7–14.

Nolen-Hoeksema, S., Wisco, B. E., & Lyubomirsky, S. (2008). Rethinking rumination. *Perspectives on Psychological Science, 3*, 400–424.

Onton, J., Delorme, A., & Makeig, S. (2005). Frontal midline EEG dynamics during working memory. *NeuroImage, 27*, 341–356.

Owen, A. M., McMillan, K. M., Laird, A. R., & Bullmore, E. (2005). N-back working memory paradigm: A meta-analysis of normative functional neuroimaging studies. *Human Brain Mapping, 25*(1), 46–59.

Park, S., Kim, M. S., & Chun, M. M. (2007). Concurrent working memory load can facilitate selective attention: Evidence for specialized load. *Journal of Experimental Psychology: Human Perception and Performance, 33*, 1062–1075.

Paulesu, E., Frith, C. D., & Frackowiak, R. S. (1993). The neural correlates of the verbal component of working memory. *Nature, 362*(6418), 342–345.

Perner, J., & Lang, B. (1999). Development of theory of mind and executive control. *Trends in Cognitive Sciences, 3*, 337–344.

Perner, J., & Ruffman, T. (1995). Episodic memory and autonoetic consciousness: Developmental evidence and a theory of childhood amnesia. *Journal of Experimental Child Psychology, 59*, 516–548.

Pillemer, D. B., & White, S. H. (1989). Childhood events recalled by children and adults. In H. W. Reese (Ed.), *Advances in child development and behavior* (Vol. 21, pp. 297–340). San Diego, CA: Academic Press.

Poole, B. J., & Kane, M. J. (2009). Working memory capacity predicts the executive control of visual search among distractors: The influences of sustained and selective attention. *Quarterly Journal of Experimental Psychology, 62*, 1430–1454.

Posner, M. I., & Petersen, S. E. (1990). The attention system of the human brain. *Annual Review of Neuroscience, 13*, 25–42.

Posner, M. I., & Rothbart, M. K. (2007). *Educating the human brain.* Washington, DC: American Psychological Association.

Postle, B. R., & D'Esposito, M. (1999). "What"-then-"where" in visual working memory: An event-related fMRI study. *Journal of Cognitive Neuroscience, 11*(6), 585–597.

Postle, B. R., Stern, C. E., Rosen, B. R., & Corkin, S. (2000). An fMRI investigation of cortical contributions to spatial and nonspatial visual working memory. *Neuroimage, 11*(5), 409–423.

Povinelli, D. J., & Simon, B. B. (1998). Young children's understanding of briefly versus extremely delayed images of the self: Emergence of the autobiographical stance. *Developmental Psychology, 34*, 188–194.

Raichle, M. E., MacLeod, A. M., Snyder, A., Powers, W. J., Gusnard, D. A., & Shulman, G. L. (2001). A default mode of brain function. *PNAS, 98*, 676–682.

Redick, T. S., & Engle, R. W. (2006). Working memory capacity and attention network test performance. *Applied Cognitive Psychology, 20*, 713–721.

Reimann, B., & McNelly, R. (1995). Cognitive processing of personally relevant information. *Cognition and Emotion, 9*, 324–340.

Revelle, W. (1993). Individual differences in personality and motivation: non-cognitive determinants of cognitive performance. In A. Baddeley & L. Weiskrantz (Eds.), *Attention: Selection, awareness and control: A tribute to Donald Broadbent* (pp. 346–373). Oxford: Oxford University Press.

Revelle, W., & Loftus, D. A. (1990). Individual differences and arousal: Implications for study of mood and memory. *Cognition and Emotion, 4*, 209–237.

Rypma, B., Berger, J. S., & D'Esposito, M. (2002). The influence of working-memory demand and participant performance on prefrontal cortical activity. *Journal of Cognitive Neuroscience, 14*, 721–731.

Rypma, B., & D'Esposito, M. (1999). The roles of prefrontal brain regions in components of working memory: Effects of memory load and individual differences. *Proceedings of the National Academy of Sciences of the United States of America, 96*(11), 6558–6563.

Schneider, W., Körkel, J., & Wienert, F. E. (1989). Domain-specific knowledge and memory performance: A comparison of high- and low-aptitude children. *Journal of Educational Psychology, 81*, 306–312.

Sedek, G., & von Hecker, U. (2004). Effects of subclinical depression and aging on generative reasoning about linear orders: Same or different processing limitations? *Journal of Experimental Psychology. General, 133*, 237–260.

Shallice, T. (1988). *From neuropsychology to mental structure.* New York: Cambridge University Press.

Smallwood, J., O'Connor, R. C., Sudbery, M. V., & Obonsawin, M. (2007). Mind-wandering and dysphoria. *Cognition and Emotion, 21*, 816–842.

Smith, E. E., & Jonides, J. (1999). Storage and executive processes in the frontal lobes. *Science, 283*, 1657–1661.

Smith, E. E., Jonides, J., Koeppe, R. A., Awh, R., Schumacher, E. H., & Minoshima, S. (1995). Spatial versus Object Working Memory: PET Investigations. *Journal of Cognitive Neuroscience, 7(3)*, 337–356.

Smyth, M. M., & Scholey, K. A. (1994). Interference in immediate spatial memory. *Memory and Cognition, 22(1)*, 1–13.

Sobel, K. V., Gerrie, M. P., Poole, B. J., & Kane, M. J. (2007). Individual differences in working memory capacity and visual search: The roles of top-down and bottom-up processing. *Psychonomic Bulletin and Review, 14*, 840–845.

Stern, C. E., Owen, A. M., Tracey, I., Look, R. B., Rosen, B. R., & Petrides, M. (2000). Activity in ventrolateral and mid-dorsolateral prefrontal cortex during nonspatial visual working memory processing: Evidence from functional magnetic resonance imaging. *NeuroImage, 11*(5 I), 392–399.

Strelau, J. (1994). The concepts of arousal and arousability as used in temperament studies. In J. E. Bates & T. D. Wachs (Eds.), *Temperament: Individual differences at the interface of biology and behavior* (pp. 117–141). Washington, DC: American Psychological Association.

Usher, J. A., & Neisser, U. (1993). Childhood amnesia and the beginnings of memory for four early life events. *Journal of Experimental Psychology. General, 122*, 155–165.

Vaish, A., & Striano, T. (2004). Is visual reference necessary? Vocal versus facial cues in social referencing. *Developmental Science, 7*, 261–269.

Waltz, J. A. (2005). Impairments of memory and reasoning in patients with neuropsychiatric illness: disruptions in dynamic cognitive binding? In R. W. Engle, G. Sedek, U. von Hecker, & D. N. McIntosh (Eds.), *Cognitive limitations in aging and psychopathology* (pp. 275–312). New York: Cambridge University Press.

Watkins, E. R. (2008). Constructive and unconstructive repetitive thought. *Psychological Bulletin, 134*, 163–206.

Webster, D. M. (1993). Motivated augmentation and reduction of the overattribution bias. *Journal of Personality and Social Psychology, 65*, 261–271.

Webster, D., Richter, L., & Kruglanski, A. W. (1995). On leaping to conclusions when feeling tired: Mental fatigue effects on impression primacy. *Journal of Experimental Social Psychology, 32*, 181–195.

Willatts, P. (1990). Development of problem-solving strategies in infancy. In D. Bjorklund (Ed.), *Children's strategies: Contemporary views of cognitive development.* Hillsdale, NJ: Erlbaum.

Williams, J. M. G., Barnhofer, T., Crane, C., Hermans, D., Raes, F., Watkins, E., et al. (2007). Autobiographical memory specificity and emotional disorder. *Psychological Bulletin, 133*, 122–148.

Williams, J. M. G., Matthews, A., & McLeod, C. (1996). The emotional Stroop task and psychopathology. *Psychological Bulletin, 120*, 3–24.

Chapter 26
Conclusion: The State of the Art in Research on Individual Differences in Executive Control and Cognition

Gerald Matthews, Aleksandra Gruszka, and Błażej Szymura

The chapters in this book illustrate the richness and diversity of research on individual differences (IDs) in executive control. Our aim in this summary chapter is to identify some of the major themes in this research area, and to discuss how the various chapters address these themes. This chapter is not intended to provide a general synthesis of the field, which would be premature. The reader is referred to the preceding chapters and the commentary sections for the various theoretical perspectives on IDs in executive control. The chapter is organized around three sets of topics. First, we outline the major research issues that provide the foundation for the study of IDs in executive control. Next, we identify some areas of reasonable consensus, at least in terms of general approaches (although significant differences in detail may remain). We finish with a survey of some areas of controversy, where some more fundamental differences between researchers may reside.

Executive Control: The Key Research Issues

The emergence of IDs in executive control as a coherent research field rests on a number of rather separate lines of research. Indeed, it attests to the increasingly multidisciplinary nature of differential psychology and studies of exceptionality. The first steps are to conceptualize executive control and the relevant personality and ability factors, and to derive valid measures of the key constructs. We also need to integrate the structural models for ability and personality factors derived from psychometrics with the process-based understanding of executive functioning emerging from cognitive neuroscience. (The structure-process issue is a familiar trope for ID research). It is important also to establish that the research has some consequential validity and relevance to IDs in everyday functioning and adaptation. Next, we outline the critical issues as they emerge from the chapter contributions to this book.

G. Matthews (✉)
Department of Psychology, University of Cincinnati, Cincinnati, OH 45221, USA
e-mail: gerald.matthews@uc.edu

A. Gruszka and B. Szymura
Institute of Psychology, Jagiellonian University, Kraków, Poland

The Nature of Executive Control

Like many psychological terms, "executive control" is often fuzzily defined. Theoretically, the clearest definition may be the cybernetic one, in terms of a closed-loop controller that analyzes input and generates a corrective response on detection of error or other challenge to attaining some goal (e.g., Carver & Scheier, 2000). The controller is not just a simple servo. It is assumed to have capabilities to perform complex analysis of inputs, and to refer to multiple goals and relevant information in long-term memory in selecting a corrective action.

The basic idea has played out in multiple domains of psychology. Neurological research was initially inspired by the selective impairments in planning, decision-making, and sound judgment produced by frontal lobe damage. Alexander Luria's identification of the dysexecutive syndrome was a landmark in the neuropsychology of the frontal lobes (see Kustubayeva, this volume). Such clinical observations provide the foundation for modern cognitive neuroscience, which has made great progress in identifying the specific circuits involved. A different tradition derives from cognitive psychology, pioneered by Donald Broadbent, Michael Posner, Richard Shiffrin, and Walter Schneider. Behavioral data, often from selective attention studies, showed that people direct attention flexibly according to some voluntary plan or strategy. Norman and Shallice's (1986) account of supervisory attention was especially influential because of its integration of cognitive–psychological and neurological accounts of control. Strategy choice raises the issue of how people select between different strategies in striving to attain a goal (or multiple goals). A third line of research then relates to cognitive–social studies of how individuals access goal-relevant knowledge in order to make such decisions (Carver & Scheier, 2000; Kossowska et al., this volume).

Thus, although researchers naturally work within a specific paradigm, research on executive control is intrinsically multileveled. In fact, the main perspectives correspond to the three explanatory levels of cognitive science (Pylyshyn, 1999), which may be roughly identified as the neural hardware, the virtual cognitive architecture, and the meaning-based regulation of system goals. Control models may provide a means for integrating multiple perspectives on human adaptation to environmental "disturbances," ranging from the neurology to high-level cognition (Matthews, 2000).

Measurement Strategies

Different theoretical perspectives generate different approaches to measurement, but one of the strengths of the field has been the mutual methodological support provided by complementary cognitive and neuropsychological perspectives. In fact, cognitive psychologists are indebted to clinical neuropsychologists for providing some of the first performance-based assessments such as the Wisconsin Card Sorting Test. Conversely, tasks developed for basic cognitive research on attention and memory have become standard tools for cognitive neuropsychologists. Two critical trends in current research are the precise operationalization of executive processes using cognitive-experimental paradigms, and the implementation of advanced neuroscience techniques, including fMRI and other neuroimaging techniques (Gruszka, Hampshire & Owen, Yarkonis & Braver, this volume).

There is considerable research supporting measurement of executive functions through neuropsychological tests, through information-processing tasks, and through brain-imaging and other psychophysiological techniques. Each has validity, but the open question is the extent to which different measures converge on common latent constructs. Matthews, Schwean, Campbell, Saklofske, and Mohamed (2000) application of psychometrics to performance tasks has been deservedly influential, but whether these measures correspond directly to factors that might be identified from neuroscience studies remains to be seen.

Laboratory research is rightly concerned with highly constrained settings, in which task instructions are designed to reduce variance in strategy choice. However, in real-life settings, people have greater freedom in choosing goals and strategies. Indeed, activating personal goals may provoke mind-wandering and errors (McVay & Kane, this volume). Given that personality may have greater influence on behavior in unconstrained settings (Buss, 1989), such issues require more attention.

Issues and Challenges

Research on executive control is now well enough established that it typically proceeds as "normal science" based on a set of generally accepted principles (e.g., Norman & Shallice, 1986). However, we briefly note some more fundamental issues. One such issue is how we decide which regulative mechanisms should be excluded from the definition of "executive control." Informally, researchers tend to assume that the concept implies some infusion of high-level cognition, insight and explicit planning, but executive control may be integrated into some more complex hierarchy of control mechanisms including those that are lower level and noncognitive (Corr, Kustubayeva, this volume). In personality research, the revival of the unconscious and implicit aspects of personality may pose a particular challenge (Schnabel, Asendorpf, & Greenwald, 2008). Integral to the executive control concept is that control may be initiated by implicit processing, and control operates through biasing implicit processes (Norman & Shallice, 1986). What is less clear is whether implicit processes possess their own executive control mechanisms, as might be suggested by work on unconscious motivation (Gollwitzer & Bargh, 2005).

We may also dispense with the notion of executive control at all, as suggested by the notion of attention being an "effect" rather than a "cause" (Johnston & Dark, 1986). Crudely, the brain may be wired to resolve processing conflicts adaptively, without there being any separate top-down control mechanism. An allied issue (Orzechowski, this volume) is the homunculus problem, the lurking ghost in the machine that pulls the levers of the regulative machinery in magical fashion. In fact, the thrust of contemporary research is to exorcise the ghost by specifying the computational mechanisms for control, ideally to the point at which control might be rigorously simulated. It remains difficult to capture personal goals and self-knowledge within such models, however. Finally, as Corr (this volume) discusses, consciousness remains problematic, although he suggests that it may be understood in a functional sense as a concomitant of "off-line" control of behavior.

Individual Difference Factors

On the other side of the equation, research also depends on good conceptual and measurement models for IDs. We need not reiterate the history of ability and personality assessment here, other than to note that there is a reasonable (though incomplete) level of consensus around multistratum models of intelligence (Carroll, 1993) and personality (McCrae, in press). Such models provide a systematic framework for identifying those ID constructs that relate to executive functioning.

Psychometric Models of Ability and Personality

It is now uncontroversial that major dimensions such as general ability and trait anxiety relate to executive processes, but issues in conceptualizing IDs remain. As explored in this volume by Kaczmarek et al., the nature of the typically modest associations between personality and intelligence remains to be fully elucidated. Working within the framework of neo-Pavlovian temperament theory,

Kaczmarek et al., uncover some nonlinear relations. The association between personality and intelligence may vary with factors such as level of intelligence, age and gender. Research from the Western perspective has pointed toward similar subtleties (Chamorro-Premuzic & Furnham, 2005).

Other psychometric fissures may also be important. Although much research has employed broad factors such as general intelligence and the Five Factor Model (FFM), executive functioning might relate to more specific, lower-level facets of ability and personality. For example, there is a rich tradition of research on impulsive personality and performance (e.g., Barratt, 1987) that does not easily fit into an FFM perspective. Traits more narrowly geared toward IDs in cognitive and motivational functioning (Kossowska et al., this volume) may also be important. Likewise, creativity and its subcomponents may be separated from general ability (Neubauer & Fink, this volume). Finding a definitive set of "primary" factors has been especially problematic for structural models of personality, perhaps because of the large number of dimensions that may potentially be discriminated. Revelle et al. (this volume) offer a novel methodological approach to the problem. The "Synthetic Aperture Personality Assessment" (SAPA) technique uses the internet to construct large correlation matrices by collecting subsets of data from multiple samples. This method has the potential to support the large-scale data analyzes needed to develop a comprehensive primary level account of personality traits, opening up more fine-grained accounts of the relationships between traits and executive functioning.

Another fundamental distinction is that between traits and states. In anxiety research, for example, the idea of a causal chain from trait anxiety to state anxiety to performance disturbance is familiar (cf. Ilkowska & Engle, this volume). However, states are more than an adjunct to anxiety research. Mind-wandering appears to influence both working memory (WM) and attention (McVay & Kane, this volume), and several situational stressors also have deleterious effects (Ilkowska & Engle, this volume). Furthermore, emotional as well as cognitive processes are a target for executive control, as demonstrated by studies of mood-regulation (Marszał-Wiśniewska & Zajusz, this volume).

In performance settings, we can identify broad-based, integrative dimensions of task engagement, distress, and worry (Matthews et al., 2002), which relate to a variety of objective performance measures, including attentional and WM tasks (Matthews et al., this volume). In terms of Revelle et al.'s (this volume) ABCD conceptualization, states integrate affect, cognition and desire, influencing behavior. As states are often only modestly correlated with the major traits (Matthews et al., 2002), research focusing primarily on state factors may represent a new frontier for work on IDs in executive control. State factors in intelligence may also be worth exploring. Although we know of no convincing operationalization of "state intelligence," the ability trait may influence state variables related to task motivation and intellectual engagement (cf. Ackerman & Heggestad, 1997).

From Structure to Process

There is quite commonly a tension in IDs research between structure and process accounts. In the ability domain, the resolution of the issue through information-processing models may be seen as one of the victories of the cognitive revolution. It is a sign of the current vigor of the field that research has moved on from collecting "cognitive correlates" to developing more detailed process models that are increasingly informed by neuropsychology. Information-processing models of personality traits are perhaps less well articulated, in part because the effect sizes for associations between traits and indices of information-processing components are substantially smaller, and more context-dependent (Matthews, in press).

It is important to differentiate short- and long-term process models. Short-term models may assume that ability and trait factors are essentially fixed, corresponding to variations in the operating parameters of neural and/or cognitive architectures (e.g., working memory capacity). The issue is then how parameter variation influences the output of the architecture as it responds dynamically to task stimuli, generating observable IDs in performance (Hudlicka, 2004).

Historically, the main research areas display a progression toward increasing precision in modeling. For example, in the early days of cognitive studies, researchers often linked ID factors to broadly defined, somewhat vague, constructs such as attentional capacity. Several of the contributions to this book illustrate how research has moved onto defining and differentiating multiple cognitive constructs, so that alternative explanations of IDs in attention and performance may be tested. Chuderski and Nęcka (this volume) list several alternative hypotheses for intelligence, concluding that cognitive (executive) control may play a critical role in ability. Similarly, major personality traits appear to have influenced different attentional processes (Szymura, this volume). Eysenck (this volume) builds on the general statement that anxiety impairs WM to differentiate multiple executive processes. Anxiety is more reliably related to deficits in shifting and inhibition than to updating. A further example is provided by Lubow and Kaplan (this volume). The impairment in latent inhibition linked to schizophrenia can be decomposed into several candidate mechanisms, based on attentional/association deficit and retrieval-competition, respectively.

Although broadly defined constructs such as WM capacity (Ilkowska & Engle, this volume) and neural processing efficiency (Neubauer & Fink, this volume) continue to be useful, we expect the trend toward more differentiated processing models to continue. The next step may be to develop connectionist models that bridge the gap between cognition and neurology (Siegle & Hasselmo, 2002). Fine-grained modeling of this kind does not negate the need to accommodate strategic influences, but it is essential for understanding individual variation in the constraints on processing.

Short-term process models fit easily into experimental methods for cognitive psychology. By contrast, modeling the interplay between ID factors and longer-term developmental processes is more difficult. Data collection requires prolonged longitudinal studies, and distinctions between traits and cognition become increasingly blurred (Corr, commentary). The key issue is that, especially in childhood, learning feeds back to influence ability and personality, so that these constructs are themselves seen as dynamic (Corno et al., 2002). Trait anxiety, for example, influences the content of the self schema and the social interactions that the child experiences, which in turn influence personality development (Wells & Matthews, 2006).

The current volume is focused more on short- than long-term process models, but the importance of the latter is clear. Researchers continue to investigate the influence of biologically based temperaments on development within varying sociocultural contexts (Kaczmarek et al., this volume). The development of autobiographical memory exemplifies the multiple influences at work. The "cognitive self" emerging at age 2 is critical, but self-development depends on both biological and culture-bound sociolinguistic factors (Courage and Howe, this volume).

Consequences and Applications

This book focuses primarily on the basic science of IDs in executive control, but we briefly signal the real-life significance of the topic. The consequences of impairment are best known from neuropsychology, and the difficulties in decision-making, planning, and impulse control evident in frontal patients such as the famous Phineas Gage. More recently, the role of other and sometimes more subtle executive impairments has been demonstrated for anxiety (Eysenck, this volume), depression (Sedek et al., this volume), schizophrenia and related personality disorders (Lubow, this volume), Parkinson's Disease (Gruszka et al., this volume), and other clinical conditions. The continued study of these various abnormalities – especially in the light of modern process models – promises to improve the diagnosis and treatment of maladaptive executive processing.

Research is also demonstrating a wide range of nonclinical applications of this research. The importance of stable ability factors, including general intelligence, for educational and organizational factors is now beyond serious dispute. The intimate relationship between ability and WM discussed by several contributors to this book places executive processes at the heart of these areas of applied psychology. Historically, ability testing has been used as a selection device in identifying academically gifted students and for hiring personnel for cognitively demanding jobs. Modern process-based accounts may succeed in going beyond selection to support interventions. For example, Ilkowska and Engle (this volume) refer to prospects for overcoming capacity limits through training, and for supporting operators vulnerable to distraction and stress.

The importance of managing operational stress is demonstrated by the sensitivity of executive control to state factors including state anxiety (Eysenck, this volume), fatigue (Matthews et al., this volume), mind-wandering (McVay & Kane, this volume), and positive and negative moods (Marszał-Wiśniewska & Zajusz, this volume). Human factors practitioners may also address the design of systems to avoid overloading executive functioning, or to provide adaptive support, such as automation, to augment the human operator (Matthews et al., this volume).

Towards Consensus on Individual Differences in Executive Control

It is encouraging that a consensus is emerging on some of the critical aspects of IDs in executive control. In this and the following sections, we summarize those issues on which most researchers agree, at least in broad outline. More specifically, we identify common ground on the key dimensions of executive control, on mappings between personality, ability and control functions, and on process models. These advances provide a solid platform for applications of the research, especially in clinical psychology.

The Importance of Fractionation

Fractionating executive control into distinct functions and processes has been critical for the field (Eysenck, this volume). There is a reasonable – though not complete – agreement on what some of the main aspects of executive control may be. Importantly, researchers are starting to model dimensions of executive control as latent factors using modern psychometric methods. There seem to be at least three levels of analysis. First, similar to Miyake, Friedman, Emerson, Witzki, and Howerter (2000), specific dimensions of executive control may be identified, including inhibition, shifting and updating functions. Dual-task control may require additional processes (Chuderski & Nęcka, this volume). These functions may themselves be fractionated; for example, we can separate perseveration and learned irrelevance as distinct elements of set-shifting (Gruszka et al., this volume). As Eysenck (commentary) indicates, further work is needed to isolate tasks or task sets that correspond more closely to the latent factors, but the factor model provides a solid empirical basis for future work.

A second level identifies broader dimensions that integrate multiple executive factors. Indeed, given that the first-order control factors are themselves correlated, there may be a unitary executive control factor (Eysenck, commentary; Friedman et al., 2006; Schweizer, this volume). We may also be able to build models that differentiate executive control from other factors for attention, as in Schweizer's (this volume) differentiation of executive and perceptual control factors. Similarly, Fan, McCandliss, Sommer, Raz, and Posner (2002) separate executive control from orienting and alertness dimensions. We should not declare a consensus prematurely (see Yarkonis & Braver, commentary). Both Chuderski and Nęcka (this volume) and Orzechowski (this volume) draw attention to nontrivial differences between various dimensional models in the field. However, as Chuderski and Nęcka (this volume) also point out, these differences may reflect different task-specific requirements. It seems reasonable that modeling data from larger sets of tasks, as Eysenck (commentary) advocates, will provide stronger convergence between different models.

Another somewhat open question is the extent to which a common executive control factor might emerge from studies of attention and WM (see Ilkowska & Engle, this volume, commentary). Kossowska et al. (commentary) describe attention as part of WM, whereas McVay and Kane (commentary) see some aspects of visual search as distinct from WM. Despite differing views, the issue seems tractable for future research.

At the third and highest level, executive control (along with additional dimensions for attention, memory and information-processing) may be seen as a facet of broad abilities, including general intelligence or fluid ability. Models of this kind may be developed using a variety of indices attentional and WM and appear to be quite robust (Ilkowska & Engle, this volume; Kane et al., 2004; Schweizer, this volume). The correlation between latent factors for general ability and control appears to be about 0.5, although the association is smaller if perceptual control is treated as a separate factor from executive control (Schweizer, this volume). Chuderski and Nęcka (this volume) suggest that the control factor may be better defined by tasks for specific executive functions. In their structural modeling study (Paulewicz, Chuderski, & Nęcka, 2007), control and ability factors were even more strongly associated.

Mapping Individual Differences in Multiple Executive Functions

The fractionation strategy sets the stage for a more fine-grained account of mappings between ability and executive control, going beyond general statements that intelligence relates to attention and WM. As several of the contributors discuss, we can now aim to map general (or fluid) intelligence onto specific executive functions (e.g., Chuderski & Nęcka, this volume). Notably, Friedman et al. (2006) used a structural modeling approach to argue that intelligence relates strongly to memory updating but not to inhibition or shifting, although this conclusion is open to question (Syzmura, commentary). We can also establish mappings between intelligence and multiple dimensions of attention and WM (Schweizer, this volume). The chapter authors appear to agree that intelligence is best treated as a broad, high-level construct, but we may also ask what might be learnt from using more differentiated ability models, and linking executive functions to primary abilities. It is also of value to contrast general cognitive ability with other high-level ability constructs including creativity (Neubauer & Fink, this volume) and emotional intelligence (Jaušovec & Jaušovec, this volume).

There are two possible challenges to such an approach. First, to the extent that fluid intelligence "is" superior WM or cognitive control, then separating the constructs may be artificial, and psychometrically a function of method rather than substantive factors. Increased precision in developing and testing structural models is needed, especially in relation to the measurement models for ability and control factors. Second, Szymura (commentary) makes the provocative observation that differentiating executive functions may be more important for personality and ability research, on the grounds that, when tasks are chosen suitably, intelligence may relate to the full spectrum of executive functions. Such a perspective suggests a more high-level approach of relating ability to a general factor of cognitive control or WM (e.g., Ilkowska & Engle, this volume), or to a general factor of neural efficiency (Neubauer & Fink, Jaušovec & Jaušovec, this volume). Again, careful structural modeling may help to address the issue.

Personality and Emotion

Ability is strongly associated with attention and WM; personality rather less so. The smaller effect sizes typical of studies of personality and performance can make it difficult to make definitive statements about mappings between traits and cognition (Matthews, in press). Nevertheless, chapters in this volume show the progress that is being made. The value of fractionating executive functions is most evident in research on trait anxiety. Attentional control theory (Eysenck, this volume; Eysenck, Derakshan, Santos, & Calvo, 2007) links anxiety to inhibition and shifting, rather than to updating. This account leaves open the question of whether anxiety relates to the specific control mechanisms engaged by dual-task performance. By contrast, Szymura (this volume) uses dual-task methods to explore the effects of a range of broad personality traits on executive control of attention (see also Szymura & Nęcka, 2005). Each trait had a highly specific effect on performance, implying that they may relate to different elements of attentional functioning. Broadly, Szymura (this volume) links neuroticism to increased selectivity of attention under stress, psychoticism to deficits in inhibition (cf., Lubow & Kaplan this volume), and extraversion to greater attentional capacity for handling competing tasks. This approach demonstrates the importance of focusing personality research on specific cognitive functions, which may be a necessary remedy for the inconsistency of the field (Matthews & Gilliland, 1999).

Traits also relate to states of emotion and arousal (e.g., Eysenck, this volume; Szymura, this volume). Traditionally, states have been studied as factors mediating trait effects, as in trait-state anxiety theory. However, the influence of stress factors such as sleep deprivation and threat on attention and WM (Ilkowska & Engle, this volume) suggests that states may productively be investigated in their own right, rather than as an adjunct to trait research. Research on anxiety has typically implicated states of worry as detrimental to executive functioning. As McVay and Kane (this volume) discuss, mind-wandering and task-unrelated thoughts (TUTs) represent failures of control that relate to impairments in performance. Matthews et al. (this volume) showed that states of fatigue or low task engagement reliably relate to deficits on a range of demanding attentional tasks, consistent with an executive impairment. Interestingly, states of task engagement are not very well predicted by standard trait measures.

A further facet of personality research is the exploration of inter-relationships between personality and ability. Although these two major fields of differential psychology occupy rather separate psychometric domains, they are not fully independent (Chamorro-Premuzic & Furnham, 2005; Zeidner & Matthews, 2000). Consistent with previous findings, Revelle et al. (this volume) used the SAPA technique previously described to show that Openness is the Big Five trait most strongly associated with cognitive ability. A further step would be to test whether Openness is associated with executive functioning, or whether the Openness – ability association is mediated by motivational and interest factors (Ackerman & Heggestad, 1997).

As Kustubayeva (this volume) discusses, there is an important Eastern European tradition of conceptualizing IDs in terms of regulation of neural excitation and inhibition processes. Kaczmarek et al. (this volume) address associations between temperament and ability from such a neo-Pavlovian perspective, identifying temperamental mobility as the most consistent correlate of intelligence. Mobility, referring to speed of response and speed of adaptation to environmental changes, correlates with Openness (as well as extraversion and emotional stability: Michielsen, De Vries, & Van Heck, 2003), so this finding appears consistent with Western data. Executive processes should support rapid adaptation to external change, and so again the data raise the questions about the relationship between this element of temperament and executive control. Indeed, Western research places self-control at the heart of one of the major temperamental dimensions, effortful control (Rothbart, Sheese, & Conradt, in press). Kaczmarek et al. (this volume) also discuss how temperament – ability relations may vary with age, gender, and level of intelligence. Revelle et al.'s (this volume) SAPA technique, with its capacity for compiling large data sets, may be well suited to further exploration of these rather subtle effects.

Neuroscience Process Models

The previous section focused on primarily structural issues related to the construction of multivariate models for inter-relating personality, ability, and measures of executive functioning. Next, we survey areas of broad consensus on complementary process models that seek to explain IDs in the sequence of neural responses and cognitive operations that mediate performance on tasks requiring executive processing. This is a rich literature to which it is difficult to do justice in a short passage. We will aim to identify some central themes, within the tri-level explanatory framework (Matthews, 2000, 2008; Pylyshyn, 1999) introduced earlier. That is, we will look in successive sections at IDs in neural functioning, in "virtual" information-processing, and in self-regulation. The main focus will be on the short-term processes through which ID factors relate to biases in executive functioning. A further section takes a brief look at longer-term developmental processes.

Neural Circuits for Control

Research on IDs in executive function has made good progress in differentiating multiple neural circuits for attention, WM and cognitive control, and it is common for models to be explicitly neurological (e.g., Fan et al., 2002; Gruszka et al., this volume). Research has moved far beyond a loose identification of executive control with the frontal lobes. There is consensus on the key structures for control and their relationship with specific control functions. Ilkowska and Engle (this volume) summarize the major associations. The prefrontal cortex (PFC) is generally important for WM and other cognitive processes related to goal-directed behavior. Dorsolateral PFC is especially related to executive control processes including planning, decision-making, resisting interference and distraction, managing dual-tasks, and other functions. The anterior cingulate cortex (ACC) supports monitoring and resolution of conflict followed by error correction, working closely with the PFC. The basal ganglia (BG) controls access to WM, via a selective gating mechanisms that is activated in planning and set shifting.

Such accounts are necessarily somewhat simplified, and, bearing in mind the methodological challenges of the research (Yarkonis & Braver, this volume), more work is needed to arrive at a definitive account of the relevant brain circuits. Triangulation of the neural models with latent factor models, and with specific tasks also needs further articulation. However, we can be optimistic that research in this area is on a trajectory toward increasingly sophisticated cognitive neuroscience models.

Studies of executive functioning in Parkinson's Disease illustrate the explanatory power of cognitive neuroscience models (Gruszka et al., this volume). Cognitive symptoms of this condition loosely resemble frontal lobe deficits, in that patients have difficulty in shifting attentional set, especially when shifting between different perceptual dimensions. Gruszka et al. argue that the deficit may reflect impairment in both the ability to shift attention from a previously relevant perceptual dimension ("perseveration"), and in the ability to shift to an alternative but previously irrelevant dimension ("learned irrelevance"). The learned irrelevance effects appears to be specific to Parkinson's but not to frontal lobe patients. Broadly, set shifting is supported by neural networks similar to those already described for generic executive control, with posterior parietal cortical involvement. Recent neuroimaging data (Gruszka et al., this volume) tentatively suggest that the ACC and caudate, both structures implicated in Parkinson's Disease, may selectively relate to learned irrelevance but not perseveration.

Despite increasing sophistication of the neuroscience of executive function, it remains challenging to develop neurological models for higher-level constructs such as ability factors, assuming that we wish to distinguish executive control from general ability within a multistratum model (e.g., Schweizer, this volume). Historically, the arousal construct has been influential, and it still has its advocates. As the commentaries indicate (Yarkonis & Braver, Kustubayeva, Gruszka), opinions vary on its value for contemporary research. There may be more agreement over the contribution of newer measures of brain activation parameters (Neubauer & Fink, commentary). These authors argue in favor of IDs in general neural efficiency, which relate to intelligence (Neubauer & Fink, this volume). A similar perspective is presented by Jaušovec and Jaušovec (this volume). Similarly, Kustubayeva (this volume) reviews Eastern European conceptions of broad functional systems that may integrate multiple brain areas. All the authors cited discuss how electroencephalographic (EEG) indices may be used to assess broad qualities of brain functioning, as a counterpoint to the localization of functioning for which fMRI and other imaging techniques are best suited. Of course, the existence of higher level parameters is not inconsistent with topographic differentiation, associated with lateralization (Jaušovec & Jaušovec, this volume), frontal–parietal differences (Neubauer & Fink, this volume) and a vertical hierarchy of levels of organization reflecting phylogeny (Kustubayeva, this volume).

It is difficult to develop strong latent factor models from psychophysiological data because of the methodological difficulties discussed by Yarkonis and Braver (this volume), including small Ns, reliability issues, and the discrimination of trait and state factors. The sheer volume of data available through multichannel recording may also be daunting. A familiar complaint about arousal is the lack of psychometric rigor surrounding the construct. Similar challenges await newer psychophysiological constructs (see Yarkoni & Braver, this volume). Assuming psychometric obstacles are overcome, it will be critical to integrate psychophysiological and performance-based factors into common structural models. While there is reasonable agreement on the importance of general attributes of brain functioning, it is currently unclear how the differentiated view of attentional and WM circuitry supported by behavioral and within-subjects analyzes can best be integrated with between-subjects variation in arousal, neural efficiency, and allied constructs.

Neural Processes for Ability

How does ability relate to the neural processes specified in the models just described? Historically, the dominant view has been that intelligence relates to some basic neural efficiency (e.g., Haier, Siegel, Tang, Abel, & Buchsbaum, 1992). This neural efficiency hypothesis (NEH) is supported by studies using a variety of measurement techniques, including PET, fMRI, and EEG. As Neubauer and Fink (this volume) point out, the majority of studies show that intelligence is associated with reduced metabolic activity during cognitive task performance, suggesting more efficient processing. The relationship also seems to be evident in frontal but not parietal areas, consistent with the link between ability and executive functioning. Although there is some variation with gender and task complexity (Neubauer & Fink, this volume), the major challenge to the NEH comes from studies showing positive associations between ability and brain activation. It is a little troubling that one of the larger studies of IDs in fRMI (Gray, Chabris, & Braver, 2003) showed a *positive* correlation between fluid intelligence and activity in a variety of brain areas, including frontal and parietal sites, and dorsal anterior cingulate. As Neubauer and Fink (this volume) discuss, other evidence for positive ability – activation associations comes from studies of long term memory (e.g., Klimesch, 1999), but the Gray et al. (2003) study used a standard WM task.

Inconsistencies in the data may be resolved by adopting more fine-grained topographical approaches. If intelligence is differentially related to specific executive functions (Friedman et al., 2006), and different functions are supported by distinct brain regions (Ilkowska & Engle, this volume), intelligence should relate differentially to brain activations in the regions concerned. Ability research has yet to capitalize fully on the fine-grained accounts of multiple executive functions that are arising from cognitive neuroscience. Braver, Gray, and Burgess' (2007) dual-mechanism control theory shows the promise of such approaches. Proactive control (sustained goal-directed preparedness) is differentiated from reactive control (transient, postevent corrections). The two forms of control are implemented by different networks of brain structures, including lateral PFC and ACC. Developing the ideas of Kane and Engle (2002) and Braver et al. (2007) propose that fluid intelligence relates to the use of proactive control, supported by lateral PFC. Consistent with this hypothesis, they cite evidence from fMRI studies that intelligence relates to increased brain activity specifically when WM performance is vulnerable to interference. Importantly, from the control theory perspective, it is expectancy of interference rather than actual incidence of interference that seems critical. An important feature of the theory is that control emerges out of the interaction of multiple brain systems. Such an approach may help to clarify the role of intelligence in other examples of such interaction such as frontal–parietal interactions (see Jaušovec & Jaušovec, this volume).

Progress may also require closer attention to the temporal dynamics of IDs in brain activation. Jaušovec and Jaušovec (this volume) discuss EEG approaches that involve measurement of either power or amplitude, or indices of network connections including coherence, phase delays, and nonlinear dynamical models of network complexity. Several intriguing, but not fully substantiated, hypotheses have arisen from EEG work. Jaušovec and Jaušovec discuss studies linking ability to faster visual integration of information (evidenced by IDs in the gamma band), to faster brain oscillation (higher alpha peak frequency), and to greater coherence (coupling of brain areas). Broadly, similar hypotheses have also been proposed by post-Soviet researchers: see Kustubeya (this volume) for a review. However, inconsistencies in findings point to the need to replicate findings and to attend to methodological issues (cf. Yarkonis & Braver, this volume). Jaušovec and Jaušovec also propose that the EEG correlates of ability may vary considerably in males and females, although the behavioral consequences of these gender differences remain to be established.

Neural Processes for Personality

Traditionally, psychobiological accounts of personality were shaped by models of brain functioning that focused on broad-based IDs in arousability, or in sensitivity of brain systems for reward and punishment (Corr, this volume). The value of such theories continues to be debated, but it is fair to conclude that major personality traits show only rather weak associations with traditional indices such as EEG alpha power (Matthews & Gilliland, 1999; Neubauer & Fink, this volume). It is generally agreed that neurological accounts of personality must accommodate motivational and emotional bases for traits punishment (Corr, this volume), many of which are subcortical. Thus, keeping a focus on executive processes, the issue here is not how to develop a comprehensive neurological account of personality, but how to apply growing understanding of executive functioning to personality theory.

Some of the arguments here parallel those introduced in the context of ability. If traits are mapped onto specific executive functions, traits should also relate also to the brain substrates for those functions. For example, Eysenck's (this volume) attentional control theory implies that anxiety should be linked to the brain areas supporting inhibition and switching functions, and such evidence is starting to emerge (Eysenck, this volume; Eysenck et al., 2007). Brain-imaging studies are also increasingly important for more fine-grained analyzes of executive functioning that may be relevant to personality effects, exemplified in this book by Gruszka et al.'s analysis of the neural structures corresponding to the various elements of set-shifting. In general, personality traits are more weakly related to the spectrum of executive functions than is general ability, and so it may be easier to narrow down the particular executive processes linked to a specific trait than for ability (Szymura, this volume, commentary).

Beyond linking traits to regional brain processes, we can also apply to personality the more sophisticated analyzes of IDs in temporal dynamics reviewed by Jaušovec and Jaušovec (this volume). For example, several studies of event-related desynchronization in the EEG (Neubauer & Fink, this volume) suggest that extraversion may be differentially related to different frequency bands within the alpha range, depending on task demands. Dynamic models have been prominent in post-Soviet psychology (Kustubayeva, this volume). Traits for emotionality may be associated with IDs in brain plasticity as assessed by patterns of transition between different EEG components (Soroko & Leonov, 1992). Similarly, Knyazev, Schutter, and van Honk (2006) related anxiety to IDs in the coupling of EEG rhythms; alpha–delta anticorrelation was a general feature of trait anxiety that may indicate inhibition of a reward system (delta) by a vigilance system (alpha).

Personality models may differ from those for ability in having a greater focus on cognitive control of emotion and motivation. Brain systems for reward and punishment may support executive control over the prioritization of goals (Yarkoni & Braver, commentary). For example, threat biases in anxiety are moderated by attentional control (Derryberry & Reed, 2002). Indeed, studies of IDs in processing stimuli of positive and negative valence have become increasingly prominent in personality traits. Whereas Reinforcement Sensivity Theory (Corr, in press, this volume) has traditionally focused on subcortical motivational systems, its current concerns with multiple levels of behavioral control are also compatible with this perspective. Indeed, the "off-line," reflective level of control described by Corr may represent such a control mechanism. Post-Soviet psychology too frequently relates personality to IDs in cortical regulation of subcortical systems (Kustubayeva, this volume; Razoumnikova, 2003).

Such approaches are already providing fruitful for understanding major personality traits. Extraversion is frequently related to reward sensitivity, mediated by ascending dopaminergic pathways, but the evidence for a general association of this kind is questionable (Matthews & Gilliland, 1999). It may be more productive to focus on more specific relationships between extraversion and executive control, as suggested by fMRI studies linking the trait to dopaminergic modulation of WM (Wacker, Chavanon, & Stemmler, 2006). In Braver et al. (2007) control theory, dopaminergic projections modulate the context- and goal-maintenance functions of the PFC, producing a bias toward proactive control in individuals high in extraversion and related traits. Many specific questions remain. Behavioral evidence may suggest that conscientious rather than extraversion is more strongly linked to proactive control (Matthews, Deary, & Whiteman, in press), and the consequences for observed performance of IDs in the neural control mechanisms remain to be worked out. However, the general approach seems highly promising.

Canli (in press) outlines a somewhat similar perspective on anxious neuroticism, which may be related to the ACC, typically seen as regulating error correction and conflict. One study (Haas, Omura, Constable, & Canli, 2007) showed that anxious neuroticism correlated positively with subgenual ACC and amygdale activation during trials of high emotional conflict, on a modified version of the emotional Stroop task. Extraversion may also relate to ACC response to positive stimuli (Canli, in press). Functional connectivity analyzes identify distributed networks of brain structures sensitive to reward and punishment stimuli. However, Canli (in press) cautions that data so far have not shown any moderating effect of extraversion and neuroticism on functional connectivity in these networks. Again, the implication may be that effects of these traits are somewhat subtle, and progress may require investigation of their roles in specific cognitive–emotional regulative processes, rather than generic reward and punishment sensitivities (though cf., Corr, in press, this volume).

Finally, neurological work contributes to understanding relationships between personality and ability, complementing the psychometric studies already described (Kaczmarek et al., Revelle et al., this volume; see also commentaries). Studies may dissociate personality and ability effects; arguably, intelligence relates to updating but not to shifting and inhibition (Friedman et al., 2006), whereas trait anxiety shows the opposite pattern of associations (Eysenck, this volume). Note, however, that a good case can be made for relating intelligence to inhibition (Chuderski & Nęcka, this volume).

Extraversion and intelligence may predominantly relate to different alpha bands (Neubauer & Fink, this volume). Studies may also identify the circumstances under which ability and personality jointly influence a specific executive function, depending on task demands and the emotive content of stimuli (Neubauer & Fink, this volume). Personality and ability may interact especially when cognitive and emotional control must be integrated (Kustubayeva, this volume). Similarly, neurological studies are contributing to understanding constructs at the personality–ability crossroads including creativity and emotional intelligence (Jaušovec & Jaušovec, Neubauer & Fink, this volume).

Information-Processing Models

Ability and Information-Processing

The psychometric studies already reviewed provide some clues toward relating ability to information-processing. The general logic is articulated by Schweizer (this volume), in relation to attentional processing. We may develop a taxonomy of components of attention, find measures of these components, collect data on both attentional and ability measures, and then model the variance–covariance structure. Such models may suggest that ability is more strongly related to some elements of attention, including control elements, than to others.

However, modeling covariances alone is not sufficient to develop process models, which requires an integration of experimental and correlational approaches (Chuderski & Nęcka, this volume). Linking intelligence to memory updating processes, for example, requires not only an association between latent factors for the constructs. It also requires demonstrations that experimentally varying updating requirements influences (1) correlations between intelligence and memory tasks, and (2) performance on intellectual tasks such as reasoning. Sternberg (1977) initiated work of this kind, which was subsequently pursued by other researchers (see Chuderski & Nęcka, this volume). The researcher constructs and validates a fully specified computational model of some task domain, such as analogical reasoning. Such models include parameters of component processes such as completion time. Intelligence can then be related to IDs in those parameters. In other words, process models are concerned with how intelligence is expressed in IDs on specific tasks, rather than with broadly defined latent constructs (although process modeling may still usefully employ structural modeling). Models may also be informed by findings from neuroscience, and make use of neural network approaches as the basis for the cognitive architecture (e.g., Braver et al., 2007).

Studies of IDs in dual-task performance may benefit from a process-based approach. IDs in this task domain have proved difficult to capture in psychometric models (e.g., Ackerman, Schneider, & Wickens, 1984), perhaps because of the multitude of different processes that may or may not be engaged in any given dual-task study, and lack of control over their sequencing. Chuderski and Nęcka (this volume) report two studies, in which participants were required to control the order of processing of two task components (letter and digit processing tasks). They found that fluid intelligence was not related in any general way to costs of dual-tasking, but intelligence was related to performance on the second of the two tasks, when order of processing was specified. Intelligence may then relate specifically to the controlled sequential scheduling of mental operations. Findings of this kind provide a platform for more detailed cognitive modeling of dual-task performance.

Other contributors discuss the processes contributing to IDs in higher-order cognition. Orzechowski (this volume) points out that studies of IDs in reasoning have moved on from demonstrating WM–reasoning correlations to probing the underlying mechanisms. Research has addressed both deductive and inductive reasoning. In both cases, a key question is whether a general, domain-independent WM process can be identified, or whether there are also domain-specific processes (e.g., verbal and spatial). To some degree, both overall reasoning performance and WM–reasoning correlation are determined by WM load, consistent with its importance as a general process (Ilkowska & Engle, this volume). Clearly, general WM capacity is an important parameter for a range of high-level cognitive tasks. Indeed, WM may function to provide a means for integrating the many elements of such tasks into a new structural representation (Oberauer, Süß, Wilhelm, & Sander, 2007).

At the same time, IDs in reasoning and other tasks may be depend on a little bit more than just WM. Orzechowski (this volume) discusses some of the more promising processes, including domain-specific processes, specific control mechanisms, and processes for abstraction of information from complex stimuli. Sedek et al. (this volume) similarly highlight IDs in the processes of constructing on-line mental models in support of complex and multistep tasks. Cognitive models of the self that develop early in childhood play a critical role in IDs in autobiographical memory (Courage & Howe, this volume).

Personality and Information-Processing

Previous reviews (Matthews, 2008, in press) suggest that the major personality traits are associated with multiple biases in a variety of processing components distributed across the main subsystems of the cognitive architecture. Many of these biases, such as those in peripheral sensory and motor processes are unrelated to executive control. However, control biases form an important subset of personality effects, including links between extraversion and impulsive behaviors, and between neuroticism/anxiety and motivational regulation of attention. The goal is to go beyond establishing associations between traits and performance on specific tasks to develop fully specified models of how traits bias theoretically justified parameters of executive functioning. As Szymura (this volume) discusses, traits typically do not relate to global deficits in attentional control, and tasks must be carefully designed to provide reliable findings.

Trait anxiety and neuroticism. Trait anxiety research suggests two broad types of effect on executive functioning. First, anxiety relates to difficulties in managing concurrent streams of processing, as evidenced by increased vulnerability to distraction and impairments in dual-task performance (Eysenck et al., 2007). Second, anxiety is also associated with vulnerability to diversion of the focus of attention onto potentially threatening stimuli, as shown in studies of the emotional Stroop and dot-probe tasks (Bar-Haim, Lamy, Pergamin, Bakermans-Kranenburg, & van IJzendoorn, 2007). Eysenck's (this volume; Eysenck et al., 2007) attentional control theory brings out the role of control processes in these effects. Deficits in inhibition and shifting plausibly mediate effects of anxiety on selective and divided attention. Eysenck et al. (2007) attribute increased selectivity in anxiety to weakness in attentional control rendering the anxious individual more vulnerable to capture of attention by salient or conspicuous stimuli. This hypothesis contrasts with the traditional view (Easterbrook, 1959) that there is an automatic shift of attention from secondary to primary task stimuli in anxiety. However, given that effects of anxiety and related traits on dual-task performance appear to be highly sensitive to task parameters (Szymura, this volume), more work is needed to identify the specific processes that mediate anxiety effects on divided attention.

The role of executive processes in bias in selective attention to threat has been controversial. Demonstrations that bias can be shown with "subliminal" stimuli has been taken as indicating the bias is localized in preattentive processes (Bar-Haim et al., 2007; Mathews, 2004). On the other hand, sensitivity of anxiety bias to contextual effects and its apparent dependence on relatively slow-acting processes suggests a role for voluntary strategy choice (Matthews & Wells, 1999; Phaf & Kan, 2007). Bias may also reflect the interaction of preattentive and strategic processes (Mathews, 2004). Eysenck et al. (2007) account of selective attention bias follows this general principle. They distinguish between goal-directed and stimulus-driven attentional systems broadly corresponding to Posner and DiGirolamo's (1998) anterior and posterior systems. Enhanced attention to threat in anxiety may be attributed both to a preattentive enhancement of stimulus-driven (preattentive) threat processing, and to weaker goal-directed inhibitory control which limits voluntary resistance to distraction.

Fractionation of attentional mechanisms also helps to understand sources of bias. The posterior system supports multiple functions of disengaging from the location attended initially, moving to a new spatial location, and then engaging the new location. Anxiety appears to relate specifically to slow disengagement from threat (Derryberry & Reed, 2002).

The role of negative affectivity in executive processing has also been investigated in relation to subclinical depression. As Sedek et al. (this volume) discuss, studies of depression raise issues similar to those featuring in research on anxiety and neuroticism. Broadly, depression seems to relate to reduced cognitive capacity, but it may be argued that the deficit is specific to certain strategies (Hertel, 2004). Sedek et al. (this volume) propose a cognitive exhaustion model of depression. It is said to relate to a generalized deficit in constructive and integrative mental processing, which impairs the formation of new ideas and hypothesis generation. Thus, depression is most damaging to problem-solving tasks that are complex, cognitively demanding, and open-ended. Sedek et al. review studies supporting this hypothesis that also suggest that depression specifically impairs the integrative processes necessary for on-line generation of social mental models, a deficit that may impair social functioning.

Psychoticism. Szymura (this volume; Szymura & Nęcka, 2005) also identifies characteristic effects of two further traits, psychoticism and extraversion. Effects of psychoticism in dual-task performance were identified with poor cognitive inhibition, which is sometimes advantageous and sometimes disadvantageous. Similarly, Corr (this volume) discusses studies that suggest psychoticism is related to lack of flexibility in rule updating on a decision-making task. Lubow and Kaplan (this volume) pursue a similar theme in reviewing effects of schizotypal personality (overlapping with psychoticism). Broadly, schizotypy (as well as clinical schizophrenia) relates to deficits in latent inhibition, consistent with the positive symptoms of these conditions. Latent inhibition is demonstrated by preexposing a stimulus in a given task context. It is then shown that new associations to the stimulus are formed relatively slowly, by comparison with a novel stimulus. An impairment in latent inhibition may cause the person to be more vulnerable to unusual thoughts and images that would normally be suppressed as being irrelevant.

However, identifying latent inhibition as a feature of schizotypy is not very informative about processing (Lubow & Kaplan, this volume). Latent inhibition may reflect both attentional and retrieval-based mechanisms, and further work is needed to differentiate the roles these processes may play in schizotypy. However, schizotypy may also relate to the retrieval of associations to stimuli that are irrelevant to the current context. The trait has also been linked to other attentional phenomena associated with inhibitory control, including negative priming (Claridge, 2009) and learned irrelevance (Gruszka et al., this volume). Again, more detailed study is needed to determine how many separate inhibitory processing mechanisms are involved.

Extraversion–introversion. Szymura (this volume) found that extraverts perform better than introverts when they have to handle competing tasks under high cognitive workload (high set size), consistent with an association between extraversion and attentional capacity. Such findings are consistent with both a behavioral tendency for extraverts to perform better than introverts on demanding, symbolically coded tasks (Matthews, 2008, in press), and with fMRI evidence suggesting that extraverts show greater neural efficiency than introverts in relevant brain areas while using WM (Gray et al., 2005). Similar conclusions may be derived from EEG studies (Fink & Neubauer, 2004; Neubauer & Fink, this volume).

Further work is needed on the relationship between extraversion and behavioral impulsivity. Personality effects on impulsive performance are fairly well-documented (Matthews et al., in press), but they are sufficiently elusive as to suggest that extraversion and other traits relate to specific executive processes, rather than some general deficit in control of speed-accuracy tradeoff.

Stress and Emotion

IDs in emotionality are important for traits such as anxiety, depression, and extraversion. However, research is increasingly focusing on affective states as important variables in their own right, and not just as adjuncts to stable traits. Various factors associated with stress and fatigue impair executive functioning (Ilkowksa & Engle, this volume). Thus far, research on states of stress has rather lacked the comprehensive dimensional models that characterize trait research. As with traits, it may be useful to organize research around different broad dimensions, such as the task engagement, distress and worry axes proposed by Matthews et al. (2002). Different state dimensions may have influenced different executive processes.

McVay and Kane's (this volume) account of mind-wandering elucidates this feature of states such as worry and cognitive interference. It is naïve to suppose that human subjects focus attention exclusively on the tasks they are asked to perform; their extra-experimental goals and concerns influence attentional focus, use of WM and executive control. TUTs may be measured using probes that interrupt ongoing thought to evaluate the contents of attention. Research reviewed by McVay and Kane (this volume) suggests that IDs in propensity for mind-wandering influence both WM capacity and executive-control tasks. Mind-wandering may signal failure of proactive goal-maintenance processes that prevent conflict between on- and off-task processes.

Matthews et al. (this volume) reviews studies that show subjective task engagement (energy, motivation, concentration) predicts performance on a wide range of demanding attentional tasks. Task engagement may index availability of resources, but this hypothesis leaves open the question of whether engagement relates to any specific executive processes required for performance of high-workload tasks. Subjective energy relates to attentional selectivity (Matthews & Margetts, 1991), implying a role for executive control, but a systematic analysis of the relationship between engagement and control functions awaits further studies. Also of interest is whether the "cognitive exhaustion" that Sedek et al. (this volume) attribute to depression is mediated by lack of task engagement.

Self-Regulative Models

The third facet of executive control identified within Pylyshyn's (1999) tri-level framework is that of self-knowledge and self-regulation. We cannot understand the voluntary deployment of executive control without reference to the person's goals, self-beliefs and rational choice of strategies for goal attainment. Such issues have been more prominent in personality than in ability research. Studies of self-rated intelligence and intellectual interests (Chamorro-Premuzic & Furnham, 2005; Revelle et al., this volume) suggest future research avenues; presumably, beliefs about one's intellectual competence may influence control strategies on cognitive tasks. The social–psychological literature on the issue (e.g., Dweck, 1999) has shown performance effects without probing what executive processes might mediate them. Self-regulative processes may also be important in emotional intelligence (cf., Jaušovec & Jaušovec, this volume).

Generally, self-regulation has been a greater concern for personality researchers. It is straightforward to show that the major traits relate to a wide variety of self-regulative constructs, including self-esteem, self-efficacy, self-focus of attention, and various constructs related to management of task demands (Matthews et al., 2000; Robinson & Sedikides, in press). For example, attentional bias in anxiety may in part result from top-down control of attention driven by the anxious person's beliefs about personal vulnerability to threat and necessary "hypervigilant" coping strategies (Matthews & Wells, 1999).

In addition to studies of broad traits, research has also focused on more narrowly defined constructs that relate to task motivations. Need for closure (Kruglanski, 1989; Kossowska et al., this volume) refers to needs for quick, decisive resolutions of problems, coupled with intolerance of ambiguity. It may be as either a stable personality disposition, or a transient state elicited by external pressures. Kossowska et al. (this volume) review their recent studies of relationships between dispositional need for closure and processing speed and WM. Data supported their hypothesis that need for closure relates to limitations in executive control that are expressed as poorer performance on WM and other tasks.

Self-regulation may also be closely related to mood. The two standard perspectives are described by Ketelaar and Clore (1997). The "affect-as-information" hypothesis states that moods provide a useful source of information when making evaluative judgments. Happy moods may promote heuristic processing, whereas unpleasant moods may elicit systematic processing (presumably requiring more executive control). The "affect-as-motivation" hypothesis proposes that affective states may also operate as incentives and disincentives that motivate action. In this case, the person's beliefs about how to regulate mood effectively will influence behavior.

Marszał-Wiśniewska and Zajusz (this volume) contrast the affect-as-information position with the more recent affect-as-input hypothesis (Martin, 2001). It is argued that moods do not provide any intrinsic evaluative information; instead mood is analyzed for its implications alongside other relevant inputs. Similarly, moods have no intrinsic effect on the control of cognition. Choices such as starting or stopping processing, or using heuristic or systematic processing, are made on a contextual basis. Marszał-Wiśniewska and Zajusz (this volume) conducted a study in which subjects formed impressions about a target individual by reading information from a series of cards until they felt they had sufficient information. When given a "stop-rule" emphasizing acquiring sufficient information, subjects in a negative mood read more cards. When the stop-rule referred to task enjoyment, positive mood was related to greater persistence. That is, the motivational implications of moods depend on the person's goals. Furthermore, mood effects are moderated by temperamental and motivational traits.

The relationship between affective states and self-regulation may also be approached from the perspective of the transactional theory of stress and emotion (Lazarus, 1999). Matthews et al. (this volume) review evidence suggesting a reciprocal relationship between cognitive stress processes and the task engagement state. High pretask engagement encourages more constructive self-regulation (e.g., challenge appraisal, task-focused coping), but the appraisal and coping processes concerned appear to feed back to influence engagement. The mode of self-regulation adopted appears to influence control of task-directed effort, as evidenced by data on the inter-relationships of engagement, coping and objective performance.

Dynamic Processing Models

Most of the empirical research already reviewed is based on straightforward experimental paradigms, in which IDs are treated as fixed factors that may bias neural response, information-processing, or goal-directed self-regulation. However, these short-term processing biases are embedded in prolonged dynamic interactions between person and environment. The importance of dynamic interactions has already been introduced in relation to self-regulation. Because processing of feedback is critical to self-regulation, the dynamic perspective is necessary. For example, if action is directed toward improving mood (affect-as-motivation), then evaluation of mood change will influence whether mood-regulative action is continued or changed (mood-as-information or -as-input; see Marszał-Wiśniewska & Zajusz, this volume). Again, the perception–action cycles that are engaged are typically studied over short time periods only.

Developmental Processes

Longer-term processes are typically studied from a developmental perspective, focusing on the influence of childhood temperament on adult personality (cf., Kaczmarek et al., this volume) or on cognitive development (Courage & Howe, this volume). In the present context, a pivotal issue is that major temperament dimensions correspond to styles of self-regulation. Maturation overlays the child's reactive tendencies with a set of control mechanisms including inhibition, attentional control, and the elicitation of help from caregivers, whose effectiveness varies with dimensions of emotionality and self-control (Rothbart et al., in press). Such mechanisms can be understood in relation to neuroscience, cognition, and self-regulation. In the current context, Rothbart et al.'s (in press) effortful control dimension is of particular relevance because it relates to executive attention skills, within the Posner and DiGirolamo (1998) model. Temperamental factors feed forward into IDs in social development, but the child's environmental exposures in turn feed back into temperament change. These interactions may again be understood at multiple levels, including gene–environment interaction, and the shaping of social cognition (Caspi, Roberts, & Shiner, 2005).

Courage and Howe (this volume, commentary) discuss the dynamic processes that shape autobiographical memory. They propose a cognitive developmental account beginning with the emergence of the "cognitive self" at age 2 or so that will come to represent the self as an independent object that persists in time. Maturation of the PFC and basic cognitive processes support increasing sophistication in organizing and personalizing autobiographical memories. IDs in memory partly reflect IDs in the extent to which the child establishes an early and stable self-identity. Temperamental factors such as those linked to attachment may also play a role in IDs, especially for emotionally charged memories. IDs in cognitive development also interact with language-based social interactions, shaped by culture. For example, the autonomous sense of self-valued in Western cultures may promote earlier autobiographical memories in American children than in Chinese children, in whom the self-concept is more strongly linked to community.

Dynamic interaction between the child and others, including family and peers, is likely to influence both the development of the self and the social environments to which the child is exposed (Caspi et al., 2005). Indeed, while IDs in executive functioning in part reflect the expression of the genes for the relevant brain structures, gene expression will also be modulated by environmental exposures during maturation. The social context for development will especially influence the motivational processes that set the goals for executive control.

Pathology as a Dynamic Process

The dynamic perspective may be especially important for understanding the role of executive dysfunction in psychopathology. The Self-Referent Executive Function (S-REF) model of emotional disorder proposed by Wells and Matthews (Matthews & Wells, 1999, 1994) attributes pathology to excessive and mis-directed executive processing, which serves to focus attention on threat and cope through perserverative worry. Maladaptive executive processing is driven by faulty self-knowledge (both explicit and implicit). The model is dynamic both internally and externally. Internal processes such as worry block the constructive reorganization of self-knowledge. The person's interactions with the external world are frequently dysfunctional, in that the anxious or depressed person elicits negative feedback from others, and may cope through avoidance of feared situations, perpetuating negative self-beliefs and blocking the acquisition of effective coping strategies. Dynamic factors are also implicated in the fatigue effects described by Matthews et al. (this volume), supported by a comparable Task-Referent Executive Function (T-REF).

The S-REF model (Wells & Matthews, 1994) also illustrates how executive processing may malfunction at different levels. Attentional control theory (Eysenck, this volume) implies that even when the anxious person may access an effective strategy for task performance, impairment in executive function may lead to performance deficits and perhaps more pervasive maladaptation (e.g., distractibility in situations requiring concentration). By contrast, the S-REF model highlights the (knowledge-level) constructs that may produce misdirection of executive processing, even if executive processes work normally. (Of course, both the intent and implementation of executive function may be impaired).

Accommodating different levels of malfunction requires the more differentiated view of executive processing described by contributors to this volume. Sedek et al.'s (this volume) proposal that depression relates to impairments in building social mental models also suggests a dynamic perspective. The impairment will guide inappropriate behaviors to which others will react; processing of negative social feedback is likely to maintain faulty mental models. Studies of team performance (Salas, Sims, & Burke, 2005) suggest that construction of shared mental models is critical for success – how do depressed and nondepressed individuals negotiate the task of arriving at a shared mental model in social settings? Abnormalities in latent inhibition in both schizophrenia and various anxiety disorders (Lubow & Kaplan, this volume) raise parallel questions. How do individuals vulnerable to overload by relatively unprocessed stimuli manage their lives to avoid such disruptive mental events? How are their social behaviors reflected back to them by others, so as to perpetuate or alleviate pathology?

Controversies and Challenges

Methodological Issues

Various methodological limitations of current work continue to act as a brake on progress. The commentaries on methodological issues provide specific recommendations for future research. Some problems reflect limits on the resources typically available for research, such as lack of statistical power in small-N studies (Yarkoni & Braver, this volume). Other limitations, such as reliability of ID measures derived from fMRI will likely be resolved through increasing statistical and technical sophistication, as described by the latter authors and in the commentaries. A provocative forthcoming article (Vul, Harris, Winkielman, & Pashler, in press) proposes that much extant research systematically over-estimated correlations between brain activity and personality through biased selection of the BOLD signal voxels for analysis; the authors recommend methods for correcting the problem.

Other issues may be rather more profound. Yarkoni and Braver (this volume) point out that, on occasion, within- and between-subjects analyzes of executive functioning may fail to converge. Indeed, the analyzes may even identify dissociated spatial regions. As the authors point out, we need an integrative approach that recognizes different types of evidence these analyzes provide. A related issue is the fundamental ambiguity of correlations between observed performance and brain activity. Does high activation of the brain region concerned indicate that it is operating more powerfully – or less efficiently? As described above, work on IDs in neural efficiency (Neubauer & Fink, this volume) continues to grapple with this issue.

Resolving the issue may require more detailed process models of neural functioning. We also reiterate Yarkoni and Braver's (this volume) recommendation that brain activations should be shown to be functionally related to behavioral performance. It may be risky to attribute, say, a negative correlation between brain activity and a personality trait to an efficiency mechanism in the absence of any corroborative behavioral evidence.

Another pressing issue is the choice of appropriate tasks for assessing IDs in executive function. It becomes apparent that several of the traditional tasks used by researchers, such as the Wisconsin Card Sorting Task, do not map well onto underlying functions and processes (Gruszka et al., this volume). A fundamental problem is that researchers agree approximately but not in detail on a taxonomy of control functions (Orzechowski, this volume). Furthermore, an illusory multiplicity of functions may arise from a common set of control mechanisms supporting different task-specific requirements (Chuderski & Nęcka, this volume). Correlations between different "executive" tasks are often quite small, so that psychometric analyzes are vulnerable to identifying method factors based on similar task versions. WM research faces the special problem of separating control from storage factors (Oberauer et al., 2007; Orzechowski, this volume). Given that many tasks in research use were designed on a rather ad hoc basis, it is also unclear how best to sample systematically the executive domain, although the commentators on this issue provide some suggestions. No doubt, increasing psychometric sophistication will make progress in articulating factor models, but the development of an optimal task battery for executive function may require better understanding of underlying neurocognitive processes.

Finding a Level: Granularity Issues

We have already raised the issue of the appropriate grain size for conceptualizing IDs. Should we work with broad constructs like resources, WM capacity, and brain motivational systems? Or should we work with fine-grained neural or information-processing models which may discriminate a multiplicity of separate IDs? The psychometric evidence is not decisive. Work on general WM capacity (Ilkowska & Engle, this volume) and on IDs in neural efficiency (Neubauer & Fink, this volume) suggests that broad ID factors may be identified. The Miyake et al. (2000) factors appear to be substantially intercorrelated (Friedman et al., 2006). Nevertheless, we have also seen that processes such as latent inhibition (Lubow & Kaplan, this volume) and set-shifting (Gruszka et al., this volume) may be partitioned into multiple processes that are differentially related to IDs. The attentional bias literature also shows the importance of fine-grained differentiation of critical processes (Derryberry & Reed, 2002).

The limitation of the psychometric evidence is that performance measures may be correlated for a variety of different reasons (Jensen, 1998). Processes that are not functionally related may be correlated because they are influenced by common genetic and environmental factors. Indeed, a recent behavioral genetics study (Friedman et al., 2008) suggests that the three Miyake executive functions are correlated because they are influenced by a highly heritable common factor. Thus, as Chuderski and Nęcka (this volume) advocate, models that seek to specify how IDs in executive processes are functionally related to one another require evidence from experimental as well as correlational studies. Although hierarchical structural models (Schweizer, this volume) offer a partial resolution to the granularity issue, the issue requires further specification of both neural and cognitive process models.

Involuntary and Voluntary Processes

It is well-understood that there is no place for homunculi in contemporary research. At the same time, there appears to be a reasonably sound set of criteria that differentiate voluntary and involuntary processing (Norman & Shallice, 1986), without any reference to some autonomous, internal agency. As recognized rather early in the modern era (Broadbent, 1984), if on-line executive decision is guided by retrieval of relevant information from memory (cf., Wells & Matthews, 1994), there is no need for a homunculus. There is no basic difficulty in developing processing models that instantiate executive control on this basis, much as we might program an autonomous robot equipped to resolve conflicting goals. At the neurological level, there is interest in how the self-organizing properties of populations of neurons may generate control functions (Braver et al., 2007).

Dealing with the "why" rather than the "how" of control may be more challenging. Several of the chapters in this volume demonstrate the significance of goals, motivations, and self-related constructs. McVay and Kane (this volume) show that priming personal concerns triggers TUTs and impairment of executive control and WM. This source of performance variation is typically uncontrolled in psychological experiments. Courage and Howe (this volume) describe how social and cultural factors influence the cognitive self, which in turn regulates autobiographical memory (and other cognitive functions). Motivations themselves may be directed toward cognitive outcomes such as the need for cognitive closure described by Kossowka et al. (this volume). In psychopathology, metacognitions such as beliefs about the importance of attending to worries shape various emotional disorders (Wells, 2000). Understanding the IDs in goals that drive efforts at executive control requires a knowledge-level analysis. However, predicting how these IDs are expressed in observed performance requires a detailed model of the cognitive architecture that specifies how goals are represented computationally, and interactions between voluntary and involuntary processes (Matthews & Wells, 1999).

A final point here is the need for caution in equating voluntary control with consciousness, given that conscious awareness seems to lag in time the mental and neural processes that have causal force (Corr, this volume). According to Corr, consciousness is an attribute of an "off-line" control system that may serve to regulate reflexive routine processing. A critique of Corr's argument is beyond the scope of this chapter, but we will make three brief comments. First, it is unclear whether consciousness is a *necessary* element of off-line control, or merely a typical epiphenomenon. Second, the distinction between on- and off-line control may be difficult to sustain in practice. Expectancy-based priming operates over fairly short intervals of 500 ms or (Neely, 1991), which may be compared with the 150 ms or so interval for automatic priming. Whether the expectancy mechanism is considered "off-line" depends on a seemingly arbitrary choice of duration. Indeed, functional analyzes of controlled processing (Norman & Shallice, 1986) suggest that it may be elicited precisely when there is a need for rapid action to deal with some unforeseen emergency. Third, whatever the limitations of consciousness, self-report remains useful for investigating the influence of state factors on cognition, as shown by research on TUTs (McVay & Kane, this volume) and subjective task engagement (Matthews et al., this volume).

More generally, as discussed by the commentators on this issue (Corr, Revelle et al.) both conscious and unconscious mechanisms contribute to cognitive control, and further work is needed to separate their roles in IDs in control. However, researchers should also recognize that automatic and controlled processes may exist on a continuum of automaticity, rather than being entirely discrete, and can be modeled computationally on that basis (Cohen, Dunbar, & McClelland, 1990).

Causal Issues

Corr's (this volume) contribution also raises the important issue of causal mechanisms for IDs, which may seem increasingly equivocal as our models rise further from the physical, neural substrate. Neural reductionism offers a coherent approach, which is likely to gain impetus from increased understanding of neurotransmitter and genetic influences on IDs (Ilkowska & Engle, this volume). Arguments against a solely neurological explanation for IDs are presented elsewhere (Matthews, 2008). In brief, it may be useful to treat mental constructs as being as "real" as physical ones (Sperry, 1993), given that we can establish nomological networks for such constructs that support hypothesis-testing within the normal scientific method.

Current research, that employs constructs at different levels of explanation, continues to face challenges in developing causal models. We have already mentioned the different perspectives derived from studying ID factors in 1-h experiments versus longitudinal studies lasting for months or years. The straightforward default position that derives from typical experimental studies is that stable ID constructs are fixed attributes that moderate the neural, cognitive, and behavioral outputs of the individual's response to stimuli. This assumption is built into structural models of IDs in executive processes, in which intelligence is treated as a latent independent factor (e.g., Schweizer, this volume). As Revelle et al. (commentary) discuss, the assumption also supports trait-state models of the kind familiar from anxiety research, in which traits refer to system parameters that govern the fluctuating state response (e.g., rate of change in response to threat). Certainly, the idea of traits as unitary, latent, stable factors has been central to both psychometric and experimental research.

However, the true picture may not be so simple. Several of the commentaries (Corr, Nęcka & Chuderski, Schweizer) point to the difficulty of treating ID constructs as separate from their constituent parts. If intelligence is, in part, an expression of IDs in executive processes, it makes little sense to talk about an effect of intelligence on executive processing. There may also be some difficulties for personality traits. Most would agree that IDs in cognition are central to intelligence, but personality traits are distributed across all the major domains of psychological functioning (Matthews, 2008). Revelle et al.'s (this volume) ABCD model differentiates affect, behavior, cognition, and desire (motivation) as separable elements of personality.

Where might such a critique of conventional thinking take us? A radical possibility is to ditch traits altogether, in favor of a truly multifactorial conception of IDs specified as a set of functionally separate endophenotypes (which might or might not be intercorrelated), including executive functions. We could then model IDs in behavior without attributing any causal status to overarching traits at all. (The practical difficulty is to develop good measurement models for a multitude of "micro-traits" that may not be amenable to self-report assessment.)

An alternative is to attribute some coherence to traits that goes beyond the sum of their parts. We will discuss this issue with relevance to personality, but similar arguments would apply to intelligence (cf., Sternberg, 1985), if we can assume that intelligence relates to IDs in multiple processing components. Traits may emerge from multiple neurological foundations, in the absence of any direct isomorphism between trait and brain system (Zuckerman, 1991). Corr (commentary) describes traits and cognition as forming an integrated psychological package, but the principle for the integration needs further specification.

Matthews (2008) proposes one resolution to the dilemma within a cognitive-adaptive theory of traits. Traits do indeed refer to numerous independent biases in neural and cognitive architectures. However, they derive coherence and functional unity from their role as IDs in adaptation; the various micro-traits support common adaptive goals. Thus, the IDs in executive processing that support superior multitasking in extraverts (Szymura, this volume) may equip these individuals to handle the cognitive demands of social situations. "Deficiencies" in inhibition typical of anxiety (Eysenck, this volume) may serve to maintain awareness and early warning of threat in those high in trait anxiety. The cognitive-adaptive model (Matthews, 2008) also addresses the longer-term dynamic features of traits; processing components, self-knowledge and selection, and shaping of external environments function synergistically to maintain the individual's adaptive stance (personality).

Conclusions

This book has aimed to present the state-of-the-art in research on IDs in executive processes. Individual exceptionality in cognition derives in large part from more effective control of attention and WM. In this concluding chapter, the editors have summarized the main contributions of diverse lines of research. Any research on IDs requires a solid psychometric foundation. Although structural models of personality and ability have a long history of provoking contention, we have seen that good progress is being made in identifying the key constructs relevant to executive functioning. These include fluid intelligence, standard personality traits such as anxiety and extraversion, more specialized cognitive traits such as need for control, and newer constructs including emotional intelligence. Personality research increasingly overlaps with studies of emotion, and state constructs related to stress, fatigue, and worry are also important for executive processing. Structural modeling is also being used to differentiate different executive functions, and to build common structural models that include both conventional ID constructs and executive functions defined by performance task measures.

Structural models are a required platform for research, but they do not tell us about IDs in processing, within a particular task environment. Contemporary research has also made great strides in delineating IDs in neural response and cognition while people perform tasks requiring WM, inhibition of irrelevant information, multitasking and switching of attention. It is becoming clearer how specific traits relate to IDs in processing, and how researchers can use this understanding to refine methodology. Most research has focused on the milliseconds-to-seconds time intervals of the typical experiment, but researchers are also beginning to study development of IDs in executive processing over the lifespan. We also saw that IDs in processing are evident at multiple levels of description, including the neural "hardware," the virtual "software," and the motivational and self-regulative processes that determine the goals of executive control. Theory is advancing to the point where it may usefully guide interventions such as treating psychopathology, supporting learning and training, and countering overload in human factors applications.

Any vigorous scientific inquiry will generate argument, and we end the chapter with a look at some of the controversies of the field. Both neuroscientific and behavioral studies have raised methodological challenges. Some are familiar issues in a new guise, such as questions of reliability and statistical power. Others are particular to the field, such as sampling experimental tasks systematically in psychometric studies. Researchers are also searching for the appropriate grain size for theory, contrasting "macro" constructs (resources, neural efficiency, general intelligence) with more fine-grained variables (specific processing components, brain regions, narrow traits). The tension between structural and process-based accounts in ID research is paralleled by uncertainties about the causal status of ID constructs, and, specifically, whether ID constructs may be treated as casual entities. Finally, the very idea of an executive process invokes a sense of voluntary control, and researchers must deal with the difficulties of volition and consciousness.

References

Ackerman, P. L. & Heggestad, E. D. (1997) Intelligence, personality and interests: evidence for overlapping traits. *Psychological Bulletin*, 121, 219–245.

Ackerman, P. L., Schneider, W., & Wickens, C. D. (1984). Deciding the existence of a time-sharing ability: A combined theoretical and methodological approach. *Human Factors, 26*, 71–82.

Bar-Haim, Y., Lamy, D., Pergamin, L., Bakermans-Kranenburg, M. J., & van IJzendoorn, M. H. (2007). Threat-related attentional bias in anxious and nonanxious individuals: A meta-analytic study. *Psychological Bulletin, 133*, 1–24.

Barratt, E. S. (1987). Impulsiveness and anxiety: Information processing and electroencephalograph topography. *Journal of Research in Personality, 21*, 453–463.

Braver, T. S., Gray, J. R., & Burgess, G. C. (2007). Explaining the many varieties of working memory variation: Dual mechanisms of cognitive control. In A. R. A. Conway, C. Jarrold, M. J. Kane, A. Miyake, & J. N. Towse (Eds.), *Variation in working memory* (pp. 76–108). Oxford: Oxford University Press.

Broadbent, D. E. (1984). The maltese cross: A new simplistic model for memory. *Behavioral and Brain Sciences, 7*, 55–94.

Buss, A. H. (1989). Personality as traits. *American Psychologist, 44*, 1378–1388.

Canli, T. (2009). Neuroimaging of personality. In P. J. Corr & G. Matthews (Eds.), *Cambridge handbook of personality* (pp. 305–346). Cambridge: Cambridge University Press.

Carroll, J. B. (1993). *Human cognitive abilities: A survey of factor-analytic studies*. Cambridge: Cambridge University Press.

Carver, C. S., & Scheier, M. F. (2000). On the structure of behavioral self-regulation. In M. Boekarts, P. R. Pintrich, & M. Zeidner (Eds.), *Handbook of self-regulation* (pp. 41–84). New York: Academic Press.

Caspi, A., Roberts, B. W., & Shiner, R. L. (2005). Personality development: Stability and change. *Annual Review of Psychology, 56*, 453–484.

Chamorro-Premuzic, T., & Furnham, A. (2005). *Personality and intellectual competence*. Mahwah, NJ: Lawrence Erlbaum Associates.

Claridge, G. (2009). Personality and psychosis. In P. L. Corr & G. Matthews (Eds.), *The Cambridge Handbook of Personality Psychology* (pp. 631–648). Cambridge: Cambridge University Press.

Cohen, J. D., Dunbar, K., & McClelland, J. L. (1990). On the control of automatic processes: A parallel distributed processing account of the Stroop effect. *Psychological Review, 97*, 332–361.

Corno, L., Cronbach, L., Kupermintz, H., Lohman, D., Mandinach, E., Porteus, A., et al. (2002). *Remaking the concept of aptitude: Extending the legacy of Richard E. Snow*. Mahwah, NJ: Lawrence Erlbaum Associates.

Corr, P. J. (2009). The reinforcement sensitivity theory of personality. In P. J. Corr & G. Matthews (Eds.), *Cambridge handbook of personality* (pp. 347–376). Cambridge: Cambridge University Press.

Derryberry, D., & Reed, A. (2002). Anxiety-related attentional biases and their regulation by attentional control. *Journal of Abnormal Psychology, 111*, 225–236.

Dweck, C. S. (1999). *Self-theories: Their role in motivation, personality, and development*. New York: Psychology Press.

Easterbrook, J. A. (1959). The effect of emotion on cue utilisation and the organisation of behavior. *Psychological Review, 66*, 183–201.

Eysenck, M. W., Derakshan, N., Santos, R., & Calvo, M. G. (2007). Anxiety and cognitive performance: Attentional control theory. *Emotion, 7*, 409–434.

Fan, J., McCandliss, B. D., Sommer, T., Raz, A., & Posner, M. I. (2002). Testing the efficiency and independence of attentional networks. *Journal of Cognitive Neuroscience, 14*, 340–347.

Fink, A., & Neubauer, A. C. (2004). Extraversion and cortical activation: Effects of task complexity. *Personality and Individual Differences, 36*, 333–347.

Friedman, N. P., Miyake, A., Corley, R. P., Young, S. E., DeFries, J. C., & Hewitt, J. K. (2006). Not all executive functions are related to intelligence. *Psychological Science, 17*, 172–179.

Friedman, N. P., Miyake, A., Young, S. E., DeFries, J. C., Corley, R. P., & Hewitt, J. K. (2008). Individual differences in executive functions are almost entirely genetic in origin. *Journal of Experimental Psychology. General, 137*, 201–225.

Gollwitzer, P. M., & Bargh, J. A. (2005). Automaticity in goal pursuit. In A. J. Elliot & C. S. Dweck (Eds.), *Handbook of competence and motivation* (pp. 624–646). New York: Guilford Press.

Gray, J. R., Burgess, G. C., Schaefer, A., Yarkoni, T., Larsen, R. J., & Braver, T. S. (2005). Affective personality differences in neural processing efficiency confirmed using fMRI. *Cognitive, Affective and Behavioral Neuroscience, 5*, 182–190.

Gray, J. R., Chabris, C. F., & Braver, T. S. (2003). Neural mechanisms of general fluid intelligence. *Nature Neuroscience, 6*, 316–322.

Haas, B. W., Omura, K., Constable, R. T., & Canli, T. (2007). Emotional conflict and neuroticism: Personality-dependent activation in the amygdala and subgenual anterior cingulate. *Behavioral Neuroscience, 121*, 249–256.

Haier, R. J., Siegel, B., Tang, C., Abel, L., & Buchsbaum, M. S. (1992). Intelligence and changes in regional cerebral glucose metabolic rate following learning. *Intelligence, 16*, 415–426.

Hertel, P. T. (2004). Memory for emotional and nonemotional events in depression: A question of habit? In D. Reisberg & P. Hertel (Eds.), *Memory and emotion* (pp. 186–216). New York: Oxford University Press.

Hudlicka, E. (2004). Beyond cognition: Modeling emotion in cognitive architectures. In M. Lovett, C. Schunn, C. Lebiere, & P. Munro (Eds.), *Proceedings of the sixth international conference on cognitive modeling: ICCCM 2004: Integrating models* (pp. 118–123). Mahwah, NJ: Lawrence Erlbaum.

Jensen, A. R. (1998). *The g factor: The science of mental ability*. Westport, CT: Praeger Publishers/Greenwood Publishing Group, Inc.

Johnston, W. A., & Dark, V. J. (1986). Selective attention. *Annual Review of Psychology, 37*, 43–75.

Kane, M. J., & Engle, R. W. (2002). The role of prefrontal cortex in working-memory capacity, executive attention, and general fluid intelligence: An individual differences perspective. *Psychonomic Bulletin & Review, 9*, 637–671.

Kane, M. J., Hambrick, D. Z., Tuholski, S. W., Wilhelm, O., Payne, T. W., & Engle, R. W. (2004). The generality of working memory capacity: A latent variable approach to verbal and visuospatial memory span and reasoning. *Journal of Experimental Psychology. General, 133*, 189–217.

Ketelaar, T., & Clore, G. L. (1997). Emotion and reason: The proximate effects and ultimate functions of emotion. In G. Matthews (Ed.), *Cognitive science perspectives on personality and emotion* (pp. 355–396). Amsterdam: Elsevier.

Klimesch, W. (1999). EEG alpha and theta oscillations reflect cognitive and memory performance: A review and analysis. *Brain Research Reviews, 29*, 169–195.

Knyazev, G. G., Schutter, D. J. L. G., & van Honk, J. (2006). Anxious apprehension increases coupling of delta and beta oscillations. *International Journal of Psychophysiology, 61*, 283–287.

Kruglanski, A. W. (1989). *Lay epistemics and human knowledge*. New York: Plenum Press.

Lazarus, R. S. (1999). *Stress and emotion: A new synthesis*. New York: Springer.

Martin, L. L. (2001). Mood as input: A configural view of mood effect. In J. P. Forgas (Ed.), *Feeling and thinking: The role of affect in social cognition* (pp. 135–157). New York: Cambridge University Press.

Mathews, A. (2004). On the malleability of emotional encoding. *Behaviour Research and Therapy, 42*, 1019–1036.

Matthews, G. (2000). A cognitive science critique of biological theories of personality traits. *History and Philosophy of Psychology, 2*, 1–17.

Matthews, G. (2008). Personality and information processing: A cognitive-adaptive theory. In G. J. Boyle, G. Matthews, & D. H. Saklofske (Eds.), *Sage handbook of personality theory and testing: Volume 1: Personality theories and models* (pp. 56–79). Thousand Oaks, CA: Sage.

Matthews, G. (2009). Cognitive processes and models. In P. L. Corr & G. Matthews (Eds.), *Cambridge handbook of personality* (pp. 400–426). Cambridge: Cambridge University Press.

Matthews, G., Campbell, S. E., Falconer, S., Joyner, L., Huggins, J., Gilliland, K., et al. (2002). Fundamental dimensions of subjective state in performance settings: Task engagement, distress and worry. *Emotion, 2*, 315–340.

Matthews, G., Deary, I. J., & Whiteman, M. C. (2009). *Personality traits* (3rd ed.). Cambridge: Cambridge University Press.

Matthews, G., & Gilliland, K. (1999). The personality theories of H. J. Eysenck and J. A. Gray: A comparative review. *Personality and Individual Differences, 26*, 583–626.

Matthews, G., & Margetts, I. (1991). Self-report arousal and divided attention: A study of performance operating characteristics. *Human Performance, 4*, 107–125.

Matthews, G., Schwean, V. L., Campbell, S. E., Saklofske, D. H., & Mohamed, A. A. R. (2000). Personality, self-regulation and adaptation: A cognitive-social framework. In M. Boekarts, P. R. Pintrich, & M. Zeidner (Eds.), *Handbook of self-regulation* (pp. 171–207). New York: Academic.

Matthews, G., & Wells, A. (1999). The cognitive science of attention and emotion. In T. Dalgleish & M. Power (Eds.), *Handbook of cognition and emotion* (pp. 171–192). New York: Wiley.

Michielsen, H. J., De Vries, J., & Van Heck, G. L. (2003). In search of personality and temperament predictors of chronic fatigue: A prospective study. *Personality and Individual Differences, 35*, 1073–1087.

Miyake, A., Friedman, N. P., Emerson, M. J., Witzki, A. H., & Howerter, A. (2000). The unity and diversity of executive functions and their contributions to complex "frontal lobe" tasks: A latent variable analysis. *Cognitive Psychology, 41*, 49–100.

Neely, J. H. (1991). Semantic priming effects in visual word recognition: A selective review of current findings and theories. In D. E. Besner & G. Humphreys (Eds.), *Basic processes in reading* (pp. 264–336). Hillsdale, NJ: Erlbaum.

Norman, D. A., & Shallice, T. (1986). Attention to action: Willed and automatic control of behavior. In R. J. Davidson, G. E. Schwartz, & D. Shapiro (Eds.), *Consciousness and self-regulation: Advances in research and theory* (Vol. 4, pp. 1–18). New York: Plenum.

Oberauer, K., Süß, H.-M., Wilhelm, O., & Sander, N. (2007). Individual differences in working memory capacity and reasoning ability. In A. R. A. Conway, C. Jarrold, M. J. Kane, A. Miyake, & N. Towse (Eds.), *Variation in working memory* (pp. 49–75). Oxford: Oxford University Press.

Paulewicz, B., Chuderski, A., & Nęcka, E. (2007). Insight problem solving, fluid intelligence, and executive control: A structural equation modeling approach. In S. Vosniadou, D. Kayser, & A. Protopapas (Eds.), *Proceedings of the 2nd European cognitive science conference* (pp. 586–591). Hove, United Kingdom: Lawrence Erlbaum.

Phaf, R. H., & Kan, K. (2007). The automaticity of emotional Stroop: A meta-analysis. *Journal of Behavior Therapy and Experimental Psychiatry, 38*, 184–199.

Posner, M. I., & DiGirolamo, G. J. (1998). Executive attention: Conflict, target detection and cognitive control. In R. Parasuraman (Ed.), *The attentive brain* (pp. 401–423). Cambridge, MA: MIT Press.

Pylyshyn, Z. W. (1999). What's in your mind? In E. Lepore & Z. W. Pylyshyn (Eds.), *What is cognitive science?* (pp. 1–25). Oxford: Blackwell.

Razoumnikova, O. (2003). Interaction of personality and intelligence factors in cortex activity modulation. *Personality and Individual Differences, 35*, 135–162.

Robinson, M. D., & Sedikides, C. (2009). Traits and the self: Toward an integration. In P. J. Corr & G. Matthews (Eds.), *Cambridge handbook of personality* (pp. 457–472). Cambridge: Cambridge University Press.

Rothbart, M. K., Sheese, B. E., & Conradt, E. D. (2009). Childhood temperament. In P. Corr & G. Matthews (Eds.), *Cambridge handbook of personality* (pp. 177–190). Cambridge: Cambridge University Press.

Salas, E., Sims, D. E., & Burke, C. S. (2005). Is there a "Big Five" in teamwork? *Small Group Research, 36,* 555–599.

Schnabel, K., Asendorpf, J. B., & Greenwald, A. G. (2008). Using implicit association tests for the assessment of implicit personality self-concept. In G. J. Boyle, G. Matthews, & D. H. Saklofske (Eds.), *Sage handbook of personality theory and testing: Volume 2: Personality measurement and testing.* Thousand Oaks, CA: Sage.

Siegle, G. J., & Hasselmo, E. (2002). Using connectionist models to guide assessment of psychological disorder. *Psychological Assessment, 14,* 263–278.

Soroko, S. I., & Leonov, V. (1992). Neurodynamic plasticity as a prognostic test of stability of operative activity under contrasting climatic conditions. *Human Physiology, 18,* 332–338.

Sperry, R. W. (1993). The impact and promise of the cognitive revolution. *American Psychologist, 48,* 878–885.

Sternberg, R. J. (1977). *Intelligence, information processing and analogical reasoning: The componential analysis of human abilities.* Hillsdale, NJ: Erlbaum.

Sternberg, R. J. (1985). *Beyond IQ: A triarchic theory of intelligence.* New York: Cambridge University Press.

Szymura, B., & Nęcka, E. (2005). Three superfactors of personality and three aspects of attention. In A. Eliasz, S. E. Hampson, & B. de Raad (Eds.), *Advances in personality psychology* (pp. 75–90). Hove, United Kingdom: Psychology Press.

Vul, E., Harris, C., Winkielman, P., & Pashler, H. (2009). Puzzlingly high correlations in fMRI studies of emotion, personality, and social cognition. *Perspectives on Psychological Science, 4,* 274–290.

Wacker, J., Chavanon, M.-L., & Stemmler, G. (2006). Investigating the dopaminergic basis of extraversion in humans: A multilevel approach. *Journal of Personality and Social Psychology, 91,* 171–187.

Wells, A. (2000). *Emotional disorders and metacognition: Innovative cognitive therapy.* New York: John Wiley.

Wells, A., & Matthews, G. (1994). *Attention and emotion: A clinical perspective.* Hove: Erlbaum.

Wells, A., & Matthews, G. (2006). Cognitive vulnerability to anxiety disorders: An integration. In L. B. Alloy & J. H. Riskind (Eds.), *Cognitive vulnerability to emotional disorders* (pp. 303–325). Hillsdale, NJ: Lawrence Erlbaum.

Zeidner, M., & Matthews, G. (2000). Personality and intelligence. In R. J. Sternberg (Ed.), *Handbook of human intelligence* (2nd ed., pp. 581–610). Cambridge: Cambridge University Press.

Zuckerman, M. (1991). *Psychobiology of personality.* Cambridge: Cambridge University Press.

Author Index

A

Aalto, S., 432
Aarela, E., 111
Aaslid, R., 218
Abad, F.J., 357, 425
Abele, A., 389
Abel, L., 74, 111, 112, 446
Abend, T., 389, 391
Abramovich, P., 182
Abramson, L.Y., 338
Achee, J.W., 389, 391–394, 396, 398
Achille, N.M., 28
Ackerman, P.L., 51, 52, 67, 235, 252, 264, 356, 362, 444, 449
Acuna, B.D., 343
Adam, S., 22
Adams, D.K., 30
Adolfsson, R., 305, 421
Adorno, T.W., 36
Aftanas, L.I., 156, 157
Agid, Y., 134
Aguirre, G.K., 89
Ahearn, M.B., 249, 253
Ahutina, T.V., 153, 156
Aiken, L., 99
Akbudak, E., 102
Albin, R.L., 303, 304
Alderman, N., 266
Aleksandrov, U.I., 157
Alexander, G.E., 128
Alexander, J.E., 112, 113
Alexander, K.W., 412
Alfonso, V.C., 257
Algom, D., 312, 377
Alkire, M.T., 89, 112, 113, 116
Alley, D., 404, 412
Allik, J., 384
Alloway, T.P., 309, 419
Alloy, L.B., 305, 308, 335, 336
Allport, A., 233, 271
Allred, K.D., 387
Almeroth, K., 40
Alonso, A., 111
Altemeyer, B., 36
Altgassen, M., 310

Alves, C.R.R., 184
Alves, S.E., 121
Amabile, T.M., 77
Ambridge, B., 354
Amelang, M., 111, 206, 221, 235
Amsterdam, B., 407
Ananiev, B.G., 152, 161, 162
Anderson, A.W., 101
Anderson, C.V., 128
Anderson, D., 406
Anderson, J.R., 269, 271
Anderson, K.J., 233, 235, 243, 427
Anderson, N.D., 91
Anderson, S.V., 128
Ando, J., 304
Andrade, J., 328
Andreasen, N.C., 74
Andrews, T.C., 137
Angleitner, A., 54
Angrist, B., 184
Annerbrink, K., 305, 421
Anokhin, A.P., 111, 112, 115, 155
Anokhin, P.K., 146, 151, 153, 161
Ansari, T.L., 200, 201
Anscombe, R., 186
Anthony, B.J., 249, 253
Antonis, B., 233
Antrobus, J.S., 325, 326, 330, 331
Arabie, P., 30
Arce, C., 116
Arcediano, F., 186
Armitage, P., 97
Armstrong, C., 303
Aron, A.R., 92, 100, 101, 127, 128
Artemenko, O.I., 154
Asendorpf, J.B., 406, 407, 439
Ashbrook, P.W., 336
Ashby, F.G., 428
Ashcraft, M.H., 302, 311
Ashton, M.C., 32, 35, 38
Aston-Jones, G., 169
Atash, M.N., 371
Atkinson, J.W., 28
Atwater, G., 184
Auerbach, P.P., 182

Auinger, P., 75
Aurlien, H., 121
Awh, E., 303, 355, 425, 426, 430
Azouvi, P., 310

B

Baars, B.J., 15, 429
Babchuk, W.A., 111
Bachner-Melman, R., 305
Bäckman, L., 111, 309
Baddeley, A.D., 15, 197, 250, 251, 253, 297, 303, 322, 325, 329, 353, 354, 372, 377, 428–430
Baddeley, B.T., 328
Badre, D., 101
Bagby, R.M., 111
Bahrick, L., 406
Baird, A.A., 307
Baird, J.A., 170
Bakay, R.A., 128
Baker, A.G., 130
Baker, J.E., 336
Bakermans-Kranenburg, M.J., 68, 450
Baker, S.C., 354
Baker, T.J., 60
Balkin, T.J., 306
Banaji, M.R., 31
Bandura, A., 224, 226
Banfield, R.F., 176
Banich, M.T., 310
Baraciaia, S.F., 325, 329
Barbaranelli, C., 118
Barcelo, F., 129
Barch, D.M., 181, 303, 304, 421
Bargh, J.A., 369, 376, 439
Bar-Haim, Y., 68, 450
Barker, R.A., 127, 131–135, 305
Barkley, R.A., 296
Barnard, P.J., 308, 424
Barnette, W.L., 55
Barnett, V., 102
Barnhofer, T., 424
Bar-On, R., 109
Baron, R.S., 377
Barratt, E.S., 440
Barrett, L.F., 222, 424, 429
Barrett, P., 249
Barrouillet, P., 354, 358, 360
Barta, S.G., 330, 427
Bartels, C., 128
Bartfai, A., 309
Bartussek, D., 79
Baruch, I., 181–183
Basak, C., 309
Ba ar, E., 113, 118, 121, 170
Basar-Eroglu, C., 114
Bassok, M., 375
Bastow, A., 176
Bates, J.E., 6
Bates, T.C., 183

Batterman-Faunce, J.M., 409, 411, 412
Baudonniere, P.-M., 406, 407
Bauer, A., 411
Bauer, C., 248
Bauer, H., 74
Bauer, P.J., 404, 406, 410, 420
Baumeister, R.F., 266, 289, 383, 387
Bayen, U.J., 329
Bazana, P.G., 74
Beatie, O., 405
Beaton, A., 308
Beauvale, A., 235
Bechtereva, N.P., 78, 147, 148
Beck, A.T., 29, 340
Becker, A.S., 336
Becker, G., 79
Beckmann, J., 427
Beeghly, M., 406
Behbehani, J., 53
Beh, H.C., 235, 248, 249
Behrend, D. A., 404
Beier, M.E., 235, 252, 264, 356, 362
Beike, D.R, 404
Beilock, S.L., 306–308, 311, 427
Bekhtereva, N.P., 147, 148
Belehov, Y.N., 154
Bell, C.J., 184
Belleville, S., 310
Bell, R., 184
Belongie, C., 326
Ben-Artzi, E., 29
Benbow, C.P., 74, 111–113, 116
Benedek, M., 77, 78, 172
Bener, J., 235
Bennett, C.H., 130, 188
Bennett, E.S., 111
Bennett, P.J., 90
Ben-Shakhar, G., 270
Bentler, P.M., 90
Benton, S.L., 310
Bercken, J.H., 130
Berenbaum, H., 111
Berenbaum, S.A., 122
Berendsen, E., 375
Berg, E.A., 127
Berger, H.J.C., 130
Berger, J.S., 89, 425
Berg, J., 37
Bergman, S., 308, 309
Berman, K.F., 93, 354
Berman, M.G., 91, 93
Bernardin, S., 354
Bernat, E., 121
Bernet, C.Z., 386
Bernstein, N.B., 154, 161
Berridge, K.C., 222, 223
Berti, S., 372
Bertolino, A., 305
Bertrand, O., 113, 114, 121
Bettman, J., 377

Author Index

Betz, A.L., 340, 405
Bezinovic, P., 371
Bezrukikh, M.M., 156
Bhattacharya, J., 113, 114
Bichsel, J., 60
Biener, L., 30
Bigler, E.D., 128
Bikov, N.B., 156
Bilder, R.M., 305
Billino, J., 310
Bimber, B., 40
Binder, J.R., 325, 326
Birbaumer, N., 111–113, 115, 155
Birch, D., 28
Biringer, E., 423
Birukov, S.D., 154
Bishop, S., 302, 304
Bjorklund, D.F., 406
Blackmore, S., 8
Blankstein, K.R., 196
Blasi, G., 305
Blatter, D.D., 128
Bleckley, K.M., 297, 300, 372, 374, 375
Bleckley, M.K., 323
Bless, B., 385, 389
Bless, H., 383, 389
Blumenthal, O., 185
Boals, A., 307, 308
Boase, P., 196
Boben, D., 118
Bobrow, D.G., 300
Bobrow, D.J., 376
Bodenhausen, G., 389
Boden, M.T., 111
Bodunov, M.V., 151
Bogomolova, I.V., 155
Bohlin, G., 308, 309
Bohner, G., 389
Bohnet, I., 37
Boiko, E.I., 150
Boise, S.J., 253
Boksem, M.A.S., 306, 307
Bollen, K.A., 90
Bolton, D., 185
Bonardi, C., 130
Bookheimer, S.Y., 343
Bookstein, F.L., 90
Boomsma, D.I., 115
Bopp, K.L., 427
Borgogni, L., 118
Borkovec, T.D., 311
Born, J., 77
Bornstein, B.H., 411
Botvinick, M.M., 303, 421
Bourdon, B., 251
Bouton, M.E., 185
Bovin, B.G., 155
Bowden, E.M., 172
Bower, G.H., 385, 386
Bowlby, J., 412

Bowling, L.E., 321
Boyce, W.T., 411
Boyle, M.O., 235, 252, 264, 356, 362
Bradley, B.P., 386
Bradley, M.M., 118
Bradley, M.T., 96
Braff, D.L., 185, 186
Braine, M.D.S., 358
Brannan, S.K., 423
Bratslavsky, E., 383
Braunstein-Bercovitz, H., 183–186
Braverman, D.L., 386
Braver, T.S., 75, 80, 83, 89–93, 95, 97, 176, 177, 272, 303, 304, 322, 356, 421, 446–449, 451, 457
Brebner, J., 53, 152
Breitenstein, C., 309
Brett, M., 302, 304
Brewer, W.F., 335, 349, 404, 405
Brewin, C.R., 308
Broadbent, D.E., 28, 231, 233, 250, 291, 456
Broadhurst, P.L., 205
Broks, P., 183
Brooks, D.J., 137
Brooks-Gunn, J., 407
Broussard, J.L., 306
Brouwer, W.H., 251
Brown, J.A., 301
Brown, L.H., 326, 327, 331
Brown, R.D., 406
Brown, R.G., 127
Brown, S.M., 101
Brown, V.J., 131, 132
Brück, A., 432
Brunner, R.P., 278
Bryden, M.P., 111
Brzezicka-Rotkiewicz, A., 338, 423
Bshary, R., 37
Bucciarelli, M., 344
Buchel, C., 360
Buchner, M., 361
Buchsbaum, B.R., 93
Buchsbaum, M.S., 74, 91, 111, 112, 116, 446
Bucik, V., 118
Buckner, J.P., 410
Buckner, R.L., 91
Budescu, D., 377
Buehner, M., 258
Bühner, M., 250, 251
Bullen, J.G., 241
Bullmore, E., 93, 425
Bulloch, K., 121
Bullock, M., 407
Bundesen, C., 254, 255, 270, 271
Bunge, S.A., 91, 92, 100
Bunting, M.F., 73, 90, 268, 298–300, 302, 311, 322, 356, 363, 429
Burch, G.S.J., 182, 183, 188
Burgdorf, J., 222
Burgess, G.C., 80, 83, 89, 91, 93, 95, 97, 266, 322, 447–449, 451, 457

Burgess, P.W., 250, 251, 297, 303
Burke, C.S., 455
Burke, M., 386
Burock, M.A., 91
Burt, D.B., 335
Buschkuehl, M., 278, 303, 308, 309, 431
Bush, G., 303, 304, 421
Bushuven, S., 309
Buss, A.H., 439
Butcher, L.M., 431
Butler, J.C., 36
Butterworth, G.E., 406
Buxton, R.B., 94
Buytenhuijs, E.L., 130
Byasheva, Z.G., 155, 156
Byrne, M.D., 269, 271
Byrne, R.M.J., 358

C

Cabeza, R., 91, 114
Cacioppo, J.T., 121
Cahill, L., 121, 410
Calamia, M., 423
Callicott, J.H., 89, 91, 95, 305
Calvo, M.G., 184, 195, 197–201, 206, 284, 286, 428, 444, 447, 450
Camos, V., 354
Campbell, J., 40
Campbell, L., 29
Campbell, S.E., 205, 206, 213, 221, 224, 438, 452
Canavan, A.G.M., 128
Canli, T., 80, 92, 101, 448
Cantor, J., 302, 354
Cantor, N., 109
Caplan, D., 309
Caplan, J.B., 90
Capon, A., 360
Caprara, G.V., 118
Caroll, J.B., 263
Carpenter, M., 420
Carpenter, P.A., 298, 310, 322, 356, 371, 376, 431
Carretta, T.R., 110
Carriedo, N., 359
Carr, L.A., 296
Carroll, J.B., 256, 439
Carroll, J.D., 30
Carr, T.H., 307, 308, 311, 427
Carter, C.S., 91, 181, 303–305, 421
Carullo, J.J., 302, 354
Caruso, D.R., 110, 111, 117, 118
Carver, C.S., 6, 7, 210, 221, 223, 225, 384, 438
Casa, G., 182, 186
Casa, L.G., 184, 186, 187
Casement, M.D., 306
Case, R., 356
Caseras, X., 307
Caspi, A., 67, 454
Caspy, T., 186
Castellan, N.J., 102, 103

Castelli, P., 404, 412
Castile, C.M., 406
Cattell, R.B., 54, 55, 263
Cerella, J., 309
Ceschi, G., 22
Chabris, C.F., 75, 89–91, 93, 95, 356, 446
Chae, J-H., 304
Chae, Y., 411, 412
Chaiken, S., 369, 375, 376
Chajut, E., 312, 377
Chalmers, D.J., 15
Chamberlain, A.G., 210, 222, 384, 392, 428
Chamorro-Premuzic, T., 51, 52, 440, 444, 452
Chang, J.J., 30
Chang, L., 90
Chang, W.L., 93
Channon, S., 336
Chapman, J.P., 181, 183
Chapman, L.J., 183
Charlot, V., 74
Chase, W.G., 431
Chavanon, M.-L., 80, 82, 448
Chee, M.W., 306
Chein, J.M., 297, 298, 304, 311, 422
Chen, P.Y., 102
Chen, Y., 375
Chernigovskaya, T.V., 156
Cherry, E.C., 299
Chertkow, H., 310
Chi, M.T.H., 431
Choi, Y.Y., 304
Choo, W.C., 306
Cho, R.Y., 272, 303, 304
Cho, S.H., 304
Choynowski, M., 55
Chrisley, R., 28
Christal, R.E., 75, 235, 311, 322, 354, 356, 358, 362, 372
Christensen, H., 384
Christianson, S.-A., 411
Chuderska, A., 269, 270, 277
Chuderski, A., 268–270, 277, 279, 443
Chun, D., 40
Chun, M.M., 430
Chun, W.Y., 371
Ciaramelli, E., 309
Ciarrochi, J.V., 111, 386
Cicchetti, D., 406, 407
Ciener, H.-C., 303
Claridge, G., 183, 235, 338, 451
Clarke, B.R., 406
Clark, L.A., 38, 384
Clark, M., 385
Clevberger, P., 309
Cleveland, W.S., 103
Cloninger, C.R., 32, 35
Clore, G.L., 29, 30, 111, 216, 383, 385, 389, 453
Coffey, E., 111
Cohen, D., 410
Cohen, E., 181, 182

Cohen, J.D., 88, 91, 99, 169, 181, 272, 303, 304, 421, 457
Cohen, L., 93
Cohen, M.S., 343
Cohen, P., 99
Coleman, R., 325
Colflesh, G.J.H., 93, 299
Collette, F., 73, 266
Cologen, J., 384
Colombo, J., 420
Colom, R., 111, 116, 264, 357, 362, 425
Conradt, E.D., 444, 454
Constable, R.T., 448
Conturo, T.E., 102
Conway, A.R.A., 73, 90, 93, 253, 268, 270, 278, 297–300, 308, 311, 322, 323, 342, 353–356, 363, 372, 374, 375, 421, 424, 429
Conway, M.A., 337, 404, 405, 409, 412
Conway, N., 372, 375, 376
Cools, A.R., 130
Cools, R., 127, 304, 305, 375
Cooper, A.J., 23
Cooper, J.A., 131
Cooper, Z., 336
Copeland, D.E., 344, 346, 348, 349
Corbetta, M., 92, 355
Corcoran, K.J., 217
Cordon, I.M., 411
Corkill, A.J., 269
Corkin, S., 308, 426
Corley, R.P., 199, 203, 431, 442, 443, 446, 448, 456
Corno, L., 441
Corr, Ph. J., 146
Corr, P.J.J., 3–5, 9, 12, 13, 16–18, 20, 21, 23, 63, 65, 66, 212, 221, 223, 225, 238, 241, 287, 458
Corsi-Cabrera, M., 116
Corwin, J., 347
Cosmides, L., 358
Costa, P.T., 38, 66, 212
Coull, J.T., 80, 250, 251, 255
Courage, M.L., 403–413, 420
Courten-Myers, G.M., 116
Court, J.H., 54, 88, 357
Courtney, S.M., 430
Cowan, N., 90, 252, 264, 268, 269, 278, 297–300, 311, 353, 354, 356, 363, 371, 410, 419, 422, 429
Cowan, P.J., 184
Cowan, W.B., 265
Cowen, N., 73
Cowen, P.J., 182, 184
Cox, J.R., 358
Cox, T., 213, 221
Cox, W.M., 330
Craig, A., 79
Craigie, M., 96
Craig, I.W., 431
Crane, C., 424
Crawford, J.D., 248
Crawford, T.J., 310
Crawley, R.A., 405, 420

Crede, M., 40
Cristal, R.E., 263
Crittenden, N., 111
Crockett, W.H., 339
Croizet, J.C., 307
Cronbach, L.J., 3, 35, 248, 322, 332, 441
Croson, R., 37
Csikszentmihalkyi, M., 405
Curiel, J.M., 346, 349
Cuthbert, B.N., 118

D

D'Agostino, P.R., 338
Dahlin, E., 309
Dahlström, K., 308, 309, 427
Dale, A.M., 91
Dale, M., 310
Dalgleish, T., 308, 424
Dalley, J.W., 208
Damasio, A.R., 128, 408
Damasio, H., 128
Damen, M.D.C., 129
Damon, W., 406
Daneman, M., 298, 310, 322, 354, 356, 376
D'Angelo, B.R., 325, 326
Danilova, N.N., 151, 156
Danko, S.G., 147, 156, 157
Dark, V.J., 439
Dar, R., 185
Das, S., 305
Das-Small, A., 248, 252
David, A.S., 81
David, O., 171
Davidson, G., 410
Davidson, R.J., 307, 423
Davies, B., 389–391
Davies, D.R., 205–210, 216, 221, 224, 392
Davies, J.B., 325, 328, 329
Davies, J.D., 325, 329
Davis, C.G., 338
Davis, M.A., 196
Dawling, S., 184, 186
Dawson, M.E., 186
Deary, I.J., 53, 54, 73, 221, 243, 251, 384, 392, 399, 427, 448
De Bellis, M. D., 116
Debner, J.A., 18
DeCaro, M.S., 306, 311
DeCoster, J., 378
De Courten-Myers, G. M., 116
Deffenbacher, K.A., 411
de Fockert, J.W., 430
de Frias, C.M., 421
DeFries, J.C., 199, 203, 431, 442, 443, 446, 448, 456
De Geus, E., 311
DeGrada, E., 371
Dehaene, S., 93–95
De Jong, P.F., 248, 252
De Jong, R., 375

De la Casa, L.G., 182, 184, 186
Della Casa, V., 186
Della-Maggiore, V., 90
Delong, M.R., 128
Delorme, A., 423
Delucia, R., 184
Demakis, G.J., 128
Dember, W.N., 207, 208, 211, 215–217, 221, 224, 225
Dempster, F.N., 269
De Neys, W., 361
Denis, M., 74
Dennett, D.C., 3
Dennis, I., 360
De Pisapia, N., 303
De Raad, B., 110
Derakshan, N., 184, 195, 197–201, 284, 286, 444, 447, 450
Derryberry, D., 386, 448, 451, 456
Desmond, J.E., 91, 92, 94, 95, 101, 365
Desmond, P.A., 210, 215, 216, 221, 226, 232
D'Esposito, M., 303–305, 309, 425, 426
Despres, G., 307
Detweiler, M., 297
Deutsch, M., 30
De Vooght, G., 361
De Vries, J., 444
DeYoung, C.G., 38, 173, 311, 422
Diamond, A., 310, 420
Dias, R., 128, 129
DiBiase, R., 407
Dickhaut, J., 37
Dickman, S.J., 209
Diehl, I., 311
Diener, E., 28, 38
Dienes, B., 389
Dienstbier, R.A., 38
Dierckx, V., 361
Dietrich, A., 79
DiGirolamo, G.J., 451, 454
Digman, J.M., 38
Dijksterhuis, A., 369, 370, 377
DiMaio, S., 305
Dimentman-Ashkenazi, I., 184
Di Santantonio, A., 309
Dissou, G., 51
Dixit, N.K., 303, 304
Dodson, J.D., 233, 235
Dolan, R.J., 360
Dolcos, F., 303
Donoghue, J.P., 343
Doppelmayr, M., 75, 112, 113, 115
Dorn, L., 291
Doumas, L.A.A., 278
Downes, J.J., 127, 129–131
Downing, P.E., 430
Doyon, C., 359
Dressler, R., 133, 185
Drewe, E.A., 128, 129
Dritschel, B.H., 325, 329
Driver, J., 267

Druzhinin, V.N., 154
Dubrovinskaya, N.V., 155, 156
Dudycha, G.L., 410
Dudycha, M.M., 410
Duffy, E., 234
Dugdale, B., 385
Dukes, C., 406
Dumas, F., 377
Dunbar, K.N., 361, 457
Duncan, C.C., 186, 249, 253
Duncan, J., 93, 268, 269, 302, 304, 323, 377, 426
Dunn, L.A., 184
Durham, R.L., 253, 255
Dvorayashkina, M.D., 152
Dweck, C.S., 224, 226, 452
d'Ydewalle, D., 361
Dykman, B., 305, 308
Dykman, D., 335, 336

E

Eacott, M.J., 405, 420
Eagly, A., 375
Easterbrook, J.A., 233, 450
Eber, H.W., 32, 35
Ebert, A.D., 128
Ebstein, R.P., 305
Ebsworthy, G., 29
Eckstein, D., 303
Edell, W.S., 183
Edison, S.E., 403, 405–407, 412
Edwards, J.A., 340
Efron, B., 102
Egeth, H.E., 254
Eimer, M., 265
Einstein, G.O., 329
Eisenberg, J., 305
Eisenberg, N., 7
Ekman, P., 217
Elbert, T., 112, 113, 115, 121, 303, 304
Elia, G., 181
Eliassen, J.C., 343
Eliasz, A., 390, 397, 399
Eling, P.A.T.M., 129
Ellinwood, E.H.J., 184
Elliot, A.J., 28, 225, 384
Elliott, E.M., 269, 278, 357
Elliott, R., 423
Ellis, H.C., 336
Elman, J., 354
Elvevag, B., 305
Embretson, S.E., 40, 60, 267, 278, 372
Emerson, M.J., 198, 201, 203, 265, 266, 268, 283, 296, 355, 442, 456
Emo, A., 209, 217
Emslie, H., 266, 268, 269, 377
Enders, P., 251
Engle, R.E., 298, 369, 372, 374–377, 429
Engle, R.W., 73, 88, 90, 100, 250–253, 255, 256, 258, 263, 264, 266, 268, 270, 278, 297, 298, 300, 301,

302, 303, 306, 308, 311, 322–324, 327, 342, 354, 356, 363, 364, 421, 422, 424, 425, 429, 430, 443, 445, 447, 456, 457
Epstein, C.M., 128
Epstein, S., 6
Erber, R., 306
Ericsson, K.A., 354, 431
Erikkson, E., 305, 421
Eriksen, B.A., 270, 291, 300
Eriksen, C.W., 270, 291, 300
Ernst, T., 90
Ershov, P.M., 176
Ertl, J., 73
Escobar, M., 186
Eslinger, P.J., 128
Essen, D.C., 92
Etienne, A., 303, 308, 309
Etlinger, S.C., 147
Ettinger, U., 200
Evans, A.M., 37
Evans, J.J., 266
Evans, J.St.B.T., 7, 358
Evans, L.H., 183
Evans, T.W., 386
Evenden, J.L., 127, 129–131
Everitt, B.J., 129
Extremera, N., 111
Eysenck, H.J., 4, 38, 39, 63, 79, 82, 118, 183, 206, 232, 234, 235, 236, 244, 384
Eysenck, M.W., 80, 118, 184, 195– 201, 206, 231, 234–236, 243, 284–287, 428, 444, 447, 450
Eysenck, S.B.G., 39, 183

F
Fadil, C., 406
Fairclough, S.H., 218, 225, 226
Falconer, S., 211, 215, 452
Fales, C.L., 343
Fallon, S.J., 134
Fangmeier, T., 74, 343, 423
Fan, J., 176, 304, 305, 421, 442, 445
Farah, M.J., 89, 129
Farber, D.A., 155, 156
Fassbender, C., 91, 95
Fazio, R.H., 68
Fehm, H.L., 77
Feldman-Barrett, L., 297, 298, 308, 369, 377
Feldon, J., 130, 140, 182, 184, 186
Fellner, A., 217
Fellows, L.K., 129
Ferguson, E., 213, 221
Fernandez-Berrocal, P., 111
Fernandez-Duque, D., 171, 249
Fernandez, G., 100
Fernandez, M., 182, 183, 187
Fernell, E., 308, 309, 427
Ferrell, R.E., 305
Ffytche, D.H., 80, 89
Fiebach, C.J., 95

Figar, S., 121
Filion, D., 185
Filler, M.S., 325
Fink, A., 64, 74, 75, 77, 78, 80–82, 112, 113, 115, 117, 122, 172, 173, 451
Finkenauer, C., 383
Finnigan, F., 325, 328, 329
Finomore, V.S., 207, 208
Fischer, T.R., 184
Fiske, S., 375
Fiss, W.H., 309
Fitzgerald, K.D., 177
Fivush, R., 405, 406, 408–410, 412
Flanagan, D.P., 257
Flashman, L.A., 128
Fleck, J., 172
Fleeson, W., 28
Flett, G.L., 196, 335
Flodman, P., 305
Flöel, A., 309
Flombaum, J.I., 176
Flor, H., 112, 113, 115
Flory, J.D., 305
Flowers, K.A., 131
Fockert, J.W., 430
Fogarty, G., 248
Fojas, S., 338
Foldi, N.S., 134
Folkard, S., 377
Forbes, E.E., 101
Ford, T.E., 369, 370
Forgas, J.P., 386
Fork, M., 128
Forssberg, H., 308, 309
Forster, S., 311
Fortgang, M., 325
Fossella, J., 176, 304, 305, 421
Fox, C.R., 90
Fox, M.D., 92
Frackowiak, R.S.J., 325, 326, 354, 426
Fraley, R.C., 31, 33, 412
Franklin, M., 89, 91, 101
Frank, L.R., 94
Freer, C., 268, 269
Freides, D., 128
Freimer, N.B., 304
French, C.C., 311, 386
Freudenthaler, H.H., 112, 113, 117, 122
Freud, S., 403
Freund, T., 370, 371, 374, 427
Frias, C.M., 305, 421
Friedman, N.P., 90, 198, 199, 201, 203, 265, 266, 268, 283, 296, 355, 431, 442, 443, 446, 448, 456
Fristoe, N., 270
Fristoe, N.M., 270, 278
Friston, K.J., 94, 170, 171
Frith, C.D., 94, 188, 325, 326, 354, 360, 426, 430
Fthenaki, A., 404
Fugelsang, J.A., 361
Fujita, F., 28

Fukuda, H., 305
Fukuyama, H., 90
Fulcher, E.P., 311
Funke, G.J., 209, 217
Furnham, A., 51, 52, 111, 241, 440, 444, 452
Fuster, J.M., 254, 259
Fux, M., 185

G
Gable, S.L., 384
Gabrieli, J.D.E., 91, 92, 101, 365
Galanter, E., 236, 353
Gale, A., 79, 234
Gal, G., 133
Galloway, M., 328
Galton, F., 73
Galvaing, M.P., 377
Ganey, N., 206
Gannon, K.M., 340
Garai, J., 110, 115
Garavan, H., 91, 94, 95, 308
García-Madruga, J. A., 359
Garner, J.P., 412
Garnham, A., 349
Gaschke, Y.N., 386
Gasper, K., 29, 30, 389
Gatenby, J.C., 101
Gathercole, S.E., 309, 322, 354
Gauggel, S., 310
Gauntlett-Gilbert, J., 131, 132
Gaunt, R., 7
Gauthier, S., 310
Gauzins, M.E., 307
Gavanski, I., 338
Gavrilova, T.A., 156
Geake, J.G., 89
Geaney, D.P., 182, 184
Geen, R.G., 234
Geffen, G.M., 304
Geffen, L.B., 304
Gehring, W.J., 177
Gerlič, I., 112, 117, 122
Gernand, W., 81
Gerrie, M.P., 429
Gershon, S., 184
Geus, E.J.C., 115
Gevins, A., 75, 112, 113, 306
Gewirtz, J.C., 181, 183, 186
Geyer, M.A., 185
Ghiselli, E.E., 173
Ghisletta, P., 427
Giambra, L.M., 321, 325, 326
Giampietro, V., 307
Giannitrapani, D., 115
Giannopoulos, C., 337
Gibbons, H., 183, 184
Gibbs, S.E.B., 89, 304, 305, 309
Giesbrecht, B., 303
Giesbrecht, T., 306

Gilbert, D.T., 7
Gilboa, E., 29, 335, 336, 348
Gilboa-Schechtman, E., 29
Gilinski, A., 344, 349
Gillath, O., 100
Gilligan, S.G., 385
Gilliland, K., 79, 206, 234, 285, 444, 447, 448, 452
Ginton, A., 186
Gittler, G., 74
Gizewski, E. R., 303
Glabus, M.F., 90
Glaser, J., 370
Glaser, R., 32
Glatt, C.E., 304
Glavanow, D., 346
Gleicher, F., 340
Glover, G.H., 91, 92, 94, 95, 365
Gluck, M.A., 92, 100, 101, 130
Gobbo, C., 411
Goel, V., 360
Gohm, C.L., 111, 389
Goldberg, J., 356
Goldberg, L.R., 32, 34, 35, 38, 66, 67
Golden, A.J., 308, 424
Goldhammer, F., 249, 251–255, 257, 289
Gold, J., 354
Goldman-Rakic, P.S., 303–305
Goldstein, S., 325
Golisano, V., 383
Gollwitzer, P.M., 439
Golosheykin, S., 111, 112, 115
Golubeva, E.A., 149, 150
Goodale, M.A., 14
Good, M.A., 135, 187
Goodman, G.S., 404, 409, 411, 412
Gordon, H.L., 307
Gordon, R.D., 254, 255, 269, 271
Gore, J.C., 101
Gorev, A.S., 156
Gorsuch, R.L., 184, 195
Gorunova, N.B., 154
Gory ska, E., 392
Goschke, T., 265, 266
Gosling, S.D., 31, 33, 36, 37
Gosselin, G., 184
Goswami, U., 419
Gotham, A.-M., 127
Gotlib, I.H., 29, 101, 335, 336, 338, 348
Grabner, R.H., 74, 75, 77, 78, 80–82, 172, 173
Grada, E., 370
Grady, C.L., 90
Grafman, D., 423
Grafton, S.T., 326
Graham, S., 186
Grant, D.A., 127
Grasby, P.M., 137
Gray, B., 278
Gray, C.M., 114
Gray, J.A., 6, 8, 12, 15–17, 20, 29, 68, 80, 89, 135, 140, 181, 182, 183, 184, 186, 384, 391

Gray, J.R., 75, 80, 83, 89–91, 93, 95, 97, 303, 304, 307, 311, 322, 356, 421, 446, 447, 448, 449, 451, 457
Gray, N.S., 181–184, 186, 187
Green, A.E., 311, 361
Greenberg, S., 325, 326, 330, 331
Green, I., 310
Green, J.D., 389, 391
Green, L., 90
Greenlee, M.W., 343, 423
Greeno, J.G., 335, 349
Greenwald, A.G., 31, 439
Greer, S., 93
Griggs, R.A., 358
Grigoryan, G.A., 135, 140
Grizenko, N., 305
Grob, A., 38
Groborz, M., 243, 244, 287
Grodsky, A., 325, 326
Groner, R., 303
Gross, J.J., 101, 308
Grossman, M., 303
Gruber, T., 121
Gruber, W., 75
Grubich, C., 128
Grucza, R.A., 32
Grudnik, J.L., 256
Gruszka, A., 134, 241
Grutter, A.S., 37
Guevara, M.A., 116
Guida, A., 431
Guilford, J.P., 76, 78
Gujar, N., 306
Gunter, T.C., 88, 303
Gunz, A., 410
Gur, R.C., 116
Guseva, E.P., 150, 151, 153
Gusnard, D.A., 326, 421
Gustafsson, J.E., 257
Gustafsson, P., 308, 309, 427
Gutbrod, K., 303
Gutiérrez, F., 359

H
Haas, B.W., 448
Habib, R., 116
Hachten, P.C., 181
Haden, C.A., 405, 406, 408, 409
Hagemann, D., 79
Hager, L.D., 265
Haier, R.J., 74, 88, 89, 91, 111–113, 116, 172, 446
Haight, J.C., 410
Haine, R.A., 409
Halford, G.S., 256, 264, 267, 270, 278, 363, 371
Hallet, M., 118
Hallett, P.E., 300
Hall, G., 130, 185
Hall, J.A., 111
Halpern, D.F., 110
Halpern, D.V., 326, 327

Hamamura, T., 184
Hambrick, D.Z., 90, 252, 258, 268, 270, 278, 298, 322, 323, 356, 363, 372, 421, 429, 443
Hames, R.B., 111
Hammar, A., 423
Hammen, C., 338
Hampshire, A., 134, 135, 137–139, 305
Hampson, E., 122
Hancock, P.A., 206, 215–217, 221, 224, 225
Handley, S., 360
Han, J.J., 410
Hansard, M., 200, 201
Hansen, P.C., 89
Hanslmayr, S., 75, 78, 173
Hardin, T.S., 335, 336
Hardisson, H., 310
Hariri, A.R., 101
Harlaar, N., 431
Harley, K., 408
Harley, T.A., 221
Harnish, R.M., 5
Harris, C., 455
Harris, J.A., 60
Harris, M., 369
Harrison, L., 171
Harrison, Y., 306
Harrod, M.-E., 235
Harshman, R.A., 122
Hart, D., 406
Hartlage, S., 305, 308, 335, 336
Hartman, P.L., 184
Hart, S.G., 213
Hartston, H.J., 184, 185
Harvey, N.S., 131
Harvey, P.D., 253
Hasenfus, N., 76
Hasher, L., 231, 302, 303, 335, 336, 354
Hasselmo, E., 441
Hawkins, K., 328
Haxby, J.V., 90, 430
Hayashi, T., 135
Hayne, H., 409, 410, 420
Hazen, K., 88, 91
Head, D., 185
Head, K., 116
Heatherton, T.F., 304, 307, 311
Hecker, U., 335, 338–344, 348, 349, 423
Heck, G.L., 444
Heggestad, E.D., 51, 52, 67, 440, 444
Heider, F., 338
Heim, D., 325, 326, 329
Heine, C., 112, 113, 115
Heinz, A., 100
Heinz, S.P., 291
Heit, E., 279
Heitz, R.C., 322
Heitz, R.P., 100, 250, 251, 255, 297, 300, 364
Heller, D., 28
Heller, W., 79
Helm-Estabrooks, N., 134

Helton, W.S., 215–217, 221
Hemenover, S.H., 38
Hemsley, D.R., 181–184, 186, 188
Henderson, A.S., 384
Henderson, J.M., 296
Hen, I., 186
Henley, N.M., 111
Henri, C., 403
Henri, V., 403
Henson, R.N., 425, 431
Herlitz, A., 111, 116
Hermann, B.P., 128
Hermans, D., 424
Hermesh, H., 29, 185
Heron, C., 265
Hertel, P.T., 335, 336, 348, 451
Hertwig, R., 358
Hess, T., 372, 376
Hester, R., 91, 95, 308
Heubeck, B.G., 384
Hewitt, J.K., 199, 203, 431, 442, 443, 446, 448, 456
Heyden, M., 252
Hiel, A., 370, 371
Higgins, D.M., 173, 422
Higgins, E.T., 389, 390
Higham, S., 310
Hikosaka, K., 305
Hilgard, E.R., 28
Himmelweit, H.T., 38
Himsley, D.R., 241
Hines, D., 76, 235
Hinson, J.N., 267
Hinton, E., 343
Hirsh, R., 6
Hirst, A., 430
Hirst, W., 231
Hirvikoski, T., 309
Hismjatullina, A., 269, 357
Hitchcock, E.M., 218, 219
Hitchcock, J.M., 184
Hitch, G.J., 251, 297, 353, 354, 356, 428–430
Hoaglin, D.C., 102
Hockey, G.R., 312
Hodges, J.R., 127, 129, 131–135
Hödlmoser, K., 75
Hoefer, I., 186
Hoeller, G., 248
Hoff, E., 114
Hoffman, J.M., 90
Hoffmann, H., 188
Hofstee, W.K., 38
Hogan, R., 32, 35
Holker, L., 29
Holland, J.H., 349
Holland, J.J., 266
Hollands, J.G., 209
Holland, S.K., 116
Holley, P.J., 208, 209, 216, 221, 392
Holmes, A.P., 94, 102, 103
Holmes, J., 96
Holt, L.E., 308

Holyoak, K.J., 278, 343, 349, 361
Honey, R.C., 135
Honk, J., 448
Horne, J.A., 306
Horner, M.D., 128
Horn, J.L., 55
Horstink, M.W.I.M., 130
Horwitz, B., 90
Hou, Y., 409
Howe, M.L., 403–408, 411, 412
Howerter, A., 198, 201, 203, 265, 266, 268, 283, 296, 355, 442, 456
Howe, S.R., 208
Hübner, R., 312
Hudlicka, E., 441
Hudson, J.A., 408
Huey, E.D., 423
Hugdahl, K., 423
Huggins, J., 452
Huguet, P., 307, 377
Hummel, J.E., 278
Hummert, M.L., 339
Humphreys, M.S., 65, 206–209, 218, 221, 222, 225, 226, 231–233, 243
Hunt, E., 236, 238, 244, 248, 249, 251, 376
Hunt, M., 405, 411
Hu, P.T., 306
Hutchings, C.H., 196
Huttenlocher, J., 335, 340
Hutton, S.B., 200
Hutton, U., 356
Hyde, J.S., 111
Hymas, N., 185
Hynes, K., 111
Hyyppa, M.T., 111

I

Iglewicz, B., 102
IJzendoorn, M.H., 450
Ijzendoorn, M.H., 68, 450
Ilin, E.P., 153
Ingberg-Sachs, Y., 183, 186
Ingram, R.E., 386
Inhelder, B., 340
Inoue, O., 305
Insler, R.Z., 101
Inz, I., 311
Irwing, P., 109, 111
Isbell, L., 389
Isen, A.M., 385, 428
Itoh, T., 305
Ito, T.A., 121
Ivanov-Smolensky, A.G., 146
Izumova, S.A., 153

J

Jackendorff, R., 5, 15, 16
Jackson, N.D., 109
Jacobaeus, H., 309

Author Index

Jacobs, G.A., 195
Jacoby, L.L., 18, 22, 23
Jacomb, P.A., 384
Jaeggi, S.M., 278, 303, 308, 309, 431
Jaencke, L., 92, 100, 101
Jagust, W., 304
Jameson, T.L., 267
James, W., 250, 327, 405
Janelle, C.M., 200
Jang, K.L., 57
Jarrold, C., 353–355
Jaskir, J., 407
Jaušovec, K., 74, 75, 77–79, 111, 112–118, 121, 122, 174
Jaušovec, N., 74, 75, 77–80, 111–118, 121, 122, 174, 235
Javoy Agid, F., 134
Jaworowska, A., 54
Jeczemien, P., 29
Jelicic, M., 306
Jellison, W.A., 307
Jenike, M.A., 303, 304
Jensen, A.R., 53, 73, 111, 244, 248, 255, 256, 264, 289, 456
Jermann, F., 22
Jiang, Q., 207, 208
John, O.P., 31, 33
Johns, M., 307, 311
Johnson, A.M., 116
Johnson, E., 377
Johnson, J.A., 32, 34–36
Johnson-Laird, P.N., 335, 336, 340, 344, 346, 348, 349, 358, 359
Johnson, M., 308, 309, 427
Johnson, M.L., 249
Johnson, M.R., 311
Johnson, R., 268, 269
Johnson, W., 304, 386
Johnstone, T., 101
Johnston, W.A., 200, 291, 439
Jolesz, F.A., 306
Jones, A.D., 272
Jones, B., 129
Jones, D.M., 210, 222, 384, 392, 427
Jones, K.S., 207, 217
Jones, R.D., 128
Jones, S.H., 183
Jong, P.F., 248, 252
Jong, R., 375
Jonides, J., 73, 89, 91, 93, 101–103, 197, 198, 202, 266, 278, 303, 307–309, 425, 426, 431
Joober, R., 305
Joormann, J., 335
Jordan, N., 131
Jorm, A.F., 384
Joseph, M.H., 135, 140, 182, 183, 184, 188
Josephson, B.R., 388
Josephs, R.A., 302
Josman, Z.E., 185
Jost, J., 370
Jouffray, C., 427

Joyner, L., 452
Juan-Espinosa, M., 264, 362
Judd, B.B., 344, 349
Jung-Beeman, M., 77, 78, 80, 172
Jung, R.E., 74, 116, 172
Just, M.A., 310, 371, 376, 431

K

Kabardov, M.K., 156
Kaczmarek, M., 51–53, 55
Kagan, J., 406
Kahneman, D., 196, 231–233, 236, 238, 243, 252, 266, 269, 376
Kaiser, J., 156, 235
Kalmar, D., 231
Kammer, D., 398
Kamping, S., 309
Kane, M.J., 90, 93, 251, 252, 256, 258, 264, 266, 268, 270, 278, 297, 298, 300–303, 306, 308, 311, 322–324, 326–328, 331, 353–356, 363, 372, 374–376, 421, 424, 429, 443, 447
Kanfer, R., 385
Kang, E., 101
Kan, K., 450
Kaplan, O., 133, 181, 182, 184, 185
Karakaş, S., 113, 118, 121, 122
Kareev, Y., 357
Karp, L., 385
Kasprow, W.J., 185
Kassubek, J., 343, 423
Katz, S., 426
Kaufman, J.N., 325, 326
Kaufmann, G., 383
Kauhanen, J., 111
Keil, A., 121
Keil, K., 430
Kellam, S.G., 249, 253
Kellendonk, C., 305
Keller, M.C., 102, 103
Kelley, W.M., 304, 311
Kemper, S., 339
Kenney, R., 411
Kensinger, E.A., 308
Keogh, E., 311
Keppel, G., 301
Kerns, J.G., 303, 304
Kerns, J.K., 111
Kerwin, R.W., 182
Ketelaar, T., 216, 453
Khachaturyan, E.V., 151
Kholodnaya, M.A., 153, 154, 162
Kieras, D.E., 354
Kiewra, K.A., 310
Kihlstrom, J.F., 109
Killgore, W.D.S., 306
Kilts, C., 184
Kimberg, D.Y., 89, 309
Kim, H.S., 122
Kim, J., 90
Kim, K., 304

Kim, M.S., 430
Kincade, J.M., 355
Kinchla, R.A., 250, 255
King, D.J., 184
King, J., 310
Kintsch, W., 346, 354, 431
Kirk, E.P., 302, 311
Kiroi, V.N., 151
Klauer, K.C., 358
Klein, K., 307–309
Klem, A., 369–371, 375, 427
Kliegel, M., 310
Klimesch, W., 75, 78, 79, 81, 82, 112, 113, 115, 116, 173, 446
Kline, R.B., 90
Klingberg, T., 303, 304, 308, 309, 421
Klinger, E.C., 329, 330, 348, 349, 427
Klirs, E.G., 29, 31
Klonowicz, T., 390, 397, 399
Kluckhohn, C., 27
Knauff, M., 74, 343, 423
Knecht, S., 309
Knippenberg, A., 369, 370, 377
Knouse, L., 326
Knyazeva, M.G., 155, 156
Knyazev, G.G., 156, 448
Kobayashi, S., 133
Koch, W., 248, 251, 252, 256
Kodama, T., 305
Koelega, H.S., 206
Koenigs, M., 423
Koeppe, R.A., 426
Kofta, M., 336–338, 340, 343
Kola czyk, A., 386
Kolodny, J., 377
Komar, J., 28
Kondo, H., 90
Konishi, S., 135
Konopkin, O.A., 158
Kopp, U., 310
Körkel, J., 431
Korotkov, A.D., 78
Korten, A.E., 384
Kossowska, M., 369–373, 375, 377, 379, 427
Kostrikina, I.S., 153
Kotler, M., 305
Kounios, J., 172
Kraemer, D.J., 361
Kral, V.A., 28
Kramer, G., 389
Kramses, L., 335
Kranzler, J.H., 256
Krendl, A.C., 311
Kringelbach, L., 222, 223
Kringelbach, M.L., 222, 223
Kris, E., 76
Kroger, J.K., 343
Kropotov, J.D., 147, 175
Kruglanski, A.W., 369–371, 373–375, 377–379, 427, 453

Krumm, S., 258, 361
Krupnov, A.I., 151
Kucharska-Pietura, K., 81
Kuhl, J., 338, 385, 392, 393, 427
Kuhn, J., 409, 412
Kulp, C.A., 308
Kumari, V., 80, 89
Kuncel, N.R., 40, 67
Kunze, Ch., 116
Kupermintz, H., 441
Kurland, M., 356
Kustubayeva, A.M., 160
Kwapil, T.R., 327, 331
Kyllonen, P.C., 75, 235, 263, 310, 311, 322, 354, 356, 358, 362, 372

L

LaCasse, L., 88, 91
Lacey, S.C., 89, 91, 101–103
Lachman, H.M., 305
Ladavas, E., 309
LaGrange, C.M., 207, 217
Laine, M., 432
Laird, A.R., 93, 425
Lampien, J.M., 404
Lamy, D., 68, 450
Landau, K.R., 406
Landry, A.M., 406
Lang, A.E., 130, 131
Lang, B., 420
Lange, E., 354
Langheim, L., 217, 218, 221
Lang, P.J., 118
Lansman, M., 236, 238, 244, 248, 249, 376
Laor, N., 182, 184
La Pointe, L., 375
Larsen, R.J., 80, 83, 89, 91, 97, 451
Larsen, W.A., 102
Larson, G.E., 88, 91, 265
Larson, R.P., 404, 412
Larsson, A., 309
Latane, B., 389
Lauber, E., 303
Laughlin, J.E., 73, 90, 253, 268, 297, 298, 311, 322, 342, 356, 372, 375, 376, 421
Laun, G., 36
Lavie, N., 311, 430
Lavric, A., 307, 311
Lawrence, A.D., 302, 304
Lazarus, R.S., 206, 210, 212, 213, 220, 453
Lease, J., 89
Lebedev, A.N., 154, 155
Lecas, J.F., 358, 360
Lecerf, T., 427
Lee, K.H., 38, 75, 88, 89, 91, 304
Lee, S., 304, 372
Lees, J.L., 207–209, 221
Lee, W.B., 28
Legerstee, M., 406

Legierski, J., 375, 379, 427
Lehtinen, V., 111
Lehtovirta, M., 115
Leichtman, M.D., 409, 410
Leiman, J.M., 43
Leitchman, M.D., 410
Leites, N.S., 153
Leodolter, M., 74
Leodolter, U., 74
Leon, M.R., 32
Leonov, V., 448
Leppink, J., 306
Leroy, A.M., 103
Leue, A., 80, 82
Leumann, L., 182
Levenson, R.W., 308
Lewandowsky, S., 279
Lewin, K., 30
Lewis, M., 406, 407
Lewis, S.J.G., 127, 131–135
Lewis, T., 102
Leyens, J.P., 307
Liao, I., 236
Liberman, A., 375
Libet, B., 7, 8
Libin, A., 153, 158
Lieberman, M.D., 7, 28
Liebert, M., 40
Lindholm, T., 111
Lindqvist, S., 308, 309
Linn, M.C., 111
Linton, M., 405
Linville, P., 348
Lipp, O.V., 186
Lister, S., 184
Litle, P., 37
Little, J.C., 327, 331
Liu, T.T., 94
Livanov, M.N., 151
Li, W., 35, 38
Lloyd, C.A., 325, 329
Lobaugh, N.J., 90
Locantore, J.K., 91
Locke, H.S., 92, 176, 177
Lockwood, C.M., 90
Loftus, D.A., 243, 427
Logan, G.D., 248, 254, 255, 265, 269–271, 301, 323
Lohman, D., 441
Look, R.B., 426
Lorist, M.M., 306, 307
Lottenberg, S., 91
Lowe, M., 325, 329
Lubart, T., 76
Lubow, R.E., 130, 133, 181–188
Lucas, R.E., 28, 38
Luce, R.D., 236
Luciano, M., 304
Luckii, V.A., 154
Ludewig, K., 182
Lukas, K., 372

Lukomskaia, S.A., 151
Luria, A.R., 146, 157, 161
Lurken, A., 79
Lushene, R.E., 184, 195
Lustig, C., 302
Lutkenhaus, P., 407
Lutzenberger, W., 111–113, 115, 155, 156
Luu, P., 421
Lynch, M.J., 427
Lynn, R., 109, 111, 116
Lyonfields, J.D., 311
Lyubomirsky, S., 387, 427

M

MacCallum, R.C., 88
MacDonald, A.W., 91, 303–305
MacDonald, S., 409, 410
Mac Gregor, J.N., 354
Machinskaya, R.I., 155, 156
Mackie, D.M., 385, 389
MacKinnon, D.P., 90
Mackintosh, B., 311, 422
Mackintosh, N.J., 111, 127, 129, 130, 185, 188
Mackworth, N.H., 205, 207
MacLachlan, A., 91
MacLean, P.D., 28
MacLeod, A.M., 326, 421
MacLeod, C., 29, 265, 284, 286
Macrae, C.N., 326
Maes, J.H.R., 129
Magoun, H.W., 234
Magulac, M., 185
Mahurin, R.K., 423
Maier, M.A., 225, 312
Maier, S., 79
Main, M., 412
Maitland, S.B., 111
Makeig, S., 423
Malagu, S., 309
Malanos, A.B., 28
Malceva, I.V., 154
Malizia, A.L., 184
Malleret, G., 305
Mamin, R.A., 151
Mandinach, E., 441
Mangan, G.L., 235
Mangun, G.R., 303
Manly, T., 328
Mannetti, L., 370, 371
Manoach, D.S., 101
Manor, I., 305
Mans, L., 407
Mansour, C.S., 116
Manuck, S.B., 101, 305
Margetts, I., 209, 210, 217, 452
Markina, A.V., 154, 156
Markovits, H., 359
Marom, S., 29
Marsden, C.D., 127, 128

Marshall, L., 77
Marsh, E., 372
Marsh, K.L., 340
Marszal-Wisniewska, M., 385, 392, 397–399
Martel, M.M., 296
Martindale, C., 76, 78, 232, 235, 236, 349
Martin, L.L., 383, 385, 389–394, 396, 398, 399, 453
Martin, N.G., 304
Marx, E.M., 338
Mason, M.F., 326
Masters, M.S., 111
Mataix-Cols, D., 307
Mathews, A., 29, 284, 286, 311, 386, 422, 450
Matova, M.A., 156
Matsuda, M., 130
Mattay, V.S., 89, 95, 305
Matthews, A., 428
Matthews, G., 4, 5, 79, 205–213, 215–217, 221–226, 232, 234, 235, 243, 286, 291, 384, 392, 399, 427, 428, 438, 441, 444, 445, 447, 448, 450–452, 454–458
Mattox, S., 269
Matushkin, A.M., 153
Matzel, L.D., 130
Mavaddat, N., 89
Maxeiner, M.E., 330, 427
Maxwell, J.S., 307
Maxwell, S.E., 94
Mayberg, H.S., 423
May, C.P., 302
Mayer, J.D., 110, 111, 117, 118, 386
Mayer, R.E., 40
Mayes, J.T., 265, 356
Mayseless, O., 375
Mazoyer, B., 74
McAdams, D.P., 404
McCabe, K., 37
McCandliss, B.D., 176, 442, 445
McCartan, D., 184
McCarthy, G., 303
McClelland, J.L., 457
McClure, E.B., 111
McConnell, A.R., 307, 308, 311
McCormick, L.J., 386
McCrae, C.N., 304
McCrae, R.R., 38, 66, 212
McDaniel, M.A., 329
McDonald, B., 385
McDonald, R.P., 35
McErlee, B., 265
McEvoy, L.K., 306
McEwen, B.S., 121
McGaugh, J.L., 410
McGee, M., 115
McGhie, A., 181
McGill, R., 102
McGinnis, S., 423
McGorty, E.K., 411
McGrew, K.S., 257
McGuigan, F., 412

McGuinnes, D., 252
McGuire, P.K., 325, 326
McGuthry, K.E., 270
McInerney, S.C., 303, 304
McIntosh, A.R., 90, 91
McIntosh, D.N., 337, 338, 340
McIsaac, P., 79
McKiernan, K.A., 325, 326
McKinstry, R.C., 102
Mclaren, I.P.L., 186
McLaughlin, S.C., 386
McLeod, C., 428
McMillan, K.M., 93, 425,
McNab, F., 303, 304, 421
McNaughton, N., 4, 5, 9, 16–18, 21, 65
McNeil, T.F., 183
McNelly, R., 428
McPherson, C.K., 97
McVay, J.C., 328, 331
Meaburn, E., 431
Mecklinger, A., 88, 303
Mednick, S.A., 76, 183
Medvedev, S.V., 78
Meffert, R., 310
Mega, C., 411
Mehta, M.A., 89, 304, 305, 309
Meier, B.P., 28
Meiser, T., 348, 358
Melinder, A., 411
Meltzoff, A.N., 406
Mendelsohn, G.A., 76
Meneses, A., 305
Meot, A., 307
Merckelbach, H., 306
Mériaux, S., 94, 95
Merike, P., 376
Merikle, P.M., 322, 354
Merlin, V.S., 152, 153
Merritt, C.R., 265
Merwin, M., 253, 255
Metcalfe, J., 7
Meyer, D.E., 354
Meyer, G.J., 96
Michaels, E.J., 28
Michielsen, H.J., 444
Migasiewicz, K., 127, 131–135
Miklewska, A., 51–53, 55
Mikulincer, M., 100
Miller, E.K., 303
Miller, G.A., 353, 354
Miller, L., 372
Miller, R.R., 130, 185, 186
Milner, A.D., 14
Milner, B., 129
Milstein, J.A., 208
Mineka, S., 29, 31
Minkoff, S.R.B., 73, 90, 268, 298, 300, 311, 356, 363
Minoshima, S., 303, 426
Mirsky, A.F., 186, 249, 253
Mischel, W., 7

Mishkin, I.Y., 155
Mishkin, M., 129
Mitchell, J.P., 304, 326
Mitchell, R.F., 75, 80, 238
Mitchell, R.L.C., 428
Mitchell, T., 369
Mitchel, R.F., 291
Miura, T.K., 93
Miyakawa, A., 304
Miyake, A., 90, 198, 199, 201, 203, 265, 266, 268, 283, 296, 353–355, 362, 372, 429, 431, 442, 443, 446, 448, 456
Miyake, T.M., 322
Miyashita, Y., 135
Mizoguchi, H., 211, 217
Mogg, K., 386
Mohamed, A.A.R., 205, 206, 221, 224, 438, 452
Mohr, B., 113
Molen, M.W., 129
Molina, V., 129
Mölle, M., 77
Monk, T., 377
Monsell, S., 201, 265, 267
Monteil, J.M., 377
Montiero, K.P., 385
Moore, A.U., 181
Moore, B.A., 336
Moore, K., 235
Moosbrugger, H., 248, 249, 251–255, 257, 264, 288
Moran, P.M., 135, 140, 182, 184
Moray, N., 236, 299
Moreno, S., 359
Morey, C.C., 269
Mori, M., 74
Morishita, M., 90
Morosanova, V.I., 153, 158
Morris, L.W., 196
Morris, N., 358
Morris, R.G., 127, 129–131
Morton, J.B., 355
Moruzzi, G., 234
Moser, P.C., 184
Moskowitz, G., 369, 376
Moss, L., 406
Mountain, M.A., 128
Mulack, T., 343, 423
Mulholland, T.M., 32
Mullen, M.K., 409, 410
Muller, J., 310
Müller, M.M., 121
Mullington, J.M., 306
Muly, E.C., 305
Mumford, J.A., 94
Munakata, Y., 355
Muncer, S.J., 96
Munk, M.H.J., 156
Muraven, M., 369
Murias, M., 305
Murphy, K., 94, 95
Murray, H.A., 27

Murray, M.J., 335, 336, 348
Murray, N.P., 200
Mycielska, K., 327
Myers, C., 130
Myin-Germeys, I., 327, 331
Myors, B., 249

N

Näätänen, R., 175
Nabatame, H., 130
Nadal, R., 184
Nagahama, Y., 130
Nagell, K., 420
Nagornova, Z.V., 147, 156
Någren, K., 432
Nakahara, K., 135
Naparstek, J., 386
Narayanan, N.S., 425
Naumann, E., 79
Navon, D., 31, 231, 250, 265
N cka, E., 203, 208, 209, 231, 232, 235–238, 240, 243, 244, 248, 249, 264, 268, 270, 277, 287, 291, 357, 372, 376, 392, 443, 444, 451
Neale, M.C., 115
Nebel, K., 303
Nebilitcyn, V.D., 146, 148–150, 161, 162
Nee, D.E., 89, 91, 93, 101, 303
Neely, J.H., 457
Neisser, U., 404–406, 420
Nelson, J.B., 187
Nelson, K., 406, 408, 412, 419
Neubauer, A.C., 64, 74, 75, 77, 78, 80–82, 112, 113, 115, 117, 122, 172, 173, 248, 259, 451
Neubauer, V., 112, 113
Neuberg, S., 375
Neumann, O., 252, 253
Neuper, C., 74, 75, 78, 80–82, 173
Newberry, B.H., 54
Newell, A., 5
Neys, W., 361
Nicewander, W.A., 88
Nichols, T.E., 94, 102, 103
Nickel, D.G., 134
Niedenthal, P.A., 386
Niedenthal, P.M., 338
Niederehe, G., 335
Nielson, M., 406
Niemivirta, M., 312
Nigg, J.T., 198, 296
Nilsson, G., 305, 421
Nilsson, L.G., 111
Nimmo-Smith, I., 325, 329
Ninio, A., 233
Nirkko, A.C., 303, 308, 309
Nisbett, R.E., 321, 349, 361
Nolan, K.A., 305
Nolen-Hoeksema, S., 387, 427
Noll, D.C., 91, 303, 304
Nordby, H., 181

Norman, D.A., 7, 28, 65, 210, 220, 223, 226, 250, 251, 253, 265, 266, 297, 376, 438, 439, 456, 457
Norman, W.T., 38
Norton, M.I., 326
Nosek, B.A., 31, 68
Ntsmmrt, M., 307
Nuechterlein, K.H., 186, 207, 208
Numachi, Y., 184
Nunez, P.L., 113, 114
Nutt, D.J., 184
Nyberg, L., 111, 114, 116, 309
Nyborg, H., 109, 110
Nystrom, L.E., 91, 272

O

Oakeshott, S.M., 130
Oatley, K., 348, 349
Oberauer, K., 264, 270, 274, 296, 309, 354–357, 360–364, 372, 450, 456
Oberling, P., 184
Obonsawin, M.C., 325, 329, 424
O'Boyle, M.W., 112, 113
Ochsner, K.N., 91, 92
O'Connor, R.C., 325, 326, 328, 329, 424
Oehlberg, K., 4
Ogle, C.M, 411
Ohman, A., 181
Oh, S.H., 355, 425
Ojemann, J.G., 102
Okina, T., 130
Olesen, P.J., 308, 309, 427
Oliphant, G., 249
Olson, M.A., 68
Omura, K., 92, 448
Onishi, K., 303
Ono, Y., 304, 311
Onton, J., 423
Oosterlaan, J., 305
O'Reilly, R. C., 355
Ortony, A., 7, 28, 65
Orzechowski, J., 279, 357
Osaka, M., 90
Osaka, N., 90
Osborne, J.W., 307, 311
Östensson, M.-L., 309
Ostrem, J.L., 354
Ottaway, S.A., 336
Owen, A.M., 89, 93, 127, 129, 131–135, 137–139, 305, 425, 426
Ozdoba, C., 303, 308, 309
Ozonoff, S., 310

P

Pachinger, T., 75
Pajares, F., 224
Pakhomov, S.V., 78
Palacios, A., 362
Palei, I.M., 152

Panksepp, J., 222
Parasuraman, R., 205, 207–209, 219
Paré-Blagoev, E.J., 101
Parker, J.D.A., 111
Park, S., 430
Parsons, K.S., 216, 220, 225
Pashina, A.Kh., 156
Pashler, H.E., 208, 247, 250, 266, 268, 269, 271
Passingham, R.E., 128
Patel, J., 310
Paulesu, E., 325, 326, 426
Paulewicz, B., 268, 277, 443
Paulhus, D.L., 37
Paunonen, S.V., 28, 38
Pavlov, I.P., 54, 145, 161
Payne, J., 377
Payne, S., 197, 284
Payne, T.W., 90, 252, 258, 268, 298, 421, 443
Paz-Alonzo, P.M., 404, 412
Pearce, J.M., 185
Pechenkov, V.V., 150
Pekrun, R., 225
Pellegrino, J.W., 32
Pelling, E.L., 23
Penney, J.B., 303, 304
Pennington, B.F., 310
Penrod, S.D., 411
Peoples, M., 182
Pereda, E., 113, 114
Perez-Garcia, G., 305
Pergamin, L., 68, 450
Perilloux, H.K., 406
Perkins, A.M., 146
Perkins, N., 308
Perkins, R., 424
Perlstein, W.M., 303, 304
Perner, J., 406, 419, 420
Perrig, W.J., 278, 303, 308, 309, 431
Perroud, A., 22
Perry, W., 185
Persson, J., 307, 309
Pervin, L.A., 390, 399
Petersen, S.E., 80, 253, 422
Peterson, A.C., 111
Peterson, B.S., 101
Peterson, J.B., 38, 173, 422
Peterson, L.R., 301
Peterson, M.J., 301
Peters, S.L., 135, 140, 184
Petrakis, E., 122
Petrides, K.V., 52, 111
Petrides, M., 304, 426
Petrosova, T.A., 151
Petsche, H., 113, 114
Petty, R.E., 387, 388
Petzold, P., 389
Pfaff, D.W., 304, 421
Pfleiderer, B., 116, 121
Pflieger, M.E., 118
Pfurtscheller, G., 75, 112, 113, 118

Phaf, R.H., 450
Phan, K.L., 177
Phillips, L.H., 310, 428
Phillips, M.L., 81
Phillips, S., 256, 264, 267, 270, 278, 363, 371
Piaget, J., 340
Piazza, M., 93
Pickard, J.D., 89
Pickering, A.D., 184, 186, 223
Pickering, S.J., 322, 354
Pick, M., 258
Pierro, A., 370, 371
Pillemer, D.B., 406, 419
Pilowsky, L.S., 182
Pinel, P., 93–95
Pineno, O., 186
Piotrowska, A., 52, 53
Pipe, M.-E., 411
Pirogov, Y.A., 156
Pisapia, N., 303
Pittman, T.S., 338
Pizzagalli, D.A., 307
Plante, E., 116
Pleydell-Price, C.W., 404, 409
Plomin, R., 431
Pluecken, T., 258
Pochon, J.B., 177
Pocock, S.J., 97
Pogge, D.L., 253
Pointe, L., 375
Polan, H.J., 305
Poldrack, R.A., 90, 92, 100, 101
Poline, J.B., 94, 95
Polkey, C.E., 127–129, 131–135, 305
Pöllhuber, D., 112, 113, 115
Polonskaya, N.N., 153, 156
Polson, P.G., 431
Poltrock, S., 248, 249
Ponomarev, V.A., 147
Poole, B.J., 429
Poon, L.W., 404, 405
Popovich, P.M., 102
Porteus, A., 441
Portrat, S., 354
Posner, M.I., 75, 80, 170, 176, 223, 248, 252, 253, 291, 297, 305, 420, 422, 442, 445, 451, 454
Posner, M.J., 238
Posthuma, D., 115, 311
Postle, B.R., 175, 426
Potts, G.R., 340
Povinelli, D.J., 406, 419
Powers, W.J., 326, 421
Prabhakaran, V., 365, 425
Pradat-Diehl, P., 310
Prados, J., 188
Preacher, K.J., 88
Press, D.Z., 306
Previc, F.H., 304
Pribram, K.H., 252, 353
Price, C.J., 94

Proctor, L., 325, 329
Prudhomme, N., 408
Pulvermüller, F., 113
Pusateri, T.P., 389
Puukka, P., 111
Pylyshyn, Z.W., 5, 222, 438, 445, 452
Pytlik Zillig, L.M., 38

Q
Quas, J.A., 409, 411, 412
Quilty, L.C., 38
Quinn, D.M., 307
Quinn, N., 128

R
Raad, B., 38, 110
Rabel, C., 383
Radilovà, J., 121
Radil, T., 121
Radvansky, G.A., 344, 346, 348, 349
Radwan, S., 257
Raes, F., 424
Rafal, R.D., 252, 253
Rahhal, T.A., 404, 405
Raichle, M.E., 92, 102, 326, 421
Raine, A., 183
Ramachandran, V.S., 11
Ramesar, R., 304, 305
Rammsayer, T., 183, 184
Ramos, J., 116
Ramsay, D.S., 407
Randolph, C., 354
Rapee, R.M., 196
Rapoport, A., 377
Rapoport, S.I., 90
Rappaport, J.L., 184
Rappelsberger, P., 116
Rascle, C., 182
Ratcliff, R., 102
Rauch, S.L., 303, 304
Raven, J.C., 32, 54, 88, 357
Rawlins, J.N.P., 182, 184
Raymont, V., 423
Raz, A., 442, 445
Razoumnikova, O.M., 77, 78, 115, 155, 448
Reading, S., 93, 202
Realo, A., 384
Reason, J.T., 327
Rebollo, I., 264, 362, 425
Redfield, J., 134
Redick, T.S., 297, 422
Reed, A., 448, 451, 456
Reed, M.A., 386
Reed, T.E., 116
Ree, M.J., 110
Reese, E., 406, 408–410, 412
Rees, G., 430
Reichle, E.D., 326, 327

Reid, H., 325, 329
Reik, P., 116
Reimann, B., 428
Reinerman, L.E., 205–227
Reis, D.L., 311
Reiser, B.J., 358
Reise, S.P., 40
Reis, H.T., 384
Reitan, R.M., 128, 303
Rentfrow, P.J., 36, 37
Renvoize, T., 310
Rescher, B., 116
Reuter-Lorenz, P.A., 91, 307, 309
Revelle, W., 4, 7, 27–29, 31, 32, 35, 37, 38, 41, 42, 65, 67, 206–209, 218, 221, 222, 225, 226, 231–233, 243, 422, 427
Reynolds, G., 420
Reynolds, J.R., 89, 95
Reynolds, P., 233
Rholes, W.S., 389, 390, 412
Ribalko, E.F., 151
Riby, L., 325, 329
Richards, A., 386
Richards, J.E., 420
Richards, J.M., 308
Richeson, J.A., 65, 90, 307, 311
Richey, E.T., 128
Richter, L., 370, 371, 427
Ridderinkhof, K.R., 129, 306, 307
Riddlesberger, M.M., 409, 412
Riedel, W.J., 304, 305, 309
Rimes, K.S., 307
Rinne, J.O., 432
Ripper, B., 75
Rippon, G., 307, 311
Rips, L.J., 358, 359
Rissman, J., 95
Robbins, T.W., 89, 127–135, 137, 208, 305
Roberts, A.C., 127–135
Roberts, B.W., 28, 67, 454
Roberts, J.E., 310, 335, 336, 348
Robertson, C., 131
Robertson, I.H., 328
Robertson, M.M., 336
Roberts, R., 248, 251
Roberts, R.C., 131, 132
Roberts, R.D., 248, 249, 256
Roberts, R.J., 265
Robinson, D.L., 53
Robinson, K., 303
Robinson, M.D., 28, 221, 224, 452
Robins, R.W., 28
Rochat, P., 406
Roche, A., 94, 95
Rocklin, T., 37, 41
Rockstroh, B., 112, 113, 115
Rockstroh, S., 248
Rodgers, B., 384
Rodrigues, S., 200
Roediger, H., 372

Rogers, G.M., 29
Rogers, R.D., 137, 265, 305
Rogers, R. D., 354
Rolls, E.T., 7
Roman, R., 369, 376
Rooksby, M., 403, 404
Rooy, D.L., 111
Roper, D.W., 310
Rosa, E., 90
Rosenberg, E.H., 326
Rosen, B.P., 303, 304
Rosen, B.R., 91, 426
Rosenthal, L., 185
Rosenthal, R., 28
Rosen, V.M., 298, 301, 302, 308, 323
Ross, M., 404, 409
Rothbart, M.K., 6, 176, 223, 420, 444, 454
Roth, E., 73
Rothman, S., 247
Rothwell, A., 306
Rotrosen, J., 184
Roudas, M.S., 78
Rousseeuw, P.J., 103
Rowe, B.C., 97
Ruberg, M., 134
Rubia, J.F., 129
Rubin, D.C., 404, 405, 410
Rucker, D.D., 88
Ruddle, R.A., 182, 183, 187
Rude, S.S., 336, 348
Rudnick, A., 182
Ruff, C.C., 74, 343, 423
Ruffman, T., 406, 419, 420
Rumain, B., 358
Rumanova, N.B., 156
Runco, M.A., 76
Rusalova, M.N., 156
Rusalov, V.M., 149, 151, 156, 161
Rushton, J.P., 109
Russegger, H., 75
Rusting, C.L., 386–388, 392
Rutherford, E.M., 29, 286
Rydell, R.J., 307, 308, 311
Rypma, B., 75, 89, 95, 425, 426

S
Saarijarvi, S., 111
Sabb, F.W., 343
Safonceva, S.V., 154
Sagar, H.J., 131
Sahakian, B.J., 89, 127, 129–131, 305
Saint-Cyr, J.A., 130, 131
Saklofske, D.H., 205, 206, 221, 224, 438, 452
Salas, E., 455
Salih, H.R., 343, 423
Salminen, J.K., 111
Salmon, K., 412
Salovey, P., 110, 111, 117, 118, 388
Salovy, P., 404

Salthouse, T.A., 255, 270, 349, 354, 371, 372
Sams, M.E., 157
Sander, N., 264, 270, 274, 354, 355, 360–362, 364, 450, 456
Sanders, B., 111
Sandhofer, C.M., 278
Sanes, J.N., 343
Sange, G., 75, 112, 113
Sanjuan, M.D.C., 187
Santantonio, A., 309
Santome-Calleja, A., 129
Santos, R., 184, 195, 197–201, 284–286, 444, 447, 450
Sanz, M., 129
Sarason, I.G., 196, 210
Sargis, E.G., 31, 33
Sarinopoulos, I., 307
Sato, M., 184
Sauer, H., 90
Saults, J.S., 269, 278, 357
Sauseng, P., 75, 78, 173
Savitz, J., 304, 305
Saxby, D.J., 205–227
Sayfan, L., 411
Scala, G., 184
Schaaf, J.M., 411
Schachtman, T.R., 130, 185
Schaefer, A., 80, 83, 89, 91, 95, 97, 451
Schaeken, W., 361
Schafer, E., 73
Schaffer, A., 406
Schaper, C., 369, 370, 377
Scheier, M.F., 210, 221, 223, 225, 438
Scheinfeld, A., 110, 115
Scheutz, M., 28
Schimke, H., 75
Schlegel, R.E., 285
Schlossberg, A., 182
Schlösser, R.G.M., 90
Schmader, T., 307, 311
Schmalhofer, F., 346
Schmeichel, B.J., 296, 306, 308
Schmid, J.J., 43
Schmidt-Atzert, L., 250, 251
Schmidtke, J.I., 79
Schmidt, M., 253, 255
Schmithorst, V.J., 116
Schmuckler, M.A., 406
Schnabel, K., 439
Schneider-Rosen, K., 407
Schneider, W., 208, 248, 256, 297, 298, 304, 311, 421, 431, 449
Schnur, P., 186
Scholey, K.A., 430
Schooler, J.W., 321, 325–327
Schrausser, D.G., 75, 80–82, 112, 113, 115
Schrock, J.C., 100, 300, 322, 323
Schroger, E., 372
Schroth, G., 303
Schuck, S., 305
Schulte, M.J., 110

Schulze, R., 264, 356, 361–363
Schumacher, E.G., 303
Schumacher, E.H., 426
Schumann, D.W., 395
Schunk, D.H., 224
Schürmann, M., 113
Schutter, D.J.L.G., 448
Schwaiger, J., 75
Schwarz, N., 383, 385, 389
Schwean, V.L., 205, 206, 221, 224, 438, 452
Schweizer, K., 244, 247–259, 264, 270, 288
Schwitzgebel, E., 321
Sedek, G., 335–350, 423
Sedikides, C., 389, 391
See, J.E., 208, 219
Seewer, R., 303
Sekuler, A.B., 90
Sekuler, R., 90
Seligman, M.E.P., 338
Sergienko, E.A., 157, 158
Serino, A., 309
Serra, A.M., 183
Servadei, F., 309
Setchenov, I.M., 161
Setterlund, M.B., 386
Seyfarth, J., 303
Shackman, A.J., 307
Shadach, E., 184
Shadrikov, V.D., 153
Shah, J., 370
Shah, N.J., 92, 100, 101
Shah, P., 296, 362, 372, 429
Shalker, T.E., 385
Shallice, T., 250, 251, 265, 266, 297, 303, 419, 438, 439, 456, 457
Shamosh, N.A., 361
Sham, P., 431
Shao, L., 38
Sharp, R., 182
Shaver, P.R., 100, 412
Shaw, G.A., 326
Shaw, T.H., 215–217
Sheese, B.E., 223, 444, 454
Sheets, V., 90
Sheffer, L., 270
Shelton, J.N., 307, 311
Shibasaki, H., 90
Shiffrin, R.M., 208, 248, 256, 297
Shimamura, A.P., 296, 303
Shih, P.C., 357, 425
Shiner, R.L., 67, 454
Shisler, R.J., 308
Shoker, L., 200, 201
Shulman, G.L., 326, 355, 421
Shvecova, E.V., 155
Siddle, D.A.T., 186
Siegel, B.V., 74, 91, 111, 112, 446
Siegel, S., 102, 103
Siegle, G.J., 441
Silberstein, R.B., 113, 114

Silva, J.A., 423
Silva, M.T.A., 184
Silver, R.C., 338
Silver, W., 369
Silvia, P.J., 327, 331
Simcock, G., 420
Simon, B.B., 406, 419
Simoneau, M., 359
Simon, H.A., 431
Simonov, P.V., 176
Simpson, E.H., 305
Simpson, J.A., 412
Sims, D.E., 455
Singer, J.A., 388, 404
Singer, J.L., 325, 326, 330, 331
Singer, W., 114
Singh, K., 343
Sirevaag, E., 111, 112, 115
Sivers, H., 101
Skitka, L.J., 31, 33
Skowronski, J.J., 340, 404, 405
Skrandies, W., 116
Skudlarski, P., 101
Slabosz, A., 127, 131–135
Slaughter, V., 406
Slessareva, E., 369
Slobodskaya, H.R., 156
Sloman, A., 28
Slomski, J.A., 303
Sloutsky, V., 343, 423
Smallwood, J., 321, 325, 328, 329, 424
Smart, L., 308
Smeets, T., 306
Smekal, V., 146
Śmigasiewicz, K., 23, 127, 131–135, 238, 241, 287
Smillie, L.D., 23, 223
Smith, A.P., 211, 217
Smith, D., 96
Smith, E.E., 73, 91, 197, 198, 266, 303, 378, 425, 426
Smith, G.A., 304
Smith, J.A.L., 365
Smith, J.D., 335, 336, 348
Smith, M.E., 75, 112, 113, 306
Smith, R.E., 329
Smith, S.M., 387, 388
Smith, T.W., 387
Smyth, M.M., 430
Snodgrass, J.G., 236, 347
Snowden, R.J., 182, 183, 187
Snow, R., 52
Snow, W.G., 128
Snyder, A.Z., 92, 102, 326, 421
Snyder, C.R.R., 248, 297
Snyderman, M., 247
Sobel, K.V., 429
Soderling, E., 91
Sokolov, E.N., 156, 161
Solms, M., 304, 305
Sommer, T., 304, 305, 421, 442, 445
Song, A.W., 303

Soroko, S.I., 151, 158–160, 162, 448
Spaendonck, K.P.M., 130
Span, M.M., 129
Spearman, C., 247, 263
Spear, N.E., 188
Specht, K., 92, 100, 101
Speelman, R., 372
Spence, M.A., 305
Spencer, S.J., 307
Sperling, G., 372
Sperry, R.W., 457
Spielberger, C.D., 184, 195
Spilsbury, G., 248, 249, 251
Spreer, J., 74
Srivastava, S., 31, 33
Sroufe, L.A., 407
Stadler, M., 114
Stadler, W., 112, 113, 115
Stammers, R.B., 205, 206, 221, 224
Stanger, C., 407
Stankov, L., 80, 235, 236, 244, 248–251, 255, 256, 270, 271, 289, 376
Stanovich, K.E., 364
Stanton, N.A., 231
Starchenko, M.G., 78
Staudt, B., 77, 78, 172
Staveland, L.E., 213
Stavridou, A., 241
Steele, C.M., 302
Stefanatos, G.A., 185
Stegmaier, R., 358
Steinhauser, M., 312
Steinmayr, R., 111
Stein, M.I., 76
Stein, S., 109
Stelmack, R.M., 74, 234
Stemmler, G., 80, 82, 448
Stenger, V.A., 91, 303, 304
Stennes, L., 410
Stephan, K.E., 170
Stephany, N., 182
Stephens, D.L., 310, 322
Sternberg, R.J., 76, 244, 340, 449, 458
Sternberg, S., 372
Stern, C.E., 426
Stettner, Z., 279
Stigsdotter Nelly, A., 309
Stipacek, A., 74, 81, 82
Stoica, G., 96
Stokes, J.M., 253
Stolarova, M., 121
Stoltzfus, E.R., 354
Stoner, P., 389, 391
Stough, C., 53, 152
Strelau, J., 51–54, 392, 393, 396, 397, 427
Strelnikov, K.N., 156
Striano, T., 406, 420
Strick, P.L., 128
Strong, S.E., 386
Stroobant, N., 219

Author Index

Stroop, J.R., 301
Strube, M.J., 97, 98
Strüber, D., 114
Stude, P., 303
Stull, A.T., 40
Stuss, D. T., 129
Sudberry, M.V., 325, 328, 329
Sudbery, M.V., 424
Suddendorf, T., 406
Suhara, T., 305
Suh, E.M., 38
Sullaway, F., 370
Sullivan, E.V., 131
Sullivan, M., 407
Summers, B.A., 127–141, 305
Suriya, A., 310
Süß, H-M., 264, 270, 274, 354–356, 360–364, 450, 456
Süß, K-M., 296
Susser, K., 389
Suss, H., 372
Suzuki, K., 305
Suzuki, N., 130
Sviderskaya, N.E., 151
Svyatogor, I.A., 151
Swainson, J., 305
Swainson, R., 305
Swanson, J.M., 421
Swerdlow, N.R., 182, 184, 185
Sylvester, C.Y.C., 89, 91, 101
Synowitz, H., 128
Szalma, J.L., 206, 216, 220, 221, 224, 225
Szustrowa, T., 54
Szymura, B., 23, 127, 131–135, 231–244, 249, 287, 291, 392, 444, 451

T
Talledo, J., 182
Tallon-Baudry, C., 113, 114, 121
Tang, C., 74, 111, 112, 446
Tangney, J.P., 338
Tang, Y., 223
Tardieu, H., 431
Taris, T., 371
Taylor, A.E., 130, 131
Taylor, G.J., 111
Taylor, M.J., 325, 327, 329
Taylor, S.F., 177
Teasdale, J.D., 325, 329
Tekell, J.L., 423
Tellegen, A., 384
Temple, J.G., 207, 217
Teplov, B.M., 146, 148
Tessier, C., 310
Tetlock, P., 375
Tetrick, L., 369
Thagard, P.R., 349
Tharp, I.J., 23
Thatcher, R.W., 118
Thayer, R.E., 206–208, 212, 216, 224, 225, 234

Theall, L.A., 406
Therriault, D.J., 73, 90, 268, 298, 300, 311, 356, 363
Thirion, B., 94, 95
Thomas, L.L., 40
Thompson, C.L., 184
Thompson, E., 369, 370, 376
Thompson, H., 303
Thompson, P.M., 75, 304
Thompson, R.A., 111
Thompson, S.C., 338
Thorell, L.B., 308, 309
Thorndike, E.L., 109
Thorndike, R.L., 109
Thrash, T.M., 28
Thurstone, L.L., 55, 263
Tibshirani, R., 102
Tice, D.M., 387
Toates, F., 6, 19
Todd, P.M., 358
Toga, A.W., 304
Toikka, T., 111
Tolegenova, A., 161
Tomasello, M., 420
Toms, M., 358
Tom, S.M., 90
Toner, B.B., 196
Tooby, J., 358
Toone, B., 183
Toren, P., 184, 185
Toro, C., 118
Toth, J.P., 22, 23
Toth, S.L., 411
Towse, J.N., 353–356
Tracey, I., 426
Tracy, J.I., 335, 336, 348
Tranel, D., 128, 423
Tran, Y., 79
Trawalter, S., 65, 307, 311
Treisman, A., 252
Tremain, M., 188
Trepel, C., 90
Trimble, K.M., 184
Trope, Y., 7, 375
Trueblood, W., 253, 255
Tsuchiya, H., 133
Tugade, M.M., 297, 298, 369, 377, 429
Tuholski, S.W., 73, 90, 252, 253, 258, 268, 297, 298, 308, 311, 322, 342, 354, 356, 363, 372, 375, 376, 421, 430, 443
Tukey, J.W., 102
Tulving, E., 407
Turken, A.U., 428
Turley-Ames, K.J., 306
Turner, M.L., 263, 268, 298, 342, 356
Tyano, S., 305
Tyler, L.E., 122
Tyszka, T., 336, 337
Tzourio-Mazoyer, N., 139
Tzourio, N., 74
Tzschentke, T.M., 184

U

Uesiliana, K., 409, 410
Underwood, B.J., 301
Ungerleider, L.G., 430
Unsworth, N., 100, 250, 251, 255, 256, 264, 268, 297, 300, 301, 322, 323, 364
Urca, G., 186
Usher, J.A., 404, 405, 420
Usher, M., 181
Uziel, L., 28

V

Vagg, P.R., 195
Vaish, A., 420
Vaitl, D., 186
Vallat, C., 310
Van der Linden, M., 22, 73, 266
Vandierendonck, A., 361, 377
Van Heck, G.L., 444
Van Hiel, A., 370
Van Honk, J., 448
Van Horn, J.D., 326
Van Ijzendoorn, M.H., 68, 450
Van Knippenberg, A., 369
van Spaendonck, K.P.M., 130, 131
Van Zomeren, A.H., 251
Vargas, P.T., 28
Varner, L.J., 336
Vazire, S., 31, 33
Vazquez, C., 305, 308, 335, 336
Velichkovsky, B.M., 154, 157, 161, 162
Velmans, M., 7, 248
Venables, L., 218
Verhaeghen, P., 309, 427
Vernescu, R., 405, 411
Vernon, P.A., 60, 74, 116, 372
Vich, J., 129
Vickers, J., 200
Viding, E., 430
Vincent, J.L., 92
Vingerhoets, G., 219
Viswesvaran, C., 111
Vitouch, O., 74
Vogel, E.K., 355, 425
Vogel, F., 115
Vogel, S., 109
Vohs, K.D., 176, 266, 307, 383
Voinov, A.V., 156
Volavka, J., 305
Volf, N.V., 155
Vollenweider, F.X., 182
Von Hecker, U., 349, 423
Vooght, G., 361
Voronin, A.N., 154
Vosburg, S.K., 383
Voyer, D., 111
Voyer, S., 111
Vredenburg, K., 335
Vries, J., 444

Vronskaya, S., 305
Vul, E., 455

W

Wachtel, P.L., 249
Wacker, J., 80, 82, 448
Wagenaar, W.A., 377
Wagenmakers, E.J., 97
Wager, D., 222
Wager, T.D., 89, 91, 93, 101–103, 177, 198, 201–203, 284, 355
Wagner, A.D., 101
Wagner, G., 90
Wailke, S., 309
Walker, M.P., 306
Wallesch, C.W., 128
Waltz, J.A., 423
Wang, M., 375
Wang, Q., 409, 410, 412
Ward, D.W., 358, 389, 391–394, 396, 398
Warkentin, V., 407
Warm, J.S., 207–209, 211, 215–217, 219, 221, 224, 225
Wasserman, L.C., 182
Wasserstein, J., 185
Watanabe, M., 305
Waters, G.S., 309
Watkins, E.R., 424, 427
Watson, D., 38, 383, 384
Watts, F.N., 284, 336
Wearing, H., 354
Weary, G., 340
Weber, K., 88, 303
Webster, D.M., 369–371, 373–375, 378, 379, 427
Wechsler, D., 109
Wegner, D.M., 304, 306, 310, 312, 321
Weiland, N.G., 121
Weiler, M.A., 29
Weinbruch, C., 121
Weiner, I., 130, 140, 182, 184, 186
Weingartner, H., 335
Weishaar, M.E., 29
Weiskrantz, L., 13
Weis, S., 423
Weiss, E., 116
Weiss, M., 407
Weissman, D.H., 303
Weitz, S., 111
Wellman, N.A., 182, 184
Wells, A., 223, 225, 286, 441, 450, 452, 454–457
Welsh, K.M., 307
Welsh, R.C., 177
Wendelken, C., 100
Wenzlaff, R.M., 310
Wesensten, N.J., 306
Wesman, A.G., 122
West, A.N., 235
Westberg, L., 305, 421
Westerberg, H., 308, 309
Westerman, S.J., 205, 206, 209, 221, 224

Author Index

Westernberg, H., 309
West, R.F., 364
West, S.G., 90, 99
Whalen, P.J., 303, 304
Whiteman, M.C., 221, 384, 392, 399
White, N.S., 89, 112, 113
White, R., 404
White, S.H., 406, 409, 419
White, T.L., 384
Whitfield, M.M., 306
Whitfield, S.L., 101
Whitmer, A.J., 310
Whitney, P., 267
Wickens, C.D., 209, 231, 449
Wickett, J.C., 74
Wieland, R., 383
Wienert, F.E., 431
Wiese, H., 303
Wilhelm, O., 90, 252, 258, 264, 268, 270, 274, 296, 298, 311, 322, 354–356, 360–364, 372, 421, 429, 443, 450, 456
Wilkinson, R.B., 384
Willatts, P., 420
Williams, A.M., 200
Williams-Gray, C.H., 305
Williams, G.V., 305
Williams, J., 182, 183, 187, 386
Williams, J.H., 182, 184
Williams, J.M.G., 29, 284, 308, 338, 424, 428
Williams, K.M., 37
Williams, P., 268, 269
Williams, S.C., 80, 89
Williams, S.E., 265
Willmes, K., 92, 100, 101
Wills, S.J., 130
Wilson, A.E., 404, 409
Wilson, B.A., 266
Wilson, E.J., 286
Wilson, T.D., 321
Wilson, W.H., 256, 264, 267, 270, 278, 363, 371
Wilt, J., 28, 38, 65
Wingeier, B.M., 113, 114
Winiger, V., 305
Winkielman, P., 455
Winkler, T., 75
Wisco, B.E., 427
Wise, R., 343
Wiser, S.L., 311
Wish, M., 30
Wittman, W.W., 296, 355, 356, 360, 361
Wittmann, W.W., 67, 264, 356, 361, 363
Witzki, A.H., 198, 201, 203, 265, 266, 268, 296, 355, 442, 456
Wizki, A.H., 283
Wodniecka, Z., 238, 241
Woldorff, M.G., 91, 303
Wolf, B., 77
Wolfson, D., 128, 303
Wong, E.C., 94

Worth, L.T., 385
Wortman, C.B., 338
Wright, M.J., 304
Wright, W.F., 386
Wuthrich, V., 183
Wu, Y., 305, 421
Wyer, R.S., 389, 391–394, 396, 398
Wyke, M., 128
Wyland, C.L., 304
Wyler, A.R., 128
Wylie, G., 271

Y

Yablokova, L.V., 153, 156
Yamaguchi, S., 133
Yamasaki, T., 305
Yantis, S., 254
Yarkoni, T., 80, 83, 89–91, 95, 97, 451
Yeo, R.A., 116
Yerkes, R.M., 233, 235
Yiend, J., 328
Yi, S., 410
Yonelinas, A.P., 22, 23
Yoon, K.L., 29
Yoo, S.-S., 306
Young, A.B., 303, 304
Young, A.M.J., 135, 140, 182
Young, M.S., 231
Young, S.E., 199, 203, 431, 442, 443, 446, 448, 456
Yovel, I., 29, 31, 35, 38

Z

Zacks, R.T., 231, 303, 335, 336, 354
Zahn, T., 184
Zalstein-Orda, N., 182, 183, 186, 187
Zanakos, S., 306
Zawadzki, B., 52, 53, 392, 396
Zbrodoff, N.J., 301, 323
Zeidner, M., 216, 444
Zelaya, F., 307
Zembar, M.J., 335
Zener, K.E., 30
Zhang, H., 101
Zhang, S., 88
Zhao, Z., 101
Zhu, J., 8
Zhu, W., 90
Ziegler, M., 258
Zientecka, 346
Zilbovicius, M., 74
Zimmermann, P., 248
Zinbarg, R.E., 29, 35, 38, 42
Zinner, S., 185
Zomeren, A.H., 251
Zubin, J., 253
Zuckerman, M., 37, 234, 458
Zwaan, R.A., 346, 349

Subject Index

A

Ability
  cognitive, xvii, 36, 38, 40, 46, 52, 65, 73, 74, 82, 87, 89, 100, 122, 148–153, 173, 288, 307, 346, 369, 370, 376–379, 407, 443, 444
  crystallized, 82, 263
  factor, general (g factor), 41, 53, 54, 362, 428
  figural-spatial, 111, 117
  fluid, 287, 311, 356, 362, 363, 422, 443
  intellectual, xiii, xvi, 32, 43, 54, 78, 82, 109, 153, 154, 174, 236, 267, 278, 362, 363, 369
  spatial, 55, 89, 111, 169, 359, 363
  verbal, 55, 78, 110, 150
Abstraction, 27, 267, 353, 358, 361, 450
Abstract reasoning test, 267
Abstract rule theory, 358–360
Achievement tests, 306, 309–311
Action
  forms of, 146
  orientation, 253, 385, 393, 396, 397
  planning, 252, 303, 304
Activation, autonomic, 234, 235
Activity style, 152, 153
Addendum, 248, 259
Adrenal stress hormones, 410
Affect, xvii, xviii, 7, 15, 21, 27, 29–31, 38–40, 46, 65, 101, 111, 134, 183, 188, 189, 210, 211, 221–223, 225, 227, 233, 301, 306, 308, 332, 344, 385–387, 404, 409–413, 421, 427, 429, 430, 440, 453, 458
Affect infusion model (AIM), 386
Age, xiii, xvii, xviii, 33, 34, 37, 42, 43, 52–55, 57, 59, 60, 75, 78, 88, 116, 130, 134, 152–155, 253, 273–275, 303, 306, 342, 346, 403–410, 420, 427, 440, 441, 454
Agreeableness, 37, 43, 44, 60, 174, 212, 221, 384
Alertness, 81, 82, 251, 253, 306
Alpha
  activity, 76–78, 80
  band, 80–82, 116, 117, 122, 449
  lower activity, 80–82
  synchronisation, 78, 79, 173
Alpha inhibition hypothesis, 78
Ambiguity, intolerance of, 371, 453
Amygdala, 101, 173

Antisaccade task, 200, 201, 203, 265, 300, 301, 323, 324
Anxiety, xi, xv, xvii, 16, 21, 29, 52, 53, 65, 67, 68, 156, 183–185, 188, 195–203, 206, 207, 210, 225, 284–290, 295, 302, 306–309, 311, 384–387, 421, 422, 424, 427, 439–441, 444, 447, 448, 450–452, 455, 458, 459
Appraisal, xv, 4, 21, 29, 63, 206, 207, 210, 213–216, 221–226, 389, 453
Appraisal of life events scale (ALE), 213, 214, 221
Approach
  differential, 64, 248, 249, 385, 388, 391, 399
  differential-dispositional, 388
  experimental, 64, 248, 249, 383, 449, xvii
  process-oriented, 388, 391
  tendencies, behavioral, 80, 97
  transactional, 399
Arousal
  constitutional, 243, 244
  energetic, xv, 67, 206–212, 216, 217, 222, 225, 226, 234–236, 384
  general, xiv, 169, 170, 205, 206, 234
  optimal level of, 208, 233–236
  state, 207, 233–236, 240, 243, 244
  tense, 67, 206–208, 211, 234, 384
Arousal theory, 76, 79, 170, 171, 206–208
A-theories, 185, 186, 189
Attachment
  insecure, 412
  secure, 412
Attention
  ability to control, xvi, 298, 300, 376, 429
  controlled, 23, 219, 251, 252, 290, 296, 299, 301, 302, 323
  control of
    goal-directed, 254
  deficits, xv, 184, 185, 244, 253, 289, 296, 419
  defocused, 76, 348–349
  divisible, 233
  executive, xvii, 176, 251, 252, 254, 256, 287, 297, 303, 305, 309, 323–324, 327, 342, 420, 422, 425, 429, 454
  as executive control, 256–258
  focal allocation of, 250

Attention (*cont.*)
  focused, 207, 251, 253, 299
  focus of, xvi, 135, 251, 253, 264, 265, 269, 296, 297, 307, 309, 323, 354, 355, 363, 364, 422, 450
  general factor, xvi, 254, 255
  as limited resource, 249
  metaphors of, 249, 250
  perceptual, 254
  as perceptual control, 255, 257, 258
  selective, 118, 156, 197, 198, 251, 285, 299, 425, 429–431, 438, 450
  self-focused, 211, 452
  shared allocation of, 250
  spatial, 251, 253, 355
  stimulus-driven control of, 254
  structure of, xvi, 252, 253, 255, 285
  sustained, 207, 219, 220, 250, 253, 255, 291, 328
  switching, 137, 250, 251, 265
  as time-sharing mechanism, 249
Attentional deficits, 185, 244, 289
Attentional lability, 233
Attentional narrowing, 233
Attention deficit and hyperactivity disorder (ADHD), 176, 184, 185, 289, 296, 305, 309, 310
Avoidance, 16, 17, 210, 213, 215, 216, 221, 223, 224, 226, 370, 384, 396, 454
Awareness
  conscious, xii, 5–10, 12–21, 24, 66–68, 322, 331, 457
  emotional, 111

B

Basal ganglia (BG), 176, 303, 304, 421, 445
Behavioral activation system (BAS), 212, 221, 223, 384
Behavioral inhibition system (BIS), 6, 13, 16, 17, 19, 177, 384
Behavior, overt, 93, 321
Beta, waves, 151
Bias
  attentional, 29, 135, 283, 284, 289, 290, 310, 452, 456
  belief, 344–346
  cognitive, 29
Binding mechanism, 114
BOLD signal, 87, 91, 92, 100–102, 173, 455
Brain
  activity, xiii, xiv, 7, 74–82, 87, 91, 100, 101, 109, 112–118, 122, 146, 155, 156, 160, 170, 172–174, 331, 420, 447, 455
  functional activation, 304
  imaging, 73, 74, 128, 266, 343, 423, 425, 438, 447
  networks, 90, 170, 175, 327
  plasticity, xiv, 158–161, 448
  visceral (VB), 234
Brainstem, 146, 152, 156, 159, 160, 162, 170

C

Capacity
  attentional, 232, 250, 287, 441, 444, 451
  capacity-limited system, 354
  cognitive, reduction, 336, 371
Catechol-*O*-methyl transferase (COMT), 305
Caudate nucleus, 139, 177
Central control unit, 296, 297
Central executive, 73, 197, 198, 251, 297, 322, 342, 355, 359, 360, 376, 429
Cerebral blood flow velocity (CBFV), 218–220, 225
Challenge, xviii, 5, 27, 207, 213, 215–216, 219, 221, 222, 224, 285–287, 310, 325, 328, 438, 439, 443, 446, 453, 455–459
CHC model, 257
Choking under pressure, 307–308, 311, 312
Classification learning task, 100
Closed mindedness, tendency toward, 371
Closure, costs of, 370
Cocktail party effect, 299
Cognition
  higher-level, 66, 353–365, 419
  primary process, 76
  social, xvii, 377, 388, 403, 408, 412, 413, 454
Cognitive closure, need for, xvii, 369–379, 423–424, 427, 457
Cognitive commitment, 370
Cognitive exhaustion, 336–338, 340, 423, 424, 451
Cognitive failures, 221, 328
Cognitive initiative, 335
Cognitive load, 113, 115, 161, 302, 306, 308, 377, 379, 421
Cognitive science, 5, 28, 157, 222, 225, 226, 278, 438
Cognitive style, xi, 153–154, 158, 162, 174
Coherence, 114–117, 151, 155–157, 161, 162, 172, 393, 396–398, 447, 458
Cold infection, 217
Comparator, 15, 68
Competition resolution, 322–324
Complexity
  dimensional, 115
  relational, 267
Complex span tasks, 298, 322, 323, 356, 362, 429
Computational modeling, 267, 278
Computational strategies, 93
Concentration, xv, 149, 207, 210, 211, 226, 248–250, 253, 312, 328, 452, 455
Configural processing system, 383, 389
Confirmatory factor analysis, 253, 266
Conflict resolution, 266, 269, 274, 304, 422
Conscientiousness, xii, 36, 37, 43, 52, 212, 221, 384
Consciousness, xv, xviii, 7–10, 12–24, 63, 67–69, 148, 157, 161, 189, 248, 286, 331, 353, 364, 420, 439, 457, 459
Consolidation, 411
Constituent, 247, 248, 258, 404
Context
  dependent effect of mood, xvii, 383, 390–393, 396–399

Subject Index

Control
    behavior, xii, 146, 158, 324, 327
    behavioral, 54, 59, 266, 448
    cognitive, xi, xiii, xvi, xvii, 7, 60, 92, 175, 176, 263–279, 287, 298, 303, 304, 307, 308, 312, 328, 355, 365, 376, 419–422, 443, 445, 448, 457
    cybernetic, 5
    endogenous, 265, 273, 274, 420
    executive
        theory of, 254, 256
    exogenous, 265
    full, 265
    personal, 216, 266, 267
    proactive, 266, 447, 448
    reactive, 7, 266, 447
    theory of, 195, 203
    volitional, 270, 385, 393
Coordination
    attentional control, of, 254
Coping, xv, 160, 206, 207, 210, 213, 216, 219–226, 290, 452–454
Coping inventory for task stress (CITS), 213, 214, 219
Cortex
    anterior
        cingulated (ACC), 91, 97, 139, 140, 176, 202, 303–307, 311, 421, 422, 445, 447, 448
    medial posterior parietal (PPC), 89, 92, 93
    mediobasal, 146, 170
    orbitofrontal, 128, 176, 222, 223
    posterior, 146, 155
    prefrontal
        dorsolateral (DLPFC), 89, 128, 175–177, 303, 423, 425, 426, 445
        ventromedial, 129, 176
Corticoreticular loop, 234
Creativity, xiii, xv, 76–79, 153–155, 157, 174, 231, 235, 236, 239, 243, 244, 287, 290, 349, 375, 440, 443, 449
Culture, 111, 154, 409–410, 454
Current concerns theory, 329, 330

D

Daydreams, 321, 329
Decision-making, 63, 93, 121, 135, 176, 303, 306, 438, 441, 445, 451
Decision-related action orientation, 393, 396, 399
Decision-related state orientation, 393, 396, 399
Decisiveness, 371, 373, 399
Default mode network, 326, 331
Defensive processes, 411
Delta, 156, 158, 161, 177, 448
Depression, xvii, 22, 23, 29, 67, 284–286, 290, 305, 308, 310, 335–350, 386, 387, 398, 423–425, 441, 451, 455
Desynchronization, 74, 75, 80, 113, 114, 155, 156, 161, 175, 448
Development, xiii, xvii, xviii, 24, 52, 54, 60, 145–148, 152, 153, 156–161, 171, 182, 195–203, 206, 220, 251, 303, 353, 360, 365, 403–409, 412, 419–423, 430, 431, 441, 454, 456, 459
Dichotic listening, 299, 386
Dieting, 22
Differential cognitology, 153–158
Differential psychophysiology, 146, 148–153, 161, 162
Distraction, 200, 202, 237, 238, 241, 290, 303, 308, 322, 363, 387, 429, 442, 450, 451
Distress, 211–213, 221, 225, 440, 452
Domain-specific factors, 263, 360
Dopamine
    antagonist, 184
Dopaminergic drugs, 89, 305
Dopaminergic system, 134, 182, 304
Dot probe task, 29, 286, 450
Dual task
    condition, 23, 209, 210, 236, 238–241, 243, 244, 271, 275, 276
    coordination, xv, xvi, 273, 274
    performance, xi, 209, 233, 236, 271–274, 278, 444, 449–451
Dundee stress state questionnaire (DSSQ), 210–213, 216, 219, 221

E

Education, 33, 34, 37, 42–44, 76, 364, 407
Effect
    size, xiv, 88, 94–99, 103, 440, 444
    size inflation, xiv, 96, 103
Efficiency theory, xv, 113, 117, 197, 199
Effort
    cognitive, 16, 93, 337, 340, 388, 424
    mental, 113, 150, 232–234, 236, 241, 243, 250, 255, 302, 303, 424
Electroencephalography (EEG)
    methodology, 113, 148
Elementary cognitive tasks (ECTs), 73, 75, 263
Emotion
    focus, 213, 224
    micro-expressions of, 217
Emotional responsiveness, 235
Emotional stability, 44, 45, 110, 444
Encoding, 113, 114, 156, 188, 189, 208, 255, 296, 304–306, 349, 403, 406, 408, 411–413, 421
Epistemic motivation, xvii, 369, 370
Error
    type I, 97–99
    type II, 99
Event
    distinctive, 404, 405, 411
    emotional, 404, 411
    stressful, 308, 407, 410–412
Event-related desynchronization/synchronization (ERD/ERS), 75, 77, 80, 82, 114, 117, 448
Event-related potential (ERP)
    P1 component, 121
    P3 component, 118, 121
Excitability, 234

Excitation
  functions, 173
Experience-sampling method, 326, 327
Extraversion, xiii, xv, 23, 28–30, 37–40, 45, 52, 65, 79–82, 89, 118, 152, 155, 158, 160, 170, 171, 206, 212, 221, 234–236, 239, 240, 243, 244, 285, 288, 384, 422, 444, 448–452, 459

F
Family, 183, 336, 379, 409, 454
Fatigue
  active, 215
  mental, 306, 307, 371, 378, 427
  passive, 213, 215
Features, central, 411
Feelings as information, 389
Fight–flight–freeze system (FFFS), xii, 16–19
Five factor model, 52, 174, 212, 285, 440
Flanker task, 300, 301
Frontoparietal network, 92, 93, 137, 305
Functional magnetic resonance imaging (fMRI), 73–75, 87–101, 103, 114, 116, 134, 135, 140, 157, 171–173, 176, 177, 199, 202, 219, 326, 343, 360, 365, 421, 423, 425, 431, 438, 446–448, 451, 455
Functional networks, 90
Functional systems, 146, 147, 151, 153, 162, 174, 446

G
Gamma
  band
    induced, 113, 114, 117, 118
    responses, evoked, 113, 118, 119, 121, 122
Gender, xiii, xiv, xviii, 37, 43, 44, 51–60, 88, 109–122, 154, 155, 174, 311, 410, 440, 446, 447
Genes, 304, 312, 421, 454
Goal
  maintenance, 322–324, 327, 328, 448
  management, 267
  neglect, xvii, 269, 323, 324, 327–329, 421
  relevant information, 175, 322, 354, 374
Go/no-go task, 326, 328
Gyrus, frontal left inferior, 93

H
Hard problem, 15
Hardware, 5, 33–34, 74, 438, 459
Hedonic tone, 211, 222, 225, 384
High-elaborative, 408, 412
Higher nervous system
  general properties of, 149, 161, 174, 175
  specific properties of, 149, 150

I
Ideational fluency, 76, 78
ID/ED visual discrimination learning paradigm, 127

Impulsivity, 6, 7, 52, 65, 67, 154, 221, 287, 422, 451
Inattention, 181
Infant, 111, 403–410, 412, 420
Infantile amnesia, 403, 404
Information
  diagnostic, 339, 340, 375, 376
  processing
    limitations, 232
  prototypical, 375
  rate of, 372, 373
Inhibition
  behavioural, 13, 16, 198, 252
  function, 198–201, 284, 288
  prepotent responses, of, 199, 265, 296
Inhibitory mechanisms, 308, 310, 354
Inoculations, 411
Insight, xiv, 24, 46, 76–78, 89, 94, 145, 172, 174, 269, 350, 412, 439
Intelligence
  chronometry of, theory, 244
  crystallized (Gc factor), 53, 55, 57, 82, 263, 422
  emotional, xiv, 109–122, 150, 174, 443, 449, 452, 459
  fluid, xvi, 54, 82, 88–91, 251, 252, 256–258, 263, 267, 269–274, 277, 278, 286, 287, 322, 356, 357, 361–365, 422, 443, 445, 447, 449, 459
  general
    fluid (Gf factor), 263, 267, 269, 272, 273, 278, 287, 322, 356
  performance, 114, 118
  social, 109, 110
  tests, 52, 115, 235, 267, 311, 357, 364
  verbal, 78, 82, 116, 169
Interference
  cognitive, xv, 93, 196, 197, 210, 211, 452
  proactive (PI), 90, 91, 93, 301
  resistance to, 354
  skill-based, 252
Internal working models, 412
Introversion, 79, 80, 82, 155, 244, 384, 422, 427, 451
Investment game, 37

J
Jacoby exclusion task, 18–19

K
Knowledge
  of results (KR), 216
Kuhl's action control theory, 385, 393

L
Language, xvii, 4, 7, 9, 15, 21, 34, 54, 113, 146, 150, 176, 278, 310, 322, 325, 329, 353, 359, 403, 405, 408, 412, 413, 420, 454
Latent activation variables, 101
Latent inhibition (LI), xiv, xv, 23, 130, 135, 181–189, 286, 451, 455, 456

Latent variables, 90, 254, 257–258, 264, 268–270, 277, 278, 362, 432
Lay epistemics, theory of, 370
Learned irrelevance (LI), xiv, 127–135, 137–140, 442, 445, 451
Learning, 4, 6, 7, 16, 19, 23, 32, 53, 63, 100, 113, 127–131, 134, 135, 152–154, 156, 170, 171, 174, 181–186, 188, 205, 207, 217, 224, 263, 278, 300, 309–311, 322, 336, 339, 342, 343, 357, 441, 459
Level
 reactive, 7, 28
 routine, 7, 28
Limbic system, 146, 149, 155, 156, 161, 170, 423
Linear order, xvii, 340–343, 349
Low-elaborative, 408, 412

M

Machiavellianism, 37–38, 386
Maintenance, 171, 256, 264, 266, 296, 297, 301, 322–324, 327, 328, 342, 344, 355, 374, 375, 404, 405, 421, 425, 429, 430, 448
Maltreatment, 411
Masking task, 181, 182, 186–187
Measurement
 impurity in, 249
 reliability, 94, 99, 103, 171
Memory
 autobiographical, xvii, xviii, 388, 403–413, 419, 420, 424, 441, 450, 454, 457
 counters task, 265
 long-term, xviii, 75, 223, 297, 323, 354, 422, 438
 primary, 264, 297, 298
 prospective, 329
 search, 209, 379, 424, 425
 secondary, 297, 298, 302
 short term (STM), 65, 156, 199, 206, 207, 209, 235, 251, 264, 268, 354, 356, 357, 362, 363, 426, 428, 431
Mental arithmetic, 93
Mental concentration, 250
Mental rotation, 111, 323
Metacognition, 9, 225, 267, 286, 406, 420
Meta-worry, 225
Mind wandering, 321, 325–332, 423–424, 427, 439, 440, 442, 444, 452
Mirror self-recognition (MSR) test, 405–408
Models
 bottom-up, 388, 399
 dual-process, 6, 24
 mental, social, xvii, 338, 340, 451, 455
 situation, 335, 346–349
 top-down, 385, 388, 399
Moderator, xiii, 52, 53, 74, 75, 81, 342, 344, 423–424
Monitoring, 91, 114, 128, 129, 198, 205, 207, 217, 232, 233, 265, 268, 287, 296, 299, 303–305, 312, 325, 328, 348, 349, 355, 357, 359, 419, 445
Monoamine oxidase A (MAOA), 305

Mood
 disorders, 22, 308, 310
 as information model, 389
 as input model, xvii, 383, 388–391, 398, 399
 mood-congruency hypothesis, 386
 three-dimensional model of, 384
Music preferences, 34, 36–37

N

Narrative(s), 205, 404–410, 413
 construction, 404
 reconstruction, 404, 409
 skill, 420
NASA-TLX workload scale, 213
Natural disasters, 411
Navon task, 243, 269
n-back task, 268, 269, 278, 303, 356, 426
Need for closure scale, 373, 375, 377, 378
Nervous system, types of, 146
Neural efficiency, xiv, 73–75, 82, 91, 113, 115, 117, 443, 446, 451, 455, 456
Neuroendocrine reactions, 411
Neuroimaging
 studies, xiv, 74, 87, 94, 102, 103, 129, 170, 172, 222, 326
Neurons, additional, recruitment of, 255
Neurophysiology, xiv, 73–76, 79, 146, 150, 425
Neuroscience, xi, xiii, xiv, xviii, 73, 87–103, 128, 169–172, 175–177, 220, 222, 285, 287, 321, 332, 350, 421, 422, 425, 437, 438, 445–449, 454
Neuroticism, xi, xv, 21, 23, 29, 30, 37, 52, 53, 89, 118, 152, 155, 158, 171, 174, 206, 212, 231, 234–236, 240–241, 243, 244, 287, 384, 387, 388, 422, 427, 444, 448, 450–451
Neurotransmitters, 173, 304, 305, 309, 421, 457
Noise, 173, 205, 206, 217, 222, 237, 238, 242, 265, 299, 332, 371, 378, 379, 427
Novelty, 19, 76, 131–133, 150, 175, 176, 263

O

Obsessive compulsive disorder (OCD), 17–18, 184–185, 310
Off-task thoughts, 331, 332
Openness, 36, 37, 44, 52, 65–67, 173, 370, 384, 386, 422, 444
Operation span, 100, 268, 298, 322, 342–346, 348, 356, 375
Operation-word span task (OSPAN), 298, 301, 322, 323, 342, 344–346, 348, 375, 376
Optimism, 16, 221, 385
Order and predictability, preference for, 371
Originality, 77, 78, 81, 158
Outliers, treatment of, 103

P

Parent-child interaction, 403, 408, 411
Parent conversational style, 408

Parkinson's disease (PD), idiopathic, 130
Patients
 frontal-lobe, 131, 134
 schizophrenic, 133, 181–183, 188
Perceived controllability, 213
Perception
 spatial, 111, 114
Perceptual process, 146, 196, 208, 248, 255, 259
Performance
 effectiveness, 197, 199
 maximum, 51, 52
 typical, 51
Performance operating characteristics (POCs), 209
Peripherals details, 411
Perseveration, 129, 131, 134–137, 139–140, 310, 442
Personality
 authoritarian, 36
 Big Five, dimensions of, 110, 384
 research, 4, 29, 32, 51, 52, 223, 439, 444, 452, 459
Personal life story, 406
Pessimism, 221
Phonological loop, 197, 251, 359, 360, 363, 431
Planning, 7, 17, 103, 158, 197, 252, 253, 265, 266, 303–305, 310, 353, 365, 421, 438, 439, 441, 445
Positron emission tomography (PET), 73, 74, 87, 103, 114, 116, 137, 147, 157, 171, 172, 326, 425, 431, 432, 446
Power calculations, 98–99
Primary caretaker hypothesis, 111
Probe technique, 200, 202, 325, 431
Problem solving, general, 110
Process
 cognitive, xii–xiv, xvii, 3–6, 8, 9, 13, 15, 18, 19, 21, 29–31, 63–68, 79, 80, 93, 113, 130, 131, 146, 150, 155, 173, 197, 202, 212, 213, 215, 221, 222, 225, 248, 250, 264, 266, 271, 277, 278, 287, 297, 303, 304, 321, 343, 350, 355–357, 369, 371, 379, 385, 398, 410, 422, 423, 426, 440, 445, 454, 456
 reflective, xii, 9, 13, 16, 20–23
 reflexive, 9, 13, 16, 20
 role-fulfillment, 390
 transformation, 248
Processing
 automatic, 6, 23, 248, 256, 271, 298, 301
 controlled, 6, 22, 23, 248, 256, 268, 290, 298, 322, 376–379, 457
 data-driven, 250, 255
 efficiency, xv, 197, 199–202, 206, 399, 441
 preconscious, 7, 8
Prosaccade, 201, 300, 301
Psychological refractory period (PRP), 269, 271, 272, 274, 276, 277
Psychology
 differential, xii, 3, 4, 145, 148, 153, 158, 160, 206, 437, 444
 disciplines of, 4, 248
Psychoticism, 23, 231, 234–236, 241–242, 244, 287, 444, 451

Q
Qualia, 10, 12, 16, 22, 68

R
Random generation of intervals (RIG) task, 377
Raven's progressive matrices, 53, 54, 267, 275
Reading span, 298, 322, 356
Reasoning
 deductive, 343, 358–362, 387
 inductive, xvii, 357, 361–364, 449
Reflective layer, 28
Reflex, 6, 145, 146, 148, 161, 175
Region
 frontal, 78, 91, 113, 128, 130, 311
 of-interest (ROI), 92
 parietal, xiv, 77, 80–82, 88, 92, 113, 343
Regulation
 effort, 232
 emotional, 156, 157, 161, 176
Regulation, behavioral, 145
Regulative theory of temperament, 392
Rehearsal, 197, 301, 302, 409, 412, 413, 425, 431, 432
Reinforcement sensitivity theory (RST), xii, 16, 22, 29, 63, 66, 68, 223
Resources
 allocation
  policy, 232, 233, 236, 239
 attentional, xv, 18, 170, 196, 207, 225, 231–233, 235, 237, 239, 243, 244, 251, 285, 291, 302, 311, 336, 354, 429
 cognitive, 65, 66, 154, 335, 338, 369–379, 420, 428, 430
 concept of, 250
 management, 231–233, 239, 243, 244, 291
 resource-sharing framework, 376
Response, prepotent, 128, 198, 199, 265, 267, 296, 298–300, 421
Retention interval, 187
Reticular formation, 79, 146, 149, 170
Retrieval, 114, 116, 185–187, 189, 207, 224, 296–298, 302, 304, 323, 338, 341, 374, 405, 408, 411–413, 421, 422, 425, 431, 441, 451, 456
Rhythm, 150, 151, 154–156, 158, 160, 161, 177, 212, 218, 255, 377, 378, 448
R-theories, 185–189
Ruminations, 13, 17, 23, 306, 308, 310, 387, 421, 427
Running memory task, 269, 356

S
Sample size, 31, 88, 90, 94–99, 102, 103, 171, 249
Schizophrenia, xiv, xv, 22, 23, 133, 134, 151, 181–189, 253, 286, 303, 305, 310, 441, 451, 455
Schizotypal, 181–189, 451
Schizotypy, 183, 186, 221, 286, 451
SciPic decision task, 377

Temperamental traits, xiii, xv, 52, 53, 57, 59, 60, 236, 239, 384, 388, 392, 393, 395, 397, 398
Text comprehension, 346–348, 423
Therapy
    cognitive-behavioural, 22
    talk, 22
Theta
    band, 113, 150, 155
Thinking, divergent, 76, 77, 155, 235
Threat, 17, 23, 29, 30, 65, 122, 201, 205, 213, 234, 284–287, 289, 290, 304, 306–307, 310–311, 384, 386, 421, 444, 448, 450–452, 454, 458
Threshold, statistical, 94, 95, 98, 99
Time of the day, 243
Time-pressure, 243
Toddlers, 406–408, 420
Tourette's disorder, 184
Trade-off, 94, 98, 255, 266
Training, 16, 160, 217, 265, 272, 275, 278, 308, 309, 340, 431, 442, 459
Trait-congruency hypothesis, 386
Transactional model of temperament, 397
Transcranial Doppler sonography (TCD), 218–220
Trust, 37
Trustworthiness, 37

U
Uncertainty, 19, 93, 152, 197, 337, 361, 369, 370, 373
Uncontrollability, 337, 338, 340
Updating, xv, xvi, 23, 197–199, 203, 265, 266, 268, 269, 277, 278, 284–288, 295–298, 300, 305, 306, 355, 421, 424, 425, 441–444, 448, 449, 451
Upper alpha activity, 80, 81

V
Ventral striatum, 222
Verbal fluency task, 302
Vigilance, 82, 160, 170, 205–209, 211, 215–221, 250, 251, 253, 285, 325–327, 330, 448
Virtual reality, 20
Visual attention, theory of, 254
Visuo-spatial sketch-pad, 197
Voiding cystourethrogram fluoroscopy (VCUG), 411
Volitional properties, 385, 393

W
Wisconsin card sorting task (WCST), xiv, 23, 123, 127–129, 456
Working memory
    capacity, xvi, 66, 67, 75, 235, 264, 295–312, 321–332, 342, 343, 345, 349, 353–365, 374–376, 379, 421, 441
    models, 296–297, 322, 358
    process, xvii, 80, 82
    span tasks, 268, 298, 322, 323, 358, 362, 374
    as a state and trait, 298, 312
    updating of, 265
    verbal, 359, 360, 363, 365
    visual, 359, 360
Workload, 160, 207, 213, 215, 216, 219, 451, 452
Worry, 17, 18, 21, 23, 66, 102, 196, 206, 211–213, 225, 321, 427, 440, 444, 452, 454, 459

Y
Yerkes-Dodson law, 205, 206, 208, 233, 235

Search
    visual, 181, 184, 185, 208, 217, 301, 429, 443
Selection-for-action, 252
Selective gating mechanism, 304, 445
Selectivity, xi, 97, 99, 152, 237–239, 243, 338, 444, 450, 452
Self
    awareness, 406
    cognitive, xvii, 225, 403, 405–408, 412, 413, 420, 421, 441, 454, 457
    concept, 224, 226, 403, 404, 406, 409, 413, 454
    efficacy, 225, 226, 369, 452
    esteem, 211, 387, 388, 391, 452
    knowledge, 223, 224, 226, 227, 286, 406, 439, 452, 454, 458
    recognition skill, 408
    regulation, xviii, 151, 153, 158–162, 171, 210–216, 221, 223–225, 419, 420, 445, 452–454
    style, 152–154, 158, 160–162, 408–410, 454
    working, 404, 413
Self-referent executive (S-REF), 223–226, 454, 455
Self-regulatory systems, 5
Sensitivity
    of the data, 94
    to pleasant, 29–30
    to unpleasant, 29
Sex differences, 78
Sexual abuse, 411
Shift
    extradimensional (EDS), 129–135, 137, 139
    intradimensional (IDS), 129–133, 135, 137, 139, 437, 439–442, 444–450, 452–459
Shifting
    attentional, 130, 135, 445
    function, 198, 199, 201–203, 284, 285
    reversal, 129
Similarity judgments, 29
Single-channel bottleneck, 233
Sleep deprivation, 65, 295, 306–307, 421, 428, 444, xvi
Sociability, 29
Social dominance, 36
Social skills, 111, 290
Sociolinguistic interactions, 404, 407–410, 412
Sociolinguistic perspective, 406–408
Software, 5, 32–34, 69, 103, 459
Span tasks, 268, 298, 322, 323, 356, 362, 374, 429
Spatial dissociations, 92
Spatial visualization, 111
Speed
    attention-paced, 255, 256
    biology-based, 255, 256
    information processing, of, 73, 248, 264, 275, 354
    mental, 81, 255, 256, 259, 302, 342, 349
Spotlight metaphor, 249
State orientation, 385, 393, 396–399, 427
Statistical power limitations, 103
Stereotype threat, 307, 310–311, 421
Sternberg's task, 372
Stimulation processing capabilities, 393, 395, 396, 398

Stimulus
    emotional, 7, 151, 176, 217, 234, 303, 348, 428
    hunger, 234
    irrelevant, 23, 129, 185, 189, 349
    preexposure, 181, 185–189
    salience, 181
    specificity, 188
Stop rules
    enjoy stop-rule, 394, 397
    enough information stop-rule, 394, 396
Stop-signal task, 265
Storage, 197, 198, 250, 287, 296–298, 342, 353, 355, 361, 363, 372, 373, 405, 408, 413, 421, 429, 456
Strategies, heuristic, 94, 385, 389
Stream of thought, 321–332
Stress
    life event, 213, 307
    reactivity, 407, 411
    transactional model of, 206
Stroop task, 287, 289, 301, 310, 323, 324, 386, 448
Structural equation modeling (SEM), 90, 101, 264, 269, 277, 422, 432
Structuring, 162, 371
Substance intake, 233, 243
Supervision, 248, 296, 355
Supervisory attentional system (SAS), 251, 297
Surgency, 29
Sustained attention to response task (SART), 328–330
Syllogisms, categorical, xvii, 344, 349
Symmetry span, 2298
Symptoms
    negative, xv, 182, 183, 188, 189
    positive, xv, 182–184, 188, 189, 451
Synchronization, 77–79, 114, 151, 155, 156, 161, 173
Synthetic aperture personality assessment (SAPA), xii, xiii, 27, 31–46, 440, 444

T
Task
    complexity, 75, 232, 233, 289, 325, 446
    demands, xv, 78, 80–82, 199, 207, 213, 219, 222, 231–233, 235, 243, 244, 250, 252, 255, 256, 307, 337, 448, 449, 452
    engagement, xv, 67, 205–227, 440, 444, 452, 453, 457
    focused coping, 207, 210, 213, 215, 219–222, 224–226
    motivation, 207, 211, 325, 440, 453
    switching, 201, 202, 266, 268, 270, 271, 277, 278, 287, 296, 301, 310, 355
    unrelated thought (TUT), xvii, 298, 324–327, 329–332, 444
Task-referent executive processing (T-REF), 223, 224, 226
Temperament
    temperament-personality coherence, 396, 397
    temperament-volition incoherence, 398